MODERN BRITISH LITERATURE

THE OXFORD ANTHOLOGY OF ENGLISH LITERATURE

General Editors: Frank Kermode and John Hollander

Medieval English Literature
J. B. TRAPP, Librarian, Warburg Institute, London

The Literature of Renaissance England
JOHN HOLLANDER, Hunter College;
and FRANK KERMODE, University College London

The Restoration and the Eighteenth Century
MARTIN PRICE, Yale University

Romantic Poetry and Prose
HAROLD BLOOM, Yale University;
and LIONEL TRILLING, Columbia University

Victorian Prose and Poetry
LIONEL TRILLING and HAROLD BLOOM

Modern British Literature
FRANK KERMODE and JOHN HOLLANDER

Modern British Literature

FRANK KERMODE
University College London

JOHN HOLLANDER
Hunter College

New York   OXFORD UNIVERSITY PRESS
London   Toronto   1973

Selections from works by the following authors were made possible by the kind permission of their respective publishers and representatives:

Kingsley Amis: *A Case of Samples*, reprinted by permission of Curtis Brown Ltd. and Victor Gollancz Ltd.

W. H. Auden: *Collected Shorter Poems, 1927–1957*, poems copyright 1934 (renewed 1962), 1937 (renewed 1965), 1940 (renewed 1968), 1947, 1951, and 1954 by W. H. Auden; *City Without Walls and Other Poems*, copyright © 1966 by W. H. Auden, all reprinted by permission of Random House, Inc., and Faber and Faber Ltd. *Collected Longer Poems*, copyright 1944 by W. H. Auden; *The Collected Poetry of W. H. Auden*, copyright 1934 and renewed 1961 by W. H. Auden; reprinted by permission of Random House, Inc. *For the Time Being* and *The Orators*, reprinted by permission of Faber and Faber Ltd.

Samuel Beckett: *Watt*, reprinted by permission of Grove Press, Inc., all rights reserved, and Calder and Boyars Ltd.

John Betjeman: *Collected Poems*, reprinted by permission of John Murray (Publishers) Ltd. and Houghton Mifflin Co.

Robert Bridges: *The Poetical Works of Robert Bridges*, reprinted by permission of The Clarendon Press, Oxford.

Basil Bunting: *Collected Poems*, reprinted by permission of Fulcrum Press.

Joseph Conrad: *Heart of Darkness*, reprinted by permission of J. M. Dent & Sons Ltd. and The Trustees of the Joseph Conrad Estate.

Donald Davie: *Collected Poems, 1950–1970*, copyright © 1971 by Donald Davie; reprinted by permission of Oxford University Press, Inc., and Routledge & Kegan Paul Ltd.

Walter de la Mare: *The Collected Poems*, reprinted by permission of The Literary Trustees of Walter de la Mare and The Society of Authors as their representative.

T. S. Eliot: *Collected Poems, 1909–1962*, copyright 1936 by Harcourt Brace Jovanovich, Inc.; copyright © 1943, 1963, 1964 by T. S. Eliot; copyright 1971 by Esme Valerie Eliot; *Selected Essays: New Edition* by T. S. Eliot, copyright 1932, 1936, 1950 by Harcourt Brace Jovanovich, Inc.; copyright 1960, 1964 by T. S. Eliot; reprinted by permission of Harcourt Brace Jovanovich, Inc., and Faber and Faber Ltd.

William Empson: *Collected Poems of William Empson*, copyright 1949 by William Empson; reprinted by permission of Harcourt Brace Jovanovich, Inc., and Chatto and Windus Ltd.

E. M. Forster: *Two Cheers for Democracy*, copyright 1939, 1967 by E. M. Forster; reprinted by permission of Harcourt Brace Jovanovich, Inc., and Edward Arnold (Publishers) Ltd.

Robert Graves: *Collected Poems*, copyright © 1955 by Robert Graves; reprinted by permission of Collins-Knowlton-Wing, Inc.

Thom Gunn: *The Sense of Movement*, reprinted by permission of Faber and Faber Ltd.

Thomas Hardy: *The Dynasts*, copyright 1904 by The Macmillan Company, renewed 1931 by Florence E. Hardy; *Collected Poems*, copyright 1925 by The Macmillan Company, renewed 1953 by Lloyds Bank Ltd.; reprinted by permission of The Macmillan Company, New York, the Trustees of the Hardy Estate, The Macmillan Company of Canada Limited, and Macmillan London and Basingstoke.

John Heath-Stubbs: *Selected Poems*, reprinted by permission of Oxford University Press, New York.

Geoffrey Hill: *For the Unfallen*, reprinted by permission of Dufour Editions, Inc., and Andre Deutsch Ltd.

A. E. Housman: From "A Shropshire Lad," Authorised Edition, from *The Collected Poems of A. E. Housman*, copyright 1939, 1940, © 1959 by Holt, Rinehart and Winston, Inc.; copyright © 1967, 1968 by Robert E. Symons; *The Collected Poems of A. E. Housman*, copyright 1922 by Holt, Rinehart and Winston, Inc.; copyright 1936, 1950 by Barclays Bank Limited; copyright © 1964 by Robert E. Symons; reprinted by permission of Holt, Rinehart and Winston, Inc., The Society of Authors as the literary representative of the Estate of A. E. Housman, and Jonathan Cape Ltd.

Ted Hughes: *Wodwo*, copyright © 1961 by Ted Hughes; *Crow*, copyright © 1971 by Ted Hughes; reprinted by permission of Harper & Row, Publishers, Inc., and Faber and Faber Ltd.

Aldous Huxley: "Wordsworth in the Tropics" from *Collected Essays*, copyright 1929, 1957 by Aldous Huxley; reprinted by permission of Harper & Row, Publishers, Inc., Mrs. Laura Huxley, and Chatto and Windus Ltd.

David Jones: *In Parenthesis*, reprinted by permission of Chilmark Press and Faber and Faber Ltd.

James Joyce: *Dubliners*, copyright © 1967 by the Estate of James Joyce; originally published in 1916 by B. W. Huebsch, Inc.; *A Portrait of the Artist as a Young Man*, copyright © 1964 by The Estate of James Joyce; all rights reserved; reprinted by permission of The Viking Press, Inc., the Executors of the James Joyce Estate, and Jonathan Cape Ltd. *Finnegans Wake*, copyright 1939 by James Joyce, © 1967 by George Joyce and Lucia Joyce; reprinted by permission of The Viking Press, Inc., and The Society of Authors as the literary representative of the Estate of James Joyce. *Ulysses*, copyright 1914, 1918 by Margaret Caroline Anderson and renewed 1942, 1946 by Nora Joseph Joyce; reprinted by permission of Random House, Inc., and The Bodley Head.

Rudyard Kipling: "Mary Postgate," copyright 1915 by Rudyard Kipling from *A Diversity of Creatures*; reprinted by permission of Mrs. George Bambridge, Doubleday and Company, Inc., and the Macmillan Companies of London and Canada.

Philip Larkin: *The Less Deceived*, copyright © 1955, 1973 by the Marvell Press; reprinted by permission of The Marvell Press, England.

D. H. Lawrence: "The Prussian Officer" from *The Complete Short Stories of D. H. Lawrence*, reprinted by permission of The Viking Press, Inc., all rights reserved, Laurence Pollinger Ltd., and the Estate of the late Mrs. Frieda Lawrence Ravagli. From *Apocalypse*, copyright 1931 by The Estate of D. H. Lawrence, all rights reserved; reprinted by permission of The Viking Press, Inc., Laurence Pollinger Ltd., and the Estate of the late Mrs. Frieda Lawrence Ravagli. Eleven poems from *The Complete Poems of D. H. Lawrence*, edited by Vivian de Sola Pinto and F. Warren Roberts, copyright © 1964, 1971 by Angelo Ravagli and C. M. Weekley, Executors of The Estate of Frieda Lawrence Ravagli; reprinted by permission of The Viking Press, Inc., Laurence Pollinger

Ltd., and the Estate of the late Mrs. Frieda Lawrence Ravagli. "St. Mawr" from *The Man Who Died*, copyright 1925 and renewed 1953 by Frieda Lawrence Ravagli, reprinted by permission of Alfred A. Knopf, Inc.; and from *The Short Novels of D. H. Lawrence*, reprinted by permission of Laurence Pollinger Ltd., and the Estate of the late Mrs. Frieda Lawrence Ravagli. From *Pornography and Obscenity*, copyright 1930 by Alfred A. Knopf, Inc.; reprinted by permission of the publisher; and from *Phoenix*, reprinted by permission of Laurence Pollinger Ltd., and the Estate of the late Mrs. Frieda Lawrence Ravagli.

Hugh MacDiarmid: *Collected Poems*, copyright © 1948, 1962 by Christopher Murray Grieve; reprinted by permission of The Macmillan Company. *Lucky Poet*, reprinted by permission of Oliver and Boyd Ltd.

Louis MacNeice: *The Collected Poems of Louis MacNeice*, edited by E. R. Dodds, copyright © 1966 by The Estate of Louis MacNeice; reprinted by permission of Oxford University Press, Inc.

Edwin Muir: *Collected Poems, 1921–1958*, copyright © 1960 by Willa Muir; reprinted by permission of Oxford University Press, Inc., and Faber and Faber Ltd.

George Orwell: *The Collected Essays, Journalism and Letters of George Orwell*, Volume 2, copyright © 1968 by Sonia Brownell Orwell; reprinted by permission of Harcourt Brace Jovanovich, Inc., Miss Sonia Brownell, and Secker & Warburg.

Wilfred Owen: *Collected Poems*, copyright 1946, © 1963 by Chatto & Windus, Ltd.; all rights reserved; reprinted by permission of New Directions Publishing Corporation, the Estate of the late Harold Owen, and Chatto & Windus.

Isaac Rosenberg: *Collected Poems*, copyright © 1949 by Schocken Books Inc., reprinted by permission of Schocken Books Inc., the Author's Literary Estate, and Chatto & Windus.

Bernard Shaw: *Saint Joan*, copyright 1924, 1930 by George Bernard Shaw; copyright 1951, 1957 by The Public Trustee as Executor of the Estate of George Bernard Shaw; reprinted by permission of Dodd, Mead & Company, Inc., and the Society of Authors, for the Estate of Bernard Shaw.

Edith Sitwell: *The Collected Poems of Edith Sitwell*, copyright 1954 by Edith Sitwell; reprinted by permission of The Vanguard Press and The Macmillan Company.

Stevie Smith: *Selected Poems*, copyright © 1962 by Stevie Smith and © 1964 by Stevie Smith; reprinted by permission of New Directions Publishing Corporation and Longman Group Limited.

Stephen Spender: *Selected Poems*, poems copyright 1934 (renewed 1962), 1942 by Stephen Spender; reprinted by permission of Random House, Inc., and Faber and Faber Ltd.

Dylan Thomas: *Collected Poems*, copyright 1938, 1939, 1946 by New Directions Publishing Corporation; copyright 1952 by Dylan Thomas; reprinted by permission of New Directions Publishing Corporation, J. M. Dent & Sons Ltd., and the Trustees for the Copyrights of the late Dylan Thomas.

Edward Thomas: *Collected Poems*, reprinted by permission of Mrs. Myfanwy Thomas and Faber and Faber Ltd.

Charles Tomlinson: *The Necklace*, copyright © 1966 by Oxford University Press; reprinted by permission of the publisher.

William Butler Yeats: *Autobiographies*, copyright 1916, 1936 by The Macmillan Company, renewed 1944 by Bertha Georgie Yeats; "Adam's Curse," copyright 1903 by The Macmillan Company, renewed 1931 by William Butler Yeats; "The Two Trees," "The Sorrow of Love," copyright 1906 by The Macmillan Company, renewed 1934 by William Butler Yeats; "No Second Troy," "A Drinking Song," "The Cold Heaven," copyright 1912 by The Macmillan Company, renewed 1940 by Bertha Georgie Yeats; "To A Friend Whose Work Has Come to Nothing," "The Magi," copyright 1916 by The Macmillan Company, renewed 1944 by Bertha Georgie Yeats; "In Memory of Major Robert Gregory," "A Thought from Propertius," "A Deep-Sworn Vow," and "The Scholars," copyright 1919 by The Macmillan Company, renewed 1947 by Bertha Georgie Yeats; "Michael Robartes and the Dancer," "Easter, 1916," "On a Political Prisoner," "The Second Coming," copyright 1924 by The Macmillan Company, renewed 1952 by Bertha Georgie Yeats; "Sailing to Byzantium," "Ancestral Houses," "Two Songs from a Play," "Leda and the Swan," "Among School Children," copyright 1928 by The Macmillan Company, renewed 1956 by Georgie Yeats; "In Memory of Eva Gore-Booth . . . ," "Coole Park, 1929," "Byzantium," "Crazy Jane Talks with the Bishop," "After Long Silence," "A Last Confession," copyright 1933 by The Macmillan Company, renewed 1961 by Bertha Georgie Yeats; "Meru," copyright 1934 by The Macmillan Company, renewed 1962 by Bertha Georgie Yeats; "Lapis Lazuli," "The Statues," "John Kinsella's Lament for Mrs. Mary Moore," "The Circus Animals' Desertion," "Cuchulian Comforted," copyright 1940 by Georgie Yeats, renewed 1968 by Bertha Georgie Yeats, Michael Butler Yeats and Anne Yeats; in *Collected Poems*; reprinted by permission of The Macmillan Company, New York, M. B. Yeats, Macmillan & Co. (London), and The Macmillan Company of Canada.

A selection from *Picture Show* by Siegfried Sassoon is reprinted by permission of G. T. Sassoon.

General Editors' Preface

The purpose of the Oxford Anthology is to provide students with a selective canon of the entire range of English Literature from the beginnings to recent times, with introductory matter and authoritative annotation. Its method is historical, in the broadest sense, and its arrangement, commentary, and notes, both analytic and contextual, have benefited not only from the teaching experience of the several editors, but from a study of the virtues and shortcomings of comparable works. A primary aim has been to avoid the insulation of any one section from the influence of others, and more positively, to allow both student and instructor to come to terms with the manner in which English literature has generated its own history. This aim has been accomplished in several ways.

First, a reorganization of chronological phases has allowed the Tudor and Stuart periods to be unified under the broad heading of the English Renaissance, with two editors collaborating over the whole extended period. Similarly, the nineteenth century has two editors, one for the poetry of the whole period, and one for the prose. This arrangement seemed appropriate in every way, especially since neither of these scholars could be called a narrow specialist in "Romantic" or "Victorian," as these terms are used in semester- or course-labels.

Every contributing editor has worked and taught in at least one period or field outside the one for which he is, in this anthology, principally responsible, and none has ever allowed specialization to reduce his broader commitment to humane studies more largely considered. Thus we were able to plan a work which called for an unusual degree of cross reference and collaboration. During a crucial phase in the preparation of the text, the editors held daily discussions of their work for a period of months. By selection, allusion, comparison, by direction and indirection, we contrived to preserve continuity between epochs, and to illuminate its character. At the same time, the close co-operation of the various editors has precluded the possibility of common surrender to any single dominating literary theory; and the teacher need have no fear that he must prepare to do battle with some critical Hydra showing a head on every page.

The method of selecting text was consistent with these principles. In the eighteenth- and nineteenth-century sections it was our general policy to exclude the novel, for obvious reasons of length; but in the twentieth, where short fiction becomes more prominent and more central, we have included entire works of fiction, or clearly defined parts of them—for example, *Heart of Darkness*, "The Dead," the "Nausicaa" episode of *Ulysses*, and *St. Mawr*. On the other hand we were persuaded, after much reflection, that a different principle must apply in the cases of Spenser and Milton, where we waived the requirement of completeness. To have given the whole of one book—say, the First of *The Faerie Queene*—would have been a solution as easy as it is, no doubt, defensible; but it is asking a great deal of students to see that portion of the poem as an epitome of the rest, which is often so delightfully different; and we decided that we must provide selections from the whole poem, with linking commentary. We did the same for *Paradise Lost* though without abandoning the practice of providing complete texts when this was both possible and desirable; for example, *Comus* is reprinted entire, and so is a lesser-known but still very important masque, Jonson's *Pleasure Reconciled to Virtue*, which is interesting not only in relation to *Comus* but as an illustration of the part poetry can play in political spectacle and—more generally—in the focusing of the moral vision. Minor texts have been chosen for their exemplary force and their beauty, as well as to embody thematic concerns. If the teacher wishes, he or she may work, both within and across periods, with recurrent patterns as large as the conception of the Earthly Paradise, or with sub-genres as small but as fascinating as the Mad Song. It will also be evident from certain patterns of selection—*The Tempest* as the Shakesperean play, the very large amount of Blake, the emphasis given to D. H. Lawrence's poems as well as his fiction—that a genuinely modern taste, rather than an eager modishness, has helped to shape our presentation of the historical canon. It is also hoped that the unusually generous sampling of material in certain sections—notably the Renaissance, eighteenth century, and the Romantics—will allow the teacher to use secondary or minor works, if he so chooses, to highlight these newer concerns or to fill in contextual background.

As for the annotations, the editors have never been afraid to be lively or even speculative. They have consistently tried to avoid usurping the teacher's role, as providing standard or definitive readings might do. On the other hand, the commentary goes beyond merely providing a lowest common denominator of information by suggesting interpretive directions and levels along which the teacher is free to move or not; and of course he always has the freedom to disagree. The editors have been neither prudish nor portentous in their tone, nor have they sought—in the interests of some superficial consistency, but with leaden effect—to efface their personal styles.

Texts have all been based on the best modern editions, which happen quite often to be published by the Oxford University Press. Spelling and punctuation have been modernized throughout, save in three instances: portions of the medieval period, and the texts of Spenser and Blake, two poets whose spelling and punctuation are so far from idiosyncrasies to be silently normalized that they constitute attempts to refashion poetic language. In the medieval section, modern verse translations of *Beowulf* (by C. W. Kennedy) and of *Gawain* (by Brian Stone) have been adopted. Glossaries of literary and historical terms in all periods have been provided, sometimes keyed to the annotations, sometimes supplementing the larger headnotes. These, it will be noticed, seek to illuminate the immediate contexts of the literature of a period rather than to provide a dense précis of its social, political, and economic history. Similarly, the reading lists at the end of each volume are not exhaustive bibliographies; in the happy instance where a teacher finds an extensive bibliography advisable, he or she will want to supply one.

A word about the pictures. They are not to be thought of simply as illustrations, and certainly not as mere decorations, but rather as part of the anthologized material, like the musical examples and the special sections (such as the one on Ovidian mythology in the Renaissance and on the Urban Scene in the eighteenth century). Throughout, the reader is introduced to the relations between poem as speaking picture, and picture as mute poem. Aside from contextual and anecdotal illustration, of which there is indeed a good deal, the pictorial examples allow teachers, or students on their own, to explore some of the interrelations of texts and the visual arts in all periods, whether exemplified in Renaissance emblems or in contemporary illustrations of Victorian poems.

Finally, an inevitable inadequate word of acknowledgment. To the English Department of Dartmouth College the editors are deeply indebted for having so generously and hospitably provided a place in which to work together for a sustained period. The staff of the Dartmouth College Library was extraordinarily helpful and attentive.

All of the editors would like to extend a note of gratitude to the many academics throughout the United States who willingly made suggestions as to what should be included as well as excluded. A special note of thanks to Jim Cox of Dartmouth College and Paul Dolan of the State University of New York at Stony Brook for their challenging and always helpful comments.

And finally to the entire staff of the New York branch of the Oxford University Press who have done more than could be humanly expected in connection with the planning and execution of this book. We would especially like to thank our editor John Wright, as well as Leona Capeless and her staff, Mary Ellen Evans, Patricia Cristol, Joyce Berry, Deborah Zwecher, and Jean Shapiro. An unusual but very deserved note of thanks to the Production people, especially Gerard S. Case and Leslie Phillips and to the designer, Frederick Schneider, whose excellent work speaks for itself.

New York
September 1972

Frank Kermode
John Hollander

BRITISH ISLES

N

Atlantic
Ocean

North Sea

SCOTLAND

Glasgow Clyde Edinburgh

Belfast

IRELAND Shannon

Dublin

Irish Sea

LAKE
DISTRICT YORKSHIRE

Blackpool York
Leeds Hull

Manchester
Liverpool Sheffield

WALES MERCIA

Trent

Nottingham Norwich

Birmingham EAST
ANGLIA

Avon

ENGLAND

Severn Oxford

Thames London

Bristol
Southampton KENT

WESSEX

English Channel

FRANCE

Miles

0   50   100   150

Contents

* An asterisk is used to indicate that a work does not appear in its entirety.

English Literary History in Process, 660

MODERN BRITISH LITERATURE

Modern British Literature

AT THE TURN OF THE CENTURY

When Queen Victoria died in 1901 people found it easy to think that an age had ended, but the Edwardians nevertheless preserved much of their heritage intact. It included the consequences of the great spiritual and intellectual discoveries of the Victorians, and capitalized their material gains. English society was as firmly as ever dominated by class; English wealth was still in a few hands, despite a growing suspicion that it was unfairly gained at the expense of the industrial workers; the British Empire was firm, well serviced, showing some respect for the rights of "lesser breeds without the law"; it was powerfully represented in literature by Kipling. Life, for the rich, was full of possibilities but also of restrictions; the early novels of Galsworthy and E. M. Forster well document the latter. Since the Education Act of 1870 the poor were literate or semi-literate, but they remained poor, and the new cheap papers were preparing them for the age of full democracy and advertising.

The legacy of Darwin, and of the whole complex Victorian loss of Christian faith, grew more troublesome, and so did the different versions of Socialism that had grown up during the century, whether native or Marxist. The Fabian Society, which stood for reformist, not revolutionary, socialism, was an important intellectual focus. The position of women, their lack of freedom and lack of votes, became an urgent question. There was a growing awareness of external threats to England's wealth and security, especially threats emanating from Germany. The Boer War, in the opening years of the century, had something of the effect of the Vietnam War in the American Sixties: the forces of the most powerful country on earth had great difficulty in defeating the small and ill-equipped Boer forces. There was much talk of decadence, and it could be substantiated by pointing to such figures as those which proved a rapid rise in the insanity rate, and those which indicated that half the volunteers for military service in South Africa were unfit. The arts were impeded by prudery and censorship, yet the decade saw the production of some of Shaw's best plays and the publication of the best novels of Conrad. The Irish Yeats had made of the Abbey a great playhouse, and was about to come into his full strength as an artist, while in England the artists of this "tragic generation" were dying.

Edward VII, symbol of the self-indulgence but also of the peace of his period, died in 1910; the war with Germany, which seemed preventable but was not prevented, begin on August 4, 1914. Some would give that as the true date for the ending of the old world; others say 1916, when the better part of a generation of Englishmen died on the Somme. The Great War produced a few good books, and some good resolutions, quickly abandoned. Politically, it broke Europe into pieces and gave rise to the first Communist state.

NEW IDEAS

The first decade of the century saw several crucial developments in the field of ideas, so new and so far-reaching in their implications that we may think the new world was born after all in 1901. In December of the previous year the foundations of quantum theory were laid; in 1905 Einstein published his Special Theory of Relativity. Freud's *Interpretation of Dreams,* in some ways his fundamental work, appeared in 1900, and *The Psychopathology of Everyday Life* in 1901. Edmund Husserl was preparing one revolution in philosophy—a very modern one, involving an entirely new way of considering the relation between the mind and phenomena; and Bertrand Russell was preparing another, in the field of logic, which would also change the whole course of twentieth-century philosophical thought and make possible the further revolutions brought about by Ludwig Wittgenstein.

In the visual arts perhaps the greatest single crisis in the history of the subject—the introduction of Cubism in 1907—preceded by three years the first showing in England of the paintings of its forerunner, Post-Impressionist movement. Changes were pending also in music; the arts were preparing for some huge alteration, some decisive break with the past. Marinetti (1876–1944) issued his Futurist Manifesto in 1909, calling the arts to a recognition of modern technology, speed, noise; demanding the abolition of syntax in poetry and of the representation of movement in painting, as the Russian Futurists demanded the abolition of the past. In Paris Guillaume Apollinaire, publicist of poetry and painting alike, propagated scorn for all that was *passéiste.* In London T. E. Hulme sketched, with Wyndham Lewis and Ezra Pound, a movement called Vortex, which had some of the aims of Futurism; but it was cut off, like its magazine BLAST, by the war, which brought also the death of its most gifted visual artist, Henri Gaudier-Brzeska. With the war at its most terrible stage in 1916, Tristan Tzara and others in neutral Switzerland founded the most radical and influential of all these "abolitionist" movements, and called it "Dada," denying progress, knowledge, morality, the family, logic, memory, the past, all that is not "the immediate product of spontaneity," all that is not "indifferent" in a Buddhist sense, that does not reflect the fact that "everything happens in a completely idiotic way"; and affirming that the emotion we need most of, the Dada emotion, is disgust.

MODERNISM: TOWARD A DEFINITION

There is a danger of making "Modernism" too inclusive; and it must be said that many good writers—some represented in this anthology—were largely unaffected by these turbulences. Nevertheless the "revolution" of the Modern did occur, and we may understand it better if we isolate a few of its recurrent themes. One such theme, obviously, is the demand for an open breach with the past, or even the abolition of the past. This professes to be more than a simple reaction against the art of the preceding generation: it is a whole new thing. Such, at any rate, is the case with such extreme positions as Dada, and others more recent which are sometimes called Neo-Dada. This may be seen—in part at any rate—as a reaction against the crushing weight of an artistic past which cannot be surveyed any longer by any one person, which may be thought tainted by the cruelty and injustice of the civilizations which produced it, or which is simply handed down with the uncritical approval of the establishment. But it is rather more than that; it is the extreme statement of a view which derives from genuine discontinuities discovered in the world, of which the quantum theory is an example. New conceptions of the operations of the human mind were coming to birth; like other instruments, it was beginning to be seen as other than had been supposed, and as having a different relation to objective reality.

The Modern *was* so different from the past that one could fairly easily think it discontinuous with the past. One measure of that difference, more obvious than phenomenology or quantum theory, is technology. The technology of the first decade of the century was much more advanced than might be thought; as Buckminster Fuller says, if you can throw a missile weighing a ton from one platform moving forward at twenty-five miles an hour and also rolling and pitching, and hit another sixteen miles away and moving in a different direction, you have already solved most of the real problems of a moonshot; and this could be done in 1907. Such technology was, whether desirable or not, *modern;* so was the increasingly rapid supersession, especially in weaponry, of one model by another. In some degree the arts imitated the technology—not with the same rapidity of obsolescence that obtains in our time, but one can see it beginning. The New had always played some part in aesthetic appreciation—even classical artists do not exactly repeat the performances of their classical predecessors—but newness now become essential. So the language of the arts changed more and more rapidly in this new age; and to change rapidly, and to abolish the precedents, became a program for artists.

But this is a very partial view of the Modern, because full discontinuity is never achieved by anything that remains recognizably part of the constantly changing language of art; this is true of Cubism and of twelve-tone music as well as of poetry. There is a continuity of languages; and there is also a continuity of ideologies. Baudelaire in the 1850's already spoke of going to the depths of the unknown to find the New. Many of the ideas and techniques of "abolitionism" were invented by Rimbaud in the Seventies. The whole French Symbolist movement underprops Modernism, as Romanticism underprops Symbolism. If you follow the Modern to its roots you go back to the seventeenth century and beyond. Equally, if you believe that reality is not something given, but something imposed on the world by human fictions, you go back to Nietzsche at least, for an authoritative expression of the theory. If you interpret the Modern as that which has the power to make an impressive engagement with the finest minds of your own time, you will find it throughout history, as Matthew Arnold found it in Athens, and others in Byzantine painting, African statues, Dante, or the seventeenth-century poets. The Modern soon acquires a Tradition of its own. It is related to the sense of the artists of the early part of the century that certain apparent laws were merely arbitrary conventions, to be overthrown as the religious and ethical establishment had been overthrown; but this does not and cannot entail a breach with the past, or even with all conventions, unless one can believe in a wholly random art. This situation accounts for the number of different dates given for the birth of Modernism: 1857, Baudelaire's *Les*

Fleurs du mal (Flowers of Evil) and Flaubert's *Madame Bovary;* 1859, Darwin's *Origin of Species,* and so on. As good a date as any, for English literature, would be 1899, the year Arthur Symons's *The Symbolist Movement in France* was published.

This particular Modernism has historical limits, for it may be said to have ended in the middle Twenties. If we look at the great works of those years we will be struck not only by their novelty but also by their respect for the past they had chosen out of all possible pasts. They include the great novels of Joseph Conrad, D. H. Lawrence, E. M. Forster, Ford Madox Ford, and James Joyce, together with much of the best poetry of W. B. Yeats and Ezra Pound. In French literature there was Marcel Proust. In American Gertrude Stein was characteristically more extreme. In the visual arts there were Pablo Picasso, a great ransacker of the past, and Wassily Kandinsky, the theorist of abstraction but no abolitionist; in music Igor Stravinsky was a classicist innovator. As Richard Ellmann and Charles Feidelson, collecting the relevant documents (and going back two centuries to do so) remark: "Modernism strongly implies some sort of historical discontinuity, either a liberation from inherited patterns or, at another extreme, deprivation and disinheritance"; but then they have to add that the "modernists have been as much imbued with a feeling for their historical role, their relation to the past, as with a feeling of historical discontinuity" (*The Modern Tradition,* 1965).

MYTHOLOGY AND PSYCHOLOGY

But there is another recurrent theme, one that involved a return, if not to the past, then to the primitive.

The poets of the Renaissance commanded easily a large syncretic body of myth, which, in combination with the teaching of the church and the whole range of Christian learning, gave them a remarkably rich and flexible body of materials. By the middle of the seventeenth century this had lost elasticity. Truth, identified either with revealed religion or with discoveries of natural science or empirical thinking, was divorced from myth; the epic poets of the 1650's tried to get along without myth, and later poets tended to use it only decoratively. The difference can be measured by looking at Bacon's use of myth at the beginning of the new science, and the handbook *Polymetis* of Joseph Spence (1699–1768), which is a relatively undynamic and decorative handling of the material. Romantic poets rebelled against this; and myth—in various new formulations—came back as the substance of poetry in Blake, Shelley, Keats. The nineteenth century, especially in France, accumulated a great deal of occultist mythological study which was important to poets partly in its own right and partly as an instrument of their fervent anti-rationalism; the great example in English is Yeats. By the turn of the century the need for a mythological repository was strongly felt; and it was supplied in various ways characteristic of a time when much more was known about societies outside Europe, about the ancient world, and above all about the human mind.

There are, broadly speaking, three main sources of modern mythology: exotic societies, classical scholarship, and psychiatry. Cubism, which broke up the conventional European picture surface, owed a debt to African primitive carving, which, at the turn of the century, suddenly became of great interest to eyes which had formerly ignored it or regarded it as simply curious. The primitive quite suddenly became a concern of the civilized, and in a wholly new way. It was also of increasing interest to scholars who sought behind the classical texts the origins of Greek poetry in religion. Of this "Cambridge School of Anthropology" Sir James G. Frazer (1854–1941) had the most powerful effect on literature. His huge composite book *The Golden Bough*—completed in twelve volumes, 1911–15, and abridged in 1922—is important not only because of the use Eliot made of it, but also because it gave a coherent ritual pattern to a huge mass of disparate mythical material. It became, as it were, the *Metamorphoses* of the twentieth century, because it appeared to indicate possibilities of a new commerce between the primitive and the civilized. Further, Frazer seemed to show that the Christian myth of a dying and resurrected god was merely one of an enormous class of such myths, invented everywhere by the primitive mind. So he strengthened the sense that underneath our own skeptical and rationalizing intellects there are remnants of such mythical thinking; that the primitive affects our conduct insofar as it is not, for good or ill, repressed by our civilization; and this, in other hands, became almost the most important single idea of the new century.

Not that it originated then; magicians of the kind cultivated by Yeats and other poets had assumed a primordial shared body of "archetypes" some time before C. G. Jung, with whom we usually associate the idea. Nevertheless, it was in this century that it became important to scientists, namely doctors, and therefore validated for others. Here the key name is Sigmund Freud (1856–1938). Freud quarreled with the Jungian position that in dream and neurosis we re-create or remember the primitive myths and cosmogonies, but he did believe that primitive myth afforded the best explanations for much of our behavior. The antiquity with which we each live is in the first place our own individual, our private childhood; but as that childhood is an abbreviated version of the development of the human race, we are, whether we remember or forget it, behaving in accordance with universal patterns. Here the two theories converge, but that of Freud has been more successful.

Freud elaborated his theory and terminology over many years, and he was not always well understood; but the general proposition that there are hidden layers of the mind which exert an enormous effect on human conduct certainly got through, and has had a profound influence not only on our views of human motive and the operation of the mind but also on the production and interpretation of works of art. In the process such a myth as that of Oedipus becomes a universal explanation of certain aspects of human behavior, both "normal" and "abnormal." Our views of the operation of time are changed, since the id, the deepest instinctual level of our personality, has nothing to do with concepts of time or space. Our views of authority are changed, since our egos (that part of the id which has been modified to deal with the external world and exhibits reason and circumspection) are supervised by a severe super-ego, the agent of external authority and repression. "Goaded on by the id, hemmed in by the super-ego, and rebuffed by reality, the ego struggles to cope with its economic task of reducing the forces and influences which work in it and upon it to some kind of harmony; and we may well understand how it is that we so often cannot repress the cry: 'Life is not easy' " (*New Introductory Lecture on Psychoanalysis,* 1933).

Dreams allow us to sleep by dealing with the problem that arises when the powers that normally repress unwelcome impulses are no longer alert; the "dream-work" entertains and modifies these impulses and makes them acceptable images. They are "censored," they are "condensed" and "displaced"—"dream-distortion" makes them tolerable, but uses means of combining and rendering unintelligible the subjects of the dream that have nothing to do with logic, and can be explained rationally only by a long process of interpretation which will recover the primitive material. The implications of all this, and of Freud's clinical techniques—such as free-association—for literature, are immense. They are not confined to Surrealism—a movement descended partly from Dada and proclaimed in 1924—which is expressly Freudian, seeking truth by the suspension of reason and by making works of art conform to a logic only of dreams. The Freudian movement restored to Modernism in general a confidence in the reasonableness of irrationality, a mistrust of what had formerly seemed the artistic equivalents of logical thinking.

Freud is not the whole story, but he is an index of this important change; he knew that some of his roots were in literature, and that literature (Dostoevsky, for example) also exerted a direct influence on later writers. It is possible that the alogical structure of The Waste Land or of Pound's Cantos, or the "stream-of-consciousness" techniques of Ulysses could not have been achieved without him; though there are the precedents of Symbolism and even earlier works. The point is not to establish Freud's direct influence but his symptomatic quality. In different ways the influence of Freud and other students of the primitive has continued to affect later kinds of Modernism. They provide us with a necessary past but one that is very different from that of the Victorians or any society before them. They have also created for twentieth-century art the possibility of a diversity of theme and treatment never before imaginable, and this is one of the most obvious and least mentioned aspects of the subject. A walk around a gallery that is arranged historically, or a glance at an anthology of twentieth-century literature, or a moment's thought about the varieties of modern philosophy, or indeed theology, will sufficiently confirm that it exists.

SOCIETY AND THE ARTS

Socially the twenties was an age of relaxation following the war. At the level of manners there were changes; the quest for a self-conscious modernity affected even the most trivial aspects of behavior. The implications of the Russian Revolution, and the Fascist revolution in Italy, were naturally of concern. Yet in England there was no profound change. The early twenties saw great industrial unrest, especially in the mines, but the General Strike of 1926 lasted only a few days, and the upper-class fear that the British worker was ripe for revolution was certainly exaggerated. Britain had its first brief spells of Labour Government, frustrated from the outset by economic crises; but the general political tone of the years was set by Stanley Baldwin, the amazingly dull Conservative politician who was Prime Minister, with intervals, from 1924 up to 1937, when Neville Chamberlain began his inglorious administration. Baldwin is associated with Britain's settling down into tranquility; he handled the General Strike; but he could not control the plunge Britain took, with the rest of the world, into the financial crisis, war, unemployment—in short, into the Great Depression. There had been no revolution, but conservatism was not working either.

In the arts, however, there was revolutionary activity. The great years of literary Modernism (anni mirabiles, as the critic R. P. Blackmur called them) were 1922–25. It is important to remember that there is only a negative correlation between this movement and any idea of political revolution. The politics of its leaders was of the right; they saw the world of the modern city and the democratic state with its half-literate population with the same horror that Yeats expressed for it. Indeed, reactionary politics is one important characteristic of the great early Modernists, Pound, Eliot, Wyndham Lewis; and not only Yeats but also D. H. Lawrence was with them in this. Their views were naturally not identical. Yeats believed in an Irish aristocracy to which he himself, in his opinion, belonged, and although he flirted with European dictatorship, the focus of his politics was Ireland. Lawrence talked about the need for aristocracy and a leader, the submission of women and the threat of Jews, but shared almost none of the ideas of Eliot, which in the end crystallized as Tory and Anglo-Catholic, or of Pound, who identified himself with the cause of Italian Fascism, or of Lewis, whose aesthetic was as abhorrent to Lawrence as Lawrence's to him. Still, a strenuous anti-egalitarianism, coupled with a powerful sense that the true politics as well as the true poetic were to be sought *in the past,* formed part of all their attitudes.

One important center of English Modernism, though dissolved by the war of 1914, continued to exert influence later. This was the group which had T. E. Hulme as its philosopher, Wyndham Lewis as its publicist and painter, Pound as its poet, and which developed the aesthetic of Vortex in prewar London. Hulme, who was killed in France in 1917 (b. 1883), was a disciple of Albert Sorel, the philosopher of anti-Liberalism, and of Henri Bergson and Wilhelm Worringer. Hulme's aesthetic, which he thought anti-Romantic, derives from Bergson the notion of an image out of the flux of time (which is, fundamentally, Romantic). From Worringer's *Abstraction and Empathy* he borrowed the idea that periods which place a low value on the individual person and imagine a universe authoritatively ordered, produce an art of "abstraction" (formal, geometric, impersonal), while others, which overvalue the human, an art of "empathy." Archaic Greek art, Byzantine art, exemplify the abstract; the Renaissance and all that has followed it—the decay of dogmatic, ritualistic religion, the rise of individualism and democracy, the history of painting—exemplify empathy. Romanticism—"spilt religion"—Hulme especially abhorred. Out of this mix he produced an extremely influential aesthetic; the art object must be dry, hard, clearly defined, unique, and discontinuous with ordinary space and time. It must lack any facile humanity or "life." Such were the teachings enshrined at first in Imagism—"An 'Image' is that which presents an intellectual and emotional complex in an instant of time" is Pound's definition—and later, in a more dynamic form, in Vorticism. Hulme's essays were published after his death as *Speculations* (1924), and his thought resumed its influential career; but most of his ideas had long been affecting Pound and, through him, Eliot. The presentation of *The Waste Land* (1922) as a non-temporal set of interrelated images owes something therefore to the aesthetic of Hulme. The practical recommendations of Imagism—to avoid sloppy diction and Romantic "feeling," to achieve "the exact curve of the thing" and not a ready-made approximation to it—had an astringent effect on the diction of the new poetry. As Ford Madox Ford liked to say, it should be "at least as well written as prose."

Ford's point was that in the early years of the century, before Imagism, most of the radical thinking about literature had been done in relation to the novel. He was remembering the late Henry James, and his own passionate researches into the novel form, sometimes in collaboration with Conrad. And it is true that if we think of the latest work of James, of Conrad's extraordinary inventions in his great novels of the first decade (e.g. *Nostromo* and *Under Western Eyes*), and of Ford's superb *The Good Soldier* (1916), we must agree that this is where thinking was productively in progress.

Lawrence published *The Rainbow* in 1915 and finished *Women in Love* in 1916, and these works have an originality of form within the native tradition far in excess of anything the poets were achieving. It was only in the twenties that there seemed at last to be a Modernism that belonged to all literature: *Ulysses*, which was well known to Eliot and others long before its publication, and *The Waste Land* appeared in the same year, 1922. Nor was this efflorescence confined to members of a group. Other works, less strikingly novel in manner but original in conception, also belong to these years. They produced some remarkable books: Yeats's *The Trembling of the Veil* (1922), Arnold Bennett's *Riceyman Steps* (1923), Lawrence's *Studies in Classic American Literature* (1923), Ford's *Some Do Not*, Forster's *A Passage to India*, as well as Hulme's *Speculations* and I. A. Richards's *Principles of Literary Criticism* (1924). That year also saw the publication of Thomas Mann's *Magic Mountain*, and André Breton's *Surrealist Manifesto*. 1925 was the year of F. Scott Fitzgerald's *The Great Gatsby*, André Gide's *Counterfeiters*, Franz Kafka's *The Trial*, of Lawrence's *St. Mawr*, Virginia Woolf's *Mrs. Dalloway*, Sean O'Casey's *Juno and the Paycock*, and Pound's first *Cantos*. In these *anni mirabiles* Modern literature as we know it was fully launched. The twenties became one of the epochal moments of literary development; one could list more works by Yeats and Lawrence and Eliot, by Robert Graves and Wyndham Lewis and Pound, by Hart Crane and Robert Musil, Ernest Hemingway, Christopher Isherwood and Evelyn Waugh, Kafka and Virginia Woolf. And the explosion in a sense ended with the Twenties; many of the writers went on writing in their own ways (some had always kept to them), but the sense of a great moment, when literature had as it were caught up with the Modern in the other arts, faded. The Twenties themselves ended with the business slump and the beginning of the age of depression.

THE THIRTIES

Mass unemployment, the rise of the Nazis, rearmament, the threat of war everywhere from Japan to Western Europe, and finally world war, the fall of France, and the battle of Britain: this was the world of the thirties. Something can be learned from the success of Victor Gollancz's Left Book Club, a highly successful operation which circulated cheap editions of left-wing publications to its members, and for which Orwell wrote *The Road to Wigan Pier* (1937). The intelligentsia was, on the whole, moving rapidly leftward. The Depression and the Spanish Civil War, which looked like a straight confrontation between the government of the Left, and the Fascist insurgents, rapidly polarized political opinion. Marxism made some way, but not in terms of political power; England was governed by a government made by coalition between the two chief parties, non-Marxist Labour and Conservative, but mostly Conservative. But reports from Spain, and from the new Germany, sent young men into or near the Communist Party and the campaign for a popular front against Fascism. The group of poets which was for a time dominated by W. H. Auden took this line, though without losing their respect for their Tory seniors such as Eliot, who was also incidentally their publisher. But the moment represented by Auden's *Spain*—a pamphlet poem of 1936 which with poster-like stridency directed everybody's attention to Spain as the center of the world crisis—and by poems about derelict industry and the poor, soon passed; the poets went their own ways, Auden into Christianity, Stephen Spender into editorship and anti-Communism, Louis MacNeice into broadcasting.

The Thirties was not a barren period; but people did go their own ways, and the sense of a politico-poetic movement was soon lost. Waugh, Graham Greene, the remarkable and neglected novelist Henry Green, Ivy Compton-Burnett, Hugh Mac-Diarmid, Isherwood (Catholics, Communists, traditionalists, experimenters) were publishing books; Elizabeth Bowen's *The Death of the Heart,* Greene's *Brighton Rock,* Richard Hughes's *In Hazard,* Isherwood's *Lions and Shadows,* Waugh's *Scoop,* Cyril Connolly's *Enemies of Promise,* Samuel Beckett's *Murphy,* and Orwell's *Homage to Catalonia,* all appeared in one year, 1938. It was certainly not a slump; but it was not a movement.

THE SECOND WORLD WAR AND AFTER

The war years 1939–45 were in one sense marked by a great interest in literature, as indicated by the success of literary magazines and the great demand for books—paper was scarce, huge stocks were destroyed by bombing, and at the time when people most wanted them books were not to be had; nor, though people wanted them also, and there was no shortage of volunteers, were there any very important war poets. The great poetry of the second war is "Little Gidding," written in 1941; there are other poems by Dylan Thomas, for example and other minor poets—Keith Douglas, Sidney Keyes, Alun Lewis—but the terrible experience did not yield poets or poems. A barren movement of Neo-Apocalyptics rose and fell; it was not a time for movements. Thousands recorded their wartime experiences, some competently; few had the time, whether in the service or not, to concentrate on writing. The best novel of the war is Virginia Woolf's *Between the Acts,* a still underestimated masterpiece which came direct out of her reaction to the crisis of 1940 after which she killed herself.

On the condition of post-war English literature a note and examples are found at the end of the book. In spite of the "Movement" of the fifties—which was hardly more than association-by-journalism of a few writers who never pretended to be a school—it does appear that in poetry and the novel English writers have continued to go their own way. The major post-war novelists—we may name Iris Murdoch, Muriel Spark, William Golding, Anthony Powell, and Henry Green, with contributions from Graham Greene, Anthony Burgess, Ivy Compton-Burnett, Joyce Cary, Evelyn Waugh, and Angus Wilson—have very little in common; perhaps if they had, their impact would be greater, our valuation of them higher. The second wave of Modernism, the Neo-Dada of the Sixties, has had little effect. English poets became more conscious of American literature than of French, their traditional source; they grew susceptible to the influence of Wallace Stevens, then of William Carlos Williams, then of Louis Zukofsky and the American Black Mountain school. There has been a strong vogue of spoken poetry, a return to those looser, more allusive or more rhetorical forms deplored by the Movement and especially its best poet, Philip Larkin. A few novelists have tried to learn from the French *nouveau roman,* but this has led to no fierce conflict, no forming of schools, no manifestos. The ferment of modern Paris has no parallel in London. Only in the drama has any sort of Modern movement occurred, partly inspired by Antonin Artaud in France and Bertolt Brecht in Germany, and more directly by Samuel Beckett.

The "new" psychiatry of R. D. Laing, the "new" cultural history of Marshall McLuhan, the "new" anthropology of Claude Lévi-Strauss, have been much discussed in the last few years, but seem to bring about no great change in the literary arts, though music and the visual arts have responded more readily, as they usually do, to the challenge of this new New. The truth is that insofar as Modernism is a matter of concerted programs and manifestos, it hardly exists in contemporary Britain. It can and should be argued that most of the neo-Modernisms—aleatory techniques, concrete poetry, and the rest—are in fact only belated developments of the old. In England, where literary history has never centered itself on a manifesto or a literary line-up of party against party, this seems to be taken for granted. We had Modernism in the twenties, as we had Romanticism at the turn of the eighteenth century; and we are not quite ready for another Copernican revolution. The history of French literature since the war is vastly more involved in creeds and manifestos than British, and modern American literature is certainly more adventurous, readier to realize theory, grasp new thought. In England there is even a feeling that the last Modernism was only a transient import —none of its practitioners were really English anyway. That this view is wrong is clear from the relation between the Tradition and the individual talents outlined above. But meanwhile English literature takes its unpredictable course, depending, as Matthew Arnold complained it did, more on the individual genius than any corporate intellectual and artistic effort. And ours is not the first period in which, with genius in short supply, it has contented itself with a reasonable abundance of scattered talents.

THOMAS HARDY
1840–1928

Thomas Hardy was born in Dorchester, the country town of Dorset, on June 12, 1840. His early education was in the classics and in architecture, and it was as an architect that he left his native Wessex—the name he gave in his fiction to an area of the West Country—for London in 1862. He worked and studied there and published his first novel, *Desperate Remedies*, in 1871. From then on for more than twenty years he produced prose fiction and was recognized as one of the greatest Victorian novelists. Among the major novels are: *Far from the Madding Crowd* (1874), *The Return of the Native* (1878), *The Mayor of Casterbridge* (1887), and *Tess of the D'Urbervilles* (1891). By the time (1896) of the hostile reception of his great, unrelentingly gloomy last novel *Jude the Obscure* (a crafty, stupid woman reviewing it for a New York newspaper called it "Jude the Obscene") he had started to devote himself exclusively to the corpus of over nine hundred poems which occupied the rest of his long creative life.

Hardy's career as a poet lies mainly within the first quarter of the twentieth century, and his qualified and peculiar modernism makes him one of the most problematic of the truly major poets of our age. He had written verse since his middle twenties and had begun to absorb the English Romantic poetic tradition, reading Keats, Shelley, Browning, and later, Swinburne, allowing their worlds to enter an inner landscape of his own. His first book of verse, *Wessex Poems*, was published in 1898; and in 1904, 1906, and 1908, the three parts of *The Dynasts*—a huge, visionary treatment in unperformable dramatic form (deriving from *Prometheus Unbound* more than from actual Greek tragedy) of the Napoleonic Wars, a project toward which Hardy had been working for forty years. *The Dynasts* is one of those works which, like Browning's *The Ring and the Book*, newer fashions of changing response to literary surface and format (a novel in verse; a historical mythology in an unsingable, non musical opera) have caused to be unfairly neglected.

It is in Hardy's short lyrics that his greatness lies, however, and it is just here that he seems such an anomaly in the history of twentieth-century poetry. His poems range widely over so many genres: narratives; dramatic lyrics; imitations of folksong and of regional balladry; brilliant, tough short stories condensed into carefully polished verse; satirical epigrams couched in unexpectedly intricate and seemingly irrelevant stanza forms; starkly personal evocations of sorrow or bitterness; occasional poems celebrating and distrusting local and international events—these and many more defy the challenge of the age to the poetic imagination to produce a *sui generis* mode, a total kind of all-encompassing lyric, approaching the condition of music in its avoidance of exposition, argument, and prosaic truth. Hardy is often expository. His poetic language seems far less experimental than that of a genuinely Victorian poet like Gerard Manley Hopkins; the latter's highly personalized revision of accentual-syllabic meter in his "sprung rhythm," the highly poetic language in which he talked about his formal inventions—these all would be taken by a later age as prophetic marks, or even as those of premature membership in that age.

Hardy's verse is traditional in almost every sense of the word: his experiments are with arrays of forms and patterns, and with the intensifications of language which come from an archaized vocabulary employed in advanced ways. He was much influenced by the Dorchester poet William Barnes (1800–1886), who wrote both in standard English and in the dialect of Dorset. Wessex usage abounds in his poems, but so do Elizabethanisms, biblical echoes, reflections of Latin and Greek and slightly strange coinages out of existing words. Spenser in *The Faerie Queene* had to invent a poetic language, one component of which would be Chaucerian, in order to root his imaginative project in an English, as well as a classical, antiquity; the young Milton deliberately used Spenserian and Shakespearan words; the Elizabethan elements in Keats's vocabulary are mirrored by the Keatsian ones in Tennyson's. This process of classicizing the language of the English poetic past has gone on for centuries, and if T. S. Eliot would find his resonating language in Jacobean English, in Dante's Italian, and in Baudelaire's French, Hardy's tongue was a composite of other sorts. The West Country landscape is full of suggestions of history—many ruins and relics of Roman Britain are there, and the Celtic presence has always been stronger in the western parts of the island toward which Roman and Saxon conquerors drove the native Britons. It is also the country of Hardy's childhood (to which he permanently returned to live in 1883), and it is the world of his novels. In his poems the local landscape, like the unique vocabulary, forms a mediating screen between the interior, private, even autobiographical references and occasions of most of these poems, and the vastly general human rhythms that lie beyond, and around, them.

Many of Hardy's poems were written during, and about, World War I; the profound skepticism which marks the world of his novels and which late Victorian readers, still anxious for their ebbing faith, dismissed as "pessimistic," seems to some readers of today almost benign. It marks many of his poems, particularly the episodic pieces and condensed narratives fixed in a moment of time. It is when the past—a personal one, England's, the planet's—wells up in what Hardy himself calls a "moment of vision," that the poems develop another dimension. And it is in this dimension that their unpredictable, sometimes arbitrary-seeming, use of the intricate verse forms more usually associated with tripping "society-verse," or their constant echoing of the stanzas of church hymns and old songs, becomes most effective. Hardy's short poems are often highly patterned in ways that are immediately apparent: seasonal or daily rhythms will be disposed among stanzas, or the two halves of a poem will embody two opposed principles in a bald and even brutal dialectic; sestet will correct octave in a sonnet like "Hap," where the anti-providential assertion of its conclusion paradoxically has a strong Miltonic resonance. Old forms of verse provide Hardy with old tunes on which to brood, and with schematic patterns upon which to drape those ironies whose patterns are not contrived (the poet will always insist), but are the work of some great Neatener who keeps making life look so much, so much like tragic art.

Hap°

If but some vengeful god would call to me
From up the sky, and laugh: 'Thou suffering thing,
Know that thy sorrow is my ecstasy,
That thy love's loss is my hate's profiting!'

Hap chance (the title of the poem in Hardy's manuscript), thought of as the guiding principle, or the substitute for one, of Darwin's "natural selection." Unlike Tennyson in *In Memoriam*, Hardy accepts it and contemplates its ironies.

Then would I bear it, clench myself, and die,
Steeled by the sense of ire unmerited;
Half-eased in that a Powerfuller than I
Had willed and meted me the tears I shed.

But not so. How arrives it joy lies slain,
And why unblooms the best hope ever sown?
—Crass Casualty° obstructs the sun and rain,
And dicing Time for gladness casts a moan. . . .
These purblind Doomsters had as readily strown
Blisses about my pilgrimage as pain.
1866   1898

Neutral Tones°

We stood by a pond that winter day,
And the sun was white, as though chidden of God,
And a few leaves lay on the starving sod;
    —They had fallen from an ash, and were grey.

Your eyes on me were as eyes that rove
Over tedious riddles of years ago;
And some words played between us to and fro
    On which lost the more by our love.

The smile on your mouth was the deadest thing
Alive enough to have strength to die;
And a grin of bitterness swept thereby
    Like an ominous bird a-wing. . . .

Since then, keen lessons that love deceives,
And wrings with wrong, have shaped to me
Your face, and the God-curst sun, and a tree,
    And a pond edged with greyish leaves.
1867   1898

The Subalterns°

I

'Poor wanderer,' said the leaden sky,
    'I fain would lighten thee,

Crass Casualty unthinking, or insensible (not coarse or brutal) contingency or circumstance; along with "dicing Time," the "Doomsters" whose carelessness is even less consoling to consider than a malicious, but at least purposeful, demonic deity might be.
Neutral Tones not the grays of photography, but of etching or wood engraving. The scene of souring love drains everything of color, and even the green ash leaves are ashen as well, as the tree's name, in the poem, takes on a new significance.
The Subalterns "Subalterns" (accent on *sub*) are junior officers (lieutenants); here, various types of force upon which human misery can be blamed, all profess to be acting under orders, from general earth, or fallen nature (as a Christian would see it), or reality. Hardy might have spoken of earth, itself subject to Will. Note the ironic use of the common meter of hymns here.

But there are laws in force on high
Which say it must not be.'

II
—'I would not freeze thee, shorn one,' cried
The North, 'knew I but how
To warm my breath, to slack my stride;
But I am ruled as thou.'

III
—'To-morrow I attack thee, wight,'°
Said Sickness. 'Yet I swear
I bear thy little ark no spite,
But am bid enter there.'

IV
—'Come hither, Son,' I heard Death say;
'I did not will a grave
Should end thy pilgrimage to-day,
But I, too, am a slave!'

V
We smiled upon each other then,
And life to me had less
Of that fell look it wore ere when
They owned their passiveness.
                    1902

The Darkling Thrush°

I leant upon a coppice gate°
    When Frost was spectre-grey,
And Winter's dregs made desolate
    The weakening eye of day.
The tangled bine-stems scored the sky
    Like strings of broken lyres.
And all mankind that haunted nigh
    Had sought their household fires.

wight archaic for "person"
The Darkling Thrush originally entitled "By the Century's Death-bed," published before the date of December 31, 1900, affixed to the final version. This is a secular ode, a celebration of the onset of a 20th century which can bring no cause for rejoicing, save for the cylic moment itself, the continuance of nature which cannot, eventually, go uncelebrated. "Darkling" is a word derived through Keats from Milton ("Ode to a Nightingale"; *Paradise Lost* III. 39), who both used it for their nightingale myths, singing out of the darkness and thereby releasing a kind of light. In "Dover Beach" Matthew Arnold uses it simply to mean "darkened." Here, the scruffy, unprepossessing thrush is a version of the poetic nightbird, but a demythologized one.
coppice gate gate to a copse, or wooded grove

The land's sharp features seemed to be
        The Century's corpse outleant,
His crypt the cloudy canopy,
        The wind his death-lament.
The ancient pulse of germ and birth
        Was shrunken hard and dry,
And every spirit upon earth
        Seemed fervourless as I.

At once a voice arose among
        The bleak twigs overhead
In a full-hearted evensong
        Of joy illimited;
An agèd thrush, frail, gaunt, and small,
        In blast-beruffled plume,
Had chosen thus to fling his soul
        Upon the growing gloom.

So little cause for carolings
        Of such ecstatic sound
Was written on terrestrial things
        Afar or nigh around,
That I could think there trembled through
        His happy good-night air
Some blessèd Hope, whereof he knew
        And I was unaware.
        1900   1902

In Tenebris° (I)

'Percussus sum sicut foenum, et aruit cor meum.'—
                                        Ps. ci

        Wintertime nighs;
But my bereavement-pain
It cannot bring again:
        Twice no one dies.

        Flower-petals flee;
But, since it once hath been,
No more that severing scene
        Can harrow me.

        Birds faint in dread:
I shall not lose old strength
In the lone frost's black length:
        Strength long since fled!

In Tenebris "In Darkness"; one of three poems originally entitled "De Profundis" ("out of the depths"). The epigraph is from the Vulgate

Bible: "I am smitten like dry grass, and my heart is dry" (in the King James version, Psalms 102:4).

Leaves freeze to dun;
But friends can not turn cold
This season as of old
    For him with none.

Tempests may scath;
But love can not make smart
Again this year his heart
20   Who no heart hath.

Black is night's cope;°
But death will not appal
One who, past doubtings all,
    Waits in unhope.
1896   1902

In Tenebris (III)

'Heu mihi, quia incolatus meus prolongatus est! Habitavi cum habitantibus
Cedar; multum incola fuit anima mea.'°—
                    Ps. cxix.

There have been times when I well might have passed and the ending have
    come—
Points in my path when the dark might have stolen on me, artless, unrueing—
Ere I had learnt that the world was a welter of futile doing:
Such had been times when I well might have passed, and the ending have come!
Say, on the noon when the half-sunny hours told that April was nigh,
And I upgathered and cast forth the snow from the crocus-border,
Fashioned and furbished the soil into a summer-seeming order,
Glowing in gladsome faith that I quickened the year thereby.
Or on that loneliest of eves when afar and benighted we stood,
10 She who upheld me and I, in the midmost of Egdon° together,
Confident I in her watching and ward through the blackening heather,
Deeming her matchless in might and with measureless scope endued.
Or on that winter-wild night when, reclined by the chimney-nook quoin,°
Slowly a drowse overgat me, the smallest and feeblest of folk there,
Weak from my baptism of pain; when at times and anon I awoke there—
Heard of a world wheeling on, with no listing or longing to join.
Even then! while unweeting that vision could vex or that knowledge could numb,
That sweets to the mouth in the belly are bitter, and tart, and untoward,°
Then, on some dim-coloured scene should my briefly raised curtain have lowered,
20 Then might the Voice that is law have said 'Cease!' and the ending have come.
1896   1902

cope ecclesiastical cape
Heu . . . mea "Woe to me that my habitation
is prolonged! I have dwelt with the dwellers of
Cedar; my soul has been a longtime inhabitant"
from the Vulgate Bible (Psalms 120:5–6 of
the King James version).
Egdon "Egdon Heath" is the fictional name,
in Hardy's novels, for a whole area of rolling

land, wild and sparse, in Dorset (described
with power in the first chapter of *The Return
of the Native*).
quoin exterior corner
That sweets . . . untoward See Revelation
10:9–10; what was sweet to eat once was the
books, read with hope when he was young.

The Schreckhorn°

(With thoughts of Leslie Stephen)

(June 1897)
Aloof, as if a thing of mood and whim;
Now that its spare and desolate figure gleams
Upon my nearing vision, less it seems
A looming Alp-height than a guise of him
Who scaled its horn with ventured life and limb,
Drawn on by vague imaginings, maybe,
Of semblance to his personality
In its quaint glooms, keen lights, and rugged trim.
At his last change, when Life's dull coils unwind,
Will he, in old love, hitherward escape,
And the eternal essence of his mind
Enter this silent adamantine shape,
And his low voicing haunt its slipping snows
When dawn that calls the climber dyes them rose?

1906

From The Dynasts°

[Chorus on the Eve of Waterloo]
>   Fires begin to shine up from the English bivouacs. Camp
> kettles are slung, and the men pile arms and stand
> round the blaze to dry themselves. The French opposite
> lie down like dead men in the dripping green wheat and
> rye, without supper and without fire.
>   By and by the English army also lies down, the men
> huddling together on the ploughed mud in their wet
> blankets, while some sleep sitting round the dying fires.

Chorus of the Years (aerial music)
The eyelids of eve fall together at last,
And the forms so foreign to plain and tree
Lie down as though native, and slumber fast!

Chorus of the Pities
Sore are the thrills of misgiving we see
In the artless champaign at this harlequinade,
Distracting a vigil where calm should be!

Schreckhorn A 13,000-foot peak in the Swiss Alps, first climbed by Leslie Stephen (1832–1904), ex-clergyman, writer, and editor whose more famous daughter was Virginia Woolf. The poem was written after Stephen's death, the date on the epigraph recording Hardy's moment of vision while visiting the environs of the mountain, a reduced and particularized version of Shelley's perception of the interaction of mind and object in "Mont Blanc."

The Dynasts This selection is from Pt. III, vi, 8. In The Dynasts, a visionary pageantry covers all of Europe, and the characters are historical ones, save for various Spirits, whose expository and lyrical comments interpret the significance of the Napoleonic wars on a cosmic scale, particularly as the manifestations of an Immanent Will. The Spirits of the Years are a kind of voice of reason, and those of the Pities, of human sympathy.

The trees seem opprest, and the Plain afraid
Of a Something to come, whereof these are the proofs,—
Neither earthquake, nor storm, nor eclipse's shade!

    Chorus of the Years
Yea, the coneys° are scared by the thud of hoofs,
And their white scuts flash at their vanishing heels,
And swallows abandon the hamlet-roofs.

The mole's tunnelled chambers are crushed by wheels,
The lark's eggs scattered, their owners fled,
And the hare's hid litter the sapper unseals.

The snail draws in at the terrible tread,
But in vain; he is crushed by the felloe-rim;°
The worm asks what can be overhead,

And wriggles deep from a scene so grim,
And guesses him safe; for he does not know
What a foul red flood will soak down to him!

Beaten about by the heel and the toe
Are butterflies, sick of the day's long rheum,
To die of a worse than the weather-foe.

Trodden and bruised to a miry tomb
Are ears that have greened but will never be gold,
And flowers in the bud that will never bloom.

    Chorus of the Pities
So the season's intent, ere its fruit unfold,
Is frustrate, and mangled, and made succumb,°
Like a youth of promise struck stark and cold! . . .

And what of these who to-night have come?

    Chorus of the Years
The young sleep sound; but the weather awakes
In the veteran, pains from the past that numb;

Old stabs of Ind., old Peninsular aches,
Old Friedland chills, haunt his moist mud bed,
Cramps from Austerlitz; till his slumber breaks.

    Chorus of Sinister Spirits
And each soul shivers as sinks his head
On the loam he's to lease with the other dead
From to-morrow's mist-fall till Time be sped!

    The fires of the English go out, and silence prevails, save for the soft hiss of the rain that falls impartially on both the sleeping armies.
(1882–1908)   1908

coneys rabbits
felloe-rim wheel rim

succumb used adjectivally; "dead" (or elliptically, "made to succumb")

The Convergence of the Twain

(Lines on the loss of the 'Titanic'°)

I

In a solitude of the sea
Deep from human vanity,
And the Pride of Life that planned her, stilly couches she.

II

Steel chambers, late the pyres
Of her salamandrine° fires,
Cold currents thrid,° and turn to rhythmic tidal lyres.

III

Over the mirrors meant
To glass the opulent
The sea-worm crawls—grotesque, slimed, dumb, indifferent.

IV

Jewels in joy designed
To ravish the sensuous mind
Lie lightless, all their sparkles bleared and black and blind.

V

Dim moon-eyed fishes near
Gaze at the gilded gear
And query: 'What does this vaingloriousness down here?' . . .

VI

Well: while was fashioning
This creature of cleaving wing,
The Immanent Will that stirs and urges everything

VII

Prepared a sinister mate
For her—so gaily great—
A Shape of Ice, for the time far and dissociate.

VIII

And as the smart ship grew
In stature, grace, and hue,
In shadowy silent distance grew the Iceberg too.

'Titanic' the famous luxury liner, touted as unsinkable, which hit an iceberg and sank on her maiden voyage, with more than 1500 persons aboard (fewer than half of that number were rescued) on April 15, 1912

salamandrine "Salamanders" were mythical dragon-like spirits that inhabited flames.
thrid threaded themselves among

IX
Alien they seemed to be:
No mortal eye could see
The intimate welding of their later history.

X
Or sign that they were bent
By paths coincident
30   On being anon twin halves of one august event,

XI
Till the Spinner of the Years
Said 'Now!' And each one hears,
And consummation comes, and jars two hemispheres.
(1912)   1912

Wessex Heights

There are some heights in Wessex, shaped as if by a kindly hand
For thinking, dreaming, dying on, and at crises when I stand,
Say, on Ingpen Beacon° eastward, or on Wylls-Neck westwardly,
I seem where I was before my birth, and after death may be.

In the lowlands I have no comrade, not even the lone man's friend—
Her who suffereth long and is kind; accepts what he is too weak to mend:
Down there they are dubious and askance; there nobody thinks as I,
But mind-chains do not clank where one's next neighbour is the sky.

In the towns I am tracked by phantoms having weird detective ways—
Shadows of beings who fellowed with myself of earlier days:
They hang about at places, and they say harsh heavy things—
Men with a wintry sneer, and women with tart disparagings.

Down there I seem to be false to myself, my simple self that was,
And is not now, and I see him watching, wondering what crass cause
Can have merged him into such a strange continuator as this,
Who yet has something in common with himself, my chrysalis.°

I cannot go to the great grey Plain;° there's a figure against the moon,
Nobody sees it but I, and it makes my breast beat out of tune;
I cannot go to the tall-spired town,° being barred by the forms now passed
For everybody but me, in whose long vision they stand there fast.

There's a ghost at Yell'ham Bottom chiding loud at the fall of the night,
There's a ghost in Froom-side Vale, thin lipped and vague, in a shroud of white,

Ingpen Beacon All the high places named in
the poem are in Hardy's Wessex—in Wiltshire,
Hampshire, Dorset, Somerset—associated with
high moments in youth.
chrysalis The cocoon-spinning stage of meta-
morphosis, whose "continuator" he is. Avoiding
the ghosts of his women, he meets those of
himself.
Plain possibly Salisbury Plain; possibly Egdon
Heath
town Salisbury, with its great, tall, cathedral
spire

There is one in the railway train whenever I do not want it near,
I see its profile against the pane, saying what I would not hear.

As for one rare fair woman, I am now but a thought of hers,
I enter her mind and another thought succeeds me that she prefers;
Yet my love for her in its fulness she herself even did not know;
Well, time cures hearts of tenderness, and now I can let her go.

So I am found on Ingpen Beacon, or on Wylls-Neck to the west,
Or else on homely Bulbarrow, or little Pilsdon Crest,
Where men have never cared to haunt, nor women have walked with me,
And ghosts then keep their distance; and I know some liberty.
1896   1914

'I Found Her Out There'°

I found her out there
On a slope few see,
That falls westwardly
To the salt-edged air,
Where the ocean breaks
On the purple strand,
And the hurricane shakes
The solid land.

I brought her here,
And have laid her to rest
In a noiseless nest
No sea beats near.
She will never be stirred
In her loamy cell
By the waves long heard
And loved so well.

So she does not sleep
By those haunted heights
The Atlantic smites
And the blind gales sweep,
Whence she often would gaze
At Dundagel's famed head,°
While the dipping blaze
Dyed her face fire-red;

'I Found Her Out There' This and the following poem are part of the group, published in *Poems of 1912–13*, which confronts the sudden death, in November 1912, of Hardy's first wife, Emma Gifford; here, as in many other poems, he remembers visiting her in her native Cornwall in 1870. The epigraph to the whole group of poems is the Virgilian *Veteris vestigia flammae*: "relics of the old flames" (*Aeneid* IV.23). **Dundagel's . . . head** Tintagel Head, site of the ruins today called King Arthur's Castle; Arthur is supposed to have been born there.

And would sigh at the tale
Of sunk Lyonnesse,°
As a wind-tugged tress
Flapped her cheek like a flail;
Or listen at whiles
30 With a thought-bound brow
To the murmuring miles
She is far from now.

Yet her shade, maybe,
Will creep underground
Till it catch the sound
Of that western sea

As it swells and sobs
Where she once domiciled,
And joy in its throbs
40 With the heart of a child.
    1912   1912

The Voice°

Woman much missed, how you call to me, call to me,
Saying that now you are not as you were
When you had changed from the one who was all to me,
But as at first, when our day was fair.

Can it be you that I hear? Let me view you, then,
Standing as when I drew near to the town
Where you would wait for me: yes, as I knew you then,
Even to the original air-blue gown!

Or is it only the breeze, in its listlessness
10 Travelling across the wet mead° to me here,
Your being ever dissolved to wan wistlessness,°
Heard no more again far and near?

    Thus I; faltering forward,
    Leaves around me falling,
Wind oozing thin through the thorn from norward,°
    And the woman calling.
            1913

sunk Lyonnesse A local Cornish tradition has
it that the southern coast was once Arthur's
Lyonnesse; all the losses in this poem, Emma's
lost childhood of myth, that western sea remembered from further inland, seem to center on
this historical missing past.
The Voice again, a memory of an 1870 meeting
with Emma Gifford, the dactyllic lines and

triple rhymes deliberately evoking old songs
mead meadow
wistlessness heedlessness
norward northward; the north wind blows death.
Notice the return, in the penultimate line of
the poem, to the jingly rhythm of the first
eight, after the rhythmic hardening just before.

Channel Firing

That night your great guns, unawares,
Shook all our coffins as we lay,°
And broke the chancel window-squares,
We thought it was the Judgment-day

And sat upright. While drearisome
Arose the howl of wakened hounds:
The mouse let fall the altar-crumb,
The worms drew back into the mounds,

The glebe° cow drooled. Till God called, 'No;
It's gunnery practice out at sea
Just as before you went below;
The world is as it used to be:

All nations striving strong to make
Red war yet redder. Mad as hatters
They do no more for Christés sake
Than you who are helpless in such matters.

That this is not the judgment-hour
For some of them's a blessed thing,
For if it were they'd have to scour
Hell's floor for so much threatening. . . .

Ha, ha. It will be warmer when
I blow the trumpet if indeed
I ever do; for you are men,
And rest eternal sorely need).'

So down we lay again. 'I wonder,
Will the world ever saner be,'
Said one, 'than when He sent us under
In our indifferent century!'

And many a skeleton shook his head.
'Instead of preaching forty year,'
My neighbour Parson Thirdly said,
'I wish I had stuck to pipes and beer.'

Again the guns disturbed the hour,
Roaring their readiness to avenge,
As far inland as Stourton Tower,
And Camelot, and starlit Stonehenge.°

April 1914   1914

---

we lay The narrator is a corpse, "wakened from the dead," as the saying goes, by the English warships' gunnery practice in the English Channel.
glebe a parson's field
Stourton . . . Stonehenge The resonances of warfare over the Channel reach a tower commemorating Alfred the Great's repulsion of a Danish invasion (879), King Arthur's Camelot (thought to be in or near Glastonbury), and finally, the earlier, pre-Celtic, mysterious Stonehenge.

The Oxen°

Christmas Eve, and twelve of the clock.
  'Now they are all on their knees,'
An elder said as we sat in a flock
  By the embers in hearthside ease.

We pictured the meek mild creatures where
  They dwelt in their strawy pen,
Nor did it occur to one of us there
  To doubt they were kneeling then.

So fair a fancy few would weave
  In these years! Yet, I feel,
If someone said on Christmas Eve,
  'Come; see the oxen kneel,

In the lonely barton° by yonder coomb°
  Our childhood used to know,'
I should go with him in the gloom,
  Hoping it might be so.
    1915   1915

During Wind and Rain°

    They sing their dearest songs—
    He, she, all of them—yea,
    Treble and tenor and bass,
      And one to play;°
    With the candles mooning each face. . .
      Ah, no; the years O!
How the sick leaves reel down in throngs!

    They clear the creeping moss—
    Elders and juniors—aye,
    Making the pathways neat
      And the garden gay;
    And they build a shady seat. . . .
      Ah, no; the years, the years;
See, the white storm-birds wing across!

    They are blithely breakfasting all--
    Men and maidens—yea,
    Under the summer tree,
      With a glimpse of the bay,

The Oxen invoking an old legend that oxen will kneel in their stables at midnight on Christmas Eve
barton farmyard
coomb valley
During Wind and Rain a bleak, contemplative November, a miserable human season intruding in the last two lines of each stanza, the beginning of which will present, in turn, a natural and social cycle from winter to autumn
play the piano (this is family music indoors)

While pet fowl come to the knee. . . .
    Ah, no; the years O!
And the rotten rose is ript from the wall.

They change to a high new house,
He, she, all of them—aye,
Clocks and carpets and chairs
    On the lawn all day,
And brightest things that are theirs. . . .
    Ah, no; the years, the years;
Down their carved names the rain-drop ploughs.
                        1917

In Time of 'The Breaking of Nations'°

I
Only a man harrowing clods
    In a slow silent walk
With an old horse that stumbles and nods
    Half asleep as they stalk.

II
Only thin smoke without flame
    From the heaps of couch-grass;
Yet this will go onward the same
    Though Dynasties pass.

III
Yonder a maid and her wight°
    Come whispering by:
War's annals will fade into night
    Ere their story die.
    1915   1916

Moments of Vision

    That mirror
Which makes of men a transparency,
    Who holds that mirror
And bids us such a breast-bare spectacle see
    Of you and me?

    That mirror
Whose magic penetrates like a dart,

In Time of . . . Nations "Thou art my battle axe and weapons of war: for with thee will I break in pieces the nations, and with thee will I destroy kingdoms" (Jeremiah 51:20); a poem of World War I, based on a memory of a moment in 1870, during the Franco-Prussian War
wight man

Who lifts that mirror
And throws our mind back on us, and our heart,
10   Until we start?

That mirror
Works well in these night hours of ache;
Why in that mirror
Are tincts° we never see ourselves once take
When the world is awake?

That mirror
Can test each mortal when unaware;
Yea, that strange mirror
May catch his last thoughts, whole life foul or fair,
20   Glassing° it—where?

Afterwards°

When the Present has latched its postern° behind my tremulous stay,
And the May month flaps its glad green leaves like wings,
Delicate-filmed as new-spun silk, will the neighbours say,
'He was a man who used to notice such things'?

If it be in the dusk when, like an eyelid's soundless blink,
The dewfall-hawk comes crossing the shades to alight
Upon the wind-warped upland thorn, a gazer may think,
'To him this must have been a familiar sight.'

If I pass during some nocturnal blackness, mothy and warm,
10   When the hedgehog travels furtively over the lawn,
One may say, 'He strove that such innocent creatures should come to no harm,
But he could do little for them; and now he is gone.'

If, when hearing that I have been stilled at last, they stand at the door,
Watching the full-starred heavens that winter sees,
Will this thought rise on those who will meet my face no more,
'He was one who had an eye for such mysteries'?

And will any say when my bell of quittance° is heard in the gloom,
And a crossing breeze cuts a pause in its outrollings,
Till they rise again, as they were a new bell's boom,
20   'He hears it not now, but used to notice such things?'
1917   1917

tincts shades of color
Glassing mirroring
Afterwards written as a closing poem for the

volume entitled *Moments of Vision* (1917)
postern a backyard gate
quittance departure

'And There Was a Great Calm'°

(On the Signing of the Armistice, Nov. 11, 1918)

I

There had been years of Passion—scorching, cold,
And much Despair, and Anger heaving high,
Care whitely watching, Sorrows manifold,
Among the young, among the weak and old,
And the pensive Spirit of Pity whispered, 'Why?'

II

Men had not paused to answer. Foes distraught
Pierced the thinned peoples in a brute-like blindness,
Philosophies that sages long had taught,
And Selflessness, were as an unknown thought,
And 'Hell!' and 'Shell!' were yapped at Lovingkindness.

III

The feeble folk at home had grown full-used
To 'dug-outs,' 'snipers,' 'Huns,' from the war-adept
In the mornings heard, and at evetides perused;
To day-dreamt men in millions, when they mused—
To nightmare-men in millions when they slept.

IV

Waking to wish existence timeless, null,
Sirius° they watched above where armies fell;
He seemed to check his flapping when, in the lull
Of night a boom came thencewise, like the dull
Plunge of a stone dropped into some deep well.

V

So, when old hopes that earth was bettering slowly
Were dead and damned, there sounded 'War is done!'
One morrow. Said the bereft, and meek, and lowly,
'Will men some day be given to grace? yea, wholly,
And in good sooth, as our dreams used to run?'

VI

Breathless they paused. Out there men raised their glance
To where had stood those poplars lank and lopped,
As they had raised it through the four years' dance
Of Death in the now familiar flats of France;
And murmured, 'Strange, this! How? All firing stopped?'

Great Calm "And he arose and rebuked the wind, and said unto the sea, Peace, be still. And the wind ceased, and there was a great calm" (Matthew 8:26).

Sirius the Dog Star, rising after Orion, early on late-autumn evenings

VII

Aye; all was hushed. The about-to-fire fired not,
The aimed-at moved away in trance-lipped song,
One checkless regiment slung a clinching shot
And turned. The Spirit of Irony smirked out, 'What?
Spoil peradventures° woven of Rage and Wrong?'

VIII

Thenceforth no flying fires inflamed the grey,
No hurtlings shook the dewdrop from the thorn,
No moan perplexed the mute bird on the spray;
Worn horses mused: 'We are not whipped to-day';
40   No weft-winged engines blurred the moon's thin horn.

IX

Calm fell. From Heaven distilled a clemency;
There was peace on earth, and silence in the sky;
Some could, some could not, shake off misery:
The Sinister Spirit sneered: 'It had to be!'
And again the Spirit of Pity whispered, 'Why?'
1920   1920

Snow in the Suburbs

Every branch big with it,
Bent every twig with it;
Every fork like a white web-foot;
Every street and pavement mute;
Some flakes have lost their way, and grope back upward, when
Meeting those meandering down they turn and descend again.
The palings are glued together like a wall,
And there is no waft of wind with the fleecy fall.

A sparrow enters the tree,
10   Whereon immediately
A snow-lump thrice his own slight size
Descends on him and showers his head and eyes,
And overturns him,
And near inurns him,
And lights on a nether twig, when its brush
Starts off a volley of other lodging lumps with a rush.

The steps are a blanched slope,
Up which, with feeble hope,
A black cat comes, wide-eyed and thin;
And we take him in.
1925

peradventures used in an archaic sense: per-
haps-es, what might have been

GEORGE BERNARD SHAW

1856–1950

The twentieth century is now old enough so that the brightness of some who had looked to be its eternal sages has somewhat paled. Shaw was one of the great Irish writers—Wilde, Yeats, Joyce, and perhaps Samuel Beckett being the others—who contributed so much to English wisdom, vision, and eloquence in the first half of the century, and for young people growing up after World War I, he was for many decades a kind of absentee schoolmaster. His plays, the prefaces to them, and some of his writing on music and theater were for a whole intellectual generation part of an introduction both to the life of the mind and to a vision of what civilization might possibly be said to mean. His kind of wit, and his approach to dialectic may have receded from a position of what looked to be moral centrality into a more totally stagey existence, but it remains true that, short of the imminence of apocalypse, he had something to teach the old and the young about each other.

Shaw left his native Dublin, as he wrote, "at the age of twenty; and forty years later [I] have learned from the books of Mr. Joyce that Dublin is still what it was, and young men are still drivelling in slackjawed blackguardism just as they were in 1870." Shaw's mother was a singer—his early education was more musical than literary—and she went with her children to study in London. There, Shaw read widely in the British Museum, tried unsuccessfully for many years to make himself into a novelist, and did some reviewing—his musical criticism published under the pseudonym of Corno di Bassetto remains some of the finest writing on musical performance that we possess. It was not until 1893 that the first of his plays, *Widowers' Houses,* was published, two years after his long, programmatic study *The Quintessence of Ibsenism* had appeared in its first form.

For the next thirty years, his plays and tracts appeared with great frequency, the former purportedly being written in aid of, and to publicize and explicate, the latter. One of the founders of the Fabian Society, with Beatrice and Sidney Webb, in 1884, Shaw was committed to evolutionary socialism brought about by legal and democratic means, to the right sort of rationalistic education, and to both the liberation of women and the liberation of men from unliberated females. His political views, in short, remained a not unpleasant amalgam of John Stuart Mill, William Morris (whom he knew personally), and a residue of Romantic hopefulness. Shaw's moral vision was more revolutionary: he was a Nietzschean, and a champion of Wagner when that still meant taking a moral as well as an aesthetic stance. In *The Perfect Wagnerite* of 1898 he gives a Marxist reading of the significance of *The Ring of the Niebelungs,* too reductive to be totally serious, too brilliant to be totally frivolous. Yet he was more concerned with the continuing operation of Will in the individual and collective psyche than with any Marxist Historical Process in the individual and collective action. Suspended somewhere between describing the world (to use the terms by which Marx had criticized philosophy for its historical inertness) and changing it, Shaw became in his major plays a unique kind of satirical explainer, his secular sermonizing and aphoristic mode deriving in some measure from Samuel Butler, and occasionally resembling Oscar Wilde's.

It is not merely that the sorts of hero and heroine Shaw invented were refreshing combinations of candor, ironic perception, and energy—Ibsenian figures of Resolution but less crippled by a slightly more southern moral climate and not totally humorless.

That Shaw should turn to the London stage of Sir Arthur Wing Pinero and Arthur Henry Jones, manipulators of the surface of stagecraft, and to the realm of the so-called "well-made play" was strange enough: his perception of the dramatic, after all, could be typified by Mozart's *Don Giovanni*, a cult masterpiece of the romantic tradition, and by Wagner's *Ring* cycle. But starting with his *Plays Pleasant and Unpleasant* (1898), he evolved a use of stage comedy as a framework for the demonstration of ideas in the only kind of action ideas can have—the dialectic of confrontation, revision, and self-criticism of a position. At the same time, his dramatic types—handsome, candid girls, clever older men, industrialists who turn out to be more revolutionary and humane than the would-be redistributors of their wealth, working-class snobs, and in general, open minds where the open mind in his audience would expect closed ones—began to take shape, and to lend form in turn to a kind of comedy all their own. Just as the action in major opera may truly be said to be taking place in the music itself, so, in one tradition of English stage comedy, the action is in the language. From Ben Jonson's *Epicoene*, through Congreve and Sheridan to Oscar Wilde and Shaw (and, ultimately, to Samuel Beckett), there stretches a line of drama in which the forward motion consists not in the unrolling of plot (which is often virtually held in contempt) but in a far less mechanical operation of the spirit of discourse. One sits on the edge of one's seat, as a member of the audience of such theater, waiting to hear what will be said next, in response to what has just been uttered. In Wilde, such dialogue is often made of a succession of aphorisms; in Shaw, character and argument are always intertwined.

In his earlier plays, he was intent on revealing the flaws, hypocrisies, traps, inner horrors, and ailments of society in the way a true Ibsenite should: prostitution was not evil for official Christian reasons, nor even only because its practitioners were largely wretched, but because their misery was so hugely profitable to proper entrepreneurs whose respectability would not countenance the production of plays like *Mrs. Warren's Profession* (1898) which exposed it. His plays needed no structural apparatus for the playing of ideas off each other when keeping to the mode of the social problem drama. But beginning with *Caesar and Cleopatra* (published 1901), a new, quizzical direction opens up. It is not merely the second-guessing of history in reworkings of famous themes and episodes of the past that were treated so tediously by nineteenth-century historical stage pageantry. It is also the way in which Shaw starts to pit his own ideas against each other, to surprise himself not with the soundness, but even with the imagination and generosity behind a position which he is in the process of showing to be wrong. This is not the mere technological cynicism of the debating team's view of argument, but something as close to a sense of humanity as Shaw's celebrated coldness seemed ever to allow.

Major Barbara, Pygmalion, and *Man and Superman* are all triumphs in this mode. *Heartbreak House* (1919) is puzzlingly Chekhovian, a lyrical meditation on the breaking-up of nineteenth-century Europe mirrored in a single weird household. *Saint Joan* is a masterpiece of another sort. Joan of Arc was finally canonized in 1920, culminating a lengthy process of rehabilitation which had started in 1455, and Shaw's play is in some measure a response not to the historical figure but to the historical process of mythologizing heroes. Joan is his greatest hero, a saint in his own non-Christian sense of an embodiment of Genius, not so much crudely super-human as quintessentially so. The opening of his own Preface to the play puts the historical matter as he saw it:

Joan the Original and Presumptuous

Joan of Arc, a village girl from the Vosges, was born about 1412; burnt for heresy, witchcraft, and sorcery in 1431; rehabilitated after a fashion in 1456; designated Venerable in 1904; declared Blessed in 1908; and finally canonized in 1920. She is the most notable Warrior Saint in the Christian calendar, and the queerest fish among the eccentric worthies of the Middle Ages. Though a professed and most pious Catholic, and the projector of a Crusade against the Husites, she was in fact one of the first Protestant martyrs. She was also one of the first apostles of Nationalism, and the first French practitioner of Napoleonic realism in warfare as distinguished from the sporting ransom-gambling chivalry of her time. She was the pioneer of rational dressing for women, and, like Queen Christina of Sweden two centuries later, to say nothing of Catalina de Erauso and innumerable obscure heroines who have disguised themselves as men to serve as soldiers and sailors, she refused to accept the specific woman's lot, and dressed and fought and lived as men did.

As she contrived to assert herself in all these ways with such force that she was famous throughout western Europe before she was out of her teens (indeed she never got out of them), it is hardly surprising that she was judicially burnt, ostensibly for a number of capital crimes which we no longer punish as such, but essentially for what we call unwomanly and insufferable presumption. At eighteen Joan's pretensions were beyond those of the proudest Pope or the haughtiest emperor. She claimed to be the ambassador and plenipotentiary of God, and to be, in effect, a member of the Church Triumphant whilst still in the flesh on earth. She patronized her own king, and summoned the English king to repentance and obedience to her commands. She lectured, talked down, and overruled statesmen and prelates. She pooh-poohed the plans of generals, leading their troops to victory on plans of her own. She had an unbounded and quite unconcealed contempt for official opinion, judgment, and authority, and for War Office tactics and strategy. Had she been a sage and monarch in whom the most venerable hierarchy and the most illustrious dynasty converged, her pretensions and proceedings would have been as trying to the official mind as the pretensions of Caesar were to Cassius. As her actual condition was pure upstart, there were only two opinions about her. One was that she was miraculous: the other that she was unbearable.

Joan of Arc had been given a variety of literary treatments in the past. She was a hypocritical and treacherous whore in British tradition (see, for example, the partly Shakespearean I *King Henry VI*); Voltaire took a high irreverent glee in reducing her to a lewd hoyden, the daughter of a priest, no less; Schiller, in *Die Jungfrau von Orleans*, had made her a pious heroine; various later nineteenth-century writers had attempted historical portraits of some accuracy. Even after Shaw's play, one can have the serious proposal of an anthropological scholar like Margaret Murray that Joan (as well as Gilles de Rais, the "Bluebeard" of fact and fairy-tale fiction) was in fact a witch, and the member of a powerful coven. Shaw is not so much interested in the history lesson he so amusingly works out as in the ironies of the human response to an instance of what humanity might itself generally be. He is playing throughout against his English audience's expectations of how the play will take sides in the Hundred Years' War. In the Middle Ages and Renaissance, the English reader would identify totally with the Trojans rather than the Greeks (because the story was read through Virgil, rather than through Homer, whom no one knew); an audience reared on Shakespeare's history plays might expect to know where to look for good sense and where for folly.

One of the great successes of the play is the way in which Joan's major antagonists —the Earl of Warwick, totally political, distantly hedonistic, and scrupulously amoral;

the Bishop of Beauvais; Peter Cauchon; and the Inquisitor at her trial, whose long speech is more magnificent than any single utterance of Joan's—are shown to be right about almost everything. If the crudest kind of hero is great in direct proportion to the size of the dragon he kills, another stage of heroism (as the Danish philosopher Søren Kierkegaard defined it), that of the moral hero, would be evaluated by the correctness, consistency, and all but ultimate truth of the position it resisted. Joan has her straw men (like the wretched English chaplain, De Stogumber, who knows that archangels must speak English), but they are there to test our characters, our prior dispositions to think along conventional and unheroic lines. It is the De Stogumber in every sincere person whom Cauchon rebukes in the Epilogue, when, after the chaplain has just confessed that seeing Joan actually burned changed his life, made him see how moralistic and narrow he had been ("But I have been a different man ever since . . ."), he produces that most resonant line of the play, perhaps: "Must then a Christ perish in torment in every age to save those that have no imagination?"

Saint Joan is, ultimately, a comedy of the historical processes which themselves can never wither away. The double catastrophe of her trial scene, the redemptive ending of the Epilogue, are both put in a final perspective by the schematic rejection of the responsibilities that accepting her sainthood would, for each of the penitents in the scene, entail. In a series of moments that surely must have influenced T. S. Eliot in the speeches of the assassins in *Murder in the Cathedral,* practical reason kneels to what transcends it, then finally slips away, in each of its aspects, one by one. Only brute human feeling, unable to make its own decisions, would just as soon remain, in the person of the soldier. But it has no choice.

Saint Joan

Scene I

A fine spring morning on the river Meuse, between Lorraine and Champagne, in the year 1429 A.D., in the castle of Vaucouleurs.

Captain Robert de Baudricourt, a military squire, handsome and physically energetic, but with no will of his own, is disguising that defect in his usual fashion by storming terribly at his steward, a trodden worm, scanty of flesh, scanty of hair, who might be any age from 18 to 55, being the sort of man whom age cannot wither because he has never bloomed.

The two are in a sunny stone chamber on the first floor of the castle. At a plain strong oak table, seated in chair to match, the captain presents his left profile. The steward stands facing him at the other side of the table, if so deprecatory a stance as his can be called standing. The mullioned thirteenth-century window is open behind him. Near it in the corner is a turret with a narrow arched doorway leading to a winding stair which descends to the courtyard. There is a stout fourlegged stool under the table, and a wooden chest under the window.

ROBERT   No eggs! No eggs!! Thousand thunders, man, what do you mean by
          no eggs?
STEWARD   Sir: it is not my fault. It is the act of God.

ROBERT   Blasphemy. You tell me there are no eggs; and you blame your Maker for it.

STEWARD   Sir: what can I do? I cannot lay eggs.

ROBERT [*sarcastic*]   Ha! You jest about it.

STEWARD   No, sir, God knows. We all have to go without eggs just as you have, sir. The hens will not lay.

ROBERT   Indeed! [*rising*] Now listen to me, you.

STEWARD [*humbly*]   Yes, sir.

ROBERT   What am I?

STEWARD   What are you, sir?

ROBERT [*coming at him*]   Yes: what am I? Am I Robert, squire of Baudricourt and captain of this castle of Vaucouleurs; or am I a cowboy?

STEWARD   Oh, sir, you know you are a greater man here than the king himself.

ROBERT   Precisely. And now, do you know what you are?

STEWARD   I am nobody, sir, except that I have the honor to be your steward.

ROBERT [*driving him to the wall, adjective by adjective*]   You have not only the honor of being my steward, but the privilege of being the worst, most incompetent, drivelling snivelling jibbering jabbering idiot of a steward in France. [*He strides back to the table.*]

STEWARD [*cowering on the chest*]   Yes, sir: to a great man like you I must seem like that.

ROBERT [*turning*]   My fault, I suppose. Eh?

STEWARD [*coming to him deprecatingly*]   Oh, sir: you always give my most innocent words such a turn!

ROBERT   I will give your neck a turn if you dare tell me when I ask you how many eggs there are that you cannot lay any.

STEWARD [*protesting*]   Oh sir, oh sir—

ROBERT   No: not oh sir, oh sir, but no sir, no sir. My three Barbary hens and the black are the best layers in Champagne. And you come and tell me that there are no eggs! Who stole them? Tell me that, before I kick you out through the castle gate for a liar and a seller of my goods to thieves. The milk was short yesterday, too: do not forget that.

STEWARD [*desperate*]   I know, sir. I know only too well. There is no milk: there are no eggs: tomorrow there will be nothing.

ROBERT   Nothing! You will steal the lot: eh?

STEWARD   No, sir: nobody will steal anything. But there is a spell on us: we are bewitched.

ROBERT   That story is not good enough for me. Robert de Baudricourt burns witches and hangs thieves. Go. Bring me four dozen eggs and two gallons of milk here in this room before noon, or Heaven have mercy on your bones! I will teach you to make a fool of me. [*He resumes his seat with an air of finality.*]

STEWARD   Sir: I tell you there are no eggs. There will be none— not if you were to kill me for it—as long as The Maid is at the door.

ROBERT   The Maid! What maid? What are you talking about?

STEWARD   The girl from Lorraine, sir. From Domrémy.

ROBERT [*rising in fearful wrath*]   Thirty thousand thunders! Fifty thousand devils! Do you mean to say that that girl, who had the impudence to ask to see me two days ago, and whom I told you to send back to her father with my orders that he was to give her a good hiding, is here still?

STEWARD   I have told her to go, sir. She wont.

ROBERT   I did not tell you to tell her to go: I told you to throw her out. You have fifty men-at-arms and a dozen lumps of able-bodied servants to carry out my orders. Are they afraid of her?

STEWARD   She is so positive, sir.

ROBERT   [*seizing him by the scruff of the neck*]   Positive! Now see here. I am going to throw you downstairs.

STEWARD   No, sir. Please.

ROBERT   Well, stop me by being positive. It's quite easy: any slut of a girl can do it.

STEWARD   [*hanging limp in his hands*]   Sir, sir: you cannot get rid of her by throwing me out. [*Robert has to let him drop. He squats on his knees on the floor, contemplating his master resignedly.*] You see, sir, you are much more positive than I am. But so is she.

ROBERT   I am stronger than you are, you fool.

STEWARD   No, sir: it isnt that: it's your strong character, sir. She is weaker than we are: she is only a slip of a girl; but we cannot make her go.

ROBERT   You parcel of curs: you are afraid of her.

STEWARD   [*rising cautiously*]   No sir: we are afraid of you; but she puts courage into us. She really doesnt seem to be afraid of anything. Perhaps you could frighten her, sir.

ROBERT   [*grimly*]   Perhaps. Where is she now?

STEWARD   Down in the courtyard, sir, talking to the soldiers as usual. She is always talking to the soldiers except when she is praying.

ROBERT   Praying! Ha! You believe she prays, you idiot. I know the sort of girl that is always talking to soldiers. She shall talk to me a bit. [*He goes to the window and shouts fiercely through it.*] Hallo, you there!

A GIRL's VOICE   [*bright, strong and rough*]   Is it me, sir?

ROBERT   Yes, you.

THE VOICE   Be you captain?

ROBERT   Yes, damn your impudence, I be captain. Come up here. [*to the soldiers in the yard*] Shew her the way, you. And shove her along quick. [*He leaves the window, and returns to his place at the table, where he sits magisterially.*]

STEWARD   [*whispering*]   She wants to go and be a soldier herself. She wants you to give her soldier's clothes. Armor, sir! And a sword! Actually! [*He steals behind Robert.*]

Joan appears in the turret doorway. She is an ablebodied country girl of 17 or 18, respectably dressed in red, with an uncommon face; eyes very wide apart and bulging as they often do in very imaginative people, a long well-shaped nose with wide nostrils, a short upper lip, resolute but full-lipped mouth, and handsome fighting chin. She comes eagerly to the table, delighted at having penetrated to Baudricourt's presence at last, and full of hope as to the results. His scowl does not *check or frighten her in the least. Her voice is normally a hearty coaxing voice, very confident, very appealing, very hard to resist.*

JOAN [*bobbing a curtsey*]   Good morning, captain squire. Captain: you are to give me a horse and armor and some soldiers, and send me to the Dauphin. Those are your orders from my Lord.

ROBERT [*outraged*]   Orders from your lord! And who the devil may your lord be? Go back to him, and tell him that I am neither duke nor peer at his orders: I am squire of Baudricourt; and I take no orders except from the king.

JOAN [*reassuringly*]   Yes, squire: that is all right. My Lord is the King of Heaven.

ROBERT   Why, the girl's mad. [*to the steward*] Why didnt you tell me so, you blockhead?

STEWARD   Sir: do not anger her: give her what she wants.

JOAN [*impatient, but friendly*]   They all say I am mad until I talk to them, squire. But you see that it is the will of God that you are to do what He has put into my mind.

ROBERT   It is the will of God that I shall send you back to your father with orders to put you under lock and key and thrash the madness out of you. What have you to say to that?

JOAN   You think you will, squire; but you will find it all coming quite different. You said you would not see me; but here I am.

STEWARD [*appealing*]   Yes, sir. You see, sir.

ROBERT   Hold your tongue, you.

STEWARD [*abjectly*]   Yes, sir.

ROBERT [*to Joan, with a sour loss of confidence*]   So you are presuming on my seeing you, are you?

JOAN [*sweetly*]   Yes, squire.

ROBERT [*feeling that he has lost ground, brings down his two fists squarely on the table, and inflates his chest imposingly to cure the unwelcome and only too familiar sensation*]   Now listen to me. I am going to assert myself.

JOAN [*busily*]   Please do, squire. The horse will cost sixteen francs. It is a good deal of money: but I can save it on the armor. I can find a soldier's armor that will fit me well enough: I am very hardy; and I do not need beautiful armor made to my measure like you wear. I shall not want many soldiers: the Dauphin will give me all I need to raise the siege of Orleans.

ROBERT [*flabbergasted*]   To raise the siege of Orleans!

JOAN [*simply*]   Yes, squire: that is what God is sending me to do. Three men will be enough for you to send with me if they are good men and gentle to me. They have promised to come with me. Polly and Jack and —

ROBERT   Polly!! You impudent baggage, do you dare call squire Bertrand de Poulengey Polly to my face?

JOAN   His friends call him so, squire: I did not know he had any other name. Jack —

ROBERT   That is Monsieur John of Metz, I suppose?

JOAN   Yes, squire. Jack will come willingly: he is a very kind gentleman, and gives me money to give to the poor. I think John Godsave will come, and Dick the Archer, and their servants John of Honecourt and Julian. There will be no trouble for you, squire: I have arranged it all: you have only to give the order.

ROBERT   [*contemplating her in a stupor of amazement*]   Well, I am damned!

JOAN   [*with unruffled sweetness*]   No, squire: God is very merciful; and the blessed saints Catherine and Margaret, who speak to me every day [*he gapes*], will intercede for you. You will go to paradise; and your name will be remembered for ever as my first helper.

ROBERT   [*to the steward, still much bothered, but changing his tone as he pursues a new clue*]   Is this true about Monsieur de Poulengey?

STEWARD   [*eagerly*]   Yes, sir, and about Monsieur de Metz too. They both want to go with her.

ROBERT   [*thoughtful*]   Mf! [*He goes to the window, and shouts into the courtyard.*] Hallo! You there: send Monsieur de Poulengey to me, will you? [*He turns to Joan*] Get out; and wait in the yard.

JOAN   [*smiling brightly at him*]   Right, squire. [*She goes out.*]

ROBERT   [*to the steward*]   Go with her, you, you dithering imbecile. Stay within call; and keep your eye on her. I shall have her up here again.

STEWARD   Do so in God's name, sir. Think of those hens, the best layers in Champagne; and—

ROBERT   Think of my boot; and take your backside out of reach of it.

The steward retreats hastily and finds himself confronted in the doorway by Bertrand de Poulengey, a lymphatic [1] *French gentleman-at-arms, aged 36 or thereabout, employed in the department of the provost-marshal, dreamily absent-minded, seldom speaking unless spoken to, and then slow and obstinate in reply; altogether in contrast to the self-assertive, loud-mouthed, superficially energetic, fundamentally will-less Robert. The steward makes way for him, and vanishes.*

Poulengey salutes, and stands awaiting orders.

ROBERT   [*genially*]   It isnt service, Polly. A friendly talk. Sit down. [*He hooks the stool from under the table with his instep.*]

Poulengey, relaxing, comes into the room: places the stool between the table and the window: and sits down ruminatively. Robert, half sitting on the end of the table, begins the friendly talk.

ROBERT   Now listen to me, Polly. I must talk to you like a father.

Poulengey looks up at him gravely for a moment, but says nothing.

ROBERT   It's about this girl you are interested in. Now, I have seen her. I have talked to her. First, she's mad. That doesnt matter. Second, she's not a farm wench. She's a bourgeoise. That matters a good deal. I know her class exactly. Her father came here last year to represent his village in a lawsuit: he is one of their notables. A farmer. Not a gentleman farmer: he makes money by it, and lives by it. Still, not a laborer. Not a mechanic. He might have a cousin a lawyer, or in the Church. People of this sort may be of no account socially; but they can give a lot of

1. Sluggish.

bother to the authorities. That is to say, to me. Now no doubt it seems to you a very simple thing to take this girl away, humbugging her into the belief that you are taking her to the Dauphin. But if you get her into trouble, you may get me into no end of a mess, as I am her father's lord, and responsible for her protection. So friends or no friends, Polly, hands off her.

POULENGEY [*with deliberate impressiveness*]   I should as soon think of the Blessed Virgin herself in that way, as of this girl.

ROBERT [*coming off the table*]   But she says you and Jack and Dick have offered to go with her. What for? You are not going to tell me that you take her crazy notion of going to the Dauphin seriously, are you?

POULENGEY [*slowly*]   There is something about her. They are pretty foul-mouthed and foulminded down there in the guardroom, some of them. But there hasnt been a word that has anything to do with her being a woman. They have stopped swearing before her. There is something. Something. It may be worth trying.

ROBERT   Oh, come, Polly! pull yourself together. Commonsense was never your strong point; but this is a little too much. [*He retreats disgustedly.*]

POULENGEY [*unmoved*]   What is the good of commonsense? If we had any commonsense we should join the Duke of Burgundy and the English king. They hold half the country, right down to the Loire. They have Paris. They have this castle: you know very well that we had to sur-render it to the Duke of Bedford, and that you are only holding it on parole. The Dauphin is in Chinon, like a rat in a corner, except that he wont fight. We dont even know that he is the Dauphin: his mother says he isnt; and she ought to know. Think of that! the queen denying the legitimacy of her own son!

ROBERT   Well, she married her daughter to the English king. Can you blame the woman?

POULENGEY   I blame nobody. But thanks to her, the Dauphin is down and out; and we may as well face it. The English will take Orleans: the Bastard[2] will not be able to stop them.

ROBERT   He beat the English the year before last at Montargis. I was with him.

POULENGEY   No mattter: his men are cowed now; and he cant work miracles. And I tell you that nothing can save our side now but a miracle.

ROBERT   Miracles are all right, Polly. The only difficulty about them is that they dont happen nowadays.

POULENGEY   I used to think so. I am not so sure now. [*rising, and moving ruminatively towards the window*] At all events this is not a time to leave any stone unturned. There is something about the girl.

ROBERT   Oh! You think the girl can work miracles, do you?

POULENGEY   I think the girl herself is a bit of a miracle. Anyhow, she is the last card left in our hand. Better play her than throw up the game. [*He wanders to the turret.*]

ROBERT [*wavering*]   You really think that?

POULENGEY [*turning*]   Is there anything else left for us to think?

2. Jean Dunois (1403–68), military leader, bastard son of the Duc d'Orleans; throughout the play, his status is never referred to as a reproach, but as a proper title. After Joan's death he went on to take Paris (1536) and to liberate Normandy from the English.

ROBERT [*going to him*]   Look here, Polly. If you were in my place would you let a girl like that do you out of sixteen francs for a horse?

POULENGEY   I will pay for the horse.

ROBERT   You will!

POULENGEY   Yes: I will back my opinion.

ROBERT   You will really gamble on a forlorn hope to the tune of sixteen francs?

POULENGEY   It is not a gamble.

ROBERT   What else is it?

POULENGEY   It is a certainty. Her words and her ardent faith in God have put fire into me.

ROBERT [*giving him up*]   Whew! You are as mad as she is.

POULENGEY [*obstinately*]   We want a few mad people now. See where the sane ones have landed us!

ROBERT [*his irresoluteness now openly swamping his affected decisiveness*] I shall feel like a precious fool. Still, if you feel sure—?

POULENGEY   I feel sure enough to take her to Chinon—unless you stop me.

ROBERT   This is not fair. You are putting the responsibility on me.

POULENGEY   It is on you whichever way you decide.

ROBERT   Yes: thats just it. Which way am I to decide? You dont see how awkward this is for me. [*snatching at a dilatory step with an unconscious hope that Joan will make up his mind for him*]   Do you think I ought to have another talk to her?

POULENGEY [*rising*]   Yes. [*He goes to the window and calls.*] Joan!

JOAN's VOICE   Will he let us go, Polly?

POULENGEY   Come up. Come in. [*turning to Robert*] Shall I leave you with her?

ROBERT   No: stay here; and back me up.

Poulengey sits down on the chest. Robert goes back to his magisterial chair, but remains standing to inflate himself more imposingly. Joan comes in, full of good news.

JOAN   Jack will go halves for the horse.

ROBERT   Well!! [*He sits, deflated.*]

POULENGEY [*gravely*]   Sit down, Joan.

JOAN [*checked a little, and looking to Robert*]   May I?

ROBERT   Do what you are told.

Joan curtsies and sits down on the stool between them. Robert outfaces his perplexity with his most peremptory air.

ROBERT   What is your name?

JOAN [*chattily*]   They always call me Jenny in Lorraine. Here in France I am Joan. The soldiers call me The Maid.

ROBERT   What is your surname?

JOAN   Surname? What is that? My father sometimes calls himself d'Arc; but I know nothing about it. You met my father. He—

ROBERT   Yes, yes; I remember. You come from Domrémy in Lorraine, I think.

JOAN   Yes; but what does it matter? we all speak French.

ROBERT   Don't ask questions: answer them. How old are you?

JOAN   Seventeen: so they tell me. It might be nineteen. I dont remember.

ROBERT   What did you mean when you said that St Catherine and St Margaret talked to you every day?

JOAN   They do.

ROBERT   What are they like?

JOAN   [*suddenly obstinate*]   I will tell you nothing about that: they have not given me leave.

ROBERT   But you actually see them; and they talk to you just as I am talking to you?

JOAN   No: it is quite different. I cannot tell you: you must not talk to me about my voices.

ROBERT   How do you mean? voices?

JOAN   I hear voices telling me what to do. They come from God.

ROBERT   They come from your imagination.

JOAN   Of course. That is how the messages of God come to us.

POULENGEY.   Checkmate.

ROBERT   No fear! [*to Joan*] So God says you are to raise the siege of Orleans?

JOAN   And to crown the Dauphin in Rheims Cathedral.

ROBERT [*gasping*]   Crown the D—! Gosh!

JOAN   And to make the English leave France.

ROBERT [*sarcastic*]   Anything else?

JOAN [*charming*]   Not just at present, thank you, squire.

ROBERT   I suppose you think raising a siege is as easy as chasing a cow out of a meadow. You think soldiering is anybody's job?

JOAN   I do not think it can be very difficult if God is on your side, and you are willing to put your life in His hand. But many soldiers are very simple.

ROBERT [*grimly*]   Simple! Did you ever see English soldiers fighting?

JOAN   They are only men. God made them just like us; but He gave them their own country and their own language; and it is not His will that they should come into our country and try to speak our language.

ROBERT   Who has been putting such nonsense into your head? Dont you know that soldiers are subject to their feudal lord, and that it is nothing to them or to you whether he is the duke of Burgundy or the king of England or the king of France? What has their language to do with it?

JOAN   I do not understand that a bit. We are all subject to the King of Heaven; and He gave us our countries and our languages, and meant us to keep to them. If it were not so it would be murder to kill an Englishman in battle; and you, squire, would be in great danger of hell fire. You must not think about your duty to your feudal lord, but about your duty to God.

POULENGEY   It's no use, Robert: she can choke you like that every time.

ROBERT   Can she, by Saint Dennis! We shall see. [*to Joan*] We are not talking about God: we are talking about practical affairs. I ask you again, girl, have you ever seen English soldiers fighting? Have you ever seen them plundering, burning, turning the countryside into a desert? Have you heard no tales of their Black Prince [3] who was blacker than the devil himself, or of the English king's father?

JOAN   You must not be afraid, Robert—

3. Edward, Prince of Wales (1330–76), son of Edward III, famed as a soldier, and ruler of parts of the south of France, captured in behalf of his father's claim to the French crown.

ROBERT   Damn you, I am not afraid. And who gave you leave to call me Robert?

JOAN   You were called so in church in the name of our Lord. All the other names are your father's or your brother's or anybody's.

ROBERT   Tcha!

JOAN   Listen to me, squire. At Domrémy we had to fly to the next village to escape from the English soldiers. Three of them were left behind, wounded. I came to know these three poor goddams quite well. They had not half my strength.

ROBERT   Do you know why they are called goddams?

JOAN   No. Everyone calls them goddams.

ROBERT   It is because they are always calling on their God to condemn their souls to perdition. That is what goddam means in their language. How do you like it?

JOAN   God will be merciful to them; and they will act like His good children when they go back to the country He made for them, and made them for. I have heard the tales of the Black Prince. The moment he touched the soil of our country the devil entered into him, and made him a black fiend. But at home, in the place made for him by God, he was good. It is always so. If I went into England against the will of God to conquer England, and tried to live there and speak its language, the devil would enter into me; and when I was old I should shudder to remember the wickedness I did.

ROBERT   Perhaps. But the more devil you were the better you might fight. That is why the goddams will take Orleans. And you cannot stop them, nor ten thousand like you.

JOAN   One thousand like me can stop them. Ten like me can stop them with God on our side. [*She rises impetuously, and goes at him, unable to sit quiet any longer.*] You do not understand, squire. Our soldiers are always beaten because they are fighting only to save their skins; and the shortest way to save your skin is to run away. Our knights are thinking only of the money they will make in ransoms: it is not kill or be killed with them, but pay or be paid. But I will teach them all to fight that the will of God may be done in France; and then they will drive the poor goddams before them like sheep. You and Polly will live to see the day when there will not be an English soldier on the soil of France; and there will be but one king there: not the feudal English king, but God's French one.

ROBERT   [*to Poulengey*]   This may be all rot, Polly; but the troops might swallow it, though nothing that we can say seems able to put any fight into them. Even the Dauphin might swallow it. And if she can put fight into him, she can put it into anybody.

POULENGEY   I can see no harm in trying. Can you? And there is something about the girl—

ROBERT   [*turning to Joan*]   Now listen you to me; and [*desperately*] dont cut in before I have time to think.

JOAN   [*plumping down on the stool again, like an obedient schoolgirl*] Yes, squire.

ROBERT   Your orders are, that you are to go to Chinon under the escort of this gentleman and three of his friends.

JOAN [*radiant, clasping her hands*]   Oh, squire! Your head is all circled with light, like a saint's.

POULENGEY   How is she to get into the royal presence?

ROBERT [*who has looked up for his halo rather apprehensively*]   I dont know: how did she get into my presence? If the Dauphin can keep her out he is a better man than I take him for. [*rising*] I will send her to Chinon; and she can say I sent her. Then let come what may: I can do no more.

JOAN   And the dress? I may have a soldier's dress, maynt I, squire?

ROBERT   Have what you please. I wash my hands of it.

JOAN [*wildly excited by her success*]   Come, Polly. [*She dashes out.*]

ROBERT [*shaking Poulengey's hand*]   Goodbye, old man, I am taking a big chance. Few other men would have done it. But as you say, there is something about her.

POULEGNEY   Yes: there is something about her. Goodbye. [*He goes out.*]

Robert, still very doubtful whether he has not been made a fool of by a crazy female, and a social inferior to boot, scratches his head and slowly comes back from the door.

The steward runs in with a basket.

STEWARD   Sir, sir—

ROBERT   What now?

STEWARD   The hens are laying like mad, sir. Five dozen eggs!

ROBERT [*stiffens convulsively: crosses himself: and forms with his pale lips the words*]   Christ in heaven! [*aloud but breathless*] She did come from God.

Scene II

Chinon, in Touraine. An end of the throne room in the castle, curtained off to make an antechamber. The Archbishop of Rheims, close on 50, a full-fed prelate with nothing of the ecclesiastic about him except his imposing bearing, and the Lord Chamberlain, Monseigneur de la Trémouille, a monstrous arrogant wineskin of a man, are waiting for the Dauphin. There is a door in the wall to the right of the two men. It is late in the afternoon on the 8th of March, 1429. The Archbishop stands with dignity whilst the Chamberlain, on his left, fumes about in the worst of tempers.

LA TRÉMOUILLE   What the devil does the Dauphin mean by keeping us waiting like this? I dont know how you have the patience to stand there like a stone idol.

THE ARCHBISHOP   You see, I am an archbishop; and an archbishop is a sort of idol. At any rate he has to learn to keep still and suffer fools patiently. Besides, my dear Lord Chamberlain, it is the Dauphin's royal privilege to keep you waiting, is it not?

LA TRÉMOUILLE   Dauphin be damned! saving your reverence. Do you know how much money he owes me?

THE ARCHBISHOP   Much more than he owes me, I have no doubt, because you are a much richer man. But I take it he owes you all you could afford to lend him. That is what he owes me.

LA TRÉMOUILLE   Twenty-seven thousand: that was his last haul. A cool twenty-seven thousand!

THE ARCHBISHOP   What becomes of it all? He never has a suit of clothes that I would throw to a curate.

LA TRÉMOUILLE   He dines on a chicken or a scrap of mutton. He borrows my last penny; and there is nothing to shew for it. [*A page appears in the doorway.*] At last!

THE PAGE   No, my lord: it is not His Majesty. Monsieur de Rais is approaching.

LA TRÉMOUILLE   Young Bluebeard! Why announce him?

THE PAGE   Captain La Hire is with him. Something has happened, I think.

> *Gilles de Rais, a young man of 25, very smart and self-possessed, and sporting the extravagance of a little curled beard dyed blue at a clean-shaven court, comes in. He is determined to make himself agreeable, but lacks natural joyousness, and is not really pleasant. In fact when he defies the Church some eleven years later he is accused of trying to extract pleasure from horrible cruelties, and hanged. So far, however, there is no shadow of the gallows on him. He advances gaily to the Archbishop. The page withdraws.*

BLUEBEARD   Your faithful lamb, Archbishop. Good day, my lord. Do you know what has happened to La Hire?

LA TRÉMOUILLE   He has sworn himself into a fit, perhaps.

BLUEBEARD   No: just the opposite. Foul Mouthed Frank, the only man in Touraine who could beat him at swearing, was told by a soldier that he shouldnt use such language when he was at the point of death.

THE ARCHBISHOP   Nor at any other point. But was Foul Mouthed Frank on the point of death?

BLUEBEARD   Yes: he has just fallen into a well and been drowned. La Hire is frightened out of his wits.

> *Captain La Hire comes in: a war dog with no court manners and pronounced camp ones.*

BLUEBEARD   I have just been telling the Chamberlain and the Archbishop. The Archbishop says you are a lost man.

LA HIRE   [*striding past Bluebeard, and planting himself between the Archbishop and La Trémouille*]   This is nothing to joke about. It is worse than we thought. It was not a soldier, but an angel dressed as a soldier.

THE ARCHBISHOP ⎱
THE CHAMBERLAIN ⎰ [*exclaiming all together*] An angel!
BLUEBEARD ⎰

LA HIRE   Yes, an angel. She has made her way from Champagne with half a dozen men through the thick of everything: Burgundians, Goddams, deserters, robbers, and Lord knows who; and they never met a soul except the country folk. I know one of them: de Poulengey. He says she's an angel. If ever I utter an oath again may my soul be blasted to eternal damnation!

THE ARCHBISHOP   A very pious beginning, Captain.

> *Bluebeard and La Trémouille laugh at him. The page returns.*

THE PAGE   His Majesty.

They stand perfunctorily at court attention. The Dauphin, aged 26, really King Charles the Seventh since the death of his father, but as yet uncrowned, comes in through the curtains with a paper in his hands. He is a poor creature physically; and the current fashion of shaving closely, and hiding every scrap of hair under the headcovering or head-dress, both by women and men, makes the worst of his appearance. He has little narrow eyes, near together, a long pendulous nose that droops over his thick short upper lip, and the expression of a young dog accustomed to be kicked, yet incorrigible and irrepressible. But he is neither vulgar nor stupid; and he has a cheeky humor which enables him to hold his own in conversation. Just at present he is excited, like a child with a new toy. He comes to the Archbishop's left hand. Bluebeard and La Hire retire towards the curtains.

CHARLES   Oh, Archbishop, do you know what Robert de Baudricourt is sending me from Vaucouleurs?

THE ARCHBISHOP   [*contemptuously*]   I am not interested in the newest toys.

CHARLES   [*indignantly*]   It isnt a toy. [*sulkily*] However, I can get on very well without your interest.

THE ARCHBISHOP   Your Highness is taking offence very unnecessarily.

CHARLES   Thank you. You are always ready with a lecture, arent you?

LA TRÉMOUILLE   [*roughly*]   Enough grumbling. What have you got there?

CHARLES   What is that to you?

LA TRÉMOUILLE   It is my business to know what is passing between you and the garrison at Vaucouleurs. [*He snatches the paper from the Dauphin's hand, and begins reading it with some difficulty, following the words with his finger and spelling them out syllable by syllable.*]

CHARLES   [*mortified*]   You all think you can treat me as you please because I owe you money, and because I am no good at fighting. But I have the blood royal in my veins.

THE ARCHBISHOP   Even that has been questioned, your Highness. One hardly recognizes in you the grandson of Charles the Wise.

CHARLES   I want to hear no more of my grandfather. He was so wise that he used up the whole family stock of wisdom for five generations, and left me the poor fool I am, bullied and insulted by all of you.

THE ARCHBISHOP   Control yourself, sir. These outbursts of petulance are not seemly.

CHARLES   Another lecture! Thank you. What a pity it is that though you are an archbishop saints and angels dont come to see you!

THE ARCHBISHOP   What do you mean?

CHARLES   Aha! Ask that bully there [*pointing to La Trémouille*].

LA TRÉMOUILLE   [*furious*]   Hold your tongue. Do you hear?

CHARLES   Oh, I hear. You neednt shout. The whole castle can hear. Why dont you go and shout at the English, and beat them for me?

LA TRÉMOUILLE   [*raising his fist*]   You young—

CHARLES   [*running behind the Archbishop*]   Dont you raise your hand to me. It's high treason.

LA HIRE   Steady, Duke! Steady!

THE ARCHBISHOP [*resolutely*]   Come, come! this will not do. My Lord Chamberlain: please! please! we must keep some sort of order. [*to the Dauphin*] And you, sir: if you cannot rule your kingdom, at least try to rule yourself.

CHARLES   Another lecture! Thank you.

LA TRÉMOUILLE [*handing over the paper to the Archbishop*]   Here: read the accursed thing for me. He has sent the blood boiling into my head: I cant distinguish the letters.

CHARLES [*coming back and peering round La Trémouille's left shoulder*]   I will read it for you if you like. I can read, you know.

LA TRÉMOUILLE [*with intense contempt, not at all stung by the taunt*]   Yes: reading is about all you are fit for. Can you make it out, Archbishop?

THE ARCHBISHOP   I should have expected more commonsense from De Baudricourt. He is sending some cracked country lass here—

CHARLES [*interrupting*]   No: he is sending a saint: an angel. And she is coming to me: to me, the king, and not to you, Archbishop, holy as you are. She knows the blood royal if you dont. [*He struts up to the curtains between Bluebeard and La Hire.*]

THE ARCHBISHOP   You cannot be allowed to see this crazy wench.

CHARLES [*turning*]   But I am the king; and I will.

LA TRÉMOUILLE [*brutally*]   Then she cannot be allowed to see you. Now!

CHARLES   I tell you I will. I am going to put my foot down—

BLUEBEARD [*laughing at him*]   Naughty! What would your wise grandfather say?

CHARLES   That just shews your ignorance, Bluebeard. My grandfather had a saint who used to float in the air when she was praying, and told him everything he wanted to know. My poor father had two saints, Marie de Maillé and the Gasque of Avignon. It is in our family; and I dont care what you say: I will have my saint too.

THE ARCHBISHOP   This creature is not a saint. She is not even a respectable woman. She does not wear women's clothes. She is dressed like a soldier, and rides round the country with soldiers. Do you suppose such a person can be admitted to your Highness's court?

LA HIRE   Stop. [*going to the Archbishop*] Did you say a girl in armor, like a soldier?

THE ARCHBISHOP   So De Baudricourt describes her.

LA HIRE   But by all the devils in hell—Oh, God forgive me, what am I saying?—by Our Lady and all the saints, this must be the angel that struck Foul Mouthed Frank dead for swearing.

CHARLES [*triumphant*]   You see! A miracle!

LA HIRE   She may strike the lot of us dead if we cross her. For Heaven's sake, Archbishop, be careful what you are doing.

THE ARCHBISHOP [*severely*]   Rubbish! Nobody has been struck dead. A drunken blackguard who has been rebuked a hundred times for swearing has fallen into a well, and been drowned. A mere coincidence.

LA HIRE   I do not know what a coincidence is. I do know that the man is dead, and that she told him he was going to die.

THE ARCHBISHOP   We are all going to die, Captain.

LA HIRE [*crossing himself*]   I hope not. [*He backs out of the conversation.*]

BLUEBEARD   We can easily find out whether she is an angel or not. Let us arrange when she comes that I shall be the Dauphin, and see whether she will find me out.

CHARLES   Yes: I agree to that. If she cannot find the blood royal I will have nothing to do with her.

THE ARCHBISHOP   It is for the Church to make saints: let De Baudricourt mind his own business, and not dare usurp the function of his priest. I say the girl shall not be admitted.

BLUEBEARD   But, Archbishop—

THE ARCHBISHOP   [*sternly*]   I speak in the Church's name. [*to the Dauphin*] Do you dare say she shall?

CHARLES   [*intimidated but sulky*]   Oh, if you make it an excommunication matter, I have nothing more to say, of course. But you havnt read the end of the letter. De Baudricourt says she will raise the siege of Orleans, and beat the English for us.

LA TRÉMOUILLE   Rot!

CHARLES   Well, will you save Orleans for us, with all your bullying?

LA TRÉMOUILLE   [*savagely*]   Do not throw that in my face again: do you hear? I have done more fighting than you ever did or ever will. But I cannot be everywhere.

THE DAUPHIN   Well, thats something.

BLUEBEARD   [*coming between the Archbishop and Charles*]   You have Jack Dunois at the head of your troops in Orleans: the brave Dunois, the handsome Dunois, the wonderful invincible Dunois, the darling of all the ladies, the beautiful bastard.[1] Is it likely that the country lass can do what he cannot do?

CHARLES   Why doesnt he raise the siege, then?

LA HIRE   The wind is against him.

BLUEBEARD   How can the wind hurt him at Orleans? It is not on the Channel.

LA HIRE   It is on the river Loire; and the English hold the bridgehead. He must ship his men across the river and upstream, if he is to take them in the rear. Well, he cannot, because there is a devil of a wind blowing the other way. He is tired of paying the priests to pray for a west wind. What he needs is a miracle. You tell me that what the girl did to Foul Mouthed Frank was no miracle. No matter: it finished Frank. If she changes the wind for Dunois, that may not be a miracle either; but it may finish the English. What harm is there in trying?

THE ARCHBISHOP   [*who has read the end of the letter and become more thoughtful*]   It is true that De Baudricourt seems extraordinarily impressed.

LA HIRE   De Baudricourt is a blazing ass; but he is a soldier; and if he thinks she can beat the English, all the rest of the army will think so too.

LA TRÉMOUILLE   [*to the Archbishop, who is hesitating*]   Oh, let them have their way. Dunois' men will give up the town in spite of him if somebody does not put some fresh spunk into them.

THE ARCHBISHOP   The Church must examine the girl before anything decisive

1. See Scene I, n. 2.

is done about her. However, since his Highness desires it, let her attend the Court.

LA HIRE   I will find her and tell her. [*He goes out.*]

CHARLES   Come with me, Bluebeard; and let us arrange so that she will not know who I am. You will pretend to be me. [*He goes out through the curtains.*]

BLUEBEARD   Pretend to be that thing! Holy Michael! [*He follows the Dauphin.*]

LA TRÉMOUILLE   I wonder will she pick him out!

THE ARCHBISHOP   Of course she will.

LA TRÉMOUILLE   Why? How is she to know?

THE ARCHBISHOP   She will know what everybody in Chinon knows: that the Dauphin is the meanest-looking and worst-dressed figure in the Court, and that the man with the blue beard is Gilles de Rais.

LA TRÉMOUILLE   I never thought of that.

THE ARCHBISHOP   You are not so accustomed to miracles as I am. It is part of my profession.

LA TRÉMOUILLE   [*puzzled and a little scandalized*]   But that would not be a miracle at all.

THE ARCHBISHOP   [*calmy*]   Why not?

LA TRÉMOUILLE   Well, come! what is a miracle?

THE ARCHBISHOP   A miracle, my friend, is an event which creates faith. That is the purpose and nature of miracles. They may seem very wonderful to the people who witness them, and very simple to those who perform them. That does not matter: if they confirm or create faith they are true miracles.

LA TRÉMOUILLE   Even when they are frauds, do you mean?

THE ARCHBISHOP   Frauds deceive. An event which creates faith does not deceive: therefore it is not a fraud, but a miracle.

LA TRÉMOUILLE   [*scratching his neck in his perplexity*]   Well, I suppose as you are an archbishop you must be right. It seems a bit fishy to me. But I am no churchman, and dont understand these matters.

THE ARCHBISHOP   You are not a churchman; but you are a diplomatist and a soldier. Could you make our citizens pay war taxes, or our soldiers sacrifice their lives, if they knew what is really happening instead of what seems to them to be happening?

LA TRÉMOUILLE   No, by Saint Dennis: the fat would be in the fire before sundown.

THE ARCHBISHOP   Would it not be quite easy to tell them the truth?

LA TRÉMOUILLE   Man alive, they wouldnt believe it.

THE ARCHBISHOP   Just so. Well, the Church has to rule men for the good of their souls as you have to rule them for the good of their bodies. To do that, the Church must do as you do: nourish their faith by poetry.

LA TRÉMOUILLE   Poetry! I should call it humbug.

THE ARCHBISHOP   You would be wrong, my friend. Parables are not lies because they describe events that have never happened. Miracles are not frauds because they are often—I do not say always—very simple and innocent contrivances by which the priest fortifies the faith of his flock. When this girl picks out the Dauphin among his courtiers, it will not be a miracle for me, because I shall know how it has been done, and my faith will not be increased. But as for the others, if they feel the thrill of the supernatural, and forget their sinful clay in a sudden sense of the glory of God, it will be a miracle and a blessed one. And you will find that the girl herself will be more affected than anyone else. She will forget how she really picked him out. So, perhaps, will you.

LA TRÉMOUILLE   Well, I wish I were clever enough to know how much of you is God's archbishop and how much the most artful fox in Touraine. Come on, or we shall be late for the fun; and I want to see it, miracle or no miracle.

THE ARCHBISHOP [detaining him a moment] Do not think that I am a lover of crooked ways. There is a new spirit rising in men: we are at the dawning of a wider epoch. If I were a simple monk, and had not to rule men, I should seek peace for my spirit with Aristotle and Pythagoras rather than with the saints and their miracles.

LA TRÉMOUILLE   And who the deuce was Pythagoras?

THE ARCHBISHOP A sage who held that the earth is round, and that it moves round the sun.

LA TRÉMOUILLE   What an utter fool! Couldnt he use his eyes?

They go out together through the curtains, which are presently withdrawn, revealing the full depth of the throne room with the Court assembled. On the right are two Chairs of State on a dais. Bluebeard is standing theatrically on the dais, playing the king, and, like the courtiers, enjoying the joke rather obviously. There is a curtained arch in the wall behind the dais; but the main door, guarded by men-at-arms, is at the other side of the room; and a clear path across is kept and lined by the courtiers. Charles is in this path in the middle of the room. La Hire is on his right. The Archbishop, on his left, has taken his place by the dais: La Trémouille at the other side of it. The Duchess de la Trémouille, pretending to be the Queen, sits in the Consort's chair, with a group of ladies in waiting close by, behind the Archbishop.

The chatter of the courtiers makes such a noise that nobody notices the appearance of the page at the door.

THE PAGE The Duke of—[*Nobody listens.*] The Duke of—[*The chatter continues. Indignant at his failure to command a hearing, he snatches the halberd of the nearest man-at-arms, and thumps the floor with it. The chatter ceases; and everybody looks at him in silence.*] Attention! [*He restores the halberd to the man-at-arms.*] The Duke of Vendôme presents Joan the Maid to his Majesty.

CHARLES [*putting his finger on his lip*] Ssh! [*He hides behind the nearest courtier, peering out to see what happens.*]

BLUEBEARD [*majestically*] Let her approach the throne.

Joan, dressed as a soldier, with her hair bobbed and hanging thickly round her face, is led in by a bashful and speechless nobleman, from whom she detaches herself to stop and look round eagerly for the Dauphin.

THE DUCHESS [*to the nearest lady in waiting*] My dear! her hair!

All the ladies explode in uncontrollable laughter.

BLUEBEARD [*trying not to laugh, and waving his hand in deprecation of their merriment*] Ssh—ssh! Ladies! Ladies!!

JOAN [*not at all embarrassed*] I wear it like this because I am a soldier. Where be Dauphin?

A titter runs through the Court as she walks to the dais.

BLUEBEARD [*condescendingly*] You are in the presence of the Dauphin.

Joan looks at him sceptically for a moment, scanning him hard up and down to make sure. Dead silence, all watching her. Fun dawns in her face.

JOAN Coom,[2] Bluebeard! Thou canst not fool me. Where be Dauphin?

A roar of laughter breaks out as Gilles, with a gesture of surrender, joins in the laugh, and jumps down from the dais beside La Trémouille. Joan, also on the broad grin, turns back, searching along the row of courtiers, and presently makes a dive and drags out Charles by the arm.

JOAN [*releasing him and bobbing him a little curtsey*] Gentle little Dauphin, I am sent to you to drive the English away from Orleans and from France, and to crown you king in the cathedral at Rheims, where all true kings of France are crowned.

CHARLES [*triumphant, to the Court*] You see, all of you: she knew the blood royal. Who dare say now that I am not my father's son? [*To Joan*] But if you want me to be crowned at Rheims you must talk to the Archbishop, not to me. There he is [*He is standing behind her.*]!

JOAN [*turning quickly, overwhelmed with emotion*] Oh, my lord! [*She falls on both knees before him, with bowed head, not daring to look up.*] My lord: I am only a poor country girl; and you are filled with the blessedness and glory of God Himself; but you will touch me with your hands, and give me your blessing, wont you?

BLUEBEARD [*whispering to La Trémouille*] The old fox blushes.

LA TRÉMOUILLE Another miracle!

THE ARCHBISHOP [*touched, putting his hand on her head*] Child: you are in love with religion.

JOAN [*startled: looking up at him*] Am I? I never thought of that. Is there any harm in it?

THE ARCHBISHOP There is no harm in it, my child. But there is danger.

JOAN [*rising, with a sunflush of reckless happiness irradiating her face*] There is always danger, except in heaven.[3] Oh, my lord, you have given me such strength, such courage. It must be a most wonderful thing to be Archbishop.

The Court smiles broadly: even titters a little.

THE ARCHBISHOP [*drawing himself up sensitively*] Gentlemen: your levity is rebuked by this maid's faith. I am, God help me, all unworthy; but your mirth is a deadly sin.

Their faces fall. Dead silence.

BLUEBEARD My lord: we were laughing at her, not at you.

THE ARCHBISHOP What? Not at my unworthiness but at her faith! Gilles de

2. With "oo" sounded as in "book"; one of several Northern usages given to Joan to establish her dialect as being provincial.

3. This is an echo of Nietzsche's famous aphorism, "Live dangerously."

Rais: this maid prophesied that the blasphemer should be drowned in his sin—

JOAN [*distressed*] No!

THE ARCHBISHOP [*silencing her by a gesture*] I prophesy now that you will be hanged in yours if you do not learn when to laugh and when to pray.

BLUEBEARD My lord: I stand rebuked. I am sorry: I can say no more. But if you prophesy that I shall be hanged, I shall never be able to resist temptation, because I shall always be telling myself that I may as well be hanged for a sheep as a lamb.

The courtiers take heart at this. There is more tittering.

JOAN [*scandalized*] You are an idle fellow, Bluebeard; and you have great impudence to answer the Archbishop.

LA HIRE [*with a huge chuckle*] Well said, lass! Well said!

JOAN [*impatiently to the Archbishop*] Oh, my lord, will you send all these silly folks away so that I may speak to the Dauphin alone?

LA HIRE [*goodhumoredly*] I can take a hint. [*He salutes; turns on his heel; and goes out.*]

THE ARCHBISHOP Come, gentlemen. The Maid comes with God's blessing, and must be obeyed.

The courtiers withdraw, some through the arch, others at the opposite side. The Archbishop marches across to the door, followed by the Duchess and La Trémouille. As the Archbishop passes Joan, she falls on her knees, and kisses the hem of his robe fervently. He shakes his head in instinctive remonstrance; gathers the robe from her; and goes out. She is left kneeling directly in the Duchess's way.

THE DUCHESS [*coldly*] Will you allow me to pass, please?

JOAN [*hastily rising, and standing back*] Beg pardon, maam, I am sure.

The Duchess passes on. Joan stares after her; then whispers to the Dauphin.

JOAN Be that Queen?

CHARLES No. She thinks she is.

JOAN [*again staring after the Duchess*] Oo-oo-ooh! [*Her awestruck amazement at the figure cut by the magnificently dressed lady is not wholly complimentary.*]

LA TRÉMOUILLE [*very surly*] I'll trouble your Highness not to gibe at my wife. [*He goes out. The others have already gone.*]

JOAN [*to the Dauphin*] Who be old Gruff-and-Grum?

CHARLES He is the Duke de la Trémouille.

JOAN What be his job?

CHARLES He pretends to command the army. And whenever I find a friend I can care for, he kills him.

JOAN Why dost let him?

CHARLES [*petulantly moving to the throne side of the room to escape from her magnetic field*] How can I prevent him? He bullies me. They all bully me.

JOAN Art afraid?

CHARLES Yes: I am afraid. It's no use preaching to me about it. It's all very well for these big men with their armor that is too heavy for me, and their swords that I can hardly lift, and their muscle and their shouting and their bad tempers. They like fighting: most of them are making fools of themselves all the time they are not fighting; but I am quiet and sensible; and I dont want to kill people: I only want to be left alone to enjoy myself in my own way. I never asked to be a king: it was pushed on me. So if you are going to say 'Son of St Louis: gird on the sword of your ancestors, and lead us to victory' you may spare your breath to cool your porridge; for I cannot do it. I am not built that way; and there is an end of it.

JOAN [*trenchant and masterful*]   Blethers! [4] We are all like that to begin with. I shall put courage into thee.

CHARLES   But I dont want to have courage put into me. I want to sleep in a comfortable bed, and not live in continual terror of being killed or wounded. Put courage into the others, and let them have their bellyful of fighting; but let me alone.

JOAN   It's no use, Charlie: thou must face what God puts on thee. If thou fail to make thyself king, thoult be a beggar: what else art fit for? Come! Let me see thee sitting on the throne. I have looked forward to that.

CHARLES   What is the good of sitting on the throne when the other fellows give all the orders? However! [*he sits enthroned, a piteous figure*] here is the king for you! Look your fill at the poor devil.

JOAN   Thourt not king yet, lad: thourt but Dauphin. Be not led away by them around thee. Dressing up dont fill empty noddle. I know the people: the real people that make thy bread for thee; and I tell thee they count no man king of France until the holy oil has been poured on his hair, and himself consecrated and crowned in Rheims Cathedral. And thou needs new clothes, Charlie. Why does not Queen look after thee properly?

CHARLES   We're poor. She wants all the money we can spare to put on her own back. Besides, I like to see her beautifully dressed; and I dont care what I wear myself: I should look ugly anyhow.

JOAN   There is some good in thee, Charlie; but it is not yet a king's good.

CHARLES   We shall see. I am not such a fool as I look. I have my eyes open; and I can tell you that one good treaty is worth ten good fights. These fighting fellows lose all on the treaties that they gain on the fights. If we can only have a treaty, the English are sure to have the worst of it, because they are better at fighting than at thinking.

JOAN   If the English win, it is they that will make the treaty: and then God help poor France! Thou must fight, Charlie, whether thou will or no. I will go first to hearten thee. We must take our courage in both hands: aye, and pray for it with both hands too.

CHARLES [*descending from his throne and again crossing the room to escape from her dominating urgency*]   Oh do stop talking about God and praying. I cant bear people who are always praying. Isnt it bad enough to have to do it at the proper times?

4. Scots for "blather" or "nonsense."

JOAN [*pitying him*]   Thou poor child, thou hast never prayed in thy life. I must teach thee from the beginning.

CHARLES   I am not a child: I am a grown man and a father; and I will not be taught any more.

JOAN   Aye, you have a little son. He that will be Louis the Eleventh when you die. Would you not fight for him?

CHARLES   No: a horrid boy. He hates me. He hates everybody, selfish little beast! I dont want to be bothered with children. I dont want to be a father; and I dont want to be a son: especially a son of St. Louis. I dont want to be any of these fine things you all have your heads full of: I want to be just what I am. Why cant you mind your own business, and let me mind mine?

JOAN [*again contemptuous*]   Minding your own business is like minding your own body; it's the shortest way to make yourself sick. What is my business? Helping mother at home. What is thine? Petting lapdogs and sucking sugar-sticks. I call that muck. I tell thee it is God's business we are here to do: not our own. I have a message to thee from God; and thou must listen to it, though thy heart break with the terror of it.

CHARLES   I dont want a message; but can you tell me any secrets? Can you do any cures? Can you turned lead into gold, or anything of that sort?

JOAN   I can turn thee into a king, in Rheims Cathedral; and that is a miracle that will take some doing, it seems.

CHARLES   If we go to Rheims, and have a coronation, Anne will want new dresses. We cant afford them. I am all right as I am.

JOAN   As you are! And what is that? Less than my father's poorest shepherd. Thourt not lawful owner of thy own land of France till thou be consecrated.

CHARLES   But I shall not be lawful owner of my own land anyhow. Will the consecration pay off my mortgages? I have pledged my last acre to the Archbishop and that fat bully. I owe money even to Bluebeard.

JOAN [*earnestly*]   Charlie: I come from the land, and have gotten my strength working on the land; and I tell thee that the land is thine to rule righteously and keep God's peace in, and not to pledge at the pawnshop as a drunken woman pledges her children's clothes. And I come from God to tell thee to kneel in the cathedral and solemnly give thy kingdom to Him for ever and ever, and become the greatest king in the world as His steward and His bailiff, His soldier and His servant. The very clay of France will become holy: her soldiers will be the soldiers of God: the rebel dukes will be rebels against God: the English will fall on their knees and beg thee let them return to their lawful homes in peace. Wilt be a poor little Judas, and betray me and Him that sent me?

CHARLES [*tempted at last*]   Oh, if I only dare!

JOAN   I shall dare, dare, and dare again, in God's name! Art for or against me?

CHARLES [*excited*]   I'll risk it, I warn you I shant be able to keep it up; but I'll risk it. You shall see. [*running to the main door and shouting*] Hallo! Come back, everybody. [*to Joan, as he runs back to the arch opposite*] Mind you stand by and dont let me be bullied. [*through the arch*]

Come along, will you: the whole Court. [*He sits down in the royal chair as they all hurry in to their former places, chattering and wondering.*] Now I'm in for it; but no matter: here goes! [*to the page*] Call for silence, you little beast, will you?

THE PAGE [*snatching a halberd as before and thumping with it repeatedly*] Silence for His Majesty the King. The King speaks. [*peremptorily*] Will you be silent there? [*Silence*].

CHARLES [*rising*]   I have given the command of the army to The Maid. The Maid is to do as she likes with it. [*He descends from the dais*].

General amazement. La Hire, delighted, slaps his steel thighpiece with his gauntlet.

LA TRÉMOUILLE [*turning threateningly towards Charles*]   What is this? I command the army.

Joan quickly puts her hand on Charles's shoulder as he instinctively recoils. Charles, with a grotesque effort culminating in an extravagant gesture, snaps his fingers in the Chamberlain's face.

JOAN   Thourt answered, old Gruff-and-Grum. [*suddenly flashing out her sword as she divines that her moment has come*] Who is for God and His Maid? Who is for Orleans with me?

LA HIRE [*carried away, drawing also*]   For God and His Maid! To Orleans!

ALL THE KNIGHTS [*following his lead with enthusiasm*]   To Orleans!

Joan, radiant, falls on her knees in thanksgiving to God. They all kneel, except the Archbishop, who gives his benediction with a sigh, and La Trémouille, who collapses, cursing.

Scene III

Orleans, April 29th, 1429. Dunois, aged 26, is pacing up and down a patch of ground on the south bank of the silver Loire, commanding a long view of the river in both directions. He has had his lance stuck up with a pennon, which streams in a strong east wind. His shield with its bend sinister [1] *lies beside it. He has his commander's baton in his hand. He is well built, carrying his armor easily. His broad brow and pointed chin give him an equilaterally triangular face, already marked by active service and responsibility, with the expression of a good-natured and capable man who has no affectations and no foolish illusions. His page is sitting on the ground, elbows on knees, cheeks on fists, idly watching the water. It is evening; and both man and boy are affected by the loveliness of the Loire.*

DUNOIS [*halting for a moment to glance up at the streaming pennon and shake his head wearily before he resumes his pacing*]   West wind, west wind, west wind. Strumpet: steadfast when you should be wanton, wanton when you should be steadfast. West wind on the silver Loire: what rhymes to Loire? [*He looks again at the pennon, and shakes his fist at it.*] Change, curse you, change, English harlot of a wind, change. West, west, I tell you. [*With a growl he resumes his march in silence, but soon begins again.*] West wind, wanton wind, wilful wind, womanish wind, wind from over the water, will you never blow again?

1. A heraldic device (diagonal stripe like that in the letter "N"), denoting illegitimacy.

THE PAGE [*bounding to his feet*]   See! There! There she goes!

DUNOIS [*startled from his reverie: eagerly*]   Where? Who? The Maid?

THE PAGE   No: the kingfisher. Like blue lightning. She went into that bush.

DUNOIS [*furiously disappointed*]   Is that all? You infernal young idiot: I have a mind to pitch you into the river.

THE PAGE [*not afraid, knowing his man*]   It looked frightfully jolly, that flash of blue. Look! There goes the other!

DUNOIS [*running eagerly to the river brim*]   Where? Where?

THE PAGE [*pointing*]   Passing the reeds.

DUNOIS [*delighted*]   I see.

> *They follow the flight till the bird takes cover.*

THE PAGE   You blew me up because you were not in time to see them yesterday.

DUNOIS   You knew I was expecting The Maid when you set up your yelping. I will give you something to yelp for next time.

THE PAGE   Arnt they lovely? I wish I could catch them.

DUNOIS   Let me catch you trying to trap them, and I will put you in the iron cage for a month to teach you what a cage feels like. You are an abominable boy.

THE PAGE [*laughs, and squats down as before*]

DUNOIS [*pacing*]   Blue bird, blue bird, since I am friend to thee, change thou the wind for me. No: it does not rhyme. He who has sinned for thee: thats better. No sense in it, though. [*He finds himself close to the page.*] You abominable boy! [*He turns away from him*] Mary in the blue snood,[2] kingfisher color: will you grudge me a west wind?

A SENTRY'S VOICE WESTWARD   Halt! Who goes there?

JOAN'S VOICE   The Maid.

DUNOIS   Let her pass. Hither, Maid! To me!

> *Joan, in splendid armor, rushes in in a blazing rage. The wind drops; and the pennon flaps idly down the lance; but Dunois is too much occupied with Joan to notice it.*

JOAN [*bluntly*]   Be you Bastard of Orleans?

DUNOIS [*cool and stern, pointing to his shield*]   You see the bend sinister. Are you Joan the Maid?

JOAN   Sure.

DUNOIS   Where are your troops?

JOAN   Miles behind. They have cheated me. They have brought me to the wrong side of the river.

DUNOIS   I told them to.

JOAN   Why did you? The English are on the other side!

DUNOIS   The English are on both sides.

JOAN   But Orleans is on the other side. We must fight the English there. How can we cross the river?

DUNOIS [*grimly*]   There is a bridge.

JOAN   In God's name, then, let us cross the bridge, and fall on them.

DUNOIS   It seems simple; but it cannot be done.

JOAN   Who says so?

2. Her hair band, proper to a virgin.

DUNOIS   I say so; and older and wiser heads than mine are of the same opinion.

JOAN   [*roundly*]   Then your older and wiser heads are fatheads: they have made a fool of you; and now they want to make a fool of me too, bringing me to the wrong side of the river. Do you not know that I bring you better help than ever came to any general or any town?

DUNOIS   [*smiling patiently*]   Your own?

JOAN   No: the help and counsel of the King of Heaven. Which is the way to the bridge?

DUNOIS   You are impatient, Maid.

JOAN   Is this a time for patience? Our enemy is at our gates; and here we stand doing nothing. Oh, why are you not fighting? Listen to me: I will deliver you from fear. I—

DUNOIS   [*laughing heartily, and waving her off*]   No, no, my girl: if you delivered me from fear I should be a good knight for a story book, but a very bad commander of the army. Come! let me begin to make a soldier of you. [*He takes her to the water's edge.*] Do you see those two forts at this end of the bridge? the big ones?

JOAN   Yes. Are they ours or the goddams'?

DUNOIS   Be quiet, and listen to me. If I were in either of those forts with only ten men I could hold it against an army. The English have more than ten times ten goddams in those forts to hold them against us.

JOAN   They cannot hold them against God. God did not give them the land under those forts: they stole it from Him. He gave it to us. I will take those forts.

DUNOIS   Single-handed?

JOAN   Our men will take them. I will lead them.

DUNOIS   Not a man will follow you.

JOAN   I will not look back to see whether anyone is following me.

DUNOIS   [*recognizing her mettle, and clapping her heartily on the shoulder*]   Good. You have the makings of a soldier in you. You are in love with war.

JOAN   [*startled*]   Oh! And the Archbishop said I was in love with religion.

DUNOIS   I, God forgive me, am a little in love with war myself, the ugly devil! I am like a man with two wives. Do you want to be like a woman with two husbands?

JOAN   [*matter-of-fact*]   I will never take a husband. A man in Toul took an action against me for breach of promise; but I never promised him. I am a soldier: I do not want to be thought of as a woman. I will not dress as a woman. I do not care for the things women care for. They dream of lovers, and of money. I dream of leading a charge, and of placing the big guns. You soldiers do not know how to use the big guns: you think you can win battles with a great noise and smoke.

DUNOIS   [*with a shrug*]   True. Half the time the artillery is more trouble than it is worth.

JOAN   Aye, lad; but you cannot fight stone walls with horses: you must have guns, and much bigger guns too.

DUNOIS   [*grinning at her familiarity, and echoing it*]   Aye, lass; but a good heart and a stout ladder will get over the stoniest wall.

JOAN   I will be first up the ladder when we reach the fort, Bastard. I dare you to follow me.

DUNOIS   You must not dare a staff officer, Joan: only company officers are allowed to indulge in displays of personal courage. Besides, you must know that I welcome you as a saint, not as a soldier. I have daredevils enough at my call, if they could help me.

JOAN   I am not a daredevil: I am a servant of God. My sword is sacred: I found it behind the altar in the church of St Catherine, where God hid it for me; and I may not strike a blow with it. My heart is full of courage, not of anger. I will lead, and your men will follow: that is all I can do. But I must do it: you shall not stop me.

DUNOIS   All in good time. Our men cannot take those forts by a sally across the bridge. They must come by water, and take the English in the rear on this side.

JOAN [her military sense asserting itself]   Then make rafts and put big guns on them; and let your men cross to us.

DUNOIS   The rafts are ready; and the men are embarked. But they must wait for God.

JOAN   What do you mean? God is waiting for them.

DUNOIS   Let Him send us a wind then. My boats are downstream: they cannot come up against both wind and current. We must wait until God changes the wind. Come: let me take you to the church.

JOAN   No. I love church; but the English will not yield to prayers: they understand nothing but hard knocks and slashes. I will not go to church until we have beaten them.

DUNOIS   You must: I have business for you there.

JOAN   What business?

DUNOIS   To pray for a west wind. I have prayed; and I have given two silver candlesticks; but my prayers are not answered. Yours may be: you are young and innocent.

JOAN   Oh yes: you are right. I will pray: I will tell St Catherine: she will make God give me a west wind. Quick: shew me the way to the church.

THE PAGE [sneezes violently]   At-cha!!!

JOAN   God bless you, child! Coom, Bastard.
    They go out. The page rises to follow. He picks up the shield, and is taking the spear as well when he notices the pennon, which is now streaming eastward.

THE PAGE [dropping the shield and calling excitedly after them]   Seigneur! Seigneur! Mademoiselle!

DUNOIS [running back]   What is it? The kingfisher? [He looks eagerly for it up the river.]

JOAN [joining them]   Oh, a kingfisher! Where?

THE PAGE   No: the wind, the wind, the wind [pointing to the pennon]: that is what made me sneeze.

DUNOIS [looking at the pennon]   The wind has changed. [He crosses himself.] God has spoken. [kneeling and handing his baton to Joan]   You command the king's army. I am your soldier.

THE PAGE [*looking down the river*]   The boats have put off. They are ripping upstream like anything.

DUNOIS [*rising*]   Now for the forts. You dared me to follow. Dare you lead?

JOAN [*bursting into tears and flinging her arms round Dunois, kissing him on both cheeks*]   Dunois, dear comrade in arms, help me. My eyes are blinded with tears. Set my foot on the ladder, and say 'Up, Joan.'

DUNOIS [*dragging her out*]   Never mind the tears: make for the flash of the guns.

JOAN [*in a blaze of courage*]   Ah!

DUNOIS [*dragging her along with him*]   For God and Saint Dennis!

THE PAGE [*shrilly*]   The Maid! The Maid! God and The Maid! Hurray-ay-ay! [*He snatches up the shield and lance, and capers out after them, mad with excitement.*]

Scene IV

A tent in the English camp. A bullnecked English chaplain of 50 is sitting on a stool at a table, hard at work writing. At the other side of the table an imposing nobleman, aged 46, is seated in a handsome chair turning over the leaves of an illuminated Book of Hours.[1] The nobleman is enjoying himself: the chaplain is struggling with suppressed wrath. There is an unoccupied leather stool on the nobleman's left. The table is on his right.

THE NOBLEMAN   Now this is what I call workmanship. There is nothing on earth more exquisite than a bonny book, with well-placed columns of rich black writing in beautiful borders, and illuminated pictures cunningly inset. But nowadays, instead of looking at books, people read them. A book might as well be one of those orders for bacon and bran that you are scribbling.

THE CHAPLAIN   I must say, my lord, you take our situation very coolly. Very coolly indeed.

THE NOBLEMAN [*supercilious*]   What is the matter?

THE CHAPLAIN   The matter, my lord, is that we English have been defeated.

THE NOBLEMAN   That happens, you know. It is only in history books and ballads that the enemy is always defeated.

THE CHAPLAIN   But we are being defeated over and over again. First, Orleans—

THE NOBLEMAN [*poohpoohing*]   Oh, Orleans!

THE CHAPLAIN   I know what you are going to say, my lord: that was a clear case of witchcraft and sorcery. But we are still being defeated. Jargeau, Meung, Beaugency, just like Orleans. And now we have been butchered at Patay, and Sir John Talbot [2] taken prisoner. [*He throws down his pen, almost in tears.*] I feel it, my lord: I feel it very deeply. I cannot bear to see my countrymen defeated by a parcel of foreigners.

THE NOBLEMAN   Oh! you are an Englishman, are you?

1. A manuscript book containing the prayers and offices to be said at the canonical hours of the day (prime, terce, sext, none, compline); they were often illuminated with brilliantly colored miniatures of calendrical subjects and scenes of daily life.
2. First Earl of Shrewsbury (1388–1453), fought in 40 battles before being stopped at Orléans, and taken prisoner by Joan's forces at Patay in 1429.

THE CHAPLAIN   Certainly not, my lord: I am a gentleman. Still, like your lordship, I was born in England; and it makes a difference.

THE NOBLEMAN   You are attached to the soil, eh?

THE CHAPLAIN   It pleases your lordship to be satirical at my expense: your greatness privileges you to be so with impunity. But your lordship knows very well that I am not attached to the soil in a vulgar manner, like a serf. Still, I have a feeling about it; [*with growing agitation*] and I am not ashamed of it; and [*rising wildly*] by God, if this goes on any longer I will fling my cassock to the devil, and take arms myself, and strangle the accursed witch with my own hands.

THE NOBLEMAN   [*laughing at him good naturedly*]   So you shall, chaplain: so you shall, if we can do nothing better. But not yet, not quite yet.

The Chaplain resumes his seat very sulkily.

THE NOBLEMAN   [*airily*]   I should not care very much about the witch—you see, I have made my pilgrimage to the Holy Land; and the Heavenly Powers, for their own credit, can hardly allow me to be worsted by a village sorceress—but the Bastard of Orleans is a harder nut to crack; and as he has been to the Holy Land too, honors are easy between us as far as that goes.

THE CHAPLAIN   He is only a Frenchman, my lord.

THE NOBLEMAN   A Frenchman! Where did you pick up that expression? Are these Burgundians and Bretons and Picards and Gascons beginning to call themselves Frenchmen, just as our fellows are beginning to call themselves Englishmen? They actually talk of France and England as their countries. Theirs, if you please! What is to become of me and you if that way of thinking comes into fashion?

THE CHAPLAIN   Why, my lord? Can it hurt us?

THE NOBLEMAN   Men cannot serve two masters. If this cant of serving their country once takes hold of them, goodbye to the authority of their feudal lords, and goodbye to the authority of the Church. That is, goodbye to you and me.

THE CHAPLAIN   I hope I am a faithful servant of the Church; and there are only six cousins between me and the barony of Stogumber, which was created by the Conqueror. But is that any reason why I should stand by and see Englishmen beaten by a French bastard and a witch from Lousy Champagne?

THE NOBLEMAN   Easy, man, easy: we shall burn the witch and beat the bastard all in good time. Indeed I am waiting at present for the Bishop of Beauvais, to arrange the burning with him. He has been turned out of his diocese by her faction.

THE CHAPLAIN   You have first to catch her, my lord.

THE NOBLEMAN   Or buy her. I will offer a king's ransom.

THE CHAPLAIN   A king's ransom! For that slut!

THE NOBLEMAN   One has to leave a margin. Some of Charles's people will sell her to the Burgundians; the Burgundians will sell her to us; and there will probably be three or four middlemen who will expect their little commissions.

THE CHAPLAIN   Monstrous. It is all those scoundrels of Jews: they get in every time money changes hands.[3] I would not leave a Jew alive in Christendom if I had my way.

THE NOBLEMAN   Why not? The Jews generally give value. They make you pay; but they deliver the goods. In my experience the men who want something for nothing are invariably Christians.

A page appears.

THE PAGE   The Right Reverend the Bishop of Beauvais: Monseigneur Cauchon.

Cauchon, aged about 60, comes in. The page withdraws. The two Englishmen rise.

THE NOBLEMAN [*with effusive courtesy*]   My dear Bishop, how good of you to come! Allow me to introduce myself: Richard de Beauchamp, Earl of Warwick, at your service.

CAUCHON   Your lordship's fame is well known to me.

WARWICK   This reverend cleric is Master John de Stogumber.

THE CHAPLAIN [*glibly*]   John Bowyer Spenser Neville de Stogumber, at your service, my lord: Bachelor of Theology, and Keeper of the Private Seal to His Eminence the Cardinal of Winchester.

WARWICK [*to Cauchon*]   You call him the Cardinal of England, I believe. Our king's uncle.

CAUCHON   Messire John de Stogumber: I am always the very good friend of His Eminence. [*He extends his hand to the chaplain, who kisses his ring.*]

WARWICK   Do me the honor to be seated. [*He gives Cauchon his chair, placing it at the head of the table.*]

Cauchon accepts the place of honor with a grave inclination. Warwick fetches the leather stool carelessly, and sits in his former place. The chaplain goes back to his chair.

Though Warwick has taken second place in calculated deference to the Bishop, he assumes the lead in opening the proceedings as a matter of course. He is still cordial and expansive; but there is a new note in his voice which means that he is coming to business.

WARWICK   Well, my Lord Bishop, you find us in one of our unlucky moments. Charles is to be crowned at Rheims, practically by the young woman from Lorraine; and—I must not deceive you, nor flatter your hopes—we cannot prevent it. I suppose it will make a great difference to Charles's position.

CAUCHON   Undoubtedly. It is a masterstroke of The Maid's.

THE CHAPLAIN [*again agitated*]   We were not fairly beaten, my lord. No Englishman is ever fairly beaten.

Cauchon raises his eyebrow slightly, then quickly composes his face.

WARWICK   Our friend here takes the view that the young woman is a sorceress. It would, I presume, be the duty of your reverend lordship to denounce her to the Inquisition, and have her burnt for that offence.

CAUCHON   If she were captured in my diocese: yes.

WARWICK [*feeling that they are getting on capitally*]   Just so. Now I suppose there can be no reasonable doubt that she is a sorceress.

3. In the Middle Ages in Europe, Jews were forbidden by law to engage in any other business than money-lending at interest, usury being forbidden by the Church, and money borrowed at interest being constantly in demand.

THE CHAPLAIN   Not the least. An arrant witch.

WARWICK [*gently reproving the interruption*]   We are asking for the Bishop's opinion, Messire John.

CAUCHON   We shall have to consider not merely our own opinions here, but the opinions—the prejudices, if you like—of a French court.

WARWICK [*correcting*]   A Catholic court, my lord.

CAUCHON   Catholic courts are composed of mortal men, like other courts, however sacred their function and inspiration may be. And if the men are Frenchmen, as the modern fashion calls them, I am afraid the bare fact that an English army has been defeated by a French one will not convince them that there is any sorcery in the matter.

THE CHAPLAIN   What! Not when the famous Sir Talbot himself has been defeated and actually taken prisoner by a drab from the ditches of Lorraine!

CAUCHON   Sir John Talbot, we all know, is a fierce and formidable soldier, Messire; but I have yet to learn that he is an able general. And though it pleases you to say that he has been defeated by this girl, some of us may be disposed to give a little of the credit to Dunois.

THE CHAPLAIN [*contemptuously*]   The Bastard of Orleans!

CAUCHON   Let me remind—

WARWICK [*interposing*]   I know what you are going to say, my lord. Dunois defeated me at Montargis.

CAUCHON [*bowing*]   I take that as evidence that the Seigneur Dunois is a very able commander indeed.

WARWICK   Your lordship is the flower of courtesy. I admit, on our side, that Talbot is a mere fighting animal, and that it probably served him right to be taken at Patay.

THE CHAPLAIN [*chafing*]   My lord: at Orleans this woman had her throat pierced by an English arrow, and was seen to cry like a child from the pain of it. It was a death wound; yet she fought all day; and when our men had repulsed all her attacks like true Englishmen, she walked alone to the wall of our fort with a white banner in her hand; and our men were paralyzed, and could neither shoot nor strike whilst the French fell on them and drove them on to the bridge, which immediately burst into flames and crumbled under them, letting them down into the river, where they were drowned in heaps. Was this your bastard's generalship? or were those flames the flames of hell, conjured up by witchcraft?

WARWICK   You will forgive Messire John's vehemence, my lord; but he has put our case. Dunois is a great captain, we admit; but why could he do nothing until the witch came?

CAUCHON   I do not say that there were no supernatural powers on her side. But the names on that white banner were not the names of Satan and Beelzebub, but the blessed names of our Lord and His holy mother. And your commander who was drowned—Clahz-da I think you call him—

WARWICK   Glasdale. Sir William Glasdale.

CAUCHON   Glass-dell, thank you. He was no saint; and many of our people think that he was drowned for his blasphemies against The Maid.

WARWICK [*beginning to look very dubious*]   Well, what are we to infer from all this, my lord? Has The Maid converted you?

CAUCHON   If she had, my lord, I should have known better than to have trusted myself here within your grasp.

WARWICK [*blandly deprecating*]   Oh! oh! My lord!

CAUCHON   If the devil is making use of this girl—and I believe he is—

WARWICK [*reassured*]   Ah! You hear, Messire John? I knew your lordship would not fail us. Pardon my interruption. Proceed.

CAUCHON   If it be so, the devil has longer views than you give him credit for.

WARWICK   Indeed? In what way? Listen to this, Messire John.

CAUCHON   If the devil wanted to damn a country girl, do you think so easy a task would cost him the winning of half a dozen battles? No, my lord: any trumpery imp could do that much if the girl could be damned at all. The Prince of Darkness does not condescend to such cheap drudgery. When he strikes, he strikes at the Catholic Church, whose realm is the whole spiritual world. When he damns, he damns the souls of the entire human race. Against that dreadful design The Church stands ever on guard. And it is as one of the instruments of that design that I see this girl. She is inspired, but diabolically inspired.

THE CHAPLAIN   I told you she was a witch.

CAUCHON [*fiercely*]   She is not a witch. She is a heretic.

THE CHAPLAIN   What difference does that make?

CAUCHON   You, a priest, ask me that! You English are strangely blunt in the mind. All these things that you call witchcraft are capable of a natural explanation. The woman's miracles would not impose on a rabbit: she does not claim them as miracles herself. What do her victories prove but that she has a better head on her shoulders than your swearing Glass-dells and mad bull Talbots, and that the courage of faith, even though it be a false faith, will always outstay the courage of wrath?

THE CHAPLAIN [*hardly able to believe his ears*]   Does your lordship compare Sir John Talbot, three times Governor of Ireland, to a mad bull?!!!

WARWICK   It would not be seemly for you to do so, Messire John, as you are still six removes from a barony. But as I am an earl, and Talbot is only a knight, I may make bold to accept the comparison. [*to the Bishop*] My lord: I wipe the slate as far as the witchcraft goes. None the less, we must burn the woman.

CAUCHON   I cannot burn her. The Church cannot take life. And my first duty is to seek this girl's salvation.

WARWICK   No doubt. But you do burn people occasionally.

CAUCHON   No. When The Church cuts off an obstinate heretic as a dead branch from the tree of life, the heretic is handed over to the secular arm. The Church has no part in what the secular arm may see fit to do.

WARWICK   Precisely. And I shall be the secular arm in this case. Well, my lord, hand over your dead branch; and I will see that the fire is ready for it. If you will answer for The Church's part, I will answer for the secular part.

CAUCHON [*with smouldering anger*]   I can answer for nothing. You great lords are too prone to treat The Church as a mere political convenience.

WARWICK [*smiling and propitiatory*]   Not in England, I assure you.

CAUCHON   In England more than anywhere else. No, my lord: the soul of this village girl is of equal value with yours or your king's before the throne of God; and my first duty is to save it. I will not suffer your lordship to smile at me as if I were repeating a meaningless form of words, and it were well understood between us that I should betray the girl to you. I am no mere political bishop: my faith is to me what your honor is to you; and if there be a loophole through which this baptized child of God can creep to her salvation, I shall guide her to it.

THE CHAPLAIN [*rising in a fury*]   You are a traitor.

CAUCHON [*springing up*]   You lie, priest. [*trembling with rage*]   If you dare do what this woman has done—set your country above the holy Catholic Church—you shall go to the fire with her.

THE CHAPLAIN   My lord: I—Iwent too far. I—[*He sits down with a submissive gesture.*]

WARWICK [*who has risen apprehensively*]   My lord: I apologize to you for the word used by Messire John de Stogumber. It does not mean in England what it does in France. In your language traitor means betrayer: one who is perfidious, treacherous, unfaithful, disloyal. In our country it means simply one who is not wholly devoted to our English interests.

CAUCHON   I am sorry: I did not understand. [*He subsides into his chair with dignity.*]

WARWICK [*resuming his seat, much relieved*]   I must apologize on my own account if I have seemed to take the burning of this poor girl too lightly. When one has seen whole countrysides burnt over and over again as mere items in military routine, one has to grow a very thick skin. Otherwise one might go mad: at all events, I should. May I venture to assume that your lordship also, having to see so many heretics burned from time to time, is compelled to take—shall I say a professional view of what would otherwise be a very horrible incident?

CAUCHON   Yes: it is a painful duty: even, as you say, a horrible one. But in comparison with the horror of heresy it is less than nothing. I am not thinking of this girl's body, which will suffer for a few moments only, and which must in any event die in some more or less painful manner, but of her soul, which may suffer to all eternity.

WARWICK   Just so; and God grant that her soul may be saved! But the practical problem would seem to be how to save her soul without saving her body. For we must face it, my lord: if this cult of The Maid goes on, our cause is lost.

THE CHAPLAIN [*his voice broken like that of a man who has been crying*]   May I speak, my lord?

WARWICK   Really, Messire John, I had rather you did not, unless you can keep your temper.

THE CHAPLAIN   It is only this. I speak under correction; but The Maid is full of deceit: she pretends to be devout. Her prayers and confessions are endless. How can she be accused of heresy when she neglects no observance of a faithful daughter of The Church?

CAUCHON [*flaming up*]   A faithful daughter of The Church! The Pope himself at his proudest dare not presume as this woman presumes. She acts as if she herself were The Church. She brings the message of God to

Charles; and The Church must stand aside. She will crown him in the cathedral of Rheims: she, not The Church! She sends letters to the king of England giving him God's command through her to return to his island on pain of God's vengeance, which she will execute. Let me tell you that the writing of such letters was the practice of the accursed Mahomet, the anti-Christ. Has she ever in all her utterances said one word of The Church? Never. It is always God and herself.

WARWICK   What can you expect? A beggar on horseback! Her head is turned.

CAUCHON   Who has turned it? The devil. And for a mighty purpose. He is spreading this heresy everywhere. The man Hus,[4] burnt only thirteen years ago at Constance, infected all Bohemia with it. A man named WcLeef,[5] himself an anointed priest, spread the pestilence in England; and to your shame you let him die in his bed. We have such people here in France too: I know the breed. It is cancerous: if it be not cut out, stamped out, burnt out, it will not stop until it has brought the whole body of human society into sin and corruption, into waste and ruin. By it an Arab camel driver [6] drove Christ and His Church out of Jerusalem, and ravaged his way west like a wild beast until at last there stood only the Pyrenees and God's mercy between France and damnation. Yet what did the camel driver do at the beginning more than this shepherd girl is doing? He had his voices from the angel Gabriel: she has her voices from St Catherine and St Margaret and the Blessed Michael. He declared himself the messenger of God, and wrote in God's name to the kings of the earth. Her letters to them are going forth daily. It is not the Mother of God now to whom we must look for intercession, but to Joan the Maid. What will the world be like when The Church's accumulated wisdom and knowledge and experience, its councils of learned, venerable, pious men, are thrust into the kennel by every ignorant laborer or dairymaid whom the devil can puff up with the monstrous self-conceit of being directly inspired from heaven? It will be a world of blood, of fury, of devastation, of each man striving for his own hand: in the end a world wrecked back into barbarism. For now you have only Mahomet and his dupes, and the Maid and her dupes; but what will it be when every girl thinks herself a Joan and every man a Mahomet? I shudder to the very marrow of my bones when I think of it. I have fought it all my life; and I will fight it to the end. Let all this woman's sins be forgiven her except only this sin; for it is the sin against the Holy Ghost; and if she does not recant in the dust before the world, and submit herself to the last inch of her soul to her Church, to the fire she shall go if she once falls into my hand.

WARWICK [unimpressed]   You feel strongly about it, naturally.

CAUCHON   Do not you?

WARWICK   I am a soldier, not a churchman. As a pilgrim I saw something of the Mahometans. They were not so ill-bred as I had been led to believe. In some respects their conduct compared favorably with ours.

4. Jan Hus (1373–1415), Bohemian church reformer, burned at the stake.
5. John Wyclif (1320–84), English church reformer and heretic; Hus was one of his followers.
6. Mohammed (570–632).

CAUCHON [*displeased*] I have noticed this before. Men go to the East to convert the infidels. And the infidels pervert them. The Crusader comes back more than half a Saracen. Not to mention that all Englishmen are born heretics.

THE CHAPLAIN Englishmen heretics!!! [*appealing to Warwick*] My lord: must we endure this? His lordship is beside himself. How can what an Englishman believes be heresy? It is a contradiction in terms.

CAUCHON I absolve you, Messire de Stogumber, on the ground of invincible ignorance. The thick air of your country does not breed theologians.

WARWICK You would not say so if you heard us quarrelling about religion, my lord! I am sorry you think I must be either a heretic or a blockhead because, as a travelled man, I know that the followers of Mahomet profess great respect for our Lord, and are more ready to forgive St Peter for being a fisherman than your lordship is to forgive Mahomet for being a camel driver. But at least we can proceed in this matter without bigotry.

CAUCHON When men call the zeal of the Christian Church bigotry I know what to think.

WARWICK They are only east and west views of the same thing.

CAUCHON [*bitterly ironical*] Only east and west! Only!!

WARWICK Oh, my Lord Bishop, I am not gainsaying you. You will carry The Church with you; but you have to carry the nobles also. To my mind there is a stronger case against The Maid than the one you have so forcibly put. Frankly, I am not afraid of this girl becoming another Mahomet, and superseding The Church by a great heresy. I think you exaggerate that risk. But have you noticed that in these letters of hers, she proposes to all the kings of Europe, as she has already pressed on Charles, a transaction which would wreck the whole social structure of Christendom?

CAUCHON Wreck The Church. I tell you so.

WARWICK [*whose patience is wearing out*] My lord: pray get The Church out of your head for a moment; and remember that there are temporal institutions in the world as well as spiritual ones. I and my peers represent the feudal aristocracy as you represent The Church. We are the temporal power. Well, do you not see how this girl's idea strikes at us?

CAUCHON How does her idea strike at you, except as it strikes at all of us, through The Church?

WARWICK Her idea is that the kings should give their realms to God, and then reign as God's bailiffs.

CAUCHON [*not interested*] Quite sound theologically, my lord. But the king will hardly care, provided he reign. It is an abstract idea: a mere form of words.

WARWICK By no means. It is a cunning device to supersede the aristocracy, and make the king sole and absolute autocrat. Instead of the king being merely the first among his peers, he becomes their master. That we cannot suffer: we call no man master. Nominally we hold our lands and dignities from the king, because there must be a keystone to the arch of human society; but we hold our lands in our own hands, and defend them with our own swords and those of our own tenants. Now by The Maid's doctrine the king will take our lands—our lands!—and make them a present to God; and God will then vest them wholly in the king.

CAUCHON   Need you fear that? You are the makers of kings after all. York or Lancaster in England, Lancaster or Valois in France: they reign according to your pleasure.

WARWICK   Yes; but only as long as the people follow their feudal lords, and know the king only as a travelling show, owning nothing but the highway that belongs to everybody. If the people's thoughts and hearts were turned to the king, and their lords became only the king's servants in their eyes, the king could break us across his knee one by one; and then what should we be but liveried courtiers in his halls?

CAUCHON   Still you need not fear, my lord. Some men are born kings; and some are born statesmen. The two are seldom the same. Where would the king find counsellors to plan and carry out such a policy for him?

WARWICK   [*with a not too friendly smile*]   Perhaps in the Church, my lord.
          Cauchon, with an equally sour smile, shrugs his shoulders, and does not contradict him.

WARWICK   Strike down the barons; and the cardinals will have it all their own way.

CAUCHON   [*conciliatory, dropping his polemical tone*]   My lord: we shall not defeat The Maid if we strive against one another. I know well that there is a Will to Power [7] in the world. I know that while it lasts there will be a struggle between the Emperor and the Pope, between the dukes and the political cardinals, between the barons and the kings. The devil divides us and governs. I see you are no friend to The Church: you are an earl first and last, as I am a churchman first and last. But can we not sink our differences in the face of a common enemy? I see now that what is in your mind is not that this girl has never once mentioned The Church, and thinks only of God and herself, but that she has never once mentioned the peerage, and thinks only of the king and herself.

WARWICK   Quite so. These two ideas of hers are the same idea at bottom. It goes deep, my lord. It is the protest of the individual soul against the interference of priest or peer between the private man and his God. I should call it Protestantism if I had to find a name for it.

CAUCHON   [*looking hard at him*]   You understand it wonderfully well, my lord. Scratch an Englishman, and find a Protestant.

WARWICK   [*playing the pink of courtesy*]   I think you are not entirely void of sympathy with The Maid's secular heresy, my lord. I leave you to find a name for it.

CAUCHON   You mistake me, my lord. I have no sympathy with her political presumptions. But as a priest I have gained a knowledge of the minds of the common people; and there you will find yet another most dangerous idea. I can express it only by such phrases as France for the French, England for the English, Italy for the Italians, Spain for the

---

7. The phrase is Friedrich Wilhelm Nietzsche's (1844–1900); *Der Wille zur Macht* was the title of an unfinished work, a vast collection of aphorisms. The invocation to "live dangerously," quoted above, comes from one of these passages beginning "I am writing for a race of men not yet in existence."

Spanish, and so forth. It is sometimes so narrow and bitter in country folk that it surprises me that this country girl can rise above the idea of her village for its villagers. But she can. She does. When she threatens to drive the English from the soil of France she is undoubtedly thinking of the whole extent of country in which French is spoken. To her the French-speaking people are what the Holy Scriptures describe as a nation. Call this side of her heresy Nationalism if you will: I can find you no better name for it. I can only tell you that it is essentially anti-Catholic and anti-Christian; for the Catholic Church knows only one realm, and that is the realm of Christ's kingdom. Divide that kingdom into nations, and you dethrone Christ. Dethrone Christ, and who will stand between our throats and the sword? The world will perish in a welter of war.

WARWICK Well, if you will burn the Protestant, I will burn the Nationalist, though perhaps I shall not carry Messire John with me there. England for the English will appeal to him.

THE CHAPLAIN Certainly England for the English goes without saying: it is the simple law of nature. But this woman denies to England her legitimate conquests, given her by God because of her peculiar fitness to rule over less civilized races for their own good. I do not understand what your lordships mean by Protestant and Nationalist: you are too learned and subtle for a poor clerk like myself. But I know as a matter of plain commonsense that the woman is a rebel; and that is enough for me. She rebels against Nature by wearing man's clothes, and fighting. She rebels against The Church by usurping the divine authority of the Pope. She rebels against God by her damnable league with Satan and his evil spirits against our army. And all these rebellions are only excuses for her great rebellion against England. That is not to be endured. Let her perish. Let her burn. Let her not infect the whole flock. It is expedient that one woman die for the people.

WARWICK [rising] My lord: we seem to be agreed.

CAUCHON [rising also, but in protest] I will not imperil my soul. I will uphold the justice of the Church. I will strive to the utmost for this woman's salvation.

WARWICK I am sorry for the poor girl. I hate these severities. I will spare her if I can.

THE CHAPLAIN [implacably] I would burn her with my own hands.

CAUCHON [blessing him] Sancta simplicitas! [8]

Scene V

The ambulatory [1] in the cathedral of Rheims, near the door of the vestry. A pillar bears one of the stations of the cross.[2] The organ is playing the people

8. "Holy simplicity!" A legendary anecdote about the burning of the Protestant martyr Jan Hus (see note 4) tells that, while he was tied to the stake, "a little old woman was bearing not merely one, but two fagots to the fire. On seeing her, Hus is said to have exclaimed 'Sancta simplicitas'" (quoted from the life of Hus by Benito Mussolini). It is hard to believe that Shaw did not have Hus's irony in mind.

1. The semi-circular aisle behind the apse of a Norman church, with chapels opening off it.
2. One of 14 carved or painted representations of stages in Christ's passion and death.

out of the nave after the coronation. Joan is kneeling in prayer before the station. She is beautifully dressed, but still in male attire. The organ ceases as Dunois, also splendidly arrayed, comes into the ambulatory from the vestry.

DUNOIS   Come, Joan! you have had enough praying. After that fit of crying you will catch a chill if you stay here any longer. It is all over: the cathedral is empty; and the streets are full. They are calling for The Maid. We have told them you are staying here alone to pray; but they want to see you again.

JOAN   No: let the king have all the glory.

DUNOIS   He only spoils the show, poor devil. No, Joan: you have crowned him; and you must go through with it.

JOAN [*shakes her head reluctantly.*]

DUNOIS [*raising her*]   Come, come! it will be over in a couple of hours. It's better than the bridge at Orleans: eh?

JOAN   Oh, dear Dunois, how I wish it were the bridge at Orleans again! We lived at that bridge.

DUNOIS   Yes, faith, and died too: some of us.

JOAN   Isnt it strange, Jack? I am such a coward: I am frightened beyond words before a battle; but it is so dull afterwards when there is no danger: oh, so dull! dull! dull!

DUNOIS   You must learn to be abstemious in war, just as you are in your food and drink, my little saint.

JOAN   Dear Jack: I think you like me as a soldier likes his comrade.

DUNOIS   You need it, poor innocent child of God. You have not many friends at court.

JOAN   Why do all these courtiers and knights and churchmen hate me? What have I done to them? I have asked nothing for myself except that my village shall not be taxed; for we cannot afford war taxes. I have brought them luck and victory: I have set them right when they were doing all sorts of stupid things: I have crowned Charles and made him a real king; and all the honors he is handing out have gone to them. Then why do they not love me?

DUNOIS [*rallying her*]   Sim-ple-ton! Do you expect stupid people to love you for shewing them up? Do blundering old military dug-outs love the successful young captains who supersede them? Do ambitious politicians love the climbers who take the front seats from them? Do archbishops enjoy being played off their own altars, even by saints? Why, I should be jealous of you myself if I were ambitious enough.

JOAN   You are the pick of the basket here, Jack: the only friend I have among all these nobles. I'll wager your mother was from the country. I will go back to the farm when I have taken Paris.

DUNOIS   I am not so sure that they will let you take Paris.

JOAN [*startled*]   What!

DUNOIS   I should have taken it myself before this if they had all been sound about it. Some of them would rather Paris took you, I think. So take care.

JOAN   Jack: the world is too wicked for me. If the goddams and the Burgundians do not make an end of me, the French will. Only for my voices I should lose all heart. That is why I had to steal away to pray here alone after the coronation. I'll tell you something, Jack. It is in the bells I hear my voices. Not to-day, when they all rang: that was nothing but jangling. But here in this corner, where the bells come down from heaven, and the echoes linger, or in the fields, where they come from a distance through the quiet of the countryside, my voices are in them. [*The cathedral clock chimes the quarter.*] Hark! [*She becomes rapt.*] Do you hear? 'Dear-child-of-God': just what you said. At the half-hour they will say 'Be-brave-go-on.' At the three-quarters they will say 'I-am-thy-Help.' But it is at the hour, when the great bell goes after 'God-will-save-France': it is then that St Margaret and St Catherine and sometimes even the blessed Michael will say things that I cannot tell beforehand. Then, oh then—

DUNOIS [*interrupting her kindly but not sympathetically*]   Then, Joan, we shall hear whatever we fancy in the booming of the bell. You make me uneasy when you talk about your voices: I should think you were a bit cracked if I hadnt noticed that you give me very sensible reasons for what you do, though I hear you tell others you are only obeying Madame Saint Catherine.

JOAN [*crossly*]   Well, I have to find reasons for you, because you do not believe in my voices. But the voices come first; and I find the reasons after: whatever you may choose to believe.

DUNOIS   Are you angry, Joan?

JOAN   Yes. [*Smiling*] No: not with you. I wish you were one of the village babies.

DUNOIS   Why?

JOAN   I could nurse you for awhile.

DUNOIS   You are a bit of a woman after all.

JOAN   No: not a bit: I am a soldier and nothing else. Soldiers always nurse children when they get a chance.

DUNOIS   That is true. [*He laughs.*]

   King Charles, with Bluebeard on his left and La Hire on his right, comes from the vestry, where he has been disrobing. Joan shrinks away behind the pillar. Dunois is left between Charles and La Hire.

DUNOIS   Well, your Majesty is an anointed king at last. How do you like it?

CHARLES   I would not go through it again to be emperor of the sun and moon. The weight of those robes! I thought I should have dropped when they loaded that crown on to me. And the famous holy oil they talked so much about was rancid: phew! The Archbishop must be nearly dead: his robes must have weighed a ton: they are stripping him still in the vestry.

DUNOIS [*drily*]   Your Majesty should wear armor oftener. That would accustom you to heavy dressing.

CHARLES   Yes: the old jibe! Well, I am not going to wear armor: fighting is not my job. Where is The Maid?

JOAN [*coming forward between Charles and Bluebeard, and falling on her knee*]   Sire: I have made you king: my work is done. I am going back to my father's farm.

CHARLES [*surprised, but relieved*]   Oh, are you? Well, that will be very nice.

   Joan rises, deeply discouraged.

CHARLES [*continuing heedlessly*]   A healthy life, you know.

DUNOIS   But a dull one.

BLUEBEARD   You will find the petticoats tripping you up after leaving them off for so long.

LA HIRE   You will miss the fighting. It's a bad habit, but a grand one, and the hardest of all to break yourself of.

CHARLES [*anxiously*]   Still, we dont want you to stay if you would really rather go home.

JOAN [*bitterly*]   I know well that none of you will be sorry to see me go. [*She turns her shoulder to Charles and walks past him to the more congenial neighborhood of Dunois and La Hire.*]

LA HIRE   Well, I shall be able to swear when I want to. But I shall miss you at times.

JOAN   La Hire: in spite of all your sins and swears we shall meet in heaven; for I love you as I love Pitou, my old sheep dog. Pitou could kill a wolf. You will kill the English wolves until they go back to their country and become good dogs of God, will you not?

LA HIRE   You and I together: yes.

JOAN   No: I shall last only a year from the beginning.

ALL THE OTHERS   What!

JOAN   I know it somehow.

DUNOIS   Nonsense!

JOAN   Jack: do you think you will be able to drive them out?

DUNOIS [*with quiet conviction*]   Yes: I shall drive them out. They beat us because we thought battles were tournaments and ransom markets. We played the fool while the goddams took war seriously. But I have learnt my lesson, and taken their measure. They have no roots here. I have beaten them before; and I shall beat them again.

JOAN   You will not be cruel to them, Jack?

DUNOIS   The goddams will not yield to tender handling. We did not begin it.

JOAN [*suddenly*]   Jack: before I go home, let us take Paris.

CHARLES [*terrified*]   Oh no no. We shall lose everything we have gained. Oh dont let us have any more fighting. We can make a very good treaty with the Duke of Burgundy.

JOAN   Treaty! [*She stamps with impatience.*]

CHARLES   Well, why not, now that I am crowned and anointed? Oh, that oil! *The Archbishop comes from the vestry, and joins the group between Charles and Bluebeard.*

CHARLES   Archbishop: The Maid wants to start fighting again.

THE ARCHBISHOP   Have we ceased fighting, then? Are we at peace?

CHARLES   No: I suppose not; but let us be content with what we have done. Let us make a treaty. Our luck is too good to last; and now is our chance to stop before it turns.

JOAN   Luck! God has fought for us; and you call it luck! And you would stop while there are still Englishmen on this holy earth of dear France!

THE ARCHBISHOP [*sternly*]   Maid: the king addressed himself to me, not to you. You forget yourself. You very often forget yourself.

JOAN [*unabashed, and rather roughly*]   Then speak, you; and tell him that it is not God's will that he should take his hand from the plough.

THE ARCHBISHOP   If I am not so glib with the name of God as you are, it is because I interpret His will with the authority of the Church and of my sacred office. When you first came you respected it, and would not have dared to speak as you are now speaking. You came clothed with the virtue of humility; and because God blessed your enterprises accordingly, you have stained yourself with the sin of pride. The old Greek tragedy is rising among us. It is the chastisement of hubris.[3]

CHARLES   Yes: she thinks she knows better than everyone else.

JOAN [*distressed, but naïvely incapable of seeing the effect she is producing*] But I do know better than any of you seem to. And I am not proud: I never speak unless I know I am right.

BLUEBEARD   Ha ha!
                         [*exclaiming together*]
CHARLES   Just so.

THE ARCHBISHOP   How do you know you are right?

JOAN   I always know. My voices—

CHARLES   Oh, your voices, your voices. Why dont the voices come to me? I am king, not you.

JOAN   They do come to you; but you do not hear them. You have not sat in the field in the evening listening for them. When the angelus rings you cross yourself and have done with it; but if you prayed from your heart, and listened to the thrilling of the bells in the air after they stop ringing, you would hear the voices as well as I do. [*turning brusquely from him*] But what voices do you need to tell you what the blacksmith can tell you: that you must strike while the iron is hot? I tell you we must make a dash at Compiègne and relieve it as we relieved Orleans. Then Paris will open its gates; or if not, we will break through them. What is your crown worth without your capital?

LA HIRE   That is what I say too. We shall go through them like a red hot shot through a pound of butter. What do you say, Bastard?

DUNOIS   If our cannon balls were all as hot as your head, and we had enough of them, we should conquer the earth, no doubt. Pluck and impetuosity are good servants in war, but bad masters: they have delivered us into the hands of the English every time we have trusted to them. We never know when we are beaten: that is our great fault.

JOAN   You never know when you are victorious: that is a worse fault. I shall have to make you carry looking-glasses in battle to convince you that the English have not cut off all your noses. You would have been besieged in Orleans still, you and your councils of war, if I had not made you attack. You should always attack; and if you only hold on long enough the enemy will stop first. You dont know how to begin a battle; and you dont know how to use your cannons. And I do.

She squats down on the flags with crossed ankles, pouting.

DUNOIS   I know what you think of us, General Joan.

JOAN   Never mind that, Jack. Tell them what you think of me.

DUNOIS   I think that God was on your side; for I have not forgotten how the wind changed, and how our hearts changed when you came; and by

---

3. The particular kind of noble pride associated with the *hamartia* or flaw in the Greek tragic hero. Needless to say, it is a comic anachronism on Shaw's part, as the archbishop would have known no Greek, nor anything of its tragedy.

my faith I shall never deny that it was in your sign that we conquered. But I tell you as a soldier that God is no man's daily drudge, and no maid's either. If you are worthy of it He will sometimes snatch you out of the jaws of death and set you on your feet again; but that is all: once on your feet you must fight with all your might and all your craft. For He has to be fair to your enemy too: dont forget that. Well, He set us on our feet through you at Orleans; and the glory of it has carried us through a few good battles here to the coronation. But if we presume on it further, and trust to God to do the work we should do ourselves, we shall be defeated; and serve us right!

JOAN   But—

DUNOIS   Sh! I have not finished. Do not think, any of you, that these victories of ours were won without generalship. King Charles: you have said no word in your proclamations of my part in this campaign; and I make no complaint of that; for the people will run after The Maid and her miracles and not after the Bastard's hard work finding troops for her and feeding them. But I know exactly how much God did for us through The Maid, and how much He left me to do by my own wits; and I tell you that your little hour of miracles is over, and that from this time on he who plays the war game best will win—if the luck is on his side.

JOAN   Ah! if, if if, if! If ifs and ands were pots and pans there'd be no need of tinkers. [rising impetuously] I tell you, Bastard, your art of war is no use, because your knights are no good for real fighting. War is only a game to them, like tennis and all their other games: they make rules as to what is fair and what is not fair, and heap armor on themselves and on their poor horses to keep out the arrows; and when they fall they cant get up, and have to wait for their squires to come and lift them to arrange about the ransom with the man that has poked them off their horse. Cant you see that all the like of that is gone by and done with? What use is armor against gunpowder? And if it was, do you think men that are fighting for France and for God will stop to bargain about ransoms, as half your knights live by doing? No: they will fight to win; and they will give up their lives out of their own hand into the hand of God when they go into battle, as I do. Common folks understand this. They cannot afford armor and cannot pay ransoms; but they followed me half naked into the moat and up the ladder and over the wall. With them it is my life or thine, and God defend the right! You may shake your head, Jack; and Bluebeard may twirl his billygoat's beard and cock his nose at me; but remember the day your knights and captains refused to follow me to attack the English at Orleans! You locked the gates to keep me in; and it was the townsfolk and the common people that followed me, and forced the gate, and shewed you the way to fight in earnest.

BLUEBEARD   [offended]   Not content with being Pope Joan,[4] you must be Caesar and Alexander as well.

4. A widely believed medieval legend held that, about the year 1100, a woman in male disguise, after a career as a scholar, became pope; after reigning for two years, she gave birth to a child during a procession and died immediately thereafter.

THE ARCHBISHOP   Pride will have a fall, Joan.

JOAN   Oh, never mind whether it is pride or not: is it true? is it commonsense?

LA HIRE   It is true. Half of us are afraid of having our handsome noses broken; and the other half are out for paying off their mortgages. Let her have her way, Dunois: she does not know everything; but she has got hold of the right end of the stick. Fighting is not what it was; and those who know least about it often make the best job of it.

DUNOIS   I know all that. I do not fight in the old way: I have learnt the lesson of Agincourt, of Poitiers and Crecy.[5] I know how many lives any move of mine will cost; and if the move is worth the cost I make it and pay the cost. But Joan never counts the cost at all: she goes ahead and trusts to God: she thinks she has God in her pocket. Up to now she has had the numbers on her side; and she has won. But I know Joan; and I see that some day she will go ahead when she has only ten men to do the work of a hundred. And then she will find that God is on the side of the big battalions. She will be taken by the enemy. And the lucky man that makes the capture will receive sixteen thousand pounds from the Earl of Ouareek.[6]

JOAN   [flattered]   Sixteen thousand pounds! Eh, laddie, have they offered that for me? There cannot be so much money in the world.

DUNOIS   There is, in England. And now tell me, all of you, which of you will lift a finger to save Joan once the English have got her? I speak first, for the army. The day after she has been dragged from her horse by a goddam or a Burgundian, and he is not struck dead: the day after she is locked in a dungeon, and the bars and bolts do not fly open at the touch of St Peter's angel: the day when the enemy finds out that she is as vulnerable as I am and not a bit more invincible, she will not be worth the life of a single soldier to us; and I will not risk that life, much as I cherish her as a companion-in-arms.

JOAN   I dont blame you, Jack: you are right. I am not worth one soldier's life if God lets me be beaten; but France may think me worth my ransom after what God has done for her through me.

CHARLES   I tell you I have no money; and this coronation, which is all your fault, has cost me the last farthing I can borrow.

JOAN   The Church is richer than you. I put my trust in the Church.

THE ARCHBISHOP   Woman: they will drag you through the streets, and burn you as a witch.

JOAN   [running to him]   Oh, my lord, do not say that. It is impossible. I a witch!

THE ARCHBISHOP   Peter Cauchon knows his business. The University of Paris has burnt a woman for saying that what you have done was well done, and according to God.

JOAN   [bewildered]   But why? What sense is there in it? What I have done is according to God. They could not burn a woman for speaking the truth.

THE ARCHBISHOP   They did.

5. Major English victories in the Hundred Years' War.
6. An unnecessary French phonetic representation of "Warwick"; since Dunois is presumably speaking standard stage British, this is almost silly. But Shaw was a spelling crank, and this may be in the background.

JOAN   But you know that she was speaking the truth. You would not let them burn me.

THE ARCHBISHOP   How could I prevent them?

JOAN   You would speak in the name of the Church. You are a great prince of the Church. I would go anywhere with your blessing to protect me.

THE ARCHBISHOP   I have no blessing for you while you are proud and disobedient.

JOAN   Oh, why will you go on saying things like that? I am not proud and disobedient. I am a poor girl, and so ignorant that I do not know A from B. How could I be proud? And how can you say that I am disobedient when I always obey my voices, because they come from God.

THE ARCHBISHOP   The voice of God on earth is the voice of the Church Militant; and all the voices that come to you are the echoes of your own wilfulness.

JOAN   It is not true.

THE ARCHBISHOP [*flushing angrily*]   You tell the Archbishop in his cathedral that he lies; and yet you say you are not proud and disobedient.

JOAN   I never said you lied. It was you that as good as said my voices lied. When have they ever lied? If you will not believe in them: even if they are only the echoes of my own commonsense, are they not always right? and are not your earthly counsels always wrong?

THE ARCHBISHOP [*indignantly*]   It is a waste of time admonishing you.

CHARLES   It always comes back to the same thing. She is right; and everyone else is wrong.

THE ARCHBISHOP   Take this as your last warning. If you perish through setting your private judgment above the instructions of your spiritual directors, the Church disowns you, and leaves you to whatever fate your presumption may bring upon you. The Bastard has told you that if you persist in setting up your military conceit above the counsels of your commanders—

DUNOIS [*interposing*]   To put it quite exactly, if you attempt to relieve the garrison in Compiègne without the same superiority in numbers you had at Orleans—

THE ARCHBISHOP   The army will disown you, and will not rescue you. And His Majesty the King has told you that the throne has not the means of ransoming you.

CHARLES   Not a penny.

THE ARCHBISHOP   You stand alone: absolutely alone, trusting to your own conceit, your own ignorance, your own headstrong presumption, your own impiety in hiding all these sins under the cloak of a trust in God. When you pass through these doors into the sunlight, the crowd will cheer you. They will bring you their little children and their invalids to heal: they will kiss your hands and feet, and do what they can, poor simple souls, to turn your head, and madden you with the self-confidence that is leading you to your destruction. But you will be none the less alone: they cannot save you. We and we only can stand between you and the stake at which our enemies have burnt that wretched woman in Paris.

JOAN [*her eyes skyward*]   I have better friends and better counsel than yours.

THE ARCHBISHOP   I see that I am speaking in vain to a hardened heart. You reject our protection, and are determined to turn us all against you. In future, then, fend for yourself; and if you fail, God have mercy on your soul.

DUNOIS   That is the truth, Joan. Heed it.

JOAN   Where would you all have been now if I had heeded that sort of truth? There is no help, no counsel, in any of you. Yes: I am alone on earth: I have always been alone. My father told my brothers to drown me if I would not stay to mind his sheep while France was bleeding to death: France might perish if only our lambs were safe. I thought France would have friends at the court of the king of France; and I find only wolves fighting for pieces of her poor torn body. I thought God would have friends everywhere, because He is the friend of everyone; and in my innocence I believed that you who now cast me out would be like strong towers to keep harm from me. But I am wiser now; and nobody is any the worse for being wiser. Do not think you can frighten me by telling me that I am alone. France is alone; and God is alone; and what is my loneliness before the loneliness of my country and my God? I see now that the loneliness of God is His strength: what would He be if He listened to your jealous little counsels? Well, my loneliness shall be my strength too; it is better to be alone with God; His friendship will not fail me, nor His counsel, nor His love. In His strength I will dare, and dare, and dare, until I die. I will go out now to the common people, and let the love in their eyes comfort me for the hate in yours. You will all be glad to see me burnt; but if I go through the fire I shall go through it to their hearts for ever and ever. And so, God be with me!

She goes from them. They stare after her in glum silence for a moment. Then Gilles de Rais twirls his beard.

BLUEBEARD   You know, the woman is quite impossible. I dont dislike her, really; but what are you to do with such a character?

DUNOIS   As God is my judge, if she fell into the Loire I would jump in in full armor to fish her out. But if she plays the fool at Compiègne, and gets caught, I must leave her to her doom.

LA HIRE   Then you had better chain me up; for I could follow her to hell when the spirit rises in her like that.

THE ARCHBISHOP   She disturbs my judgment too: there is a dangerous power in her outbursts. But the pit is open at her feet; and for good or evil we cannot turn her from it.

CHARLES   If only she would keep quiet, or go home!

They follow her dispiritedly.

Scene VI

Rouen, 30th May 1431. A great stone hall in the castle, arranged for a trial-at-law, but not a trial-by-jury, the court being the Bishop's court with the Inquisition participating: hence there are two raised chairs side by side for the Bishop and the Inquisitor as judges. Rows of chairs radiating from them at an obtuse angle are for the canons, the doctors of law and theology, and the Dominican monks, who act as assessors. In the angle is a table for the scribes, with stools.

There is also a heavy rough wooden stool for the prisoner. All these are at the inner end of the hall. The further end is open to the courtyard through a row of arches. The court is shielded from the weather by screens and curtains.

Looking down the great hall from the middle of the inner end, the judicial chairs and scribes' table are to the right. The prisoner's stool is to the left. There are arched doors right and left. It is a fine sunshiny May morning.

Warwick comes in through the arched doorway on the judges' side, followed by his page.

THE PAGE [*pertly*]   I suppose your lordship is aware that we have no business here. This is an ecclesiastical court; and we are only the secular arm.

WARWICK   I am aware of that fact. Will it please your impudence to find the Bishop of Beauvais for me, and give him a hint that he can have a word with me here before the trial, if he wishes?

THE PAGE [*going*]   Yes, my lord.

WARWICK   And mind you behave yourself. Do not address him as Pious Peter.

THE PAGE   No, my lord. I shall be kind to him, because, when The Maid is brought in, Pious Peter will have to pick a peck of pickled pepper.

Cauchon enters through the same door with a Dominican monk and a canon, the latter carrying a brief.

THE PAGE   The Right Reverend his lordship the Bishop of Beauvais. And two other reverend gentlemen.

WARWICK   Get out; and see that we are not interrupted.

THE PAGE   Right, my lord [*He vanishes airily.*]

CAUCHON   I wish your lordship good-morrow.

WARWICK   Good-morrow to your lordship. Have I had the pleasure of meeting your friends before? I think not.

CAUCHON [*introducing the monk, who is on his right*]   This, my lord, is Brother John Lemaître, of the order of St Dominic. He is acting as deputy for the Chief Inquisitor into the evil of heresy in France. Brother John: the Earl of Warwick.

WARWICK   Your Reverence is most welcome. We have no Inquisitor in England, unfortunately; though we miss him greatly, especially on occasions like the present.

The Inquisitor smiles patiently, and bows. He is a mild elderly gentleman, but has evident reserves of authority and firmness.

CAUCHON [*introducing the canon, who is on his left*]   This gentleman is Canon John D'Estivet, of the Chapter of Bayeux. He is acting as Promoter.

WARWICK   Promoter?

CAUCHON   Prosecutor, you would call him in civil law.

WARWICK   Ah! prosecutor. Quite, quite. I am very glad to make your acquaintance, Canon D'Estivet.

D'Estivet bows. [He is on the young side of middle age, well mannered, but vulpine beneath his veneer.]

WARWICK   May I ask what stage the proceedings have reached? It is now more than nine months since The Maid was captured at Compiègne by the Burgundians. It is fully four months since I bought her from the Burgundians for a very handsome sum, solely that she might be brought to justice. It is very nearly three months since I delivered her up to you, my Lord Bishop, as a person suspected of heresy. May I suggest that you are taking a rather unconscionable time to make up your minds about a very plain case? Is this trial never going to end?

THE INQUISITOR [*smiling*]   It has not yet begun, my lord.

WARWICK   Not yet begun! Why, you have been at it eleven weeks!

CAUCHON   We have not been idle, my lord. We have held fifteen examinations of The Maid: six public and nine private.

THE INQUISITOR [*always patiently smiling*]   You see, my lord, I have been present at only two of these examinations. They were proceedings of the Bishop's court solely, and not of the Holy Office. I have only just decided to associate myself—that is, to associate the Holy Inquisition —with the Bishop's court. I did not at first think that this was a case of heresy at all. I regarded it as a political case, and The Maid as a prisoner of war. But having now been present at two of the examinations, I must admit that this seems to be one of the gravest cases of heresy within my experience. Therefore everything is now in order, and we proceed to trial this morning. [*He moves towards the judicial chairs.*]

CAUCHON   This moment, if your lordship's convenience allows.

WARWICK [*graciously*]   Well, that is good news, gentlemen. I will not attempt to conceal from you that our patience was becoming strained.

CAUCHON   So I gathered from the threats of your soldiers to drown those of our people who favor The Maid.

WARWICK   Dear me! At all events their intentions were friendly to you, my lord.

CAUCHON [*sternly*]   I hope not. I am determined that the woman shall have a fair hearing. The justice of the Church is not a mockery, my lord.

THE INQUISITOR [*returning*]   Never has there been a fairer examination within my experience, my lord. The Maid needs no lawyers to take her part: she will be tried by her most faithful friends, all ardently desirous to save her soul from perdition.

D'ESTIVET   Sir: I am the Promoter; and it has been my painful duty to present the case against the girl; but believe me, I would throw up my case today and hasten to her defence if I did not know that men far my superiors in learning and piety, in eloquence and persuasiveness, have been sent to reason with her, to explain to her the danger she is running, and the ease with which she may avoid it. [*suddenly bursting into forensic eloquence, to the disgust of Cauchon and the Inquisitor, who have listened to him so far with patronizing approval*] men have dared to say that we are acting from hate; but God is our witness that they lie. Have we tortured her? No. Have we ceased to exhort her; to implore her to have pity on herself; to come to the bosom of her Church as an erring but beloved child? Have we—

CAUCHON [*interrupting drily*]   Take care, Canon. All that you say is true; but if you make his lordship believe it I will not answer for your life, and hardly for my own.

WARWICK [*deprecating, but by no means denying*]   Oh, my lord, you are very hard on us poor English. But we certainly do not share your pious desire to save The Maid: in fact I tell you now plainly that her death is a political necessity which I regret but cannot help. If the Church lets her go—

CAUCHON [*with fierce and menacing pride*] If the Church lets her go, woe to the man, were he the Emperor himself, who dares lay a finger on her! The Church is not subject to political necessity, my lord.

THE INQUISITOR [*interposing smoothly*] You need have no anxiety about the result, my lord. You have an invincible ally in the matter: one who is far more determined than you that she shall burn.

WARWICK And who is this very convenient partisan, may I ask?

THE INQUISITOR The Maid herself. Unless you put a gag in her mouth you cannot prevent her from convicting herself ten times over every time she opens it.

D'ESTIVET That is perfectly true, my lord. My hair bristles on my head when I hear so young a creature utter such blasphemies.

WARWICK Well, by all means do your best for her if you are quite sure it will be of no avail. [*looking hard at Cauchon*] I should be sorry to have to act without the blessing of the Church.

CAUCHON [*with a mixture of cynical admiration and contempt*] And yet they say Englishmen are hypocrites! You play for your side, my lord, even at the peril of your soul. I cannot but admire such devotion; but I dare not go so far myself. I fear damnation.

WARWICK If we feared anything we could never govern England, my lord. Shall I send your people in to you?

CAUCHON Yes: it will be very good of your lordship to withdraw and allow the court to assemble.

>   *Warwick turns on his heel, and goes out through the courtyard. Cauchon takes one of the judicial seats; and D'Estivet sits at the scribes' table, studying his brief.*

CAUCHON [*casually, as he makes himself comfortable*] What scoundrels these English nobles are!

THE INQUISITOR [*taking the other judicial chair on Cauchon's left*] All secular power makes men scoundrels. They are not trained for the work; and they have not the Apostolic Succession. Our own nobles are just as bad.

>   *The Bishop's assessors hurry into the hall, headed by Chaplain de Stogumber and Canon de Courcelles, a young priest of 30. The scribes sit at the table, leaving a chair vacant opposite D'Estivet. Some of the assessors take their seats: other stand chatting, waiting for the proceedings to begin formally. De Stogumber, aggrieved and obstinate, will not take his seat: neither will the Canon, who stands on his right.*

CAUCHON Good morning, Master de Stogumber. [*to the Inquisitor*] Chaplain to the Cardinal of England.

THE CHAPLAIN [*correcting him*] Of Winchester, my lord. I have to make a protest, my lord.

CAUCHON You make a great many.

THE CHAPLAIN I am not without support, my lord. Here is Master de Courcelles, Canon of Paris, who associates himself with me in my protest.

CAUCHON   Well, what is the matter?

THE CHAPLAIN [*sulkily*]   Speak you, Master de Courcelles, since I do not seem to enjoy his lordship's confidence. [*He sits down in dudgeon next to Cauchon, on his right.*]

COURCELLES   My lord: we have been at great pains to draw up an indictment of The Maid on sixty-four counts. We are now told that they have been reduced, without consulting us.

THE INQUISITOR   Master de Courcelles: I am the culprit. I am overwhelmed with admiration for the zeal displayed in your sixty-four counts; but in accusing a heretic, as in other things, enough is enough. Also you must remember that all the members of the court are not so subtle and profound as you, and that some of your very great learning might appear to them to be very great nonsense. Therefore I have thought it well to have your sixty-four articles cut down to twelve—

COURCELLES [*thunderstruck*]   Twelve!!!

THE INQUISITOR   Twelve will, believe me, be quite enough for your purpose.

THE CHAPLAIN   But some of the most important points have been reduced almost to nothing. For instance, The Maid has actually declared that the blessed saints Margaret and Catherine, and the holy Archangel Michael, spoke to her in French. That is a vital point.

THE INQUISITOR   You think, doubtless, that they should have spoken in Latin?

CAUCHON   No: he thinks they should have spoken in English.

THE CHAPLAIN   Naturally, my lord.

THE INQUISITOR   Well, as we are all here agreed, I think, that these voices of The Maid are the voices of evil spirits tempting her to her damnation, it would not be very courteous to you, Master de Stogumber, or to the King of England, to assume that English is the devil's native language. So let it pass. The matter is not wholly omitted from the twelve articles. Pray take your places, gentlemen; and let us proceed to business.

All who have not taken their seats, do so.

THE CHAPLAIN   Well, I protest. That is all.

COURCELLES   I think it hard that all our work should go for nothing. It is only another example of the diabolical influence which this woman exercises over the court. [*He takes his chair, which is on the Chaplain's right.*]

CAUCHON   Do you suggest that I am under diabolical influence?

COURCELLES   I suggest nothing, my lord. But it seems to me that there is a conspiracy here to hush up the fact that The Maid stole the Bishop of Senlis's horse.

CAUCHON [*keeping his temper with difficulty*]   This is not a police court. Are we to waste our time on such rubbish?

COURCELLES [*rising, shocked*]   My lord: do you call the Bishop's horse rubbish?

THE INQUISITOR [*blandly*]   Master de Courcelles: The Maid alleges that she paid handsomely for the Bishop's horse, and that if he did not get the money the fault was not hers. As that may be true, the point is one on which The Maid may well be acquitted.

COURCELLES   Yes, if it were an ordinary horse. But the Bishop's horse! how can she be acquitted for that? [*He sits down again, bewildered and discouraged.*]

THE INQUISITOR   I submit to you, with great respect, that if we persist in trying The Maid on trumpery issues on which we may have to declare her innocent, she may escape us on the great main issue of heresy, on which she seems so far to insist on her own guilt. I will ask you, therefore, to say nothing, when The Maid is brought before us, of these stealings of horses, and dancings round fairy trees with the village children, and prayings at haunted wells, and a dozen other things which you were diligently inquiring into until my arrival. There is not a village girl in France against whom you could not prove such things: they all dance around haunted trees, and pray at magic wells. Some of them would steal the Pope's horse if they got the chance. Heresy, gentlemen, heresy is the charge we have to try. The detection and suppression of heresy is my peculiar business: I am here as an inquisitor, not as an ordinary magistrate. Stick to the heresy, gentlemen; and leave the other matters alone.

CAUCHON   I may say that we have sent to the girl's village to make inquiries about her, and there is practically nothing serious against her.

THE CHAPLAIN   [*rising and clamoring together*]   Nothing serious, my lord—
COURCELLES   What! The fairy tree not—

CAUCHON   [*out of patience*]   Be silent, gentlemen; or speak one at a time.
   Courcelles collapses into his chair, intimidated.

THE CHAPLAIN   [*sulkily resuming his seat*]   That is what The Maid said to us last Friday.

CAUCHON   I wish you had followed her counsel, sir. When I say nothing serious, I mean nothing that men of sufficiently large mind to conduct an inquiry like this would consider serious. I agree with my colleague the Inquisitor that it is on the count of heresy that we must proceed.

LADVENU   [*a young but ascetically fine-drawn Dominican who is sitting next Courcelles, on his right*]   But is there any great harm in the girl's heresy? Is it not merely her simplicity? Many saints have said as much as Joan.

THE INQUISITOR   [*dropping his blandness and speaking very gravely*]   Brother Martin: if you had seen what I have seen of heresy, you would not think it a light thing even in its most apparently harmless and even lovable and pious origins. Heresy begins with people who are to all appearance better than their neighbors. A gentle and pious girl, or a young man who has obeyed the command of our Lord by giving all his riches to the poor, and putting on the garb of poverty, the life of austerity, and the rule of humility and charity, may be the founder of a heresy that will wreck both Church and Empire if not ruthlessly stamped out in time. The records of the Holy Inquisition are full of histories we dare not give to the world, because they are beyond the belief of honest men and innocent women; yet they all began with saintly simpletons. I have seen this again and again. Mark what I say: the woman who quarrels with her clothes, and puts on the dress of a man, is like the man who throws off his fur gown and dresses like John the Baptist: they are followed, as surely as the night follows the day, by bands of wild women and men who refuse to wear any clothes at all. When maids will neither marry nor take regular vows, and men reject marriage and exalt their lusts into divine inspirations, then, as surely as the summer follows the spring, they begin with polygamy, and end by incest. Heresy at first seems innocent and even laudable; but it ends in such a monstrous horror of unnatural wickedness that the most tender-hearted among you, if you saw it at work as I have seen it, would clamor against the mercy of the Church in dealing with it. For two hundred years the Holy Office has striven with these diabolical madnesses; and it knows that they begin always by vain and ignorant persons setting up their own judgment against the Church, and taking it upon themselves to be the interpreters of God's will. You must not fall into the common error of mistaking these simpletons for liars and hypocrites. They believe honestly and sincerely that their diabolical inspiration is divine. Therefore you must be on your guard against your natural compassion. You are all, I hope, merciful men: how else could you have devoted your lives to the service of our gentle Savior? You are going to see before you a young girl, pious and chaste; for I must tell you, gentlemen, that the things said of her by our English friends are supported by no evidence, whilst there is abundant testimony that her excesses have been excesses of religion and charity and not of worldliness and wantonness. This girl is not one of those whose hard features are the sign of hard hearts, and whose brazen looks and lewd demeanor condemn them before they are accused. The devilish pride that has led her into her present peril has left no mark on her countenance. Strange as it may seem to you, it has even left no mark on her character outside those special matters in which she is proud; so that you will see a diabolical pride and a natural humility seated side by side in the selfsame soul. Therefore be on your guard. God forbid that I should tell you to harden your hearts; for her punishment if we condemn her will be so cruel that we should forfeit our own hope of divine mercy were there one grain of malice against her in our hearts. But if you hate cruelty—and if any man here does not hate it I command him on his soul's salvation to quit this holy court— I say, if you hate cruelty, remember that nothing is so cruel in its consequences as the toleration of heresy. Remember also that no court of law can be so cruel as the common people are to those whom they suspect of heresy. The heretic in the hands of the Holy Office is safe from violence, is assured of a fair trial, and cannot suffer death, even when guilty, if repentance follows sin. Innumerable lives of heretics have been saved because the Holy Office has taken them out of the hands of the people, and because the people have yielded them up, knowing that the Holy Office would deal with them. Before the Holy Inquisition existed, and even now when its officers are not within reach, the unfortunate wretch suspected of heresy, perhaps quite ignorantly and unjustly, is stoned, torn in pieces, drowned, burned in his house with all his innocent children, without a trial, unshriven, unburied save as a dog is buried: all of them deeds hateful to God and most cruel to man. Gentlemen: I am compassionate by nature as well as by my profession; and though the work I have to do may seem cruel to those who do not know how much more cruel it would be to leave it undone, I would go to the stake myself sooner than do it if I did not know its righteousness, its necessity, its essential mercy. I ask you to address yourself to this trial in that conviction. Anger is a bad counsellor: cast out anger. Pity is sometimes worse: cast out pity. But do not cast out mercy. Remember only that justice comes first. Have you anything to say, my lord, before we proceed to trial?

CAUCHON   You have spoken for me, and spoken better than I could. I do not see how any sane man could disagree with a word that has fallen from you. But this I will add. The crude heresies of which you have told us are horrible; but their horror is like that of the black death: they rage for a while and then die out, because sound and sensible men will not under any incitement be reconciled to nakedness and incest and polygamy and the like. But we are confronted today throughout Europe with a heresy that is spreading among men not weak in mind nor diseased in brain: nay, the stronger the mind, the more obstinate the heretic. It is neither discredited by fantastic extremes nor corrupted by the common lusts of the flesh; but it, too, sets up the private judgment of the single erring mortal against the considered wisdom and experience of the Church. The mighty structure of Catholic Christendom will never be shaken by naked madmen or by the sins of Moab and Ammon.[1] But it may be betrayed from within, and brought to barbarous ruin and desolation, by this arch heresy which the English Commander calls Protestantism.[2]

THE ASSESSORS [whispering]   Protestantism! What was that? What does the Bishop mean? Is it a new heresy? The English Commander, he said. Did you ever hear of Protestantism? etc., etc.

CAUCHON [continuing]   And that reminds me. What provision has the Earl of Warwick made for the defence of the secular arm should The Maid prove obdurate, and the people be moved to pity her?

THE CHAPLAIN   Have no fear on that score, my lord. The noble earl has eight hundred men-at-arms at the gates. She will not slip through our English fingers even if the whole city be on her side.

CAUCHON [revolted]   Will you not add, God grant that she repent and purge her sin?

THE CHAPLAIN   That does not seem to me to be consistent; but of course I agree with your lordship.

CAUCHON [giving him up with a shrug of contempt]   The court sits.

THE INQUISITOR   Let the accused be brought in.

LADVENU [calling]   The accused. Let her be brought in.

    Joan, chained by the ankles, is brought in through the arched door behind the prisoner's stool by a guard of English soldiers. With them

---

1. Pride and carnality, for which their destruction is elaborately prophesied in Jeremiah 48 and 49, among other places.
2. For the effect of this mild, anachronistic joke, the word should be pronounced "Protéstantism."

is the Executioner and his assistants. They lead her to the prisoner's stool, and place themselves behind it after taking off her chain. She wears a page's black suit. Her long imprisonment and the strain of the examinations which have preceded the trial have left their mark on her; but her vitality still holds; she confronts the court unabashed, without a trace of the awe which their formal solemnity seems to require for the complete success of its impressiveness.

THE INQUISITOR [kindly] Sit down, Joan. [She sits on the prisoner's stool.] You look very pale today. Are you not well?

JOAN   Thank you kindly: I am well enough. But the Bishop sent me some carp; and it made me ill.

CAUCHON   I am sorry. I told them to see that it was fresh.

JOAN   You meant to be good to me, I know; but it is a fish that does not agree with me. The English thought you were trying to poison me—

CAUCHON   [together]   What!
THE CHAPLAIN   No, my lord.

JOAN [continuing] They are determined that I shall be burnt as a witch; and they sent their doctor to cure me; but he was forbidden to bleed me because the silly people believe that a witch's witchery leaves her if she is bled; so he only called me filthy names. Why do you leave me in the hands of the English? I should be in the hands of the Church. And why must I be chained by the feet to a log of wood? Are you afraid I will fly away?

D'ESTIVET [harshly] Woman: it is not for you to question the court: it is for us to question you.

COURCELLES   When you were left unchained, did you not try to escape by jumping from a tower sixty feet high?[3] If you cannot fly like a witch, how is it that you are still alive?

JOAN   I suppose because the tower was not so high then. It has grown higher every day since you began asking me questions about it.

D'ESTIVET   Why did you jump from the tower?

JOAN   How do you know that I jumped?

D'ESTIVET   You were found lying in the moat. Why did you leave the tower?

JOAN   Why would anybody leave a prison if they could get out?

D'ESTIVET   You tried to escape?

JOAN   Of course I did; and not for the first time either. If you leave the door of the cage open the bird will fly out.

D'ESTIVET [rising] That is a confessioin of heresy. I call the attention of the court to it.

JOAN   Heresy, he calls it! Am I a heretic because I try to escape from prison?

D'ESTIVET   Assuredly, if you are in the hands of the Church, and you wilfully take yourself out of its hands, you are deserting the Church; and that is heresy.

JOAN   It is great nonsense. Nobody could be such a fool as to think that.

D'ESTIVET   You hear, my lord, how I am reviled in the execution of my duty by this woman. [He sits down indignantly.]

3. At Beaurevoir Castle, when she heard that Compiègne (where she had been captured by the Duke of Burgundy and sold to the English) would fall.

CAUCHON   I have warned you before, Joan, that you are doing yourself no good by these pert answers.

JOAN   But you will not talk sense to me. I am reasonable if you will be reasonable.

THE INQUISITOR [*interposing*]   This is not yet in order. You forget, Master Promoter, that the proceedings have not been formally opened. The time for questions is after she has sworn on the Gospels to tell us the whole truth.

JOAN   You say this to me every time. I have said again and again that I will tell you all that concerns this trial. But I cannot tell you the whole truth: God does not allow the whole truth to be told. You do not understand it when I tell it. It is an old saying that he who tells too much truth is sure to be hanged. I am weary of this argument: we have been over it nine times already. I have sworn as much as I will swear; and I will swear no more.

COURCELLES   My lord: she should be put to the torture.

THE INQUISITOR   You hear, Joan? That is what happens to the obdurate. Think before you answer. Has she been shewn the instruments?

THE EXECUTIONER   They are ready, my lord. She has seen them.

JOAN   If you tear me limb from limb until you separate my soul from my body you will get nothing out of me beyond what I have told you. What more is there to tell that you could understand? Besides, I cannot bear to be hurt; and if you hurt me I will say anything you like to stop the pain. But I will take it all back afterwards; so what is the use of it?

LADVENU   There is much in that. We should proceed mercifully.

COURCELLES   But the torture is customary.

THE INQUISITOR   It must not be applied wantonly. If the accused will confess voluntarily, then its use cannot be justified.

COURCELLES   But this is unusual and irregular. She refuses to take the oath.

LADVENU [*disgusted*]   Do you want to torture the girl for the mere pleasure of it?

COURCELLES [*bewildered*] [4]   But it is not a pleasure. It is the law. It is customary. It is always done.

THE INQUISITOR   That is not so, Master, except when the inquiries are carried on by people who do not know their legal business.

COURCELLES   But the woman is a heretic. I assure you it is always done.

CAUCHON [*decisively*]   It will not be done today if it is not necessary. Let there be an end of this. I will not have it said that we proceeded on forced confessions. We have sent our best preachers and doctors to this woman to exhort and implore her to save her soul and body from the fire: we shall not now send the executioner to thrust her into it.

COURCELLES   Your lordship is merciful, of course. But it is a great responsibility to depart from the usual practice.

JOAN   Thou art a rare noodle, Master. Do what was done last time is thy rule, eh?

4. He is truly bewildered, and not in the least hypocritical; only a writer of cheap propaganda would have distorted Joan's trial, or her accusers, into caricatures. The ironies of history are played out, Shaw has been saying, by everyone acting in good faith; if everyone were pragmatically hypocritical, nobody would ever have been burned for anything.

COURCELLES [*rising*]   Thou wanton: dost thou dare call me noodle?

THE INQUISITOR   Patience, Master, patience: I fear you will soon be only too terribly avenged.

COURCELLES [*mutters*]   Noodle indeed! [*He sits down, much discontented.*]

THE INQUISITOR   Meanwhile, let us not be moved by the rough side of a shepherd lass's tongue.

JOAN   Nay: I am no shepherd lass, though I have helped with the sheep like anyone else. I will do a lady's work in the house—spin or weave—against any woman in Rouen.

THE INQUISITOR   This is not a time for vanity, Joan. You stand in great peril.

JOAN   I know it: have I not been punished for my vanity? If I had not worn my cloth of gold surcoat in battle like a fool, that Burgundian soldier would never have pulled me backwards off my horse; and I should not have been here.

THE CHAPLAIN   If you are so clever at woman's work why do you not stay at home and do it?

JOAN   There are plenty of other women to do it; but there is nobody to do my work.

CAUCHON   Come! we are wasting time on trifles. Joan: I am going to put a most solemn question to you. Take care how you answer; for your life and salvation are at stake on it. Will you for all you have said and done, be it good or bad, accept the judgment of God's Church on earth? More especially as to the acts and words that are imputed to you in this trial by the Promoter here, will you submit your case to the inspired interpretation of the Church Militant?

JOAN   I am a faithful child of the Church. I will obey the Church—

CAUCHON [*hopefully leaning forward*]   You will?

JOAN   —provided it does not command anything impossible.

Cauchon sinks back in his chair with a heavy sigh. The Inquisitor purses his lips and frowns. Ladvenu shakes his head pitifully.

D'ESTIVET   She imputes to the Church the error and folly of commanding the impossible.

JOAN   If you command me to declare that all that I have done and said, and all the visions and revelations I have had, were not from God, then that is impossible: I will not declare it for anything in the world. What God made me do I will never go back on; and what He has commanded or shall command I will not fail to do in spite of any man alive. That is what I mean by impossible. And in case the Church should bid me do anything contrary to the command I have from God, I will not consent to it, no matter what it may be.

THE ASSESSORS [*shocked and indignant*]   Oh! The Church contrary to God! What do you say now? Flat heresy. This is beyond everything, etc., etc.

D'ESTIVET [*throwing down his brief*]   My lord: do you need anything more than this?

CAUCHON   Woman: you have said enough to burn ten heretics. Will you not be warned? Will you not understand?

THE INQUISITOR   If the Church Militant tells you that your revelations and visions are sent by the devil to tempt you to your damnation, will you not believe that the Church is wiser than you?

JOAN   I believe that God is wiser than I; and it is His commands that I will do. All the things that you call my crimes have come to me by the command of God. I say that I have done them by the order of God: it is impossible for me to say anything else. If any Churchman says the contrary I shall not mind him: I shall mind God alone, whose command I always follow.

LADVENU [*pleading with her urgently*]   You do not know what you are saying, child. Do you want to kill yourself? Listen. Do you not believe that you are subject to the Church of God on earth?

JOAN   Yes. When have I ever denied it?

LADVENU   Good. That means, does it not, that you are subject to our Lord the Pope, to the cardinals, the archbishops, and the bishops for whom his lordship stands here today?

JOAN   God must be served first.

D'ESTIVET   Then your voices command you not to submit yourself to the Church Militant?

JOAN   My voices do not tell me to disobey the Church; but God must be served first.

CAUCHON   And you, and not the Church, are to be the judge?

JOAN   What other judgment can I judge by but my own?

THE ASSESSORS [*scandalized*]   Oh! [*They cannot find words.*]

CAUCHON   Out of your own mouth you have condemned yourself. We have striven for your salvation to the verge of sinning ourselves: we have opened the door to you again and again; and you have shut it in our faces and in the face of God. Dare you pretend, after what you have said, that you are in a state of grace?

JOAN   If I am not, may God bring me to it: if I am, may God keep me in it!

LADVENU   That is a very good reply, my lord.

COURCELLES   Were you in a state of grace when you stole the Bishop's horse?

CAUCHON [*rising in a fury*]   Oh, devil take the Bishop's horse and you too! We are here to try a case of heresy; and no sooner do we come to the root of the matter than we are thrown back by idiots who understand nothing but horses. [*Trembling with rage, he forces himself to sit down.*]

THE INQUISITOR   Gentlemen, gentlemen: in clinging to these small issues you are The Maid's best advocates. I am not surprised that his lordship has lost patience with you. What does the Promoter say? Does he press these trumpery matters?

D'ESTIVET   I am bound by my office to press everything; but when the woman confesses a heresy that must bring upon her the doom of excommunication, of what consequence is it that she has been guilty also of offences which expose her to minor penances? I share the impatience of his lordship as to these minor charges. Only, with great respect, I must emphasize the gravity of two very horrible and blasphemous crimes which she does not deny. First, she has intercourse with evil spirits, and is therefore a sorceress. Second, she wears men's clothes, which is indecent, unnatural, and abominable; and in spite of our most earnest remonstrances and entreaties, she will not change them even to receive the sacrament.

JOAN   Is the blessed St Catherine an evil spirit? Is St Margaret? Is Michael the Archangel?

COURCELLES   How do you know that the spirit which appears to you is an archangel? Does he not appear to you as a naked man?

JOAN   Do you think God cannot afford clothes for him?

The assessors cannot help smiling, especially as the joke is against Courcelles.

LADVENU   Well answered, Joan.

THE INQUISITOR   It is, in effect, well answered. But no evil spirit would be so simple as to appear to a young girl in a guise that would scandalize her when he meant her to take him for a messenger from the Most High. Joan: the Church instructs you that these apparitions are demons seeking your soul's perdition. Do you accept the instruction of the Church?

JOAN   I accept the messenger of God. How could any faithful believer in the Church refuse him?

CAUCHON   Wretched woman: again I ask you, do you know what you are saying?

THE INQUISITOR   You wrestle in vain with the devil for her soul, my lord: she will not be saved. Now as to this matter of the man's dress. For the last time, will you put off that impudent attire, and dress as becomes your sex?

JOAN   I will not.

D'ESTIVET [*pouncing*]   The sin of disobedience, my lord.

JOAN [*distressed*]   But my voices tell me I must dress as a soldier.

LADVENU   Joan, Joan: does not that prove to you that the voices are the voices of evil spirits? Can you suggest to us one good reason why an angel of God should give you such shameless advice?

JOAN   Why, yes: what can be plainer commonsense? I was a soldier living among soldiers. I am a prisoner guarded by soldiers. If I were to dress as a woman they would think of me as a woman; and then what would become of me? If I dress as a soldier they think of me as a soldier, and I can live with them as I do at home with my brothers. That is why St Catherine tells me I must not dress as a woman until she gives me leave.

COURCELLES   When will she give you leave?

JOAN   When you take me out of the hands of the English soldiers. I have told you that I should be in the hands of the Church, and not left night and day with four soldiers of the Earl of Warwick. Do you want me to live with them in petticoats?

LADVENU   My lord: what she says is, God knows, very wrong and shocking; but there is a grain of worldly sense in it such as might impose on a simple village maiden.

JOAN   If we were as simple in the village as you are in your courts and palaces, there would soon be no wheat to make bread for you.

CAUCHON   That is the thanks you get for trying to save her, Brother Martin.

LADVENU   Joan: we are all trying to save you. His lordship is trying to save you. The Inquisitor could not be more just to you if you were his own daughter. But you are blinded by a terrible pride and self-sufficiency.

JOAN   Why do you say that? I have said nothing wrong. I cannot understand.

THE INQUISITOR   The blessed St Athanasius has laid it down in his creed [5] that those who cannot understand are damned. It is not enough to be simple. It is not enough even to be what simple people call good. The simplicity of a darkened mind is no better than the simplicity of a beast.

JOAN   There is great wisdom in the simplicity of a beast, let me tell you; and sometimes great foolishness in the wisdom of scholars.

LADVENU   We know that, Joan: we are not so foolish as you think us. Try to resist the temptation to make pert replies to us. Do you see that man who stands behind you [*He indicates the Executioner.*]?

JOAN [*turning and looking at the man*]   Your torturer? But the Bishop said I was not to be tortured.

LADVENU   You are not to be tortured because you have confessed everything that is necessary to your condemnation. That man is not only the torturer: he is also the Executioner. Executioner: let The Maid hear your answers to my questions. Are you prepared for the burning of a heretic this day?

THE EXECUTIONER   Yes, Master.

LADVENU   Is the stake ready?

THE EXECUTIONER   It is. In the market-place. The English have built it too high for me to get near her and make the death easier. It will be a cruel death.

JOAN [*horrified*]   But you are not going to burn me now?

THE INQUISITOR   You realize it at last.

LADVENU   There are eight hundred English soldiers waiting to take you to the market-place the moment the sentence of excommunication has passed the lips of your judges. You are within a few short moments of that doom.

JOAN [*looking round desperately for rescue*]   Oh God!

LADVENU   Do not despair, Joan. The Church is merciful. You can save yourself.

JOAN [*hopefully*]   Yes: my voices promised me I should not be burnt. St Catherine bade me be bold.

CAUCHON   Woman: are you quite mad? Do you not yet see that your voices have deceived you?

JOAN   Oh no: that is impossible.

CAUCHON   Impossible! They have led you straight to your excommunication, and to the stake which is there waiting for you.

LADVENU [*pressing the point hard*]   Have they kept a single promise to you since you were taken at Compiègne? The devil has betrayed you. The Church holds out its arms to you.

JOAN [*despairing*]   Oh, it is true: it is true: my voices have deceived me. I have been mocked by devils: my faith is broken. I have dared and dared; but only a fool will walk into a fire: God, who gave me my commonsense, cannot will me to do that.

5. St. Athanasius (296–373), Bishop of Alexandria, was probably not the author of the so-called Athanasian Creed, used only secondarily, in the Western churches, to the Apostles' and Nicene Creeds as professions of faith.

LADVENU   Now God be praised that He has saved you at the eleventh hour! [*He hurries to the vacant seat at the scribes' table, and snatches a sheet of paper, on which he sets to work writing eagerly.*]

CAUCHON   Amen!

JOAN   What must I do?

CAUCHON   You must sign a solemn recantation of your heresy.

JOAN   Sign? That means to write my name. I cannot write.

CAUCHON   You have signed many letters before.

JOAN   Yes; but someone held my hand and guided the pen. I can make my mark.

THE CHAPLAIN [*who has been listening with growing alarm and indignation*] My lord: do you mean that you are going to allow this woman to escape us?

THE INQUISITOR   The law must take its course, Master de Stogumber. And you know the law.

THE CHAPLAIN [*rising, purple with fury*] I know that there is no faith in a Frenchman. [*tumult, which he shouts down*] I know what my lord the Cardinal of Winchester will say when he hears of this. I know what the Earl of Warwick will do when he learns that you intend to betray him. There are eight hundred men at the gate who will see that this abominable witch is burnt in spite of your teeth.

THE ASSESSORS [*meanwhile*] What is this? What did he say? He accuses us of treachery! This is past bearing. No faith in a Frenchman! Did you hear that? This is an intolerable fellow. Who is he? Is this what English Churchmen are like? He must be mad or drunk, etc., etc.

THE INQUISITOR [*rising*] Silence, pray! Gentlemen: pray silence! Master Chaplain: bethink you a moment of your holy office: of what you are, and where you are. I direct you to sit down.

THE CHAPLAIN [*folding his arms doggedly, his face working convulsively*] I will NOT sit down.

CAUCHON   Master Inquisitor: this man has called me a traitor to my face before now.

THE CHAPLAIN   So you are a traitor. You are all traitors. You have been doing nothing but begging this damnable witch on your knees to recant all through this trial.

THE INQUISITOR [*placidly resuming his seat*] If you will not sit, you must stand: that is all.

THE CHAPLAIN   I will NOT stand [*He flings himself back into his chair.*]

LADVENU [*rising with the paper in his hand*] My lord: here is the form of recantation for The Maid to sign.

CAUCHON   Read it to her.

JOAN   Do not trouble. I will sign it.

THE INQUISITOR   Woman: you must know what you are putting your hand to. Read it to her, Brother Martin. And let all be silent.

LADVENU [*reading quietly*] 'I, Joan, commonly called The Maid, a miserable sinner, do confess that I have most grievously sinned in the following articles. I have pretended to have revelations from God and the angels and the blessed saints, and perversely rejected the Church's warnings that these were temptations by demons. I have blasphemed abominably by wearing an immodest dress, contrary to the Holy Scripture and the canons of the Church. Also I have clipped my hair in the style of a man, and, against all the duties which have made my sex specially acceptable in heaven, have taken up the sword, even to the shedding of human blood, inciting men to slay each other, invoking evil spirits to delude them, and stubbornly and most blasphemously imputing these sins to Almighty God. I confess to the sin of sedition, to the sin of idolatry, to the sin of disobedience, to the sin of pride, and to the sin of heresy. All of which sins I now renounce and abjure and depart from, humbly thanking you Doctors and Masters who have brought me back to the truth and into the grace of our Lord. And I will never return to my errors, but will remain in communion with our Holy Church and in obedience to our Holy Father the Pope of Rome. All this I swear by God Almighty and the Holy Gospels, in witness whereto I sign my name to this recantation.'

THE INQUISITOR   You understand this, Joan?

JOAN [listless]   It is plain enough, sir.

THE INQUISITOR   And it is true?

JOAN   It may be true. If it were not true, the fire would not be ready for me in the market-place.

LADVENU [taking up his pen and a book, and going to her quickly lest she should compromise herself again]   Come, child: let me guide your hand. Take the pen. [She does so; and they begin to write, using the book as a desk] J.E.H.A.N.E. So. Now make your mark by yourself.

JOAN [makes her mark, and gives him back the pen, tormented by the rebellion of her soul against her mind and body]   There!

LADVENU [replacing the pen on the table, and handing the recantation to Cauchon with a reverence]   Praise be to God, my brothers, the lamb has returned to the flock; and the shepherd rejoices in her more than in ninety and nine just persons. [He returns to his seat].

THE INQUISITOR [taking the paper from Cauchon]   We declare thee by this act set free from the danger of excommunication in which thou stoodest. [He throws the paper down to the table.]

JOAN   I thank you.

THE INQUISITOR   But because thou has sinned most presumptuously against God and the Holy Church, and that thou mayst repent thy errors in solitary contemplation, and be shielded from all temptation to return to them, we, for the good of thy soul, and for a penance that may wipe out thy sins and bring thee finally unspotted to the throne of grace, do condemn thee to eat the bread of sorrow and drink the water of afflic-tion to the end of thy earthly days in perpetual imprisonment.

JOAN [rising in consternation and terrible anger]   Perpetual imprisonment! Am I not then to be set free?

LADVENU [mildly shocked]   Set free, child, after such wickedness as yours! What are you dreaming of?

JOAN   Give me that writing. [She rushes to the table; snatches up the paper; and tears it into fragments.] Light your fire: do you think I dread it as much as the life of a rat in a hole? My voices were right.

LADVENU   Joan! Joan!

JOAN   Yes: they told me you were fools [*the word gives great offence*], and that I was not to listen to your fine words nor trust to your charity. You promised me my life; but you lied [*indignant exclamations*]. You think that life is nothing but not being stone dead. It is not the bread and water I fear: I can live on bread: when have I asked for more? It is no hardship to drink water if the water be clean. Bread has no sorrow for me, and water no affliction. But to shut me from the light of the sky and the sight of the fields and flowers; to chain my feet so that I can never again ride with the soldiers nor climb the hills; to make me breathe foul damp darkness, and keep from me everything that brings me back to the love of God when your wickedness and foolishness tempt me to hate Him: all this is worse than the furnace in the Bible that was heated seven times. I could do without my warhorse; I could drag about in a skirt; I could let the banners and the trumpets and the knights and soldiers pass me and leave me behind as they leave the other women, if only I could still hear the wind in the trees, the larks in the sunshine, the young lambs crying through the healthy frost, and the blessed blessed church bells that send my angel voices floating to me on the wind. But without these things I cannot live; and by your wanting to take them away from me, or from any human creature, I know that your counsel is of the devil, and that mine is of God.

THE ASSESSORS [*in great commotion*]   Blasphemy! blasphemy! She is possessed. She said our counsel was of the devil. And hers of God. Monstrous! The devil is in our midst, etc., etc.

D'ESTIVET [*shouting above the din*]   She is a relapsed heretic, obstinate, incorrigible, and altogether unworthy of the mercy we have shewn her. I call for her excommunication.

THE CHAPLAIN [*to the Executioner*]   Light your fire, man. To the stake with her.

The Executioner and his assistants hurry out through the courtyard.

LADVENU   You wicked girl: if your counsel were of God would He not deliver you?

JOAN   His ways are not your ways. He wills that I go through the fire to His bosom; for I am His child, and you are not fit that I should live among you. That is my last word to you.

The soldiers seize her.

CAUCHON [*rising*]   Not yet.

They wait. There is a dead silence. Cauchon turns to the Inquisitor with an inquiring look. The Inquisitor nods affirmatively. They rise solemnly, and intone the sentence antiphonally.

CAUCHON   We decree that thou art a relapsed heretic.

THE INQUISITOR   Cast out from the unity of the Church.

CAUCHON   Sundered from her body.

THE INQUISITOR   Infected with the leprosy of heresy.

CAUCHON   A member of Satan.

THE INQUISITOR   We declare that thou must be excommunicate.

CAUCHON   And now we do cast thee out, segregate thee, and abandon thee to the secular power.

THE INQUISITOR   Admonishing the same secular power that it moderate its judgment of thee in respect of death and division of the limbs. [*He resumes his seat.*]

CAUCHON   And if any true sign of penitence appear in thee, to permit our Brother Martin to administer to thee the sacrament of penance.

THE CHAPLAIN   Into the fire with the witch [*He rushes at her, and helps the soldiers to push her out.*]

> *Joan is taken away through the courtyard. The assessors rise in disorder, and follow the soldiers, except Ladvenu, who has hidden his face in his hands.*

CAUCHON   [*rising again in the act of sitting down*]   No, no: this is irregular. The representative of the secular arm should be here to receive her from us.

THE INQUISITOR   [*also on his feet again*]   That man is an incorrigible fool.

CAUCHON   Brother Martin: see that everything is done in order.

LADVENU   My place is at her side, my lord. You must exercise your own authority. [*He hurries out.*]

CAUCHON   These English are impossible: they will thrust her straight into the fire. Look!

> *He points to the courtyard, in which the glow and flicker of fire can now be seen reddening the May daylight. Only the Bishop and the Inquisitor are left in the court.*

CAUCHON   [*turning to go*]   We must stop that.

THE INQUISITOR   [*calmly*]   Yes; but not too fast, my lord.

CAUCHON   [*halting*]   But there is not a moment to lose.

THE INQUISITOR   We have proceeded in perfect order. If the English choose to put themselves in the wrong, it is not our business to put them in the right. A flaw in the procedure may be useful later on: one never knows. And the sooner it is over, the better for that poor girl.

CAUCHON   [*relaxing*]   That is true. But I suppose we must see this dreadful thing through.

THE INQUISITOR   One gets used to it. Habit is everything. I am accustomed to the fire: it is soon over. But it is a terrible thing to see a young and innocent creature crushed between these mighty forces, the Church and the Law.

CAUCHON   You call her innocent!

THE INQUISITOR   Oh, quite innocent. What does she know of the Church and the Law? She did not understand a word we were saying. It is the ignorant who suffer. Come, or we shall be late for the end.

CAUCHON   [*going with him*]   I shall not be sorry if we are: I am not so accustomed as you.

> *They are going out when Warwick comes in, meeting them.*

WARWICK   Oh, I am intruding. I thought it was all over. [*He makes a feint of retiring.*]

CAUCHON   Do not go, my lord. It is all over.

THE INQUISITOR   The execution is not in our hands, my lord; but it is desirable that we should witness the end. So by your leave—[*He bows, and goes out through the courtyard.*]

CAUCHON   There is some doubt whether your people have observed the forms of law, my lord.

WARWICK   I am told that there is some doubt whether your authority runs in this city, my lord. It is not in your diocese. However, if you will answer for that I will answer for the rest.

CAUCHON   It is to God that we both must answer. Good morning, my lord.

WARWICK   My lord: good morning.

They look at one another for a moment with unconcealed hostility. Then Cauchon follows the Inquisitor out. Warwick looks round. Finding himself alone, he calls for attendance.

WARWICK   Hallo: some attendance here! [*Silence*]. Hallo, there! [*Silence*]. Hallo! Brian, you young blackguard, where are you? [*Silence*]. Guard! [*Silence*]. They have all gone to see the burning: even that child.

The silence is broken by someone frantically howling and sobbing.

WARWICK   What in the devil's name—?

The Chaplain staggers in from the courtyard like a demented creature, his face streaming with tears, making the piteous sounds that Warwick has heard. He stumbles to the prisoner's stool, and throws himself upon it with heartrending sobs.

WARWICK [*going to him and patting him on the shoulder*]   What is it, Master John? What is the matter?

THE CHAPLAIN [*clutching at his hand*]   My lord, my lord: for Christ's sake pray for my wretched guilty soul.

WARWICK [*soothing him*]   Yes, yes: of course I will. Calmly, gently—

THE CHAPLAIN [*blubbering miserably*]   I am not a bad man, my lord.

WARWICK   No, no: not at all.

THE CHAPLAIN   I meant no harm. I did not know what it would be like.

WARWICK [*hardening*]   Oh! You saw it, then?

THE CHAPLAIN   I did not know what I was doing. I am a hotheaded fool; and I shall be damned to all eternity for it.

WARWICK   Nonsense! Very distressing, no doubt; but it was not your doing.

THE CHAPLAIN [*lamentably*]   I let them do it. If I had known, I would have torn her from their hands. You dont know: you havnt seen: it is so easy to talk when you dont know. You madden yourself with words: you damn yourself because it feels grand to throw oil on the flaming hell of your own temper. But when it is brought home to you; when you see the thing you have done; when it is blinding your eyes, stifling your nostrils, tearing your heart, then—then—[*Falling on his knees*] O God, take away this sight from me! O Christ, deliver me from this fire that is consuming me! She cried to Thee in the midst of it: Jesus! Jesus! Jesus! She is in Thy bosom; and I am in hell for evermore.

WARWICK [*summarily hauling him to his feet*]   Come come, man! you must pull yourself together. We shall have the whole town talking of this. [*He throws him not too gently into a chair at the table.*] If you have not the nerve to see these things, why do you not do as I do, and stay away?

THE CHAPLAIN [*bewildered and submissive*]   She asked for a cross. A soldier gave her two sticks tied together. Thank God he was an Englishman!

I might have done it; but I did not: I am a coward, a mad dog, a fool. But he was an Englishman too.

WARWICK   The fool! they will burn him too if the priests get hold of him.

THE CHAPLAIN [*shaken with a convulsion*]   Some of the people laughed at her. They would have laughed at Christ. They were French people, my lord: I know they were French.

WARWICK   Hush! someone is coming. Control yourself.

Ladvenu comes back through the courtyard to Warwick's right hand, carrying a bishop's cross which he has taken from a church. He is very grave and composed.

WARWICK   I am informed that it is all over, Brother Martin.

LADVENU [*enigmatically*]   We do not know, my lord. It may have only just begun.

WARWICK   What does that mean, exactly?

LADVENU   I took this cross from the church for her that she might see it to the last: she had only two sticks that she put into her bosom. When the fire crept round us, and she saw that if I held the cross before her I should be burnt myself, she warned me to get down and save myself. My lord: a girl who could think of another's danger in such a moment was not inspired by the devil. When I had to snatch the cross from her sight, she looked up to heaven. And I do not believe that the heavens were empty. I firmly believe that her Savior appeared to her then in His tenderest glory. She called to Him and died. This is not the end for her, but the beginning.

WARWICK   I am afraid it will have a bad effect on the people.

LADVENU   It had, my lord, on some of them. I heard laughter. Forgive me for saying that I hope and believe it was English laughter.

THE CHAPLAIN [*rising frantically*]   No: it was not. There was only one Englishman there that disgraced his country; and that was the mad dog, de Stogumber. [*He rushes wildly out, shrieking*] Let them torture him. Let them burn him. I will go pray among her ashes. I am no better than Judas: I will hang myself.

WARWICK   Quick, Brother Martin: follow him: he will do himself some mischief. After him, quick.

Ladvenu hurries out, Warwick urging him. The Executioner comes in by the door behind the judges' chairs; and Warwick, returning, finds himself face to face with him.

WARWICK   Well, fellow: who are you?

THE EXECUTIONER [*with dignity*]   I am not addressed as fellow, my lord. I am the Master Executioner of Rouen: it is a highly skilled mystery. I am come to tell your lordship that your orders have been obeyed.

WARWICK   I crave your pardon, Master Executioner; and I will see that you lose nothing by having no relics to sell. I have your word, have I, that nothing remains, not a bone, not a nail, not a hair?

THE EXECUTIONER   Her heart would not burn, my lord; but everything that was left is at the bottom of the river. You have heard the last of her.

WARWICK [*with a wry smile, thinking of what Ladvenu said*]   The last of her? Hm! I wonder!

Epilogue

A restless fitfully windy night in June 1456, full of summer lightning after many days of heat. King Charles the Seventh of France, formerly Joan's Dauphin, now Charles the Victorious, aged 51, is in bed in one of his royal chateaux. The bed, raised on a dais of two steps, is towards the side of the room so as to avoid blocking a tall lancet window in the middle. Its canopy bears the royal arms in embroidery. Except for the canopy and the huge down pillows there is nothing to distinguish it from a broad settee with bed-clothes and a valance. Thus its occupant is in full view from the foot.

Charles is not asleep: he is reading in bed, or rather looking at the pictures in Fouquet's Boccaccio [1] *with his knees doubled up to make a reading desk. Beside the bed on his left is a little table with a picture of the Virgin, lighted by candles of painted wax. The walls are hung from ceiling to floor with painted curtains which stir at times in the draughts. At first glance the prevailing yellow and red in these hanging pictures is somewhat flamelike when the folds breathe in the wind.*

The door is on Charles's left, but in front of him close to the corner farthest from him. A large watchman's rattle, handsomely designed and gaily painted, is in the bed under his hand.

Charles turns a leaf. A distant clock strikes the half-hour softly. Charles shuts the book with a clap; throws it aside; snatches up the rattle; and whirls it energetically, making a deafening clatter. Ladvenu enters, 25 years older, strange and stark in bearing, and still carrying the cross from Rouen. Charles evidently does not expect him; for he springs out of bed on the farther side from the door.

CHARLES   Who are you? Where is my gentleman of the bedchamber? What do you want?

LADVENU [*solemnly*]   I bring you glad tidings of great joy. Rejoice, O king; for the taint is removed from your blood, and the stain from your crown. Justice, long delayed, is at last triumphant.

CHARLES   What are you talking about? Who are you?

LADVENU   I am Brother Martin.

CHARLES   And who, saving your reverence, may Brother Martin be?

LADVENU   I held this cross when The Maid perished in the fire. Twenty-five years have passed since then: nearly ten thousand days. And on every one of those days I have prayed to God to justify His daughter on earth as she is justified in heaven.

CHARLES [*reassured, sitting down on the foot of the bed*]   Oh, I remember now. I have heard of you. You have a bee in your bonnet about The Maid. Have you been at the inquiry?

LADVENU   I have given my testimony.

CHARLES   Is it over?

LADVENU   It is over.

CHARLES   Satisfactorily?

1. A magnificent manuscript of the works of Giovanni Boccaccio (1313–75) with miniatures possibly by Jean Fouquet (1416–80), still extant. Fouquet was painter to the French court, and Shaw probably mentions him because he painted Agnes Sorel, Charles's mistress, as the Virgin in a famous altarpiece.

LADVENU   The ways of God are very strange.

CHARLES   How so?

LADVENU   At the trial which sent a saint to the stake as a heretic and a sorceress, the truth was told; the law was upheld; mercy was shewn beyond all custom; no wrong was done but the final and dreadful wrong of the lying sentence and the pitiless fire. At this inquiry from which I have just come, there was shameless perjury, courtly corruption, calumny of the dead who did their duty according to their lights, cowardly evasion of the issue, testimony made of idle tales that could not impose on a ploughboy. Yet out of this insult to justice, this defamation of the Church, this orgy of lying and foolishness, the truth is set in the noonday sun on the hilltop; the white robe of innocence is cleansed from the smirch of the burning faggots; the holy life is sanctified; the true heart that lived through the flame is consecrated; a great lie is silenced for ever; and a great wrong is set right before all men.

CHARLES   My friend: provided they can no longer say that I was crowned by a witch and a heretic, I shall not fuss about how the trick has been done. Joan would not have fussed about it if it came all right in the end: she was not that sort: I knew her. Is her rehabilitation complete? I made it pretty clear that there was to be no nonsense about it.

LADVENU   It is solemnly declared that her judges were full of corruption, cozenage, fraud, and malice. Four falsehoods.

CHARLES   Never mind the falsehoods: her judges are dead.

LADVENU   The sentence on her is broken, annulled, annihilated, set aside as non-existent, without value or effect.

CHARLES   Good. Nobody can challenge my consecration now, can they?

LADVENU   Not Charlemagne nor King David himself was more sacredly crowned.

CHARLES [rising]   Excellent. Think of what that means to me!

LADVENUE   I think of what it means to her!

CHARLES   You cannot. None of us ever knew what anything meant to her. She was like nobody else; and she must take care of herself wherever she is; for I cannot take care of her; and neither can you, whatever you may think: you are not big enough. But I will tell you this about her. If you could bring her back to life, they would burn her again within six months, for all their present adoration of her. And you would hold up the cross, too, just the same. So [crossing himself] let her rest; and let you and I mind our own business, and not meddle with hers.

LADVENU   God forbid that I should have no share in her, nor she in me! [He turns and strides out as he came, saying] Henceforth my path will not lie through palaces, nor my conversation be with kings.

CHARLES [following him towards the door, and shouting after him]   Much good may it do you, holy man! [He returns to the middle of the chamber, where he halts, and says quizzically to himself] That was a funny chap. How did he get in? Where are my people? [He goes impatiently to the bed, and swings the rattle. A rush of wind through the open door sets the walls swaying agitatedly. The candles go out. He calls in the darkness.] Hallo! Someone come and shut the windows: everything is being blown all over the place. [A flash of summer lightning shews up the

lancet window. A figure is seen in silhouette against it.] Who is there?
Who is that? Help! Murder! [*Thunder. He jumps into bed, and hides
under the clothes.*]

JOAN'S VOICE   Easy, Charlie, easy. What art making all that noise for? No one
can hear thee. Thourt asleep. [*She is dimly seen in a pallid greenish light
by the bedside.*]

CHARLES [*peeping out*]   Joan! Are you a ghost, Joan?

JOAN   Hardly even that, lad. Can a poor burnt-up lass have a ghost? I am but
a dream that thourt dreaming. [*The light increases: they become plainly
visible as he sits up.*] Thou looks older, lad.

CHARLES   I am older. Am I really asleep?

JOAN   Fallen asleep over thy silly book.

CHARLES   That's funny.

JOAN   Not so funny as that I am dead, is it?

CHARLES   Are you really dead?

JOAN   As dead as anybody ever is, laddie. I am out of the body.

CHARLES   Just fancy! Did it hurt much?

JOAN   Did what hurt much?

CHARLES   Being burnt.

JOAN   Oh, that! I cannot remember very well. I think it did at first; but then
it all got mixed up; and I was not in my right mind until I was free of
the body. But do not thou go handling fire and thinking it will not hurt
thee. How hast been ever since?

CHARLES   Oh, not so bad. Do you know, I actually lead my army out and win
battles? Down into the moat up to my waist in mud and blood. Up the
ladders with the stones and hot pitch raining down. Like you.

JOAN   No! Did I make a man of thee after all, Charlie?

CHARLES   I am Charles the Victorious now. I had to be brave because you
were. Agnes put a little pluck into me too.

JOAN   Agnes! Who was Agnes?

CHARLES   Agnes Sorel. A woman I fell in love with. I dream of her often. I
never dreamed of you before.

JOAN   Is she dead, like me?

CHARLES   Yes. But she was not like you. She was very beautiful.

JOAN [*laughing heartily*]   Ha ha! I was no beauty: I was always a rough one:
a regular soldier. I might almost as well have been a man. Pity I wasnt:
I should not have bothered you all so much then. But my head was in
the skies; and the glory of God was upon me; and, man or woman, I
should have bothered you as long as your noses were in the mud. Now
tell me what has happened since you wise men knew no better than to
make a heap of cinders of me?

CHARLES   Your mother and brothers have sued the courts to have your case
tried over again. And the courts have declared that your judges were
full of corruption and cozenage, fraud and malice.

JOAN   Not they. They were as honest a lot of poor fools as ever burned their
betters.

CHARLES   The sentence on you is broken, annihilated, annulled: null, non-
existent, without value or effect.

JOAN   I was burned, all the same. Can they unburn me?

CHARLES   If they could, they would think twice before they did it. But they have decreed that a beautiful cross be placed where the stake stood, for your perpetual memory and for your salvation.

JOAN   It is the memory and the salvation that sanctify the cross, not the cross that sanctifies the memory and the salvation. [*She turns away, forgetting him.*] I shall outlast that cross. I shall be remembered when men will have forgotten where Rouen stood.

CHARLES   There you go with your self-conceit, the same as ever! I think you might say a word of thanks to me for having had justice done at last.

CAUCHON [*appearing at the window between them*]   Liar!

CHARLES   Thank you.

JOAN   Why, if it isnt Peter Cauchon! How are you, Peter? What luck have you had since you burned me?

CAUCHON   None. I arraign the justice of Man. It is not the justice of God.

JOAN   Still dreaming of justice, Peter? See what justice came to with me! But what has happened to thee? Art dead or alive?

CAUCHON   Dead. Dishonored. They pursued me beyond the grave. They excommunicated my dead body: they dug it up and flung it into the common sewer.

JOAN   Your dead body did not feel the spade and the sewer as my live body felt the fire.

CAUCHON   But this thing that they have done against me hurts justice; destroys faith; saps the foundation of the Church. The solid earth sways like the treacherous sea beneath the feet of men and spirits alike when the innocent are slain in the name of law, and their wrongs are undone by slandering the pure of heart.

JOAN   Well, well, Peter, I hope men will be the better for remembering me; and they would not remember me so well if you had not burned me.

CAUCHON   They will be the worse for remembering me: they will see in me evil triumphing over good, falsehood over truth, cruelty over mercy, hell over heaven. Their courage will rise as they think of you, only to faint as they think of me. Yet God is my witness I was just: I was merciful: I was faithful to my light: I could do no other than I did.

CHARLES [*scrambling out of the sheets and enthroning himself on the side of the bed*]   Yes: it is always you good men that do the big mischiefs. Look at me! I am not Charles the Good, nor Charles the Wise, nor Charles the Bold. Joan's worshippers may even call me Charles the Coward because I did not pull her out of the fire. But I have done less harm than any of you. You people with your heads in the sky spend all your time trying to turn the world upside down; but I take the world as it is, and say that top-side-up is right-side-up; and I keep my nose pretty close to the ground. And I ask you, what king of France has done better, or been a better fellow in his little way?

JOAN   Art really king of France, Charlie? Be the English gone?

DUNOIS [*coming through the tapestry on Joan's left, the candles relighting themselves at the same moment, and illuminating his armor and surcoat cheerfully*]   I have kept my word: the English are gone.

JOAN   Praised be God! now is fair France a province in heaven. Tell me all about the fighting, Jack. Was it thou that led them? Wert thou God's captain to thy death?

DUNOIS   I am not dead. My body is very comfortably asleep in my bed at Chateaudun; but my spirit is called here by yours.

JOAN   And you fought them my way, Jack: eh? Not the old way, chaffering for ransoms; but The Maid's way: staking life against death, with the heart high and humble and void of malice, and nothing counting under God but France free and French. Was it my way, Jack?

DUNOIS   Faith, it was any way that would win. But the way that won was always your way. I give you best, lassie. I wrote a fine letter to set you right at the new trial. Perhaps I should never have let the priests burn you; but I was busy fighting; and it was the Church's business, not mine. There was no use in both of us being burned, was there?

CAUCHON   Ay! put the blame on the priests. But I, who am beyond praise and blame, tell you that the world is saved neither by its priests nor its soldiers, but by God and His Saints. The Church Militant sent this woman to the fire; but even as she burned, the flames whitened into the radiance of the Church Triumphant.

The clock strikes the third quarter. A rough male voice is heard trolling an improvised tune.

Rum tum trumpledum,
Bacon fat and rumpledum,
Old Saint mumpledum,
Pull his tail and stumpledum
    O my Ma—ry Ann!

A ruffianly English soldier comes through the curtains and marches between Dunois and Joan.

DUNOIS   What villainous troubadour taught you that doggrel?

THE SOLDIER   No troubadour. We made it up ourselves as we marched. We were not gentlefolks and troubadours. Music straight out of the heart of the people, as you might say. Rum tum trumpledum, Bacon fat and rumpledum, Old Saint mumpledum, Pull his tail and stumpledum: that dont mean anything, you know; but it keeps you marching. Your servant, ladies and gentlemen. Who asked for a saint?

JOAN   Be you a saint?

THE SOLDIER   Yes, lady, straight from hell.

DUNOIS   A saint, and from hell!

THE SOLDIER   Yes, noble captain: I have a day off. Every year, you know. Thats my allowance for my one good action.

CAUCHON   Wretch! In all the years of your life did you do only one good action?

THE SOLDIER   I never thought about it: it came natural like. But they scored it up for me.

CHARLES   What was it?

THE SOLDIER   Why, the silliest thing you ever heard of. I—

JOAN   [*interrupting him by strolling across to the bed, where she sits beside Charles*]   He tied two sticks together, and gave them to a poor lass that was going to be burned.

THE SOLDIER   Right. Who told you that?

JOAN   Never mind. Would you know her if you saw her again?

THE SOLDIER   Not I. There are so many girls! and they all expect you to re-member them as if there was only one in the world. This one must have been a prime sort; for I have a day off every year for her; and so, until twelve o'clock punctually, I am a saint, at your service, noble lords and lovely ladies.

CHARLES   And after twelve?

THE SOLDIER   After twelve, back to the only place fit for the likes of me.

JOAN [rising]   Back there! You! that gave the lass the cross!

THE SOLDIER [excusing his unsoldierly conduct]   Well, she asked for it; and they were going to burn her. She had as good a right to a cross as they had; and they had dozens of them. It was her funeral, not theirs. Where was the harm in it?

JOAN   Man: I am not reproaching you. But I cannot bear to think of you in torment.

THE SOLDIER [cheerfully]   No great torment, lady. You see I was used to worse.

CHARLES   What! worse than hell?

THE SOLDIER   Fifteen years' service in the French wars. Hell was a treat after that.

    Joan throws up her arms, and takes refuge from despair of humanity before the picture of the Virgin.

THE SOLDIER [continuing]—   Suits me somehow. The day off was dull at first, like a wet Sunday. I dont mind it so much now. They tell me I can have as many as I like as soon as I want them.

CHARLES   What is hell like?

THE SOLDIER   You wont find it so bad, sir. Jolly. Like as if you were always drunk without the trouble and expense of drinking. Tip top company too: emperors and popes and kings and all sorts. They chip me about giving that young judy the cross; but I dont care: I stand up to them proper, and tell them that if she hadnt a better right to it than they, she'd be where they are. That dumbfounds them, that does. All they can do is gnash their teeth, hell fashion; and I just laugh, and go off singing the old chanty: Rum tum trumple—Hullo! Who's that knocking at the door?

    They listen. A long gentle knocking is heard.

CHARLES   Come in.

    The door opens; and an old priest, white-haired, bent, with a silly but benevolent smile, comes in and trots over to Joan.

THE NEWCOMER   Excuse me, gentle lords and ladies. Do not let me disturb you. Only a poor old harmless English rector. Formerly chaplain to the cardinal: to my lord of Winchester. John de Stogumber, at your service. [He looks at them inquiringly.] Did you say anything? I am a little deaf, unfortunately. Also a little—well, not always in my right mind, perhaps; but still, it is a small village with a few simple people. I suffice: I suffice: they love me there; and I am able to do a little good. I am well con-nected, you see; and they indulge me.

JOAN   Poor old John! What brought thee to this state?

DE STOGUMBER   I tell my folks they must be very careful. I say to them, 'If you only saw what you think about you would think quite differently about it. It would give you a great shock. Oh, a great shock.' And they all say 'Yes, parson: we all know you are a kind man, and would not harm a fly.' That is a great comfort to me. For I am not cruel by nature, you know.

THE SOLDIER   Who said you were?

DE STOGUMBER   Well, you see, I did a very cruel thing once because I did not know what cruelty was like. I had not seen it, you know. That is the great thing: you must see it. And then you are redeemed and saved.

CAUCHON   Were not the sufferings of our Lord Christ enough for you?

DE STOGUMBER   No. Oh no; not at all, I had seen them in pictures, and read of them in books, and been greatly moved by them, as I thought. But it was no use: it was not our Lord that redeemed me, but a young woman whom I saw actually burned to death. It was dreadful: oh, most dreadful. But it saved me. I have been a different man ever since, though a little astray in my wits sometimes.

CAUCHON   Must then a Christ perish in torment in every age to save those that have no imagination?

JOAN   Well, if I saved all those he would have been cruel to if he had not been cruel to me, I was not burnt for nothing, was I?

DE STOGUMBER   Oh no; it was not you. My sight is bad: I cannot distinguish your features: but you are not she: oh no: she was burned to a cinder: dead and gone, dead and gone.

THE EXECUTIONER [stepping from behind the bed curtains on Charles's right, the bed being between them]   She is more alive than you, old man. Her heart would not burn; and it would not drown. I was a master at my craft: better than the master of Paris, better than the master of Toulouse; but I could not kill The Maid. She is up and alive everywhere.

THE EARL OF WARWICK [sallying from the bed curtains on the other side, and coming to Joan's left hand]   Madam: my congratulations on your rehabilitation. I feel that I owe you an apology.

JOAN   Oh, please don't mention it.

WARWICK [pleasantly]   The burning was purely political. There was no personal feeling against you, I assure you.

JOAN   I bear no malice, my lord.

WARWICK   Just so. Very kind of you to meet me in that way: a touch of true breeding. But I must insist on apologizing very amply. The truth is, these political necessities sometimes turn out to be political mistakes; and this one was a veritable howler; for your spirit conquered us, madam, in spite of our faggots. History will remember me for your sake, though the incidents of the connection were perhaps a little unfortunate.

JOAN   Ay, perhaps just a little, you funny man.

WARWICK   Still, when they make you a saint, you will owe your halo to me, just as this lucky monarch owes his crown to you.

JOAN [turning from him]   I shall owe nothing to any man: I owe everything to the spirit of God that was within me. But fancy me a saint! What would St Catherine and St Margaret say if the farm girl was cocked up [2] beside them!

2. Celebrated and venerated.

A clerical-looking gentleman in black frockcoat and trousers, and tall hat, in the fashion of the year 1920, suddenly appears before them in the corner on their right. They all stare at him. Then they burst into uncontrollable laughter.

THE GENTLEMAN   Why this mirth, gentlemen?

WARWICK   I congratulate you on having invented a most extraordinarily comic dress.

THE GENTLEMAN   I do not understand. You are all in fancy dress: I am properly dressed.

DUNOIS   All dress is fancy dress, is it not, except our natural skins?

THE GENTLEMAN   Pardon me: I am here on serious business, and cannot engage in frivolous discussions. [*He takes out a paper, and assumes a dry official manner.*] I am sent to announce to you that Joan of Arc, formerly know as The Maid, having been the subject of an inquiry instituted by the Bishop of Orleans—

JOAN [*interrupting*]   Ah! They remember me still in Orleans.

THE GENTLEMAN [*emphatically, to mark his indignation at the interruption*]— by the Bishop of Orleans into the claim of the said Joan of Arc to be canonized as a saint—

JOAN [*again interrupting*]   But I never made any such claim.

THE GENTLEMAN [*as before*]—   the Church has examined the claim exhaustively in the usual course, and, having admitted the said Joan successively to the ranks of Venerable and Blessed,—

JOAN [*chuckling*]   Me venerable!

THE GENTLEMAN—   has finally declared her to have been endowed with heroic virtues and favored with private revelations, and calls the said Venerable and Blessed Joan to the communion of the Church Triumphant as Saint Joan.

JOAN [*rapt*]   Saint Joan!

THE GENTLEMAN   On every thirtieth day of May, being the anniversary of the death of the said most blessed daughter of God, there shall in every Catholic church to the end of time be celebrated a special office in commemoration of her; and it shall be lawful to dedicate a special chapel to her, and to place her image on its altar in every such church. And it shall be lawful and laudable for the faithful to kneel and address their prayers through her to the Mercy Seat.

JOAN   Oh no. It is for the saint to kneel. [*She falls on her knees, still rapt.*]

THE GENTLEMAN [*putting up his paper, and retiring beside the Executioner*] In Basilica Vaticana, the sixteenth day of May, nineteen hundred and twenty.

DUNOIS [*raising Joan*]   Half an hour to burn you, dear Saint, and four centuries to find out the truth about you!

DE STOGUMBER   Sir: I was chaplain to the Cardinal of Winchester once. They always would call him the Cardinal of England. It would be a great comfort to me and to my master to see a fair statue of The Maid in Winchester Cathedral. Will they put one there, do you think?

THE GENTLEMAN   As the building is temporarily in the hands of the Anglican heresy, I cannot answer for that.

A vision of the statue in Winchester Cathedral is seen through the window.

DE STOGUMBER   Oh look! look! that is Winchester.

JOAN   Is that meant to be me? I was stiffer on my feet.
The vision fades.

THE GENTLEMAN   I have been requested by the temporal authorities of France to mention that the multiplication of public statues to The Maid threatens to become an obstruction to traffic. I do so as a matter of courtesy to the said authorities, but must point out on behalf of the Church that The Maid's horse is no greater obstruction to traffic than any other horse.

JOAN   Eh! I am glad they have not forgotten my horse.
A vision of the statue before Rheims Cathedral appears.

JOAN   Is that funny little thing me too?

CHARLES   That is Rheims Cathedral where you had me crowned. It must be you.

JOAN   Who has broken my sword? My sword was never broken. It is the sword of France.

DUNOIS   Never mind. Swords can be mended. Your soul is unbroken; and you are the soul of France.
The vision fades. The Archbishop and the Inquisitor are now seen on the right and left of Cauchon.

JOAN   My sword shall conquer yet: the sword that never struck a blow. Though men destroyed my body, yet in my soul I have seen God.

CAUCHON [*kneeling to her*]   The girls in the field praise thee; for thou hast raised their eyes; and they see that there is nothing between them and heaven.

DUNOIS [*kneeling to her*]   The dying soldiers praise thee, because thou art a shield of glory between them and the judgment.

THE ARCHBISHOP [*kneeling to her*]   The princes of the Church praise thee, because thou hast redeemed the faith their worldlinesses have dragged through the mire.

WARWICK [*kneeling to her*]   The cunning counsellors praise thee, because thou hast cut the knots in which they have tied their own souls.

DE STOGUMBER [*kneeling to her*]   The foolish old men on their deathbeds praise thee, because their sins against thee are turned into blessings.

THE INQUISITOR [*kneeling to her*]   The judges in the blindness and bondage of the law praise thee, because thou hast vindicated the vision and the freedom of the living soul.

THE SOLDIER [*kneeling to her*]   The wicked out of hell praise thee, because thou hast shewn them that the fire that is not quenched is a holy fire.

THE EXECUTIONER [*kneeling to her*]   The tormentors and executioners praise thee, because thou hast shewn that their hands are guiltless of the death of the soul.

CHARLES [*kneeling to her*]   The unpretending praise thee, because thou hast taken upon thyself the heroic burdens that are too heavy for them.

JOAN   Woe unto me when all men praise me! I bid you remember that I am a saint, and that saints can work miracles. And now tell me: shall I rise from the dead, and come back to you a living woman?

A sudden darkness blots out the walls of the room as they all spring to their feet in consternation. Only the figures and the bed remain visible.

JOAN   What! Must I burn again? Are none of you ready to receive me?

CAUCHON   The heretic is always better dead. And mortal eyes cannot distinguish the saint from the heretic. Spare them. [*He goes out as he came.*]

DUNOIS   Forgive us, Joan: we are not yet good enough for you. I shall go back to my bed. [*He also goes.*]

WARWICK   We sincerely regret our little mistake; but political necessities, though occasionally erroneous, are still imperative; so if you will be good enough to excuse me—[*He steals discreetly away.*]

THE ARCHBISHOP   Your return would not make me the man you once thought me. The utmost I can say is that though I dare not bless you, I hope I may one day enter into your blessedness. Meanwhile, however—[*He goes.*]

THE INQUISITOR   I who am of the dead, testified that day that you were innocent. But I do not see how The Inquisition could possibly be dispensed with under existing circumstances. Therefore—[*He goes.*]

DE STOGUMBER   Oh, do not come back: you must not come back. I must die in peace. Give us peace in our time, O Lord! [*He goes.*]

THE GENTLEMAN   The possibility of your resurrection was not contemplated in the recent proceedings for your canonization. I must return to Rome for fresh instructions. [*He bows formally, and withdraws.*]

THE EXECUTIONER   As a master in my profession I have to consider its interests. And, after all, my first duty is to my wife and children. I must have time to think over this. [*He goes.*]

CHARLES   Poor old Joan! They have all run away from you except this blackguard who has to go back to hell at twelve o'clock. And what can I do but follow Jack Dunois' example, and go back to bed too? [*He does so.*]

JOAN [*sadly*]   Goodnight, Charlie.

CHARLES [*mumbling in his pillows*]   Goo ni. [*He sleeps. The darkness envelops the bed.*]

JOAN [*to the soldier*]   And you, my one faithful? What comfort have you for Saint Joan?

THE SOLDIER   Well, what do they all amount to, these kings and captains and bishops and lawyers and such like? They just leave you in the ditch to bleed to death; and the next thing is, you meet them down there, for all the airs they give themselves. What I say is, you have as good a right to your notions as they have to theirs, and perhaps better. [*settling himself for a lecture on the subject*] You see, it's like this. If—[*The first stroke of midnight is heard softly from a distant bell.*] Excuse me: a pressing appointment—[*He goes on tiptoe.*]

The last remaining rays of light gather into a white radiance descending on Joan. The hour continues to strike.

JOAN   O God that madest this beautiful earth, when will it be ready to receive Thy saints? How long, O Lord, how long? [3]

3. "How long, O Lord" is a formula used in Psalms and by the prophets, and echoed in Revelation.

JOSEPH CONRAD

1857–1924

Conrad was born Teodor Josef Konrad Korzeniowski in the Ukraine. His father, Appollo Korzeniowski, was a man of letters and a leader of the Polish revolt against Russia in 1863; after a period of exile he died in Cracow in 1869. The young Conrad had early expressed interest in travel, and would in any case probably have had to emigrate to make his way in the world; but his family did not approve of his taking to the sea. This he did In 1874, when he went to Marseille and helped in a gun-running operation in behalf of the Carlists (supporters of the claim of Don Carlos of Spain to the Spanish throne). Here he had an almost fatal adventure, and fell in love, gambled, and attempted suicide. Thenceforth he followed a more normal seafaring life. In 1878 he joined an English merchant vessel, and followed the sea for sixteen years, rising to command his own ship.

In 1889, in his forty-second year, he began to write the novel *Almayer's Folly;* in the following year he undertook the Congo trip which is the source of *Heart of Darkness.* He gave up the sea only in 1894, and began his career as a novelist, using a language he had not learned till in his twenties. A painful writer, he nevertheless produced thirty-one books and a vast number of letters. He married in 1896, and settled to a life of drudgery and poverty, lightened only by a distinguished circle of friends, notably H. G. Wells, Henry James, John Galsworthy, Stephen Crane, and his collaborator Ford Madox Hueffer (later and better known as Ford Madox Ford). Suffering and complaining almost ceaselessly, Conrad struggled with a novel (*The Rescuer,* later *The Rescue*) which would not come right, and then turned away from it to write his great early stories *The Nigger of the "Narcissus"* (1897), *Heart of Darkness* (1899), and the first of the major novels, *Lord Jim* (1900). While the importance of all of these in the development of the artist is enormous, he reached his full stature in the years of the three great novels *Nostromo* (1904), *The Secret Agent* (1906), and *Under Western Eyes* (1910). Somewhat surprisingly, a very complicated and on the whole inferior novel, *Chance* (1912), brought him the income which had eluded him as his fame grew. *Victory,* the last of the first-rate books, followed in 1914.

This account omits comment on some of the remarkable shorter works—early and late—such as *The End of the Tether* and *The Shadow Line;* and some relatively unsuccessful novels—*The Rescue, The Outcast of the Islands, The Arrow of Gold* (an autobiographical work about his Carlist period)—and *The Rover.* So large a body of work makes generalization difficult; but two things at least may be said. First, Conrad's fiction is related with unusual closeness to his own experience; and second, he was from the outset an artist, never accepting conventional forms or conventional judgments. The closeness of the novels to Conrad's own experience is something that scholarship increasingly confirms, but in the writing process this experience is developed, transfigured, and shaped in extraordinary ways. No writer did more to establish in the English novel the strict necessity to find new forms for every undertaking. This may seem strange when we consider that Conrad used to be thought of as a master of exotic scenes and narratives, the South Seas and romantic adventure; yet it was a habit of brooding creatively on such adventures that produced *Lord Jim, The End of the Tether, Heart of Darkness*—all closely related to Conrad's own biography and all "good stories" of the kind the narrator is talking about when, in *Heart of Darkness,* he says to Marlow that "the meaning of an episode was not inside like a kernel but outside, enveloping the tale which brought it out only as a glow brings out a haze, in the likeness of one of those misty halos that sometimes are made visible by the spectral illumination of moonshine."

Although the shorter pieces have not, as a rule, the structural complexity of the major novels, they share their fidelity to art and experience. This was to Conrad a moral issue; he is concerned with the truth, the truth as it appeared to his somber imagination. In some famous lines in the Preface to The Nigger of the "Narcissus" he expresses thus the peculiar adventure of the artist, and its purpose:

> A work that aspires, however humbly, to the condition of art should carry its justification in every line. And art itself may be defined as a single-minded attempt to render the highest kind of justice to the visible universe, by bringing to light the truth, manifold and one, underlying its every aspect. It is an attempt to find in its forms, in its colours, in its light, in its shadows, in the aspects of matter and in the facts of life what of each is fundamental, what is enduring and essential—their one illuminating and convincing quality—the very truth of their existence. The artist, then, like the thinker or the scientist, seeks the truth and makes his appeal. Impressed by the aspect of the world the thinker plunges into ideas, the scientist into facts—whence, presently, emerging they make their appeal to those qualities of our being that fit us best for the hazardous enterprise of living. They speak authoritatively to our commonsense, to our intelligence, to our desire of peace or to our desire of unrest; not seldom to our prejudices, sometimes to our fears, often to our egoism—but always to our credulity. And their words are heard with reverence, for their concern is with weighty matters: with the cultivation of our minds and the proper care of our bodies, with the attainment of our ambitions, with the perfection of the means and the glorification of our precious aims.
>
> It is otherwise with the artist.
>
> Confronted by the same enigmatical spectacle the artist descends within himself, and in that lonely region of stress and strife, if he be deserving and fortunate, he finds the terms of his appeal. His appeal is made to our less obvious capacities: to that part of our nature which, because of the warlike conditions of existence, is necessarily kept out of sight within the more resisting and hard qualities—like the vulnerable body within a steel armour. His appeal is less loud, more profound, less distinct, more stirring—and sooner forgotten. Yet its effect endures forever. The changing wisdom of successive generations discards ideas, questions facts, demolishes theories. But the artist appeals to that part of our being which is not dependent on wisdom; to that in us which is a gift and not an acquisition—and, therefore, more permanently enduring. He speaks to our capacity for delight and wonder, to the sense of mystery surrounding our lives; to our sense of pity, and beauty, and pain; to the latent feeling of fellowship with all creation—and to the subtle but invincible conviction of solidarity that knits together the loneliness of innumerable hearts, to the solidarity in dreams, in joy, in sorrow, in aspirations, in illusions, in hope, in fear, which binds men to each other, which binds together all humanity—the dead to the living and the living to the unborn.

In the rhetoric of this opening manifesto there are one or two very characteristic phrases: the emphasis on truth, the artist's descent "within himself," the appeal to human nature as it exists universally but concealed by "the warlike conditions of [our] existence." Conrad goes on to argue that fiction achieves this end by its appeal to the senses.

> All art . . . appeals primarily to the senses, and the artistic aim when expressing itself in written words must also make its appeal through the senses, if its high desire is to reach the secret spring of responsive emotions. It must

strenuously aspire to the plasticity of sculpture, to the colour of painting, and to the magic suggestiveness of music—which is the art of arts. And it is only through complete, unswerving devotion to the perfect blending of form and substance; it is only through an unremitting never-discouraged care for the shape and ring of sentences that an approach can be made to plasticity, to colour, and that the light of magic suggestiveness may be brought to play for an evanescent instant over the commonplace surface of words: of the old, old words, worn thin, defaced by ages of careless usage.

The sincere endeavour to accomplish that creative task, to go as far on that road as his strength will carry him, to go undeterred by faltering, weariness or reproach, is the only valid justification for the worker in prose. And if his conscience is clear, his answer to those who in the fulness of a wisdom which looks for immediate profit, demand specifically to be edified, consoled, amused; who demand to be promptly improved, or encouraged, or frightened, or shocked, or charmed, must run thus:—My task which I am trying to achieve is, by the power of the written word to make you hear, to make you feel—it is, before all, to make you see. That—and no more, and it is everything. If I succeed, you shall find there according to your deserts: encouragement, consolation, fear, charm—all you demand—and, perhaps, also that glimpse of truth for which you have forgotten to ask.

To snatch in a moment of courage, from the remorseless rush of time, a passing phase of life, is only the beginning of the task. The task approached in tenderness and faith is to hold up unquestioningly, without choice and without fear, the rescued fragment before all eyes in the light of a sincere mood. It is to show its vibration, its colour, its form; and through its movement, its form, and its colour, reveal the substance of its truth—disclose its inspiring secret: the stress and passion within the core of each convincing moment. In a single-minded attempt of that kind, if one be deserving and fortunate, one may perchance attain to such clearness of sincerity that at last the presented vision of regret or pity, of terror or mirth, shall awaken in the hearts of the beholders that feeling of unavoidable solidarity; of the solidarity in mysterious origin, in toil, in joy, in hope, in uncertain fate, which binds men to each other and all mankind to the visible world.

It is evident that he who, rightly or wrongly, holds by the convictions expressed above cannot be faithful to any one of the temporary formulas of his craft. The enduring part of them—the truth which each only imperfectly veils—should abide with him as the most precious of his possessions, but they all: Realism, Romanticism, Naturalism, even the unofficial sentimentalism (which like the poor, is exceedingly difficult to get rid of), all these gods must, after a short period of fellowship, abandon him—even on the very threshold of the temple—to the stammerings of his conscience and to the outspoken consciousness of the difficulties of his work.

This is not merely the familiar late-nineteenth-century aspiration to the condition of music; it is a declaration of the immense formal difficulty of the novelist's task. Fiction is a mode of truth-telling but also an art: "Fiction is history, human history, or it is nothing," said Conrad elsewhere, but added, "it is also more than that . . . being based on the reality of forms." The art lies in "perfect blending of form and substance." This is why Conrad studied Flaubert and Maupassant, and why he and Ford Madox Ford labored to work out a whole new practice as well as a new aesthetic of the novel, one that required the most intense study of the form. The result is in a new sense "to make you see." What you "see" may be that "glimpse of the truth for which you have forgotten to ask," and it will certainly be what you could not have seen at all without the aid of the novel, which Conrad, like Lawrence, regarded as one of the great instruments of knowledge.

This explains not only Conrad's unremitting experiment but also the suffering and labor he complained of. He was always looking, not for some startling novelty, but for the light that plays "over the commonplace surface of words." His own life contained incidents to which imagination gave ambiguous meanings that a man of his sensibility might spend the rest of it exploring: his attempted suicide as a youth, his behavior in certain emergencies at sea, his relation to Poland. All life was made up of such incidents, of solitude and fear relieved, for some, by society, and for some by the simple and difficult virtues, such as fidelity. By the time Conrad's opinions and attitudes have been changed under the pressure of his constructive imagination, they are not as they appear in his straightforward expressions of opinion: the view of Russia in *Under Western Eyes* is not that held by the "waking" Conrad; *The Secret Agent* is not "a simple tale"—whatever the subtitle says—about a police trick played on anarchists, but an ironic, tragic meditation on the darkness at the heart of the world. The technical devices he invents are instruments devised "to make you see" more than you bargained for. *Heart of Darkness* shows him using such devices quite early in his career.

Heart of Darkness

First written to appear as a three-part serial in *Blackwood's Magazine, Heart of Darkness* was published in book form with *Youth* and *The End of the Tether* in 1902. Its material derives from Conrad's time in the Congo in 1890, a brief period rightly thought of as the turning point of his career. Conrad had wanted to visit the blank on the map since he was a child; now, thanks to the good offices of an aunt who lived in Brussels, he was able to do so. As a consequence his health suffered badly, but—after "the descent into the self" which the visit entailed—he was transformed into a great writer. He himself says he was "a perfect animal" till that time.

The entire Congo area—nearly one million square miles—belonged personally, by a freak of European diplomacy, to Leopold II, King of the Belgians. The King spoke of opening it to civilization, and of bringing in Christianity to "pierce the darkness which envelops the entire population," but this was merely a cover for ruthless exploitation. The fine talk of high purposes was accompanied by a barbarous labor policy, savage punishments (from flogging to amputation), and a rankling contempt for the savages supposedly to be saved. This was the Congo Conrad found himself in after the long sea trip from England. Later he called it "the vilest scramble for loot that ever disfigured the history of human conscience," but at the time he probably expected something quite different. The period of his stay in Africa is by now well researched, most notably and recently by Norman Sherry in *Conrad's Western World* (1971). So small a detail as the death of Captain Fresleven, which gave Marlow his command, is based on the murder of a real Captain Freisleben, and so is the detail of the grass growing up through his ribs. Conrad himself left a diary covering part of the voyage and revealing, among other things, that he omitted some of the more agreeable early encounters that befell him; and in general he departs from the facts, or stays close to them, as best suits his purposes. The steamer he was sent to had been wrecked like Marlow's; but unlike Marlow he did not stay to repair it. There *was* a brickmaker, but he managed to make bricks. Kurtz is based on a man named

A. E. C. Hodister (though not in minute detail), and the Harlequin, on Hodister's champion Jacques Doré. And the settlement at Stanley Falls was a large one, quite unlike Kurtz's.

None of this is essential to the study of *Heart of Darkness,* though the ironic contrast between the professions of colonists and missionaries, and the actual conduct of the "explorers" and "pilgrims" and "managers" are of course part of the conception. Mr. Sherry even finds that the opening sequence, in which the Thames in Roman times is compared to the modern Congo, owes something to a speech of the famous explorer and journalist Henry Morton Stanley—a speech quoting in turn the question raised by Prime Minister Pitt in 1799, as to whether a Roman senator might not have said of ancient Britain what men now said about Africa (that it was incapable of civilization, and so on): "Sir, we were once as obscure among the nations of the earth, as debased in our morals, as savage in our manners, as degraded in our understandings as these unhappy Africans are at present." Further, the *Nellie* was an actual yawl, and Conrad knew what he was doing when he set Marlow's tale aboard it, and in the salt water of the estuary; for Conrad's primary image of the ordered society, of fidelity, of courage and endurance in human crisis, was a well-found sailing ship in salt water. To explore the heart of darkness both Conrad and Marlow sailed up a river into the heart of a continent.

Marlow is not a mere mouthpiece. Neither is he a veil between author and reader. He contributes, here and everywhere, to Conrad's object, which is to make one see; see more, perhaps, than Marlow. Does he, for instance, see Kurtz as we are made to? He has limitations which, at important points, make his narrative suggestive rather than explicit. He provides the commonplace words over which the haze of meanings develops. What Marlow does is to alter the perspectives in the way which Conrad described as that "wherein almost all my 'art' consists." The setting does the same thing: the yawl with its head to the open sea, and dark London—"devourer of the world's light," he called it in the Preface to *The Secret Agent*—behind; and when Marlow has finished his account of a trip to the edge of the heart of darkness, the tide has turned and the Thames flows out into a darkness of which we have now learned something. It is an alteration of perspectives, and, like the acuteness and limitations of Marlow, it is an instrument to make us see.

The mass of interpretive and critical comment on *Heart of Darkness* cannot be reviewed here. The chief complaint is that Conrad overdoes the "unspeakable," "monstrous," "atrocious," "inconceivable" in his rendering of the story: "adjectival and worse than supererogatory insistence," says F. R. Leavis. Others explain this as a consequence of Conrad's need to keep the heart of the meaning dark; he himself claimed "an inalienable right to the use of all my epithets." In a sense all these views are defensible. Where the story proceeds by means of bizarre colonial vignettes— the doctor, the ship shelling a continent, the objectless dynamiting, the hole, the flogging, the admirable correctness of the accountant's dress, the lack of rivets, the beautiful dull order of the manual of seamanship—such language is not called for. It is needed when Marlow is not equal to the experience described.

Marlow, who feels his affinity with Kurtz, nevertheless contents himself with the lie, "the great and saving illusion." To do otherwise would have been "too dark altogether." And yet, says Marlow ambiguously to the girl, "His words will remain"; these words are "the horror, the horror." We see, in all the anxiety and terror of this, why the narrator entrusts the story to Marlow, who for all his virtues cannot quite tell all, and how we are made to work for our glimpse of a truth we have perhaps not bargained for. It is an instance of how Conrad thought truth may be told in fiction: by "unswerving devotion to the perfect blending of form and substance."

Heart of Darkness

I

The *Nellie*, a cruising yawl, swung to her anchor without a flutter of the sails, and was at rest. The flood had made, the wind was nearly calm, and being bound down the river, the only thing for it was to come to and wait for the turn of the tide.

The sea-reach of the Thames stretched before us like the beginning of an interminable waterway. In the offing the sea and the sky were welded together without a joint, and in the luminous space the tanned sails of the barges drifting up with the tide seemed to stand still in red clusters of canvas sharply peaked, with gleams of varnished spirits. A haze rested on the low shores that ran out to sea in vanishing flatness. The air was dark above Gravesend,[1] and farther back still seemed condensed into a mournful gloom, brooding motionless over the biggest, and the greatest, town on earth.

The Director of Companies was our captain and our host. We four affectionately watched his back as he stood in the bows looking to seaward. On the whole river there was nothing that looked half so nautical. He resembled a pilot, which to a seaman is trustworthiness personified. It was difficult to realise his work was not out there in the luminous estuary, but behind him, within the brooding gloom.

Between us there was, as I have already said somewhere, the bond of the sea. Besides holding our hearts together through long periods of separation, it had the effect of making us tolerant of each other's yarns—and even convictions. The Lawyer—the best of old fellows—had, because of his many years and many virtues, the only cushion on deck, and was lying on the only rug. The Accountant had brought out already a box of dominoes, and was toying architecturally with the bones. Marlow sat cross-legged right aft, leaning against the mizzen-mast. He had sunken cheeks, a yellow complexion, a straight back, an ascetic aspect, and, with his arms dropped, the palms of hands outwards, resembled an idol. The Director, satisfied the anchor had good hold, made his way aft and sat down amongst us. We exchanged a few words lazily. Afterwards there was silence on board the yacht. For some reason or other we did not begin that game of dominoes. We felt meditative, and fit for nothing but placid staring. The day was ending in a serenity of still and exquisite brilliance. The water shone pacifically; the sky, without a speck, was a benign immensity of unstained light; the very mist on the Essex marshes was like a gauzy and radiant fabric, hung from the wooded rises inland, and draping the low shores in diaphanous folds. Only the gloom to the west, brooding over the upper reaches, became more sombre every minute, as if angered by the approach of the sun.

1. Town on the Kent (south) bank of the Thames, 26 miles east of London.

And at last, in its curved and imperceptible fall, the sun sank low, and from glowing white changed to a dull red without rays and without heat, as if about to go out suddenly, stricken to death by the touch of that gloom brooding over a crowd of men.

Forthwith a change came over the waters, and the serenity became less brilliant but more profound. The old river in its broad reach rested unruffled at the decline of day, after ages of good service done to the race that peopled its banks, spread out in the tranquil dignity of a waterway leading to the uttermost ends of the earth. We looked at the venerable stream not in the vivid flush of a short day that comes and departs for ever, but in the august light of abiding memories. And indeed nothing is easier for a man who has, as the phrase goes, 'followed the sea' with reverence and affection, than to evoke the great spirit of the past upon the lower reaches of the Thames. The tidal current runs to and fro in its unceasing service, crowded with memories of men and ships it has borne to the rest of home or to the battles of the sea. It had known and served all the men of whom the nation is proud, from Sir Francis Drake [2] to Sir John Franklin,[3] knights all, titled and untitled—the great knights-errant of the sea. It had borne all the ships whose names are like jewels flashing in the night of time, from the *Golden Hind* returning with her round flanks full of treasure, to be visited by the Queen's Highness and thus pass out of the gigantic tale, to the *Erebus* and *Terror,* bound on other conquests—and that never returned. It had known the ships and the men. They had sailed from Deptford, from Greenwich, from Erith [4]—the adventurers and the settlers; kings' ships and the ships of men on 'Change; [5] captains, admirals, the dark 'interlopers' of the Eastern trade, and the commissioned 'generals' of East India fleets.[6] Hunters for gold or pursuers of fame, they all had gone out on that stream, bearing the sword, and often the torch,[7] messengers of the might within the land, bearers of a spark from the sacred fire. What greatness had not floated on the ebb of that river into the mystery of an unknown earth! . . . The dreams of men, the seed of commonwealths, the germs of empires.

The sun set; the dusk fell on the stream, and lights began to appear along the shore. The Chapman lighthouse, a three-legged thing erect on a mud-flat, shone strongly. Lights of ships moved in the fairway—a great stir of lights going up and going down. And farther west on the upper reaches the place of the monstrous town was still marked ominously on the sky, a brooding gloom in sunshine, a lurid glare under the stars.

'And this also,' said Marlow suddenly, 'has been one of the dark places of the earth.'

2. Sir Francis Drake (c. 1540–96) in 1577 sailed *The Golden Hind* around the world, made enormous profits for shareholders, and was knighted by the Queen at Deptford on his return.
3. Sir John Franklin (1786–1847) set out with the *Erebus* and the *Terror* to find a northwest passage, and died in the ice of Victoria Strait.
4. Estuary ports east of London.
5. 'Change Alley was the scene of 18th-century speculation in Eastern trade.
6. The East India Company, founded by royal charter in 1600, was by the 18th century the ruler of India; only in 1858 did the British government take over.
7. Conrad often allowed some disinterested motives to British imperialists; hence they bear not only the "sword" but "often the torch."

He was the only man of us who still 'followed the sea.' The worst that could be said of him was that he did not represent his class. He was a seaman, but he was a wanderer too, while most seamen lead, if one may so express it, a sedentary life. Their minds are of the stay-at-home order, and their home is always with them—the ship; and so is their country—the sea. One ship is very much like another, and the sea is always the same. In the immutability of their surroundings the foreign shores, the foreign faces, the changing immensity of life, glide past, veiled not by a sense of mystery but by a slightly disdainful ignorance; for there is nothing mysterious to a seaman unless it be the sea itself, which is the mistress of his existence and as inscrutable as Destiny. For the rest, after his hours of work, a casual stroll or a casual spree on shore suffices to unfold for him the secret of a whole continent, and generally he finds the secret not worth knowing. The yarns of seamen have a direct simplicity, the whole meaning of which lies within the shell of a cracked nut. But Marlow was not typical (if his propensity to spin yarns be excepted), and to him the meaning of an episode was not inside like a kernel but outside,[8] enveloping the tale which brought it out only as a glow brings out a haze, in the likeness of one of those misty halos that sometimes are made visible by the spectral illumination of moonshine.

His remark did not seem at all surprising. It was just like Marlow. It was accepted in silence. No one took the trouble to grunt even; and presently he said, very slow:

'I was thinking of very old times, when the Romans first came here, nineteen hundred years ago—the other day. . . . Light came out of this river since— you say Knights? Yes; but it is like a running blaze on a plain, like a flash of lightning in the clouds. We live in the flicker—may it last as long as the old earth keeps rolling! But darkness was here yesterday. Imagine the feelings of a commander of a fine—what d'ye call 'em?—trireme [9] in the Mediterranean, ordered suddenly to the north; run overland across the Gauls in a hurry; put in charge of one of these craft the legionaries—a wonderful lot of handy men they must have been too—used to build, apparently by the hundred, in a month or two, if we may believe what we read. Imagine him here—the very end of the world, a sea the colour of lead, a sky the colour of smoke, a kind of ship about as rigid as a concertina—and going up this river with stores, or orders, or what you like. Sandbanks, marshes, forests, savages—precious little to eat fit for a civilised man, nothing but Thames water to drink. No Falernian wine [10] here, no going ashore. Here and there a military camp lost in a wilderness, like a needle in a bundle of hay—cold, fog, tempests, disease, exile, and death —death skulking in the air, in the water, in the bush. They must have been dying like flies here. Oh yes—he did it. Did it very well, too, no doubt, and without thinking much about it either, except afterwards to brag of what he had gone through in his time, perhaps. They were men enough to face the darkness. And perhaps he was cheered by keeping his eye on a chance of

8. A useful account of Conrad's technique in such stories as this, which make a straight-forward narrative suggestive.
9. Galley with three banks of oars.
10. A wine celebrated by the Latin poets.

promotion to the fleet at Ravenna [11] by and by, if he had good friends in Rome and survived the awful climate. Or think of a decent young citizen in a toga— perhaps too much dice, you know—coming out here in the train of some prefect, or tax-gatherer, or trader, even, to mend his fortunes. Land in a swamp, march through the woods, and in some inland post feel the savagery, the utter savagery, had closed round him—all that mysterious life of the wilderness that stirs in the forest, in the jungles, in the hearts of wild men. There's no initiation either into such mysteries. He has to live in the midst of the incomprehensible, which is also detestable. And it has a fascination, too, that goes to work upon him. The fascination of the abomination [12]—you know. Imagine the growing regrets, the longing to escape, the powerless disgust, the surrender, the hate.' He paused.

'Mind,' he began again, lifting one arm from the elbow, the palm of the hand outwards, so that, with his legs folded before him, he had the pose of a Buddha preaching in European clothes and without a lotus-flower—'Mind, none of us would feel exactly like this. What saves us is efficiency—the devotion to efficiency. But these chaps were not much account, really. They were no colonists; their administration was merely a squeeze,[13] and nothing more, I suspect. They were conquerors, and for that you want only brute force— nothing to boast of, when you have it, since your strength is just an accident arising from the weakness of others. They grabbed what they could get for the sake of what was to be got. It was just robbery with violence, aggravated murder on a great scale, and men going at it blind—as is very proper for those who tackle a darkness. The conquest of the earth, which mostly means the taking it away from those who have a different complexion or slightly flatter noses than ourselves, is not a pretty thing when you look into it too much. What redeems it is the idea only. An idea at the back of it; not a sentimental pretence but an idea; and an unselfish belief in the idea—something you can set up, and bow down before, and offer a sacrifice to. . . .'

He broke off. Flames glided in the river, small green flames, red flames, white flames, pursuing, overtaking, joining, crossing each other—then separating slowly or hastily. The traffic of the great city went on in the deepening night upon the sleepless river. We looked on, waiting patiently—there was nothing else to do till the end of the flood; but it was only after a long silence, when he said, in a hesitating voice, 'I suppose you fellows remember I did once turn fresh-water sailor for a bit,' that we knew we were fated, before the ebb began to run, to hear about one of Marlow's inconclusive experiences.

'I don't want to bother you much with what happened to me personally,' he began, showing in this remark the weakness of many tellers of tales who seem so often unaware of what their audience would best like to hear; 'yet to understand the effect of it on me you ought to know how I got out there, what I saw, how I went up that river to the place where I first met the poor chap. It was the farthest point of navigation and the culminating point of my

11. Ravenna, on the Adriatic, then a port.
12. "When ye therefore shall see the abomination of desolation, spoken of by Daniel the prophet, stand in the holy place (whoso readeth, let him understand) . . ."(Matthew 24:15).
13. A means of exploitation.

experience.[14] It seemed somehow to throw a kind of light on everything about me—and into my thoughts. It was sombre enough too—and pitiful—not extraordinary in any way—not very clear either. No, not very clear. And yet it seemed to throw a kind of light.

'I had then, as you remember, just returned to London after a lot of Indian Ocean, Pacific, China Seas—a regular dose of the East—six years or so, and I was loafing about, hindering you fellows in your work and invading your homes, just as though I had got a heavenly mission to civilise you. It was very fine for a time, but after a bit I did get tired of resting. Then I began to look for a ship—I should think the hardest work on earth. But the ships wouldn't even look at me. And I got tired of that game too.

'Now when I was a little chap I had a passion for maps. I would look for hours at South America, or Africa, or Australia, and lose myself in all the glories of exploration. At that time there were many blank spaces on the earth, and when I saw one that looked particularly inviting on a map (but they all look that) I would put my finger on it and say, When I grow up I will go there. The North Pole was one of these places, I remember. Well, I haven't been there yet, and shall not try now. The glamour's off. Other places were scattered about the Equator, and in every sort of latitude all over the two hemispheres. I have been in some of them, and . . . well, we won't talk about that. But there was one yet—the biggest, the most blank,[15] so to speak —that I had a hankering after.

'True, by this time it was not a blank space any more. It had got filled since my boyhood with rivers and lakes and names. It had ceased to be a blank space of delightful mystery—a white patch for a boy to dream gloriously over. It had become a place of darkness. But there was in it one river especially, a mighty big river, that you could see on the map, resembling an immense snake uncoiled, with its head in the sea, its body at rest curving afar over a vast country, and its tail lost in the depths of the land. And as I looked at the map of it in a shop-window, it fascinated me as a snake would a bird—a silly little bird. Then I remembered there was a big concern, a Company for trade on that river. Dash it all! I thought to myself, they can't trade without using some kind of craft on that lot of fresh water—steamboats! Why shouldn't I try to get charge of one? I went on along Fleet Street,[16] but could not shake off the idea. The snake had charmed me.

'You understand it was a Continental concern, that Trading Society; but I have a lot of relations living on the Continent, because it's cheap and not so nasty as it looks, they say.

'I am sorry to own I began to worry them. This was already a fresh departure for me. I was not used to get things that way, you know. I always went my own road and on my own legs where I had a mind to go. I wouldn't have believed it of myself; but, then—you see—I felt somehow I must get there by

14. An important indication of the multiple sense Conrad intends to impose on the simple narrative.
15. The "white space" in the middle of maps of Africa before the exploration of the Congo; see Headnote.
16. Runs from the western limit of the City of London eastward towards St. Paul's and the docks; it is the center of newspaper publishing.

hook or by crook. So I worried them. The men said, "My dear fellow," and did nothing. Then—would you believe it?—I tried the women. I, Charlie Marlow, set the women to work—to get a job. Heavens! Well, you see, the notion drove me. I had an aunt, a dear enthusiastic soul. She wrote: "It will be delightful. I am ready to do anything, anything for you. It is a glorious idea. I know the wife of a very high personage in the Administration, and also a man who has lots of influence with," etc. etc. She was determined to make no end of fuss to get me appointed skipper of a river steamboat, if such was my fancy.

'I got my appointment—of course; and I got it very quick. It appears the Company had received news that one of their captains had been killed in a scuffle with the natives. This was my chance, and it made me the more anxious to go. It was only months and months afterwards, when I made the attempt to recover what was left of the body, that I heard the original quarrel arose from a misunderstanding about some hens. Yes, two black hens. Fresleven [17]— that was the fellow's name, a Dane—thought himself wronged somehow in the bargain, so he went ashore and started to hammer the chief of the village with a stick. Oh, it didn't surprise me in the least to hear this, and at the same time to be told that Fresleven was the gentlest, quietest creature that ever walked on two legs. No doubt he was; but he had been a couple of years already out there engaged in the noble cause, you know, and he probably felt the need at last of asserting his self-respect in some way. Therefore he whacked the old nigger mercilessly, while a big crowd of his people watched him, thunderstruck, till some man—I was told the chief's son—in desperation at hearing the old chap yell, made a tentative jab with a spear at the white man —and of course it went quite easy between the shoulder-blades. Then the whole population cleared into the forest, expecting all kinds of calamities to happen, while, on the other hand, the steamer Fresleven commanded left also in a bad panic, in charge of the engineer, I believe. Afterwards nobody seemed to trouble much about Fresleven's remains, till I got out and stepped into his shoes. I couldn't let it rest, though; but when an opportunity offered at last to meet my predecessor, the grass growing through his ribs was tall enough to hide his bones. They were all there. The supernatural being had not been touched after he fell. And the village was deserted, the huts gaped black, rotting, all askew within the fallen enclosures. A calamity had come to it, sure enough. The people had vanished. Mad terror had scattered them, men, women, and children, through the bush, and they had never returned. What became of the hens I don't know either. I should think the cause of progress got them, anyhow. However, through this glorious affair I got my appointment, before I had fairly begun to hope for it.

'I flew around like mad to get ready, and before forty-eight hours I was crossing the Channel to show myself to my employers, and sign the contract. In a very few hours I arrived in a city that always makes me think of a whited sepulchre.[18] Prejudice no doubt. I had no difficulty in finding the Com-

17. For details of origin see Headnote.
18. Christ said the scribes and Pharisees were "like unto whited sepulchres, which indeed appear beautiful outward, but are within full of dead men's bones, and of all uncleanness" (Matthew 23:27). Conrad uses the expression of Brussels, center of the colonial adminis- tration.

pany's offices. It was the biggest thing in the town, and everybody I met was full of it. They were going to run an oversea empire, and make no end of coin by trade.

'A narrow and deserted street in deep shadow, high houses, innumerable windows with venetian blinds, a dead silence, grass sprouting between the stones, imposing carriage archways right and left, immense double doors standing ponderously ajar. I slipped through one of these cracks, went up a swept and ungarnished staircase, as arid as a desert, and opened the first door I came to. Two women, one fat and the other slim, sat on straw-bottomed chairs, knitting black wool. The slim one got up and walked straight at me—still knitting with downcast eyes—and only just as I began to think of getting out of her way, as you would for a somnambulist, stood still, and looked up. Her dress was as plain as an umbrella-cover, and she turned round without a word and preceded me into a waiting-room. I gave my name, and looked about. Deal table in the middle, plain chairs all round the walls, on one end a large shining map, marked with all the colours of a rainbow. There was a vast amount of red—good to see at any time, because one knows that some real work is done in there, a deuce of a lot of blue, a little green, smears of orange, and, on the East Coast, a purple patch, to show where the jolly pioneers of progress drink the jolly lager-beer. However, I wasn't going into any of these. I was going into the yellow. Dead in the centre. And the river was there—fascinating—deadly—like a snake. Ough! A door opened, a white-haired secretarial head, but wearing a compassionate expression, appeared, and a skinny forefinger beckoned me into the sanctuary. Its light was dim, and a heavy writing-desk squatted in the middle. From behind that structure came out an impression of pale plumpness in a frock-coat. The great man himself. He was five feet six, I should judge, and had his grip on the handle-end of ever so many millions. He shook hands, I fancy, murmured vaguely, was satisfied with my French. *Bon voyage.*

'In about forty-five seconds I found myself again in the waiting-room with the compassionate secretary, who, full of desolation and sympathy, made me sign some document. I believe I undertook amongst other things not to disclose any trade secrets. Well, I am not going to.

'I began to feel slightly uneasy. You know I am not used to such ceremonies, and there was something ominous in the atmosphere. It was just as though I had been let into some conspiracy—I don't know—something not quite right; and I was glad to get out. In the outer room the two women knitted black wool feverishly. People were arriving, and the younger one was walking back and forth introducing them. The old one sat on her chair. Her flat cloth slippers were propped up on a foot-warmer, and a cat reposed on her lap. She wore a starched white affair on her head, had a wart on one cheek, and silver-rimmed spectacles hung on the tip of her nose. She glanced at me above the glasses. The swift and indifferent placidity of that look troubled me. Two youths with foolish and cheery countenances were being piloted over, and she threw at them the same quick glance of unconcerned wisdom. She seemed to know all about them and about me too. An eerie feeling came over me. She seemed uncanny and fateful. Often far away there I thought of these two, guarding the door of Darkness, knitting black wool as for a warm pall, one introducing,

introducing continuously to the unknown, the other scrutinising the cheery and foolish faces with unconcerned old eyes. *Ave!* Old knitter of black wool. *Morituri te salutant*.[19] Not many of those she looked at ever saw her again—not half, by a long way.

'There was yet a visit to the doctor. "A simple formality," assured me the secretary, with an air of taking an immense part in all my sorrows. Accordingly a young chap wearing his hat over the left eyebrow, some clerk I suppose— there must have been clerks in the business, though the house was as still as a house in a city of the dead—came from somewhere upstairs, and led me forth. He was shabby and careless, with ink-stains on the sleeves of his jacket, and his cravat was large and billowy, under a chin shaped like the toe of an old boot. It was a little too early for the doctor, so I proposed a drink, and thereupon he developed a vein of joviality. As we sat over our vermouths he glorified the Company's business, and by and by I expressed casually my surprise at him not going out there. He became very cool and collected all at once. "I am not such a fool as I look, quoth Plato to his disciples," he said sententiously, emptied his glass with great resolution, and we rose.

'The old doctor felt my pulse, evidently thinking of something else the while. "Good, good for there," he mumbled, and then with a certain eagerness asked me whether I would let him measure my head. Rather surprised, I said Yes, when he produced a thing like callipers and got the dimensions back and front and every way, taking notes carefully. He was an unshaven little man in a thread-bare coat like a gaberdine, with his feet in slippers, and I thought him a harmless fool. "I always ask leave, in the interests of science, to measure the crania of those going out there," he said. "And when they come back too?" I asked. "Oh, I never see them," he remarked; "and, moreover, the changes take place inside, you know." He smiled, as if at some quiet joke. "So you are going out there. Famous. Interesting too." He gave me a searching glance, and made another note. "Ever any madness in your family?" he asked, in a matter-of-fact tone. I felt very annoyed. "Is that question in the interests of science too?" "It would be," he said, without taking notice of my irritation, "interesting for science to watch the mental changes of individuals, on the spot, but . . ." "Are you an alienist?"[20] I interrupted. "Every doctor should be—a little," answered that original imperturbably. "I have a little theory which you Messieurs who go out there must help me to prove. This is my share in the advantages my country shall reap from the possession of such a magnificent dependency. The mere wealth I leave to others. Pardon my questions, but you are the first Englishman coming under my observation . . ." I hastened to assure him I was not in the least typical. "If I were," said I, "I wouldn't be talking like this with you." "What you say is rather profound, and probably erroneous," he said, with a laugh. "Avoid irritation more than exposure to the sun. Adieu. How do you English say, eh? Good-bye. Ah! Good-bye. Adieu. In the tropics one must before everything keep calm.". . . He lifted a warning forefinger. . . . *"Du calme, du calme. Adieu."*

'One thing more remained to do—say good-bye to my excellent aunt. I found

19. "Those who are about to die salute you" (the greeting of Roman gladiators at the games).
20. Specialist in mental illness.

her triumphant. I had a cup of tea—the last decent cup of tea for many days —and in a room that most soothingly looked just as you would expect a lady's drawing-room to look, we had a long quiet chat by the fireside. In the course of these confidences it became quite plain to me I had been represented to the wife of the high dignitary, and goodness knows to how many more people besides, as an exceptional and gifted creature—a piece of good fortune for the Company—a man you don't get hold of every day. Good Heavens! and I was going to take charge of a two-penny-half-penny river-steamboat with a penny whistle attached! It appeared, however, I was also one of the Workers, with a capital—you know. Something like an emissary of light, something like a lower sort of apostle. There had been a lot of such rot let loose in print and talk just about that time, and the excellent woman, living right in the rush of all that humbug, got carried off her feet. She talked about "weaning those ignorant millions from their horrid ways," till, upon my word, she made me quite uncomfortable. I ventured to hint that the Company was run for profit.

' "You forget, dear Charlie, that the labourer is worthy of his hire," she said brightly. It's queer how out of touch with truth women are. They live in a world of their own, and there had never been anything like it, and never can be. It is too beautiful altogether, and if they were to set it up it would go to pieces before the first sunset. Some confounded fact we men have been living contentedly with ever since the day of creation would start up and knock the whole thing over.

'After this I got embraced, told to wear flannel, be sure to write often, and so on—and I left. In the street—I don't know why—a queer feeling came to me that I was an impostor. Odd thing that I, who used to clear out for any part of the world at twenty-four hours' notice, with less thought than most men give to the crossing of a street, had a moment—I won't say of hesitation, but of startled pause, before this commonplace affair. The best way I can explain it to you is by saying that, for a second or two, I felt as though, instead of going to the centre of a continent, I were about to set off for the centre of the earth.

'I left in a French steamer, and she called in every blamed port they have out there, for, as far as I could see, the sole purpose of landing soldiers and custom-house officers. I watched the coast. Watching a coast as it slips by the ship is like thinking about an enigma. There it is before you—smiling, frowning, inviting, grand, mean, insipid, or savage, and always mute with an air of whispering, Come and find out. This one was almost featureless, as if still in the making, with an aspect of monotonous grimness. The edge of a colossal jungle, so dark green as to be almost black, fringed with white surf, ran straight, like a ruled line, far, far away along a blue sea whose glitter was blurred by a creeping mist. The sun was fierce, the land seemed to glisten and drip with steam. Here and there greyish-whitish specks showed up clustered inside the white surf, with a flag flying above them perhaps—settlements some centuries old, and still no bigger than pin-heads on the untouched expanse of their background. We pounded along, stopped, landed soldiers; went on, landed custom-house clerks to levy toll in what looked like a God-forsaken wilderness, with a tin shed and a flag-pole lost in it; landed more soldiers—to take care of the custom-house clerks presumably. Some, I heard, got drowned in the surf; but whether they did or not, nobody seemed particularly to care. They were just flung out there, and on we went. Every day the coast looked the same, as though we had not moved; but we passed various places—trading places—with names like Gran' Bassam, Little Popo; names that seemed to belong to some sordid farce acted in front of a sinister back-cloth. The idleness of a passenger, my isolation amongst all these men with whom I had no point of contact, the oily and languid sea, the uniform sombreness of the coast, seemed to keep me away from the truth of things, within the toil of a mournful and senseless delusion. The voice of the surf heard now and then was a positive pleasure, like the speech of a brother. It was something natural, that had its reason, that had a meaning. Now and then a boat from the shore gave one a momentary contact with reality. It was paddled by black fellows. You could see from afar the white of their eyeballs glistening. They shouted, sang; their bodies streamed with perspiration; they had faces like grotesque masks—these chaps; but they had bone, muscle, a wild vitality, an intense energy of movement, that was as natural and true as the surf along their coast. They wanted no excuse for being there. They were a great comfort to look at. For a time I would feel I belonged still to a world of straightforward facts; but the feeling would not last long. Something would turn up to scare it away. Once, I remember, we came upon a man-of-war anchored off the coast. There wasn't even a shed there, and she was shelling the bush. It appears the French had one of their wars going on thereabouts. Her ensign dropped limp like a rag; the muzzles of the long six-inch guns stuck out all over the low hull; the greasy, slimy swell swung her up lazily and let her down, swaying her thin masts. In the empty immensity of earth, sky, and water, there she was, incomprehensible, firing into a continent. Pop, would go one of the six-inch guns; a small flame would dart and vanish, a little white smoke would disappear, a tiny projectile would give a feeble screech—and nothing happened. Nothing could happen. There was a touch of insanity in the proceeding, a sense of lugubrious drollery in the sight; and it was not dissipated by somebody on board assuring me earnestly there was a camp of natives—he called them enemies!—hidden out of sight somewhere.

'We gave her her letters (I heard the men in that lonely ship were dying of fever at the rate of three a day) and went on. We called at some more places with farcical names, where the merry dance of death and trade goes on in a still and earthy atmosphere as of an overheated catacomb; all along the formless coast bordered by dangerous surf, as if Nature herself had tried to ward off intruders; in and out of rivers, streams of death in life, whose banks were rotting into mud, whose waters, thickened into slime, invaded the contorted mangroves, that seemed to writhe at us in the extremity of an impotent despair. Nowhere did we stop long enough to get a particularised impression, but the general sense of vague and oppressive wonder grew upon me. It was like a weary pilgrimage amongst hints for nightmares.

'It was upward of thirty days before I saw the mouth of the big river. We anchored off the seat of the government. But my work would not begin till some two hundred miles farther on. So as soon as I could I made a start for a place thirty miles higher up.

'I had my passage on a little sea-going steamer. Her captain was a Swede, and knowing me for a seaman, invited me on the bridge. He was a young man, lean, fair, and morose, with lanky hair and a shuffling gait. As we left the miserable little wharf, he tossed his head contemptuously at the shore. "Been living there?" he asked. I said, "Yes." "Fine lot these government chaps—are they not?" he went on, speaking English with great precision and considerable bitterness. "It is funny what some people will do for a few francs a month. I wonder what becomes of that kind when it goes up country?" I said to him I expected to see that soon. "So-o-o!" he exclaimed. He shuffled athwart, keeping one eye ahead vigilantly. "Don't be too sure," he continued. "The other day I took up a man who hanged himself on the road. He was a Swede, too." "Hanged himself! Why, in God's name?" I cried. He kept on looking out watchfully. "Who knows? The sun too much for him, or the country perhaps."

'At last we opened a reach. A rocky cliff appeared, mounds of turned-up earth by the shore, houses on a hill, others with iron roofs, amongst a waste of excavations, or hanging to the declivity. A continuous noise of the rapids above hovered over this scene of inhabited devastation. A lot of people, mostly black and naked, moved about like ants. A jetty projected into the river. A blinding sunlight drowned all this at times in a sudden recrudescence of glare. "There's your Company's station," said the Swede, pointing to three wooden barrack-like structures on the rocky slope. "I will send your things up. Four boxes did you say? So. Farewell."

'I came upon a boiler wallowing in the grass, then found a path leading up the hill. It turned aside for the boulders, and also for an undersized railway truck lying there on its back with its wheels in the air. One was off. The thing looked as dead as the carcass of some animal. I came upon more pieces of decaying machinery, a stack of rusty rails. To the left a clump of trees made a shady spot, where dark things seemed to stir feebly. I blinked, the path was steep. A horn tooted to the right, and I saw the black people run. A heavy and dull detonation shook the ground, a puff of smoke came out of the cliff, and that was all. No change appeared on the face of the rock. They were building a railway. The cliff was not in the way or anything; but this objectless blasting was all the work going on.

'A slight clinking behind me made me turn my head. Six black men advanced in a file, toiling up the path. They walked erect and slow, balancing small baskets full of earth on their heads, and the clink kept time with their footsteps. Black rags were wound round their loins, and the short ends behind waggled to and fro like tails. I could see every rib, the joints of their limbs were like knots in a rope; each had an iron collar on his neck, and all were connected together with a chain whose bights swung between them, rhythmically clinking. Another report from the cliff made me think suddenly of that ship of war I had seen firing into a continent. It was the same kind of ominous voice; but these men could by no stretch of imagination be called enemies. They were called criminals, and the outraged law, like the bursting shells, had come to them, an insoluble mystery from the sea. All their meagre breasts panted together, the violently dilated nostrils quivered, the eyes stared stonily uphill. They passed me within six inches, without a glance, with that complete, death-like indifference of unhappy savages. Behind this raw matter one of the reclaimed, the product of the new forces at work, strolled despondently, carrying a rifle by its middle. He had a uniform jacket with one button off, and seeing a white man on the path, hoisted his weapon to his shoulder with alacrity. This was simple prudence, white men being so much alike at a distance that he could not tell who I might be. He was speedily reassured, and with a large, white, rascally grin, and a glance at his charge, seemed to take me into partnership in his exalted trust. After all, I also was a part of the great cause of these high and just proceedings.

'Instead of going up, I turned and descended to the left. My idea was to let that chain-gang get out of sight before I climbed the hill. You know I am not particularly tender, I've had to strike and to fend off. I've had to resist and to attack sometimes—that's only one way of resisting—without counting the exact cost, according to the demands of such sort of life as I had blundered into. I've seen the devil of violence, and the devil of greed, and the devil of hot desire; but, by all the stars! these were strong, lusty, red-eyed devils, that swayed and drove men—men, I tell you. But as I stood on this hillside, I foresaw that in the blinding sunshine of that land I would become acquainted with a flabby, pretending, weak-eyed devil of a rapacious and pitiless folly. How insidious he could be, too, I was only to find out several months later and a thousand miles farther. For a moment I stood appalled, as though by a warning. Finally I descended the hill, obliquely, towards the trees I had seen.

'I avoided a vast artificial hole somebody had been digging on the slope, the purpose of which I found it impossible to divine. It wasn't a quarry or a sandpit, anyhow. It was just a hole. It might have been connected with the philanthropic desire of giving the criminals something to do. I don't know. Then I nearly fell into a very narrow ravine, almost no more than a scar in the hill-side. I discovered that a lot of imported drainage-pipes for the settlement had been tumbled in there. There wasn't one that was not broken. It was a wanton smash-up. At last I got under the trees. My purpose was to stroll into the shade for a moment; but no sooner within than it seemed to me I had stepped into the gloomy circle of some Inferno. The rapids were near, and an uninterrupted, uniform, headlong, rushing noise filled the mournful stillness of the grove, where not a breath stirred, not a leaf moved, with a mysterious sound—as though the tearing pace of the launched earth had suddenly become audible.

'Black shapes crouched, lay, sat between the trees, leaning against the trunks, clinging to the earth, half coming out, half effaced within the dim light, in all the attitudes of pain, abandonment, and despair. Another mine [21] on the cliff went off, followed by a slight shudder of the soil under my feet. The work was going on. The work! And this was the place where some of the helpers had withdrawn to die.

'They were dying slowly— it was very clear. They were not enemies, they were not criminals, they were nothing earthly now—nothing but black shadows of disease and starvation, lying confusedly in the greenish gloom. Brought from all the recesses of the coast in all the legality of time contracts, lost in uncongenial surroundings, fed on unfamiliar food, they sickened, became inefficient, and were then allowed to crawl away and rest. These moribund shapes were free as air—and nearly as thin. I began to distinguish the gleam of the eyes under the trees. Then, glancing down, I saw a face near my hand. The black

21. Explosive charge.

bones reclined at full length with one shoulder against the tree, and slowly the eyelids rose and the sunken eyes looked up at me, enormous and vacant, a kind of blind, white flicker in the depths of the orbs, which died out slowly. The man seemed young—almost a boy—but you know with them it's hard to tell. I found nothing else to do but to offer him one of my good Swede's ship's biscuits I had in my pocket. The fingers closed slowly on it and held—there was no other movement and no other glance. He had tied a bit of white worsted round his neck—Why? Where did he get it? Was it a badge—an ornament—a charm—a propitiatory act? Was there any idea at all connected with it? It looked startling round his black neck, this bit of white thread from beyond the seas.

'Near the same tree two more bundles of acute angles sat with their legs drawn up. One, with his chin propped on his knees, stared at nothing, in an intolerable and appalling manner: his brother phantom rested its forehead, as if overcome with a great weariness; and all about others were scattered in every pose of contorted collapse, as in some picture of a massacre or a pestilence. While I stood horror-struck, one of these creature rose to his hands and knees, and went off on all-fours towards the river to drink. He lapped out of his hand, then sat up in the sunlight, crossing his shins in front of him, and after a time let his woolly head fall on his breastbone.

'I didn't want any more loitering in the shade, and I made haste towards the station. When near the buildings I met a white man, in such an unexpected elegance of get-up that in the first moment I took him for a sort of vision. I saw a high starched collar, white cuffs, a light alpaca jacket, snowy trousers, a clean necktie, and varnished boots. No hat. Hair parted, brushed, oiled, under a green-lined parasol held in a big white hand. He was amazing, and had a pen-holder behind his ear.

'I shook hands with this miracle, and I learned he was the Company's chief accountant, and that all the book-keeping was done at this station. He had come out for a moment, he said, "to get a breath of fresh air." The expression sounded wonderfully odd, with its suggestion of sedentary desk-life. I wouldn't have mentioned the fellow to you at all, only it was from his lips that I first heard the name of the man who is so indissolubly connected with the memories of that time. Moreover, I respected the fellow. Yes; I respected his collars, his vast cuffs, his brushed hair. His appearance was certainly that of a hair-dresser's dummy; but in the great demoralisation of the land he kept up his appearance. That's backbone. His starched collars and got-up shirt-fronts were achievements of character. He had been out nearly three years; and, later, I could not help asking him how he managed to sport such linen. He had just the faintest blush, and said modestly, "I've been teaching one of the native women about the station. It was difficult. She had a distaste for the work." Thus this man had verily accomplished something. And he was devoted to his books, which were in apple-pie order.

'Everything else in the station was in a muddle,—heads, things, buildings. Strings of dusty niggers with splay feet arrived and departed; a stream of manu-factured goods, rubbishy cottons, beads, and brass-wire set into the depths of darkness, and in return came a precious trickle of ivory.

'I had to wait in the station for ten days—an eternity. I lived in a hut in the yard, but to be out of the chaos I would sometimes get into the accountant's office. It was built of horizontal planks, and so badly put together that, as he bent over his high desk, he was barred from neck to heels with narrow strips of sunlight. There was no need to open the big shutter to see. It was hot there too; big flies buzzed fiendishly, and did not sting, but stabbed. I sat generally on the floor, while, of faultless appearance (and even slightly scented), perching on a high stool, he wrote, he wrote. Sometimes he stood up for exercise. When a truckle-bed with a sick man (some invalided agent from up-country) was put in there, he exhibited a gentle annoyance. "The groans of this sick person," he said, "distract my attention. And without that it is extremely difficult to guard against clerical errors in this climate."

'One day he remarked, without lifting his head, "In the interior you will no doubt meet Mr. Kurtz." On my asking who Mr. Kurtz was, he said he was a first-class agent; and seeing my disappointment at this information, he added slowly, laying down his pen, "He is a very remarkable person." Further questions elicited from him that Mr. Kurtz was at present in charge of a trading-post, a very important one, in the true ivory-country, at "the very bottom of there. Sends in as much ivory as all the others put together . . ." He began to write again. The sick man was too ill to groan. The flies buzzed in a great peace.

'Suddenly there was a growing murmur of voices and a great tramping of feet. A caravan had come in. A violent babble of uncouth sounds burst out on the other side of the planks. All the carriers were speaking together, and in the midst of the uproar the lamentable voice of the chief agent was heard "giving it up" tearfully for the twentieth time that day. . . . He rose slowly. "What a frightful row," he said. He crossed the room gently to look at the sick man, and returning, said to me, "He does not hear." "What! Dead?" I asked, startled. "No, not yet," he answered, with great composure. Then, alluding with a toss of the head to the tumult in the station-yard, "When one has got to make correct entries, one comes to hate those savages—hate them to the death." He remained thoughtful for a moment. "When you see Mr. Kurtz," he went on, "tell him from me that everything here"—he glanced at the desk—"is very satisfactory. I don't like to write to him—with those messengers of ours you never know who may get hold of your lettter—at that Central Station." He stared at me for a moment with his mild, bulging eyes. "Oh, he will go far, very far," he began again. "He will be a somebody in the Administration before long. They, above—the Council in Europe, you know —mean him to be."

'He turned to his work. The noise outside had ceased, and presently in going out I stopped at the door. In the steady buzz of flies the homeward-bound agent was lying flushed and insensible; the other, bent over his books, was making correct entries of perfectly correct transactions; and fifty feet below the doorstep I could see the still tree-tops of the grove of death.

'Next day I left that station at last, with a caravan of sixty men, for a two-hundred-mile tramp.

'No use telling you much about that. Paths, paths, everywhere; a stamped-in network of paths spreading over the empty land, through long grass, through burnt grass, through thickets, down and up chilly ravines, up and down stony hills ablaze with heat; and a solitude, a solitude, nobody, not a hut. The population had cleared out a long time ago. Well, if a lot of mysterious niggers armed with all kinds of fearful weapons suddenly took to travelling on the road between Deal and Gravesend, catching the yokels right and left to carry heavy loads for them, I fancy every farm and cottage thereabouts would get empty very soon. Only here the dwellings were gone too. Still, I passed through several abandoned villages. There's something pathetically childish in the ruins of grass walls. Day after day, with the stamp and shuffle of sixty pair of bare feet behind me, each pair under a 6o-lb. load. Camp, cook, sleep; strike camp, march. Now and then a carrier dead in harness, at rest in the long grass near the path, with an empty water-gourd and his long staff lying by his side. A great silence around and above. Perhaps on some quiet night the tremor of far-off drums, sinking, swelling, a tremor vast, faint; a sound weird, appealing, suggestive, and wild—and perhaps with as profound a meaning as the sound of bells in a Christian country. Once a white man in an unbuttoned uniform, camping on the path with an armed escort of lank Zanzibaris,[22] very hospitable and festive—not to say drunk. Was looking after the upkeep of the road, he declared. Can't say I saw any road or any upkeep, unless the body of a middle-aged negro, with a bullet-hole in the forehead, upon which I absolutely stumbled three miles farther on,[23] may be considered as a permanent improvement. I had a white companion too, not a bad chap, but rather too fleshy and with the exasperating habit of fainting on the hot hillsides, miles away from the least bit of shade and water. Annoying, you know, to hold your own coat like a parasol over a man's head while he is coming to. I couldn't help asking him once what he meant by coming there at all. "To make money, of course. What do you think?" he said scornfully. Then he got fever, and had to be carried in a hammock slung under a pole. As he weighed sixteen stone [24] I had no end of rows with the carriers. They jibbed, ran away, sneaked off with their loads in the night—quite a mutiny. So, one evening, I made a speech in English with gestures, not one of which was lost to the sixty pairs of eyes before me, and the next morning I started the hammock off in front all right. An hour afterwards I came upon the whole concern wrecked in a bush—man, hammock, groans, blankets, horrors. The heavy pole had skinned his poor nose. He was very anxious for me to kill somebody, but there wasn't the shadow of a carrier near. I remembered the old doctor— "It would be interesting for science to watch the mental changes of individuals, on the spot." I felt I was becoming scientifically interesting. However, all that is to no purpose. On the fifteenth day I came in sight of the big river again, and hobbled into the Central Station. It was on a back water surrounded by scrub and forest, with a pretty border of smelly mud on one side, and on the three others enclosed by a crazy fence of rushes. A neglected gap was all the gate it had, and the first glance at the place was enough to let you see the flabby devil was running that show. White men with long staves [25] in their

22. Natives of Zanzibar used as mercenaries.
23. Modified from an actual experience of Conrad's; see Headnote.
24. 224 pounds.
25. It was the custom for white men to carry these staves, which gave rise to Conrad's ironical description of them as "pilgrims."

hands appeared languidly from amongst the buildings, strolling up to take a look at me, and then retired out of sight somewhere. One of them, a stout, excitable chap with black moustaches, informed me with great volubility and many digressions, as soon as I told him who I was, that my steamer was at the bottom of the river. I was thunderstruck. What, how, why? Oh, it was "all right." The "manager himself" was there. All quite correct. "Everybody had behaved splendidly! splendidly!"—"You must," he said in agitation, "go and see the general manager at once. He is waiting."

"I did not see the real significance of that wreck at once. I fancy I see it now, but I am not sure—not at all. Certainly the affair was too stupid—when I think of it—to be altogether natural. Still . . . But at the moment it presented itself simply as a confounded nuisance. The steamer was sunk. They had started two days before in a sudden hurry up the river with the manager on board, in charge of some volunteer skipper, and before they had been out three hours they tore the bottom out of her on stones, and she sank near the south bank. I asked myself what I was to do there, now my boat was lost. As a matter of fact, I had plenty to do in fishing my command out of the river. I had to set about it the very next day. That, and the repairs when I brought the pieces to the station, took some months.

'My first interview with the manager was curious. He did not ask me to sit down after my twenty-mile walk that morning. He was commonplace in complexion, in feature, in manners, and in voice. He was of middle size and of ordinary build. His eyes, of the usual blue, were perhaps remarkably cold, and he certainly could make his glance fall on one as trenchant and heavy as an axe. But even at these times the rest of his person seemed to disclaim the intention. Otherwise there was only an indefinable, faint expression of his lips, something stealthy—a smile—not a smile—I remember it, but I can't explain. It was unconscious, this smile was, though just after he had said something it got intensified for an instant. It came at the end of his speeches like a seal applied on the words to make the meaning of the commonest phrase appear absolutely inscrutable. He was a common trader, from his youth up employed in these parts—nothing more. He was obeyed, yet he inspired neither love nor fear, nor even respect. He inspired uneasiness. That was it! Uneasiness. Not a definite mistrust—just uneasiness—nothing more. You have no idea how effective such a . . . a . . . faculty can be. He had no genius for organising, for initiative, or for order even. That was evident in such things as the deplorable state of the station. He had no learning, and no intelligence. His position had come to him—why? Perhaps because he was never ill . . . He had served three terms of three years out there . . . Because triumphant health in the general rout of constitutions is a kind of power in itself. When he went home on leave he rioted on a large scale—pompously. Jack ashore—with a difference—in externals only. This one could gather from his casual talk. He originated nothing, he could keep the routine going—that's all. But he was great. He was great by this little thing that it was impossible to tell what could control such a man. He never gave that secret away. Perhaps there was nothing within him. Such a suspicion made one pause—for out there there were no external checks. Once when various tropical diseases had laid low almost every "agent" in the station, he was heard to say, "Men who come out here should have no entrails." He sealed the utterance with that smile of his, as though it had been a door opening into a darkness he had in his keeping. You fancied you had seen things—but the seal was on. When annoyed at meal-times by the constant quarrels of the white men about precedence, he ordered an immense round table to be made, for which a special house had to be built. This was the station's mess-room. Where he sat was the first place —the rest were nowhere. One felt this to be his unalterable conviction. He was neither civil or uncivil. He was quiet. He allowed his "boy"—an overfed young negro from the coast—to treat the white men, under his very eyes, with provoking insolence.

'He began to speak as soon as he saw me. I had been very long on the road. He could not wait. Had to start without me. The up-river stations had to be relieved. There had been so many delays already that he did not know who was dead and who was alive, and how they got on—and so on, and so on. He paid no attention to my explanations, and, playing with a stick of sealing-wax, repeated several times that the situation was "very grave, very grave." There were rumours that a very important station was in jeopardy, and its chief, Mr. Kurtz, was ill. Hoped it was not true. Mr. Kurtz was . . . I felt weary and irritable. Hang Kurtz, I thought. I interrupted him by saying I had heard of Mr. Kurtz on the coast, "Ah! So they talk of him down there," he murmured to himself. Then he began again, assuring me Mr. Kurtz was the best agent he had, an exceptional man, of the greatest importance to the Company; therefore I could understand his anxiety. He was, he said, "very, very uneasy." Certainly he fidgeted on his chair a good deal, exclaimed, "Ah, Mr. Kurtz!" broke the stick of sealing-wax and seemed dumbfounded by the accident. Next thing he wanted to know "how long it would take to". . . I interrupted him again. Being hungry, you know, and kept on my feet too, I was getting savage. "How can I tell?" I said. "I haven't even seen the wreck yet—some months, no doubt." All this talk seemed to me so futile. "Some months," he said. "Well, let us say three months before we can make a start. Yes. That ought to do the affair." I flung out of his hut (he lived all alone in a clay hut with a sort of verandah) muttering to myself my opinion of him. He was a chattering idiot. Afterwards I took it back when it was borne in upon me startlingly with what extreme nicety he had estimated the time requisite for the "affair."

'I went to work the next day, turning, so to speak, my back on that station. In that way only it seemed to me I could keep my hold on the redeeming facts of life. Still, one must look about sometimes; and then I saw this station, these men strolling aimlessly about in the sunshine of the yard. I asked myself sometimes what it all meant. They wandered here and there with their absurd long staves in their hands, like a lot of faithless pilgrims bewitched inside a rotten fence. The word "ivory" rang in the air, was whispered, was sighed. You would think they were praying to it. A taint of imbecile rapacity blew through it all, like a whiff from some corpse. By Jove! I've never seen anything so unreal in my life. And outside, the silent wilderness surrounding this cleared speck on the earth struck me as something great and invincible, like evil or truth, waiting patiently for the passing away of this fantastic invasion.

'Oh, those months! Well, never mind. Various things happened. One evening a grass shed full of calico, cotton prints, beads, and I don't know what else, burst into a blaze so suddenly that you would have thought the earth had opened to let an avenging fire consume all that trash. I was smoking my pipe quietly by my dismantled steamer, and saw them all cutting capers in the light, with their arms lifted high, when the stout man with moustaches came tearing down to the river, a tin pail in his hand, assured me that everybody was "behaving splendidly, splendidly," dipped about a quart of water and tore back again. I noticed there was a hole in the bottom of his pail.

'I strolled up. There was no hurry. You see the thing had gone off like a box of matches. It had been hopeless from the very first. The flame had leaped high, driven everybody back, lighted up everything—and collapsed. The shed was already a heap of embers glowing fiercely. A nigger was being beaten near by. They said he had caused the fire in some way; be that as it may, he was screeching most horribly. I saw him, later, for several days, sitting in a bit of shade looking very sick and trying to recover himself: afterwards he arose and went out—and the wilderness without a sound took him into its bosom again. As I approached the glow from the dark I found myself at the back of two men, talking. I heard the name of Kurtz pronounced, then the words, "take advantage of this unfortunate accident." One of the men was the manager. I wished him a good evening. "Did you ever see anything like it—eh? it is incredible." he said, and walked off. The other man remained. He was a first-class agent, young, gentlemanly, a bit reserved, with a forked little beard and a hooked nose. He was stand-offish with the other agents, and they on their side said he was the manager's spy upon them. As to me, I had hardly ever spoken to him before. We got into talk, and by and by we strolled away from the hissing ruins. Then he asked me to his room, which was in the main building of the station. He struck a match, and I perceived that this young aristocrat had not only a silver-mounted dressing-case but also a whole candle all to himself. Just at that time the manager was the only man supposed to have any right to candles. Native mats covered the clay walls; a collection of spears, assegais,[26] shields, knives, was hung up in trophies. The business entrusted to this fellow was the making of bricks—so I had been informed; but there wasn't a fragment of a brick anywhere in the station, and he had been there more than a year—waiting. It seems he could not make bricks without something, I don't know what—straw maybe. Anyway, it could not be found there, and as it was not likely to be sent from Europe, it did not appear clear to me what he was waiting for. An act of special creation [27] perhaps. However, they were all waiting—all the sixteen or twenty pilgrims of them—for something; and upon my word it did not seem an uncongenial occupation, from the way they took it, though the only thing that ever came to them was disease—as far as I could see. They beguiled the time by back-biting and intriguing against each other in a foolish kind of way. There was an air of plotting about that station, but nothing came of it, of course. It was as unreal as everything else—as the philanthropic pretence of the whole concern, as their talk, as their government, as their show of work. The only real

26. Zulu throwing-spears.
27. The doctrine that God created all things according to their kinds ("special creation") was overthrown by 19th-century evolutionism. Here the use is facetious.

feeling was a desire to get appointed to a trading-post where ivory was to be had, so that they could earn percentages. They intrigued and slandered and hated each other only on that account—but as to effectually lifting a little finger—oh no. By Heavens! there is something after all in the world allowing one man to steal a horse while another must not look at a halter. Steal a horse straight out. Very well. He has done it. Perhaps he can ride. But there is a way of looking at a halter that would provoke the most charitable of saints into a kick.

'I had no idea why he wanted to be sociable, but as we chatted in there it suddenly occurred to me the fellow was trying to get at something—in fact, pumping me. He alluded constantly to Europe, to the people I was supposed to know there—putting leading questions as to my acquaintances in the sepulchral city, and so on. His little eyes glittered like mica discs—with curiosity—though he tried to keep up a bit of superciliousness. At first I was astonished, but very soon I became awfully curious to see what he would find out from me. I couldn't possibly imagine what I had in me to make it worth his while. It was very pretty to see how he baffled himself, for in truth my body was full only of chills, and my head had nothing in it but that wretched steamboat business. It was evident he took me for a perfectly shameless prevaricator. At last he got angry, and, to conceal a movement of furious annoyance, he yawned. I rose. Then I noticed a small sketch in oils, on a panel, representing a woman, draped and blindfolded, carrying a lighted torch. The background was sombre—almost black. The movement of the woman was stately, and the effect of the torchlight on the face was sinister.

'It arrested me, and he stood by civilly, holding an empty half-pint champagne bottle (medical comforts) with the candle stuck in it. To my question he said Mr. Kurtz had painted this—in this very station more than a year ago—while waiting for means to go to his trading-post. "Tell me, pray," said I, "who is this Mr. Kurtz?"

' "The chief of the Inner Station," he answered in a short tone, looking away. "Much obliged," I said, laughing. "And you are the brickmaster of the Central Station. Every one knows that." He was silent for a while. "He is a prodigy," he said at last. "He is an emissary of pity, and science, and progress, and devil knows what else. We want," he began to declaim suddenly, "for the guidance of the cause entrusted to us by Europe, so to speak, higher intelligence, wide sympathies, a singleness of purpose." "Who says that?" I asked. "Lots of them," he replied. "Some even write that; and so *he* comes here, a special being, as you ought to know." "Why ought I to know?" I interrupted, really surprised. He paid no attention. "Yes. To-day he is chief of the best station, next year he will be assistant-manager, two years more and . . . but I daresay you know what he will be in two years' time. You are of the new gang—the gang of virtue. The same people who sent him specially also recommended you. Oh, don't say no. I've my own eyes to trust." Light dawned upon me. My dear aunt's influential acquaintances were producing an unexpected effect upon that young man. I nearly burst into a laugh. "Do you read the Company's confidential correspondence?" I asked. He hadn't a word to say. It was great fun. "When Mr. Kurtz," I continued severely, "is General Manager, you won't have the opportunity."

'He blew the candle out suddenly, and we went outside. The moon had risen. Black figures strolled about listlessly, pouring water on the glow, whence proceeded a sound of hissing; steam ascended in the moonlight; the beaten nigger groaned somewhere. "What a row the brute makes!" said the indefatigable man with the moustaches, appearing near us. "Serve him right. Transgression—punishment—bang! Pitiless, pitiless. That's the only way. This will prevent all conflagrations for the future. I was just telling the manager . . ." He noticed my companion, and became crestfallen all at once. "Not in bed yet," he said, with a kind of servile heartiness; "It's so natural. Ha! Danger—agitation." He vanished. I went on to the river-side, and the other followed me. I heard a scathing murmur at my ear, "Heaps of muffs—go to." The pilgrims could be seen in knots gesticulating, discussing. Several had still their staves in their hands. I verily believe they took these sticks to bed with them. Beyond the fence the forest stood up spectrally in the moonlight, and through the dim stir, through the faint sounds of that lamentable courtyard, the silence of the land went home to one's very heart—its mystery, its greatness, the amazing reality of its concealed life. The hurt nigger moaned feebly somewhere near by, and then fetched a deep sigh that made me mend my pace away from there. I felt a hand introducing itself under my arm. "My dear sir," said the fellow, "I don't want to be misunderstood, and especially by you, who will see Mr. Kurtz long before I can have that pleasure. I wouldn't like him to get a false idea of my disposition. . . ."

'I let him run on, this papier-mâché Mephistopheles, and it seemed to me that if I tried I could poke my forefinger through him, and would find nothing inside but a little loose dirt, maybe. He, don't you see, had been planning to be assistant-manager by and by under the present man, and I could see that the coming of that Kurtz had upset them both not a little. He talked precipitately, and I did not try to stop him. I had my shoulders against the wreck of my steamer, hauled up on the slope like a carcass of some big river animal. The smell of mud, of primeval mud, by Jove! was in my nostrils, the high stillness of primeval forest was before my eyes; there were shiny patches on the black creek. The moon had spread over everything a thin layer of silver—over the rank grass, over the mud, upon the wall of matted vegetation standing higher than the wall of a temple, over the great river I could see through a sombre gap glittering, glittering, as it flowed broadly by without a murmur. All this was great, expectant, mute, while the man jabbered about himself. I wondered whether the stillness on the face of the immensity looking at us two were meant as an appeal or as a menace. What were we who had strayed in here? Could we handle that dumb thing, or would it handle us? I felt how big, how confoundedly big, was that thing that couldn't talk and perhaps was deaf as well. What was in there? I could see a little ivory coming out from there, and I had heard Mr. Kurtz was in there. I had heard enough about it too—God knows! Yet somehow it didn't bring any image with it—no more than if I had been told an angel or a fiend was in there. I believed it in the same way one of you might believe there are inhabitants in the planet Mars. I knew once a Scotch sailmaker who was certain, dead sure, there were people in Mars. If you asked him for some idea how they looked and behaved, he would get shy and mutter something about "walking on all fours." If you as much as smiled, he would

—though a man of sixty—offer to fight you. I would not have gone so far as to fight for Kurtz, but I went for him near enough to a lie. You know I hate, detest, and can't bear a lie, not because I am straighter than the rest of us, but simply because it appals me. There is a taint of death, a flavour of mortality in lies—which is exactly what I hate and detest in the world—what I want to forget. It makes me miserable and sick, like biting something rotten would do. Temperament, I suppose. Well, I went near enough to it by letting the young fool there believe anything he liked to imagine as to my influence in Europe. I became in an instant as much of a pretence as the rest of the bewitched pilgrims. This simply because I had a notion it somehow would be of help to that Kurtz whom at the time I did not see—you understand. He was just a word for me. I did not see the man in the name any more than you do. Do you see him? Do you see the story? Do you see anything? It seems to me I am trying to tell you a dream—making a vain attempt, because no relation of a dream can convey the dream-sensation, that commingling of absurdity, surprise, and bewilderment in a tremor of struggling revolt, that notion of being captured by the incredible which is of the very essence of dreams. . . .'

He was silent for a while.

'. . . No, it is impossible; it is impossible to convey the life-sensation of any given epoch of one's existence—that which makes its truth, its meaning —its subtle and penetrating essence. It is impossible. We live, as we dream— alone. . . .'

He paused again as if reflecting, then added:

'Of course in this you fellows see more than I could then. You see me, whom you know. . . .'

It had become so pitch dark that we listeners could hardly see one another. For a long time already he, sitting apart, had been no more to us than a voice. There was not a word from anybody. The others might have been asleep, but I was awake. I listened, I listened on the watch for the sentence, for the word, that would give me the clue to the faint uneasiness inspired by this narrative that seemed to shape itself without human lips in the heavy night-air of the river.

'. . . Yes—I let him run on,' Marlow began again, 'and think what he pleased about the powers that were behind me. I did! And there was nothing behind me! There was nothing but that wretched, old, mangled steamboat I was leaning against, while he talked fluently about "the necessity for every man to get on." "And when one comes out here, you conceive, it is not to gaze at the moon." Mr. Kurtz was a "universal genius," but even a genius would find it easier to work with "adequate tools—intelligent men." He did not make bricks—why, there was a physical impossibility in the way—as I was well aware; and if he did secretarial work for the manager, it was because "no sensible man rejects wantonly the confidence of his superiors." Did I see it? I saw it. What more did I want? What I really wanted was rivets, by Heaven! Rivets. To get on with the work—to stop the hole. Rivets I wanted. There were cases of them down at the coast—cases—piled up—burst—split! You kicked a loose rivet at every second step in that station yard on the hillside. Rivets had rolled into the grove of death. You could fill your pockets with rivets for the trouble of stooping down—and there wasn't one rivet to be found where it was wanted. We had plates that would do, but nothing to fasten them with. And every week the messenger, a lone negro, letter-bag on shoulder and staff in hand, left our station for the coast. And several times a week a coast caravan came in with trade goods—ghastly glazed calico that made you shudder only to look at it, glass beads value about a penny a quart, confounded spotted cotton handkerchiefs. And no rivets. Three carriers could have brought all that was wanted to set that steamboat afloat.

'He was becoming confidential now, but I fancy my unresponsive attitude must have exasperated him at last, for he judged it necessary to inform me he feared neither God nor devil, let alone any mere man. I said I could see that very well, but what I wanted was a certain quantity of rivets—and rivets were what really Mr. Kurtz wanted, if he had only known it. Now letters went to the coast every week. . . . "My dear sir," he cried, "I write from dictation." I demanded rivets. There was a way—for an intelligent man. He changed his manner; became very cold, and suddenly began to talk about a hippopotamus; wondered whether sleeping on board the steamer (I stuck to my salvage night and day) I wasn't disturbed. There was an old hippo that had the bad habit of getting out on the bank and roaming at night over the station grounds. The pilgrims used to turn out in a body and empty every rifle they could lay hands on at him. Some even had sat up o' nights for him. All this energy was wasted, though. "That animal has a charmed life," he said; "but you can say this only of brutes in this country. No man—you apprehend me? —no man here bears a charmed life." He stood there for a moment in the moonlight with his delicate hooked nose set a little askew, and his mica eyes glittering without a wink, then, with a curt Good-night, he strode off. I could see he was disturbed and considerably puzzled, which made me feel more hopeful than I had been for days. It was a great comfort to turn from that chap to my influential friend, the battered, twisted, ruined, tin-pot steamboat. I clambered on board. She rang under my feet like an empty Huntley & Palmer biscuit-tin kicked along a gutter; she was nothing so solid in make, and rather less pretty in shape, but I had expended enough hard work on her to make me love her. No influential friend would have served me better. She had given me a chance to come out a bit—to find out what I could do. No, I don't like work. I had rather laze about and think of all the fine things that can be done. I don't like work—no man does—but I like what is in the work—the chance to find yourself. Your own reality—for yourself, not for others—what no other man can ever know. They can only see the mere show, and never can tell what it really means.

'I was not surprised to see somebody sitting aft, on the deck, with his legs dangling over the mud. You see I rather chummed with the few mechanics there were in that station, whom the other pilgrims naturally despised—on account of their imperfect manners, I suppose. This was the foreman—a boiler-maker by trade—a good worker. He was a lank, bony, yellow-faced man, with big intense eyes. His aspect was worried, and his head was as bald as the palm of my hand; but his hair in falling seemed to have stuck to his chin, and had prospered in the new locality, for his beard hung down to his waist. He was a widower with six young children (he had left them in charge of a sister of his to come out there), and the passion of his life was pigeon-flying. He was an enthusiast and a connoisseur. He would rave about pigeons. After work hours he used sometimes to come over from his hut for a talk about his children and his pigeons; at work, when he had to crawl in the mud under the bottom of the steamboat, he would tie up that beard of his in a kind of white serviette [28] he brought for the purpose. It had loops to go over his ears. In the evening he could be seen squatted on the bank rinsing that wrapper in the creek with great care, then spreading it solemnly on a bush to dry.

'I slapped him on the back and shouted "We shall have rivets!" He scrambled to his feet exclaiming "No! Rivets!" as though he couldn't believe his ears. Then in a low voice, "You . . . eh?" I don't know why we behaved like lunatics. I put my finger to the side of my nose and nodded mysteriously. "Good for you!" he cried, snapped his fingers above his head, lifting one foot. I tried a jig. We capered on the iron deck. A frightful clatter came out of that hulk, and the virgin forest on the other bank of the creek sent it back in a thundering roll upon the sleeping station. It must have made some of the pilgrims sit up in their hovels. A dark figure obscured the lighted doorway of the manager's hut, vanished, then, a second or so after, the doorway itself vanished too. We stopped, and the silence driven away by the stamping of our feet flowed back again from the recesses of the land. The great wall of vegetation, an exuberant and entangled mass of trunks, branches, leaves, boughs, festoons, motionless in the moonlight, was like a rioting invasion of soundless life, a rolling wave of plants, piled up, crested, ready to topple over the creek, to sweep every little man of us out of his little existence. And it moved not. A deadened burst of mighty splashes and snorts reached us from afar, as though an ichthyosaurus [29] had been taking a bath of glitter in the great river. "After all," said the boiler-maker in a reasonable tone, "why shouldn't we get the rivets?" Why not, indeed! I did not know of any reason why we shouldn't. "They'll come in three weeks," I said confidently.

'But they didn't. Instead of rivets there came an invasion, an infliction, a visitation. It came in sections during the next three weeks, each section headed by a donkey carrying a white man in new clothes and tan shoes, bowing from that elevation right and left to the impressed pilgrims. A quarrelsome band of footsore sulky niggers trod on the heels of the donkey; a lot of tents, camp-stools, tin boxes, white cases, brown bales would be shot down in the court-yard, and the air of mystery would deepen a little over the muddle of the station. Five such instalments came, with their absurd air of disorderly flight with the loot of innumerable outfit shops and provision stores, that, one would think, they were lugging, after a raid, into the wilderness for equitable division. It was an inextricable mess of things decent in themselves but that human folly made look like the spoils of thieving.

'This devoted band called itself the Eldorado Exploring Expedition, and I believe they were sworn to secrecy. Their talk, however, was the talk of sordid buccaneers: it was reckless without hardihood, greedy without audacity, and cruel without courage; there was not an atom of foresight or of serious inten-

28. Napkin.
29. Extinct marine reptile.

tion in the whole batch of them, and they did not seem aware these things are wanted for the work of the world. To tear treasure out of the bowels of the land was their desire, with no more moral purpose at the back of it than there is in burglars breaking into a safe. Who paid the expenses of the noble enterprise I don't know; but the uncle of our manager was leader of that lot. 'In exterior he resembled a butcher in a poor neighbourhood, and his eyes had a look of sleepy cunning. He carried his fat paunch with ostentation on his short legs, and during the time his gang infested the station spoke to no one but his nephew. You could see these two roaming about all day long with their heads close together in an everlasting confab.

'I had given up worrying myself about the rivets. One's capacity for that kind of folly is more limited than you would suppose. I said Hang!—and let things slide. I had plenty of time for meditation, and now and then I would give some thought to Kurtz. I wasn't very interested in him. No. Still, I was curious to see whether this man, who had come out equipped with moral ideas of some sort, would climb to the top after all, and how he would set about his work when there.'

II

'One evening as I was lying flat on the deck of my steamboat, I heard voices approaching—and there were the nephew and the uncle strolling along the bank. I laid my head on my arm again, and had nearly lost myself in a doze, when somebody said in my ear, as it were: "I am as harmless as a little child, but I don't like to be dictated to. Am I the manager—or am I not? I was ordered to send him there. It's incredible.". . . I became aware that the two were standing on the shore alongside the forepart of the steamboat, just below my head. I did not move; it did not occur to me to move: I was sleepy. "It is unpleasant," grunted the uncle. "He has asked the Administration to be sent there," said the other, "with the idea of showing what he could do; and I was instructed accordingly. Look at the influence that man must have. Is it not frightful?" They both agreed it was frightful, then made several bizarre remarks: "Make rain and fine weather—one man—the Council—by the nose" —bits of absurd sentences that got the better of my drowsiness, so that I had pretty near the whole of my wits about me when the uncle said, "The climate may do away with this difficulty for you. Is he alone there?" "Yes," answered the manager; "he sent his assistant down the river with a note to me in these terms: 'Clear this poor devil out of the country, and don't bother sending more of that sort. I had rather be alone than have the kind of men you can dispose of with me.' It was more than a year ago. Can you imagine such impudence?" "Anything since then?" asked the other hoarsely. "Ivory," jerked the nephew; "lots of it—prime sort—lots—most annoying, from him." "And with that?" questioned the heavy rumble. "Invoice," was the reply fired out, so to speak. Then silence. They had been talking about Kurtz.

'I was broad awake by this time, but, lying perfectly at ease, remained still, having no inducement to change my position. "How did that ivory come all this way?" growled the elder man, who seemed very vexed. The other explained that it had come with a fleet of canoes in charge of an English half-caste clerk Kurtz had with him; that Kurtz had apparently intended to return himself, the station being by that time bare of goods and stores, but after coming three hundred miles, had suddenly decided to go back, which he started to do alone in a small dugout with four paddlers, leaving the half-caste to continue down the river with the ivory. The two fellows there seemed astounded at anybody attempting such a thing. They were at a loss for an adequate motive. As for me, I seemed to see Kurtz for the first time. It was a distinct glimpse: the dugout, four paddling savages, and the lone white man turning his back suddenly on the headquarters, on relief, on thoughts of home—perhaps; setting his face towards the depths of the wilderness, towards his empty and desolate station. I did not know the motive. Perhaps he was just simply a fine fellow who stuck to his work for its own sake. His name, you understand, had not been pronounced once. He was "that man." The half-caste, who, as far as I could see, had conducted a difficult trip with great prudence and pluck, was invariably alluded to as "that scoundrel." The "scoundrel" had reported that the "man" had been very ill—had recovered imperfectly. . . . The two below me moved away then a few paces, and strolled back and forth at some little distance. I heard: "Military post—doctor—two hundred miles—quite alone now—unavoidable delays—nine months—no news—strange rumours." They approached again, just as the manager was saying, "No one, as far as I know, unless a species of wandering trader—a pestilential fellow, snapping ivory from the natives." Who was it they were talking about now? I gathered in snatches that this was some man supposed to be in Kurtz's district, and of whom the manager did not approve. "We will not be free from unfair competition till one of these fellows is hanged for an example," he said. "Certainly," grunted the other; "get him hanged! Why not? Anything—anything can be done in this country. That's what I say; nobody here, you understand, *here*, can endanger your position. And why? You stand the climate—you outlast them all. The danger is in Europe; but there before I left I took care to——" They moved off and whispered, then their voices rose again. "The extraordinary series of delays is not my fault. I did my possible." The fat man sighed, "Very sad." "And the pestiferous absurdity of his talk," continued the other; "he bothered me enough when he was here. 'Each station should be like a beacon on the road towards better things, a centre for trade of course, but also for humanising, improving, instructing.' Conceive you—that ass! And he wants to be manager! No, it's——" Here he got choked by excessive indignation, and I lifted my head the least bit. I was surprised to see how near they were—right under me. I could have spat upon their hats. They were looking on the ground, absorbed in thought. The manager was switching his leg with a slender twig: his sagacious relative lifted his head. "You have been well since you came out this time?" he asked. The other gave a start. "Who? I? Oh! Like a charm—like a charm. But the rest—oh, my goodness! All sick. They die so quick, too, that I haven't the time to send them out of the country—it's incredible!" "H'm. Just so," grunted the uncle. "Ah! my boy, trust to this—I say, trust to this." I saw him extend his short flipper of an arm for a gesture that took in the forest, the creek, the mud, the river—seemed to beckon with a dishonouring flourish before the sunlit face of the land a treacherous appeal to the lurking death, to the hidden evil, to the profound darkness of its heart. It was so startling that I leaped to my feet and looked

back at the edge of the forest, as though I had expected an answer of some
sort to that black display of confidence. You know the foolish notions that
come to one sometimes. The high stillness confronted these two figures with
its ominous patience, waiting for the passing away of a fantastic invasion.

'They swore aloud together—out of sheer fright, I believe—then, pretending
not to know anything of my existence, turned back to the station. The sun
was low; and leaning forward side by side, they seemed to be tugging painfully uphill their two ridiculous shadows of unequal length, that trailed behind
them slowly over the tall grass without bending a single blade.

'In a few days the Eldorado Expedition went into the patient wilderness,
that closed upon it as the sea closes over a diver. Long afterwards the news
came that all the donkeys were dead. I know nothing as to the fate of the less
valuable animals. They, no doubt, like the rest of us, found what they deserved.
I did not inquire. I was then rather excited at the prospect of meeting Kurtz
very soon. When I say very soon I mean it comparatively. It was just two
months from the day we left the creek when we came to the bank below
Kurtz's station.

'Going up that river was like travelling back to the earliest beginnings of
the world, when vegetation rioted on the earth and the big trees were kings.
An empty stream, a great silence, an impenetrable forest. The air was warm,
thick, heavy, sluggish. There was no joy in the brilliance of sunshine. The
long stretches of the waterway ran on, deserted, into the gloom of overshadowed distances. On silvery sandbanks hippos and alligators sunned themselves side by side. The broadening waters flowed through a mob of wooded
islands; you lost your way on that river as you would in a desert, and butted
all day long against shoals, trying to find the channel, till you thought yourself
bewitched and cut off for ever from everything you had known once—somewhere—far away—in another existence perhaps. There were moments when
one's past came back to one, as it will sometimes when you have not a
moment to spare to yourself; but it came in the shape of an unrestful and
noisy dream, remembered with wonder amongst the overwhelming realities
of this strange world of plants, and water, and silence. And this stillness of
life did not in the least resemble a peace. It was the stillness of an implacable
force brooding over an inscrutable intention. It looked at you with a vengeful
aspect. I got used to it afterwards; I did not see it any more; I had no time.
I had to keep guessing at the channel; I had to discern, mostly by inspiration,
the signs of hidden banks; I watched for sunken stones; I was learning to
clap my teeth smartly before my heart flew out, when I shaved by a fluke
some infernal sly old snag that would have ripped the life out of the tin-pot
steamboat and drowned all the pilgrims; I had to keep a look-out for the
signs of dead wood we could cut up in the night for next day's steaming.[30]
When you have to attend to things of that sort, to the mere incidents of the
surface, the reality—the reality, I tell you—fades. The inner truth is hidden
—luckily, luckily. But I felt it all the same; I felt often its mysterious stillness
watching me at my monkey tricks, just as it watches you fellows performing
on your respective tight-ropes for—what it is? half a crown a tumble——'

30. A detail based on Conrad's Congo experience.

'Try to be civil, Marlow,' growled a voice, and I knew there was at least one listener awake besides myself.

'I beg your pardon. I forgot the heartache which makes up the rest of the price. And indeed what does the price matter, if the trick be well done? You do your tricks very well. And I didn't do badly either, since I managed not to sink that steamboat on my first trip. It's a wonder to me yet. Imagine a blindfolded man set to drive a van over a bad road. I sweated and shivered over that business considerably, I can tell you. After all, for a seaman, to scrape the bottom of the thing that's supposed to float all the time under his care is the unpardonable sin. No one may know of it, but you never forget the thump—eh? A blow on the very heart. You remember it, you dream of it, you wake up at night and think of it—years after—and go hot and cold all over. I don't pretend to say that steamboat floated all the time. More than once she had to wade for a bit, with twenty cannibals splashing around and pushing. We had enlisted some of these chaps on the way for a crew. Fine fellows—cannibals—in their place. They were men one could work with, and I am grateful to them. And, after all, they did not eat each other before my face: they had brought along a provision of hippo-meat which went rotten, and made the mystery of the wilderness stink in my nostrils. Phoo! I can sniff it now. I had the manager on board and three or four pilgrims with their staves—all complete. Sometimes we came upon a station close by the bank, clinging to the skirts of the unknown, and the white men rushing out of a tumble-down hovel, with great gestures of joy and surprise and welcome, seemed very strange—had the appearance of being held there captive by a spell. The word "ivory" would ring in the air for a while—and on we went again into the silence, along empty reaches, round the still bends, between the high walls of our winding way, reverberating in hollow claps the ponderous beat of the stern-wheel. Trees, trees, millions of trees, massive, immense, running up high; and at their foot, hugging the bank against the stream, crept the little begrimed steamboat, like a sluggish beetle crawling on the floor of a lofty portico. It made you feel very small, very lost, and yet it was not altogether depressing, that feeling. After all, if you were small, the grimy beetle crawled on—which was just what you wanted it to do. Where the pilgrims imagined it crawled to I don't know. To some place where they expected to get something, I bet! For me it crawled towards Kurtz—exclusively; but when the steam-pipes started leaking we crawled very slow. The reaches opened before us and closed behind, as if the forest had stepped leisurely across the water to bar the way for our return. We penetrated deeper and deeper into the heart of darkness. It was very quiet there. At night sometimes the roll of drums behind the curtain of trees would run up the river and remain sustained faintly, as if hovering in the air high over our heads, till the first break of day. Whether it meant war, peace, or prayer we could not tell. The dawns were heralded by the descent of a chill stillness; the woodcutters slept, their fires burned low; the snapping of a twig would make you start. We were wanderers on a prehistoric earth, on an earth that wore the aspect of an unknown planet. We could have fancied ourselves the first of men taking possession of an accursed inheritance, to be subdued at the cost of profound anguish and of excessive toil. But suddenly, as we struggled round a bend, there would be a glimpse of rush walls, of peaked grass-roofs, a burst of yells, a whirl of black limbs, a mass of hands clapping, of feet stamping, of bodies swaying, of eyes rolling, under the droop of heavy and motionless foliage. The steamer toiled along slowly on the edge of a black and incomprehensible frenzy. The prehistoric man was cursing us, praying to us, welcoming us—who could tell? We were cut off from the comprehension of our surroundings; we glided past like phantoms, wondering and secretly appalled, as sane men would be before an enthusiastic [31] outbreak in a mad-house. We could not understand because we were too far and could not remember, because we were travelling in the night of first ages, of those ages that are gone, leaving hardly a sign—and no memories.

'The earth seemed unearthly. We are accustomed to look upon the shackled form of a conquered monster, but there—there you could look at a thing monstrous and free. It was unearthly, and the men were—— No, they were not inhuman. Well, you know, that was the worst of it—this suspicion of their not being inhuman. It would come slowly to one. They howled and leaped, and spun, and made horrid faces; but what thrilled you was just the thought of their humanity—like yours—the thought of your remote kinship with this wild and passionate uproar. Ugly. Yes, it was ugly enough; but if you were man enough you would admit to yourself that there was in you just the faintest trace of a response to the terrible frankness of that noise, a dim suspicion of there being a meaning in it which you—you so remote from the night of first ages—could comprehend. And why not? The mind of man is capable of anything—because everything is in it, all the past as well as all the future. What was there after all? Joy, fear, sorrow, devotion, valour, rage—who can tell?—but truth—truth stripped of its cloak of time. Let the fool gape and shudder—the man knows, and can look on without a wink. But he must at least be as much of a man as these on the shore. He must meet that truth with his own true stuff—with his own inborn strength. Principles? Principles won't do. Acquisitions, clothes, pretty rags—rags that would fly off at the first good shake. No; you want a deliberate belief. An appeal to me in this fiendish row—is there? Very well; I hear; I admit, but I have a voice too, and for good or evil mine is the speech that cannot be silenced. Of course, a fool, what with sheer fright and fine sentiments, is always safe. Who's that grunting? You wonder I didn't go ashore for a howl and a dance? Well, no— I didn't. Fine sentiments, you say? Fine sentiments be hanged! I had no time. I had to mess about with white-lead and strips of woollen blanket helping to put bandages on those leaky steam-pipes—I tell you. I had to watch the steering, and circumvent those snags, and get the tin-pot along by hook or by crook. There was surface-truth enough in these things to save a wiser man. And between whiles I had to look after the savage who was fireman. He was an improved specimen; he could fire up a vertical boiler. He was there below me, and, upon my word, to look at him was as edifying as seeing a dog in a parody of breeches and a feather hat, walking on his hind legs. A few months of training had done for that really fine chap. He squinted at the steam-gauge and at the water-gauge with an evident effort of intrepidity—and he had filed

31. In the older sense of "fanatical," suffering from religious mania.

teeth too, the poor devil, and the wool of his pate shaved into queer patterns, and three ornamental scars on each of his cheeks. He ought to have been clapping his hands and stamping his feet on the bank, instead of which he was hard at work, a thrall to strange witchcraft, full of improving knowledge. He was useful because he had been instructed; and what he knew was this— that should the water in that transparent thing disappear, the evil spirit inside the boiler would get angry through the greatness of his thirst, and take a terrible vengeance. So he sweated and fired up and watched the glass fearfully (with an impromptu charm, made of rags, tied to his arm, and a piece of polished bone, as big as a watch, stuck flatways through his lower lip), while the wooded banks slipped past us slowly, the short noise was left behind, the interminable miles of silence—and we crept on, towards Kurtz. But the snags were thick, the water was treacherous and shallow, the boiler seemed indeed to have a sulky devil in it, and thus neither that fireman nor I had any time to peer into our creepy thoughts.

'Some fifty miles below the Inner Station we came upon a hut of reeds, an inclined and melancholy pole, with the unrecognisable tatters of what had been a flag of some sort flying from it, and a neatly stacked wood-pile. This was unexpected. We came to the bank, and on the stack of firewood found a flat piece of board with some faded pencil-writing on it. When deciphered it said: "Wood for you. Hurry up. Approach cautiously." There was a signature, but it was illegible—not Kurtz—a much longer word. "Hurry up." Where? Up the river? "Approach cautiously." We had not done so. But the warning could not have been meant for the place where it could be only found after approach. Something was wrong above. But what—and how much? That was the question. We commented adversely upon the imbecility of that telegraphic style. The bush around said nothing, and would not let us look very far, either. A torn curtain of red twill hung in the doorway of the hut, and flapped sadly in our faces. The dwelling was dismantled; but we could see a white man had lived there not very long ago. There remained a rude table—a plank on two posts; a heap of rubbish reposed in a dark corner, and by the door I picked up a book. It had lost its covers, and the pages had been thumbed into a state of extremely dirty softness; but the back had been lovingly stitched afresh with white cotton thread, which looked clean yet. It was an extraordinary find. Its title was, *An Inquiry into some Points of Seamanship,* by a man Towser, Towson—some such name—Master in His Majesty's Navy. The matter looked dreary reading enough, with illustrative diagrams and repulsive tables of figures, and the copy was sixty years old. I handled this amazing antiquity with the greatest possible tenderness, lest it should dissolve in my hands. Within, Towson or Towser was inquiring earnestly into the breaking strain of ships' chains and tackle, and other such matters. Not a very enthralling book; but at the first glance you could see there a singleness of intention, an honest concern for the right way of going to work, which made these humble pages, thought out so many years ago, luminous with another than a professional light. The simple old sailor, with his talk of chains and purchases, made me forget the jungle and the pilgrims in a delicious sensation of having come upon something unmistakably real. Such a book being there was wonderful enough; but still more astounding were the notes pencilled in the margin, and plainly referring to the text. I couldn't believe my eyes! They were in cipher! Yes, it looked like cipher. Fancy a man lugging with him a book of that description into this nowhere and studying it—and making notes —in cipher at that! It was an extravagant mystery.

'I had been dimly aware for some time of a worrying noise, and when I lifted my eyes I saw the wood-pile was gone, and the manager, aided by all the pilgrims, was shouting at me from the river-side. I slipped the book into my pocket. I assure you to leave off reading was like tearing myself away from the shelter of an old and solid friendship.

'I started the lame engine ahead. "It must be this miserable trader—this intruder," exclaimed the manager, looking back malevolently at the place we had left. "He must be English," I said. "It will not save him from getting into trouble if he is not careful," muttered the manager darkly. I observed with assumed innocence that no man was safe from trouble in this world.

'The current was more rapid now, the steamer seemed at her last gasp, the stern-wheel flopped languidly, and I caught myself listening on tiptoe for the next beat of the float,[32] for in sober truth I expected the wretched thing to give up every moment. It was like watching the last flickers of a life. But still we crawled. Sometimes I would pick out a tree a little way ahead to measure our progress towards Kurtz by, but I lost it invariably before we got abreast. To keep the eyes so long on one thing was too much for human patience. The manager displayed a beautiful resignation. I fretted and fumed and took to arguing with myself whether or no I would talk openly with Kurtz; but before I could come to any conclusion it occurred to me that my speech or my silence, indeed any action of mine, would be a mere futility. What did it matter what any one knew or ignored? What did it matter who was manager? One gets sometimes such a flash of insight. The essentials of this affair lay deep under the surface, beyond my reach, and beyond my power of meddling.

'Towards the evening of the second day we judged ourselves about eight miles from Kurtz's station. I wanted to push on; but the manager looked grave, and told me the navigation up there was so dangerous that it would be advisable, the sun being very low already, to wait where we were till next morning. Moreover, he pointed out that if the warning to approach cautiously were to be followed, we must approach in daylight—not at dusk, or in the dark. This was sensible enough. Eight miles meant nearly three hours' steaming for us, and I could also see suspicious ripples at the upper end of the reach. Nevertheless, I was annoyed beyond expression at the delay, and most unreasonably too, since one night more could not matter much after so many months. As we had plenty of wood, and caution was the word, I brought up in the middle of the stream. The reach was narrow, straight, with high sides like a railway cutting. The dusk came gliding into it long before the sun had set. The current ran smooth and swift, but a dumb immobility sat on the banks. The living trees, lashed together by the creepers and every living bush of the undergrowth, might have been changed into stone, even to the slenderest twig, to the lightest leaf. It was not sleep—it seemed unnatural, like a state of trance. Not the faintest sound of any kind could be heard. You looked on

32. Floating device to keep water level steady.

amazed, and began to suspect yourself of being deaf—then the night came suddenly, and struck you blind as well. About three in the morning some large fish leaped, and the loud splash made me jump as though a gun had been fired. When the sun rose there was a white fog, very warm and clammy, and more blinding than the night. It did not shift or drive; it was just there, standing all round you like something solid. At eight or nine, perhaps, it lifted as a shutter lifts. We had a glimpse of the towering multitude of trees, of the immense matted jungle, with the blazing little ball of the sun hanging over it—all perfectly still—and then the white shutter came down again, smoothly, as if sliding in greased grooves. I ordered the chain, which we had begun to heave in, to be paid out again. Before it stopped running with a muffled rattle, a cry, a very loud cry, as of infinite desolation, soared slowly in the opaque air. It ceased. A complaining clamour, modulated in savage discords, filled our ears. The sheer unexpectedness of it made my hair stir under my cap. I don't know how it struck the others: to me it seemed as though the mist itself had screamed, so suddenly, and apparently from all sides at once, did this tumultuous and mournful uproar arise. It culminated in a hurried outbreak of almost intolerably excessive shrieking, which stopped short, leaving us stiffened in a variety of silly attitudes, and obstinately listening to the nearly as appalling and excessive silence. "Good God! What is the meaning——?" stammered at my elbow one of the pilgrims—a little fat man, with sandy hair and red whiskers, who wore side-spring boots, and pink pyjamas tucked into his socks. Two others remained open-mouthed a whole minute, then dashed into the little cabin, to rush out incontinently and stand darting scared glances, with Winchesters at "ready" in their hands. What we could see was just the steamer we were on, her outlines blurred as though she had been on the point of dissolving, and a misty strip of water, perhaps two feet broad, around her—and that was all. The rest of the world was nowhere, as far as our eyes and ears were concerned. Just nowhere. Gone, disappeared; swept off without leaving a whisper or a shadow behind.

'I went forward, and ordered the chain to be hauled in short, so as to be ready to trip the anchor and move the steamboat at once if necessary. "Will they attack?" whispered an awed voice. "We will all be butchered in this fog," murmured another. The faces twitched with the strain, the hands trembled slightly, the eyes forgot to wink. It was very curious to see the contrast of expressions of the white men and of the black fellows of our crew, who were as much strangers to that part of the river as we, though their homes were only eight hundred miles away. The whites, of course greatly discomposed, had besides a curious look of being painfully shocked by such an outrageous row. The others had an alert, naturally interested expression; but their faces were essentially quiet, even those of the one or two who grinned as they hauled at the chain. Several exchanged short, grunting phrases, which seemed to settle the matter to their satisfaction. Their head-man, a young, broad-chested black, severely draped in dark-blue fringed cloths, with fierce nostrils and his hair all done up artfully in oily ringlets, stood near me. "Aha!" I said, just for good fellowship's sake. "Catch 'im," he snapped, with a bloodshot widening of his eyes and a flash of sharp teeth—"catch 'im. Give 'im to us." "To you, eh?" I asked; "what would you do with them?" "Eat 'im!" he said curtly, and, leaning his elbow on the rail, looked out into the fog in a dignified and profoundly pensive attitude. I would no doubt have been properly horri- fied, had it not occurred to me that he and his chaps must be very hungry: that they must have been growing increasingly hungry for at least this month past. They had been engaged for six months (I don't think a single one of them had any clear idea of time, as we at the end of countless ages have. They still belonged to the beginnings of time—had no inherited experience to teach them, as it were), and of course, as long as there was a piece of paper written over in accordance with some farcical law or other made down the river, it didn't enter anybody's head to trouble how they would live. Certainly they had brought with them some rotten hippo-meat, which couldn't have lasted very long, anyway, even if the pilgrims hadn't, in the midst of a shocking hullabaloo, thrown a considerable quantity of it overboard. It looked like a high-handed proceeding; but it was really a case of legitimate self-defence. You can't breathe dead hippo waking, sleeping, and eating, and at the same time keep your pre- carious grip on existence. Besides that, they had given them every week three pieces of brass wire,[33] each about nine inches long; and the theory was they were to buy their provisions with that currency in river-side villages. You can see how *that* worked. There were either no villages, or the people were hostile, or the director, who like the rest of us fed out of tins, with an occasional old he-goat thrown in, didn't want to stop the steamer for some more or less recon- dite reason. So, unless they swallowed the wire itself, or made loops of it to snare the fishes with, I don't see what good their extravagant salary could be to them. I must say it was paid with a regularity worthy of a large and hon- ourable trading company. For the rest, the only thing to eat—though it didn't look eatable in the least—I saw in their possession was a few lumps of some stuff like half-cooked dough, of a dirty lavender colour, they kept wrapped in leaves, and now and then swallowed a piece of, but so small that it seemed done more for the look of the thing than for any serious purpose of sustenance.[34] Why in the name of all the gnawing devils of hunger they didn't go for us— they were thirty to five—and have a good tuck-in for once, amazes me now when I think of it. They were big powerful men, with not much capacity to weigh the consequences, with courage, with strength, even yet, though their skins were no longer glossy and their muscles no longer hard. And I saw that something restraining, one of those human secrets that baffle probability, had come into play there. I looked at them with a swift quickening of interest— not because it occurred to me I might be eaten by them before very long, though I own to you that just then I perceived—in a new light, as it were— how unwholesome the pilgrims looked, and I hoped, yes, I positively hoped, that my aspect was not so—what shall I say?—so—unappetising: a touch of fantastic vanity which fitted well with the dream-sensation that pervaded all my days at that time. Perhaps I had a little fever too. One can't live with one's finger everlastingly on one's pulse. I had often "a little fever," or a little touch of other things—the playful paw-strokes of the wilderness, the preliminary trifling before the more serious onslaught which came in due course. Yes; I

33. Such wire was used as currency in the Congo at the time.
34. Cassava, manioc root ground to flour, mixed into a dough, and wrapped in banana leaves (not, as has been suggested, human flesh).

looked at them as you would on any human being, with a curiosity of their impulses, motives, capacities, weaknesses, when brought to the test of an inexorable physical necessity. Restraint! What possible restraint? Was it superstition, disgust, patience, fear—or some kind of primitive honour? No fear can stand up to hunger, no patience can wear it out, disgust simply does not exist where hunger is; and as to superstition, beliefs, and what you may call principles, they are less than chaff in a breeze. Don't you know the devilry of lingering starvation, its exasperating torment, its black thoughts, its sombre and brooding ferocity? Well, I do. It takes a man all his inborn strength to fight hunger properly. It's really easier to face bereavement, dishonour, and the perdition of one's soul—than this kind of prolonged hunger. Sad, but true. And these chaps too had no earthly reason for any kind of scruple. Restraint! I would just as soon have expected restraint from a hyena prowling amongst the corpses of a battlefield. But there was the fact facing me—the fact dazzling, to be seen, like the foam on the depths of the sea, like a ripple on an unfathomable enigma, a mystery greater—when I thought of it—than the curious. inexplicable note of desperate grief in this savage clamour that had swept by us on the river-bank, behind the blind whiteness of the fog.

'Two pilgrims were quarrelling in hurried whispers as to which bank. "Left." "No, no; how can you? Right, right, of course." "It is very serious," said the manager's voice behind me; "I would be desolated if anything should happen to Mr. Kurtz before we came up." I looked at him, and had not the slightest doubt he was sincere. He was just the kind of man who would wish to preserve appearances. That was his restraint. But when he muttered something about going on at once, I did not even take the trouble to answer him. I knew, and he knew, that it was impossible. Were we to let go our hold of the bottom, we would be absolutely in the air—in space. We wouldn't be able to tell where we were going to—whether up or down stream, or across—till we fetched against one bank or the other—and then we wouldn't know at first which it was. Of course I made no move. I had no mind for a smash-up. You couldn't imagine a more deadly place for a shipwreck. Whether drowned at once or not, we were sure to perish speedily in one way or another. "I authorise you to take all the risks," he said, after a short silence. "I refuse to take any," I said shortly; which was just the answer he expected, though its tone might have surprised him. "Well, I must defer to your judgment. You are captain," he said, with marked civility. I turned my shoulder to him in sign of my appreciation, and looked into the fog. How long would it last? It was the most hopeless look-out. The approach to this Kurtz grubbing for ivory in the wretched bush was beset by as many dangers as though he had been an enchanted princess sleeping in a fabulous castle. "Will they attack, do you think?" asked the manager, in a confidential tone.

'I did not think they would attack, for several obvious reasons. The thick fog was one. If they left the bank in their canoes they would get lost in it, as we would be if we attempted to move. Still, I had also judged the jungle of both banks quite impenetrable—and yet eyes were in it, eyes that had seen us. The river-side bushes were certainly very thick; but the undergrowth behind was evidently penetrable. However, during the short lift I had seen no canoes anywhere in the reach—certainly not abreast of the steamer. But what made the idea of attack inconceivable to me was the nature of the noise—of the cries we had heard. They had not the fierce character boding of immediate hostile intention. Unexpected, wild, and violent as they had been, they had given me an irresistible impression of sorrow. The glimpse of the steamboat had for some reason filled those savages with unrestrained grief. The danger, if any, I expounded, was from our proximity to a great human passion let loose. Even extreme grief may ultimately vent itself in violence—but more generally takes the form of apathy. . . .

'You should have seen the pilgrims stare! They had no heart to grin, or even to revile me; but I believe they thought me gone mad—with fright, maybe. I delivered a regular lecture. My dear boys, it was no good bothering. Keep a look-out? Well, you may guess I watched the fog for the signs of lifting as a cat watches a mouse; but for anything else our eyes were of no more use to us than if we had been buried miles deep in a heap of cotton-wool. It felt like it too—choking, warm, stifling. Besides, all I said, though it sounded extravagant, was absolutely true to fact. What we afterwards alluded to as an attack was really an attempt at repulse. The action was very far from being aggressive—it was not even defensive, in the usual sense: it was undertaken under the stress of desperation, and in its essence was purely protective.

'It developed itself, I should say, two hours after the fog lifted, and its commencement was at a spot, roughly speaking, about a mile and a half below Kurtz's station. We had just floundered and flopped round a bend, when I saw an islet, a mere grassy hummock of bright green, in the middle of the stream. It was the only thing of the kind; but as we opened the reach more, I perceived it was the head of a long sandbank, or rather of a chain of shallow patches stretching down the middle of the river. They were discoloured, just awash, and the whole lot was seen just under the water, exactly as a man's backbone is seen running down the middle of his back under the skin. Now, as far as I did see, I could go to the right or to the left of this. I didn't know either channel, of course. The banks looked pretty well alike, the depth appeared the same; but as I had been informed the station was on the west side, I naturally headed for the western passage.

'No sooner had we fairly entered it than I became aware it was much narrower than I had supposed. To the left of us there was the long uninterrupted shoal, and to the right a high steep bank heavily overgrown with bushes. Above the bush the trees stood in serried ranks. The twigs overhung the current thickly, and from distance to distance a large limb of some tree projected rigidly over the stream. It was then well on in the afternoon, the face of the forest was gloomy, and a broad strip of shadow had already fallen on the water. In this shadow we steamed up—very slowly, as you may imagine. I sheered her well inshore—the water being deepest near the bank, as the sounding-pole informed me.

'One of my hungry and forbearing friends was sounding in the bows just below me. This steamboat was exactly like a decked scow. On the deck there were two little teak-wook houses, with doors and windows. The boiler was in the fore-end, and the machinery right astern. Over the whole there was a light roof, supported on stanchions. The funnel projected through that roof, and in front of the funnel a small cabin built of light planks served for a pilot-house.

It contained a couch, two camp-stools, a loaded Martini-Henry [35] leaning in one corner, a tiny table, and the steering-wheel. It had a wide door in front and a broad shutter at each side. All these were always thrown open, of course. I spent my days perched up there on the extreme fore-end of that roof, before the door. At night I slept, or tried to, on the couch. An athletic black belonging to some coast tribe, and educated by my poor predecessor, was the helmsman. He sported a pair of brass earrings, wore a blue cloth wrapper from the waist to the ankles, and thought all the world of himself. He was the most unstable kind of fool I had ever seen. He steered with no end of a swagger while you were by; but if he lost sight of you, he became instantly the prey of an abject funk, and would let that cripple of a steamboat get the upper hand of him in a minute.

'I was looking down at the sounding-pole, and feeling much annoyed to see at each try a little more of it stick out of that river, when I saw my poleman give up the business suddenly, and stretch himself flat on the deck, without even taking the trouble to haul his pole in. He kept hold on it though, and it trailed in the water. At the same time the fireman, whom I could also see below me, sat down abruptly before his furnace and ducked his head. I was amazed. Then I had to look at the river mighty quick, because there was a snag in the fairway. Sticks, little sticks, were flying about—thick: they were whizzing before my nose, dropping below me, striking behind me against my pilot-house. All this time the river, the shore, the woods, were very quiet—perfectly quiet. I could only hear the heavy splashing thump of the stern-wheel and the patter of these things. We cleared the snag clumsily. Arrows, by Jove! We were being shot at! I stepped in quickly to close the shutter on the land-side. That fool-helmsman, his hands on the spokes, was lifting his knees high, stamping his feet, champing his mouth, like a reined-in horse. Confound him! And we were staggering within ten feet of the bank. I had to lean right out to swing the heavy shutter, and I saw a face amongst the leaves on the level with my own, looking at me very fierce and steady; and then suddenly, as though a veil had been removed from my eyes, I made out, deep in the tangled gloom, naked breasts, arms, legs, glaring eyes—the bush was swarming with human limbs in movement, glistening, of bronze colour. The twigs shook, swayed, and rustled, the arrows flew out of them, and then the shutter came to. "Steer her straight," I said to the helmsman. He held his head rigid, face forward; but his eyes rolled, he kept on lifting and setting down his feet gently, his mouth foamed a little. "Keep quiet!" I said in a fury. I might just as well have ordered a tree not to sway in the wind. I darted out. Below me there was a great scuffle of feet on the iron deck; confused exclamations; a voice screamed, "Can you turn back?" I caught sight of a V-shaped ripple on the water ahead. What? Another snag! A fusillade burst out under my feet. The pilgrims had opened with their Winchesters, and were simply squirting lead into that bush.[36] A deuce of a lot of smoke came up and drove slowly forward. I swore at it. Now I couldn't see the ripple or the snag either. I stood in the doorway, peering, and the arrows came in swarms. They might have been poisoned, but they looked as though

---

35. Rifle (more powerful than a Winchester).
36. Repeats the image of the gunboat shelling a continent.

they wouldn't kill a cat. The bush began to howl. Our wood-cutters raised a war-like whoop; the report of a rifle just at my back deafened me. I glanced over my shoulder, and the pilot-house was yet full of noise and smoke when I made a dash at the wheel. The fool-nigger had dropped everything, to throw the shutter open and let off that Martini-Henry. He stood before the wide opening, glaring, and I yelled at him to come back, while I straightened the sudden twist out of that steamboat. There was no room to turn even if I had wanted to, the snag was somewhere very near ahead in that confounded smoke, there was no time to lose, so I just crowded her into the bank—right into the bank, where I knew the water was deep.

'We tore slowly along the overhanging bushes in a whirl of broken twigs and flying leaves. The fusillade below stopped short, as I had foreseen it would when the squirts got empty. I threw my head back to a glinting whiz that traversed the pilot-house, in at one shutter-hole and out at the other. Looking past that mad helmsman, who was shaking the empty rifle and yelling at the shore, I saw vague forms of men running bent double, leaping, gliding, distinct, incomplete, evanescent. Something big appeared in the air before the shutter, the rifle went overboard, and the man stepped back swiftly, looked at me over his shoulder in an extraordinary, profound, familiar manner, and fell upon my feet. The side of his head hit the wheel twice, and the end of what appeared a long cane clattered round and knocked over a little camp-stool. It looked as though after wrenching that thing from somebody ashore he had lost his balance in the effort. The thin smoke had blown away, we were clear of the snag, and looking ahead I could see that in another hundred yards or so I would be free to sheer off, away from the bank; but my feet felt so very warm and wet that I had to look down. The man had rolled on his back and stared straight up at me; both his hands clutched that cane. It was the shaft of a spear that, either thrown or lunged through the opening, had caught him in the side just below the ribs; the blade had gone in out of sight, after making a frightful gash; my shoes were full; a pool of blood lay very still, gleaming dark-red under the wheel; his eyes shone with an amazing lustre. The fusillade burst out again. He looked at me anxiously, gripping the spear like something precious, with an air of being afraid I would try to take it away from him. I had to make an effort to free my eyes from his gaze and attend to the steering. With one hand I felt above my head for the line of the steam whistle, and jerked out screech after screech hurriedly. The tumult of angry and warlike yells was checked instantly, and then from the depths of the woods went out such a tremulous and prolonged wail of mournful fear and utter despair as may be imagined to follow the flight of the last hope from the earth. There was a great commotion in the bush; the shower of arrows stopped, a few dropping shots rang out sharply—then silence, in which the languid beat of the stern-wheel came plainly to my ears. I put the helm hard a-starboard at the moment when the pilgrim in pink pyjamas, very hot and agitated, appeared in the dorway. "The manager sends me——" he began in an official tone, and stopped short. "Good God!" he said, glaring at the wounded man.

'We two whites stood over him, and his lustrous and inquiring glance enveloped us both. I declare it looked as though he would presently put to us some question in an understandable language; but he died without uttering a sound, without moving a limb, without twitching a muscle. Only in the very last moment, as though in response to some sign we could not see, to some whisper we could not hear, he frowned heavily, and that frown gave to his black death-mask an inconceivably sombre, brooding, and menacing expression. The lustre of inquiring glance faded swiftly into vacant glassiness. "Can you steer?" I asked the agent eagerly. He looked very dubious; but I made a grab at his arm, and he understood at once I meant him to steer whether or no. To tell you the truth, I was morbidly anxious to change my shoes and socks. "He is dead," murmured the fellow, immensely impressed. "No doubt about it," said I, tugging like mad at the shoe-laces. "And by the way, I suppose Mr. Kurtz is dead as well by this time."

'For the moment that was the dominant thought. There was a sense of extreme disappointment, as though I had found out I had been striving after something altogether without a substance. I couldn't have been more disgusted if I had travelled all this way for the sole purpose of talking with Mr. Kurtz. Talking with . . . I flung one shoe overboard, and became aware that that was exactly what I had been looking forward to—a talk with Kurtz. I made the strange discovery that I had never imagined him as doing, you know, but as discoursing. I didn't say to myself, "Now I will never see him," or "Now I will never shake him by the hand," but, "Now I will never hear him." The man presented himself as a voice. Not of course that I did not connect him with some sort of action. Hadn't I been told in all the tones of jealousy and admiration that he had collected, bartered, swindled, or stolen more ivory than all the other agents together? That was not the point. The point was in his being a gifted creature, and that of all his gifts the one that stood out pre-eminently, that carried with it a sense of real presence, was his ability to talk, his words— the gift of expression, the bewildering, the illuminating, the most exalted and the most contemptible, the pulsating stream of light, or the deceitful flow from the heart of an impenetrable darkness.

'The other shoe went flying unto the devil-god of that river. I thought, By Jove! it's all over. We are too late; he has vanished—the gift has vanished, by means of some spear, arrow, or club. I will never hear that chap speak after all —and my sorrow had a startling extravagance of emotion, even such as I had noticed in the howling sorrow of these savages in the bush. I couldn't have felt more of lonely desolation somehow, had I been robbed of a belief or had missed my destiny in life. . . . Why do you sigh in this beastly way, somebody? Absurd? Well, absurd. Good Lord! mustn't a man ever——Here, give me some tobacco.' [37]. . .

There was a pause of profound stillness, then a match flared, and Marlow's lean face appeared, worn, hollow, with downward folds and dropped eyelids, with an aspect of concentrated attention; and as he took vigorous draws at his pipe, it seemed to retreat and advance out of the night in the regular flicker of the tiny flame. The match went out.

'Absurd!' he cried. 'This is the worst of trying to tell . . . Here you all are, each moored with two good addresses, like a hulk with two anchors, a butcher

37. Here Conrad, who in other works has a much less straightforward time-scheme than in *Heart of Darkness,* breaks off the story and allows Marlow to anticipate what has not yet been described.

round one corner, a policeman round another, excellent appetites, and temperature normal—you hear—normal from year's end to year's end. And you say, Absurd! Absurd be—exploded! Absurd! My dear boys, what can you expect from a man who out of sheer nervousness had just flung overboard a pair of new shoes? Now I think of it, it is amazing I did not shed tears. I am, upon the whole, proud of my fortitude. I was cut to the quick at the idea of having lost the inestimable privilege of listening to the gifted Kurtz. Of course I was wrong. The privilege was waiting for me. Oh yes, I heard more than enough. And I was right, too. A voice. He was very little more than a voice. And I heard—him—it—this voice—other voices—all of them were so little more than voices—and the memory of that time itself lingers around me, impalpable, like a dying vibration of one immense jabber, silly, atrocious, sordid, savage, or simply mean, without any kind of sense. Voices, voices—even the girl herself—now—'

He was silent for a long time.

'I laid the ghost of his gifts at last with a lie,' he began suddenly. 'Girl! What? Did I mention a girl? Oh, she is out of it—completely. They—the women I mean—are out of it—should be out of it. We must help them to stay in that beautiful world of their own, lest ours gets worse. Oh, she had to be out of it. You should have heard the disinterred body of Mr. Kurtz saying, "My Intended." You would have perceived directly then how completely she was out of it. And the lofty frontal bone of Mr. Kurtz! They say the hair goes on growing sometimes, but this—ah—specimen was impressively bald. The wilderness had patted him on the head, and, behold, it was like a ball—an ivory ball; it had caressed him, and—lo!—he had withered; it had taken him, loved him, embraced him, got into his veins, consumed his flesh, and sealed his soul to its own by the inconceivable ceremonies of some devilish initiation. He was its spoiled and pampered favourite. Ivory? I should think so. Heaps of it, stacks of it. The old mud shanty was bursting with it. You would think there was not a single tusk left either above or below the ground in the whole country. "Mostly fossil," the manager had remarked disparagingly. It was no more fossil than I am; but they call it fossil when it is dug up. It appears these niggers do bury the tusks sometimes—but evidently they couldn't bury this parcel deep enough to save the gifted Mr. Kurtz from his fate. We filled the steamboat with it, and had to pile a lot on the deck. Thus he could see and enjoy as long as he could see, because the appreciation of this favour had remained with him to the last. You should have heard him say, "My ivory." Oh yes, I heard him. "My Intended, my ivory, my station, my river, my——" everything belonged to him. It made me hold my breath in expectation of hearing the wilderness burst into a prodigious peal of laughter that would shake the fixed stars in their places. Everything belonged to him—but that was a trifle. The thing was to know what he belonged to, how many powers of darkness claimed him for their own. That was the reflection that made you creepy all over. It was impossible—it was not good for one either—trying to imagine. He had taken a high seat amongst the devils of the land—I mean literally. You can't understand. How could you?—with solid pavement under your feet, surrounded by kind neighbours ready to cheer you or to fall on you, stepping delicately between the butcher and the policeman, in the holy terror of scandal and gallows and lunatic asylums—how can you imagine what particular region of the first ages a man's untrammelled feet may take him into by the way of solitude—utter solitude without a police-man—by the way of silence—utter silence, where no warning voice of a kind neighbour can be heard whispering of public opinion? These little things make all the great difference. When they are gone you must fall back upon your own innate strength, upon your own capacity for faithfulness.[38] Of course you may be too much of a fool to go wrong—too dull even to know you are being as-saulted by the powers of darkness. I take it, no fool ever made a bargain for his soul with the devil: the fool is too much of a fool, or the devil too much of a devil—I don't know which. Or you may be such a thunderingly exalted crea-ture as to be altogether deaf and blind to anything but heavenly sights and sounds. Then the earth for you is only a standing place—and whether to be like this is your loss or your gain I won't pretend to say. But most of us are neither one nor the other. The earth for us is a place to live in, where we must put up with sights, with sounds, with smells, too, by Jove!—breathe dead hippo, so to speak, and not be contaminated. And there, don't you see? your strength comes in, the faith in your ability for the digging of unostentatious holes to bury the stuff in—your power of devotion, not to yourself, but to an obscure, back-breaking business. And that's difficult enough. Mind, I am not trying to excuse or even explain—I am trying to account to myself for—for—Mr. Kurtz—for the shade of Mr. Kurtz. This initiated wraith from the back of Nowhere hon-oured me with its amazing confidence before it vanished altogether. This was because it could speak English to me. The original Kurtz had been educated partly in England, and—as he was good enough to say himself—his sympathies were in the right place. His mother was half-English, his father was half-French. All Europe contributed to the making of Kurtz; and by and by I learned that, most appropriately, the International Society for the Suppression of Savage Customs had entrusted him with the making of a report, for its future guidance. And he had written it too. I've seen it. I've read it. It was eloquent, vibrating with eloquence, but too high-strung, I think. Seventeen pages of close writing he had found time for! But this must have been before his—let us say—nerves went wrong, and caused him to preside at certain midnight dances ending with unspeakable rites,[39] which—as far as I reluctantly gathered from what I heard at various times—were offered up to him—do you understand?—to Mr. Kurtz himself. But it was a beautiful piece of writing. The opening paragraph, how-ever, in the light of later information, strikes me now as ominous. He began with the argument that we whites, from the point of development we had arrived at, "must necessarily appear to them [savages] in the nature of super-natural beings—we approach them with the might as of a deity," and so on, and so on. "By the simple exercise of our will we can exert a power for good practically unbounded," etc. etc. From that point he soared and took me with him. The peroration was magnificent, though difficult to remember, you know. It gave me the notion of an exotic Immensity ruled by an august Benevolence. It made me tingle with enthusiasm. This was the unbounded power of elo-quence—of words—of burning noble words. There were no practical hints to

38. However Marlow comes out of this story, he is here stating the essence of Conrad's ethic, and continues to do so in condemning those who are too spiritually inert to "go wrong," and in praising work.
39. For speculation on these rites see Headnote.

interrupt the magic current of phrases, unless a kind of note at the foot of the last page, scrawled evidently much later, in an unsteady hand, may be regarded as the exposition of a method. It was very simple, and at the end of that moving appeal to every altruistic sentiment it blazed at you, luminous and terrifying, like a flash of lightning in a serene sky: "Exterminate all the brutes!" The curious part was that he had apparently forgotten all about that valuable post-scriptum, because, later on, when he in a sense came to himself, he repeatedly entreated me to take good care of "my pamphlet" (he called it), as it was sure to have in the future a good influence upon his career. I had full information about all these things, and, besides, as it turned out, I was to have the care of his memory. I've done enough for it to give me the indisputable right to lay it, if I choose, for an everlasting rest in the dust-bin of progress, amongst all the sweepings and, figuratively speaking, all the dead cats of civilisation. But then, you see, I can't choose. He won't be forgotten. Whatever he was, he was not common. He had the power to charm or frighten rudimentary souls into an aggravated witch-dance in his honour; he could also fill the small souls of the pilgrims with bitter misgivings: he had one devoted friend at least, and he had conquered one soul in the world that was neither rudimentary nor tainted with self-seeking. No; I can't forget him, though I am not prepared to affirm the fellow was exactly worth the life we lost in getting to him. I missed my late helmsman awfully—I missed him even while his body was still lying in the pilot-house. Perhaps you will think it passing strange this regret for a savage who was no more account than a grain of sand in a black Sahara. Well, don't you see, he had done something, he had steered; for months I had him at my back—a help—an instrument. It was a kind of partnership. He steered for me— I had to look after him, I worried about his deficiencies, and thus a subtle bond had been created, of which I only became aware when it was suddenly broken. And the intimate profundity of that look he gave me when he received his hurt remains to this day in my memory—like a claim of distant kinship affirmed in a supreme moment.

'Poor fool! If he had only left that shutter alone. He had no restraint, no restraint—just like Kurtz—a tree swayed by the wind. As soon as I had put on a dry pair of slippers, I dragged him out, after first jerking the spear out of his side, which operation I confess I performed with my eyes shut tight. His heels leaped together over the little door-step; his shoulders were pressed to my breast; I hugged him from behind desperately. Oh! he was heavy, heavy; heavier than any man on earth, I should imagine. Then without more ado I tipped him overboard. The current snatched him as though he had been a wisp of grass, and I saw the body roll over twice before I lost sight of it for ever. All the pilgrims and the manager were then congregated on the awning-deck about the pilot-house, chattering at each other like a flock of excited magpies, and there was a scandalised murmur at my heartless promptitude. What they wanted to keep that body hanging about for I can't guess. Embalm it, maybe. But I had also heard another, and a very ominous, murmur on the deck below. My friends the wood-cutters were likewise scandalised, and with a better show of reason—though I admit that the reason itself was quite inadmissible. Oh, quite! I had made up my mind that if my late helmsman was to be eaten, the fishes alone should have him. He had been a very second-rate helmsman while alive, but now he was dead he might have become a first-class temptation, and possibly cause some startling trouble. Besides, I was anxious to take the wheel, the man in pink pyjamas showing himself a hopeless duffer at the business.

'This I did directly the simple funeral was over. We were going half-speed, keeping right in the middle of the stream, and I listened to the talk about me. They had given up Kurtz, they had given up the station; Kurtz was dead, and the station had been burnt—and so on, and so on. The red-haired pilgrim was beside himself with the thought that at least this poor Kurtz had been properly revenged. "Say! We must have made a glorious slaughter of them in the bush. Eh? What do you think? Say?" He positively danced, the bloodthirsty little gingery beggar. And he had nearly fainted when he saw the wounded man! I could not help saying, "You made a glorious lot of smoke, anyhow." I had seen, from the way the tops of the bushes rustled and flew, that almost all the shots had gone too high. You can't hit anything unless you take aim and fire from the shoulder; but these chaps fired from the hip with their eyes shut. The retreat, I maintained—and I was right—was caused by the screeching of the steam-whistle. Upon this they forgot Kurtz, and began to howl at me with indignant protests.

'The manager stood by the wheel murmuring confidentially about the necessity of getting well away down the river before dark at all events, when I saw in the distance a clearing on the river-side and the outlines of some sort of building. "What's this?" I asked. He clapped his hands in wonder. "The station!" he cried. I edged in at once, still going half-speed.

'Through my glasses I saw the slope of a hill interspersed with rare trees and perfectly free from undergrowth. A long decaying building on the summit was half buried in the high grass; the large holes in the peaked roof gaped black from afar; the jungle and the woods made a background. There was no enclosure or fence of any kind; but there had been one apparently, for near the house half a dozen slim posts remained in a row, roughly trimmed, and with their upper ends ornamented with round carved balls. The rails, or whatever there had been between, had disappeared. Of course the forest surrounded all that. The river-bank was clear, and on the water side I saw a white man under a hat like a cart-wheel beckoning persistently with his whole arm. Examining the edge of the forest above and below, I was almost certain I could see movements—human forms gliding here and there. I steamed past prudently, then stopped the engines and let her drift down. The man on the shore began to shout, urging us to land. "We have been attacked," screamed the manager. "I know—I know. It's all right," yelled back the other, as cheerful as you please. "Come along. It's all right. I am glad."

'His aspect reminded me of something I had seen—something funny I had seen somewhere. As I manœuvred to get alongside, I was asking myself, "What does this fellow look like?" Suddenly I got it. He looked like a harlequin. His clothes had been made of some stuff that was brown holland probably, but it was covered with patches all over, with bright patches, blue, red, and yellow—patches on the back, patches on the front, patches on elbows, on knees; coloured binding round his jacket, scarlet edging at the bottom of his trousers; and the sunshine made him look extremely gay and wonderfully neat withal, because you could see how beautifully all this patching had been done. A beardless, boyish face, very fair, no features to speak of, nose peeling, little blue eyes, smiles and frowns chasing each other over that open countenance like sunshine and shadow on a wind-swept plain. "Look out, captain!" he cried; "there's a snag lodged in here last night." What! Another snag? I confess I swore shamefully. I had nearly holed my cripple, to finish off that charming trip. The harlequin on the bank turned his little pug-nose up to me. "You English?" he asked, all smiles. "Are you?" I shouted from the wheel. The smiles vanished, and he shook his head as if sorry for my disappointment. Then he brightened up. "Never mind!" he cried encouragingly. "Are we in time?" I asked. "He is up there," he replied, with a toss of the head up the hill, and becoming gloomy all of a sudden. His face was like the autumn sky, overcast one moment and bright the next.

'When the manager, escorted by the pilgrims, all of them armed to the teeth, had gone to the house, this chap came on board. "I say, I don't like this. These natives are in the bush," I said. He assured me earnestly it was all right. "They are simple people," he added; "well, I am glad you came. It took me all my time to keep them off." "But you said it was all right," I cried. "Oh, they meant no harm," he said; and as I stared he corrected himself, "Not exactly." Then vivaciously, "My faith, your pilot-house wants a clean-up!" In the next breath he advised me to keep enough steam on the boiler to blow the whistle in case of any trouble. "One good screech will do more for you than all your rifles. They are simple people," he repeated. He rattled away at such a rate he quite overwhelmed me. He seemed to be trying to make up for lots of silence, and actually hinted, laughing, that such was the case. "Don't you talk with Mr. Kurtz?" I said. "You don't talk with that man—you listen to him," he exclaimed with severe exaltation. "But now——" He waved his arm, and in the twinkling of an eye was in the uttermost depths of despondency. In a moment he came up again with a jump, possessed himself of both my hands, shook them continuously, while he gabbled: "Brother sailor . . . honour . . . pleasure . . . delight . . . introduce myself . . . Russian . . . son of an arch-priest . . . Government of Tambov . . . What? Tobacco! English tobacco; the excellent English tobacco! Now, that's brotherly. Smoke? Where's a sailor that does not smoke?"

'The pipe soothed him, and gradually I made out he had run away from school, had gone to sea in a Russian ship; ran away again; served some time in English ships; was now reconciled with the arch-priest. He made a point of that. "But when one is young one must see things, gather experience, ideas; enlarge the mind." "Here!" I interrupted. "You can never tell! Here I met Mr. Kurtz," he said, youthfully solemn and reproachful. I held my tongue after that. It appears he had persuaded a Dutch trading-house on the coast to fit him out with stores and goods, and had started for the interior with a light heart, and no more idea of what would happen to him than a baby. He had been wandering about that river for nearly two years alone, cut off from everybody and everything. "I am not so young as I look. I am twenty-five," he said. "At first old Van Shuyten would tell me to go to the devil," he narrated with keen enjoyment; "but I stuck to him, and talked and talked, till at last he got afraid I would talk the hind-leg off his favourite dog, so he gave me some cheap things and a few guns, and told me he hoped he would never see my face again. Good old Dutchman, Van Shuyten. I sent him one small lot of ivory a year ago, so that he can't call me a little thief when I get back. I hope he got it. And for the rest, I don't care. I had some wood stacked for you. That was my old house. Did you see?" 'I gave him Towson's book. He made as though he would kiss me, but restrained himself. "The only book I had left, and I thought I had lost it," he said, looking at it ecstatically. "So many accidents happen to a man going about alone, you know. Canoes get upset sometimes—and sometimes you've got to clear out so quick when the people get angry." He thumbed the pages. "You made notes in Russian?" I asked. He nodded. "I thought they were written in cipher," I said. He laughed, then became serious. "I had lots of trouble to keep these people off," he said. "Did they want to kill you?" I asked. "Oh no!" he cried, and checked himself. "Why did they attack us?" I pursued. He hesitated, then said shamefacedly, "They don't want him to go." "Don't they?" I said curiously. He nodded a nod full of mystery and wisdom. "I tell you," he cried, "this man has enlarged my mind." He opened his arms wide, staring at me with his little blue eyes that were perfectly round.'

III

'I looked at him, lost in astonishment. There he was before me, in motley, as though he had absconded from a troupe of mimes, enthusiastic, fabulous. His very existence was improbable, inexplicable, and altogether bewildering. He was an insoluble problem. It was inconceivable how he had existed, how he had succeeded in getting so far, how he had managed to remain—why he did not instantly disappear. "I went a little farther," he said, "then still a little farther—till I had gone so far that I don't know how I'll ever get back. Never mind. Plenty time. I can manage. You take Kurtz away quick—quick—I tell you." The glamour of youth enveloped his parti-coloured rags, his destitution, his loneliness, the essential desolation of his futile wanderings. For months— for years—his life hadn't been worth a day's purchase; and there he was gallantly, thoughtlessly alive, to all appearance indestructible solely by the virtue of his few years and of his unreflecting audacity. I was seduced into something like admiration—like envy. Glamour urged him on, glamour kept him unscathed. He surely wanted nothing from the wilderness but space to breathe in and to push on through. His need was to exist, and to move onwards at the greatest possible risk, and with a maximum of privation. If the absolutely pure, uncalculating, unpractical spirit of adventure had ever ruled a human being, it ruled this be-patched youth. I almost envied him the possession of this modest and clear flame. It seemed to have consumed all thought of self so completely, that, even while he was talking to you, you forget that it was he—the man before your eyes—who had gone through these things. I did not envy him his devotion to Kurtz, though. He had not meditated over it. It came to him, and he accepted it with a sort of eager fatalism. I must say that to me it appeared about the most dangerous thing in every way he had come upon so far.

'They had come together unavoidably, like two ships becalmed near each other, and lay rubbing sides at last. I suppose Kurtz wanted an audience, because on a certain occasion, when encamped in the forest, they had talked all night, or more probably Kurtz had talked. "We talked of everything," he said, quite transported at the recollection. "I forgot there was such a thing as sleep. The night did not seem to last an hour. Everything! Everything! . . . Of love too." "Ah, he talked to you of love!" I said, much amused. "It isn't what you think," he cried, almost passionately. "It was in general. He made me see things—things."

'He threw his arms up. We were on deck at the time, and the head-man of my wood-cutters, lounging near by, turned upon him his heavy and glittering eyes. I looked around, and I don't know why, but I assure you that never, never before, did this land, this river, this jungle, the very arch of this blazing sky, appear to me so hopeless and so dark, so impenetrable to human thought, so pitiless to human weakness. "And, ever since, you have been with him, of course?" I said.

'On the contrary. It appears their intercourse had been very much broken by various causes. He had, as he informed me proudly, managed to nurse Kurtz through two illnesses (he alluded to it as you would to some risky feat), but as a rule Kurtz wandered alone, far in the depths of the forest. "Very often coming to this station, I had to wait days and days before he would turn up," he said. "Ah, it was worth waiting for!—sometimes." "What was he doing? exploring or what?" I asked. "Oh yes, of course"; he had discovered lots of villages, a lake too—he did not know exactly in what direction; it was dangerous to inquire too much—but mostly his expeditions had been for ivory. "But he had no goods to trade with by that time," I objected. "There's a good lot of cartridges left even yet," he answered, looking away. "To speak plainly, he raided the country," I said. He nodded. "Not alone, surely!" He muttered something about the villages round that lake. "Kurtz got the tribe to follow him, did he?" I suggested. He fidgeted a little. "They adored him," he said. The tone of these words was so extraordinary that I looked at him searchingly. It was curious to see his mingled eagerness and reluctance to speak of Kurtz. The man filled his life, occupied his thoughts, swayed his emotions. "What can you expect?" he burst out; "he came to them with thunder and lightning, you know—and they had never seen anything like it—and very terrible. He could be very terrible. You can't judge Mr. Kurtz as you would an ordinary man. No, no, no! Now—just to give you an idea—I don't mind telling you, he wanted to shoot me too one day—but I don't judge him." "Shoot you!" I cried. "What for?" "Well, I had a small lot of ivory the chief of that village near my house gave me. You see I used to shoot game for them. Well, he wanted it, and wouldn't hear reason. He declared he would shoot me unless I gave him the ivory and then cleared out of the country, because he could do so, and had a fancy for it, and there was nothing on earth to prevent him killing whom he jolly well pleased. And it was true too. I gave him the ivory. What did I care! But I didn't clear out. No, no. I couldn't leave him. I had to be careful, of course, till we got friendly again for a time. He had his second illness then. Afterwards I had to keep out of the way; but I didn't mind. He was living for the most part in those villages on the lake. When he came down to the river, sometimes he would take to me, and sometimes it was better for me to be careful. This man suffered too much. He hated all this, and somehow he couldn't get away. When

I had a chance I begged him to try and leave while there was time: I offered to go back with him. And he would say yes, and then he would remain; go off on another ivory hunt; disappear for weeks; forget himself amongst these people—forget himself—you know." "Why! he's mad," I said. He protested indignantly. Mr. Kurtz couldn't be mad. If I had heard him talk, only two days ago, I wouldn't dare hint at such a thing. . . . I had taken up my binoculars while we talked, and was looking at the shore, sweeping the limit of the forest at each side and at the back of the house. The consciousness of there being people in that bush, so silent, so quiet—as silent and quiet as the ruined house on the hill—made me uneasy. There was no sign on the face of nature of this amazing tale that was not so much told as suggested to me in desolate exclamations, completed by shrugs, in interrupted phrases, in hints ending in deep sighs. The woods were unmoved, like a mask—heavy, like the closed door of a prison—they looked with their air of hidden knowledge, of patient expectation, of unapproachable silence. The Russian was explaining to me that it was only lately that Mr. Kurtz had come down to the river, bringing along with him all the fighting men of that lake tribe. He had been absent for several months—getting himself adored, I suppose—and had come down unexpectedly, with the intention to all appearance of making a raid either across the river or down stream. Evidently the appetite for more ivory had got the better of the—what shall I say?—less material aspirations. However, he had got much worse suddenly. "I heard he was lying helpless, and so I came up—took my chance," said the Russian. "Oh, he is bad, very bad." I directed my glass to the house. There were no signs of life, but there were the ruined roof, the long mud wall peeping above the grass, with three little square window-holes, no two of the same size; all this brought within reach of my hand, as it were. And then I made a brusque movement, and one of the remaining posts of that vanished fence leaped up in the field of my glass. You remember I told you I had been struck at the distance by certain attempts at ornamentation, rather remarkable in the ruinous aspect of the place. Now I had suddenly a nearer view, and its first result was to make me throw my head back as if before a blow. Then I went carefully from post to post with my glass, and I saw my mistake. These round knobs were not ornamental but symbolic; they were expressive and puzzling, striking and disturbing—food for thought and also for vultures if there had been any looking down from the sky; but at all events for such ants as were industrious enough to ascend the pole. They would have been even more impressive, those heads on the stakes, if their faces had not been turned to the house. Only one, the first I had made out, was facing my way. I was not so shocked as you may think. The start back I had given was really nothing but a movement of surprise. I had expected to see a knob of wood there, you know. I returned deliberately to the first I had seen— and there it was, black, dried, sunken, with closed eyelids—a head that seemed to sleep at the top of that pole, and, with the shrunken dry lips showing a narrow white line of the teeth, was smiling too, smiling continuously at some endless and jocose dream of that eternal slumber.

'I am not disclosing any trade secrets. In fact the manager said afterwards that Mr. Kurtz's methods had ruined the district. I have no opinion on that point, but I want you clearly to understand that there was nothing exactly profitable in these heads being there. They only showed that Mr. Kurtz lacked restraint in the gratification of his various lusts, that there was something wanting in him—some small matter which, when the pressing need arose, could not be found under his magnificent eloquence. Whether he knew of this deficiency himself I can't say. I think the knowledge came to him at last— only at the very last. But the wilderness had found him out early, and had taken on him a terrible vengeance for the fantastic invasion. I think it had whispered to him things about himself which he did not know, things of which he had no conception till he took counsel with this great solitude—and the whisper had proved irresistibly fascinating. It echoed loudly within him because he was hollow at the core. . . . I put down the glass, and the head that had appeared near enough to be spoken to seemed at once to have leaped away from me into inaccessible distance.

'The admirer of Mr. Kurtz was a bit crestfallen. In a hurried, indistinct voice he began to assure me he had not dared to take these—say, symbols—down. He was not afraid of the natives; they would not stir till Mr. Kurtz gave the word. His ascendancy was extraordinary. The camps of these people sur- rounded the place, and the chiefs came every day to see him. They would crawl . . . "I don't want to know anything of the ceremonies used when approaching Mr. Kurtz," I shouted. Curious, this feeling that came over me that such details would be more intolerable than those heads drying on the stakes under Mr. Kurtz's windows. After all, that was only a savage sight, while I seemed at one bound to have been transported into some lightless region of subtle horrors, where pure, uncomplicated savagery was a positive relief, being something that had a right to exist—obviously—in the sunshine. The young man looked at me with surprise. I suppose it did not occur to him that Mr. Kurtz was no idol of mine. He forgot I hadn't heard any of these splendid monologues on, what was it? on love, justice, conduct of life—or what not. If it had come to crawling before Mr. Kurtz, he crawled as much as the veriest savage of them all. I had no idea of the conditions, he said: these heads were the heads of rebels. I shocked him excessively by laughing. Rebels! What would be the next definition I was to hear? There had been enemies, criminals, workers—and these were rebels. Those rebellious heads looked very subdued to me on their sticks. "You don't know how such a life tries a man like Kurtz," cried Kurtz's last disciple. "Well, and you?" I said. "I! I! I am a simple man. I have no great thoughts. I want nothing from any- body. How can you compare me to . . .?" His feelings were too much for speech, and suddenly he broke down. "I don't understand," he groaned. "I've been doing my best to keep him alive, and that's enough. I had no hand in all this. I have no abilities. There hasn't been a drop of medicine or a mouth- ful of invalid food for months here. He was shamefully abandoned. A man like this, with such ideas. Shamefully! Shamefully! I—I—haven't slept for the last ten nights. . . ."

'His voice lost itself in the calm of the evening. The long shadows of the forest had slipped downhill while we talked, had gone far beyond the ruined hovel, beyond the symbolic row of stakes. All this was in the gloom, while we down there were yet in the sunshine, and the stretch of the river abreast of the clearing glittered in a still and dazzling splendour, with a murky and overshadowed bend above and below. Not a living soul was seen on the shore. The bushes did not rustle.

'Suddenly round the corner of the house a group of men appeared, as though they had come up from the ground. They waded waist-deep in the grass, in a compact body, bearing an improvised stretcher in their midst. Instantly, in the emptiness of the landscape, a cry arose whose shrillness pierced the still air like a sharp arrow flying straight to the very heart of the land; and, as if by enchantment, streams of human beings—of naked human beings—with spears in their hands, with bows, with shields, with wild glances and savage movements, were poured into the clearing by the dark-faced and pensive forest. The bushes shook, the grass swayed for a time, and then everything stood still in attentive immobility.

' "Now, if he does not say the right thing to them we are all done for," said the Russian at my elbow. The knot of men with the stretcher had stopped too, half-way to the steamer, as if petrified. I saw the man on the stretcher sit up, lank and with an uplifted arm, above the shoulders of the bearers. "Let us hope that the man who can talk so well of love in general will find some particular reason to spare us this time," I said. I resented bitterly the absurd danger of our situation, as if to be at the mercy of that atrocious phantom had been a dishonouring necessity. I could not hear a sound, but through my glasses I saw the thin arm extended commandingly, the lower jaw moving, the eyes of that apparition shining darkly far in its bony head that nodded with grotesque jerks. Kurtz—Kurtz—that means "short" in German—don't it? Well, the name was as true as everything else in his life—and death. He looked at least seven feet long. His covering had fallen off, and his body emerged from it pitiful and appalling as from a winding-sheet. I could see the cage of his ribs all astir, the bones of his arm waving. It was as though an animated image of death carved out of old ivory had been shaking its hand with menaces at a motionless crowd of men made of dark and glittering bronze. I saw him open his mouth wide—it gave him a weirdly voracious aspect, as though he had wanted to swallow all the air, all the earth, all the men before him. A deep voice reached me faintly. He must have been shouting. He fell back suddenly. The stretcher shook as the bearers staggered forward again, and almost at the same time I noticed that the crowd of savages was vanishing without any perceptible movement of retreat, as if the forest that had ejected these beings so suddenly had drawn them in again as the breath is drawn in a long aspiration.

'Some of the pilgrims behind the stretcher carried his arms—two shot-guns, a heavy rifle, and a light revolver-carbine—the thunderbolts of that pitiful Jupiter. The manager bent over him murmuring as he walked beside his head. They laid him down in one of the little cabins—just a room for a bed-place and a camp-stool or two, you know. We had brought his belated correspondence, and a lot of torn envelopes and open letters littered his bed. His hand roamed feebly amongst these papers. I was struck by the fire of his eyes and the composed languor of his expression. It was not so much the exhaustion of disease. He did not seem in pain. This shadow looked satiated and calm, as though for the moment it had had its fill of all the emotions.

'He rustled one of the letters, and looking straight in my face said, "I am

glad." Somebody had been writing to him about me. These special recommendations were turning up again. The volume of tone he emitted without
effort, almost without the trouble of moving his lips, amazed me. A voice! a
voice! It was grave, profound, vibrating, while the man did not seem capable
of a whisper. However, he had enough strength in him—factitious no doubt—
to very nearly make an end of us, as you shall hear directly.

'The manager appeared silently in the doorway; I stepped out at once and
he drew the curtain after me. The Russian, eyed curiously by the pilgrims, was
staring at the shore. I followed the direction of his glance.

'Dark human shapes could be made out in the distance, flitting indistinctly
against the gloomy border of the forest, and near the river two bronze figures,
leaning on tall spears, stood in the sunlight under fantastic head-dresses of
spotted skins, warlike and still in statuesque repose. And from right to left
along the lighted shore moved a wild and gorgeous apparition of a woman.

'She walked with measured steps, draped in striped and fringed cloths,
treading the earth proudly, with a slight jingle and flash of barbarous orna-
ments. She carried her head high; her hair was done in the shape of a helmet;
she had brass leggings to the knees, brass wire gauntlets to the elbow, a crimson
spot on her tawny cheek, innumerable necklaces of glass beads on her neck;
bizarre things, charms, gifts of witch-men, that hung about her, glittered and
trembled at every step. She must have had the value of several elephant
tusks upon her. She was savage and superb, wild-eyed and magnificent; there
was something ominous and stately in her deliberate progress. And in the
hush that had fallen suddenly upon the whole sorrowful land, the immense
wilderness, the colossal body of the fecund and mysterious life seemed to
look at her, pensive, as though it had been looking at the image of its own
tenebrous and passionate soul.

'She came abreast of the steamer, stood still, and faced us. Her long shadow
fell to the water's edge. Her face had a tragic and fierce aspect of wild sorrow and of dumb pain mingled with the fear of some struggling, half-shaped
resolve. She stood looking at us without a stir, and like the wilderness itself,
with an air of brooding over an inscrutable purpose. A whole minute passed,
and then she made a step forward. There was a low jingle, a glint of yellow
metal, a sway of fringed draperies, and she stopped as if her heart had failed
her. The young fellow by my side growled. The pilgrims murmured at my
back. She looked at us all as if her life had depended upon the unswerving
steadiness of her glance. Suddenly she opened her bared arms and threw them
up rigid above her head, as though in an uncontrollable desire to touch the
sky, and at the same time the swift shadows darted out on the earth, swept
around on the river, gathering the steamer in a shadowy embrace. A formidable
silence hung over the scene.

'She turned away slowly, walked on, following the bank, and passed into the
bushes to the left. Once only her eyes gleamed back at us in the dusk of the
thickets before she disappeared.

' "If she had offered to come aboard I really think I would have tried to
shoot her," said the man of patches nervously. "I had been risking my life
every day for the last fortnight to keep her out of the house. She got in one
day and kicked up a row about those miserable rags I picked up in the store-

room to mend my clothes with. I wasn't decent. At least it must have been that, for she talked like a fury to Kurtz for an hour, pointing at me now and then. I don't understand the dialect of this tribe. Luckily for me, I fancy Kurtz felt too ill that day to care, or there would have been mischief. I don't understand. . . . No—it's too much for me. Ah, well, it's all over now."

'At this moment I heard Kurtz's deep voice behind the curtain: "Save me!—save the ivory, you mean. Don't tell me. Save *me!* Why, I've had to save you. You are interrupting my plans now. Sick! Sick! Not so sick as you would like to believe. Never mind. I'll carry my ideas out yet—I will return. I'll show you what can be done. You with your little peddling notions—you are interfering with me. I will return. I . . ."

'The manager came out. He did me the honour to take me under the arm and lead me aside. "He is very low, very low," he said. He considered it necessary to sigh, but neglected to be consistently sorrowful. "We have done all we could for him—haven't we? But there is no disguising the fact, Mr. Kurtz has done more harm than good to the Company. He did not see the time was not ripe for vigorous action. Cautiously, cautiously—that's my principle. We must be cautious yet. The district is closed to us for a time. Deplorable! Upon the whole, the trade will suffer. I don't deny there is a remarkable quantity of ivory—mostly fossil. We must save it, at all events—but look how precarious the position is—and why? Because the method is unsound." "Do you," said I, looking at the shore, "call it 'unsound method'?" "Without doubt," he exclaimed hotly. "Don't you?" . . . "No method at all," I murmured after a while. "Exactly," he exulted. "I anticipated this. Shows a complete want of judgment. It is my duty to point it out in the proper quarter." "Oh," said I, "that fellow—what's his name?—the brickmaker, will make a readable report for you." He appeared confounded for a moment. It seemed to me I had never breathed an atmosphere so vile, and I turned mentally to Kurtz for relief—positively for relief. "Nevertheless, I think Mr. Kurtz is a remarkable man," I said with emphasis. He started, dropped on me a cold heavy glance, said very quietly, "He *was*," and turned his back on me. My hour of favour was over; I found myself lumped along with Kurtz as a partisan of methods for which the time was not ripe: I was unsound! Ah! but it was something to have at least a choice of nightmares.

'I had turned to the wilderness really, not to Mr. Kurtz, who, I was ready to admit, was as good as buried. And for a moment it seemed to me as if I also [40] were buried in a vast grave full of unspeakable secrets. I felt an intolerable weight oppressing my breast, the smell of the damp earth, the unseen presence of victorious corruption, the darkness of an impenetrable night. . . . The Russian tapped me on the shoulder. I heard him mumbling and stammering something about "brother seaman—couldn't conceal—knowledge of matters that would affect Mr. Kurtz's reputation." I waited. For him evidently Mr. Kurtz was not in his grave; I suspect that for him Mr. Kurtz was one of the immortals. "Well!" said I at last, "speak out. As it happens, I am Mr. Kurtz's friend—in a way."

'He stated with a good deal of formality that had we not been "of the same

40. Again suggesting the "double" theme.

profession," he would have kept the matter to himself without regard to consequences. He suspected "there was an active ill-will towards him on the part of these white men that——" "You are right," I said, remembering a certain conversation I had overheard. "The manager thinks you ought to be hanged." He showed a concern at this intelligence which amused me at first. "I had better get out of the way quietly," he said earnestly. "I can do no more for Kurtz now, and they would soon find some excuse. What's to stop them? There's a military post three hundred miles from here." "Well, upon my word," said I, "perhaps you had better go if you have any friends amongst the savages near by." "Plenty," he said. "They are simple people—and I want nothing, you know." He stood biting his lip, then: "I don't want any harm to happen to these whites here, but of course I was thinking of Mr. Kurtz's reputation—but you are a brother seaman and——" "All right," said I, after a time. "Mr. Kurtz's reputation is safe with me." I did not know how truly I spoke.

'He informed me, lowering his voice, that it was Kurtz who had ordered the attack to be made on the steamer. "He hated sometimes the idea of being taken away—and then again . . . But I don't understand these matters. I am a simple man. He thought it would scare you away—that you would give it up, thinking him dead. I could not stop him. Oh, I had an awful time of it this last month." "Very well," I said. "He is all right now." "Ye-e-es," he muttered, not very convinced apparently. "Thanks," said I; "I shall keep my eyes open." "But quiet—eh?" he urged anxiously. "It would be awful for his reputation if anybody here——" I promised a complete discretion with great gravity. "I have a canoe and three black fellows waiting not very far. I am off. Could you give me a few Martini-Henry cartridges?" I could, and did, with proper secrecy. He helped himself, with a wink at me, to a handful of my tobacco. "Between sailors—you know—good English tobacco." At the door of the pilot-house he turned round—"I say, haven't you a pair of shoes you could spare?" He raised one leg. "Look." The soles were tied with knotted strings sandal-wise under his bare feet. I rooted out an old pair, at which he looked with admiration before tucking it under his left arm. One of his pockets (bright red) was bulging with cartridges, from the other (dark blue) peeped "Towson's Inquiry," etc. etc. He seemed to think himself excellently well equipped for a renewed encounter with the wilderness. "Ah! I'll never, never meet such a man again. You ought to have heard him recite poetry— his own too it was, he told me. Poetry!" He rolled his eyes at the recollection of these delights. "Oh, he enlarged my mind! "Good-bye," said I. He shook hands and vanished in the night. Sometimes I ask myself whether I had ever really seen him—whether it was possible to meet such a phenomenon! . . .

'When I woke up shortly after midnight his warning came to my mind with its hint of danger that seemed, in the starred darkness, real enough to make me get up for the purpose of having a look round. On the hill a big fire burned, illuminating fitfully a crooked corner of the station-house. One of the agents with a picket of a few of our blacks, armed for the purpose, was keeping guard over the ivory; but deep within the forest, red gleams that wavered, that seemed to sink and rise from the ground amongst confused columnar shapes of intense blackness, showed the exact position of the camp where Mr. Kurtz's adorers were keeping their uneasy vigil. The monotonous beating of a big drum filled the air with muffled shocks and a lingering vibration. A steady droning sound of many men chanting each to himself some weird incantation came out from the black, flat wall of the woods as the humming of bees comes out of a hive, and had a strange narcotic effect upon my half-awake senses. I believe I dozed off leaning over the rail, till an abrupt burst of yells, an overwhelming outbreak of a pent-up and mysterious frenzy, woke me up in a bewildered wonder. It was cut short all at once, and the low droning went on with an effect of audible and soothing silence. I glanced casually into the little cabin. A light was burning within, but Mr. Kurtz was not there.

'I think I would have raised an outcry if I had believed my eyes. But I didn't believe them at first—the thing seemed so impossible. The fact is, I was completely unnerved by a sheer blank fright, pure abstract terror, unconnected with any distinct shape of physical danger. What made this emotion so overpowering was—how shall I define it?—the moral shock I received, as if something altogether monstrous, intolerable to thought and odious to the soul, had been thrust upon me unexpectedly. This lasted of course the merest fraction of a second, and then the usual sense of commonplace, deadly danger, the possibility of a sudden onslaught and massacre, or something of the kind, which I saw impending, was positively welcome and composing. It pacified me, in fact, so much, that I did not raise an alarm.

'There was an agent buttoned up inside an ulster and sleeping on a chair on deck within three feet of me. The yells had not awakened him; he snored very slightly; I left him to his slumbers and leaped ashore. I did not betray Mr. Kurtz—it was ordered I should never betray him—it was written I should be loyal to the nightmare of my choice. I was anxious to deal with this shadow by myself alone—and to this day I don't know why I was so jealous of sharing with any one the peculiar blackness of that experience.

'As soon as I got on the bank I saw a trail—a broad trail through the grass. I remember the exultation with which I said to myself, "He can't walk—he is crawling on all-fours—I've got him." The grass was wet with dew. I strode rapidly with clenched fists. I fancy I had some vague notion of falling upon him and giving him a drubbing. I don't know. I had some imbecile thoughts. The knitting old woman with the cat obtruded herself upon my memory as a most improper person to be sitting at the other end of such an affair. I saw a row of pilgrims squirting lead in the air out of Winchesters held to the hip. I thought I would never get back to the steamer, and imagined myself living alone and unarmed in the woods to an advanced age. Such silly things—you know. And I remember I confounded the beat of the drum with the beating of my heart, and was pleased at its calm regularity.

'I kept to the track though—then stopped to listen. The night was very clear; a dark blue space, sparkling with dew and starlight, in which black things stood very still. I thought I could see a kind of motion ahead of me. I was strangely cocksure of everything that night. I actually left the track and ran in a wide semicircle (I verily believe chuckling to myself) so as to get in front of that stir, of that motion I had seen—if indeed I had seen anything. I was circumventing Kurtz as though it had been a boyish game.

'I came upon him, and, if he had not heard me coming, I would have fallen over him too, but he got up in time. He rose, unsteady, long, pale, indistinct, like a vapour exhaled by the earth, and swayed slightly, misty and silent before me; while at my back the fires loomed between the trees, and the murmur of many voices issued from the forest. I had cut him off cleverly; but when actually confronting him I seemed to come to my senses, I saw the danger in its right proportion. It was by no means over yet. Suppose he began to shout? Though he could hardly stand, there was still plenty of vigour in his voice. "Go away—hide yourself," he said, in that profound tone. It was very awful. I glanced back. We were within thirty yards from the nearest fire. A black figure stood up, strode on long black legs, waving long black arms, across the glow. It had horns—antelope horns, I think—on its head. Some sorcerer, some witch-man, no doubt: it looked fiend-like enough. "Do you know what you are doing?" I whispered. "Perfectly," he answered, raising his voice for that single word: it sounded to me far off and yet loud, like a hail through a speaking-trumpet. If he makes a row we are lost, I thought to myself. This clearly was not a case for fisticuffs, even apart from the very natural aversion I had to beat that Shadow—this wandering and tormented thing. "You will be lost," I said—"utterly lost." One gets sometimes such a flash of inspiration, you know. I did say the right thing, though indeed he could not have been more irretrievably lost than he was at this very moment, when the foundations of our intimacy were being laid—to endure—to endure— even to the end—even beyond.

'"I had immense plans," he muttered irresolutely. "Yes," said I; "but if you try to shout I'll smash your head with——" There was not a stick or a stone near. "I will throttle you for good," I corrected myself. "I was on the threshold of great things," he pleaded, in a voice of longing, with a wistfulness of tone that made my blood run cold. "And now for this stupid scoundrel——" "Your success in Europe is assured in any case," I affirmed steadily. I did not want to have the throttling of him, you understand—and indeed it would have been very little use for any practical purpose. I tried to break the spell—the heavy, mute spell of the wilderness—that seemed to draw him to its pitiless breast by the awakening of forgotten and brutal instincts, by the memory of gratified and monstrous passions. This alone, I was convinced, had driven him out to the edge of the forest, to the bush, towards the gleam of fires, the throb of drums, the drone of weird incantations; this alone had beguiled his unlawful soul beyond the bounds of permitted aspirations. And, don't you see, the terror of the position was not in being knocked on the head—though I had a very lively sense of that danger too—but in this, that I had to deal with a being to whom I could not appeal in the name of anything high or low. I had, even like the niggers, to invoke him—himself—his own exalted and incredible degradation. There was nothing either above or below him, and I knew it. He had kicked himself loose of the earth. Confound the man! he had kicked the very earth to pieces. He was alone, and I before him did not know whether I stood on the ground or floated in the air. I've been telling you what we said—repeating the phrases we pronounced—but what's the good? They were common everyday words—the familiar, vague sounds exchanged on every waking day of life. But what of that? They had behind them, to my mind, the terrific suggestiveness of words heard in dreams, of phrases spoken in nightmares. Soul! If anybody had ever struggled with a soul, I am the man. And I wasn't arguing with a lunatic either. Believe me or not, his intelligence was perfectly clear—concentrated, it is true, upon himself with horrible intensity, yet clear; and therein was my only chance—barring, of course, the killing him there and then, which wasn't so good, on account of unavoidable noise. But his soul was mad. Being alone in the wilderness, it had looked within itself, and, by Heavens! I tell you, it had gone mad. I had—for my sins, I suppose, to go through the ordeal of looking into it myself. No eloquence could have been so withering to one's belief in mankind as his final burst of sincerity. He struggled with himself too. I saw it— I heard it. I saw the inconceivable mystery of a soul that knew no restraint, no faith, and no fear, yet struggling blindly with itself. I kept my head pretty well; but when I had him at last stretched on the couch, I wiped my forehead, while my legs shook under me as though I had carried half a ton on my back down that hill. And yet I had only supported him, his bony arm clasped round my neck—and he was not much heavier than a child.

'When next day we left at noon, the crowd, of whose presence behind the curtain of trees I had been acutely conscious all the time, flowed out of the woods again, filled the clearing, covered the slope with a mass of naked, breathing, quivering, bronze bodies. I steamed up a bit, then swung downstream, and two thousand eyes followed the evolutions of the splashing, thumping, fierce river-demon beating the water with its terrible tail and breathing black smoke into the air. In front of the first rank, along the river, three men, plastered with bright red earth from head to foot, strutted to and fro restlessly. When we came abreast again, they faced the river, stamped their feet, nodded their horned heads, swayed their scarlet bodies; they shook towards the fierce river-demon a bunch of black feathers, a mangy skin with a pendent tail—something that looked like a dried gourd; they shouted periodically together strings of amazing words that resembled no sounds of human language; and the deep murmurs of the crowd, interrupted suddenly, were like the responses of some satanic litany.

'We had carried Kurtz into the pilot-house: there was more air there. Lying on the couch, he stared through the open shutter. There was an eddy in the mass of human bodies, and the woman with helmeted head and tawny cheeks rushed out to the very brink of the stream. She put out her hands, shouted something, and all that wild mob took up the shout in a roaring chorus of articulated, rapid, breathless utterance.

' "Do you understand this?" I asked.

'He kept on looking out past me with fiery, longing eyes, with a mingled expression of wistfulness and hate. He made no answer, but I saw a smile, a smile of indefinable meaning, appear on his colourless lips that a moment after twitched convulsively. "Do I not?" he said slowly, gasping, as if the words had been torn out of him by a supernatural power.

'I pulled the string of the whistle, and I did this because I saw the pilgrims on deck getting out their rifles with an air of anticipating a jolly lark. At the sudden screech there was a movement of abject terror through that wedged mass of bodies. "Don't! don't you frighten them away," cried some one on deck disconsolately. I pulled the string time after time. They broke and ran, they leaped, they crouched, they swerved, they dodged the flying terror of the sound. The three red chaps had fallen flat, face down on the shore, as though they had been shot dead. Only the barbarous and superb woman did not so much as flinch, and stretched tragically her bare arms after us over the sombre and glittering river.

'And then that imbecile crowd down on the deck started their little fun, and I could see nothing more for smoke.

"The brown current ran swiftly out of the heart of darkness, bearing us down towards the sea with twice the speed of our upward progress; and Kurtz's life was running swiftly too, ebbing, ebbing out of his heart into the sea of inexorable time. The manager was very placid, he had no vital anxieties now, he took us both in with a comprehensive and satisfied glance: the "affair" had come off as well as could be wished. I saw the time approaching when I would be left alone of the party of "unsound method." The pilgrims looked upon me with disfavour. I was, so to speak, numbered with the dead. It is strange how I accepted this unforeseen partnership, this choice of nightmares forced upon me in the tenebrous land invaded by these mean and greedy phantoms.

'Kurtz discoursed. A voice! a voice! It rang deep to the very last. It survived his strength to hide in the magnificent folds of eloquence the barren darkness of his heart. Oh, he struggled! he struggled! The wastes of his weary brain were haunted by shadowy images now—images of wealth and fame revolving obsequiously round his unextinguishable gift of noble and lofty expression. My Intended, my station, my career, my ideas—these were the subjects for the occasional utterances of elevated sentiments. The shade of the original Kurtz frequented the bedside of the hollow sham, whose fate it was to be buried presently in the mould of primeval earth. But both the diabolic love and the unearthly hate of the mysteries it had penetrated fought for the possession of that soul satiated with primitive emotions, avid of lying fame, of sham distinction, of all the appearances of success and power.

'Sometimes he was contemptibly childish. He desired to have kings meet him at railway stations on his return from some ghastly Nowhere, where he intended to accomplish great things. "You show them you have in you something that is really profitable, and then there will be no limits to the recognition of your ability," he would say. "Of course you must take care of the motives—right motives—always." The long reaches that were like one and the same reach, monotonous bends that were exactly alike, slipped past the steamer with their multitude of secular [41] trees looking patiently after this grimy fragment of another world, the forerunner of change, of conquest, of trade, of massacres, of blessings. I looked ahead—piloting. "Close the shutter," said Kurtz suddenly one day; "I can't bear to look at this." I did so. There was a silence. "Oh, but I will wring your heart yet!" he cried at the invisible wilderness.

'We broke down—as I had expected—and had to lie up for repairs at the head of an island. This delay was the first thing that shook Kurtz's confidence.

41. Living through ages.

One morning he gave me a packet of papers and a photograph—the lot tied together with a shoe-string. "Keep this for me," he said. "This noxious fool" (meaning the manager) "is capable of prying into my boxes when I am not looking." In the afternoon I saw him. He was lying on his back with closed eyes, and I withdrew quietly, but I heard him mutter, "Live rightly, die, die . . ." I listened. There was nothing more. Was he rehearsing some speech in his sleep, or was it a fragment of a phrase from some newspaper article? He had been writing for the papers and meant to do so again, "for the furthering of my ideas. It's a duty."

'His was an impenetrable darkness. I looked at him as you peer down at a man who is lying at the bottom of a precipice where the sun never shines. But I had not much time to give him, because I was helping the engine-driver to take to pieces the leaky cylinders, to straighten a bent connecting-rod, and in other such matters. I lived in an infernal mess of rust, filings, nuts, bolts, spanners, hammers, ratchet-drills—things I abominate, because I don't get on with them. I tended the little forge we fortunately had aboard; I toiled wearily in a wretched scrap-heap—unless I had the shakes too bad to stand.

'One evening coming in with a candle I was startled to hear him say a little tremulously, "I am lying here in the dark waiting for death." The light was within a foot of his eyes. I forced myself to murmur, "Oh, nonsense!" and stood over him as if transfixed.

'Anything approaching the change that came over his features I have never seen before, and hope never to see again. Oh, I wasn't touched. I was fascinated. It was as though a veil had been rent. I saw on that ivory face the expression of sombre pride, of ruthless power, of craven terror—of an intense and hopeless despair. Did he live his life again in every detail of desire, temptation, and surrender during that supreme moment of complete knowledge? He cried in a whisper at some image, at some vision—he cried out twice, a cry that was no more than a breath:

' "The horror! The horror!" [42]

'I blew the candle out and left the cabin. The pilgrims were dining in the mess-room, and I took my place opposite the manager, who lifted his eyes to give me a questioning glance, which I successfully ignored. He leaned back, serene, with that peculiar smile of his sealing the unexpressed depths of his meanness. A continuous shower of small flies streamed upon the lamp, upon the cloth, upon our hands and faces. Suddenly the manager's boy put his insolent black head in the doorway, and said in a tone of scathing contempt:

' "Mistah Kurtz—he dead."

'All the pilgrims rushed out to see. I remained, and went on with my dinner. I believe I was considered brutally callous. However, I did not eat much. There was a lamp in there—light, don't you know—and outside it was so beastly, beastly dark. I went no more near the remarkable man who had pronounced a judgment upon the adventures of his soul on this earth. The voice was gone. What else had been there? But I am of course aware that next day the pilgrims buried something in a muddy hole.

42. The expression Eliot had wished to use as epigraph to *The Waste Land*. Later he used "Mistah Kurtz—he dead" as epigraph to "The Hollow Men," a poem imbued with the atmosphere of *Heart of Darkness*.

'And then they very nearly buried me.

'However, as you see, I did not go to join Kurtz there and then.[43] I did not. I remained to dream the nightmare out to the end, and to show my loyalty to Kurtz once more. Destiny. My destiny! Droll thing life is—that mysterious arrangement of merciless logic for a futile purpose. The most you can hope from it is some knowledge of yourself—that comes too late—a crop of unextinguishable regrets. I have wrestled with death. It is the most unexciting contest you can imagine. It takes place in an impalpable greyness, with nothing underfoot, with nothing around, without spectators, without clamour, without glory, without the great desire of victory, without the great fear of defeat, in a sickly atmosphere of tepid scepticism, without much belief in your own right, and still less in that of your adversary. If such is the form of ultimate wisdom, then life is a greater riddle than some of us think it to be. I was within a hair's-breadth of the last opportunity for pronouncement, and I found with humiliation that probably I would have nothing to say. This is the reason why I affirm that Kurtz was a remarkable man. He had something to say. He said it. Since I had peeped over the edge myself, I understand better the meaning of his stare, that could not see the flame of the candle, but was wide enough to embrace the whole universe, piercing enough to penetrate all the hearts that beat in the darkness. He had summed up—he had judged. "The horror!" He was a remarkable man. After all, this was the expression of some sort of belief; it had candour, it had conviction, it had a vibrating note of revolt in its whisper, it had the appalling face of a glimpsed truth—the strange commingling of desire and hate. And it is not my own extremity I remember best—a vision of greyness without form filled with physical pain, and a careless contempt for the evanescence of all things—even of this pain itself. No! It is his extremity that I seem to have lived through. True, he had made that last stride, he had stepped over the edge, while I had been permitted to draw back my hesitating foot. And perhaps in this is the whole difference; perhaps all the wisdom, and all truth, and all sincerity, are just compressed into that inappreciable moment of time in which we step over the threshold of the invisible. Perhaps! I like to think my summing-up would not have been a word of careless contempt. Better his cry—much better. It was an affirmation, a moral victory paid for by innumerable defeats, by abominable terrors, by abominable satisfactions. But it was a victory! That is why I have remained [44] loyal to Kurtz to the last, and even beyond, when a long time after I heard once more, not his own voice, but the echo of his magnificent eloquence thrown to me from a soul as translucently pure as a cliff of crystal.

'No, they did not bury me, though there is a period of time which I remember mistily, with a shuddering wonder, like a passage through some inconceivable world that had no hope in it and no desire. I found myself back in the sepulchral city resenting the sight of people hurrying through the streets to filch a little money from each other, to devour their infamous cookery, to gulp their unwholesome beer, to dream their insignificant and silly dreams. They trespassed upon my thoughts. They were intruders whose knowledge

43. With the odd implication that later he will.
44. "I remained" (one of Conrad's slight confusions of English tense).

of life was to me an irritating pretence, because I felt so sure they could not possibly know the things I knew. Their bearing, which was simply the bearing of commonplace individuals going about their business in the assurance of perfect safety, was offensive to me like the outrageous flauntings of folly in the face of a danger it is unable to comprehend. I had no particular desire to enlighten them, but I had some difficulty in restraining myself from laughing in their faces, so full of stupid importance. I daresay I was not very well at that time. I tottered about the streets—there were various affairs to settle—grinning bitterly at perfectly respectable persons. I admit my behaviour was inexcusable, but then my temperature was seldom normal in these days. My dear aunt's endeavours to "nurse up my strength" seemed altogether beside the mark. It was not my strength that wanted nursing, it was my imagination that wanted soothing. I kept the bundle of papers given me by Kurtz, not knowing exactly what to do with it. His mother had died lately, watched over, as I was told, by his Intended. A clean-shaved man, with an official manner and wearing gold-rimmed spectacles, called on me one day and made inquiries, at first circuitous, afterwards suavely pressing, about what he was pleased to denominate certain "documents." I was not surprised, because I had had two rows with the manager on the subject out there. I had refused to give up the smallest scrap out of that package, and I took the same attitude with the spectacled man. He became darkly menacing at last, and with much heat argued that the Company had the right to every bit of information about its "territories." And, said he, "Mr. Kurtz's knowledge of unexplored regions must have been necessarily extensive and peculiar—owing to his great abilities and to the deplorable circumstances in which he had been placed: there-fore——" I assured him Mr. Kurtz's knowledge, however extensive, did not bear upon the problems of commerce or administration. He invoked then the name of science. "It would be an incalculable loss if," etc. etc. I offered him the report on the "Suppression of Savage Customs," with the postscriptum torn off. He took it up eagerly, but ended by sniffing at it with an air of contempt. "This is not what we had a right to expect," he remarked. "Expect nothing else," I said. "There are only private letters." He withdrew upon some threat of legal proceedings, and I saw him no more; but another fellow, calling himself Kurtz's cousin, appeared two days later, and was anxious to hear all the details about his dear relative's last moments. Incidentally he gave me to understand that Kurtz had been essentially a great musician. "There was the making of an immense success," said the man, who was an organist, I believe, with lank grey hair flowing over a greasy coat-collar. I had no reason to doubt his statement; and to this day I am unable to say what was Kurtz's profession, whether he ever had any—which was the greatest of his talents. I had taken him for a painter who wrote for the papers, or else for a journalist who could paint—but even the cousin (who took snuff during the interview) could not tell me what he had been—exactly. He was a uni-versal genius—on that point I agreed with the old chap, who thereupon blew his nose noisily into a large cotton handkerchief and withdrew in senile agita-tion, bearing off some family letters and memoranda without importance. Ultimately a journalist anxious to know something of the fate of his "dear colleague" turned up. This visitor informed me Kurtz's proper sphere ought to have been politics "on the popular side." He had furry straight eyebrows, bristly hair cropped short, an eyeglass on a broad ribbon, and, becoming expansive, confessed his opinion that Kurtz really couldn't write a bit—"but Heavens! how that man could talk! He electrified large meetings. He had faith —don't you see?—he had the faith. He could get himself to believe anything— anything. He would have been a splendid leader of an extreme party." "What party?" I asked. "Any party," answered the other. "He was an—an—extremist." Did I not think so? I assented. Did I know, he asked, with a sudden flash of curiosity, "what it was that had induced him to go out there?" "Yes," said I, and forthwith handed him the famous Report for publication, if he thought fit. He glanced through it hurriedly, mumbling all the time, judged "it would do," and took himself off with this plunder.

'Thus I was left at last with a slim packet of letters and the girl's portrait. She struck me as beautiful—I mean she had a beautiful expression. I know that the sunlight can be made to lie too, yet one felt that no manipulation of light and pose could have conveyed the delicate shade of truthfulness upon those features. She seemed ready to listen without mental reservation, without suspicion, without a thought for herself. I concluded I would go and give her back her portrait and those letters myself. Curiosity? Yes; and also some other feeling perhaps. All that had been Kurtz's had passed out of my hands: his soul, his body, his station, his plans, his ivory, his career. There remained only his memory and his Intended—and I wanted to give that up too to the past, in a way—to surrender personally all that remained of him with me to that oblivion which is the last word of our common fate. I don't defend myself. I had no clear perception of what it was I really wanted. Perhaps it was an impulse of unconscious loyalty, or the fulfilment of one of those ironic necessities that lurk in the facts of human existence. I don't know. I can't tell. But I went.

'I thought his memory was like the other memories of the dead that accumulate in every man's life—a vague impress on the brain of shadows that had fallen on it in their swift and final passage; but before the high and ponderous door, between the tall houses of a street as still and decorous as a well-kept alley in a cemetery, I had a vision of him on the stretcher, opening his mouth voraciously, as if to devour all the earth with all its mankind. He lived then before me; he lived as much as he had ever lived—a shadow insatiable of splendid appearances, of frightful realities; a shadow darker than the shadow of the night, and draped nobly in the folds of a gorgeous eloquence. The vision seemed to enter the house with me—the stretcher, the phantom-bearers, the wild crowd of obedient worshippers, the gloom of the forests, the glitter of the reach between the murky bends, the beat of the drum, regular and muffled like the beating of a heart—the heart of a conquering darkness. It was a moment of triumph for the wilderness, an invading and vengeful rush which, it seemed to me, I would have to keep back alone for the salvation of another soul. And the memory of what I had heard him say afar there, with the horned shapes stirring at my back, in the glow of fires, within the patient woods, those broken phrases came back to me, were heard again in their ominous and terrifying simplicity. I remembered his abject pleading, his abject threats, the colossal scale of his vile desires, the meanness, the torment, the tempestuous anguish of his soul. And later on I seemed to see his collected languid manner, when he said one day, "This lot of ivory now is really mine. The Company did not pay for it. I collected it myself at a very great personal risk. I am afraid they will try to claim it as theirs though. H'm. It is a difficult case. What do you think I ought to do—resist? Eh? I want no more than justice.". . . He wanted no more than justice—no more than justice. I rang the bell before a mahogany door on the first floor, and while I waited he seemed to stare at me out of the glassy panel—stare with that wide and immense stare embracing, condemning, loathing all the universe. I seemed to hear the whispered cry, "The horror! The horror!"

'The dusk was falling. I had to wait in a lofty drawing-room with three long windows from floor to ceiling that were like three luminous and bedraped columns. The bent gilt legs and backs of the furniture shone in indistinct curves. The tall marble fireplace had a cold and monumental whiteness. A grand piano stood massively in a corner; with dark gleams on the flat surfaces like a sombre and polished sarcophagus. A high door opened—closed. I rose.

'She came forward, all in black, with a pale head, floating towards me in the dusk. She was in mourning. It was more than a year since his death, more than a year since the news came; she seemed as though she would remember and mourn for ever. She took both my hands in hers and murmured, "I had heard you were coming." I noticed she was not very young—I mean not girlish. She had a mature capacity for fidelity, for belief, for suffering. The room seemed to have grown darker, as if all the sad light of the cloudy evening had taken refuge on her forehead. This fair hair, this pale visage, this pure brow, seemed surrounded by an ashy halo from which the dark eyes looked out at me. Their glance was guileless, profound, confident, and trustful. She carried her sorrowful head as though she were proud of that sorrow, as though she would say, I—I alone know how to mourn for him as he deserves. But while we were still shaking hands, such a look of awful desolation came upon her face that I perceived she was one of those creatures that are not the playthings of Time. For her he had died only yesterday. And, by Jove! the impression was so powerful that for me too he seemed to have died only yesterday—nay, this very minute. I saw her and him in the same instant of time—his death and her sorrow—I saw her sorrow in the very moment of his death. Do you understand? I saw them together—I heard them together. She had said, with a deep catch of the breath, "I have survived"; while my strained ears seemed to hear distinctly, mingled with her tone of despairing regret, the summing-up whisper of his eternal condemnation. I asked myself what I was doing there, with a sensation of panic in my heart as though I had blundered into a place of cruel and absurd mysteries not fit for a human being to behold. She motioned me to a chair. We sat down. I laid the packet gently on the little table, and she put her hand over it. . . . "You knew him well," she murmured, after a moment of mourning silence.

'"Intimacy grows quickly out there," I said. "I knew him as well as it is possible for one man to know another."

'"And you admired him," she said. "It was impossible to know him and not to admire him. Was it?"

' "He was a remarkable man," I said unsteadily. Then before the appealing fixity of her gaze, that seemed to watch for more words on my lips, I went on, "It was impossible not to——"

' "Love him," she finished eagerly, silencing me into an appalled dumbness. "How true! how true! But when you think that no one knew him so well as I! I had all his noble confidence. I knew him best."

' "You knew him best," I repeated. And perhaps she did. But with every word spoken the room was growing darker, and only her forehead, smooth and white, remained illumined by the unextinguishable light of belief and love.

' "You were his friend," she went on. "His friend," she repeated, a little louder. "You must have been, if he had given you this, and sent you to me. I feel I can speak to you—and oh! I must speak. I want you—you who have heard his last words—to know I have been worthy of him. . . . It is not pride. . . . Yes! I am proud to know I understood him better than any one on earth—he told me so himself. And since his mother died I have had no one—no one—to—to——"

'I listened. The darkness deepened. I was not even sure whether he had given me the right bundle. I rather suspect he wanted me to take care of another batch of his papers which, after his death, I saw the manager examining under the lamp. And the girl talked, easing her pain in the certitude of my sympathy; she talked as thirsty men drink. I had heard that her engagement with Kurtz had been disapproved by her people. He wasn't rich enough or something. And indeed I don't know whether he had not been a pauper all his life. He had given me some reason to infer that it was his impatience of comparative poverty that drove him out there.

' ". . . Who was not his friend who had heard him speak once?" she was saying. "He drew men towards him by what was best in them." She looked at me with intensity. "It is the gift of the great," she went on, and the sound of her low voice seemed to have the accompaniment of all the other sounds, full of mystery, desolation, and sorrow, I had ever heard—the ripple of the river, the soughing of the trees swayed by the wind, the murmurs of the crowds, the faint ring of incomprehensible words cried from afar, the whisper of a voice speaking from beyond the threshold of an eternal darkness. "But you have heard him! You know!" she cried.

' "Yes, I know," I said with something like despair in my heart, but bowing my head before the faith that was in her, before that great and saving illusion that shone with an unearthly glow in the darkness, in the triumphant darkness from which I could not have defended her—from which I could not even defend myself.

' "What a loss to me—to us!"—she corrected herself with beautiful generosity; then added in a murmur, "To the world." By the last gleams of twilight I could see the glitter of her eyes, full of tears—of tears that would not fall.

' "I have been very happy—very fortunate—very proud," she went on. "Too fortunate. Too happy for a little while. And now I am unhappy for—for life."

'She stood up; her fair hair seemed to catch all the remaining light in a glimmer of gold. I rose too.

' "And of all this," she went on mournfully, "of all his promise, and of all his greatness, of his generous mind, of his noble heart, nothing remains—nothing but a memory. You and I——"

' "We shall always remember him," I said hastily.

' "No!" she cried. "It is impossible that all this should be lost—that such a life should be sacrificed to leave nothing—but sorrow. You know what vast plans he had. I knew of them too—I could not perhaps understand—but others knew of them. Something must remain. His words, at least, have not died."

' "His words will remain," I said.

' "And his example," she whispered to herself. "Men looked up to him—his goodness shone in every act. His example——"

' "True," I said; "his example too. Yes, his example. I forgot that."

' "But I do not. I cannot—I cannot believe—not yet. I cannot believe that I shall never see him again, that nobody will see him again, never, never, never."

'She put out her arms as if after a retreating figure, stretching them back and with clasped pale hands across the fading and narrow sheen of the window. Never see him! I saw him clearly enough then. I shall see this eloquent phantom as long as I live, and I shall see her too, a tragic and familiar Shade, resembling in this gesture another one, tragic also, and bedecked with powerless charms, stretching bare brown arms over the glitter of the infernal stream, the stream of darkness. She said suddenly very low, "He died as he lived."

' "His end," said I, with dull anger stirring in me, "was in every way worthy of his life."

' "And I was not with him," she murmured. My anger subsided before a feeling of infinite pity.

' "Everything that could be done——" I mumbled.

' "Ah, but I believed in him more than any one on earth—more than his own mother, more than—himself. He needed me! Me! I would have treasured every sigh, every word, every sign, every glance."

'I felt like a chill grip on my chest. "Don't," I said, in a muffled voice.

' "Forgive me. I—I—have mourned so long in silence—in silence. . . . You were with him—to the last? I think of his loneliness. Nobody near to understand him as I would have understood. Perhaps no one to hear . . ."

' "To the very end," I said shakily. "I heard his very last words. . . ." I stopped in a fright.

' "Repeat them," she murmured in a heart-broken tone. "I want—I want—something—something—to—to live with."

'I was on the point of crying at her, "Don't you hear them?" The dusk was repeating them in a persistent whisper all around us, in a whisper that seemed to swell menacingly like the first whisper of a rising wind. "The horror! The horror!"

' "His last word—to live with," she insisted. "Don't you understand I loved him—I loved him—I loved him!"

'I pulled myself together and spoke slowly.

' "The last word he pronounced was—your name."

'I heard a light sigh and then my heart stood still, stopped dead short by an exulting and terrible cry, by the cry of inconceivable triumph and of unspeakable pain. "I knew it—I was sure!". . . She knew. She was sure. I heard her weeping; she had hidden her face in her hands. It seemed to me that the house would collapse before I could escape, that the heavens would fall upon my head. But nothing happened. The heavens do not fall for such a trifle. Would they have fallen, I wonder, if I had rendered Kurtz that justice which was his due? Hadn't he said he wanted only justice? But I couldn't. I could not tell her. It would have been too dark—too dark altogether. . . .'

Marlow ceased, and sat apart, indistinct and silent, in the pose of a meditating Buddha. Nobody moved for a time. 'We have lost the first of the ebb,' said the Director suddenly. I raised my head. The offing was barred by a black bank of clouds, and the tranquil waterway leading to the uttermost ends of the earth flowed sombre under an overcast sky—seemed to lead into the heart of an immense darkness.

1899   1902

WILLIAM BUTLER YEATS
1865–1939

William Butler Yeats, eldest child of the painter John Butler Yeats, was born in Dublin on June 13, 1865. Two years later the Yeatses moved to London, but frequently visited County Sligo, where lived the family of the poet's mother, the Pollexfens. Yeats went to school first in London and, from 1880 to 1883, in Dublin. He then entered the Dublin School of Art, grew interested in the occult and, through the patriot John O'Leary, in the cause of Irish independence. Back in London in 1887, he made the acquaintance of William Morris, Oscar Wilde, and others, including Edwin J. Ellis, with whom he began work on an edition of William Blake. In 1889 appeared hs book *The Wanderings of Oisin;* and in the same year he met and fell in love with Maud Gonne, who was to figure so prominently in his poetry. In 1890 he joined the Order of the Golden Dawn, a secret society in which he held important office. The Rhymers' Club—a group of poets meeting in inns (of whom Yeats made the famous remark, "The one thing certain is that we are too many")—was founded in 1891, and Yeats became the friend of fellow members Lionel Johnson and Ernest Dowson (see Headnote to *Autobiographies*). *The Countess Cathleen,* a verse play for Maud Gonne (who in the previous year had issued the first of her many refusals to marry Yeats), appeared in 1892, and the essays called *The Celtic Twilight,* with the Blake edition, in the following year. In 1894 he visited Paris, and grew acquainted with some modern French poetry; the Symbolist aesthetic was explained to him by the poet-critic Arthur Symons, with whom he shared rooms for a time in 1895. This new interest was not inconsistent either with an interest in Blake or continuing research into the occult. *Poems* (1895) collected the lyrics of the early years. In 1896 he met Lady Augusta Gregory and John Millington Synge, both to have a profound effect on his life; in the following year he paid the first of his many visits to Lady Gregory's house at Coole in County Galway. He now had political and theatrical interests, and was writing a good deal of prose, but produced another volume of lyrics, *The Wind Among the Reeds,* in 1899. The theatrical interest resulted in his becoming president of the Irish National Dramatic Society and eventually, in 1904, opening, with Lady Gregory, the Abbey Theatre.

Poems 1895 1905 appeared in 1906, but this was mainly a period of "theatre business, management of men," of box-office takings and training actors, of handling many crises, notably the disturbances at the performance of Synge's *Playboy of the Western World* in 1907. In 1908 Bullen's eight-volume edition of the *Collected Works* was published, though Yeats had as yet written none of the poetry that established him as a major author. His father, who settled permanently in New York in that year, had always urged his son to interest himself in the concrete, for which, he said, Willie had a special gift that Celtic-twilight abstractions tended to conceal. Yeats was aware of this; as a poet he had always understood the need for concreteness, freshness, and flexibility, however tempted into fashionable vagueness. His involvement in the heated day-to-day business of the Dublin theater and politics, though he complained that it interfered with his poetry, may have helped him finally to approach his own and his father's ideal.

A new note is audible in *The Green Helmet and Other Poems* (1910); and, after an American tour with the Abbey troupe in 1911, he met another poet who would influence him decisively, Ezra Pound. Their relation is the nearest in literature to that of Haydn and Mozart in music, for the influence went both ways, and Pound's was perhaps the stronger, although he was twenty years Yeats's junior. In 1914 Pound married the daughter of Olivia Shakespear, Yeats's old friend; and Yeats, at the time working on the first part of his *Autobiographies,* published his most important volume of poetry so far, *Responsibilities.* Pound introduced him to the Japanese Nōh plays, and Yeats began to produce his plays for dancers, the first being *At the Hawk's Well* (1916). This was also the year of the Easter Rising in Dublin, and of Yeats's poem on the subject; he was to write many more about the troubles of Ireland. In 1917 he bought (for £35) an old Norman tower at Ballylee in Galway, near Lady Gregory's house. Again he proposed marriage to Maud Gonne, whose husband, Major Mac-Bride, had been executed by the British for his part in the Rising. Turned down, he proposed to Maud's daughter Iseult; turned down again, he proposed to and was accepted by Georgie Hyde-Lees, October 21, 1917.

This same year of 1917 marked the publication of the collection *The Wild Swans at Coole,* which is headed by the great elegy for Lady Gregory's son Robert and which contains a number of "system" poems: he was "hammering his thoughts into unity," working out an all-inclusive system of personality and history, as a means to realizing himself as an artist. A daughter was born in 1919, and a son in 1921, the year of the volumes *Michael Robartes and the Dancer* and *Four Plays for Dancers.* In 1922 Yeats bought a house in Dublin, but continued to spend his summers at the Tower in Ballylee. He became a senator of the new Irish Free State. Now he published a collection, *Later Poems,* and the part of his autobiography dealing with his life in the Nineties, *The Trembling of the Veil.* In 1923 he was awarded a Nobel Prize. At this time he was working on the first version of *A Vision,* his systematic world-philosophy, and reading widely if eccentrically in history and philosophy. After a winter in Sicily and Italy he returned to Ballylee and Dublin, and made a bold speech to the Senate in favor of divorce. The prose work *A Vision* appeared in January 1926. Though his health was now poor he produced what is probably his greatest single volume, *The Tower* (1928). He spent some time at Coole with the dying Lady Gregory, and wrote the poems that appeared in *The Winding Stair* (1933). In 1934 he underwent a Steinach operation for rejuvenation; it had certainly some such effect.

Yeats now produced an abundance of verse, prose, and plays, and in 1936 published the *Oxford Book of Modern Verse,* an idiosyncratic but fascinating anthology, and the dance-play *A Full Moon in March.* He formed new friendships, notably with the poet Dorothy Wellesley, began the extraordinary "Rabelaisian" verse-play *The Herne's Egg,* and gave a radio lecture on modern poetry; his correspondence is especially rich at this time. Adoption of a new "mask," that of the wild old man, recruited his physical energy, and he gave exciting broadcasts of his poetry. The fuller revised version of *A Vision* appeared in 1937. In 1938 he moved to the south of France, and wrote the pamphlet *On the Boiler,* a miscellany of opinions reflecting his flirtation with fascism and with eugenics. He wrote the play *Purgatory,* performed in his presence at the Abbey in August 1938, and at the end of the year began his last play, *The Death of Cuchulain,* in which a wild old man like Yeats himself speaks an excited prologue. He fell ill at the beginning of 1939 and died on January 28. He was buried at Roquebrune; the body was taken to Drumcliffe Churchyard near Sligo in September 1948.

There are many aspects of Yeats's work that cannot be represented in a selection of thirty-odd poems and a few short prose extracts—a whole corpus of plays of many kinds, a lifework of speculation on politics, verse, the occult. And it is in the hammered unity of all this that his greatness lies. Nevertheless his poems—even when they are not expressly "system" poems—refer to his occult beliefs, as well as to his personal life and the politics of Ireland. The notes explain particular allusions, but a general word of introduction may be useful.

Yeats needed a system not because he needed abstract and systematic thought, but because he saw that the *oeuvre* of a writer is fragmentary and multiple unless one poem "lights up another"—unless all refer, somehow, to an integral whole, namely, the poet; so that the poet needs also to be possessed of some arrangement of beliefs that suggests and promotes the sense of his unity. The world itself, at the period of history he found himself in, was "but a bundle of fragments," and the establishment of some fiction of integrity that would serve a poet in such a world was his own responsibility: it could not, he felt, be done by a church, or by science. It would be achieved at great cost, and as the *Autobiographies* and other works demonstrate, Yeats was so keenly aware of this cost that he judged his own life, and those of his friends, by asking how they paid the cost as well as how near they came to their goal. What was needed in the poet was something the world had lost: confidence in that universal humanity represented by the stored images of the unconscious, the complementary dreams of noble and beggarman that had been destroyed, like all the fine things of traditional civilization, by the rise of the middle classes, the "shopkeeping logicians." Yeats made a remarkably clear statement of what he was after in the opening sentences of an essay on magic, written as early as 1901.

> I believe in the practice and the philosophy of what we have agreed to call magic . . . in the vision of truth in the depths of the mind when the eyes are closed; and I believe in three doctrines, which have, as I think, been handed down from early times, and been the foundation of nearly all magical practices. These doctrines are:
> (1) That the borders of the mind are ever shifting, and that many minds can flow into one another, as it were, and create or reveal a single mind, a single energy.
> (2) That the borders of our memories are a part of one great memory, the memory of Nature herself.
> (3) That this great mind and great memory can be evoked by symbols. . . .
> *Essays and Introductions,* 1961, p. 28

Yeats first thought to reach down to this Great Memory through Irish folktale and, in ever more sophisticated forms, continued to do so, as we see for example from the late poem "The Statues," the last play, *The Death of Cuchulain,* and the last poem, "Cuchulain Comforted." But he also extended his interest far beyond any national boundary, and—although he was not a learned man in the usual sense—sought to include in one package an interpretation of the whole of history and the whole range of human personality. Steeped in the symbolism of Shelley and Blake—he had edited Blake, and knew what a poet's "system" might involve—he had also before him the example of many occult traditions, all seeking some unitary explanation of the world and the soul.

One such system was that of Mme. H. P. Blavatsky (1831–91) and the Theosophical Society, which Yeats had joined in 1887. Madame Blavatsky's elaborate system (expounded in *Isis Unveiled,* 1877) was adapted from Indian philosophy and involved cyclical time and reincarnation, among other things. Although Yeats later broke with the Theosophists, their influence on his thought was considerable. Another system was that of the Cabbalist and ritualist MacGregor Mathers, who introduced Yeats to the society of the Hermetic Students of the Order of the Golden Dawn. With symbol and system Yeats sought access to a place he later called simply, after Plotinus, "There," some center where everything came together. What he was trying to get together, for the sake of major poetry, was himself. He was convinced that his was the age of "the trembling of the veil" (see notes on *Autobiographies*)—that in a disintegrating world, a world near some terrible apocalypse, the way to stand up to the terrors, to resist the appeals of the decadence, was to renew oneself. Hence his system of belief, thought necessary to the avoidance of "multiplicity" in the personality, grew ever more elaborate; and there was a decisive development when it emerged that his new wife, married in 1917, had the gift of automatic writing.

Yeats had been melancholy; now he had "Instructors," who elaborated his thought for him in communications from the spirit world, from "There." These communications led to the doctrinal poems of *Michael Robartes and the Dancer* (1921) and eventually to the system explained in the first and second versions of *A Vision* (1925, 1937). These books assume that *everything* is interrelated, all history, theology, biography; and so all poetry, and in particular all Yeats's poetry, may be. Of the elements of this system the primary and antithetical gyres, the Great Wheel, the Mask, and the Daimon, there is no need to say anything here. Yeats called it his "lunar parable." "Some will ask whether I believe in the actual existence of my circuits of the sun and moon," he wrote, evidently aware that all this raised a problem of belief.

> To such a question I can but answer that if sometimes, overwhelmed by miracle as all men must be when in the midst of it, I have taken such periods literally, my reason has soon recovered; and now that the system stands out clearly in my imagination I regard them as stylistic arrangements of experience comparable to the cubes in the drawings of Wyndham Lewis and to the ovoids in the sculpture of Brancusi. They have helped me to hold in a single thought reality and justice.

The system gave point to Yeats's profound belief in the apocalyptic character of his time, and in his own role and that of the artist in general. That is its justification; it gave him, as he said of his spirit "Instructors," "metaphors for poetry," and for a poetry that should be founded on a single intelligible world in his mind. In this world, as Yeats said in that most memorable sentence, reality and justice constitute but a single thought. Elsewhere they are perpetually at odds. So *A Vision* makes great poetry a project the visionary can sustain; it is, as Yeats said, "a last defence against the chaos of the world."

What is the direct effect on the poetry? There are some poems—"The Phases of the Moon" and "Ego Dominus Tuus" are examples, both written in the first flush of the new "instructions" mediated by his wife—in which Yeats is frankly doctrinal; yet in spite of that they are still, and primarily, poems; the doctrines give Yeats some memorable metaphors and sonorities. He was, even in these extremities, an artist first. There are other poems—"Leda and the Swan," for instance, or "The Second Coming" —which have established themselves as memorable with readers who know and care nothing about the doctrines they certainly do contain. It may be said that in some others—e.g., "Byzantium" with its "Hades' bobbin," or "The Statues," where some very unfamiliar cultural propositions are presented only elliptically—Yeats's allusions to doctrine are too curt, too idiosyncratic, and that the casual technicality of the references damages the poem. It may be so; it grew more probable that such things should happen when Yeats, in old age, deliberately cultivated a dashing, nonchalant attitude toward the reader. His *Last Poems*, which struck everybody dumb with admiration when they appeared (1940), now seem to fall too often into intellectual or rhetorical posturing; the precision of his work in the 1920's is a world ill lost if the reward is the self-indulgent rant of "Under Ben Bulben." And by the same token it may be that at times, in the late poems, the system mastered its master. But how rarely this occurred!

Yeats's passion for making and remaking himself led him to revise his early work; it might contain elements of later thought, and be made, by a few touches, to conform to a later pattern. These revisions are sometimes substantial, when an old essay or story is integrated into a pattern later evolved; sometimes they are matters of detail, the artist in search of the concrete, the flexible, hating the tired or conventional rhythm. Some instances of revision are mentioned in the notes. The process was not always, in the opinions of other readers than its author, successful. But it was part of the process of making oneself whole from moment to moment. The need for stylistic changes in the early poetry is thus part of the same process that led Yeats to revise and expand his system. What developed—perhaps at the cost of a few spoiled poems—was the extraordinary certainty and range of the mature Yeatsian style. This style became an instrument equal to the demands of a great variety of themes— personal, political, doctrinal—and of kinds—song, ballad, romantic meditation, elegy, tragedy—without the loss of what Yeats himself regarded as essential: the powerful and true impression of the whole poet at work behind it.

The Sorrow of Love

The quarrel of the sparrows in the eaves,
The full round moon and the star-laden sky,
And the loud song of the ever-singing leaves
Had hid away earth's old and weary cry.

And then you came with those red mournful lips,
And with you came the whole of the world's tears,

And all the sorrows of her labouring ships,
And all the burden of her myriad years.

And now the sparrows warring in the eaves,
10   The crumbling moon, the white stars in the sky,
And the loud chanting of the unquiet leaves,
Are shaken with earth's old and weary cry.
1891   1892

[This version of "The Sorrow of Love" was written in 1891 and went through several
revisions before it appeared in its final form—given below—in *Early Poems and Stories*
(1927). Yeats mentions it as an instance of a new poem produced by rewriting an old
one. In the revision he was avoiding what came to strike him as inert diction (*star-
laden, ever-singing, weary*) and evidently thought *brawling* tougher than *quarrel*. He
gave up the gentle, relaxed anaphora of the second stanza; the moon, which had been
crumbling and then *curd-pale,* was set in action. Yeats liked to use *famous* in a semi-
journalistic way from the 1920's on, and does so in line 3. Some florid alliterations are
introduced. The last line is so changed as to give the poem a different and obscurer
sense. Yeats's search for a harsher and more modern diction went on through these
years, and these versions are a slight indication of its direction.]

The Sorrow of Love

The brawling of a sparrow in the eaves,
The brilliant moon and all the milky sky,
And all that famous harmony of leaves,
Had blotted out man's image and his cry.

A girl° arose that had red mournful lips
And seemed the greatness of the world in tears,
Doomed like Odysseus° and the labouring ships
And proud as Priam° murdered with his peers;

Arose, and on the instant clamorous eaves,
10   A climbing moon upon an empty sky,
And all that lamentation of the leaves,
Could but compose man's image and his cry.
1922   1927

The Two Trees

"The Two Trees" was much altered between its first appearance in 1892 and the
definitive version, which was established in *Selected Poems* (1929): e.g., lines 13–16:

girl Helen of Troy, who often occurs in Yeat's
poetry, usually standing for Maud Gonne
Odysseus After successfully planning the capture of Troy Odysseus (Ulysses) spent ten
years wandering about the Mediterranean on
his way home to Thrace.
Priam king of Troy killed by Neoptolemus, the
son of Achilles

"There, through bewildered branches, go / Winged Loves borne on in gentle strife, / Tossing and tossing to and fro / The flaming circle of our life." The revisions emphasize the difference between the anti-intellectual tree of life and the dead rottenness of the other tree. Yeats had in mind one of Blake's *Poetical Sketches:* "Love and harmony combine, / And around our souls entwine, / While thy branches meet with mine, / And our roots together join. / Joys upon our branches sit, / Chirping loud and singing sweet; / Like gentle streams beneath our feet / Innocence and virtue meet. . . ." He remembered also Blake's later comment: "Art is the Tree of Life . . . Science is the Tree of Death" (*The Laocoon Group*).

His second tree is introspection, thought, the ruin of the body by the abstract mind which Yeats especially deplored in women (see "Michael Robartes and the Dancer," "In Memory of Eva Gore-Booth . . . ," "Easter 1916," as examples). In *Ideas of Good and Evil*, a Blakean book with a Blakean title, he asserts that "men who sought their food among the green leaves of the Tree of Life condemned none but the unimaginative and the idle, and those who forget that even love and death and old age are an imaginative art." Another source is the Cabbala, in which the Sephirotic Tree has two aspects, one benign, one malign. Yeats records in an essay on magic that he found in MacGregor Mathers's book *The Kabbalah Unveiled* this passage: "The Tree . . . is the Tree of the Knowledge of Good and Evil . . . in its branches the birds lodge and build their nests. . . ." He may have remembered Milton's Satan, who "on the tree of Life, . . . / Sat like a cormorant" (*Paradise Lost* IV.194–96).

The Two Trees

Belovèd, gaze in thine own heart,
The holy tree is growing there;
From joy the holy branches start,
And all the trembling flowers they bear.
The changing colours of its fruit
Have dowered the stars with merry light;
The surety of its hidden root
Has planted quiet in the night;
The shaking of its leafy head
Has given the waves their melody,
And made my lips and music wed,
Murmuring a wizard song for thee.
There the Loves a circle go,
The flaming circle of our days,
Gyring, spiring to and fro
In those great ignorant° leafy ways;
Remembering all that shaken hair
And how the wingèd sandals dart,
Thine eyes grow full of tender care:
Belovèd, gaze in thine own heart.

ignorant This revision enables Yeats to emphasize
the vital absence of abstraction and intellect
in the good tree.

Gaze no more in the bitter glass
The demons, with their subtle guile,
Lift up before us when they pass,
Or only gaze a little while;
For there a fatal image grows
That the stormy night receives,
Roots half hidden under snows,
Broken boughs and blackened leaves.
For all things turn to barrenness
30 In the dim glass the demons hold,
The glass of outer weariness,
Made when God slept in times of old.
There, through the broken branches, go
The ravens of unresting thought;
Flying, crying, to and fro,
Cruel claw and hungry throat,
Or else they stand and sniff the wind,
And shake their ragged wings; alas!
Thy tender eyes grow all unkind:
40 Gaze no more in the bitter glass.

1929

Adam's Curse°

We sat together at one summer's end,
That beautiful mild woman, your close friend,
And you and I, and talked of poetry.
I said, 'A line will take us hours maybe;
Yet if it does not seem a moment's thought,
Our stitching and unstitching has been naught.

Better go down upon your marrow-bones
And scrub a kitchen pavement, or break stones
Like an old pauper, in all kinds of weather;
10 For to articulate sweet sounds together
Is to work harder than all these, and yet
Be thought an idler by the noisy set
Of bankers, schoolmasters, and clergymen
The martyrs call the world.'

And thereupon

That beautiful mild woman for whose sake
There's many a one shall find out all heartache
On finding that her voice is sweet and low
Replied, 'To be born woman is to know—

Adam's Curse Adam's curse is the need to labor
(Genesis 3:19). The poem is for Maud Gonne,
who recounts in her autobiography (*A Servant*
of the Queen, 1938) the occasion commemorated; the friend had remarked that it "was
hard work being beautiful."

Although they do not talk of it at school°—
That we must labour to be beautiful.'°

I said, 'It's certain there is no fine thing
Since Adam's fall but needs much labouring.
There have been lovers who thought love should be
So much compounded of high courtesy
That they would sigh and quote with learned looks
Precedents out of beautiful old books;°
Yet now it seems an idle trade enough.'

We sat grown quiet at the name of love;
We saw the last embers of daylight die,
And in the trembling blue-green of the sky
A moon, worn as if it had been a shell
Washed by time's waters as they rose and fell
About the stars and broke in days and years.

I had a thought for no one's but your ears:
That you were beautiful, and that I strove
To love you in the old high way of love;
That it had all seemed happy, and yet we'd grown
As weary-hearted as that hollow moon.
1902?   1902

No Second Troy°

Why should I blame her that she filled my days
With misery, or that she would of late
Have taught to ignorant men most violent ways,
Or hurled the little streets upon the great,°
Had they but courage equal to desire?°
What could have made her peaceful with a mind
That nobleness made simple as a fire,
With beauty like a tightened bow, a kind
That is not natural in an age like this,
Being high and solitary and most stern?°

at school See concluding line of "Michael Robartes and the Dancer."
labour . . . beautiful In *Discoveries* (1907) Yeats has a passage called "The Looking Glass," telling of a girl fresh from school, where she has had her memory, but not her imagination, cultivated; hence her awkward movements and monotonous voice. She should have been taught "the heroic discipline of the looking-glass."
So much . . . books Yeats is thinking of the elaborate Renaissance cult of love and courtesy, which we now associate chiefly with Castiglione, a writer Yeats was to grow more interested in later on.
No Second Troy From Yeats's diary; the second Helen is Maud Gonne.

hurled . . . great called out the mob against its aristocratic betters
Had . . . desire Reference is to Maud Gonne's revolutionary activities. In various ways she stirred up the Irish against the English, though in Yeats's view of the Catholic middle class and urban poor (often expressed) the Irish lacked the nerve to carry out this violence. When they did Yeats recanted ("Easter 1916" and elsewhere).
high . . . stern One of several such allusions to Maud Gonne; see the mention of her in *Autobiographies*: ". . . great stature . . . solitary . . . her face, like the face of some Greek statue, showed little thought" (p. 364).

Why, what could she have done, being what she is?
Was there another Troy for her to burn?
1908   1910

A Drinking Song°

Wine comes in at the mouth
And love comes in at the eye;
That's all we shall know for truth
Before we grow old and die.
I lift the glass to my mouth,
I look at you, and I sigh.
1910   1910

To a Friend Whose Work Has Come to Nothing°

Now all the truth is out,
Be secret and take defeat
From any brazen throat,
For how can you compete,
Being honour bred, with one°
Who, were it proved he lies,
Were neither shamed in his own
Nor in his neighbours' eyes?
Bred to a harder thing
10   Than Triumph, turn away
And like a laughing string
Whereon mad fingers play
Amid a place of stone,
Be secret and exult,
Because of all things known
That is most difficult.
1913   1914

The Cold Heaven°

Suddenly I saw the cold and rook-delighting heaven
That seemed as though ice burned and was but the more ice,
And thereupon imagination and heart were driven
So wild that every casual thought of that and this
Vanished, and left but memories, that should be out of season
With the hot blood of youth, of love crossed long ago;
And I took all the blame out of all sense and reason,
Until I cried and trembled and rocked to and fro,
Riddled with light. Ah! when the ghost begins to quicken,
Confusion of the death-bed over, is it sent
Out naked on the roads, as the books say, and stricken
By the injustice of the skies for punishment?
1910   1910

The Magi°

Now as at all times I can see in the mind's eye,
In their stiff, painted clothes, the pale unsatisfied ones
Appear and disappear in the blue depth of the sky
With all their ancient faces like rain-beaten stones,
And all their helms of silver hovering side by side,
And all their eyes still fixed, hoping to find once more,
Being by Calvary's turbulence unsatisfied,
The uncontrollable mystery on the bestial floor.
1913   1914

In Memory of Major Robert Gregory

Yeats admired Lady Gregory's son Robert (1881–1918) as scholar, horseman, and painter, and when he was killed fighting with the English on the Italian front as a Royal Flying Corps major (January 23, 1918) the poet sought to make a fitting elegy. Preparations were going forward to make the Tower habitable for Yeats and his wife, and its associations with the Gregory family and Coole brought it into his thoughts. It took half a year to produce the poem we now have. Yeats wrote about Gregory in his diary and in letters, and also composed, for the London *Observer*, an obituary containing many of the germs of the poem he eventually produced: it celebrates the

The Cold Heaven A poem partly about Yeats's lost love Maud Gonne, and partly on the theme (to which he returns later) that at death we live our lives again backward (the "dreaming back") and so "live it all again"—all the indignities and suffering; in this moment he seems to be enduring again the pains of his youth, as the dead must.

The Magi The new life found by the Magi at the Epiphany (see Matthew 2:9), with its sequel, the Crucifixion, is not the annunciation of a new cycle of time which will end only with the end of the world; there will be more such "uncontrollable mysteries" because time is cyclical (a notion that later grew very important to Yeats). The Magi, therefore, are perpetually seeking a recurrence. Contrast Eliot's "Journey of the Magi," where what disconcerts the wise men is precisely the finality of what they have witnessed. See the second of "Two Songs from a Play" (below) for further associations of violence with the birth of Christ.

young man's courage and athletic prowess, and discusses his genius as a painter in the line of "visionary landscape" which, according to Yeats, originated with Blake. He sees Gregory as using action to escape from contemplation, from "the growing absorption of his dream."

Yeats heard the news of Gregory's death when he was in Oxford working on Palmer and Calvert, the heirs of Blake and continuators of the tradition of visionary landscape; but he did not at once build a poem on this foundation. First he tried—struck by a resemblance between Gregory and Sir Philip Sidney—to write a pastoral elegy on the pattern of Spenser's *Astrophel,* which mourns Sidney's death in action. This version, which includes a passage on the doctrine of "dreaming-back" at death, stands in Yeats's *Collected Poems,* but is not a success. Yeats then wrote "An Irish Airman Foresees His Death," a short poem about Gregory's delight in action, even on behalf of an alien power. In the present poem, finished by June 14, Yeats moved on from Spenser to Cowley's "Ode on the Death of Mr. William Harvey," the stanza of which he exactly imitates (he uses it again in "A Prayer for My Daughter" and the second poem of *The Tower* sequence).

Yeats's poem is basically about an artist who broke out of that dream into a brief life of action. The eighth stanza was inserted at the request of Gregory's widow, who thought the poem said too little about her husband's physical courage; and it is arguable that the poem is better without it, since the seventh and ninth stanzas are obviously related. Gregory is refined into a symbolic artist, breaking out of the horror of the artist's isolation into activity and death, achieving the condition Yeats called Unity of Being, something more easily achieved in the period 1450–1550 A.D. than in the collapsing modern world. Other artists and contemplatives appear in the poem as a means of measuring the plight and the achievement of its hero. And as is usual in such elegies, the hero is as it were a mask of the poet himself; this poem is as much about Yeats as *Lycidas* is about Milton.

In Memory of Major Robert Gregory

I

Now that we're almost settled in our house°
I'll name the friends that cannot sup with us
Beside a fire of turf° in th' ancient tower,
And having talked to some late hour
Climb up the narrow winding stair to bed:
Discoverers of forgotten truth°
Or mere companions of my youth,
All, all are in my thoughts to-night being dead.

II

Always we'd have the new friend meet the old
10   And we are hurt if either friend seem cold,

---

house the Tower (Thoor Ballylee)
turf peat (commonly cut from the bogs as fuel in Ireland)

Discoverers . . . truth the occultist friends of his youth

And there is salt to lengthen out the smart
In the affections of our heart,
And quarrels are blown up upon that head;
But not a friend that I would bring
This night can set us quarrelling,
For all that come into my mind are dead.

III

Lionel Johnson comes the first to mind,
That loved his learning better than mankind,
Though courteous to the worst; much falling he
Brooded upon sanctity
Till all his Greek and Latin learning seemed
A long blast upon the horn that brought
A little nearer to his thought
A measureless consummation that he dreamed.°

IV

And that enquiring man John Synge comes next,
That dying chose the living world for text
And never could have rested in the tomb
But that, long travelling, he had come
Towards nightfall upon certain set apart
In a most desolate stony place,
Towards nightfall upon a race
Passionate and simple like his heart.°

V

And then I think of old George Pollexfen,
In muscular youth well known to Mayo men
For horsemanship at meets or at racecourses,
That could have shown how pure-bred horses
And solid men, for all their passion, live
But as the outrageous stars incline
By opposition, square and trine:
Having grown sluggish and contemplative.°

Lionel . . . dreamed Lionel Johnson (1867–1902), learned poet, member of the Rhymers' Club, devout Catholic, and believer in the poet as the third order of priesthood (with priest and deacon). He drank heavily and often fell down stairs; he died by falling off a barstool. But he also wrote, in "Mystic and Cavalier," "Go from me: I am one of those who fall."
And that . . . heart (ll.25–32) Yeats met Synge (1871–1909) in Paris in 1896, and persuaded him to go to the Aran Islands off the west coast of Ireland, having recently been there himself. Synge went, and listened to the talk of the islanders; one of the results was *The Playboy of the Western World* (1907), which caused riots when Yeats staged it at the Abbey; Yeats defended it fiercely. Placing Synge in the Twenty-third Phase of his lunar division of personalities, Yeats observed that he was one of those "who must not pursue an image, but fly from it. . . . He had to take the first plunge into the world beyond himself" (*Autobiographies*, p. 344).
And then . . . contemplative (ll. 33–40) George Pollexfen, Yeats's maternal uncle, lived near Sligo, and as a boy Yeats had discussed occult and folk beliefs with him. He was a gloomy man, yet he kept himself fit with Indian clubs when he gave up riding, and became interested in astrology (*incline, opposition, square, trine* are technical terms in that discipline). The first two friends escape the contemplative by excessive action; Pollexfen does not.

VI

They were my close companions many a year,
A portion of my mind and life, as it were,
And now their breathless faces seem to look
Out of some old picture-book;
I am accustomed to their lack of breath,
But not that my dear friend's dear son,
Our Sidney and our perfect man,
Could share in that discourtesy of death.

VII

For all things the delighted eye now sees
50   Were loved by him:° the old storm-broken trees
That cast their shadows upon road and bridge;
The tower set on the stream's edge;
The ford where drinking cattle make a stir
Nightly, and startled by that sound
The water-hen must change her ground;
He might have been your heartiest welcomer.

VIII

When with the Galway foxhounds he would ride
From Castle Taylor to the Roxborough side
Or Esserkelly plain, few kept his pace;
60   At Mooneen he had leaped a place
So perilous that half the astonished meet
Had shut their eyes; and where was it
He rode a race without a bit?
And yet his mind outran the horses' feet.

IX

We dreamed that a great painter had been born
To cold Clare rock and Galway rock and thorn,
To that stern colour and that delicate line
That are our secret discipline
Wherein the gazing heart doubles her might.
70   Soldier, scholar, horseman, he,
And yet he had the intensity
To have published all to be a world's delight.

X

What other could so well have counselled us
In all lovely intricacies of a house
As he that practised or that understood
All work in metal or in wood,

loved by him Gregory, who studied at the
Slade, a London art school, made some drawings of the Tower and its surroundings.

In moulded plaster or in carven stone?
Soldier, scholar, horseman, he,
And all he did done perfectly,
As though he had but that one trade alone.

XI

Some burn damp faggots, others may consume
The entire combustible world in one small room
As though dried straw, and if we turn about
The bare chimney is gone black out
Because the work had finished in that flare.
Soldier, scholar, horseman, he,
As 'twere all life's epitome.
What made us dream that he could comb grey hair?

XII

I had thought, seeing how bitter is that wind
That shakes the shutter, to have brought to mind
All those that manhood tried, or childhood loved
Or boyish intellect approved,
With some appropriate commentary on each;
Until imagination brought
A fitter welcome; but a thought
Of that late death took all my heart for speech.
1918   1919

The Scholars

Bald heads forgetful of their sins,
Old, learned, respectable bald heads
Edit and annotate the lines
That young men, tossing on their beds,
Rhymed out in love's despair
To flatter beauty's ignorant ear.

All shuffle there; all cough in ink;
All wear the carpet with their shoes;
All think what other people think;
All know the man their neighbour knows.
Lord, what would they say
Did their Catullus° walk that way?
1914–1915   1919

Catullus Gaius Valerius Catullus (84–54 B.C.),   obscene love poetry addressed to "Lesbia"
Roman author of passionate and sometimes   (Clodia, wife of a consul)

A Thought from Propertius°

She might, so noble from head
To great shapely knees
The long flowing line,
Have walked to the altar
Through the holy images
At Pallas Athene's° side,
Or been fit spoil for a centaur
Drunk with the unmixed wine.°
1915   1919

A Deep-Sworn Vow°

Others because you did not keep
That deep-sworn vow have been friends of mine;
Yet always when I look death in the face,
When I clamber to the heights of sleep,
Or when I grow excited with wine,
Suddenly I meet your face.
1915   1919

Michael Robartes and the Dancer°

HE   Opinion° is not worth a rush;
     In this altar-piece° the knight,
     Who grips his long spear so to push
     That dragon through the fading light,
     Loved the lady; and it's plain
     The half-dead dragon was her thought,
     That every morning rose again
     And dug its claws and shrieked and fought.
     Could the impossible come to pass
10   She would have time to turn her eyes,
     Her lover thought, upon the glass
     And on the instant would grow wise.°

SHE   You mean they argued.

HE   Put it so;
But bear in mind your lover's wage
Is what your looking-glass can show,
And that he will turn green with rage
At all that is not pictured there.

SHE   May I not put myself to college?

HE   Go pluck Athene by the hair;°
For what mere book can grant a knowledge
With an impassioned gravity
Appropriate to that beating breast,
That vigorous thigh, that dreaming eye?
And may the Devil take the rest.

SHE   And must no beautiful woman be
Learned like a man?

HE   Paul Veronese°
And all his sacred company
Imagined bodies all their days
By the lagoon you love so much,
For proud, soft, ceremonious proof
That all must come to sight and touch;
While Michael Angelo's Sistine roof,
His 'Morning' and his 'Night'° disclose
How sinew that has been pulled tight,
Or it may be loosened in repose,
Can rule by supernatural right
Yet be but sinew.

SHE   I have heard said
There is great danger in the body.

HE   Did God in portioning wine and bread
Give man His thought or His mere body?°

SHE   My wretched dragon° is perplexed.

HE   I have principles to prove me right.
It follows from this Latin text

Go . . . hair Seize (the goddess of) wisdom by violence. Yeats was opposed to orthodox education for girls, believing that it caused a separation of body and mind.
Veronese (1525–88), last of the great Venetian painters. Here he is commended (as Yeats always commended the High Renaissance artists) for his power to combine thought and feeling, sense and intellect.
Michael Angelo's . . . 'Night' Michelangelo Buonarroti (1475–1564) painted the Sistine ceiling (1508–12) for Pope Julius II; Yeats may be thinking of the figure of Adam touched into life by God. "Morning" and "Night" are statues in the Medici chapel in Florence: "Morning" a male figure, awakening and angry; "Night" a female in uneasy sleep—hence the "sinews pulled tight" and "loosened."
Did . . . body A reference to the Eucharist, the blood and body of Christ present in the wine and bread. This sacramental defense of the argument gives it a surprising seriousness. *Mere* is used almost in the old sense of *pure* (uncontaminated by thought)—as Queen Elizabeth claimed to be "mere English."
dragon her intellect

> That blest souls are not composite,°
> And that all beautiful women may
> Live in uncomposite blessedness,
> And lead us to the like—if they
> Will banish every thought, unless
> The lineaments that please their view
> When the long looking-glass is full,
> Even from the foot-sole think it too.°

50

SHE   They say such different things at school.°
1916   1921

Easter 1916°

I have met them° at close of day
Coming with vivid faces
From counter or desk among grey
Eighteenth-century houses.°
I have passed with a nod of the head
Or polite meaningless words,
Or have lingered awhile and said
Polite meaningless words,
And thought before I had done
Of a mocking tale or a gibe
To please a companion
Around the fire at the club,
Being certain that they and I
But lived where motley° is worn:
All changed, changed utterly:
A terrible beauty is born.

10

That woman's° days were spent
In ignorant good-will,

not composite One soul is diffused throughout
the body; there are not separate compartments
for body and mind.
unless . . . too That is, no thought is allowed
unless the body thinks it; as in Donne's famous
lines, which Yeats knew and admired: ". . .
her pure and eloquent blood / Spoke in her
cheeks, and so distinctly wrought" / That one
might almost say, her body thought" (The Second Anniversary, ll. 243–45).
They . . . school See note on "Adam's Curse."
Yeats's condemnation of education for girls was
perfectly serious.
Easter 1916 On April 24, 1916, the Irish
Republican Brotherhood organized a rebellion
against the English. They proclaimed an Irish
Republic and, after much fighting, occupied
central Dublin. The rebellion collapsed on
April 29 and its leaders were subsequently executed. One of them was Major John MacBride,
estranged husband of Maud Gonne. Another
military commander was Constance Markiewicz
(née Gore-Booth), daughter of the great house
at Lissadell near Sligo, whom Yeats had known

since 1894; she was sentenced to penal servitude for life but was later released. The Rising,
though fundamentally a miscalculation, gave a
new aura of heroism to the cause of Irish
freedom. Yeats was with Maud Gonne in France
when he heard the news, and felt at first "that
all the work of the years has been overturned."
But Maud Gonne told him that "tragic dignity
has returned to Ireland." And he was moved as
never before by a public event. The poem is
dated September 25, 1916, in the manuscript,
and appeared both in a periodical and in a
privately printed edition before publication in
Michael Robartes and the Dancer. In the interim
it was greatly improved by revision.
them the revolutionary leaders
Eighteenth-century houses Central Dublin was
largely an 18th-century city, and is still strongly
Georgian in appearance.
motley parti-colored dress of the fool
woman's Constance Markiewicz (1868–1927),
the daughter of the Gore-Booths and wife of a
Polish count. See also "On a Political Prisoner"
and "In Memory of Eva Gore-Booth and Con

Her nights in argument
Until her voice grew shrill.
What voice more sweet than hers
When, young and beautiful,
She rode to harriers?
This man° had kept a school
And rode our wingèd horse;
This other° his helper and friend
Was coming into his force;
He might have won fame in tho end,
So sensitive his nature seemed,
So daring and sweet his thought.
This other man I had dreamed
A drunken, vainglorious lout.°
He had done most bitter wrong
To some who are near my heart,
Yet I number him in the song;
He, too, has resigned his part
In the casual comedy;
He, too, has been changed in his turn,
Transformed utterly:
A terrible beauty is born.

Hearts with one purpose alone
Through summer and winter seem
Enchanted to a stone
To trouble the living stream.
The horse that comes from the road,
The rider, the birds that range
From cloud to tumbling cloud,
Minute by minute they change;
A shadow of cloud on the stream
Changes minute by minute;
A horse-hoof slides on the brim,
And a horse plashes within it;
The long-legged moor-hens dive,
And hens to moor-cocks call;
Minute by minute they live:
The stone's in the midst of all.°

Markiewicz." She was an officer in the Volunteers of the Irish Republican Brotherhood. Yeats dwelt on the loss of beauty involved in her conversion to fanatical politics.
This man Patrick Pearse (1879–1916), schoolmaster, lawyer, poet in Gaelic and English, and President of the Republic for the few days leading up to his capture by British troops in the Dublin Post Office. Shot as a leader of the Rising, as were those mentioned below.
This other Thomas MacDonagh (1878–1916), poet, dramatist, and critic, English professor at University College Dublin

This . . . lout Major John MacBride, husband of Maud Gonne
Hearts . . . all (ll. 41–56) In this bold metaphor Yeats suggests the rigidity and lack of feeling imposed upon people who dedicate themselves exclusively to some intellectual or political end, their stoniness contrasting with the perpetual change observable in life and nature. This, for him, is the sacrifice made by these people who fought steadfastly for Ireland. As we see in other poems, he had especially in mind the militant women, Constance Markiewicz and Maud Gonne.

Too long a sacrifice
Can make a stone of the heart.
O when may it suffice?
60 That is Heaven's part, our part
To murmur name upon name,
As a mother names her child
When sleep at last has come
On limbs that had run wild.
What is it but nightfall?
No, no, not night but death;
Was it needless death° after all?
For England may keep faith°
For all that is done and said.
70 We know their dream; enough
To know they dreamed and are dead;
And what if excess of love
Bewildered them till they died?
I write it out in a verse—
MacDonagh and MacBride
And Connolly° and Pearse
Now and in time to be,
Wherever green is worn,
Are changed, changed utterly:
80 A terrible beauty is born.
1916   1921

On a Political Prisoner°

She that but little patience knew,
From childhood on, had now so much
A grey gull lost its fear and flew
Down to her cell and there alit,
And there endured her fingers' touch
And from her fingers ate its bit.

Did she in touching that lone wing
Recall the years before her mind
Became a bitter, an abstract thing,°
10 Her thought some popular enmity:

needless death Many Irishmen thought the Rebellion a terrible mistake, but it had the value, which Yeats's poem helps to promote, of endowing the cause with martyrs.
England . . . faith The English Parliament had passed an act for Home Rule in Ireland in 1913; it was shelved at the beginning of World War I, and rumors that the British government meant to rescind it were partly responsible for the Rising.
Connolly James Connolly (1870–1916), the

great Irish Labor leader, who organized the Citizen Army. He led the forces in the Post Office, was wounded, and had to be allowed to recover sufficiently for the death sentence to be carried out.
On . . . Prisoner Countess Markiewicz was in Holloway, a woman's prison in London, serving a life sentence for her part in the Easter Rising.
bitter . . . thing a recurrence of this preoccupation of Yeats's, often expressed with special reference to the Countess and Maud Gonne

Blind and leader of the blind
Drinking the foul ditch where they lie?

When long ago I saw her ride
Under Ben Bulben° to the meet,
The beauty of her country-side
With all youth's lonely wildness stirred,
She seemed to have grown clean and sweet
Like any rock-bred, sea-borne bird:

Sea-borne, or balanced on the air
When first it sprang out of the nest
Upon some lofty rock to stare
Upon the cloudy canopy,
While under its storm-beaten breast
Cried out the hollows of the sea.°
1919   1921

The Second Coming

The title of this poem is derived from the Christian belief in the second coming of
Christ (see Matthew 24), but the god to be born in the second Bethlehem is a beast,
and not a beast like that in Revelation, for it will not be subdued. As in "The Magi"
there is a succession of "uncontrollable mysteries," and this is antithetical to that of
the Christian Nativity. A new age is to be born, a reversal of the last. Some of Yeats's
poems are rendered very obscure by the presence of allusions to his developing
system of occult beliefs, which came to systematize all his thinking about history, civilization, and personality. There are several such poems in Michael Robartes; but "The
Second Coming" is not one of them. For all its occult freight, it is lucid. Yeats believed that the relation between objectivity and subjectivity in personality could be
represented by a figure of two cones, one with its apex on the other's base, so that
a personality envisaged as nearing one or other apex would be confronted with the
breadth of the antithetical base. So with historical epochs:

> The end of an age, which always receives the revelation of the character of the
> next age, is represented by the coming of one gyre [the circling around the
> surfaces of the cones] to its place of greatest expansion and of the other to
> that of its greatest contraction. At the present moment the life gyre is sweeping
> outward, unlike that before the birth of Christ which was narrowing, and has
> almost reached its greatest expansion. The revelation which approaches will,
> however, take its character from the contrary movement of the interior gyre.
> All our scientific, democratic, fact-accumulating, heterogeneous civilization
> belongs to the outward gyre and prepares not the continuance of itself but
> the revelation as in a lightning flash. . . .

Ben Bulben A mountain near Sligo and Lissadell, the Gore-Booth house; Constance Gore-
Booth was reckoned, in youth, the finest horsewoman in Ireland.
Like any . . . sea (ll. 18–24) A beautifully
elaborate and successful example of the mature

Yeatsian use of images; the seabird not only
represents lost youth and physical grace but
also rides over an image of terror and destruction; so that the coming together of woman and
gull at the opening is fully exploited.

So Yeats in his own note, in *Michael Robartes*. Later, when he developed this approach in more detail, Yeats said that it, or the "instructors" who communicated it to him, gave him "metaphors for poetry." This is true of the present case. In general the poem meets an understanding response not because we accept its peculiar doctrine but because its apocalytic feeling—the terror and decadence of the last days of an epoch— is widely shared.

The Second Coming

Turning and turning in the widening gyre
The falcon cannot hear the falconer;°
Things fall apart; the centre cannot hold;
Mere anarchy is loosed upon the world,
The blood-dimmed tide is loosed,° and everywhere
The ceremony of innocence° is drowned;
The best lack all conviction, while the worst
Are full of passionate intensity.

Surely some revelation is at hand;
10   Surely the Second Coming is at hand.
The Second Coming! Hardly are those words out
When a vast image out of *Spiritus Mundi*°
Troubles my sight: somewhere in sands of the desert
A shape with lion body and the head of a man,°
A gaze blank and pitiless as the sun,
Is moving its slow thighs, while all about it
Reel shadows of the indignant desert birds.
The darkness drops again; but now I know
That twenty centuries of stony sleep°
20   Were vexed to nightmare by a rocking cradle,
And what rough beast, its hour come round at last,
Slouches towards Bethlehem to be born?

1919   1921

Turning . . . falconer The falcon circles in such wide sweeps that it no longer answers its master's call; at the same time this is a figure for the widening base of the cone at the end of an age.
the . . . loosed thinking perhaps of the recent war and the Russian revolution as well as the Irish Troubles
ceremony of innocence Ceremony here, as in "A Prayer for My Daughter," is an image of order and obedience.
Spiritus Mundi "A general storehouse of images which have ceased to be the property of any personality or spirit" (Yeats's words in a note on "An Image from Past Life," also in *Michael Robartes*). He had long believed in a Great

Memory, a reservoir of images on which we all draw.
A shape . . . man This Sphinx-like creature derives from an early magical experiment in which Yeats held an occult symbol and when he closed his eyes had these mental images: "a desert, and a black Titan raising himself up by his hands from the middle of a heap of ancient ruins" (*Autobiographies*, p. 186). Later (*Explorations*, 1962, p. 393) he spoke of an image "at my left side just out of the range of sight, a brazen winged beast that I associated with laughing destruction," and added that he had described it in "The Second Coming."
twenty . . . sleep i.e. before Christ was born

Sailing to Byzantium°

I

That° is no country for old men. The young
In one another's arms, birds in the trees
—Those dying generations—at their song,
The salmon-falls, the mackerel-crowded seas,
Fish, flesh, or fowl, commend all summer long
Whatever is begotten, born, and dies.
Caught in that sensual music all neglect
Monuments of unageing intellect.°

II

An aged man is but a paltry thing,
A tattered coat upon a stick, unless
Soul clap its hands and sing, and louder sing
For every tatter in its mortal dress,
Nor is there singing school but studying
Monuments of its own magnificence;
And therefore I have sailed the seas and come
To the holy city of Byzantium.

III

O sages standing in God's holy fire°
As in the gold mosaic of a wall,
Come from the holy fire, perne in a gyre,°
And be the singing-masters of my soul.
Consume my heart away; sick with desire
And fastened to a dying animal
It knows not what it is; and gather me
Into the artifice of eternity.

IV

Once out of nature I shall never take
My bodily form from any natural thing,

Sailing to Byzantium In his 63rd year Yeats felt great power and bitterness; the volume *The Tower*, of which this is the first poem, deals with war, old age, the Anglo-Irish inheritance, the decay of the world. Byzantium, the modern Istanbul, housed the Platonic Academy until the 15th century, and was the capital of Eastern (Greek) Christianity. Yeats makes it an image of eternity, a paradise without the growth and change which are the sorrow and the delight of life. Here the artist, free of the distortions wrought by age and labor, finds his place; whereas the young, caught up in natural generation, belong to another country. Yeats says in *A Vision* that if he could choose to spend time in antiquity he would go to Byzantium in the 6th century. When he was in Sicily in 1924 he saw the Byzantine mosaics, and long before he had visited St. Apollinare Nuovo at Ravenna and seen the sages and saints in its walls. In early drafts Yeats describes the voyage to Byzantium, and the title reflects the pre-history of the poem.
That Ireland, and the natural world
sensual . . . intellect The basic opposition of the poem, which contains more than a celebration of spirit and art; Yeats always resented the loss of youth and natural beauty of the body.
sages . . . fire remembered from Ravenna
perne in a gyre A *perne* is a spool, a *gyre* a spiral: he asks them to spiral down the cone to him.

But such a form as Grecian goldsmiths make°
Of hammered gold and gold enamelling
To keep a drowsy Emperor awake;
³⁰ Or set upon a golden bough to sing
To lords and ladies of Byzantium
Of what is past, or passing, or to come.
1926   1928

Ancestral Houses°

Surely among a rich man's flowering lawns,
Amid the rustle of his planted hills,
Life overflows without ambitious pains;
And rains down life until the basin spills,
And mounts more dizzy high the more it rains
As though to choose whatever shape it wills
And never stoop to a mechanical
Or servile shape, at others' beck and call.

Mere dreams, mere dreams! Yet Homer had not sung
¹⁰ Had he not found it certain beyond dreams
That out of life's own self-delight° had sprung
The abounding glittering jet; though now it seems
As if some marvellous empty sea-shell flung
Out of the obscure dark of the rich streams,
And not a fountain, were the symbol which
Shadows the inherited glory of the rich.

Some violent bitter man, some powerful man
Called architect and artist in, that they,
Bitter and violent men, might rear in stone
²⁰ The sweetness that all longed for night and day,
The gentleness none there had ever known;

such . . . make Yeats, in a note, writes, "I have read somewhere that in the Emperor's palace at Byzantium was a tree made of gold and silver, and artificial birds that sang." One suggested explanation is that he was thinking of Hans Christian Andersen's story *The Emperor's Nightingale.*
Ancestral Houses This is the first poem of the sequence *Meditations in Time of Civil War.* It is one of those meditations on the decline of the aristocracy that fed Yeats's own aristocratic pretensions and at the same time supported his view that "leveling" was a symptom of the rapid collapse of the good society, in which aristocrat and peasant each knew his place. He believed that sweetness, gentleness, art and courtesy, were possible only where power and violence had made them so; that the inheritors of sweetness and gentleness, art and courtesy, might lack the vigor or violence to preserve these qualities, so that their creation undermined the class that made them possible, by in-capacitating the heirs from defending them against a new and baser exercise of violence. Later in the sequence he speaks of his own powerlessness against the soldiers who would blow up his bridge; of the breeding-out of aristocratic violence; of his envy: "We are closed in, and the key is turned / On our uncertainty."
self-delight Yeats was fond of such compounds as this: *self-delighting, self-appeasing, self-begotten, self-born.* They all suggest what the fountain symbolizes: a continual supply of energy and vitality without recourse to abstract systems that have nothing to do with the life of the body. The basin of a fountain, perpetually brimming, was for him an image of Unity of Being, the perfection of life, when thought and sensation are one. The seashell is an image of what has been wrought in the past, no longer changing, and fished up by others from the depths of the past.

But when the master's buried mice can play,
And maybe the great-grandson of that house,
For all its bronze and marble,° 's but a mouse.

O what if gardens where the peacock strays
With delicate feet upon old terraces,
Or else all Juno from an urn displays
Before the indifferent garden deities;
O what if levelled lawns and gravelled ways
Where slippered Contemplation finds his ease
And Childhood a delight for every sense,
But take our greatness with our violence?

What if the glory of escutcheoned doors,
And buildings that a haughtier age designed,
The pacing to and fro on polished floors
Amid great chambers and long galleries, lined
With famous portraits of our ancestors;
What if those things the greatest of mankind
Consider most to magnify, or to bless,
But take our greatness with our bitterness?
1921   1928

Two Songs from a Play°

I

I saw a staring virgin stand
Where holy Dionysus° died,
And tear the heart out of his side,
And lay the heart upon her hand
And bear that beating heart away;
And then did all the Muses sing
Of Magnus Annus° at the spring,
As though God's death were but a play.

Another Troy must rise and set,
Another lineage feed the crow,

bronze and marble a favored image of the completeness and lack of change in works of art: see "Among School Children" (below) and also "The Living Beauty"
Two Songs . . . Play Sung by the Chorus of Musicians in the play, Resurrection. The figure of Christ appears, and a Greek, sure that it is a phantom, is horrified to find that it has a beating heart. This is what the musicians presage in their first song, which opens the play. The Syrian character is more like Yeats, asking "What if the irrational return? What if the circle begin again?" —and that is the theme of the second stanza. The first stanza of the second and closing song more or less restates this, and the second states another Yeatsian theme: "Our love-letters wear out our love . . . every stroke of the brush exhausts the impulse," he says in Autobiographies, and, in A Vision: "Exhausted by the cry that it can never end, my love ends."
Dionysus When he was torn to pieces by the Titans, Athene, the virgin goddess, snatched his heart and bore it to Zeus, who swallowed it and then re-begot Dionysus on Semele, daughter of Cadmus.
Magnus Annus The Great Year; when all the heavenly bodies return to their original places this year is complete (a notion as old as Plato's Timaeus). The values vary from 18,000 to 36,000 years. The Muses sing because, given this cyclical time, the god will be killed and reborn as if in a play often repeated.

Another Argo's painted prow
Drive to a flashier bauble yet.
The Roman Empire stood appalled:
It dropped the reigns of peace and war
When that fierce virgin and her Star
Out of the fabulous darkness called.°

II

In pity for man's darkening thought
He walked that room and issued thence
In Galilean turbulence;°
20   The Babylonian starlight brought
A fabulous, formless darkness in;°
Odour of blood when Christ was slain
Made all Platonic tolerance° vain
And vain all Doric° discipline.

Everything that man esteems
Endures a moment or a day.
Love's pleasure drives his love away,
The painter's brush consumes his dreams;
The herald's cry, the soldier's tread
30   Exhaust his glory and his might:
Whatever flames upon the night
Man's own resinous heart has fed.°
1927   1931

Leda and the Swan°

A sudden blow: the great wings beating still
Above the staggering girl, her thighs caressed

Another Troy . . . called (ll. 9–16) Virgil's
Fourth Eclogue, long regarded as a prophecy
of the birth of Christ, speaks of the return of
Astraea, goddess of Justice, who was last to
leave earth at the end of the Golden Age, and
will inaugurate a new one. Virgil speaks of
another voyage of the *Argo,* another fall of
Troy, in the new cycle of time. Yeats must
also have recalled Shelley's drama *Hellas,*
ll. 1060–79. *Fabulous* is a word that was in
Yeats's head at the time of the *Tower* poems;
it occurs four times in that volume, out of six
in his whole work. Here Yeats adapts a description of Christianity by a fourth-century
Neoplatonist and anti-Christian philosopher,
Proclus, whom Yeats knew in Thomas Taylor's
version of his *Six Books . . . on the Theology
of Plato* (1816). The Roman Empire is appalled because Christianity will be its ruin.
turbulence Yeats sees the arrival of the Christian
age as a deep disturbance of the world.
fabulous . . . darkness The Babylonian astron-
omers foretold a world in which man would
be as nothing compared with God.

Platonic tolerance A god actually killed by
violence (not merely a myth) ends the free
philosophical speculation of the Greek Academy.
Doric Greek
Whatever . . . fed That is, he consumes himself; he is the fuel of his own splendid conceptions.
Leda and the Swan Yeats may have had in
mind the painting of the subject by Michelangelo,
or some other version. Leda had by Zeus the
twins Castor and Pollux, and also Helen and
Clytemnestra. So her eggs produced the cause
of the fall of Troy and the death of Agamemnon.
Yeats saw the rape of Leda as a "violent annunciation" such as might be expected in our own
day; an annunciation parallel to the Christian,
and involving the union of a god and a woman
as the Christian does. The outcome is terror, but
the poem dwells on the strangeness of Leda's
experience, feeling "the strange heart," and the
question whether such a visitation of the divine
means an access only of power or also of the
knowledge of a new cycle of history which it
inaugurates.

By the dark webs, her nape caught in his bill,
He holds her helpless breast upon his breast.

How can those terrified vague fingers push
The feathered glory from her loosening thighs?
And how can body, laid in that white rush,
But feel the strange heart beating where it lies?

A shudder in the loins engenders there
The broken wall, the burning roof and tower°
And Agamemnon dead.°
            Being so caught up,
So mastered by the brute blood of the air,
Did she put on his knowledge with his power
Before the indifferent beak could let her drop?
1923   1928

Among School Children

In his capacity as senator, Yeats visited a Montessori school in February 1926. In March of that year he noted in his diary as a topic for a poet, "school children and the thought that life will waste them, perhaps that no possible life can fulfill their own dreams or even their teacher's hope. Bring in the old thought that life prepares for what never happens." Later he sent a version of stanza VI to Olivia Shakespear with the comment: ". . . a fragment of my last curse on old age. It means that even the greatest men are owls, scarecrows, by the time their fame has come. Aristotle, remember, was Alexander's tutor, hence the taws [a leather strap used for whipping]. . . . Pythagoras made some measurement of the intervals between notes on a stretched string" (Letters, ed. Wade, 1954). The development of this poem from a form in which there was nothing to suggest "the rhapsodic resolution" of stanza VIII is memorably studied in T. R. Parkinson, W. B. Yeats, The Later Poetry (1964). The topic, and even the account of it sent to Mrs. Shakespear, is transcended, but the labor involved, as Parkinson shows by a study of the drafts, is extraordinary: "puzzlement, self-analysis, revelation, lurching mistake, refinement, recovery, and ultimately, triumph" (p. 113).

Among School Children

I

I walk through the long schoolroom questioning;
A kind old nun in a white hood replies;
The children learn to cipher° and to sing,
To study reading-books and histories,
To cut and sew, be neat in everything

The broken . . . tower the sack of Troy   **cipher** do arithmetic
Agamemnon dead murdered by his wife Cly-
temnestra on his return from Troy

In the best modern way—the children's eyes
In momentary wonder stare upon
A sixty-year-old smiling public man.

II

I dream of a Ledaean° body, bent
10   Above a sinking fire, a tale that she
Told of a harsh reproof, or trivial event
That changed some childish day to tragedy—
Told, and it seemed that our two natures blent
Into a sphere from youthful sympathy,
Or else, to alter Plato's parable,°
Into the yolk and white of the one shell.

III

And thinking of that fit of grief or rage
I look upon one child or t'other there
And wonder if she stood so at that age—
20   For even daughters of the swan can share
Something of every paddler's heritage—
And had that colour upon cheek or hair,
And thereupon my heart is driven wild:
She stands before me as a living child.

IV

Her present image° floats into the mind—
Did Quattrocento° finger fashion it
Hollow of cheek as though it drank the wind
And took a mess of shadows for its meat?
And I though never of Ledaean kind
30   Had pretty plumage once—enough of that,
Better to smile on all that smile, and show
There is a comfortable kind of old scarecrow.°

V

What youthful mother, a shape upon her lap
Honey of generation° had betrayed,

Ledaean   Helen-like, referring to Helen the
daughter of Leda. The reverie is of Maud
Gonne.
Plato's parable   In *Symposium* 190, Plato has
Aristophanes suggest that man was originally
double, with two faces, four hands, and so on,
and that after the halves were divided they
strive toward one another in love.
Her present image   the woman as she now was,
in her sixties
Quattrocento   15th-century. Among earlier versions there is the nonexistent *quinto-cento* and
also *Da Vinci' finger;* so Yeats was perhaps
thinking of Leonardo da Vinci (1452–1519)
as painter.

scarecrow   See "Sailing to Byzantium," l. 9 ff.
Honey of generation   taken from *On the Cave of
the Nymphs* by Porphyry, 3rd-century Neoplatonist, a commentary on the cave in *Odyssey*
XIII. There were bowls of honey, allegorized as
"the pleasure which draws souls downward to
generation." Yeats, in a note, suggests that he
meant a drug that destroyed the recollection
of prenatal freedom, but adds that he found
no warrant for this in Porphyry. Certainly
honey of generation has betrayed applies in the
poem to the child, not the mother. It will either
recollect its prenatal state or it will not, depending on whether the drug works.

And that must sleep, shriek, struggle to escape
As recollection or the drug decide,
Would think her son, did she but see that shape
With sixty or more winters on its head,
A compensation for the pang of his birth,°
Or the uncertainty of his setting forth?

VI

Plato thought nature but a spume that plays
Upon a ghostly paradigm of things;°
Solider Aristotle played the taws
Upon the bottom of a king of kings;°
World-famous golden-thighed Pythagoras
Fingered upon a fiddle-stick or strings
What a star sang and careless Muses heard:°
Old clothes upon old sticks to scare a bird.°

VII

Both nuns and mothers worship images,
But those the candles light are not as those
That animate a mother's reveries,
But keep a marble or a bronze repose.°
And yet they too break hearts—O Presences
That passion, piety or affection knows,
And that all heavenly glory symbolise—
O self-born° mockers of man's enterprise;

VIII

Labour is blossoming or dancing where
The body is not bruised to pleasure soul,
Nor beauty born out of its own despair,
Nor blear-eyed wisdom out of midnight oil.
O chestnut-tree, great-rooted blossomer,
Are you the leaf, the blossom or the bole?

A compensation . . . birth See *At The Hawk's Well:* "A mother that saw her son / Doubled over a speckled shin, / Cross-grained with ninety years, / Would cry, 'How little worth / Were all my hopes and fears / And the hard pain of his birth'."
Plato . . . things Plato thought the world of appearance a mere veil over the real mathematical structure of the forms.
Solider . . . kings Aristotle was Alexander's tutor.
World-famous . . . heard In working out the ratios of the notes of the scale Pythagoras discovered the music of the spheres, the harmony of the cosmos. Pythagoras (late 6th to early 5th century B.C.) was an important precursor of Plato; Iamblichus, a 4th-century A.D. Neoplatonist who wrote a life of Pythagoras, credits him with a golden thigh.
Old . . . bird These great thinkers are still mere scarecrows.
marble . . . repose This points up the distinction so frequent in Yeats between the natural body that ages and warps, and the perpetual work of art. But at this point the poem takes off in a new, unexpected, and somewhat obscure direction; and Yeats ends with an image of the natural body as having—in some paradise out of time—identity with the permanent work of art.
self-born See note on "Ancestral Houses."

O body swayed to music, O brightening glance,
How can we know the dancer from the dance?°
1926   1928

In Memory of Eva Gore-Booth and Con Markiewicz°

The light of evening, Lissadell,°
Great windows open to the south,
Two girls in silk kimonos, both
Beautiful, one a gazelle.
But a raving autumn shears
Blossom from the summer's wreath;
The older° is condemned to death,
Pardoned, drags out lonely years
Conspiring among the ignorant.°
10 I know not what the younger dreams—
Some vague Utopia—and she seems,
When withered old and skeleton-gaunt,
An image of such politics.
Many a time I think to seek
One or the other out and speak
Of that old Georgian mansion, mix
Pictures of the mind, recall
That table and the talk of youth,
Two girls in silk kimonos, both
20 Beautiful, one a gazelle.
Dear shadows, now you know it all,
All the folly of a fight
With a common wrong or right.
The innocent and the beautiful
Have no enemy but time;
Arise and bid me strike a match
And strike another till time catch;

Labour . . . dance? (ll. 57–64) *Labour* in both senses: physical work and childbirth. In an ideal world where there is no division between soul and body, where it is untrue that "whatever flames upon the night / Man's own resinous heart has fed," labor is identified with product. The *blossoming* and *dancing* look forward to the chestnut tree and the dancer later in the stanza. Goethe, in *Wilhelm Meister*, compares the unity of *Hamlet* to that of a tree: "It is a trunk with boughs, leaves, buds, blossoms and fruit. Are they not all one, and thereby means of one another?" One part of the tree does not precede, or produce, another. The dancer is a favorite image of Yeats; here her labor *is* her dance, the movement of her body is dancing, not labor. Mallarmé, the Symbolist poet (1842–98) whom Yeats studied years before, says that a dancer "is not a woman

who dances, for these related reasons: she *is not a woman* but a metaphor summing up elemental aspects of our form, sword, bowl, flower; and *she does not dance*, suggesting [what can be summed up as] *the poem freed of all the apparatus of the writer."*
In Memory . . . Markiewicz This poem heads Yeats's 1933 collection, *The Winding Stair,* named for the staircase in the Tower. Eva Gore-Booth (b. 1870) died in 1926, Constance (b. 1868) in 1927. See note on "Easter 1916."
Lissadell early 19th-century mansion near Sligo, home of the Gore-Booths; first visited by Yeats in 1894
The older Constance (see note on "Easter 1916")
Conspiring . . . ignorant She returned to revolutionary politics after her release and fought in the Irish Civil War.

Should the conflagration climb,
Run till all the sages know.
We the great gazebo° built,
They convicted us of guilt;
Bid me strike a match and blow.

1927   1933

Coole Park, 1929°

I meditate upon a swallow's flight,
Upon an agèd woman° and her house,
A sycamore and lime-tree lost in night
Although that western cloud is luminous,
Great works constructed there in nature's spite
For scholars and for poets after us,
Thoughts long knitted into a single thought,
A dance-like glory that those walls begot.

There Hyde° before he had beaten into prose
That noble blade the Muses buckled on,
There one° that ruffled in a manly pose
For all his timid heart, there that slow man,
That meditative man, John Synge,° and those
Impetuous men, Shawe-Taylor° and Hugh Lane°
Found pride established in humility,
A scene well set and excellent company.

They came like swallows and like swallows went,
And yet a woman's powerful character
Could keep a swallow to its first intent;
And half a dozen in formation there,
That seemed to whirl upon a compass-point,
Found certainty upon the dreaming air,

gazebo A summer house on the grounds of a mansion, such as the one at Lissadell. In Irish slang "to make a gazebo of yourself" is to make yourself look ridiculous. The sense seems to be of an aristocratic, elegant structure that time and politics have made anachronistic.
Coole Park, 1929 A prose draft survives: "Here Synge came, Hugh Lane, Shawe-Taylor, many names. I too in my timid youth. Coming and going like migratory birds. Then address the swallows fluttering in their dream like circles. Speak of the rarity of the circumstances that bring together such concords of men. Each man more than himself through whom an unknown life speaks. A circle ever returning into itself." This is of interest because it illustrates Yeats's habit of beginning poems with a prose draft, and also because of the transformation of the idea in the writing of the poem, studied by T. R. Parkinson (*W. B. Yeats, The Later Poetry*, (1964), pp. 80–81).

agèd woman Lady Augusta Gregory (1852–1932), close friend of Yeats for almost 40 years, mother of Robert Gregory (see "In Memory of Major Robert Gregory") and aunt of Hugh Lane and John Shawe-Taylor. She translated from the Gaelic, wrote plays, and was co-founder of the Abbey Theatre with Yeats, who believed that this was their role in the liberation of Ireland.
Hyde Dr. Douglas Hyde (1860–1949), Gaelic poet, scholar, first president of Eire (1938–45). He gave up writing poetry because it affected his health.
one Yeats himself
John Synge See note on "In Memory of Major Robert Gregory."
Shawe-Taylor (1866–1911) Anglo-Irish politician
Hugh Lane (1874–1915) See note on "To a Friend Whose Work Has Come to Nothing."

The intellectual sweetness of those lines
That cut through time or cross it withershins.°

Here, traveller, scholar, poet, take your stand
When all those rooms and passages are gone,°
When nettles wave upon a shapeless mound
And saplings root among the broken stone,
And dedicate—eyes bent upon the ground,
30   Back turned upon the brightness of the sun
And all the sensuality of the shade—
A moment's memory to that laurelled head.
1928–29   1933

Byzantium

A poem written in 1930 and included in the collections *Words for Music Perhaps* (1932) and *The Winding Stair* (1933). Yeats had intended to title *The Winding Stair* volume *Byzantium,* and asked the artist T. Sturge Moore (1870–1944), who designed the symbolic covers of several of his later books, for an appropriate drawing. Moore had said in a letter that "Sailing to Byzantium" "let him down" at the end since "such a goldsmith's bird is as much nature as man's body" and Yeats told him that "Byzantium" originated in this criticism, which proved that "the idea needed exposition." Moore had also sent Yeats a poem by James Elroy Flecker (1884–1915), "A Queen's Song," about magically turning living beauty into gold in order to preserve it.

The bird in this second Byzantium poem is contrasted with "common bird or petal" more explicitly than before. Byzantium itself has been developed and made obscure as a symbol, but is essentially the same as in the earlier poem: the completed image of art liberated from all connection with human labor and intellect. The focus is no longer on the poignant contrast between the vigor and beauty of the living and the still permanence of art; nature is now "mere complexities, / The fury and the mire," and is converted into art which though dead has more life and being than the living— echoing Blake's "This World of Imagination is Infinite & Eternal, whereas the world of Generation, or Vegetation, is Finite and Temporal . . . The Human Imagination . . . appear'd to Me . . . throwing off the Temporal that the Eternal might be Establish'd." There is a surviving prose draft: "Describe Byzantium as it is in the system [Yeats's *A Vision*] toward the end of the first Christian millennium. A walking mummy. Flames at the street corners where the soul is purified, birds of hammered gold singing in the golden trees, in the harbour [dolphins] offering their backs to the wailing dead that they may carry them to Paradise."

withershins counterclockwise, backward

rooms . . . gone Coole was demolished some years later, after the death of Lady Gregory.

Byzantium

The unpurged images of day recede;
The Emperor's drunken soldiery are abed;
Night resonance recedes, night-walkers' song°
After great cathedral gong;°
A starlit or a moonlit dome° disdains
All that man is,
All mere complexities,
The fury and the mire of human veins

Before me floats an image, man or shade,
Shade more than man, more image than a shade;
For Hades' bobbin bound in mummy-cloth
May unwind the winding path;°
A mouth that has no moisture and no breath
Breathless mouths may summon;
I hail the superhuman;
I call it death-in-life and life-in-death.

Miracle, bird or golden handiwork,
More miracle than bird or handiwork,°
Planted on the star-lit golden bough,°
Can like the cocks of Hades° crow,
Or, by the moon embittered, scorn aloud
In glory of changeless metal
Common bird or petal
And all complexities of mire or blood.

At midnight on the Emperor's pavement° flit
Flames that no faggot feeds, nor steel has lit,
Nor storm disturbs, flames begotten of flame,
Where blood-begotten spirits° come
And all complexities of fury leave,
Dying into a dance,

night-walkers' song the call of the prostitutes
gong suspended in Byzantine church porches
and struck with mallets
dome that of the cathedral of St. Sophia, begun
in 532 A.D.; a mosque after the Turkish conquest (1453); now a museum of Byzantine
art
Before . . . path This is the mummy of the
draft. Yeats imagines it as wound around like
wool on a perne or "bobbin" (see "The Second
Coming" and "Sailing to Byzantium"). The
man has become a shade, "dreaming back" or
unwinding his natural life, and so an image
of the passage from life into eternity, representing the point that is both life in death and
death in life.
Miracle . . . handiwork removing the bird
from the human context it still had in "Sailing
to Byzantium"

golden bough The tree is artificial. Yeats may
be looking back to his Cabbalistic tree (see
"The Two Trees") and also remembering that
the golden bough was used to achieve entry
into the underworld.
cocks of Hades These do not signal the continuity of existence or, as in some occult writing
earthly cocks do, the Resurrection, but rather
despise those commonplace heralds of life and
rebirth.
Emperor's pavement mosaic pavement in the
Forum of Constantine
blood-begotten spirits The spirits of the recently
dead, they are blood-begotten in contrast to
the self-begotten flames of Byzantium which
will purge them of their complexities of fury,
the mire of human veins.

An agony of trance,
An agony of flame that cannot singe a sleeve.°

Astraddle on the dolphin's mire and blood,°
Spirit after spirit! The smithies break the flood,°
The golden smithies of the Emperor!
Marbles of the dancing floor
Break bitter furies of complexity,
Those images that yet
Fresh images beget,
⁴⁰ That dolphin-torn, that gong-tormented sea.
1930   1933

Crazy Jane Talks with the Bishop°

I met the Bishop on the road
And much said he and I.
'Those breasts are flat and fallen now,
Those veins must soon be dry;
Live in a heavenly mansion,
Not in some foul sty.'

'Fair and foul are near of kin,
And fair needs foul,' I cried.
'My friends are gone, but that's a truth
¹⁰ Nor grave nor bed denied,
Learned in bodily lowliness
And in the heart's pride.

'A woman can be proud and stiff
When on love intent;
But love has pitched his mansion in
The place of excrement;
For nothing can be sole or whole
That has not been rent.'
1929   1932, 1933

An agony . . . sleeve This figure was suggested to Yeats by a Japanese Nōh play, *Motomezuka*, in which a girl dances the agony of her burning in flames that are the subjective creation of her guilt and have no reality. He also knew the famous Fire Dance of Loie Fuller, in which, by means of underfloor electric lighting and other devices, she seemed to be dancing in flames that did not burn her.
dolphin's mire and blood Yeats here and elsewhere follows a tradition that the dead are conveyed to the afterlife on the backs of dolphins; being themselves natural—having *mire and blood*—they are another image of the transition from life to death.
smithies . . . flood The Emperor's workshops convert the natural into the eternal, like the mosaic pavement or dancing floor.
Crazy Jane Talks with the Bishop Yeats wrote

the poems in *Words for Music Perhaps and Other Poems* (1932), in a burst of creative energy after a serious illness, during the spring of 1929. Among them is the sequence first called the Cracked Mary, later the Crazy Jane, poems. The original Crazy Jane was an old woman who lived at Gort, near Lady Gregory's estate, and was much admired for her audacity of speech. This is the sixth of the poems and the second involving the Bishop. They belong to a period when Yeats, "full of desire" as he said, was engaged in giving a strong sexual dimension to his occult thinking. Crazy Jane did as Yeats thought he should: she cast out remorse, and in old age did not turn against the sensuality of youth but embraced and defended it against the orthodox advice of the Bishop.

After Long Silence°

Speech after long silence; it is right,
All other lovers being estranged or dead,
Unfriendly lamplight hid under its shade,
The curtains drawn upon unfriendly night,
That we descant and yet again descant
Upon the supreme theme of Art and Song:
Bodily decrepitude is wisdom; young
We loved each other and were ignorant.
1929   1933

A Last Confession°

What lively lad most pleasured me
Of all that with me lay?
I answer that I gave my soul
And loved in misery,
But had great pleasure with a lad
That I loved bodily.

Flinging from his arms I laughed
To think his passion such,
He fancied that I gave a soul
Did but our bodies touch,
And laughed upon his breast to think
Beast gave beast as much.

I gave what other women gave
That stepped out of their clothes,
But when this soul, its body off,
Naked to naked goes,
He it has found shall find therein
What none other knows,

And give his own and take his own
And rule in his own right;
And though it loved in misery
Close and cling so tight,
There's not a bird of day° that dare
Extinguish that delight.
1926   1933

After Long Silence This is number XVII of
Words for Music Perhaps. The last lines memo-
rably repeat what the reader will now recognize
as a leading theme of Yeats's poetry.
A Last Confession from the sequence *A Woman
Young and Old*

bird of day the bird song at dawn that ends
lovemaking in the ancient type of poem called
the *aubade*

Meru°

Civilisation is hooped together, brought
Under a rule, under the semblance of peace
By manifold illusion; but man's life is thought,
And he, despite his terror, cannot cease
Ravening through century after century,
Ravening, raging, and uprooting that he may come
Into the desolation of reality:
Egypt and Greece, good-bye, and good-bye, Rome!
Hermits upon Mount Meru° or Everest,
10   Caverned in night under the drifted snow,
Or where that snow and winter's dreadful blast
Beat down upon their naked bodies, know
That day brings round the night, that before dawn
His glory and his monuments are gone.

1933–34   1935

Lapis Lazuli

This poem was included in the posthumous *Last Poems and Plays* (1940). In July 1935 Yeats wrote to Dorothy Wellesley that "people much occupied with morality always lose heroic ecstasy" and quoted Dowson's lines "Wine and women and song, / To us they belong / To us the bitter and gay," adding " 'Bitter and gay,' that is the heroic mood." The Dowson poem, "Villanelle of the Poet's Road," was included by Yeats in *The Oxford Book of Modern Verse* (1936), his anthology. He also mentioned in the letter Harry Clifton's gift to him of a carved piece of lapis lazuli (a stone of deep blue color): it was "carved by some Chinese sculptor into the semblance of a mountain with temple, trees, paths and an ascetic and pupil about to climb the mountain. Ascetic, pupil, hard stone, eternal theme of the sensual east. The heroic cry in the midst of despair. But no, I am wrong, the east has its solutions always and therefore knows nothing of tragedy. It is we, not the east, that must raise the heroic cry." He had recently received a letter from his friend the artist Edmund Dulac expressing terror as to the consequences if London were to be bombed from the air. There is a study of the manuscript drafts in Jon Stallworthy, *Vision and Revision in Yeats's Last Poems* (1969).

Meru This sonnet is the twelfth and last in the sequence *Supernatural Songs*, which first appeared in *The King of the Great Clock Tower* (1934, limited edition) and *A Full Moon in March* (1935). There are songs are accompanied by a note explaining the relevance to the sequence of certain affinities between Oriental religion and Irish Christianity; he invents a character Ribh who is critical of St. Patrick ("An abstract Greek absurdity has crazed the man— / Recall that masculine Trinity"). The sequence represents a theological phase of Yeats's thought, and ends with "Meru," which he mentions in the note as a "legendary" place of pilgrimage for Indian holy men. He was interested in a book called *The Holy Mountain* (1934) by his friend Shri Purohit Swami, and prepared his introduction to it at about the time of the poem.

Mount Meru Shri Purohit Swami speaks of advanced meditation by ascetics on Mount Kailas, Yeats's "legendary Meru."

Lapis Lazuli

(For Harry Clifton)

I have heard that hysterical women say
They are sick of the palette and fiddle-bow,
Of poets that are always gay,
For everybody knows or else should know
That if nothing drastic is done
Aeroplane and Zeppelin° will come out,
Pitch like King Billy bomb-balls in°
Until the town lie beaten flat.

All perform their tragic play,
There struts Hamlet, there is Lear,
That's Ophelia, that Cordelia;
Yet they, should the last scene be there,
The great stage curtain about to drop,
If worthy their prominent part in the play,
Do not break up their lines to weep.
They know that Hamlet and Lear are gay;°
Gaiety transfiguring all that dread.
All men have aimed at, found and lost;
Black out; Heaven blazing into the head:
Tragedy wrought to its uttermost.
Though Hamlet rambles and Lear rages,
And all the drop-scenes drop at once
Upon a hundred thousand stages,
It° cannot grow by an inch or an ounce.

On their own feet they came, or on shipboard,
Camel-back, horse-back, ass-back, mule-back,
Old civilisations put to the sword.
Then they and their wisdom went to rack:
No handiwork of Callimachus,°
Who handled marble as if it were bronze,
Made draperies that seemed to rise
When sea-wind swept the corner, stands;
His long lamp-chimney shaped like the stem
Of a slender palm, stood but a day;

Zeppelin a World War I lighter-than-air bomber, obsolete by the time of writing
Pitch . . . in Recalls an Irish ballad about the Battle of the Boyne, during which "King William threw his bomb-balls in." William III, who was married to James II's daughter Mary, became joint sovereign with her by invitation of Parliament in 1689, after the flight of James II, king from 1685. William decisively defeated James at the Battle of the Boyne in Ireland, July 1, 1690.
Hamlet . . . gay In "A General Introduction for My Work" (*Essays and Introductions*, 1961, p. 522) Yeats writes· "The heroes of Shakespeare convey to us through their looks, or through the metaphorical patterns of their speech, the sudden enlargement of their vision, their ecstasy at the approach of death", and he quotes Lady Gregory's remark, "Tragedy must be a joy to the man who dies."
It presumably tragedy
Callimachus Sculptor of 5th century B.C. who is said to have invented the Corinthian column and a method of sculpting the folds of drapery with a rolling drill. Yeats uses him as one who tried to keep up the formal purity of earlier Greek sculpture when Greece was being submerged in Asiatic influences; the lamp he found mentioned in Pausanias' *Description of Greece* (a 2nd-century A.D. tourist guide).

All things fall and are built again,
And those that build them again are gay.

Two Chinamen, behind them a third,
Are carved in lapis lazuli,
Over them flies a long-legged bird,
40   A symbol of longevity;
The third, doubtless a serving-man,
Carries a musical instrument.

Every discoloration of the stone,
Every accidental crack or dent,
Seems a water-course or an avalanche,
Or lofty slope where it still snows
Though doubtless plum or cherry-branch
Sweetens the little half-way house
Those Chinamen climb towards, and I
50   Delight to imagine them seated there;
There, on the mountain and the sky,
On all the tragic scene they stare.
One asks for mournful melodies;
Accomplished fingers begin to play.
Their eyes mid many wrinkles, their eyes,
Their ancient, glittering eyes, are gay.
1936   1940

The Statues

In early prose drafts Yeats is already contrasting the mathematical proportions of Greek sculpture, based on Pythagoras, with the formlessness of the Asiatic, the flood temporarily stemmed at Salamis (the Athenian naval victory over the Persians in 480 B.C.). Yeats says that "Apollo forgot Pythagoras and took the name of Buddha" and that Apollo should return under the name of Cuchulain to give us back Pythagorean number in the formless chaos of the modern world. In his topical pamphlet *On the Boiler* (1939) Yeats has this passage:

> There are moments when I am certain that art must once again accept those Greek proportions which carry into plastic art the Pythagorean numbers, those faces which are divine because all there is empty and measured. Europe was not born when Greek galleys defeated the Persian hordes at Salamis; but when the Doric studios sent out those broad-backed marble statues against the multiform, vague, expressive Asiatic sea, they gave to the sexual instinct of Europe its goal, its fixed type.

Elsewhere in the same booklet he advises that Greek and mathematics be taught in Irish schools, the latter "because being certainty without reality it is the modern key to power. . . ." Yeats's elevation of the Greek statue to a European physical norm is not unrelated to his interest, also expressed in *On the Boiler,* in eugenics, which in turn was, in the formulations then current, related to his interest in the European dictatorships.

The Statues

Pythagoras planned it. Why did the people stare?
His numbers, though they moved or seemed to move
In marble or in bronze,° lacked character.°
But boys and girls, pale from the imagined love
Of solitary beds, knew what they were,
That passion could bring character enough,
And pressed at midnight in some public place
Live lips upon a plummet-measured face.

No! Greater than Pythagoras,° for the men
That with a mallet or a chisel modelled these
Calculations that look but casual flesh, put down
All Asiatic vague immensities,
And not the banks of oars that swam upon
The many-headed foam at Salamis.
Europe put off that foam when Phidias
Gave women dreams and dreams their looking-glass.

One image crossed the many-headed,° sat
Under the tropic shade, grew round and slow,
No Hamlet thin from eating flies,° a fat
Dreamer of the Middle Ages. Empty eyeballs knew
That knowledge increases unreality, that
Mirror on mirror mirrored is all the show.
When gong and conch declare the hour to bless
Grimalkin crawls to Buddha's emptiness.°

When Pearse summoned Cuchulain to his side,
What stalked through the Post Office?° What intellect,
What calculation, number, measurement, replied?
We Irish, born into that ancient sect

marble . . . bronze See note on "Among School Children."
lacked character For Yeats *character* was undesirable, a sign of old age, growing "like the ash of a burning stick" (essay, "The Tragic Theatre," 1910); the valuable possession was *personality*, more vital, less uselessly differentiated; thus in art personal emotion is expressed not by quirks of character but by "a mask from whose eyes the disembodied looks."
No . . . Pythagoras On second thought, the sculptors are greater than the mathematician who made their measurements possible; for they rather than the warships at Salamis kept the Persians out, making the sexual ideal that of proportions discovered or created by man, not natural formlessness.
One . . . many-headed Refers to the effect on Persian and Indian art of Greek influence brought in by Alexander the Great when he invaded those regions (4th century B.C.); the Ghandara (Pakistan) Buddhas of the North West frontier are Greek in style; *many-headed* from a Greek epithet for the sea.
Hamlet . . . flies Hamlet says he eats "the air, promise-crammed" like the chameleon, thought to live on air (*Hamlet* III.ii.91). Yeats substitutes flies; cats that eat flies are said to grow thin, hence perhaps Grimalkin in the last line of the stanza.
Empty . . . emptiness The eyeballs of the statues, which the Greeks painted, are now empty; even in India there is a coming together of the European and the Asiatic spirit. Here the wilder, more wantonly allusive manner of Yeats's later poetry has obscured the meaning almost completely, except that it is plain there is a call for Greek proportion in the modern version of the Asiatic tide.
When . . . Office? Pearse, according to Yeats himself, "had a cult" of Cuchulain, the ancient Irish hero, and called on him during the siege of the Post Office at Easter 1916. (There is a statue of Cuchulain in the Dublin Post Office to commemorate this.) Yeats, imagining the Irish as belonging to a world earlier than the Christian dispensation now coming to an end, reads Cuchulain as Apollo and imagines him bringing back the principles of measurement implicit in the Greek statues.

But thrown upon this filthy modern tide
30   And by its formless spawning fury wrecked,
Climb to our proper dark, that we may trace
The lineaments of a plummet-measured face.
1938   1940

John Kinsella's Lament for Mrs. Mary Moore°

A bloody and a sudden end,
    Gunshot or a noose,
For Death who takes what man would keep,
    Leaves what man would lose.
He might have had my sister,
    My cousins by the score,
But nothing satisfied the fool
    But my dear Mary Moore,
None other knows what pleasures man
10   At table or in bed.
    What shall I do for pretty girls
      Now my old bawd is dead?°

Though stiff to strike a bargain,
    Like an old Jew man,
Her bargain struck we laughed and talked
    And emptied many a can;
And O! but she had stories,
    Though not for the priest's ear,
To keep the soul of man alive,
20   Banish age and care,
And being old she put a skin
    On everything she said.
    What shall I do for pretty girls
      Now my old bawd is dead?

The priests have got a book that says
    But for Adam's sin
Eden's Garden would be there
    And I there within.
No expectation fails there,
30   No pleasing habit ends,
No man grows old, no girl grows cold,
    But friends walk by friends.
Who quarrels over halfpennies
    That plucks the trees for bread?

John . . . Moore written July 1938 as "A
Strong Farmer's Complaint about Death"
What . . . dead "I have just thought of a
chorus for a ballad. A strong farmer is mourning over the shortness of life and changing
times, and every stanza ends "What . . .
dead?" (letter of July 1938).

What shall I do for pretty girls
   Now my old bawd is dead?
   1938   1940

The Circus Animals' Desertion°

I

I sought a theme and sought for it in vain,
I sought it daily for six weeks or so.
Maybe at last, being but a broken man,
I must be satisfied with my heart, although
Winter and summer till old age began
My circus animals were all on show,
Those stilted boys, that burnished chariot,
Lion and woman° and the Lord knows what.

II

What can I but enumerate old themes?
First that sea-rider Oisin° led by the nose
Through three enchanted islands, allegorical dreams,
Vain gaiety, vain battle, vain repose,
Themes of the embittered heart, or so it seems,
That might adore old songs or courtly shows;
But what cared I that set him on to ride,
I, starved for the bosom of his faery bride?

And then a counter-truth filled out its play,
The Countess Cathleen° was the name I gave it;
She, pity-crazed, had given her soul away,
But masterful Heaven had intervened to save it.
I thought my dear must her own soul destroy,
So did fanaticism and hate enslave it,
And this brought forth a dream and soon enough
This dream itself had all my thought and love.°

And when the Fool and Blind Man stole the bread
Cuchulain fought the ungovernable sea;°

The Circus . . . Desertion This is a poem somewhat like Coleridge's "Dejection" ode, a poem about no longer being able to write poems. The "Circus Animals" are his usual themes.
Lion and woman In a visionary poem, "The Double Vision of Michael Robartes," Yeats sees "A Sphinx with woman breast and lion paw" and a Buddha, with a girl dancing between, symbolizing the Fifteenth Phase of his system, or Unity of Being.
Oisin (pronounced Usheen) was carried off to fairyland by Niamh on her horse (see Yeats's early long poem in three parts, *The Wanderings of Oisin*).
The Countess Cathleen This is a play (first version 1889) written for Maud Gonne in which the devil's agents tempt starving peasants to sell their souls for gold. The Countess sacrifices her wealth and then her soul to save them, but in the end is herself saved. Yeats thought this an allegory of Maud Gonne's ruining herself for the sake of politics.
This . . love The poetic invention takes possession of its creator and cuts him off from the pain of his own being.
And when . . . sea In Yeats's play *On Baile's Strand* (pronounced Bala) Cuchulain dies fighting the waves, and the Fool and Blind Man steal bread from the full ovens of the empty houses nearby.

Heart-mysteries there,° and yet when all is said
It was the dream itself enchanted me:
Character isolated by a deed
30 To engross the present and dominate memory.
Players and painted stage took all my love,
And not those things that they were emblems of.°

III
Those masterful images because complete
Grew in pure mind, but out of what began?
A mound of refuse or the sweepings of a street,
Old kettles, old bottles, and a broken can,
Old iron, old bones, old rags, that raving slut
Who keeps the till. Now that my ladder's gone,
I must lie down where all the ladders start,
40 In the foul rag-and-bone shop of the heart.°
1938?   1940

Cuchulain Comforted

This is probably Yeats's last work. From *On Baile's Strand* (1903) Cuchulain (pronounced Cohullan) is a recurring feature in Yeats's plays, of which five include him.
In *The Green Helmet* he is a figure of fearless creative joy; in *On Baile's Strand* his
integrity is impaired through lamentation for the lack of a son. In Yeats's first adaptation
of a Japanese Nōh play, *At the Hawk's Well,* he returns as part of a "system" allegory,
lured away from the fountain that represents Unity of Being; and in another dance
play, *The Only Jealousy of Emer,* an evil spirit occupies his body (wears his mask) and
Cuchulain is redeemed from death (after fighting the waves) by Emer's self-sacrifice.
Cuchulain appears once again in the very late dance play, *The Death of Cuchulain*
(1938), a remarkable work in which Cuchulain is finally killed by the Fool, and has a
vision of his departing soul as "a soft feathery shape." The last poem is closely related
to the final Cuchulain play; Yeats called it "a kind of sequel—strange, too, something
new." On January 7 he dictated a prose draft, which is close to the resulting poem.
Yeats uses Dante's *terza rima* (see Glossary, *Meter: versification*) and also imitates his
diction and imagery with unparalleled closeness; he means the poem to sound like an
encounter in the *Inferno*.

Heart-mysteries there Again Yeats apparently
finds this story allegorical of his own life.
Players . . . emblems of Yeats managed the
Abbey Theatre, and wrote much for it, between
1902 and 1910, neglecting (he implies) the
personal life of which the stage and the plays
were emblems.

Those . . . heart (ll. 33–40) The images he
speaks of belonged to the mind, but started in
the heart; now, with no access to them, he is
left lying in the "mire" of his experience,
unredeemed by dream.

Cuchulain Comforted

A man that had six mortal wounds, a man
Violent and famous, strode among the dead;
Eyes stared out of the branches and were gone.

Then certain Shrouds that muttered head to head
Came and were gone. He leant upon a tree
As though to meditate on wounds and blood.

A Shroud that seemed to have authority
Among those bird-like things came, and let fall
A bundle of linen. Shrouds by two and three

Came creeping up because the man was still.
And thereupon that linen-carrier said:
'Your life can grow much sweeter if you will

Obey our ancient rule and make a shroud;
Mainly because of what we only know
The rattle of those arms makes us afraid.

We thread the needles' eyes, and all we do
All must together do.' That done, the man
Took up the nearest and began to sew.°

'Now must we sing and sing the best we can,
But first you must be told our character:
Convicted cowards all, by kindred slain

Or driven from home and left to die in fear.'
They sang, but had nor human tunes nor words,
Though all was done in common as before,

They had changed their throats and had the throats of birds.
1938–39   1940

Autobiographies

Yeats's output of prose was very large, ranging from journalism of small importance to the long excogitated and central document of his thought, A Vision, of which the final revision appeared in 1937. Few, however, would disagree that his most impressive work of art in prose is the accumulation of autobiographical material which, over the years, he shaped into a strange unity and called Autobiographies (later The Autobiography). This work reflects his intense and continuous effort to shape himself as man and poet; to escape from the destructive "multiplicity" of his youth and give his life and work the power and authority that come only from relatedness and unity. In a lecture of 1910 Yeats defended the position that knowledge of a poet's life is

---

We thread . . . sew (ll. 16–18) recalling a famous passage in Inferno XV; e si ver noi aguzzevan le ciglia / come vecchio sartor fu

nella cruna ("and knitted their brows at us like an old tailor peering at his needle")

relevant to his work, for the reader ought to see the work as "no rootless flower but the speech of a man." The life and the poetry will have the same symbolic patterns. Yeats labored over the successive sections of the work (concealing their sources in letters and diaries), and making them conform to the state of his thought and poetry at the time of writing. The first section, *Reveries over Childhood and Youth*, was written in 1914. *The Trembling of the Veil*, the second section, came out in 1922, and included some reworked earlier material. *Dramatis Personae*, covering Yeats's life from 1896 to 1902, and including *Estrangement* (from a diary of 1909), *The Death of Synge*, and *The Bounty of Sweden*, also earlier pieces, the last inspired by his Nobel Prize, appeared in 1936. These were added to *Reveries* and *Trembling* (which were revised in 1926), and the whole was published as *Autobiographies* (1938). There are accordingly six autobiographies, all in different ways what Yeats called "stylistic arrangements of experience." The first, *Reveries*, is about childhood in Ireland and London, youthful dealings with his occultist uncle George Pollexfen, and early reading —the abandonment of conventional knowledge for "psychical research and mystical philosophy." This takes him up to the period described in the first section (Four Years, 1887–91) of *The Trembling of the Veil*. The title he explains thus: "I have found in an old diary a saying from Stéphane Mallarmé, that his epoch was troubled by the trembling of the veil of the Temple" (the allusion is to Matthew 27:51, the rending of the Temple veil at the time of the Crucifixion). The figure is apocalyptic; during the years covered in the book, says Yeats, Mallarmé's words were still true. The beginning of the end was at hand, the change to a new historical epoch that Yeats predicted for 1927.

The selections below are from the third and fourth of the five sections of *The Trembling of the Veil*. At the time described Yeats had a full life; he was deep in occult studies and practices, and in 1891 helped to found the Rhymers' Club, which included Lionel Johnson, Ernest Dowson, John Davidson, Arthur Symons, and others. He was still unhappily in love with Maud Gonne, and this obsession survived love affairs with other women as well as her marriage to John MacBride in 1903. Yet during these years he was, with that marvelous energy which underlies all the affectations of languor in life and work, "hammering his thoughts into unity" (see the essay "If I Were Four and Twenty" in *Explorations* (1962), p. 263).

As in the theoretical elaborations of *A Vision*, Yeats's purpose was "getting one's mind into order," so enabling it to be creative. Lost on the "Path of the Cameleon" it could not free itself of useless multiplicity, or "choose from among [generalizations] those that belonged" to his life. So too with his friends: they also had to be set in order, even, in the end, distributed among the Twenty-eight Phases of the Moon in his system. In this system the Fifteenth Phase represents a Unity of Being toward which artists aspire, though they never attain it. Subjective types, including artists, belong to phases Nine to Twenty-one, and seek fulfillment in an inner self, called a mask; objective types seek fulfillment in the outside world. In *Trembling* he considers his friends in the light of such preoccupations.

The first selection is part of a discussion of the reservoir of souls and images, the Platonic *anima mundi* to which poets, like others, have access ("I know now that revelation is from the self, but from that age-long memoried self, that shapes the elaborate shell of the mollusc and the child in the womb, that teaches the birds to make their nests"). Poets achieve it by crises of despair. "What portion in the world can the artist have, / Who has awakened from the common dream, / But dissipation and despair?"—asks Yeats, quoting his own "Ego Dominus Tuus" (written 1915). And in the fourth section of *Trembling* he considers those artist friends who "had to face their ends when young" (*The Grey Rock*, 1913). Yeats himself was not given to drugs, drink, or harlots; yet around him were men who seemed to reflect in their personalities the disaster of the artist in a world hurrying on to an apocalypse of the objective era. They are his "Tragic Generation," and Lionel Johnson was the most characteristic. Johnson and Dowson alike lacked any objective relation with the world. They, together with the more objective Symons, the victimized Beardsley, and Verlaine, are all systematically placed, all organized in relation to the image of poetry and revelation. This Yeats called the Fifteenth Phase; its image was a Salome-like dancer calling for the head of the victim. Yet Yeats, in his account of these men's struggle for vision, is not solemn or unduly schematic; the strength and conviction of what he says do not preclude humor, or stifle his acute sense of anecdote. When that Unity of Being which he admired in the Renaissance (1450 A.D. and somewhat later, he says) was no longer possible because of the widening gyre of the age, when soul and body began to fall apart, and the quest for the Image required secret study and difficult poetry, men could still be fascinating and even funny. Wilde's tragic life did not prevent his being a great comedian; and the last mention of him in Yeats's book is the ribald story about his exploit with Dowson in Dieppe. This blend of high seriousness and a sense of the comic is one of the many attributes that place Yeats's among the greatest of all autobiographies.

From The Trembling of the Veil: III

Hodos Chameliontos

III

At Sligo we walked twice every day, once after lunch and once after dinner, to the same gate on the road to Knocknarea;[1] and at Rosses Point, to the same rock upon the shore; and as we walked we exchanged those thoughts that never rise before me now without bringing some sight of mountain or of shore. Considering that Mary Battle[2] received our thoughts in sleep, though coarsened or turned to caricature, do not the thoughts of the scholar or the hermit, though they speak no word, or something of their shape and impulse, pass into the general mind? Does not the emotion of some woman of fashion, caught in the subtle torture of self-analysing passion, pass down, although she speak no word, to Joan with her Pot, Jill with her Pail and, it may be, with one knows not what nightmare melancholy to Tom the Fool?

Seeing that a vision could divide itself in divers complementary portions, might not the thought of philosopher or poet or mathematician depend at every moment of its progress upon some complementary thought in minds perhaps at a great distance? Is there nation-wide multiform reverie, every mind passing through a stream of suggestion, and all streams acting and reacting upon one another no matter how distant the minds, how dumb the

1. Mountain near Sligo.
2. Servant of Yeats's uncle, George Pollexfen; she had "second sight."

lips? A man walked, as it were, casting a shadow, and yet one could never say which was man and which was shadow, or how many the shadows that he cast. Was not a nation, as distinguished from a crowd of chance comers, bound together by this interchange among streams or shadows; that Unity of Image, which I sought in national literature, being but an originating symbol? From the moment when these speculations grew vivid, I had created for myself an intellectual solitude, most arguments that could influence action had lost something of their meaning. How could I judge any scheme of education, or of social reform, when I could not measure what the different classes and occupations contributed to that invisible commerce of reverie and of sleep: and what is luxury and what necessity when a fragment of gold braid, or a flower in the wallpaper may be an originating impulse to revolution or to philosophy? I began to feel myself not only solitary but helpless.

IV

I had not taken up these subjects wilfully, nor through love of strangeness, nor love of excitement, nor because I found myself in some experimental circle, but because unaccountable things had happened even in my childhood, and because of an ungovernable craving. When supernatural events begin, a man first doubts his own testimony, but when they repeat themselves again and again, he doubts all human testimony. At least he knows his own bias, and may perhaps allow for it, but how trust historian and psychologist that have for some three hundred years ignored in writing of the history of the world, or of the human mind, so momentous a part of human experience? What else had they ignored and distorted? When Mesmerists [3] first travelled about as public entertainers, a favourite trick was to tell a mesmerised man that some letter of the alphabet had ceased to exist, and after that to make him write his name upon the blackboard. Brown, or Jones, or Robinson would become upon the instant, and without any surprise or hesitation, Rown, or Ones, or Obinson.

Was modern civilisation a conspiracy of the subconscious? Did we turn away from certain thoughts and things because the Middle Ages lived in terror of the dark, or had some seminal illusion been imposed upon us by beings greater than ourselves for an unknown purpose? Even when no facts of experience were denied, might not what had seemed logical proof be but a mechanism of change, an automatic impulse? Once in London, at a dinner party, where all the guests were intimate friends, I had written upon a piece of paper, 'In five minutes York Powell [4] will talk of a burning house,' thrust the paper under my neighbour's plate, and imagined my fire symbol, and waited in silence. Powell shifted conversation from topic to topic and within the five minutes was describing a fire he had seen as a young man. When Locke's French translator Coste [5] asked him how, if there were no 'innate ideas,' he could explain the skill shown by a bird in making its nest, Locke replied,

3. Franz Anton Mesmer (1734?–1815), an Austrian physician, developed a theory of animal magnetism and gave his name to hypnotists.
4. Frederick York Powell (1850–1904), historian and Icelandic scholar.
5. Pierre Coste (1668–1747) translated Locke's *Reasonableness of Christianity* (1696) and his *Essay on Human Understanding* (1700).

'I did not write to explain the actions of dumb creatures,' and his translator thought the answer 'very good, seeing that he had named his book *A Philosophical Essay upon Human Understanding.*' Henry More,[6] upon the other hand, considered that the bird's instinct proved the existence of the Anima Mundi,[7] with its ideas and memories. Did modern enlightenment think with Coste that Locke had the better logic, because it was not free to think otherwise?

v

I ceased to read modern books that were not books of imagination, and if some philosophic idea interested me, I tried to trace it back to its earliest use, believing that there must be a tradition of belief older than any European Church, and founded upon the experience of the world before the modern bias. It was this search for a tradition that urged George Pollexfen[8] and myself to study the visions and thoughts of the country people, and some country conversation, repeated by one or the other, often gave us a day's discussion. These visions, we soon discovered, were very like those we called up by symbol. Mary Battle, looking out of the window at Rosses Point, saw coming from Knocknarea, where Queen Maeve, according to local folklore, is buried under a great heap of stones, 'the finest woman you ever saw travelling right across from the mountains and straight to here.'—I quote a record written at the time. 'She looked very strong, but not wicked' (that is to say, not cruel). 'I have seen the Irish Giant' (some big man shown at a fair). 'And though he was a fine man he was nothing to her, for he was round and could not have stepped out so soldierly . . . she had no stomach on her but was slight and broad in the shoulders, and was handsomer than any one you ever saw; she looked about thirty.' And when I asked if she had seen others like her, she said, 'Some of them have their hair down, but they look quite different, more like the sleepy-looking ladies one sees in the papers. Those with their hair up are like this one. The others have long white dresses, but those with their hair up have short dresses, so that you can see their legs right up to the calf.' And when I questioned her, I found that they wore what might well be some kind of buskin. 'They are fine and dashing-looking, like the men one sees riding their horses in twos and threes on the slopes of the mountains with their swords swinging. There is no such race living now, none so finely proportioned. . . . When I think of her and the ladies now they are like little children running about not knowing how to put their clothes on right . . . why, I would not call them women at all.'

Not at this time, but some three or four years later, when the visions came without any conscious use of symbol for a short time, and with much greater vividness, I saw two or three forms of this incredible beauty, one especially that must always haunt my memory. Then, too, the Master Pilot told us of meeting at night close to the Pilot House a procession of women in what seemed the costume of another age. Were they really people of the past, revisiting, perhaps, the places where they lived, or must I explain them, as

6. English Platonist (1614–87).
7. The Platonists' World Soul, provider of principle of growth in the creation, and reservoir of unconscious images.
8. See note on "In Memory of Major Robert Gregory."

I explained that vision of Eden as a mountain garden, by some memory of the race, as distinct from living memory? Certainly these Spirits, as the country people called them, seemed full of personality; were they not capricious, generous, spiteful, anxious, angry, and yet did that prove them more than images and symbols? When I used a combined earth and fire and lunar symbol my seer, a girl of twenty-five, saw an obvious Diana and her dogs, about a fire in a cavern. Presently, judging from her closed eyes, and from the tone of her voice, that she was in trance, not in reverie, I wished to lighten the trance a little, and made through carelessness or hasty thinking a symbol of dismissal; and at once she started and cried out, 'She says you are driving her away too quickly. You have made her angry.' Then, too, if my visions had a subjective element, so had Mary Battle's, for her fairies had but one tune, *The Distant Waterfall*, and she never heard anything described in a sermon at the Cathedral that she did not 'see it after,' and spoke of seeing in this way the gates of Purgatory.

Furthermore, if my images could affect her dreams, the folk-images could affect mine in turn, for one night I saw between sleeping and waking a strange long-bodied pair of dogs, one black and one white, that I found presently in some country tale. How, too, could one separate the dogs of the country tale from those my uncle heard bay in his pillow? In order to keep myself from nightmare, I had formed the habit of imagining four watch-dogs, one at each corner of my room, and, though I had not told him or anybody, he said, 'Here is a very curious thing; most nights now, when I lay my head upon the pillow, I hear a sound of dogs baying—the sound seems to come up out of the pillow.' A friend of Strindberg's,[9] in *delirium tremens*,[10] was haunted by mice, and a friend in the next room heard the squealing of the mice.

VI

I have much evidence that these images, or the symbols that call them up, can influence the bodily health. My uncle told me one evening that there were cases of smallpox—it turned out to be untrue—somewhere under Knocknarea, and that the doctor was coming to vaccinate him. Vaccination, probably from some infection in the lymph, brought on a very serious illness, blood-poisoning I heard it called, and presently he was delirious and a second doctor called in consultation. Between eleven and twelve one night when the delirium was at its height, I sat down beside his bed and said, 'What do you see, George?' He said, 'Red dancing figures,' and without commenting, I imagined the cabalistic symbol of water and almost at once he said, 'There is a river running through the room,' and a little later, 'I can sleep now.' I told him what I had done and that, if the dancing figures came again, he was to bid them go in the name of the Archangel Gabriel. Gabriel is angel of the Moon in the Cabala and might, I considered, command the waters at a pinch. The doctor found him much better and heard that I had driven the delirium away and given him such a word of command that when the red men came again in the middle of the night, they looked greatly startled, and fled.

9. August Strindberg (1849–1912), Swedish playwright.
10. A pathological condition resulting from excessive use of alcohol.

The doctor came, questioned, and said, 'Well, I suppose it is a kind of hypnotism, but it is very strange, very strange.' The delirium did not return.

VII

To that multiplicity of interest and opinion, of arts and sciences, which had driven me to conceive a Unity of Culture defined and evoked by Unity of Image, I had but added a multiplicity of images, and I was the more troubled because, the first excitement over, I had done nothing to rouse George Pollexfen from the gloom and hypochondria always thickening about him. I asked no help of books, for I believed that the truth I sought would come to me like the subject of a poem, from some moment of passionate experience, and that if I filled my exposition with other men's thought, other men's investigation, I would sink into all that multiplicity of interest and opinion. That passionate experience could never come—of that I was certain—until I had found the right image or right images. From what but the image of Apollo, fixed always in memory and passion, did his priesthood get that occasional power, a classical historian has described, of lifting great stones and snapping great branches; and did not Gemma Galgani,[11] like many others that had gone before, in 1889 cause deep wounds to appear in her body by contemplating her crucifix? In the essay that Wilde read to me one Christmas Day, occurred these words —'What does not the world owe to the imitation of Christ, what to the imitation of Caesar?' and I had seen Macgregor Mathers [12] paint little pictures combining the forms of men, animals, and birds, according to a rule which provided a combination for every possible mental condition, and I had heard him say, upon what authority I do not remember, that citizens of ancient Egypt assumed, when in contemplation, the images of their gods.

But now image called up image in an endless procession, and I could not always choose among them with any confidence; and when I did choose, the image lost its intensity, or changed into some other image. I had but exchanged the temptation of Flaubert's *Bouvard et Pecuchet* for that of his *St. Anthony*,[13] and I was lost in that region a cabalistic manuscript, shown me by Macgregor Mathers, had warned me of; astray upon the Path of the Cameleon, upon *Hodos Chameliontos*.[14]

11. 1878–1903; modern Christian mystic and canonized saint of the Catholic Church. The phenomenon mentioned by Yeats is known as the *stigmata*.
12. 1854–1918; occultist, Freemason, member of the Magical Order of the Golden Dawn, which Yeats joined; he introduced Yeats to symbol-induced trances.
13. Gustave Flaubert (1821–80), French novelist, author of *Madame Bovary* (1857). His *Temptation of Saint Anthony* (1874) is a highly wrought and symbolic account of the sensual temptations besetting the ascetic saint, founder of Christian monasticism; *Bouvard et Pécuchet* (published posthumously and unfinished, 1881) is the story of two clerks who experiment absurdly in various branches of human knowledge—an expression of disgust at human stupidity.
14. The chameleon, which changes color to match its environment, is here a symbol of intellectual instability and multiplicity.

From The Trembling of the Veil: IV

The Tragic Generation

III

Somewhere about 1450, though later in some parts of Europe by a hundred years or so, and in some earlier, men attained to personality in great numbers, 'Unity of Being,' and became like a 'perfectly proportioned human body,' and as men so fashioned held places of power, their nations had it too, prince and ploughman sharing that thought and feeling. What afterwards showed for rifts and cracks were there already, but imperious impulse held all together. Then the scattering came, the seeding of the poppy, bursting of pea-pod, and for a time personality seemed but the stronger for it. Shakespeare's people make all things serve their passion, and that passion is for the moment the whole energy of their being—birds, beasts, men, women, landscape, society, are but symbols, and metaphors, nothing is studied in itself, the mind is a dark well, no surface, depth only. The men that Titian [1] painted, the men that Jongsen [2] painted, even the men of Van Dyck,[3] seemed at moments like great hawks at rest. In the Dublin National Gallery there hung, perhaps there still hang, upon the same wall, a portrait of some Venetian gentleman by Strozzi [4] and Mr. Sargent's [5] painting of President Wilson. Whatever thought broods in the dark eyes of that Venetian gentleman, has drawn its life from his whole body; it feeds upon it as the flame feeds upon the candle—and should that thought be changed, his pose would change, his very cloak would rustle for his whole body thinks. President Wilson lives only in the eyes, which are steady and intent; the flesh about the mouth is dead, and the hands are dead, and the clothes suggest no movement of his body, nor any movement but that of the valet, who has brushed and folded in mechanical routine. There, all was an energy flowing outward from the nature itself; here, all is the anxious study and slight deflection of external force; there man's mind and body were predominantly subjective; here all is objective, using those words not as philosophy uses them, but as we use them in conversation.

The bright part of the moon's disk, to adopt the symbolism of a certain poem, is subjective mind, and the dark, objective mind, and we have eight and twenty Phases for our classification of mankind, and of the movement

---

1. Tiziano Vecelli (1477?–1576) greatest of the Venetian painters.
2. In all editions of the work this name appears as *Jongsen*, but there was no such painter. A check of the manuscripts in Dublin, kindly made for us by Professor Denis Donoghue, reveals that in one Yeats has left a blank, and in the other written an indecipherable name beginning with J. (Yeats had some uncertainty about which painters to put in, and at first wrote "Velasquez" instead of Van Dyke.) The likeliest conjecture (J. B. Trapp's) is *Jonson*. Cornelius Jonson or Johnson van Ceulen (1593–1661), born in London of Dutch parents, was a portrait painter who, like Van Dyke, worked for Charles I and for other English patrons before settling in Holland in 1643. Possibly Yeats was uncertain about the spelling of the name, but Professor Donoghue says he cannot see how anybody could have read it as *Jongsen*.
3. Sir Anthony Vandyke or Van Dyck (1599–1641), Flemish artist, court painter to Charles I of England.
4. Bernardo Strozzi ("Il Cappucino"; 1581–1644), painter of the Venetian school, and a Capuchin friar.
5. John Singer Sargent (1856–1925), American painter celebrated for his portraits.

of its thought. At the first Phase—the night where there is no moonlight—all is objective, while when, upon the fifteenth night, the moon comes to the full, there is only subjective mind. The mid-renaissance could but approximate to the full moon 'For there's no human life at the full or the dark,' [6] but we may attribute to the next three nights of the moon the men of Shakespeare, of Titian, of Strozzi, and of Van Dyck, and watch them grow more reasonable, more orderly, less turbulent, as the nights pass; and it is well to find before the fourth—the nineteenth moon counting from the start—a sudden change, as when a cloud becomes rain, or water freezes, for the great transitions are sudden; popular, typical men have grown more ugly and more argumentative; the face that Van Dyck called a fatal face [7] has faded before Cromwell's warty opinionated head. Henceforth no mind made like 'a perfectly proportionated human body' shall sway the public, for great men must live in a portion of themselves, become professional and abstract; but seeing that the moon's third quarter is scarce passed; that abstraction has attained but not passed its climax; that a half, as I affirm it, of the twenty-second night still lingers, they may subdue and conquer, cherish even some Utopian dream, spread abstraction ever further till thought is but a film, and there is no dark depth any more, surface only. But men who belong by nature to the nights near to the full are still born, a tragic minority, and how shall they do their work when too ambitious for a private station, except as Wilde [8] of the nineteenth Phase, as my symbolism has it, did his work? He understood his weakness, true personality was impossible, for that is born in solitude, and at his moon one is not solitary; he must project himself before the eyes of others, and, having great ambition, before some great crowd of eyes; but there is no longer any great crowd that cares for his true thought. He must humour and cajole and pose, take worn-out stage situations, for he knows that he may be as romantic as he please, so long as he does not believe in his romance, and all that he may get their ears for a few strokes of contemptuous wit in which he does believe.

We Rhymers did not humour and cajole; but it was not wholly from demerit, it was in part because of different merit, that he refused our exile. Shaw, as I understand him, has no true quarrel with his time, its moon and his almost exactly coincide. He is quite content to exchange Narcissus and his Pool for the signal-box at a railway junction, where goods and travellers pass perpetually upon their logical glittering road. Wilde was a monarchist, though content that monarchy should turn demagogue for its own safety, and he held a theatre by the means whereby he held a London dinner-table. 'He who can dominate a London dinner-table,' he had boasted, 'can dominate the world.' While Shaw has but carried his street-corner socialist eloquence on to the stage, and in him one discovers, in his writing and his public speech, as once —before their outline had been softened by prosperity or the passage of the years—in his clothes and in his stiff joints, the civilisation that Sargent's

6. Yeats is quoting his own "system" poem, *The Phases of the Moon*, written 1918.
7. That of Charles I.
8. Oscar Wilde (1854–1900), flamboyant wit, dramatist, novelist, poet, and essayist, whose tragic life (convicted of sodomy, he was in prison 1895–97 and lived in exile thereafter) made a deep impression on his friend Yeats.

picture has explored. Neither his crowd nor he have yet made a discovery that brought President Wilson so near his death, that the moon draws to its fourth quarter. But what happens to the individual man whose moon has come to that fourth quarter, and what to the civilisation . . . ?

I can but remember pipe music to-night, though I can half hear beyond it in the memory a weightier music, but this much at any rate is certain—the dream of my early manhood, that a modern nation can return to Unity of Culture, is false; though it may be we can achieve it for some small circle of men and women, and there leave it till the moon bring round its century. . . .

XI

Gradually Arthur Symons [9] came to replace in my intimate friendship, Lionel Johnson [10] from who I was slowly separated by a scruple of conscience. If he came to see me he sat tongue-tied unless I gave him the drink that seemed necessary to bring his vitality to but its normal pitch, and if I called upon him he drank so much that I became his confederate. Once, when a friend and I had sat long after our proper bed-time at his constantly repeated and most earnest entreaty, knowing what black melancholy would descend upon him at our departure, and with the unexpressed hope of getting him to his bed, he fixed upon us a laughing and whimsical look, and said:—'I want you two men to understand that you are merely two men that I am drinking with.' That was the only time that I was to hear from him an imaginary conversation that had not an air of the most scrupulous accuracy. He gave two accounts of a conversation with Wilde in prison; in one Wilde wore his hair long, and in the other it had been cropped by the prison barber. He was gradually losing, too, the faculty of experience, and in his prose and verse repeated the old ideas and emotions, but faintly, as though with fading interest. I am certain that he prayed much, and on those rare days that I came upon him dressed and active before mid-day or but little after, I concluded that he had been to morning Mass at Farm Street.[11]

When with Johnson I had tuned myself to his mood, but Arthur Symons, more than any man I have ever known, could slip as it were into the mind of another, and my thoughts gained in richness and in clearness from his sympathy, nor shall I ever know how much my practice and my theory owe to the passages that he read me from Catullus and from Verlaine and Mallarmé.[12] I had read *Axel* [13] to myself or was still reading it, so slowly, and with

9. Arthur Symons (1865–1946), a prolific poet and writer on poetry; a dramatist, exponent of Wagner, the dance, and French Symbolist poetry, which he virtually introduced into England and the United States. His strong influence on Yeats is recorded here. He suffered a serious breakdown in middle life; he recovered his sanity but not his vigor or influence.
10. See note on "In Memory of Major Robert Gregory."
11. Immaculate Conception church, London, where artists and intellectuals forgathered.
12. Paul Verlaine (1844–95), Symbolist and Decadent poet; his disorderly life and subtle verse fascinated Yeats, who had met him in Paris and London. Stéphane Mallarmé (1842–98), the greatest of the Symbolist poets in France; Yeats attended some of his Tuesday salons.
13. Comte Philippe Auguste Mathias de Villiers de l'Isle-Adam (1838–89), pioneer Symbolist, whose drama *Axël* (1890) provided Yeats with his early motto: "As to living, our servants will do that for us."

so much difficulty, that certain passages had an exaggerated importance, while all remained so obscure that I could without much effort imagine that here at last was the Sacred Book I longed for. An Irish friend of mine lives in a house where beside a little old tower rises a great new Gothic hall and stair, and I have sometimes got him to extinguish all light but a little Roman lamp, and in that faint light and among great vague shadows, blotting away the unmeaning ornament, have imagined myself partaking in some incredible romance. Half-a-dozen times, beginning in boyhood with Shelley's *Prometheus Unbound*, I have in that mood possessed for certain hours or months the book that I long for; and Symons, without ever being false to his own impressionist view of art and of life, deepened as I think my longing.

It seems to me, looking backward, that we always discussed life at its most intense moment, that moment which gives a common sacredness to the Song of Songs, and to the Sermon on the Mount, and in which one discovers something supernatural, a stirring as it were of the roots of the hair. He was making those translations from Mallarmé and from Verlaine, from Calderon,[14] from St. John of the Cross,[15] which are the most accomplished metrical translations of our time, and I think that those from Mallarmé may have given elaborate form to my verses of those years, to the latter poems of *The Wind Among the Reeds*, to *The Shadowy Waters*, while Villiers de L'Isle Adam had shaped whatever in my *Rosa Alchemica*[16] Pater[17] had not shaped. I can remember the day in Fountain Court when he first read me Herodiade's address to some Sibyl who is her nurse and it may be the moon also:

> The horror of my virginity
> Delights me, and I would envelope me
> In the terror of my tresses, that, by night,
> Inviolate reptile, I might feel the white
> And glimmering radiance of thy frozen fire,
> Thou that art chaste and diest of desire,
> White night of ice and of the cruel snow!
> Eternal sister, my lone sister, lo
> My dreams uplifted before thee! now, apart,
> So rare a crystal is my dreaming heart,
> And all about me lives but in mine own
> Image, the idolatrous mirror of my pride,
> Mirroring this Herodiade diamond-eyed.

Yet I am certain that there was something in myself compelling me to attempt creation of an art as separate from everything heterogeneous and casual, from all character and circumstance, as some Herodiade[18] of our

14. Pedro Calderón de la Barca (1600–81), Spanish dramatist and poet.
15. San Juan de la Cruz (1542–91), Spanish mystic and author of a poem called *The Dark Night of the Soul*, of which Symons had made a good translation.
16. An essay included in *The Secret Rose* (1897).
17. Walter Horatio Pater (1839–94), Oxford don whose writings on the Renaissance and aesthetics, and especially his *Marius the Epicurean* (1885), powerfully affected the thought and prose of the young Yeats and his contemporaries.
18. Hérodiade (Salome) recurs frequently in late 19th-century poetry after Mallarmé; Yeats made her a complicated symbol of art.

theatre, dancing seemingly alone in her narrow moving luminous circle. Certainly I had gone a great distance from my first poems, from all that I had copied from the folk-art of Ireland, as from the statue of Mausolus [19] and his Queen, where the luminous circle is motionless and contains the entire popular life; and yet why am I so certain? I can imagine an Aran Islander who had strayed into the Luxembourg Gallery, turning bewildered from Impressionist or Post-Impressionist, but lingering at Moreau's 'Jason,' [20] to study in mute astonishment the elaborate background, where there are so many jewels, so much wrought stone and moulded bronze. Had not lover promised mistress in his own island song, 'A ship with a gold and silver mast, gloves of the skin of a fish, and shoes of the skin of a bird, and a suit of the dearest silk in Ireland'?

XII

Hitherto when in London I had stayed with my family in Bedford Park,[21] but now I was to live for some twelve months in chambers in the Temple [22] that opened through a little passage into those of Arthur Symons. If anybody rang at either door, one or other would look through a window in the connecting passage, and report. We would then decide whether one or both should receive the visitor, whether his door or mine should be opened, or whether both doors were to remain closed. I have never liked London, but London seemed less disagreeable when one could walk in quiet, empty places after dark, and upon a Sunday morning sit upon the margin of a fountain almost as alone as if in the country. I was already settled there, I imagine, when a publisher called and proposed that Symons should edit a Review [23] or Magazine, and Symons consented on the condition that Beardsley [24] were Art Editor—and I was delighted at his condition, as I think were all his other proposed contributors. Aubrey Beardsley had been dismissed from the Art editorship of The Yellow Book [25] under circumstances that had made us indignant. He had illustrated Wilde's Salome,[26] his strange satiric art had raised the popular press to fury, and at the height of the excitement aroused by Wilde's condemnation, a popular novelist, a woman who had great influence among the most conventional part of the British public, had written demanding his dismissal. 'She owed it to her position before the British people,' she had said. Beardsley was not even a friend of Wilde's—they even disliked each

19. 4th-century B.C. king in Asia Minor, enemy of Athens; his tomb at Halicarnassus is called the Mausoleum.
20. Gustave Moreau (1826–98), French artist much admired by the Yeats circle; he painted Hérodiade.
21. Bedford Park, a section near Chiswick in London, laid out by its architect, Norman Shaw, as a sort of Pre-Raphaelite village for people who wanted to escape Victorian taste. The Yeats family moved there in 1876.
22. The Temple (consisting of the Inner and Middle Temples) lies between Fleet Street and the Thames; accommodation is primarily for lawyers.
23. The Savoy was first issued in January 1896, and ceased publication in December 1896.
24. Aubrey Vincent Beardsley (1872–98), artist who worked in black and white; his book illustrations are inseparably associated with the Nineties.
25. In 1894 Beardsley was art editor of The Yellow Book (1894–97), which represented the Modernism checked by Wilde's trial.
26. Play, originally in French (1894), on which the libretto of Richard Strauss's opera (1905) was based.

other—he had no sexual abnormality, but he was certainly unpopular, and the moment had come to get rid of unpopular persons. The public at once concluded—they could hardly conclude otherwise, he was dismissed by telegram—that there was evidence against him, and Beardsley, who was some twenty-three years old, being embittered and miserable, plunged into dissipation. We knew that we must face an infuriated press and public, but being all young we delighted in enemies and in everything that had an heroic air.

XIII

We might have survived but for our association with Beardsley; perhaps, but for his *Under the Hill*,[27] a Rabelaisian fragment promising a literary genius as great maybe as his artistic genius; and for the refusal of the bookseller who controlled the railway bookstalls to display our wares. The bookseller's manager, no doubt looking for a design of Beardsley's, pitched upon Blake's *Anteus setting Virgil and Dante upon the verge of Cocytus* as the ground of refusal, and when Arthur Symons pointed out that Blake was considered 'a very spiritual artist,' replied, 'O, Mr. Symons, you must remember that we have an audience of young ladies as well as an audience of agnostics.' However, he called Arthur Symons back from the door to say, 'If contrary to our expectations the *Savoy* should have a large sale, we should be very glad to see you again.' As Blake's design illustrated an article of mine, I wrote a letter upon that remarkable saying to a principal daily newspaper. But I had mentioned Beardsley, and I was told that the editor had made it a rule that his paper was never to mention Beardsley's name. I said upon meeting him later, 'Would you have made the same rule in the case of Hogarth?'[28] against whom much the same objection could be taken, and he replied with what seemed to me a dreamy look, as though suddenly reminded of a lost opportunity—'Ah, there was no popular press in Hogarth's day.' We were not allowed to forget that in our own day there was a popular press, and its opinions began to affect our casual acquaintance, and even our comfort in public places. At some well-known house, an elderly man to whom I had just been introduced, got up from my side and walked to the other end of the room; but it was as much my reputation as an Irish rebel as the evil company that I was supposed to keep, that excited some young men in a railway carriage to comment upon my general career in voices raised that they might catch my attention. I discovered, however, one evening that we were perhaps envied as well as despised. I was in the pit at some theatre, and had just noticed Arthur Symons a little in front of me, when I heard a young man, who looked like a shop-assistant or clerk, say, 'There is Arthur Symons. If he can't get an order, why can't he pay for a stall?' Clearly we were supposed to prosper upon iniquity, and to go to the pit added a sordid parsimony. At another theatre I caught sight of a woman that I once liked, the widow of some friend of my father's youth, and tried to attract her attention, but she had no eyes for anything but the stage curtain; and at some house where I met no hostility to myself, a popular novelist snatched out of my hand a copy of the *Savoy*, and opening it at Beardsley's

27. A comic erotic fantasy first published in extracts in *The Savoy*, and with other writings in a volume of 1904.

28. William Hogarth (1697–1764), painter, engraver, pictorial satirist.

drawing, called *The Barber,* expounded what he called its bad drawing and
wound up with, 'Now if you want to admire really great black and white
art, admire the *Punch* [29] Cartoons of Mr. Lindley Sambourne.' Our hostess,
after making peace between us, said, 'O, Mr. Yeats, why do you not send
your poems to the *Spectator* [30] instead of to the *Savoy?*' The answer, 'My friends
read the *Savoy* and they do not read the *Spectator,*' called up a puzzled,
disapproving look.

Yet, even apart from Beardsley, we were a sufficiently distinguished body:
Max Beerbohm,[31] Bernard Shaw, Ernest Dowson, Lionel Johnson, Arthur
Symons, Charles Conder,[32] Charles Shannon,[33] Havelock Ellis,[34] Selwyn
Image,[35] Joseph Conrad; but nothing counted but the one hated name. I think
that had we been challenged we might have argued something after this
fashion: 'Science through much ridicule and some persecution has won its
right to explore whatever passes before its corporeal eye, and merely because
it passes: to set as it were upon an equality the beetle and the whale though
Ben Jonson could find no justification for the entomologist in *The New Inn,*[36]
but that he had been crossed in love. Literature now demands the same right
of exploration of all that passes before the mind's eye, and merely because it
passes.' Not a complete defence, for it substitutes a spiritual for a physical
objectivity, but sufficient it may be for the moment, and to settle our place
in the historical process.

The critic might well reply that certain of my generation delighted in writing with an unscientific partiality for subjects long forbidden. Yet is it not
most important to explore especially what has been long forbidden, and to
do this not only 'with the highest moral purpose,' like the followers of Ibsen,[37]
but gaily, out of sheer mischief, or sheer delight in that play of the mind?
Donne could be as metaphysical as he pleased, and yet never seemed unhuman
and hysterical as Shelley often does, because he could be as physical as he
pleased; and besides who will thirst for the metaphysical, who have a parched
tongue, if we cannot recover the Vision of Evil?

I have felt in certain early works of my own which I have long abandoned,
and here and there in the work of others of my generation, a slight, sentimental
sensuality which is disagreeable, and does not exist in the work of Donne,
let us say, because he, being permitted to say what he pleased, was never
tempted to linger, or rather to pretend that we can linger, between spirit and
sense.[38] How often had I heard men of my time talk of the meeting of spirit

---

29. British weekly, very roughly equivalent to *The New Yorker,* founded 1841 and originally radical.
30. British Conservative weekly, founded 1828.
31. Sir Max Beerbohm (1872–1956), caricaturist, novelist, critic.
32. Charles Conder (1868–1909), fan painter.
33. Charles Shannon (1863–1937), painter and lithographer.
34. Henry Havelock Ellis (1859–1939), author of the famous *Studies in the Psychology
of Sex* (1897–1928).
35. Selwyn Image, illustrator and designer (1849–1930).
36. A play of 1629.
37. Henrik Ibsen (1828–1906), greatest Norwegian playwright; his work was admired by
Shaw and Joyce but not by Wilde and Yeats.
38. Despite the priority attributed to Eliot's essay *The Metaphysical Poets* (see below), it
was quite common to speak thus of Donne in Yeats's youth.

and sense, yet there is no meeting but only change upon the instant, and it is by the perception of a change, like the sudden 'blacking out' of the lights of the stage, that passion creates its most violent sensation.[39]

XIV

Dowson was now at Dieppe, now at a Normandy village. Wilde, too, was at Dieppe; and Symons, Beardsley, and others would cross and recross, returning with many tales, and there were letters and telegrams. Dowson wrote a protest against some friend's too vivid essay upon the disorder of his life, and explained that in reality he was living a life of industry in a little country village; but before the letter arrived that friend received a wire, 'arrested, sell watch and send proceeds.' Dowson's watch had been left in London—and then another wire, 'Am free.' Dowson, or so ran the tale as I heard it ten years after, had got drunk and fought the baker, and a deputation of villagers had gone to the magistrate and pointed out that Monsieur Dowson was one of the most illustrious of English poets. 'Quite right to remind me,' said the magistrate, 'I will imprison the baker.'

A Rhymer had seen Dowson at some café in Dieppe with a particularly common harlot, and as he passed, Dowson, who was half drunk, caught him by the sleeve and whispered, 'She writes poetry—it is like Browning and Mrs. Browning.' Then there came a wonderful tale, repeated by Dowson himself, whether by word of mouth or by letter I do not remember. Wilde had arrived in Dieppe, and Dowson pressed upon him the necessity of acquiring 'a more wholesome taste.' They emptied their pockets on to the café table, and though there was not much, there was enough if both heaps were put into one. Meanwhile the news had spread, and they set out accompanied by a cheering crowd. Arrived at their destination, Dowson and the crowd remained outside, and presently Wilde returned. He said in a low voice to Dowson, 'The first these ten years, and it will be the last. It was like cold mutton'—always, as Henley had said, 'a scholar and a gentleman' he now remembered that the Elizabethan dramatists used the words 'Cold mutton' [40]—and then aloud so that the crowd might hear him, 'But tell it in England, for it will entirely restore my character.'

1922, 1926, 1938

JAMES JOYCE
1882–1941

Like Yeats, another truly great writer of our age, Joyce was an Irishman who had to escape from Ireland in order that his imagination might be able to cope with it. Both his life, and the literary career which that life produced and which fed back into it, were directed toward an escape from isolation into universality: in the first instance, an escape from Ireland into Europe, which in his youthful reading and studies had been an earthly paradise within, but hemmed in on all sides by narrowness, bigotry, puritanism, and gray despair. In the second instance, the journey of his imaginative life was from small forms to large, from lyric to epic, from literature to myth. His life

---

39. See "Lapis Lazuli."
40. Mutton was Elizabethan slang for "prostitute."

and art were so programmatically intertwined that it is hard to comment on his biography without referring to his books, particularly the earlier two, *Dubliners*, and *A Portrait of the Artist as a Young Man.* This is as he might have wished.

Joyce was born to a middle-class Dublin family somewhat come down in the world; his father, as reflected in Simon Daedalus of the autobiographical *A Portrait of the Artist as a Young Man* (1916), had been and done many things but was, like Joyce's own vision of Ireland itself, "at present a praiser of his own past." Joyce attended two Jesuit schools, Clongowes Wood School and, thereafter, Belvedere College, and at sixteen started studying at University College, Dublin, the institution for which John Henry Newman wrote *The Idea of a University.* He had rejected the possibility of entering the Jesuit order, and experienced an early vocation of another sort, a Paterian call to self-fulfillment in art. He read modern languages in college and in 1900 wrote an essay on Ibsen which earned him a certain amount of notoriety (he had learned Norwegian in order to read and correspond with this writer, who spoke so directly to the condition of an artistic temperament struggling to break free from an oppressive society).

Like Stephen Daedalus, Joyce chose "silence, exile and cunning" as his mode of action. After graduating from the university in 1902, he went to Paris, returned briefly to Dublin at his mother's death, and then left Ireland for ever. Nora Barnacle, his girl, went with him. They went to Trieste, where he taught English in a Berlitz school, and then to Zurich, where they remained until 1920. Then they moved to Paris and lived there until the fall of France in 1940, when they returned to Zurich. Although Joyce and Nora had several children, they were married only in 1931, maintaining their irregular alliance with a kind of religious devotion. From about 1917 on, Joyce was the recipient of various kinds and amounts of patronage, both in Zurich and in Paris; and his cause, as an uncommercial writer and as a kind of saint of modernism in literature, was taken up by Ezra Pound, by T. S. Eliot, and by a close and adoring circle of friends in Paris, who made of him and his work something of a cult.

Dubliners, published in 1914, was his second finished book (*Chamber Music,* early lyric poems, had appeared in 1907). It is a collection of fifteen stories, each representing some instance of a failure of self-realization on the part of an inhabitant of the city. "My intention was to write a chapter of the moral history of my country," wrote Joyce to his publisher about this book, "and I chose Dublin for the scene because the city seemed to me to be the centre of paralysis." Indeed, the opening story of the book, about a failing priest, centers on a sensitive boy's apprehension without understanding of the magical sounds of the polysyllabic "paralysis." *Dubliners* starts out in the first person, and moves into the third person narration as though to carry out in miniature Joyce's plan for developing from lyrical art through dramatic to epic —an example of the hard-edged, neo-Aristotelian conceptualizing that his Thomistic education had led him to. And yet *Dubliners* ends, ironically, in lyric: the last story, "The Dead," a summation and concentration of all that has gone before, dissolves into magnificently resonant lyric in its last paragraph.

The "Dead" of the title are all the Dubliners of the preceding stories, and they are the ghosts of the past, sharing present moments with living consciousness. Gabriel Conroy, the story's hero, is the epitome of all the failed Dubliners in that he is aware of his predicament, knows where its solution lies (in journeys eastward, toward Europe, toward all that he holds civilization to be). He is what Joyce would have been had he remained, and the story is all the more powerful for being able to reveal his sensitivity and spiritual generosity.

But Joyce did transcend the condition of his characters in *Dubliners,* and he was able, from the spiritual safety of the Continent, to write of them in a manner both brilliantly and delicately naturalistic (the actual geography and business directory of Dublin pervades these stories), but seeded with symbolic germ everywhere. Whether or not a registering consciousness is present in the story (and often, it must be the reader or even the narrator himself), the resonances of words and phrases, clichés taken literally to reveal unavowed ironies, universal themes transubstantial in the ordinary, all flare up into prominence after more than a casual reading. Joyce himself theorized about this kind of poetic revelation; like the moments of intensification Walter Pater describes, or like the revelations of the "inscapes" in Gerard Manley Hopkins, the "epiphanies" of Stephen Daedalus—Joyce's youthful self in his fiction—are like momentary rips in a gray curtain of hopelessness. In an early manuscript called *Stephen Hero* and, later, more subtly worked out in *A Portrait of the Artist as a Young Man,* Joyce led Stephen, his Gabriel Conroy, his artist-intellectual who could fly out of the labyrinth of insularity on wings of language, through his crucial years. These are years of education, and of renunciation of the status of Dubliner for that of artist.

A Portrait (published in 1916) starts out lyrically and subjectively, and its longish sections cover discontinuous tableaus in Stephen's life. Joyce named him for St. Stephen the Deacon, the first martyr, and for St. Stephen's Green, the park outside University College. Daedalus was the master craftsman of Greek myth who built the famous labyrinth for King Minos; and, to escape it, fashioned wax wings for himself and for his son, Icarus, who came to an unfortunate end when he flew too near the sun. But Stephen is not Icarus, and Simon Daedalus is not Stephen's true father, but merely his biological one. It is his quest for a true, rather than merely an actual, familial identity, which occupies the book. It moves through a youthful sentimental amour, a refusal to become a Jesuit, and a remarkable perception—at twilight along a beach where a girl is standing in the water—of the possibilities of art for transcending the narrowness and spiritual suffocation that religion has become for him and (he feels) for his country.

Yet *A Portrait* still belonged to a known genre of the novel of adolescent awakening. With the exception of his Ibsenish play, *Exiles,* and some later lyric and satiric verses, his mature work would elude easy classification. *Ulysses* and *Finnegans Wake* are both monuments of comprehensiveness; and both books, centering totally on the Dublin Joyce had fled, make of their city an *omphalos,* as Joyce called it, a navel of the world, an oracular pit from which more than Delphic prophecies emerge. Both works, purged of the relentless bitterness of Stephen's self-protectiveness, achieve grandeur through comedy, and through the kind of complexity into which Joyce's early use of symbolic and mythological association (woven into the naturalistic fabric of *Dubliners*) had expanded. In the first of these works the very boundary between naturalism and epic poetry is redrawn at every moment, as is, in the second, that between languages, ages, cultures, and identities. And both works are quintessential examples of their age in that they absorb into themselves the annotations and footnotes on what they are: glosses that, in older books, lie ranged about their texts like borders.

Ulysses is not only Joyce's masterpiece but one of the major works in the entire epic tradition as well. Its germ lay in a possible story idea for *Dubliners,* of a day in the life of a Dublin citizen, but it was put aside until after *A Portrait* was completed. *Ulysses* plants that germ in the great cyclic epic of the *Odyssey,* the Homeric poem of wandering and return, of the hero's movements through different realms and distractions back to his native land and his wife. Even in classical times the *Odyssey* had begun to be read allegorically as a vision of the journey of every man: "Man," indeed, is its opening word. And for Joyce's "man" he chose an embodied joke, an Irish Jew named Leopold Bloom. *Ulysses* is a day in his life (specifically, June 16, 1904) and in the life of Dublin, itself a provincial island city standing for the world. Just as Stephen Daedalus's mythical father, rather than Simon Daedalus, his real one, assumes importance at the end of *A Portrait*, so Bloom's own dead infant son, Rudy, is symbolically supplanted in the novel by Stephen, now returned to Ireland from abroad, as Telemachus to Bloom's Odysseus. The Penelope is an unfaithful wife, Marion Tweedy Bloom ("Molly"), and there is a daughter named Milly.

The events of the day are banal, and universal. Bloom gets up, goes to a Turkish bath, then to the funeral of a friend, Paddy Dignam, shows up at his newspaper office (where he works selling advertising), has lunch, wanders about, goes to a library, makes some purchases, encounters other people, hears some singing, goes to a pub (where he is insulted), sits at twilight along a beach (where he stares up the skirts of a girl he does not know), masturbates, visits a lying-in hospital to inquire about the birth of a friend's baby, ends up in Nighttown, in a whorehouse where at midnight he meets up with Stephen Daedalus and takes him home with him. Meanwhile his wife Molly (with whom he has not slept since Rudy's death) has been cuckolding him with one Blazes Boylan, her concert manager. Molly is a singer; and singing—and particularly opera—plays a complex and vital role in *Ulysses:* an aria from Mozart's *Don Giovanni* and a popular late-nineteenth-century song by J. L. Molloy, "Love's Old Sweet Song," run throughout the book in various ways.

The most audacious element of Joyce's triumph is the style and construction of his comic masterpiece. Each section of the book parallels an incident in Homer, and the relation of each scene to its parallel is slightly different, in a variety of parodistic ways. The first three sections involve Telemachus, and are about Stephen's morning: getting up, teaching a history class at a boys' school (parallel to Nestor's advice in Homer), and walking along the beach, wrestling in his mind with the sea and a sea of thoughts that constantly change (as with Proteus, the old man of the sea) under the grip of intellect. Bloom's day moves through other sorts of parodies: thus Circe, who transforms men into beasts, is seen as Bella Cohen, the owner of a brothel, in a great scene of transformations in which all the events of the day become actualized in forms they might have taken, as well as in those they did.

The section of *Ulysses* given below is the episode Joyce referred to as *Nausicaa,* inasmuch as it parallels the Homeric scene in which the shipwrecked Odysseus is washed up on the strand of Phaeacia, an idyllic kingdom, and is discovered by Nausicaa, the king's daughter, who has gone down to the sea with her handmaidens to wash linen and (unofficially) to play ball. Joyce's episode occurs at dusk. Its style is a hilarious parody of sentimental fiction that is, in its own nastily evasive way, pornographic; in it, the world is seen through the horrendous clichés and coy rhetoric of the bad novels that its Nausicaa, a girl named Gerty MacDowell, would have read and absorbed. Gerty has gone to the beach with her friends Cissy and Edy and their assorted infant brothers; she sees Bloom and romanticizes his tired presence. Halfway through the chapter, an amazing reversal occurs, and we are given a deflating, debunking reduction of the sentimentality in the first part by shifting to the stream-of-consciousness technique with which Bloom's thoughts have been presented to us all along. Joyce referred, half-jokingly, to the technique of the chapter as "tumescencedetumescence," by which he meant not only the literal sexual event in it (Bloom's voyeuristic excitement and his orgasm) but the inflating-deflating of the language in the two halves. It typifies the comic brilliance of the book, which consists in some measure in never totally reducing its classical prototype by comparing it with the modern, and by never showing up the modern as sleazy in comparison with the original (it is not, in fact, mock- or anti-heroic like *The Waste Land*). Throughout *Nausicaa*, the reader is probably to think of the words of the chorus of "Love's Old Sweet Song," for the whole section is, jokingly, "Just a song at twilight / When the lamps are low." If its words are the comic deflation of sentimentally conceived, vulgarized romantic love, its melody unveils Bloom's sexual and domestic loneliness —estranged from Molly, separated from Milly, not actually linked even to Martha, with whom he has been trying to start an affair—embedded in his intellectual and mythological universality.

From Dubliners

The Dead

Lily, the caretaker's daughter, was literally run off her feet. Hardly had she brought one gentleman into the little pantry behind the office on the ground floor and helped him off with his overcoat than the wheezy hall-door bell clanged again and she had to scamper along the bare hallway to let in another guest. It was well for her she had not to attend to the ladies also. But Miss Kate and Miss Julia had thought of that and had converted the bathroom upstairs into a ladies' dressing-room. Miss Kate and Miss Julia were there, gossiping and laughing and fussing, walking after each other to the head of the stairs, peering down over the banisters and calling down to Lily to ask her who had come.

It was always a great affair, the Misses Morkan's annual dance. Everybody who knew them came to it, members of the family, old friends of the family, the members of Julia's choir, any of Kate's pupils that were grown up enough and even some of Mary Jane's pupils too. Never once had it fallen flat. For years and years it had gone off in splendid style as long as anyone could remember; ever since Kate and Julia, after the death of their brother Pat, had left the house in Stoney Batter and taken Mary Jane, their only niece, to live with them in the dark gaunt house on Usher's Island,[1] the upper part of which they had rented from Mr Fulham, the corn-factor [2] on the ground floor. That was a good thirty years ago if it was a day. Mary Jane, who was then a little girl in short clothes, was now the main prop of the household for she had the organ [3] in Haddington Road. She had been through the Academy and gave a pupils' concert every year in the upper room of the Antient Concert Rooms. Many of her pupils belonged to better-class families on the Kingstown and

1. One of the banks of the Liffey, in the city itself.
2. Crain merchant.
3. Was the organist.

Dalkey line. Old as they were, her aunts also did their share. Julia, though she was quite grey, was still the leading soprano in Adam and Eve's,[4] and Kate, being too feeble to go about much, gave music lessons to beginners on the old square piano in the back room. Lily, the caretaker's daughter, did housemaid's work for them. Though their life was modest they believed in eating well; the best of everything: diamond-bone sirloins, three-shilling tea and the best bottled stout. But Lily seldom made a mistake in the orders so that she got on well with her three mistresses. They were fussy, that was all. But the only thing they would not stand was back answers.

Of course they had good reason to be fussy on such a night. And then it was long after ten o'clock and yet there was no sign of Gabriel and his wife. Besides they were dreadfully afraid that Freddy Malins might turn up screwed.[5] They would not wish for worlds that any of Mary Jane's pupils should see him under the influence; and when he was like that it was sometimes very hard to manage him. Freddy Malins always came late but they wondered what could be keeping Gabriel: and that was what brought them every two minutes to the banisters to ask Lily had Gabriel or Freddy come.

—O, Mr Conroy, said Lily to Gabriel when she opened the door for him, Miss Kate and Miss Julia thought you were never coming. Good-night, Mrs Conroy.

—I'll engage they did, said Gabriel, but they forget that my wife here takes three mortal hours to dress herself.

He stood on the mat, scraping the snow from his goloshes, while Lily led his wife to the foot of the stairs and called out:

—Miss Kate, here's Mrs Conroy.

Kate and Julia came toddling down the dark stairs at once. Both of them kissed Gabriel's wife, said she must be perished alive and asked was Gabriel with her.

—Here I am as right as the mail, Aunt Kate! Go on up. I'll follow, called out Gabriel from the dark.

He continued scraping his feet vigorously while the the three women went upstairs, laughing, to the ladies' dressing-room. A light fringe of snow lay like a cape on the shoulders of his overcoat and like toecaps on the toes of his goloshes; and, as the buttons of his overcoat slipped with a squeaking noise through the snow-stiffened frieze, a cold fragrant air from out-of-doors escaped from crevices and folds.

—Is it snowing again, Mr Conroy? asked Lily.

She had preceded him into the pantry to help him off with his overcoat. Gabriel smiled at the three syllables she had given his surname and glanced at her. She was a slim, growing girl, pale in complexion and with hay-coloured hair. The gas in the pantry made her look still paler. Gabriel had known her when she was a child and used to sit on the lowest step nursing a rag doll.

—Yes, Lily, he answered, and I think we're in for a night of it.

He looked up at the pantry ceiling, which was shaking with the stamping and shuffling of feet on the floor above, listened for a moment to the piano

4. A parish church in Dublin.
5. Drunk.

and then glanced at the girl, who was folding his overcoat carefully at the end of a shelf.

—Tell me, Lily, he said in a friendly tone, do you still go to school?

—O no, sir, she answered. I'm done schooling this year and more.

—O, then, said Gabriel gaily, I suppose we'll be going to your wedding one of these fine days with your young man, eh?

The girl glanced back at him over her shoulder and said with great bitterness:

—The men that is now is only all palaver and what they can get out of you.

Gabriel coloured as if he felt he had made a mistake and, without looking at her, kicked off his goloshes and flicked actively with his muffler at his patent-leather shoes.

He was a stout tallish young man. The high colour of his cheeks pushed upwards even to his forehead where it scattered itself in a few formless patches of pale red; and on his hairless face there scintillated restlessly the polished lenses and the bright gilt rims of the glasses which screened his delicate and restless eyes. His glossy black hair was parted in the middle and brushed in a long curve behind his ears where it curled slightly beneath the groove left by his hat.

When he had flicked lustre into his shoes he stood up and pulled his waistcoat down more tightly on his plump body. Then he took a coin rapidly from his pocket.

—O Lily, he said, thrusting it into her hands, it's Christmastime, isn't it? Just . . . here's a little. . . .

He walked rapidly towards the door.

—O no, sir! cried the girl, following him. Really, sir, I wouldn't take it.

—Christmas-time! Christmas-time! said Gabriel, almost trotting to the stairs and waving his hand to her in deprecation.

The girl, seeing that he had gained the stairs, called out after him:

—Well, thank you, sir.

He waited outside the drawing-room door until the waltz should finish, listening to the skirts that swept against it and to the shuffling of feet. He was still discomposed by the girl's bitter and sudden retort. It had cast a gloom over him which he tried to dispel by arranging his cuffs and the bows of his tie. Then he took from his waistcoat pocket a little paper and glanced at the headings he had made for his speech. He was undecided about the lines from Robert Browning for he feared they would be above the heads of his hearers. Some quotation that they could recognise from Shakespeare or from the Melodies [6] would be better. The indelicate clacking of the men's heels and the shuffling of their soles reminded him that their grade of culture differed from his. He would only make himself ridiculous by quoting poetry to them which they could not understand. They would think that he was airing his superior education. He would fail with them just as he had failed with the girl in the

6. The *Irish Melodies* of Thomas Moore (1779–1852), romantic lyrics sung throughout the 19th century ("Believe me, if all those endearing young charms," for one, is still popular today). One of them, "O Ye Dead," begins "It is true, it is true, we are shadows cold and wan; / And the fair and the brave whom we loved on earth are gone." Joyce had it in mind while writing the story.

pantry. He had taken up a wrong tone. His whole speech was a mistake from first to last, an utter failure.

Just then his aunts and his wife came out of the ladies' dressing-room. His aunts were two small plainly dressed old women. Aunt Julia was an inch or so the taller. Her hair, drawn low over the tops of her ears, was grey; and grey also, with darker shadows, was her large flaccid face. Though she was stout in build and stood erect her slow eyes and parted lips gave her the appearance of a woman who did not know where she was or where she was going. Aunt Kate was more vivacious. Her face, healthier than her sister's, was all puckers and creases, like a shrivelled red apple, and her hair, braided in the same old-fashioned way, had not lost its ripe nut colour.

They both kissed Gabriel frankly. He was their favourite nephew, the son of their dead elder sister, Ellen, who had married T. J. Conroy of the Port and Docks.

—Gretta tells me you're not going to take a cab back to Monkstown to-night, Gabriel, said Aunt Kate.

—No, said Gabriel, turning to his wife, we had quite enough of that last year, hadn't we? Don't you remember, Aunt Kate, what a cold Gretta got out of it? Cab windows rattling all the way, and the east wind blowing in after we passed Merrion. Very jolly it was. Gretta caught a dreadful cold.

Aunt Kate frowned severely and nodded her head at every word.

—Quite right, Gabriel, quite right, she said. You can't be too careful.

—But as for Gretta there, said Gabriel, she'd walk home in the snow if she were let.

Mrs Conroy laughed.

—Don't mind him, Aunt Kate, she said. He's really an awful bother, what with green shades for Tom's eyes at night and making him do the dumb-bells, and forcing Eva to eat the stirabout.[7] The poor child! And she simply hates the sight of it! . . . O, but you'll never guess what he makes me wear now!

She broke out into a peal of laughter and glanced at her husband, whose admiring and happy eyes had been wandering from her dress to her face and hair. The two aunts laughed heartily too, for Gabriel's solicitude was a standing joke with them.

—Goloshes! said Mrs Conroy. That's the latest. Whenever it's wet underfoot I must put on my goloshes. Tonight even he wanted me to put them on, but I wouldn't. The next thing he'll buy me will be a diving suit.

Gabriel laughed nervously and patted his tie reassuringly while Aunt Kate nearly doubled herself, so heartily did she enjoy the joke. The smile soon faded from Aunt Julia's face and her mirthless eyes were directed towards her nephew's face. After a pause she asked:

—And what are goloshes, Gabriel?

—Goloshes, Julia! exclaimed her sister. Goodness me, don't you know what goloshes are? You wear them over your . . . over your boots, Gretta, isn't it?

—Yes, said Mrs Conroy. Guttapercha things. We both have a pair now. Gabriel says everyone wears them on the continent.

—O, on the continent, murmured Aunt Julia, nodding her head slowly.

7. Porridge.

Gabriel knitted his brows and said, as if he were slightly angered:

—It's nothing very wonderful but Gretta thinks it very funny because she says the word reminds her of Christy Minstrels.[8]

—But tell me, Gabriel, said Aunt Kate, with brisk tact. Of course, you've seen about the room. Gretta was saying . . .

—O, the room is all right, replied Gabriel. I've taken one in the Gresham.[9]

—To be sure, said Aunt Kate, by far the best thing to do. And the children, Gretta, you're not anxious about them?

—O, for one night, said Mrs Conroy. Besides, Bessie will look after them.

—To be sure, said Aunt Kate again. What a comfort it is to have a girl like that, one you can depend on! There's that Lily, I'm sure I don't know what has come over her lately. She's not the girl she was at all.

Gabriel was about to ask his aunt some questions on this point but she broke off suddenly to gaze after her sister who had wandered down the stairs and was craning her neck over the banisters.

—Now, I ask you, she said, almost testily, where is Julia going? Julia! Julia! Where are you going?

Julia, who had gone halfway down one flight, came back and announced blandly:

—Here's Freddy.

At the same moment a clapping of hands and a final flourish of the pianist told that the waltz had ended. The drawing-room door was opened from within and some couples came out. Aunt Kate drew Gabriel aside hurriedly and whispered into his ear:

—Slip down, Gabriel, like a good fellow and see if he's all right, and don't let him up if he's screwed. I'm sure he's screwed. I'm sure he is.

Gabriel went to the stairs and listened over the banisters. He could hear two persons talking in the pantry. Then he recognised Freddy Malins' laugh. He went down the stairs noisily.

—It's such a relief, said Aunt Kate to Mrs Conroy, that Gabriel is here. I always feel easier in my mind when he's here. . . . Julia, there's Miss Daly and Miss Power will take some refreshment. Thanks for your beautiful waltz, Miss Daly. It made lovely time.

A tall wizen-faced man, with a stiff grizzled moustache and swarthy skin, who was passing out with his partner said:

—And may we have some refreshment, too, Miss Morkan?

—Julia, said Aunt Kate summarily, and here's Mr Browne and Miss Furlong. Take them in, Julia, with Miss Daly and Miss Power.

—I'm the man for the ladies, said Mr Browne, pursing his lips until his moustache bristled and smiling in all his wrinkles. You know, Miss Morkan, the reason they are so fond of me is—

He did not finish his sentence, but, seeing that Aunt Kate was out of earshot, at once led the three young ladies into the back room. The middle of the room was occupied by two square tables placed end to end, and on these Aunt Julia and the caretaker were straightening and smoothing a large cloth.

8. A famous blackface minstrel show troupe.
9. Not the most elegant hotel in Dublin, but comfortable and respectable.

On the sideboard were arrayed dishes and plates, and glasses and bundles of knives and forks and spoons. The top of the closed square piano served also as a sideboard for viands and sweets. At a smaller sideboard in one corner two young men were standing, drinking hop-bitters.[10]

Mr Browne led his charges thither and invited them all, in jest, to some ladies' punch, hot, strong and sweet. As they said they never took anything strong he opened three bottles of lemonade for them. Then he asked one of the young men to move aside, and, taking hold of the decanter, filled out for himself a goodly measure of whisky. The young men eyed him respectfully while he took a trial sip.

—God help me, he said, smiling, it's the doctor's orders.

His wizened face broke into a broader smile, and the three young ladies laughed in musical echo to his pleasantry, swaying their bodies to and fro, with nervous jerks of their shoulders. The boldest said:

—O, now, Mr Browne, I'm sure the doctor never ordered anything of the kind.

Mr Browne took another sip of his whisky and said, with sidling mimicry:

—Well, you see, I'm like the famous Mrs Cassidy, who is reported to have said: *Now, Mary Grimes, if I don't take it, make me take it, for I feel I want it.*

His hot face had leaned forward a little too confidentially and he had assumed a very low Dublin accent so that the young ladies, with one instinct, received his speech in silence. Miss Furlong, who was one of Mary Jane's pupils, asked Miss Daly what was the name of the pretty waltz she had played; and Mr Browne, seeing that he was ignored, turned promptly to the two young men who were more appreciative.

A red-face young woman, dressed in pansy, came into the room, excitedly clapping her hands and crying:

—Quadrilles! Quadrilles![11]

Close on her heels came Aunt Kate, crying:

—Two gentlemen and three ladies, Mary Jane!

—O, here's Mr Bergin and Mr Kerrigan, said Mary Jane. Mr Kerrigan, will you take Miss Power? Miss Furlong, may I get you a partner, Mr Bergin. O, that'll just do now.

—Three ladies, Mary Jane, said Aunt Kate.

The two young gentlemen asked the ladies if they might have the pleasure, and Mary Jane turned to Miss Daly.

—O, Miss Daly, you're really awfully good, after playing for the last two dances, but really we're so short of ladies to-night.

—I don't mind in the least, Miss Morkan.

—But I've a nice partner for you, Mr Bartell D'Arcy, the tenor. I'll get him to sing later on. All Dublin is raving about him.

—Lovely voice, lovely voice! said Aunt Kate.

As the piano had twice begun the prelude to the first figure Mary Jane led

10. A soft drink flavored with hops.
11. One of many kinds of figured dances, like reels, in which dancers pair off only temporarily, partners change, and complex groupings emerge. The "lancers" mentioned farther on is another. Square dances are country versions of the more elegant 19th-century ballroom forms.

her recruits quickly from the room. They had hardly gone when Aunt Julia wandered slowly into the room, looking behind her at something.

—What is the matter, Julia? asked Aunt Kate anxiously. Who is it?

Julia, who was carrying in a column of table-napkins, turned to her sister and said, simply, as if the question had surprised her:

—It's only Freddy, Kate, and Gabriel with him.

In fact right behind her Gabriel could be seen piloting Freddy Malins across the landing. The latter, a young man of about forty, was of Gabriel's size and build, with very round shoulders. His face was fleshy and pallid, touched with colour only at the thick hanging lobes of his ears and at the wide wings of his nose. He had coarse features, a blunt nose, a convex and receding brow, tumid and protruded lips. His heavy-lidded eyes and the disorder of his scanty hair made him look sleepy. He was laughing heartily in a high key at a story which he had been telling Gabriel on the stairs and at the same time rubbing the knuckles of his left fist backwards and forwards into his left eye.

—Good-evening, Freddy, said Aunt Julia.

Freddy Malins bade the Misses Morkan good-evening in what seemed an offhand fashion by reason of the habitual catch in his voice and then, seeing that Mr Browne was grinning at him from the sideboard, crossed the room on rather shaky legs and began to repeat in an undertone the story he had just told to Gabriel.

—He's not so bad, is he? said Aunt Kate to Gabriel.

Gabriel's brows were dark but he raised them quickly and answered:

—O no, hardly noticeable.

—Now, isn't he a terrible fellow! she said. And his poor mother made him take the pledge [12] on New Year's Eve. But come on, Gabriel, into the drawing-room.

Before leaving the room with Gabriel she signalled to Mr Browne by frowning and shaking her forefinger in warning to and fro. Mr Browne nodded in answer and, when she had gone, said to Freddy Malins:

—Now, then, Teddy, I'm going to fill you out a good glass of lemonade just to buck you up.

Freddy Malins, who was nearing the climax of his story, waved the offer aside impatiently but Mr Browne, having first called Freddy Malins' attention to a disarray in his dress, filled out and handed him a full glass of lemonade. Freddy Malins' left hand accepted the glass mechanically, his right hand being engaged in the mechanical readjustment of his dress. Mr Browne, whose face was once more wrinkling with mirth, poured out for himself a glass of whisky while Freddy Malins exploded, before he had well reached the climax of his story, in a kink of high-pitched bronchitic laughter and, setting down his untasted and overflowing glass, began to rub the knuckles of his left fist backwards and forwards into his left eye, repeating words of his last phrase as well as his fit of laughter would allow him.

Gabriel could not listen while Mary Jane was playing her Academy piece,[13] full of runs and difficult passages, to the hushed drawing-room. He liked music

12. A temperance pledge, taken by one who solemnly "swears off" drink.
13. A difficult display piece, learned as a qualifying exercise in a musical conservatory.

but the piece she was playing had no melody for him and he doubted whether it had any melody for the other listeners, though they had begged Mary Jane to play something. Four young men, who had come from the refreshment-room to stand in the doorway at the sound of the piano, had gone away quietly in couples after a few minutes. The only persons who seemed to follow the music were Mary Jane herself, her hands racing along the keyboard or lifted from it at the pauses like those of a priestess in momentary imprecation, and Aunt Kate standing at her elbow to turn the page.

Gabriel's eyes, irritated by the floor, which glittered with beeswax under the heavy chandelier, wandered to the wall above the piano. A picture of the balcony scene in *Romeo and Juliet* hung there and beside it was a picture of the two murdered princes in the Tower which Aunt Julia had worked in red, blue and brown wools when she was a girl. Probably in the school they had gone to as girls that kind of work had been taught, for one year his mother had worked for him as a birthday present a waistcoat of purple tabinet,[14] with little foxes' heads upon it, lined with brown satin and having round mulberry buttons. It was strange that his mother had had no musical talent though Aunt Kate used to call her the brains carrier of the Morkan family. Both she and Julia had always seemed a little proud of their serious and matronly sister. Her photograph stood before the pierglass.[15] She held an open book on her knees and was pointing out something in it to Constantine who, dressed in a man-o'-war suit, lay at her feet. It was she who had chosen the names for her sons for she was very sensible of the dignity of family life. Thanks to her, Constantine was now senior curate in Balbriggan and, thanks to her, Gabriel himself had taken his degree in the Royal University. A shadow passed over his face as he remembered her sullen opposition to his marriage. Some slighting phrases she had used still rankled in his memory; she had once spoken of Gretta as being country cute and that was not true of Gretta at all. It was Gretta who had nursed her during all her last long illness in their house at Monkstown.

He knew that Mary Jane must be near the end of her piece for she was playing again the opening melody with runs of scales after every bar and while he waited for the end the resentment died down in his heart. The piece ended with a trill of octaves in the treble and a final deep octave in the bass. Great applause greeted Mary Jane as, blushing and rolling up her music nervously, she escaped from the room. The most vigorous clapping came from the four young men in the doorway who had gone away to the refreshment-room at the beginning of the piece but had come back when the piano had stopped.

Lancers [16] were arranged. Gabriel found himself partnered with Miss Ivors. She was a frank-mannered talkative young lady, with a freckled face and prominent brown eyes. She did not wear a low-cut bodice and the large brooch which was fixed in the front of her collar bore on it an Irish device.

When they had taken their places she said abruptly:

—I have a crow to pluck [17] with you.

14. A kind of Irish cotton cloth, a poplin with a watered surface.
15. Tall vertical mirror, set along a wall.
16. See note 11 above.
17. The American expression would be "a bone to pick."

—With me? said Gabriel.

She nodded her head gravely.

—What is it? asked Gabriel, smiling at her solemn manner.

—Who is G. C.? answered Miss Ivors, turning her eyes upon him.

Gabriel coloured and was about to knit his brows, as if he did not understand, when she said bluntly:

—O, innocent Amy! I have found out that you write for *The Daily Express*. Now, aren't you ashamed of yourself?

—Why should I be ashamed of myself? asked Gabriel, blinking his eyes and trying to smile.

—Well, I'm ashamed of you, said Miss Ivors frankly. To say you'd write for a rag like that. I didn't think you were a West Briton.[18]

A look of perplexity appeared on Gabriel's face. It was true that he wrote a literary column every Wednesday in *The Daily Express,* for which he was paid fifteen shillings. But that did not make him a West Briton surely. The books he received for review were almost more welcome than the paltry cheque. He loved to feel the covers and turn over the pages of newly printed books. Nearly every day when his teaching in the college was ended he used to wander down the quays to the second-hand booksellers, to Hickey's on Bachelor's Walk, to Webb's or Massey's on Aston's Quay, or to O'Clohissey's in the by-street. He did not know how to meet her charge. He wanted to say that literature was above politics. But they were friends of many years' standing and their careers had been parallel, first at the University and then as teachers: he could not risk a grandiose phrase with her. He continued blinking his eyes and trying to smile and murmured lamely that he saw nothing political in writing reviews of books.

When their turn to cross had come he was still perplexed and inattentive. Miss Ivors promptly took his hand in a warm grasp and said in a soft friendly tone:

—Of course, I was only joking. Come, we cross now.

When they were together again she spoke of the University question and Gabriel felt more at ease. A friend of hers had shown her his review of Browning's poems. That was how she had found out the secret: but she liked the review immensely. Then she said suddenly:

—O, Mr Conroy, will you come for an excursion to the Aran Isles [19] this summer? We're going to stay there a whole month. It will be splendid out in the Atlantic. You ought to come. Mr Clancy is coming, and Mr Kilkelly and Kathleen Kearney. It would be splendid for Gretta too if she'd come. She's from Connacht, isn't she?

—Her people are, said Gabriel shortly.

—But you will come, won't you? said Miss Ivors, laying her warm hand eagerly on his arm.

—The fact is, said Gabriel, I have already arranged to go—

18. Meaning one whose "Irish consciousness" had not been sufficiently "raised"—*i.e.* an Irishman who still thought of himself as a subject of the United Kingdom of England and Ireland, rather than as an Irish nationalist. Miss Ivors is a tough and humorless ideologue.
19. Islands off the Galway coast, one of the few places where Gaelic was still spoken. A militant nationalist like Miss Ivors would, in her dedicated way, want to go there.

—Go where? asked Miss Ivors.

—Well, you know, every year I go for a cycling tour with some fellows and so—

—But where? asked Miss Ivors.

—Well, we usually go to France or Belgium or perhaps Germany, said Gabriel awkwardly.

—And why do you go to France and Belgium, said Miss Ivors, instead of visiting your own land?

—Well, said Gabriel, it's partly to keep in touch with the languages and partly for a change.

—And haven't you your own language to keep in touch with—Irish? asked Miss Ivors.

—Well, said Gabriel, if it comes to that, you know, Irish is not my language.

Their neighbours had turned to listen to the cross-examination. Gabriel glanced right and left nervously and tried to keep his good humour under the ordeal which was making a blush invade his forehead.

—And haven't you your own land to visit, continued Miss Ivors, that you know nothing of, your own people, and your own country?

—O, to tell you the truth, retorted Gabriel suddenly, I'm sick of my own country, sick of it!

—Why? asked Miss Ivors.

Gabriel did not answer for his retort had heated him.

—Why? repeated Miss Ivors.

They had to go visiting together and, as he had not answered her, Miss Ivors said warmly:

—Of course, you've no answer.

Gabriel tried to cover his agitation by taking part in the dance with great energy. He avoided her eyes for he had seen a sour expression on her face. But when they met in the long chain he was surprised to feel his hand firmly pressed. She looked at him from under her brows for a moment quizzically until he smiled. Then, just as the chain was about to start again, she stood on tiptoe and whispered into his ear:

—West Briton!

When the lancers were over Gabriel went away to a remote corner of the room where Freddy Malins' mother was sitting. She was a stout feeble old woman with white hair. Her voice had a catch in it like her son's and she stuttered slightly. She had been told that Freddy had come and that he was nearly all right. Gabriel asked her whether she had had a good crossing. She lived with her married daughter in Glasgow and came to Dublin on a visit once a year. She answered placidly that she had had a beautiful crossing and that the captain had been most attentive to her. She spoke also of the beautiful house her daughter kept in Glasgow, and of all the nice friends they had there. While her tongue rambled on Gabriel tried to banish from his mind all memory of the unpleasant incident with Miss Ivors. Of course the girl or woman, or whatever she was, was an enthusiast but there was a time for all things. Perhaps he ought not to have answered her like that. But she had no right to call him a West Briton before people, even in joke. She had tried to make him ridiculous before people, heckling him and staring at him with her rabbit's eyes.

He saw his wife making her way towards him through the waltzing couples. When she reached him she said into his ear:

—Gabriel, Aunt Kate wants to know won't you carve the goose as usual. Miss Daly will carve the ham and I'll do the pudding.

—All right, said Gabriel.

—She's sending in the younger ones first as soon as this waltz is over so that we'll have the table to ourselves.

—Were you dancing? asked Gabriel.

—Of course I was. Didn't you see me? What words had you with Molly Ivors?

—No words. Why? Did she say so?

—Something like that. I'm trying to get that Mr D'Arcy to sing. He's full of conceit, I think.

—There were no words, said Gabriel moodily, only she wanted me to go for a trip to the west of Ireland and I said I wouldn't.

His wife clasped her hands excitedly and gave a little jump.

—O, do go, Gabriel, she cried. I'd love to see Galway again.

—You can go if you like, said Gabriel coldly.

She looked at him for a moment, then turned to Mrs Malins and said:

—There's a nice husband for you, Mrs Malins.

While she was threading her way back across the room Mrs Malins, without adverting to the interruption, went on to tell Gabriel what beautiful places there were in Scotland and beautiful scenery. Her son-in-law brought them every year to the lakes and they used to go fishing. Her son-in-law was a splendid fisher. One day he caught a fish, a beautiful big big fish, and the man in the hotel boiled it for their dinner.

Gabriel hardly heard what she said. Now that supper was coming near he began to think again about his speech and about the quotation. When he saw Freddy Malins coming across the room to visit his mother Gabriel left the chair free for him and retired into the embrasure of the window. The room had already cleared and from the back room came the clatter of plates and knives. Those who still remained in the drawing-room seemed tired of dancing and were conversing quietly in little groups. Gabriel's warm trembling fingers tapped the cold pane of the window. How cool it must be outside! How pleasant it would be to walk out alone, first along by the river and then through the park! The snow would be lying on the branches of the trees and forming a bright cap on the top of the Wellington Monument. How much more pleasant it would be there than at the supper-table!

He ran over the headings of his speech: Irish hospitality, sad memories, the Three Graces, Paris, the quotation from Browning. He repeated to himself a phrase he had written in his review: One feels that one is listening to a thought-tormented music. Miss Ivors had praised the review. Was she sincere? Had she really any life of her own behind all her propagandism? There had never been any ill-feeling between them until that night. It unnerved him to think that she would be at the supper-table, looking up at him while he spoke with her critical quizzing eyes. Perhaps she would not be sorry to see him fail in his speech. An idea came into his mind and gave him courage. He would say, alluding to Aunt Kate and Aunt Julia: Ladies and Gentlemen, the generation which is now on the wane among us may have had its faults but for my part I think it had certain *qualities of hospitality, of humour, of humanity, which the new and very serious and hypereducated generation that is growing up around us seems to me to lack.* Very good: that was one for Miss Ivors. What did he care that his aunts were only two ignorant old women?

A murmur in the room attracted his attention. Mr Browne was advancing from the door, gallantly escorting Aunt Julia, who leaned upon his arm, smiling and hanging her head. An irregular musketry of applause escorted her also as far as the piano and then, as Mary Jane seated herself on the stool, and Aunt Julia, no longer smiling, half turned so as to pitch her voice fairly into the room, gradually ceased. Gabriel recognised the prelude. It was that of an old song of Aunt Julia's—*Arrayed for the Bridal.* Her voice, strong and clear in tone, attacked with great spirit the runs which embellish the air and though she sang very rapidly she did not miss even the smallest of the grace notes. To follow the voice, without looking at the singer's face, was to feel and share the excitement of swift and secure flight. Gabriel applauded loudly with all the others at the close of the song and loud applause was borne in from the invisible supper-table. It sounded so genuine that a little colour struggled into Aunt Julia's face as she bent to replace in the music-stand the old leather-bound songbook that had her initials on the cover. Freddy Malins, who had listened with his head perched sideways to hear her better, was still applauding when everyone else had ceased and talking animatedly to his mother who nodded her head gravely and slowly in acquiescence. At last, when he could clap no more, he stood up suddenly and hurried across the room to Aunt Julia whose hand he seized and held in both his hands, shaking it when words failed him or the catch in his voice proved too much for him.

—I was just telling my mother, he said, I never heard you sing so well, never. No, I never heard your voice so good as it is to-night. Now! Would you believe that now? That's the truth. Upon my word and honour that's the truth. I never heard your voice sound so fresh and so . . . so clear and fresh, never.

Aunt Julia smiled broadly and murmured something about compliments as she released her hand from his grasp. Mr Browne extended his open hand towards her and said to those who were near him in the manner of a showman introducing a prodigy to an audience:

—Miss Julia Morkan, my latest discovery!

He was laughing very heartily at this himself when Freddy Malins turned to him and said:

—Well, Browne, if you're serious you might make a worse discovery. All I can say is I never heard her sing half so well as long as I am coming here. And that's the honest truth.

—Neither did I, said Mr Browne. I think her voice has greatly improved.

Aunt Julia shrugged her shoulders and said with meek pride:

—Thirty years ago I hadn't a bad voice as voices go.

—I often told Julia, said Aunt Kate emphatically, that she was simply thrown away in that choir. But she never would be said by me.

She turned as if to appeal to the good sense of the others against a refractory child while Aunt Julia gazed in front of her, a vague smile of reminiscence playing on her face.

—No, continued Aunt Kate, she wouldn't be said or led by anyone, slaving there in that choir night and day, night and day. Six o'clock on Christmas morning! And all for what?

—Well, isn't it for the honour of God, Aunt Kate? asked Mary Jane, twisting round on the piano-stool and smiling.

Aunt Kate turned fiercely on her niece and said:

—I know all about the honour of God, Mary Jane, but I think it's not at all honourable for the pope to turn out the women out of the choirs that have slaved there all their lives and put little whipper-snappers of boys over their heads. I suppose it is for the good of the Church if the pope does it. But it's not just, Mary Jane, and it's not right.

She had worked herself into a passion and would have continued in defence of her sister for it was a sore subject with her but Mary Jane, seeing that all the dancers had come back, intervened pacifically:

—Now, Aunt Kate, you're giving scandal to Mr Browne who is of the other persuasion.[20]

Aunt Kate turned to Mr Browne, who was grinning at this allusion to his religion, and said hastily:

—O, I don't question the pope's being right. I'm only a stupid old woman and I wouldn't presume to do such a thing. But there's such a thing as common everyday politeness and gratitude. And if I were in Julia's place I'd tell that Father Healy straight up to his face . . .

—And besides, Aunt Kate, said Mary Jane, we really are all hungry and when we are hungry we are all very quarrelsome.

—And when we are thirsty we are also quarrelsome, added Mr Browne.

—So that we had better go to supper, said Mary Jane, and finish the discussion afterwards.

On the landing outside the drawing-room Gabriel found his wife and Mary Jane trying to persuade Miss Ivors to stay for supper. But Miss Ivors, who had put on her hat and was buttoning her cloak, would not stay. She did not feel in the least hungry and she had already overstayed her time.

—But only for ten minutes, Molly, said Mrs Conroy. That won't delay you.

—To take a pick itself, said Mary Jane, after all your dancing.

—I really couldn't, said Miss Ivors.

—I am afraid you didn't enjoy yourself at all, said Mary Jane hopelessly.

—Ever so much, I assure you, said Miss Ivors, but you really must let me run off now.

—But how can you get home? asked Mrs Conroy.

—O, it's only two steps up the quay.

Gabriel hesitated a moment and said:

—If you will allow me, Miss Ivors, I'll see you home if you really are obliged to go.

But Miss Ivors broke away from them.

—I won't hear of it, she cried. For goodness sake go in to your suppers and don't mind me. I'm quite well able to take care of myself.

—Well, you're the comical girl, Molly, said Mrs Conroy frankly.

20. She is saying, delicately, that he is a Protestant.

—*Beannacht libh*,[21] cried Miss Ivors, with a laugh, as she ran down the stair-case.

Mary Jane gazed after her, a moody puzzled expression on her face, while Mrs Conroy leaned over the banisters to listen for the hall-door. Gabriel asked himself was he the cause of her abrupt departure. But she did not seem to be in ill humour: she had gone away laughing. He stared blankly down the stair-case.

At that moment Aunt Kate came toddling out of the supper-room, almost wringing her hands in despair.

—Where is Gabriel? she cried. Where on earth is Gabriel? There's everyone waiting in there, stage to let, and nobody to carve the goose!

—Here I am, Aunt Kate! cried Gabriel, with sudden animation, ready to carve a flock of geese, if necessary.

A fat brown goose lay at one end of the table and at the other end, on a bed of creased paper strewn with sprigs of parsley, lay a great ham, stripped of its outer skin and peppered over with crust crumbs, a neat paper frill round its shin; and beside this was a round of spiced beef. Between these rival ends ran parallel lines of side-dishes: two little minsters of jelly, red and yellow; a shallow dish full of blocks of blancmange and red jam, a large green leaf-shaped dish with a stalk-shaped handle, on which lay bunches of purple raisins and peeled almonds, a companion dish on which lay a solid rectangle of Smyrna figs, a dish of custard topped with grated nutmeg, a small bowl full of chocolates and sweets wrapped in gold and silver papers and a glass vase in which stood some tall celery stalks. In the centre of the table there stood, as sentries to a fruit-stand which upheld a pyramid of oranges and American apples, two squat old-fashioned decanters of cut glass, one containing port and the other dark sherry. On the closed square piano a pudding in a huge yellow dish lay in waiting and behind it were three squads of bottles of stout and ale and minerals, drawn up according to the colours of their uniforms, the first two black, with brown and red labels, the third and smallest squad white, with transverse green sashes.

Gabriel took his seat boldly at the head of the table and, having looked to the edge of the carver, plunged his fork firmly into the goose. He felt quite at ease now for he was an expert carver and liked nothing better than to find himself at the head of a well-laden table.

—Miss Furlong, what shall I send you? he asked. A wing or a slice of the breast?

—Just a small slice of the breast.

—Miss Higgins, what for you?

—O, anything at all, Mr Conroy.

While Gabriel and Miss Daly exchanged plates of goose and plates of ham and spiced beef Lily went from guest to guest with a dish of hot floury potatoes wrapped in a white napkin. This was Mary Jane's idea and she had also sug-gested apple sauce for the goose but Aunt Kate had said that plain roast goose without apple sauce had always been good enough for her and she hoped she might never eat worse. Mary Jane waited on her pupils and saw that they got the best slices and Aunt Kate and Aunt Julia opened and carried across from

21. "A blessing on you" (Gaelic).

the piano bottles of stout and ale for the gentlemen and bottles of minerals for the ladies. There was a great deal of confusion and laughter and noise, the noise of orders and counter-orders, of knives and forks, of corks and glass-stoppers. Gabriel began to carve second helpings as soon as he had finished the first round without serving himself. Everyone protested loudly so that he compromised by taking a long draught of stout for he had found the carving hot work. Mary Jane settled down quietly to her supper but Aunt Kate and Aunt Julia were still toddling round the table, walking on each other's heels, getting in each other's way and giving each other unheeded orders. Mr Browne begged of them to sit down and eat their suppers and so did Gabriel but they said there was time enough so that, at last, Freddy Malins stood up and, capturing Aunt Kate, plumped her down on her chair amid general laughter.

When everyone had been well served Gabriel said, smiling:

—Now, if anyone wants a little more of what vulgar people call stuffing let him or her speak.

A chorus of voices invited him to begin his own supper and Lily came forward with three potatoes which she had reserved for him.

—Very well, said Gabriel amiably, as he took another preparatory draught, kindly forget my existence, ladies and gentlemen, for a few minutes.

He set to his supper and took no part in the conversation with which the table covered Lily's removal of the plates. The subject of talk was the opera company which was then at the Theatre Royal. Mr Bartell D'Arcy, the tenor, a dark-complexioned young man with a smart moustache, praised very highly the leading contralto of the company but Miss Furlong thought she had a rather vulgar style of production. Freddy Malins said there was a negro chieftain singing in the second part of the Gaiety pantomime [22] who had one of the finest tenor voices he had ever heard.

—Have you heard him? he asked Mr Bartell D'Arcy across the table.

—No, answered Mr Bartell D'Arcy carelessly.

—Because, Freddy Malins explained, now I'd be curious to hear your opinion of him. I think he has a grand voice.

—It takes Teddy to find out the really good things, said Mr Browne familiarly to the table.

—And why couldn't he have a voice too? asked Freddy Malins sharply. Is it because he's only a black?

Nobody answered this question and Mary Jane led the table back to the legitimate opera. One of her pupils had given her a pass for *Mignon*. Of course it was very fine, she said, but it made her think of poor Georgina Burns. Mr Browne could go back farther still, to the old Italian companies that used to come to Dublin—Tietjens, Ilma de Murzka, Campanini, the great Trebelli, Giuglini, Ravelli, Aramburo. Those were the days, he said, when there was something like singing to be heard in Dublin. He told too of how the top gallery of the old Royal used to be packed night after night, of how one night an Italian tenor had sung five encores to *Let Me Like a Soldier Fall*, introducing a high C every time, and of how the gallery boys would sometimes in their

22. In England and Ireland, a kind of formalized musical comedy, using fairy-tale plots such as that of Aladdin but with new song and-dance routines.

enthusiasm unyoke the horses from the carriage of some great *prima donna* and pull her themselves through the streets to her hotel. Why did they never play the grand old operas now, he asked, *Dinorah, Lucrezia Borgia?* Because they could not get the voices to sing them: that was why.

—O, well, said Mr Bartell D'Arcy, I presume there are as good singers to-day as there were then.

—Where are they? asked Mr Browne defiantly.

—In London, Paris, Milan, said Mr Bartell D'Arcy warmly. I suppose Caruso, for example, is quite as good, if not better than any of the men you have mentioned.

—Maybe so, said Mr Browne. But I may tell you I doubt it strongly.

—O, I'd give anything to hear Caruso sing, said Mary Jane.

—For me, said Aunt Kate, who had been picking a bone, there was only one tenor. To please me, I mean. But I suppose none of you ever heard of him.

—Who was he, Miss Morkan? asked Mr Bartell D'Arcy politely.

—His name, said Aunt Kate, was Parkinson. I heard him when he was in his prime and I think he had then the purest tenor voice that was ever put into a man's throat.

—Strange, said Mr Bartell D'Arcy. I never even heard of him.

—Yes, yes, Miss Morkan is right, said Mr Browne. I remember hearing of old Parkinson but he's too far back for me.

—A beautiful pure sweet mellow English tenor, said Aunt Kate with enthusiasm.

Gabriel having finished, the huge pudding was transferred to the table. The clatter of forks and spoons began again. Gabriel's wife served out spoonfuls of the pudding and passed the plates down the table. Midway down they were held up by Mary Jane, who replenished them with raspberry or orange jelly or with blancmange and jam. The pudding was of Aunt Julia's making and she received praises for it from all quarters. She herself said that it was not quite brown enough.

—Well, I hope, Miss Morkan, said Mr Browne, that I'm brown enough for you because, you know, I'm all brown.

All the gentlemen, except Gabriel, ate some of the pudding out of compliment to Aunt Julia. As Gabriel never ate sweets the celery had been left for him. Freddy Malins also took a stalk of celery and ate it with his pudding. He had been told that celery was a capital thing for the blood and he was just then under doctor's care. Mrs Malins, who had been silent all through the supper, said that her son was going down to Mount Melleray in a week or so. The table then spoke of Mount Melleray, how bracing the air was down there, how hospitable the monks were and how they never asked for a penny-piece from their guests.

—And do you mean to say, asked Mr Browne incredulously, that a chap can go down there and put up there as if it were a hotel and live on the fat of the land and then come away without paying a farthing?

—O, most people give some donation to the monastery when they leave, said Mary Jane.

—I wish we had an institution like that in our Church, said Mr. Browne candidly.

He was astonished to hear that the monks never spoke, got up at two in the morning and slept in their coffins. He asked what they did it for.

—That's the rule of the order, said Aunt Kate firmly.

—Yes, but why? asked Mr Browne.

Aunt Kate repeated that it was the rule, that was all. Mr Browne still seemed not to understand. Freddy Malins explained to him, as best he could, that the monks were trying to make up for the sins committed by all the sinners in the outside world. The explanation was not very clear for Mr Browne grinned and said:

—I like that idea very much but wouldn't a comfortable spring bed do them as well as a coffin?

—The coffin, said Mary Jane, is to remind them of their last end.[23]

As the subject had grown lugubrious it was buried in a silence of the table during which Mrs Malins could be heard saying to her neighbour in an indistinct undertone:

—They are very good men, the monks, very pious men.

The raisins and almonds and figs and apples and oranges and chocolates and sweets were now passed about the table and Aunt Julia invited all the guests to have either port or sherry. At first Mr Bartell D'Arcy refused to take either but one of his neighbours nudged him and whispered something to him upon which he allowed his glass to be filled. Gradually as the last glasses were being filled the conversation ceased. A pause followed, broken only by the noise of the wine and by unsettlings of chairs. The Misses Morkan, all three, looked down at the tablecloth. Someone coughed once or twice and then a few gentlemen patted the table gently as a signal for silence. The silence came and Gabriel pushed back his chair and stood up.

The patting at once grew louder in encouragement and then ceased altogether. Gabriel leaned his ten trembling fingers on the tablecloth and smiled nervously at the company. Meeting a row of upturned faces he raised his eyes to the chandelier. The piano was playing a waltz tune and he could hear the skirts sweeping against the drawing-room door. People, perhaps, were standing in the snow on the quay outside, gazing up at the lighted windows and listening to the waltz music. The air was pure there. In the distance lay the park where the trees were weighted with snow. The Wellington Monument [24] wore a gleaming cap of snow that flashed westward over the white field of Fifteen Acres.

He began:

—Ladies and Gentlemen.

—It has fallen to my lot this evening, as in years past, to perform a very pleasing task but a task for which I am afraid my poor powers as a speaker are all too inadequate.

—No, no! said Mr Browne.

—But, however that may be, I can only ask you tonight to take the will for the deed and to lend me your attention for a few moments while I endeavour to express to you in words what my feelings are on this occasion.

23. The strangeness and resonance of the phrase ("last end" sounds either archaic or awkwardly redundant) are not lost on Gabriel: see the final paragraph of the story.
24. A tall obelisk in Phoenix Park, Dublin, unavowedly but commandingly phallic. Here it is only visualized by Gabriel; later on, we see it.

—Ladies and Gentlemen. It is not the first time that we have gathered to-gether under this hospitable roof, around this hospitable board. It is not the first time that we have been the recipients—or perhaps, I had better say, the victims—of the hospitality of certain good ladies.

He made a circle in the air with his arm and paused. Everyone laughed or smiled at Aunt Kate and Aunt Julia and Mary Jane who all turned crimson with pleasure. Gabriel went on more boldly:

—I feel more strongly with every recurring year that our country has no tradition which does it so much honour and which it should guard so jealously as that of its hospitality. It is a tradition that is unique as far as my experience goes (and I have visited not a few places abroad) among the modern nations. Some would say, perhaps, that with us it is rather a failing than anything to be boasted of. But granted even that, it is, to my mind, a princely failing, and one that I trust will long be cultivated among us. Of one thing, at least, I am sure. As long as this one roof shelters the good ladies aforesaid—and I wish from my heart it may do so for many and many a long year to come—the tra-dition of genuine warm-hearted courteous Irish hospitality, which our fore-fathers have handed down to us and which we in turn must hand down to our descendants, is still alive among us.

A hearty murmur of assent ran round the table. It shot through Gabriel's mind that Miss Ivors was not there and that she had gone away discourteously: and he said with confidence in himself:

—Ladies and Gentlemen.

—A new generation is growing up in our midst, a generation actuated by new ideas and new principles. It is serious and enthusiastic for these new ideas and its enthusiasm, even when it is misdirected, is, I believe, in the main sincere. But we are living in a sceptical and, if I may use the phrase, a thought-tormented age: and sometimes I fear that this new generation, educated or hypereducated as it is, will lack those qualities of humanity, of hospitality, of kindly humour which belonged to an older day. Listening to-night to the names of all those great singers of the past it seemed to me, I must confess, that we were living in a less spacious age. Those days might, without exaggeration, be called spa-cious days: and if they are gone beyond recall let us hope, at least, that in gatherings such as this we shall still speak of them with pride and affection, still cherish in our hearts the memory of those dead and gone great ones whose fame the world will not willingly let die.

—Hear, hear! said Mr Browne loudly.

—But yet, continued Gabriel, his voice falling into a softer inflection, there are always in gatherings such as this sadder thoughts that will recur to our minds: thoughts of the past, of youth, of changes, of absent faces that we miss here to-night. Our path through life is strewn with many such sad memories: and were we to brood upon them always we could not find the heart to go on bravely with our work among the living. We have all of us living duties and living affections which claim, and rightly claim, our strenuous endeavours.

—Therefore, I will not linger on the past. I will not let any gloomy moralising intrude upon us here to-night. Here we are gathered together for a brief moment from the bustle and rush of our everyday routine. We are met here as friends, in the spirit of good-fellowship, as colleagues also to a certain extent, in the true spirit of *camaraderie*,[25] and as the guests of—what shall I call them?—the Three Graces of the Dublin musical world.

The table burst into applause and laughter at this sally. Aunt Julia vainly asked each of her neighbours in turn to tell her what Gabriel had said.

—He says we are the Three Graces, Aunt Julia, said Mary Jane.

Aunt Julia did not understand but she looked up, smiling, at Gabriel, who continued in the same vein:

—Ladies and Gentlemen.

—I will not attempt to play to-night the part that Paris played on another occasion. I will not attempt to choose between them. The task would be an invidious one and one beyond my poor powers. For when I view them in turn, whether it be our chief hostess herself, whose good heart, whose too good heart, has become a byword with all who know her, or her sister, who seems to be gifted with perennial youth and whose singing must have been a surprise and a revelation to us all to-night, or, last but not least, when I consider our youngest hostess, talented, cheerful, hard-working and the best of nieces, I confess, Ladies and Gentlemen, that I do not know to which of them I should award the prize.

Gabriel glanced down at his aunts and, seeing the large smile on Aunt Julia's face and the tears which had risen to Aunt Kate's eyes, hastened to his close. He raised his glass of port gallantly, while every member of the company fingered a glass expectantly, and said loudly:

—Let us toast them all three together. Let us drink to their health, wealth, long life, happiness and prosperity and may they long continue to hold the proud and self-won position which they hold in their profession and the position of honour and affection which they hold in our hearts.

All the guests stood up, glass in hand, and, turning towards the three seated ladies, sang in unison, with Mr Browne as leader:

> *For they are jolly gay fellows,*
> *For they are jolly gay fellows,*
> *For they are jolly gay fellows,*
> *Which nobody can deny.*

Aunt Kate was making frank use of her handkerchief and even Aunt Julia seemed moved. Freddy Malins beat time with his pudding-fork and the singers turned towards one another, as if in melodious conference, while they sang, with emphasis:

> *Unless he tells a lie,*
> *Unless he tells a lie.*

Then, turning once more towards their hostesses, they sang:

> *For they are jolly gay fellows,*
> *For they are jolly gay fellows,*
> *For they are jolly gay fellows,*
> *Which nobody can deny.*

25. Good fellowship.

The acclamation which followed was taken up beyond the door of the supper-room by many of the other guests and renewed time after time, Freddy Malins acting as officer with his fork on high.

The piercing morning air came into the hall where they were standing so that Aunt Kate said:

—Close the door, somebody. Mrs Malins will get her death of cold.

—Browne is out there, Aunt Kate, said Mary Jane.

—Browne is everywhere, said Aunt Kate, lowering her voice.

Mary Jane laughed at her tone.

—Really, she said archly, he is very attentive.

—He has been laid on here like the gas, said Aunt Kate in the same tone, all during the Christmas.

She laughed herself this time good-humouredly and then added quickly:

—But tell him to come in, Mary Jane, and close the door. I hope to goodness he didn't hear me.

At that moment the hall-door was opened and Mr Browne came in from the doorstep, laughing as if his heart would break. He was dressed in a long green overcoat with mock astrakhan cuffs and collar and wore on his head an oval fur cap. He pointed down the snow-covered quay from where the sound of shrill prolonged whistling was borne in.

—Teddy will have all the cabs in Dublin out, he said.

Gabriel advanced from the little pantry behind the office, struggling into his overcoat and, looking round the hall, said:

—Gretta not down yet?

—She's getting on her things, Gabriel, said Aunt Kate.

—Who's playing up there? asked Gabriel.

—Nobody. They're all gone.

—O no, Aunt Kate, said Mary Jane. Bartell D'Arcy and Miss O'Callaghan aren't gone yet.

—Someone is strumming at the piano, anyhow, said Gabriel.

Mary Jane glanced at Gabriel and Mr Browne and said with a shiver:

—It makes me feel cold to look at you two gentlemen muffled up like that. I wouldn't like to face your journey home at this hour.

—I'd like nothing better this minute, said Mr Browne stoutly, than a rattling fine walk in the country or a fast drive with a good spanking goer between the shafts.

—We used to have a very good horse and trap at home, said Aunt Julia sadly.

—The never-to-be-forgotten Johnny, said Mary Jane, laughing.

Aunt Kate and Gabriel laughed too.

—Why, what was wonderful about Johnny? asked Mr Browne.

—The late lamented Patrick Morkan, our grandfather, that is, explained Gabriel, commonly known in his later years as the old gentleman, was a glue-boiler.

—O, now, Gabriel, said Aunt Kate, laughing, he had a starch mill.

—Well, glue or starch, said Gabriel, the old gentleman had a horse by the name of Johnny. And Johnny used to work in the old gentleman's mill, walking round and round in order to drive the mill. That was all very well; but now comes the tragic part about Johnny. One fine day the old gentleman thought he'd like to drive out with the quality to a military review in the park.

—The Lord have mercy on his soul, said Aunt Kate compassionately.

—Amen, said Gabriel. So the old gentleman, as I said, harnessed Johnny and put on his very best tall hat and his very best stock collar and drove out in grand style from his ancestral mansion somewhere near Back Lane, I think.

Everyone laughed, even Mrs Malins, at Gabriel's manner and Aunt Kate said:

—O now, Gabriel, he didn't live in Back Lane, really. Only the mill was there

—Out from the mansion of his forefathers, continued Gabriel, he drove with Johnny. And everything went on beautifully until Johnny came in sight of King Billy's statue: [26] and whether he fell in love with the horse King Billy sits on or whether he thought he was back again in the mill, anyhow he began to walk round the statue.

Gabriel paced in a circle round the hall in his goloshes amid the laughter of the others.

—Round and round he went, said Gabriel, and the old gentleman, who was a very pompous old gentleman, was highly indignant. *Go on, sir! What do you mean, sir? Johnny! Johnny! Most extraordinary conduct! Can't understand the horse!*

The peals of laughter which followed Gabriel's imitation of the incident were interrupted by a resounding knock at the hall-door. Mary Jane ran to open it and let in Freddy Malins. Freddy Malins, with his hat well back on his head and his shoulders humped with cold, was puffing and steaming after his exertions.

—I could only get one cab, he said.

—O, we'll find another along the quay, said Gabriel.

—Yes, said Aunt Kate. Better not keep Mrs Malins standing in the draught.

Mrs Malins was helped down the front steps by her son and Mr Browne and, after many manœuvres, hoisted into the cab. Freddy Malins clambered in after her and spent a long time settling her on the seat, Mr Browne helping him with advice. At last she was settled comfortably and Freddy Malins invited Mr Browne into the cab. There was a good deal of confused talk, and then Mr Browne got into the cab. The cabman settled his rug over his knees, and bent down for the address. The confusion grew greater and the cabman was directed differently by Freddy Malins and Mr Browne, each of whom had his head out through a window of the cab. The difficulty was to know where to drop Mr Browne along the route and Aunt Kate, Aunt Julia and Mary Jane helped the discussion from the doorstep with cross-directions and contradictions and abundance of laughter. As for Freddy Malins he was speechless with laughter. He popped his head in and out of the window every moment, to the great danger of his hat, and told his mother how the discussion was progressing till at last Mr

26. King William III (1650–1700), following Cromwell, conquered Ireland for the English for the last time at the end of the 17th century. In 1701 an equestrian statue of the King was erected in front of Trinity College. From then on, it was systematically defaced, daubed, smeared, wrecked, rebuilt, protected, and finally, in 1929, blown up, as an emblem of oppression.

Browne shouted to the bewildered cabman above the din of everybody's laughter:

—Do you know Trinity College?

—Yes, sir, said the cabman.

—Well, drive bang up against Trinity College gates, said Mr Browne, and then we'll tell you where to go. You understand now?

—Yes, sir, said the cabman.

—Make like a bird for Trinity College.

—Right, sir, cried the cabman.

The horse was whipped up and the cab rattled off along the quay amid a chorus of laughter and adieus.

Gabriel had not gone to the door with the others. He was in a dark part of the hall gazing up the staircase. A woman was standing near the top of the first flight, in the shadow also. He could not see her face but he could see the terracotta and salmonpink panels of her skirt which the shadow made appear black and white. It was his wife. She was leaning on the banisters, listening to something. Gabriel was surprised at her stillness and strained his ear to listen also. But he could hear little save the noise of laughter and dispute on the front steps, a few chords struck on the piano and a few notes of a man's voice singing.

He stood still in the gloom of the hall, trying to catch the air that the voice was singing and gazing up at his wife. There was grace and mystery in her attitude as if she were a symbol of something. He asked himself what is a woman standing on the stairs in the shadow, listening to distant music, a symbol of. If he were a painter he would paint her in that attitude. Her blue felt hat would show off the bronze of her hair against the darkness and the dark panels of her skirt would show off the light ones. *Distant Music* he would call the picture if he were a painter.[27]

The hall-door was closed; and Aunt Kate, Aunt Julia and Mary Jane came down the hall, still laughing.

—Well, isn't Freddy terrible? said Mary Jane. He's really terrible.

Gabriel said nothing but pointed up the stairs towards where his wife was standing. Now that the hall-door was closed the voice and the piano could be heard more clearly. Gabriel held up his hand for them to be silent. The song seemed to be in the old Irish tonality and the singer seemed uncertain both of his words and of his voice. The voice, made plaintive by distance and by the singer's hoarseness, faintly illuminated the cadence of the air with words expressing grief:

> *O, the rain falls on my heavy locks*
> *And the dew wets my skin,*
> *My babe lies cold . . .*

—O, exclaimed Mary Jane. It's Bartell D'Arcy singing and he wouldn't sing all the night. O, I'll get him to sing a song before he goes.

—O do, Mary Jane, said Aunt Kate.

27. This title is strikingly resonant. Not only will "The Lass of Aughrim" be that distant music (see below), but it will stand also for the general voice of the dead calling the living. Gabriel's question as to what the woman listening to the distant music symbolizes may, of course, be answered "Ireland."

Mary Jane brushed past the others and ran to the staircase but before she reached it the singing stopped and the piano was closed abruptly.

—O, what a pity! she cried. Is he coming down, Gretta?

Gabriel heard his wife answer yes and saw her come down towards them. A few steps behind her were Mr Bartell D'Arcy and Miss O'Callaghan.

—O, Mr D'Arcy, cried Mary Jane, it's downright mean of you to break off like that when we were all in raptures listening to you.

—I have been at him all the evening, said Miss O'Callaghan, and Mrs Conroy too and he told us he had a dreadful cold and couldn't sing.

—O, Mr D'Arcy, said Aunt Kate, now that was a great fib to tell.

—Can't you see that I'm as hoarse as a crow? said Mr D'Arcy roughly.

He went into the pantry hastily and put on his overcoat. The others, taken aback by his rude speech, could find nothing to say. Aunt Kate wrinkled her brows and made signs to the others to drop the subject. Mr D'Arcy stood swathing his neck carefully and frowning.

—It's the weather, said Aunt Julia, after a pause.

—Yes, everybody has colds, said Aunt Kate readily, everybody.

—They say, said Mary Jane, we haven't had snow like it for thirty years; and I read this morning in the newspapers that the snow is general all over Ireland.[28]

—I love the look of snow, said Aunt Julia sadly.

—So do I, said Miss O'Callaghan. I think Christmas is never really Christmas unless we have the snow on the ground.

—But poor Mr D'Arcy doesn't like the snow, said Aunt Kate, smiling.

Mr D'Arcy came from the pantry, fully swathed and buttoned, and in a repentant tone told them the history of his cold. Everyone gave him advice and said it was a great pity and urged him to be very careful of his throat in the night air. Gabriel watched his wife who did not join in the conversation. She was standing right under the dusty fanlight and the flame of the gas lit up the rich bronze of her hair which he had seen her drying at the fire a few days before. She was in the same attitude and seemed unaware of the talk about her. At last she turned towards them and Gabriel saw that there was colour on her cheeks and that her eyes were shining. A sudden tide of joy went leaping out of his heart.

—Mr D'Arcy, she said, what is the name of that song you were singing?

—It's called *The Lass of Aughrim,* said Mr D'Arcy, but I couldn't remember it properly. Why? Do you know it?

—*The Lass of Aughrim,* she repeated. I couldn't think of the name.

—It's a very nice air, said Mary Jane. I'm sorry you were not in voice to-night.

—Now, Mary Jane, said Aunt Kate, don't annoy Mr D'Arcy. I won't have him annoyed.

Seeing that all were ready to start she shepherded them to the door where good-night was said:

—Well, good-night, Aunt Kate, and thanks for the pleasant evening.

—Good-night, Gabriel. Good-night, Gretta!

—Good-night, Aunt Kate, and thanks ever so much. Good-night, Aunt Julia.

28. Gabriel has noticed this phrase of Mary Jane's as well; see final paragraph of story.

—O, good-night, Gretta, I didn't see you.

—Good-night, Mr D'Arcy. Good-night, Miss O'Callaghan.

—Good-night, Miss Morkan.

—Good-night, again.

—Good night, all. Safe home.

—Good-night. Good-night.

The morning was still dark. A dull yellow light brooded over the houses and the river; and the sky seemed to be descending. It was slushy underfoot; and only streaks and patches of snow lay on the roofs, on the parapets of the quay and on the area railings. The lamps were still burning redly in the murky air and, across the river, the palace of the Four Courts stood out menacingly against the heavy sky.

She was walking on before him with Mr Bartell D'Arcy, her shoes in a brown parcel tucked under one arm and her hands holding her skirt up from the slush. She had no longer any grace of attitude but Gabriel's eyes were still bright with happiness. The blood went bounding along his veins; and the thoughts went rioting through his brain, proud, joyful, tender, valorous.

She was walking on before him so lightly and so erect that he longed to run after her noiselessly, catch her by the shoulders and say something foolish and affectionate into her ear. She seemed to him so frail that he longed to defend her against something and then to be alone with her. Moments of their secret life together burst like stars upon his memory. A heliotrope envelope was lying beside his breakfast-cup and he was caressing it with his hand. Birds were twittering in the ivy and the sunny web of the curtain was shimmering along the floor: he could not eat for happiness. They were standing on the crowded platform and he was placing a ticket inside the warm palm of her glove. He was standing with her in the cold, looking in through a grated window at a man making bottles in a roaring furnace. It was very cold. Her face, fragrant in the cold air, was quite close to his; and suddenly she called out to the man at the furnace:

—Is the fire hot, sir?

But the man could not hear her with the noise of the furnace. It was just as well. He might have answered rudely.

A wave of yet more tender joy escaped from his heart and went coursing in warm flood along his arteries. Like the tender fires of stars moments of their life together, that no one knew of or would ever know of, broke upon and illumined his memory. He longed to recall to her those moments, to make her forget the years of their dull existence together and remember only their moments of ecstasy. For the years, he felt, had not quenched his soul or hers. Their children, his writing, her household cares had not quenched all their souls' tender fire. In one letter that he had written to her then he had said: *Why is it that words like these seem to me so dull and cold? Is it because there is no word tender enough to be your name?*

Like distant music these words that he had written years before were borne towards him from the past. He longed to be alone with her. When the others had gone away, when he and she were in their room in the hotel, then they would be alone together. He would call her softly:

—Gretta!

Perhaps she would not hear at once: she would be undressing. Then something in his voice would strike her. She would turn and look at him. . . .

At the corner of Winetavern Street they met a cab. He was glad of its rattling noise as it saved him from conversation. She was looking out of the window and seemed tired. The others spoke only a few words, pointing out some building or street. The horse galloped along wearily under the murky morning sky, dragging his old rattling box after his heels, and Gabriel was again in a cab with her, galloping to catch the boat, galloping to their honeymoon.

As the cab drove across O'Connell Bridge Miss O'Callaghan said:

—They say you never cross O'Connell Bridge without seeing a white horse.

—I see a white man this time, said Gabriel.

—Where? asked Mr Bartell D'Arcy.

Gabriel pointed to the statue, on which lay patches of snow. Then he nodded familiarly to it and waved his hand.

—Good-night, Dan, he said gaily.

When the cab drew up before the hotel Gabriel jumped out and, in spite of Mr Bartell D'Arcy's protest, paid the driver. He gave the man a shilling over his fare. The man saluted and said:

—A prosperous New Year to you, sir.

—The same to you, said Gabriel cordially.

She leaned for a moment on his arm in getting out of the cab and while standing at the curbstone, bidding the others good-night. She leaned lightly on his arm, as lightly as when she had danced with him a few hours before. He had felt proud and happy then, happy that she was his, proud of her grace and wifely carriage. But now, after the kindling again of so many memories, the first touch of her body, musical and strange and perfumed, sent through him a keen pang of lust. Under cover of her silence he pressed her arm closely to his side; and, as they stood at the hotel door, he felt that they had escaped from their lives and duties, escaped from home and friends and run away together with wild and radiant hearts to a new adventure.

An old man was dozing in a great hooded chair in the hall. He lit a candle in the office and went before them to the stairs. They followed him in silence, their feet falling in soft thuds on the thickly carpeted stairs. She mounted the stairs behind the porter, her head bowed in the ascent, her frail shoulders curved as with a burden, her skirt girt tightly about her. He could have flung his arms about her hips and held her still for his arms were trembling with desire to seize her and only the stress of his nails against the palms of his hands held the wild impulse of his body in check. The porter halted on the stairs to settle his guttering candle. They halted too on the steps below him. In the silence Gabriel could hear the falling of the molten wax into the tray and the thumping of his own heart against his ribs.

The porter led them along a corridor and opened a door. Then he set his unstable candle down on a toilet-table and asked at what hour they were to be called in the morning.

—Eight, said Gabriel.

The porter pointed to the tap of the electric-light and began a muttered apology but Gabriel cut him short.

—We don't want any light. We have light enough from the street. And

I say, he added, pointing to the candle, you might remove that handsome article, like a good man.

The porter took up his candle again, but slowly for he was surprised by such a novel idea. Then he mumbled good-night and went out. Gabriel shot the lock to.

A ghostly light from the street lamp lay in a long shaft from one window to the door. Gabriel threw his overcoat and hat on a couch and crossed the room towards the window. He looked down into the street in order that his emotion might calm a little. Then he turned and leaned against a chest of drawers with his back to the light. She had taken off her hat and cloak and was standing before a large swinging mirror, unhooking her waist.[29] Gabriel paused for a few moments, watching her, and then said:

—Gretta!

She turned away from the mirror slowly and walked along the shaft of light towards him. Her face looked so serious and weary that the words would not pass Gabriel's lips. No, it was not the moment yet.

—You looked tired, he said.

—I am a little, she answered.

—You don't feel ill or weak?

—No, tired: that's all.

She went on to the window and stood there, looking out. Gabriel waited again and then, fearing that diffidence was about to conquer him, he said abruptly:

—By the way, Gretta!

—What is it?

—You know that poor fellow Malins? he said quickly.

—Yes. What about him?

—Well, poor fellow, he's a decent sort of chap after all, continued Gabriel in a false voice. He gave me back that sovereign I lent him and I didn't expect it really. It's a pity he wouldn't keep away from that Browne, because he's not a bad fellow at heart.

He was trembling now with annoyance. Why did she seem so abstracted? He did not know how he could begin. Was she annoyed, too, about something? If she would only turn to him or come to him of her own accord! To take her as she was would be brutal. No, he must see some ardour in her eyes first. He longed to be master of her strange mood.

—When did you lend him the pound? she asked, after a pause.

Gabriel strove to restrain himself from breaking out into brutal language about the sottish Malins and his pound. He longed to cry to her from his soul, to crush her body against his, to overmaster her. But he said:

—O, at Christmas, when he opened that little Christmas-card shop in Henry Street.

He was in such a fever of rage and desire that he did not hear her come from the window. She stood before him for an instant, looking at him strangely. Then, suddenly raising herself on tiptoe and resting her hands lightly on his shoulders, she kissed him.

29. Shirtwaist, or blouse.

—You are a very generous person, Gabriel, she said.

Gabriel, trembling with delight at her sudden kiss and at the quaintness of her phrase, put his hands on her hair and began smoothing it back, scarcely touching it with his fingers. The washing had made it fine and brilliant. His heart was brimming over with happiness. Just when he was wishing for it she had come to him of her own accord. Perhaps her thoughts had been running with his. Perhaps she had felt the impetuous desire that was in him and then the yielding mood had come upon her. Now that she had fallen to him so easily he wondered why he had been so diffident.

He stood, holding her head between his hands. Then, slipping one arm swiftly about her body and drawing her towards him, he said softly:

—Gretta dear, what are you thinking about?

She did not answer nor yield wholly to his arm. He said again, softly:

—Tell me what it is, Gretta. I think I know what is the matter. Do I know?

She did not answer at once. Then she said in an outburst of tears:

—O, I am thinking about that song, *The Lass of Aughrim*.

She broke loose from him and ran to the bed and, throwing her arms across the bed-rail, hid her face. Gabriel stood stock-still for a moment in astonishment and then followed her. As he passed in the way of the cheval-glass [30] he caught sight of himself in full length, his broad, well-filled shirt-front, the face whose expression always puzzled him when he saw it in a mirror and his glimmering gilt-rimmed eyeglasses. He halted a few paces from her and said:

—What about the song? Why does that make you cry?

She raised her head from her arms and dried her eyes with the back of her hand like a child. A kinder note than he had intended went into his voice.

—Why, Gretta? he asked.

—I am thinking about a person long ago who used to sing that song.

—And who was the person long ago? asked Gabriel, smiling.

—It was a person I used to know in Galway when I was living with my grandmother, she said.

The smile passed away from Gabriel's face. A dull anger began to gather again at the back of his mind and the dull fires of his lust began to glow angrily in his veins.

—Someone you were in love with? he asked ironically.

—It was a young boy I used to know, she answered, named Michael Furey. He used to sing that song, *The Lass of Aughrim*.[31] He was very delicate.

Gabriel was silent. He did not wish her to think that he was interested in this delicate boy.

—I can see him so plainly, she said after a moment. Such eyes as he had: big dark eyes! And such an expression in them—an expression!

—O then, you were in love with him? said Gabriel.

—I used to go out walking with him, she said, when I was in Galway.

A thought flew across Gabriel's mind.

30. A long mirror framed so that it can tilt.

31. The song is gaining in significance. Aughrim is a village near Galway, in the west of Ireland from which Gretta comes, and away from which, spiritually, Gabriel would like to be able to move. The ballad is about a girl who drowns herself after her betrayal by one Lord Gregory who will not admit her to his house.

—Perhaps that was why you wanted to go to Galway with that Ivors girl?
he said coldly.

She looked at him and asked in surprise:

—What for?

Her eyes made Gabriel feel awkward. He shrugged his shoulders and said:

—How do I know? To see him perhaps.

She looked away from him along the shaft of light towards the window in
silence.

—He is dead, she said at length. He died when he was only seventeen.
Isn't it a terrible thing to die so young as that?

—What was he? asked Gabriel, still ironically.

—He was in the gasworks, she said.

Gabriel felt humiliated by the failure of his irony and by the evocation of
this figure from the dead, a boy in the gasworks. While he had been full of
memories of their secret life together, full of tenderness and joy and desire,
she had been comparing him in her mind with another. A shameful consciousness of his own person assailed him. He saw himself as a ludicrous figure,
acting as a pennyboy [32] for his aunts, a nervous well-meaning sentimentalist,
orating to vulgarians and idealising his own clownish lusts, the pitiable fatuous
fellow he had caught a glimpse of in the mirror. Instinctively he turned his
back more to the light lest she might see the shame that burned upon his
forehead.

He tried to keep up his tone of cold interrogation but his voice when he
spoke was humble and indifferent.

—I suppose you were in love with this Michael Furey, Gretta, he said.

—I was great with him at that time, she said.

Her voice was veiled and sad. Gabriel, feeling now how vain it would be to
try to lead her whither he had purposed, caressed one of her hands and said,
also sadly:

—And what did he die of so young, Gretta? Consumption, was it?

—I think he died for me,[33] she answered.

A vague terror seized Gabriel at this answer as if, at that hour when he had
hoped to triumph, some impalpable and vindictive being was coming against
him, gathering forces against him in its vague world. But he shook himself
free of it with an effort of reason and continued to caress her hand. He did
not question her again for he felt that she would tell him of herself. Her
hand was warm and moist: it did not respond to his touch but he continued
to caress it just as he had caressed her first letter to him that spring morning.

—It was in the winter, she said, about the beginning of the winter when
I was going to leave my grandmother's and come up here to the convent. And
he was ill at the time in his lodgings in Galway and wouldn't be let out and
his people in Oughterard were written to. He was in decline, they said, or
something like that. I never knew rightly.

She paused for a moment and sighed.

32. Toady.

33. It has already been established that he was consumptive. Joyce may be letting Gretta
echo a phrase from Yeats's play *Cathleen ni Houlihan* (1902): "He died for love of me;
many a man has died for love of me," in which the spirit of Ireland is speaking.

—Poor fellow, she said. He was very fond of me and he was such a gentle boy. We used to go out together, walking, you know, Gabriel, like the way they do in the country. He was going to study singing only for his health. He had a very good voice, poor Michael Furey.

—Well; and then? asked Gabriel.

—And then when it came to the time for me to leave Galway and come up to the convent he was much worse and I wouldn't be let see him so I wrote a letter saying I was going up to Dublin and would be back in the summer and hoping he would be better then.

She paused for a moment to get her voice under control and then went on:

—Then the night before I left I was in my grandmother's house in Nuns' Island, packing up, and I heard gravel thrown up against the window. The window was so wet I couldn't see so I ran downstairs as I was and slipped out the back into the garden and there was the poor fellow at the end of the garden, shivering.

—And did you not tell him to go back? asked Gabriel.

—I implored of him to go home at once and told him he would get his death in the rain. But he said he did not want to live. I can see his eyes as well as well! He was standing at the end of the wall where there was a tree.

—And did he go home? asked Gabriel.

—Yes, he went home. And when I was only a week in the convent he died and he was buried in Oughterard where his people came from. O, the day I heard that, that he was dead!

She stopped, choking with sobs, and, overcome by emotion, flung herself face downward on the bed, sobbing in the quilt. Gabriel held her hand for a moment longer, irresolutely, and then, shy of intruding on her grief, let it fall gently and walked quietly to the window.

She was fast asleep.

Gabriel, leaning on his elbow, looked for a few moments unresentfully on her tangled hair and half-open mouth, listening to her deep-drawn breath. So she had had that romance in her life: a man had died for her sake. It hardly pained him now to think how poor a part he, her husband, had played in her life. He watched her while she slept as though he and she had never lived together as man and wife. His curious eyes rested long upon her face and on her hair: and, as he thought of what she must have been then, in that time of her first girlish beauty, a strange friendly pity for her entered his soul. He did not like to say even to himself that her face was no longer beautiful but he knew that it was no longer the face for which Michael Furey had braved death.

Perhaps she had not told him all the story.[34] His eyes moved to the chair over which she had thrown some of her clothes. A petticoat string dangled to the floor. One boot stood upright, its limp upper fallen down: the fellow of it lay upon its side. He wondered at his riot of emotions of an hour before. From what had it proceeded? From his aunt's supper, from his own foolish speech, from the wine and dancing, the merry-making when saying good-night in the hall, the pleasure of the walk along the river in the snow. Poor Aunt

34. With almost a cinematic technique, the transition from this feeling of jealous doubt (had Gretta over slept with Michael Furey?) dissolves into an erotic image of underclothes flung across a chair, an empty boot, and such items.

Julia! She too, would soon be a shade with the shade of Patrick Morkan and his horse. He had caught that haggard look upon her face for a moment when she was singing *Arrayed for the Bridal*.[35] Soon, perhaps, he would be sitting in that same drawing-room, dressed in black, his silk hat on his knees. The blinds would be drawn down and Aunt Kate would be sitting beside him, crying and blowing her nose and telling him how Julia had died. He would cast about in his mind for some words that might console her, and would find only lame and useless ones. Yes, yes: that would happen very soon.

The air of the room chilled his shoulders. He stretched himself cautiously along under the sheets and lay down beside his wife. One by one they were all becoming shades. Better pass boldly into that other world, in the full glory of some passion, than fade and wither dismally with age. He thought of how she who lay beside him had locked in her heart for so many years that image of her lover's eyes when he had told her that he did not wish to live.

Generous tears filled Gabriel's eyes. He had never felt like that himself towards any woman but he knew that such a feeling must be love. The tears gathered more thickly in his eyes and in the partial darkness he imagined he saw the form of a young man standing under a dripping tree. Other forms were near. His soul had approached that region where dwell the vast hosts of the dead. He was conscious of, but could not apprehend, their wayward and flickering existence. His own identity was fading out into a grey impalpable world: the solid world itself which these dead had one time reared and lived in was dissolving and dwindling.

A few light taps upon the pane made him turn to the window. It had begun to snow again. He watched sleepily the flakes, silver and dark, falling obliquely against the lamplight. The time had come for him to set out on his journey westward.[36] Yes, the newspapers were right: snow was general all over Ireland. It was falling on every part of the dark central plain, on the treeless hills, falling softly upon the Bog of Allen and, farther westward, softly falling into the dark mutinous Shannon waves. It was falling, too, upon every part of the lonely churchyard on the hill where Michael Furey lay buried. It lay thickly drifted on the crooked crosses and headstones, on the spears of the little gate, on the barren thorns. His soul swooned slowly as he heard the snow falling faintly through the universe and faintly falling, like the descent of their last end, upon all the living and the dead.

1906–7   1914

---

35. What is unstated involves his perception of how Aunt Julia was never arrayed for any bridal, and of how the phrase modulates into "arrayed for the burial."

36. To Connaught, to Gretta's home town. But more than that, a journey of renewal in his insularity, of affiliation with the dead around him, both literal and figurative dead who, in this last great paragraph of lyrical dissolution, are becoming each other. The snow that has lurked in the corners of the story now emerges openly and symbolically. Mary Jane's remembered phrases are now recomposed into their true meanings, and lyric permutations of phrase and syntax bring the story to a close in a moment of compensatory beauty and expansion of feeling.

From A Portrait of the Artist as a Young Man

[Stephen's Epiphany]

He turned seaward [1] from the road at Dollymount and as he passed on to the thin wooden bridge he felt the planks shaking with the tramp of heavily shod feet. A squad of christian brothers was on its way back from the Bull and had begun to pass, two by two, across the bridge. Soon the whole bridge was trembling and resounding. The uncouth faces passed him two by two, stained yellow or red or livid by the sea, and as he strove to look at them with ease and indifference, a faint stain of personal shame and commiseration rose to his own face. Angry with himself he tried to hide his face from their eyes by gazing down sideways into the shallow swirling water under the bridge but he still saw a reflection therein of their topheavy silk hats, and humble tapelike collars and loosely hanging clerical clothes.

—Brother Hickey.

Brother Quaid.

Brother MacArdle.

Brother Keogh.

Their piety would be like their names, like their faces, like their clothes, and it was idle for him to tell himself that their humble and contrite hearts,[2] it might be, paid a far richer tribute of devotion than his had ever been, a gift tenfold more acceptable than his elaborate adoration. It was idle for him to move himself to be generous towards them, to tell himself that if he ever came to their gates, stripped of his pride, beaten and in beggar's weeds, that they would be generous towards him, loving him as themselves. Idle and embittering, finally, to argue, against his own dispassionate certitude, that the commandment of love bade us not to love our neighbour as ourselves with the same amount and intensity of love but to love him as ourselves with the same kind of love.

He drew forth a phrase from his treasure and spoke it softly to himself:

—A day of dappled seaborne clouds.

The phrase and the day and the scene harmonised in a chord. Words. Was it their colours? He allowed them to glow and fade, hue after hue: sunrise gold, the russet and green of apple orchards, azure of waves, the greyfringed fleece of clouds. No, it was not their colours: it was the poise and balance of the period itself. Did he then love the rhythmic rise and fall of words better than their associations of legend and colour? Or was it that, being as weak of sight as he was shy of mind, he drew less pleasure from the reflection of the glowing sensible world through the prism of a language manycoloured and richly storied than from the contemplation of an inner world of individual emotions mirrored perfectly in a lucid supple periodic prose?

1. In the previous section Stephen Daedalus has just declined an invitation to prepare himself to enter the Jesuit community. Still asking himself why he had refused, he sets out on a walk along a seawall on Dublin Bay. "The Bull" is the spit of land along which that wall is built.

2. The reference may be to the priest's prayer "In a humble spirit and contrite heart," in the Offertory of the mass, or to its source in Isaiah 57:15: ". . . to revive the spirit of the humble, and to revive the heart of the contrite ones"; or, possibly and more ironically, to its echo in Kipling's "Recessional" (1897): "Still stands Thine ancient sacrifice, / An humble and a contrite heart."

He passed from the trembling bridge on to firm land again. At that instant, as it seemed to him, the air was chilled and looking askance towards the water he saw a flying squall darkening and crisping suddenly the tide. A faint click at his heart, a faint throb in his throat told him once more of how his flesh dreaded the cold infrahuman odour of the sea: yet he did not strike across the downs on his left but held straight on along the spine of rocks that pointed against the river's mouth.

A veiled sunlight lit up faintly the grey sheet of water where the river was embayed. In the distance along the course of the slowflowing Liffey [3] slender masts flecked the sky and, more distant still, the dim fabric of the city lay prone in haze. Like a scene on some vague arras, old as man's weariness, the image of the seventh city of christendom [4] was visible to him across the timeless air, no older nor more weary nor less patient of subjection than in the days of the thingmote.[5]

Disheartened, he raised his eyes towards the slowdrifting clouds, dappled and seaborne. They were voyaging across the deserts of the sky, a host of nomads on the march, voyaging high over Ireland, westward bound. The Europe they had come from lay out there beyond the Irish Sea, Europe of strange tongues and valleyed and woodbegirt and citadelled and of entrenched and marshalled races. He heard a confused music within him as of memories and names which he was almost conscious of but could not capture even for an instant; then the music seemed to recede, to recede, to recede: and from each receding trail of nebulous music there fell always one longdrawn calling note, piercing like a star the dusk of silence. Again! Again! Again! A voice from beyond the world was calling.

—Hello, Stephanos!

—Here comes The Dedalus!

—Ao! . . . Eh, give it over, Dwyer, I'm telling you or I'll give you a stuff in the kisser for yourself. . . . Ao!

—Good man, Towser! Duck him!

—Come along, Dedalus! Bous Stephanoumenos! Bous Stephaneforos! [6]

—Duck him! Guzzle him now, Towser!

—Help! Help! . . . Ao!

He recognised their speech collectively before he distinguished their faces. The mere sight of that medley of wet nakedness chilled him to the bone. Their bodies, corpsewhite or suffused with a pallid golden light or rawly tanned by the suns, gleamed with the wet of the sea. Their divingstone, poised on its rude supports and rocking under their plunges, and the roughhewn stones of the sloping breakwater over which they scrambled in their horseplay, gleamed with cold wet lustre. The towels with which they smacked their bodies were heavy with cold seawater: and drenched with cold brine was their matted hair.

He stood still in deference to their calls and parried their banter with easy

---

3. The river flowing through Dublin, its Thames, its Tiber. Joyce mythologizes the Liffey in *Finnegans Wake* as the great mothering entity.
4. Dublin.
5. Ancient Danish governmental council; in the 9th and 10th centuries parts of Ireland as well as of England were under Danish occupation.
6. In Greek, *stephanes* means "crown," and *bous*, "ox"; the phrases mean "garlanded ox" —*i.e.* crowned for a sacrifice.

words. How characterless they looked: Shuley without his deep unbuttoned collar, Ennis without his scarlet belt with the snaky clasp, and Connolly without his Norfolk coat [7] with the flapless sidepockets! It was a pain to see them and a swordlike pain to see the signs of adolescence that made repellent their pitiable nakedness. Perhaps they had taken refuge in number and noise from the secret dread in their souls. But he, apart from them and in silence, remembered in what dread he stood of the mystery of his own body.

—Stephanos Dedalos! Bous Stephanoumenos! Bous Stephaneforos!

Their banter was not new to him and now it flattered his mild proud sovereignty. Now, as never before, his strange name seemed to him a prophecy.[8] So timeless seemed the grey warm air, so fluid and impersonal his own mood, that all ages were as one to him. A moment before the ghost of the ancient kingdom of the Danes had looked forth through the vesture of the hazewrapped city. Now, at the name of the fabulous artificer,[9] he seemed to hear the noise of dim waves and to see a winged form flying above the waves and slowly climbing the air. What did it mean? Was it a quaint device opening a page of some medieval book of prophecies and symbols, a hawklike man flying sunward above the sea, a prophecy of the end he had been born to serve and had been following through the mists of childhood and boyhood, a symbol of the artist forging anew in his workshop out of the sluggish matter of the earth a new soaring impalpable imperishable being?

His heart trembled; his breath came faster and a wild spirit passed over his limbs as though he were soaring sunward. His heart trembled in an ecstasy of fear and his soul was in flight. His soul was soaring in an air beyond the world and the body he knew was purified in a breath and delivered of incertitude and made radiant and commingled with the element of the spirit. An ecstasy of flight made radiant his eyes and wild his breath and tremulous and wild and radiant his windswept limbs.

—One! Two! . . . Look out!

—O, cripes, I'm drownded!

—One! Two! Three and away!

—Me next! Me next!

—One! . . . Uk!

—Stephaneforos!

His throat ached with a desire to cry aloud, the cry of a hawk or eagle on high, to cry piercingly of his deliverance to the winds. This was the call of

7. A fashionable jacket, belted in back.

8. Throughout this book the strangeness of Stephen's name has passed without comment (as, in the earlier pages, has that of an aunt named "Dante"). Here, at the point where Stephen is struck by the possible hidden significance of his name, Joyce tacitly alludes to a great heroic tradition, in which the hero receives a new name, or discovers his actual one. Thus, Jacob wrestles with an angel and becomes "Israel"; John Little fights with Robin Hood and becomes "Little John"; Redcross fights with a dragon in Book I of *The Faerie Queene* and becomes St. George.

9. Stephen's true father, he feels, is not his actual father, Simon Daedalus, but the more real mythological figure, the Daedalus of antiquity. This phrase comes up again at the very end of the book, when, in one of the most famous passages of dedicated resolve in modern literature, Stephen notes in his journal as he sets off for Europe and freedom: "I go to encounter for the millionth time the reality of experience and to forge in the smithy of my soul the uncreated conscience of my race. . . . Old father, old artificer, stand me now and ever in good stead."

life to his soul not the dull gross voice of the world of duties and despair, not the inhuman voice that had called him to the pale service of the altar. An instant of wild flight had delivered him and the cry of triumph which his lips withheld cleft his brain.

—Stephaneforos!

What were they now but cerements [10] shaken from the body of death—the fear he had walked in night and day, the incertitude that had ringed him round, the shame that had abased him within and without—cerements, the linens of the grave?

His soul had arisen from the grave of boyhood, spurning her graveclothes. Yes! Yes! Yes! He would create proudly out of the freedom and power of his soul, as the great artificer whose name he bore, a living thing, new and soaring and beautiful, impalpable, imperishable.

He started up nervously from the stoneblock for he could no longer quench the flame in his blood. He felt his cheeks aflame and his throat throbbing with song. There was a lust of wandering in his feet that burned to set out for the ends of the earth. On! On! his heart seemed to cry. Evening would deepen above the sea, night fall upon the plains, dawn glimmer before the wanderer and show him strange fields and hills and faces. Where?

He looked northward towards Howth. The sea had fallen below the line of seawrack on the shallow side of the breakwater and already the tide was running out fast along the foreshore. Already one long oval bank of sand lay warm and dry amid the wavelets. Here and there warm isles of sand gleamed above the shallow tide, and about the isles and around the long bank and amid the shallow currents of the beach were lightclad gayclad figures, wading and delving.

In a few moments he was barefoot, his stockings folded in his pockets and his canvas shoes dangling by their knotted laces over his shoulders: and, picking a pointed salteaten stick out of the jetsam among the rocks, he clambered down the slope of the breakwater.

There was a long rivulet in the strand: and, as he waded slowly up its course, he wondered at the endless drift of seaweed. Emerald and black and russet and olive, it moved beneath the current, swaying and turning. The water of the rivulet was dark with endless drift and mirrored the high-drifting clouds. The clouds were drifting above him silently and silently the seatangle was drifting below him; and the grey warm air was still: and a new wild life was singing in his veins.

Where was his boyhood now? Where was the soul that had hung back from her destiny, to brood alone upon the shame of her wounds and in her house of squalor and subterfuge to queen it in faded cerements and in wreaths that withered at the touch? Or where was he?

He was alone. He was unheeded, happy and near to the wild heart of life. He was alone and young and wilful and wildhearted, alone amid a waste of wild air and brackish waters and the seaharvest of shells and tangle and veiled grey sunlight and gayclad lightclad figures, of children and girls and voices childish and girlish in the air.

10. Waxed cloth used for wrapping corpses.

A girl stood before him in midstream, alone and still, gazing out to sea. She seemed like one whom magic had changed into the likeness of a strange and beautiful seabird. Her long slender bare legs were delicate as a crane's and pure save where an emerald trail of seaweed had fashioned itself as a sign upon the flesh. Her thighs, fuller and softhued as ivory, were bared almost to the hips where the white fringes of her drawers were like featherings of soft white down. Her slateblue skirts were kilted boldly about her waist and dovetailed behind her. Her bosom was as a bird's soft and slight, slight and soft as the breast of some darkplumaged dove. But her long fair hair was girlish: and girlish, and touched with the wonder mortal beauty, her face.

She was alone and still, gazing out to sea; and when she felt his presence and the worship of his eyes her eyes turned to him in quiet sufferance of his gaze, without shame or wantonness. Long, long she suffered his gaze and then quietly withdrew her eyes from his and bent them towards the stream, gently stirring the water with her foot hither and thither. The first faint noise of gently moving water broke the silence, low and faint and whispering, faint as the bells of sleep; hither and thither, hither and thither: and a faint flame trembled on her cheek.

—Heavenly God! cried Stephen's soul, in an outburst of profane joy.

He turned away from her suddenly and set off across the strand. His cheeks were aflame; his body was aglow; his limbs were trembling. On and on and on and on he strode, far out over the sands, singing wildly to the sea, crying to greet the advent of the life that had cried to him.

Her image had passed into his soul for ever and no word had broken the holy silence of his ecstasy. Her eyes had called him and his soul had leaped at the call. To live, to err, to fall, to triumph, to recreate life out of life! A wild angel had appeared to him, the angel of mortal youth and beauty, an envoy from the fair courts of life, to throw open before him in an instant of ecstasy the gates of all the ways of error and glory. On and on and on and on!

He halted suddenly and heard his heart in the silence. How far had he walked? What hour was it?

There was no human figure near him nor any sound borne to him over the air. But the tide was near the turn and already the day was on the wane. He turned landward and ran towards the shore and, running up the sloping beach, reckless of the sharp shingle, found a sandy nook amid a ring of tufted sand-knolls and lay down there that the peace and silence of the evening might still the riot of his blood.

He felt above him the vast indifferent dome and the calm processes of the heavenly bodies; and the earth beneath him, the earth that had borne him, had taken him to her breast.

He closed his eyes in the languor of sleep. His eyelids trembled as if they felt the vast cyclic movement of the earth and her watchers, trembled as if they felt the strange light of some new world. His soul was swooning into some new world,[11] fantastic, dim, uncertain as under sea, traversed by cloudy

11. At the peak of this visual epiphany of the girl in the water, which complements the aural epiphany of his own name, Stephen "swoons" very much as Gabriel Conroy does, in an overwhelming surge of spiritual generosity, in which subject and object merge, outlines are blurred by feeling, and a total spiritual fulfillment is glimpsed.

shapes and beings. A world, a glimmer, or a flower? Glimmering and trembling, trembling and unfolding, a breaking light, an opening flower, it spread in endless succession to itself, breaking in full crimson and unfolding and fading to palest rose, leaf by leaf and wave of light by wave of light, flooding all the heavens with its soft flushes, every flush deeper than other.

Evening had fallen when he woke and the sand and arid grasses of his bed glowed no longer. He rose slowly and, recalling the rapture of his sleep, sighed at its joy.

He climbed to the crest of the sandhill and gazed about him. Evening had fallen. A rim of the young moon cleft the pale waste of sky like the rim of a silver hoop embedded in grey sand; and the tide was flowing in fast to the land with a low whisper of her waves, islanding a few last figures in distant pools.

[Stephen's Poem [12]]

Towards dawn he awoke. O what sweet music! His soul was all dewy wet. Over his limbs in sleep pale cool waves of light had passed. He lay still, as if his soul lay amid cool waters, conscious of faint sweet music. His mind was waking slowly to a tremulous morning knowledge, a morning inspiration. A spirit filled him, pure as the purest water, sweet as dew, moving as music. But how faintly it was inbreathed, how passionlessly, as if the seraphim themselves were breathing upon him! His soul was waking slowly, fearing to awake wholly. It was that windless hour of dawn when madness wakes and strange plants open to the light and the moth flies forth silently.

An enchantment of the heart! The night had been enchanted. In a dream or vision he had known the ecstasy of seraphic life. Was it an instant of enchantment only or long hours and days and years and ages?

The instant of inspiration seemed now to be reflected from all sides at once from a multitude of cloudy circumstance of what had happened or of what might have happened. The instant flashed forth like a point of light and now from cloud on cloud of vague circumstance confused form was veiling softly its afterglow. O! In the virgin womb of the imagination the word was made flesh. Gabriel the seraph had come to the virgin's chamber. An afterglow deepened within his spirit, whence the white flame had passed, deepening to a rose and ardent light. That rose and ardent light was her strange wilful heart, strange that no man had known or would know, wilful from before the beginning of the world: and lured by that ardent roselike glow the choirs of the seraphim were falling from heaven.

> Are you not weary of ardent ways,
> Lure of the fallen seraphim?
> Tell no more of enchanted days.

The verses passed from his mind to his lips and, murmuring them over, he felt the rhythmic movement of a villanelle [13] pass through them. The roselike

---

12. In this section we observe and overhear the inner creative processes as Stephen writes a lyric and observes himself as he is writing.

13. The originally French lyric form (featuring repeated refrain lines), as exemplified by Stephen's poem, was used by Victorian poets for easy sentimental effects. But see the way William Empson and Dylan Thomas manipulate the form (below).

glow sent forth its rays of rhyme; ways, days, blaze, praise, raise. Its rays burned up the world, consumed the hearts of men and angels: the rays from the rose that was her wilful heart.

Your eyes have set man's heart ablaze
And you have had your will of him.
Are you not weary of ardent ways?

And then? The rhythm died away, ceased, began again to move and beat. And then? Smoke, incense ascending from the altar of the world.

Above the flame the smoke of praise
Goes up from ocean rim to rim.
Tell no more of enchanted days.

Smoke went up from the whole earth, from the vapoury oceans, smoke of her praise. The earth was like a swinging smoking swaying censer, a ball of incense, an ellipsoidal ball. The rhythm died out at once; the cry of his heart was broken. His lips began to murmur the first verses over and over; then went on stumbling through half verses, stammering and baffled; then stopped. The heart's cry was broken.

The veiled windless hour had passed and behind the panes of the naked window the morning light was gathering. A bell beat faintly very far away. A bird twittered; two birds, three. The bell and the bird ceased: and the dull white light spread itself east and west, covering the world, covering the rose-light in his heart.

Fearing to lose all, he raised himself suddenly on his elbow to look for paper and pencil. There was neither on the table; only the soupplate he had eaten the rice from for supper and the candlestick with its tendrils of tallow and its paper socket, singed by the last flame. He stretched his arm wearily towards the foot of the bed, groping with his hand in the pockets of the coat that hung there. His fingers found a pencil and then a cigarette packet. He lay back and, tearing open the packet, placed the last cigarette on the windowledge and began to write out the stanzas of the villanelle in small neat letters on the rough cardboard surface.

Having written them out he lay back on the lumpy pillow, murmuring them again. The lumps of knotted flock under his head reminded him of the lumps of knotted horsehair in the sofa of her parlour on which he used to sit, smiling or serious, asking himself why he had come, displeased with her and with himself, confounded by the print of the Sacred Heart above the untenanted sideboard. He saw her approach him in a lull of the talk and beg him to sing one of his curious songs. Then he saw himself sitting at the old piano, striking chords softly from its speckled keys and singing, amid the talk which had risen again in the room, to her who leaned beside the mantlepiece a dainty song of the Elizabethans, a sad and sweet loth to depart,[14] the victory chant of Agincourt, the happy air of Greensleeves. While he sang and she listened,

14. A "Loth to Depart" was a kind of Elizabethan keyboard piece based on a song form. All the pieces mentioned might be found in some late 19th-century collection of musical antiquities arranged for piano.

or feigned to listen, his heart was at rest but when the quaint old songs had ended and he heard again the voices in the room he remembered his own sarcasm: the house where young men are called by their christian names a little too soon.

At certain instants her eyes seemed about to trust him but he had waited in vain. She passed now dancing lightly across his memory as she had been that night at the carnival ball, her white dress a little lifted, a white spray nodding in her hair. She danced lightly in the round. She was dancing towards him and, as she came, her eyes were a little averted and a faint glow was on her cheek. At the pause in the chain of hands her hand had lain in his an instant, a soft merchandise.

—You are a great stranger now.

—Yes. I was born to be a monk.

—I am afraid you are a heretic.

—Are you much afraid?

For answer she had danced away from him along the chain of hands, dancing lightly and discreetly, giving herself to none. The white spray nodded to her dancing and when she was in shadow the glow was deeper on her cheek.

A monk! His own image started forth a profaner of the cloister, a heretic Franciscan, willing and willing not to serve, spinning like Gherardino da Borgo San Donnino,[15] a lithe web of sophistry and whispering in her ear.

No, it was not his image. It was like the image of the young priest in whose company he had seen her last, looking at him out of dove's eyes, toying with the pages of her Irish phrase-book.

—Yes, yes, the ladies are coming round to us. I can see it every day. The ladies are with us. The best helpers the language has.

—And the church, Father Moran?

—The church too. Coming round too. The work is going ahead there too. Don't fret about the church.

Bah! he had done well to leave the room in disdain. He had done well not to salute her on the steps of the library. He had done well to leave her to flirt with her priest, to toy with a church which was the scullerymaid of christendom.

Rude brutal anger routed the last lingering instant of ecstasy from his soul. It broke up violently her fair image and flung the fragments on all sides. On all sides distorted reflections of her image started from his memory: the flower-girl in the ragged dress with damp coarse hair and a hoyden's face who had called herself his own girl and begged his handsel,[16] the kitchengirl in the next house who sang over the clatter of her plates with the drawl of a country singer the first bars of *By Killarney's Lakes and Fells*, a girl who had laughed gaily to see him stumble when the iron grating in the footpath near Cork Hill had caught the broken sole of his shoe, a girl he had glanced at, attracted by her small ripe mouth as she passed out of Jacob's biscuit factory, who had cried to him over her shoulder:

15. A 13th-century Franciscan spiritual, follower of the Cistercian Joachim of Fiore (1132–1202) who had founded a group whose views of the absolute poverty of Christ were later declared heretical. Gherardino published Joachim's writings and developed his doctrines, which Stephen would have been taught to distrust.

16. Gift (price paid for a girl).

—Do you like what you seen of me, straight hair and curly eyebrows?

And yet he felt that, however he might revile and mock her image, his anger was also a form of homage. He had left the classroom in disdain that was not wholly sincere, feeling that perhaps the secret of her race lay behind those dark eyes upon which her long lashes flung a quick shadow. He had told himself bitterly as he walked through the streets that she was a figure of the womanhood of her country, a batlike soul waking to the consciousness of itself in darkness and secrecy and loneliness, tarrying awhile, loveless and sinless, with her mild lover and leaving him to whisper of innocent transgressions in the latticed ear of a priest.[17] His anger against her found vent in coarse railing at her paramour, whose name and voice and features offended his baffled pride: a priested peasant, with a brother a policeman in Dublin and a brother a potboy in Moycullen. To him she would unveil her soul's shy nakedness, to one who was but schooled in the discharging of a formal rite rather than to him, a priest of eternal imagination, transmuting the daily bread of experience into the radiant body of everliving life.

The radiant image of the eucharist united again in an instant his bitter and despairing thoughts, their cries arising unbroken in a hymn of thanksgiving.

> Our broken cries and mournful lays
> Rise in one eucharistic hymn.
> Are you not weary of ardent ways?
>
> While sacrificing hands upraise
> The chalice flowing to the brim,
> Tell no more of enchanted days.

He spoke the verses aloud from the first lines till the music and rhythm suffused his mind, turning it to quiet indulgence; then copied them painfully to feel them the better by seeing them; then lay back on his bolster.

The full morning light had come. No sound was to be heard: but he knew that all around him life was about to awaken in common noises, hoarse voices, sleepy prayers. Shrinking from that life he turned towards the wall, making a cowl of the blanket and staring at the great overblown scarlet flowers of the tattered wallpaper. He tried to warm his perishing joy in their scarlet glow, imagining a roseway from where he lay upwards to heaven all strewn with scarlet flowers. Weary! Weary! He too was weary of ardent ways.

A gradual warmth, a languorous weariness passed over him, descending along his spine from his closely cowled head. He felt it descend and, seeing himself as he lay, smiled. Soon he would sleep.

He had written verses for her again after ten years. Ten years before she had worn her shawl cowlwise about her head, sending sprays of her warm breath into the night air, tapping her foot upon the glassy road. It was the last tram; the lank brown horses knew it and shook their bells to the clear night in admonition. The conductor talked with the driver, both nodding often in the green light of the lamp. They stood on the steps of the tram, he on the upper, she on the lower. She came up to his step many times between their phrases

17. I.e. in the confessional, in which a curtained grille separates priest from penitent to preserve penitent's anonymity.

and went down again and once or twice remained beside him forgetting to go down and then went down. Let be! Let be!

Ten years from that wisdom of children to his folly. If he sent her the verses? They would be read out at breakfast amid the tapping of eggshells. Folly indeed! The brothers would laugh and try to wrest the page from each other with their strong hard fingers. The suave priest, her uncle, seated in his armchair, would hold the page at arm's length, read it smiling and approve of the literary form.

No, no: that was folly. Even if he sent her the verses she would not show them to others. No, no: she could not.

He began to feel that he had wronged her. A sense of her innocence moved him almost to pity her, an innocence he had never understood till he had come to the knowledge of it through sin, an innocence which she too had not understood while she was innocent or before the strange humiliation of her nature had first come upon her. Then first her soul had begun to live as his soul had when he had first sinned: and a tender compassion filled his heart as he remembered her frail pallor and her eyes, humbled and saddened by the dark shame of womanhood.

While his soul had passed from ecstasy to languor where had she been? Might it be, in the mysterious ways of spiritual life, that her soul at those same moments had been conscious of his homage? It might be.

A glow of desire kindled again his soul and fired and fulfilled all his body. Conscious of his desire she was waking from odorous sleep, the temptress of his villanelle. Her eyes, dark and with a look of languor, were opening to his eyes. Her nakedness yielded to him, radiant, warm, odorous and lavish-limbed, enfolded him like a shining cloud, enfolded him like water with a liquid life: and like a cloud of vapour or like waters circumfluent in space the liquid letters of speech, symbols of the element of mystery, flowed forth over his brain.

> *Are you not weary of ardent ways,*
> *Lure of the fallen seraphim?*
> *Tell no more of enchanted days.*
>
> *Your eyes have set man's heart ablaze*
> *And you have had your will of him.*
> *Are you not weary of ardent ways?*
>
> *Above the flame the smoke of praise*
> *Goes up from ocean rim to rim.*
> *Tell no more of enchanted days.*
>
> *Our broken cries and mournful lays*
> *Rise in one eucharistic hymn.*
> *Are you not weary of ardent ways?*
>
> *While sacrificing hands upraise*
> *The chalice flowing to the brim,*
> *Tell no more of enchanted days.*
>
> *And still you hold our longing gaze*
> *With languorous look and lavish limb!*

Are you not weary of ardent ways?
Tell no more of enchanted days.

      *   *   *

What birds were they? He stood on the steps of the library to look at them,
leaning wearily on his ashplant. They flew round and round the jutting shoulder
of a house in Molesworth Street. The air of the late March evening made clear
their flight, their dark darting quivering bodies flying clearly against the sky
as against a limphung cloth of smoky tenuous blue.

He watched their flight; bird after bird: a dark flash, a swerve, a flash again,
a dart aside, a curve, a flutter of wings. He tried to count them before all their
darting quivering bodies passed: six, ten, eleven: and wondered were they odd
or even in number. Twelve, thirteen: for two came wheeling down from the
upper sky. They were flying high and low but ever round and round in straight
and curving lines and ever flying from left to right, circling about a temple
of air.

He listened to the cries: like the squeak of mice behind the wainscot: a
shrill twofold note. But the notes were long and shrill and whirring, unlike
the cry of vermin, falling a third or a fourth and trilled as the flying beaks clove
the air. Their cry was shrill and clear and fine and falling like threads of silken
light unwound from whirring spools.

The inhuman clamour soothed his ears in which his mother's sobs and
reproaches murmured insistently and the dark frail quivering bodies wheeling
and fluttering and swerving round an airy temple of the tenuous sky soothed
his eyes which still saw the image of his mother's face.

Why was he gazing upwards from the steps of the porch, hearing their
shrill twofold cry, watching their flight? For an augury of good or evil? A phrase
of Cornelius Agrippa[18] flew through his mind and then there flew hither and
thither shapeless thoughts from Swedenborg[19] on the correspondence of birds
to things of the intellect and of how the creatures of the air have their knowledge and know their times and seasons because they, unlike man, are in the
order of their life and have not perverted that order by reason.

And for ages man had gazed upward as he was gazing at birds in flight.
The colonnade above him made him think vaguely of an ancient temple and the
ashplant on which he leaned wearily of the curved stick of an augur. A sense
of fear of the unknown moved in the heart of his weariness, a fear of symbols
and portents, of the hawklike man whose name he bore soaring out of his
captivity on osierwoven wings, of Thoth,[20] the god of writers, writing with a
reed upon a tablet and bearing on his narrow ibis head the cusped moon.

He smiled as he thought of the god's image for it made him think of a
bottlenosed judge in a wig, putting commas into a document which he held at
arm's length and he knew that he would not have remembered the god's name
but that it was like an Irish oath. It was folly. But was it for this folly that he
was about to leave for ever the house of prayer and prudence into which he
had been born and the order of life out of which he had come?

18. Cornelius Agrippa von Nettesheim (1486–1535), German alchemist and philosopher.
19. Emanuel Swedenborg (1688–1722), Swedish theologian and philosopher.
20. The Egyptian god who served as scribe to the other gods, and was later identified with
the Greek Hermes (founder of "hermetic" knowledge). Thoth was represented as having
the head of an ibis.

They came back with shrill cries over the jutting shoulder of the house, flying darkly against the fading air. What birds were they? He thought that they must be swallows who had come back from the south. Then he was to go away for they were birds ever going and coming, building ever an unlasting home under the eaves of men's houses and ever leaving the homes they had built to wander.

> Bend down your faces, Oona and Aleel,
> I gaze upon them as the swallow gazes
> Upon the nest under the eave before
> He wander the loud waters.[21]

A soft liquid joy like the noise of many waters flowed over his memory and he felt in his heart the soft peace of silent spaces of fading tenuous sky above the waters, of oceanic silence, of swallows flying through the seadusk over the flowing waters.

A soft liquid joy flowed through the words[22] where the soft long vowels hurtled noiselessly and fell away, lapping and flowing back and ever shaking the white bells of their waves in mute chime and mute peal and soft low swooning cry; and he felt that the augury he had sought in the wheeling darting birds and in the pale space of sky above him had come forth from his heart like a bird from a turret quietly and swiftly.

Symbol of departure or of loneliness? The verses crooned in the ear of his memory composed slowly before his remembering eyes the scene of the hall on the night of the opening of the national theatre. He was alone at the side of the balcony, looking out of jaded eyes at the culture of Dublin in the stalls and at the tawdry scenecloths and human dolls framed by the garish lamps of the stage. A burly policeman sweated behind him and seemed at every moment about to act. The catcalls and hisses and mocking cries ran in rude gusts round the hall from his scattered fellowstudents.

—A libel on Ireland!

—Made in Germany!

—Blasphemy!

—We never sold our faith!

—No Irish woman ever did it!

—We want no amateur atheists.

—We want no budding buddhists.

A sudden swift hiss fell from the windows above him and he knew that the electric lamps had been switched on in the reader's room. He turned into the pillared hall, now calmly lit, went up the staircase and passed in through the clicking turnstile.

1904–1914   1916

---

21. Lines from Yeats's play *The Countess Cathleen* (1895).

22. The very words he had just uttered internally to describe the scene. This response to the physical actuality of words, their meanings aside, is part of the Joycean sensibility, and occupies his world from the very first study of *Dubliners* on through *Finnegans Wake*'s world of words. In this scene Stephen is reading the swallows for their symbolic meaning; compare this twilight moment with that in D. H. Lawrence's poem "Bat."

From Ulysses

[Nausicaa]

The summer evening had begun to fold the world in its mysterious embrace. Far away in the west the sun was setting and the last glow of all too fleeting day lingered lovingly on sea and strand, on the proud promontory of dear old Howth guarding as ever the waters of the bay, on the weedgrown rocks along Sandymount [1] shore and, last but not least, on the quiet church whence there streamed forth at times upon the stillness the voice of prayer to her who is in her pure radiance a beacon ever to the storm-tossed heart of man, Mary, star of the sea.[2]

The three girl friends were seated on the rocks, enjoying the evening scene and the air which was fresh but not too chilly. Many a time and oft were they wont to come there to that favourite nook to have a cosy chat beside the sparkling waves and discuss matters feminine, Cissy Caffrey and Edy Boardman with the baby in the pushcar and Tommy and Jacky Caffrey, two little curly-headed boys, dressed in sailor suits with caps to match and the name H.M.S. Belleisle printed on both. For Tommy and Jacky Caffrey were twins, scarce four years old and very noisy and spoiled twins sometimes but for all that darling little fellows with bright merry faces and endearing ways about them. They were dabbling in the sand with their spades and buckets, building castles as children do, or playing with their big coloured ball, happy as the day was long. And Edy Boardman was rocking the chubby baby to and fro in the pushcar while that young gentleman fairly chuckled with delight. He was but eleven months and nine days old and, though still a tiny toddler, was just beginning to lisp his first babyish words. Cissy Caffrey bent over him to tease his fat little plucks and the dainty dimple in his chin.

—Now, baby, Cissy Caffrey said. Say out big, big. I want a drink of water. And baby prattled after her:

—A jink a jink a jawbo.

Cissy Caffrey cuddled the wee chap for she was awfully fond of children, so patient with little sufferers and Tommy Caffrey could never be got to take his castor oil unless it was Cissy Caffrey that held his nose and promised him the scatty heel of the loaf of brown bread with golden syrup on. What a persuasive power that girl had! But to be sure baby was as good as gold, a perfect little dote in his new fancy bib. None of your spoilt beauties, Flora MacFlimsy sort, was Cissy Caffrey. A truerhearted lass never drew the breath of life, always with a laugh in her gipsylike eyes and a frolicsome word on her cherryripe red lips, a girl lovable in the extreme. And Edy Boardman laughed too at the quaint language of little brother.

But just then there was a slight altercation between Master Tommy and

1. Near the beginning of the book, Stephen Daedalus had taken a solitary and introspective morning walk here on the beach along Dublin Bay. Now, at 8 P.M., the evening falling, near Leahy's Terrace and the church of St. Mary's Star of the Sea, the absurd, sentimental narration of the *Nausicaa* episode begins.
2. The parish church, incidentally, of the dead Paddy Dignam, as well as of Gerty MacDowell, the transformed Nausicaa.

Master Jacky. Boys will be boys and our two twins were no exception to this golden rule. The apple of discord [3] was a certain castle of sand which Master Jacky had built and Master Tommy would have it right go wrong that it was to be architecturally improved by a frontdoor like the Martello tower had. But if Master Tommy was headstrong Master Jacky was selfwilled too and, true to the maxim that every little Irishman's house is his castle, he fell upon his hated rival and to such purpose that the wouldbe assailant came to grief and (alas to relate!) the coveted castle too. Needless to say the cries of discomfited Master Tommy drew the attention of the girl friends.

—Come here, Tommy, his sister called imperatively, at once! And you, Jacky, for shame to throw poor Tommy in the dirty sand. Wait till I catch you for that.

His eyes misty with unshed tears Master Tommy came at her call for their big sister's word was law with the twins. And in a sad plight he was after his misadventure. His little man-o'-war top and unmentionables [4] were full of sand but Cissy was a past mistress in the art of smoothing over life's tiny troubles and very quickly not one speck of sand was to be seen on his smart little suit. Still the blue eyes were glistening with hot tears that would well up so she kissed away the hurtness and shook her hand at Master Jacky the culprit and said if she was near him she wouldn't be far from him, her eyes dancing in admonition.

—Nasty bold Jacky! she cried.

She put an arm round the little mariner and coaxed winningly:

—What's your name? Butter and cream?

—Tell us who is your sweetheart, spoke Edy Boardman. Is Cissy your sweetheart?

—Nao, tearful Tommy said.

—Is Edy Boardman your sweetheart? Cissy queried.

—Nao, Tommy said.

—I know, Edy Boardman said none too amiably with an arch glance from her shortsighted eyes. I know who is Tommy's sweetheart, Gerty is Tommy's sweetheart.

—Nao, Tommy said on the verge of tears.

Cissy's quick motherwit guessed what was amiss and she whispered to Edy Boardman to take him there behind the pushcar where the gentlemen couldn't see and to mind he didn't wet his new tan shoes.

But who was Gerty?

Gerty MacDowell who was seated near her companions, lost in thought, gazing far away into the distance, was in very truth as fair a specimen of winsome Irish girlhood as one could wish to see. She was pronounced beautiful by all who knew her though, as folks often said, she was more a Giltrap than a MacDowell. Her figure was slight and graceful, inclining even to fragility but those iron jelloids she had been taking of late had done her a world of good much better than the Widow Welch's female pills and she was much better of those discharges she used to get and that tired feeling. The waxen pallor of her face was almost spiritual in its ivorylike purity though her rosebud mouth

---

3. A mechanical literary reference to the apple Paris awarded to Venus (in exchange for being given Helen of Troy)—thus precipitating the Trojan War.
4. Underpants. This introduces the attention paid to underwear (mostly Gerty's) throughout the episode and connected to the *Odyssey* through the fact that Nausicaa and her handmaidens were out washing dirty linen on the rocks when they saw Odysseus.

was a genuine Cupid's bow, Greekly perfect. Her hands were of finely veined alabaster with tapering fingers and as white as lemon juice and queen of ointments could make them though it was not true that she used to wear kid gloves in bed or take a milk footbath either. Bertha Supple told that once to Edy Boardman, a deliberate lie, when she was black out at daggers drawn with Gerty (the girl chums had of course their little tiffs from time to time like the rest of mortals) and she told her not let on whatever she did that it was her that told her or she'd never speak to her again. No. Honour where honour is due. There was an innate refinement, a languid queenly *hauteur* [5] about Gerty which was unmistakably evidenced in her delicate hands and higharched instep. Had kind fate but willed her to be born a gentlewoman of high degree in her own right and had she only received the benefit of a good education Gerty MacDowell might easily have held her own beside any lady in the land and have seen herself exquisitely gowned with jewels on her brow and patrician suitors at her feet vying with one another to pay their devoirs to her. Mayhap it was this, the love that might have been, that lent to her softlyfeatured face at whiles a look, tense with suppressed meaning, that imparted a strange yearning tendency to the beautiful eyes a charm few could resist. Why have women such eyes of witchery? Gerty's were of the bluest Irish blue, set off by lustrous lashes and dark expressive brows. Time was when those brows were not so silkilyseductive. It was Madame Vera Verity, directress of the Woman Beautiful page of the Princess novelette, who had first advised her to try eyebrowleine which gave that haunting expression to the eyes, so becoming in leaders of fashion, and she had never regretted it. Then there was blushing scientifically cured and how to be tall increase your height and you have a beautiful face but your nose? That would suit Mrs Dignam [6] because she had a button one. But Gerty's crowning glory was her wealth of wonderful hair. It was dark brown with a natural wave in it. She had cut it that very morning on account of the new moon and it nestled about her pretty head in a profusion of luxuriant clusters and pared her nails too, Thursday for wealth. And just now at Edy's words as a telltale flush, delicate as the faintest rosebloom, crept into her cheeks she looked so lovely in her sweet girlish shyness that of a surety God's fair land of Ireland did not hold her equal.

For an instant she was silent with rather sad downcast eyes. She was about to retort but something checked the words on her tongue. Inclination prompted her to speak out: dignity told her to be silent. The pretty lips pouted a while but then she glanced up and broke out into a joyous little laugh which had in it all the freshness of a young May morning. She knew right well, no-one better, what made squinty Edy say that because of him cooling in his attentions when it was simply a lovers' quarrel. As per usual somebody's nose was out of joint about the boy that had the bicycle always riding up and down in front of her window. Only now his father kept him in the evenings studying hard to get an exhibition [7] in the intermediate that was on and he was going to Trinity college [8] to study for a doctor when he left the high school like his brother W. E. Wylie

5. Lofty manner; haughtiness.
6. The widow of Paddy Dignam.
7. A fellowship.
8. Trinity College (Dublin), founded for, and at that time still attended largely by, Anglo-Irish (Protestant) "gentry."

who was racing in the bicycle races in Trinity college university. Little recked he perhaps for what she felt, that dull aching void in her heart sometimes, piercing to the core. Yet he was young and perchance he might learn to love her in time. They were protestants in his family and of course Gerty knew Who came first and after Him the blessed Virgin and then Saint Joseph. But he was undeniably handsome with an exquisite nose and he was what he looked, every inch a gentleman, the shape of his head too at the back without his cap on that she would know anywhere something off the common and the way he turned the bicycle at the lamp with his hands off the bars and also the nice perfume of those good cigarettes and besides they were both of a size and that was why Edy Boardman thought she was so frightfully clever because he didn't go and ride up and down in front of her bit of a garden.

Gerty was dressed simply but with the instinctive taste of a votary of Dame Fashion for she felt that there was just a might that he might be out. A neat blouse of electric blue, selftinted by dolly dyes (because it was expected in the *Lady's Pictorial* that electric blue would be worn), with a smart vee opening down to the division and kerchief pocket (in which she always kept a piece of cottonwool scented with her favourite perfume because the handkerchief spoiled the sit) and a navy threequarter skirt cut to the stride showed off her slim graceful figure to perfection. She wore a coquettish little love of a hat of wide-leaved nigger straw contrast trimmed with an underbrim of eggblue chenille and at the side a butterfly bow to tone. All Tuesday week afternoon she was hunting to match that chenille but at last she found what she wanted at Clery's summer sales, the very it, slightly shopsoiled but you would never notice, seven fingers two and a penny. She did it up all by herself and what joy was hers when she tried it on then, smiling at the lovely reflection which the mirror gave back to her! And when she put it on the waterjug to keep the shape she knew that that would take the shine out of some people she knew. Her shoes were the newest thing in footwear (Edy Boardman prided herself that she was very *petite* but she never had a foot like Gerty MacDowell, a five, and never would ash, oak or elm) with patent toecaps and just one smart buckle at her high-arched instep. Her wellturned ankle displayed its perfect proportions beneath her skirt and just the proper amount and no more of her shapely limbs encased in finespun hose with high spliced heels and wide garter tops. As for undies they were Gerty's chief care and who that knows the fluttering hopes and fears of sweet seventeen (though Gerty would never see seventeen again) can find it in his heart to blame her? She had four dinky [9] sets, with awfully pretty stichery, three garments and nighties extra, and each set slotted with different coloured ribbons, rosepink, pale blue, mauve and peagreen and she aired them herself and blued them when they came home from the wash and ironed them and she had a brickbat to keep the iron on because she wouldn't trust those washerwomen as far as she'd see them scorching the things. She was wearing the blue for luck, hoping against hope, her own colour and the lucky colour too for a bride to have a bit of blue somewhere on her because the green she wore that day week brought grief because his father brought him in to study for the intermediate exhibition and because she thought perhaps he might be

9. Nifty.

out because when she was dressing that morning she nearly slipped up the old pair on her inside out and that was for luck and lovers' meetings if you put those things on inside out so long as it wasn't on a Friday. And yet and yet! That strained look on her face! A gnawing sorrow is there all the time. Her very soul is in her eyes and she would give worlds to be in the privacy of her own familiar chamber where, giving way to tears, she could have a good cry and relieve her pentup feelings. Though not too much because she knew how to cry nicely before the mirror. You are lovely, Gerty, it said. The paly light of evening falls upon a face infinitely sad and wistful. Gerty Mac-Dowell yearns in vain. Yes, she had known from the first that her daydream of a marriage has been arranged and the weddingbells ringing for Mrs Reggy Wylie T. C. D.[10] (because the one who married the elder brother would be Mrs Wylie) and in the fashionable intelligence Mrs Gertrude Wylie was wearing a sumptuous confection of grey trimmed with expensive blue fox was not to be. He was too young to understand. He would not believe in love, a woman's birthright. The night of the party long ago in Stoers' (he was still in short trousers) when they were alone and he stole an arm round her waist she went white to the very lips. He called her little one in a strangely husky voice and snatched a half kiss (the first!) but it was only the end of her nose and then he hastened from the room with a remark about refreshments. Impetuous fellow! Strength of character had never been Reggy Wylie's strong point and he who would woo and win Gerty MacDowell must be a man among men. But waiting, always waiting to be asked and it was leap year too and would soon be over. No prince charming is her beau ideal to lay a rare and wondrous love at her feet but rather a manly man with a strong quiet face who had not found his ideal, perhaps his hair slightly flecked with grey, and who would understand, take her in his sheltering arms, strain her to him in all the strength of his deep passionate nature and comfort her with a long long kiss. It would be like heaven. For such a one she yearns this balmy summer eve. With all the heart of her she longs to be his only, his affianced bride for riches for poor,[11] in sickness in health, till death us two part, from this to this day forward.

And while Edy Boardman was with little Tommy behind the pushcar she was just thinking would the day ever come when she could call herself his little wife to be. Then they could talk about her till they went blue in the face, Bertha Supple too, and Edy, the spitfire, because she would be twenty-two in November. She would care for him with creature comforts too for Gerty was womanly wise and knew that a mere man liked that feeling of hominess. Her griddlecakes done to a golden-brown hue and queen Ann's pudding of delightful creaminess had won golden opinions from all because she had a lucky hand also for lighting a fire, dredge in the fine selfraising flour and always stir in the same direction then cream the milk and sugar and whisk well the white of eggs though she didn't like the eating part when there were any people that made her shy and often she wondered why you couldn't eat something poetical like violets or roses and they would have a beautifully appointed drawingroom with pictures and engravings and the photograph of grandpapa

10. Trinity College, Dublin.
11. "For richer, for poorer," which she has garbled, as from the marriage ceremony, "till death us do part."

Giltrap's lovely dog Garryowen that almost talked, it was so human, and chintz covers for the chairs and that silver toastrack in Clery's summer jumble sales [13] like they have in rich houses. He would be tall with broad shoulders (she had always admired tall men for a husband) with glistening white teeth under his carefully trimmed sweeping moustache and they would go on the continent for their honeymoon (three wonderful weeks!) and then, when they settled down in a nice snug and cosy little homely house, every morning they would both have brekky, simple but perfectly served, for their own two selves and before he went out to business he would give his dear little wifey a good hearty hug and gaze for a moment deep down into her eyes.

Edy Boardman asked Tommy Caffrey was he done and he said yes, so then she buttoned up his little knickerbockers for him and told him to run off and play with Jacky and to be good now and not to fight. But Tommy said he wanted the ball and Edy told him no that baby was playing with the ball and if he took it there'd be wigs on the green [13] but Tommy said it was his ball and he wanted his ball and he pranced on the ground, if you please. The temper of him! O, he was a man already was little Tommy Caffrey since he was out of pinnies.[14] Edy told him no, no and to be off now with him and she told Cissy Caffrey not to give in to him.

—You're not my sister, naughty Tommy said. It's my ball.

But Cissy Caffrey told baby Boardman to look up, look up high at her finger and she snatched the ball quickly and threw it along the sand and Tommy after it in full career, having won the day.

—Anything for a quiet life, laughed Ciss.

And she tickled tiny tot's two cheeks to make him forget and played here's the lord mayor, here's his two horses, here's his gingerbread carriage and here he walks in, chinchopper, chinchopper, chinchopper chin. But Edy got as cross as two sticks about him getting his own way like that from everyone always petting him.

—I'd like to give him something, she said, so I would, where I won't say.

—On the beetoteetom, laughed Cissy merrily.

Gerty MacDowell bent down her head and crimsoned at the idea of Cissy saying an unladylike thing like that out loud she'd be ashamed of her life to say, flushing a deep rosy red, and Edy Boardman said she was sure the gentleman opposite heard what she said. But not a pin cared Ciss.

—Let him! she said with a pert toss of her head and a piquant tilt of her nose. Give it to him too on the same place as quick as I'd look at him.

Madcap Ciss with her golliwog [15] curls. You had to laugh at her sometimes. For instance when she asked you would you have some more Chinese tea and jaspberry ram and when she drew the jugs too and the men's faces on her nails with red ink make you split your sides or when she wanted to go where you know she said she wanted to run and pay a visit to the Miss White. That was just like Cissycums. O, and will you ever forget the evening she dressed up in her father's suit and hat and the burned cork moustache and

12. Clearance sales.
13. There'd be trouble, a row.
14. Pinafore. At this date very young boys were still dressed in girls' clothes.
15. A grotesque black doll.

walked down Tritonville road, smoking a cigarette? There was none to come up to her for fun. But she was sincerity itself, one of the bravest and truest hearts heaven ever made, not one of your twofaced things, too sweet to be wholesome.

And then there came out upon the air the sound of voices and the pealing anthem of the organ. It was the men's temperance retreat conducted by the missioner, the reverend John Hughes S.J., rosary, sermon and benediction of the Most Blessed Sacrament. They were there gathered together without distinction of social class (and a most edifying spectacle it was to see) in that simple fane beside the waves, after the storms of this weary world, kneeling before the feet of the immaculate, reciting the litany of Our Lady of Loreto,[16] beseeching her to intercede for them, the old familiar words, holy Mary, holy virgin of virgins. How sad to poor Gerty's ears! Had her father only avoided the clutches of the demon drink, by taking the pledge or those powders the drink habit cured in Pearson's Weekly, she might now be rolling in her carriage, second to none. Over and over had she told herself that as she mused by the dying embers in a brown study without the lamp because she hated two lights or oftentimes gazing out of the window dreamily by the hour at the rain falling on the rusty bucket, thinking. But that vile decoction which has ruined so many hearts and homes had cast its shadow over her childhood days. Nay, she had even witnessed in the home circle deeds of violence caused by intemperance and had seen her own father, a prey to the fumes of intoxication, forget himself completely for if there was one thing of all things that Gerty knew it was the man who lifts his hand to a woman save in the way of kindness deserves to be branded as the lowest of the low.

And still the voices sang in supplication to the Virgin most powerful, Virgin most merciful. And Gerty, wrapt in thought, scarce saw or heard her companions or the twins at their boyish gambols or the gentleman off Sandymount green that Cissy Caffrey called the man that was so like himself passing along the strand taking a short walk. You never saw him anyway screwed but still and for all that she would not like him for a father because he was too old or something or on account of his face (it was a palpable case of doctor Fell [17]) or his carbuncly nose with the pimples on it and his sandy moustache a bit white under his nose. Poor father! With all his faults she loved him still when he sang *Tell me, Mary, how to woo thee* or *My love and cottage near Rochelle* and they had stewed cockles and lettuce with Lazenby's salad dressing for supper and when he sang *The moon hath raised* with Mr Dignam that died suddenly and was buried, God have mercy on him, from a stroke. Her mother's birthday that was and Charley was home on his holidays and Tom and Mr Dignam and Mrs and Patsy and Freddy Dignam and they were to have had a

16. The Litany of the Virgin, which will be sung in the course of the service, is intercut with the gooey narration throughout, to underline the relation between the primary and parodied forms of the Virgin. Also, the sermon on temperance ironically reverses a Homeric event: Alcinous, Nausicaa's father, overdrank.

17. From the nursery rhyme: "I do not like thee, Doctor Fell, / The reason why I cannot tell; / But this I know, and know full well, / I do not like thee Doctor Fell," originally improvised by the 18th-century satirist Tom Brown when the Dr. Fell in question, the dean of his Oxford college, demanded that he translate an epigram of Martial saying much the same thing.

group taken. No-one would have thought the end was so near. Now he was
laid to rest. And her mother said to him to let that be a warning to him for the
rest of his days and he couldn't even go to the funeral on account of the gout
and she had to go into town to bring him the letters and samples from his
office about Catesby's cork lino, artistic standard designs, fit for a palace, gives
tiptop wear and always bright and cheery in the home.

A sterling good daughter was Gerty just like a second mother in the house,
a ministering angel too with a little heart worth its weight in gold. And when
her mother had those raging splitting headaches who was it rubbed on the
menthol cone on her forehead but Gerty though she didn't like her mother
taking pinches of snuff and that was the only single thing they ever had words
about, taking snuff. Everyone thought the world of her for her gentle ways.
It was Gerty who turned off the gas at the main every night and it was Gerty
who tacked up on the wall of that place where she never forgot every fortnight
the chlorate of lime Mr Tunney the grocer's christmas almanac the picture of
halcyon days where a young gentleman in the costume they used to wear
then with a three-cornered hat was offering a bunch of flowers to his ladylove
with oldtime chivalry through her lattice window. You could see there was a
story behind it. The colours were done something lovely. She was in a soft
clinging white in a studied attitude and the gentleman was in chocolate and
he looked a thorough aristocrat. She often looked at them dreamily when
there for a certain purpose and felt her own arms that were white and soft
just like hers with the sleeves back and thought about those times because
she had found out in Walker's pronouncing dictionary that belonged to grandpapa Giltrap about the halcyon days what they meant.

The twins were now playing in the most approved brotherly fashion, till
at last Master Jacky who was really as bold as brass there was no getting
behind that deliberately kicked the ball as hard as ever he could down towards
the seaweedy rocks. Needless to say poor Tommy was not slow to voice his
dismay but luckily the gentleman in black who was sitting there by himself [18]
came gallantly to the rescue and intercepted the ball. Our two champions
claimed their plaything with lusty cries and to avoid trouble Cissy Caffrey
called to the gentleman to throw it to her please. The gentleman aimed the
ball once or twice and then threw it up the strand towards Cissy Caffrey but
it rolled down the slope and stopped right under Gerty's skirt near the little
pool by the rock. The twins clamoured again for it and Cissy told her to kick
it away and let them fight for it so Gerty drew back her foot but she wished
their stupid ball hadn't come rolling down to her and she gave a kick but she
missed and Edy and Cissy laughed.

—If you fail try again, Edy Boardman said.

Gerty smiled assent and bit her lip. A delicate pink crept into her pretty
cheek but she was determined to let them see so she just lifted her skirt a little
but just enough and took good aim and gave the ball a jolly good kick and
it went ever so far and the two twins after it down towards the shingle. Pure
jealousy of course it was nothing else to draw attention on account of the
gentleman opposite looking. She felt the warm flush, a danger signal always

18. Leopold Bloom, our hero.

with Gerty MacDowell, surging and flaming into her cheeks. Till then they had only exchanged glances of the most casual but now under the brim of her new hat she ventured a look at him and the face that met her gaze there in the twilight, wan and strangely drawn, seemed to her the saddest she had ever seen.

Through the open window of the church the fragrant incense was wafted and with it the fragrant names of her who was conceived without stain of original sin,[19] spiritual vessel, pray for us, honourable vessel, pray for us, vessel of singular devotion, pray for us, mystical rose. And careworn hearts were there and toilers for their daily bread and many who had erred and wandered, their eyes wet with contrition but for all that bright with hope for the reverend father Hughes had told them what the great saint Bernard said in his famous prayer of Mary, the most pious Virgin's intercessory power that it was not recorded in any age that those who implored her powerful protection were ever abandoned by her.

The twins were now playing again right merrily for the troubles of childhood are but as fleeting summer showers. Cissy played with baby Boardman till he crowed with glee, clapping baby hands in air. Peep she cried behind the hood of the pushcar and Edy asked where was Cissy gone and then Cissy popped up her head and cried ah! and, my word, didn't the little chap enjoy that! And then she told him to say papa.

—Say papa, baby. Say pa pa pa pa pa pa pa.

And baby did his level best to say it for he was very intelligent for eleven months everyone said and big for his age and the picture of health, a perfect little bunch of love, and he would certainly turn out to be something great, they said.

—Haja ja ja haja.

Cissy wiped his little mouth with the dribbling bib and wanted him to sit up properly, and say pa pa pa but when she undid the strap she cried out, holy saint Denis, that he was possing[20] wet and to double the half blanket the other way under him. Of course his infant majesty was most obstreperous at such toilet formalities and he let everyone know it:

—Habaa baaaahabaaa baaaa.

And two great big lovely big tears coursing down his cheeks. It was all no use soothering him with no, nono, baby, no and telling him about the geegee and where was the puffpuff but Ciss, always readywitted, gave him in his mouth the teat of the suckingbottle and the young heathen was quickly appeased.

Gerty wished to goodness they would take their squalling baby home out of that and not get on her nerves no hour to be out and the little brats of twins. She gazed out towards the distant sea. It was like the paintings that man used to do on the pavement with all the coloured chalks and such a pity too leaving

---

19. "Fragrant names . . . ," further invocations in the litany. "Conceived without stain of original sin" is a reference to the dogma of the Immaculate Conception of the Blessed Virgin Mary, who is here a kind of parody on Gerty, the other virgin of the story. They are both associated with blue, both "stars of the sea" (the latter, for Bloom). The litany is being sung in Gerty's parish church. The "famous prayer" mentioned below is known as the "Memorare."
20. From the same word "poss-tub," in which the washing is churned with a stick.

them there to be all blotted out, the evening and the clouds coming out and
the Bailey light on Howth and to hear the music like that and the perfume of
those incense they burned in the church like a kind of waft. And while she
gazed her heart went pitapat. Yes, it was her he was looking at and there was
meaning in his look. His eyes burned into her as though they would search
her through and through, read her very soul. Wonderful eyes they were,
superbly expressive, but could you trust them? People were so queer. She
could see at once by his dark eyes and his pale intellectual face that he was a
foreigner, the image of the photo she had of Martin Harvey, the matinée idol,
only for the moustache which she preferred because she wasn't stagestruck
like Winny Rippingham that wanted they two to always dress the same on
account of a play but she could not see whether he had an aquiline nose or
a slightly retroussé from where [s]he was sitting. He was in deep mourning, she
could see that, and the story of a haunting sorrow was written on his face. She
would have given worlds to know what it was. He was looking up so intently,
so still and he saw her kick the ball and perhaps he could see the bright steel
buckles of her shoes if she swung them like that thoughtfully with the toes
down. She was glad that something told her to put on the transparent stockings
thinking Reggy Wylie might be out but that was far away. Here was that of
which she had so often dreamed. It was he who mattered and there was joy
on her face because she wanted him because she felt instinctively that he was
like no-one else. The very heart of the girlwoman went out to him, her dream-
husband, because she knew on the instant it was him. If he had suffered, more
sinned against than sinning, or even, even, if he had been himself a sinner, a
wicked man, she cared not. Even if he was a protestant or methodist she could
convert him easily if he truly loved her. There were wounds that wanted healing
with heartbalm. She was a womanly woman not like other flighty girls, un-
feminine, he had known, those cyclists showing off what they hadn't got and
she just yearned to know all, to forgive all if she could make him fall in love
with her, make him forget the memory of the past. Then mayhap he would
embrace her gently, like a real man, crushing her soft body to him, and love
her, his ownest girlie, for herself alone.

Refuge of sinners. Comfortress of the afflicted. *Ora pro nobis.*[21] Well has it
been said that whosoever prays to her with faith and constancy can never be
lost or cast away: and fitly is she too a haven of refuge for the afflicted because
of the seven dolours which transpierced her own heart. Gerty could picture the
whole scene in the church, the stained glass windows lighted up, the candles,
the flowers and the blue banners of the blessed Virgin's sodality and Father
Conroy was helping Canon O'Hanlon at the altar, carrying things in and out
with his eyes cast down. He looked almost a saint and his confession-box was
so quiet and clean and dark and his hands were just like white wax and if
ever she became a Dominican nun in their white habit perhaps he might come
to the convent for the novena of Saint Dominic. He told her that time when
she told him about that in confession crimsoning up to the roots of her hair
for fear he could see, not to be troubled because that was only the voice of
nature and we were all subject to nature's laws, he said, in this life and that

21. "Pray for us," the response said after each invocation of the litany.

that was no sin because that came from the nature of woman instituted by God, he said, and that Our Blessed Lady herself said to the archangel Gabriel be it done unto me according to Thy Word. He was so kind and holy and often and often she thought and thought could she work a ruched teacosy with embroidered floral design for him as a present or a clock but they had a clock she noticed on the mantlepiece white and gold with a canary bird that came out of a little house to tell the time the day she went there about the flowers for the forty hours' adoration because it was hard to know what sort of a present to give or perhaps an album of illuminated views of Dublin or some place.

The exasperating little brats of twins began to quarrel again and Jacky threw the ball out towards the sea and they both ran after it. Little monkeys common as ditchwater. Someone ought to take them and give them a good hiding for themselves to keep them in their places, the both of them. And Cissy and Edy shouted after them to come back because they were afraid the tide might come in on them and be drowned.

—Jacky! Tommy!

Not they! What a great notion they had! So Cissy said it was the very last time she'd ever bring them out. She jumped up and called them and she ran down the slope past him, tossing her hair behind her which had a good enough colour if there had been more of it but with all the thingamerry she was always rubbing into it she couldn't get it to grow long because it wasn't natural so she could just go and throw her hat at it. She ran with long gandery strides it was a wonder she didn't rip up her skirt at the side that was too tight on her because there was a lot of the tomboy about Cissy Caffrey and she was a forward piece whenever she thought she had a good opportunity to show off and just because she was a good runner she ran like that so that he could see all the end of her petticoat running and her skinny shanks up as far as possible. It would have served her just right if she had tripped up over something accidentally on purpose with her high crooked French heels on her to make her look tall and got a fine tumble. *Tableau!* [22] That would have been a very charming exposé for a gentleman like that to witness.

Queen of angels, queen of patriarchs, queen of prophets, of all saints, they prayed, queen of the most holy rosary and then Father Conroy handed the thurible to Canon O'Hanlon and he put in the incense and censed the Blessed Sacrament and Cissy Caffrey caught the two twins and she was itching to give them a ringing good clip on the ear but she didn't because she thought he might be watching but she never made a bigger mistake in all her life because Gerty could see without looking that he never took his eyes off of her and then Canon O'Hanlon handed the thurible back to Father Conroy and knelt down looking up at the Blessed Sacrament and the choir began to sing *Tantum ergo* and she just swung her foot in and out in time as the music rose and fell to the *Tantumer gosa cramen tum.* [23] Three and eleven she paid for those stockings in Sparrow's of George's street on the Tuesday, no the Monday

22. Stage direction to indicate a frozen pictured group at the opening or end of a scene. Today one might make the same joke by saying "Cut!" or "Print that!"

23. Gerty's fractured version of *Tantum ergo sacramentum* (literally, "So great a sacrament, therefore . . ."), opening line of a Benediction hymn by St. Thomas Aquinas (actually the last two stanzas of the *Pange Lingua* he composed for the feast of Corpus Christi).

before Easter and there wasn't a brack[24] on them and that was what he was looking at, transparent, and not at her insignificant ones that had neither shape nor form (the cheek of her!) because he had eyes in his head to see the difference for himself.

Cissy came up along the strand with the two twins and their ball with her hat anyhow on her to one side after her run and she did look a streel[25] tugging the two kids along with the flimsy blouse she bought only a fortnight before like a rag on her back and bit of her petticoat hanging like a caricature. Gerty just took off her hat for a moment to settle her hair and a prettier, a daintier head of nutbrown tresses was never seen on a girl's shoulders, a radiant little vision, in sooth, almost maddening in its sweetness. You would have to travel many a long mile before you found a head of hair the like of that. She could almost see the swift answering flush of admiration in his eyes that set her tingling in every nerve. She put on her hat so that she could see from underneath the brim and swung her buckled shoe faster for her breath caught as she caught the expression in his eyes. He was eyeing her as a snake eyes its prey. Her woman's instinct told her that she had raised the devil in him and at the thought a burning scarlet swept from throat to brow till the lovely colour of her face became a glorious rose.

Edy Boardman was noticing it too because she was squinting at Gerty, half smiling, with her specs, like an old maid, pretending to nurse[26] the baby. Irritable little gnat she was and always would be and that was why no-one could get on with her, poking her nose into what was no concern of hers. And she said to Gerty:

—A penny for your thoughts.

—What? replied Gerty with a smile reinforced by the whitest of teeth. I was only wondering was it late.

Because she wished to goodness they'd take the snottynosed twins and their baby home to the mischief out of that so that was why she just gave a gentle hint about its being late. And when Cissy came up Edy asked her the time and Miss Cissy, as glib as you like, said it was half past kissing time, time to kiss again. But Edy wanted to know because they were told to be in early.

—Wait, said Cissy, I'll ask my uncle Peter over there what's the time by his conundrum.

So over she went and when he saw her coming she could see him take his hand out of his pocket, getting nervous, and beginning to play with his watchchain, looking at the church. Passionate nature though he was Gerty could see that he had enormous control over himself. One moment he had been there, fascinated by a loveliness that made him gaze, and the next moment it was the quiet gravefaced gentleman, selfcontrol expressed in every line of his distinguishedlooking figure.

Cissy said to excuse her would he mind telling her what was the right time and Gerty could see him taking out his watch, listening to it and looking up and clearing his throat and he said he was very sorry his watch was stopped but he thought it must be after eight because the sun was set. His voice had a

24. A run or, in Ireland, a "ladder."
25. Slattern.
26. Dandle, not give suck.

cultured ring in it and though he spoke in measured accents there was a suspicion of a quiver in the mellow tones. Cissy said thanks and came back with her tongue out and said uncle said his waterworks were out of order.

Then they sang the second verse of the *Tantum ergo* and Canon O'Hanlon got up again and censed the Blessed Sacrament and knelt down and he told Father Conroy that one of the candles was just going to set fire to the flowers and Father Conroy got up and settled it all right and she could see the gentleman winding his watch and listening to the works and she swung her leg more in and out in time. It was getting darker but he could see and he was looking all the time that he was winding the watch or whatever he was doing to it and then he put it back and put his hands back into his pockets. She felt a kind of a sensation rushing all over her and she knew by the feel of her scalp and that irritation against her stays that that thing must be coming on because the last time too was when she clipped her hair on account of the moon. His dark eyes fixed themselves on her again drinking in her every contour, literally worshipping at her shrine. If ever there was undisguised admiration in a man's passionate gaze it was there plain to be seen on that man's face. It is for you, Gertrude MacDowell, and you know it.

Edy began to get ready to go and it was high time for her and Gerty noticed that that little hint she gave had the desired effect because it was a long way along the strand to where there was the place to push up the pushcar and Cissy took off the twins' caps and tidied their hair to make herself attractive of course and Canon O'Hanlon stood up with his cope poking up at his neck and Father Conroy handed him the card to read off and he read out *Panem de cœlo præstitisti eis*[27] and Edy and Cissy were talking about the time all the time and asking her but Gerty could pay them back in their own coin and she just answered with scathing politeness when Edy asked her was she heartbroken about her best boy throwing her over. Gerty winced sharply. A brief cold blaze shone from her eyes that spoke volumes of scorn immeasurable. It hurt. O yes, it cut deep because Edy had her own quiet way of saying things like that she knew would wound like the confounded little cat she was. Gerty's lips parted swiftly to frame the word but she fought back the sob that rose to her throat, so slim, so flawless, so beautifully moulded it seemed one an artist might have dreamed of. She had loved him better than he knew. Lighthearted deceiver and fickle like all his sex he would never understand what he had meant to her and for an instant there was in the blue eyes a quick stinging of tears. Their eyes were probing her mercilessly but with a brave effort she sparkled back in sympathy as she glanced at her new conquest for them to see.

—O, responded Gerty, quick as lightning, laughing, and the proud head flashed up, I can throw my cap at who I like because it's leap year.

Her words rang out crystalclear, more musical than the cooing of the ringdove, but they cut the silence icily. There was that in her young voice that told that she was not a one to be lightly trifled with. As for Mr Reggy with his swank and his bit of money she could just chuck him aside as if he was so much filth and never again would she cast as much as a second thought

27. "You have given them bread from heaven," versicle chanted by celebrant after the *Tantum ergo*.

on him and tear his silly postcard into a dozen pieces. And if ever after he dared to presume she could give him one look of measured scorn that would make him shrivel up on the spot. Miss puny little Edy's countenance fell to no slight extent and Gerty could see by her looking as black as thunder that she was simply in a towering rage though she hid it, the little kinnatt,[28] because that shaft had struck home for her petty jealousy and they both knew that she was something aloof, apart in another sphere, that she was not of them and there was somebody else too that knew it and saw it so they could put that in their pipe and smoke it.

Edy straightened up baby Boardman to get ready to go and Cissy tucked in the ball and the spades and buckets and it was high time too because the sandman was on his way for Master Boardman junior and Cissy told him too that Billy Winks was coming and that baby was to go deedaw and baby looked just too ducky, laughing up out of his gleeful eyes, and Cissy poked him like that out of fun in his wee fat tummy and baby, without as much as by your leave, sent up his compliments on to his brandnew dribbling bib.

—O my! Puddeny pie! protested Ciss. He has his bib destroyed.

The slight *contretemps* claimed her attention but in two twos she set that little matter to rights.

Gerty stifled a smothered exclamation and gave a nervous cough and Edy asked what and she was just going to tell her to catch it while it was flying but she was ever ladylike in her deportment so she simply passed it off with consummate tact by saying that that was the benediction because just then the bell rang out from the steeple over the quiet seashore because Canon O'Hanlon was up on the altar with the veil that Father Conroy put round him round his shoulders giving the benediction with the blessed Sacrament in his hands.

How moving the scene there in the gathering twilight, the last glimpse of Erin, the touching chime of those evening bells and at the same time a bat flew forth from the ivied belfry through the dusk, hither, thither, with a tiny lost cry. And she could see far away the lights of the lighthouses so picturesque she would have loved to do with a box of paints because it was easier than to make a man and soon the lamplighter would be going his rounds past the presbyterian church grounds and along by shady Tritonville avenue where the couples walked and lighting the lamp near her window where Reggy Wylie used to turn his freewheel like she read in that book *The Lamplighter*[29] by Miss Cummins, author of *Mabel Vaughan* and other tales. For Gerty had her dreams that no-one knew of. She loved to read poetry and when she got a keepsake from Bertha Supple of that lovely confession album with the coralpink cover to write her thoughts in she laid it in the drawer of her toilettable which, though it did not err on the side of luxury, was scrupulously neat and clean. It was there she kept her girlish treasures trove, the tortoiseshell combs, her

28. Probably Joyce's transcription of the way "gnat" is pronounced in Ireland.
29. A sentimental American bestseller by Maria S. Cummins, first published in 1854. A sample of its style suggests that Joyce was using it, among other texts, as the basis of his parody: "It was a stormy evening. Gerty was standing at the window, watching for True's return from his lamplighting. She was neatly and comfortably dressed, her hair smooth, her face and hands clean. She was now quite well—better than for years before her sickness. . . ."

child of Mary badge, the whiterose scent, the eyebrowleine, her alabaster pouncetbox and the ribbons to change when her things came home from the wash and there were some beautiful thoughts written in it in violet ink that she bought in Hely's of Dame Street for she felt that she too could write poetry if she could only express herself like that poem that appealed to her so deeply that she had copied out of the newspaper she found one evening round the potherbs. *Art thou real, my ideal?* it was called by Louis J. Walsh, Magherafelt, and after there was something about *twilight, wilt thou ever?* and ofttimes the beauty of poetry, so sad in its transient loveliness, had misted her eyes with silent tears that the years were slipping by for her, one by one, and but for that one shortcoming she knew she need fear no competition and and that was an accident coming down Dalkey hill and she always tried to conceal it. But it must end she felt. If she saw that magic lure in his eyes there would be no holding back for her. Love laughs at locksmiths. She would make the great sacrifice. Her every effort would be to share his thoughts. Dearer than the whole world would she be to him and gild his days with happiness. There was the allimportant question and she was dying to know was he a married man or a widower who had lost his wife or some tragedy like the nobleman with the foreign name from the land of song had to have her put into a madhouse, cruel only to be kind. But even if—what then? Would it make a very great difference? From everything in the least indelicate her finebred nature instinctively recoiled. She loathed that sort of person, the fallen women off the accommodation walk beside the Dodder [30] that went with the soldiers and coarse men, with no respect for a girl's honour, degrading the sex and being taken up to the police station. No, no: not that. They would be just good friends like a big brother and sister without all that other in spite of the conventions of Society with a big ess. Perhaps it was an old flame he was in mourning for from the days beyond recall. She thought she understood. She would try to understand him because men were so different. The old love was waiting, waiting with little white hands stretched out, with blue appealing eyes. Heart of mine! She would follow her dream of love, the dictates of her heart that told her he was her all in all, the only man in all the world for her for love was the master guide. Nothing else mattered. Come what might she would be wild, untrammelled, free.

Canon O'Hanlon put the Blessed Sacrament back into the tabernacle and the choir sang *Laudate Dominum omnes gentes* [31] and then he locked the tabernacle door because the benediction was over and Father Conroy handed him his hat to put on and crosscat Edy asked wasn't she coming but Jacky Caffrey called out:

—O, look, Cissy!

And they all looked was it sheet lightning but Tommy saw it too over the trees beside the church, blue, and then green and purple.

—It's fireworks, Cissy Caffrey said.

And they all ran down the strand to see over the houses and the church, helterskelter, Edy with the pushcar with baby Boardman in it and Cissy holding Tommy and Jacky by the hand so they wouldn't fall running.

30. Another Dublin river, flowing into the Bay from the south.
31. "Praise the Lord, all ye people," Psalm 116, sung at the end of Benediction.

—Come on, Gerty, Cissy called. It's the bazaar fireworks.

But Gerty was adamant. She had no intention of being at their beck and call. If they could run like rossies she could sit so she said she could see from where she was. The eyes that were fastened upon her set her pulses tingling. She looked at him a moment, meeting his glance, and a light broke in upon her. Whitehot passion was in that face, passion silent as the grave, and it had made her his. At last they were left alone without the others to pry and pass remarks and she knew he could be trusted to the death, steadfast, a sterling man, a man of inflexible honour to his fingertips. His hands and face were working and a tremor went over her. She leaned back far to look up where the fireworks were and she caught her knee in her hands so as not to fall back looking up and there was no one to see only him and her when she revealed all her graceful beautifully shaped legs like that, supply soft and delicately rounded, and she seemed to hear the panting of his heart, his hoarse breathing, because she knew about the passion of men like that, hot-blooded, because Bertha Supple told her once in dead secret and made her swear she'd never about the gentleman lodger that was staying with them out of the Congested Districts Board that had pictures cut out of papers of those skirtdancers and highkickers and she said he used to do something not very nice that you could imagine sometimes in the bed. But this was altogether different from a thing like that because there was all the difference because she could almost feel him draw her face to his and the first quick hot touch of his handsome lips. Besides there was absolution so long as you didn't do the other thing before being married and there ought to be women priests that would under- stand without your telling out and Cissy Caffrey too sometimes had that dreamy kind of dreamy look in her eyes so that she too, my dear, and Winny Ripping- ham so mad about actors' photographs and besides it was on account of that other thing coming on the way it did.

And Jack Caffrey shouted to look, there was another and she leaned back and the garters were blue to match on account of the transparent and they all saw it and shouted to look, look there it was and she leaned back ever so far to see the fireworks and something queer was flying about through the air, a soft thing to and fro, dark. And she saw a long Roman candle going up over the trees up, up, and, in the tense hush, they were all breathless with excite- ment as it went higher and higher and she had to lean back more and more to look up after it, high, high, almost out of sight, and her face was suffused with a divine, an entrancing blush from straining back and he could see her other things too, nainsook [32] knickers, the fabric that caresses the skin, better than those other pettiwidth, the green, four and eleven, on account of being white and she let him and she saw that he saw and then it went so high it went out of sight a moment and she was trembling in every limb from being bent so far back he had a full view high up above her knee no-one ever not even on the swing or wading and she wasn't ashamed and he wasn't either to look in that immodest way like that because he couldn't resist the sight of the wondrous revealment half offered like those skirtdancers behaving so immodest before gentlemen looking and he kept on looking, looking. She would fain have cried to him chokingly, held out her snowy slender arms to him to come, to

32. A fine white cotton, used for underwear.

feel his lips laid on her white brow the cry of a young girl's love, a little strangled cry, wrung from her, that cry that has rung through the ages. And then a rocket sprang and bang shot blind and O! then the Roman candle burst and it was like a sigh of O! and everyone cried O! O! in raptures and it gushed out of it a stream of rain gold hair threads and they shed and ah! they were all greeny dewy stars falling with golden, O so lively! O so soft, sweet, soft! [33]

Then all melted away dewily in the grey air: all was silent. Ah! She glanced at him as she bent forward quickly, a pathetic little glance of piteous protest, of shy reproach under which he coloured like a girl. He was leaning back against the rock behind. Leopold Bloom (for it is he) stands silent, with bowed head before those young guileless eyes. What a brute he had been! At it again? A fair unsullied soul had called to him and, wretch that he was, how had he answered? An utter cad he had been. He of all men! But there was an infinite store of mercy in those eyes, for him too a word of pardon even though he had erred and sinned and wandered. Should a girl tell? No, a thousand times no. That was their secret, only theirs, alone in the hiding twilight and there was none to know or tell save the little bat that flew so softly through the evening to and fro and little bats don't tell.

Cissy Caffrey whistled, imitating the boys in the football field to show what a great person she was: and then she cried:

—Gerty! Gerty! We're going. Come on. We can see from farther up.

Gerty had an idea, one of love's little ruses. She slipped a hand into her kerchief pocket and took out the wadding and waved in reply of course without letting him and then slipped it back. Wonder if he's too far to. She rose. Was it goodbye? No. She had to go but they would meet again, there, and she would dream of that till then, tomorrow, of her dream of yester eve. She drew herself up to her full height. Their souls met in a last lingering glance and the eyes that reached her heart, full of a strange shining, hung enraptured on her sweet flowerlike face. She half smiled at him wanly, a sweet forgiving smile, a smile that verged on tears, and then they parted.

Slowly without looking back she went down the uneven strand to Cissy, to Edy, to Jacky and Tommy Caffrey, to little baby Boardman. It was darker now and there were stones and bits of wood on the strand and slippy seaweed. She walked with a certain quiet dignity characteristic of her but with care and very slowly because Gerty MacDowell was . . .

Tight boots? No. She's lame! O! [34]

Mr Bloom watched her as she limped away. Poor girl! That's why she's left on the shelf and the others did a sprint. Thought something was wrong by the cut of her jib. Jilted beauty. A defect is ten times worse in a woman. But makes them polite. Glad I didn't know it when she was on show. Hot little devil all the same. Wouldn't mind. Curiosity like a nun or a negress or a girl

33. The softness is of the visionary lights of the fireworks, and of Gerty's own underclothing and flesh. It is at this point in the story that the sentimental evasions of the directly sexual will give way, in the very image of the exploding Roman candle that is a counterpart of Bloom's sexual climax. The "outer" explosion in the world of Gerty's rhetoric is matched by an inner one, and the chapter now moves into that world, undercutting the parody of the first part.

34. The introduction of Bloom's interior monologue is characteristic of him; his practical, even (within its means) scientific, curiosity is always at work, Sherlock Holmes-like, on the phenomena he observes. And so is his memory.

with glasses. That squinty one is delicate. Near her monthlies, I expect, makes them feel ticklish. I have such a bad headache today. Where did I put the letter?[35] Yes, all right. All kinds of crazy longings. Licking pennies. Girl in Tranquilla convent that nun told me liked to smell rock oil. Virgins go mad in the end I suppose. Sister? How many women in Dublin have it today? Martha, she. Something in the air. That's the moon. But then why don't all women menstruate at the same time with same moon, I mean? Depends on the time they were born, I suppose. Or all start scratch then get out of step. Sometimes Molly and Milly together. Anyhow I got the best of that. Damned glad I didn't do it in the bath this morning over her silly I will punish you letter. Made up for that tramdriver this morning. That gouger M'Coy stopping me to say nothing.[36] And his wife engagement in the country valise, voice like a pickaxe. Thankful for small mercies. Cheap too. Yours for the asking. Because they want it themselves. Their natural craving. Shoals of them every evening poured out of offices. Reserve better. Don't want it they throw it at you. Catch em alive, O. Pity they can't see themselves. A dream of wellfilled hose. Where was that? Ah, yes. Mutoscope pictures in Capel street: for men only. Peeping Tom. Willy's hat and what the girls did with it. Do they snapshot those girls or is it all a fake? *Lingerie* does it. Felt for the curves inside her *deshabillé*. Excites them also when they're. I'm all clean come and dirty me. And they like dressing one another for the sacrifice. Milly delighted with Molly's new blouse. At first. Put them all on to take them all off. Molly. Why I bought her the violet garters. Us too: the tie he wore, his lovely socks and turnedup trousers. He wore a pair of gaiters the night that first we met. His lovely shirt was shining beneath his what? of jet. Say a woman loses a charm with every pin she takes out. Pinned together. O Mairy lost the pin of her. Dressed up to the nines for somebody. Fashion part of their charm. Just changes when you're on the track of the secret. Except the east: Mary, Martha: now as then. No reasonable offer refused. She wasn't in a hurry either. Always off to a fellow when they are. They never forget an appointment. Out on spec probably. They believe in chance because like themselves. And the others inclined to give her an odd dig. Girl friends at school, arms round each other's neck or with ten fingers locked, kissing and whispering secrets about nothing in the convent garden. Nuns with whitewashed faces, cool coif and their rosaries going up and down, vindictive too for what they can't get. Barbed wire. Be sure now and write to me. And I'll write to you. Now won't you? Molly and Josie Powell. Till Mr Right comes along then meet once in a blue moon. *Tableau!*[37] O, look who it is for the love of God! How are you at all? What have you been doing with yourself? Kiss and delighted to, kiss, to see you. Picking holes in each other's appearance. You're looking splendid. Sister souls showing their teeth at one another. How many have you left? Wouldn't lend each other a pinch of salt.

Ah!

35. From Martha Clifford, a typist with whom he is corresponding, under the pseudonym "Henry Flower." In his brooding about menstruation he will revert to Martha a few lines farther along.

36. A bore who had stopped Bloom earlier in the day to cadge a suitcase from him.

37. This reciprocates Gerty's identical joke earlier. See note 22.

Devils they are when that's coming on them.[38] Dark devilish appearance. Molly often told me feel things a ton weight. Scratch the sole of my foot. O that way! O, that's exquisite! Feel it myself too. Good to rest once in a way. Wonder if it's bad to go with them then. Safe in one way. Turns milk, makes fiddlestrings snap. Something about withering plants I read in a garden. Besides they say if the flower withers she wears she's a flirt. All are. Daresay she felt I. When you feel like that you often meet what you feel. Liked me or what? Dress they look at. Always know a fellow courting: collars and cuffs. Well cocks and lions do the same and stags. Same time might prefer a tie undone or something. Trousers? Suppose I when I was? No. Gently does it. Dislike rough and tumble. Kiss in the dark and never tell. Saw something in me. Wonder what. Sooner have me as I am than some poet chap with bearsgrease, plastery hair lovelock over his dexter optic.[39] To aid gentleman in literary. Ought to attend to my appearance my age. Didn't let her see me in profile. Still, you never know. Pretty girls and ugly men marrying. Beauty and the beast. Besides I can't be so if Molly. Took off her hat to show her hair. Wide brim bought to hide her face, meeting someone might know her, bend down or carry a bunch of flowers to smell. Hair strong in rut. Ten bob I got for Molly's combings when we were on the rocks in Holles street. Why not? Suppose he gave her money. Why not? All a prejudice. She's worth ten, fifteen, more a pound. All that for nothing. Bold hand. Mrs Marion. Did I forget to write address on that lettter like the postcard I sent to Flynn? And the day I went to Drimmie's without a necktie. Wrangle with Molly it was put me off. No, I remember. Richie Goulding.[40] He's another. Weighs on his mind. Funny my watch stopped at half past four.[41] Dust. Shark liver oil they use to clean could do it myself. Save. Was that just when he, she?

O, he did. Into her. She did. Done.

Ah! [42]

Mr. Bloom with careful hand recomposed his wet shirt. O Lord, that little limping devil. Begins to feel cold and clammy. Aftereffect not pleasant. Still you have to get rid of it someway. They don't care. Complimented perhaps. Go home to nicey bread and milky and say night prayers with the kiddies. Well, aren't they. See her as she is spoil all. Must have the stage setting, the rouge, costume, position, music. The name too. *Amours* of actresses. Nell Gwynn, Mrs Bracegirdle, Maud Branscombe.[43] Curtain up. Moonlight silver effulgence. Maiden discovered with pensive bosom. Little sweetheart come and kiss me. Still I feel. The strength it gives a man. That's the secret of it. Good job I let off there behind coming out of Dignam's. Cider that was. Otherwise I couldn't have. Makes you want to sing after. *Lacaus esant taratara.*[44] Suppose I spoke to her. What about? Bad plan however if you don't

38. Again, menstruation, and remembered superstitions about it.
39. Right eye.
40. Stephen Daedalus's uncle, brother of his dead mother.
41. The moment of Molly Bloom's adultery with Blazes Boylan, her concert manager. Bloom is almost aware of this.
42. The moment of his ejaculation.
43. Famous actresses of the Restoration stage.
44. Bloom is garbling the words ("*La causa è santa*") of an aria from Meyerbeer's *The*

know how to end the conversation. Ask them a question they ask you another. Good idea if you're in a cart. Wonderful of course if you say: good evening, and you see she's on for it: good evening. O but the dark evening in the Appian way I nearly spoke to Mrs Clinch O thinking she was. Whew! Girl in Meath street that night. All the dirty things I made her say all wrong of course. My arks she called it. It's so hard to find one who. Aho! If you don't answer when they solicit must be horrible for them till they harden. And kissed my hand when I gave her the extra two shillings. Parrots. Press the button and the bird will squeak. Wish she hadn't called me sir. Oh, her mouth in the dark! And you a married man with a single girl! That's what they enjoy. Taking a man from another woman. Or even hear of it. Different with me. Glad to get away from other chap's wife. Eating off his cold plate. Chap in the Burton [45] today spitting back gumchewed gristle. French letter [46] still in my pocketbook. Cause of half the trouble. But might happen sometime, I don't think. Come in. All is prepared. I dreamt. What? [47] Worst is beginning. How they change the venue [48] when it's not what they like. Ask you do you like mushrooms because she once knew a gentleman who. Or ask you what someone was going to say when he changed his mind and stopped. Yet if I went the whole hog, say: I want to, something like that. Because I did. She too. Offend her. Then make it up. Pretend to want something awfully, then cry off for her sake. Flatters them. She must have been thinking of someone else all the time. What harm? Must since she came to the use of reason, he, he and he. First kiss does the trick. The propitious moment. Something inside them goes pop. Mushy like, tell by their eye, on the sly. First thoughts are best. Remember that till their dying day. Molly, lieutenant Mulvey that kissed her under the Moorish wall beside the gardens.[49] Fifteen she told me. But her breasts were developed. Fell asleep then. After Gencree dinner that was when we drove home the featherbed mountain. Gnashing her teeth in sleep. Lord mayor had his eye on her too. Val Dillon.[50] Apoplectic.

There she is with them down there for the fireworks. My fireworks. Up like a rocket, down like a stick. And the children, twins they must be, waiting for something to happen. Want to be grownups. Dressing in mother's clothes. Time enough, understand all the ways of the world. And the dark one with the mop head and the nigger mouth. I knew she could whistle. Mouth made for that. Like Molly. Why that high class whore in Jammet's wore her veil only to her nose. Would you mind, please, telling me the right time? I'll tell you the right time up a dark lane. Say prunes and prisms forty times every morning, cure for fat lips. Caressing the little boy too. Onlookers see most of the game. Of course they understand birds, animals, babies. In their line.

Huguenots: La cause est juste et sainte, through an Italian translation; the "taratara" may be Bloom's version of the famous "Rataplan Chorus" from that opera, although Tara is the name of a hill where the Irish kings were crowned.

45. A restaurant Bloom had entered at lunchtime, only to be revolted by the sight of men eating meat (in the Laestrygonians episode); he went elsewhere for a cheese sandwich.
46. A condom.
47. He is aware of a dream that he does not remember until the end of this episode.
48. In court cases, a change of venue brings about a removal of the trial to another court.
49. Bloom is thinking of an early erotic incident in Molly Bloom's life, in Gibraltar (where she grew up) with an early lover, Lieut. Henry Mulvey.
50. The mayor of Dublin.

Didn't look back when she was going down the strand. Wouldn't give that satisfaction. Those girls, those girls, those lovely seaside girls. Fine eyes she had, clear. It's the white of the eye brings that out not so much the pupil. Did she know what I? Course. Like a cat sitting beyond a dog's jump. Women never meet one like that Wilkins in the high school drawing a picture of Venus with all his belongings on show. Call that innocence? Poor idiot! His wife has her work cut out for her. Never see them sit on a bench marked *Wet Paint.* Eyes all over them. Look under the bed for what's not there. Longing to get the fright of their lives. Sharp as needles they are. When I said to Molly the man at the corner of Cuffe street was goodlooking, thought she might like, twigged at once he had a false arm. Had too. Where do they get that? Typist going up Roger Greene's stairs two at a time to show her understandings. Handed down from father to mother to daughter, I mean. Bred in the bone. Milly for example drying her handkerchief on the mirror to save the ironing. Best place for an ad to catch a woman's eye on a mirror. And when I sent her [51] for Molly's Paisley shawl to Prescott's, by the way that ad I must, carrying home the change in her stocking. Clever little minx! I never told her. Neat way she carried parcels too. Attract men, small thing like that. Holding up her hand, shaking it, to let the blood flow back when it was red. Who did you learn that from? Nobody. Something the nurse taught me. O, don't they know? Three years old she was in front of Molly's dressingtable just before we left Lombard street west. Me have a nice face. Mullingar.[52] Who knows? Ways of the world. Young student. Straight on her pins anyway not like the other. Still she was game. Lord, I am wet. Devil you are. Swell of her calf. Transparent stockings, stretched to breaking point. Not like that frump today. A. E.[53] Rumpled stockings. Or the one in Grafton street. White. Wow! Beef to the heel.

A monkey puzzle rocket burst, spluttering in darting crackles. Zrads and zrads, zrads, zrads. And Cissy and Tommy ran out to see and Edy after with the pushcar and then Gerty beyond the curve of the rocks. Will she? Watch! Watch! See! Looked round. She smelt an onion. Darling, I saw your. I saw all.

Lord!

Did me good all the same. Off colour after Kiernan's, Dignam's. For this relief much thanks.[54] In *Hamlet,* that is. Lord! It was all things combined. Excitement. When she leaned back felt an ache at the butt of my tongue. Your head it simply swirls. He's right. Might have made a worse fool of myself however. Instead of talking about nothing. Then I will tell you all. Still it was a kind of language between us. It couldn't be? No, Gerty they called her. Might be false name however like my and the address Dolphin's barn a blind.

> *Her maiden name was Jemina Brown*
> *And she lived with her mother in Irishtown.*

Place made me think of that I suppose. All tarred with the same brush. Wiping pens in their stockings. But the ball rolled down to her as if it under-

51. He goes on thinking of Milly.
52. Where Milly is currently working for a photographer.
53. Earlier in the day, Bloom had encountered the poet "A.E." (George Russell, 1867–1935) talking to a woman ("Her stockings are loose over her ankles. I detest that: so tasteless"), and then goes on to brood on Russell's vegetarian habits (in the *Laestrygonians* chapter). Here he remembers this and another incident.
54. *Hamlet* I.i.8.

stood. Every bullet has its billet. Course I never could throw anything straight at school. Crooked as a ram's horn. Sad however because it lasts only a few years till they settle down to potwalloping and papa's pants will soon fit Willy and fullers' earth [55] for the baby when they hold him out to do ah ah. No soft job. Saves them. Keeps them out of harm's way. Nature. Washing child, washing corpse. Dignam. Children's hands always round them. Cocoanut skulls, monkeys, not even closed at first, sour milk in their swaddles and tainted curds. Oughtn't to have given that child an empty teat to suck. Fill it up with wind. Mrs Beaufoy, Purefoy.[56] Must call to the hospital. Wonder is nurse Callan there still. She used to look over some nights when Molly was in the Coffee Palace. That young doctor O'Hare I noticed her brushing his coat. And, Mrs Breen and Mrs Dignam once like that too, marriageable. Worst of all at night Mrs Duggan told me in the City Arms.[57] Husband rolling in drunk, stink of pub off him like a polecat. Have that in your nose in the dark, whiff of stale boose. Then ask in the morning: was I drunk last night? Bad policy however to fault the husband. Chickens come home to roost. They stick by one another like glue. Maybe the women's fault also. That's where Molly can knock spots off them. It is the blood of the south. Moorish.[58] Also the form, the figure. Hands felt for the opulent. Just compare for instance those others. Wife locked up at home, skeleton in the cupboard. Allow me to introduce my. Then they trot you out some kind of a nondescript, wouldn't know what to call her. Always see a fellow's weak point in his wife. Still there's destiny in it, falling in love. Have their own secrets between them. Chaps that would go to the dogs if some woman didn't take them in hand. Then little chits of girls, height of a shilling in coppers, with little hubbies. As God made them He matched them. Sometimes children turn out well enough. Twice nought makes one. Or old rich chap of seventy and blushing bride. Marry in May and repent in December. This wet is very unpleasant. Stuck. Well the foreskin is not back. Better detach.

Ow!

Other hand a sixfooter with a wifey up to his watchpocket. Long and the short of it. Big he and little she. Very strange about my watch.[59] Wristwatches are always going wrong. Wonder is there any magnetic influence between the person because that was about the time he. Yes, I suppose at once. Cat's away the mice will play. I remember looking in Pill lane. Also that now is magnetism. Back of everything magnetism. Earth for instance pulling this and being pulled. That causes movement. And time? Well that's the time the movement takes. Then if one thing stopped the whole ghesabo [60] would stop bit by bit. Because it's arranged. Magnetic needle tells you what's going on in

55. Talc, so named for its use in cleaning clothes, but here used as baby powder. "Papa's pants will soon fit Willy"—a well-known music-hall song.

56. Philip Beaufoy was the author of a story Bloom had read that morning in the privy. In the next chapter Mrs. Purefoy, a friend of Bloom's, will be delivered of a baby in the Lying-in Hospital in Holles Street. Earlier in the day, Bloom, in chatting with Mrs. Breen, a youthful flame, got the names mixed up in a Freudian slip, as he does again here.

57. A pub.

58. The Moorish wall in Gibraltar, scene of Molly's early love.

59. It had stopped at 4:30.

60. Contraption.

the sun, the stars. Little piece of steel iron. When you hold out the fork. Come. Come. Tip. Woman and man that is. Fork and steel. Molly, he. Dress up and look and suggest and let you see and see more and defy you if you're a man to see that and, like a sneeze coming, legs, look, look and if you have any guts in you. Tip. Have to let fly.

Wonder how is she feeling in that region. Shame all put on before third person. More put out about a hole in her stocking. Molly, her underjaw stuck out head back, about the farmer in the ridingboots and spurs at the horse show. And when the painters were in Lombard street west. Fine voice that fellow had. How Giuglini [61] began. Smell that I did, like flowers. It was too. Violets. Came from the turpentine probably in the paint. Make their own use of everything. Same time doing it scraped her slipper on the floor so they wouldn't hear. But lots of them can't kick the beam, I think. Keep that thing up for hours. Kind of a general all round over me and half down my back. Wait. Hm. Hm. Yes. That's her perfume. Why she waved her hand. I leave you this to think of me when I'm far away on the pillow. What is it? Heliotrope? No, Hyacinth? Hm. Roses, I think. She'd like scent of that kind. Sweet and cheap: soon sour. Why Molly likes opoponax.[62] Suits her with a little jessamine mixed. Her high notes and her low notes. At the dance night she met him, dance of the hours. Heat brought it out. She was wearing her black and it had the perfume of the time before. Good conductor, is it? Or bad? Light too. Suppose there's some connection. For instance if you go into a cellar where it's dark. Mysterious thing too. Why did I smell it only now? Took its time in coming like herself, slow but sure. Suppose it's ever so many millions of tiny grains blown across. Yes, it is. Because those spice islands, Cinghalese this morning,[63] smell them leagues off. Tell you what it is. It's like a fine veil or web they have all over the skin, fine like what do you call it gossamer and they're always spinning it out of them, fine as anything, rainbow colours without knowing it. Clings to everything she takes off. Vamp of her stockings. Warm shoe. Stays.[64] Drawers: little kick, taking them off. Byby till next time. Also the cat likes to sniff in her shift on the bed. Know her smell in a thousand. Bathwater too. Reminds me of strawberries and cream. Wonder where it is really. There or the armpits or under the neck. Because you get it out of all holes and corners. Hyacinth perfume made of oil or ether or something. Muskrat. Bag under their tails one grain pour off odour for years. Dogs at each other behind. Good evening. Evening. How do you sniff? Hm. Hm. Very well, thank you. Animals go by that. Yes now, look at it that way. We're the same. Some women for instance warn you off when they have their period. Come near. Then get a hogo [65] you could hang your hat on. Like what? Potted herrings gone stale or. Boof! Please keep off the grass.

61. Antonio Giuglini (1827-65), opera tenor.
62. Resin used in perfumes.
63. At about 10 A.M. Bloom had passed a shop with "finest Ceylon" tea advertised; it sent him into a reverie of the exotic, erotic, spice-laden, mysterious East: "Those Cinghalese lobbing around the sun in *dolce far niente*. Not doing a hand's turn all day. Sleep six months out of the twelve. Too hot to quarrel. Influence of the climate. Lethargy. Flowers of idleness. . . ."
64. Corsets.
65. A stink.

Perhaps they get a man smell off us. What though? Cigary gloves Long John had on his desk the other. Breath? What you eat and drink gives that. No. Mansmell, I mean. Must be connected with that because priests that are supposed to be are different. Women buzz round it like flies round treacle. Railed off the altar get on to it at any cost. The tree of forbidden priest. O father, will you? Let me be the first to. That diffuses itself all through the body, permeates. Source of life and it's extremely curious the smell. Celery sauce. Let me.

Mr Bloom inserted his nose. Hm. Into the. Hm. Opening of his waistcoat. Almonds or. No. Lemons it is. Ah, no, that's the soap.[66]

O by the by that lotion. I knew there was something on my mind. Never went back and the soap not paid. Dislike carrying bottles like that hag this morning. Hynes might have paid me [67] that three shillings. I could mention Meagher's just to remind him. Still if he works that paragraph. Two and nine. Bad opinion of me he'll have. Call tomorrow. How much do I owe you? Three and nine? Two and nine, sir. Ah. Might stop him giving credit another time. Lose your customers that way. Pubs do. Fellow run up a bill on the slate and then slinking around the back streets into somewhere else.

Here's this nobleman passed before. Blown in from the bay. Just went as far as turn back. Always at home at dinnertime. Looks mangled out: had a good tuck in. Enjoying nature now. Grace after meals. After supper walk a mile. Sure he has a small bank balance somewhere, government sit. Walk after him now make him awkward like those newsboys me today. Still you learn something. See ourselves as others see us. So long as women don't mock what matter? That's the way to find out. Ask yourself who is he now. *The Mystery Man on the Beach*,[68] prize titbit story by Mr Leopold Bloom. Payment at the rate of one guinea per column. And that fellow today at the graveside in the brown macintosh. Corns on his kismet [69] however. Healthy perhaps absorb all the. Whistle brings rain they say. Must be some somewhere. Salt in the Ormond [70] damp. The body feels the atmosphere. Old Betty's joints are on the rack. Mother Shipton's [71] prophecy that is about ships around they fly in the twinkling. No. Signs of rain it is. The royal reader. And distant hills seem coming nigh.

Howth.[72] Bailey light. Two, four, six, eight, nine. See. Has to change or they

---

66. Bloom had bought a bar of "sweet lemony" soap at a chemist's (pharmacy), forgetting to pay for it (he had gone in originally to buy some lotion for Molly). He carries the soap about in his pocket all day.

67. A newspaper reporter who owes Bloom a small sum. Bloom has encountered him several times during the day.

68. The "titbit story" was the one by Beaufoy that Bloom had read earlier; the man in the brown macintosh at Dignam's funeral is the "mystery man" of *Ulysses:* we never learn who he is.

69. "Fate," derived from the Turkish.

70. The Ormond Hotel, where all the singing takes place in *Sirens*.

71. A 17th-century prophetess, credited, in an 1862 book about her, with having prophesied the steam engine, telegraphy, and other scientific marvels, as well as the end of the world (to occur in 1881).

72. Bloom is looking across Dublin Bay at the Hill of Howth (mentioned in the epening sentences) and its lighthouse.

might think it a house. Wreckers. Grace Darling.[73] People afraid of the dark. Also glowworms, cyclists: lightingup time. Jewels diamonds flash better. Light is a kind of reassuring. Not going to hurt you. Better now of course than long ago. Country roads. Run you through the small guts for nothing. Still two types there are you bob against. Scowl or smile. Pardon! Not at all. Best time to spray plants too in the shade after the sun. Some light still. Red rays are longest. Roygbiv Vance taught us: red, orange, yellow, green, blue, indigo, violet. A star I see. Venus? Can't tell yet. Two, when three it's night.[74] Were those nightclouds there all the time? Looks like a phantom ship. No. Wait. Trees are they. An optical illusion. Mirage. Land of the setting sun this. Homerule [75] sun setting in the southeast. My native land, goodnight.

Dew falling. Bad for you, dear, to sit on that stone. Brings on white fluxions.[76] Never have little baby then less he was big strong fight his way up through. Might get piles myself. Sticks too like a summer cold, sore on the mouth. Cut with grass or paper worst. Friction of the position. Like to be that rock she sat on. O sweet little, you don't know how nice you looked. I begin to like them at that age. Green apples. Grab at all that offer. Suppose it's the only time we cross legs, seated. Also the library today: those girl graduates. Happy chairs under them. But it's the evening influence. They feel all that. Open like flowers, know their hours, sunflowers, Jerusalem artichokes, in ballrooms, chandeliers, avenues under the lamps. Nightstock [77] in Mat Dillon's garden where I kissed her shoulder. Wish I had a full length oil-painting of her then. June that was too I wooed. The year returns. History repeats itself. Ye crags and peaks I'm with you once again. Life, love, voyage round your own little world. And now? Sad about her lame of course but must be on your guard not to feel too much pity. They take advantage.

All quiet on Howth now. The distant hills seem. Where we. The rhododendrons. I am a fool perhaps. He gets the plums and I the plumstones. Where I come in. All that old hill has seen. Names change: that's all. Lovers: yum yum.

Tired I feel now. Will I get up? O wait. Drained all the manhood out of me, little wretch. She kissed me. My youth. Never again. Only once it comes. Or hers. Take the train there tomorrow. No. Returning not the same. Like kids your second visit to a house. The new I want. Nothing new under the sun. Care of P. O. Dolphin's barn. Are you not happy in your? Naughty darling. At Dolphin's barn charades in Luke Doyle's house. Mat Dillon and his bevy of daughters: Tiny, Atty, Floey, Maimy, Louy, Hetty. Molly too. Eightyseven that was. Year before we. And the old major partial to his drop of spirits. Curious she an only child, I an only child. So it returns. Think you're escaping and run into yourself. Longest way round is the shortest way home. And just when he and she. Circus horse walking in a ring. Rip van Winkle we played. Rip: tear

73. Heroine (1815–42), daughter of a lighthouse keeper who saved people from drowning. Wordsworth wrote a poem about her.

74. According to canonical Jewish law, night (and, thus, the next day) starts when three stars are visible. The evening star that Bloom sees, along with the starry fireworks, is yet another *stella maris*, "star of the sea."

75. Southeast of Dublin is London, and Parliament, which refused to grant Ireland home rule.

76. Discharges.

77. A plant also called garden rocket. Bloom is thinking of his first meeting with Molly.

in Henny Doyle's overcoat. Van: breadvan delivering. Winkle: cockles and peri-
winkles. Then I did Rip van Winkle coming back. She leaned on the sideboard
watching. Moorish eyes. Twenty years asleep in Sleepy Hollow. All changed.
Forgotten. The young are old. His gun rusty from the dew.
    Ba. What is that flying about? Swallow? Bat probably.[78] Thinks I'm a tree,
so blind. Have birds no smell? Metempsychosis.[79] They believed you could be
changed into a tree from grief. Weeping willow. Ba. There he goes. Funny
little beggar. Wonder where he lives. Belfry up there. Very likely. Hanging by
his heels in the odour of sanctity. Bell scared him out, I suppose. Mass seems
to be over. Could hear them all at it. Pray for us. And pray for us. And pray
for us. Good idea the repetition. Same thing with ads. Buy from us. And buy
from us. Yes, there's the light in the priest's house. Their frugal meal. Remember
about the mistake in the valuation when I was in Thom's. Twentyeight it is.
Two houses they have. Gabriel Conroy's brother is curate.[80] Ba. Again. Wonder
why they come out at night like mice. They're a mixed breed. Birds are like
hopping mice. What frightens them, light or noise? Better sit still. All instinct
like the bird in drouth got water out of the end of a jar by throwing in pebbles.
Like a little man in a cloak he is with tiny hands. Weeny bones. Almost see
them shimmering, kind of a bluey white. Colours depend on the light you see.
Stare the sun for example like the eagle then look at a shoe see a blotch blob
yellowish. Wants to stamp his trademark on everything. Instance, that cat this
morning on the staircase. Colour of brown turf. Say you never see them with
three colours. Not true. That half tabbywhite tortoiseshell in the *City Arms*
with the letter em on her forehead. Body fifty different colours. Howth a while
ago amethyst. Glass flashing. That's how that wise man what's his name with
the burning glass. Then the heather goes on fire. It can't be tourists' matches.
What? Perhaps the sticks dry rub together in the wind and light. Or broken
bottles in the furze act as a burning glass in the sun. Archimedes. I have it![81]
My memory's not so bad.
    Ba. Who knows what they're always flying for. Insects? That bee last week
got into the room playing with his shadow on the ceiling. Might be the one bit
me, come back to see. Birds too never find out what they say. Like our small
talk. And says she and says he. Nerve? they have to fly over the ocean and
back. Lot must be killed in storms, telegraph wires. Dreadful life sailors have
too. Big brutes of ocean-going steamers floundering along in the dark, lowing
out like seacows. *Faugh a ballagh.*[82] Out of that, bloody curse to you. Others in
vessels, bit of a handkerchief sail, pitched about like snuff at a wake when the
stormy winds do blow. Married too. Sometimes away for years at the ends of
the earth somewhere. No ends really because it's round. Wife in every port they
say. She has a good job if she minds it till Johnny comes marching home again.

78. Compare a similar moment of twilight for the young Stephen Daedalus at the end of
our excerpt from *A Portrait of the Artist as a Young Man,* and the D. H. Lawrence "Bat" poem
referred to there; compare its protagonist's reaction with the same discovery Bloom is making.
79. The word means the transmigration of souls, the doctrine of reincarnation. The word,
and the concept (connected as it is with historical repetition; see "History repeats itself,"
above), have been thematic in *Ulysses.*
80. That is, the Father Conroy referred to in Gerty's half of the chapter; see *The Dead.*
81. "Eureka!" the famous cry of Archimedes on discovering how to measure weight by
water displacement.
82. A worthless person (Gaelic).

If ever he does. Smelling the tail end of ports. How can they like the sea? Yet they do. The anchor's weighed. Off he sails with a scapular or a medal on him for luck. Well? And the tephilim [83] no what's this they call it poor papa's father had on his door to touch. That brought us out of the land of Egypt and into the house of bondage.[84] Something in all those superstitions because when you go out never know what dangers. Hanging on to a plank or astride of a beam for grim life, lifebelt round round him, gulping salt water, and that's the last of his nibs till the sharks catch hold of him. Do fish ever get seasick?

Then you have a beautiful calm without a cloud, smooth sea, placid, crew and cargo in smithereens, Davy Jones' locker. Moon looking down. Not my fault, old cockalorum.

A lost long candle wandered up the sky from Mirus bazaar in search of funds for Mercer's hospital and broke, drooping, and shed a cluster of violet but one white stars. They floated, fell: they faded. The shepherd's hour: the hour of holding: hour of tryst. From house to house, giving his everwelcome double knock, went the nine o'clock postman, the glowworm's lamp at his belt gleaming here and there through the laurel hedges. And among the five young trees a hoisted lintstock lit the lamp at Leahy's terrace.[85] By screens of lighted windows, by equal gardens a shrill voice went crying, wailing: *Evening Telegraph, stop press edition! Result of the Gold Cup race!* [86] and from the door of Dignam's house a boy ran out and called. Twittering the bat flew here, flew there. Far out over the sands the coming surf crept, grey. Howth settled for slumber tired of long days, of yumyum rhododendrons (he was old) and felt gladly the night breeze lift, ruffle his fell of ferns. He lay but opened a red eye unsleeping, deep and slowly breathing, slumberous but awake. And far on Kish bank [87] the anchored lightship twinkled, winked at Mr Bloom.

Life those chaps out there must have, stuck in the same spot. Irish Lights board. Penance for their sins. Coastguards too. Rocket and breeches buoy and lifeboat. Day we went out for the pleasure cruise in the Erin's King, throwing them the sack of old papers. Bears in the zoo. Filthy trip. Drunkards out to shake up their livers. Puking overboard to feed the herrings. Nausea. And the women, fear of God in their faces. Milly, no sign of funk. Her blue scarf loose, laughing. Don't know what death is at that age. And then their stomachs clean. But being lost they fear. When we hid behind the tree at Crumlin. I didn't want to. Mamma! Mamma! Babes in the wood. Frightening them with masks too. Throwing them up in the air to catch them. I'll murder you. Is it only half fun? Or children playing battle. Whole earnest. How can people aim guns at each other? Sometimes they go off. Poor kids. Only troubles wildfire and nettle-rash. Calomel [88] purge I got her for that. After getting better asleep with Molly. Very same teeth she has. What do they love? Another themselves? But the

83. *Tefillin*, phylacteries, small containers of written prayers wrapped around the head and hands of orthodox Jews during daily prayers. Bloom confuses these with a *mezuzzah*, an analogous container of the same text put up on the doorposts of one's house and upon one's gates.
84. He deliberately misquotes the text of the First Commandment: ". . . out of the land of Egypt, out of the house of bondage" (Exodus 20.2).
85. Behind the beach along which he has been sitting.
86. This race has figured prominently in the book.
87. Out across the bay.
88. Mercury salts formerly used in laxatives.

morning she chased her with the umbrella. Perhaps so as not to hurt. I felt her pulse. Ticking. Little hand it was: now big. Dearest Papli.[89] All that the hand says when you touch. Loved to count my waistcoat buttons. Her first stays I remember. Made me laugh to see. Little paps to begin with. Left one is more sensitive, I think. Mine too. Nearer the heart. Padding themselves out if fat is in fashion. Her growing pains at night, calling, wakening me. Frightened she was when her nature came on her first.[90] Poor child! Strange moment for the mother too. Brings back her girlhood. Gibraltar. Looking from Buena Vista. O'Hara's tower. The seabirds screaming. Old Barbary ape that gobbled all his family. Sundown, gunfire for the men to cross the lines. Looking out over the sea she told me. Evening like this, but clear, no clouds. I always thought I'd marry a lord or a gentleman with a private yacht. *Buenas noches, señorita. El hombre ama la muchacha hermosa.*[91] Why me? Because you were so foreign from the others.

Better not stick here all night like a limpet. This weather makes you dull. Must be getting on for nine by the light. Go home. Too late for *Leah, Lily of Killarney.*[92] No. Might be still up. Call to the hospital to see. Hope she's over. Long day I've had. Martha,[93] the bath,[94] funeral,[95] house of keys,[96] museum with those goddesses,[97] Dedalus' song.[98] Then that bawler in Barney Kiernan's.[99] Got my own back there. Drunken ranters. What I said about his God made him wince. Mistake to hit back. Or? No. Ought to go home and laugh at themselves. Always want to be swilling in company. Afraid to be alone like a child of two. Suppose he hit me. Look at it other way round. Not so bad then. Perhaps not to hurt he meant. Three cheers for Israel. Three cheers for the sister-in-law he hawked about, three fangs in her mouth. Same style of beauty. Particularly nice old party for a cup of tea. The sister of the wife of the wild man of Borneo has just come to town. Imagine that in the early morning at close range. Everyone to his taste as Morris said when he kissed the cow. But Dignam's put the boots on it. Houses of mourning so depressing because you never know. Anyhow she wants the money. Must call to those Scottish widows [100] as I promised. Strange name. Takes it for granted we're going to pop off first.

89. Milly had written her father like this.
90. Again, thinking of Milly's first menstruation.
91. "Good evening, Miss. The man loves the pretty girl" (Spanish).
92. Earlier, Bloom had wondered whether to see a play called *Leah, or the Jewish Maiden,* by the American playwright T. A. Daly, that evening, or an operetta called *Lily of Killarney.*
93. Bloom now goes through a résumé of his day, summing up the previous chapters in which he has appeared; Martha Clifford, his secret correspondent (see note 35).
94. The Turkish bath in which Bloom had reclined, in the *Lotus-Eaters* episode.
95. Paddy Dignam's funeral, the *Hades* chapter.
96. At the newspaper office, thinking of an advertisement for the House of Keys. The House of Keys is the legislature of the Isle of Man, the name of which, in the context of *Ulysses,* cannot help but resonate symbolically for us.
97. The museum stands next to the National Library, in which the *Scylla and Charybdis* scene occurs.
98. The *Sirens* episode at the Ormond Hotel, where Simon Daedalus, Stephen's father, sings an aria from Flotow's opera *Martha.*
99. In Barney Kiernan's pub (*Cyclops*), Bloom has suffered rhetorically elaborate anti-Semitic abuse. In a later recapitulation of the episodes of *Ulysses* the present *Nausicaa* section is called "rite of Onan," centering on Bloom's masturbation.
100. A well-known life-insurance company.

That widow on Monday was it outside Cramer's that looked at me. Buried the poor husband but progressing favourably on the premium. Her widow's mite. Well? What do you expect her to do? Must wheedle her way along. Widower I hate to see. Looks so forlorn. Poor man O'Connor wife and five children poisoned by mussels here. The sewage. Hopeless. Some good matronly woman in a porkpie hat to mother him. Take him in tow, platter face and a large apron. Ladies' grey flannelette bloomers, three shillings a pair, astonishing bargain. Plain and loved, loved for ever, they say. Ugly: no woman thinks she is. Love, lie and be handsome for tomorrow we die. See him sometimes walking about trying to find out who played the trick. U, p.: up.[101] Fate that is. He, not me. Also a shop often noticed. Curse seems to dog it. Dream last night?[102] Wait Something confused. She had red slippers on. Turkish. Wore the breeches. Suppose she does. Would I like her in pyjamas? Damned hard to answer. Nannetti's gone. Mailboat. Near Holyhead[103] by now. Must nail that ad of Keyes's.[104] Work Hynes and Crawford. Petticoats for Molly.[105] She has something to put in them. What's that? Might be money.

Mr Bloom stooped and turned over a piece of paper on the strand. He brought it near his eyes and peered. Letter? No. Can't read. Better go. Better. I'm tired to move. Page of an old copybook. All those holes and pebbles. Who could count them? Never know what you find. Bottle with story of a treasure in it thrown from a wreck. Parcels post. Children always want to throw things in the sea. Trust? Bread cast on the waters. What's this? Bit of stick.

O! Exhausted that female has me. Not so young now. Will she come here tomorrow? Wait for her somewhere for ever. Must come back. Murderers do. Will I?

Mr Bloom with his stick gently vexed the thick sand at his foot. Write a message for her. Might remain. What?

I.

Some flatfoot tramp on it in the morning. Useless. Washed away. Tide comes here a pool near her foot. Bend, see my face there, dark mirror, breathe on it, stirs. All these rocks with lines and scars and letters. O, those transparent! Besides they don't know. What is the meaning of that other world. I called you naughty boy because I do not like.

AM. A[106]

No room. Let it go.

Mr Bloom effaced the letters with his slow boot. Hopeless thing sand. Nothing grows in it. All fades. No fear of big vessels coming up here. Except Guinness's barges. Round the Kish in eighty days. Done half by design.

He flung his wooden pen away. The stick fell in silted sand, stuck. Now if you were trying to do that for a week on end you couldn't. Chance. We'll never

---

101. An anonymous postcard sent to an acquaintance of Bloom contained this crude pun on the spelling of "up" as "You pee up."
102. Bloom is remembering his dream of Molly in Turkish trousers.
103. Holyhead, across the Irish Sea in Wales. Bloom's longest voyage ended there.
104. The House of Keys, from which Bloom had been trying to solicit an advertisement.
105. Here again, the underwear that has been thematic, in Bloom's thoughts, in the Victorian erotic imagination, and in this *Nausicaa* episode.
106. A what? Was Bloom going to write "Jew"? "cuckold"?

meet again. But it was lovely. Goodbye, dear. Thanks. Made me feel so young. Short snooze now if I had. Must be near nine. Liverpool boat long gone. Not even the smoke. And she can do the other. Did too. And Belfast. I won't go. Race there, race back to Ennis. Let him. Just close my eyes a moment. Won't sleep though. Half dream. It never comes the same. Bat again. No harm in him. Just a few.

O sweety all your little girlwhite up I saw dirty bracegirdle made me do love sticky we two naughty Grace darling she him half past the bed met him pike hoses [107] frillies for Raoul [108] to perfume your wife black hair heave under embon [109] *señorita* young eyes Mulvey [110] plump years dreams return tail end Agendath [111] swoony love showed me her next year [112] in drawers return next in her next her next.[113]

A bat flew. Here. There. Here. Far in the grey a bell chimed. Mr Bloom with open mouth, his left boot sanded sideways, leaned, breathed. Just for a few.

> *Cuckoo* [113]
> *Cuckoo*
> *Cuckoo*

The clock on the mantelpiece in the priest's house cooed where Canon O'Hanlon and Father Conroy and the reverend John Hughes S. J. were taking tea and sodabread and butter and fried mutton chops with catsup and talking about

> *Cuckoo*
> *Cuckoo*
> *Cuckoo*

Because it was a little canarybird bird that came out of its little house to tell the time that Gerty MacDowell noticed the time she was there because she was as quick as anything about a thing like that, was Gerty MacDowell, and she noticed at once that that foreign gentleman that was sitting on the rocks looking was

> *Cuckoo*
> *Cuckoo*
> *Cuckoo*

1920   1922

107. Molly had thus mispronounced the word "metempsychosis" earlier in the day; now, the "hose" part of her word leads to more underwear thoughts.

108. Raoul was a character in *Sweets of Sin*, a cheap, semi-pornographic book Bloom had bought for Molly. In it, the heroine thought of "costliest frillies. For him. For Raoul!" Throughout, Bloom associates Raoul with Boylan.

109. For *embonpoint*, round belly (French).

110. Lieut. Mulvey, Molly's lover in Gibraltar.

111. "*Agendath Netaim*" (Joyce's mistaken Hebrew for *Agudath Netaim*), a Zionist planters' association whose advertisement Bloom had noticed earlier in the day. Its address was on the actual but inadvertently symbolic *Bleibtreustrasse* ("Keep Faithful Street") in Berlin.

112. "Next year in Jerusalem"—a formula at the Passover Seder feast.

113. The cuckoo's cry ("Oh word of fear/ Unpleasing to a married ear," in the spring song in *Love's Labour's Lost*) has been associated, along with the emblem of horns, with a cuckold.

Finnegans Wake

Finnegans Wake, the last and most problematic of Joyce's works, belongs to a genre of mythological anatomies, of handbooks for the ordering of a poet's fictions, that includes Burton's *Anatomy of Melancholy* in the seventeenth century and, in the twentieth, Yeats's *A Vision* and Robert Grave's *The White Goddess.* It is a greater, more important, and yet less available work than the last two mentioned, containing such visions in its totality of story, pattern, and relation.

Renaissance poetic imagination had its mythology in a number of related works, along with instructions known by everyone about how to connect them. Thus, the Old and New Testaments were related typologically, and Ovid's *Metamorphoses* and Homer and other cycles of classic myth were related to Scripture in a complex figural way, foreshadowing in a distorted but retrievable form the truths of Christian biblical narrative. William Blake created a mythological world of his own (rather than being "enslaved by another man's") in his long poems. His system is not easy to grasp, in part because the instructions for putting patterns together, widely known though unstated within the Renaissance fictions themselves, became with Blake elements of the narrative and descriptive material. Dialectical process, that Enlightenment vision of how, in human history, institutions and actions and principles could in time become their own opposites, the cycle of youth and age, the warfare of moral and other contraries—all became thematic for Blake.

Every major modern author has had to do something like this. For a great novelist like Balzac or Dickens or Proust, his fictional world becomes the map of everything: London or Paris is a rich micro-macrocosm. Dublin became, in *Ulysses,* one of these cities. But event and thought and name—the elements of Bloom's and Stephen's world in the book—were finally for Joyce to seem too secondary, too molecular; he wanted to get to the atoms of poetry, and he did so by trying to articulate the pattern out of which all conceptual patterns themselves evolved. That pattern was, on the one hand, historical repetition: the way in which, for the mythological imagination as influenced by the cyclic theory of history of the eighteenth-century thinker Giambattista Vico, everything is a version of something else. In space rather than in time, on the other hand, that pattern was the Freudian one of family romance: ultimately, the oppositions of father-mother, father-son, and son-rival brother, with a peculiarly ancillary father-daughter one, could be used to generate a map of all relations, all events.

Joyce's family is that of an innkeeper named Humphrey Chimpden Earwicker, in Chapelizod (named for Isolde), his wife Anna Livia Plurabella (Ana Liffey is the river Liffey in Irish), their sons Shem and Shaun, and their daughter, Issy. Earwicker (referred to as H.C.E.) is, however, identified with the great sleeping giant Finn MacCool, supposedly buried (as many heroes and kings are buried all over Europe) under the city of Dublin, his head under the Hill of Howth and his feet in Phoenix Park. His wife is the river Liffey, and all women, as he is all men. Shem and Shaun—James and John—are the dialectical pair of Dionysian and Apollonian, organized and lyrical, beloved of mother and of father, antithetical and primary; their rivalry is also an eternal process.

Joyce, delighting in universalizing what was most provincial and peculiar, took his title from an Irish-American ballad that tells how a hodcarrier named Finnegan fell from a ladder to his death, and how everyone became so drunk as his wake that the corpse himself was resurrected. Joyce called his book a "funferal" (made up out of *funeral* and *fun for all*, like the "portmanteau" words of Humpty Dumpty in *Alice in Wonderland*). Finn's awakening, throughout history, at every moment of reality, *is* the book, as well as its subject. The format allows for a total compendium of all the truths and lies and languages Joyce had ever heard of. If the epic style of *Ulysses* involves parodies of all styles, the encyclopedic style of *Finnegans Wake* contains all lists and catalogues, all languages simultaneously. It has the "form" of Earwicker's dream, during which certain Bloomsday-like events appear to happen (such as accusations about sexual transgression); and there are clearly defined sections in which various characters take over in various modes, from learned lecture to parable to song to radio script. Joyce put into the work everything he could think of or find out about; its layers of significance are such that, whenever the surface is scratched, something ironically and comically significant emerges.

A few small excerpts have been given below, in order that the student may realize that Joyce's intention was to create a quasi-scriptural work, one whose reading would have to be a continuing historical process (as it has been a cooperative one among scholars, a kind of rabbinical or patristic continuum). First, there is the opening of Shaun's fable of the *Ondt and the Gracehoper*, adapted from Aesop's ant and grasshopper, the one a diligent and hard-working puritan, the other a carefree (and careless) musician who fiddles all summer long and dies of hunger in the winter. Shaun is an ant, and tells the parable in praise of ant-hood. Joyce intends the opposition to stand also for space (Shaun, *ondt*) and time (Shem, also the artist "Jim the Penman," *gracehoper*). *Ondt* is also an anagram for "don't." The section quoted is the beginning of a description of the grasshopper. The whole tale is full of references to insects and bugs of all sorts: what is sometimes called "entymology" (from *etym-* + *entom-ology*).

From Finnegans Wake

—I apologuise,[1] Shaun began, but I would rather spinooze [2] you one from the grimm gests [3] of Jacko and Esaup,[4] fable one, feeble too. Let us here consider the casus,[5] my dear little cousis (husstenhasstencaffincoffintussemtossemda-mandamnacosaghcusaghhobixhatouxpeswchbechoscashlcarcarcaract) [6] of the Ondt [7] and the Gracehoper.

The Gracehoper was always jigging ajog, hoppy on akkant [8] of his joyicity, (he had a partner pair of findlestilts [9] to supplant him), or, if not, he was always

1. Shaun, the tight, crafty son, would indeed always "guise" an apology.
2. Spinoza is the first philosopher of time and space, good and evil, to be mentioned; also *spin* + *ooze* a tale.
3. Grimm's fairy tales + *geste* (story).
4. *Jacob* and *Esau*, instances of Shem and Shaun + Jacob (Grimm) + Aesop of the fables.
5. In Latin, "fall;" also "case."
6. One of ten occurrences in *Finnegans Wake* of a hundred-letter word, this one indicating the voice of thunder, and marking a cyclical progression in the vision of phased history.
7. In Danish, "evil" (Shaun, *vs.* the gracehoping Shem) + *ont-* (pertaining to being).
8. *Account* + *Kant* (another philosopher).
9. The grasshopper's legs are indeed fiddlesticks.

making ungraceful overtures [10] to Floh and Luse and Bienie and Vespatilla [11] to play pupa-pupa [12] and pulicy-pulicy [13] and langtennas and pushpygyddyum and to commence insects with him, there mouthparts to his orefice [14] and his gambills [15] to there airy processes, even if only in chaste, ameng [16] the everlistings, behold a waspering pot. He would of curse melissciously,[17] by his fore feelhers. flexors, contractors, depressors and extensors, lamely, harry me, marry me, bury me, bind me, till she was puce [18] for shame and allso fourmish [19] her in Spinner's housery [20] at the earthsbest schoppinhour [21] so summery as his cottage, which was cald fourmillierly [22] Tingsomingenting,[23] groped up. Or, if he was always striking up funny funereels [24] with Resterfarther Zeuts,[25] the Aged One, with all his wigeared corollas, albedinous [26] and oldbuoyant, inscythe his elytri cal [27] wormcasket and Dehlia and Peonia,[28] his druping [29] nymphs, bewheedling him, compound eyes [30] on hornitosehead,[31] and Auld Letty Plussiboots [32] to scratch his cacumen and cackle his tramsitus,[33] diva deborah [34] . . .

[Next follows a part of the *Anna Livia Plurabelle* section, one of the titled parts previously published in separate form. It is the last paragraph of the remarkable dialogue of two washerwomen on the banks of the Liffey, "washing the dirty linen" of the Earwicker family in public, gossiping until darkness falls and their voices become as indistinguishable from the sound of the river herself as objects from each other in the darkness.]

Can't hear with the waters of. The chittering waters of. Flittering bats, fieldmice bawk talk. Ho! Are you not gone ahome? What Thom Malone? [35] Can't

10. In a musical sense. The grasshopper as happy fiddler, as artist, is thematic here as in Aesop; he is also sexually joyful.
11. *Flea* and *Louse* and *Bee* and *Wasp*.
12. From insect pupal stage of development.
13. *Policy* + Latin *pulex* (flea).
14. *Orifice* + *ore* + *ora-* (pray, say) + *-fice* (doing, making).
15. *Gambols* + *gams* (legs) + *bills*.
16. *Among* + German *Mengen* (crowds, collections), *"waspering"* (*wasp* + *whispering*).
17. *Maliciously* + Greek *melissa*, (bee).
18. French for "flea" + the color purple.
19. *Furnish* + *fourmi* (French), "ant."
20. Also *hosiery*.
21. *Shopping hour* + *Schopenhauer* (still another philosopher).
22. *Familiarly* + *fourmi* (ant).
23. "A thing like no thing" (Danish).
24. *Funerals* + *reels* (dances) + *reels* (of movie film).
25. Grandfather Zeus, an instance of H.C.E. (note the "earwig" immediately following).
26. *All-being* + *libidinous*.
27. *Electrical* + *elytron* (beetle's hard wing-covering).
28. *Dahlia* and *Peony* + *Delia* (Artemis, from Delos) and *Peona*, a shepherdess in Keats's *Endymion*.
29. Drupes are fruits of the peach, cherry, plum family.
30. Flies have compound eyes.
31. From *hornito* (Spanish): oven-shaped hill.
32. An instance of A.L.P., with Puss-in-Boots.
33. "Cacumen" is "tip" in Latin. "Tramsitus" is *transit* + *trama* + *site* (*trama* being Latin for the weft of a spider web).
34. Hebrew for "bee."
35. A character in one of the *Dubliners* stories.

hear with bawk of bats, all thim liffeying waters of. Ho,[36] talk save us! My foos [37] won't moos.[38] I feel as old as yonder elm. A tale told of Shaun or Shem? All Livia's daughtersons. Dark hawks hear us. Night! Night! My ho head halls. I feel as heavy as yonder stone. Tell me of John or Shaun? Who were Shem and Shaun the living sons or daughters of? Night now! Tell me, tell me, tell me, elm! Night night! Telmetale of stem or stone.[39] Beside the rivering waters of, hitherandthithering waters of. Night!

[This final quotation is from the very end of the book, when A.L.P. (now totally submerged into her identity as the river of life, of flow and process, moving about the fixity of the land-mass of H.C.E.) forsakes husband, sons, and daughter, and all the past as well, and flows down to meet the sea, her father. To maintain the total circularity of the book itself, her last sentence breaks off, to be completed only by the fragmentary opening sentence of *Finnegans Wake*. The whole passage is one of singular lyrical beauty, suggesting the final paragraph of *The Dead* in its lyrical purification of the complexities of the earlier part of the work in each case, as well as being reminiscent of Molly Bloom's final long soliloquy at the end of *Ulysses*, a flow of more than 45 pages of scarcely broken stream-of-consciousness.]

Try not to part. Be happy, dear ones! May I be wrong! For she'll be sweet for you as I was sweet when I came down out of me mother. My great blue bedroom, the air so quiet, scarce a cloud. In peace and silence. I could have stayed up there for always only. It's something fails us. First we feel. Then we fall. And let her rain now if she likes. Gently or strongly as she likes. Anyway let her rain for my time is come. I done me best when I was let. Thinking always if I go all goes. A hundred cares, a tithe of troubles and is there one who understands me? One in a thousand of years of the nights? All me life I have been lived among them but now they are becoming lothed to me. And I am lothing their little warm tricks. And lothing their mean cosy turns. And all the greedy gushes out through their small souls. And all the lazy leaks down over their brash bodies. How small it's all! And me letting on to meself always. And lilting on all the time. I thought you were all glittering with the noblest of carriage. You're only a bumpkin. I thought you the great in all things, in guilt and in glory. You're but a puny. Home! My people were not their sort out beyond there so far as I can. For all the bold and bad and bleary they are blamed, the seahags. No! Nor for all our wild dances in all their wild din. I can seen meself among them, allaniuvia pulchrabelled.[40] How she was handsome, the wild Amazia,[41] when she would seize to my other breast! And what is she weird, haughty

36. Chinese for "river."
37. In German, "foot."
38. *Move + moss* (her foot is turning to moss).
39. Thematically, a stone and an elm tree have been an important dyad of fixity and process; here they merge with Shaun and Shem.
40. The last version of her name, Anna Livia Plurabella, in the book: *A.L.P.* + *all new via* (way) + *alluvial* (the soil of her bed) + (Latin) *pulchra* (beautiful) + *bella + bell*.
41. *Amazon + amaze +* etymological, "breastless"; Amazon and Nile are the two rivers, attendant nymphs of Anna Livia.

Niluna,[42] that she will snatch from my ownest hair! For 'tis they are the stormies. Ho hang! Hang ho![43] And the clash of our cries till we spring to be free. Auravoles,[44] they says, never heed of your name! But I'm loothing them that's here and all I lothe. Loonely in me loneness. For all their faults. I am passing out. O bitter ending! I'll slip away before they're up. They'll never see. Nor know. Nor miss me. And it's old and old it's sad and old it's sad and weary I go back to you, my cold father, my cold mad father, my cold mad feary father, till the near sight of the mere [45] size of him, the moyles [46] and moyles of it, moananoaning, makes me seasilt saltsick and I rush, my only, into your arms. I see them rising! Save me from those therrble prongs! Two more. Onetwo moremens more. So. Avelaval.[47] My leaves havo drifted from me. All. But one clings still. I'll bear it on me. To remind me of. Lff! [48] So soft this morning ours. Yes. Carry me along, taddy, like you done through the toy fair. If I seen him bearing down on me now under whitespread wings like he'd come from Arkangels,[49] I sink I'd die down over his feet, humbly dumbly, only to washup. Yes, tid. There's where. First. We pass through grass behush the bush to. Whish! A gull. Gulls. Far calls. Coming, far! End here. Us then. Finn, again! [50] Take. Bussoftlhee, mememormee! Till thousendsthee. Lps. The keys to. Given! A way a lone a last a loved a long the [51]

[The opening sentence of Finnegans Wake]
riverrun, past Eve and Adam's,[52] from swerve of shore to bend of bay, brings us by a commodious [53] vicus [54] of recirculation back to Howth Castle and Environs.[55]

42. *Nile* + *Luna* (moon); another etymology of "Amazon" was also from a Circassian word for "moon."
43. *Hwang Ho*, the Yellow River of China.
44. *Au revoir* (as "goodbye" and, more literally in the eternally cyclic context, "to the seeing again") + *aureole* (halo) + "thou desirest gold" (Latin) + *volare* (flying or moving rapidly).
45. With pun on German *Meer* (sea) + Latin *mare* + French *mère* (mother).
46. Miles, spelled phonetically for Irish pronunciation + *Magh* (pronounced "moy"), "life."
47. Latin *Ave* (farewell) + *lava* (derived from the meaning "sliding down") + *lave* (wash) + *lave* (the past) (from Germanic, cognate "leave") + *Livia* (Liffey).
48. Liffey.
49. *Archangel* + *angel of the ark* + Russian northern port of *Archangelsk*.
50. Finally, the name of the ever-living, repeatedly resurrected form of H.C.E., as the giant Finn, again, Finnegan has awakened.
51. The sentence ends only with the opening sentence of *Finnegans Wake*, which follows below.
52. A Dublin parish church, but also the first parents. The Liffey flows past this church into Dublin Bay, and back past the Hill of Howth, where the sleeping giant Finn lies buried.
53. "Spacious" + *commode* (chamber pot), into which a city river empties, also called a "Jordan," hence another river; also the Christian name of Giordano Bruno, the Renaissance philosopher of dialectical synthesis of polar opposites, one of the two basic patterns of *Finnegans Wake*. ("A terrible heretic," Stephen Daedalus is told in *A Portrait*; "He was terribly burned," Stephen answers.)
54. Latin for "lane," "vicinity" + Vico Way, the shore road along Dublin Bay + Giambattista Vico, the other philosopher of the cyclic theory of history.
55. The first given instance of H.C.E. Later ones include "Haveth Childers Everywhere" and "Heinz cans everywhere."

D. H. LAWRENCE
1885–1930

David Herbert Lawrence was born at Eastwood, Nottinghamshire, on September 11, 1885. His father was a miner, his mother of somewhat higher class; and her social regrets and aspirations affected the children, especially this son, who, after the death of an elder brother, became her favorite. The conflict between the earthy, careless, often drunk and dirty father and the refined mother was crucial for Lawrence, and he records it, and his escape from his mother, in *Sons and Lovers* (1913). Later he turned against her, and also against the girl represented as Miriam, persuaded that such women were particularly responsible for the prevalence of a consciousness divorced from the life of the body; and he railed furiously against mother-love.

A somewhat sickly child, Lawrence was a little cut off from other boys, and thus early acquired his intimacy with the countryside and with books. But the background life of the mining town, with its blend of the sinister and the genial, stamped him permanently, and emerges throughout his work. Life in such an area was, however, less limited than might be thought. Lawrence and "Miriam" (Jessie Chambers) read very seriously and adventurously; Lawrence knew personally some quite important political thinkers, mostly radical; and after some preliminary teaching he was able to go to what was then Nottingham University College (1906). He had already produced his first poems, and was working on his first novel, *The White Peacock* (finished in 1910 and published in 1911), and on several stories. In 1908 he taught in Croydon (an outer suburb of London), made new friends, and enjoyed something of metropolitan entertainment, including the operas of Wagner; his Croydon novel, *The Trespasser* (1912), is a strangely Wagnerian work.

The year 1910 was a turning point; he broke his engagement with Jessie Chambers, became engaged to Louie Burrows, began the first version of *Sons and Lovers,* and saw his mother die. When a serious illness forced him to give up teaching he returned to Eastwood in 1912, and met Frieda von Richthofen Weekley, the wife of a former professor of his. Eloping in May 1912, they lived first in Germany and then in Italy. At this time Lawrence finished *Sons and Lovers,* and wrote the poems called *Look! We Have Come Through* (a poetic record of the early days with Frieda) and the play *The Widowing of Mrs. Holroyd,* only recently (and successfully) produced on the stage. He began the novel called *The Lost Girl* (completed after the war), wrote the travel sketches later revised for *Twilight in Italy* (1916), and took the first tentative steps toward his major work, a novel called *The Sisters,* which later split into *The Rainbow* (1915) and *Women in Love* (1921). He also produced short stories, of which *The Prussian Officer* is the best.

Lawrence returned to England with Frieda in June 1914, in time for what he was to call the "nightmare" of the war. Struggling against poverty and sickness, taken for a German spy in Cornwall, in profound trouble with the draft, and, above all, hating the hideous decadence typified by the war, with its bogus emotions and universal ugliness, Lawrence nevertheless worked at his writing—philosophical essays, his novel *The Sisters,* short stories—and made and broke friendships with, among others, Bertrand Russell and Lady Ottoline Morell, the original of Hermione in *Women in Love.* He passionately wanted to leave England, preferably for the United States; and his wide reading in American literature at this time came to fruition in 1923 with the publication of his major critical work, *Studies in Classic American Literature.* He also turned out a school history of Europe (under a pseudonym), the novel *Aaron's Rod* (1922), and the important novella *The Fox*. At last, in November 1919, he was able to leave England; and he never again returned for more than visits.

In Italy and Sicily between 1919 and 1922 he wrote his reply to Freud, *Psychoanalysis and the Unconscious* and *Fantasia of the Unconscious* (1921, 1922); he translated the Sicilian novelist Verga, wrote some of the poems in *Birds, Beasts and Flowers,* and finished two more novellas, *The Captain's Doll* and *The Ladybird*. In 1922 the Lawrences went to Ceylon, and then to Australia for a few months during which Lawrence wrote a long novel, *Kangaroo* (1923), and eventually another, *The Boy in the Bush* (1924)—Lawrence's revision of an original by the Australian writer Molly Skinner. In 1923 he accepted the invitation of Mabel Dodge Luhan (an American admirer of his work) to live near her ranch in Taos, New Mexico; and there he stayed, off and on, until February 1925. While visiting Mexico he was almost fatally ill; yet these years in America produced a long novel, *The Plumed Serpent,* the sketches that became *Mornings in Mexico,* the stories called *The Princess* and *The Woman Who Rode Away,* and the greatest of his short novels, *St. Mawr*. He returned to Europe in September 1925. The last years were also prolific of what he called "metaphysical" work, such as the study of the Book of Revelation called *Apocalypse,* published incomplete and posthumously. But there were also more stories, and his best novel after *Women in Love,* namely, *Lady Chatterley's Lover*. Many poems, mostly epigrammatic and satirical, a number of paintings, the brilliant defense of *Lady Chatterley's Lover* called first *My Skirmish with Jolly Roger* and later *A Propos of Lady Chatterley's Lover,* and the pamphlet *Pornography and Obscenity* (1929) also belong to this period. Lawrence died in the south of France on March 2, 1930, aged forty-four, of the tuberculosis that had dogged him through his life.

Such a summary says little about this tempestuous and controversial writer and prophet, albeit a prophet partly unarmed by his own talent; that is, a man given to working out in extraordinary detail his apocalyptic images and predictions, but—because he was a writer of fiction who believed in fiction as a method of achieving truth—allowing the fiction to qualify what he called the "metaphysic." Many times he praised the novel as "the one bright book of life," as the best means to restore some quality of livingness—"quickness" as he called it—to the disastrous modern world. What he said in his famous comment on Hawthorne is equally true of his own work: "Never trust the artist, trust the tale." Lawrence held astonishing opinions—on the strength of his non-fictional writings you might take him to be an anti-Semitic, childbeating, woman-hating fascist; yet these opinions are transfigured when they appear in his fictions. Again and again it is the character in the novel closest in ideas to the author who is put down by another character, usually a woman. But his disgust with the modern world—especially after the war had shown it in its true colors—is very deep, and affects his fiction.

Lawrence had a slightly fearful admiration for miners, with their underground life and distorted bodies, the instruments of rich men and yet their own men, gay and without greed, dedicated to pleasure, until the blight that industry brought to the countryside struck them also. And this admiration for people whose life was not conducted wholly from the head accounts for his use of other primitive figures: gamekeepers, gypsies, Italian peasants. He thought that the illness which divorced our minds and bodies, though originating in male shame, was now inflicted on men by women as mothers and lovers; and, especially when entertaining fantasies about his own role as a political or spiritual leader, he usually wanted to put women in a place subordinate to men.

Just as he wanted an educational system which would make society a rigid aristocracy of merit, he called for permanent stable marriages with dominant men. (This is to simplify opinions which changed over the years.) In a full sexual relation, achievable only in marriage, he saw the only means of redemption, a reversal of the death-flow of the modern world. He worked up these views to a level of great complexity; and as qualified by other pressures in his greatest book, *Women in Love,* they become both serious and mysterious. And though we must trust the tale, we cannot but remember that the artist was a man of powerful ideas and violent temperament. The fact is that Lawrence thinks, and also thinks with his story—which is a different matter and a richer, because he was a great artist. In *The Rainbow* and *Women in Love,* especially the latter, he invented a new kind of novel and a new way of treating human personality. He was a poet—some say a great one—and alive in all his senses; his travel writings, especially the remarkable *Etruscan Places* and *The Sea and Sardinia,* are strong testimony to the union of his mind and his eye. His literary criticism is notably creative, and even in his driest "metaphysical" work he is an exciting writer.

After his death Lawrence's reputation sank low for many years. Its revival, helped in part by the eventual publication—openly and legally—of *Lady Chatterley's Lover,* is now complete. Lawrence is an acknowledged master, and not only in the literary sense. There is controversy about his views on women, politics, and writing; he provides texts for those who think him extravagantly repressive, and also for their opponents. Lawrence lived through the years when many modern attitudes were being formed on a basis which made them less easily distinguished from one another than they have later become. Some of the roots of modern left-wing radicalism and those of Fascism were largely the same; the other ideas of Lawrence, though developed in a different way, have enough in common with Freud's to have made him anxious to emphasize the differences. Lawrence would have abhorred the more sharply sexually oriented revision of Freud by Wilhelm Reich ((1897–1957), and yet he resembled Reich strongly, if fleetingly.

In these and many other ways Lawrence belongs to early modernism. A newcomer to his work, expecting it to look "modern," may be surprised to observe that it has no obvious marks of modernism: his poems are not like Eliot's, he knew but did not imitate the Futurists, he largely ignored the kind of experiments with presentation and time-sequence found in Conrad, and he hated Joyce. The revolutionary tactics of Dada and the dream images of Surrealism had no effect on him. He made his own innovations, and discovered his own tradition. For all their novelty, *The Rainbow* and *Women in Love* are closer to George Eliot and Hardy than to the other great experimental fiction of the time—Joyce's, Proust's, Kafka's. He is more prolific, more untidy, more spontaneous than any of these; he has much more design on the reader, and, despite his exiles and wanderings, he gave himself a more urgent social role. Given that our notions of modernism were formed on the evidence of quite different writers, we have here an explanation of why it took so long for Lawrence to achieve his place as a master of the modern. But it is now, though not beyond discussion, beyond denial.

The Prussian Officer

Lawrence saw something of the Prussian military caste when he went to Germany in 1912; he disliked Metz, a garrison town where he stayed, and was aware that Frieda's family was aristocratic and military. It was in the following year, in Bavaria (which he also disliked), that he wrote this story. He called it *Honour and Arms,* and wrote to his publisher Edward Garnett that it was his best story so far. Garnett, to Lawrence's annoyance, changed the title to *The Prussian Officer.* By the time it appeared, in a volume of the same title, England was at war with Germany, and the change was doubtless made to appeal to anti-Prussian sentiment. Lawrence already believed that soldiers, herded together in all-male company, "men without women, never being satisfied by a woman, as a man never is from a street affair, get their surplus sex and their frustration and dissatisfaction into the blood, and *love* cruelty. It is sex lust fermented makes atrocity." Another story, somewhat similar but inferior, which Garnett entitled *The Thorn in the Flesh,* appeared in the same 1914 volume. Lawrence's strong reaction to German militarism was not merely a matter of disliking Germans; his portraits of English military men, particularly the ones he met when under suspicion of spying in Cornwall and in the course of his short visits to barracks for physical examinations, are equally hostile and more contemptuous. In any case, the virtues of *The Prussian Officer* are independent of these circumstances.

The Prussian Officer

They had marched more than thirty kilometres since dawn, along the white, hot road where occasional thickets of trees threw a moment of shade, then out into the glare again. On either hand, the valley, wide and shallow, glittered with heat; dark green patches of rye, pale young corn, fallow and meadow and black pine woods spread in a dull, hot diagram under a glistening sky. But right in front the mountains ranged across, pale blue and very still, snow gleaming gently out of the deep atmosphere. And towards the mountains, on and on, the regiment marched between the rye fields and the meadows, between the scraggy fruit trees set regularly on either side the high road. The burnished, dark green rye threw off a suffocating heat, the mountains drew gradually nearer and more distinct. While the feet of the soldiers grew hotter, sweat ran through their hair under their helmets, and their knapsacks could burn no more in contact with their shoulders, but seemed instead to give off a cold, prickly sensation.

He walked on and on in silence, staring at the mountains ahead, that rose sheer out of the land and stood fold behind fold, half earth, half heaven, the heaven, the barrier with slits of soft snow, in the pale, bluish peaks.

He could now walk almost without pain. At the start, he had determined not to limp. It had made him sick to take the first steps, and during the first mile or so, he had compressed his breath, and the cold drops of sweat had stood on his forehead. But he had walked it off. What were they after all but bruises! He had looked at them, as he was getting up: deep bruises on the backs of his thighs. And since he had made his first step in the morning, he had been conscious of them, till now he had a tight, hot place in his chest, with suppressing the pain, and holding himself in. There seemed no air when he breathed. But he walked almost lightly.

The Captain's hand had trembled at taking his coffee at dawn: his orderly saw it again. And he saw the fine figure of the Captain wheeling on horseback at the farm-house ahead, a handsome figure in pale blue uniform with facings of scarlet, and the metal gleaming on the black helmet and the sword-scabbard, and dark streaks of sweat coming on the silky bay horse. The orderly felt he was connected with that figure moving so suddenly on horseback: he followed it like a shadow, mute and inevitable and damned by it. And the officer was always aware of the tramp of the company behind, the march of his orderly among the men.

The Captain was a tall man of about forty, grey at the temples. He had a handsome, finely knit figure, and was one of the best horsemen in the West. His orderly, having to rub him down, admired the amazing riding-muscles of his loins.

For the rest, the orderly scarcely noticed the officer any more than he noticed himself. It was rarely he saw his master's face: he did not look at it. The Captain had reddish-brown, stiff hair that he wore short upon his skull. His moustache was also cut short and bristly over a full, brutal mouth. His face was rather rugged, the cheeks thin. Perhaps the man was the more handsome for the deep lines in his face, the irritable tension of his brow, which gave him the look of a man who fights with life. His fair eyebrows stood bushy over light blue eyes that were always flashing with cold fire.

He was a Prussian aristocrat, haughty and overbearing. But his mother had been a Polish Countess. Having made too many gambling debts when he was young, he had ruined his prospects in the Army, and remained an infantry captain. He had never married: his position did not allow of it, and no woman had ever moved him to it. His time he spent riding—occasionally he rode one of his own horses at the races—and at the officers' club. Now and then he took himself a mistress. But after such an event, he returned to duty with his brow still more tense, his eyes still more hostile and irritable. With the men, however, he was merely impersonal, though a devil when roused; so that, on the whole, they feared him, but had no great aversion from him. They accepted him as the inevitable.

To his orderly he was at first cold and just and indifferent: he did not fuss over trifles. So that his servant knew practically nothing about him, except just what orders he would give, and how he wanted them obeyed. That was quite simple. Then the change gradually came.

The orderly was a youth of about twenty-two, of medium height, and well built. He had strong, heavy limbs, was swarthy, with a soft, black, young moustache. There was something altogether warm and young about him. He had firmly marked eyebrows over dark, expressionless eyes that seemed never to have thought, only to have received life direct through his senses, and acted straight from instinct.[1]

1. This distinction—between the instinctual integrity of the boy and the officer's divided mind and body—is important not only in Lawrence but in the general thought of artists in the period. Later we hear of the boy's "unmeaning dark eyes" and the officer's head-centered power lust; of the boy's sexual satisfaction and the officer's frustration in his liai-

Gradually the officer had become aware of his servant's young, vigorous, unconscious presence about him. He could not get away from the sense of the youth's person, while he was in attendance. It was like a warm flame upon the older man's tense, rigid body, that had become almost unliving, fixed. There was something so free and self-contained about him, and something in the young fellow's movement, that made the officer aware of him. And this irritated the Prussian. He did not choose to be touched into life by his servant. He might easily have changed his man, but he did not. He now very rarely looked direct at his orderly, but kept his face averted, as if to avoid seeing him. And yet as the young soldier moved unthinking about the apartment, the elder watched him, and would notice the movement of his strong young shoulders under the blue cloth, the bend of his neck. And it irritated him. To see the soldier's young, brown, shapely peasant's hand grasp the loaf or the wine-bottle sent a flash of hate or of anger through the elder man's blood. It was not that the youth was clumsy: it was rather the blind, instinctive sureness of movement of an unhampered young animal that irritated the officer to such a degree.

Once, when a bottle of wine had gone over, and the red gushed out on to the tablecloth, the officer had started up with an oath, and his eyes, bluey like fire, had held those of the confused youth for a moment. It was a shock for the young soldier. He felt something sink deeper, deeper into his soul, where nothing had ever gone before. It left him rather blank and wondering. Some of his natural completeness in himself was gone, a little uneasiness took its place. And from that time an undiscovered feeling had held between the two men.

Henceforward the orderly was afraid of really meeting his master. His sub-consciousness remembered those steely blue eyes and the harsh brows, and did not intend to meet them again. So he always stared past his master and avoided him. Also, in a little anxiety, he waited for the three months to have gone, when his time would be up. He began to feel a constraint in the Captain's presence, and the soldier even more than the officer wanted to be left alone, in his neutrality as servant.

He had served the Captain for more than a year, and knew his duty. This he performed easily, as if it were natural to him. The officer and his commands he took for granted, as he took the sun and the rain, and he served as a matter of course. It did not implicate him personally.

But now if he were going to be forced into a personal interchange with his master he would be like a wild thing caught, he felt he must get away.

But the influence of the young soldier's being had penetrated through the officer's stiffened discipline, and perturbed the man in him. He, however, was a gentleman, with long, fine hands and cultivated movements, and was not going to allow such a thing as the stirring of his innate self. He was a man of passionate temper, who had always kept himself suppressed. Occasionally

son. Even the boy's revulsions—e.g. from creeping birds—are instinctive, whereas the officer's revulsion from the boy is a kind of love corrupted by his will. Lawrence's emphasis on stimuli such as scent and color reinforces the orderly's, not the officer's, natural acquiescence in the world of sense.

there had been a duel, an outburst before the soldiers. He knew himself to be always on the point of breaking out. But he kept himself hard to the idea of the Service. Whereas the young soldier seemed to live out his warm, full nature, to give it off in his very movements, which had a certain zest, such as wild animals have in free movement. And this irritated the officer more and more.

In spite of himself, the Captain could not regain his neutrality of feeling towards his orderly. Nor could he leave the man alone. In spite of himself, he watched him, gave him sharp orders, tried to take up as much of his time as possible. Sometimes he flew into a rage with the young soldier, and bullied him. Then the orderly shut himself off, as it were out of earshot, and waited, with sullen, flushed face, for the end of the noise. The words never pierced to his intelligence, he made himself, protectively, impervious to the feelings of his master.

He had a scar on his left thumb, a deep seam going across the knuckle. The officer had long suffered from it, and wanted to do something to it. Still it was there, ugly and brutal on the young, brown hand. At last the Captain's reserve gave way. One day, as the orderly was smoothing out the tablecloth, the officer pinned down his thumb with a pencil, asking:

'How did you come by that?'

The young man winced and drew back at attention.

'A wood axe, Herr Hauptmann,' [2] he answered.

The officer waited for further explanation. None came. The orderly went about his duties. The elder man was sullenly angry. His servant avoided him. And the next day he had to use all his will-power to avoid seeing the scarred thumb. He wanted to get hold of it and——A hot flame ran in his blood.

He knew his servant would soon be free, and would be glad. As yet, the soldier had held himself off from the elder man. The Captain grew madly irritable. He could not rest when the soldier was away, and when he was present, he glared at him with tormented eyes. He hated those fine black brows over the unmeaning dark eyes, he was infuriated by the free movement of the handsome limbs, which no military discipline could make stiff. And he became harsh and cruelly bullying, using contempt and satire. The young soldier only grew more mute and expressionless.

'What cattle were you bred by, that you can't keep straight eyes? Look me in the eyes when I speak to you.'

And the soldier turned his dark eyes to the other's face, but there was no sight in them: he stared with the slightest possible cast, holding back his sight, perceiving the blue of his master's eyes, but receiving no look from them. And the elder man went pale, and his reddish eyebrows twitched. He gave his order, barrenly.

Once he flung a heavy military glove into the young soldier's face. Then he had the satisfaction of seeing the black eyes flare up into his own, like a blaze when straw is thrown on a fire. And he had laughed with a little tremor and a sneer.

But there were only two months more. The youth instinctively tried to keep

2. Captain.

himself intact: he tried to serve the officer as if the latter were an abstract authority and not a man. All his instinct was to avoid personal contact, even definite hate. But in spite of himself the hate grew, responsive to the officer's passion. However, he put it in the background. When he had left the Army he could dare acknowledge it. By nature he was active, and had many friends. He thought what amazing good fellows they were. But, without knowing it, he was alone. Now this solitariness was intensified. It would carry him through his term. But the officer seemed to be going irritably insane, and the youth was deeply frightened.

The soldier had a sweetheart, a girl from the mountains, independent and primitive. The two walked together, rather silently. He went with her, not to talk, but to have his arm round her, and for the physical contact. This eased him, made it easier for him to ignore the Captain; for he could rest with her held fast against his chest. And she, in some unspoken fashion, was there for him. They loved each other.

The Captain perceived it, and was mad with irritation. He kept the young man engaged all the evenings long, and took pleasure in the dark look that came on his face. Occasionally, the eyes of the two men met, those of the younger sullen and dark, doggedly unalterable, those of the elder sneering with restless contempt.

The officer tried hard not to admit the passion that had got hold of him. He would not know that his feeling for his orderly was anything but that of a man incensed by his stupid, perverse servant. So, keeping quite justified and conventional in his consciousness, he let the other thing run on. His nerves, however, were suffering. At last he slung the end of a belt in his servant's face. When he saw the youth start back, the pain-tears in his eyes and the blood on his mouth, he had felt at once a thrill of deep pleasure and of shame.

But this, he acknowledged to himself, was a thing he had never done before. The fellow was too exasperating. His own nerves must be going to pieces. He went away for some days with a woman.

It was a mockery of pleasure. He simply did not want the woman. But he stayed on for his time. At the end of it, he came back in an agony of irritation, torment, and misery. He rode all the evening, then came straight in to supper. His orderly was out. The officer sat with his long, fine hands lying on the table, perfectly still, and all his blood seemed to be corroding.

At last his servant entered. He watched the strong, easy young figure, the fine eyebrows, the thick black hair. In a week's time the youth had got back his old well-being. The hands of the officer twitched and seemed to be full of mad flame. The young man stood at attention, unmoving, shut off.

The meal went in silence. But the orderly seemed eager. He made a clatter with the dishes.

'Are you in a hurry?' asked the officer, watching the intent, warm face of his servant. The other did not reply.

'Will you answer my question?' said the Captain.

'Yes, sir,' replied the orderly, standing with his pile of deep Army plates. The Captain waited, looked at him, then asked again:

'Are you in a hurry?'

'Yes, sir,' came the answer, that sent a flash through the listener.

'For what?'

'I was going out, sir.'

'I want you this evening.'

There was a moment's hesitation. The officer had a curious stiffness of countenance.

'Yes, sir,' replied the servant, in his throat.

'I want you tomorrow evening also—in fact, you may consider your evenings occupied, unless I give you leave.'

The mouth with the young mustache set close.

'Yes, sir,' answered the orderly, loosening his lips for a moment. He again turned to the door.

'And why have you a piece of pencil in your ear?'

The orderly hesitated, then continued on his way without answering. He set the plates in a pile outside the door, took the stump of pencil from his ear, and put it in his pocket. He had been copying a verse for his sweetheart's birthday card. He returned to finish clearing the table. The officer's eyes were dancing, he had a little, eager smile.

'Why have you a piece of pencil in your ear?' he asked.

The orderly took his hands full of dishes. His master was standing near the great green stove, a little smile on his face, his chin thrust forward. When the young soldier saw him his heart suddenly ran hot. He felt blind. Instead of answering, he turned dazedly to the door. As he was crouching to set down the dishes, he was pitched forward by a kick from behind. The pots went in a stream down the stairs, he clung to the pillar of the banisters. And as he was rising he was kicked heavily again, and again, so that he clung sickly to the post for some moments. His master had gone swiftly into the room and closed the door. The maid-servant downstairs looked up the staircase and made a mocking face at the crockery disaster.

The officer's heart was plunging. He poured himself a glass of wine, part of which he spilled on the floor, and gulped the remainder, leaning against the cool, green stove. He heard his man collecting the dishes from the stairs. Pale, as if intoxicated, he waited. The servant entered again. The Captain's heart gave a pang, as of pleasure, seeing the young fellow bewildered and uncertain on his feet, with pain.

'Schöner!' [3] he said.

The soldier was a little slower in coming to attention.

'Yes, sir!'

The youth stood before him, with pathetic young moustache, and fine eyebrows very distinct on his forehead of dark marble.

'I asked you a question.'

'Yes, sir.'

The officer's tone bit like acid.

'Why had you a pencil in your ear?'

Again the servant's heart ran hot, and he could not breathe. With dark, strained eyes, he looked at the officer, as if fascinated. And he stood there sturdily planted, unconscious. The withering smile came into the Captain's eyes, and he lifted his foot.

3. The orderly's name (recalling with some irony the German meaning, "beautiful one").

'I—I forgot it—sir,' panted the soldier, his dark eyes fixed on the other man's dancing blue ones.

'What was it doing there?'

He saw the young man's breast heaving as he made an effort for words.

'I had been writing.'

'Writing what?'

Again the soldier looked him up and down. The officer could hear him panting. The smile came into the blue eyes. The soldier worked his dry throat, but could not speak. Suddenly the smile lit like a flame on the officer's face, and a kick came heavily against the orderly's thigh. The youth moved a pace sideways. His face went dead, with two black, staring eyes.

'Well?' said the officer.

The orderly's mouth had gone dry, and his tongue rubbed in it as on dry brown-paper. He worked his throat. The officer raised his foot. The servant went stiff.

'Some poetry, sir,' came the crackling, unrecognizable sound of his voice.

'Poetry, what poetry?' asked the Captain, with a sickly smile.

Again there was the working in the throat. The Captain's heart had suddenly gone down heavily, and he stood sick and tired.

'For my girl, sir,' he heard the dry, inhuman sound.

'Oh!' he said, turning away. 'Clear the table.'

'Click!' went the soldier's throat; then again, 'Click!' and then the half-articulate:

'Yes, sir.'

The young soldier was gone, looking old, and walking heavily.

The officer, left alone, held himself rigid, to prevent himself from thinking. His instinct warned him that he must not think. Deep inside him was the intense gratification of his passion, still working powerfully. Then there was a counter-action, a horrible breaking down of something inside him, a whole agony of reaction. He stood there for an hour motionless, a chaos of sensations, but rigid with a will to keep blank his consciousness, to prevent his mind grasping. And he held himself so until the worst of the stress had passed, when he began to drink, drank himself to an intoxication, till he slept obliterated. When he woke in the morning he was shaken to the base of his nature. But he had fought off the realization of what he had done. He had prevented his mind from taking it in, had suppressed it along with his instincts, and the conscious man had nothing to do with it. He felt only as after a bout of intoxication, weak, but the affair itself all dim and not to be recovered. Of the drunkenness of his passion he successfully refused remembrance. And when his orderly appeared with coffee, the officer assumed the same self he had had the morning before. He refused the event of the past night—denied it had ever been—and was successful in his denial. He had not done any such thing—not he himself. Whatever blame there might be, lay at the door of a stupid, insubordinate servant.

The orderly had gone about in a stupor all the evening. He drank some beer because he was parched, but not much, the alcohol made his feeling come back, and he could not bear it. He was dulled, as if nine-tenths of the ordinary man in him were inert. He crawled about disfigured. Still, when he thought of the kicks, he went sick, and when he thought of the threat of more kicking, in the room afterwards, his heart went hot and faint, and he panted, remembering the one that had come. He had been forced to say, 'For my girl.' He was much too done even to want to cry. His mouth hung slightly open, like an idiot's. He felt vacant, and wasted. So, he wandered at his work, painfully, and very slowly and clumsily, fumbling blindly with the brushes, and finding it difficult, when he sat down, to summon the energy to move again. His limbs, his jaw, were slack and nerveless. But he was very tired. He got to bed at last, and slept inert, relaxed, in a sleep that was rather stupor than slumber, a dead night of stupefaction shot through with gleams of anguish.

In the morning were the manœuvres. But he woke even before the bugle sounded. The painful ache in his chest, the dryness of his throat, the awful steady feeling of misery made his eyes come awake and dreary at once. He knew, without thinking, what had happened. And he knew that the day had come again, when he must go on with his round. The last bit of darkness was being pushed out of the room. He would have to move his inert body and go on. He was so young, and had known so little trouble, that he was bewildered. He only wished it would stay night, so that he could lie still, covered up by the darkness. And yet nothing would prevent the day from coming, nothing would save him from having to get up and saddle the Captain's horse, and make the Captain's coffee. It was there, inevitable. And then, he thought, it was impossible. Yet they would not leave him free. He must go and take the coffee to the Captain. He was too stunned to understand it. He only knew it was inevitable—inevitable, however long he lay inert.

At last, after heaving at himself, for he seemed to be a mass of inertia, he got up. But he had to force every one of his movements from behind, with his will. He felt lost, and dazed, and helpless. Then he clutched hold of the bed, the pain was so keen. And looking at his thighs, he saw the darker bruises on his swarthy flesh and he knew that, if he pressed one of his fingers on one of the bruises, he should faint. But he did not want to faint—he did not want anybody to know. No one should ever know. It was between him and the Captain. There were only the two people in the world now—himself and the Captain.

Slowly, economically, he got dressed and forced himself to walk. Everything was obscure, except just what he had his hands on. But he managed to get through his work. The very pain revived his dull senses. The worst remained yet. He took the tray and went up to the Captain's room. The officer, pale and heavy, sat at the table. The orderly, as he saluted, felt himself put out of existence. He stood still for a moment submitting to his own nullification—then he gathered himself, seemed to regain himself, and then the Captain began to grow vague, unreal, and the younger soldier's heart beat up. He clung to this situation—that the Captain did not exist—so that he himself might live. But when he saw his officer's hand tremble as he took the coffee, he felt everything falling shattered. And he went away, feeling as if he himself were coming to pieces, disintegrated. And when the Captain was there on horse-back, giving orders, while he himself stood, with rifle and knapsack, sick with pain, he felt as if he must shut his eyes—as if he must shut his eyes on every-thing. It was only the long agony of marching with a parched throat that filled him with one single, sleep-heavy intention: to save himself.

II

He was getting used even to his parched throat. That the snowy peaks were radiant among the sky, that the whity-green glacier-river twisted through its pale shoals in the valley below, seemed almost supernatural. But he was going mad with fever and thirst. He plodded on uncomplaining. He did not want to speak, not to anybody. There were two gulls, like flakes of water and snow, over the river. The scent of green rye soaked in sunshine came like a sickness. And the march continued, monotonously, almost like a bad sleep.

At the next farm-house, which stood low and broad near the high road, tubs of water had been put out. The soldiers clustered round to drink. They took off their helmets, and the steam mounted from their wet hair. The Captain sat on horseback, watching. He needed to see his orderly. His helmet threw a dark shadow over his light, fierce eyes, but his moustache and mouth and chin were distinct in the sunshine. The orderly must move under the presence of the figure of the horseman. It was not that he was afraid, or cowed. It was as if he was disembowelled, made empty, like an empty shell. He felt himself as nothing, a shadow creeping under the sunshine. And, thirsty as he was, he could scarcely drink, feeling the Captain near him. He would not take off his helmet to wipe his wet hair. He wanted to stay in shadow, not to be forced into consciousness. Starting, he saw the light heel of the officer prick the belly of the horse; the Captain cantered away, and he himself could relapse into vacancy.

Nothing, however, could give him back his living place in the hot, bright morning. He felt like a gap among it all. Whereas the Captain was prouder, overriding. A hot flash went through the young servant's body. The Captain was firmer and prouder with life, he himself was empty as a shadow. Again the flash went through him, dazing him out. But his heart ran a little firmer.

The company turned up the hill, to make a loop for the return. Below, from among the trees, the farm-bell clanged. He saw the labourers, mowing bare-foot at the thick grass, leave off their work and go downhill, their scythes hanging over their shoulders, like long, bright claws curving down behind them. They seemed like dream-people, as if they had no relation to himself. He felt as in a blackish dream: as if all the other things were there and had form, but he himself was only a consciousness, a gap that could think and perceive.

The soldiers were tramping silently up the glaring hillside. Gradually his head began to revolve, slowly, rhythmically. Sometimes it was dark before his eyes, as if he saw this world through a smoked glass, frail shadows and unreal. It gave him a pain in his head to walk.

The air was too scented, it gave no breath. All the lush green-stuff seemed to be issuing its sap, till the air was deathly, sickly with the smell of greenness. There was the perfume of clover, like pure honey and bees. Then there grew a faint acrid tang—they were near the beeches; and then a queer clattering noise, and a suffocating, hideous smell; they were passing a flock of sheep, a shepherd in a black smock, holding his crook. Why should the sheep huddle together under this fierce sun? He felt that the shepherd would not see him, though he could see the shepherd.

At last there was the halt. They stacked rifles in a conical stack, put down their kit in a scattered circle around it, and dispersed a little, sitting on a small knoll high on the hillside. The chatter began. The soldiers were steaming with heat, but were lively. He sat still, seeing the blue mountains rising upon the land, twenty kilometres away. There was a blue fold in the ranges, then out of that, at the foot, the broad, pale bed of the river, stretches of whity-green water between pinkish-grey shoals among the dark pine woods. There it was, spread out a long way off. And it seemed to come downhill, the river. There was a raft being steered, a mile away. It was a strange country. Nearer, a red-roofed, broad farm with white base and square dots of windows crouched beside the wall of beech foliage on the wood's edge. There were long strips of rye and clover and pale green corn. And just at his feet, below the knoll, was a darkish bog, where globe flowers stood breathless still on their slim stalks. And some of the pale gold bubbles were burst, and a broken fragment hung in the air. He thought he was going to sleep.

Suddenly something moved into this coloured mirage before his eyes. The Captain, a small, light-blue and scarlet figure, was trotting evenly between the strips of corn, along the level brow of the hill. And the man making flag-signals was coming on. Proud and sure moved the horseman's figure, the quick, bright thing, in which was concentrated all the light of this morning, which for the rest lay a fragile, shining shadow. Submissive, apathetic, the young soldier sat and stared. But as the horse slowed to a walk, coming up the last steep path, the great flash flared over the body and soul of the orderly. He sat waiting. The back of his head felt as if it were weighted with a heavy piece of fire. He did not want to eat. His hands trembled slightly as he moved them. Meanwhile the officer on horseback was approaching slowly and proudly. The tension grew in the orderly's soul. Then again, seeing the Captain ease himself on the saddle, the flash blazed through him.

The Captain looked at the patch of light blue and scarlet, and dark heads, scattered closely on the hill-side. It pleased him. The command pleased him. And he was feeling proud. His orderly was among them in common subjection. The officer rose a little on his stirrups to look. The young soldier sat with averted, dumb face. The Captain relaxed on his seat. His slim-legged, beautiful horse, brown as a beech nut, walked proudly uphill. The Captain passed into the zone of the company's atmosphere: a hot smell of men, of sweat, of leather. He knew it very well. After a word with the lieutenant, he went a few paces higher, and sat there, a dominant figure, his sweat-marked horse swishing its tail, while he looked down on his men, on his orderly, a nonentity among the crowd.

The young soldier's heart was like fire in his chest, and he breathed with difficulty. The officer, looking downhill, saw three of the young soldiers, two pails of water between them, staggering across a sunny green field. A table had been set up under a tree, and there the slim lieutenant stood, importantly busy. Then the Captain summoned himself to an act of courage. He called his orderly.

The flame leapt into the young soldier's throat as he heard the command, and he rose blindly, stifled. He saluted, standing below the officer. He did not look up. But there was the flicker in the Captain's voice.

'Go to the inn and fetch me . . .' the officer gave his commands. 'Quick!' he added.

At the last word, the heart of the servant leapt with a flash, and he felt the strength come over his body. But he turned in mechanical obedience, and set off at a heavy run downhill, looking almost like a bear, his trousers bagging over his military boots. And the officer watched this blind, plunging run all the way.

But it was only the outside of the orderly's body that was obeying so humbly and mechanically. Inside had gradually accumulated a core into which all the energy of that young life was compact and concentrated. He executed his commission, and plodded quickly back uphill. There was a pain in his head, as he walked, that made him twist his features unknowingly. But hard there in the centre of his chest was himself, himself, firm, and not to be plucked to pieces.

The Captain had gone up into the wood. The orderly plodded through the hot, powerfully smelling zone of the company's atmosphere. He had a curious mass of energy inside him now. The Captain was less real than himself. He approached the green entrance to the wood. There, in the half-shade, he saw the horse standing, the sunshine and the flickering shadow of leaves dancing over his brown body. There was a clearing where timber had lately been felled. Here, in the gold-green shade beside the brilliant cup of sunshine, stood two figures, blue and pink, the bits of pink showing out plainly. The Captain was talking to his lieutenant.

The orderly stood on the edge of the bright clearing, where great trunks of trees, stripped and glistening, lay stretched like naked, brown-skinned bodies. Chips of wood littered the trampled floor, like splashed light, and the bases of the felled trees stood here and there, with their raw, level tops. Beyond was the brilliant, sunlit green of a beech.

'Then I will ride forward,' the orderly heard his Captain say. The lieutenant saluted and strode away. He himself went forward. A hot flash passed through his belly, as he tramped towards his officer.

The Captain watched the rather heavy figure of the young soldier stumble forward, and his veins, too, ran hot. This was to be man to man between them. He yielded before the solid, stumbling figure with bent head. The orderly stooped and put the food on a level-sawn tree-base. The Captain watched the glistening, sun-inflamed, naked hands. He wanted to speak to the young soldier but could not. The servant propped a bottle against his thigh, pressed open the cork, and poured out the beer into the mug. He kept his head bent. The Captain accepted the mug.

'Hot!' he said, as if amiably.

The flame sprang out of the orderly's heart, nearly suffocating him.

'Yes, sir,' he replied, between shut teeth.

And he heard the sound of the Captain's drinking, and he clenched his fists, such a strong torment came into his wrists. Then came the faint clang of the closing of the pot-lid. He looked up. The Captain was watching him. He glanced swiftly away. Then he saw the officer stoop and take a piece of bread from the tree-base. Again the flash of flame went through the young soldier, seeing the stiff body stoop beneath him, and his hands jerked. He looked away. He could feel the officer was nervous. The bread fell as it was being broken. The officer ate the other piece. The two men stood tense and still, the master laboriously chewing his bread, the servant staring with averted face, his fist clenched.

Then the young soldier started. The officer had pressed open the lid of the mug again. The orderly watched the lid of the mug, and the white hand that clenched the handle, as if he were fascinated. It was raised. The youth followed it with his eyes. And then he saw the thin, strong throat of the elder man moving up and down as he drank, the strong jaw working. And the instinct which had been jerking at the young man's wrists suddenly jerked free. He jumped, feeling as if it were rent in two by a strong flame.

The spur of the officer caught in a tree-root, he went down backwards with a crash, the middle of his back thudding sickeningly against a sharp-edged tree-base, the pot flying away. And in a second the orderly, with serious, earnest young face, and underlip between his teeth, had got his knee in the officer's chest and was pressing the chin backward over the farther edge of the tree-stump, pressing, with all his heart behind in a passion of relief, the tension of his wrists exquisite with relief. And with the base of his palms he shoved at the chin, with all his might. And it was pleasant, too, to have that chin, that hard jaw already slightly rough with beard, in his hands. He did not relax one hair's breadth, but, all the force of all his blood exulting in his thrust, he shoved back the head of the other man, till there was a little 'cluck' and a crunching sensation. Then he felt as if his head went to vapour. Heavy convulsions shook the body of the officer, frightening and horrifying the young soldier. Yet it pleased him, too, to repress them. It pleased him to keep his hands pressing back the chin, to feel the chest of the other man yield in expiration to the weight of his strong, young knees, to feel the hard twitchings of the prostrate body jerking his own whole frame, which was pressed down on it.

But it went still. He could look into the nostrils of the other man, the eyes he could scarcely see. How curiously the mouth was pushed out, exaggerating the full lips, and the moustache bristling up from them. Then, with a start, he noticed the nostrils gradually filled with blood. The red brimmed, hesitated, ran over, and went in a thin trickle down the face to the eyes.

It shocked and distressed him. Slowly, he got up. The body twitched and sprawled there, inert. He stood and looked at it in silence. It was a pity it was broken. It represented more than the thing which had kicked and bullied him. He was afraid to look at the eyes. They were hideous now, only the whites showing, and the blood running to them. The face of the orderly was drawn with horror at the sight. Well, it was so. In his heart he was satisfied. He had hated the face of the Captain. It was extinguished now. There was a heavy relief in the orderly's soul. That was as it should be. But he could not bear to see the long, military body lying broken over the tree-base, the fine fingers crisped. He wanted to hide it away.

Quickly, busily, he gathered it up and pushed it under the felled tree-trunks, which rested their beautiful, smooth length either end on logs. The face was horrible with blood. He covered it with the helmet. Then he pushed the limbs straight and decent, and brushed the dead leaves off the fine cloth of the uniform. So, it lay quite still in the shadow under there. A little strip of sunshine ran along the breast, from a chink between the logs. The orderly sat by it for a few moments. Here his own life also ended.

Then, through his daze, he heard the lieutenant, in a loud voice, explaining to the men outside the wood, that they were to suppose the bridge on the river below was held by the enemy. Now they were to march to the attack in such and such a manner. The lieutenant had no gift of expression. The orderly, listening from habit, got muddled. And when the lieutenant began it all again he ceased to hear.

He knew he must go. He stood up. It surprised him that the leaves were glittering in the sun, and the chips of wood reflecting white from the ground. For him a change had come over the world. But for the rest it had not—all seemed the same. Only he had left it. And he could not go back. It was his duty to return with the beer-pot and bottle. He could not. He had left all that. The lieutenant was still hoarsely explaining. He must go, or they would overtake him. And he could not bear contact with anyone now.

He drew his fingers over his eyes, trying to find out where he was. Then he turned away. He saw the horse standing in the path. He went up to it and mounted. It hurt him to sit in the saddle. The pain of keeping his seat occupied him as they cantered through the wood. He would not have minded anything, but he could not get away from the sense of being divided from the others. The path led out of the trees. On the edge of the wood he pulled up and stood watching. There in the spacious sunshine of the valley soldiers were moving in a little swarm. Every now and then, a man harrowing on a strip of fallow shouted to his oxen, at the turn. The village and the white-towered church was small in the sunshine. And he no longer belonged to it— he sat there, beyond, like a man outside in the dark. He had gone out from everyday life into the unknown, and he could not, he even did not want to go back.

Turning from the sun-blazing valley, he rode deep into the wood. Tree-trunks, like people standing grey and still, took no notice as he went. A doe, herself a moving bit of sunshine and shadow, went running through the flecked shade. There were bright green rents in the foliage. Then it was all pine wood, dark and cool. And he was sick with pain, he had an intolerable great pulse in his head, and he was sick. He had never been ill in his life. He felt lost, quite dazed with all this.

Trying to get down from the horse, he fell, astonished at the pain and his lack of balance. The horse shifted uneasily. He jerked its bridle and sent it cantering jerkily away. It was his last connection with the rest of things.

But he only wanted to lie down and not be disturbed. Stumbling through the trees, he came on a quiet place where beeches and pine trees grew on a slope. Immediately he had lain down and closed his eyes, his consciousness went racing on without him. A big pulse of sickness beat in him as if it throbbed through the whole earth. He was burning with dry heat. But he was too busy, too tearingly active in the incoherent race of delirium to observe.

III

He came to with a start. His mouth was dry and hard, his heart beat heavily, but he had not the energy to get up. His heart beat heavily. Where was he? —the barracks—at home? There was something knocking. And, making an effort, he looked round—trees, and litter of greenery, and reddish, bright, still pieces of sunshine on the floor. He did not believe he was himself, he did not believe what he saw. Something was knocking. He made a struggle towards consciousness, but relapsed. Then he struggled again. And gradually his surroundings fell into relationship with himself. He knew, and a great pang of fear went through his heart. Somebody was knocking. He could see the heavy, black rags of a fir tree overhead. Then everything went black. Yet he did not believe he had closed his eyes. He had not. Out of the blackness sight slowly emerged again. And someone was knocking. Quickly, he saw the blood-disfigured face of his Captain, which he hated. And he held himself still with horror. Yet, deep inside him, he knew that it was so, the Captain should be dead. But the physical delirium got hold of him. Someone was knocking. He lay perfectly still, as if dead, with fear. And he went unconscious.

When he opened his eyes again, he started, seeing something creeping swiftly up a tree-trunk. It was a little bird. And the bird was whistling overhead. Tap-tap-tap—it was the small, quick bird rapping the tree-trunk with its beak, as if its head were a little round hammer. He watched it curiously. It shifted sharply, in its creeping fashion. Then, like a mouse, it slid down the bare trunk. Its swift creeping sent a flash of revulsion through him. He raised his head. It felt a great weight. Then, the little bird ran out of the shadow across a still patch of sunshine, its little head bobbing swiftly, its white legs twinkling brightly for a moment. How neat it was in its build, so compact, with pieces of white on its wings. There were several of them. They were so pretty—but they crept like swift, erratic mice, running here and there among the beech-mast.

He lay down again exhausted, and his consciousness lapsed. He had a horror of the little creeping birds. All his blood seemed to be darting and creeping in his head. And yet he could not move.

He came to with a further ache of exhaustion. There was the pain in his head, and the horrible sickness, and his inability to move. He had never been ill in his life. He did not know where he was or what he was. Probably he had got sunstroke. Or what else?—he had silenced the Captain for ever—some time ago—oh, a long time ago. There had been blood on his face, and his eyes had turned upwards. It was all right, somehow. It was peace. But now he had got beyond himself. He had never been here before. Was it life, or not life? He was by himself. They were in a big, bright place, those others, and he was outside. The town, all the country, a big bright place of light: and he was outside, here, in the darkened open beyond, where each thing existed alone. But they would all have to come out there sometime, those others. Little, and left behind him, they all were. There had been father and mother and sweetheart. What did they all matter? This was the open land.

He sat up. Something scuffled. It was a little brown squirrel running in lovely, undulating bounds over the floor, its red tail completing the undulation of its body—and then, as it sat up, furling and unfurling. He watched it, pleased. It ran on again, friskily, enjoying itself. It flew wildly at another squirrel, and they were chasing each other, and making little scolding, chattering noises. The soldier wanted to speak to them. But only a hoarse sound came out of his throat. The squirrels burst away—they flew up the trees. And then he saw the one peeping round at him, half-way up a tree-trunk. A start of fear went through him, though, in so far as he was conscious, he was amused. It still stayed, its little, keen face staring at him half-way up the tree-trunk, its little ears pricked up, its clawey little hands clinging to the bark, its white breast reared. He started from it in panic.

Struggling to his feet, he lurched away. He went on walking, walking, looking for something—for a drink. His brain felt hot and inflamed for want of water. He stumbled on. Then he did not know anything. He went unconscious as he walked. Yet he stumbled on, his mouth open.

When, to his dumb wonder, he opened his eyes on the world again, he no longer tried to remember what it was. There was thick, golden light behind golden-green glitterings, and tall, grey-purple shafts, and darknesses further off, surrounding him, growing deeper. He was conscious of a sense of arrival. He was amid the reality, on the real, dark bottom. But there was the thirst burning in his brain. He felt lighter, not so heavy. He supposed it was newness. The air was muttering with thunder. He thought he was walking wonderfully swiftly and was coming straight to relief—or was it to water?

Suddenly he stood still with fear. There was a tremendous flare of gold, immense—just a few dark trunks like bars between him and it. All the young level wheat was burnished gold glaring on its silky green. A woman, full-skirted, a black cloth on her head for head-dress, was passing like a block of shadow through the glistening green corn, into the full glare. There was a farm, too, pale blue in shadow, and the timber black. And there was a church spire, nearly fused away in the gold. The woman moved on, away from him. He had no language with which to speak to her. She was the bright, solid unreality. She would make a noise of words that would confuse him, and her eyes would look at him without seeing him. She was crossing there to the other side. He stood against a tree.

When at last he turned, looking down the long, bare grove whose flat bed was already filling dark, he saw the mountains in a wonder-light, not far away, and radiant. Behind the soft, grey ridge of the nearest range the further mountains stood golden and pale grey, the snow all radiant like pure, soft gold. So still, gleaming in the sky, fashioned pure out of the ore of the sky, they shone in their silence. He stood and looked at them, his face illuminated. And like the golden, lustrous gleaming of the snow he felt his own thirst bright in him. He stood and gazed, leaning against a tree. And then everything slid away into space.

During the night the lightning fluttered perpetually, making the whole sky white. He must have walked again. The world hung livid round him for moments, fields a level sheen of grey-green light, trees in dark bulk, and the range of clouds black across a white sky. Then the darkness fell like a shutter, and the night was whole. A faint flutter of a half-revealed world, that could not quite leap out of the darkness!—Then there again stood a sweep of pallor for the land, dark shapes looming, a range of clouds hanging overhead. The world was a ghostly shadow, thrown for a moment upon the pure darkness, which returned ever whole and complete.

And the mere delirium of sickness and fever went on inside him—his brain opening and shutting like the night—then sometimes convulsions of terror from something with great eyes that stared round a tree—then the long agony of the march, and the sun decomposing his blood—then the pang of hate for the Captain, followed by a pang of tenderness and ease. But everything was distorted, born of an ache and resolving into an ache.

In the morning he came definitely awake. Then his brain flamed with the sole horror of thirstiness! The sun was on his face, the dew was steaming from his wet clothes. Like one possessed, he got up. There, straight in front of him, blue and cool and tender, the mountains ranged across the pale edge of the morning sky. He wanted them—he wanted them alone—he wanted to leave himself and be identified with them. They did not move, they were still and soft, with white, gentle markings of snow. He stool still, mad with suffering, his hands crisping and clutching. Then he was twisting in a paroxysm on the grass.

He lay still, in a kind of dream of anguish. His thirst seemed to have separated itself from him, and to stand apart, a single demand. Then the pain he felt was another single self. Then there was the clog of his body, another separate thing. He was divided among all kinds of separate beings. There was some strange, agonized connection between them, but they were drawing further apart. Then they would all split. The sun, drilling down on him, was drilling through the bond. Then they would all fall, fall through the everlasting lapse of space. Then again, his consciousness reasserted itself. He roused on to his elbow and stared at the gleaming mountains. There they ranked, all still and wonderful between earth and heaven. He stared till his eyes went black, and the mountains, as they stood in their beauty, so clean and cool, seemed to have it, that which was lost in him.

IV

When the soldiers found him, three hours later, he was lying with his face over his arm, his black hair giving off heat under the sun. But he was still alive. Seeing the open, black mouth, the young soldiers dropped him in horror.

He died in the hospital at night, without having seen again.

The doctors saw the bruises on his legs, behind, and were silent.

The bodies of the two men lay together, side by side, in the mortuary, the one white and slender, but laid rigidly at rest, the other looking as if every moment it must rouse into life again, so young and unused, from a slumber.

1913   1914

St. Mawr

Lawrence wrote *St. Mawr* on the ranch described in its closing pages. It had been given to Frieda by Mabel Dodge Luhan, and during the summer of 1924 he worked on the property and on the book. The five hundred goats, whose smell still lingered, the horses struck by lightning—these and other details are from life. Earlier in the year he had been in England, and had gone to Pontesbury in Shropshire to visit his correspondent Frederick Carter. Carter makes a brief appearance in *St. Mawr,* thinly disguised as Cartwright, the Pan-like figure with an interest in the occult. He and Lawrence discussed "a certain line of research in symbolism . . . and . . . the problem of the last end of the world."

Lawrence had always been interested in the symbolism of Apocalypse, and this interest grew in his last years. He had read Carter's manuscript, *The Dragon of the Alchemists* (published in 1926), with its astrological interpretation of the Book of Revelation, and used it in writing *The Plumed Serpent* in the following year. Later he wrote a preface, posthumously published, to Carter's book, and worked on his own *Apocalypse,* which remained unfinished and was also published posthumously. Carter himself noted that from Lawrence's visit to Shropshire came not only the landscape of that section of the "little novel" (as Lawrence called it) but also the red horse, an apocalyptic symbol. Thus *St. Mawr,* like *Women in Love, The Plumed Serpent,* and *Lady Chatterley's Lover,* reflects Lawrence's concern with the apocalyptic symbols and patterns; they are all, in a sense, about the end of the world, and the possibility of regeneration. Since Lawrence believed that the modern world was a betrayal of true life, he often set against it an image of the regenerate; he took St. John's Apocalypse to be a corrupt account of an ancient ritual of rebirth. Thus Lawrence's treatment of the theme, like much of his thought, has a strong but not exclusive sexual connotation. What he contrives to do in this, the masterpiece among his shorter fictions, is to establish, in his account of the modern world of death, images of a primeval and somehow still accessible life.

An instance of the indirectness with which Lawrence could use apocalyptic symbolism occurs in the description of the night journey of Mrs. Witt and Lewis; a star falls in heaven, and though Mrs. Witt offers the rational explanation—this is a frequent occurrence in August when the earth passes through a certain region—Lewis sticks to a different one: *There's movement in the sky. The world is going to change again.* This is based on Revelation: "And the stars of heaven fell unto the earth" (6:13) at the time of the opening of the Sixth Seal, when men cower in caves and dens—"For the great day of his wrath is come; and who shall be able to stand?" (6:17) Lawrence associates this with other primitive beliefs of Lewis, and emphasizes the Welshness of the groom: an ancient Briton, he belongs to an earlier time, before the modern sophistication of religion, astronomy, technology. He is closer to the world of St. Mawr, symbol of the world of Pan. Elsewhere—in *Apocalypse,* for example—he also gave horses this role.

In this book Lawrence has to represent both the wasteland of modern life, its joyless gaiety, its dissociation of mind and body, its death wish, and also the true dark integral life by which its fatuity can be measured. Civilization and the flight from it—London, Havana; Rico and his friends—are his subject. He had himself felt this disgust and made this flight. What is remarkable is the skill and varied emphasis with which he renders it. Mrs. Witt, anxious for the experience of death, Lou deciding that love and sex in such a world are to be given up (chastity as preferable to all but true sexuality is also a theme of *Lady Chatterley's Lover*)—all this is given a sort of unemphatic, actual quality. Even the great concluding set piece, the totally unsentimental account of the ranch and its New Mexican setting, is rooted in fact. Yet this does not prevent Lawrence's bold symbolic flights, and it does not prevent his directly expressing his own view of the world in a manner which the context makes perfectly acceptable. Both Lewis and the half-Indian Phoenix reflect Lawrence's opinions on race—but not aggressively, qualified as they are by the narrative. In themselves these views are often offensive. "Trust the tale." The long condemnation of the world that follows Lou's recognition of the adder which made first St. Mawr and then her own mare rear is not intrusive. It belongs to the same narrative that, a moment earlier, showed St. Mawr on his back and thrashing his legs, a vision of panic and evil. Lou's vision is of the true evil, the "break," the loosing of the uncontrollable tide which Lawrence saw happening in his own time, correctly predicting worse for the near future; while Rico and his friends in their nervous, brittle way, devoted themselves to illusions of art, pleasure, and thought.

St Mawr is not about the need for a return to the primitive, but about the need for an end to human ignobility, for a new civilization that remembers the body and relates men to the rest of the creation. That is what is hinted at in the end, despite Mrs. Witt's acid comments. The story of the ranch is the story of a genuine human effort to make a life in nature; it is not a wishing away of the sordid and terrible that nature includes. The flight to it—across the world to the American Southwest—was Lawrence's own; he had looked to America as the country where he might find it. It was there, in part; it was also—and rapidly—being ruined, like Phoenix. But Lawrence's passion for a true America still existing under the false was important; it animates his studies in American fiction, and, as developed by others, has had a profound effect on later American thought and art. If the first claim of the "little novel" on our attention is, as Leavis rightly says, that it treats the theme of the waste land with "a creative and technical originality more remarkable" than Eliot's, its second may be that it reflects, more directly than any other work of the period, the thought and the imagery of a later generation of moderns. As a narrative achievement, and as a portent, it is more than worthy to compare with those two other seminal works of the modern mind, Eliot's poem and Conrad's Heart of Darkness.

St. Mawr

Lou Witt had had her own way so long that by the age of twenty-five she didn't know where she was. Having one's own way landed one completely at sea.

To be sure, for a while she had failed in her grand love affair with Rico. And then she had had something really to despair about. But even that had worked out as she wanted. Rico had come back to her, and was dutifully married to her. And now, when she was twenty-five and he was three months older, they were a charming married couple. He flirted with other women still, to be sure. He wouldn't be the handsome Rico if he didn't. But she had 'got' him. Oh, yes! You had only to see the uneasy backward glance at her, from his big blue eyes: just like a horse that is edging away from its master: to know how completely he was mastered.

She, with her odd little *museau*,[1] not exactly pretty, but very attractive; and her quaint air of playing at being well-bred, in a sort of charade game;

1. Literally "muzzle," face.

and her queer familiarity with foreign cities and foreign languages; and the lurking sense of being an outsider everywhere, like a sort of gipsy, who is at home anywhere and nowhere: all this made up her charm and her failure. She didn't quite belong.

Of course she was American: Louisiana family, moved down to Texas. And she was moderately rich, with no close relation except her mother. But she had been sent to school in France when she was twelve, and since she had finished school, she had drifted from Paris to Palermo, Biarritz to Vienna and back via Munich to London, then down again to Rome. Only fleeting trips to her America.

So what sort of American was she, after all?

And what sort of European was she either? She didn't 'belong' anywhere. Perhaps most of all in Rome, among the artists and the Embassy people.

It was in Rome she had met Rico. He was an Australian, son of a government official in Melbourne, who had been made a baronet.[2] So one day Rico would be Sir Henry, as he was the only son. Meanwhile he floated around Europe on a very small allowance—his father wasn't rich in capital—and was being an artist.

They met in Rome when they were twenty-two, and had a love affair in Capri. Rico was handsome, elegant, but mostly he had spots of paint on his trousers and he ruined a necktie pulling it off. He behaved in a most floridly elegant fashion, fascinating to the Italians. But at the same time he was canny and shrewd and sensible as any young poser could be, and, on principle, goodhearted, anxious. He was anxious for his future, and anxious for his place in the world, he was poor, and suddenly wasteful in spite of all his tension of economy, and suddenly spiteful in spite of all his ingratiating efforts, and suddenly ungrateful in spite of all his burden of gratitude, and suddenly rude in spite of all his good manners, and suddenly detestable in spite of all his suave, courtier-like amiability.

He was fascinated by Lou's quaint aplomb, her experiences, her 'knowledge,' her *gamine*[3] knowingness, her aloneness, her pretty clothes that were sometimes an utter failure, and her southern 'drawl' that was sometimes so irritating. That sing-song which was so American. Yet she used no Americanisms at all, except when she lapsed into her odd spasms of acid irony, when she was very American indeed!

And she was fascinated by Rico. They played to each other like two butterflies at one flower. They pretended to be very poor in Rome—he *was* poor: and very rich in Naples. Everybody stared their eyes out at them. And they had that love affair in Capri.

But they reacted badly on each other's nerves. She became ill. Her mother appeared. He couldn't stand Mrs. Witt, and Mrs. Witt couldn't stand him. There was a terrible fortnight. Then Lou was popped into a convent nursing-home in Umbria, and Rico dashed off to Paris. Nothing would stop him. He must go back to Australia.

He went to Melbourne, and while there his father died, leaving him a

2. Rank between knight and baron, the lowest hereditary honor.
3. Urchin, waif.

baronet's title and an income still very moderate. Lou visited America once more, as the strangest of strange lands to her. She came aways disheartened, panting for Europe, and, of course, doomed to meet Rico again.

They couldn't get away from one another, even though in the course of their rather restrained correspondence he informed her that he was 'probably' marrying a very dear girl, friend of his childhood, only daughter of one of the oldest families in Victoria.[4] Not saying much.

He didn't commit the probability, but reappeared in Paris, wanting to paint his head off, terribly inspired by Cézanne and by old Renoir. He dined at the Rotonde with Lou and Mrs. Witt, who, with her queer democratic New Orleans sort of conceit, looked round the drinking-hall with savage contempt, and at Rico as part of the show. Certainly, she said, 'when these people here have got any money, they fall in love on a full stomach. And when they've got no money, they fall in love with a full pocket. I never was in a more disgusting place. They take their love like some people take after-dinner pills.'

She would watch with her arching, full, strong grey eyes, sitting there erect and silent in her well-bought American clothes. And then she would deliver some such charge of grape-shot. Rico always writhed.

Mrs. Witt hated Paris: 'this sordid, unlucky city,' she called it. 'Something unlucky is bound to happen to me in this sinister, unclean town,' she said. 'I feel *contagion* in the air of this place. For heaven's sake, Louise, let us go to Morocco or somewhere.'

'No, mother dear, I can't now. Rico has proposed to me, and I have accepted him. Let us think about a wedding, shall we?'

'There!' said Mrs. Witt. 'I said it was an unlucky city!'

And the peculiar look of extreme New Orleans annoyance came round her sharp nose. But Lou and Rico were both twenty-four years old, and beyond management. And anyhow, Lou would be Lady Carrington. But Mrs. Witt was exasperated beyond exasperation. She would almost rather have preferred Lou to elope with one of the great, evil porters at Les Halles.[5] Mrs. Witt was at the age when the malevolent male in man, the old Adam, begins to loom above all the social tailoring. And yet—and yet—it was better to have Lady Carrington for a daughter, seeing Lou was that sort.

There was a marriage, after which Mrs. Witt departed to America. Lou and Rico leased a little old house in Westminster, and began to settle into a certain layer of English society. Rico was becoming an almost fashionable portrait-painter. At least, *he* was almost fashionable, whether his portraits were or not. And Lou too was almost fashionable: almost a hit. There was some flaw somewhere. In spite of their appearances, both Rico and she would never quite go down in any society. They were the drifting artist sort. Yet neither of them was content to be of the drifting artist sort. They wanted to fit in, to make good.

Hence the little house in Westminster, the portraits, the dinners, the friends, and the visits. Mrs. Witt came and sardonically established herself in a suite in a quiet but good-class hotel not far off. Being on the spot. And her terrible grey eyes with the touch of a leer looked on at the hollow mockery of things. As if *she* knew of anything better!

---

4. Australian state, capital Melbourne.
5. Central Paris market (demolished in the 1970's).

Lou and Rico had a curious exhausting effect on one another: neither knew why. They were fond of one another. Some inscrutable bond held them together. But it was a strange vibration of the nerves, rather than of the blood. A nervous attachment, rather than a sexual love. A curious tension of will, rather than a spontaneous passion. Each was curiously under the domination of the other. They were a pair—they had to be together. Yet quite soon they shrank from one another. This attachment of the will and the nerves was destructive. As soon as one felt strong, the other felt ill. As soon as the ill one recovered strength, down went the one who had been well.

And soon, tacitly, the marriage became more like a friendship, Platonic. It was a marriage, but without sex. Sex was shattering and exhausting, they shrank from it, and became like brother and sister. But still they were husband and wife. And the lack of physical relation was a secret source of uneasiness and chagrin to both of them. They would neither of them accept it. Rico looked with contemplative, anxious eyes at other women.

Mrs. Witt kept track of everything, watching, as it were, from outside the fence, like a potent well-dressed demon, full of uncanny energy and a shattering sort of sense. She said little: but her small, occasionally biting remarks revealed her attitude of contempt for the *ménage*.[6]

Rico entertained clever and well-known people. Mrs. Witt would appear, in her New York gowns and few good jewels. She was handsome, with her vigorous grey hair. But her heavy-lidded grey eyes were the despair of any hostess. They looked too many shattering things. And it was but too obvious that these clever, well-known English people got on her nerves terribly, with their finickiness and their fine-drawn discriminations. She wanted to put her foot through all these fine-drawn distinctions. She thought continually of the house of her girlhood, the plantation, the Negroes, the planters: the sardonic grimness that underlay all the big, shiftless life. And she wanted to cleave with some of this grimness of the big, dangerous America, into the safe, finicky drawing-rooms of London. So naturally she was not popular.

But being a woman of energy, she had to do *something*. During the latter part of the war she had worked with the American Red Cross in France, nursing. She loved men—real men. But, on close contact, it was difficult to define what she meant by 'real' men. She never met any.

Out of the debacle of the war she had emerged with an odd piece of debris, in the shape of Geronimo Trujillo. He was an American, son of a Mexican father and a Navajo Indian mother, from Arizona. When you knew him well, you recognized the real half-breed, though at a glance he might pass as a sunburnt citizen of any nation, particularly of France. He looked like a certain sort of Frenchman, with his curiously set dark eyes, his straight black hair, his thin black moustache, his rather long cheeks, and his almost slouching, diffident, sardonic bearing. Only when you knew him, and looked right into his eyes, you saw that unforgettable glint of the Indian.

He had been badly shell-shocked, and was for a time a wreck. Mrs. Witt, having nursed him into convalescence, asked him where he was going next. He didn't know. His father and mother were dead, and he had nothing to take him back to Phoenix, Arizona. Having had an education in one of the Indian high

6. Establishment, domestic arrangements.

schools, the unhappy fellow had now no place in life at all. Another of the many misfits.

There was something of the Paris *Apache* [7] in his appearance: but he was all the time withheld, and nervously shut inside himself. Mrs. Witt was intrigued by him.

'Very well, Phœnix,' she said, refusing to adopt his Spanish name, 'I'll see what I can do.'

What she did was to get him a place on a sort of manor farm, with some acquaintances of hers. He was very good with horses, and had a curious success with turkeys and geese and fowls.

Some time after Lou's marriage, Mrs. Witt reappeared in London, from the country, with Phœnix in tow, and a couple of horses. She had decided that she would ride in the Park in the morning, and see the world that way. Phœnix was to be her groom.

So, to the great misgiving of Rico, behold Mrs. Witt in splendidly tailored habit and perfect boots, a smart black hat on her smart grey hair, riding a grey gelding as smart as she was, and looking down her conceited, inquisitive, scornful, aristocratic-democratic Louisiana nose at the people in Piccadilly, as she crossed to the Row,[8] followed by the taciturn shadow of Phœnix, who sat on a chestnut with three white feet as if he had grown there.

Mrs. Witt, like many other people, always expected to find the real *beau monde* and the real *grand monde* [9] somewhere or other. She didn't quite give in to what she saw in the Bois de Boulogne,[10] or in Monte Carlo, or on the Pincio; [11] all a bit shoddy, and not very *beau* and not at all *grand*. There she was, with her grey eagle eye, her splendid complexion and her weapon-like health of a woman of fifty, dropping her eyelids a little, very slightly nervous, but completely prepared to despise the *monde* she was entering in Rotten Row.

In she sailed, and up and down that regatta-canal of horsemen and horsewomen under the trees of the Park. And yes, there were lovely girls with fair hair down their backs, on happy ponies. And awfully well-groomed papas, and tight mammas who looked as if they were going to pour tea between the ears of their horses, and converse with banal skill, one eye on the teapot, one on the visitor with whom she was talking, and all the rest of her hostess' argus-eyes [12] upon everybody in sight. That alert argus capability of the English matron was startling and a bit horrifying. Mrs. Witt would at once think of the old Negro mammies, away in Louisiana. And her eyes became dagger-like as she watched the clipped, shorn, mincing young Englishmen. She refused to look at the prosperous Jews.

It was still the days before motor-cars were allowed in the Park, but Rico and Lou, sliding round Hyde Park Corner and up Park Lane in their car, would

7. Hooligan, tough.
8. Rotten Row, track in Hyde Park set aside for riding.
9. Fashionable society, high society.
10. Park on outskirts of Paris.
11. Terrace overlooking Rome, favorite walking place.
12. Argus, in Greek myth, had eyes all over his body; Juno transferred them at his death to the peacock's tail.

watch the steely horsewoman and the saturnine groom with a sort of dismay. Mrs. Witt seemed to be pointing a pistol at the bosom of every other horseman or horsewoman, and announcing: *Your virility or your life! Your femininity or your life!* She didn't know herself what she really wanted them to be: but it was something as democratic as Abraham Lincoln, and as aristocratic as a Russian Czar, as highbrow as Arthur Balfour,[13] and as taciturn and unideal as Phœnix. Everything at once.

There was nothing for it: Lou had to buy herself a horse and ride at her mother's side, for very decency's sake. Mrs. Witt was *so* like a smooth, levelled, gun-metal pistol, Lou had to be a sort of sheath. And she really looked pretty, with her clusters of dark, curly, New Orleans hair, like grapes, and her quaint brown eyes that didn't quite match, and that looked a bit sleepy and vague, and at the same time quick as a squirrel's. She was slight and elegant, and a tiny bit rakish, and somebody suggested she might be in the movies.

Nevertheless, they were in the society columns next morning—*two new and striking figures in the Row this morning were Lady Henry Carrington* [14] *and her mother Mrs. Witt,* etc. And Mrs. Witt liked it, let her say what she might. So did Lou. Lou liked it immensely. She simply luxuriated in the sun of publicity.

'Rico dear, you must get a horse.'

The tone was soft and southern and drawling, but the overtone had a decisive finality. In vain Rico squirmed—he had a way of writhing and squirming which perhaps he had caught at Oxford. In vain he protested that he couldn't ride, and that he didn't care for riding. He got quite angry, and his handsome arched nose tilted and his upper lip lifted from his teeth, like a dog that is going to bite. Yet daren't quite bite.

And that was Rico. He daren't quite bite. Not that he was really afraid of the others. He was afraid of himself, once he let himself go. He might rip up in an eruption of lifelong anger all this pretty-pretty picture of a charming young wife and a delightful little home and a fascinating success as a painter of fashionable and, at the same time, 'great' portraits: with colour, wonderful colour, and, at the same time, form, marvellous form. He had composed this little *tableau vivant* [15] with great effort. He didn't want to erupt like some suddenly wicked horse—Rico was really more like a horse than a dog, a horse that might go nasty any moment. For the time, he was good, very good, dangerously good.

'Why, Rico dear, I thought you used to ride so much, in Australia, when you were young? Didn't you tell me all about it, hm?'—and as she ended on that slow, singing *hm?* which acted on him like an irritant and a drug, he knew he was beaten.

Lou kept the sorrel mare in a mews just behind the house in Westminster and she was always slipping round to the stables. She had a funny little nostalgia for the place: something that really surprised her. She had never had the

13. Arthur James, 1st Earl of Balfour (1848–1930), British philosopher and statesman, prime minister 1902–6, associated with Balfour Declaration (1917), which promised the Jews a national home in Palestine.
14. A slip for which Lawrence is sometimes castigated: Lou, as the wife of a baronet, would be known as Lady Carrington.
15. Living picture.

faintest notion that she cared for horses and stables and grooms. But she did. She was fascinated. Perhaps it was her childhood's Texas associations come back. Whatever it was, her life with Rico in the elegant little house, and all her social engagements, seemed like a dream, the substantial reality of which was those mews in Westminster, her sorrel mare, the owner of the mews, Mr. Saintsbury, and the grooms he employed. Mr. Saintsbury was a horsy elderly man like an old maid, and he loved the sound of titles.

'Lady Carrington!—well, I never! You've come to us for a bit of company again, I see. I don't know whatever we shall do if you go away, we shall be that lonely!' and he flashed his old-maid's smile at her. 'No matter how grey the morning, your Ladyship would make a beam of sunshine. Poppy is all right, I think . . .'

Poppy was the sorrel mare with the three white feet and the startled eye, and she was all right. And Mr. Saintsbury was smiling with his old-maid's mouth, and showing all his teeth.

'Come across with me, Lady Carrington, and look at a new horse just up from the country? I think he's worth a look, and I believe you have a moment to spare, your Ladyship.'

Her Ladyship had too many moments to spare. She followed the sprightly, elderly, clean-shaven man across the yard to a loose box, and waited while he opened the door.

In the inner dark she saw a handsome bay horse with his clean ears pricked like daggers from his naked head as he swung handsomely round to stare at the open doorway. He had big, black, brilliant eyes, with a sharp questioning glint, and that air of tense, alert quietness which betrays an animal that can be dangerous.

'Is he quiet?' Lou asked.

'Why—yes—my Lady! He's quiet, with those that know how to handle him. *Cup! my boy! Cup my beauty! Cup then! St. Mawr!*'

Loquacious even with the animals, he went softly forward and laid his hand on the horse's shoulder, soft and quiet as a fly settling. Lou saw the brilliant skin of the horse crinkle a little in apprehensive anticipation, like the shadow of the descending hand on a bright red-gold liquid. But then the animal relaxed again.

'Quiet with those that know how to handle him, and a bit of a ruffian with those that don't. Isn't that the ticket, eh, St. Mawr?'

'What is his name?' Lou asked.

The man repeated it, with a slight Welsh twist. 'He's from the Welsh borders, belonging to a Welsh gentleman, Mr. Griffith Edwards. But they're wanting to sell him.'

'How old is he?' asked Lou.

'About seven years—seven years and five months,' said Mr. Saintsbury, dropping his voice as if it were a secret.

'Could one ride him in the Park?'

'Well—yes! I should say a gentleman who knew how to handle him could ride him very well and make a very handsome figure in the Park.'

Lou at once decided that this handsome figure should be Rico's. For she was already half in love with St. Mawr. He was of such a lovely red-gold colour, and a dark, invisible fire seemed to come out of him. But in his big black eyes there was a lurking afterthought. Something told her that the horse was not quite happy: that somewhere deep in his animal consciousness lived a dangerous, half-revealed resentment, a diffused sense of hostility. She realized that he was sensitive, in spite of his flaming, healthy strength, and nervous with a touchy uneasiness that might make him vindictive.

'Has he got any tricks?' she asked.

'Not that I know of, my Lady: not tricks exactly. But he's one of these temperamental creatures, as they say. Though *I* say, every horse is temperamental, when you come down to it. But this one, it is as if he was a trifle raw somewhere. Touch this raw spot, and there's no answering for him.'

'Where is he raw?' asked Lou, somewhat mystified. She thought he might really have some physical sore.

'Why, that's hard to say, my Lady. If he was a human being, you'd say something had gone wrong in his life. But with a horse, it's not that, exactly. A highbred animal like St. Mawr needs understanding, and I don't know as anybody has quite got the hang of him. I confess I haven't myself. But I do realize that he is a special animal and needs a special sort of touch, and I'm willing he should have it, did I but know exactly what it is.'

She looked at the glowing bay horse that stood there with his ears back, his face averted, but attending as if he were some lightning-conductor. He was a stallion. When she realized this, she became more afraid of him.

'Why does Mr. Griffith Edwards want to sell him?' she asked.

'Well—my Lady—they raised him for stud purposes—but he didn't answer. There are horses like that: don't seem to fancy the mares, for some reason. Well, anyway, they couldn't keep him for the stud. And as you see, he's a powerful, beautiful hackney, clean as a whistle, and eaten up with his own power. But there's no putting him between the shafts. He won't stand it. He's a fine saddle-horse, beautiful action, and lovely to ride. But he's got to be handled, and there you are.'

Lou felt there was something behind the man's reticence.

'Has he ever made a break?' she asked, apprehensive.

'Made a break?' replied the man. 'Well, if I must admit it, he's had two accidents. Mr. Griffith Edwards' son rode him a bit wild, away there in the forest of Deane,[16] and the young fellow had his skull smashed in, against a low oak bough. Last autumn, that was. And some time back, he crushed a groom against the side of the stall—injured him fatally. But they were both accidents, my Lady. Things will happen.'

The man spoke in a melancholy, fatalistic way. The horse, with his ears laid back, seemed to be listening tensely, his face averted. He looked like something finely bred and passionate, that has been judged and condemned.

'May I say *how do you do?*' she said to the horse, drawing a little nearer in her white, summery dress, and lifting her hand that glittered with emeralds and diamonds.

He drifted away from her, as if some wind blew him. Then he ducked his head, and looked sideways at her, from his black, full eye.

'I think I'm all right,' she said, edging nearer, while he watched her.

She laid her hand on his side, and gently stroked him. Then she stroked his

16. On the border of Wales and Gloucestershire.

shoulder, and then the hard, tense arch of his neck. And she was startled to feel the vivid heat of his life come through to her, through the lacquer of red-gold gloss. So slippery with vivid, hot life!

She paused, as if thinking, while her hand rested on the horse's sun-arched neck. Dimly, in her weary young-woman's soul, an ancient understanding seemed to flood in.

She wanted to buy St. Mawr.

'I think,' she said to Saintsbury, 'if I can, I will buy him.'

The man looked at her long and shrewdly.

'Well, my Lady,' he said at last, 'there shall be nothing kept from you. But what would your Ladyship do with him, if I may make so bold?'

'I don't know,' she replied, vaguely. 'I might take him to America.'

The man paused once more, then said:

'They say it's been the making of some horses, to take them over the water, to Australia or such places. It might repay you—you never know.'

She wanted to buy St. Mawr. She wanted him to belong to her. For some reason the sight of him, his power, his alive, alert intensity, his unyieldingness, made her want to cry.

She never did cry: except sometimes with vexation, or to get her own way. As far as weeping went, her heart felt as dry as a Christmas walnut. What was the good of tears, anyhow? You had to keep on holding on, in this life, never give way, and never give in. Tears only left one weakened and ragged.

But now, as if that mysterious fire of the horse's body had split some rock in her, she went home and hid herself in her room, and just cried. The wild, brilliant, alert head of St. Mawr seemed to look at her out of another world. It was as if she had had a vision, as if the walls of her own world had suddenly melted away, leaving her in a great darkness, in the midst of which the large, brilliant eyes of that horse looked at her with demonish question, while his naked ears stood up like daggers from the naked lines of his inhuman head, and his great body glowed red with power.

What was it? Almost like a god looking at her terribly out of the everlasting dark, she had felt the eyes of that horse; great, glowing, fearsome eyes, arched with a question, and containing a white blade of light like a threat. What was his non-human question, and his uncanny threat? She didn't know. He was some splendid demon, and she must worship him.

She hid herself away from Rico. She could not bear the triviality and super-ficiality of her human relationships. Looming like some god out of the darkness was the head of that horse, with the wide, terrible, questioning eyes. And she felt that it forbade her to be her ordinary, commonplace self. It forbade her to be just Rico's wife, young Lady Carrington, and all that.

It haunted her, the horse. It had looked at her as she had never been looked at before: terrible, gleaming, questioning eyes arching out of darkness, and backed by all the fire of that great ruddy body. What did it mean, and what ban did it put upon her? She felt it put a ban on her heart: wielded some uncanny authority over her, that she dared not, could not understand.

No matter where she was, what she was doing, at the back of her conscious-ness loomed a great, over-aweing figure out of a dark background: St. Mawr, looking at her without really seeing her, yet gleaming a question at her, from his wide terrible eyes, and gleaming a sort of menace, doom. Master of doom, he seemed to be!

'You are thinking about something, Lou dear!' Rico said to her that evening. He was so quick and sensitive to detect her moods—so exciting in this respect. And his big, slightly prominent blue eyes, with the whites a little bloodshot, glanced at her quickly, with searching, and anxiety, and a touch of fear, as if his conscience were always uneasy. He, too, was rather like a horse—but forever quivering with a sort of cold, dangerous mistrust, which he covered with anxious love.

At the middle of his eyes was a central powerlessness, that left him anxious. It used to touch her to pity, that central look of powerlessness in him. But now, since she had seen the full, dark, passionate blaze of power and of different life in the eyes of the thwarted horse, the anxious powerlessness of the man drove her mad. Rico was so handsome, and he was so self-controlled, he had a gallant sort of kindness and a real worldly shrewdness. One had to admire him: at least *she* had to.

But after all, and after all, it was a bluff, an attitude. He kept it all working in himself, deliberately. It was an attitude. She read psychologists who said that everything was an attitude. Even the best of everything. But now she realized that, with men and women, everything is an attitude only when something else is lacking. Something is lacking and they are thrown back on their own devices. That black fiery flow in the eyes of the horse was not 'attitude.' It was something much more terrifying, and real, the only thing that was real. Gushing from the darkness in menace and question, and blazing out in the splendid body of the horse.

'Was I thinking about something?' she replied, in her slow, amused, casual fashion. As if everything was so casual and easy to her. And so it was, from the hard, polished side of herself. But that wasn't the whole story.

'I think you were, Loulina. May we offer the penny?'

'Don't trouble,' she said. 'I was thinking, if I was thinking of anything, about a bay horse called St. Mawr.'—Her secret *almost* crept into her eyes.

'The name is awfully attractive,' he said with a laugh.

'Not so attractive as the creature himself. I'm going to buy him.'

'Not really!' he said. 'But why?'

'He *is* so attractive. I'm going to buy him for you.'

'For *me! Darling!* how you do take me for granted! He may not be in the least attractive to me. As you know, I have hardly any feeling for horses at all. — Besides, how much does he cost?'

'That I don't know, Rico dear. But I'm sure you'll love him, for my sake.'— She felt, now, she was merely playing for her own ends.

'Lou dearest, *don't* spend a fortune on a horse for me, which I *don't* want. Honestly, I prefer a car.'

'Won't you ride with me in the Park, Rico?'

'Honestly, dear Lou, I don't want to.'

'Why not, dear boy? You'd look so beautiful. I wish you would.—And anyhow, come with me to look at St. Mawr.'

Rico was divided. He had a certain uneasy feeling about horses. At the same time, he *would* like to cut a handsome figure in the Park.

They went across to the mews. A little Welsh groom was watering the brilliant horse.

'Yes, dear, he certainly *is* beautiful: such a marvellous colour! Almost orange! But rather large, I should say, to ride in the Park.'

'No, for you he's perfect. You are so tall.'

'He'd be marvellous in a composition. That colour!'

And all Rico could do was to gaze with the artist's eye at the horse, with a glance at the groom.

'Don't you think the man is rather fascinating too?' he said, nursing his chin artistically and penetratingly.

The groom, Lewis, was a little, quick, rather bow-legged, loosely built fellow of indeterminate age, with a mop of black hair and little black beard. He was grooming the brilliant St. Mawr, out in the open. The horse was really glorious: like a marigold, with a pure golden sheen, a shimmer of green-gold lacquer, upon a burning red-orange. There on the shoulder you saw the yellow lacquer glisten. Lewis, a little scrub of a fellow, worked absorbedly, unheedingly, at the horse, with an absorption that was almost ritualistic. He seemed the attendant shadow of the ruddy animal.

'He goes with the horse,' said Lou. 'If we buy St. Mawr, we get the man thrown in.'

'They'd be *so* amusing to paint: such an extraordinary contrast! But, darling, I *hope* you won't insist on buying the horse. It's so frightfully expensive.'

'Mother will help me. —You'd look so well on him, Rico.'

'If ever I dared take the liberty of getting on his back—!'

'Why not?' She went quickly across the cobbled yard.

'Good morning, Lewis. How is St. Mawr?'

Lewis straightened himself and looked at her from under the falling mop of his black hair.

'All right,' he said.

He peered straight at her from under his overhanging black hair. He had pale-grey eyes, that looked phosphorescent, and suggested the eyes of a wildcat peering intent from under the darkness of some bush where it lies unseen. Lou, with her brown, unmatched, oddly perplexed eyes, felt herself found out.—'He's a common little fellow,' she thought to herself. 'But he knows a woman and a horse, at sight.'—Aloud she said, in her southern drawl:

'How do you think he'd be with Sir Henry?'

Lewis turned his remote, coldly watchful eyes on the young baronet. Rico was tall and handsome and balanced on his hips. His face was long and well-defined, and with the hair taken straight back from the brow. It seemed as well-made as his clothing, and as perpetually presentable. You could not imagine his face dirty, or scrubby and unshaven, or bearded, or even moustached. It was perfectly prepared for social purposes. If his head had been cut off, like John the Baptist's, it would have been a thing complete in itself, would not have missed the body in the least.[17] The body was perfectly tailored. The head was one of the famous 'talking heads' of modern youth, with eyebrows

17. A recurrent figure in Lawrence, and also in Yeats and other contemporaries, for the modern divorce of mind and body.

a trifle Mephistophelian, large blue eyes a trifle bold, and curved mouth thrilling to death to kiss.

Lewis, the groom, staring from between his bush of hair and his beard, watched like an animal from the underbrush. And Rico was still sufficiently a colonial to be uneasily aware of the underbrush, uneasy under the watchfulness of the pale-grey eyes, and uneasy in that man-to-man exposure which is characteristic of the democratic colonies and of America. He knew he must ultimately be judged on his merits as a man, alone without a background: an ungarnished colonial.

This lack of background, this defenceless man-to-man business which left him at the mercy of every servant, was bad for his nerves. For he was *also* an artist. He bore up against it in a kind of desperation, and was easily moved to rancorous resentment. At the same time he was free of the Englishman's watertight *suffisance*.[18] He really was aware that he would have to hold his own all alone, thrown alone on his own defences in the universe. The extreme democracy of the colonies had taught him this.

And this the little aboriginal Lewis recognized in him. He recognized also Rico's curious hollow misgiving, fear of some deficiency in himself, beneath all his handsome, young-hero appearance.

'He'd be all right with anybody as would meet him half-way,' said Lewis, in the quick Welsh manner of speech, impersonal.

'You hear, Rico!' said Lou in her sing-song, turning to her husband.

'Perfectly, darling.'

'Would you be willing to meet St. Mawr half-way, hmm?'

'All the way, darling! Mahomet would go *all* the way to that mountain.[19] Who would dare to do otherwise?'

He spoke with a laughing, yet piqued sarcasm.

'Why, I think St. Mawr would understand perfectly,' she said in the soft voice of a woman haunted by love. And she went and laid her hand on the slippery, life-smooth shoulder of the horse. He, with his strange equine head lowered, its exquisite fine lines reaching a little snake-like forward, and his ears a little back, was watching her sideways, from the corner of his eye. He was in a state of absolute mistrust, like a cat crouching to spring.

'St. Mawr!' she said. 'St. Mawr! What is the matter? Surely you and I are all right!'

And she spoke softly, dreamily stroked the animal's neck. She could feel a response gradually coming from him. But he would not lift up his head. And when Rico suddenly moved nearer, he sprang with a sudden jerk backwards, as if lightning exploded in his four hoofs.

The groom spoke a few low words in Welsh. Lou, frightened, stood with lifted hand arrested. She had been going to stroke him.

'Why did he do that?' she said.

'They gave him a beating once or twice,' said the groom in a neutral voice, 'and he doesn't forget.'

18. Self-sufficiency, conceit.
19. Mahomet, asked for a miracle, summoned a mountain to him; when it did not come he thanked God for sparing the people the destruction such a move would have brought, and went to it.

She could hear a neutral sort of judgment in Lewis' voice. And she thought of the 'raw spot.'

Not any raw spot at all. A battle between two worlds. She realized that St. Mawr drew his hot breaths in another world from Rico's, from our world. Perhaps the old Greek horses had lived in St. Mawr's world. And the old Greek heroes, even Hippolytus,[20] had known it.

With their strangely naked equine heads, and something of a snake in their way of looking round, and lifting their sensitive, dangerous muzzles, they moved in a prehistoric twilight where all things loomed phantasmagoric, all on one plane, sudden presences suddenly jutting out of the matrix. It was another world, an older, heavily potent world. And in this world the horse was swift and fierce and supreme, undominated and unsurpassed.—'Meet him half-way,' Lewis said. But half-way across from our human world to that terrific equine twilight was not a small step. It was a step, she knew, that Rico could never take. She knew it. But she was prepared to sacrifice Rico.

St. Mawr was bought, and Lewis was hired along with him. At first, Lewis rode him behind Lou, in the Row,[21] to get him going. He behaved perfectly.

Phœnix, the half-Indian, was very jealous when he saw the black-bearded Welsh groom on St. Mawr.

'What horse you got there?' he asked, looking at the other man with the curious unseeing stare in his hard, Navajo eyes, in which the Indian glint moved like a spark upon a dark chaos. In Phœnix's high-boned face there was all the race-misery of the dispossessed Indian, with an added blankness left by shell-shock. But at the same time, there was that unyielding, save to death, which is characteristic of his tribe: his mother's tribe. Difficult to say what subtle thread bound him to the Navajo, and made his destiny a Red Man's destiny still.

They were a curious pair of grooms, following the correct, and yet extraordinary, pair of American mistresses. Mrs. Witt and Phœnix both rode with long stirrups and straight leg, sitting close to the saddle, without posting. Phœnix looked as if he and the horse were all one piece, he never seemed to rise in the saddle at all, neither trotting nor galloping, but sat like a man riding bareback. And all the time he stared around, at the riders in the Row, at the people grouped outside the rail, chatting, at the children walking with their nurses, as if he were looking at a mirage, in whose actuality he never believed for a moment. London was all a sort of dark mirage to him. His wide, nervous-looking brown eyes, with a smallish brown pupil that showed the white all round, seemed to be focused on the far distance, as if he could not see things too near. He was watching the pale deserts of Arizona shimmer with moving light, the long mirage of a shallow lake ripple, the great pallid concave of earth and sky expanding with interchanged light. And a horse-shape loom large and portentous in the mirage, like some prehistoric beast.

20. Son of Theseus and the Amazon Hippolyta; devoted to chastity, he rejected the advances of Phaedra, his stepmother, who then charged him with seducing her; Theseus invoked the vengeance of Poseidon (Neptune) on his son; Poseidon sent a monster who terrified Hippolytus's horses as he drove his chariot along the beach, so that he was thrown and killed.

21. Another mistake: stallions are not permitted in Rotten Row.

That was real to him: the phantasm of Arizona. But this London was something his eye passed over, as a false mirage.

He looked too smart in his well-tailored groom's clothes, so smart, he might have been one of the satirized new-rich. Perhaps it was a sort of half-breed physical assertion that came through his clothing, the savage's physical assertion of himself. Anyhow, he looked 'common,' rather horsy and loud.

Except his face. In the golden suavity of his high-boned Indian face, that was hairless, with hardly any eyebrows, there was a blank, lost look that was almost touching. The same startled blank look was in his eyes. But in the smallish dark pupils the dagger-point of light still gleamed unbroken.

He was a good groom, watchful, quick, and on the spot in an instant if anything went wrong. He had a curious, quiet power over the horses, unemotional, unsympathetic, but silently potent. In the same way, watching the traffic of Piccadilly with his blank, glinting eye, he would calculate everything instinctively, as if it were an enemy, and pilot Mrs. Witt by the strength of his silent will. He threw around her the tense watchfulness of her own America, and made her feel at home.

'Phoenix,' she said, turning abruptly in her saddle as they walked the horses past the sheltering policeman at Hyde Park Corner, 'I can't tell you how glad I am to have something a hundred per cent American at the back of me, when I go through these gates.'

She looked at him from dangerous grey eyes as if she meant it indeed, in vindictive earnest. A ghost of a smile went up to his high cheek-bones, but he did not answer.

'Why, mother?' said Lou, sing-song. 'It feels to me so friendly—!'

'Yes, Louise, it does. So friendly! That's why I mistrust it so entirely—'

And she set off at a canter up the Row, under the green trees, her face like the face of Medusa [22] at fifty, a weapon in itself. She stared at everything and everybody, with that stare of cold dynamite waiting to explode them all. Lou posted trotting at her side, graceful and elegant, and faintly amused. Behind came Phoenix, like a shadow, with his yellowish, high-boned face still looking sick. And at his side, on the big brilliant bay horse, the smallish, black-bearded Welshman.

Between Phoenix and Lewis there was a latent but unspoken and wary sympathy. Phoenix was terribly impressed by St. Mawr, he could not leave off staring at him. And Lewis rode the brilliant, handsome-moving stallion so very quietly, like an insinuation.

Of the two men, Lewis looked the darker, with his black beard coming up to his thick black eyebrows. He was swarthy, with a rather short nose, and the uncanny pale-green eyes that watched everything and cared about nothing. He cared about nothing in the world, except, at the present, St. Mawr. People did not matter to him. He rode his horse and watched the world from the vantage-ground of St. Mawr, with a final indifference.

'You have been with that horse long?' asked Phoenix.

'Since he was born.'

22. One of the three Gorgons, with faces so hideous that the sight of them turned the beholder to stone.

Phœnix watched the action of St. Mawr as they went. The bay moved proud and springy, but with perfect good sense, among the stream of riders. It was a beautiful June morning, the leaves overhead were thick and green; there came the first whiff of lime-tree scent. To Phœnix, however, the city was a sort of nightmare mirage, and to Lewis it was a sort of prison. The presence of people he felt as a prison around him.

Mrs. Witt and Lou were turning, at the end of the Row, bowing to some acquaintances. The grooms pulled aside. Mrs. Witt looked at Lewis with a cold eye.

'It seems an extraordinary thing to me, Louise,' she said, 'to see a groom with a beard.'

'It isn't usual, mother,' said Lou. 'Do you mind?'

'Not at all. At least, I think I don't. I get very tired of modern bare-faced young men, very! The clean, pure boy, don't you know! Doesn't it make you tired?—No, I think a groom with a beard is quite attractive.'

She gazed into the crowd defiantly, perching her finely shod toe with warlike firmness on the stirrup-iron. Then suddenly she reined in, and turned her horse towards the grooms.

'Lewis!' she said. 'I want to ask you a question. Supposing, now, that Lady Carrington wanted you to shave off that beard, what should you say?'

Lewis instinctively put up his hand to the said beard.

'They've wanted me to shave it off, Mam,' he said. 'But I've never done it.'

'But why? Tell me why.'

'It's part of me, Mam.'

Mrs. Witt pulled on again.

'Isn't that extraordinary, Louise?' she said. 'Don't you like the way he says Mam? It sounds so impossible to me. Could any woman think of herself as Mam? Never, since Queen Victoria! But—do you know?—it hadn't occurred to me that a man's beard was really part of him. It always seemed to me that men wore their beards, like they wear their neckties, for show. I shall always re-member Lewis for saying his beard was part of him. Isn't it curious, the way he rides? He seems to sink himself in the horse. When I speak to him, I'm not sure whether I'm speaking to a man or to a horse.'

A few days later, Rico himself appeared on St. Mawr, for the morning ride. He rode self-consciously, as he did everything, and he was just a little nervous. But his mother-in-law was benevolent. She made him ride between her and Lou, like three ships slowly sailing abreast.

And that very day, who should come driving in an open carriage through the Park but the Queen Mother! Dear old Queen Alexandra, there was a flutter everywhere. And she bowed expressly to Rico, mistaking him, no doubt, for somebody else.

'Do you know,' said Rico as they sat at lunch, he and Lou and Mrs. Witt, in Mrs. Witt's sitting-room in the dark, quiet hotel in Mayfair, 'I really like riding St. Mawr so much. He really is a noble animal.—If ever I am made a Lord—which heaven forbid!—I shall be Lord St. Mawr.'

'You mean,' said Mrs. Witt, 'his real lordship would be the horse?'

'Very possible, I admit,' said Rico, with a curl of his long upper lip.

'Don't you think, mother,' said Lou, 'there is something quite noble about St. Mawr? He strikes me as the first noble thing I have ever seen.'

'Certainly I've not seen any *man* that could compare with him. Because these English noblemen—well! I'd rather look at a Negro Pullman-boy, if I was looking for what *I* call nobility.'

Poor Rico was getting crosser and crosser. There was a devil in Mrs. Witt. She had a hard, bright devil inside her, that she seemed to be able to let loose at will.

She let it loose the next day, when Rico and Lou joined her in the Row. She was silent but deadly with the horses, balking them in every way. She suddenly crowded over against the rail, in front of St. Mawr, so that the stallion had to rear to pull himself up. Then, having a clear track, she suddenly set off at a gallop, like an explosion, and the stallion, all on edge, set off after her.

It seemed as if the whole Park, that morning, were in a state of nervous tension. Perhaps there was thunder in the air. But St. Mawr kept on dancing and pulling at the bit, and wheeling sideways up against the railing, to the terror of the children and the onlookers, who squealed and jumped back suddenly, sending the nerves of the stallion into a rush like rockets. He reared and fought as Rico pulled him round.

Then he went on: dancing, pulling, springily progressing sideways, possessed with all the demons of perversity. Poor Rico's face grew longer and angrier. A fury rose in him, which he could hardly control. He hated his horse, and viciously tried to force him to a quiet, straight trot. Up went St. Mawr on his hind legs, to the terror of the Row. He got the bit in his teeth, and began to fight.

But Phœnix, cleverly, was in front of him.

'You get off, Rico!' called Mrs. Witt's voice, with all the calm of her wicked exultance.

And almost before he knew what he was doing, Rico had sprung lightly to the ground, and was hanging on to the bridle of the rearing stallion.

Phœnix also lightly jumped down, and ran to St. Mawr, handing his bridle to Rico. Then began a dancing and a splashing, a rearing and a plunging. St. Mawr was being wicked. But Phœnix, the indifference of conflict in his face, sat tight and immovable, without any emotion, only the heaviness of his impersonal will settling down like a weight, all the time, on the horse. There was, perhaps, a curious barbaric exultance in bare, dark will devoid of emotion or personal feeling.

So they had a little display in the Row for almost five minutes, the brilliant horse rearing and fighting. Rico, with a stiff long face, scrambled on to Phœnix's horse, and withdrew to a safe distance. Policemen came, and an officious mounted police rode up to save the situation. But it was obvious that Phœnix, detached and apparently unconcerned, but barbarically potent in his will, would bring the horse to order.

Which he did, and rode the creature home. Rico was requested not to ride St. Mawr in the Row any more, as the stallion was dangerous to public safety. The authorities knew all about him.

Where ended the first fiasco of St. Mawr.

'We didn't get on very well with his lordship this morning,' said Mrs. Witt triumphantly.

'No, he didn't like his company *at all!*' Rico snarled back.

He wanted Lou to sell the horse again.

'I doubt if anyone would buy him, dear,' she said. 'He's a known character.'

'Then make a gift of him—to your mother,' said Rico with venom.

'Why to mother?' asked Lou innocently.

'She might be able to cope with him—or he with her!' The last phrase was deadly. Having delivered it, Rico departed.

Lou remained at a loss. She felt almost always a little bit dazed, as if she could not see clear nor feel clear. A curious deadness upon her, like the first touch of death. And through this cloud of numbness, or deadness, came all her muted experiences.

Why was it? She did not know. But she felt that in some way it came from a battle of wills. Her mother, Rico, herself, it was always an unspoken, unconscious battle of wills, which was gradually numbing and paralysing her. She knew Rico meant nothing but kindness by her. She knew her mother only wanted to watch over her. Yet always there was this tension of will, that was so numbing. As if at the depths of him, Rico were always angry, though he seemed so 'happy' on the top. And Mrs. Witt was organically angry. So they were like a couple of bombs, timed to explode some day, but ticking on like two ordinary timepieces in the meanwhile.

She had come definitely to realize this: that Rico's anger was wound up tight at the bottom of him, like a steel spring that kept his works going, while he himself was 'charming,' like a bomb-clock with Sèvres paintings or Dresden figures on the outside. But his very charm was a sort of anger, and his love was a destruction in itself. He just couldn't help it.

And she? Perhaps she was a good deal the same herself. Wound up tight inside, and enjoying herself being 'lovely.' But wound up tight on some tension that, she realized now with wonder, was really a sort of anger. This, the mainspring that drove her on the round of 'joys.'

She used really to enjoy the tension, and the *élan* [23] it gave her. While she knew nothing about it. So long as she felt it really was life and happiness, this *élan*, this tension and excitement of 'enjoying oneself.'

Now suddenly she doubted the whole show. She attributed to it the curious numbness that was overcoming her, as if she couldn't feel any more.

She wanted to come unwound. She wanted to escape this battle of wills.

Only St. Mawr gave her some hint of the possibility. He was so powerful, and so dangerous. But in his dark eye, that looked, with its cloudy brown pupil, a cloud within a dark fire, like a world beyond our world, there was a dark vitality glowing, and within the fire, another sort of wisdom. She felt sure of it: even when he put his ears back, and bared his teeth, and his great eyes came bolting out of his naked horse's head, and she saw demons upon demons in the chaos of his horrid eyes.

Why did he seem to her like some living background, into which she wanted to retreat? When he reared his head and neighed from his deep chest, like deep wind-bells resounding, she seemed to hear the echoes of another darker, more spacious, more dangerous, more splendid world than ours, that was beyond her. And there she wanted to go.

23. Drive, lift.

She kept it utterly a secret, to herself. Because Rico would just have lifted his long upper lip, in his bare face, in a condescending sort of 'understanding.' And her mother would, as usual, have suspected her of sidestepping. People, all the people she knew, seemed so entirely contained within their cardboard let's-be-happy world. Their wills were fixed like machines on happiness, or fun, or the-best-ever. This ghastly cheery-o! touch, that made all her blood go numb.

Since she had really seen St. Mawr looming fiery and terrible in an outer darkness, she could not believe the world she lived in. She could not believe it was actually happening, when she was dancing in the afternoon at Claridge's, or in the evening at the Carlton, sliding about with some suave young man who wasn't like a man at all to her. Or down in Sussex for the week-end with the Enderleys: the talk, the eating and drinking, the flirtation, the endless dancing: it all seemed far more bodiless and, in a strange way, wraith-like, than any fairy-story. She seemed to be eating Barmecide [24] food, that had been conjured up out of thin air, by the power of words. She seemed to be talking to handsome young bare-faced unrealities, not men at all: as she slid about with them, in the perpetual dance, they too seemed to have been conjured up out of air, merely for this soaring, slithering dance-business. And she could not believe that, when the lights went out, they wouldn't melt back into thin air again, and complete nonentity. The strange nonentity of it all! Everything just conjured up, and nothing real. *Isn't this the best ever!* they would beamingly assert, like the wraiths of enjoyment, without any genuine substance. And she would beam back: *Lots of fun!*

She was thankful the season was over and everybody was leaving London. She and Rico were due to go to Scotland, but not till August. In the meantime they would go to her mother.

Mrs. Witt had taken a cottage in Shropshire, on the Welsh border, and had moved down there with Phœnix and her horses. The open, heather-and-bilberry-covered hills were splendid for riding.

Rico consented to spend the month in Shropshire, because for near neighbours Mrs. Witt had the Manbys, at Corrabach Hall. The Manbys were rich Australians returned to the old country and set up as Squires, all in full blow. Rico had known them in Victoria: they were of good family: and the girls made a great fuss of him.

So down went Lou and Rico, Lewis, Poppy and St. Mawr, to Shrewsbury, then out into the country. Mrs. Witt's 'cottage' was a tall red-brick Georgian house looking straight on to the churchyard, and the dark, looming big church.

'I never knew what a comfort it would be,' said Mrs. Witt, 'to have gravestones under my drawing-room windows, and funerals for lunch.'

She really did take a strange pleasure in sitting in her panelled room, that was painted grey, and watching the Dean or one of the curates officiating at the graveside, among a group of black country mourners with black-bordered handkerchiefs luxuriantly in use.

'Mother!' said Lou. 'I think it's gruesome!'

24. An illusory banquet served by a prince of the Barmecide family to a poor man (*Arabian Nights*).

She had a room at the back, looking over the walled garden and the stables. Nevertheless there was the *boom! boom!* of the passing-bell, and the chiming and pealing on Sundays. The shadow of the church, indeed! A very audible shadow, making itself heard insistently.

The Dean was a big, burly fat man with a pleasant manner. He was a gentleman, and a man of learning in his own line. But he let Mrs. Witt know that he looked down on her just a trifle—as a parvenu American, a Yankee—though she never was a Yankee: and at the same time he had a sincere respect for her, as a rich woman. Yes, a sincere respect for her, as a rich woman.

Lou knew that every Englishman, especially of the upper classes, has a wholesome respect for riches. But then, who hasn't?

The Dean was more *impressed* by Mrs. Witt than by little Lou. But to Lady Carrington he was charming: she was *almost* 'one of us,' you know. And he was very gracious to Rico: 'your father's splendid colonial service.'

Mrs. Witt had now a new pantomime to amuse her: the Georgian house, her own pew in church—it went with the old house: a village of thatched cottages—some of them with corrugated iron over the thatch: the cottage people, farm labourers and their families, with a few, very few, outsiders: the wicked little group of cottages down at Mile End, famous for ill living. The Mile-Enders were all Allisons and Jephsons, and inbred, the Dean said: result of working through the centuries at the quarry, and living isolated there at Mile End.

Isolated! Imagine it! A mile and a half from the railway station, ten miles from Shrewsbury. Mrs. Witt thought of Texas, and said:

'Yes, they are *very* isolated, away down there!'

And the Dean never for a moment suspected sarcasm.

But there she had the whole thing staged complete for her: English village life. Even miners breaking in to shatter the rather stuffy, unwholesome harmony.—All the men touched their caps to her, all the women did a bit of a reverence, the children stood aside for her, if she appeared in the street.

They were all poor again: the labourers could no longer afford even a glass of beer in the evenings, since the Glorious War.

'Now I think that *is* terrible,' said Mrs. Witt. 'Not to be able to get away from those stuffy, squalid, picturesque cottages for an hour in the evening, to drink a glass of beer.'

'It's a pity, I do agree with you, Mrs. Witt. But Mr. Watson has organized a men's reading-room, where the men can smoke and play dominoes, and read if they wish.'

'But that,' said Mrs. Witt, 'is not the same as that cosy parlour in the "Moon and Stars".'

'I quite agree,' said the Dean. 'It isn't.'

Mrs. Witt marched to the landlord of the 'Moon and Stars,' and asked for a glass of cider.

'I want,' she said, in her American accent, 'these poor labourers to have their glass of beer in the evenings.'

'They want it themselves,' said Harvey.

'Then they must have it—'

The upshot was, she decided to supply one large barrel of beer per week and the landlord was to sell it to the labourers at a penny a glass.

'My own country has gone dry,' she asserted. 'But not because we can't *afford* it.'

By the time Lou and Rico appeared, she was deep in. She actually interfered very little: the barrel of beer was her one public act. But she *did* know everybody by sight, already, and she *did* know everybody's circumstances. And she had attended one prayer-meeting, one mother's meeting, one sewing-bee, one 'social,' one Sunday School meeting, one Band of Hope meeting, and one Sunday School treat. She ignored the poky little Wesleyan and Baptist chapels, and was true-blue Episcopalian.

'How strange these picturesque old villages are, Louise!' she said, with a duskiness around her sharp, well-bred nose. 'How *easy* it all seems, all on a definite pattern. And how false! And underneath, *how corrupt!*'

She gave that queer, triumphant leer from her grey eyes, and queer demonish wrinkles seemed to twitter on her face.

Lou shrank away. She was beginning to be afraid of her mother's insatiable curiosity, that always looked for the snake under the flowers. Or rather, for the maggots.

Always this same morbid interest in other people and their doings, their privacies, their dirty linen. Always this air of alertness for personal happenings, personalities, personalities, personalities. Always this subtle criticism and appraisal of other people, this analysis of other people's motives. If anatomy presupposes a corpse, then psychology presupposes a world of corpses. Personalities, which means personal criticism and analysis, presupposes a whole world-laboratory of human psyches waiting to be vivisected. If you cut a thing up, of course it will smell. Hence, nothing raises such an infernal stink, at last, as human psychology.

Mrs. Witt was a pure psychologist, a fiendish psychologist. And Rico, in his way, was a psychologist too. But he had a formula. 'Let's *know* the worst, dear! But let's look on the bright side, and believe the best.'

'Isn't the Dean a priceless old darling!' said Rico at breakfast.

And it had begun. Work had started in the psychic vivisection laboratory.

'Isn't he wonderful!' said Lou vaguely.

'So delightfully worldly!—*Some of us are not born to make money, dear boy. Luckily for us, we can marry it.*'—Rico made a priceless face.

'Is Mrs. Vyner so rich?' asked Lou.

'She is, quite a wealthy woman—in coal,' replied Mrs. Witt. 'But the Dean is surely worth his weight, even in gold. And he's a massive figure. I can imagine there would be great satisfaction in having him for a husband.'

'Why, mother?' asked Lou.

'Oh, such a presence! One of these old Englishmen, that nobody can put in their pocket. You can't imagine his wife asking him to thread her needle. Something, after all, so *robust!* So different from *young* Englishmen, who all seem to me like ladies, perfect ladies.'

'*Somebody* has to keep up the tradition of the perfect lady,' said Rico.

'I know it,' said Mrs. Witt. 'And if the women won't do it, the young gentlemen take on the burden. They bear it very well.'

It was in full swing, the cut and thrust. And poor Lou, who had reached the point of stupefaction in the game, felt she did not know what to do with herself.

Rico and Mrs. Witt were deadly enemies, yet neither could keep clear of the other. It might have been they who were married to one another, their duel and their duet were so relentless.

But Rico immediately started the social round: first the Manbys: then motor twenty miles to luncheon at Lady Tewkesbury's: then young Mr. Burns came flying down in his aeroplane from Chester: then they must motor to the sea, to Sir Edward Edwards' place, where there was a moonlight bathing-party. Everything intensely thrilling, and so innerly wearisome, Lou felt.

But back of it all was St. Mawr, looming like a bonfire in the dark. He really was a tiresome horse to own. He worried the mares, if they were in the same paddock with him, always driving them round. And with any other horse he just fought with definite intent to kill. So he had to stay alone.

'That St. Mawr, he's a bad horse,' said Phœnix.

'Maybe!' said Lewis.

'You don't like quiet horses?' said Phœnix.

'Most horses *is* quiet,' said Lewis. 'St. Mawr, he's different.'

'Why don't he never get any foals?'

'Doesn't want to, I should think. Same as me.'

'What good is a horse like that? Better shoot him, before he kill somebody.'

'What good'll they get, shooting St. Mawr?' said Lewis.

'If he kills somebody!' said Phœnix.

But there was no answer.

The two grooms both lived over the stables, and Lou, from her window, saw a good deal of them. They were two quiet men, yet she was very much aware of their presence, aware of Phœnix's rather high square shoulders and his fine, straight, vigorous black hair that tended to stand up assertively on his head, as he went quietly drifting about his various jobs. He was not lazy, but he did everything with a sort of diffidence, as if from a distance, and handled his horses carefully, cautiously, and cleverly, but without sympathy. He seemed to be holding something back, all the time, unconsciously, as if in his very being there was some secret. But it was a secret of *will*. His quiet, reluctant movements, as if he never really wanted to do anything; his long flat-stepping stride; the permanent challenge in his high cheek-bones, the Indian glint in his eyes, and his peculiar stare, watchful and yet unseeing, made him unpopular with the women servants.

Nevertheless, women had a certain fascination for him: he would stare at the pretty young maids with an intent blank stare, when they were not looking. Yet he was rather overbearing, domineering with them, and they resented him. It was evident to Lou that he looked upon himself as belonging to the Master, not to the servant class. When he flirted with the maids, as he very often did, for he had a certain crude ostentatiousness, he seemed to let them feel that he despised them as inferiors, servants, while he admired their pretty charms, as fresh country maids.

'I'm fair nervous of that Phœnix,' said Fanny, the fair-haired maid. 'He makes you feel what he'd do to you if he could.'

'He'd better not try with me,' said Mabel. 'I'd scratch his cheeky eyes out. Cheek!—for it's nothing else! He's nobody—common as they're made!'

'He makes you feel you was there for him to trample on,' said Fanny.

'Mercy, you *are* soft! If anybody's that, it's him. Oh, my, Fanny, you've no right to let a fellow make you feel like *that!* Make *them* feel that *they're* dirt, for *you* to trample on: which they are!'

Fanny, however, being a shy little blond thing, wasn't good at assuming the trampling rôle. She was definitely nervous of Phœnix. And he enjoyed it. An invisible smile seemed to creep up his cheek-bones, and the glint moved in his eyes as he teased her. He tormented her by his very presence, as he knew.

He would come silently up when she was busy, and stand behind her perfectly still, so that she was unaware of his presence. Then, silently, he would *make* her aware. Till she glanced nervously round and, with a scream, saw him.

One day Lou watched this little play. Fanny had been picking over a bowl of black currants, sitting on the bench under the maple tree in a corner of the yard. She didn't look round till she had picked up her bowl to go to the kitchen. Then there was a scream and a crash.

When Lou came out, Phœnix was crouching down silently gathering up the currants, which the little maid, scarlet and trembling, was collecting into another bowl. Phœnix seemed to be smiling down his back.

'Phœnix!' said Lou. 'I wish you wouldn't startle Fanny!'

He looked up, and she saw the glint of ridicule in his eyes.

'Who, me?' he said.

'Yes, you. You go up behind Fanny, to startle her. You're not to do it.'

He slowly stood erect, and lapsed into his peculiar invisible silence. Only for a second his eyes glanced at Lou's, and then she saw the cold anger, the gleam of malevolence and contempt. He could not bear being commanded, or reprimanded, by a woman.

Yet it was even worse with a man.

'What's that, Lou?' said Rico, appearing all handsome and in the picture, in white flannels with an apricot silk shirt.

'I'm telling Phœnix he's not to torment Fanny!'

'Oh!' and Rico's voice immediately became his father's, the important government official's. 'Certainly *not!* Most certainly *not!*' He looked at the scattered currants and the broken bowl. Fanny melted into tears. 'This, I suppose, is some of the results! Now look here, Phœnix, you're to leave the maids strictly alone. I shall ask them to report to me whenever, or *if* ever, you interfere with them. But I hope you *won't* interfere with them—in any way. You understand?'

As Rico became more and more Sir Henry and the government official, Lou's bones melted more and more into discomfort. Phœnix stood in his peculiar silence, the invisible smile on his cheek-bones.

'You understand what I'm saying to you?' Rico demanded, in intensified acid tones.

But Phœnix only stood there, as it were behind a cover of his own will, and looked back at Rico with a faint smile on his face and the glint moving in his eyes.

'Do you intend to answer?' Rico's upper lip lifted nastily.

'Mrs. Witt is my boss,' came from Phœnix.

The scarlet flew up Rico's throat and flushed his face, his eyes went glaucous. Then quickly his face turned yellow.

Lou looked at the two men: her husband, whose rages, over-controlled, were organically terrible; the half-breed, whose dark-coloured lips were widened in a faint smile of derision, but in whose eyes caution and hate were playing against one another. She realized that Phœnix would accept *her* reprimand, or her mother's, because he could despise the two of them as mere women. But Rico's bossiness aroused murder pure and simple.

She took her husband's arm.

'Come, dear!' she said, in her half-plaintive way. 'I'm sure Phœnix understands. We all understand. Go to the kitchen, Fanny, never mind the currants. There are plenty more in the garden.'

Rico was always thankful to be drawn quickly, submissively away from his own rage. He was afraid of it. He was afraid lest he should fly at the groom in some horrible fashion. The very thought horrified him. But in actuality he came very near to it.

He walked stiffly, feeling paralysed by his own fury. And those words, *Mrs. Witt is my boss*, were like hot acid in his brain. An insult!

'By the way, Belle-Mère!' [25] he said when they joined Mrs. Witt—she hated being called Belle-Mère, and once said: 'If I'm the bell-mare, are you one of the colts?'—she also hated his voice of smothered fury—'I had to speak to Phœnix about persecuting the maids. He took the liberty of informing me that you were his boss, so perhaps you had better speak to him.'

'I certainly will. I believe they're my maids, and nobody else's, so it's my duty to look after them. Who was he persecuting?'

'I'm the responsible one, mother,' said Lou—

Rico disappeared in a moment. He must get out: get away from the house. How? Something was wrong with the car. Yet he must get away, away. He would go over to Corrabach. He would ride St. Mawr. He had been talking about the horse, and Flora Manby was dying to see him. She had said: 'Oh, I can't *wait* to see that marvellous horse of yours.'

He would ride him over. It was only seven miles. He found Lou's maid Flena, and sent her to tell Lewis. Meanwhile, to soothe himself, he dressed himself most carefully in white riding-breeches and a shirt of purple silk crêpe, with a flowing black tie spotted red like a ladybird, and black riding-boots. Then he took a *chic* little white hat with a black band.

St. Mawr was saddled and waiting, and Lewis had saddled a second horse.

'Thanks, Lewis, I'm going alone!' said Rico.

This was the first time he had ridden St. Mawr in the country, and he was nervous. But he was also in the hell of a smothered fury. All his careful dressing had not really soothed him. So his fury consumed his nervousness.

He mounted with a swing, blind and rough. St. Mawr reared.

'Stop that!' snarled Rico, and put him to the gate.

Once out in the village street, the horse went dancing sideways. He insisted on dancing at the sidewalk, to the exaggerated terror of the children. Rico, exasperated, pulled him across. But no, he wouldn't go down the centre of the village street. He began dancing and edging on to the other sidewalk, so the foot-passengers fled into the shops in terror.

The devil was in him. He would turn down every turning where he was not

25. Mother-in-law.

meant to go. He reared with panic at a furniture van. He *insisted* on going down the wrong side of the road. Rico was riding him with a martingale, and he could see the rolling, bloodshot eye.

'Damn you, *go!*' said Rico, giving him a dig with the spurs.

And away they went, down the high road, in a thunderbolt. It was a hot day, with thunder threatening, so Rico was soon in a flame of heat. He held on tight, with fixed eyes, trying all the time to rein in the horse. What he really was afraid of was that the brute would shy suddenly, as he galloped. Watching for this, he didn't care when they sailed past the turning to Corrabach.

St. Mawr flew on, in a sort of *élan*. Marvellous, the power and life in the creature! There was really a great joy in the motion. If only he wouldn't take the corners at a gallop, nearly swerving Rico off! Luckily the road was clear. To ride, to ride at this terrific gallop, on into eternity!

After several miles, the horse slowed down, and Rico managed to pull him into a lane that might lead to Corrabach. When all was said and done, it was a wonderful ride. St. Mawr could go like the wind, but with that luxurious heavy ripple of life which is like nothing else on earth. It seemed to carry one at once into another world, away from the life of the nerves.

So Rico arrived after all something of a conqueror at Corrabach. To be sure, he was perspiring, and so was his horse. But he was a hero from another, heroic world.

'Oh, such a hot ride!' he said, as he walked on to the lawn at Corrabach Hall. 'Between the sun and the horse, really!—between two fires!'

'Don't you trouble, you're looking dandy, a bit hot and flushed like,' said Flora Manby. 'Let's go and see your horse.'

And her exclamation was: 'Oh, he's *lovely!* He's *fine!* I'd love to try him once—'

Rico decided to accept the invitation to stay overnight at Corrabach. Usually he was very careful, and refused to stay, unless Lou was with him. But they telephoned to the post office at Chomesbury, would Mr. Jones please send a message to Lady Carrington that Sir Henry was staying the night at Corrabach Hall, but would be home next day? Mr. Jones received the request with unction, and said he would go over himself to give the message to Lady Carrington.

Lady Carrington was in the walled garden. The peculiarity of Mrs. Witt's house was that, for grounds proper, it had the churchyard.

'I never thought, Louise, that one day I should have an old English churchyard for my lawns and shrubbery and park, and funeral mourners for my herds of deer. It's curious. For the first time in my life a funeral has become a real thing to me. I feel I could write a book on them.'

But Louise only felt intimidated.

At the back of the house was a flagged court-yard, with stables and a maple tree in a corner, and big doors opening on to the village street. But at the side was a walled garden, with fruit trees and currant bushes and a great bed of rhubarb, and some tufts of flowers, peonies, pink roses, sweet-williams. Phœnix, who had a certain taste for gardening, would be out there thinning the carrots or tying up the lettuce. He was not lazy. Only he would not take work seriously, as a job. He would be quite amused tying up lettuce, and would tie up head after head, quite prettily. Then, becoming bored, he would abandon his task, light a cigarette, and go and stand on the threshold of the big doors, in full view of the street, watching, and yet completely indifferent.

After Rico's departure on St. Mawr, Lou went into the garden. And there she saw Phœnix working in the onion-bed. He was bending over, in his own silence, busy with nimble, amused fingers among the grassy young onions. She thought he had not seen her, so she went down another path to where a swing bed hung under the apple trees. There she sat with a book and a bundle of magazines. But she did not read.

She was musing vaguely. Vaguely, she was glad that Rico was away for a while. Vaguely, she felt a sense of bitterness, of complete futility: the complete futility of her living. This left her drifting in a sea of utter chagrin. And Rico seemed to her the symbol of the futility. Vaguely, she was aware that something else existed, but she didn't know where it was or what it was.

In the distance she could see Phœnix's dark, rather tall-built head, with its black, fine, intensely living hair tending to stand on end, like a brush with long, very fine black bristles. His hair, she thought, betrayed him as an animal of a different species. He was growing a little bored by weeding onions: that also she could tell. Soon he would want some other amusement.

Presently Lewis appeared. He was small, energetic, a little bit bow-legged, and he walked with a slight strut. He wore khaki riding-breeches, leather gaiters, and a blue shirt. And, like Phœnix, he rarely had any cap or hat on his head. His thick black hair was parted at the side and brushed over heavily sideways, dropping on his forehead at the right. It was very long, a real mop, under which his eyebrows were dark and steady.

'Seen Lady Carrington?' he asked of Phœnix.

'Yes, she's sitting on that swing over there—she's been there quite a while.'

The wretch—he had seen her from the very first!

Lewis came striding over, looking towards her with his pale-grey eyes, from under his mop of hair.

'Mr. Jones from the post office wants to see you, my Lady, with a message from Sir Henry.'

Instantly alarm took possession of Lou's soul.

'Oh!—Does he want to see me personally?—What message? Is anything wrong?'—And her voice trailed out over the last word, with a sort of anxious nonchalance.

'I don't think it's anything amiss,' said Lewis reassuringly.

'Oh! You don't'—the relief came into her voice. Then she looked at Lewis with a slight, winning smile in her unmatched eyes. 'I'm so afraid of St. Mawr, you know.' Her voice was soft and cajoling. Phœnix was listening in the distance.

'St. Mawr's all right, if you don't do nothing to him,' Lewis replied.

'I'm sure he is!—But how is one to know when one is doing something to him?—Tell Mr. Jones to come here, please,' she concluded, on a changed tone.

Mr. Jones, a man of forty-five, thickset, with a fresh complexion and rather foolish brown eyes, and a big brown moustache, came prancing down the path, smiling rather fatuously, and doffing his straw hat with a gorgeous bow the moment he saw Lou sitting in her slim white frock on the coloured swing bed under the trees with their hard green apples.

'Good morning, Mr. Jones!'

'Good morning, Lady Carrington.—If I may say so, what a picture you make —a beautiful picture—'

He beamed under his big brown moustache like the greatest lady-killer.

'Do I! Did Sir Henry say he was all right?'

'He didn't *say* exactly, but I should expect he is all right—' and Mr. Jones delivered his message, in the mayonnaise of his own unction.

'Thank you so much, Mr. Jones. It's awfully good of you to come and tell me. Now I shan't worry about Sir Henry *at all.*'

'It's a great pleasure to come and deliver a satisfactory message to Lady Carrington. But it won't be kind to Sir Henry if you don't worry about him *at all* in his absence. We all enjoy being worried about by those we love—so long as there is nothing to worry about of course!'

'Quite!' said Lou. 'Now won't you take a glass of port and a biscuit, or a whisky and soda? And thank you ever so much.'

'Thank *you*, my Lady. I might drink a whisky and soda, since you are so good.'

And he beamed fatuously.

'Let Mr. Jones mix himself a whisky and soda, Lewis,' said Lou.

'Heavens!' she thought, as the postmaster retreated a little uncomfortably down the garden path, his bald spot passing in and out of the sun, under the trees. 'How ridiculous everything is, how ridiculous, ridiculous!' Yet she didn't really dislike Mr. Jones and his interlude.

Phœnix was melting away out of the garden. He had to follow the fun.

'Phœnix!' Lou called. 'Bring me a glass of water, will you? Or send somebody with it.'

He stood in the path looking round at her.

'All right!' he said.

And he turned away again.

She did not like being alone in the garden. She liked to have the men working somewhere near. Curious how pleasant it was to sit there in the garden when Phœnix was about, or Lewis. It made her feel she could never be lonely or jumpy. But when Rico was there, she was all aching nerve.

Phœnix came back with a glass of water, lemon juice, sugar, and a small bottle of brandy. He knew Lou liked a spoonful of brandy in her iced lemonade.

'How thoughtful of you, Phœnix!' she said. 'Did Mr. Jones get his whisky?'

'He was just getting it.'

'That's right.—By the way, Phœnix, I wish you wouldn't get mad if Sir Henry speaks to you. He is *really* so kind.'

She looked up at the man. He stood there watching her in silence, the invisible smile on his face, and the inscrutable Indian glint moving in his eyes. What was he thinking? There was something passive and almost submissive about him, but, underneath this, an unyielding resistance and cruelty: yes, even cruelty. She felt that, on top, he was submissive and attentive, bringing her her lemonade as she liked it, without being told: thinking for her quite subtly. But underneath there was an unchanging hatred. He submitted circumstantially, he worked for a wage. And, even circumstantially, he *liked* his mistress—*la patrona*—and her daughter. But much deeper than any circumstance, or any circumstantial liking, was the categorical hatred upon which he was founded, and with which he was powerless. His liking for Lou and for Mrs. Witt, his serving them and working for a wage, was all side-tracking his own nature, which was grounded on hatred of their very existence. But what was he to do? He had to live. Therefore he had to serve, to work for a wage, and even to be faithful.

And yet *their* existence made his own existence negative. If he was to exist, positively, they would have to cease to exist. At the same time, a fatal sort of tolerance made him serve these women, and go on serving.

'Sir Henry is *so* kind to everybody,' Lou insisted.

The half-breed met her eyes, and smiled uncomfortably.

'Yes, he's a kind man,' he replied, as if sincerely.

'Then why do you mind if he speaks to you?'

'I don't mind,' said Phœnix glibly.

'But you do. Or else you wouldn't make him so angry.'

'Was he angry?—I don't know,' said Phœnix.

'He was very angry. And you *do* know.'

'No, I don't know if he's angry. I don't know,' the fellow persisted. And there was a glib sort of satisfaction in his tone.

'That's awfully unkind of you, Phœnix,' she said, growing offended in her turn.

'No, I don't know if he's angry. I don't want to make him angry. I don't know—'

He had taken on a tone of naïve ignorance, which at once gratified her pride as a woman, and deceived her.

'Well, you believe me when I tell you you *did* make him angry, don't you?'

'Yes, I believe when you tell me.'

'And you promise me, won't you, not to do it again? It's *so* bad for him— so bad for his nerves, and for his eyes. It makes them inflamed, and injures his eyesight. And you know, as an artist, it's terrible if anything happens to his eyesight—'

Phœnix was watching her closely, to take it in. He still was not good at understanding continuous, logical statement. Logical connection in speech seemed to stupefy him, make him stupid. He understood in disconnected assertions of fact. But he had gathered what she said. 'He gets mad at you. When he gets mad, it hurts his eyes. His eyes hurt him. He can't see, because his eyes hurt him. He want to paint a picture, he can't. He can't paint a picture, he can't see clear—'

Yes, he had understood. She saw he had understood. The bright glint of satisfaction moved in his eyes.

'So now promise me, won't you, you won't make him mad again: you won't make him angry?'

'No, I won't make him angry. I don't do anything to make him angry,' Phœnix answered, rather glibly.

'And you do understand, don't you? You know how kind he is: how he'd do a good turn to anybody?'

'Yes, he's a kind man,' said Phœnix.

'I'm so glad you realize.—There, that's luncheon! How nice it is to sit here in the garden, when everybody is nice to you! No, I can carry the tray, don't you bother.'

But he took the tray from her hand, and followed her to the house. And as he walked behind her, he watched the slim white nape of her neck, beneath the clustering of her bobbed hair, something as a stoat watches a rabbit he is following.

In the afternoon Lou retreated once more to her place in the garden. There she lay, sitting with a bunch of pillows behind her, neither reading nor working, just musing. She had learned the new joy: to do absolutely nothing, but to lie and let the sunshine filter through the leaves, to see the bunch of red-hot-poker flowers pierce scarlet into the afternoon, beside the comparative neutrality of some foxgloves. The mere colour of hard red, like the big oriental poppies that had fallen, and these poker flowers, lingered in her consciousness like a communication.

Into this peaceful indolence, when even the big, dark-grey tower of the church beyond the wall and the yew trees was keeping its bells in silence, advanced Mrs. Witt, in a broad panama hat and the white dress.

'Don't you want to ride, or do something, Louise?' she asked ominously.

'Don't you want to be peaceful, mother?' retorted Louise.

'Yes—an *active* peace.—I can't *believe* that my daughter can be content to lie on a hammock and do *nothing*, not even read or improve her mind, the greater part of the day.'

'Well, your daughter *is* content to do that. It's her greatest pleasure.'

'I know it. I can see it. And it surprises me *very* much. When I was your age, I was never still. I had so much go—'

> ' "Those maids, thank God,
> Are 'neath the sod,
> And all their generation." [26]

'No, but mother, I only take life differently. Perhaps you used up that sort of *go*. I'm the harem type, mother: only I never want the men inside the lattice.'

'Are you really my daughter?—Well! A woman never knows what will happen to her.—I'm an *American* woman, and I suppose I've got to remain one, no matter where I am.—What did you want, Lewis?'

The groom had approached down the path.

'If I am to saddle Poppy?' said Lewis.

'No, apparently *not!*' replied Mrs. Witt. 'Your mistress prefers the hammock to the saddle.'

'Thank you, Lewis. What mother says is true this afternoon, at least.' And she gave him a peculiar little cross-eyed smile.

'Who,' said Mrs. Witt to the man, 'has been cutting at your hair?'

There was a moment of silent resentment.

'I did it myself, Mam! Sir Henry said it was too long.'

'He certainly spoke the truth.—But I believe there's a barber in the village on Saturdays—or you could ride over to Shrewsbury.—Just turn round, and let me look at the back. Is it the money?'

'No, Mam. I don't like these fellows touching my head.'

He spoke coldly, with a certain hostile reserve that at once piqued Mrs. Witt.

26. From an early lyric by William Carlos Williams (1883–1963).

'Don't you really!' she said. 'But it's quite *impossible* for you to go about as you are. It gives you a half-witted appearance. Go now into the yard, and get a chair and dust-sheet. I'll cut your hair.'

The man hesitated, hostile.

'Don't be afraid, I know how it's done. I've cut the hair of many a poor wounded boy in hospital: and shaved them too. *You've got such a touch, nurse!* Poor fellow, he was dying, though none of us knew it.—Those are compliments I value, Louise.—Get that chair now, and a dust-sheet. I'll borrow your hair-scissors from Elena, Louise.'

Mrs. Witt, happily on the war path, was herself again. She didn't care for work, actual work. But she loved trimming. She loved arranging unnatural and pretty salads, devising new and piquant-looking ice-creams, having a turkey stuffed exactly as she knew a stuffed turkey in Louisiana, with chestnuts and butter and stuff, or showing a servant how to turn waffles on a waffle-iron, or to bake a ham with brown sugar and cloves and a moistening of rum. She liked pruning rose trees, or beginning to cut a yew-hedge into shape. She liked ordering her own and Louise's shoes, with an exactitude and a knowledge of shoe-making that sent the salesmen crazy. She was a demon in shoes. Reappearing from America, she would pounce on her daughter. 'Louise, throw those shoes away. Give them to one of the maids.'—'But, mother, they are some of the best French shoes. I like them.'—'Throw them away. A shoe has only two excuses for existing: perfect comfort or perfect appearance. Those have neither. I have brought you some shoes.'—Yes, she had brought ten pairs of shoes from New York. She knew her daughter's foot as she knew her own.

So now she was in her element, looming behind Lewis as he sat in the middle of the yard swathed in a dust-sheet. She had on an overall and a pair of wash-leather gloves, and she poised a pair of long scissors like one of the Fates.[27] In her big hat she looked curiously young, but with the youth of a bygone generation. Her heavy-lidded, laconic grey eyes were alert, studying the groom's black mop of hair. Her eyebrows made thin, uptilting black arches on her brow. Her fresh skin was slightly powdered, and she was really handsome, in a bold, bygone, eighteenth-century style. Some of the curious, adventurous stoicism of the eighteenth century: and then a certain blatant American efficiency.

Lou, who had strayed into the yard to see, looked so much younger and so many thousands of years older than her mother, as she stood in her wisp-like diffidence, the clusters of grape-like bobbed hair hanging beside her face, with its fresh colouring and its ancient weariness, her slightly squinting eyes, that were so disillusioned they were becoming faun-like.

'Not too short, mother, not too short,' she remonstrated, as Mrs. Witt, with a terrific flourish of efficiency, darted at the man's black hair, and the thick flakes fell like black snow.

'Now, Louise, I'm right in this job, please don't interfere.—Two things I hate to see: a man with his wool in his neck and ears: and a bare-faced young man who looks as if he'd bought his face as well as his hair from a men's beauty-specialist.'

27. Of the three Fates Clotho held the distaff, Lachesis drew off the thread, and Atropos cut it; in this way they controlled each human life. One of the many passages associating Mrs. Witt with death.

And efficiently she bent down, clip—clip—clipping! while Lewis sat utterly immobile, with sunken head, in a sort of despair.

Phoenix stood against the stable door, with his restless, eternal cigarette. And in the kitchen doorway the maids appeared and fled, appeared and fled in delight. The old gardener, a fixture who went with the house, creaked in and stood with his legs apart, silent in intense condemnation.

'First time I ever see such a thing!' he muttered to himself, as he creaked on into the garden. He was a bad-tempered old soul, who thoroughly disapproved of the household, and would have given notice, but that he knew which side his bread was buttered: and there was butter unstinted on his bread, in Mrs. Witt's kitchen.

Mrs. Witt stood back to survey her handiwork, holding those terrifying shears with their beak erect. Lewis lifted his head and looked stealthily round, like a creature in a trap.

'Keep still!' she said. 'I haven't finished.'

And she went for his front hair, with vigour, lifting up long layers and snipping off the ends artistically: till at last he sat with a black aureole upon the floor, and his ears standing out with curious new alertness from the sides of his clean-clipped head.

'Stand up,' she said, 'and let me look.'

He stood up, looking absurdly young, with the hair all cut away from his neck and ears, left thick only on top. She surveyed her work with satisfaction.

'You look so much younger,' she said, 'you would be surprised. Sit down again.'

She clipped the back of his neck with the shears, and then, with a very slight hesitation, she said:

'Now about the beard!'

But the man rose suddenly from the chair, pulling the dust-cloth from his neck with desperation.

'No, I'll do that myself,' he said, looking her in the eyes with a cold light in his pale-grey, uncanny eyes.

She hesitated in a kind of wonder at his queer male rebellion.

'Now, listen, I shall do it much better than you—and besides,' she added hurriedly, snatching at the dust-cloth he was flinging on the chair, 'I haven't quite finished round the ears.'

'I think I shall do,' he said, again looking her in the eyes, with a cold, white gleam of finality. 'Thank you for what you've done.'

And he walked away to the stable.

'You'd better sweep up here,' Mrs. Witt called.

'Yes, Mam,' he replied, looking round at her again with an odd resentment, but continuing to walk away.

'However!' said Mrs. Witt. 'I suppose he'll do.'

And she divested herself of gloves and overall, and walked indoors to wash and to change. Lou went indoors too.

'It is extraordinary what hair that man has!' said Mrs. Witt. 'Did I tell you when I was in Paris I saw a woman's face in the hotel that I thought I knew? I couldn't place her, till she was coming towards me. *Aren't you Rachel Fannière?* she said. *Aren't you Janette Leroy?* We hadn't seen each other since we were girls of twelve and thirteen, at school in New Orleans. *Oh! she said to me. Is every illusion doomed to perish? You had such wonderful golden curls! All my life I've said: Oh, if only I had such lovely hair as Rachel Fannière! I've seen those beautiful golden curls of yours all my life. And now I meet you, you're grey!* Wasn't that terrible, Louise? Well, that man's hair made me think of it—so thick and curious. It's strange what a difference there is in hair, I suppose it's because he's just an animal—no mind! There's nothing I admire in a man like a good *mind*. Your father was a very clever man, and all the men I've admired have been clever. But isn't it curious now, I've never cared much to touch their hair. How strange life is! If it gives one thing, it takes away another.—And even those poor boys in hospital: I have shaved them, or cut their hair, like a mother, never thinking anything of it. Lovely, intelligent, clean boys most of them were. Yet it never did anything to me. I never knew before that something could happen to one from a person's *hair!* Like to Janette Leroy from my curls when I was a child. And now I'm grey, as she says.—I wonder how old a man Lewis is, Louise! Didn't he look absurdly young, with his ears pricking up?'

'I think Rico said he was forty or forty-one.'

'And never been married?'

'No—not as far as I know.'

'Isn't that curious now!—just an animal! no mind! A man with no mind! I've always thought that the *most* despicable thing. Yet such wonderful hair to touch. Your Henry has quite a good mind, yet I would simply shrink from touching his hair.—I suppose one likes stroking a cat's fur, just the same. Just the animal in man. Curious that I never seem to have met it, Louise. Now I come to think of it, he has the eyes of a human cat: a human tom-cat. Would you call him stupid? Yes, he's very stupid.'

'No, mother, he's not stupid. He only doesn't care about our sort of things.'

'Like an animal! But what a strange look he has in his eyes! a strange sort of intelligence! and a confidence in himself. Isn't that curious, Louise, in a man with as little mind as he has? Do you know, I should say he could see through a woman pretty well.'

'Why, mother!' said Lou impatiently. 'I think one gets so tired of your men with mind, as you call it. There are so many of that sort of clever men. And there are lots of men who aren't very clever, but are rather nice: and lots are stupid. It seems to me there's something else besides mind and cleverness, or niceness or cleanness. Perhaps it is the animal. Just think of St. Mawr! I've thought so much about him. We call him an animal, but we never know what it means. He seems a far greater mystery to me than a clever man. He's a horse. Why can't one say in the same way, of a man: *He's a man?* There seems no mystery in being a man. But there's a terrible mystery in St. Mawr.'

Mrs. Witt watched her daughter quizzically.

'Louise,' she said, 'you won't tell me that the mere animal is all that counts in a man. I will never believe it. Man is wonderful because he is able to *think.*'

'But is he?' cried Lou, with sudden exasperation. 'Their thinking seems to me all so childish: like stringing the same beads over and over again. Ah, men! They and their thinking are all so *paltry*. How can you be impressed?'

Mrs. Witt raised her eyebrows sardonically.

'Perhaps I'm not—any more,' she said with grim smile.

'But,' she added, 'I still can't see that I am to be impressed by the mere animal in man. The animals are the same as we are. It seems to me they have the same feelings and wants as we do, in a commonplace way. The only difference is that they have no minds: no human minds, at least. And no matter what you say, Louise, lack of mind makes the commonplace.'

Lou knitted her brows nervously.

'I suppose it does, mother.—But men's minds *are* so commonplace: look at Dean Vyner and his mind! Or look at Arthur Balfour, as a shining example. Isn't *that* commonplace, that cleverness? I would hate St. Mawr to be spoilt by such a mind.'

'Yes, Louise, so would I. Because the men you mention are really old women, knitting the same pattern over and over again. Nevertheless, I shall never alter my belief that real mind is all that matters in a man, and it's *that* that we women love.'

'Yes, mother!—But what *is* real mind? The old woman who knits the most complicated pattern? Oh, I can hear all their needles clicking, the clever men! As a matter of fact, mother, I believe Lewis has far more real mind than Dean Vyner or any of the clever ones. He has a good intuitive mind, he knows things without thinking them.'

'That may be, Louise! But he is a servant. He is *under*. A real man should never be under. And then you could never be intimate with a man like Lewis.'

'I don't want intimacy, mother. I'm too tired of it all. I love St. Mawr because he isn't intimate. He stands where one can't get at him. And he burns with life. And where does his life come from, to him? That's the mystery. That great burning life in him, which never is dead. Most men have a deadness in them that frightens me so, because of my own deadness. Why can't men get their life straight, like St. Mawr, and then think? Why can't they think quick, mother: quick as a woman: only farther than we do? Why isn't men's thinking quick like fire, mother? Why is it so slow, so dead, so deadly dull?'

'I can't tell you, Louise. My own opinion of the men of to-day has grown very small. But I can live in spite of it.'

'No, mother. We seem to be living off old fuel, like the camel when he lives off his hump. Life doesn't rush into us, as it does even into St. Mawr, and he's a dependent animal. I can't live, mother. I just can't.'

'I don't see why not. *I'm* full of life.'

'I know you are, mother. But I'm not, and I'm your daughter.—And don't misunderstand me, mother. I don't want to be an animal like a horse or a cat or a lioness, though they all fascinate me, the way they get their life *straight*, not from a lot of old tanks, as we do. I don't admire the cave-man, and that sort of thing. But think, mother, if we could get our lives straight from the source, as the animals do, and still be ourselves. You don't like men yourself. But you've no idea how men just tire me out: even the very thought of them. You say they are too animal. But they're not, mother. It's the animal in them has gone perverse, or cringing, or humble, or domesticated, like dogs. I don't know one single man who is a proud living animal. I know they've left off really thinking. But then men always do leave off really thinking, when the last bit of wild animal dies in them.'

'Because we have minds—'

'We have no minds once we are tame, mother. Men are all women, knitting and crocheting words together.'

'I can't altogether agree, you know, Louise.'

'I know you don't.—You like clever men. But clever men are mostly such unpleasant *animals*. As animals, so very unpleasant. And in men like Rico, the animal has gone queer and wrong. And in those nice clean boys you liked so much in the war, there is no wild animal left in them. They're all tame dogs, even when they're brave and well-bred. They're all tame dogs, mother, with human masters. There's no mystery in them.'

'What do you want, Louise? You *do* want the cave-man who'll knock you on the head with a club.'

'Don't be silly, mother. That's much more your subconscious line, you admirer of Mind.—I don't consider the cave-man is a real human animal at all. He's a brute, a degenerate. A pure animal man would be as lovely as a deer or a leopard, burning like a flame fed straight from underneath. And he'd be part of the unseen, like a mouse is, even. And he'd never cease to wonder, he'd breathe silence and unseen wonder, as the partridges do, running in the stubble. He'd be all the animals in turn, instead of one fixed, automatic thing, which he is now, grinding on the nerves.—Ah, no, mother, I want the wonder back again, or I shall die. I don't want to be like you, just criticizing and annihilating these dreary people, and enjoying it.'

'My dear daughter, whatever else the human animal might be, he'd be a dangerous commodity.'

'I wish he would, mother. I'm dying of these empty, dangerless men, who are only sentimental and spiteful.'

'Nonsense, you're not dying.'

'I am, mother. And I should be dead if there weren't St. Mawr and Phœnix and Lewis in the world.'

'St. Mawr and Phœnix and Lewis! I thought you said they were servants!'

'That's the worst of it. If only they were masters! If only there were some men with as much natural life as they have, and their brave, quick minds that commanded instead of serving!'

'There are no such men,' said Mrs. Witt, with a certain grim satisfaction.

'I know it. But I'm young, and I've got to live. And the thing that is offered me as life just starves me, starves me to death, mother. What am I to do? You enjoy shattering people like Dean Vyner. But I am young, I can't live that way.'

'That may be.'

It had long ago struck Lou how much more her mother realized and understood than ever Rico did. Rico was afraid, always afraid of realizing. Rico, with his good manners and his habitual kindness, and that peculiar imprisoned sneer of his.

He arrived home next morning on St. Mawr, rather flushed and gaudy, and over-kind, with an *empressé* [28] anxiety about Lou's welfare which spoke too many volumes. Especially as he was accompanied by Flora Manby, and by Flora's sister Elsie, and Elsie's husband, Frederick Edwards. They all came on horseback.

---

28. Urgent, forced.

'Such awful ages since I saw you!' said Flora to Lou. 'Sorry if we burst in on you. We're only just saying *How do you do?* and going on to the inn. They've got rooms all ready for us there. We thought we'd stay just one night over here, and ride to-morrow to the Devil's Chair. Won't you come? Lots of fun! Isn't Mrs. Witt at home?'

Mrs. Witt was out for the moment. When she returned she had on her curious stiff face, yet she greeted the new-comers with a certain cordiality: she felt it would be diplomatic, no doubt.

'There *are* two rooms here,' she said, 'and if you care to poke into them, why, we shall be *delighted* to have you. But I'll show them to you first, because they are poor, inconvenient rooms, with no running water and *miles* from the baths.'

Flora and Elsie declared that they were 'perfectly darling sweet rooms—not overcrowded.'

'Well,' said Mrs. Witt, 'the conveniences certainly don't fill up much space. But if you like to take them for what they are—'

'Why, we feel absolutely overwhelmed, don't we, Elsie!—But we've no clothes—!'

Suddenly the silence had turned into a house-party. The Manby girls appeared to lunch in fine muslin dresses, bought in Paris, fresh as daisies. Women's clothing takes up so little space, especially in summer! Fred Edwards was one of those blond Englishmen with a little brush moustache and those strong blue eyes which were always attempting the sentimental, but which Lou, in her prejudice, considered cruel: upon what grounds, she never analysed. However, he took a gallant tone with her at once, and she had to seem to simper. Rico, watching her, was so relieved when he saw the simper coming.

It had begun again, the whole clockwork of 'lots of fun!'

'Isn't Fred flirting perfectly outrageously with Lady Carrington!—She looks so *sweet!*' cried Flora, over her coffee-cup. 'Don't you mind, Harry!'

They called Rico 'Harry'! His boy-name.

'Only a very little,' said Harry. '*L'uomo è cacciatore.*'

'Oh, now, what does that mean?' cried Flora, who always thrilled to Rico's bits of affectation.

'It means,' said Mrs. Witt, leaning forward and speaking in her most suave voice, 'that man is a hunter.'

Even Flora shrank under the smooth acid of the irony.

'Oh, well now!' she cried. 'If he is, then what is woman?'

'The hunted,' said Mrs. Witt, in a still smoother acid.

'At least,' said Rico, 'she is always *game!*'

'Ah, is she though!' came Fred's manly, well-bred tones. 'I'm not so sure.'

Mrs. Witt looked from one man to the other, as if she were dropping them down the bottomless pit.

Lou escaped to look at St. Mawr. He was still moist where the saddle had been. And he seemed a little bit extinguished, as if virtue had gone out of him.

But when he lifted his lovely naked head, like a bunch of flames, to see who it was had entered, she saw he was still himself. Forever sensitive and alert, his head lifted like the summit of a fountain. And within him the clean bones striking to the earth, his hoofs intervening between him and the ground like lesser jewels.

He knew her and did not resent her. But he took no notice of her. He would never 'respond.' At first she had resented it. Now she was glad. He would never be intimate, thank heaven.

She hid herself away till tea-time, but she could not hide from the sound of voices. Dinner was early, at seven. Dean Vyner came—Mrs. Vyner was an invalid—and also an artist who had a studio in the village and did etchings. He was a man of about thirty-eight, and poor, just beginning to accept himself as a failure, as far as making money goes. But he worked at his etchings and studied esoteric matters like astrology and alchemy.[29] Rico patronized him, and was a little afraid of him. Lou could not quite make him out. After knocking about Paris and London and Munich, he was trying to become staid, and to persuade himself that English village life, with squire and dean in the background, humble artist in the middle, and labourer in the common foreground, was a genuine life. His self-persuasion was only moderately successful. This was betrayed by the curious arrest in his body: he seemed to have to force himself into movement: and by the curious duplicity in his yellow-grey, twinkling eyes, that twinkled and expanded like a goat's; with mockery, irony, and frustration.

'Your face is curiously like Pan's,' said Lou to him at dinner.

It was true, in a commonplace sense. He had the tilted eyebrows, the twinkling goaty look, and the pointed ears of a goat-Pan.

'People have said so,' he replied. 'But I'm afraid it's not the face of the Great God Pan. Isn't it rather the Great Goat Pan!'

'I say, that's good!' cried Rico. 'The Great Goat Pan!'

'I have always found it difficult,' said the Dean, 'to see the Great God Pan in that goat-legged old father of satyrs. He may have a good deal of influence—the world will always be full of goaty old satyrs. But we find them somewhat vulgar. Even our late King Edward. The goaty old satyrs are too comprehensible to me to be venerable, and I fail to see a Great God in the father of them all.'

'Your ears should be getting red,' said Lou to Cartwright. She, too, had an odd squinting smile that suggested nymphs, so irresponsible and unbelieving.

'Oh, no, nothing personal!' cried the Dean.

'I am not sure,' said Cartwright, with a small smile. 'But don't you imagine Pan once *was* a Great God, before the anthropomorphic Greeks turned him into half a man?'

'Ah!—maybe. That is very possible. But—I have noticed the limitation in myself—my mind has no grasp whatsoever of Europe before the Greeks arose. Mr. Wells' Outline [30] does not help me there, either,' the Dean added with a smile.

'But what was Pan before he was a man with goat legs?' asked Lou.

'Before he looked like me?' said Cartwright, with a faint grin. 'I should say he was the God that is hidden in everything. In those days you saw the thing, you never saw the God in it: I mean in the tree or the fountain or the animal. If you ever saw the God instead of the thing, you died. If you saw it with the naked eye, that is. But in the night you might see the God. And you knew it was there.'

---

29. This character is drawn directly from Frederick Carter.

30. H. G. Wells (1866–1946), *Outline of History* (1920), a famous book at the time.

'The modern pantheist not only sees the God in everything, he takes photographs of it,' said the Dean.

'Oh, and the divine pictures he paints!' cried Rico.

'Quite!' said Cartwright.

'But if they never *saw* the God in the thing, the old ones, how did they know he was there? How did they have any Pan at all?' said Lou.

'Pan was the hidden mystery—the hidden cause. That's how it was a Great God. Pan wasn't *he* at all: not even a Great God. He was Pan. All: what you see when you see in full. In the daytime you see the thing. But if your third eye is open, which sees only the things that can't be seen, you may see Pan within the thing, hidden: you may see with your third eye, which is darkness.' [31]

'Do you think I might see Pan in a horse, for example?'

'Easily. In St. Mawr!'—Cartwright gave her a knowing look.

'But,' said Mrs. Witt, 'it would be difficult, I should say, to open the third eye and see Pan in a man.'

'Probably,' said Cartwright, smiling. 'In man he is over-visible: the old satyr: the fallen Pan.'

'Exactly!' said Mrs. Witt. And she fell into a muse. 'The fallen Pan!' she re-echoed. 'Wouldn't a man be wonderful in whom Pan hadn't fallen!'

Over the coffee in the grey drawing-room she suddenly asked:

'Supposing, Mr. Cartwright, one *did* open the third eye and see Pan in an actual man—I wonder what it would be like.'

She half lowered her eyelids and tilted her face in a strange way, as if she were tasting something, and not quite sure.

'I wonder!' he said, smiling his enigmatic smile. But she could see he did not understand.

'Louise!' said Mrs. Witt at bedtime. 'Come into my room for a moment, I want to ask you something.'

'What is it, mother?'

'You, you *get* something from what Mr. Cartwright said, about seeing Pan with the third eye? Seeing Pan in something?'

Mrs. Witt came rather close, and tilted her face with strange insinuating question at her daughter.

'I think I do, mother.'

'In what?'—The question came as a pistol-shot.

'I think, mother,' said Lou reluctantly, 'in St. Mawr.'

'In a horse!'—Mrs. Witt contracted her eyes slightly. 'Yes, I can see that. I know what you mean. It *is* in St. Mawr. It *is*! But in St. Mawr it makes me *afraid*—' she dragged out the word. Then she came a step closer. 'But, Louise, did you ever see it in a man?'

'What, mother?'

'Pan. Did you ever see Pan in a man, as you see Pan in St. Mawr?'

Louise hesitated.

'No, mother, I don't think I did. When I look at men with my third eye, as you call it—I think I see—mostly—a sort of—pancake.' She uttered the last word with a despairing grin, not knowing quite what to say.

'Oh, Louise, isn't that it! Doesn't one always see a pancake!—Now listen, Louise. Have you ever been in love?'

'Yes, as far as I understand it.'

'Listen now. Did you ever see Pan in the man you loved? Tell me if you did.'

'As I see Pan in St. Mawr?—no, mother.' And suddenly her lips began to tremble and the tears came to her eyes.

'Listen, Louise.—I've been in love innumerable times—and *really* in love twice. Twice!—yet for fifteen years I've left off wanting to have anything to do with a man, really. For fifteen years! And why?—Do you know?—Because I couldn't see that peculiar hidden Pan in any of them. And I became that I needed to. I needed it. But it wasn't there. Not in any man. Even when I was in love with a man, it was for other things: because I *understood* him so well, or he understood me, or we had such sympathy. Never the hidden Pan.—Do you understand what I mean? Unfallen Pan!'

'More or less, mother.'

'But now my third eye is coming open, I believe. I am tired of all these men like breakfast cakes, with a teaspoonful of mind or a teaspoonful of spirit in them, for baking-powder. Isn't it extraordinary that young man Cartwright talks about Pan, but he knows nothing of it all? He knows nothing of the unfallen Pan: only the fallen Pan with goat legs and a leer—and that sort of power, don't you know—'

'But what do you know of the unfallen Pan, mother?'

'Don't ask me, Louise! I feel all of a tremble, as if I was just on the verge.' She flashed a little look of incipient triumph, and said good night.

An excursion on horseback had been arranged for the next day, to two old groups of rocks, called the Angel's Chair and the Devil's Chair, which crowned the moor-like hills looking into Wales, ten miles away. Everybody was going—they were to start early in the morning, and Lewis would be the guide, since no one exactly knew the way.

Lou got up soon after sunrise. There was a summer scent in the trees of early morning, and monkshood flowers stood up dark and tall, with shadows. She dressed in the green linen riding-skirt her maid had put ready for her, with a close bluish smock.

'Are you going out already, dear?' called Rico from his room.

'Just to smell the roses before we start, Rico.'

He appeared in the doorway in his yellow silk pyjamas. His large blue eyes had that rolling irritable look and the slightly bloodshot whites which made her want to escape.

'Booted and spurred!—the *energy!*' he cried.

'It's a lovely day to ride,' she said.

'A lovely day to do anything *except* ride!' he said. 'Why spoil the day riding!'—A curious bitter-acid escaped into his tone. It was evident he hated the excursion.

'Why, we needn't go if you don't want to, Rico.'

'Oh, I'm sure I shall love it, once I get started. It's all this business of *starting*, with horses and paraphernalia—'

Lou went into the yard. The horses were drinking at the trough under the pump, their colours strong and rich in the shadow of the tree.

'You're not coming with us, Phœnix?' she said.

'Lewis, he's riding my horse.'

She could tell Phœnix did not like being left behind.

By half past seven everybody was ready. The sun was in the yard, the horses were saddled. They came swishing their tails. Lewis brought out St. Mawr from his separate box, speaking to him very quietly in Welsh: a murmuring, soothing little speech. Lou, alert, could see that he was uneasy.

'How is St. Mawr this morning?' she asked.

'He's all right. He doesn't like so many people. He'll be all right once he's started.'

The strangers were in the saddle: they moved out to the deep shade of the village road outside. Rico came to his horse to mount. St. Mawr jumped away as if he had seen the devil.

'Steady, fool!' cried Rico.

The bay stood with his four feet spread, his neck arched, his big dark eye glancing sideways with that watchful, frightening look.

'You shouldn't be irritable with him, Rico!' said Lou. 'Steady then, St. Mawr! Be steady.'

But a certain anger rose also in her. The creature was so big, so brilliant, and so stupid, standing there with his hind legs spread, ready to jump aside or to rear terrifically, and his great eye glancing with a sort of suspicious frenzy. What was there to be suspicious of, after all?—Rico would do him no harm.

'No one will harm you, St. Mawr,' she reasoned, a bit exasperated.

The groom was talking quietly, murmuringly, in Welsh. Rico was slowly advancing again, to put his foot in the stirrup. The stallion was watching from the corner of his eye, a strange glare of suspicious frenzy burning stupidly. Any moment his immense physical force might be let loose in a frenzy of panic— or malice. He was really very irritating.

'Probably he doesn't like that apricot shirt,' said Mrs. Witt, 'although it tones into him wonderfully well.'

She pronounced it ap-ricot,[32] and it irritated Rico terribly.

'Ought we to have *asked* him before we put it on?' he flashed, his upper lip lifting venomously.

'I should say you should,' replied Mrs. Witt coolly.

Rico turned with a sudden rush to the horse. Back went the great animal, with a sudden splashing crash of hoofs on the cobble-stones, and Lewis hanging on like a shadow. Up went the forefeet, showing the belly.

'The thing is accursed,' said Rico, who had dropped the reins in sudden shock, and stood marooned. His rage overwhelmed him like a black flood.

'Nothing in the world is so irritating as a horse that is acting up,' thought Lou.

'Say, Harry!' called Flora from the road. 'Come out here into the road to mount him.'

Lewis looked at Rico and nodded. Then, soothing the big, quivering animal, he led him springily out to the road under the trees, where the three friends

<hr/>

32. The usual British pronunciation is *ape-ricot*.

were waiting. Lou and her mother got quickly into the saddle to follow. And in another moment Rico was mounted and bouncing down the road in the wrong direction, Lewis following on the chestnut. It was some time before Rico could get St. Mawr round. Watching him from behind, those waiting could judge how the young Baronet hated it.

But at last they set off—Rico ahead, unevenly but quietly, with the two Manby girls, Lou following with the fair young man who had been in a cavalry regiment and who kept looking round for Mrs. Witt.

'Don't look round for me,' she called. 'I'm riding behind, out of the dust.'

Just behind Mrs. Witt came Lewis. It was a whole cavalcade trotting in the morning sun past the cottages and the cottage gardens, round the field that was the recreation ground, into the deep hedges of the lane.

'Why is St. Mawr so bad at starting? Can't you get him into better shape?' she asked over her shoulder.

'Beg your pardon, Mam!'

Lewis trotted a little nearer. She glanced over her shoulder at him, at his dark, unmoved face, his cool little figure.

'I think *Mam!* is so ugly. Why not leave it out!' she said. Then she repeated her question.

'St. Mawr doesn't trust anybody,' Lewis replied.

'Not you?'

'Yes, he trusts me—mostly.'

'Then why not other people?'

'They're different.'

'All of them?'

'About all of them.'

'How are they different?'

He looked at her with his remote, uncanny grey eyes.

'Different,' he said, not knowing how else to put it.

They rode on slowly, up the steep rise of the wood, then down into a glade where ran a little railway built for hauling some mysterious mineral out of the hill, in war-time, and now already abandoned. Even on this country-side the dead hand of the war lay like a corpse decomposing.

They rode up again, past the foxgloves under the trees. Ahead the brilliant St. Mawr and the sorrel and grey horses were swimming like butterflies through the sea of bracken, glittering from sun to shade, shade to sun. Then once more they were on a crest, and through the thinning trees could see the slopes of the moors beyond the next dip.

Soon they were in the open, rolling hills, golden in the morning and empty save for a couple of distant bilberry-pickers, whitish figures pick—pick—picking with curious, rather disgusting assiduity. The horses were on an old trail which climbed through the pinky tips of heather and ling, across patches of green bilberry. Here and there were tufts of harebells blue as bubbles.

They were out, high on the hills. And there to west lay Wales, folded in crumpled folds, goldish in the morning light, with its moor-like slopes and patches of corn uncannily distinct. Between was a hollow, wide valley of summer haze, showing white farms among trees, and grey slate roofs.

'Ride beside me,' she said to Lewis. 'Nothing makes me want to go back to

America like the old look of these little villages.—You have never been to America?'

'No, Mam.'

'Don't you ever want to go?'

'I wouldn't mind going.'

'But you're not just crazy to go?'

'No, Mam.'

'Quite content as you are?'

He looked at her, and his pale, remote eyes met hers.

'I don't fret myself,' he replied.

'Not about anything at all—ever?'

His eyes glanced ahead, at the other riders.

'No, Mam!' he replied, without looking at her.

She rode a few moments in silence.

'What is that over there?' she asked, pointing across the valley. 'What is it called?'

'Yon's Montgomery.'

'Montgomery! And is that *Wales*—?' She trailed the ending curiously.

'Yes, Mam.'

'Where you come from?'

'No, Mam! I come from Merioneth.'

'Not from Wales? I thought you were Welsh?'

'Yes, Mam. Merioneth *is* Wales.'

'And you are Welsh?'

'Yes, Mam.'

'I had a Welsh grandmother. But I come from Louisiana, and when I go back home, the Negroes still call me Miss Rachel. *Oh, my, it's little Miss Rachel come back home. Why, ain't I mighty glad to see you—u, Miss Rachel!* That gives me such a strange feeling, you know.'

The man glanced at her curiously, especially when she imitated the Negroes.

'Do you feel strange when you go home?' she asked.

'I was brought up by an aunt and uncle,' he said. 'I never go to see them.'

'And you don't have any home?'

'No, Mam.'

'No wife nor anything?'

'No, Mam.'

'But what do you do with your life?'

'I keep to myself.'

'And care about nothing?'

'I mind St. Mawr.'

'But you've not always had St. Mawr—and you won't always have him.— Were you in the war?'

'Yes, Mam.'

'At the front?'

'Yes, Mam—but I was a groom.'

'And you came out all right?'

'I lost my little finger from a bullet.'

He held up his small, dark left hand, from which the little finger was missing.

'And did you like the war—or didn't you?'

'I didn't like it.'

Again his pale-grey eyes met hers, and they looked so non-human and uncommunicative, so without connection, and inaccessible, she was troubled.

'Tell me,' she said. 'Did you never want a wife and a home and children, like other men?'

'No, Mam. I never wanted a home of my own.'

'Nor a wife of your own?'

'No, Mam.'

'Nor children of your own?'

'No, Mam.'

She reined in her horse.

'Now wait a minute,' she said. 'Now tell me why.'

His horse came to standstill, and the two riders faced one another.

'Tell me why—I must know why you never wanted a wife and children and a home. I must know why you're not like other men.'

'I never felt like it,' he said. 'I made my life with horses.'

'Did you hate people very much? Did you have a very unhappy time as a child?'

'My aunt and uncle didn't like me, and I didn't like them.'

'So you've never liked anybody?'

'Maybe not,' he said. 'Not to get as far as marrying them.'

She touched her horse and moved on.

'Isn't that curious!' she said. 'I've loved people, at various times. But I don't believe *I've* ever liked anybody, except a few of our Negroes. I don't like Louise, though she's my daughter and I love her. But I don't really *like* her.—I think you're the first person I've ever liked since I was on our plantation, and we had some *very fine* Negroes.—And I think that's very curious.—Now I want to know if you like *me*.'

She looked at him searchingly, but he did not answer.

'Tell me,' she said. 'I don't mind if you say no. But tell me if you like me. I feel I must know.'

The flicker of a smile went over his face—a very rare thing with him.

'Maybe I do,' he said. He was thinking that she put him on a level with a Negro slave on a plantation: in his idea, Negroes were still slaves. But he did not care where she put him.

'Well, I'm glad—I'm glad if you like me. Because you *don't* like most people I know that.'

They had passed the hollow where the old Aldecar Chapel hid in damp isolation, beside the ruined mill, over the stream that came down from the moors. Climbing the sharp slope, they saw the folded hills like great shut fingers, with steep, deep clefts between. On the near sky-line was a bunch of rocks; and away to the right another bunch.

'Yon's the Angel's Chair,' said Lewis, pointing to the nearer rocks. 'And yon' the Devil's Chair, where we're going.'

'Oh!' said Mrs. Witt. 'And aren't we going to the Angel's Chair?'

'No, Mam.'

'Why not?'

'There's nothing to see there. The other's higher, and bigger, and that's where folks mostly go.'

'Is that so!—They give the Devil the higher seat in this country, do they? I think they're right.'—And as she got no answer, she added: 'You believe in the Devil, don't you?'

'I never met him,' he answered, evasively.

Ahead, they could see the other horses twinkling in a cavalcade up the slope, the black, the bay, the two greys and the sorrel, sometimes bunching, sometimes straggling. At a gate all waited for Mrs. Witt. The fair young man fell in beside her, and talked hunting at her. He had hunted the fox over these hills, and was vigorously excited locating the spot where the hounds gave the first cry, etc.

'Really!' said Mrs. Witt. 'Really! Is that so!'

If irony could have been condensed to prussic acid, the fair young man would have ended his life's history with his reminiscences.

They came at last, trotting in file along a narrow track between heather, along the saddle of a hill, to where the knot of pale granite suddenly cropped out. It was one of those places where the spirit of aboriginal England still lingers, the old savage England, whose last blood flows still in a few Englishmen, Welshmen, Cornishmen. The rocks, whitish with weather of all the ages, jutted against the blue August sky, heavy with age-moulded roundnesses.

Lewis stayed below with the horses, the party scrambled rather awkwardly, in their riding-boots, up the foot-worn boulders. At length they stood in the place called the Chair, looking west, west towards Wales, that rolled in golden folds upwards. It was neither impressive nor a very picturesque landscape: the hollow valley with farms, and then the rather bare upheaval of hills, slopes with corn and moor and pasture, rising like a barricade, seemingly high, slantingly. Yet it had a strange effect on the imagination.

'Oh, mother,' said Lou, 'doesn't it make you feel old, old, older than anything ever was?'

'It certainly does seem aged,' said Mrs. Witt.

'It makes me want to die,' said Lou. 'I feel we've lasted almost too long.'

'Don't say that, Lady Carrington. Why, you're a spring chicken yet: or shall I say an unopened rosebud?' remarked the fair young man.

'No,' said Lou. 'All these millions of ancestors have used all the life up. We're not really alive, in the sense that they were alive.'

'But who?' said Rico. 'Who are they?'

'The people who lived on these hills, in the days gone by.'

'But the same people still live on the hills, darling. It's just the same stock.'

'No, Rico. That old fighting stock that worshipped devils among these stones —I'm sure they did—'

'But look here, do you mean they were any better than we are?' asked the fair young man.

Lou looked at him quizzically.

'We don't exist,' she said, squinting at him oddly.

'I jolly well know I do,' said the fair young man.

'I consider these days are the best ever, especially for girls,' said Flora

Manby. 'And anyhow they're our own days, so I don't jolly well see the use of crying them down.'

They were all silent, with the last echoes of emphatic *joie de vivre* trumpeting on the air, across the hills of Wales.

'Spoken like a brick, Flora,' said Rico. 'Say it again, we may not have the Devil's Chair for a pulpit next time.'

'I do,' reiterated Flora. 'I think this is the best age there ever was for a girl to have a good time in. I read all through H. G. Wells' history, and I shut it up and thanked my stars I live in nineteen-twenty odd, not in some other beastly date when a woman had to cringe before mouldy domineering men.'

After this they turned to scramble to another part of the rocks, to the famous Needle's Eye.

'Thank you so much, I am really better without help,' said Mrs. Witt to the fair young man, as she slid downwards till a piece of grey silk stocking showed above her tall boot. But she got her toe in a safe place, and in a moment stood beside him, while he caught her arm protectingly. He might as well have caught the paw of a mountain lion protectingly.

'I should like *so* much to know,' she said suavely, looking into his eyes with a demonish straight look, 'what makes you so certain that you exist.'

He looked back at her, and his jaunty blue eyes went baffled. Then a slow, hot, salmon-coloured flush stole over his face, and he turned abruptly round.

The Needle's Eye was a hole in the ancient grey rock, like a window, looking to England: England at the moment in shadow. A stream wound and glinted in the flat shadow, and beyond that the flat, insignificant hills leaped in mounds of shade. Cloud was coming—the English side was in shadow. Wales was still in the sun, but the shadow was spreading. The day was going to disappoint them. Lou was a tiny bit chilled already.

Luncheon was still several miles away. The party hastened down to the horses. Lou picked a few sprigs of ling, and some harebells, and some straggling yellow flowers: not because she wanted them, but to distract herself. The atmosphere of 'enjoying ourselves' was becoming cruel to her: it sapped all the life out of her. 'Oh, if only I needn't enjoy myself,' she moaned inwardly. But the Manby girls were enjoying themselves so much. 'I think it's frantically lovely up here,' said the other one—not Flora—Elsie.

'It *is* beautiful, isn't it! I'm *so* glad you like it,' replied Rico. And he was really relieved and gratified, because the other one said she was enjoying it so frightfully. He dared not say to Lou, as he wanted to: 'I'm afraid, Lou darling, you don't love it as much as we do.'—He was afraid of her answer: 'No, dear, I don't love it at all! I want to be away from these people.'

Slightly piqued, he rode on with the Manby group, and Lou came behind with her mother. Cloud was covering the sky with grey. There was a cold wind. Everybody was anxious to get to the farm for luncheon, and be safely home before rain came.

They were riding along one of the narrow little foot-tracks, mere grooves of grass between heather and bright green bilberry. The blond young man was ahead, then his wife, then Flora, then Rico. Lou, from a little distance, watched the glossy, powerful haunches of St. Mawr swaying with life, always too much life, like a menace. The fair young man was whistling a new dance tune.

'That's an awfully attractive tune,' Rico called. 'Do whistle it again, Fred, I should like to memorize it.'

Fred began to whistle it again.

At that moment St. Mawr exploded again, shied sideways as if a bomb had gone off, and kept backing through the heather.

'Fool!' cried Rico, thoroughly unnerved: he had been terribly sideways in the saddle, Lou had feared he was going to fall. But he got his seat, and pulled the reins viciously, to bring the horse to order, and put him on the track again. St. Mawr began to rear: his favourite trick. Rico got him forward a few yards, when up he went again.

'Fool!' yelled Rico, hanging in the air.

He pulled the horse over backwards on top of him.

Lou gave a loud, unnatural, horrible scream: she heard it herself, at the same time as she heard the crash of the falling horse. Then she saw a pale gold belly, and hoofs that worked and flashed in the air, and St. Mawr writhing, straining his head terrifically upwards, his great eyes starting from the naked lines of his nose. With a great neck arching cruelly from the ground, he was pulling frantically at the reins, which Rico still held tight.—Yes, Rico, lying strangely sideways, his eyes also starting from his yellow-white face, among the heather, still clutched the reins.

Young Edwards was rushing forward, and circling round the writhing, immense horse, whose pale-gold, inverted bulk seemed to fill the universe.

'Let him get up, Carrington! Let him get up!' he was yelling, darting warily near, to get the reins.—Another spasmodic convulsion of the horse.

Horror! The young man reeled backwards with his face in his hands. He had got a kick in the face. Red blood running down his chin!

Lewis was there, on the ground, getting the reins out of Rico's hands. St. Mawr gave a great curve like a fish, spread his forefeet on the earth and reared his head, looking round in a ghastly fashion. His eyes were arched, his nostrils wide, his face ghastly in a sort of panic. He rested thus, seated with his forefeet planted and his face in panic, almost like some terrible lizard, for several moments. Then he heaved sickeningly to his feet, and stood convulsed, trembling.

There lay Rico, crumpled and rather sideways, staring at the heavens from a yellow, dead-looking face. Lewis, glancing round in a sort of horror, looked in dread at St. Mawr again. Flora had been hovering.—She now rushed screeching to the prostrate Rico:

'Harry! Harry! you're not dead! Oh, Harry! Harry! Harry!'

Lou had dismounted.—She didn't know when. She stood a little way off, as if spellbound, while Flora cried *Harry! Harry! Harry!*

Suddenly Rico sat up.

'Where is the horse?' he said.

At the same time an added whiteness came on his face, and he bit his lip with pain, and he fell prostrate again in a faint. Flora rushed to put her arm round him.

Where was the horse? He had backed slowly away, in an agony of suspicion, while Lewis murmured to him in vain. His head was raised again, the eyes still starting from their sockets, and a terrible guilty, ghostlike look on his face.

When Lewis drew a little nearer, he twitched and shrank like a shaken steel spring, away—not to be touched. He seemed to be seeing legions of ghosts, down the dark avenues of all the centuries that have lapsed since the horse became subject to man.

And the other young man? He was still standing, at a little distance, with his face in his hands, motionless, the blood falling on his white shirt, and his wife at his side, pleading, distracted.

Mrs. Witt too was there, as if cast in steel, watching. She made no sound and did not move, only, from a fixed, impassive face, watched each thing.

'Do tell me what you think is the matter?' Lou pleaded, distracted, to Flora, who was supporting Rico and weeping torrents of unknown tears.

Then Mrs. Witt came forward and began in a very practical manner to unclose the shirt-neck and feel the young man's heart. Rico opened his eyes again, said '*Really!*' and closed his eyes once more.

'It's fainting!' said Mrs. Witt. 'We have no brandy.'

Lou, too weary to be able to feel anything, said:

'I'll go and get some.'

She went to her alarmed horse, who stood among the others with her head down, in suspense. Almost unconsciously Lou mounted, set her face ahead, and was riding away.

Then Poppy shied too, with a sudden start, and Lou pulled up. 'Why?' she said to her horse. 'Why did you do that?'

She looked round, and saw in the heather a glimpse of yellow and black.

'A snake!' she said wonderingly.

And she looked closer.

It was a dead adder that had been drinking at a reedy pool in a little depression just off the road, and had been killed with stones. There it lay, also crumpled, its head crushed, its gold-and-yellow back still glittering dully, and a bit of pale-blue belly showing, killed that morning.

Lou rode on, her face set towards the farm. An unspeakable weariness had overcome her. She could not even suffer. Weariness of spirit left her in a sort of apathy.

And she had a vision, a vision of evil. Or not strictly a vision. She became aware of evil, evil, evil, rolling in great waves over the earth. Always she had thought there was no such thing—only a mere negation of good. Now, like an ocean to whose surface she had risen, she saw the dark-grey waves of evil rearing in a great tide.

And it had swept mankind away without mankind's knowing. It had caught up the nations as the rising ocean might lift the fishes, and was sweeping them on in a great tide of evil. They did not know. The people did not know. They did not even wish it. They wanted to be good and to have everything joyful and enjoyable. Everything joyful and enjoyable: for everybody. This was what they wanted, if you asked them.

But at the same time, they had fallen under the spell of evil. It was a soft, subtle thing, soft as water, and its motion was soft and imperceptible, as the running of a tide is invisible to one who is out on the ocean. And they were all out on the ocean, being borne along in the current of the mysterious evil, creatures of the evil principle, as fishes are creatures of the sea.

There was no relief. The whole world was enveloped in one great flood. All the nations, the white, the brown, the black, the yellow, all were immersed in the strange tide of evil that was subtly, irresistibly rising. No one, perhaps, deliberately wished it. Nearly every individual wanted peace and a good time all round: everybody to have a good time.

But some strange thing had happened, and the vast, mysterious force of positive evil was let loose. She felt that from the core of Asia the evil welled up, as from some strange pole, and slowly was drowning earth.

It was something horrifying, something you could not escape from. It had come to her as in a vision, when she saw the pale-gold belly of the stallion upturned, the hoofs working wildly, the wicked curved hams of the horse, and then the evil straining of that arched, fish-like neck, with the dilated eyes of the head. Thrown backwards, and working its hoofs in the air. Reversed, and purely evil.

She saw the same in people. They were thrown backwards, and writhing with evil. And the rider, crushed, was still reining them down.

What did it mean? Evil, evil, and a rapid return to the sordid chaos. Which was wrong, the horse or the rider? Or both?

She thought with horror of St. Mawr, and of the look on his face. But she thought with horror, a colder horror, of Rico's face as he snarled *Fool!* His fear, his impotence as a master, as a rider, his presumption. And she thought with horror of those other people, so glib, so glibly evil.

What did they want to do, those Manby girls? Undermine, undermine, undermine. They wanted to undermine Rico, just as that fair young man would have liked to undermine her. Believe in nothing, care about nothing: but keep the surface easy, and have a good time. *Let us undermine one another. There is nothing to believe in, so let us undermine everything. But look out! No scenes, no spoiling the game. Stick to the rules of the game. Be sporting, and don't do anything that would make a commotion. Keep the game going smooth and jolly, and bear your bit like a sport. Never, by any chance, injure your fellow man openly. But always injure him secretly. Make a fool of him, and undermine his nature. Break him up by undermining him, if you can. It's good sport.*

The evil! The mysterious potency of evil. She could see it all the time, in individuals, in society, in the press. There it was in socialism and Bolshevism: the same evil. But Bolshevism made a mess of the outside of life, so turn it down. Try Fascism. Fascism would keep the surface of life intact, and carry on the undermining business all the better. All the better sport. Never draw blood. Keep the hæmorrhage internal, invisible.

And as soon as Fascism makes a break—which it is bound to, because all evil works up to a break—then turn it down. With gusto, turn it down.

Mankind, like a horse, ridden by a stranger, smooth-faced, evil rider. Evil himself, smooth-faced and pseudo-handsome, riding mankind past the dead snake, to the last break.

Mankind no longer its own master. Ridden by this pseudo-handsome ghoul of outward loyalty, inward treachery, in a game of betrayal, betrayal, betrayal. The last of the gods of our era, Judas supreme!

People performing outward acts of loyalty, piety, self-sacrifice. But inwardly bent on undermining, betraying. Directing all their subtle evil will against any positive living thing. Masquerading as the ideal, in order to poison the real. Creation destroys as it goes, throws down one tree for the rise of another. But ideal mankind would abolish death, multiply itself million upon million, rear up city upon city, save every parasite alive, until the accumulation of mere existence is swollen to a horror. But go on saving life, the ghastly salvation army of ideal mankind. At the same time secretly, viciously, potently undermine the natural creation, betray it with kiss after kiss, destroy it from the inside, till you have the swollen rottenness of our teeming existence.—But keep the game going. Nobody's going to make another bad break, such as Germany and Russia made.

Two bad breaks the secret evil has made: in Germany and in Russia. Watch it! Let evil keep a policeman's eye on evil! The surface of life must remain unruptured. Production must be heaped upon production. And the natural creation must be betrayed by many more kisses, yet. Judas is the last God, and, by heaven, the most potent.

But even Judas made a break: hanged himself, and his bowels gushed out. Not long after his triumph.

Man must destroy as he goes, as trees fall for trees to rise. The accumulation of life and things means rottenness. Life must destroy life, in the unfolding of creation. We save up life at the expense of the unfolding, till all is full of rottenness. Then at last, we make a break.

What's to be done? Generally speaking, nothing. The dead will have to bury their dead, while the earth stinks of corpses. The individual can but depart from the mass, and try to cleanse himself. Try to hold fast to the living thing, which destroys as it goes, but remains sweet. And in his soul fight, fight, fight to preserve that which is life in him from the ghastly kisses and poison-bites of the myriad evil ones. Retreat to the desert, and fight. But in his soul adhere to that which is life itself, creatively destroying as it goes: destroying the stiff old thing to let the new bud come through. The one passionate principle of creative being, which recognizes the natural good, and has a sword for the swarms of evil. Fights, fights, fights to protect itself. But with itself, is strong and at peace.

Lou came to the farm, and got brandy, and asked the men to come out to carry in the injured.

It turned out that the kick in the face had knocked a couple of young Edwards' teeth out, and would disfigure him a little.

'To go through the war, and then get this!' he mumbled, with a vindictive glance at St. Mawr.

And it turned out that Rico had two broken ribs and a crushed ankle. Poor Rico, he would limp for life.

'I want St. Mawr *shot!*' was almost his first word, when he was in bed at the farm and Lou was sitting beside him.

'What good would that do, dear?' she said.

'The brute is evil. I want him *shot!*'

Rico could make the last word sound like the spitting of a bullet.

'Do you want to shoot him yourself?'

'No. But I want to have him shot. I shall never be easy till I know he has a bullet through him. He's got a wicked character. I don't feel you are safe, with him down there. I shall get one of the Manbys' gamekeepers to shoot him. You might tell Flora—or I'll tell her myself, when she comes.'

'Don't talk about it now, dear. You've got a temperature.'

Was it true, St. Mawr was evil? She would never forget him writhing and lunging on the ground, nor his awful face when he reared up. But then that noble look of his: surely he was not mean? Whereas all evil had an inner meanness, mean! Was he mean? Was he meanly treacherous? Did he know he could kill, and meanly wait his opportunity?

She was afraid. And if this were true, then he *should* be shot. Perhaps he ought to be shot.

This thought haunted her. Was there something mean and treacherous in St. Mawr's spirit, the vulgar evil? If so, then have him shot. At moments, an anger would rise in her, as she thought of his frenzied rearing, and his mad, hideous writhing on the ground, and in the heat of her anger she would want to hurry down to her mother's house and have the creature shot at once. It would be a satisfaction, and a vindication of human rights. Because, after all, Rico was considerate of the brutal horse. But not a spark of consideration did the stallion have for Rico. No, it was the slavish malevolence of a domesticated creature that kept cropping up in St. Mawr. The slave, taking his slavish vengeance, then dropping back into subservience.

All the slaves of this world, accumulating their preparations for slavish vengeance, and then, when they have taken it, ready to drop back into servility. Freedom! Most slaves can't be freed, no matter how you let them loose. Like domestic animals, they are, in the long run, more afraid of freedom than of masters: and freed by some generous master, they will at last crawl back to some mean boss, who will have no scruples about kicking them. Because, for them, far better kicks and servility than the hard, lonely responsibility of real freedom.

The wild animal is at every moment intensely self-disciplined, poised in the tension of self-defence, self-preservation, and self-assertion. The moments of relaxation are rare and most carefully chosen. Even sleep is watchful, guarded, unrelaxing, the wild courage pitched one degree higher than the wild fear. Courage, the wild thing's courage to maintain itself alone and living in the midst of a diverse universe.

Did St. Mawr have this courage?

And did Rico?

Ah, Rico! He was one of mankind's myriad conspirators, who conspire to live in absolute physical safety, whilst willing the minor disintegration of all positive living.

But St. Mawr? Was it the natural wild thing in him which caused these disasters? Or was it the slave, asserting himself for vengeance?

If the latter, let him be shot. It would be a great satisfaction to see him dead.

But if the former—

When she could leave Rico with the nurse, she motored down to her mother for a couple of days. Rico lay in bed at the farm.

Everything seemed curiously changed. There was a new silence about the place, a new coolness. Summer had passed with several thunderstorms, and the blue, cool touch of autumn was about the house. Dahlias and perennial yellow sunflowers were out, the yellow of ending summer, the red coals of early autumn. First mauve tips of Michaelmas daisies were showing. Something suddenly carried her away to the great bare spaces of Texas, the blue sky, the flat, burnt earth, the miles of sunflowers. Another sky, another silence, towards the setting sun.

And suddenly, she craved again for the more absolute silence of America. English stillness was so soft, like an inaudible murmur of voices, of presences. But the silence in the empty spaces of America was still unutterable, almost cruel.

St. Mawr was in a small field by himself: she could not bear that he should be always in stable. Slowly she went through the gate towards him. And he stood there looking at her, the bright bay creature.

She could tell he was feeling somewhat subdued, after his late escapade. He was aware of the general human condemnation: the human damning. But something obstinate and uncanny in him made him not relent.

'Hello! St. Mawr!' she said, as she drew near, and he stood watching her, his ears pricked, his big eyes glancing sideways at her.

But he moved away when she wanted to touch him.

'Don't trouble,' she said. 'I don't want to catch you or do anything to you.'

He stood still, listening to the sound of her voice, and giving quick, small glances at her. His underlip trembled. But he did not blink. His eyes remained wide and unrelenting. There was a curious malicious obstinacy in him which aroused her anger.

'I don't want to touch you,' she said. 'I only want to look at you, and even you can't prevent that.'

She stood gazing hard at him, wanting to know, to settle the question of his meanness or his spirit. A thing with a brave spirit is not mean.

He was uneasy as she watched him. He pretended to hear something, the mares two fields away, and he lifted his head and neighed. She knew the powerful, splendid sound so well: like bells made of living membrane. And he looked so noble again, with his head tilted up, listening, and his male eyes looking proudly over the distance, eagerly.

But it was all a bluff.

He knew, and became silent again. And as he stood there a few yards away from her, his head lifted and wary, his body full of power and tension, his face slightly averted from her, she felt a great animal sadness come from him. A strange animal atmosphere of sadness, that was vague and disseminated through the air, and made her feel as though she breathed grief. She breathed it into her breast, as if it were a great sigh down the ages, that passed into her breast. And she felt a great woe: the woe of human unworthiness. The race of men judged in the consciousness of the animals they have subdued, and there found unworthy, ignoble.

Ignoble men, unworthy of the animals they have subjugated, bred the woe in the spirit of their creatures. St. Mawr, that bright horse, one of the kings of creation in the order below man, it had been a fulfilment for him to serve the brave, reckless, perhaps cruel men of the past, who had a flickering, rising flame of nobility in them. To serve that flame of mysterious further nobility.

Nothing matters but that strange flame, of inborn nobility that obliges men to be brave, and onward plunging. And the horse will bear him on.

But now where is the flame of dangerous, forward-pressing nobility in men? Dead, dead, guttering out in a stink of self-sacrifice whose feeble light is a light of exhaustion and *laissez-faire*.

And the horse, is he to go on carrying man forward into this?—this gutter? No! Man wisely invents motor-cars and other machines, automobile and locomotive. The horse is superannuated, for man.

But alas, man is even more superannuated, for the horse.

Dimly in a woman's muse, Lou realized this, as she breathed the horse's sadness, his accumulated vague woe from the generations of latter-day ignobility. And a grief and a sympathy flooded her, for the horse. She realized now how his sadness recoiled into these frenzies of obstinacy and malevolence. Underneath it all was grief, an unconscious, vague, pervading animal grief, which perhaps only Lewis understood, because he felt the same. The grief of the generous creature which sees all ends turning to the morass of ignoble living.

She did not want to say any more to the horse: she did not want to look at him any more. The grief flooded her soul, that made her want to be alone. She knew now what it all amounted to. She knew that the horse, born to serve nobly, had waited in vain for someone noble to serve. His spirit knew that nobility had gone out of men. And this left him high and dry, in a sort of despair.

As she walked away from him, towards the gate, slowly he began to walk after her.

Phœnix came striding through the gate towards her. 'You not afraid of that horse?' he asked sardonically, in his quiet, subtle voice.

'Not at the present moment,' she replied, even more quietly, looking direct at him. She was not in any mood to be jeered at.

And instantly the sardonic grimace left his face, followed by the sudden blankness, and the look of race-misery in the keen eyes.

'Do you want me to be afraid?' she said, continuing to the gate.

'No, I don't want it,' he replied, dejected.

'Are you afraid of him yourself?' she said, glancing round. St. Mawr had stopped, seeing Phœnix, and had turned away again.

'I'm not afraid of no horses,' said Phœnix.

Lou went on quietly. At the gate, she asked him:

'Don't you like St. Mawr, Phœnix?'

'I like him. He's a very good horse.'

'Even after what he's done to Sir Henry?'

'That don't make no difference to him being a good horse.'

'But suppose he'd done it to you?'

'I don't care. I say it my own fault.'

'Don't you think he is wicked?'

'I don't think so. He don't kick anybody. He don't bite anybody. He don't pitch, he don't buck, he don't do nothing.'

'He rears,' said Lou.

'Well, what is rearing!' said the man, with a slow, contemptuous smile.

'A good deal, when a horse falls back on you.'

'That horse don't want to fall back on you, if you don't make him. If you know how to ride him.—That horse want his own way sometime. If you don't let him, you got to fight him. Then look out!'

'Look out he doesn't kill you, you mean!'

'Look out you don't let him,' said Phœnix, with his slow, grim, sardonic smile.

Lou watched the smooth, golden face with its thin line of moustache and its sad eyes with the glint in them. Cruel—there was something cruel in him, right down in the abyss of him. But at the same time, there was an aloneness, and a grim little satisfaction in a fight, and the peculiar courage of an inherited despair. People who inherit despair may at last turn it into greater heroism. It was almost so with Phœnix. Three quarters of his blood was probably Indian and the remaining quarter, that came through the Mexican father, had the Spanish-American despair to add to the Indian. It was almost complete enough to leave him free to be heroic.

'What are we going to do with him, though?' she asked.

'Why don't you and Mrs. Witt go back to America—you never been West. You go West.'

'Where, to California?'

'No. To Arizona or New Mexico or Colorado or Wyoming, anywhere. Not to California.'

Phœnix looked at her keenly, and she saw the desire dark in him. He wanted to go back. But he was afraid to go back alone, empty-handed, as it were. He had suffered too much, and in that country his sufferings would overcome him, unless he had some other background. He had been too much in contact with the white world, and his own world was too dejected, in a sense, too hopeless for his own hopelessness. He needed an alien contact to give him relief.

But he wanted to go back. His necessity to go back was becoming too strong for him.

'What is it like in Arizona?' she asked. 'Isn't it all pale-coloured sand and alkali, and a few cactuses, and terribly hot and deathly?'

'No!' he cried. 'I don't take you there. I take you to the mountains—trees—' he lifted up his hand and looked at the sky—'big trees—pine! *Pino—real* and *pinovetes,* smell good. And then you come down, *piñon,* not very tall, and *cedro,* cedar, smell good in the fire. And then you see the desert, away below, go miles and miles, and where the canyon go, the crack where it look red! I know, I been there, working a cattle ranch.'

He looked at her with a haunted glow in his dark eyes. The poor fellow was suffering from nostalgia. And as he glowed at her in that queer mystical way, she too seemed to see that country, with its dark, heavy mountains holding in their lap the great stretches of pale, creased, silent desert that still is virgin of idea, its word unspoken.

Phœnix was watching her closely and subtly. He wanted something of her. He wanted it intensely, heavily, and he watched her as if he could force her to give it him. He wanted her to take him back to America, because, rudderless, he was afraid to go back alone. He wanted her to take him back: avidly he wanted it. She was to be the means to his end.

Why shouldn't he go back by himself? Why should he crave for her to go too? Why should he want her there?

There was no answer, except that he did.

'Why, Phœnix,' she said, 'I might possibly go back to America. But you know, Sir Henry would never go there. He doesn't like America, though he's never been. But I'm sure he'd never go there to live.'

'Let him stay here,' said Phœnix abruptly, the sardonic look on his face as he watched her face. 'You come, and let him stay here.'

'Ah, that's a whole story!' she said, and moved away.

As she went, he looked after her, standing silent and arrested and watching as an Indian watches.—It was not love. Personal love counts so little when the greater griefs, the greater hopes, the great despairs and the great resolutions come upon us.

She found Mrs. Witt rather more silent, more firmly closed within herself, than usual. Her mouth was shut tight, her brows were arched rather more imperiously than ever, she was revolving some inward problem about which Lou was far too wise to enquire.

In the afternoon Dean Vyner and Mrs. Vyner came to call on Lady Carrington.

'What bad luck this is, Lady Carrington!' said the Dean. 'Knocks Scotland on the head for you this year, I'm afraid. How did you leave your husband?'

'He seems to be doing as well as he could do!' said Lou.

'But how *very* unfortunate!' murmured the invalid Mrs. Vyner. 'Such a handsome young man, in the bloom of youth! Does he suffer much pain?'

'Chiefly his foot,' said Lou.

'Oh, I *do* so hope they'll be able to restore the ankle. Oh, how dreadful to be lamed at his age!'

'The doctor doesn't know. There *may* be a limp,' said Lou.

'That horse has certainly left his mark on two good-looking young fellows,' said the Dean. 'If you don't mind my saying so, Lady Carrington, I think he's a bad egg.'

'Who, St. Mawr?' said Lou, in her American sing-song.

'Yes, Lady Carrington,' murmured Mrs. Vyner, in her invalid's low tone. 'Don't you think he ought to be put away? He seems to me the incarnation of cruelty. His neigh. It goes through me like knives. Cruel! Cruel! Oh, I think he should be put away.'

'How put away?' murmured Lou, taking on an invalid's low tone herself.

'Shot, I suppose,' said the Dean.

'It is quite painless. He'll know nothing,' murmured Mrs. Vyner hastily. 'And think of the harm he has done already! Horrible! Horrible!' she shuddered. 'Poor Sir Henry lame for life, and Eddy Edwards disfigured. Besides all that has gone before. Ah, no, such a creature ought not to live!'

'To live, and have a groom to look after him and feed him,' said the Dean. 'It's a bit thick, while he's smashing up the very people that give him bread— or oats, since he's a horse. But I suppose you'll be wanting to get rid of him?'

'Rico does,' murmured Lou.

'Very naturally. So should I. A vicious horse is worse than a vicious man— except that you are free to put him six feet underground, and end his vice finally, by your own act.'

'Do you think St. Mawr is vicious?' said Lou.

'Well, of course—if we're driven to definitions!—I *know* he's dangerous.'

'And do you think we ought to shoot everything that is dangerous?' asked Lou, her colour rising.

'But, Lady Carrington, have you consulted your husband? Surely his wish should be law, in a matter of this sort! And on such an occasion! For *you*, who are a woman, it is enough that horse is cruel, cruel, evil! I felt it long before anything happened. That evil male cruelty! Ah!' and she clasped her hands convulsively.

'I suppose,' said Lou slowly, 'that St. Mawr is really Rico's horse: I gave him to him, I suppose. But I don't believe I could let him shoot him, for all that.'

'Ah, Lady Carrington,' said the Dean breezily, 'you can shift the responsibility. The horse is a public menace, put it at that. We can get an order to have him done away with, at the public expense. And among ourselves we can find some suitable compensation for you, as a mark of sympathy. Which, believe me, is very sincere! One hates to have to destroy a fine-looking animal. But I would sacrifice a dozen rather than have our Rico limping.'

'Yes, indeed,' murmured Mrs. Vyner.

'Will you excuse me one moment, while I see about tea?' said Lou, rising and leaving the room. Her colour was high, and there was a glint in her eye. These people almost roused her to hatred. Oh, these awful, house-bred, house-inbred human beings, how repulsive they were!

She hurried to her mother's dressing-room. Mrs. Witt was very carefully putting a touch of red on her lips.

'Mother, they want to shoot St. Mawr,' she said.

'I know,' said Mrs. Witt, as calmly as if Lou had said tea was ready.

'Well—' stammered Lou, rather put out, 'don't you think it cheek?'

'It depends, I suppose, on the point of view,' said Mrs. Witt dispassionately, looking closely at her lips. 'I don't think the English climate agrees with me. I need something to stand up against, no matter whether it's great heat or great cold. This climate, like the food and the people, is most always luke-warm or tepid, one or the other. And the tepid and the lukewarm are not really my line.' She spoke with a slow drawl.

'But they're in the drawing-room, mother, trying to force me to have St. Mawr killed.'

'What about tea?' said Mrs. Witt.

'I don't care,' said Lou.

Mrs. Witt worked the bell-handle.

'I suppose, Louise,' she said, in her most beaming eighteenth-century manner, 'that these are your guests, so you will preside over the ceremony of pouring out.'

'No, mother, you do it. I can't smile to-day.'

'I can,' said Mrs. Witt.

And she bowed her head slowly, with a faint, ceremoniously effusive smile, as if handing a cup of tea.

Lou's face flickered to a smile.

'Then you pour out for them. You can stand them better than I can.'

'Yes,' said Mrs. Witt. 'I saw Mrs. Vyner's hat coming across the churchyard. It looks so like a crumpled cup and saucer, that I have been saying to myself ever since: *Dear Mrs. Vyner, can't I fill your cup?*—and then pouring tea into that hat. And I hear the Dean responding: *My head is covered with cream, my cup runneth over.*—That is the way they make *me* feel.'

They marched downstairs, and Mrs. Witt poured tea with that devastating correctness which made Mrs. Vyner, who was utterly impervious to sarcasm, pronounce her 'indecipherably vulgar.'

But the Dean was the old bulldog, and he had set his teeth in a subject.

'I was talking to Lady Carrington about that stallion, Mrs. Witt.'

'Did you say stallion?' asked Mrs. Witt, with perfect neutrality.

'Why, yes, I presume that's what he is.'

'I presume so,' said Mrs. Witt colourlessly.

'I'm afraid Lady Carrington is a little sensitive on the wrong score,' said the Dean.

'I beg your pardon,' said Mrs. Witt, leaning forward in her most colourless polite manner. 'You mean stallion's score?'

'Yes,' said the Dean testily. 'The horse St. Mawr.'

'The stallion St. Mawr,' echoed Mrs. Witt, with utmost mild vagueness. She completely ignored Mrs. Vyner, who felt plunged like a specimen into methylated spirit. There was a moment's full stop.

'Yes?' said Mrs. Witt naïvely.

'You agree that we can't have any more of these accidents to your young men?' said the Dean rather hastily.

'I certainly do!' Mrs. Witt spoke very slowly, and the Dean's lady began to look up. She might find a loophole through which to wriggle into the contest. 'You know, Dean, that my son-in-law calls me, for preference, *belle-mère!* It sounds so awfully English when he says it; I always see myself as an old grey mare with a bell round her neck, leading a bunch of horses.' She smiled a prim little smile, *very* conversationally. 'Well!' and she pulled herself up from the aside. 'Now, as the bell-mare of the bunch of horses, I shall see to it that my son-in-law doesn't go too near that stallion again. That stallion won't stand mischief.'

She spoke so earnestly that the Dean looked at her with round wide eyes, completely taken aback.

'We all know, Mrs. Witt, that the author of the mischief is St. Mawr himself,' he said, in a loud tone.

'Really! you think *that?*' Her voice went up in American surprise. 'Why, how *strange—!*' and she lingered over the last word.

'Strange, eh?—After what's just happened?' said the Dean, with a deadly little smile.

'Why, yes! Most strange! I saw with my own eyes my son-in-law pull that stallion over backwards, and hold him down with the reins as tight as he could hold them; pull St. Mawr's head backwards on to the ground, till the groom had to crawl up and force the reins out of my son-in-law's hands. Don't you think that was mischievous on Sir Henry's part?'

The Dean was growing purple. He made an apoplectic movement with his hand. Mrs. Vyner was turned to a seated pillar of salt, strangely dressed up.

'Mrs. Witt, you are playing on words.'

'No, Dean Vyner, I am not. My son-in-law pulled that horse over backwards and pinned him down with the reins.'

'I am sorry for the horse,' said the Dean, with heavy sarcasm.

'I am *very*,' said Mrs. Witt, 'sorry for that stallion: *very!*'

Here Mrs. Vyner rose as if a chair-spring had suddenly propelled her to her feet. She was streaky pink in the face.

'Mrs. Witt,' she panted, 'you misdirect your sympathies. That poor young man—in the beauty of youth!'

'Isn't he *beautiful*—' murmured Mrs. Witt, extravagantly in sympathy. 'He is my daughter's husband!' And she looked at the petrified Lou.

'Certainly!' panted the Dean's wife. 'And you can defend that—that—'

'That stallion,' said Mrs. Witt. 'But you see, Mrs. Vyner,' she added, leaning forward female and confidential, 'if the old grey mare doesn't defend the stallion, who will? All the blooming young ladies will defend my beautiful son-in-law. You feel so *warmly* for him yourself! I'm an American woman, and I always have to stand up for the accused. And I stand up for that stallion. I say it is not right. He was pulled over backwards and then pinned down by my son-in-law—who may have meant to do it, or may not. And now people abuse him.—Just tell everybody, Mrs. Vyner and Dean Vyner'—she looked round at the Dean—'that the *belle-mère's* sympathies are with the stallion.'

She looked from one to the other with a faint and gracious little bow, her black eyebrows arching in her eighteenth-century face like black rainbows, and her full, bold grey eyes absolutely incomprehensible.

'Well, it's a peculiar message to have to hand round, Mrs. Witt,' the Dean began to boom, when she interrupted him by laying her hand on his arm and leaning forward, looking up into his face like a clinging, pleading female.

'Oh, but *do* hand it, Dean, *do* hand it,' she pleaded, gazing intently into his face.

He backed uncomfortably from that gaze.

'Since you wish it,' he said, in a chest voice.

'I most certainly *do*—' she said, as if she were wishing the sweetest wish on earth. Then, turning to Mrs. Vyner:

'Good-bye, Mrs. Vyner. We *do* appreciate your coming, my daughter and I.'

'I came out of kindness—' said Mrs. Vyner.

'Oh, I know it, I know it,' said Mrs. Witt. 'Thank you *so* much. Good-bye! Good-bye, Dean! Who is taking the morning service on Sunday? I hope it is you, because I want to come.'

'It *is* me,' said the Dean. 'Good-bye! Well, good-bye, Lady Carrington. I shall be going over to see our young man to-morrow, and will gladly take you or any thing you have to send.'

'Perhaps mother would like to go,' said Lou, softly, plaintively.

'Well, we shall see,' said the Dean. 'Good-bye for the present!'

Mother and daughter stood at the window watching the two cross the churchyard. Dean and wife knew it, but daren't look round, and daren't admit the fact to one another.

Lou was grinning with a complete grin that gave her an odd, dryad or faun look, intensified.

'It was almost as good as pouring tea into her hat,' said Mrs. Witt serenely. 'People like that tire me out. I shall take a glass of sherry.'

'So will I, mother.—It was even better than pouring tea in her hat.—You meant, didn't you, if you poured tea in her hat, to put cream and sugar in first?'

'I did,' said Mrs. Witt.

But after the excitement of the encounter had passed away, Lou felt as if her life had passed away too. She went to bed, feeling she could stand no more.

In the morning she found her mother sitting at a window watching a funeral. It was raining heavily, so that some of the mourners even wore mackintosh coats. The funeral was in the poorer corner of the churchyard, where another new grave was covered with wreaths of sodden, shrivelling flowers.—The yellowish coffin stood on the wet earth, in the rain: the curate held his hat, in a sort of permanent salute, above his head like a little umbrella, as he hastened on with the service. The people seemed too wet to weep more wet.

It was a long coffin.

'Mother, do you really *like* watching?' asked Lou irritably, as Mrs. Witt sat in complete absorption.

'I do, Louise, I really enjoy it.'

'Enjoy, mother!'—Lou was almost disgusted.

'I'll tell you why. I imagine I'm the one in the coffin—this is a girl of eighteen, who died of consumption—and those are my relatives, and I'm watching them put me away. And you know, Louise, I've come to the conclusion that hardly anybody in the world really lives, and so hardly anybody really dies. They may well say: *O Death, where is thy sting-a-ling-a-ling?* [33] Even Death can't sting those that have never really lived.—I always used to want that—to die without death stinging me.—And I'm sure the girl in the coffin is saying to herself: *Fancy Aunt Emma putting on a drab slicker, and wearing it while they bury me. Doesn't show much respect. But then my mother's family always were common!* I feel there should be a solemn burial of a roll of newspapers containing the account of the death and funeral, next week. It would be just as serious: the grave of all the world's remarks—'

'I don't want to think about it, mother. One ought to be able to laugh at it. I want to laugh at it.'

'Well, Louise, I think it's just as great a mistake to laugh at everything as to cry at everything. Laughter's not the one panacea, either. I should *really* like, before I do come to be buried in a box, to know where I am. That young girl in that coffin never was anywhere—any more than the newspaper remarks on her death and burial. And I begin to wonder if I've ever been anywhere. I seem to have been a daily sequence of newspaper remarks, myself. I'm sure I never really conceived you and gave you birth. It all happened in newspaper notices. It's a newspaper fact that you are my child, and that's about all there is to it.'

Lou smiled as she listened.

'I always knew you were philosophic, mother. But I never dreamed it would come to elegies in a country churchyard, written to your motherhood.'

'*Exactly*, Louise! Here I sit and sing the elegy to my own motherhood. I never had any motherhood, except in newspaper fact. I never was a wife, except in newspaper notices. I never was a young girl, except in newspaper

33. From a revivalist hymn ("The bells of hell go ting-aling-aling . . .").

remarks. Bury everything I ever said or that was said about me, and you've buried *me*. But since Kind Words Can Never Die, I can't be buried, and death has no sting-a-ling-a-ling for *me!*—Now listen to me, Louise: I want death to be real to me—not as it was to that young girl. I *want* it to hurt me, Louise. If it hurts me enough, I shall know I was alive.'

She set her face and gazed under half-dropped lids at the funeral, stoic, fate-like, and yet, for the first time, with a certain pure wistfulness of a young, virgin girl. This frightened Lou very much. She was so used to the matchless Amazon in her mother, that when she saw her sit there still, wistful, virginal, tender as a girl who has never taken armour, wistful at the window that only looked on graves, a serious terror took hold of the young woman. The terror of *too late!*

Lou felt years, centuries older than her mother, at that moment, with the tiresome responsibility of youth to protect and guide their elders.

'What can we do about it, mother?' she asked protectively.

'Do nothing, Louise. I'm not going to have anybody wisely steering my canoe, now I feel the rapids are near. I shall go with the river. Don't you pretend to do anything for me. I've done enough mischief myself, that way. I'm going down the stream, at last.'

There was a pause.

'But in actuality, what?' asked Lou, a little ironically.

'I don't quite know. Wait awhile.'

'Go back to America?'

'That is possible.'

'I may come too.'

'I've always waited for you to go back of your own will.'

Lou went away, wandering round the house. She was so unutterably tired of everything—weary of the house, the graveyard, weary of the thought of Rico. She would have to go back to him to-morrow, to nurse him. Poor old Rico, going on like an amiable machine from day to day. It wasn't his fault. But his life was a rattling nullity, and her life rattled in null correspondence. She had hardly strength enough to stop rattling and be still. Perhaps she had not strength enough.

She did not know. She felt so weak that unless something carried her away, she would go on rattling her bit in the great machine of human life till she collapsed, and her rattle rattled itself out, and there was a sort of barren silence where the sound of her had been.

She wandered out in the rain, to the coach-house where Lewis and Phœnix were sitting facing one another, one on a bin, the other on the inner door-step.

'Well,' she said, smiling oddly. 'What's to be done?'

The two men stood up. Outside, the rain fell steadily on the flagstones of the yard, past the leaves of trees. Lou sat down on the little iron step of the dogcart.

'That's cold,' said Phœnix. 'You sit here.' And he threw a yellow horse-blanket on the box where he had been sitting.

'I don't want to take your seat,' she said.

'All right, you take it.'

He moved across and sat gingerly on the shaft of the dogcart.—Lou seated herself, and loosened her soft tartan shawl. Her face was pink and fresh, and her dark hair curled almost merrily in the damp. But under her eyes were the finger-prints of deadly weariness.

She looked up at the two men, again smiling in her odd fashion.

'What are we going to do?' she asked.

They looked at her closely, seeking her meaning.

'What about?' said Phœnix, a faint smile reflecting on his face, merely because she smiled.

'Oh, everything,' she said, hugging her shawl again. 'You know what they want? They want to shoot St. Mawr.'

The two men exchanged glances.

'Who want it?' said Phœnix.

'Why—all our *friends!*' she made a little *moue.*[34] 'Dean Vyner does.'

Again the men exchanged glances. There was a pause. Then Phœnix said, looking aside:

'The boss is selling him.'

'Who?'

'Sir Henry.'—The half-breed always spoke the title with difficulty, and with a sort of sneer. 'He sell him to Miss Manby.'

'How do you know?'

'The man from Corrabach told me last night. Flora, she say it.' Lou's eyes met the sardonic, empty-seeing eyes of Phœnix direct. There was too much sarcastic understanding. She looked aside.

'What else did he say?' she asked.

'I don't know,' said Phœnix, evasively. 'He say they cut him—else shoot him. Think they cut him—and if he die, he die.'

Lou understood. He meant they would geld St. Mawr—at his age.

She looked at Lewis. He sat with his head down, so she could not see his face.

'Do you think it is true?' she asked. 'Lewis? Do you think they would try to geld St. Mawr—to make him a gelding?'

Lewis looked up at her. There was a faint deadly glimmer of contempt on his face.

'Very likely, Mam,' he said.

She was afraid of his cold, uncanny pale eyes, with their uneasy grey dawn of contempt. These two men, with their silent, deadly inner purpose, were not like other men. They seemed like two silent enemies of all the other men she knew. Enemies in the great white camp, disguised as servants, waiting the incalculable opportunity. What the opportunity might be, none knew.

'Sir Henry hasn't mentioned anything to me about selling St. Mawr to Miss Manby,' she said.

The derisive flicker of a smile came on Phœnix's face.

'He sell him first, and tell you then,' he said, with his deadly impassive manner.

'But do you really think so?' she asked.

It was extraordinary how much corrosive contempt Phœnix could convey, saying nothing. She felt it almost as an insult. Yet it was a relief to her.

34. Pout.

'You know, I can't believe it. I can't believe Sir Henry would want to have St. Mawr mutilated. I believe he'd rather shoot him.'

'You think so?' said Phœnix, with a faint grin.

Lou turned to Lewis.

'Lewis, will you tell me what you truly think?'

Lewis looked at her with a hard, straight, fearless British [35] stare.

'That man Philips was in the "Moon and Stars" last night. He said Miss Manby told him she was buying St. Mawr, and she asked him if he thought it would be safe to cut him, and make a horse of him. He said it would be better, take some of the nonsense out of him. He's no good for a sire, anyhow—'

Lewis dropped his head again, and tapped a tattoo with the toe of his rather small foot.

'And what do you think?' said Lou.—It occurred to her how sensible and practicable Miss Manby was, so much more so than the Dean.

Lewis looked up at her with his pale eyes.

'It won't have anything to do with me,' he said. 'I shan't go to Corrabach Hall.'

'What will you do, then?'

Lewis did not answer. He looked at Phœnix.

'Maybe him and me go to America,' said Phœnix, looking at the void.

'Can he get in?' said Lou.

'Yes, he can. I know how,' said Phœnix.

'And the money?' she said.

'We got money.'

There was a silence, after which she asked of Lewis:

'You'd leave St. Mawr to his fate?'

'I can't help his fate,' said Lewis. 'There's too many people in the world for me to help anything.'

'Poor St. Mawr!'

She went indoors again, and up to her room: then higher, to the top rooms of the tall Georgian house. From one window she could see the fields in the rain. She could see St. Mawr himself, alone as usual, standing with his head up, looking across the fences. He was streaked dark with rain. Beautiful, with his poised head and massive neck, and his supple hindquarters. He was neighing to Poppy. Clear on the wet wind came the sound of his bell-like, stallion's calling, that Mrs. Vyner called cruel. It was a strange noise, with a splendour that belonged to another world-age. The mean cruelty of Mrs. Vyner's humanitarianism, the barren cruelty of Flora Manby, the eunuch cruelty of Rico. Our whole eunuch civilization, nasty-minded as eunuchs are, with their kind of sneaking, sterilizing cruelty.

Yet even she herself, seeing St. Mawr's conceited march along the fence, could not help addressing him:

'Yes, my boy! If you knew what Miss Flora Manby was preparing for you! She'll sharpen a knife that will settle you.'

And Lou called her mother.

The two American women stood high at the window, overlooking the wet,

35. Here meaning "Celtic," "ancient British."

close, hedged-and-fenced English landscape. Everything enclosed, enclosed, to stifling. The very apples on the trees looked so shut in, it was impossible to imagine any speck of 'Knowledge' lurking inside them. Good to eat, good to cook, good even for show. But the wild sap of untamable and inexhaustible knowledge—no! Bred out of them. Geldings, even the apples.

Mrs. Witt listened to Lou's half-humorous statements.

'You must admit, mother, Flora is a sensible girl,' she said.

'I admit it, Louise.'

'She goes straight to the root of the matter.'

'And eradicates the root. Wise girl! And what is your answer?'

'I don't know, mother. What would you say?'

'I know what *I* should say.'

'Tell me.'

'I should say: *Miss Manby, you may have my husband, but not my horse. My husband won't need emasculating, and my horse I won't have you meddle with. I'll preserve one last male thing in the museum of this world, if I can.*'

Lou, listened, smiling faintly.

'That's what I will say,' she replied at length. 'The funny thing is, mother, they think all their men with their bare faces or their little quotation-marks moustaches *are* so tremendously male. That foxhunting one!'

'I know it. Like little male motor-cars. Give him a little gas, and start him on the low gear, and away he goes: all his male gear rattling, like a cheap motor-car.'

'I'm afraid I dislike men altogether, mother.'

'You may, Louise. Think of Flora Manby, and how you love the fair sex.'

'After all. St. Mawr is better. And I'm glad if he gives them a kick in the face.'

'Ah, Louise!' Mrs. Witt suddenly clasped her hands with wicked passion. '*Ay, que gozo!* [36] as our Juan used to say, on your father's ranch in Texas.' She gazed in a sort of wicked ecstasy out of the window.

They heard Lou's maid softly calling Lady Carrington from below. Lou went to the stairs.

'What is it?'

'Lewis wants to speak to you, my Lady.'

'Send him into the sitting-room.'

The two women went down.

'What is it, Lewis?' asked Lou.

'Am I to bring in St. Mawr, in case they send for him from Corrabach?'

'No,' said Lou swiftly.

'Wait a minute,' put in Mrs. Witt. 'What makes you think they will send for St. Mawr from Corrabach, Lewis?' she asked, suave as a grey leopard cat.

'Miss Manby went up to Flints Farm with Dean Vyner this morning, and they've just come back. They stopped the car, and Miss Manby got out at the field gate, to look at St. Mawr. I'm thinking if she made the bargain with Sir Henry, she'll be sending a man over this afternoon, and if I'd better brush St. Mawr down a bit, in case.'

36. "What joy!"

The man stood strangely still, and the words came like shadows of his real meaning. It was a challenge.

'I see,' said Mrs. Witt slowly.

Lou's face darkened. She too saw.

'So that is her game,' she said. 'That is why they got me down here.'

'Never mind, Louise,' said Mrs. Witt. Then to Lewis: 'Yes, please bring in St. Mawr. You wish it, don't you, Louise?'

'Yes,' hesitated Lou. She saw by Mrs. Witt's closed face that a counter-move was prepared.

'And, Lewis,' said Mrs. Witt, 'my daughter may wish you to ride St. Mawr this afternoon—not to Corrabach Hall.'

'Very good, Madam.'

Mrs. Witt sat silent for some time, after Lewis had gone, gathering inspiration from the wet, grisly gravestones.

'Don't you think it's time we made a move, daughter?' she asked.

'Any move,' said Lou desperately.

'Very well then.—My dearest friends, and my *only* friends, in this country, are in Oxfordshire. I will set off to *ride* to Merriton this afternoon, and Lewis will ride with me on St. Mawr.'

'But you can't ride to Merriton in an afternoon,' said Lou.

'I know it. I shall ride across country. I shall *enjoy* it, Louise.—Yes.—I shall consider I am on my way back to America. I am most deadly tired of this country. From Merriton I shall make my arrangements to go to America, and take Lewis and Phœnix and St. Mawr along with me. I think they want to go.— You will decide for yourself.'

'Yes, I'll come too,' said Lou casually.

'Very well. I'll start immediately after lunch, for I can't *breathe* in this place any longer. Where are Henry's automobile maps?'

Afternoon saw Mrs. Witt, in a large waterproof cape, mounted on her horse, Lewis, in another cape, mounted on St. Mawr, trotting through the rain, splashing in the puddles, moving slowly southwards. They took the open country, and would pass quite near to Flints Farm. But Mrs. Witt did not care. With great difficulty she had managed to fasten a small waterproof roll behind her, containing her night things. She seemed to breathe the first breath of freedom.

And sure enough, an hour or so after Mrs. Witt's departure, arrived Flora Manby in a splashed-up motor-car, accompanied by her sister, and bringing a groom and a saddle.

'Do you know, Harry sold me St. Mawr,' she said. 'I'm just wild to get that horse in hand.'

'How?' said Lou.

'Oh, I don't know. There are ways. Do you mind if Philips rides him over now, to Corrabach?—Oh, I forgot, Harry sent you a note.'

DEAREST LOULINA: *Have you been gone from here two days or two years? It seems the latter. You are terribly missed. Flora wanted so much to buy St. Mawr, to save us further trouble, that I have sold him to her. She is giving me what we paid: rather, what you paid; so of course the money is yours. I am thankful we are rid of the animal, and*

that he falls into competent hands—I asked her please to remove him
from your charge to-day. And I can't tell how much easier I am in my
mind, to think of him gone. You are coming back to me to-morrow, aren't
you? I shall think of nothing else but you, till I see you. A rivederti,[37]
darling dear! R.

'I'm so sorry,' said Lou. 'Mother went on horseback to see some friends, and
Lewis went with her on St. Mawr. He knows the road.'

'She'll be back this evening?' said Flora.

'I don't know. Mother is so uncertain. She may be away a day or two.'

'Well, here's the cheque for St. Mawr.'

'No, I won't take it now—no, thank you—not till mother comes back with
the goods.'

Flora was chagrined. The two women knew they hated one another. The visit
was a brief one.

Mrs. Witt rode on in the rain, which abated as the afternoon wore down, and
the evening came without rain, and with a suffusion of pale yellow light. All the
time she had trotted in silence, with Lewis just behind her. And she scarcely
saw the heather-covered hills with the deep clefts between them, nor the oak-
woods, nor the lingering foxgloves, nor the earth at all. Inside herself she felt a
profound repugnance for the English country: she preferred even the crudeness
of Central Park in New York.

And she felt an almost savage desire to get away from Europe, from everything European. Now she was really *en route,* she cared not a straw for St.
Mawr or for Lewis or anything. Something just writhed inside her, all the time,
against Europe. That closeness, that sense of cohesion, that sense of being fused
into a lump with all the rest—no matter how much distance you kept—this
drove her mad. In America the cohesion was a matter of choice and will. But
in Europe it was organic, like the helpless particles of one sprawling body. And
the great body in a state of incipient decay.

She was a woman of fifty-one: and she seemed hardly to have lived a day.
She looked behind her—the thin trees and swamps of Louisiana, the sultry,
sub-tropical excitement of decaying New Orleans, the vast bare dryness of
Texas, with mobs of cattle in an illumined dust! The half-European thrills of
New York! The false stability of Boston! A clever husband, who was a brilliant
lawyer, but who was far more thrilled by his cattle ranch than by his law: and
who drank heavily and died. The years of first widowhood in Boston, consoled
by a self-satisfied sort of intellectual courtship from clever men.—For curiously
enough, while she wanted it, she had always been able to compel men to pay
court to her. All kinds of men. Then a rather dashing time in New York—
when she was in her early forties. Then the long *visual* philandering in Europe.
She left off 'loving,' save through the eye, when she came to Europe. And when
she made her trips to America, she found it was finished there also, her 'loving.'

What was the matter? Examining herself, she had long ago decided that her
nature was a destructive force. But then, she justified herself, she had only destroyed that which was destructible. If she could have found something inde-

---

37. Italian equivalent of *Au revoir* (more commonly *Arrivederci*).

structible, especially in men, though she would have fought against it, she would have been glad at last to be defeated by it.

That was the point. She really wanted to be defeated, in her own eyes. And nobody had ever defeated her. Men were never really her match. A woman of terrible strong health, she felt even that in her strong limbs there was far more electric power than in the limbs of any man she had met. That curious fluid electric force, that could make any man kiss her hand, if she so willed it. A queen, as far as she wished. And not having been very clever at school, she always had the greatest respect for the mental powers. Her own were not mental powers. Rather electric, as of some strange physical dynamo within her. So she had been ready to bow before Mind.

But alas! After a brief time, she had found Mind, at least the man who was supposed to have the mind, bowing before her. Her own peculiar dynamic force was stronger than the force of Mind. She could make Mind kiss her hand.

And not by any sensual tricks. She did not really care about sensualities, especially as a younger woman. Sex was a mere adjunct. She cared about the mysterious, intense, dynamic sympathy that could flow between her and some 'live' man—a man who was highly conscious, a real live wire. That she cared about.

But she had never rested until she had made the man she admired: and admiration was the root of her attraction to any man: made him kiss her hand. In both senses, actual and metaphorical. Physical and metaphysical. Conquered his country.

She had always succeeded. And she believed that, if she cared, she always *would* succeed. In the world of living men. Because of the power that was in her, in her arms, in her strong, shapely, but terrible hands, in all the great dynamo of her body.

For this reason she had been so terribly contemptuous of Rico, and of Lou's infatuation. Ye Gods! what was Rico in the scale of men!

Perhaps she despised the younger generation too easily. Because she did not see its sources of power, she concluded it was powerless. Whereas perhaps the power of accommodating oneself to any circumstance and committing oneself to no circumstance is the last triumph of mankind.

Her generation had had its day. She had had her day. The world of her men had sunk into a sort of insignificance. And with a great contempt she despised the world that had come into place instead: the world of Rico and Flora Manby, the world represented, to her, by the Prince of Wales.[38]

In such a world there was nothing even to conquer. It gave everything and gave nothing to everybody and anybody all the time. *Dio benedetto!* as Rico would say. A great complicated tangle of nonentities ravelled in nothingness. So it seemed to her.

Great God! This was the generation she had helped to bring into the world.

She had had her day. And, as far as the mysterious battle of life went, she had won all the way. Just as Cleopatra, in the mysterious business of a woman's life, won all the way.

---

38. Edward, Prince of Wales (1894–1972), for a scant year (1936) King Edward VIII, famous during the post-war years for his world tours and leadership of the smart set.

Though that bald tough Cæsar had drawn his iron from the fire without losing much of its temper. And he had gone his way. And Antony surely was splendid to die with.

In her life there had been no tough Cæsar to go his way in cold blood, away from her. Her men had gone from her like dogs on three legs, into the crowd. And certainly there was no gorgeous Antony to die for and with.

Almost she was tempted in her heart to cry: 'Conquer me, O God, before I die!'—But then she had a terrible contempt for the God that was supposed to rule this universe. She felt she could make *Him* kiss her hand. Here she was, a woman of fifty-one, past the change of life. And her great dread was to die an empty, barren death. Oh, if only Death might open dark wings of mystery and consolation! To die an easy, barren death. To pass out as she had passed in, without mystery or the rustling of darkness! That was her last, final, ashy dread.

'Old!' she said to herself. 'I am not *old!* I have lived many years, that is all. But I am as timeless as an hour-glass that turns morning and night, and spills the hours of sleep one way, the hours of consciousness the other way, without itself being affected. Nothing in all my life has ever truly affected me.—I believe Cleopatra only tried the asp, as she tried her pearls in wine, to see if it would really, really have any effect on her. Nothing had ever really had any effect on her, neither Cæsar nor Antony nor any of them. Never once had she really been lost, lost to herself. Then try death, see if that trick would work. If she would lose herself to herself that way.—Ah, death—!'

But Mrs. Witt mistrusted death too. She felt she might pass out as a bed of asters passes out in autumn, to mere nothingness.—And something in her longed to die, at least, *positively:* to be folded then at last into throbbing wings of mystery, like a hawk that goes to sleep. Not like a thing made into a parcel and put into the last rubbish-heap.

So she rode trotting across the hills, mile after mile, in silence. Avoiding the roads, avoiding everything, avoiding everybody, just trotting forwards, towards night.

And by nightfall they had travelled twenty-five miles. She had motored around this country, and knew the little towns and the inns. She knew where she would sleep.

The morning came beautiful and sunny. A woman so strong in health, why should she ride with the fact of death before her eyes? But she did.

Yet in sunny morning she must do something about it.

'Lewis!' she said. 'Come here and tell me something, please! Tell me,' she said, 'do you believe in God?'

'In God!' he said, wondering. 'I never think about it.'

'But do you say your prayers?'

'No, Mam!'

'Why don't you?'

He thought about it for some minutes.

'I don't like religion. My aunt and uncle were religious.'

'You don't like religion,' she repeated. 'And you don't believe in God.—Well, then—'

'Nay!' he hesitated. 'I never said I didn't believe in God.—Only I'm sure I'm not a Methodist. And I feel a fool in a proper church. And I feel a fool saying my prayers.—And I feel a fool when ministers and parsons come getting at me. —I never think about God, if folks don't try to make me.' He had a small, sly smile, almost gay.

'And you don't like feeling a fool?' She smiled rather patronizingly.

'No, Mam.'

'Do I make you feel a fool?' she asked, dryly.

He looked at her without answering.

'Why don't you answer?' she said, pressing.

'I think you'd like to make a fool of me sometimes,' he said.

'Now?' she pressed.

He looked at her with that slow, distant look.

'Maybe!' he said, rather unconcernedly.

Curiously, she couldn't touch him. He always seemed to be watching her from a distance, as if from another country. Even if she made a fool of him, something in him would all the time be far away from her, not implicated.

She caught herself up in the personal game, and returned to her own isolated question. A vicious habit made her start the personal tricks. She didn't want to, really.

There was something about this little man—sometimes, to herself, she called him *Little Jack Horner, Sat in a corner*—that irritated her and made her want to taunt him. His peculiar little inaccessibility, that was so tight and easy.

Then again, there was something, his way of looking at her as if he looked from out of another country, a country of which he was an inhabitant, and where she had never been: this touched her strangely. Perhaps behind this little man was the mystery. In spite of the fact that in actual life, in her world, he was only a groom, almost *chétif*,[39] with his legs a little bit horsy and bowed; and of no education, saying *Yes, Mam!* and *No, Mam!* and accomplishing nothing, simply nothing at all on the face of the earth. Strictly a nonentity.

And yet, what made him perhaps the only real entity to her, his seeming to inhabit another world than hers. A world dark and still, where language never ruffled the growing leaves, and seared their edges like a bad wind.

Was it an illusion, however? Sometimes she thought it was. Just bunkum, which she had faked up, in order to have something to mystify about.

But then, when she saw Phœnix and Lewis silently together, she knew there *was* another communion, silent, excluding her. And sometimes when Lewis was alone with St. Mawr: and once, when she saw him pick up a bird that had stunned itself against a wire: she had realized another world, silent, where each creature is alone in its own aura of silence, the mystery of power: as Lewis had power with St. Mawr, and even with Phœnix.

The visible world, and the invisible. Or rather, the audible and the inaudible. She had lived so long, and so completely, in the visible, audible world. She would not easily admit that other, inaudible. She always wanted to jeer, as she approached the brink of it.

Even now, she wanted to jeer at the little fellow, because of his holding himself inaccessible within the inaudible, silent world. And she knew he knew it.

39. Puny.

'Did you never want to be rich, and be a gentleman, like Sir Henry?' she asked.

'I would many times have liked to be rich. But I never exactly wanted to be a gentleman,' he said.

'Why not?'

'I can't exactly say. I should be uncomfortable if I was like they are.'

'And are you comfortable now?'

'When I'm let alone.'

'And do they let you alone? Does the world let you alone?'

'No, they don't.'

'Well, then—!'

'I keep to myself all I can.'

'And are you comfortable, as you call it, when you keep to yourself?'

'Yes, I am.'

'But when you keep to yourself, what do you keep to? What precious treasure have you to keep to?'

He looked, and saw she was jeering.

'None,' he said. 'I've got nothing of that sort.'

She rode impatiently on ahead.

And the moment she had done so, she regretted it. She might put the little fellow, with contempt, out of her reckoning. But no, she would not do it.

She had put so much out of her reckoning: soon she would be left in an empty circle, with her empty self at the centre.

She reined in again.

'Lewis!' she said. 'I don't want you to take offence at anything I say.'

'No, Mam.'

'I don't want you to say just *No, Mam!* all the time!' she cried impulsively. 'Promise me.'

'Yes, Mam!'

'But really! Promise me you won't be offended at whatever I say.'

'Yes, Mam!'

She looked at him searchingly. To her surprise, she was almost in tears. A woman of her years! And with a servant!

But his face was blank and stony, with a stony, distant look of pride that made him inaccessible to her emotions. He met her eyes again: with that cold, distant look, looking straight into her hot, confused, pained self. So cold and as if merely refuting her. He didn't believe her, nor trust her, nor like her even. She was an attacking enemy to him. Only he stayed really far away from her, looking down at her from a sort of distant hill where her weapons could not reach: not quite.

And at the same time, it hurt him in a dumb, living way, that she made these attacks on him. She could see the cloud of hurt in his eyes, no matter how distantly he looked at her.

They bought food in a village shop, and sat under a tree near a field where men were already cutting oats, in a warm valley. Lewis had stabled the horses for a couple of hours, to feed and rest. But he came to join her under the tree, to eat.—He sat at a little distance from her, with the bread and cheese in his small brown hands, eating silently, and watching the harvesters. She was cross with him, and therefore she was stingy, would give him nothing to eat but dry bread and cheese. Herself, she was not hungry.—So all the time he kept his face a little averted from her. As a matter of fact, he kept his whole being averted from her, away from her. He did not want to touch her, nor to be touched by her. He kept his spirit there, alert, on its guard, but out of contact. It was as if he had unconsciously accepted the battle, the old battle. He was her target, the old object of her deadly weapons. But he refused to shoot back. It was as if he caught all her missiles in full flight, before they touched him, and silently threw them on the ground behind him. And in some essential part of himself he ignored her, staying in another world.

That other world! Mere male armour of artificial imperviousness! It angered her.

Yet she knew, by the way he watched the harvesters, and the grasshoppers popping into notice, that it was another world. And when a girl went by, carrying food to the field, it was at him she glanced. And he gave that quick, animal little smile that came from him unawares. Another world!

Yet also, there was a sort of meanness about him: a *suffisance!* [40] A keep-yourself-for-yourself, and don't give yourself away.

Well!—she rose impatiently.

It was hot in the afternoon, and she was rather tired. She went to the inn and slept, and did not start again till tea-time.

Then they had to ride rather late. The sun sank, among a smell of cornfields, clear and yellow-red behind motionless dark trees. Pale smoke rose from cottage chimneys. Not a cloud was in the sky, which held the upward-floating like a bowl inverted on purpose. A new moon sparkled and was gone. It was beginning of night.

Away in the distance, they saw a curious pinkish glare of fire, probably furnaces. And Mrs. Witt thought she could detect the scent of furnace smoke, or factory smoke. But then she always said that of the English air: it was never quite free of the smell of smoke, coal-smoke.

They were riding slowly on a path through fields, down a long slope. Away below was a puther [41] of lights. All the darkness seemed full of half-spent crossing lights, a curious uneasiness. High in the sky a star seemed to be walking. It was an aeroplane with a light. Its buzz rattled above. Not a space, not a speck of this country that wasn't humanized, occupied by the human claim. Not even the sky.

They descended slowly through a dark wood, which they had entered through a gate. Lewis was all the time dismounting and opening gates, letting her pass, shutting the gate and mounting again.

So, in a while she came to the edge of the wood's darkness, and saw the open pale concave of the world beyond. The darkness was never dark. It shook with the concussion of many invisible lights, lights of towns, villages, mines, factories, furnaces, squatting in the valleys and behind all the hills.

Yet, as Rachel Witt drew rein at the gate emerging from the wood, a very big, soft star fell in heaven, cleaving the hubbub of this human night with a gleam from the greater world.

---

40. Self-sufficiency, conceit.
41. Muddle, disturbance.

'See! a star falling!' said Lewis, as he opened the gate.

'I saw it,' said Mrs. Witt, walking her horse past him.

There was a curious excitement of wonder, or magic, in the little man's voice. Even in this night something strange had stirred awake in him.

'You ask me about God,' he said to her, walking his horse alongside in the shadow of the wood's edge, the darkness of the old Pan, that kept our artificially lit world at bay. 'I don't know about God. But when I see a star fall like that out of long-distance places in the sky: and the moon sinking saying Good-bye! Good-bye! Good-bye! and nobody listening: I think I hear something, though I wouldn't call it God.'

'What then?' said Rachel Witt.

'And you smell the smell of oak-leaves now,' he said, 'now the air is cold. They smell to me more alive than people. The trees hold their bodies hard and still, but they watch and listen with their leaves. And I think they say to me: *Is that you passing there, Morgan Lewis? All right, you pass quickly, we shan't do anything to you. You are like a holly bush.*'

'Yes,' said Rachel Witt, dryly. '*Why?*'

'All the time, the trees grow, and listen. And if you cut a tree down without asking pardon, trees will hurt you some time in your life, in the night-time.'

'I suppose,' said Rachel Witt, 'that's an old superstition.'

'They say that ash trees don't like people. When the other people were most in the country—I mean like what they call fairies, that have all gone now—they liked ash trees best. And you know the little green things with little small nuts in them, that come flying down from ash trees—*pigeons,* we call them—they're the seeds—the other people used to catch them and eat them before they fell to the ground. And that made the people so they could hear trees living and feeling things.—But when all these people that there are now came to England, they liked the oak trees best, because their pigs ate the acorns. So now you can tell the ash trees are mad, they want to kill all these people. But the oak trees are many more than the ash trees.'

'And do you eat the ash-tree seeds?' she asked.

'I always ate them when I was little. Then I wasn't frightened of ash trees, like most of the others. And I wasn't frightened of the moon. If you didn't go near the fire all day, and if you didn't eat any cooked food nor anything that had been in the sun, but only things like turnips or radishes or pig-nuts, and then went without any clothes on, in the full moon, then you could see the people in the moon, and go with them. They never have fire, and they never speak, and their bodies are clear almost like jelly. They die in a minute if there's a bit of fire near them. But they know more than we. Because unless fire touches them, they never die. They see people live and they see people perish, and they say people are only like twigs on a tree, you break them off the tree, and kindle with them. You made a fire of them, and they are gone, the fire is gone, everything is gone. But the people of the moon don't die, and fire is nothing to them. They look at it from the distance of the sky, and see it burning things up, people all appearing and disappearing like twigs that come in spring and you cut them in autumn and make a fire of them and they are gone. And they say: what do people matter? If you want to matter, you must become a moon-boy. Then, all your life, fire can't blind you and people can't hurt you. Because at full moon you can join the moon people, and go through the air and pass any cool places, pass through rocks and through the trunks of trees, and when you come to people lying warm in bed, you punish them.'

'How?'

'You sit on the pillow where they breathe, and you put a web across their mouth, so they can't breathe the fresh air that comes from the moon. So they go on breathing the same air again and again, and that makes them more and more stupefied. The sun gives out heat, but the moon gives out fresh air. That's what the moon people do: they wash the air clean with moonlight.'

He was talking with a strange eager naïveté that amused Rachel Witt, and made her a little uncomfortable in her skin. Was he after all no more than a sort of imbecile?

'Who told you all this stuff?' she asked abruptly.

And, as abruptly, he pulled himself up.

'We used to say it, when we were children.'

'But you don't believe it? It *is* only childishness, after all.'

He paused a moment or two.

'No,' he said, in his ironical little day-voice. 'I know I shan't make anything but a fool of myself, with that talk. But all sorts of things go through our heads, and some seem to linger, and some don't. But you asking me about God put it into my mind, I suppose. I don't know what sort of things I believe in: only I know it's not what the chapel-folks believe in. We, none of us believe in them when it comes to earning a living, or, with you people, when it comes to spending your fortune. Then we know that bread costs money, and even your sleep you have to pay for.—That's work. Or, with you people, it's just owning property and seeing you get your value for your money.—But a man's mind is always full of things. And some people's mind's like my aunt and uncle, are full of religion and hell for everybody except themselves. And some people's minds are all money, money, money, and how to get hold of something they haven't got hold of yet. And some people, like you, are always curious about what everybody else in the world is after. And some people are all for enjoying themselves and being thought much of, and some, like Lady Carrington, don't know what to do with themselves. Myself, I don't want to have in my mind the things other people have in their minds. I'm one that likes my own things best. And if, when I see a bright star fall, like to-night, I think to myself: *There's movement in the sky. The world is going to change again. They're throwing something to us from the distance, and we've got to have it, whether we want it or not. To-morrow there will be a difference for everybody, thrown out of the sky upon us, whether we want it or not:* then that's how I want to think, so let me please myself.'

'You know what a shooting star actually is, I suppose?—and that there are always many in August, because we pass through a region of them?'

'Yes, Mam, I've been told. But stones don't come at us from the sky for nothing. Either it's like when a man tosses an apple to you out of his orchard, as you go by, or it's like when somebody shies a stone at you, to cut your head open. You'll never make me believe the sky is like an empty house with a slate falling from the roof. The world has its own life, the sky has a life of its own, and never is it like stones rolling down a rubbish-heap and falling into a pond.

Many things twitch and twitter within the sky, and many things happen beyond us. My own way of thinking is my own way.'

'I never knew you talk so much.'

'No, Mam. It's your asking me that about God. Or else it's the night-time. I don't believe in God and being good and going to heaven. Neither do I worship idols, so I'm not a heathen, as my aunt called me. Never from a boy did I want to believe the things they kept grinding in their guts at home, and at Sunday School, and at school. A man's mind has to be full of something, so I keep to what we used to think as lads. It's childish nonsense, I know it. But it suits me. Better than other people's stuff. Your man Phœnix is about the same, when he lets on.—Anyhow, it's my own stuff, that we believed as lads, and I like it better than other people's stuff.—You asking about God made me let on. But I would never belong to any club, or trades-union, and God's the same to my mind.'

With this he gave me a little kick to his horse, and St. Mawr went dancing excitedly along the highway they now entered, leaving Mrs. Witt to trot after as rapidly as she could.

When she came to the hotel, to which she had telegraphed for rooms, Lewis disappeared, and she was left thinking hard.

It was not till they were twenty miles from Merriton, riding through a slow morning mist, and she had a rather far-away, wistful look on her face, unusual for her, that she turned to him in the saddle and said:

'Now don't be surprised, Lewis, at what I am going to say. I am going to ask you, now, supposing I wanted to marry you, what should you say?'

He looked at her quickly, and was at once on his guard.

'That you didn't mean it,' he replied hastily.

'Yes,'—she hesitated, and her face looked wistful and tired.—'Supposing I did mean it. Supposing I did really, from my heart, want to marry you and be a wife to you—' she looked away across the fields—'then what should you say?'

Her voice sounded sad, a little broken.

'Why, Mam!' he replied, knitting his brow and shaking his head a little. 'I should say you didn't mean it, you know. Something would have come over you.'

'But supposing I wanted something to come over me?'

He shook his head.

'It would never do, Mam! Some people's flesh and blood is kneaded like bread: and that's me. And some are rolled like fine pastry, like Lady Carrington. And some are mixed with gun-powder. They're like a cartridge you put in a gun, Mam.'

She listened impatiently.

'Don't talk,' she said, 'about bread and cakes and pastry, it all means nothing. You used to answer short enough, Yes, Mam! No, Mam! That will do now. Do you mean Yes! or No?'

His eyes met hers. She was again hectoring.

'No, Mam!' he said, quite neutral.

'Why?'

As she waited for his answer, she saw the foundations of his loquacity dry up, his face go distant and mute again, as it always used to be, till these last two days, when it had had a funny touch of inconsequential merriness.

He looked steadily into her eyes, and his look was neutral, sombre, and hurt. He looked at her as if infinite seas, infinite spaces divided him and her. And his eyes seemed to put her away beyond some sort of fence. An anger congealed cold like lava, set impassive against her and all her sort.

'No, Mam. I couldn't give my body to any woman who didn't respect it.'

'But I do respect it, I do!'—she flushed hot like a girl.

'No, Mam. Not as *I* mean it,' he replied.

There was a touch of anger against her in his voice, and a distance of distaste.

'And how do *you* mean it?' she replied, the full sarcasm coming back into her tones. She could see that as a woman to touch and fondle he saw her as repellent: only repellent.

'I have to be a servant to women now,' he said, 'even to earn my wage. I could never touch with my body a woman whose servant I was.'

'You're not my servant: my daughter pays your wages.—And all that is beside the point, between a man and a woman.'

'No woman who I touched with my body should ever speak to me as you speak to me, or think of me as you think of me,' he said.

'But—' she stammered, 'I think of you—with love. And can you be so unkind as to notice the way I speak? You know it's only my way.'

'You, as a woman,' he said, 'you have no respect for a man.'

'Respect! Respect!' she cried. 'I'm likely to lose what respect I have left. I know I can *love* a man. But whether a man can love a woman—'

'No,' said Lewis. 'I never could, and I think I never shall. Because I don't want to. The thought of it makes me feel shame.'

'What do you mean?' she cried.

'Nothing in the world,' he said, 'would make me feel such shame as to have a woman shouting at me, or mocking at me, as I see women mocking and despising the men they marry. No woman shall touch my body, and mock me or despise me. No woman.'

'But men must be mocked, or despised even, sometimes.'

'No. Not this man. Not by the woman I touch with my body.'

'Are you perfect?'

'I don't know. But if I touch a woman with my body, it must put a lock on her, to respect what I will never have despised: never!'

'What will you never have despised?'

'My body! And my touch upon the woman.'

'Why insist so on your body?'—And she looked at him with a touch of contemptuous mockery, raillery.

He looked her in the eyes, steadily, and coldly, putting her away from him, and himself far away from her.

'Do you expect that any woman will stay your humble slave to-day?' she asked cuttingly.

But he only watched her, coldly, distant, refusing any connection.

'Between men and women, it's a question of give and take. A man can't expect *always* to be humbly adored.'

He watched her still, cold, rather pale, putting her far from him. Then he turned his horse and set off rapidly along the road, leaving her to follow.

She walked her horse and let him go, thinking to herself:

'There's a little bantam cock. And a groom! Imagine it! Thinking he can dictate to a woman!'

She was in love with him. And he, in an odd way, was in love with her. She had known it by the odd, uncanny merriment in him, and his unexpected loquacity. But he would not have her come physically near him. Unapproachable there as a cactus, guarding his 'body' from her contact. As if contact with her would be mortal insult and fatal injury to his marvellous 'body.'

What a little cock-sparrow!

Let him ride ahead. He would have to wait for her somewhere.

She found him at the entrance to the next village. His face was pallid and set. She could tell he felt he had been insulted, so he had congealed into stiff insentience.

'At the bottom of all men is the same,' she said to herself: 'an empty, male conceit of themselves.'

She too rode up with a face like a mask, and straight on to the hotel.

'Can you serve dinner to myself and my servant?' she asked at the inn: which, fortunately for her, accommodated motorists, otherwise they would have said No!

'I think,' said Lewis as they came in sight of Merriton, 'I'd better give Lady Carrington a week's notice.'

A complete little stranger! And an impudent one.

'Exactly as you please,' she said.

She found several letters from her daughter at Marshall Place.

> DEAR MOTHER: *No sooner had you gone off than Flora appeared, not at all in the bud, but rather in full blow. She demanded her victim: Shylock demanding the pound of flesh: and wanted to hand over the shekels.*
>
> *Joyfully I refused them. She said 'Harry' was much better, and invited him and me to stay at Corrabach Hall till he was quite well: it would be less strain on your household while he was still in bed and helpless. So the plan is that he shall be brought down on Friday, if he is really fit for the journey, and we drive straight to Corrabach. I am packing his bags and mine, clearing up our traces: his trunks to go to Corrabach, mine to stay here and make up their minds.—I am going to Flints Farm again to-morrow, dutifully, though I am no flower for the bedside.—I do so want to know if Rico has already called her Fiorita: or perhaps Florecita.[42] It reminds me of old William's joke: Now yuh tell me, little Missy: which is the best posy that grow? And the hushed whisper in which he said the answer: The Collyposy! Oh, dear, I am so tired of feeling spiteful, but how else is one to feel?*
>
> *You looked most prosaically romantic, setting off in a rubber cape, followed by Lewis. Hope the roads were not very slippery, and that you had a good time, à la Mademoiselle de Maupin.[43] Do remember, dear, not to devour little Lewis before you have got half-way—*

42. Italian and Spanish diminutives.
43. In *Mademoiselle de Maupin* (1835), a novel of somewhat risqué character by Théophile Gautier (1811–72), the heroine, dressed as a boy, travels with a young man.

DEAR MOTHER: *I half expected word from you before I left, but nothing came. Forrester drove me up here just before lunch. Rico seems much better, almost himself, and a little more than that.* He broached our staying at Corrabach very tactfully. I told him Flora had asked me, and it seemed a good plan. Then I told him about St. Mawr. He was a little piqued, and there was a pause of very disapproving silence. Then he said: Very well, darling. If you wish to keep the animal, do so by all means. I make a present of him again. Me: That's so good of you, Rico. Because I know revenge is sweet. Rico: Revenge, Loulina! I don't think I was selling him for vengeance! Merely to get rid of him to Flora, who can keep better hold over him. Me: But you know, dear, she was going to geld him! Rico: I don't think anybody knew it. We only wondered if it were possible, to make him more amenable. Did she tell you? Me: No—Phœnix did. He had it from a groom. Rico: Dear me! A concatenation of grooms! So your mother rode off with Lewis, and carried St. Mawr out of danger! I understand! Let us hope worse won't befall. Me: Whom? Rico: Never mind, dear! It's so lovely to see you. You are looking rested. I thought those Countess of Witton roses the most marvellous things in the world, till you came, now they're quite in the background. *He had some very lovely red roses, in a crystal bowl: the room smelled of roses.* Me: Where did they come from? Rico: Oh, Flora brought them! Me: Bowl and all? Rico: Bowl and all! Wasn't it dear of her? Me: Why, yes! But then she's the goddess of flowers, isn't she? *Poor darling, he was offended that I should twit him while he is ill, so I relented. He has had a couple of marvellous invalid's bed-jackets sent from London: one a pinkish yellow, with rose-arabesque facings: this one in fine cloth. But unfortunately he has already dropped soup on it. The other is a lovely silvery and blue and green soft brocade. He had that one on to receive me, and I at once complimented him on it. He has got a new ring too: sent by Aspasia Weingartner, a rather lovely intaglio of Priapus* [44] *under an apple bough, at least so he says it is.* He made a naughty face, and said: The Priapus stage is rather advanced for poor me. *I asked what the Priapus stage was, but he said: Oh, nothing! Then nurse said: There's a big classical dictionary that Miss Manby brought up, if you wish to see it. So I have been studying the Classical Gods. The world always was a queer place. It's a very queer one when Rico is the god Priapus. He would go round the orchard painting lifelike apples on the trees, and inviting nymphs to come and eat them. And the nymphs would pretend they were real: Why, Sir Prippy, what stunningly naughty apples! There's nothing so artificial as sinning nowadays. I suppose it once was real.*

I'm bored here: wish I had my horse.

DEAR MOTHER: *I'm so glad you are enjoying your ride. I'm sure it is like riding into history, like the Yankee at the Court of King Arthur,* [45] *in those old by-lanes and Roman roads. They still fascinate me: at least, more before I get there than when I am actually there. I begin to feel*

44. God of gardens and fertility, represented with a large phallus.
45. *A Connecticut Yankee at King Arthur's Court* (1889), by Mark Twain.

1. Thomas Hardy in 1923, a portrait by R. G. Eves (1876–1941).
National Portrait Gallery, London.

2. Joseph Conrad, a drawing by Sir William Rothenstein (1872–1945).
National Portrait Gallery.

3. "Central Station"—Kinshassa Station in the Belgian Congo. From H. M. Stanley, *The Congo, Founding of Its Free State* (1885).

HEART OF DARKNESS

4. "Inner Station"—The settlement at Stanley Falls photographed during a Governor-General's inspection. From Albert Chapaux, *Le Congo* (1894).

5. G. B. Shaw, a drawing by Sir Bernard Partridge.
National Portrait Gallery, © *Punch,* London 1925.

6. William Butler Yeats in 1900, a portrait by his father, John B. Yeats.
The National Gallery of Ireland, Dublin.

7. "Was there another Troy for her to burn?" (from "No Second Troy"). Maud Gonne, in a portrait by Sarah Purser. *The Granger Collection.*

8. "Human, superhuman, a bird's round eye, / Everything else withered and mummy-dead . . . " (from "A Bronze Head"). Maud Gonne, by Lawrence Campbell.
The Municipal Gallery, Dublin *(Photo Barry Mason).*

9. "An image of such politics . . . " (from "In Memory of Constance Markiewicz and Eva Gore-Booth"). Constance (Gore-Booth) Markiewicz in uniform of the Citizens' Army, c. 1914. *Photograph Keogh.*

"The innocent and the beautiful / no enemy but time . . ." (from "In ...ory . . ."). Constance Gore-Booth ...r first ball-gown, c. 1886 From the ...-Booth family album; *courtesy the ...-Booth family.*

11. Bernardo Strozzi (1581–1644), *Portrait of a Gentleman.*

"In the Dublin National Gallery there hung, perhaps there still hang, upon the same wall, a portrait of some Venetian gentleman by Strozzi, and Mr. Sargent's painting of President Wilson. Whatever thought broods in the dark eyes of that Venetian gentleman has drawn its life from his whole body; it feeds upon it as the flame feeds upon the candle —and should that thought be changed, his pose would change, his very cloak would rustle, for his whole body thinks. President Wilson lives only in the eyes, which are steady and intent; the flesh about the mouth is dead, and the hands are dead, and the clothes suggest no movement of his body, nor any movement but that of the valet, who has brushed and folded in mechanical routine." (From Yeats, *The Trembling of the Veil*).

12. John Singer Sargent (1856–1925), Portrait of Woodrow Wilson.
The National Gallery of Ireland.

13. Yeats, as drawn by the noted portraitist
Augustus John (1878–1961).
The Tate Gallery, London, *courtesy of Romilly John.*

14. William Butler Yeats broadcasting in 1937. *BBC Copyright Photograph.*

15. James Joyce, c. 1917.
The Croessman James Joyce Collection,
Southern Illinois University at Carbondale.

JOYCE'S DUBLIN

16. Usher's Island, the bank of the Liffey where Kate and Julia Morkan's house was situated (see "The Dead"). W. Y. Tindall, from his work *The Joyce Country, Pennsylvania State University Press* (1960).

17. Clongowes Wood College, Stephen's—and Joyce's—school (see *A Portrait of the Artist as a Young Man*). *Irish Tourist Board.*

JOYCE'S DUBLIN

18. The Wellington Monument
(see "The Dead").
W. Y. Tindall, from *The Joyce Country.*

19. "There was no human figure near him, nor any sound borne to him over the air. But the tide was near the turn and already the day was on the wave." Looking across the bay towards the Hill of Howth (see *A Portrait of the Artist*). W. Y. Tindall, from *The Joyce Country*.

20. St. Mary's Star of the Sea (see the "Nausicaa" section of *Ulysses*). W. Y. Tindall, from *The Joyce Country*.

JOYCE'S DUBLIN

21. 7 Eccles Street (Bloom's house),
by Nora Mitchell.
*The Croessman James Joyce Collection,
Southern Illinois University.*

22. ALP, the river Liffey (see *Finnegans Wake*). W. Y. Tindall, from *The Joyce Country*.

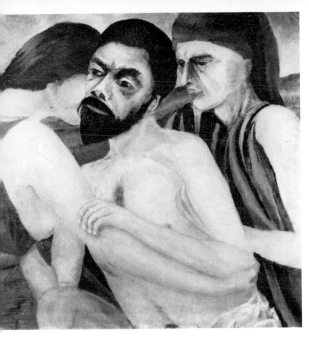

23. One of Lawrence's paintings:
Resurrection.
Humanities Research Center
The University of Texas
at Austin.

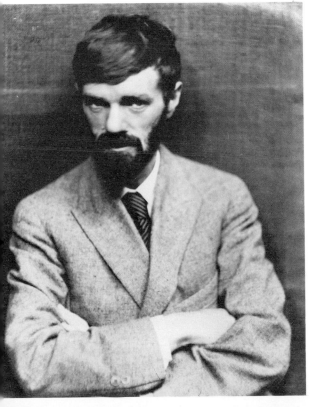

24. D. H. Lawrence.
George Eastman House,
Rochester (New York).

25. T. S. Eliot, painted in 1938 by Wyndham Lewis, novelist and painter (Eliot described him as the best contemporary writer of English prose). This portrait caused some controversy, but Eliot admired it. (See also Lewis's portrait of Edith Sitwell, Fig. 38.)
Fogg Art Museum, Harvard University Portrait Collection, Gift Mrs. Stanley B. Resor.

26. *Ennui*, the famous image of quiet desperation; Camden Town, London 1913, by Walter Sickert, R.A. (1860–1942).
The Tate Gallery.

TOWARD THE WASTE LAND

27. A crowd flowed over London Bridge, so many,
   I had not thought death had undone so many.
      From *The Waste Land*, ll. 62f. *Radio Times-Hulton Picture Library.*

. . . where the walls
Of Magnus Martyr hold
Inexplicable splendour of Ionian white and gold.
   From *The Waste Land*, ll. 263–65.

28. The Church of St. Magnus Martyr,
Lower Thames St., London.
A. F. Kersting.

After the dark dove with the flickering tongue
Had passed below the horizon of his homing . . .

From "Little Gidding," ll. 83f.

29. Bomb damage surrounding St. Paul's Cathedral, 1940, photographed by Cecil Beaton,
photographer and designer best known for his portraits of celebrities.

30. Rudyard Kipling in 1899. Portrait by Philip Burne-Jones.
National Portrait Gallery.

31. Wilfred Owen in 1917.
Oxford University Press, London.

32. The Somme Battlefield, 1916.
Imperial War Museum, London.

33. A Daylight Raid near Arras, 1917.
Imperial War Museum.

WORLD WAR I

34. Front-line Trench, the Battle of the Somme, 1916.
Imperial War Museum, London.

> Why do you lie with your legs ungainly huddled,
> And one arm bent across your sullen, cold
> Exhausted face? It hurts my heart to watch you,
> Deep-shadowed from the candle's guttering gold;
> And you wonder why I shove you by the shoulder;
> Drowsy, you mumble and sigh and turn your head . . .
> *You are too young to fall asleep for ever;*
> *And when you sleep you remind me of the dead.*

From Siegfried Sassoon (1886–1968), "The Dug-Out."

35. David Jones Vision: *Guenever* (1940), an illustration of Arthurian Legend. *The Tate Gallery.*

36. George Orwell in 1943.
BBC Copyright Photograph.

37. W. H. Auden, a recent photograph.
Jill Krementz.

38. Edith Sitwell, a portrait by Wyndham Lewis, c. 1926.
The Tate Gallery, courtesy of Ann Wyndham Lewis.

39. Dylan Thomas in 1938, by Augustus John.
The National Museum of Wales, Cardiff.

40. E. M. Forster, by Cecil Beaton (1904–   ).

41. *Shelter Scene* (1941). *Marlborough Gallery,* New York.

Henry Moore (1898–   ), one of the greatest sculptors of the twentieth century, has developed some of his major abstract forms from what Blake called, in another context, "the human form divine." In 1941 he did some remarkable drawings, in combined chalk, crayon, pen and brush, of London Underground areas in use as air-raid shelters. These drawings capture both the historical moment –patience amid horror—and the power to transcend it of visual forms themselves (here so closely related to those of his sculpture) and the eternal life they lead.

42. Francis Bacon (1909–   ), in his post-World War II painting, represents a recent kind of expressionism in his rigid control over modes of distortion. This *Study after Velasquez's Portrait of Pope Innocent X* (1953) transforms the masterful force of the seventeenth-century original into a horrific scream of the atomic age, a scream shared by wielders of power and their victims alike, the whole picture suggesting the qualities of a rubbed, scuffed news photograph.
Collection Carter Burden, New York.

real American and resent the past. Why doesn't the past decently bury itself, instead of sitting waiting to be admired by the present?

Phœnix brought Poppy. I am so fond of her: rode for five hours yesterday. I was glad to get away from this farm. The doctor came, and said Rico would be able to go down to Corrabach to-morrow. Flora came to hear the bulletin, and sailed back full of zest. Apparently Rico is going to do a portrait of her, sitting up in bed. What a mercy the bed-clothes won't be mine when Priapus wields his pallette from the pillow.

Phœnix thinks you intend to go to America with St. Mawr, and that I am coming too, leaving Rico this side.—I wonder. I feel so unreal, nowadays, as if I too were nothing more than a painting by Rico on a millboard. I feel almost too unreal even to make up my mind to anything. It is terrible when the life-flow dies out of one, and everything is like cardboard, and oneself is like cardboard. I'm sure it is worse than being dead. I realized it yesterday when Phœnix and I had a picnic lunch by a stream. You see I must imitate you in all things. He found me some watercresses, and they tasted so damp and alive, I knew how deadened I was. Phœnix wants us to go and have a ranch in Arizona, and raise horses, with St. Mawr, if willing, for Father Abraham. I wonder if it matters what one does: if it isn't all the same thing over again. Only Phœnix, his funny blank face, makes my heart melt and go sad. But I believe he'd be cruel too. I saw it in his face when he didn't know I was looking. Anything though, rather than this deadness and this paint-Priapus business. Au revoir, mother dear! Keep on having a good time—

DEAR MOTHER: I had your letter from Merriton: am so glad you arrived safe and sound in body and temper. There was such a funny letter from Lewis, too: I enclose it. What makes him take this extraordinary line? But I'm writing to tell him to take St. Mawr to London, and wait for me there. I have telegraphed Mrs. Squire to get the house ready for me. I shall go straight there.

Things developed here as they were bound to. I just couldn't bear it. No sooner was Rico put in the automobile than a self-conscious importance came over him, like when the wounded hero is carried into the middle of the stage. Why so solemn, Rico dear? I asked him, trying to laugh him out of it. Not solemn, dear, only a feeling a little transient. I don't think he knew himself what he meant. Flora was on the steps as the car drew up, dressed in severe white. She only needed an apron, to become a nurse: or a veil, to become a bride. Between the two, she had an unbearable air of a woman in seduced circumstances, as the Times said.[46] She ordered two menservants about in subdued, you would have said hushed, but competent tones. And then I saw there was a touch of the priestess about her as well: Cassandra preparing for her violation:[47] Iphigenia, with Rico for Orestes, on a stretcher:[48] he looking

46. A joke attributed apocryphally to a London *Times* misprint ("in reduced circumstances").
47. Cassandra, daughter of Priam, king of Troy, was violated by Ajax at the fall of the city.
48. Iphigenia saved her brother Orestes from execution, and fled with him.

like Adonis,[49] *fully prepared to be an unconscionable time in dying. They had given him a lovely room, downstairs, with doors opening on to a little garden all of its own. I believe it was Flora's boudoir. I left nurse and the men to put him to bed. Flora was hovering anxiously in the passage outside.* Oh, what a marvellous room! Oh, how colourful, how beautiful! *came Rico's tones, the hero behind the scenes. I must say, it was like a harvest festival, with roses and gaillardias in the shadow, and cornflowers in the light, and a bowl of grapes, and nectarines among leaves.* I'm so anxious that he should be happy, *Flora said to me in the passage.* You know him best. Is there anything else I could do for him? *Me:* Why, if you went to the piano and sang, I'm sure he'd love it. Couldn't you sing: Oh, my love is like a rred, rred rrose! [50]—*You know how Rico imitates Scotch!*

Thank goodness I have a bedroom upstairs: nurse sleeps in a little antechamber to Rico's room. The Edwards are still here, the blond young man with some very futuristic plaster on his face. Awfully good of you to come! *he said to me, looking at me out of one eye, and holding my hand fervently.* How's that for cheek? It's awfully good of Miss Manby to let me come, *said I. He:* Ah, but Flora is always a sport, a topping good sport!

I don't know what's the matter, but it just all put me into a fiendish temper. I felt I couldn't sit there at luncheon with that bright, youthful company, and hear about their tennis and their polo and their hunting and have their flirtatiousness making me sick. So I asked for a tray in my room. Do as I might, I couldn't help being horrid.

Oh, and Rico! He really is too awful. Lying there in bed with every ear open, like Adonis waiting to be persuaded not to die. Seizing a hushed moment to take Flora's hand and press it to his lips, murmuring: How awfully good you are to me, dear Flora! *And Flora:* I'd be better if I knew how, Harry! *So cheerful with it all! No, it's too much. My sense of humour is leaving me: which means, I'm getting into too bad a temper to be able to ridicule it all. I suppose I feel in the minority. It's an awful thought, to think that most all the young people in the world are like this: so bright and cheerful, and* sporting, *and so brimming with* libido.[51] *How awful!*

I said to Rico: You're very comfortable here, aren't you? *He:* Comfortable! It's comparative heaven. *Me:* Would you mind if I went away? *A deadly pause. He is deadly afraid of being left alone with Flora. He feels safe so long as I am about, and he can take refuge in his marriage ties. He:* Where do you want to go, dear? *Me:* To mother. To London. *Mother is planning to go to America, and she wants me to go. Rico:*

---

49. Adonis was beloved of Venus, but a boar killed him while hunting. King Charles II is said to have remarked on his deathbed that he was an unconscionable time a-dying.
50. From the song "A Red, Red Rose" by Robert Burns.
51. Instinctual energy deriving, in Freud's psychoanalytic theory, from the Id. Lawrence had been reading Freud and attacking him in *Psychoanalysis and the Unconscious* (1921) and *Fantasia of the Unconscious* (1922). This is an early use of the word in nontechnical writing.

But you don't want to go t—he—e—re—e! *You know, mother, how Rico can put a venomous emphasis on a word, till it suggests pure poison. It nettled me. I'm not sure, I said. Rico: Oh, but you can't stand that awful America. Me: I want to try again. Rico: But, Lou dear, it will be winter before you get there. And this is absolutely the wrong moment for me to go over there. I am only just making headway over here. When I am absolutely sure of a position in England, then we nip across the Atlantic and scoop in a few dollars, if you like. Just now, even when I am well, would be fatal. I've only just sketched in the outline of my success in London, and one ought to arrive in New York ready-made as a famous and important Artist. Me: But mother and I didn't think of going to New York. We thought we'd sail straight to New Orleans—if we could: or to Havana. And then go West to Arizona. The poor boy looked at me in such distress. But, Loulina darling, do you mean you want to leave me in the lurch for the winter season? You can't mean it. We're just getting on so splendidly, really!—I was surprised at the depth of feeling in his voice: how tremendously his career as an artist—a popular artist—matters to him. I can never believe it. —You know, mother, you and I feel alike about daubing paint on canvas: every possible daub that can be daubed has already been done, so people ought to leave off. Rico is so shrewd. I always think he's got his tongue in his cheek, and I'm always staggered once more to find that he takes it absolutely seriously. His career! The Modern British Society of Painters: perhaps even the Royal Academy! Those people we see in London, and those portraits Rico does! He may even be a second Laslow,*[52] or a thirteenth Orpen,[53] and die happy! Oh! mother! How can it really matter to* anybody!

But I was really rather upset, when I realized how his heart was fixed on his career, and that I might be spoiling everything for him. So I went away to think about it. And then I realized how unpopular you are, and how unpopular I shall be myself, in a little while. A sort of hatred for people has come over me. I hate their ways and their bunk, and I feel like kicking them in the face, as St. Mawr did that young man. Not that I should ever do it. And I don't think I should ever have made my final announcement to Rico, if he hadn't been such a beautiful pig in clover, here at Corrabach Hall. He has known the Manbys all his life; they and he are sections of one engine. He would be far happier with Flora: or I won't say happier, because there is something in him which rebels: but he would on the whole fit much better. I myself am at the end of my limit, and beyond it. I can't 'mix' any more, and I refuse to. I feel like a bit of eggshell in the mayonnaise: the only thing is to take it out, you can't beat it in. I know I shall cause a fiasco, even in Rico's career, if I stay. I shall go on being rude and hateful to people as I am at Corrabach, and Rico will lose all his nerve.

So I have told him. I said this evening, when no one was about: Rico

52. Sir Philip László (1869–1937), Hungarian-born British portrait painter.
53. Sir William Orpen (1878–1931), portrait painter, official war artist, and painter at the Peace Conference.

dear, listen to me seriously. I can't stand these people. If you ask me to endure another week of them, I shall either become ill or insult them, as mother does. And I don't want to do either. *Rico:* But, darling, isn't everybody perfect to you! *Me:* I tell you, I shall just make a break, like St. Mawr, if I don't get out. I simply can't stand people.—*The poor darling, his face goes so blank and anxious. He knows what I mean, because, except that they tickle his vanity all the time, he hates them as much as I do. But his vanity is the chief thing to him.* He: Lou darling, can't you wait till I get up, and we can go away to the Tyrol or some-where for a spell? *Me:* Won't you come with me to America, to the South-west? I believe it's marvellous country.—*I saw his face switch into hostility; quite vicious.* He: Are you so keen on spoiling everything for me? Is that what I married you for? Do you do it deliberately? *Me:* Everything is already spoilt for me. I tell you I can't stand people, your Floras and your Aspasias, and your forthcoming young Englishmen. After all, I am an American, like mother, and I've got to go back. *He:* Really! And am I to come along as part of the luggage, labelled cabin! *Me:* You do as you wish, Rico. *He:* I wish to God you did as you wished, Lou dear. I'm afraid you do as Mrs. Witt wishes. I've always heard that the holiest thing in the world was a mother. *Me:* No, dear, it's just that I can't stand people. *He (with a snarl):* And I suppose I'm lumped in as PEOPLE! *And when he'd said it, it was true. We neither of us said anything for a time. Then he said, calculating:* Very well, dear! You take a trip to the land of stars and stripes, and I'll stay here and go on with my work. And when you've seen enough of their stars and tasted enough of their stripes, you can come back and take your place again with me.—*We left it at that.*

You and I are supposed to have important business connected with our estates in Texas—it sounds so well—so we are making a hurried trip to the States, as they call them. I shall leave for London early next week—

Mrs. Witt read this long letter with satisfaction. She herself had one strange craving: to get back to America. It was not that she idealized her native country: she was a tartar of restlessness there, quite as much as in Europe. It was not that she expected to arrive at any blessed abiding-place. No, in America she would go on fuming and chafing the same. But at least she would be in America, in her own country. And that was what she wanted.

She picked up the sheet of poor paper, that had been folded in Lou's letter. It was the letter from Lewis, quite nicely written.

Lady Carrington, I write to tell you and Sir Henry that I think I had better quit your service, as it would be more comfortable all round. If you will write and tell me what you want me to do with St. Mawr, I will do whatever you tell me. With kind regards to Lady Carrington and Sir Henry, I remain, Your obedient servant, MORGAN LEWIS.

Mrs. Witt put the letter aside, and sat looking out of the window. She felt, strangely, as if already her soul had gone away from her actual surroundings.

She was there, in Oxfordshire, in the body, but her spirit had departed else-where. A listlessness was upon her. It was with an effort she roused herself, to write to her lawyer in London, to get her release from her English obliga-tions. Then she wrote to the London hotel.

For the first time in her life she wished she had a maid, to do little things for her. All her life, she had had too much energy to endure anyone hanging round her, personally. Now she gave up. Her wrists seemed numb, as if the power in her were switched off.

When she went down, they said Lewis had asked to speak to her. She had hardly seen him since they had arrived at Merriton.

'I've had a letter from Lady Carrington, Mam. She says will I take St. Mawr to London and wait for her there. But she says I am to come to you, Mam, for definite orders.'

'Very well, Lewis. I shall be going to London in a few days' time. You arrange for St. Mawr to go up one day this week, and you will take him to the Mews. Come to me for anything you want. And don't talk of leaving my daughter. We want you to go with St. Mawr to America, with us and Phœnix.'

'And your horse, Mam?'

'I shall leave him here at Merriton. I shall give him to Miss Atherton.'

'Very good, Mam!'

DEAR DAUGHTER: *I shall be in my old quarters in Mayfair next Satur-day, calling the same day at your house to see if everything is ready for you. Lewis has fixed up with the railway: he goes to town to-morrow. The reason of his letter was that I had asked him if he would care to marry me, and he turned me down with emphasis. But I will tell you about it. You and I are the scribe and the Pharisee; I never could write a letter, and you could never leave off—*

DEAREST MOTHER: *I smelt something rash, but I know it's no use say-ing: How could you? I only wonder, though, that you should think of marriage. You know, dear, I ache in every fibre to be left alone, from all that sort of thing. I feel all bruises, like one who has been assassi-nated. I do so understand why Jesus said:* Noli me tangere.[54] *Touch me not, I am not yet ascended unto the Father. Everything had hurt him so much, wearied him so beyond endurance, he felt he could not bear one little human touch on his body. I am like that. I can hardly bear even Elena to hand me a dress. As for a man—and marriage—ah, no!* Noli me tangere, homo! *I am not yet ascended unto the Father. Oh, leave me alone, leave me alone! That is all my cry to all the world.*

Curiously, I feel that Phœnix understands what I feel. He leaves me so understandingly alone, he almost gives me my sheath of aloneness: or at least, he protects me in my sheath. I am grateful for him.

Whereas Rico feels my aloneness as a sort of shame to himself. He wants at least a blinding pretence of intimacy. Ah, intimacy! The thought of it fills me with aches, and the pretence of it exhausts me beyond myself.

54. John 20:17; a quotation Lawrence was particularly prone to use, especially in his later years.

Yes, I long to go away to the West, to be away from the world like one dead and in another life, in a valley that life has not yet entered. Rico asked me: What are you doing with St. Mawr? When I said we were taking him with us, he said: Oh, the corpus delicti! [55] *Whether that means anything I don't know. But he has grown sarcastic beyond my depth.*

I shall see you to-morrow——

Lou arrived in town, at the dead end of August, with her maid and Phœnix. How wonderful it seemed to have London empty of all her set: her own little house to herself, with just the housekeeper and her own maid. The fact of being alone in those surroundings was so wonderful. It made the surroundings themselves seem all the more ghostly. Everything that had been actual to her was turning ghostly: even her little drawing-room was the ghost of a room, belonging to the dead people who had known it, or to all the dead generations that had brought such a room into being, evolved it out of their quaint domestic desires. And now, in herself, those desires were suddenly spent: gone out like a lamp that suddenly dies. And then she saw her pale, delicate room with its little green agate bowl and its two little porcelain birds and its soft, roundish chairs, turned into something ghostly, like a room set out in a museum. She felt like fastening little labels on the furniture: *Lady Louise Carrington Lounge Chair, Last used August, 1923.* Not for the benefit of posterity: but to remove her own self into another world, another realm of existence.

'My house, my house, my house, how can I ever have taken so much pains about it!' she kept saying to herself. It was like one of her old hats, suddenly discovered neatly put away in an old hatbox. And what a horror: an old 'fashionable' hat!

Lewis came to see her, and he sat there in one of her delicate mauve chairs, with his feet on a delicate old carpet from Turkestan, and she just wondered. He wore his leather gaiters and khaki breeches as usual, and a faded blue shirt. But his beard and hair were trimmed, he was tidy. There was a certain fineness of contour about him, a certain subtle gleam, which made him seem, apart from his rough boots, not at all gross, or coarse, in that setting of rather silky, Oriental furnishings. Rather he made the Asiatic, sensuous exquisiteness of her old rugs and her old white Chinese figures seem a weariness. Beauty! What was beauty, she asked herself? The Oriental exquisiteness seemed to her all like dead flowers whose hour had come, to be thrown away.

Lou could understand her mother's wanting, for a moment, to marry him. His detachedness and his acceptance of something in destiny which people cannot accept. Right in the middle of him he accepted something from destiny, that gave him a quality of eternity. He did not care about persons, people, even events. In his own odd way, he was an aristocrat, inaccessible in his aristocracy. But it was the aristocracy of the invisible powers, the greater influences, nothing to do with human society.

'You don't really want to leave St. Mawr, do you?' Lou asked him. 'You don't really want to quit, as you said?'

---

55. The material thing in respect of which a crime has been committed, whether a body or a stolen object; he means that they are removing the evidence of a crime.

He looked at her steadily, from his pale-grey eyes, without answering, not knowing what to say.

'Mother told me what she said to you.—But she doesn't mind, she says you are entirely within your rights. She has a real regard for you. But we mustn't let our regards run us into actions which are beyond our scope, must we? That makes everything unreal. But you will come with us to America with St. Mawr, won't you? We depend on you.'

'I don't want to be uncomfortable,' he said.

'Don't be,' she smiled. 'I myself hate unreal situations—I feel I can't stand them any more. And most marriages are unreal situations. But apart from anything exaggerated, you like being with mother and me, don't you?'

'Yes, I do. I like Mrs. Witt as well. But not—'

'I know. There won't be any more of that—'

'You see, Lady Carrington,' he said, with a little heat, 'I'm not by nature a marrying man. And I should feel I was selling myself.'

'Quite!—Why do you think you are not a marrying man, though?'

'Me! I don't feel myself after I've been with women.' He spoke in a low tone, looking down at his hands. 'I feel messed up. I'm better to keep to myself.—Because—' and here he looked up with a flare in his eyes—'women—they only want to make you give in to them, so that they feel almighty, and you feel small.'

'Don't you like feeling small?' Lou smiled. 'And don't you want to make them give in to you?'

'Not me,' he said. 'I don't want nothing. Nothing, I want.'

'Poor mother!' said Lou. 'She thinks if she feels moved by a man, it must result in marriage—or that kind of thing. Surely she makes a mistake. I think you and Phœnix and mother and I might live somewhere in a far-away wild place, and make a good life: so long as we didn't begin to mix up marriage, or love or that sort of thing, into it. It seems to me men and women have really hurt one another so much, nowadays, that they had better stay apart till they have learned to be gentle with one another again. Not all this forced passion and destructive philandering. Men and women should stay apart, till their hearts grow gentle towards one another again. Now, it's only each one fighting for his own—or her own—underneath the cover of tenderness.'

'Dear!—darling!—Yes, my love!' mocked Lewis, with a faint smile of amused contempt.

'Exactly. People always say dearest! when they hate each other most.'

Lewis nodded, looking at her with a sudden sombre gloom in his eyes. A queer bitterness showed on his mouth. But even then, he was so still and remote.

The housekeeper came and announced The Honourable Laura Ridley. This was like a blow in the face to Lou. She rose hurriedly—and Lewis rose, moving to the door.

'Don't go, please, Lewis,' said Lou—and then Laura Ridley appeared in the doorway. She was a woman a few years older than Lou, but she looked younger. She might have been a shy girl of twenty-two, with her fresh complexion, her hesitant manner, her round, startled brown eyes, her bobbed hair.

'Hello!' said the new-comer. 'Imagine your being back! I saw you in Paddington.'

Those sharp eyes would see everything.

'I thought everyone was out of town,' said Lou. 'This is Mr. Lewis.'

Laura gave him a little nod, then sat on the edge of her chair.

'No,' she said. 'I did go to Ireland to my people, but I came back. I prefer London when I can be more or less alone in it. I though I'd just run in for a moment, before you're gone again.—Scotland, isn't it?'

'No, mother and I are going to America.'

'America! Oh, I thought it was Scotland.'

'It was. But we have suddenly to go to America.'

'I see!—And what about Rico?'

'He is staying on in Shropshire. Didn't you hear of his accident?'

Lou told about it briefly.

'But how awful!' said Laura. 'But there! I knew it! I had a premonition when I saw that horse. We had a horse that killed a man. Then my father got rid of it. But ours was a mare, that one. Yours is a boy.'

'A full-grown man, I'm afraid.'

'Yes, of course, I remember.—But how awful! I suppose you won't ride in the Row. The awful people that ride there nowadays, anyhow! Oh, aren't they awful! Aren't people monstrous, really! My word, when I see the horses crossing Hyde Park corner, on a wet day, and coming down smash on those slippery stones, giving their riders a fractured skull!—No joke!'

She enquired details of Rico.

'Oh, I suppose I shall see him when he gets back,' she said. 'But I'm sorry you are going. I shall miss you, I'm afraid. Though you won't be staying long in America. No one stays there longer than they can help.'

'I think the winter through, at least,' said Lou.

'Oh, all the winter! So long? I'm sorry to hear *that*. You're one of the few, very few people one can talk *really* simply with. Extraordinary, isn't it, how few really simple people there are! And they get fewer and fewer. I stayed a fortnight with my people, and a week of that I was in bed. It was really horrible. They really try to take the life out of one, *really*! Just because one won't be as they are, and play their game. I simply refused, and came away.'

'But you can't cut yourself off altogether,' said Lou.

'No, I suppose not. One has to see somebody. Luckily one has a few artists for friends. They're the only real people, anyhow—' She glanced round inquisitively at Lewis, and said, with a slight, impertinent elvish smile on her virgin face:

'Are you an artist?'

'No, Mam!' he said. 'I'm a groom.'

'Oh, I see!' She looked him up and down.

'Lewis is St. Mawr's master,' said Lou.

'Oh, the horse! the terrible horse!' She paused a moment. Then again she turned to Lewis with that faint smile, slightly condescending, slightly impertinent, slightly flirtatious.

'Aren't you afraid of him?' she asked.

'No, Mam.'

'Aren't you *really!*—And can you always master him?'

'Mostly. He knows me.'

'Yes! I suppose that's it.'—She looked him up and down again, then turned away to Lou.

'What have you been painting lately?' said Lou. Laura was not a bad painter.

'Oh, hardly anything. I haven't been able to get on at all. This is one of my bad intervals.'

Here Lewis rose, and looked at Lou.

'All right,' she said. 'Come in after lunch, and we'll finish those arrangements.'

Laura gazed after the man, as he dived out of the room, as if her eyes were gimlets that could bore into his secret.

In the course of the conversation she said:

'What a curious little man that was!'

'Which?'

'The groom who was here just now. *Very* curious! Such peculiar eyes. I shouldn't wonder if he had psychic powers.'

'What sort of psychic powers?' said Lou.

'Could *see* things.—And hypnotic too. He might have hypnotic powers.'

'What makes you think so?'

'He gives me that sort of feeling. Very curious! Probably he hypnotizes the horse.—Are you leaving the horse here, by the way, in stable?'

'No, taking him to America.'

'Taking him to America! How extraordinary!'

'It's mother's idea. She thinks he might be valuable as a stock horse on a ranch. You know we still have interest in a ranch in Texas.'

'Oh, I see! Yes, probably he'd be very valuable, to improve the breed of the horses over there.—My father has some very lovely hunters. Isn't it disgraceful, he would never let me ride!'

'Why?'

'Because we girls weren't important, in his opinion.—So you're taking the horse to America! With the little man?'

'Yes, St. Mawr will hardly behave without him.'

'I see!—I see—ee—ee! Just you and Mrs. Witt and the little man. I'm sure you'll find he has psychic powers.'

'I'm afraid I'm not so good at finding things out,' said Lou.

'Aren't you? No, I suppose not. I am. I have a flair. I sort of *smell* things.— Then the horse is already here, is he? When do you think you'll sail?'

'Mother is finding a merchant-boat that will go to Galveston, Texas, and take us along with the horse. She knows people who will find the right thing. But it takes time.'

'What a much nicer way to travel than on one of those great liners! Oh, how awful they are! So vulgar! Floating palaces they call them! My word, the people inside the palaces!—Yes, I should say that would be a much pleasanter way of travelling: on a cargo-boat.'

Laura wanted to go down to the Mews to see St. Mawr. The two women went together.

St. Mawr stood in his box, bright and tense as usual.

'Yes!' said Laura Ridley, with a slight hiss. 'Yes! Isn't he beautiful! Such very perfect legs!'—She eyed him round with those gimlet, sharp eyes of hers.

'Almost a pity to let him go out of England. We need some of his perfect *bone*, I feel.—But his eye! Hasn't he got a look in it, my word!'

'I can never see that he looks wicked,' said Lou.

'Can't you!'—Laura had a slight hiss in her speech, a sort of aristocratic decision in her enunciation, that got on Lou's nerves.—'He looks wicked to me!'

'He's not *mean*,' said Lou. 'He'd never do anything mean to you.'

'Oh, mean! I dare say not. No! I'll grant him that, he gives fair warning. His eye says *Beware!*—But isn't he a beauty, *isn't* he!' Lou could feel the peculiar reverence for St. Mawr's breeding, his show qualities. Herself, all she cared about was the horse himself, his real nature. 'Isn't it extraordinary,' Laura continued, 'that you never get a *really*, perfectly satisfactory animal! There's always something wrong. And in men too. Isn't it curious? there's always something—something wrong—or something missing. Why is it?'

'I don't know,' said Lou. She felt unable to cope with any more. And she was glad when Laura left her.

The days passed slowly, quietly, London almost empty of Lou's acquaintances. Mrs. Witt was busy getting all sorts of papers and permits: such a fuss! The battle light was still in her eye. But about her nose was a dusky, pinched look that made Lou wonder.

Both women wanted to be gone: they felt they had already flown in spirit, and it was weary having the body left behind.

At last all was ready: they only awaited the telegram to say when their cargo-boat would sail. Trunks stood there packed, like great stones locked forever. The Westminster house seemed already a shell. Rico wrote and telegraphed, tenderly, but there was a sense of relentless effort in it all, rather than of any real tenderness. He had taken his position.

Then the telegram came, the boat was ready to sail.

'There now!' said Mrs. Witt, as if it had been a sentence of death.

'Why do you look like that, mother?'

'I feel I haven't an ounce of energy left in my body.'

'But how queer, for you, mother. Do you think you are ill?'

'No, Louise. I just feel that way: as if I hadn't an ounce of energy left in my body.'

'You'll feel yourself again, once you are away.'

'Maybe I shall.'

After all, it was only a matter of telephoning. The hotel and the railway porters and taxi-men would do the rest.

It was a grey, cloudy day, cold even. Mother and daughter sat in a cold first-class carriage and watched the little Hampshire country-side go past: little, old, unreal it seemed to them both, and passing away like a dream whose edges only are in consciousness. Autumn! Was this autumn? Were these trees, fields, villages? It seemed but the dim, dissolving edges of a dream, without inward substance.

At Southampton it was raining: and just a chaos, till they stepped on to a clean boat, and were received by a clean young captain, quite sympathetic, and quite a gentleman. Mrs. Witt, however, hardly looked at him, but went down to her cabin and lay down in her bunk.

There, lying concealed, she felt the engines start, she knew the voyage had begun. But she lay still. She saw the clouds and the rain, and refused to be disturbed.

Lou had lunch with the young captain, and she felt she ought to be flirty. The young man was so polite and attentive. And she wished so much she were alone.

Afterwards, she sat on deck and saw the Isle of Wight pass shadowy, in a misty rain. She didn't know it was the Isle of Wight. To her, it was just the lowest bit of the British Isles. She saw it fading away: and with it, her life, going like a clot of shadow in a mist of nothingness. She had no feelings about it, none: neither about Rico, nor her London house, nor anything. All passing in a grey curtain of rainy drizzle, like a death, and she with not a feeling left. They entered the Channel, and felt the slow heave of the sea. And soon the clouds broke in a little wind. The sky began to clear. By mid-afternoon it was blue summer, on the blue, running waters of the Channel. And soon, the ship steering for Santander, there was the coast of France, the rock twinkling like some magic world.

The magic world! And back of it, that post-war Paris which Lou knew only too well, and which depressed her so thoroughly. Or that post-war Monte Carlo, the Riviera still more depressing even than Paris. No, one must not land, even on magic coasts. Else you found yourself in a railway station and a 'centre of civilization' in five minutes.

Mrs. Witt hated the sea, and stayed, as a rule, practically the whole time of the crossing, in her bunk. There she was now, silent, shut up like a steel trap, as in her tomb. She did not even read. Just lay and stared at the passing sky. And the only thing to do was to leave her alone.

Lewis and Phœnix hung on the rail, and watched everything. Or they went down to see St. Mawr. Or they stood talking in the doorway of the wireless operator's cabin. Lou begged the captain to give them jobs to do.

The queer, transitory, unreal feeling, as the ship crossed the great, heavy Atlantic. It was rather bad weather. And Lou felt, as she had felt before, that this grey, wolf-like, cold-blooded Ocean hated men and their ships and their smoky passage. Heavy grey waves, a low-sagging sky: rain: yellow, weird evenings with snatches of sun: so it went on. Till they got way South, into the westward-running stream. Then they began to get blue weather and blue water.

To go South! Always to go South, away from the arctic horror as far as possible! That was Lou's instinct. To go out of the clutch of greyness and low skies, of sweeping rain, and of slow, blanketing snow. Never again to see the mud and rain and snow of a northern winter, nor to feel the idealistic, Christian-ized tension of the now irreligious North.

As they neared Havana, and the water sparkled at night with phosphorus, and the flying-fishes came like drops of bright water, sailing out of the massive-slippery waves, Mrs. Witt emerged once more. She still had that shut-up, deathly look on her face. But she prowled round the deck, and manifested at least a little interest in affairs not her own. Here at sea, she hardly remembered the existence of St. Mawr or Lewis or Phœnix. She was not very deeply aware even of Lou's existence.—But, of course, it would all come back, once they were on land.

They sailed in hot sunshine out of a blue, blue sea, past the castle into the harbour at Havana. There was a lot of shipping: and this was already America. Mrs. Witt had herself and Lou put ashore immediately. They took a motor-car and drove at once to the great boulevard that is the centre of Havana. Here they saw a long rank of motor-cars, all drawn up ready to take a couple of hundred American tourists for one more tour. There were the tourists, all with badges in their coats, lest they should get lost.

'They get so drunk by night,' said the driver in Spanish, 'that the policemen find them lying in the road—turn them over, see the badge—and, hup!—carry them to their hotel.' He grinned sardonically.

Lou and her mother lunched at the Hotel d'Angleterre, and Mrs. Witt watched transfixed while a couple of her countrymen, a stout successful man and his wife, lunched abroad. They had cocktails—then lobster—and a bottle of hock—then a bottle of champagne—then a half-bottle of port.—And Mrs. Witt rose in haste as the liqueurs came. For that successful man and his wife had gone on imbibing with a sort of fixed and deliberate will, apparently tasting nothing, but saying to themselves: Now we're drinking Rhine wine! Now we're drinking 1912 champagne. Yah, Prohibition! Thou canst not put it over me.—Their complexions became more and more lurid. Mrs. Witt fled, fearing a Havana debacle. But she said nothing.

In the afternoon, they motored into the country, to see the great brewery gardens, the new villa suburb, and through the lanes past the old, decaying plantations with palm trees. In one lane they met the fifty motor-cars with the two hundred tourists all with badges on their chests and self-satisfaction on their faces. Mrs. Witt watched in grim silence.

'Plus ça change, plus c'est la même chose,' said Lou, with a wicked little smile. 'On n'est pas mieux ici,[56] mother.'

'I know it,' said Mrs. Witt.

The hotels by the sea were all shut up: it was not yet the 'season.' Not till November. And then!—Why, then Havana would be an American city, in full leaf of green dollar bills. The green leaf of American prosperity shedding itself recklessly, from every roaming sprig of a tourist, over this city of sunshine and alcohol. Green leaves unfolded in Pittsburgh and Chicago, showering in winter downfall in Havana.

Mother and daughter drank tea in a corner of the Hotel d'Angleterre once more, and returned to the ferry.

The Gulf of Mexico was blue and rippling, with the phantom of islands on the south. Great porpoises rolled and leaped, running in front of the ship in the clear water, diving, travelling in perfect motion, straight, with the tip of the ship touching the tip of their tails, then rolling over, corkscrewing, and showing their bellies as they went. Marvellous! The marvellous beauty and fascination of natural wild things! The horror of man's unnatural life, his heaped-up civilization!

The flying-fishes burst out of the sea in clouds of silvery, transparent motion. Blue above and below, the Gulf seemed a silent, empty, timeless place where

---

56. "The more it changes the more it stays the same"; "things are no better here."

man did not really reach. And Lou was again fascinated by the glamour of the universe.

But bump! She and her mother were in a first-class hotel again, calling down the telephone for the bell-boy and ice-water. And soon they were in a Pullman, off towards San Antonio.

It was America, it was Texas. They were at their ranch, on the great level of yellow autumn, with the vast sky above. And after all, from the hot wide sky, and the hot, wide, red earth, there *did* come something new, something not used up. Lou *did* feel exhilarated.

The Texans were there, tall blond people, ingenuously cheerful, ingenuously, childishly intimate, as if the fact that you had never seen them before was as nothing compared to the fact that you'd all been living in one room together all your lives, so that nothing was hidden from either of you. The one room being the mere shanty of the world in which we all live. Strange, uninspired cheerfulness, filling, as it were, the blank of complete incomprehension.

And off they set in their motor-cars, chiefly high-legged Fords, rattling away down the red trails between yellow sunflowers or sere grass or dry cotton, away, away into great distances, cheerfully raising the dust of haste. It left Lou in a sort of blank amazement. But it left her amused, not depressed. The old screws of emotion and intimacy that had been screwed down so tightly upon her fell out of their holes, here. The Texan intimacy weighed no more on her than a postage stamp, even if, for the moment, it stuck as close. And there was a certain underneath recklessness, even a stoicism, in all the apparently childish people, which left one free. They might appear childish: but they stoically depended on themselves alone, in reality. Not as in England, where every man waited to pour the burden of himself upon you.

St. Mawr arrived safely, a bit bewildered. The Texans eyed him closely, struck silent, as ever, by anything pure-bred and beautiful. He was somehow too beautiful, too perfected, in this great open country. The long-legged Texan horses, with their elaborate saddles, seemed somehow more natural.

Even St. Mawr felt himself strange, as it were naked and singled out, in this rough place. Like a jewel among stones, a pearl before swine, maybe. But the swine were no fools. They knew a pearl from a grain of maize, and a grain of maize from a pearl. And they knew what they wanted. When it was pearls, it was pearls; though chiefly it was maize. Which shows good sense. They could see St. Mawr's points. Only he needn't draw the point too fine, or it would just not pierce the tough skin of this country.

The ranch-man mounted him—just threw a soft skin over his back, jumped on, and away down the red trail, raising the dust among the tall wild yellow of sunflowers, in the hot wild sun. Then back again in a fume, and the man slipped off.

'He's got the stuff in him, he sure has,' said the man.

And the horse seemed pleased with this rough handling. Lewis looked on in wonder, and a little envy.

Lou and her mother stayed a fortnight on the ranch. It was all so queer: so crude, so rough, so easy, so artificially civilized, and so meaningless. Lou could not get over the feeling that it all meant nothing. There were no roots of reality at all. No consciousness below the surface, no meaning in anything save the obvious, the blatantly obvious. It was like life enacted in a mirror. Visually, it was wildly vital. But there was nothing behind it. Or like a cinematograph: flat shapes, exactly like men, but without any substance of reality, rapidly rattling away with talk, emotions, activity, all in the flat, nothing behind it. No deeper consciousness at all.—So it seemed to her.

One moved from dream to dream, from phantasm to phantasm.

But at least this Texan life, if it had no bowels, no vitals, at least it could not prey on one's own vitals. It was this much better than Europe.

Lewis was silent, and rather piqued. St. Mawr had already made advances to the boss' long-legged, arched-necked, glossy-maned Texan mare. And the boss was pleased.

What a world!

Mrs. Witt eyed it all shrewdly. But she failed to participate. Lou was a bit scared at the emptiness of it all, and the queer, phantasmal self-consciousness. Cowboys just as self-conscious as Rico, far more sentimental, inwardly vague and unreal. Cowboys that went after their cows in black Ford motor-cars: and who self-consciously saw Lady Carrington falling to them, as elegant young ladies from the East fall to the noble cowboy of the films, or in Zane Grey. It was all film-psychology.

And at the same time, these boys led a hard, hard life, often dangerous and gruesome. Nevertheless, inwardly they were self-conscious film-heroes. The boss himself, a man over forty, long and lean and with a great deal of stringy energy, showed off before her in a strong silent manner, existing for the time being purely in his imagination of the sort of picture he made to her, the sort of impression he made on her.

So they all were, coloured up like a Zane Grey book-jacket, all of them living in the mirror. The kind of picture they made to somebody else.

And at the same time, with energy, courage, and a stoical grit getting their work done, and putting through what they had to put through.

It left Lou blank with wonder. And in the face of this strange, cheerful living in the mirror—a rather cheap mirror at that—England began to seem real to her again.

Then she had to remember herself back in England. And no, O God, England was not real either, except poisonously.

What was real? What under heaven was real?

Her mother had gone dumb and, as it were, out of range. Phœnix was a bit assured and bouncy, back more or less in his own conditions. Lewis was a bit impressed by the emptiness of everything, the *lack* of concentration. And St. Mawr followed at the heels of the boss' long-legged black Texan mare, almost slavishly.

What, in heaven's name, was one to make of it all?

Soon, she could not stand this sort of living in a film-setting, with the mechanical energy of 'making good,' that is, making money, to keep the show going. The mystic duty to 'make good,' meaning to make the ranch pay a laudable interest on the 'owners'' investment. Lou herself being one of the owners. And the interest that came to her, from her father's will, being the money she spent to buy St. Mawr and to fit up that house in Westminster. Then also the mystic duty to 'feel good.' Everybody had to *feel good, fine!* 'How are you this morning, Mr. Latham?'—'*Fine!* Eh! Don't you feel good out here, eh, Lady Carrington?' —'*Fine!*'—Lou pronounced it with the same ringing conviction. It was Coué [57] all the time!

'Shall we stay here long, mother?' she asked.

'Not a day longer than you want to, Louise. I stay entirely for your sake.'

'Then let us go, mother.'

They left St. Mawr and Lewis. But Phœnix wanted to come along. So they motored to San Antonio, got into the Pullman, and travelled as far as El Paso. Then they changed to go north, Santa Fe would be at least 'easy.' And Mrs. Witt had acquaintances there.

They found the fiesta over in Santa Fe: Indians, Mexicans, artists had finished their great effort to amuse and attract the tourists. *Welcome, Mr. Tourist,* said a great board on one side of the high road. And on the other side, a little nearer to town: *Thank You, Mr. Tourist.*

'*Plus ça change*—' Lou began.

'*Ca ne change jamais* [58]—except for the worse!' said Mrs. Witt, like a pistol going off. And Lou held her peace, after she had sighed to herself, and said in her own mind: '*Welcome Also Mrs. and Miss Tourist!*'

There was no getting a word out of Mrs. Witt, these days. Whereas Phœnix was becoming almost loquacious.

They stayed awhile in Sante Fe, in the clean, comfortable, 'homely' hotel, where 'every room had its bath': a spotless white bath, with very hot water night and day. The tourists and commercial travellers sat in the big hall down below, everybody living in the mirror! And, of course, they knew Lady Carrington down to her shoe-soles. And they all expected her to know them down to their shoe-soles. For the only object of the mirror is to reflect images.

For two days mother and daughter ate in the salad-bowl intimacy of the dining-room. Then Mrs. Witt struck, and telephoned down, every meal-time, for her meal in her room. She got to staying in bed later and later, as on the ship. Lou became uneasy. This was worse than Europe.

Phœnix was still there, as a sort of half-friend, half-servant retainer. He was perfectly happy, roving round among the Mexicans and Indians, talking Spanish all day, and telling about England and his two mistresses, rolling the ball of his own importance.

'I'm afraid we've got Phœnix for life,' said Lou.

'Not unless we wish,' said Mrs. Witt indifferently. And she picked up a novel which she didn't want to read, but which she was going to read.

'What shall we do next, mother?' Lou asked.

'As far as I am concerned, there is no next,' said Mrs. Witt.

'Come, mother! Let's go back to Italy or somewhere, if it's as bad as that.'

'Never again, Louise, shall I cross that water. I have come home to die.'

'I don't see much home about it—the Gonzales Hotel in Santa Fe.'

'Indeed not! But as good as anywhere else, to die in.'

57. Emile Coué (1857–1926), famous for his "autosuggestion"—the patient recites "Every day and in every way I'm getting better and better."
58. "It never changes."

'Oh, mother, don't be silly! Shall we look for somewhere where we can be by ourselves?'

'I leave it to you, Louise. I have made my last decision.'

'What is that, mother?'

'Never, never to make another decision.'

'Not even to decide to die?'

'No, not even that.'

'Or *not* to die?'

'Not that either.'

Mrs. Witt shut up like a trap. She refused to rise from her bed that day.

Lou went to consult Phœnix. The result was, the two set out to look at a little ranch that was for sale.

It was autumn, and the loveliest time in the South-west, where there is no spring, snow blowing into the hot lap of summer; and no real summer, hail falling in thick ice, from the thunderstorms: and even no very definite winter, hot sun melting the snow and giving an impression of spring at any time. But autumn there is, when the winds of the desert are almost still, and the mountains fume no clouds. But morning comes cold and delicate, upon the wild sunflowers and the puffing, yellow-flowered greasewood.[59] For the desert blooms in autumn. In spring it is grey ash all the time, and only the strong breath of the summer sun, and the heavy splashing of thunder-rain, succeed at last, by September, in blowing it into soft, puffy yellow fire.

It was such a delicate morning when Lou drove out with Phœnix towards the mountains, to look at this ranch that a Mexican wanted to sell. For the brief moment the high mountains had lost their snow: it would be back again in a fortnight: and stood dim and delicate with autumn haze. The desert stretched away pale, as pale as the sky, but silvery and sere, with hummock-mounds of shadow, and long wings of shadow, like the reflection of some great bird. The same eagle-shadows came like rude paintings of the outstretched bird, upon the mountains, where the aspens were turning yellow. For the moment, the brief moment, the great desert-and-mountain landscape had lost its certain cruelty, and looked tender, dreamy. And many, many birds were flickering around.

Lou and Phœnix bumped and hesitated over a long trail: then wound down into a deep canyon: and then the car began to climb, climb, climb, in steep rushes, and in long heart-breaking, uneven pulls. The road was bad, and driving was no joke. But it was the sort of road Phœnix was used to. He sat impassive and watchful, and kept on, till his engine boiled. He was *himself* in this country: impassive, detached, self-satisfied, and silently assertive. Guarding himself at every moment, but on his guard, sure of himself. Seeing no difference at all between Lou or Mrs. Witt and himself, except that they had money and he had none, while he had a native importance which they lacked. He depended on them for money, they on him for the power to live out here in the West. Intimately, he was as good as they. Money was their only advantage.

As Lou sat beside him in the front seat of the car, where it bumped less than behind, she felt this. She felt a peculiar tough-necked arrogance in him, as if he

59. Low shrub common in the West of the United States.

were asserting himself to put something over her. He wanted her to allow him to make advances to her, to allow him to suggest that he should be her lover. And then, finally, she would marry him, and he would be on the same footing as she and her mother.

In return, he would look after her, and give her his support and countenance, as a man, and stand between her and the world. In this sense, he would be faithful to her, and loyal. But as far as other women went, Mexican women or Indian women: why, that was none of her business. His marrying her would be a pact between two aliens, on behalf of one another, and he would keep his part of it all right. But himself, as a private man and a predative alien-blooded male, this had nothing to do with her. It didn't enter into her scope and count. She was one of these nervous white women with lots of money. She was very nice too. But as a *squaw*—as a real woman in a shawl whom a man went after for the pleasure of the night—why, she hardly counted. One of these white women who talk clever and know things like a man. She could hardly expect a half-savage male to acknowledge her as his female counterpart.—No! She had the bucks! And she had all the paraphernalia of the white man's civilization, which a savage can play with and so escape his own hollow boredom. But his own real female counterpart?—Phœnix would just have shrugged his shoulders, and thought the question not worth answering. How could there be any answer in *her* to the phallic male in him? Couldn't! Yet it would flatter his vanity and his self-esteem immensely, to possess her. That would be possessing the very clue to the white man's overwhelming world. And if she would let him possess her, he would be absolutely loyal to her, as far as affairs and appearances went. Only, the aboriginal phallic male in him simply couldn't recognize her as a woman at all. In this respect, she didn't exist. It needed the shawled Indian or Mexican women, with their squeaky, plaintive voices, their shuffling, watery humility, and the dark glances of their big, knowing eyes. When an Indian woman looked at him from under her black fringe, with dark, half-secretive suggestion in her big eyes: and when she stood before him hugged in her shawl, in such apparently complete quiescent humility: and when she spoke to him in her mousy squeak of a high, plaintive voice, as if it were difficult for her female bashfulness even to emit so much sound: and when she shuffled away with her legs wide apart, because of her wide-topped, white, high buckskin boots with tiny white feet, and her dark-knotted hair so full of hard, yet subtle lure: and when he remembered the almost watery softness of the Indian woman's dark, warm flesh: then he was a male, an old, secretive, rat-like male. But before Lou's straightforwardness and utter sexual incompetence, he just stood in contempt. And to him, even a French *cocotte* was utterly devoid of the right sort of sex. She couldn't really move him. She couldn't satisfy the furtiveness in him. He needed this plaintive, squeaky, dark-fringed Indian quality. Something furtive and soft and rat-like, really to rouse him.

Nevertheless he was ready to trade his sex, which, in his opinion, every white woman was secretly pining for, for the white woman's money and social privileges. In the daytime, all the thrill and excitement of the white man's motor-cars and moving pictures and ice-cream sodas and so forth. In the night, the soft, watery-soft warmth of an Indian or half-Indian woman. This was Phœnix's idea of life for himself.

Meanwhile, if a white woman gave him the privileges of the white man's world, he would do his duty by her as far as all that went.

Lou, sitting very, very still beside him as he drove the car: he was not a very good driver, not quick and marvellous as some white men are, particularly some French chauffeurs she had known, but usually a little behindhand in his movements: she knew more or less all that he felt. More or less she divined as a woman does. Even from a certain rather assured stupidity of his shoulders, and a certain rather stupid assertiveness of his knees, she knew him.

But she did not judge him too harshly. Somewhere deep, deep in herself she knew she too was at fault. And this made her sometimes inclined to humble herself, as a woman, before the furtive assertiveness of this underground, 'knowing' savage. He was so different from Rico.

Yet, after all, *was* he? In his rootlessness, his drifting, his real meaninglessness, was he different from Rico? And his childish, spellbound absorption in the motor-car, or in the moving pictures, or in an ice-cream soda—was it very different from Rico? Anyhow, was it really any better? Pleasanter, perhaps, to a woman, because of the childishness of it.

The same with his opinion of himself as a sexual male! So childish, really, it was almost thrilling to a woman. But then, so stupid also, with that furtive lurking in holes and imagining it could not be detected. He imagined he kept himself dark, in his sexual rat-holes. He imagined he was not detected!

No, no, Lou was not such a fool as she looked, in his eyes anyhow. She knew what she wanted. She wanted relief from the nervous tension and irritation of her life, she wanted to escape from the friction [60] which is the whole stimulus in modern social life. She wanted to be still: only that, to be very, very still, and recover her own soul.

When Phœnix presumed she was looking for some secretly sexual male such as himself, he was ridiculously mistaken. Even the illusion of the beautiful St. Mawr was gone. And Phœnix, roaming round like a sexual rat in promiscuous back yards!—*Merci, mon cher!* For that was all he was: a sexual rat in the great barn-yard of man's habitat, looking for female rats!

Merci, mon cher! You are had.

Nevertheless, in his very mistakenness, he was a relief to her. His mistake was amusing rather than impressive. And the fact that one-half of his intelligence was a complete dark blank, that too was a relief.

Strictly, and perhaps in the best sense, he was a servant. His very unconsciousness and his very limitation served as a shelter, as one shelters within the limitations of four walls. The very decided limits to his intelligence were a shelter to her. They made her feel safe.

But that feeling of safety did not deceive her. It was the feeling one derived from having a *true* servant attached to one, a man whose psychic limitations left him incapable of anything but service, and whose strong flow of natural life, at the same time, made him need to serve.

And Lou, sitting there so very still and frail, yet self-contained, had not lived for nothing. She no longer wanted to fool herself. She had no desire at all to fool herself into thinking that a Phœnix might be a husband and a mate. No desire

60. Another key-word of Lawrence's, used of bad, mechanical sex, and so on.

that way at all. His obtuseness was a servant's obtuseness. She was grateful to him for serving, and she paid him a wage. Moreover, she provided him with something to do, to occupy his life. In a sense, she gave him his life, and rescued him from his own boredom. It was a balance.

He did not know what she was thinking. There was a certain physical sympathy between them. His obtuseness made him think it was also a sexual sympathy.

'It's a nice trip, you and me,' he said suddenly, turning and looking her in the eyes with an excited look, and ending on a foolish little laugh.

She realized that she should have sat in the back seat.

'But it's a bad road,' she said. 'Hadn't you better stop and put the sides of the hood up? your engine is boiling.'

He looked away with a quick switch of interest to the red thermometer in front of his machine.

'She's boiling,' he said, stopping, and getting out with a quick alacrity to go to look at the engine.

Lou got out also, and went to the back seat, shutting the door decisively.

'I think I'll ride at the back,' she said; 'it gets so frightfully hot in front, when the engine heats up.—Do you think she needs some water? Have you got some in the canteen?'

'She's full,' he said, peering into the steaming valve.

'You can run a bit out, if you think there's any need. I wonder if it's much further!'

'*Quién sabe?*' [61] said he, slightly impertinent.

She relapsed in her own stillness. She realized how careful, how very careful she must be of relaxing into sympathy, and reposing, as it were, on Phœnix. He would read it as a sexual appeal. Perhaps he couldn't help it. She had only herself to blame. He was obtuse, as a man and a savage. He had only one interpretation, sex, for any woman's approach to him.

And she knew, with the last clear knowledge of weary disillusion, that she did not want to be mixed up in Phœnix's sexual promiscuities. The very thought was an insult to her. The crude, clumsy servant-male: no, no, not that. He was a good fellow, a very good fellow, as far as he went. But he fell far short of physical intimacy.

'No, no,' she said to herself, 'I was wrong to ride in the front seat with him. I must sit alone, just alone. Because sex, mere sex, is repellent to me. I will never prostitute myself again. Unless something touches my very spirit, the very quick of me, I will stay alone, just alone. Alone, and give myself only to the unseen presences, serve only the other, unseen presences.'

She understood now the meaning of the Vestal Virgins, the Virgins of the holy fire in the old temples. They were symbolic of herself, of woman weary of the embrace of incompetent men, weary, weary, weary of all that, turning to the unseen gods, the unseen spirits, the hidden fire, and devoting herself to that, and that alone. Receiving thence her pacification and her fulfilment.

Not these little, incompetent, childish, self-opionated men! Not these to touch her. She watched Phœnix's rather stupid shoulders, as he drove the car on be-

61. "Who knows?"

tween the piñon trees and the cedars of the narrow mesa ridge, to the mountain foot. He was a good fellow. But let him run among women of his own sort. Something was beyond him. And this something must remain beyond him, never allow itself to come within his reach. Otherwise he would paw it and mess it up, and be as miserable as a child that has broken its father's watch.

No, no! She had loved an American, and lived with him for a fortnight. She had had a long, intimate friendship with an Italian. Perhaps it was love on his part. And she had yielded to him. Then her love and marriage to Rico.

And what of it all? Nothing. It was almost nothing. It was as if only the outside of herself, her top layers, were human. This inveigled her into intimacies. As soon as the inimacy penetrated, or attempted to penetrate, inside her, it was a disaster. Just a humiliation and a breaking down.

Within these outer layers of herself lay the successive inner sanctuaries of herself. And these were inviolable. She accepted it.

'I am not a marrying woman,' she said to herself. 'I am not a lover nor a mistress nor a wife. It is no good. Love can't really come into me from the outside, and I can never, never mate with any man, since the mystic new man will never come to me. No, no, let me know myself and my rôle. I am one of the eternal Virgins, serving the eternal fire. My dealings with men have only broken my stillness and messed up my doorways. It has been my own fault. I ought to stay virgin, and still, very, very still, and serve the most perfect service. I want my temple and my loneliness and my Apollo mystery of the inner fire. And with men, only the delicate, subtler, more remote relations. No coming near. A coming near only breaks the delicate veils, and broken veils, like broken flowers, only lead to rottenness.'

She felt a great peace inside herself as she made this realization. And a thankfulness. Because, after all, it seemed to her that the hidden fire was alive and burning in this sky, over the desert, in the mountains. She felt a certain latent holiness in the very atmosphere, a young spring-fire of latent holiness, such as she had never felt in Europe, or in the East. 'For me,' she said, as she looked away at the mountains in shadow and the pale-warm desert beneath, with wings of shadow upon it: 'For me, this place is sacred. It is blessed.'

But as she watched Phœnix: as she remembered the motor-cars and tourists, and the rather dreary Mexicans of Santa Fe, and the lurking, invidious Indians, with something of a rat-like secretiveness and defeatedness in their bearing, she realized that the latent fire of the vast landscape struggled under a great weight of dirt-like inertia. She had to mind the dirt, most carefully and vividly avoid it and keep it away from her, here in this place that at least seemed sacred to her.

The motor-car climbed up, past the tall pine trees, to the foot of the mountains, and came at last to a wire gate, where nothing was to be expected. Phœnix opened the gate, and they drove on, through more trees, into a clearing where dried-up bean-plants were yellow.

'This man got no water for his beans,' said Phœnix. 'Not got much beans this year.'

They climbed slowly up the incline, through more pine trees, and out into another clearing, where a couple of horses were grazing. And there they saw the ranch itself, little low cabins with patched roofs, under a few pine trees, and facing the long twelve-acre clearing, or field, where the Michaelmas daisies were purple mist, and spangled with clumps of yellow flowers.

'Not got no alfalfa here neither!' said Phœnix, as the car waded past the flowers. 'Must be a dry place up here. Got no water, sure they haven't.'

Yet it was the place Lou wanted. In an instant, her heart sprang to it. The instant the car stopped, and she saw the two cabins inside the rickety fence, the rather broken corral beyond, and, behind all, tall, blue balsam pines, the round hills, the solid uprise of the mountain flank: and, getting down, she looked across the purple and gold of the clearing, downwards at the ring of pine trees standing so still, so crude and untamable, the motionless desert beyond the bristles of the pine crests, a thousand feet below: and, beyond the desert, blue mountains, and far, far-off blue mountains in Arizona: 'This is the place,' she said to herself.

This little tumble-down ranch, only a homestead of a hundred and sixty acres, was, as it were, man's last effort towards the wild heart of the Rockies, at this point. Sixty years before, a restless schoolmaster had wandered out from the East, looking for gold among the mountains. He found a very little, then no more. But the mountains had got hold of him, he could not go back.

There was a little trickling spring of pure water, a thread of treasure perhaps better than gold. So the schoolmaster took up a homestead on the lot where this little spring arose. He struggled, and got himself his log cabin erected, his fence put up, sloping at the mountain-side through the pine trees and dropping into the hollows where the ghost-white mariposa lilies stood leafless and naked in flower, in spring, on tall invisible stems. He made the long clearing for alfalfa.

And fell so into debt, that he had to trade his homestead away, to clear his debt. Then he made a tiny living teaching the children of the few American prospectors who had squatted in the valleys, beside the Mexicans.

The trader who got the ranch tackled it with a will. He built another log cabin, and a big corral, and brought water from the canyon two miles and more across the mountain-slope, in a little runnel ditch, and more water, piped a mile or more down the little canyon immediately above the cabins. He got a flow of water for his houses: for, being a true American, he felt he could not *really* say he had conquered his environment till he had got running water, taps, and wash-hand basins inside his house.

Taps, running water, and wash-hand basins he accomplished. And, un-daunted through the years, he prepared the basin for a fountain in the little fenced-in enclosure, and he built a little bath-house. After a number of years, he sent up the enamelled bath-tub to be put in the little log bath-house on the little wild ranch hung right against the savage Rockies, above the desert.

But here the mountains finished him. He was a trader down below, in the Mexican village. This little ranch was, as it were, his hobby, his ideal. He and his New England wife spent their summers there: and turned on the taps in the cabins and turned them off again, and felt really that civilization had con-quered.

All this plumbing from the savage ravines of the canyons—one of them name-less to this day—cost, however, money. In fact, the ranch cost a great deal of money. But it was all to be got back. The big clearing was to be irrigated for alfalfa, the little clearing for beans, and the third clearing, under the corral, for potatoes. All these things the trader could trade to the Mexicans, very advantageously.

And, moreover, since somebody had started a praise of the famous goat's cheese made by Mexican peasants in New Mexico, goats there should be.

Goats there were: five hundred of them, eventually. And they fed chiefly in the wild mountain hollows, the no-man's-land. The Mexicans call them firemouths, because everything they nibble dies. Not because of their flaming mouths, really, but because they nibble a live plant down, down to the quick, till it can put forth no more.

So, the energetic trader, in the course of five or six years, had got the ranch ready. The long three-roomed cabin was for him and his New England wife. In the two-roomed cabin lived the Mexican family who really had charge of the ranch. For the trader was mostly fixed to his store, seventeen miles away, down in the Mexican village.

The ranch lay over eight thousand feet up, the snows of winter came deep, and the white goats, looking dirty yellow, swam in snow with their poor curved horns poking out like dead sticks. But the corral had a long, cosy, shut-in goat-shed all down one side, and into this crowded the five hundred, their acrid goat-smell rising like hot acid over the snow. And the thin, pock-marked Mexican threw them alfalfa out of the log barn. Until the hot sun sank the snow again, and froze the surface, when patter-patter went the two thousand little goat-hoofs, over the silver-frozen snow, up at the mountain. Nibble, nibble, nibble, the fire-mouths, at every tender twig. And the goat-bell climbed, and the baa-ing came from among the dense and shaggy pine trees. And sometimes, in a soft drift under the trees, a goat, or several goats, went through, into the white depths, and some were lost thus, to reappear dead and frozen at the thaw.

By evening, they were driven down again, like a dirty yellowish-white stream carrying dark sticks on its yeasty surface, tripping and bleating over the frozen snow, past the bustling dark-green pine trees, down to the trampled mess of the corral. And everywhere, everywhere over the snow, yellow stains and dark pills of goat-droppings melting into the surface crystal. On still, glittering nights, when the frost was hard, the smell of goats came up like some uncanny acid fire, and great stars sitting on the mountain's edge seemed to be watching like the eyes of a mountain lion, brought by the scent. Then the coyotes in the near canyon howled and sobbed, and ran like shadows over the snow. But the goat corral had been built tight.

In the course of years the goat-herd had grown from fifty to five hundred, and surely that was increase. The goat-milk cheeses sat drying on their little racks. In spring, there was a great flowing and skipping of kids. In summer and early autumn, there was a pest of flies, rising from all that goat-smell and that cast-out whey of goats'-milk, after the cheese-making. The rats came, and the pack-rats, swarming.

And, after all, it was difficult to sell or trade the cheeses, and little profit to be made. And, in dry summers, no water came down in the narrow ditch-channel, that straddled in wooden runnels over the deep clefts in the mountain-side. No water meant no alfalfa. In winter the goats scarcely drank at all. In summer they could be watered at the little spring. But the thirsty land was not so easy to accommodate.

Five hundred fine white Angora goats, with their massive handsome padres! They were beautiful enough. And the trader made all he could of them. Come summer, they were run down into the narrow tank filled with the fiery dipping fluid. Then their lovely white wool was clipped. It was beautiful, and valuable, but comparatively little of it.

And it all cost, cost, cost. And a man was always let down. At one time no water. At another a poison-weed. Then a sickness. Always, some mysterious malevolence fighting, fighting against the will of man. A strange invisible influence coming out of the livid rock-fastnesses in the bowels of those uncreated Rocky Mountains, preying upon the will of man, and slowly wearing down his resistance, his onward-pushing spirit. The curious, subtle thing, like a mountain fever, got into the blood, so that the men at the ranch, and the animals with them, had bursts of queer, violent, half-frenzied energy, in which, however, they were wont to lose their wariness. And then, damage of some sort. The horses ripped and cut themselves, or they were struck by lightning, the men had great hurts, or sickness. A curious disintegration working all the time, a sort of malevolent breath, like a stupefying, irritant gas, coming out of the unfathomed mountains.

The pack-rats with their bushy tails and big ears came down out of the hills, and were jumping and bouncing about: symbols of the curious debasing malevolence that was in the spirit of the place. The Mexicans in charge, good honest men, worked all they could. But they were like most of the Mexicans in the South-west, as if they had been pithed, to use one of Kipling's words. As if the invidious malevolence of the country itself had slowly taken all the pith of manhood from them, leaving a hopeless sort of corpus of a man.

And the same happened to the white men, exposed to the open country. Slowly, they were pithed. The energy went out of them. And, more than that, the interest. An inertia of indifference invading the soul, leaving the body healthy and active, but wasting the soul, the living interest, quite away.

It was the New England wife of the trader who put most energy into the ranch. She looked on it as her home. She had a little white fence put all round the two cabins: the bright brass water-taps she kept shining in the two kitchens: outside the kitchen door she had a little kitchen garden and nasturtiums, after a great fight with invading animals, that nibbled everything away. And she got so far as the preparation of the round concrete basin which was to be a little pool, under the few enclosed pine trees between the two cabins, a pool with a tiny fountain jet.

But this, with the bath-tub, was her limit, as the five hundred goats were her man's limit. Out of the mountains came two breaths of influence: the breath of the curious, frenzied energy, that took away one's intelligence as alcohol or any other stimulus does: and then the most strange invidiousness that ate away the soul. The woman loved her ranch, almost with passion. It was she who felt the stimulus, more than the men. It seemed to enter her like a sort of sex passion, intensifying her ego, making her full of violence and of blind female energy. The energy, and the blindness of it! A strange blind frenzy, like an intoxication while it lasted. And the sense of beauty that thrilled her New England woman's soul.

Her cabin faced the slow down-slope of the clearing, the alfalfa field: her long, low cabin, crouching under the great pine tree that threw up its trunk sheer in front of the house, in the yard. That pine tree was the guardian of the place. But a bristling, almost demonish guardian, from the far-off crude ages of the world. Its great pillar of pale, flaky-ribbed copper rose there in strange callous indifference, and the grim permanence, which is in pine trees. A passionless, non-phallic column, rising in the shadows of the pre-sexual world, before the hot-blooded ithyphallic column ever erected itself. A cold, blossomless, resinous sap surging and oozing gum, from that pallid brownish bark. And the wind hissing in the needles, like a vast nest of serpents. And the pine cones falling plumb as the hail hit them. Then lying all over the yard, open in the sun like wooden roses, but hard, sexless, rigid with a blind will.

Past the column of that pine tree, the alfalfa field sloped gently down, to the circling guard of pine trees, from which silent, living barrier isolated pines rose to ragged heights at intervals, in blind assertiveness. Strange, those pine trees! In some lights all their needles glistened like polished steel, all subtly glittering with a whitish glitter among darkness, like real needles. Then again, at evening, the trunks would flare up orange-red, and the tufts would be dark, alert tufts like a wolf's tail touching the air. Again, in the morning sunlight they would be soft and still, hardly noticeable. But all the same, present, and watchful. Never sympathetic, always watchfully on their guard, and resistant, they hedged one in with the aroma and the power and the slight horror of the pre-sexual primeval world. The world where each creature was crudely limited to its own ego, crude and bristling and cold, and then crowding in packs like pine trees and wolves.

But beyond the pine trees, ah, there beyond, there was beauty for the spirit to soar in. The circle of pines, with the loose trees rising high and ragged at intervals, this was the barrier, the fence to the foreground. Beyond was only distance, the desert a thousand feet below, and beyond.

The desert swept its great fawn-coloured circle around, away beyond and below like a beach, with a long mountain-side of pure blue shadow closing in the near corner, and strange bluish hummocks of mountains rising like wet rock from a vast strand, away in the middle distance, and beyond, in the farthest distance, pale-blue crests of mountains looking over the horizon, from the west, as if peering in from another world altogether.

Ah, that was beauty!—perhaps the most beautiful thing in the world. It was pure beauty, *absolute* beauty! There! That was it. To the little woman from New England, with her tense, fierce soul and her egoistic passion of service, this beauty was absolute, a *ne plus ultra*.[62] From her doorway, from her porch, she could watch the vast, eagle-like wheeling of the daylight, that turned as the eagles which lived in the near rocks turned overhead in the blue, turning their luminous, dark-edged-patterned bellies and under-wings upon the pure air, like winged orbs. So the daylight made the vast turn upon the desert, brushing the farthest outwatching mountains. And sometimes the vast strand of the desert would float with curious undulations and exhalations amid the blue fragility of mountains, whose upper edges were harder than the floating bases. And sometimes she would see the little brown adobe houses of the village

62. "Nothing further"—the most perfect state anything can be brought to.

Mexicans, twenty miles away, like little cube crystals of insect-houses dotting upon the desert, very distinct, with a cottonwood tree or two rising near. And sometimes she would see the far-off rocks, thirty miles away, where the canyon made a gateway between the mountains. Quite clear, like an open gateway out of a vast yard, she would see the cut-out bit of the canyon-passage. And on the desert itself curious puckered folds of mesa-sides. And a blackish crack which in places revealed the otherwise invisible canyon of the Rio Grande. And beyond everything, the mountains like icebergs showing up from an outer sea. Then later, the sun would go down blazing above the shallow cauldron of simmering darkness, and the round mountain of Colorado would lump up into uncanny significance, northwards. That was always rather frightening But morning came again, with the sun peeping over the mountain-slopes and lighting the desert away in the distance long, long before it lighted on her yard. And then she would see another valley, like magic and very lovely, with green fields and long tufts of cottonwood trees, and a few long-cubical adobe houses, lying floating in shallow light below, like a vision.

Ah! It was beauty, beauty absolute, at any hour of the day: whether the perfect clarity of morning, or the mountains beyond the simmering desert at noon, or the purple lumping of northern mounds under a red sun at night. Or whether the dust whirled in tall columns, travelling across the desert far away, like pillars of cloud by day, tall, leaning pillars of dust hastening with ghostly haste: or whether, in the early part of the year, suddenly in the morning a whole sea of solid white would rise rolling below, a solid mist from melted snow, ghost-white under the mountain sun, the world below blotted out: or whether the black rain and cloud streaked down, far across the desert, and lightning stung down with sharp white stings on the horizon: or the cloud travelled and burst overhead, with rivers of fluid blue fire running out of heaven and exploding on earth, and hail coming down like a world of ice shattered above: or the hot sun rode in again: or snow fell in heavy silence: or the world was blinding white under a blue sky, and one must hurry under the pine trees for shelter against that vast, white, back-beating light which rushed up at one and made one almost unconscious, amid the snow.

It was always beauty, always! It was always great, and splendid, and, for some reason, natural. It was never grandiose or theatrical. Always, for some reason, perfect. And quite simple, in spite of it all.

So it was, when you watched the vast and living landscape. The landscape lived, and lived as the world of the gods, unsullied and unconcerned. The great circling landscape lived its own life, sumptuous and uncaring. Man did not exist for it.

And if it had been a question simply of living through the eyes, into the distance, then this would have been Paradise, and the little New England woman on her ranch would have found what she was always looking for, the earthly paradise of the spirit.

But even a woman cannot live only into the distance, the beyond. Willy-nilly she finds herself juxtaposed to the near things, the thing in itself. And willy-nilly she is caught up into the fight with the immediate object.

The New England woman had fought to make the nearness as perfect as the distance: for the distance was absolute beauty. She had been confident of success. She had felt quite assured, when the water came running out of her bright brass taps, the wild water of the hills caught, tricked into the narrow iron pipes, and led tamely to her kitchen, to jump out over her sink, into her wash-basin, at her service. *There!* she said. I have tamed the waters of the mountain to my service.

So she had, for the moment.

At the same time, the invisible attack was being made upon her. While she revelled in the beauty of the luminous world that wheeled around and below her, the grey, rat-like spirit of the inner mountains was attacking her from behind. She could not keep her attention. And, curiously, she could not keep even her speech. When she was saying something, suddenly the next word would be gone out of her, as if a pack-rat had carried it off. And she sat blank, stuttering, staring in the empty cupboard of her mind, like Mother Hubbard, and seeing the cupboard bare. And this irritated her husband intensely.

Her chickens, of which she was so proud, were carried away. Or they strayed. Or they fell sick. At first she could cope with their circumstances. But after a while, she couldn't. She couldn't care. A drug-like numbness possessed her spirit, and at the very middle of her, she couldn't care what happened to her chickens.

The same when a couple of horses were struck by lightning. It frightened her. The rivers of fluid fire that suddenly fell out of the sky and exploded on the earth near by, as if the whole earth had burst like a bomb, frightened her from the very core of her, and made her know, secretly and with cynical certainty, *that there was no merciful God in the heavens.* A very tall, elegant pine tree just above her cabin took the lightning, and stood tall and elegant as before, but with a white seam spiralling from its crest, all down its tall trunk, to earth. The perfect scar, white and long as lightning itself. And every time she looked at it, she said to herself, in spite of herself: *There is no Almighty loving God. The God there is shaggy as the pine trees, and horrible as the lightning.* Outwardly, she never confessed this. Openly, she thought of her dear New England Church as usual. But in the violent undercurrent of her woman's soul, after the storms, she would look at that living seamed tree, and the voice would say in her, almost savagely: *What nonsense about Jesus and a God of Love, in a place like this! This is more awful and more splendid. I like it better.* The very chipmunks, in their jerky helter-skelter, the blue jays wrangling in the pine tree in the dawn, the grey squirrel undulating to the tree-trunk, then pausing to chatter at her and scold her, with a shrewd fearlessness, as if she were the alien, the outsider, the creature that should not be permitted among the trees, all destroyed the illusion she cherished, of love, universal love. There was no love on this ranch. There was life, intense, bristling life, full of energy, but also with an undertone of savage sordidness.

The black ants in her cupboard, the pack-rats bouncing on her ceiling like hippopotamuses in the night, the two sick goats: there was a peculiar undercurrent of squalor, flowing under the curious *tussle* of wild life. That was it. The wild life, even the life of the trees and flowers, seemed one bristling, hair-raising tussle. The very flowers came up bristly, and many of them were fang-mouthed, like the dead-nettle: and none had any real scent. But they were very fascinating, too, in their very fierceness. In May, the curious columbines of the stream-beds, columbines scarlet outside and yellow in, like the red and yellow of a herald's uniform: farther from the dove nothing could be: then the beautiful rosy-blue of the great tufts of the flower they called bluebell, but which was really a flower of the snapdragon family: these grew in powerful beauty in the little clearing of the pine trees, followed by the flower the settlers had mysteriously called herb honeysuckle: a tangle of long drops of pure fire-red, hanging from slim invisible stalks of smoke-colour. The purest, most perfect vermilion scarlet, cleanest fire-colour, hanging in long drops like a shower of fire-rain that is just going to strike the earth. A little later, more in the open, there came another sheer fire-red flower, sparking, fierce red stars running up a bristly grey ladder, as if earth's fire-centre had blown out some red sparks, white-speckled and deadly inside, puffing for a moment in the day air.

So it was! The alfalfa field was one raging, seething conflict of plants trying to get hold. One dry year, and the bristly wild things had got hold: the spiky, blue-leaved thistle-poppy with its moon-white flowers, the low clumps of blue nettle-flower, the later rush, after the sereness of June and July, the rush of red sparks and Michaelmas daisies, and the tough wild sunflowers, strangling and choking the dark, tender green of the clover-like alfalfa! A battle, a battle, with banners of bright scarlet and yellow.

When a really defenceless flower did issue, like the moth-still, ghost-centered mariposa lily, with its inner moth-dust of yellow, it came invisible. There was nothing to be seen but a hair of greyish grass near the oak-scrub. Behold, this invisible long stalk was balancing a white, ghostly, three-petalled flower, naked out of nothingness. A mariposa lily!

Only the pink wild roses smelled sweet, like the Old World. They were sweet brier-roses. And the dark-blue harebells among the oak-scrub, like the ice-dark bubbles of the mountain flowers in the Alps, the Alpenglocken.

The roses of the desert are the cactus flowers, crystal of translucent yellow or of rose-colour. But set among spines the devil himself must have conceived in a moment of sheer ecstasy.

Nay, it was a world before and after the God of Love. Even the very humming-birds hanging about the flowering squawberry bushes, when the snow had gone, in May, they were before and after the God of Love. And the blue jays were crested dark with challenge, and the yellow-and-dark woodpecker was fearless like a warrior in war-paint, as he struck the wood. While on the fence the hawks sat motionless, like dark fists clenched under heaven, ignoring man and his ways.

Summer, it was true, unfolded the tender cottonwood leaves, and the tender aspen. But what a tangle and a ghostly aloofness in the aspen thickets high up on the mountains, the coldness that is in the eyes and the long cornelian talons of the bear.

Summer brought the little wild strawberries, with their savage aroma, and the late summer brought the rose-jewel raspberries in the valley cleft. But how lonely, how harsh-lonely and menacing it was, to be alone in that shadowy, steep cleft of a canyon just above the cabins, picking raspberries, while the thunder gathered thick and blue-purple at the mountain-tops. The many wild raspberries hanging rose-red in the thickets. But the stream-bed below all silent, waterless. And the trees all bristling in silence, and waiting like warriors at an outpost. And the berries waiting for the sharp-eyed, cold, long-snouted bear to come rambling and shaking his heavy sharp fur. The berries grew for the bears, and the little New England woman, with her uncanny sensitiveness to underlying influences, felt all the time she was stealing. Stealing the wild raspberries in the secret little canyon behind her home. And when she had made them into jam, she could almost taste the theft in her preserves.

She confessed nothing of this. She tried even to confess nothing of her dread. But she was afraid. Especially she was conscious of the prowling, intense aerial electricity all the summer, after June. The air was thick with wandering currents of fierce electric fluid, waiting to discharge themselves. And almost every day there was the rage and battle of thunder. But the air was never cleared. There was no relief. However the thunder raged, and spent itself, yet, afterwards, among the sunshine was the strange lurking and wandering of the electric currents, moving invisible, with strange menace, between the atoms of the air. She knew. Oh, she knew!

And her love for her ranch turned sometimes into a certain repulsion. The underlying rat-dirt, the everlasting bristling tussle of the wild life, with the tangle and the bones strewing. Bones of horses struck by lightning, bones of dead cattle, skulls of goats with little horns: bleached, unburied bones. Then the cruel electricity of the mountains. And then, most mysterious but worst of all, the animosity of the spirit of place: the crude, half-created spirit of place, like some serpent-bird forever attacking man, in a hatred of man's onward-struggle towards further creation.

The seething cauldron of lower life, seething on the very tissue of the higher life, seething the soul away, seething at the marrow. The vast and unrelenting will of the swarming lower life, working forever against man's attempt at a higher life, a further created being.

At last, after many years, the little woman admitted to herself that she was glad to go down from the ranch when November came with snows. She was glad to come to a more human home, her house in the village. And as winter passed by, and spring came again, she knew she did not want to go up to the ranch again. It had broken something in her. It had hurt her terribly. It had maimed her forever in her hope, her belief in paradise on earth. Now, she hid from herself her own corpse, the corpse of her New England belief in a world ultimately all for love. The belief, and herself with it, was a corpse. The gods of those inner mountains were grim and invidious and relentless, huger than man, and lower than man. Yet man could never master them.

The little woman in her flower-garden away below, by the stream-irrigated village, hid away from the thought of it all. She would not go to the ranch any more.

The Mexicans stayed in charge, looking after the goats. But the place didn't pay. It didn't pay, not quite. It had paid. It might pay. But the effort, the effort! And as the marrow is eaten out of a man's bones and the soul out of his belly, contending with the strange rapacity of savage life, the lower stage of creation, he cannot make the effort any more.

Then also, the war came, making many men give up their enterprises at civilization.

Every new stroke of civilization has cost the lives of countless brave men, who have fallen defeated by the 'dragon,' in their efforts to win the apples of the Hesperides, or the fleece of gold.[63] Fallen in their efforts to overcome the old, half-sordid savagery of the lower stages of creation, and win to the next stage.

For all savagery is half sordid. And man is only himself when he is fighting on and on, to overcome the sordidness.

And every civilization, when it loses its inward vision and its cleaner energy, falls into a new sort of sordidness, more vast and more stupendous than the old savage sort. An Augean stable of metallic filth.

And all the time, man has to rouse himself afresh, to cleanse the new accumulations of refuse. To win from the crude wild nature the victory and the power to make another start, and to cleanse behind him the century-deep deposits of layer upon layer of refuse: even of tin cans.

The ranch dwindled. The flock of goats declined. The water ceased to flow. And at length the trader gave it up.

He rented the place to a Mexican, who lived on the handful of beans he raised, and who was being slowly driven out by the vermin.

And now arrived Lou, new blood to the attack. She went back to Santa Fe, saw the trader and a lawyer, and bought the ranch for twelve hundred dollars. She was so pleased with herself.

She went upstairs to tell her mother.

'Mother, I've bought a ranch.'

'It is just as well, for I can't stand the noise of automobiles outside here another week.'

'It is quiet on my ranch, mother: the stillness simply speaks.'

'I had rather it held its tongue. I am simply drugged with all the bad novels I have read. I feel as if the sky was a big cracked bell and a million clappers were hammering human speech out of it.'

'Aren't you interested in my ranch, mother?'

'I hope I may be, by and by.'

Mrs. Witt actually got up the next morning, and accompanied her daughter in the hired motor-car, driven by Phœnix, to the ranch: which was called Las Chivas.[64] She sat like a pillar of salt, her face looking what the Indians call a False Face, meaning a mask. She seemed to have crystallized into neutrality. She watched the desert with its tufts of yellow greasewood go lurching past: she saw the fallen apples on the ground in the orchards near the adobe cottages: she looked down into the deep arroyo, and at the stream they forded in the car, and at the mountains blocking up the sky ahead, all with indifference. High on the mountains was snow: lower, blue-grey livid rock: and below the livid rock the aspens were expiring their daffodil-yellow, this year, and the oak-scrub was dark and reddish, like gore. She saw it all with a sort of stony indifference.

'Don't you think it's lovely?' said Lou.

'I can see it is lovely,' replied her mother.

The Michaelmas daisies in the clearing as they drove up to the ranch were sharp-rayed with purple, like a coming night.

Mrs. Witt eyed the two log cabins, one of which was dilapidated and prac-

63. The apples of the Hesperides, which Hercules was sent to pick, were protected by a dragon; Jason, to win the Golden Fleece, had to sow dragon's teeth from which armed men arose to combat him.
64. The She Goats (Spanish).

tically abandoned. She looked at the rather rickety corral, whose long planks had silvered and warped in the fierce sun. On one of the roof-planks a pack-rat was sitting erect like an old Indian keeping watch on a pueblo roof. He showed his white belly, and folded his hands and lifted his big ears, for all the world like an old immobile Indian.

'Isn't it for all the world as if *he* were the real boss of the place, Louise?' she said cynically.

And, turning to the Mexican, who was a rag of a man but a pleasant, courteous fellow, she asked him why he didn't shoot the rat.

'Not worth a shell!' said the Mexican, with a faint hopeless smile.

Mrs. Witt paced round and saw everything: it did not take long. She gazed in silence at the water of the spring, trickling out of an iron pipe into a barrel, under the cottonwood tree in an arroyo.

'Well, Louise,' she said, 'I am glad you feel competent to cope with so much hopelessness and so many rats.'

'But, mother, you must admit it is beautiful.'

'Yes, I suppose it is. But, to use one of your Henry's phrases, beauty is a cold egg,[65] as far as I am concerned.'

'Rico never would have said that beauty was a cold egg to him.'

'No, he wouldn't. He sits on it like a broody old hen on a china imitation.—Are you going to bring him here?'

'*Bring* him!—No. But he can come if he likes,' stammered Lou.

'*Oh—h!* won't it be beau—ti—ful!' cried Mrs. Witt, rolling her head and lifting her shoulders in savage imitation of her son-in-law.

'Perhaps he won't come, mother,' said Lou, hurt.

'He will most certainly come, Louise, to see what's doing: unless you tell him you don't want him.'

'Anyhow, I needn't think about it till spring,' said Lou, anxiously pushing the matter aside.

Mrs. Witt climbed the steep slope above the cabins, to the mouth of the little canyon. There she sat on a fallen tree, and surveyed the world beyond: a world not of men. She could not fail to be roused.

'What is your idea in coming here, daughter?' she asked.

'I love it here, mother.'

'But what do you expect to achieve by it?'

'I was rather hoping, mother, to escape achievement. I'll tell you—and you mustn't get cross if it sounds silly. As far as people go, my heart is quite broken. As far as people go, I don't want any more. I can't stand any more. What heart I ever had for it—for life with people—is quite broken. I want to be alone, mother: with you here, and Phœnix perhaps to look after horses and drive a car. But I want to be by myself, really.'

'With Phœnix in the background! Are you sure he won't be coming into the foreground before long?'

'No, mother, no more of that. If I've got to say it, Phœnix is a servant: he's really placed, as far as I can see. Always the same, playing about in the old back yard. I can't take those men seriously. I can't fool round with them, or

65. See "The Mess of Love," l. 8.

fool myself about them. I can't and I won't fool myself any more, mother, especially about men. They don't count. So why should you want them to pay me out?'

For the moment, this silenced Mrs. Witt. Then she said:

'Why, I don't want it. Why should I? But after all you've got to live. You've never *lived* yet: not in my opinion.'

'Neither, mother, in my opinion, have you,' said Lou dryly.

And this silenced Mrs. Witt altogether. She had to be silent, or angrily on the defensive. And the latter she wouldn't be. She couldn't, really, in honesty.

'What do you call life?' Lou continued. 'Wriggling half naked at a public show, and going off in a taxi to sleep with some half-drunken fool who thinks he's a man because—oh, mother, I don't even want to think of it. I know you have a lurking idea that *that is life*. Let it be so then. But leave me out. Men in that aspect simply nauseate me: so grovelling and ratty. Life in that aspect simply drains all my life away. I tell you, for all that sort of thing, I'm broken, absolutely broken: if I wasn't broken to start with.'

'Well, Louise,' said Mrs. Witt after a pause, 'I'm convinced that ever since men and women were men and women, people who took things seriously, and had time for it, got their hearts broken. Haven't I had mine broken? It's as sure as having your virginity broken: and it amounts to about as much. It's a beginning rather than an end.'

'So it is, mother. It's the beginning of something else, and the end of something that's done with. I *know*, and there's no altering it, that I've got to live differently. It sounds silly, but I don't know how else to put it. I've got to live for something that matters, way, way down in me. And I think sex would matter, to my very soul, if it was really sacred. But cheap sex kills me.'

'You have had a fancy for rather cheap men, perhaps.'

'Perhaps I have. Perhaps I should always be a fool, where people are concerned. Now I want to leave off that kind of foolery. There's something else, mother, that I want to give myself to. I know it. I know it absolutely. Why should I let myself be shouted down any more?'

Mrs. Witt sat staring at the distance, her face a cynical mask.

'What is the something bigger? And *pray*, what is it bigger than?' she asked, in that tone of honeyed suavity which was her deadliest poison. 'I want to learn. I am out to know. I'm terribly intrigued by it. Something bigger! Girls in my generation occasionally entered convents, for *something bigger*. I always wondered if they found it. They seemed to me inclined in the imbecile direction, but perhaps that was because I was *something less*—'

There was a definite pause between the mother and daughter, a silence that was a pure breach. Then Lou said:

'You know quite well I'm not conventy, mother, whatever else I am—even a bit of an imbecile. But that kind of religion seems to me the other half of men. Instead of running after them, you run away from them, and get the thrill that way. I don't hate men *because* they're men, as nuns do. I dislike them because they're not men enough: babies, and playboys, and poor things showing off all the time, even to themselves. I don't say I'm any better. I only wish, with all my soul, that some men *were* bigger and stronger and *deeper* than I am . . .'

'How do you know they're not?' asked Mrs. Witt.

'How *do* I know?—' said Lou mockingly.

And the pause that was a breach resumed itself. Mrs. Witt was teasing with a little stick the bewildered black ants among the fir-needles.

'And no doubt you are right about men,' she said at length. 'But at your age, the only sensible thing is to try and keep up the illusion. After all, as you say, you may be no better.'

'I may be no better. But keeping up the illusion means fooling myself. And I won't do it. When I see a man who is even a bit attractive to me—even as much as Phœnix—I say to myself: *Would you care for him afterwards? Does he really mean anything to you, except just a sensation?*—And I know he doesn't. No, mother, of this I am convinced: either my taking a man shall have a meaning and a mystery that penetrates my very soul, or I will keep to myself.—And what I *know* is that the time has come for me to keep to myself. No more messing about.'

'Very well, daughter. You will probably spend your life keeping to yourself.'

'Do you think I mind! There's something else for me, mother. There's something else even that loves me and wants me. I can't tell you what it is. It's a spirit. And it's here, on this ranch. It's here, in this landscape. It's something more real to me than men are, and it soothes me, and it holds me up. I don't know what it is, definitely. It's something wild, that will hurt me sometimes and will wear me down sometimes. I know it. But it's something big, bigger than men, bigger than people, bigger than religion. It's something to do with wild America. And it's something to do with me. It's a mission, if you like. I am imbecile enough for that!—But it's my mission to keep myself for the spirit that is wild, and has waited so long here: even waited for such as me. Now I've come! Now I'm here. Now I am where I want to be: with the spirit that wants me.—And that's how it is. And neither Rico nor Phœnix nor anybody else really matters to me. They are in the world's back yard. And I am here, right deep in America, where there's a wild spirit wants me, a wild spirit more than men. And it doesn't want to save me either. It needs me. It craves for me. And to it, my sex is deep and sacred, deeper than I am, with a deep nature aware deep down of my sex. It saves me from cheapness, mother. And even you could never do that for me.'

Mrs. Witt rose to her feet, and stood looking far, far away, at the turquoise ridge of mountains half sunk under the horizon.

'How much did you say you paid for Las Chivas?' she asked.

'Twelve hundred dollars,' said Lou, surprised.

'Then I call it cheap, considering all there is to it: even the name.'

1924   1925

Poems

Like Thomas Hardy, Lawrence produced, aside from his fiction, a body of major poetry. Unlike the older writer who was, indeed, his master in many ways, Lawrence did not turn to poems when the impulse to write fiction was stifled by the institutions of literary life, but kept writing verse throughout his career. His early *Love Poems* and *Others* (1913) showed a good bit of Hardy's influence, but it was not until the free-verse poetry of *Look, We Have Come Through!* (1917) that he was able to come to terms with the demands that his reading of Walt Whitman and, through him, earlier Romantic poetic tradition, was making upon him. Although at first purporting to share in the Imagist (see Glossary) revision of Victorian formal modes, Lawrence soon developed a range of keys of his own, in a verse derived from Whitman and ultimately from the English Bible. But like all programmatic and self-conscious formal choices in the history of English poetry, the form claimed to come either from on high or—its later equivalent—from within. ". . . Free verse is, or should be, direct utterance from the instant, whole man. It is the soul and the mind and the body surging at once, nothing left out," wrote Lawrence in a preface to the American edition of his *New Poems* (1918); and the arguments of Whitman, who likened his own lines to the wave motions of the sea, are not far away.

Characteristically, Lawrence does not discuss *per se the* mythopoetic quality which is so central to his greatest poetry. Much of his verse is a vehicle for a certain kind of hard, relentless ironic epigram he made his own; the volume entitled *Pansies* (1929), not for conventional floral reasons but because of the origin of the name in the French *pensée* ("thought"), is composed of these, and they constitute an impressive and subsequently influential body of what Yeats would have called "rhetoric," made out of a writer's quarrel with other men. But the larger Lawrentian poetry appears in early love poems and glimpses of childhood, and fully emerges in the great emblematic readings of *Birds, Beasts, and Flowers* (1923). The presence of life other than human evokes visions of temporarily buried human visions of the earth and its depths (as in "Snake"). Sometimes the poem's meditation drives a wedge between two aspects of a phenomenon which ordinary plain speech blurs: thus the difference between fig as fruit and apple as fruit in "Figs"; the difference between the gently sad twilight of approaching darkness seen through the swallows of Keats's "to Autumn," and a horrid, fearful bat-twilight of imminent death in "Bat."

Piano

Softly, in the dusk, a woman is singing to me;
Taking me back down the vista of years, till I see
A child sitting under the piano, in the boom of the tingling strings
And pressing the small, poised feet of a mother who smiles as she sings.

In spite of myself, the insidious mastery of song
Betrays me back, till the heart of me weeps to belong
To the old Sunday evenings at home, with winter outside
And hymns in the cozy parlour, the tinkling piano our guide.

So now it is vain for the singer to burst into clamour
With the great black piano appassionato.° The glamour
Of childish days is upon me, my manhood is cast
Down in the flood of remembrance, I weep like a child for the past.

1913

appassionato impassioned

River Roses°

By the Isar, in the twilight
We were wandering and singing,
By the Isar, in the evening
We climbed the huntsman's ladder and sat swinging
In the fir-tree overlooking the marshes,
While river met with river, and the ringing
Of their pale-green glacier water filled the evening.

By the Isar, in the twilight
We found the dark wild roses
10   Hanging red at the river; and simmering
Frogs were singing, and over the river closes
Was savour of ice and of roses; and glimmering
Fear was abroad. We whispered: 'No one knows us.
Let it be as the snake disposes
Here in this simmering marsh.'

              1917

Medlars and Sorb-Apples°

I love you, rotten,
Delicious rottenness.

I love to suck you out from your skins
So brown and soft and coming suave,
So morbid,° as the Italians say.

What a rare, powerful, reminiscent flavour
Comes out of your falling through the stages of decay:
Stream within stream.

Something of the same flavour as Syracusan muscat wine
10   Or vulgar Marsala.°

Though even the word Marsala will smack of preciosity
Soon in the pussyfoot West.°

What is it?
What is it, in the grape turning raisin,
In the medlar, in the sorb-apple,

River Roses This scene in the Bavarian Tyrol became more highly mythologized, with its Edenic overtones and its serpent, in a second version; it is instructive to compare the original second stanza from the poem's first publication in *Poetry* in 1914: "By the Isar, in the twilight / We found our warm wild roses / Hanging red at the river; and simmering / Frogs were singing, and over the river closes / Was scent of roses, and glimmering / In the twilight, our kisses across the roses / Met, and her face, and my face were roses."

Medlars and Sorb-Apples Medlars are a fruit of the apple-pear-quince family, edible only when they have started to rot; the sorb, likewise. The poem begins with a meditation on decay as promise, a reversal of the normal cycles in which spring promises, autumn fulfills.
morbid Italian *morbido* means soft (of fruit, "ripe"), although the original Latin "diseased" supplies the English meaning.
Marsala the sweet fortified wine of Sicily
pussyfoot West presumably because of the onset of Prohibition in the United States in 1920

Wineskins of brown morbidity,
Autumnal excrementa;
What is it that reminds us of white gods?

Gods nude as blanched nut-kernels,
Strangely, half-sinisterly flesh-fragrant
As if with sweat,
And drenched with mystery.

Sorb-apples, medlars with dead crowns.

I say, wonderful are the hellish experiences,
Orphic,° delicate
Dionysos of the Underworld.

A kiss, and a spasm of farewell, a moment's orgasm of rupture,
Then along the damp road alone, till the next turning.
And there, a new partner, a new parting, a new unfusing into twain,
A new gasp of further isolation,
A new intoxication of loneliness, among decaying, frost-cold leaves.

Going down the strange lanes of hell, more and more intensely alone,
The fibres of the heart parting one after the other
And yet the soul continuing, naked-footed, ever more vividly embodied
Like a flame blown whiter and whiter
In a deeper and deeper darkness
Ever more exquisite, distilled in separation.

So, in the strange retorts of medlars and sorb-apples
The distilled essence of hell.
The exquisite odour of leave-taking.
        Jamque vale!°
Orpheus, and the winding, leaf-clogged, silent lanes of hell.

Each soul departing with its own isolation,
Strangest of all strange companions,
And best.

Medlars, sorb-apples,
More than sweet
Flux of autumn
Sucked out of your empty bladders
And sipped down, perhaps, with a sip of Marsala
So that the rambling, sky-dropped grape can add its savour to yours,
Orphic farewell, and farewell, and farewell
And the *ego sum*° of Dionysos
The *sono io*° of perfect drunkenness
Intoxication of final loneliness.

                1921

Orphic pertaining to the Orphic mysteries
celebrated in late Greek times, which assimilated the Orpheus legend to the worship of
Dionysus as underworld god, and one of whose
doctrines was that of *metempsychosis*, the transmigration of souls after death
Jamque vale "and now, farewell"
ego sum "I am"
sono io "I am" (Italian)

Bat

At evening, sitting on this terrace,°
When the sun from the west, beyond Pisa, beyond the mountains of Carrara
Departs, and the world is taken by surprise . . .

When the tired flower of Florence is in gloom beneath the glowing
Brown hills surrounding . . .

When under the arches of the Ponte Vecchio
A green light enters against the stream, flush from the west,
Against the current of obscure Arno . . .

Look up, and you see things flying
10 Between the day and the night;
Swallows with spools of dark thread sewing the shadows together.

A circle swoop, and a quick parabola under the bridge arches
Where light pushes through;
A sudden turning upon itself of a thing in the air.
A dip to the water.

And you think:
'The swallows are flying so late!'

Swallows?

Dark air-life looping
20 Yet missing the pure loop . . .
A twitch, a twitter, an elastic shudder in flight
And serrated wings against the sky,
Like a glove, a black glove thrown up at the light,
And falling back.

Never swallows!
Bats!
The swallows are gone.

At a wavering instant the swallows give way to bats
By the Ponte Vecchio . . .
30 Changing guard.

Bats, and an uneasy creeping in one's scalp
As the bats swoop overhead!
Flying madly.

Pipistrello!°
Black piper on an infinitesimal pipe.
Little lumps that fly in air and have voices indefinite, wildly vindictive;
Wings like bits of umbrella.

terrace The poet is looking out over the river   bridge") crosses the river near a central square.
Arno in Florence; the Ponte Vecchio ("old   **Pipistrello** "bat" in Italian

436

Bats!

Creatures that hang themselves up like an old rag to sleep;
And disgustingly upside down.
Hanging upside down like rows of disgusting old rags
And grinning in their sleep.
Bats!

In China the bat is symbol of happiness.

Not for me!
1921   1923

Snake

A snake came to my water-trough
On a hot, hot day, and I in pyjamas for the heat,
To drink there.

In the deep, strange-scented shade of the great dark carob tree
I came down the steps with my pitcher
 And must wait, must stand and wait, for there he was at the trough before me.

He reached down from a fissure in the earth-wall in the gloom
And trailed his yellow-brown slackness soft-bellied down, over the edge of the
          stone trough

And rested his throat upon the stone bottom,
And where the water had dripped from the tap, in a small clearness,
He sipped with his straight mouth,
Softly drank through his straight gums, into his slack long body,
Silently.

Someone was before me at my water-trough,
And I, like a second comer, waiting.

He lifted his head from his drinking, like cattle do,
And looked at me vaguely, as drinking cattle do,
And flickered his two-forked tongue from his lips, and mused a moment,
And stooped and drank a little more,
Being earth-brown, earth-golden from the burning bowels of the earth
On the day of Sicilian July, with Etna° smoking.

The voice of my education said to me
He must be killed,
For in Sicily the black, black snakes are innocent, the gold are venomous.

And voices in me said, if you were a man
You would take a stick and break him now, and finish him off.

Etna the great Sicilian volcano, still active

But I must confess how I liked him,
How glad I was he had come like a guest in quiet, to drink at my water-trough
And depart peaceful, pacified, and thankless,
30   Into the burning bowels of this earth.

Was it cowardice, that I dared not kill him?
Was it perversity, that I longed to talk to him?
Was it humility, to feel so honoured?
I felt so honoured.

And yet those voices:
If you were not afraid, you would kill him!

And truly I was afraid, I was most afraid,
But even so, honoured still more
That he should seek my hospitality
40   From out the dark door of the secret earth.

He drank enough
And lifted his head, dreamily, as one who has drunken,
And flickered his tongue like a forked night on the air, so black,
Seeming to lick his lips,
And looking around like a god, unseeing, into the air,
And slowly turned his head,
And slowly, very slowly, as if thrice adream,
Proceeded to draw his slow length curving round
And climb again the broken bank of my wall-face.

50   And as he put his head into that dreadful hole,
And as he slowly drew up, snake-easing his shoulders, and entered farther,
A sort of horror, a sort of protest against his withdrawing into that horrid black
        hole,
Deliberately going into the blackness, and slowly drawing himself after,
Overcame me now his back was turned.

I looked around, I put down my pitcher,
I picked up a clumsy log
And threw it at the water-trough with a clatter.

I think I did not hit him,
But suddenly that part of him that was left behind convulsed in undignified
        haste,
60   Writhed like lightning, and was gone
Into the black hole, the earth-lipped fissure in the wall-front,
At which, in the intense still noon, I stared with fascination.

And immediately I regretted it.
I thought how paltry, how vulgar, what a mean act!
I despised myself and the voices of my accursed human education.
And I thought of the albatross,
And I wished he would come back, my snake.

For he seemed to me again like a king,
Like a king in exile, uncrowned in the underworld,
Now due to be crowned again.

And so, I missed my chance with one of the lords
Of life.
And I have something to expiate;
A pettiness.

1923

Tortoise Shell

The Cross, the Cross
Goes deeper in than we know,
Deeper into life;
Right into the marrow
And through the bone.

Along the back of the baby tortoise
The scales are locked in an arch like a bridge,
Scale-lapping, like a lobster's sections
Or a bee's.

Then crossways down his sides
Tiger-stripes and wasp-bands.

Five, and five again, and five again,
And round the edges twenty-five little ones,
The sections of the baby tortoise shell.

Four, and a keystone;
Four, and a keystone;
Four, and a keystone;
Then twenty-four, and a tiny little keystone.

It needed Pythagoras° to see life playing with counters on the living back
Of the baby tortoise;
Life establishing the first eternal mathematical tablet,
Not in stone, like the Judean Lord,° or bronze, but in life-clouded, life-rosy
            tortoise shell.

The first little mathematical gentleman
Stepping, wee mite, in his loose trousers
Under all the eternal dome of mathematical law.

Fives, and tens,
Threes and fours and twelves,
All the *volte face*° of decimals,
The whirligig of dozens and the pinnacle of seven.

Pythagoras the Greek philosopher of the 6th   Judean Lord who gave Moses stone tablets
century B.C. who was associated with numerical   volte face turnabout (Italian)
and geometric mysteries

30 Turn him on his back,
The kicking little beetle,
And there again, on his shell-tender, earth-touching belly,
The long cleavage of division, upright of the eternal cross
And on either side count five,
On each side, two above, on each side, two below
The dark bar horizontal.

The Cross!
It goes right through him, the sprottling insect,
Through his cross-wise cloven psyche,
40 Through his five-fold complex-nature.

So turn him over on his toes again;
Four pin-point toes, and a problematical thumb-piece,
Four rowing limbs, and one wedge-balancing head,
Four and one makes five, which is the clue to all mathematics.

The Lord wrote it all down on the little slate
Of the baby tortoise.
Outward and visible indication of the plan within,
The complex, manifold involvedness of an individual creature
Plotted out
50 On this small bird, this rudiment,
This little dome, this pediment
Of all creation,
This slow one.
1921   1923

Figs

The proper way to eat a fig, in society,
Is to split it in four, holding it by the stump,
And open it, so that it is a glittering, rosy, moist, honied, heavy-petalled four-
      petalled flower.

Then you throw away the skin
Which is just like a four-sepalled calyx,°
After you have taken off the blossom with your lips.

But the vulgar way
Is just to put your mouth to the crack, and take out the flesh in one bite.

Every fruit has its secret.

10 The fig is a very secretive fruit.
As you see it standing growing, you feel at once it is symbolic:

four-sepalled calyx a cup-like section behind the
petals of a flower

And it seems male.
But when you come to know it better, you agree with the Romans, it is female.

The Italians vulgarly say, it stands for the female part; the fig-fruit:
The fissure, the yoni,°
The wonderful moist conductivity towards the centre.

Involved,
Inturned,
The flowering all inward and womb-fibrilled;
And but one orifice.

The fig, the horse-shoe, the squash-blossom.
Symbols.

There was a flower that flowered inward, womb-ward;
Now there is a fruit like a ripe womb.

It was always a secret.
That's how it should be, the female should always be secret.

There never was any standing aloft and unfolded on a bough
Like other flowers, in a revelation of petals;

Silver-pink peach, venetian green glass of medlars and sorb-apples,
Shallow wine-cups on short, bulging stems
Openly pledging heaven:
Here's to the thorn in flower! Here is to Utterance!
The brave, adventurous rosaceae.

Folded upon itself, and secret unutterable,
And milky-sapped, sap that curdles milk and makes *ricotta*,°
Sap that smells strange on your fingers, that even goats won't taste it;
Folded upon itself, enclosed like any Mohammedan woman,
Its nakedness all within-walls, its flowering forever unseen,
One small way of access only, and this close-curtained from the light;
Fig, fruit of the female mystery, covert and inward,
Mediterranean fruit, with your covert nakedness,
Where everything happens invisible, flowering and fertilisation, and fruiting
In the inwardness of your you, that eye will never see
Till it's finished, and you're over-ripe, and you burst to give up your ghost.

Till the drop of ripeness exudes,
And the year is over.

And then the fig has kept her secret long enough.
So it explodes, and you see through the fissure the scarlet.
And the fig is finished, the year is over.

That's how the fig dies, showing her crimson through the purple slit
Like a wound, the exposure of her secret, on the open day.
Like a prostitute, the bursten fig, making a show of her secret.

yoni Sanskrit for vagina   **ricotta** a white pot cheese

That's how women die too.

The year is fallen over-ripe,
The year of our women.
The year of our women is fallen over-ripe.
The secret is laid bare.
And rottenness soon sets in.
The year of our women is fallen over-ripe.

60   When Eve once knew *in her mind* that she was naked
She quickly sewed fig-leaves, and sewed the same for the man.
She'd been naked all her days before,
But till then, till that apple of knowledge, she hadn't had the fact on her mind.

She got the fact on her mind, and quickly sewed fig-leaves.
And women have been sewing ever since.
But now they stitch to adorn the bursten fig, not to cover it.
They have their nakedness more than ever on their mind,
And they won't let us forget it.

Now, the secret
70   Becomes an affirmation through moist, scarlet lips
That laugh at the Lord's indignation.

What then, good Lord! cry the women.
We have kept our secret long enough.
We are a ripe fig.
Let us burst into affirmation.

They forget, ripe figs won't keep.
Ripe figs won't keep.
Honey-white figs of the north, black figs with scarlet inside, of the south.
Ripe figs won't keep, won't keep in any clime.
80   What then, when women the world over have all bursten into self-assertion?
And bursten figs won't keep?
                    1923

The American Eagle

The dove of Liberty sat on an egg
And hatched another eagle.

But didn't disown the bird.

Down with all eagles! cooed the Dove.
And down all eagles began to flutter, reeling from their perches:
Eagles with two heads, eagles with one, presently eagles with none
Fell from the hooks and were dead.

Till the American Eagle was the only eagle left in the world.

Then it began to fidget, shifting from one leg to the other,
Trying to look like a pelican,
And plucking out of his plumage a few loose feathers to feather the nest of all
The new naked little republics come into the world.

But the feathers were, comparatively, a mere flea-bite.
And the bub-eagle that Liberty had hatched was growing a startling big bird
On the roof of the world;
A bit awkward, and with a funny squawk in his voice,
His mother Liberty trying always to teach him to coo
And him always ending with a yawp°
Coo! Coo! Coo! Coo-ark! Coo-ark! Quark!! Quark!!
YAWP!!!

So he clears his throat, the young Cock-eagle!

Now if the lilies of France lick Solomon in all his glory;°
And the leopard cannot change his spots;
Nor the British lion his appetite;
Neither can a young Cock-eagle sit simpering
With an olive-sprig in his mouth.

It's not his nature.

The big bird of the Amerindian being the eagle,
Red Men still stick themselves over with bits of his fluff,
And feel absolutely IT.

So better make up your mind, American Eagle,
Whether you're a sucking dove, *Roo—coo—ooo! Quark! Yawp!!*
Or a pelican
Handing out a few loose golden breast-feathers, at moulting time;
Or a sort of prosperity-gander
Fathering endless ten-dollar golden eggs.

Or whether it actually is an eagle you are,
With a Roman nose
And claws not made to shake hands with,
And a Me-Almighty eye.

The new Proud Republic
Based on the mystery of pride.
Overweening men, full of power of life, commanding a teeming obedience.

Eagle of the Rockies, bird of men that are masters,
Lifting the rabbit-blood of the myriads up into something splendid,
Leaving a few bones;
Opening great wings in the face of the sheep-faced ewe

Who is losing her lamb,
Drinking a little blood, and loosing another royalty unto the world.

50   Is that you, American Eagle?

Or are you the goose that lays the golden egg?
Which is just a stone to anyone asking for meat.
And are you going to go on for ever
Laying that golden egg,
That addled golden egg?

                    1923

The Mess of Love

We've made a great mess of love
Since we made an ideal of it.

The moment I swear to love a woman, a certain woman, all my life
That moment I begin to hate her.

The moment I even say to a woman: I love you!—
My love dies down considerably.

The moment love is an understood thing between us, we are sure of it,
It's a cold egg,° it isn't love any more.

Love is like a flower, it must flower and fade;
10   If it doesn't fade, it is not a flower,
It's either an artificial rag blossom, or an immortelle, for the cemetery.

The moment the mind interferes with love, or the will fixes on it,
Or the personality assumes it as an attribute, or the ego takes possession of it,
It is not love any more, it's just a mess.
And we've made a great mess of love, mind-perverted, will-perverted, ego-
    perverted love.

                    1929

The Ship of Death

            I
Now it is autumn and the falling fruit
and the long journey towards oblivion.

The apples falling like great drops of dew
to bruise themselves an exit from themselves.

And it is time to go, to bid farewell
to one's own self, and find an exit
from the fallen self.

cold egg See "beauty is a cold egg" in *St.
Mawr*, n. 65.

II

Have you built your ship of death,° O have you?
O build your ship of death, for you will need it.

The grim forest is at hand, when the apples will fall
thick, almost thunderous, on the hardened earth.

And death is on the air like a smell of ashes!
Ah! can't you smell it?

And in the bruised body, the frightened soul
finds itself shrinking, wincing from the cold
that blows upon it through the orifices.

III

And can a man his own quietus make
with a bare bodkin?°

With daggers, bodkins, bullets, man can make
a bruise or break of exit for his life;
but is that a quietus, O tell me, is it quietus?

Surely not so! for how could murder, even self-murder
ever a quietus make?

IV

O let us talk of quiet that we know,
that we can know, the deep and lovely quiet
of a strong heart at peace!

How can we this, our own quietus, make?

V

Build then the ship of death, for you must take
the longest journey, to oblivion.

And die the death, the long and painful death
that lies between the old self and the new.

Already our bodies are fallen, bruised, badly bruised,
already our souls are oozing through the exit
of the cruel bruise.

Already the dark and endless ocean of the end
is washing in through the breaches of our wounds,
already the flood is upon us.

O build your ship of death, your little ark
and furnish it with food, with little cakes, and wine
for the dark flight down oblivion.

ship of death Lawrence is thinking of the ship models, with all their crew and fully supplied, put into Etruscan and Egyptian tombs to ferry the dead across final waters.

his own . . . bare bodkin "quietus," a release from life; "bodkin," here, a sword. This phrase is quoted from Hamlet's soliloquy on suicide (*Hamlet* III.i.75–76).

VI

Piecemeal the body dies, and the timid soul
has her footing washed away, as the dark flood rises.

We are dying, we are dying, we are all of us dying
and nothing will stay the death-flood rising within us
and soon it will rise on the world, on the outside world.

We are dying, we are dying, piecemeal our bodies are dying
and our strength leaves us,
and our soul cowers naked in the dark rain over the flood,
cowering in the last branches of the tree of our life.

VII

50 We are dying, we are dying, so all we can do
is now to be willing to die, and to build the ship
of death to carry the soul on the longest journey.

A little ship, with oars and food
and little dishes, and all accoutrements
fitting and ready for the departed soul.

Now launch the small ship, now as the body dies
and life departs, launch out, the fragile soul
in the fragile ship of courage, the ark of faith
with its store of food and little cooking pans
60 and change of clothes,
upon the flood's black waste
upon the waters of the end
upon the sea of death, where still we sail
darkly, for we cannot steer, and have no port.

There is no port, there is nowhere to go
only the deepening blackness darkening still
blacker upon the soundless, ungurgling flood
darkness at one with darkness, up and down
and sideways utterly dark, so there is no direction any more.
70 and the little ship is there; yet she is gone.
She is not seen, for there is nothing to see her by.
She is gone! gone! and yet
somewhere she is there.

Nowhere!

VIII

And everything is gone, the body is gone
completely under, gone, entirely gone.
The upper darkness is heavy as the lower,
between them the little ship
is gone
80 she is gone

It is the end, it is oblivion.

IX

And yet out of eternity a thread
separates itself on the blackness,
a horizontal thread
that fumes a little with pallor upon the dark.

Is it illusion? or does the pallor fume
a little highor?
Ah wait, wait, for there's the dawn,
the cruel dawn of coming back to life
out of oblivion.

Wait, wait, the little ship
drifting, beneath the deadly ashy grey
of a flood-dawn.

Wait, wait! even so, a flush of yellow
and strangely, O chilled wan soul, a flush of rose.

A flush of rose, and the whole thing starts again.

X

The flood subsides, and the body, like a worn sea-shell
emerges strange and lovely.
And the little ship wings home, faltering and lapsing
on the pink flood,
and the frail soul steps out, into her house again
filling the heart with peace.

Swings the heart renewed with peace
even of oblivion.

Oh build your ship of death. Oh build it!
for you will need it.
For the voyage of oblivion awaits you.
1929–30   1932

Bavarian Gentians°

(version of Manuscript "A")
Not every man has gentians in his house
In soft September, at slow, sad Michaelmas.

Bavarian Gentians This is the manuscript version of one of Lawrence's greatest last poems, a reading of the intensely dark blue-violet of the autumnal flowers as the color of the "darkness visible," in Milton's phase, of the underworld. The story of Persephone, daughter of Demeter (Ceres), carried off to be queen of Hades by Pluto (Dis), was a myth of the seasons: because Persephone ate some pomegranate seeds while in the underworld, she had to remain there part of each year, during which time Demeter, the grain goddess (our word "cereal" comes from her Latin name) grieves. The revised version is appended.

Bavarian gentians, tall and dark, but dark
darkening the day-time torch-like with the smoking blueness of Pluto's gloom,
ribbed hellish flowers erect, with their blaze of darkness spread blue
Blown into points, by the heavy white draught of the day.

Torch-flowers of the blue-smoking darkness, Pluto's dark-blue blaze
black lamps from the halls of Dis, smoking dark blue
giving off darkness, blue darkness, upon Demeter's yellow-pale day
10   Whom have you come for, here in the white-cast day?

Reach me a gentian, give me a torch!
let me guide myself with the blue, forked torch of a flower
down the darker and darker stairs, where blue is darkened on blueness
down the way Persephone goes, just now, in first-frosted September
to the sightless realm where darkness is married to dark
and Persephone herself is but a voice, as a bride,
a gloom invisible enfolded in the deeper dark
of the arms of Pluto as he ravishes her once again
and pierces her once more with his passion of the utter dark.
20   among the splendour of black-blue torches, shedding fathomless darkness on the
       nuptials.

Give me a flower on a tall stem, and three dark flames,
For I will go to the wedding, and be wedding-guest
At the marriage of the living dark.

Bavarian Gentians

(final version)
Not every man has gentians in his house
In Soft September, at slow, Sad Michaelmas.

Bavarian gentians, big and dark, only dark
Darkening the day-time torch-like with the smoking blueness of Pluto's gloom,
Ribbed and torch-like with their blaze of darkness spread blue
Down flattening into points, flattened under the sweep of white day
Torch-flower of the blue-smoking darkness, Pluto's dark-blue daze,
Black lamps from the halls of Dis, burning dark blue,
Giving off darkness, blue darkness, as Demeter's pale lamps give off light,
10   Lead me then, lead me the way.

Reach me a gentian, give me a torch
Let me guide myself with the blue, forked torch of this flower
Down the darker and darker stairs, where blue is darkened on blueness,
Even where Persephone goes, just now, from the frosted September
To the sightless realm where darkness is awake upon the dark
And Persephone herself is but a voice
Or a darkness invisible enfolded in the deeper dark

Of the arms Plutonic, and pierced with the passion of dense gloom,
Among the splendour of torches of darkness, shedding darkness on the lost bride
and her groom.
1929   1932

Pornography and Obscenity

Lawrence had first-hand experience of those he called the "censor-morons." *The
Rainbow* was prosecuted and withdrawn from circulation in 1915, to the great detri-
ment of his income in the following years. *Lady Chatterley's Lover*, with its deliberate
use of "shocking" words, ran head-on into censorship, and was not published in an
openly available unexpurgated edition until 1959. In his last years Lawrence painted,
and when his paintings were shown in London they were seized by the police. He
wrote the present essay in 1929, and it was published by Faber and Faber in the same
series of pamphlets as Lord Brentford's defense of censorship. William Joynson-Hicks,
1st Viscount Brentford (1865–1932), unpopularly known as Jix, was Home Secretary
(with responsibilities that in the United States are assumed partly by the Attorney
General and partly by the Secretary of the Interior), and a symbol of all that was most
repressive and sanctimonious in the administration of the laws relating to censorship.
While in his pamphlet Lawrence ridicules Jix, he has more important matters in hand
—partly the defense of his own shock tactic in *Lady Chatterley*, a tactic intended to
liberate the "four-letter words" from their bondage to dirt and secrecy, and even
more importantly to emphasize one of his main preoccupations—the need for a
revolutionary change in sexual attitudes. He distinguishes between works which deal
cleanly with sex, and those which "do dirt on it"; then, having defined pornography,
he explains the harm it does, relating it to a diseased—and very widespread—attitude
toward sex, an attitude exemplified by the puritans themselves.

Lawrence over the years developed a vigorous journalistic and polemical manner;
occasionally it sank into a kind of tabloid shouting, but this selection shows it at its
best. For many years he had speculated, sometimes in a rather highflown way, on
the consequences for human conduct of the juxtaposition of sexual and excremental
functions; here he returns to this topic in the context of his argument against puritanism, and it does not sound at all cranky, but reinforces what he is saying. He believed
that since the Renaissance we have gone badly wrong about sex, partly from fear of
disease, partly because of a dissociation of mind and bodily function which has made
for the wrong kind of secrecy. The abolition of the "dirty little secret" is necessary to
human freedom and the redevelopment of the whole man. Thus, in this lively and
lucid polemic, Lawrence attacks a specific target but also gives expression to some of
his most deeply held convictions about the modern world. That sex is degraded was
for him a catastrophe in itself, and also a symptom of the whole disease of modern life.

From Pornography and Obscenity

. . . The reaction to any word may be, in any individual, either a mob-reaction
or an individual reaction. It is up to the individual to ask himself: Is my reaction
individual, or am I merely reacting from my mob-self?

When it comes to the so-called obscene words, I should say that hardly one person in a million escapes mob-reaction. The first reaction is almost sure to be mob-reaction, mob-indignation, mob-condemnation. And the mob gets no further. But the real individual has second thoughts and says: Am I really shocked? Do I *really* feel outraged and indignant? And the answer of any individual is bound to be: No, I am not shocked, not outraged, nor indignant. I know the word, and take it for what it is, and I am not going to be jockeyed into making a mountain out of a mole-hill, not for all the law in the world.

Now if the use of a few so-called obscene words will startle man or woman out of a mob-habit into an individual state, well and good. And word prudery is so universal a mob-habit that it is time we were startled out of it.

But still we have only tackled obscenity, and the problem of pornography goes even deeper. When a man is startled into his individual self, he still may not be able to know, inside himself, whether Rabelais [1] is or is not pornographic: and over Aretino or even Boccaccio [2] he may perhaps puzzle in vain, torn between different emotions.

One essay on pornography, I remember, comes to the conclusion that pornography in art is that which is calculated to arouse sexual desire, or sexual excitement. And stress is laid on the fact, whether the author or artist *intended* to arouse sexual feelings. It is the old vexed question of intention, become so so dull today, when we know how strong and influential our unconscious intentions are. And why a man should be held guilty of his conscious intentions, and innocent of his unconscious intentions, I don't know, since every man is more made up of unconscious intentions than of conscious ones. I am what I am, not merely what I think I am.

However! We take it, I assume, that *pornography* is something base, something unpleasant. In short, we don't like it. And why don't we like it? Because it arouses sexual feelings?

I think not. No matter how hard we may pretend otherwise, most of us rather like a moderate rousing of our sex. It warms us, stimulates us like sunshine on a grey day. After a century or two of Puritanism, this is still true of most people. Only the mob-habit of condemning any form of sex is too strong to let us admit it naturally. And there are, of course, many people who are genuinely repelled by the simplest and most natural stirrings of sexual feeling. But these people are perverts who have fallen into hatred of their fellow men: thwarted, disappointed, unfulfilled people, of whom, alas, our civilization contains so many. And they nearly always enjoy some unsimple and unnatural form of sex excitement, secretly.

Even quite advanced art critics would try to make us believe that any picture or book which had 'sex appeal' was ipso facto a bad book or picture. This is just canting hypocrisy. Half the great poems, pictures, music, stories of the whole

1. François Rabelais (1495–1553), French humanist and satirist, author of *Gargantua* and *Pantagruel* (1546–64); he was against asceticism, in favor of obeying the dictates of experience rather than authority, and frequently obscene.
2. Pietro Aretino (1492–1556), humanist and poet, famous for erotic and obscene verses, for which appropriate illustrations were provided. Giovanni Boccaccio (1313–75), whose hundred tales called the *Decameron* (Greek: "10 days") include some that are indecent.

world are great by virtue of the beauty of their sex appeal. Titian [3] or Renoir,[4] the Song of Solomon or *Jane Eyre*,[5] Mozart or 'Annie Laurie,' [6] the loveliness is all interwoven with sex appeal, sex stimulus, call it what you will. Even Michelangelo,[7] who rather hated sex, can't help filling the Cornucopia with phallic acorns. Sex is a very powerful, beneficial and necessary stimulus in human life, and we are all grateful when we feel its warm, natural flow through us, like a form of sunshine.

So we can dismiss the idea that sex appeal in art is pornography. It may be so to the grey Puritan, but the grey Puritan is a sick man, soul and body sick, so why should we bother about his hallucinations? Sex appeal, of course, varies enormously. There are endless different kinds, and endless degrees of each kind. Perhaps it may be argued that a mild degree of sex appeal is not pornographical, whereas a high degree is. But this is a fallacy. Boccaccio at his hottest seems to me less pornographical than *Pamela* or *Clarissa Harlowe* [8] or even *Jane Eyre*, or a host of modern books or films which pass uncensored. At the same time Wagner's *Tristan and Isolde* [9] seems to me very near to pornography, and so, even, do some quite popular Christian hymns.

What is it, then? It isn't a question of sex appeal, merely: nor even a question of deliberate intention on the part of the author or artist to arouse sexual excitement. Rabelais sometimes had a deliberate intention, so, in a different way, did Boccaccio. And I'm sure poor Charlotte Brontë, or the authoress of *The Sheik*,[10] did not have any deliberate intention to stimulate sex feelings in the reader. Yet I find *Jane Eyre* verging towards pornography and Boccaccio seems to me always fresh and wholesome.

The late British Home Secretary,[11] who prides himself on being a very sincere Puritan, grey, grey in every fibre, said with indignant sorrow in one of his outbursts on improper books: '—and these two young people, who had been perfectly pure up till that time, after reading this book went and had sexual intercourse together!!!' *One up to them!* is all we can answer. But the grey Guardian of British Morals seemed to think that if they had murdered one another, or worn each other to rags of nervous prostration, it would have been much better. The grey disease!

---

3. Tiziano Vercelli (1490?–1576), one of the greatest Venetian painters.
4. Pierre Auguste Renoir (1841–1919), French painter celebrated for sensuous rendering of women.
5. Novel (1847) by Charlotte Brontë (1816–55), in which the passion of Mr. Rochester, who has a mad wife, remains unrequited until her death and his disfigurement in a fire.
6. Famous love song by William Douglas (1672–1748).
7. Michelangelo Buonarotti (1475–1564), greatest of the Florentine Renaissance artists; architect, sculptor, poet, and painter of the Sistine ceiling in the Vatican, in which this cornucopia and its contents appear (under the figure of Adam).
8. Samuel Richardson (1689–1761) wrote *Pamela* (1741), about the resistance of a virtuous servant-girl to her master and their subsequent marriage; and *Clarissa Harlowe* (1748), about the seduction of a virtuous woman by a rake and her subsequent noble death.
9. Richard Wagner (1813–83), after many difficulties, had his *Tristan and Isolde* performed in 1865. It is the story of a consuming erotic passion between the two, and its tragic end.
10. A bestseller of 1921, by Edith Maud Hull; later a famous film starring Rudolph Valentino.
11. See Headnote.

Then what is pornography, after all this? It isn't sex appeal or sex stimulus in art. It isn't even a deliberate intention on the part of the artist to arouse or excite sexual feelings. There's nothing wrong with sexual feelings in themselves, so long as they are straightforward and not sneaking or sly. The right sort of sex stimulus is invaluable to human daily life. Without it the world grows grey. I would give everybody the gay Renaissance stories to read, they would help to shake off a lot of grey self-importance, which is our modern civilized disease.

But even I would censor genuine pornography, rigorously. It would not be very difficult. In the first place, genuine pornography is almost always underworld, it doesn't come into the open. In the second, you can recognize it by the insult it offers, invariably, to sex, and to the human spirit.

Pornography is the attempt to insult sex, to do dirt on it. This is unpardonable. Take the very lowest instance, the picture post-card sold under hand, by the underworld, in most cities. What I have seen of them have been of an ugliness to make you cry. The insult to the human body, the insult to a vital human relationship! Ugly and cheap they make the human nudity, ugly and degraded they make the sexual act, trivial and cheap and nasty.

It is the same with the books they sell in the underworld. They are either so ugly they make you ill, or so fatuous you can't imagine anybody but a cretin or a moron reading them, or writing them.

It is the same with the dirty limericks that people tell after dinner, or the dirty stories one hears commercial travellers telling each other in a smoke-room. Occasionally there is a really funny one, that redeems a great deal. But usually they are just ugly and repellent, and the so-called 'humour' is just a trick of doing dirt on sex.

Now the human nudity of a great many modern people is just ugly and degraded, and the sexual act between modern people is just the same, merely ugly and degrading. But this is nothing to be proud of. It is the catastrophe of our civilization. I am sure no other civilization, not even the Roman, has showed such a vast proportion of ignominious and degraded nudity, and ugly, squalid, dirty sex. Because no other civilization has driven sex into the underworld, and nudity to the w.c.

The intelligent young, thank heaven, seem determined to alter in these two respects. They are rescuing their young nudity from the stuffy, pornographical, hole-and-corner underworld of their elders, and they refuse to sneak about the sexual relation. This is a change the elderly grey ones of course deplore, but it is in fact a very great change for the better, and a real revolution.

But it is amazing how strong is the will in ordinary, vulgar people to do dirt on sex. It was one of my fond illusions, when I was young, that the ordinary healthy-seeming sort of men, in railway carriages, or the smoke-room of an hotel or a pullman, were healthy in their feelings and had a wholesome rough devil-may-care attitude towards sex. All wrong! All wrong! Experience teaches that common individuals of this sort have a disgusting attitude towards sex, a disgusting contempt of it, a disgusting desire to insult it. If such fellows have intercourse with a woman, they triumphantly feel that they have done her dirt, and now she is lower, cheaper, more contemptible than she was before.

It is individuals of this sort that tell dirty stories, carry indecent picture postcards, and know the indecent books. This is the great pornographical class—

the really common men-in-the-street and women-in-the-street. They have as great a hate and contempt of sex as the greyest Puritan, and when an appeal is made to them, they are always on the side of the angels. They insist that a film-heroine shall be a neuter, a sexless thing of washed-out purity. They insist that real sex-feeling shall only be shown by the villain or villainess, low lust. They find a Titian or a Renoir really indecent, and they don't want their wives and daughters to see it.

Why? Because they have the grey disease of sex-hatred, coupled with the yellow disease of dirt-lust. The sex functions and the excrementory functions in the human body work so close together, yet they are, so to speak, utterly different in direction. Sex is a creative flow, the excrementory flow is towards dissolution, de-creation, if we may use such a word. In the really healthy human being the distinction between the two is instant, our profoundest instincts are perhaps our instincts of opposition between the two flows.

But in the degraded human being the deep instincts have gone dead, and then the two flows become identical. *This* is the secret of really vulgar and of pornographical people: the sex flow and the excrement flow is the same to them. It happens when the psyche deteriorates, and the profound controlling instincts collapse. Then sex is dirt and dirt is sex, and sexual excitement becomes a playing with dirt, and any sign of sex in a woman becomes a show of her dirt. This is the condition of the common, vulgar human being whose name is legion, and who lifts his voice and it is the *Vox populi, vox Dei*.[12] And this is the source of all pornography.

And for this reason we must admit that *Jane Eyre* or Wagner's *Tristan* are much nearer to pornography than is Boccaccio. Wagner and Charlotte Brontë were both in the state where the strongest instincts have collapsed, and sex has become something slightly obscene, to be wallowed in, but despised. Mr. Rochester's sex passion is not 'respectable' till Mr. Rochester is burned, blinded, disfigured, and reduced to helpless dependence. Then, thoroughly humbled and humiliated, it may be merely admitted. All the previous titillations are slightly indecent, as in *Pamela* or *The Mill on the Floss*[13] or *Anna Karenina*.[14] As soon as there is sex excitement with a desire to spite the sexual feeling, to humiliate it and degrade it, the element of pornography enters.

For this reason, there is an element of pornography in nearly all nineteenth century literature and very many so-called pure people have a nasty pornographical side to them, and never was the pornographical appetite stronger than it is today. It is a sign of a diseased condition of the body politic. But the way to treat the disease is to come out into the open with sex and sex stimulus. The real pornographer truly dislikes Boccaccio, because the fresh healthy naturalness of the Italian story-teller makes the modern pornographical shrimp feel the dirty worm he is. Today Boccaccio should be given to everybody, young or old, to

12. "The voice of the people is the voice of God," advice contained in a letter to Charlemagne (*c*. 800 A.D.) from his English theological consultant, Alcuin.

13. Novel (1860) by George Eliot (Mary Ann Evans; 1819–80). Lawrence is thinking of a scene in which the heroine drifts down river with a handsome young man.

14. Novel (1874–76) by Leo Tolstoy (1828–1910). Lawrence often expressed his disagreement with the conventional judgment that it is one of the greatest of novels, or perhaps even the greatest; he thought it sexually repressive.

read if they like. Only a natural fresh openness about sex will do any good, now we are being swamped by secret or semi-secret pornography. And perhaps the Renaissance story-tellers, Boccaccio, Lasca,[15] and the rest, are the best antidote we can find now, just as more plasters of Puritanism are the most harmful remedy we can resort to.

The whole question of pornography seems to me a question of secrecy. Without secrecy there would be no pornography. But secrecy and modesty are two utterly different things. Secrecy has always an element of fear in it, amounting very often to hate. Modesty is gentle and reserved. Today, modesty is thrown to the winds, even in the presence of the grey guardians. But secrecy is hugged, being a vice in itself. And the attitude of the grey ones is: Dear young ladies, you may abandon all modesty, so long as you hug your dirty little secret.

This 'dirty little secret' has become infinitely precious to the mob of people today. It is a kind of hidden sore or inflammation which, when rubbed or scratched, gives off sharp thrills that seem delicious. So the dirty little secret is rubbed and scratched more and more, till it becomes more and more secretly inflamed, and the nervous and psychic health of the individual is more and more impaired. One might easily say that half the love novels and half the love films today depend entirely for their success on the secret rubbing of the dirty little secret. You can call this sex excitement if you like, but it is sex excitement of a secretive, furtive sort, quite special. The plain and simple excitement, quite open and wholesome, which you find in some Boccaccio stories is not for a minute to be confused with the furtive excitement aroused by rubbing the dirty little secret in all secrecy in modern best-sellers. This furtive, sneaking, cunning rubbing of an inflamed spot in the imagination is the very quick of modern pornography, and it is a beastly and very dangerous thing. You can't so easily expose it, because of its very furtiveness and its sneaking cunning. So the cheap and popular modern love novel and love film flourishes and is even praised by moral guardians, because you get the sneaking thrill fumbling under all the purity of dainty underclothes, without one single gross word to let you know what is happening.

Without secrecy there would be no pornography. But if pornography is the result of sneaking secrecy, what is the result of pornography? What is the effect on the individual?

The effect on the individual is manifold, and always pernicious. But one effect is perhaps inevitable. The pornography of today, whether it be the pornography of the rubber-goods shop or the pornography of the popular novel, film, and play, is an invariable stimulant to the vice of self-abuse, onanism, masturbation, call it what you will. In young or old, man or woman, boy or girl, modern pornography is a direct provocative of masturbation. It cannot be otherwise. When the grey ones wail that the young man and the young woman went and had sexual intercourse, they are bewailing the fact that the young man and the young woman didn't go separately and masturbate. Sex must go somewhere, especially in young people. So, in our glorious civilization, it goes in masturbation. And the mass of our popular literature, the bulk of our popular amuse-

---

15. Lasca is presumably Janus Lascaris (1445–1535), Greek humanist who served as a librarian to Lorenzo de' Medici and wrote epigrams.

ments just exists to provoke masturbation. Masturbation is the one thoroughly secret act of the human being, more secret even than excrementation. It is the one functional result of sex-secrecy, and it is stimulated and provoked by our glorious popular literature of pretty pornography, which rubs on the dirty secret without letting you know what is happening.

Now I have heard men, teachers and clergymen, commend masturbation as the solution of an otherwise insoluble sex problem. This at least is honest. The sex problem is there, and you can't just will it away. There it is, and under the ban of secrecy and taboo in mother and father, teacher, friend, and foe, it has found its own solution, the solution of masturbation.

But what about the solution? Do we accept it? Do all the grey ones of this world accept it? If so, they must now accept it openly. We can none of us pretend any longer to be blind to the fact of masturbation, in young and old, man and woman. The moral guardians who are prepared to censor all open and plain portrayal of sex must now be made to give their only justification: We prefer that the people shall masturbate. If this preference is open and declared, then the existing forms of censorship are justified. If the moral guardians prefer that the people shall masturbate, then their present behaviour is correct, and popular amusements are as they should be. If sexual intercourse is deadly sin, and masturbation is comparatively pure and harmless, then all is well. Let things continue as they now are.

Is masturbation so harmless, though? Is it even comparatively pure and harmless? Not to my thinking. In the young, a certain amount of masturbation is inevitable, but not therefore natural. I think, there is no boy or girl who masturbates without feeling a sense of shame, anger, and futility. Following the excitement comes the shame, anger, humiliation, and the sense of futility. This sense of futility and humiliation deepens as the years go on, into a suppressed rage, because of the impossibility of escape. The one thing that it seems impossible to escape from, once the habit is formed, is masturbation. It goes on and on, on into old age, in spite of marriage or love affairs or anything else. And it always carries this secret feeling of futility and humiliation, futility and humiliation. And this is, perhaps, the deepest and most dangerous cancer of our civilization. Instead of being a comparatively pure and harmless vice, masturbation is certainly the most dangerous sexual vice that a society can be afflicted with, in the long run. Comparatively pure it may be—purity being what it is. But harmless!!!

The great danger of masturbation lies in its merely exhaustive nature. In sexual intercourse, there is a give and take. A new stimulus enters as the native stimulus departs. Something quite new is added as the old surcharge is removed. And this is so in all sexual intercourse where two creatures are concerned, even in the homosexual intercourse. But in masturbation there is nothing but loss. There is no reciprocity. There is merely the spending away of a certain force, and no return. The body remains, in a sense, a corpse, after the act of self-abuse. There is no change, only deadening. There is what we call dead loss. And this is not the case in any act of sexual intercourse between two people. Two people may destroy one another in sex. But they cannot just produce the null effect of masturbation.

The only positive effect of masturbation is that it seems to release a certain mental energy, in some people. But it is mental energy which manifests itself always in the same way, in a vicious circle of analysis and impotent criticism, or else a vicious circle of false and easy sympathy, sentimentalities. The sentimentalism and the niggling analysis, often self-analysis, of most of our modern literature, is a sign of self-abuse. It is the manifestation of masturbation, the sort of conscious activity stimulated by masturbation, whether male or female. The outstanding feature of such consciousness is that there is no real object, there is only subject. That is just the same whether it be a novel or a work of science. The author never escapes from himself, he pads along within the vicious circle of himself. There is hardly a writer living who gets out of the vicious circle of himself—or a painter either. Hence the lack of creation, and the stupendous amount of production. It is a masturbation result, within the vicious circle of the self. It is self-absorption made public.

And of course the process is exhaustive. The real masturbation of Englishmen began only in the nineteenth century. It has continued with an increasing emptying of the real vitality and the real *being* of men, till now people are little more than shells of people. Most of the responses are dead, most of the awareness is dead, nearly all the constructive activity is dead, and all that remains is a sort of shell, a half-empty creature fatally self-preoccupied and incapable of either giving or taking. Incapable either of giving or taking, in the vital self. And this is masturbation's result. Enclosed within the vicious circle of the self, with no vital contacts outside, the self becomes emptier and emptier, till it is almost a nullus, a nothingness.

But null or nothing as it may be, it still hangs on to the dirty little secret, which it must still secretly rub and inflame. For ever the vicious circle. And it has a weird, blind will of its own.

One of my most sympathetic critics wrote: 'If Mr. Lawrence's attitude to sex were adopted, then two things would disappear, the love lyric and the smoking-room story.' And this, I think, is true. But it depends on which love lyric he means. If it is the: *Who is Sylvia, what is she?* [16]—then it may just as well disappear. All that pure and noble and heaven-blessed stuff is only the counterpart to the smoking-room story. *Du bist wie eine Blume!* [17] Jawohl! One can see the elderly gentleman laying his hands on the head of the pure maiden and praying God to keep her for ever so pure, so clean and beautiful. Very nice for him! Just pornography! Tickling the dirty little secret and rolling his eyes to heaven! He knows perfectly well that if God keeps the maiden so clean and pure and beautiful—in his vulgar sense of clean and pure—for a few more years, then she'll be an unhappy old maid, and not pure nor beautiful at all, only stale and pathetic. Sentimentality is a sure sign of pornography. Why should 'sadness strike through the heart' of the old gentleman, because the maid was pure and beautiful? Anybody but a masturbator would have been glad and would have thought: What a lovely bride for some lucky man!—But no, not the self-enclosed, pornographic masturbator. Sadness has to strike into his beastly heart!—Away with such love lyrics, we've had too much of their pornographic poison, tickling the dirty little secret and rolling the eyes to heaven.

16. Song from Shakespeare's *Two Gentlemen of Verona;* it has a famous setting by Schubert.
17. Song by Heinrich Heine (1799–1856): "Thou art like a flower, so chaste and pure, . . ." "Yes, indeed!" adds Lawrence in German.

But if it is a question of the sound love lyric, *My love is like a red, red rose*—*!* [18] then we are on other ground. My love is like a red, red rose only when she's *not* like a pure, pure lily. And nowadays the pure, pure lilies are mostly festering, anyhow. Away with them and their lyrics. Away with the pure, pure lily lyric, along with the smoking-room story. They are counterparts, and the one is as pornographic as the other. *Du bist wie eine Blume* is really as pornographic as a dirty story: tickling the dirty little secret and rolling the eyes to heaven. But oh, if only Robert Burns had been accepted for what he is, then love might still have been like a red, red rose.

The vicious circle, the vicious circle! The vicious circle of masturbation! The vicious circle of self-consciousness that is never *fully* self-conscious, never fully and openly conscious, but always harping on the dirty little secret. The vicious circle of secrecy, in parents, teachers, friends—everybody. The specially vicious circle of family. The vast conspiracy of secrecy in the press, and, at the same time, the endless tickling of the dirty little secret. The needless masturbation! and the endless purity! The vicious circle!

How to get out of it? There is only one way: Away with the secret! No more secrecy! The only way to stop the terrible mental itch about sex is to come out quite simply and naturally into the open with it. It is terribly difficult, for the secret is cunning as a crab. Yet the thing to do is to make a beginning. The man who said to his exasperating daughter: 'My child, the only pleasure I ever had out of you was the pleasure I had in begetting you' has already done a great deal to release both himself and her from the dirty little secret.

How to get out of the dirty little secret! It is, as a matter of fact, extremely difficult for us secretive moderns. You can't do it by being wise and scientific about it, like Dr. Marie Stopes: [19] though to be wise and scientific like Dr. Marie Stopes is better than to be utterly hypocritical, like the grey ones. But by being wise and scientific in the serious and earnest manner you only tend to disinfect the dirty little secret, and either kill sex altogether with too much seriousness and intellect, or else leave it a miserable disinfected secret. The unhappy 'free and pure' love of so many people who have taken out the dirty little secret and thoroughly disinfected it with scientific words is apt to be more pathetic even than the common run of dirty-little-secret love. The danger is, that in killing the dirty little secret, you kill dynamic sex altogether, and leave only the scientific and deliberate mechanism.

This is what happens to many of those who become seriously 'free' in their sex, free and pure. They have mentalized sex till it is nothing at all, nothing at all but a mental quantity. And the final result is disaster, every time.

The same is true, in an even greater proportion, of the emancipated bohemians: and very many of the young are bohemian today, whether they ever set foot in Bohemia or not. But the bohemian is 'sex free.' The dirty little secret is no secret either to him or her. It is, indeed, a most blatantly open question. There is nothing they don't say: everything that can be revealed is revealed. And they do as they wish.

And then what? They have apparently killed the dirty little secret, but

18. Song by Robert Burns (1759–96). Lawrence admired Burns and even, at one stage, began a novel based on his life.
19. Marie Carmichael Stopes (1880–1958), pioneer birth control clinician and author of early sex manuals.

somehow, they have killed everything else too. Some of the dirt still sticks, perhaps; sex remains still dirty. But the thrill of secrecy is gone. Hence the terrible dreariness and depression of modern Bohemia, and the inward dreariness and emptiness of so many young people of today. They have killed, they imagine, the dirty little secret. The thrill of secrecy is gone. Some of the dirt remains. And for the rest, depression, inertia, lack of life. For sex is the fountainhead of our energetic life, and now the fountain ceases to flow.

Why? For two reasons. The idealists along the Marie Stopes line, and the young bohemians of today, have killed the dirty little secret as far as their personal self goes. But they are still under its dominion socially. In the social world, in the press, in literature, film, theatre, wireless, everywhere purity and the dirty little secret reign supreme. At home, at the dinner table, it is just the same. It is the same wherever you go. The young girl and the young woman is by tacit assumption pure, virgin, sexless. *Du bist wie eine Blume.* She, poor thing, knows quite well that flowers, even lilies, have tippling yellow anthers and a sticky stigma, sex, rolling sex. But to the popular mind flowers are sexless things, and when a girl is told she is like a flower, it means she is sexless and ought to be sexless. She herself knows quite well she isn't sexless and she isn't merely like a flower. But how bear up against the great social life forced on her? She can't! She succumbs, and the dirty little secret triumphs. She loses her interest in sex, as far as men are concerned, but the vicious circle of masturbation and self-consciousness encloses her even still faster.

This is one of the disasters of young life today. Personally, and among themselves, a great many, perhaps a majority, of the young people of today have come out into the open with sex and laid salt on the tail of the dirty little secret. And this is a very good thing. But in public, in the social world, the young are still entirely under the shadow of the grey elderly ones. The grey elderly ones belong to the last century, the eunuch century, the century of the mealy-mouthed lie, the century that has tried to destroy humanity, the nineteenth century. All our grey ones are left over from this century. And they rule us. They rule us with the grey, mealy-mouthed, canting lie of that great century of lies which, thank God, we are drifting away from. But they rule us still with the lie, for the lie, in the name of the lie. And they are too heavy and too numerous, the grey ones. It doesn't matter what government it is. They are all grey ones, left over from the last century, the century of mealy-mouthed liars, the century of purity and the dirty little secret.

So there is one cause for the depression of the young: the public reign of the mealy-mouthed lie, purity and the dirty little secret, which they themselves have privately overthrown. Having killed a good deal of the lie in their own private lives, the young are still enclosed and imprisoned within the great public lie of the grey ones. Hence the excess, the extravagance, the hysteria, and then the weakness, the feebleness, the pathetic silliness of the modern youth. They are all in a sort of prison, the prison of a great lie and a society of elderly liars. And this is one of the reasons, perhaps the main reason why the sex-flow is dying out of the young, the real energy is dying away. They are enclosed within a lie, and the sex won't flow. For the length of a complete lie is never more than three generations, and the young are the fourth generation of the nineteenth century lie.

The second reason why the sex-flow is dying is of course, that the young, in spite of their emancipation, are still enclosed within the vicious circle of self-conscious masturbation. They are thrown back into it, when they try to escape, by the enclosure of the vast public lie of purity and the dirty little secret. The most emancipated bohemians, who swank most about sex, are still utterly self-conscious and enclosed within the narcissus-masturbation circle. They have perhaps less sex even than the grey ones. The whole thing has been driven up into their heads. There isn't even the lurking hole of a dirty little secret. Their sex is more mental than their arithmetic; and as vital physical creatures they are more non-existent than ghosts. The modern bohemian is indeed a kind of ghost, not even narcissus, only the image of narcissus reflected on the face of the audience. The dirty little secret is most difficult to kill. You may put it to death publicly a thousand times, and still it reappears, like a crab, stealthily from under the submerged rocks of the personality. The French, who are supposed to be so open about sex, will perhaps be the last to kill the dirty little secret. Perhaps they don't want to. Anyhow, mere publicity won't do it.

You may parade sex abroad, but you will not kill the dirty little secret. You may read all the novels of Marcel Proust, with everything there in all detail. Yet you will not kill the dirty little secret. You will perhaps only make it more cunning. You may even bring about a state of utter indifference and sex-inertia, still without killing the dirty little secret. Or you may be the most wispy and enamoured little Don Juan of modern days, and still the core of your spirit merely be the dirty little secret. That is to say, you will still be in the narcissus-masturbation circle, the vicious circle of self-enclosure. For whenever the dirty little secret exists, it exists as the centre of the vicious circle of masturbation self-enclosure. And whenever you have the vicious circle of masturbation self-enclosure, you have at the core the dirty little secret. And the most high-flown sex-emancipated young people today are perhaps the most fatally and nervously enclosed within the masturbation self-enclosure. Nor do they want to get out of it, for there would be nothing left to come out.

But some people surely do want to come out of the awful self-enclosure. Today, practically everybody is self-conscious and imprisoned in self-consciousness. It is the joyful result of the dirty little secret. Vast numbers of people don't want to come out of the prison of their self-consciousness: they have so little left to come out with. But some people, surely, want to escape this doom of self-enclosure which is the doom of our civilization. There is surely a proud minority that wants once and for all to be free of the dirty little secret.

And the way to do it is, first, to fight the sentimental lie of purity and the dirty little secret wherever you meet it, inside yourself or in the world outside. Fight the great lie of the nineteenth century, which has soaked through our sex and our bones. It means fighting with almost every breath, for the lie is ubiquitous.

Then secondly, in his adventure of self-consciousness a man must come to the limits of himself and become aware of something beyond him. A man must be self-conscious enough to know his own limits, and to be aware of that which surpasses him. What surpasses me is the very urge of life that is within me, and this life urges me to forget myself and to yield to the stirring half-born impulse to smash up the vast lie of the world, and make a new world. If my life is merely to go on in a vicious circle of self-enclosure, masturbating self-consciousness, it is worth nothing to me. If my individual life is to be enclosed within the huge corrupt lie of society today, purity and the dirty little secret, then it is worth not much to me. Freedom is a very great reality. But it means, above all things, freedom from lies. It is, first, freedom from myself, from the lie of myself, from the lie of my all-importance, even to myself; it is freedom from the self-conscious masturbating thing I am, self-enclosed. And second, freedom from the vast lie of the social world, the lie of purity and the dirty little secret. All the other monstrous lies lurk under the cloak of this one primary lie. The monstrous lie of money lurks under the cloak of purity. Kill the purity-lie, and the money-lie will be defenceless.

We have to be sufficiently conscious, and self-conscious, to know our own limits and to be aware of the greater urge within us and beyond us. Then we cease to be primarily interested in ourselves. Then we learn to leave ourselves alone, in all the affective centres: not to force our feelings in any way, and never to force our sex. Then we make the great onslaught on to the outside lie, the inside lie being settled. And that is freedom and the fight for freedom. . . .

1929   1929

Apocalypse

Lawrence's interest in this subject was of long standing, and it occupied him a good deal during the last years of his life. He came to believe that the Book of Revelation was a distorted version of an older myth, itself an account of the ritual of a mystery religion such as that associated with Eleusis. This primitive text, he proposes, had been corrupted first by Jewish and then by Christian scribes. His intention is to recover the original, and use it as testimony of that condition of vital correspondence with the cosmos which has disappeared from our lives "in a time of the long slow death of the human being." In his theory the first part of the biblical text relates to the ritual directly; the rest is more a reflection of Christian power lust, the desire of the underdog for revenge. He finds in the recovered ritual a process of self-purgation very congenial to him in these years (witness the asceticism of his long late story *The Man Who Died*): a ritual death from which emerges "a new whole cloven flame of a new-bodied man with golden thighs and a face of glory," a man equipped with a third eye.

In the Bible, Lawrence feels, the imagery is corrupted; the Dragon (originally the Logos, wisdom) is now debased and becomes the insane acquisitive consciousness which entraps us all, especially women. The lurid prophecies and allegories of the later part of Revelation do not concern him; but in his final pages (among the last things Lawrence wrote) he considers the implication, religious and political, of this cult of the underdog, attacking the curse of power-seeking democracy and individualism, and asserting the need for a new collective consciousness of our relation to the universe, such as the original Apocalypse-myth embodies.

From Apocalypse

. . . Let us give up our false position as Christians, as individuals, as demo-
crats. Let us find some conception of ourselves that will allow us to be peaceful
and happy, instead of tormented and unhappy.
The Apocalypse shows us what we are resisting, unnaturally. We are unnaturally resisting our connection with the cosmos, with the world, with mankind, with the nation, with the family. All these connections are, in the
Apocalypse, anathema, and they are anathema to us. We *cannot bear connection.* That is our malady. We *must* break away, and be isolate. We call that
being free, being individual. Beyond a certain point, which we have reached,
it is suicide. Perhaps we have chosen suicide. Well and good. The Apocalypse
too chose suicide, with subsequent self-glorification.
But the Apocalypse shows, by its very resistance, the things that the human
heart secretly yearns after. By the very frenzy with which the Apocalypse
destroys the sun and the stars, the world, and all kings and all rulers, all scarlet
and purple and cinnamon, all harlots, finally all men altogether who are not
'sealed,' we can see how deeply the apocalyptists are yearning for the sun and
the stars and the earth and the waters of the earth, for nobility and lordship and
might, and scarlet and gold splendour, for passionate love, and a proper unison
with men, apart from this sealing business. What man most passionately wants
is his living wholeness and his living unison, not his own isolate salvation of
his 'soul.' Man wants his physical fulfilment first and foremost, since now, once
and once only, he is in the flesh and potent. For man, the vast marvel is to be
alive. For man, as for flower and beast and bird, the supreme triumph is to be
most vividly, most perfectly alive. Whatever the unborn and the dead may
know, they cannot know the beauty, the marvel of being alive in the flesh. The
dead may look after the afterwards. But the magnificent here and now of life
in the flesh is ours, and ours alone, and ours only for a time. We ought to dance
with rapture that we should be alive and in the flesh, and part of the living,
incarnate cosmos. I am part of the sun as my eye is part of me. That I am part
of the earth my feet know perfectly, and my blood is part of the sea. My soul
knows that I am part of the human race, my soul is an organic part of the great
human soul, as my spirit is part of my nation. In my own very self, I am part of
my family. There is nothing of me that is alone and absolute except my mind,
and we shall find that the mind has no existence by itself, it is only the glitter
of the sun on the surface of the waters.
So that my individualism is really an illusion. I am a part of the great whole,
and I can never escape. But I *can* deny my connections, break them, and become
a fragment. Then I am wretched.
What we want is to destroy our false, inorganic connections, especially those
related to money, and re-establish the living organic connections, with the
cosmos, the sun and earth, with mankind and nation and family. Start with the
sun, and the rest will slowly, slowly happen.

1929   1931

T. S. ELIOT
1888–1965

Thomas Stearns Eliot was born in St. Louis, Missouri, on September 26, 1888. The family, Unitarian in religion, was descended from one Andrew Eliot who left East Coke, Somerset, England, in the mid-seventeenth century and settled in Massachusetts. His earliest writings appeared in the magazine of Smith Academy, St. Louis, in 1905. In the following year he entered Harvard, where he edited and contributed poems to *The Advocate*. While still in college he wrote several of the poems, including the title work, published in *Prufrock and Other Observations* (1917). *Prufrock* was written in 1910–11, by which time his early taste for such poetry as the *Rubáiyát* had been qualified by the anti-Romantic teachings of Irving Babbitt. His main academic interest was philosophy, and in 1910, armed with a Harvard M.A., Eliot went to Paris for a year and studied the philosophy of Henri Bergson (1859–1941), whose theory of time and intuition—distinguishing between clock time and a duration of a different order, and between orders of experience which one analyzes with the intelligence and those which one intuits as "intensive manifolds"—left its traces on the poetry. In 1911 he was a graduate assistant in philosophy at Harvard, and in 1914 went to Germany with the intention of studying philosophy at Marburg; in September 1914, the war having begun, he went instead to Oxford, where he worked on his thesis, a study of the Oxford philosopher F. H. Bradley.

In 1915 Eliot married, and taught for some time before joining a bank, where he was to work for eight years. During this period he was an editor of *The Egoist*, a London literary magazine, and reviewed for several journals. He was writing poetry, still influenced by the French Symbolist poets and especially Jules Laforgue, of whom he had learned in 1908 from Arthur Symons's influential book, *The Symbolist Movement in Literature* (1899); he was also studying the "metaphysical" poets and the Jacobean drama. In poor health, he obtained three months' leave from his bank and, first at Margate (a seaside resort near London) and then at a clinic in Lausanne, made *The Waste Land* ready for publication. In January 1922 he stopped at Paris on his way home to consult Ezra Pound about the poem. Later in that year he founded *The Criterion*, the influential right-wing literary journal which he continued until 1939; *The Waste Land* appeared in the first number. In 1925 he became a director of Faber and Gwyer (now Faber and Faber), the publishers. Already a celebrated London critic and lecturer, he took British citizenship in 1927, and was received into the Church of England. In 1930 he published *Ash Wednesday*.

It was only after an interval of four years that Eliot's poetry appeared again, with the choruses written for a church charity pageant, *The Rock;* this was followed in 1935 by his first play, *Murder in the Cathedral*. Unused material from this work went into the making of the poem "Burnt Norton" (1936), which was to be the first of the *Four Quartets*. A second play, *The Family Reunion*, appeared in 1939, and the remaining quartets were written in 1940–42. "Little Gidding," written twenty-three years before his death, was Eliot's last important poem. In 1948 he was awarded the Nobel Prize for literature. Three more plays, *The Cocktail Party, The Confidential Clerk,* and *The Elder Statesman,* belong to 1950, 1954, and 1959. Eliot's wife, from whom he had been separated for many years, died after a long illness in 1947; he married Valerie Fletcher in 1957. Eliot died in London on January 4, 1965.

Eliot's poetry and its historical background are discussed in the Headnotes to the individual poems; the principal critical works are treated in connection with the prose selections.

The Love Song of J. Alfred Prufrock

Eliot began *Prufrock* at Harvard in 1910 and finished it in Munich in the following year. It has something in common with earlier Harvard poems, but is much more ambitious and elaborate. At this time he was much under the influence of the French poet Jules Laforgue (1860–87), whose methods of fantastic irony, free association, and deliberate bathos are here adopted. *Prufrock* is a dramatic monologue, and owes an obvious debt to Browning also, but has developed a new obliquity and reticence; there is no attempt to give the *persona* of Prufrock the interiority or solidity of a Browning *persona*. This is in part due to Eliot's current study of the philosopher F. H. Bradley (1846–1924), who treated personality as a delusion, holding that the "finite center" of the perceiving person is unknowable by other such centers. Prufrock is, it has been said, a name with a voice; the relations between his remarks are bound to seem arbitrary. It becomes a characteristic of all Eliot's poetry that it will not offer generally acceptable endorsements of its internal logic.

At the time of this poem Eliot had learned something about the Symbolist movement in literature from Arthur Symons's ground-breaking book of that title. This introduced the young poet to the bizarre alternations of cynicism and sentiment in Laforgue but also to other recent French poets, notably Mallarmé and Verlaine, who were to become important to him. The effect of Symons is in fact hard to exaggerate; this friend, contemporary, and instructor of Yeats also shaped the interests of the younger man at Harvard. Symons wrote some verse that faintly resembles *Prufrock;* but, more importantly, he handed on to Eliot a mixture of interests—in the Jacobean drama and Donne, in Wagner and the Symbolists—which, though we think it characteristic of Eliot, was a fashionable blend of the concerns of the avant-garde in the generation immediately preceding his. (The affinity between modernist and Metaphysical poetry, as Eliot saw it, is expressed in his essay "The Metaphysical Poets.")

This does not detract from the modernist virtuosity of Eliot's poem, which was first recognized by Ezra Pound. Pound was responsible for its publication in the magazine *Poetry* (Chicago) in 1915, by which time Eliot was living in London and had formed his mutually admiring and fruitful relationship with Pound. He developed his own interests in Donne, the Jacobean drama, and the French poets; they were not identical with Pound's, but the poets had much in common: Eliot's belief (stated in the essay "Tradition and the Individual Talent") that poetry involved an extinction of the personality of the author, justified the use of an inscrutable *persona;* and his other famous theory, expressed briefly in the essay on *Hamlet* (1921), of the *objective correlative,* implied that the work in its objective existence called for a collaborative effort which would be different for different readers so that it would suggest no agreed story or interpretation; its relationship to what went on in the poet's mind is impenetrably obscure and irrelevant. Since *Prufrock* is written quite expressly to exemplify this kind of poetry, it is a mistake to try to extract from it a concealed narrative, even to assert that it is the story of what is going on in the mind of a man who may or may not be on the point of issuing a marriage proposal; or at any rate to do this at the expense of all the other possibilities inherent in the impenetrable reverie. The strength of the poem lies in its apparently random transitions, its rhetorical and poetic flights, interrupted by bathos or irrelevance; its echoes of other poems. The image of the fog is *too* playful and elaborate, and the point lies partly in its being so. The indecorum of "butt-ends" tells us nothing about a character, but only helps to constitute a poem. The slight movement of disappointed erotic feeling (lines 62 ff., and at the end) like the comic inflation of "Do I dare / Disturb the universe," the Salome and Lazarus figures incongruously irrupting into an atmosphere of coffee-spoon life, all contribute to the substance of a poem, not of a personality; and the way to read it is to move with its movement, ride its little shocks, and, in a sense, live along its lines. The point is worth dwelling on here, since that is also the way to handle the much tougher poems that follow *Prufrock*.

The Love Song of J. Alfred Prufrock°

S'io credesse che mia risposta fosse
A persona che mai tornasse al mondo,
Questa fiamma staria senza più scosse.
Ma perciocché giammai di questo fondo
Non tornò vivo alcun, s'i'odo il vero,
Senza tema d'infamia ti rispondo.°

Let us go then, you and I,
When the evening is spread out against the sky
Like a patient etherised° upon a table;
Let us go, through certain half-deserted streets,
The muttering retreats
Of restless nights in one-night cheap hotels
And sawdust restaurants with oyster-shells:
Streets that follow like a tedious argument
Of insidious intent
To lead you to an overwhelming question . . .
Oh, do not ask, 'What is it?'
Let us go and make our visit.

In the room the women come and go
Talking of Michelangelo.

10

Prufrock Eliot apparently noted this name on a shopfront in the St. Louis of his youth.
S'io . . . rispondo "If I thought that my answer were being made to someone who would ever return to earth, this flame would remain without further movement; but since no one has ever returned alive from this depth, if what I hear is true, I answer you without fear of infamy" (Dante, *Inferno* XXVII.61–66). The speaker is Guido de Montefeltro, placed in the eighth circle of hell for giving evil counsel to a pope. He is wrapped in a flame and speaks from its trembling tip. The *persona* of the poem also tries to speak—though of a much less dramatic life—with a similar candor, on the assumption that whatever hell he is in, the reader is **there** also; or expecting (ll. 95 ff.) that to give such importance to his plight would simply gain him a rebuff.
etherised anesthetized

The yellow fog that rubs its back upon the window-panes,
The yellow smoke that rubs its muzzle on the window-panes,
Licked its tongue into the corners of the evening,
Lingered upon the pools that stand in drains,
Let fall upon its back the soot that falls from chimneys,
Slipped by the terrace, made a sudden leap,
And seeing that it was a soft October night,
Curled once about the house, and fell asleep.

And indeed there will be time°
For the yellow smoke that slides along the street,
Rubbing its back upon the window-panes;
There will be time, there will be time
To prepare a face to meet the faces that you meet;
There will be time to murder and create,
And time for all the works and days° of hands
That lift and drop a question on your plate;
Time for you and time for me,°
And time yet for a hundred indecisions,
And for a hundred visions and revisions,
Before the taking of a toast and tea.

In the room the women come and go
Talking of Michelangelo.

And indeed there will be time
To wonder, 'Do I dare?' and, 'Do I dare?'
Time to turn back and descend the stair,
With a bald spot in the middle of my hair—
(They will say: 'How his hair is growing thin!')
My morning coat, my collar mounting firmly to the chin,
My necktie rich and modest, but asserted by a simple pin—
(They will say: 'But how his arms and legs are thin!')
Do I dare
Disturb the universe?°
In a minute there is time
For decisions and revisions which a minute will reverse.

For I have known them all already, known them all—
Have known the evenings, mornings, afternoons,
I have measured out my life with coffee spoons;

---

there . . . time Here and in the subsequent uses of the word "time" we hear a tired allusion to Ecclesiastes 3:1–8: "To everything there is a season, and a time to every purpose under heaven: A time to be born, and a time to die; a time to plant, and a time to pluck up that which is planted; a time to kill, and a time to heal; . . . a time to weep, and a time to laugh; a time to mourn, and a time to dance; . . . a time to keep silence, and a time to speak." **works and days** title of didactic poem by the early Greek poet Hesiod (8th century B.C.) concerning rural labor
Time . . . me The theme and the rhythm drop together into pure banality. In the fogbound drawing room all the trivial issues seem important enough for solemn language, but only momentarily; their futility declares itself in various ways, this being one.
Do . . . universe? one of the poem's ironical overstatements

I know the voices dying with a dying fall°
Beneath the music from a farther room.
  So how should I presume?

And I have known the eyes already, known them all—
The eyes that fix you in a formulated phrase,
And when I am formulated, sprawling on a pin,
When I am pinned and wriggling on the wall,
Then how should I begin
60 To spit out all the butt-ends of my days and ways?
  And how should I presume?

And I have known the arms already, known them all—
Arms that are braceleted and white and bare
(But in the lamplight, downed with light brown hair!)
Is it perfume from a dress
That makes me so digress?
Arms that lie along a table, or wrap about a shawl.
  And should I then presume?
  And how should I begin?

                    *   *   *
70 Shall I say, I have gone at dusk through narrow streets
And watched the smoke that rises from the pipes
Of lonely men in shirt-sleeves, leaning out of windows? . . .

I should have been a pair of ragged claws°
Scuttling across the floors of silent seas.

                    *   *   *
And the afternoon, the evening, sleeps so peacefully!
Smoothed by long fingers,
Asleep . . . tired . . . or it malingers,
Stretched on the floor, here beside you and me.
Should I, after tea and cakes and ices,
80 Have the strength to force the moment to its crisis?°
But though I have wept and fasted, wept and prayed,
Though I have seen my head (grown slightly bald) brought in upon a platter,
I am no prophet°—and here's no great-matter;
I have seen the moment of my greatness flicker,
And I have seen the eternal Footman hold my coat, and snicker,
And in short, I was afraid.

And would it have been worth it, after all,
After the cups, the marmalade, the tea,
Among the porcelain, among some talk of you and me,

dying fall "That strain again! It had a dying fall," *Twelfth Night* I.i.4, where the lovesick Duke commends the music; here applied to affected upperclass accents
pair . . . claws A crab; thus, it would be a relief to lead a merely instinctual life, involving no moral decisions and revisions.

ices . . . crisis The comic rhyme is another deflationary device.
Though . . . prophet Salome asked the head of John the Baptist on a platter as a reward for her dance before Herod (Mark 6, Matthew 14). The story was one much used by poets as an image of the sacrifices required by art. Laforgue wrote an ironic *Salome.*

Would it have been worth while,
To have bitten off the matter with a smile,
To have squeezed the universe into a ball°
To roll it toward some overwhelming question,
To say: 'I am Lazarus,° come from the dead,
Come back to tell you all, I shall tell you all'—
If one, settling a pillow by her head,
    Should say: 'That is not what I meant at all;
    That is not it, at all.'

And would it have been worth it, after all,
Would it have been worth while,
After the sunsets and the dooryards and the sprinkled streets,
After the novels, after the teacups, after the skirts that trail along the
    floor—
And this, and so much more?—
It is impossible to say just what I mean!
But as if a magic lantern threw the nerves in patterns on a screen:°
Would it have been worth while
If one, settling a pillow or throwing off a shawl,
And turning toward the window, should say:
    'That is not it at all,
    That is not what I meant, at all.'

                 ❁   ❁   ❁

No! I am not Prince Hamlet, nor was meant to be;
Am an attendant lord, one that will do
To swell a progress,° start a scene or two,
Advise the prince; no doubt, an easy tool,
Deferential, glad to be of use,
Politic, cautious, and meticulous;
Full of high sentence,° but a bit obtuse;
At times, indeed, almost ridiculous—
Almost, at times, the Fool.°

    I grow old . . . I grow old . . .
I shall wear the bottoms of my trousers rolled.°

    Shall I part my hair behind?° Do I dare to eat a peach?
I shall wear white flannel trousers, and walk upon the beach.
I have heard the mermaids singing,° each to each.

squeezed . . . ball "Let us roll all our strength and all / Our sweetness up into one ball," Marvell, "To His Coy Mistress"—a seduction poem in which the lover *wants* something to happen
Lazarus See John 11:1–44.
as if . . . screen the equivalent of "telling all"
swell a progress A progress was a ceremonial royal journey; here he sees himself as an "extra" in a progress in a play.
Full . . . sentence expressing worthly sentiments (see Chaucer, the General Prologue, l. 306)
the Fool the Fool of Elizabethan drama, li-

censed not only to clown but to quibble with his betters
wear . . . rolled presumably, adopt the new fashion of trouser cuffs
part . . . behind a daring new hair style. He seems to contemplate a series of faintly daring gestures in defiance of advancing age, but soon gives up; the white trousers suggest the beach, the beach the mermaids, and the mermaids the myth of drowning which ends the work.
mermaids singing See Donne's "Go and Catch a Falling Star": "Teach me to hear mermaids singing" (l. 5), considered an impossibility.

I do not think that they will sing to me.

I have seen them riding seaward on the waves
Combing the white hair of the waves blown back
When the wind blows the water white and black.

We have lingered in the chambers of the sea
130   By sea-girls wreathed with seaweed red and brown
Till human voices wake us, and we drown.
1911   1917

Gerontion

This poem, which Eliot at one time wished to use as the prelude to *The Waste Land*,
heads his *Poems, 1920* and represents his mature middle style. The method is not
greatly different from *Prufrock*, but the tone of *vers de société* has been eliminated;
the stylistic transitions and imitations are even more abrupt, the allusions and pastiche
still more private and unsusceptible to "public" explanation. In the arbitrariness of
the poem there are a few forces that make for cohesion. A past is exposed and contemplated in a reverie; the reverie is proper to the fractured, spiritually moribund
world of Europe immediately after the Great War. Eliot's preoccupation with the
spiritual sterility of this world, which he saw as involved in a great doomed experiment
in heresy, a suicidal separation from the past and from religion, achieves an expression which is as far as possible *not* an expression but a statement of all these things
in a mysterious and arbitrary image. Eliot believed that the man who suffers should
be kept separate from the artist who creates, and by the same token divorced his
"thought" from his poetry; the "thought" is nevertheless there, though in extraordinary disguises; and naturally it is the thought he had in his head at the time. Hence
the echoes of his recent reading, the imitations of Jacobean dramatic verse, the use
of Lancelot Andrewes's sermons, the presentation of the past as instantaneously there
in the present, which is a condition expounded by Eliot in his essay "Tradition and
the Individual Talent." The modern idea of history as meaningless chaos, related to
the view that all nature is a chaos on which only the mind of man imposes fictions
of order, Eliot derived from *The Education of Henry Adams* (1918).

Gerontion, "little old man," is obviously in some ways the image of a moribund
civilization. He is near death, like Cardinal Newman's protagonist in *The Dream of
Gerontius*, and, it has rightly been said, shares some attributes with another modern
man to whom Eliot gave his careful attention, the Kurtz of Conrad's *Heart of Darkness*,
who said he was "lying here in the dark waiting for death." The corruption of European religion, culture, and sex are the topics here as in *The Waste Land*, the method
of which derives from "Gerontion." Eliot's prose deliberations, in his journal *The
Criterion* and in many essays and lectures, are reflections in a different mode on the
same subject.

Gerontion°

Thou hast nor youth nor age
But as it were an after dinner sleep
Dreaming of both.°

Here I am, an old man in a dry month,
Being read to by a boy, waiting for rain.°
I was neither at the hot gates°
Nor fought in the warm rain
Nor knee deep in the salt marsh, heaving a cutlass,
Bitten by flies, fought.
My house is a decayed house,
And the Jew° squats on the window sill, the owner,
Spawned in some estaminet° of Antwerp,
Blistered in Brussels, patched and peeled in London.
The goat coughs at night in the field overhead;
Rocks, moss, stonecrop, iron, merds.°
The woman keeps the kitchen,° makes tea,
Sneezes at evening, poking the peevish gutter.°
                              I an old man,
A dull head among windy spaces.

Signs are taken for wonders. 'We would see a sign!'°
The word within a word, unable to speak a word,
Swaddled with darkness.° In the juvescence° of the year

Gerontion "little old man"
Thou . . . both Shakespeare, *Measure for Measure* III.i.32–34. The Duke is counseling Claudio to accept his death sentence calmly. Later his sister Isabella explains to him that she could have had him reprieved by sleeping with his judge, Angelo, and he allows his fear of death and its consequences to overcome him. In expressing these fears he speaks of the guilty spirit after death: "imprisoned in the viewless winds / And blown with restless violence round about / The pendent world"—a speech based on the same passage in Cicero's *Somnium Scipionis* that is at the root of "Gerontion," ll. 67–69. The poem is in part a contemplation, in a dry season, of death and judgment.
in . . . rain A. C. Benson in his biography (1905) of Edward FitzGerald, the translator of Omar Khayyam, summarizes a letter describing the poet as sitting "in a dry month, old and blind, being read to by a country boy, longing for rain."
hot gates literal translation of "Thermopylae," the pass which was the scene of the famous battle in 480 B.C. between Persians and Greeks, crucial to the history of Europe.
Jew In earlier texts, this was *jew;* the word, in association with great European commercial centers, suggests perhaps the decay of culture through corrupt love of money.
estaminet cheap café
merds turds
woman . . . kitchen reminiscence of another FitzGerald letter
gutter drain
Signs . . . sign When the Scribes and Pharisees said, "Master, we would see a sign from thee,"

Christ answered, "An evil and adulterous generation seeketh after a sign" (Matthew 12:38–39). In John 4:48 Jesus says "Except ye see signs and wonders, ye will not believe"; the two words often go together in the Bible but Eliot dissociates them, quoting Andrewes (see next note).
The word . . . darkness Lancelot Andrewes (1555–1626) in a Nativity Sermon of 1618 on the text "And this shall be a sign unto you . . ." (Luke 2:12): "Signs are taken for wonders. 'Master, we would fain see a sign,' that is a miracle. And in this sense it is a sign to wonder at . . . *Verbum infans*, the Word without a word; the eternal Word not able to speak a word . . . a wonder sure. And the *sparganismus*, 'swaddled' [Luke 2:12], and that a wonder too. 'He,' that (as in the thirty-eighth of Job he saith) 'taketh the vast body of the main sea, turns it to and fro, as a little child, and rolls it about with the swaddling bands of darkness;'—He to come thus in clouts, Himself!" Eliot's admiration for Andrewes, and this passage in particular, is expressed in his essay on the preacher. Andrewes says "the Word without a word," a literal translation of the Latin *verbum infans;* Eliot says "The word within a word," and that this is an odd mistake rather than a deliberate alteration is suggested by the fact that in the essay (1926) he gives the same wrong version, quoting his poem rather than Andrewes (see *Selected Essays*, 1932, p. 307; *For Lancelot Andrewes*, 1928, p. 18).
juvescence presumably a mistake for *juvenescence*—youth, spring

20   Came Christ the tiger°

    In depraved May, dogwood and chestnut, flowering judas,°
To be eaten, to be divided, to be drunk
Among whispers; by Mr. Silvero
With caressing hands, at Limoges°
Who walked all night in the next room;

    By Hakagawa, bowing among the Titians;
By Madame de Tornquist, in the dark room
Shifting the candles; Fräulein von Kulp
Who turned in the hall, one hand on the door. Vacant shuttles
30   Weave the wind.° I have no ghosts,
An old man in a draughty house
Under a windy knob.

    After such knowledge, what forgiveness? Think now
History has many cunning passages, contrived corridors
And issues, deceives with whispering ambitions,
Guides us by vanities. Think now
She gives when our attention is distracted
And what she gives, gives with such supple confusions
That the giving famishes the craving. Gives too late
40   What's not believed in, or if still believed,
In memory only, reconsidered passion. Gives too soon
Into weak hands, what's thought can be dispensed with
Till the refusal propagates a fear. Think
Neither fear nor courage saves us. Unnatural vices
Are fathered by our heroism. Virtues
Are forced upon us by our impudent crimes.
These tears are shaken from the wrath-bearing tree.°

    The tiger springs in the new year. Us he devours. Think at last
50   We have not reached conclusion, when I
Stiffen in a rented house.° Think at last
I have not made this show purposelessly

Christ the tiger In Andrewes's Nativity Sermon of 1622 he has the people who will not hurry (as the Magi did) to see the newborn Christ, exclaim, "Christ is no wild-cat. . . . What needs such haste?" Eliot admired this passage (see *Selected Essays,* p. 307). Insofar as these people were wrong, Christ *can* be called a wildcat. In the bestiaries a panther is sometimes an emblem of Christ.
In . . . judas alluding to *The Education of Henry Adams,* a description of the Maryland spring: "the . . . intermixture of delicate grace and passionate depravity that marked the Maryland May"
Limoges French town producing fine china. Silvero and the other names appear to have no significance beyond their cosmopolitanism; all are enacting rituals which are not those of the Mass.
Vacant . . . wind "My days are swifter than a weaver's shuttle, and are spent without hope. O remember that my life is wind: mine eye shall no more see good" (Job 7:6-7).
After . . . tree (ll. 33-47) a meditation on history and the moral confusion of the times written in the manner of some Jacobean dramatic poets. Henry Adams's *Education* furnished the hint for the material. The excited ellipses of the passionate argument are Jacobean in origin. Given the confusion that disorderly knowledge has brought, the past cannot be understood with any immediacy, as is necessary to a healthy culture. Hence an ethical confusion pointed up by the vices and virtues demonstrated, for example, in war.
wrath-bearing tree Compare Blake's *Poison Tree,* where wrath produces a tree, watered by tears.
We . . . house Simply: the death of the body is not the end of the matter.

And it is not by any concitation°
Of the backward devils.
I would meet you° upon this honestly.
I that was near your heart was removed therefrom°
To lose beauty in terror, terror in inquisition.
I have lost my passion: why should I need to keep it
Since what is kept must be adulterated?
I have lost my sight, smell, hearing, taste, and touch:
How should I use them for your closer contact?

These° with a thousand small deliberations
Protract the profit of their chilled delirium,°
Excite the membrane, when the sense has cooled,
With pungent sauces, multiply variety
In a wilderness of mirrors.° What will the spider do,
Suspend its operations, will the weevil
Delay? De Bailhache, Fresca, Mrs. Cammel,° whirled
Beyond the circuit of the shuddering Bear°
In fractured atoms. Gull against the wind,° in the windy straits
Of Belle Isle,° or running on the Horn,°
White feathers in the snow, the Gulf° claims,
And an old man driven by the Trades°
To a sleepy corner.

Tenants of the house,

Thoughts of a dry brain in a dry season.

1919   1920

concitation conjuring, exciting
you He now seems to address a lover, perhaps simply the world of sense.
I . . . therefrom Middleton, *The Changeling* V.iii: "I am that of" [or, "I that am of" in that inferior reading used by Eliot] "your blood was taken from you / For your better health": quoted with admiration by Eliot in the essay on Middleton (*Selected Essays*, pp. 140–48)
These these people (as though pointing to others who will not abandon the sensual life)
Protract . . . delirium See "Little Gidding" II.
multiply . . . mirrors remembering the voluptuous Sir Epicure Mammon in Jonson's *The Alchemist:* "my glasses / Cut in more subtle angles, to disperse / And multiply the figures as I walk / Naked among my succubae" (II.i), but thinking also of brothels that specialize in mirrors
De Bailhache . . . Cammel More random cosmopolitan names, as if from a society paper; these are the rootless, the dissociated from the past, who, after death, suffer the fate foreseen by Claudio. Fresca appears again as the central figure of the pseudo-Popean section of "The

Fire Sermon" in *The Waste Land*, which Eliot canceled on Pound's advice.
whirled . . . Bear This version uses the language of George Chapman's dying superhero in *Bussy D'Ambois* V.iv: "fly where men feel / The burning axletree, and those that suffer / Beneath the chariot of the snowy Bear"—a passage commended by Eliot, who remarks that what the image meant to Seneca, to Chapman, and to himself would in each case be "too obscure" for any of them quite to understand. (*The Use of Poetry and the Use of Criticism*, pp. 46–47). The Great Bear belongs to the northern hemisphere, hence "shuddering."
Gull . . . wind The picture of the whirling souls dissolves associatively into that of the gull and the white feathers; so to the trade winds and back to the beginning. The new poetry anticipates later cinema.
Belle Isle island in North Atlantic
Horn Cape Horn, the southern tip of the South American continent
Gulf the warmer water of the Gulf Stream
Trades trade winds, blowing constantly from the northeast in the northern tropics

The Waste Land

The poem was originally a longer sequence, composed for the most part in the fall of 1921, when Eliot, on the verge of a nervous breakdown, obtained paid leave from his City of London bank and went to recuperate first in Margate and then in Lausanne, Switzerland. He was in continuous correspondence with Pound, and on the way back to London early in 1922 took the manuscript to him in Paris. Pound made extensive cuts and changes, and a few more were made later at the suggestion of the first Mrs. Eliot. The poem was published in 1922 and in the same year the manuscript was sold to the New York collector John Quinn. It was then thought to have been lost, but it is now in the Berg Collection of the New York Public Library, and an edition of the uncut poem, by Mrs. Valerie Eliot, appeared in 1971. From it we learn more of the personal crisis that Eliot underwent during the time leading up to the composition of the poem. He was exhausted by overwork and by the stress of his marriage to a brilliant but mentally unstable woman; and the writing of the poem represented both an assessment of the world as he felt it to be, and a creative transformation of it, which culminates in the final section, "What the Thunder Said." This, we now know, was as it were "given" to the poet, without the long processes of trial and error, cancellation and rewriting, that were necessary for all the others. The entire effort to find the true shape of the work was suddenly rewarded, and this section was "right" from the first draft, and written in a condition of exaltation. It formed, of course, but a small proportion of the original thousand-line manuscript he took to Pound in Paris; in helping to reduce the work to 433 lines Pound left the last section alone.

Elsewhere Pound recommended many changes of detail. He diminished, without destroying, the dependence of the poem on a basic iambic pentameter measure; he deleted what was rhythmically inert; he cut passages that seemed to belong to an earlier stage of the poet's development—lines reminiscent, for example, of *Prufrock*. Pound, as Eliot several times acknowledged, had an incalculably beneficial effect on the poem, simply in his sense of Eliot's true quality and voice. His changes are all of detail and have no direct bearing on the mythic structure and allusions. One or two instances must serve. Where Eliot wrote:

> Unreal City, I have sometimes seen and see
> Under the brown fog of a winter dawn—

Pound simply reduced it to

> Unreal City,
> Under the brown fog of a winter dawn—

cutting out, without replacement, an inert piece of filling, and economically eliminating the somewhat mannered invocation to the City (the first line does all that). In the seduction scene in "The Fire Sermon" Pound canceled lines and part-lines of the regular quatrains in which it was originally written; Eliot did not reconstitute them, but left them in their cut state. Some quatrains remain intact; the whole movement has grown more flexible without the slightest loss of weight, and the gain in authenticity and authority of tone is quite extraordinary.

There are minor changes, too many to mention; an example is the substitution by Pound of *demotic* for "abominable" in the account of Mr. Eugenides's French— the superior sharpness of the word is matched by an increase in rhythmic force.

Eliot did not by any means accept all of Pound's cuts and changes, and he preserved some fine things that were marked for deletion. But few fine things were lost by his attending to Pound's advice, and it is hard to think of any comparable instance of a great poem that owes so much to the counsel of another poet.

Eliot showed his gratitude to Pound not only in the dedication of the poem but also by remarking later that his friend's skill had "done so much to turn *The Waste Land* from a jumble of good and bad passages into a poem"; and in 1946 he paid further tribute to the man who reduced to about half its size the "sprawling, chaotic poem."

It is important to remember that however interesting we may find the original as deciphered from the Quinn manuscript, the poem we have to deal with is the one published in 1922; the other is simply a draft in which it had not found its own shape. What kind of shape did it find? In spite of the labors of the commentators, *The Waste Land* remains, and will always remain, an obscure poem. It is not a matter of cracking a code or reconstructing a suppressed narrative. When Eliot in 1956 professed to regret the inclusion of his own notes with the poem, he had in mind the fact that it is very easy to avoid the difficulties of such a poem as this by pretending that it is something other than it is.

Speaking of a French poet, Eliot once remarked that poetry uses the logic of the imagination, not the logic of concepts. "People who do not appreciate poetry always find it difficult to distinguish between order and chaos in the arrangement of images; and even those who are capable of appreciating poetry cannot depend upon first impressions. I was not convinced of Mr. Perse's imaginative order until I had read the poem five or six times" (Preface to *Anabasis: A poem by St. John Perse, with a translation into English by T. S. Eliot,* 1930, p. 8). There is no doubt that he would have said the same thing about his own poem. It is offered as an arrangement of images; their order is not expository or narrative, and one is required not to extract that order but to enter the poem and inhabit it.

This might be thought a *tall* order, and recently there have been critics willing to say that it is not so much imaginative as imaginary; that *The Waste Land* is simply a sequence of poems more or less arbitrarily brought together, and having a number of internal cross references not in excess of what might be expected of any such sequence, though the Notes, later ridiculed by Eliot himself, suggest otherwise. These same critics tend also to stress the Americanism of Eliot's culture and imagination, pointing out, for example, that his cosmopolitan range of reference, the sense he gives of inventing a cultural tradition, add up to a modernism that belongs to the New World, not the Old, or even to a characteristic American rejection of the New. Nor is this an entirely English reaction; William Carlos Williams regarded *The Waste Land* as a disaster for American poetry: "Eliot had turned his back on the possibility of reviving my world. And being an accomplished craftsman, better skilled in some ways than I could ever hope to be, I had to watch him carry my world off with him, the fool, to the enemy" (*Autobiography,* 1951, p. 174).

Yet the fact of the matter is that *The Waste Land,* for whatever reasons, is the central English poem of the twentieth century. This means that many readers have, by reading it six times, somehow intuited its order, so that it is useless to insist on the nonexistence, or the cultural instability, of that order. There can be no doubt that the best way to read it is any way that enables one to intuit its order. For some readers this may mean ignoring Eliot's notes, ignoring the supplementary notes

of his commentators, and letting the poem do its own work. Others will need help.
Even if the background of myth and ritual to which the poem alludes is perfunctory
or unnecessary or mere scaffolding, even if the network of allusions to occult materials and other poets is inessential, there is some comfort in having it pointed out.
These things are at worst useful fictions, instruments which can be thrown away once
a true encounter with the poem itself is achieved.

The myth to which the title refers us, but which asserts itself powerfully only in
the last section of the poem, is that of the country which shares the infertility of
its ruler, whose cure can only be brought about by a knight who will ask the right
questions at a ritual. Eliot refers us to Jessie L. Weston's *From Ritual to Romance*
(1920), a book in the tradition of the Cambridge school of anthropology of which
the best-known product is Sir James Frazer's vast work *The Golden Bough* (1890–
1915); Eliot also refers to this in his notes, and frequently elsewhere. In the poem he
uses Frazer's account of ancient vegetation ceremonies in the cults of Adonis, Attis,
and Osiris. Commenting on Stravinsky's *Rite of Spring* he spoke of the *Golden Bough*
as "a revelation of that vanished mind of which our mind is a continuum" (in *Dial*,
October 1921). Eliot's own notes say: "Not only the title, but a good deal of the inci-
dental symbolism of the poem were suggested by [Jessie L. Weston] . . . Indeed,
so deeply am I indebted, Miss Weston's notes will elucidate the difficulties of the
poem much better than my notes can do. . . ." He goes on to acknowledge the debt
to Frazer. "Anyone who is acquainted with these works will immediately recognize in
the poem certain references to vegetation ceremonies."

Weston's book argues that the medieval romances of the Grail derive from primitive
religious rituals and vegetation ceremonies, the Grail being a female, and the Lance
a male symbol. The Fisher King, the impotent ruler, is a romance manifestation of
another primitive myth. (See Headnote to David Jones for more discussion.) Miss
Weston's book is not well thought of by modern students of romance, and it is doubtful whether the Waste Land theme is one of the more primitive parts of the romance
cycle; but it does not matter. The basic notion of sexual sterility or the dissociation
of sexuality from the cultural and religious health of a society is in Eliot's mind, and
the anthropological material enabled him to perform for himself the act he found so
admirable in Joyce, namely the application of myth to a modern world lacking the
order of myth. The pressure of these and many related ideas on his mind and
imagination is undoubted; he was interested in the origins of Catholic ritual, in
religious dancing, and in Wagner.

That *The Waste Land* is a Wagnerian work is so obvious that only the dip in Wagner's reputation between the 1920's and the 1960's can explain the relative neglect
of the fact. Eliot, like George Moore, Shaw, Forster, and Lawrence, was a Wagnerite.
It was hard to avoid it; Wagner was venerated by the Symbolists and by all who
valued his concept of the great work which not only employed all the arts but projected a universal myth onto the chaos of modern life. If Eliot had not been reading
Miss Weston's new book—Miss Weston herself was a Wagner expert, and saw her
material *through* Wagner—he could as easily have referred us to *Parsifal,* with its
wounded impotent king, its questing knight, its Chapel Perilous and Grail ritual. He
does in fact allude briefly to the close of the opera when he quotes Verlaine's
Sonnet "Parsifal" at line 202. He also refers to *Tristan and Isolde,* the type-myth of
romantic love and its frustration, and to *The Ring,* especially to its opening section,
the *Rhinegold,* and to its last, the *Twilight of the Gods.* The body of myth is very

similar to that treated by Wagner; Eliot goes behind the German treatment, but also evokes it with great deliberation, as the notes indicate. There are other hints of Wagner, as in the reference to the Starnbergersee, powerfully associated with Wagner and also with his extraordinary patron (possibly even his lover), King Ludwig II of Bavaria, who drowned in the lake.

Eliot is, in a sense, attempting to achieve in heroic poetry (or mock-heroic: the genres are now indistinguishable) what Wagner did in music; he even imitates Wagner's verse. Above all, the effect is intended to be musical, suggestive as the interplay of leitmotifs, a complex image of a mythic integrity against a background of actual sterility and decadence. This is a better way of stating the case than to call Eliot's poem a poem about spiritual dryness or decadence. He himself denied that it was "melancholy"; later he would argue that the structures of truth persist throughout the tumults of heresy, and here he is neither merely stating decadence nor proposing remedies for it, but providing an image of an accessible integrity that somehow persists; just as the right questions exist to be asked, the right conduct is knowable, even if the questions are not asked and the knowledge not applied. This is the sense in which the past interpenetrates the present, "quick, now, here, always"; the poem is a kind of Mass, itself the image of an eternal truth in the midst of flux or chaos.

Eliot's theory of poetry, and ultimately his theories of everything, support this view; he was in 1928 to announce himself "classicist in literature, royalist in politics, and Anglo-Catholic in religion" (Preface to For Lancelot Andrewes)—all positions depending on the coexistence of modernity with truths existing in a different order of time. Such views are consistent with the opinion that modern poetry must be "difficult," since the poetry stemming from them must reflect both the ancient order and the modern disorder which normally conceals it. Of that difficulty, as of that order, The Waste Land is Eliot's supreme expression; as Eliot said of Baudelaire, it is not merely a matter of "the imagery of the sordid life of a great metropolis, but . . . the elevation of such imagery to the first intensity—presenting it as it is, and yet making it represent something much more than itself" (Selected Essays, p. 377).

It remains to be said that poetry of this kind will often in its allusions be private; nothing except the poetry itself really causes all the bric-à-brac to cohere, and the poet can use the materials that he has in his head. That the myth finds its expression in whatever material happens to be available is consistent with the teaching of a later mythographer than Frazer, namely Claude Lévi-Strauss. He calls this random material, momentarily integrated in a restatement of a myth, bricolage, and that is what we are examining when we track down the bits and pieces of Eliot's material in our notes.

The Waste Land

> Nam Sibyllam quidem Cumis ego ipse oculis meis vidi
> in ampulla pendere, et cum illi pueri dicerent Σίβυλλα
> τί θέλεις; respondebat illa: ἀποθανεῖν θέλω. °

Nam . . . thélo "For once I saw with my own eyes the Sibyl at Cumae hanging in a cage, and when the boys asked her, 'Sibyl, what do you want?' she answered, 'I want to die.'" That this is part of a drunken boast in the Satyricon of Petronius Arbiter (1st century A.D.) has no apparent relevance. The Cumaean Sibyl, who conducted Aeneas through the underworld (Virgil, Aeneid VI) was granted immortality but not youth.

For Ezra Pound
il miglior fabbro.°

i. *The Burial of the Dead*°

April is the cruellest month,° breeding
Lilacs out of the dead land, mixing
Memory and desire, stirring
Dull roots with spring rain.
Winter kept us warm, covering
Earth in forgetful snow, feeding
A little life with dried tubers.
Summer surprised us, coming over the Starnbergersee°
With a shower of rain; we stopped in the colonnade,
10   And went on in sunlight, into the Hofgarten,°
And drank coffee, and talked for an hour.
Bin gar keine Russin, stamm' aus Litauen, echt deutsch.°
And when we were children, staying at the archduke's,
My cousin's, he took me out on a sled,
And I was frightened. He said, Marie,
Marie, hold on tight. And down we went.
In the mountains, there you feel free.
I read, much of the night, and go south in the winter.

What are the roots that clutch, what branches grow
20   Out of this stony rubbish?° Son of man,°
You cannot say, or guess, for you know only
A heap of broken images,° where the sun beats,
And the dead tree gives no shelter, the cricket° no relief,
And the dry stone no sound of water. Only
There is shadow under this red rock,
(Come in under the shadow of this red rock),

il miglior fabbro "The better workman";
Dante, *Purgatorio* XXVI.117, pays this tribute
to the Provençal poet Arnaut Daniel, and Eliot
turns it into a graceful tribute to Pound.
The . . . Dead The funeral service in the
English Book of Common Prayer is called
"The Order for the Burial of the Dead."
April . . . month usually of Easter, the month
of remembered but no longer wanted divine
resurrections
Starnbergersee Lake near Munich, which Eliot
visited in 1911. It was then a fashionable
resort, and also the site of King Ludwig's
castle, Schloss Berg; in escaping from imprisonment there he drowned in the lake. The following lines to 17 borrow from *My Past,* a volume
of recollections published in 1913 by Countess
Marie Larisch, a kinswoman of the king who
had a vision of him after his death, believed
in fortune-telling by cards, and was assassinated
at Lake Leman (see l. 182). Ludwig was mad
and sick; Wagner, who had once called him
Parsifal, later called him Amfortas, the sick
king whom Parsifal (Wagner himself) will relieve with the Grail. Many further suggestions

of the importance of Countess Marie's memoirs
and other Wagnerian and Bavarian parallels
are proposed by Herbert Knust, *Wagner, The
King, and The Waste Land* (1967), a book
over-enthusiastically argued but establishing that
the Countess's memoirs provided Eliot with
more than a picture of frivolous and rootless
high society. (In the original version Eliot wrote
Königsee.)
Hofgarten public park in Munich
Bin . . . deutsch "I'm not Russian at all, I
come from Lithuania, a pure German." This, we
now learn from Mrs. Eliot, directly reports a
remark of Countess Marie Larisch to Eliot when
he met her, presumably, at Munich.
What . . . rubbish Note this unmotivated
transition, more abrupt than that at l. 8; for
the language see Job 8.
Son of man "See Ezekiel 2:1" (T.S.E.); Ezekiel
is told to preach the coming of the Messiah
to an incredulous people.
broken images Ezekiel 6:6
Cricket "Cf. Ecclesiastes 12:5" (T.S.E.): "the
grasshopper shall be a burden, and desire shall
fail. . . ."

And I will show you something different from either
Your shadow at morning striding behind you
Or your shadow at evening rising to meet you;°
I will show you fear in a handful of dust.°
    Frisch weht der Wind
    Der Heimat zu
    Mein Irisch Kind,
    Wo weilest du?°
'You gave me hyacinths° first a year ago;
They called me the hyacinth girl.'
—Yet when we came back, late, from the Hyacinth garden,
Your arms full, and your hair wet, I could not
Speak, and my eyes failed, I was neither
Living nor dead, and I knew nothing,
Looking into the heart of light, the silence.°
Oed' und leer das Meer.°

    Madame Sosostris,° famous clairvoyante,
Had a bad cold, nevertheless
Is known to be the wisest woman in Europe,
With a wicked pack of cards.° Here, said she,
Is your card, the drowned Phoenician Sailor,°
(Those are pearls that were his eyes.° Look!)
Here is Belladonna,° the Lady of the Rocks,°
The lady° of situations.

Come . . . you based on Eliot's *The Death of Saint Narcissus, c.* 1912, a poem printed but never published until it appeared, with other rejected material, in Mrs. Eliot's edition.
handful of dust "consumes himself to a handful of dust" (Donne, *Devotions,* 1624, Meditation 4)
Frisch . . . du Sailor's song which opens Wagner's *Tristan and Isolde:* he is sailing away from Ireland and singing, "Fresh blows the wind to the homeland—my Irish child, where do you wait?"
hyacinths symbols of resurrection
Yet . . . silence (ll. 37–41) This describes a moment of mystical love-recognition like that at the end of Act I of Wagner's *Tristan,* when the lovers, having drunk the potion, gaze silently at each other for a long time. This is sometimes taken to be the crucial moment; the quester meets the Grail-bearer and fails to ask the right question, so losing his chance of success. Pound tried to change this, but Eliot kept it intact.
Oed' . . . Meer At the beginning of the third and last act of *Tristan* the hero lies sick with a deadly wound, waiting for Isolde's ship; the shepherd lookout reports no sign: "Waste and empty the sea." Isolde's arrival is followed instantly by Tristan's virtually self-inflicted death. Eliot must mean some reference to the fact that passionate sexual love is not the answer to the wound and the waste.
Sosostris Eliot thinks he unconsciously bor-

rowed the name from the fake fortune-teller Madame Sesostris in Aldous Huxley's novel *Crome Yellow* (1921).
cards Eliot's note says that he was not familiar "with the exact constitution of the Tarot pack of cards. . . . The Hanged Man, a member of the traditional pack, fits my purpose in two ways: because he is associated in my mind with the Hanged God of Frazer, and because I associate him with the hooded figure in the passage of the disciples to Emmaus in Part V. The Phoenician Sailor and the Merchant appear later; also the 'crowds of people,' and Death by Water is executed in Part IV. The Man with Three Staves (an authentic member of the Tarot pack) I associate, quite arbitrarily, with the Fisher King himself." The Tarot pack of 78 cards is thought (e.g. by Jessie Weston) to use symbols of ancient ritual origin, and is used for fortune-telling.
Phoenician Sailor See Part IV.
Those . . . eyes *The Tempest* I.ii.398: Ariel's song tells Ferdinand that the king his father is drowned and transfigured.
Belladonna Italian, "beautiful lady"; also the flower Deadly Nightshade, and the poison extracted from it
Lady of the Rocks The reference to a painting of Leonardo da Vinci (Madonna of the Rocks) is ironical; these are wasteland rocks.
lady reducing the word in its new vulgar context by substituting lower-case *l*

Here is the man with three staves, and here the Wheel,°
And here is the one-eyed merchant, and this card,
Which is blank, is something he carries on his back,
Which I am forbidden to see. I do not find
The Hanged Man. Fear death by water.
I see crowds of people, walking round in a ring.
Thank you. If you see dear Mrs. Equitone,
Tell her I bring the horoscope myself:
One must be so careful these days.

60   Unreal City,°
Under the brown fog of a winter dawn,
A crowd flowed over London Bridge, so many,
I had not thought death had undone so many.°
Sighs, short and infrequent, were exhaled,°
And each man fixed his eyes before his feet.
Flowed up the hill and down King William Street,
To where Saint Mary Woolnoth° kept the hours
With a dead sound on the final stroke of nine.°
There I saw one I knew, and stopped him, crying: 'Stetson!
70   You who were with me in the ships at Mylae!°
That corpse you planted last year in your garden,
Has it begun to sprout?° Will it bloom this year?
Or has the sudden frost disturbed its bed?
Oh keep the Dog far hence, that's friend to men,
Or with his nails he'll dig it up again!°
You! hypocrite lecteur!—mon semblable,—mon frère!'°

Wheel of Fortune
Unreal City This passage begins, without transition, a City of London scene; see Headnote remarks about Baudelaire's use of metropolitan imagery. "Cf. Baudelaire: *Fourmillante cité, / cité pleine de rêves, / Où le spectre en plein jour raccroche le passant*" (T.S.E.): "Swarming city, city full of dreams, where the ghost stops the passer-by in full daylight."
so many "Cf. *Inferno* III.55–57: *sì lunga tratta / di gente, ch'io non avrei mai creduto / che morte tanta n'avesse disfatta*" (T.S.E.): "so long a stream of people that I should never have believed that death had undone so many." They are the spirits who in life knew neither good nor evil; see Eliot's essay on Baudelaire for a striking condemnation of them.
Sighs . . . exhaled "Cf. *Inferno* IV.25–27: *Quivi, secondo che per ascoltare, / non avea pianto, ma' che di sospiri, / che l'aura eterna facevan tremare*" (T.S.E.): "Here, to my hearing, there was no lamentation except sighs, which caused the eternal air to tremble." Dante is in the Limbo of the unbaptised.
St. Mary Woolnoth one of the many fine churches, mostly by Wren, in the City of London (the financial district) in which these people are going to work. Eliot joined the campaign to save these churches from destruction.

dead . . . nine "A phenomenon which I have often noticed" (T.S.E.). Nine was the hour when office work began.
Mylae a battle in the First Punic War (260 B.C.) between the Romans and the Carthaginians, fought for control of Mediterranean trade
That . . . sprout Stetson, some veteran of the Great War perhaps, has buried its memories as formerly people buried images of the dead god, but unlike them does not wish it to sprout; he is like all the others in the City procession, indifferent to the central images of religion.
Oh . . . again "Cf. the Dirge in Webster's *White Devil*" (T.S.E.). In that play, IV.iv, Cornelia, referring to "the friendless bodies of unburied men," sings: "But keep the wolf far hence that's foe to men, / For with his nails he'll dig them up again." In the tame life of Stetson there are friendly dogs, not hostile wolves; a milieu unsuited to the rising of a god. There were originally more allusions to Webster in the poem.
hypocrite . . . frère "V. Baudelaire, Preface to *Fleurs du Mal*" (T.S.E.): "Hypocrite reader! my likeness, my brother!" Baudelaire says the reader shares with him the sin of *ennui*, which, under some more modern formulation such as *anomie*, is the sin of the city-workers and of us all.

II. *A Game of Chess*°
The Chair she sat in, like a burnished throne,°
Glowed on the marble, where the glass
Held up by standards wrought with fruited vines
From which a golden Cupidon peeped out
(Another hid his eyes behind his wing)
Doubled the flames of sevenbranched candelabra
Reflecting light upon the table as
The glitter of her jewels rose to meet it,
From satin cases poured in rich profusion;
In vials of ivory and coloured glass
Unstoppered, lurked her strange synthetic perfumes,
Unguent, powdered, or liquid—troubled, confused
And drowned the sense in odours; stirred by the air
That freshened from the window, these ascended
In fattening the prolonged candle-flames,
Flung their smoke into the laquearia,°
Stirring the pattern on the coffered ceiling.
Huge sea-wood fed with copper
Burned green and orange, framed by the coloured stone,
In which sad light a carvèd dolphin swam.
Above the antique mantel was displayed
As though a window gave upon the sylvan scene°
The change of Philomel,° by the barbarous king
So rudely forced; yet there the nightingale°
Filled all the desert with inviolable voice
And still she cried, and still the world pursues,°
'Jug Jug'° to dirty ears.
And other withered stumps of time
Were told upon the walls; staring forms
Leaned out, leaning, hushing the room enclosed.
Footsteps shuffled on the stair.
Under the firelight, under the brush, her hair

A Game of Chess Referring not to Middleton's *A Game at Chess* but to his *Women Beware Women*, one of the great Jacobean tragedies. In one scene the Duke's procuress plays chess with a girl's mother while the Duke is seducing the girl upstairs; the chess moves are made to correspond to the progress of the seduction. The Chair . . . throne "Cf. *Antony and Cleopatra* II.ii.90" (T.S.E.). This is the description by Enobarbus of Cleopatra's barge at her first meeting with Antony: "The barge she sat in, like a burnished throne, / Burned on the water. . . ." Eliot is perhaps thinking also of the bedchamber in *Cymbeline* II.ii and iv, and possibly of Keats's banquet scene in *Lamia*. The luxury is an ironical setting for ennui and hysteria in a loveless marriage; later we switch to a proletarian version of the same horror.
laquearia Eliot's note refers to Virgil, *Aeneid*

I.726: ". . . flaming torches hang from the golden paneled ceiling, and the torches conquer the night with flames." This is at a banquet given by Dido to Aeneas, who makes love to her but deserts her at the call of duty.
sylvan scene "V. Milton, *Paradise Lost* IV.140" (T.S.E.). Satan sees it when he arrives in Eden.
The . . . Philomel "V. Ovid, *Metamorphoses* VI, Philomela" (T.S.E.). In Ovid Philomel is raped by the husband of her sister Procne, King Tereus, who also cut out her tongue; she was changed into the nightingale.
yet . . . nightingale "Cf. Part III, 204" (T.S.E.).
cried . . . pursues Note change of tense.
Jug Jug the nightingale's sound in Elizabethan poetry; also sexual slang, and so a dirty story to "dirty ears"

Spread out in fiery points
110   Glowed into words, then would be savagely still.

    'My nerves are bad to-night. Yes, bad. Stay with me.
Speak to me. Why do you never speak. Speak.
    What are you thinking of? What thinking? What?
I never know what you are thinking. Think.'

    I think we are in rats' alley°
Where the dead men lost their bones.

'What is that noise?'
                  The wind under the door.°
'What is that noise now? What is the wind doing?'
120   Nothing again nothing.
                          'Do
You know nothing? Do you see nothing? Do you remember
Nothing?'

    I remember
Those are pearls that were his eyes.°
'Are you alive, or not? Is there nothing in your head?'
                              But

O O O O that Shakespeherian Rag—
It's so elegant
So intelligent°
130   'What shall I do now? What shall I do?'
'I shall rush out as I am, and walk the street
With my hair down, so. What shall we do to-morrow?
What shall we ever do?'
                  The hot water at ten.
And if it rains, a closed car at four.
And we shall play a game of chess,°
Pressing lidless eyes and waiting for a knock upon the door.

    When Lil's husband got demobbed,° I said—
140   I didn't mince my words, I said to her myself,
HURRY UP PLEASE ITS TIME°
Now Albert's coming back, make yourself a bit smart.
He'll want to know what you done with that money he gave you
To get yourself some teeth. He did, I was there.

I . . . alley "Cf. Part III, 195" (T.S.E.).
wind . . . door "Cf. Webster; "Is the wind in that door still?" (T.S.E.) (*The Devil's Law Case*, III.ii).
Those . . . eyes "Cf. Part I. 37, 48" (T.S.E.). The reference to 37 is mysterious; the other is to Ariel's song in *The Tempest* I.ii, a leitmotif partly explicated in "Death by Water."
O . . . intelligent A burst of contemporary ragtime, with a sophisticated 'twenties lyric, momentarily varies the atmosphere of tense ennui.

a game of chess "Cf. the game of chess in Middleton's *Women Beware Woman*" (T.S.E.): here presumably a substitute for sexual activity, just as the rape of Tereus only figuratively represents the civilized cruelty of this marriage
demobbed Slang for "demobilized," released from the army. Eliot tries here to catch the tone of proletarian conversation.
Hurry . . . time signifying that the closing time set by the licensing laws has come, so that everybody must drink up and leave the pub

You have them all out, Lil, and get a nice set,
He said, I swear, I can't bear to look at you.
And no more can't I, I said, and think of poor Albert,
He's been in the army four years, he wants a good time,
And if you don't give it him, there's others will, I said.
Oh is there, she said. Something o' that, I said.
Then I'll know who to thank, she said, and give me a straight look.
HURRY UP PLEASE ITS TIME
If you don't like it you can get on with it,° I said.
Others can pick and choose if you can't.
But if Albert makes off, it won't be for lack of telling.
You ought to be ashamed, I said, to look so antique.
(And her only thirty-one.)
I can't help it, she said, pulling a long face,
It's them pills I took, to bring it off,° she said.
(She's had five already, and nearly died of young George.)
The chemist° said it would be all right, but I've never been the same.
You *are* a proper fool, I said.
Well, if Albert won't leave you alone, there it is, I said,
What you get married for if you don't want children?
HURRY UP PLEASE ITS TIME
Well, that Sunday Albert was home, they had a hot gammon,°
And they asked me in to dinner, to get the beauty of it hot—
HURRY UP PLEASE ITS TIME
HURRY UP PLEASE ITS TIME
Goonight Bill. Goonight Lou. Goonight May. Goonight.
Ta ta. Goonight. Goonight.
Good night, ladies, good night, sweet ladies, good night, good night.°

    III. *The Fire Sermon*°
The river's tent is broken: the last fingers of leaf
Clutch and sink into the wet bank. The wind
Crosses the brown land, unheard. The nymphs are departed.
Sweet Thames, run softly, till I end my song.°
The river bears no empty bottles, sandwich papers,
Silk handkerchiefs, cardboard boxes, cigarette ends
Or other testimony of summer nights. The nymphs are departed.
And their friends, the loitering heirs of City directors,
Departed, have left no addresses.
By the waters of Leman° I sat down and wept . . .

If you . . . get on with it Mrs. Vivien Eliot proposed this to replace "No, you needn't look old-fashioned at me" in the original. This whole section was apparently derived, in part, from the conversation of the Eliots' cleaning woman.
bring it off induce abortion
chemist pharmacist
gammon smoked ham
Good . . . night Ophelia's last words in *Hamlet* IV.v. before drowning herself
The Fire Sermon a sermon preached by the Buddha against the fires of lust

Sweet . . . song "V. Spenser, *Prothalamion*" (T.S.E.). Spenser's poem is a celebration of a noble wedding; the river and its nymphs join the celebrations. Now the river is a place of litter and loveless seduction.
By . . . Leman "By the waters of Babylon, there we sat down, yea, we wept, when we remembered Zion" (Psalms 137:1). Leman is Lake Geneva, near which Eliot worked on the poem; see l. 8n. Leman means "mistress" also, and Eliot may be using the name for the sake of the pun.

Sweet Thames, run softly till I end my song,
Sweet Thames, run softly, for I speak not loud or long.
But at my back in a cold blast I hear
The rattle of the bones, and chuckle spread from ear to ear.°
A rat crept softly through the vegetation
Dragging its slimy belly on the bank
While I was fishing° in the dull canal
190   On a winter evening round behind the gashouse
Musing upon the king my brother's wreck°
And on the king my father's death before him.
White bodies naked on the low damp ground
And bones cast in a little low dry garret,
Rattled by the rat's foot only, year to year.
But at my back from time to time I hear°
The sound of horns and motors, which shall bring
Sweeney to Mrs. Porter in the spring.°
O the moon shone bright on Mrs. Porter
200   And on her daughter
They wash their feet in soda water°
Et O ces voix d'enfants, chantant dans la coupole!°

   Twit twit twit
Jug jug jug jug jug jug°
So rudely forc'd.
Tereu°

   Unreal City°
Under the brown fog of a winter noon
Mr. Eugenides, the Smyrna merchant°

But . . . ear parodying "But at my back I always hear / Time's winged chariot hurrying near" (Marvell, "To His Coy Mistress")
fishing The notion of polluted water is even stronger when we come to the figure of the desolate Fisher.
Musing . . . wreck "Cf. *The Tempest* I.ii" (T.S.E.). Ferdinand: "Sitting upon a bank, / Weeping again the king my father's wrack, / This music crept by me upon the waters, / Allaying both their fury and my passion . . . " (I.ii.389–92). Eliot reserves the last regenerative, calming line until 257. Eliot's changes have not been satisfactorily explained, least of all by his note on l. 218.
But . . . hear "Cf. Marvell, 'To His Coy Mistress' " (T.S.E.).
The sound . . . spring "Cf. Day, *Parliament of Bees:* When of the sudden, listening, you shall hear, / A noise of horns and hunting, which shall bring / Actaeon to Diana in the spring, / Where all shall see her naked skin . . . " (T.S.E.). Actaeon surprised Diana bathing, and as a punishment was turned into a stag and killed by his own hounds; usually regarded as an allegory of how men are destroyed by their own intemperate desires. Sweeney is Eliot's natural man, and his leman Mrs. Porter is so named for the sake of the ballad. Again the effect is to take a stately mythical representation of disordered passion

and juxtapose it with a modern banality.
O . . . water "I do not know the origin of the ballad from which these lines are taken: it was reported to me from Sydney, Australia" (T.S.E.). The ballad, usually more obscene, is well known in Australia and was sung by Australian troops in World War I.
Et . . . coupole A line of the sonnet *Parsifal* by Paul Verlaine (1844–96): "And O those children's voices singing in the dome!" Verlaine refers to the choir of children in Wagner's opera near the close, when Parsifal's feet are ceremonially washed before he proceeds to the worship of the Grail.
Jug . . . jug See l. 103; the purity of Parsifal, quester, now juxtaposed with the story of rape and violence.
Tereu O Tereus!, but also the nightingale's song, as in John Lyly (1554–1606), *Alexander and Campaspe:* " 'Tis the ravished nightingale; / Jug, jug, jug, jug, tereu, she cries."
Unreal City Back in the commercial scene, Eliot describes an encounter which, he later revealed, happened to him personally.
Eugenides . . . merchant The name ironically suggests that the merchant comes of good family. Smyrna is in Turkey and a source of currants, which some take to be symbolic of the shriveling up of fruit in the hands of the modern descendants of those early Levantine merchants who spread the Grail cult.

Unshaven, with a pocket full of currants
C.i.f.° London: documents at sight,
Asked me in demotic° French
To luncheon at the Cannon Street Hotel°
Followed by a weekend at the Metropole.°

At the violet hour,° when the eyes and back
Turn upward from the desk, when the human engine waits
Like a taxi throbbing waiting,
I Tiresias,° though blind, throbbing between two lives,
Old man with wrinkled female breasts, can see
At the violet hour, the evening hour that strives
Homeward, and brings the sailor home from sea,°
The typist home at teatime, clears her breakfast, lights
Her stove, and lays out food in tins.
Out of the window perilously spread
Her drying combinations touched by the sun's last rays,
On the divan are piled (at night her bed)
Stockings, slippers, camisoles, and stays.
I Tiresias, old man with wrinkled dugs
Perceived the scene, and foretold the rest—
I too awaited the expected guest.
He, the young man carbuncular, arrives,
A small house agent's clerk, with one bold stare,
One of the low on whom assurance sits
As a silk hat on a Bradford° millionaire.
The time is now propitious, as he guesses,
The meal is ended, she is bored and tired,
Endeavours to engage her in caresses

C.i.f. "The currants were quoted at a price 'cost insurance and freight to London'; and the Bill of Lading, etc., were to be handed to the buyer upon payment of the sight draft" (T.S.E.).
demotic vulgar
Cannon Street Hotel hotel in the City (at which Wagner was banqueted when he came to London with the libretto of *Parsifal*)
Metropole Luxury hotel at Brighton, one hour from London on the south coast; the invitation seems to be sexual.
At . . . hour The hint of sexual temptation in the city will give way to this scene of loveless sex between clerks at the end of the work day.
Tiresias "Tiresias, although a mere spectator and not indeed a 'character,' is yet the most important personage in the poem, uniting all the rest. Just as the one-eyed merchant, seller of currants, melts into the Phoenician Sailor, and the latter is not wholly distinct from Ferdinand Prince of Naples [in *The Tempest*], so all the women are one woman, and the two sexes meet in Tiresias. What Tiresias *sees*, in fact, is the substance of the poem. The whole passage from Ovid is of great anthropological interest. . . ." (T.S.E.) Eliot then quotes in Latin Ovid's account of the sex change of Tiresias: Jupiter tells Juno that he believes women to have more pleasure in sex than men do; she disagrees, and they decide to consult Tiresias, who has been both man and woman. He took Jupiter's view, and Juno, in anger, blinded him. Jupiter, to compensate him, gave him the gift of prophecy. In this note Eliot identifies Tiresias with the Bradleyan finite center of consciousness that is the *persona* of his poems; he is merely saying that Tiresias has a role similar to that of Gerontion. He is *not* saying that we must construct out of the discrete episodes a continuous narrative in which Tiresias, under various disguises, has a central part. In a sense Tiresias is the poem itself, informed of, yet detached from, the life of the sexes as it discovers that life to be, bringing together all the female characters, and all the male, and eventually uniting them in one poem, one center.
sailor . . . sea "This may not appear as exact as Sappho's lines, but I had in mind the 'long-shore' or 'dory' fisherman, who returns home at nightfall" (T.S.E.). Sappho (Greek poetess of the 7th century B.C.), in Fragment 149, prays to the Evening Star, which brings "the sheep, the goat, and the child back to the mother." Eliot is more directly remembering Robert Louis Stevenson's "Requiem": "Home is the sailor, home from sea. . . ."
Bradford Yorkshire wool town with many manufacturers who were said to have made fortunes out of the war.

Which still are unreproved, if undesired.
Flushed and decided, he assaults at once;
240 Exploring hands encounter no defence;
His vanity requires no response,
And makes a welcome of indifference.
(And I Tiresias have foresuffered all
Enacted on this same divan or bed;
I who have sat by Thebes° below the wall
And walked among the lowest of the dead.°)
Bestows one final patronising kiss,
And gropes his way, finding the stairs unlit . . .

She turns and looks a moment in the glass,
250 Hardly aware of her departed lover;
Her brain allows one half-formed thought to pass:
'Well now that's done: and I'm glad it's over.'
When lovely woman stoops to folly° and
Paces about her room again, alone,
She smooths her hair with automatic hand,
And puts a record on the gramophone.

'This music crept by me upon the waters'°
And along the Strand, up Queen Victoria Street.
O City city, I can sometimes hear
260 Beside a public bar in Lower Thames Street,
The pleasant whining of a mandoline
And a clatter and a chatter from within
Where fishmen° lounge at noon: where the walls
Of Magnus Martyr hold
Inexplicable splendour of Ionian white and gold.°

The river sweats°
Oil and tar
The barges drift
With the turning tide

Thebes Tiresias (who has "foresuffered" love-less sex in both ways) is also the blind seer who knows that the curse which makes Thebes a waste land stems from the unwitting incest of Oedipus and his mother Jocasta; in Sophocles (495–406 B.C.), *Oedipus the King.*
walked . . . dead In Homer's *Odyssey* XI Odysseus meets Tiresias in the underworld.
When . . . folly "V. Goldsmith, the song in *The Vicar of Wakefield*" (T.S.E.): "When lovely woman stoops to folly, / And finds too late that men betray, / What charm can soothe her melancholy, / What art can wash her guilt away? / The only art her guilt to cover, / To hide her shame from every eye, / To give repentance to her lover / And wring his bosom—is to die."
This . . . waters "V. *The Tempest,* as above" (T.S.E.); see ll. 48 and 125.
fishmen workers from the nearby Billingsgate fishmarket

Magnus Martyr . . . gold. "The interior of St. Magnus Martyr is to my mind one of the finest among Wren interiors . . . " (T.S.E.).
The river sweats "The Song of the (three) Thames-daughters begins here. From line 292 to 306 they speak in turn. V. *Götterdämmerung* III.i: the Rhine-daughters" (T.S.E.). Wagner's Rhinemaidens in the last opera of *The Ring* flirt with Siegfried but also lament the theft of the gold of the Nibelungs and the destruction of the old world of the gods. Eliot imitates Wagner's verse, and at the end of each section the wordless cries of the Rhinemaidens' refrains. The picture of the Thames may owe something to the beginning of Conrad's *Heart of Darkness,* a work we know Eliot had in mind during the writing of *The Waste Land;* the original epigraph (vetoed by Pound) was Kurtz's exclamation "*The horror! The horror!*"

Red sails
Wide
To leeward, swing on the heavy spar.
The barges wash
Drifting logs
Down Greenwich reach°
Past the Isle of Dogs.°
   Weialala leia
   Wallala leialala

Elizabeth and Leicester°
Beating oars
The stern was formed
A gilded shell
Red and gold
The brisk swell
Rippled both shores
Southwest wind
Carried down stream
The peal of bells
White towers
   Weialala leia
   Wallala leialala

'Trams and dusty trees.°
Highbury bore me. Richmond and Kew
Undid me.° By Richmond I raised my knees
Supine on the floor of a narrow canoe.'

'My feet are at Moorgate,° and my heart
Under my feet. After the event
He wept. He promised "a new start."
I made no comment. What should I resent?'

  'On Margate Sands.°
I can connect
Nothing with nothing.
The broken fingernails of dirty hands.
My people humble people who expect

Greenwich reach the river at Greenwich, east of London
Isle of Dogs riverbank opposite Greenwich
Elizabeth and Leicester "V. Froude, *Elizabeth*, Vol. I, ch. iv, letter of De Quadra to Philip of Spain: 'In the afternoon we were in a barge, watching the games on the river. (The queen) was alone with Lord Robert and myself on the poop, when they began to talk nonsense, and went so far that Lord Robert at last said, as I was on the spot there was no reason why they should not be married if the queen pleased" (T.S.E.) (J. A. Froude, *History of England* Vol. VII, p. 349; Lord Robert Dudley, Earl of Leicester; Elizabeth had a palace at Greenwich). Elizabeth's failure to marry Leicester, or anybody, meant that she was a sterile queen.
Trams . . . trees back to the modern river and the lament of the Thames-daughters
Highbury . . . me "Cf. *Purgatorio* V.133: *Ricorditi di mi, che son la Pia; / Siena mi fe', disfecemi Maremma*" (T.S.E.): "Remember me, who am La Pia; Siena made me, Maremma unmade me." La Pia, the lady of Siena, was murdered by her husband at Maremma. Highbury is an inner suburb of North London; Richmond and Kew are on the river to the west, popular boating places.
Moorgate City area of East London
Margate seaside resort near London

Nothing.'
la la

To Carthage then I came°

Burning burning burning burning°
O Lord Thou pluckest me out°
310   O Lord Thou pluckest

burning

iv. *Death by Water*°

Phlebas the Phoenician, a fortnight dead,
Forgot the cry of gulls, and the deep sea swell
And the profit and loss.
                    A current under sea
Picked his bones in whispers. As he rose and fell
He passed the stages of his age and youth°
Entering the whirlpool.
                    Gentile or Jew
320   O you who turn the wheel and look to windward,
Consider Phlebas, who was once handsome and tall as you.

v. *What the Thunder Said*°

After the torchlight red on sweaty faces
After the frosty silence in the gardens
After the agony in stony places
The shouting and the crying
Prison and palace and reverberation

To . . . came "V. St. Augustine's *Confessions:* "to Carthage then I came, where a cauldron of unholy loves sang all about mine ears" (T.S.E.); *Confessions* III.1, on the temptations of sense that assailed the young Augustine.
Burning . . . burning Eliot refers to "the Buddha's Fire Sermon (which corresponds in importance to the Sermon on the Mount)." The Buddha condemns all the senses, which, he maintains, introduce the soul to a world of fire and prevent its becoming free of desire.
O Lord . . . out "From St. Augustine's *Confessions* again. The collocation of these two representatives of eastern and western asceticism, as the culmination of his part of the poem, is not an accident" (T.S.E.): "I entangle my steps with these outward beauties, but thou pluckest me out, O Lord, thou pluckest me out!" (*Confessions* X.34). The asceticism here celebrated is related to that required of the quester Parsifal; the poem intends it to be an abstention from the desolating indulgences of the world in general, though in the context it is easy to see it as a specific sexual disgust.
Death by Water See l. 55. These lines are adapted from the last seven of Eliot's poem in French, *Dans le Restaurant* (1916–17), here translated: "Phlebas the Phoenician, two weeks drowned, forgot the cries of gulls and the swell of Cornish seas, and the profit and the loss, and the cargo of tin: an undersea current carried him very far, taking him back through

the stages of his former life. Think of it, it was a hard fate; he was after all once handsome and tall." The main part of the poem is about an old waiter who remembers a moment of power and delight with a young girl when he was a child, a moment that ended when he ran away, in fear of a dog. He is now a dirty, frustrated old man. The Phlebas lines follow. Pound was insistent on the retention of these lines in *The Waste Land*. Their connection with the poem is obscure, though the sailor is related to Mr. Eugenides and death by water is a recurring theme, related to the *Tempest* quotations. The manuscript includes a long nautical poem of which these remaining lines form the brief conclusion.
He . . . youth This is what Yeats calls the "dreaming-back" that follows death, a return to the source.
What the Thunder Said "In the first part of Part V three themes are employed: the journey to Emmaus, the approach to the Chapel Perilous (see Miss Weston's book) and the present decay of Eastern Europe" (T.S.E.). For the Emmaus journey see Luke 24:13–31, in which the resurrected Jesus joins two disciples on the road to Emmaus and they do not recognize him; the Chapel Perilous is the critical final stage of the Grail quest; by "the present decay" Eliot means the chaos of Eastern Europe after World War I, and the success of the Bolsheviks.

Of thunder of spring over distant mountains
He who was living is now dead°
We who were living are now dying
With a little patience

    Here is no water but only rock
Rock and no water and the sandy road
The road winding above among the mountains
Which are mountains of rock without water
If there were water we should stop and drink
Amongst the rock one cannot stop or think
Sweat is dry and feet are in the sand
If there were only water amongst the rock
Dead mountain mouth of carious teeth that cannot spit
Here one can neither stand nor lie nor sit
There is not even silence in the mountains
But dry sterile thunder without rain
There is not even solitude in the mountains
But red sullen faces sneer and snarl
From doors of mudcracked houses
                    If there were water

  And no rock
  If there were rock
  And also water
  And water
  A spring
  A pool among the rock
  If there were the sound of water only
  Not the cicada°
  And dry grass singing
  But sound of water over a rock
  Where the hermit-thrush° sings in the pine trees
  Drip drop drip drop drop drop drop
  But there is no water

  Who is the third who walks always beside you?°
When I count, there are only you and I together
But when I look ahead up the white road
There is always another one walking beside you
Gliding wrapt in a brown mantle, hooded
I do not know whether a man or a woman
—But who is that on the other side you?
  What is that sound high in the air

After . . . dead (ll. 322–28) events from the betrayal of Christ to his death, the Passion story
cicada Ecclesiastes 12:5
hermit-thrush Eliot has a note on this North American bird, which ends: "Its 'water-dripping song' is justly celebrated."
the third . . . you Eliot explains that the in-spiration of these lines (360–66) was the account by Sir Ernest Shackleton, the Antarctic explorer, of a delusion suffered by exhausted men "that there was *one more member* than could actually be counted", here related to the experience of the disciples.

Murmur of maternal lamentation
Who are those hooded hordes swarming
370   Over endless plains, stumbling in cracked earth
Ringed by the flat horizon only
What is the city over the mountains
Cracks and reforms and bursts in the violet air
Falling towers
Jerusalem Athens Alexandria
Vienna London
Unreal°

A woman° drew her long black hair out tight
And fiddled whisper music on those strings
380   And bats with baby faces in the violet light
Whistled, and beat their wings
And crawled head downward down a blackened wall
And upside down in air were towers
Tolling reminiscent bells, that kept the hours
And voices singing out of empty cisterns° and exhausted wells.

In this decayed hole among the mountains
In the faint moonlight, the grass is singing
Over the tumbled graves, about the chapel
There is the empty chapel, only the wind's home.°
390   It has no windows, and the door swings,
Dry bones can harm no one.
Only a cock stood on the rooftree
Co co rico co co rico°
In a flash of lightning. Then a damp gust
Bringing rain

Ganga° was sunken, and the limp leaves
Waited for rain, while the black clouds
Gathered far distant, over Himavant.°
The jungle crouched, humped in silence.
400   Then spoke the thunder

What . . . Unreal (ll. 367–77) Eliot quotes Hermann Hesse's *Glimpse into Chaos* (1920): "Already half of Europe, already at least half of Eastern Europe, on the way to chaos, drives drunkenly in spiritual frenzy along the edge of the abyss, sings drunkenly, as though singing hymns, as Dmitri Karamazov sang. The offended bourgeois laughs at the songs; the saint and the seer hear them with tears." The reference is to Dostoevsky's *The Brothers Karamazov* (1880). The apocalyptic quality of the lines, reinforced by the repetition "Unreal" which suggests the contrast between the earthly and the heavenly city, recalls the scenes of destruction at the end of Wagner's *Götterdämmerung*.
A woman This phantasmagorical interlude (ll. 378–85) owing something to Surrealism and to the painter Hieronymous Bosch (b. 1450) con-

tinues the note of apocalyptic fantasy and horror, and looks forward to the terrifying illusions of Chapel Perilous.
And . . . cisterns In Richard Strauss's opera *Salome* John the Baptist sings out of the empty cistern in which he is imprisoned.
empty . . . home *Empty* echoes l. 385; the quester will have to give the right answers under inauspicious conditions, as St. John did. The Chapel Perilous, in medieval romance, was surrounded by deterrent horrors.
cock . . . rico The cock is a symbol of Christ and, as *Hamlet* I.i., heralds the return of light and the departure of ghosts, and evil spirits; here it announces a rainstorm, but in the next section the rain has not materialized.
Ganga Ganges, the sacred river of India
Himavant holy mountain in the Himalayas

Da
Datta:° what have we given?
My friend, blood shaking my heart
The awful daring of a moment's surrender
Which an age of prudence can never retract°
By this, and this only, we have existed
Which is not to be found in our obituaries
Or in memories draped by the beneficent spider°
Or under seals broken by the lean solicitor
In our empty rooms
Da
Dayadhvam: I have heard the key°
Turn in the door once and turn once only
We think of the key, each in his prison
Thinking of the key, each confirms a prison
Only at nightfall, aethereal rumours
Revive for a moment a broken Coriolanus°
Da
Damyata: The boat responded
Gaily, to the hand expert with sail and oar
The sea was calm, your heart would have responded
Gaily, when invited, beating obedient
To controlling hands°

I sat upon the shore
Fishing,° with the arid plain behind me
Shall I at least set my lands in order?°
London Bridge is falling down falling down falling down°

Datta "Datta, dayadhvam, damyata (Give, sympathize, control). The fable of the meaning of the Thunder is found in the *Brihadaranyaka-Upanishad* 5.1" (T.S.E.). In that fable gods, demons, and men ask the Creator to speak to them; he replies DA, and each group interprets the answer differently, using the three words employed by Eliot. *Datta* means "give" in Sanskrit, which Eliot had studied at Harvard.
The awful . . . retract presumably a sexual surrender, not the kind of giving proposed by the Thunder
spider "Cf. Webster, *The White Devil* V.vi: ". . . they'll remarry / Ere the worm pierce your winding-sheet, ere the spider / Make a thin curtain for your epitaphs" (T.S.E.). They are women.
the key "Cf. *Inferno* XXXIII.46: *ed io sentii chiavar l'uscio di sotto / all'orribile torre*" (T.S.E.): "and from below I heard the door of the horrible tower being locked." The words of Ugolino, who devoured his children when starving in captivity; the key of the tower was thrown into the river. Eliot adds in his note to this image of suffering isolation a quotation from F. H. Bradley's *Appearance and Reality* (1893), p. 346: "My external sensations are no less private to myself than are my thoughts

and feelings. In either case my experience falls within my own circle, a circle closed on the outside; and, with all its elements alike, every sphere is opaque to the others which surround it. . . . In brief, regarded as an existence which appears in the soul, the whole world for each is peculiar and private to that soul." This is an important testimony to what Eliot is doing in such poems as "Gerontion" and *The Waste Land*.
Coriolanus broken and exiled through his own pride; reviving only momentarily, as when Coriolanus is revived by the chance of fighting against Rome
controlling hands The picture provided for *control* is first a well-managed sailing boat, secondly, some moment when control could have assured a personal relation, now lost.
Fishing "V. Weston: *From Ritual to Romance;* chapter on the Fisher King" (T.S.E.). The land is still "arid."
set . . . order Isaiah to Hezekiah, the sick king whose lands lie waste: "Thus saith the Lord, Set thine house in order: for thou shalt die and not live" (Isaiah 38:1). The Fisher King contemplates death; no successful quest is recorded in the poem.
London . . . down an English nursery rhyme

Poi s'ascose nel foco che gli affina°
Quando fiam uti chelidon°—O swallow swallow
430   *Le Prince d'Aquitaine à la tour abolie*°
These fragments I have shored against my ruins°
Why then Ile fit you. Hieronymo's mad againe.°
Datta. Dayadhvam. Damyata.
Shantih shantih shantih°
1921   1922

The Hollow Men

Eliot said in an interview that "The Hollow Men" "originated out of separate poems.
. . . That's one way in which my mind does seem to have evolved through the years
poetically—doing things separately and then seeing the possibility of focusing them
together, altering them, making a kind of whole of them." The first four sections
had all appeared separately before the publication of the whole, in 1925. Some of
the material was originally in *The Waste Land*. The Hollow Men are like the city
crowds of *The Waste Land*, the damned who are so because of a lack of spiritual
reality, even their sins lacking violence and conviction. The first references are, then,
Dantean. There is a contrast with the blessed; their "direct eyes" are avoided in II,
where the hollowness of the Hollow Men begets scarecrow imagery. The landscape is
a stony desert of privation; despair and a consciousness of the necessary imperfection
of a life which resembles that of the faint-hearted damned are the other themes
developed. For the title see *Julius Caesar* IV.ii.23, where the word means "insincere";
Conrad uses "hollow" several times in *Heart of Darkness*.

Poi . . . affina "V. *Purgatorio* XXVI.148: 'Ara *vos prec, per aquella valor / que vos guida al som de l'escalina, / sovegna vos a temps de ma dolor.' / Poi s'ascose nel foco che gli affina*" (T.S.E.): " 'Now I pray you, by that virtue which leads you to the top of the stair, think of me in my time of pain.' Then he hid himself in the fire that refines them." The speaker in purgatory is the Provençal poet Arnaut Daniel, speaking his own language. The passage was especially dear to Eliot, who comments on it in his remarkable essay *"Dante"* / (*Selected Essays*, 1932, pp. 199–237), that the suffering of purgatory is embraced voluntarily, and is so distinguished from that of hell, where it is of "the very nature of the damned themselves, expresses their essence"; this reflects Eliot's views in the Baudelaire essay, and the stress in *The Waste Land* on the difference between sin actively and boldly committed and the anomie of the modern scene.
Quando . . . chelidon "V. *Pervigilium Veneris*. Cf. Philomela in Parts II and III" (T.S.E.): "When shall I be like the swallow?"—from *The Vigil of Venus*, an anonymous late Latin poem about Venus and the spring. The other references are to Philomel's sister Procne, wife of Tereus, who became a swallow.
Le Prince . . . abolie "The Prince of Aquitaine in the ruined tower"—from Gérard de Nerval's sonnet "El Deschidado" (The Disinherited). Nerval (1808–55) refers to himself as the dis-inherited prince; the troubadour poets were associated with the castles of Aquitaine in southern France. A Tarot card shows a tower struck by lightning.
These . . . ruins meaning these disjointed but obliquely relevant scraps which render the situation of the unrelieved Fisher King and support him in his isolation and loneliness
Why . . . againe "V. Kyd's *Spanish Tragedy*" (T.S.E.). In this play of Thomas Kyd (1557?–95), which is subtitled *Hieronymo's Mad Again*, Hieronymo, seeking revenge for the murder of his son, takes the opportunity offered by an invitation to stage a court entertainment, saying, "Why then, I'll fit you," meaning both "I'll give you what you want" and "I'll give you your due"; he contrives the murder of the guilty in a play made up of bits in various languages.
Shantih . . . shantih "Repeated as here, a formal ending to an Upanishad. 'The Peace which passeth understanding' is our equivalent to this word" (T.S.E.). The Upanishads are poetic dialogues commenting on the Hindu scriptures or Vedas.

The Hollow Men

Mistah Kurtz—he dead.°
A penny for the Old Guy°

I

We are the hollow men
We are the stuffed men
Leaning together
Headpiece filled with straw. Alas!
Our dried voices, when
We whisper together
Are quiet and meaningless
As wind in dry grass
Or rats' feet over broken glass
In our dry cellar°

Shape without form, shade without colour,
Paralysed force, gesture without motion;°

Those who have crossed
With direct eyes, to death's other Kingdom°
Remember us—if at all—not as lost
Violent souls, but only
As the hollow men
The stuffed men.

II

Eyes I dare not meet in dreams
In death's dream kingdom
These do not appear:
There, the eyes are
Sunlight on a broken column
There, is a tree swinging
And voices are
In the wind's singing
More distant and more solemn
Than a fading star.

Mistah . . . dead the boy's announcement of Kurtz's death in *Heart of Darkness*. The whole passage, from Marlow's visit to Kurtz, to the paragraph about Marlow's own contest with death, is relevant to "The Hollow Men"; indeed, the whole work is.
A penny . . . Guy Every year on November 5, English children burn a scarecrow effigy of the traitor Guy Fawkes, who tried to blow up the Parliament buildings in 1605; on preceding days they carry their "guys" around begging pennies for fireworks.
rats' . . . cellar See *The Waste Land*, ll. 115, 195.
Shape . . . motion These distinctions between near-synonyms (shape-form, shade-colour) and near oxymorons (paralysed force, gesture without motion) constitute a theme to be developed differently in the final section. See Conrad's "A vision of grayness without form" (*Heart of Darkness*).
death's . . . Kingdom The habitation of the hollow men is one, the other is a heaven for those who have passed into a condition in which eyes look directly, and beyond the acquaintance of lost souls—lost not for their strong sinning but for spiritual incapacity. At the end of the *Purgatorio* and in *Paradiso* IV Dante cannot meet the gaze of Beatrice (see Eliot's essay "Dante").

Let me be no nearer°
30   In death's dream kingdom
Let me also wear
Such deliberate disguises
Rat's coat, crowskin, crossed staves
In a field°
Behaving as the wind behaves
No nearer—

Not that final meeting
In the twilight kingdom°

III
This is the dead land
40   This is the cactus land
Here the stone images°
Are raised, here they receive
The supplication of a dead man's hand
Under the twinkle of a fading star.
Is it like this
In death's other kingdom
Waking alone
At the hour when we are
Trembling with tenderness°
50   Lips that would kiss
Form prayers to broken stone.

IV
The eyes are not here
There are no eyes here
In this valley of dying stars
In this hollow valley
This broken jaw of our lost kingdoms

In this last of meeting places
We grope together
And avoid speech
60   Gathered on this beach of the tumid river°

Sightless, unless
The eyes reappear
As the perpetual star

Let . . . nearer He wants to have only a distant view of such eyes, and himself to remain without decision or volition, like a scarecrow.
Rat's . . . field a typical English scarecrow, with dead birds and animals attached to it
final . . . kingdom Referring perhaps to the meeting of Dante with Beatrice after he has crossed the Lethe; he is reminded of his sin and disloyalty, but without the confrontation cannot go on to Paradise (*Purgatorio* XXX).
stone images See *The Waste Land*, l. 22.
Waking . . . tenderness In this condition the true recognition of love (as in *The Waste Land*, ll. 39 ff. and 418 ff.) is frustrated.
Gathered . . . river Dante's Acheron, encircling hell, and Conrad's Congo; they are in the "heart of darkness" unless they cross.

Multifoliate rose°
Of death's twilight kingdom
The hope only
Of empty men.

V

Here we go round the prickly pear
Prickly pear prickly pear
Here we go round the prickly pear
At five o'clock in the morning.°

Between the idea
And the reality°
Between the motion
And the act
Falls the Shadow°
                For Thine is the Kingdom°

Between the conception
And the creation
Between the emotion
And the response
Falls the Shadow
                Life is very long

Between the desire
And the spasm
Between the potency
And the existence°
Between the essence
And the descent°
Falls the Shadow
                For Thine is the Kingdom

For Thine is
Life is
For Thine is the

Multifoliate rose Dante's image of heaven (*Paradiso* XXXII)
Here . . . morning parodying the children's rhyme "Here we go round the mulberry bush on a cold frosty morning"
Between . . . reality See ll. 11–12n; developed from *Julius Caesar* II.i.63 ff.: "Between the acting of a dreadful thing / And the first motion, all the interim is / Like a phantasma or a hideous dream."
Falls the Shadow Eliot agreed that this expression probably came to him from Dowson's *Non sum qualis eram . . .* : "There fell thy shadow . . .". The Shadow divides concepts increasingly difficult to divide as the section continues.

For . . . Kingdom from the Lord's Prayer, but echoing the other uses of the word *kingdom* earlier
potency . . . existence ultimately Aristotelian philosophical terms, e.g. matter has only potency till form gives it existence (the actual possession of being)
essence . . . descent Unlike the former example, this is a false pair, brought together by serious punning. *Essence* is that which constitutes the being of a thing, that by which it is what it is; it is converted by assonance into *ascent* for the purposes of the poem. *Descent* accordingly has overtones of loss of being.

This is the way the world ends°
This is the way the world ends
This is the way the world ends
Not with a bang but a whimper.°

1924–25   1925

Little Gidding

Eliot's most notable work after "The Hollow Men" was *Ash Wednesday,* a sequence of allusive religious meditations assembled, as usual, piecemeal, and published in 1930. In 1934, he wrote choruses for *The Rock,* a church pageant; and this led to the commissioning of *Murder in the Cathedral* (1935), a verse play, for Canterbury Cathedral. He has attributed to the exercise afforded by *The Rock* the revival of his "numbed powers": he was now able to proceed to "the second half of his creative life" (H. Howarth, *Notes on Some Figures Behind T. S. Eliot,* 1965). Out of some lines left over from *Murder in the Cathedral* he developed the long sequence, meditating on time and eternity, called "Burnt Norton" (1935). This work stood alone until 1940, when an obviously parallel poem, "East Coker," appeared. In the meantime Eliot had written a second play, the highly wrought *Family Reunion* (1939), which shows some of the same preoccupations. While writing "East Coker" he conceived the notion of a set of four related works, and added "The Dry Salvages" (1941) and "Little Gidding" (1941). The *Four Quartets* were first published together in 1943.

Each of the poems is named for a place of special significance to the author; they are parallel in structure; and there is a great deal of cross reference. Eliot wrote the first two in the London borough of Kensington and first wanted to call the work *Kensington Quartets.* Mrs. Eliot says that the "place of disaffection" in "Burnt Norton" is the Gloucester Road Underground station in Kensington, and the pavement they "trod . . . in a dead patrol" in "Little Gidding" is Cromwell Road, a main artery of the borough.

Eliot dropped this idea but kept to his original intention of giving the work a musical title. He rejected "sonata" and, while admitting that there were "general objections to these musical analogies," chose *Quartets.* "I should like to indicate that these poems are all in a particular set from which I have elaborated, and the word 'quartet' does seem to me to start people on the right tack for understanding them. . . . It suggests to me the notion of making a poem by weaving in together three or four superficially unrelated themes: the 'poem' being the degree of success in making a new whole out of them" (letter to John Hayward, September 3, 1942, quoted by Valerie Eliot in a letter to the (London) *Times Literary Supplement,* July 16, 1971). Eliot also had in mind the late quartets of Beethoven (Opp. 127, 130–32, 135), with their strange transitions, intermingling of conventional and original forms, internal references and unpredicted sonorities.

This . . . ends partly from the same children's game and rhyme as ll. 68–71: "This is the way we clap our hands . . . "; mixed with the end of the *Gloria,* "as it was in the beginning, is now and ever shall be, world without end, Amen"
whimper Eliot, in his *Choice of Kipling's Verse,* commended Kipling's choice of this word in "Danny Deever" as "exactly right": Deever is executed for killing a comrade and this dialogue occurs: " 'What's that that whimpers over'ead?' said Files-on-Parade, / 'It's Danny's soul that's passin' now,' the Colour-Sergeant said."

In his lecture "The Music of Poetry" (1942, see *On Poetry and Poets*, 1957), in which he must have had his recent poems in mind, he asserts that music in poetry is not a matter of "beautiful words" but of the whole structure and does not preclude the prosaic: in fact "no poet can write a poem of amplitude unless he is a master of the prosaic." Speaking of structural music, he says that it will depend on interlinked allusions, recurrent themes. The poet should not work "too closely to musical analogies"; yet "there are possibilities for verse which bear some analogy to the development of a theme by different groups of instruments; there are possibilities of transitions in a poem comparable to the different movements of a symphony or a quartet; there are possibilities of contrapuntal arrangement of subject matter. It is in the concert room, rather than in the opera house, that the germ of a poem may be quickened." This is farewell to Wagner, welcome to Beethoven.

The four poems have strong structural similarities. The first movements are divided into three parts, like sonata form in the opening movements of classical music. The second movement varies from lyric stanzas to a "prosaic" section ("Little Gidding" is a slight exception); the third is a discursive exploration of stated themes; the fourth is lyrical and usually in stanzas, and its themes are usually explicitly Christian; the fifth (itself anomalous in the classical quartet except for Beethoven) is in two sections and recapitulates the whole.

The four poems share preoccupations most clearly enunciated in the first, and "Little Gidding," coming last, is full of references to the earlier poems. Since we have but one of the four we can do little to indicate these references. All that needs to be said on this score is that the poems are all concerned with time and eternity, history and the present, the intervention of the divine in human life. They are thus philosophical poems, and their philosophy is Christian; Eliot's acceptance into the church, predictable enough on the evidence of his early work, had happened years before. Yet the poems are *not* doctrinal and do not depend upon religious or intellectual assent from the reader. The "set" from which Eliot says they are elaborated is not the Thirty-nine Articles of his church. Its images are sometimes those private ones, inexplicably meaningful, mentioned in the notes to "The Journey of the Magi"; others—the garden, the wounded god, the sea and death by water, the chapel and the refining fire—are familiar to readers of *The Waste Land*. The *Quartets* comprise a complex poem of great transparency, virtuosity, and originality; and quite obviously they are colored by the mind of a poet, not a philosopher or theologian.

Each of the four poems has its own season and its own element; "Little Gidding" is winter and fire. Its title is the name of a village in Huntingtonshire, off the Great North Road out of London, where, in 1625, Nicholas Ferrar established the Anglican community described by Izaak Walton in his *Life of Herbert* (the description is reprinted in the Renaissance section of this anthology). The community had one, perhaps two, visits from King Charles I; it was eventually broken up by Parliamentary troops. Eliot visited it in 1936. It had not for him the personal associations of East Coker, the Somerset village from which his ancestors had set out for New England, nor of the Dry Salvages—rocks off the coast of Cape Ann, Massachusetts—where he spent boyhood summers; but its attractions, as the site of a rare experiment in Anglican piety in the days of the seventeenth-century Anglican preachers and poets he venerated, and as a spot associated with the Royal Martyr, were great. The blend of monasticism and family life, ruined by that Civil War to which Eliot in a sense attributed the "dissociation of sensibility" (see "Milton" in *On Poetry and Poets*, and

"The Metaphysical Poets," below) gave him a locus for his meditation on conflicts resolved by divine intervention.

Eliot wrote "Little Gidding" in the darkest time of the war for the British; and just as in the other poems he suggests his London, its crowds and "tubes" (subways), here he incorporates into the texture of the poem the heavy night bombing and fire raids of the winter of 1940–41. "Little Gidding" is a poem of fire, and not only Pentecostal fire but also the conflagration of cities, of St. Paul's ringed by flame as it was in December 1940 (see Fig. 29). One of the epigraphs to "Burnt Norton" is a fragment of Heraclitus: "The way up and the way down are one and the same." One is "redeemed from fire by fire." The image of a purgatorial London, set against both history and the timeless that intersects history and the present moment, is essential to the feeling of the poem.

From The Four Quartets

Little Gidding

I°

Midwinter spring is its own season
Sempiternal though sodden towards sundown,
Suspended in time, between pole and tropic.
When the short day is brightest, with frost and fire,
The brief sun flames the ice, on pond and ditches,
In windless cold that is the heart's heat,
Reflecting in a watery mirror
A glare that is blindness in the early afternoon.
And glow more intense than blaze of branch, or brazier,
10 Stirs the dumb spirit: no wind, but pentecostal fire°
In the dark time of the year. Between melting and freezing
The soul's sap quivers.° There is no earth smell
Or smell of living thing. This is the spring time
But not in time's covenant.° Now the hedgerow
Is blanched for an hour with transitory blossom
Of snow, a bloom more sudden
Than that of summer, neither budding nor fading,
Not in the scheme of generation.°

I The opening movement begins with an evocation of season and place. The season is the illusory spring of midwinter, sun reflected in ice, a moment of reconciled opposites, *sempiternal*— having some characteristics of the intemporal or eternal—and holding together as in an image heat and cold, pole and tropic, ice and fire, winter and summer.
pentecostal fire At Pentecost, commemorated on the seventh Sunday after Easter, the Holy Ghost descended on the apostles: "And there appeared unto them cloven tongues like as of fire" (Acts 2:3). The symbol for this is the Dove. These figures, here introduced, become very important in the poem.
soul's sap quivers caught in this uncanonical season between the seasons of the sap's rise and fall
There is . . . covenant (ll. 12–14) The absence of these smells establishes a difference from normal spring, the one "in time's covenant."
Not . . . generation (ll. 15–19) The blossoms of this spring are not those of the season which plays a part in the generative cycle.

Where is the summer, the unimaginable
Zero summer?°

          If you came this way,
Taking the route you would be likely to take
From the place you would be likely to come from,
If you came this way in may time,° you would find the hedges
White again, in May, with voluptuary sweetness.
It would be the same at the end of the journey,
If you came at night like a broken king,°
If you came by day not knowing what you came for,
It would be the same, when you leave the rough road
And turn behind the pig-sty to the dull façade
And the tombstone. And what you thought you came for
Is only a shell, a husk of meaning
From which the purpose breaks only when it is fulfilled
If at all. Either you had no purpose
Or the purpose is beyond the end you figured
And is altered in fulfilment. There are other places
Which also are the world's end,° some at the sea jaws,
Or over a dark lake, in a desert or a city—
But this is the nearest, in place and time,
Now and in England.

          If you came this way,
Taking any route, starting from anywhere,
At any time or at any season,
It would always be the same: you would have to put off
Sense and notion.° You are not here to verify,
Instruct yourself, or inform curiosity
Or carry report. You are here to kneel
Where prayer has been valid. And prayer is more
Than an order of words, the conscious occupation
Of the praying mind, or the sound of the voice praying.
And what the dead had no speech for, when living,
They can tell you, being dead: the communication
Of the dead is tongued with fire° beyond the language of the living.
Here, the intersection of the timeless moment°
Is England and nowhere. Never and always.

Zero summer A summer complementary to this
winter would have to appear cold as this appears
warm; but this is unimaginable. The uniqueness
of this moment is reinforced.
may time the time when the hawthorn blossoms
broken king Charles 1 is said to have visited
Little Gidding after his defeat at the Battle of
Naseby (1645).
the world's end This is not the only spot where
one can meet one's transfigured purpose, one's
true meaning realized only in this end, as the
result of a prayer.

Sense and notion modifying the more usual
"sense and motion"—the use of the senses
for trivial purposes, commonplace notional ideas
tongued with fire The Holy Ghost gave the
apostles the gift of tongues (Acts 2:4); by
the same gift the dead can now communicate
with the living.
intersection . . . moment As the midwinter
spring is a timeless moment, so is the place;
eternity crosses time, space and time are both
present and not present.

II°

Ash on an old man's sleeve
Is all the ash the burnt roses leave.
Dust in the air suspended
Marks the place where a story ended.
60   Dust inbreathed was a house—
The wall, the wainscot and the mouse.
The death of hope and despair,
     This is the death of air.

There are flood and drouth
Over the eyes and in the mouth,
Dead water and dead sand
Contending for the upper hand.
The parched eviscerate soil
Gapes at the vanity of toil,
70   Laughs without mirth.
     This is the death of earth.

Water and fire succeed
The town, the pasture and the weed.
Water and fire deride
The sacrifice that we denied.
Water and fire shall rot
The marred foundations we forgot,
Of sanctuary and choir.
     This is the death of water and fire.

80   In the uncertain hour before the morning
     Near the ending of interminable night
     At the recurrent end of the unending°
After the dark dove with the flickering tongue
     Had passed below the horizon of his homing°
     While the dead leaves still rattled on like tin
Over the asphalt where no other sound was
     Between three districts whence the smoke arose
     I met one walking, loitering and hurried
As if blown towards me like the metal leaves
90   Before the urban dawn wind unresisting.
     And as I fixed upon the down-turned face
That pointed scrutiny with which we challenge

II A lyric recapitulation of the elements, with reminiscences of the three other poems associated with them, opens the movement. The third stanza refers to the damage by fire and water in London, as well as to the desecration of Little Gidding; in the bombing of the City many churches were damaged or destroyed. This is the link with the second section, a totally original imitation, without rhyme, of Dante's *terza rima*—"the nearest equivalent to a canto of the *Inferno* or *Purgatorio*" Eliot could achieve, and "a parallel . . . between the *Inferno* and the *Purgatorio* . . . and a hallucinated scene after an air-raid" (*To Criticize the Critic*, 1965). Eliot transfers the conditions of hell and purgatory, as Dante treats them, to the streets of London in the early morning after a raid has ended.

recurrent . . . unending The short daylight of winter days provided only brief respite between night raids that began with the onset of dark.
dark dove . . . homing The *dark* dove is the German warplanes, of which exhaust flames might be visible, returning to base.

The first-met stranger in the waning dusk
    I caught the sudden look of some dead master
Whom I had known, forgotten, half recalled
    Both one and many; in the brown baked features
    The eyes of a familiar compound ghost°
Both intimate and unidentifiable.
    So I assumed a double part, and cried
    And heard another's voice cry: 'What! are *you* here?'
Although we were not. I was still the same,
    Knowing myself yet being someone other—
    And he a face still forming; yet the words sufficed
To compel the recognition they preceded.
    And so, compliant to the common wind,
    Too strange to each other for misunderstanding,
In concord at this intersection time°
Of meeting nowhere, no before and after,
    We trod the pavement in a dead patrol.
I said: 'The wonder that I feel is easy,
    Yet ease is cause of wonder. Therefore speak:
    I may not comprehend, may not remember.'
And he: 'I am not eager to rehearse
    My thought and theory which you have forgotten.
    These things have served their purpose: let them be.
So with your own, and pray they be forgiven
    By others, as I pray you to forgive
    Both bad and good. Last season's fruit is eaten
And the fullfed beast shall kick the empty pail.
    For last year's words belong to last year's language°
    And next year's words await another voice.
But, as the passage now presents no hindrance
    To the spirit unappeased and peregrine
    Between two worlds become much like each other,
So I find words I never thought to speak
    In streets I never thought I should revisit
    When I left my body on a distant shore.°
Since our concern was speech, and speech impelled us
    To purify the dialect of the tribe°

---

familiar compound ghost recalling Shakespeare, Sonnet LXXXVI: "affable familiar ghost." Eliot said that a major element in the compound "master" was Yeats, who died in France in 1939 and whose body could not be brought back to Ireland till after the war; but in the nature of the passage there are other masters present also, including perhaps Dante himself and Arnaut Daniel, recalled in l. 147 by an allusion to the passage in the *Purgatorio* Eliot used in *The Waste Land*, l. 427. The ghost is finally a double of the speaker himself. The root is in Dante's encounter (*Inferno* XV) with his damned teacher Brunetto Latini, who provides the facial type.

intersection time neither night nor morning, a moment when place and time are abolished by the simultaneity of past and present
last year's language An important preoccupation of the *Quartets* is the difficulty of finding language, or cleansing it to make it adequate to its task.
left . . . shore Palinurus, the helmsman who fell overboard, tells Aeneas in the underworld that his body was buried on a foreign shore (*Aeneid* VI.325 ff.).
To purify . . . tribe *Donner un sens plus pur aux mots de la tribu*, Mallarmé, "Le Tombeau d'Edgar Poe" (Poe's Tomb).

130   And urge the mind to aftersight and foresight,°
       Let me disclose the gifts reserved for age
       To set a crown upon your lifetime's effort.
       First, the cold friction of expiring sense
       Without enchantment, offering no promise
       But bitter tastelessness of shadow fruit°
       As body and soul begin to fall asunder.
       Second, the conscious impotence of rage
       At human folly, and the laceration°
       Of laughter at what ceases to amuse.
140   And last, the rending pain of re-enactment
       Of all that you have done, and been;° the shame
       Of motives late revealed, and the awareness
       Of things ill done and done to others' harm
       Which once you took for exercise of virtue.°
       Then fools' approval stings, and honour stains.°
       From wrong to wrong the exasperated spirit
       Proceeds, unless restored by that refining fire°
       Where you must move in measure, like a dancer.'°
       The day was breaking. In the disfigured street
150   He left me, with a kind of valediction,
       And faded on the blowing of the horn.°

                    III°
       There are three conditions which often look alike
       Yet differ completely, flourish in the same hedgerow:
       Attachment to self and to things and to persons, detachment
       From self and from things and from persons; and, growing between
           them, indifference
       Which resembles the others as death resembles life,
       Being between two lives—unflowering, between

aftersight and foresight "He that made us with such large discourse / Stretching before and after, gave us not / That capability and god-like reason / To rust in us unused" (*Hamlet* IV.iv. 36–39).
bitter . . . fruit See the Sodom apples in Milton, *Paradise Lost* X.565–66.
laceration remembering Swift's epitaph in St. Patrick's Cathedral (Dublin), *Ubi saeva indignatio ulterius cor lacerare nequit,* of which Eliot knew Yeats's translation: "Savage indignation there / Cannot lacerate his breast" ("Swift's Epitaph," *Collected Poems,* 1951)
re-enactment . . . been See Yeat's "Dialogue of Self and Soul."
shame . . . virtue See Yeats's, "Vacillation" V and the opening of "The Man and the Echo."
Then . . . stains See Samuel Johnson, *The Vanity of Human Wishes,* l. 117: "Grief aids disease, remembered folly stings."
refining fire See *The Waste Land,* l. 427n.
like a dancer remembering Yeats's "Byzantium," stanza 4
faded . . . horn "It faded on the crowing of the cock"—the departure of the Ghost in

Hamlet I.i.157; the "horn" is the air-raid siren sounding the all-clear. This episode has occurred in the interval between the end of the raid and the blowing of the siren. Eliot, who served as a civilian firewatcher, must often have experienced such moments.
III Opens with a discursive but difficult passage. As usual the "trimmers" are condemned; attachment to the world may lead to something better, in a larger pattern of eternal detachment. The intermediate condition, neither attachment nor detachment, is deadly. The second strophe quotes from the *Shewings* of Dame Julian of Norwich, one of the 14th-century English mystics, who heard a divine voice telling her that sin is necessary but that all shall be well; the "happy sin" of Adam was the cause of the Incarnation that saved us; attachment is a stage on the way to detachment. He thinks of the people at Little Gidding, and of those on the other side of the political and religious dispute. In honoring them we do not neglect men who are now dying in war; they are that attachment which, by the action of Christ, produces detachment.

The live and the dead nettle. This is the use of memory:
For liberation—not less of love but expanding
Of love beyond desire, and so liberation
From the future as well as the past. Thus, love of a country
Begins as attachment to our own field of action
And comes to find that action of little importance
Though never indifferent. History may be servitude,
History may be freedom. See, now they vanish,
The faces and places, with the self which, as it could, loved them,
To become renewed, transfigured, in another pattern.

Sin is Behovely, but
All shall be well, and
All manner of thing shall be well.°
If I think, again, of this place,
And of people, not wholly commendable,
Of no immediate kin or kindness,°
But some of peculiar genius,
All touched by a common genius,°
United in the strife which divided them;
If I think of a king at nightfall,
Of three men, and more, on the scaffold
And a few who died forgotten
In other places, here and abroad,°
And of one who died blind and quiet,°
Why should we celebrate
These dead men more than the dying?
It is not to ring the bell backward
Nor is it an incantation
To summon the spectre of a Rose.°
We cannot revive old factions
We cannot restore old policies
Or follow an antique drum.
These men, and those who opposed them
And those whom they opposed
Accept the constitution of silence
And are folded in a single party.
Whatever we inherit from the fortunate
We have taken from the defeated
What they had to leave us— a symbol:
A symbol perfected in death.
And all shall be well and

Sin . . . well "Sin is behovable, but all shall
be well & all shall be well & all manner of
thing shall be well."
kin or kindness "A little more than kin and less
than kind" (*Hamlet* I.ii.65)
peculiar . . . genius the peculiar genius of such
as Herbert, the common genius of the unique
institution

a few . . . abroad perhaps Richard Crashaw
(1613–49), convert Catholic poet who knew
Ferrar and died in Loreto
blind and quiet Milton, the opponent of king,
bishop, and the Anglican Church
spectre of a Rose referring to title of a Nijinsky
ballet

200 All manner of thing shall be well
By the purification of the motive
In the ground of our beseeching.°

IV°

The dove descending breaks the air
With flame of incandescent terror
Of which the tongues declare
The one discharge from sin and error.
The only hope, or else despair
    Lies in the choice of pyre or pyre—
    To be redeemed from fire by fire.
Who then devised the torment? Love.
210 Love is the unfamiliar Name
Behind the hands that wove
The intolerable shirt of flame
Which human power cannot remove.
    We only live, only suspire
    Consumed by either fire or fire.

V°

What we call the beginning is often the end
And to make an end is to make a beginning.
The end is where we start from. And every phrase
And sentence that is right (where every word is at home,
220 Taking its place to support the others,
The word neither diffident nor ostentatious,
An easy commerce of the old and the new,
The common word exact without vulgarity,
The formal word precise but not pedantic,
The complete consort dancing together)
Every phrase and every sentence is an end and a beginning,
Every poem an epitaph. And any action
Is a step to the block, to the fire, down the sea's throat

In . . . beseeching The voice said to Dame Julian: "I am the Ground of thy beseeching; first it is my will that thou have it; and after, I make thee to will it."
IV a gnomic lyric on the themes of the first three movements. The dove is the Holy Spirit proclaiming that only suffering—the fire that refines—can release us from sin, from attachment to the world (the fires of London, properly understood, might be an emblem of that refining fire). The tormentor is love; the torment is compared to that of the shirt of Nessus which Deianira gave her husband Hercules to wear, believing it to have the power to make him love her; the torment of the poisoned shirt was such that in order to escape it he burnt himself on a pyre and ascended to heaven.
V In this conclusion of the whole work Eliot echoes themes of all the Quartets; thus the opening line refers to the first and last lines of

"East Coker": "In my beginning is my end. . . . In my end is my beginning" (referring to the motto of Mary Queen of Scots, "In my end is my beginning"). The poem stresses the contemporaneity of the past, dismissing the illusion that the present is separated from it by time; a well-written poem, any confrontation with death, confronts the past in an order out of time. So, the first section ends, with this moment in time, in the fading light of a winter afternoon at Little Gidding, the meaningful past is present and actual. The link to the second and final section is another line from a 14th-century mystic. Then the theme of all journeying as a return to origins is restated; the children in the tree were there at the beginning of "Burnt Norton." "Quick now, here, now, always" is the timeless experience they represent at the end of that opening poem.

Or to an illegible stone: and that is where we start.
We die with the dying:
See, they depart, and we go with them.
We are born with the dead:
See, they return, and bring us with them.
The moment of the rose and the moment of the yew-tree
Are of equal duration. A people without history
Is not redeemed from time, for history is a pattern
Of timeless moments. So, while the light fails
On a winter's afternoon, in a secluded chapel
History is now and England.

With the drawing of this Love and the voice of this Calling°

We shall not cease from exploration
And the end of all our exploring
Will be to arrive where we started
And know the place for the first time.
Through the unknown, remembered gate
When the last of earth left to discover
Is that which was the beginning;
At the source of the longest river
The voice of the hidden waterfall
And the children in the apple-tree
Not known, because not looked for
But heard, half-heard, in the stillness
Between two waves of the sea.
Quick now, here, now, always—
A condition of complete simplicity
(Costing not less than everything)
And all shall be well and
All manner of thing shall be well
When the tongues of flame are in-folded
Into the crowned knot of fire
And the fire and the rose° are one.

1941   1943

Prose

Eliot was a distinguished and prolific prosewriter, editor of an important journal, *The Criterion*, which ran from 1922 to 1939. In the first number he spoke up for "the application, in literature, of principles which have their consequences also in politics and in private conduct," and this is an indication of the surprising, if not always pleasing, homogeneity of Eliot's prose, over the whole wide range of criticism, sociol-

With . . . Calling from The Cloud of *Unknowing*, an anonymous mystical work of the 14th century
rose The Dantean symbol of the Host of the Blessed (*Paradiso* XXXI ff.); the union is of the heavenly order of the purged spirit and the fire that purges it. There are here, as throughout the movement, internal allusions of much complexity.

ogy, theology, and economics which he attempted. His first published book, *The Sacred Wood* (1920), is criticism of high historical importance which is yet closely allied to the poet's own practice. Of the considerable volume of criticism he wrote in periodicals and elsewhere some was collected, some not, in *Selected Essays* (1932), *On Poetry and Poets* (1957), and *To Criticize the Critic* (1965). His Norton lectures at Harvard appeared as *The Use of Poetry and the Use of Criticism* (1933). Of his other writing the most important are: *After Strange Gods* (1934), lectures delivered at the University of Virginia, and expressing, together with an admiration for the American writers known as the Southern Agrarians, opinions so far to the right (in those days of polarized political opinions) that he later suppressed it; *The Idea of a Christian Society* (1939); and *Notes Toward a Definition of Culture* (1948).

It is not within the scope of this note to provide more than the most general idea of all this prose; all the selections are critical essays, and a word must serve by way of explanation as to how the whole thing hangs together. We have seen from the poetry that Eliot's chief horror was of life and society divorced from the stresses and torments of genuine spiritual engagement; one of his mottos might have been, though it was not, the Lutheran *pecca fortiter* (sin strongly)—rather than merely exist like the crowd flowing over London Bridge, the Hollow Men by the tumid river, the inhabitants of Baudelaire's *fourmillante cité*. There is a strong sense of *election*, of the superiority of men who are in conscious engagement with sin and reality, over those unaware of law and sunk in a bestial hedonism like Sweeney's. Speaking of Communism, which he hated but saw as a rival religion to Christianity, he says that the young who "would like to grow up and believe in something" find it a godsend, and "have joined that bitter fraternity which lives on a higher level of doubt"; and Christians live on that level also (*Criterion*, vol. 12). Feelings of this kind animate Eliot's famous choice of conservatism and a hierarchical society, his insistence on the need for *élites*, his acceptance of the authority of an established Catholic Church (the Church of England), and his interest, during the years of political crisis in Europe, in the virtually fascist, but also Catholic and Royalist, French organization called *Action Française*.

There is in Eliot a persistent requirement of *authority*—in the state, the church, the arts. The source of authority in the arts is the art of the past. He was fond of such expressions as "the mind of Europe" and "the mind of England"; he had an imperial imagination, which was fed by the notion of a continuous transmission of authority, such as what the Roman empire, duly associated with Christianity, may be said to have achieved in Europe. Politically, the consequences may strike one as having a provincial air, since the time and the place—now and England—called for acceptance of the English reformed church, the English post-Stuart royal house, and an English general culture—soccer, cheese, music hall—not his own. And in much of this the student of poetry may not be directly interested. It is the reflection of these doctrines in the sphere of literature that most concerns him. Eliot's "imperialism" led him to undertake a profound and delicate study of Dante, and to respect him and Virgil (in this second admiration he differed from his associates in the poetic revolution) as transmitters of a literary *imperium*. But of more direct importance, it led him to a consideration of the meaning of tradition in the light of the further and apparently contradictory truth that all good art is in various ways *new*, and apparently a departure from tradition. It led him further to a consideration of how the individual artist, the new sufferer and creator, stands in relation to the authority of the tradition. The answer lies in a necessary and difficult *impersonality*.

In addition to this whole complex problem of the relations of new to old, and of the individual talent to the past on which it operates, there was the further difficulty that people habitually thought of a poem as the *expression* of an individual, and as having some kind of *message*. Eliot had also to deal with this, to redefine not only the role of the artist but the mode of existence of the poem itself; and also to explain how these and other mistaken notions of poetry had grown up since—when? Since the seventeenth century; and this introduces the historical problem, of how and when all this came about. A new history of poetry was required, and Eliot sketched it; later it was filled out by others. The practical problem, of putting things right, he tackled as a poet, there were of course others—political, cultural, economic—on which he said his say in prose. But the radical diagnosis is really to be sought in a few pages of his early critical essays.

These have a "pontifical solemnity" he later came to disown, but the tone of authority is right for the material. That there are many things wrong with the arguments of the essays goes without saying and has often been said; but rarely has a powerful—and what is more, effective—poetic, aesthetic, and historical conjecture been so clearly and forcefully expressed in so few pages.

Tradition and the Individual Talent [1]

I

In English writing we seldom speak of tradition,[2] though we occasionally apply its name in deploring its absence. We cannot refer to 'the tradition' or to 'a tradition'; at most, we employ the adjective in saying that the poetry of So-and-so is 'traditional' or even 'too traditional.' Seldom, perhaps, does the word appear except in a phrase of censure. If otherwise, it is vaguely approbative, with the implication, as to the work approved, of some pleasing archaeological reconstruction. You can hardly make the word agreeable to English ears without this comfortable reference to the reassuring science of archaeology.

Certainly the word is not likely to appear in our appreciations of living or dead writers. Every nation, every race, has not only its own creative, but its own critical turn of mind; and is even more oblivious of the shortcomings and limitations of its critical habits than of those of its creative genius. We know, or think we know, from the enormous mass of critical writing that has appeared

---

1. "Tradition and the Individual Talent" appeared in the *Egoist*, 1919, and was reprinted in *The Sacred Wood* (1920). The essay re-values the idea of tradition: in the mature poet past poetry is part of his individuality; the past is part of the present, and is modified by it. Thus what is genuinely new is to be aware of, and a part of, the ever-changing "mind of Europe." To achieve this integral relation with the body of European poetry a poet must aim at the extinction of his personality. He must be not a personality but a medium for the digestion and transmutation of his material. The result is its own kind of thing; its complexity is not that of the emotions represented or suffered by the man who wrote the poem. Consequently the Romantic doctrines are rejected as too personal, too crudely related to the emotions of the poet. There is, further, a distinction between poetic value and anything "semi-ethical"; it is not the good things said, but the good saying, that marks mature poetry. The business of the poem is "emotion which has its life in the poem," not the poet's emotions or his opinions. That is why he must strive for Impersonality.

2. That this is now palpably untrue is directly attributable to the influence of Eliot's essay.

in the French language the critical method or habit of the French; we only conclude (we are such unconscious people) that the French are 'more critical' than we, and sometimes even plume ourselves a little with the fact, as if the French were the less spontaneous. Perhaps they are; but we might remind ourselves that criticism is as inevitable as breathing, and that we should be none the worse for articulating what passes in our minds when we read a book and feel an emotion about it, for criticizing our own minds in their work of criticism. One of the facts that might come to light in this process is our tendency to insist, when we praise a poet, upon those aspects of his work in which he least resembles anyone else. In these aspects or parts of his work we pretend to find what is individual, what is the peculiar essence of the man. We dwell with satisfaction upon the poet's difference from his predecessors, especially his immediate predecessors; we endeavour to find something that can be isolated in order to be enjoyed. Whereas if we approach a poet without this prejudice we shall often find that not only the best, but the most individual parts of his work may be those in which the dead poets, his ancestors, assert their immortality most vigorously. And I do not mean the impressionable period of adolescence, but the period of full maturity.

Yet if the only form of tradition, of handing down, consisted in following the ways of the immediate generation before us in a blind or timid adherence to its successes, 'tradition' should positively be discouraged. We have seen many such simple currents soon lost in the sand; and novelty is better than repetition. Tradition is a matter of much wider significance. It cannot be inherited, and if you want it you must obtain it by great labour.[3] It involves, in the first place, the historical sense, which we may call nearly indispensable to any one who would continue to be a poet beyond his twenty-fifth year; and the historical sense involves a perception, not only of the pastness of the past, but of its presence; the historical sense compels a man to write not merely with his own generation in his bones, but with a feeling that the whole of the literature of Europe from Homer and within it the whole of the literature of his own country has a simultaneous existence and composes a simultaneous order. This historical sense, which is a sense of the timeless as well as of the temporal and of the timeless and of the temporal together, is what makes a writer traditional. And it is at the same time what makes a writer most acutely conscious of his place in time, of his own contemporaneity.

No poet, no artist of any art, has his complete meaning alone. His significance, his appreciation is the appreciation of his relation to the dead poets and artists. You cannot value him alone; you must set him, for contrast and comparison, among the dead. I mean this as a principle of aesthetic, not merely historical, criticism. The necessity that he shall conform, that he shall cohere, is not onesided; what happens when a new work of art is created is something that happens simultaneously to all the works of art which preceded it. The existing monuments form an ideal order among themselves, which is modified by the introduction of the new (the really new) work of art among them. The existing order is complete before the new work arrives; for order to persist after the supervention of novelty, the *whole* existing order must be, if ever so slightly,

---

3. There is a paradox in stating that what is "handed down" cannot be inherited.

altered; and so the relations, proportions, values of each work of art toward the whole are readjusted; and this is conformity between the old and the new. Whoever has approved this idea of order, of the form of European, of English literature will not find it preposterous that the past should be altered by the present as much as the present is directed by the past. And the poet who is aware of this will be aware of great difficulties and responsibilities.

In a peculiar sense he will be aware also that he must inevitably be judged by the standards of the past. I say judged, not amputated, by them; not judged to be as good as, or worse or better than, the dead; and certainly not judged by the canons of dead critics. It is a judgment, a comparison, in which two things are measured by each other. To conform merely would be for the new work not really to conform at all; it would not be new, and would therefore not be a work of art. And we do not quite say that the new is more valuable because it fits in; but its fitting in is a test of its value—a test, it is true, which can only be slowly and cautiously applied, for we are none of us infallible judges of conformity. We say: it appears to conform, and is perhaps individual, or it appears individual, and may conform; but we are hardly likely to find that it is one and not the other.

To proceed to a more intelligible exposition of the relation of the poet to the past: he can neither take the past as a lump, an indiscriminate bolus,[4] nor can he form himself wholly on one or two private admirations, nor can he form himself wholly upon one preferred period. The first course is inadmissible, the second is an important experience of youth, and the third is a pleasant and highly desirable supplement. The poet must be very conscious of the main current, which does not at all flow invariably through the most distinguished reputations.[5] He must be quite aware of the obvious fact that art never improves, but that the material of art is never quite the same. He must be aware that the mind of Europe—the mind of his own country—a mind which he learns in time to be much more important than his own private mind—is a mind which changes, and that this change is a development which abandons nothing en route, which does not superannuate either Shakespeare, or Homer, or the rock drawing of the Magdalenian[6] draughtsmen. That this development, refinement perhaps, complication certainly,[7] is not, from the point of view of the artist, any improvement. Perhaps not even an improvement from the point of view of the psychologist or not to the extent which we imagine; perhaps only in the end based upon a complication in economics and machinery. But the difference between the present and the past is that the conscious present is an awareness of the past in a way and to an extent which the past's awareness of itself cannot show.

Someone said: 'The dead writers are remote from us because we *know* so much more than they did.' Precisely, and they are that which we know.

4. A large pill.
5. Related to Eliot's current preoccupation with the Metaphysical poets, minor Jacobean drama, and such poets as Laforgue; the implication for criticism is that the map of literary history needs redrawing; see "The Metaphysical Poets."
6. Paleolithic drawings at La Madeleine, France, gave the draftsmen this name; later the caves at Lascaux became more famous.
7. Because Eliot also held the view that modern poetry, because of the character of our civilization, must be difficult, and supported it in his verse.

I am alive to a usual objection to what is clearly part of my programme for the *métier* of poetry. The objection is that the doctrine requires a ridiculous amount of erudition (pedantry), a claim which can be rejected by appeal to the lives of poets in any pantheon. It will even be affirmed that much learning deadens or perverts poetic sensibility. While, however, we persist in believing that a poet ought to know as much as will not encroach upon his necessary receptivity and necessary laziness, it is not desirable to confine knowledge to whatever can be put into a useful shape for examinations, drawing rooms, or the still more pretentious modes of publicity. Some can absorb knowledge, the more tardy must sweat for it. Shakespeare acquired more essential history from Plutarch [8] than most men could from the whole British Museum. What is to be insisted upon is that the poet must develop or procure the consciousness of the past and that he should continue to develop this consciousness throughout his career.

What happens is a continual surrender of himself as he is at the moment to something which is more valuable. The progress of an artist is a continual self-sacrifice, a continual extinction of personality.[9]

There remains to define this process of depersonalization and its relation to the sense of tradition. It is in this depersonalization that art may be said to approach the condition of science. I, therefore, invite you to consider, as a suggestive analogy, the action which takes place when a bit of finely filiated [10] platinum is introduced into a chamber containing oxygen and sulphur dioxide.

II

Honest criticism and sensitive appreciation are directed not upon the poet but upon the poetry.[11] If we attend to the confused cries of the newspaper critics and the *susurrus* [12] of popular repetition that follows, we shall hear the names of poets in great numbers; if we seek not Blue-book [13] knowledge but the enjoyment of poetry, and ask for a poem, we shall seldom find it. I have tried to point out the importance of the relation of the poem to other poems by other authors, and suggested the conception of poetry as a living whole of all the poetry that has ever been written. The other aspect of this Impersonal theory of poetry *is* the relation of the poem to its author. And I hinted, by an analogy, that the mind of the mature poet differs from that of the immature one not precisely in any valuation of 'personality,' not being necessarily more interesting, or having 'more to say,' but rather by being a more finely perfected medium in which special, or very varied, feelings are at liberty to enter into new combinations.

The analogy was that of the catalyst.[14] When the two gases previously mentioned are mixed in the presence of a filament of platinum, they form sulphurous acid. This combination takes place only if the platinum is present; nevertheless

8. First-century A.D. Greek philosopher and biographer, whose *Lives* contain the source material of Shakespeare's Roman plays.
9. This central doctrine involves an asceticism which links it to Eliot's religious interests, and to much in *The Waste Land* and *Four Quartets*.
10. Drawn out into a fine wire.
11. Another doctrine with intensely important implications for 20th-century criticism.
12. Murmuring.
13. Official government publication.
14. Substance causing a chemical reaction in which it plays no direct part.

the newly formed acid contains no trace of platinum, and the platinum itself is apparently unaffected; has remained inert, neutral, and unchanged. The mind of the poet is the shred of platinum. It may partly or exclusively operate upon the experience of the man himself; but, the more perfect the artist, the more completely separate in him will be the man who suffers and the mind which creates; the more perfectly will the mind digest and transmute the passions which are its material.

The experience, you will notice, the elements which enter the presence of the transforming catalyst, are of two kinds: emotions and feelings. The effect of a work of art upon the person who enjoys it is an experience different in kind from any experience not of art. It may be formed out of one emotion, or may be a combination of several; and various feelings, inhering for the writer in particular words or phrases or images, may be added to compose the final result.[15] Or great poetry may be made without the direct use of any emotion whatever: composed out of feelings solely. Canto XV of the Inferno (Brunetto Latini [16]) is a working up of the emotion evident in the situation; but the effect, though single as that of any work of art, is obtained by considerable complexity of detail. The last quatrain gives an image, a feeling attaching to an image, which 'came,' which did not develop simply out of what precedes, but which was probably in suspension in the poet's mind until the proper combination arrived for it to add itself to. The poet's mind is in fact a receptacle for seizing and storing up numberless feelings, phrases, images, which remain there until all the particles which can unite to form a new compound are present together.[17]

If you compare several representative passages of the greatest poetry you see how great is the variety of types of combination, and also how completely any semi-ethical criterion of 'sublimity' misses the mark.[18] For it is not the 'greatness,' the intensity, of the emotions, the components, but the intensity of the artistic process, the pressure, so to speak, under which the fusion takes place, that counts. The episode of Paolo and Francesca [19] employs a definite emotion, but the intensity of the poetry is something quite different from whatever intensity in the supposed experience it may give the impression of. It is no more intense, furthermore, than Canto XXVI, the voyage of Ulysses,[20] which has not the direct dependence upon an emotion. Great variety is possible in the process of transmutation of emotion: the murder of Agamemnon,[21] or the agony of Othello, gives an artistic effect apparently closer to a possible original than the scenes from Dante. In the Agamemnon, the artistic emotion approximates to the

15. This has a direct relation to the method of "Gerontion" and The Waste Land. Critics have objected to the imprecision with which Eliot, in this passage and later, uses the words emotion and feeling.
16. This is the scene closely imitated by Eliot in "Little Gidding" II (see l. 98n.).
17. In representing the poet's mind as "medium" or "receptacle" Eliot provokes the criticism, e. g. of F. R. Leavis, that the connnection of the poem with a real and intense life is something we value very highly.
18. An attempt to dissociate himself from the criticism of Arnold, which in some ways his own resembles; Eliot was always shocked by the idea that poetry could be a sort of religion-substitute.
19. The illicit lovers of Inferno V; an episode famous for its pathos though the lovers are in hell.
20. Ulysses is in hell as a false counselor, and tells Dante the story of his final voyage.
21. By his wife, Clytemnestra, in Aeschylus' Agamemnon.

emotion of an actual spectator; in *Othello* to the emotion of the protagonist himself. But the difference between art and the event is always absolute; the combination which is the murder of Agamemnon is probably as complex as that which is the voyage of Ulysses. In either case there has been a fusion of elements. The ode of Keats contains a number of feelings which have nothing particular to do with the nightingale, but which the nightingale, partly, perhaps, because of its attractive name, and partly because of its reputation, served to bring together.

The point of view which I am struggling to attack is perhaps related to the metaphysical theory of the substantial unity of the soul: for my meaning is, that the poet has, not a 'personality' to express, but a particular medium, which is only a medium and not a personality, in which impressions and experiences combine in peculiar and unexpected ways. Impressions and experiences which are important for the man may take no place in the poetry, and those which become important in the poetry may play quite a negligible part in the man, the personality.

I will quote a passage which is unfamiliar enough to be regarded with fresh attention in the light—or darkness—of these observations:

> And now methinks I could e'en chide myself
> For doting on her beauty, though her death
> Shall be revenged after no common action.
> Does the silkworm expend her yellow labours
> For thee? For thee does she undo herself?
> Are lordships sold to maintain ladyships
> For the poor benefit of a bewildering minute?
> Why does yon fellow falsify highways,
> And put his life between the judge's lips,
> To refine such a thing—keeps horse and men
> To beat their valours for her? . . .[22]

In this passage (as is evident if it is taken in its context) there is a combination of positive and negative emotions: an intensely strong attraction toward beauty and an equally intense fascination by the ugliness which is contrasted with it and which destroys it. This balance of contrasted emotion is in the dramatic situation to which the speech is pertinent, but that situation alone is inadequate to it. This is, so to speak, the structural emotion, provided by the drama. But the whole effect, the dominant tone, is due to the fact that a number of floating feelings, having an affinity to this emotion by no means superficially evident, have combined with it to give us a new art emotion.

It is not in his personal emotions, the emotions provoked by particular events in his life, that the poet is in any way remarkable or interesting. His particular emotions may be simple, or crude, or flat. The emotion in his poetry will be a very complex thing, but not with the complexity of the emotions of people who have very complex or unusual emotions in life. One error, in fact, of eccentricity

---

22. Cyril Tourneur, *The Revenger's Tragedy* (1607) III.v.67–78; *bewitching* is probably the true reading in l. 73, though Eliot in his essay "Tourneur" (*Selected Essays*, p. 192) says that "*bewildering* is much the richer word here."

in poetry is to seek for new human emotions to express; and in this search for novelty in the wrong place it discovers the perverse.[23] The business of the poet is not to find new emotions, but to use the ordinary ones and, in working them up into poetry, to express feelings which are not in actual emotions at all. And emotions which he has never experienced will serve his turn as well as those familiar to him. Consequently, we must believe that 'emotion recollected in tranquillity'[24] is an inexact formula. For it is neither emotion, nor recollection, nor, without distortion of meaning, tranquillity. It is a concentration, and a new thing resulting from the concentration, of a very great number of experiences which to the practical and active person would not seem to be experiences at all; it is a concentration which does not happen consciously or of deliberation. These experiences are not 'recollected,' and they finally unite in an atmosphere which is 'tranquil' only in that it is a passive attending upon the event. Of course this is not quite the whole story. There is a great deal, in the writing of poetry, which must be conscious and deliberate. In fact, the bad poet is usually unconscious where he ought to be conscious, and conscious where he ought to be unconscious. Both errors tend to make him 'personal.' Poetry is not a turning loose of emotion, but an escape from emotion; it is not the expression of personality, but an escape from personality. But, of course, only those who have personality and emotions know what it means to want to escape from these things.[25]

III

ὁ δὲ νοῦς ἴσως Θειότερόν τι χαὶ ἀπαθές ἐστιν.[26]

This essay proposes to halt at the frontier of metaphysics or mysticism, and confine itself to such practical conclusions as can be applied by the responsible person interested in poetry. To divert interest from the poet to the poetry is a laudable aim: for it would conduce to a juster estimation of actual poetry, good and bad. There are many people who appreciate the expression of sincere emotion in verse, and there is a smaller number of people who can appreciate technical excellence. But very few know when there is an expression of *significant* emotion, emotion which has its life in the poem and not in the history of the poet. The emotion of art is impersonal. And the poet cannot reach this impersonality without surrendering himself wholly to the work to be done. And he is not likely to know what is to be done unless he lives in what is not merely the present, but the present moment of the past, unless he is conscious, not of what is dead, but of what is already living.

1920

23. Perhaps a complaint against the Dada movement which developed into Surrealism and was strong at this time; Eliot has occasional affinities with it but of course did not share its disavowal of the past.
24. Wordsworth in the Preface to the second edition of *Lyrical Ballads* (1800) said that poetry "takes its origin in emotion recollected in tranquillity," which is not quite the same thing.
25. A touch of the familiar contempt for the half-life of the non-elect.
26. "The mind is doubtless more divine and less subject to passion," Aristotle, *De Anima* (On the Soul) I.4.

The Metaphysical Poets [1]

By collecting these poems [2] from the work of a generation more often named than read, and more often read than profitably studied, Professor Grierson has rendered a service of some importance. Certainly the reader will meet with many poems already preserved in other anthologies, at the same time that he discovers poems such as those of Aurelian Townshend or Lord Herbert of Cherbury here included. But the function of such an anthology as this is neither that of Professor Saintsbury's admirable edition of Caroline poets nor that of the *Oxford Book of English Verse*. Mr. Grierson's book is in itself a piece of criticism and a provocation of criticism; and we think that he was right in including so many poems of Donne, elsewhere (though not in many editions) accessible, as documents in the case of 'metaphysical poetry.' The phrase has long done duty as a term of abuse or as the label of a quaint and pleasant taste.[3] The question is to what extent the so-called metaphysicals formed a school (in our own time we should say a 'movement'), and how far this so-called school or movement is a digression from the main current.

Not only is it extremely difficult to define metaphysical poetry, but difficult to decide what poets practise it and in which of their verses. The poetry of Donne (to whom Marvell and Bishop King are sometimes nearer than any of the other authors) is late Elizabethan, its feeling often very close to that of Chapman. The 'courtly' poetry is derivative from Jonson, who borrowed liberally from the Latin; it expires in the next century with the sentiment and witticism of Prior. There is finally the devotional verse of Herbert, Vaughan, and Crashaw (echoed long after by Christina Rossetti and Francis Thompson); Crashaw, sometimes more profound and less sectarian than the others, has a quality which returns through the Elizabethan period to the early Italians. It is difficult to find any precise use of metaphor, simile, or other conceit, which is common to all the poets and at the same time important enough as an element of style to isolate these poets as a group. Donne, and often Cowley, employ a device which is sometimes considered characteristically 'metaphysical'; the elaboration (contrasted with the condensation) of a figure of speech to the farthest stage to which ingenuity can carry it. Thus Cowley develops the commonplace comparison of the world to a chessboard through long stanzas (*To Destiny*), and Donne, with more grace, in *A Valediction*,[4] the comparison of two lovers to a pair of compasses. But elsewhere we find, instead of the mere explication of the content of a comparison, a development by rapid association of thought which requires considerable agility on the part of the reader.

1. "The Metaphysical Poets" was originally a book review in the (London) *Times Literary Supplement* in 1921. This essay bears the marks of its origin, but is very important as the central statement of the doctrine of "dissociation of sensibility" and the sketch of a new history of English poetry which acceptance of such a doctrine (and, it appeared, of the validity of Eliot's own current poetry) entailed.
2. Eliot was reviewing H. J. C. Grierson's anthology, *Metaphysical Lyrics and Poems of the Seventeenth Century* (1921).
3. This and some later passages in the essay underestimate the degree to which the Metaphysicals had already been rescued from such criticism in the late 19th century and the years leading up to Grierson's edition of Donne (1912).
4. "A Valediction: Forbidding Mourning."

On a round ball
A workman that hath copies by, can lay
An Europe, Afrique, and an Asia,
And quickly make that which was nothing, all;
So doth each tear,
Which thee doth wear,
A globe, yea world, by that impression grow,
Till thy tears mixed with mine do overflow
This world; by waters sent from thee, my heaven dissolvèd so.[5]

Here we find at least two connections which are not implicit in the first figure, but are forced upon it by the poet: from the geographer's globe to the tear, and the tear to the deluge. On the other hand, some of Donne's most successful and characteristic effects are secured by brief words and sudden contrasts:

A bracelet of bright hair about the bone,[6]

where the most powerful effect is produced by the sudden contrast of associations of 'bright hair' and of 'bone.' This telescoping of images and multiplied associations is characteristic of the phrase of some of the dramatists of the period which Donne knew: not to mention Shakespeare, it is frequent in Middleton, Webster, and Tourneur, and is one of the sources of the vitality of their language.[7]

Johnson, who employed the term 'metaphysical poets,' apparently having Donne, Cleveland, and Cowley chiefly in mind, remarks of them that 'the most heterogeneous ideas are yoked by violence together.'[8] The force of this impeachment lies in the failure of the conjunction, the fact that often the ideas are yoked but not united; and if we are to judge of styles of poetry by their abuse, enough examples may be found in Cleveland to justify Johnson's condemnation. But a degree of heterogeneity of material compelled into unity by the operation of the poet's mind is omnipresent in poetry. We need not select for illustration such a line as:

Notre âme est un trois-mâts cherchant son Icarie;[9]

we may find it in some of the best lines of Johnson himself (The Vanity of Human Wishes):

His fate was destined to a barren strand,
A petty fortress, and a dubious hand;
He left a name at which the world grew pale,
To point a moral, or adorn a tale.

where the effect is due to a contrast of ideas, different in degree but the same in principle, as that which Johnson mildly reprehended. And in one of the finest

5. "A Valediction: Of Weeping," ll. 10–18.
6. "The Relic," l. 6.
7. Here Eliot brings together two bodies of "minor" poetry to which he himself was heavily indebted.
8. In the Life of Cowley.
9. "Our soul is a three-master seeking its Icarie" (Baudelaire, "Le Voyage"). Icarie is a utopia.

poems of the age (a poem which could not have been written in any other age), the *Exequy* of Bishop King, the extended comparison is used with perfect success: the idea and the simile become one, in the passage in which the Bishop illustrates his impatience to see his dead wife, under the figure of a journey:

> Stay for me there; I will not fail
> To meet thee in that hollow Vale.
> And think not much of my delay;
> I am already on the way,
> And follow thee with all the speed
> Desire can make, or sorrows breed.
> Each minute is a short degree,
> And ev'ry hour a step towards thee.
> At night when I betake to rest,
> Next morn I rise nearer my West
> Of life, almost by eight hours sail,
> Then when sleep breathed his drowsy gale. . . .
> But hark! My pulse, like a soft drum
> Beats my approach, tells Thee I come;
> And slow howe'er my marches be,
> I shall at last sit down by Thee.

(In the last few lines there is that effect of terror which is several times attained by one of Bishop King's admirers, Edgar Poe.) Again, we may justly take these quatrains from Lord Herbert's Ode,[10] stanzas which would, we think, be immediately pronounced to be of the metaphysical school:

> So when from hence we shall be gone,
>   And be no more, nor you, nor I,
>   As one another's mystery,
> Each shall be both, yet both but one.
>
> This said, in her uplifted face,
>   Her eyes, which did that beauty crown,
>   Were like two stars, that having faln down,
> Look up again to find their place:
>
> While such a moveless silent peace
>   Did seize on their becalmèd sense,
>   One would have thought some influence
> Their ravished spirits did possess.

There is nothing in these lines (with the possible exception of the stars, a simile not at once grasped, but lovely and justified) which fits Johnson's general observations on the metaphysical poets in his essay on Cowley. A good deal resides in the richness of association which is at the same time borrowed from and given to the word 'becalmed'; but the meaning is clear, the language simple and elegant. It is to be observed that the language of these poets is as a rule simple and pure; in the verse of George Herbert this simplicity is carried as far as it

---

10. "Ode upon a Question Moved, Whether Love Should Continue for Ever," by Lord Herbert of Cherbury (1583–1648).

can go—a simplicity emulated without success by numerous modern poets. The *structure* of the sentences, on the other hand, is sometimes far from simple, but this is not a vice; it is a fidelity to thought and feeling.[11] The effect, at its best, is far less artificial than that of an ode by Gray. And as this fidelity induces variety of thought and feeling, so it induces variety of music. We doubt whether, in the eighteenth century, could be found two poems in nominally the same metre, so dissimilar as Marvell's *Coy Mistress* and Crashaw's *Saint Teresa;* the one producing an effect of great speed by the use of short syllables, and the other an ecclesiastical solemnity by the use of long ones:

> Love, thou art absolute sole lord
> Of life and death.

If so shrewd and sensitive (though so limited) a critic as Johnson failed to define metaphysical poetry by its faults, it is worth while to inquire whether we may not have more success by adopting the opposite method: by assuming that the poets of the seventeenth century (up to the Revolution [12]) were the direct and normal development of the precedent age; and, without prejudicing their case by the adjective 'metaphysical,' consider whether their virtue was not something permanently valuable, which subsequently disappeared, but ought not to have disappeared. Johnson has hit, perhaps by accident, on one of their peculiarities, when he observes that 'their attempts were always analytic'; he would not agree that, after the dissociation, they put the material together again in a new unity.

It is certain that the dramatic verse of the later Elizabethan and early Jacobean poets expresses a degree of development of sensibility which is not found in any of the prose, good as it often is. If we except Marlowe, a man of prodigious intelligence, these dramatists were directly or indirectly (it is at least a tenable theory) affected by Montaigne. Even if we except also Jonson and Chapman, these two were probably erudite, and were notably men who incorporated their erudition into their sensibility: their mode of feeling was directly and freshly altered by their reading and thought. In Chapman especially there is a direct sensuous apprehension of thought, or a recreation of thought into feeling,[13] which is exactly what we find in Donne:

> in this one thing, all the discipline
> Of manners and of manhood is contained;
> A man to join himself with th' Universe
> In his main sway, and make in all things fit
> One with that All, and go on, round as it;
> Not plucking from the whole his wretched part,

11. Here *thought* and *feeling* are brought together; later in the essay their dissociation will be discussed.

12. The Civil War, which for Eliot brought the great and continuing change in "the mind of England." Ordinarily "Revolution" would refer to the Glorious Revolution of 1688, which established a constitutional monarchy; but Eliot attached special importance to the Civil War, which, in his Marvell essay, he calls "The Great Rebellion." See "Milton II" in *On Poetry and Poets* for Eliot's later reflections on the Civil War and the "dissociation of sensibility."

13. This terminology derives from the French Symbolist writer Rémy de Gourmont (1858–1915), who uses it in a different context.

And into straits, or into nought revert,
Wishing the complete Universe might be
Subject to such a rag of it as he;
But to consider great Necessity.[14]

We compare this with some modern passage:

No, when the fight begins within himself,
A man's worth something. God stoops o'er his head,
Satan looks up between his feet—both tug—
He's left, himself, i' the middle; the soul wakes
And grows. Prolong that battle through his life![15]

It is perhaps somewhat less fair, though very tempting (as both poets are concerned with the perpetuation of love by offspring), to compare with the stanzas already quoted from Lord Herbert's Ode the following from Tennyson:

One walked between his wife and child,
With measured footfall firm and mild,
And now and then he gravely smiled.
The prudent partner of his blood
Leaned on him, faithful, gentle, good,
Wearing the rose of womanhood.
And in their double love secure,
The little maiden walked demure,
Pacing with downward eyelids pure.
These three made unity so sweet,
My frozen heart began to beat,
Remembering its ancient heat.[16]

The difference is not a simple difference of degree between poets. It is something which had happened to the mind of England between the time of Donne or Lord Herbert of Cherbury and the time of Tennyson and Browning;[17] it is the difference between the intellectual poet and the reflective poet. Tennyson and Browning are poets, and they think; but they do not feel their thought as immediately as the odor of a rose. A thought to Donne was an experience; it modified his sensibility. When a poet's mind is perfectly equipped for its work, it is constantly amalgamating disparate experience; the ordinary man's experience is chaotic, irregular, fragmentary. The latter falls in love, or reads Spinoza, and these two experiences have nothing to do with each other, or with the noise of the typewriter or the smell of cooking; in the mind of the poet these experiences are always forming new wholes.[18]

We may express the difference by the following theory: The poets of the

14. George Chapman (1559?–1634), *The Revenge of Bussy d'Ambois* IV.i.137 ff.
15. Robert Browning (1812–89), *Bishop Blougram's Apology*, ll. 693–97.
16. *The Two Voices*, ll. 412–23.
17. The heart of Eliot's doctrine, historically considered. Are the examples chosen fairly? Is this the right way to project a modern, post-Symbolist doctrine of the poem as non-discursive image onto the past? These and other questions have been cogently raised by subsequent critics.
18. As in the passage in "Tradition and the Individual Talent" on the "medium . . . in which impressions and experiences combine in peculiar and unexpected ways."

seventeenth century, the successors of the dramatists of the sixteenth, possessed a mechanism of sensibility which could devour any kind of experience. They are simple, artificial, difficult, or fantastic, as their predecessors were; no less nor more than Dante, Guido Cavalcanti, Guinicelli, or Cino.[19] In the seventeenth century a dissociation of sensibility [20] set in, from which we have never recovered; and this dissociation, as is natural, was aggravated by the influence of the two most powerful poets of the century, Milton and Dryden. Each of these men performed certain poetic functions so magnificently well that the magnitude of the effect concealed the absence of others. The language went on and in some respects improved; the best verse of Collins, Gray, Johnson, and even Goldsmith satisfies some of our fastidious demands better than that of Donne or Marvell or King. But while the language became more refined, the feeling became more crude. The feeling, the sensibility, expressed in the *Country Churchyard* (to say nothing of Tennyson and Browning) is cruder than that in the *Coy Mistress*.

The second effect of the influence of Milton and Dryden followed from the first, and was therefore slow in manifestation. The sentimental age began early in the eighteenth century, and continued. The poets revolted against the ratiocinative, the descriptive; they thought and felt by fits, unbalanced; they reflected. In one or two passages of Shelley's *Triumph of Life*, in the second *Hyperion*, there are traces of a struggle toward unification of sensibility. But Keats and Shelley died, and Tennyson and Browning ruminated.

After this brief exposition of a theory—too brief, perhaps, to carry conviction—we may ask, what would have been the fate of the 'metaphysical' had the current of poetry descended in a direct line from them, as it descended in a direct line to them? They would not, certainly, be classified as metaphysical. The possible interests of a poet are unlimited; the more intelligent he is the better; the more intelligent he is the more likely that he will have interests: our only condition is that he turn them into poetry, and not merely meditate on them poetically. A philosophical theory which has entered into poetry is established, for its truth or falsity in one sense ceases to matter, and its truth in another sense is proved. The poets in question have, like other poets, various faults. But they were, at best, engaged in the task of trying to find the verbal equivalent for states of mind and feeling. And this means both that they are more mature, and that they wear better, than later poets of certainly not less literary ability.

It is not a permanent necessity that poets should be interested in philosophy, or in any other subject. We can only say that it appears likely that poets in our civilization, as it exists at present, must be *difficult*. Our civilization comprehends great variety and complexity, and this variety and complexity, playing upon a refined sensibility, must produce various and complex results. The poet must become more and more comprehensive, more allusive, more indirect, in order to force, to dislocate if necessary, language into his meaning.[21] (A brilliant and

---

19. Cavalcanti, Guinicelli, and Cino da Pistoia were poets of the *dolce stil nuovo* ("sweet new style"), predecessors and contemporaries of Dante (late 13th, early 14th century). Pound sets his date for the "dissociation of sensibility" between them and Petrarch (1304–74).

20. The first use of the phrase in English (borrowed from De Gourmont).

21. An influential idea, later labeled by the American critic Yvor Winters "the fallacy of imitative form."

extreme statement of this view, with which it is not requisite to associate one-self, is that of M. Jean Epstein, *La Poésie d' aujourd'hui.*[22]) Hence we get something which looks very much like the conceit—we get, in fact, a method curiously similar to that of the 'metaphysical poets,' similar also in its use of obscure words and of simple phrasing.

> *O géraniums diaphanes, guerroyeurs sortilèges,*
> *Sacrilèges monomanes!*
> *Emballages, dévergondages, douches! O pressoirs*
> *Des vendanges des grands soirs!*
> *Layettes aux abois,*
> *Thyrses au fond des bois!*
> *Transfusions, représailles,*
> *Relevailles, compresses et l'éternal potion,*
> *Angélus! n'en pouvoir plus*
> *De débâcles nuptiales! de débâcles nuptiales!* [23]

The same poet could write also simply:

> *Elle est bien loin, elle pleure,*
> *Le grand vent se lamente aussi . . .*[24]

Jules Laforgue, and Tristan Corbière [25] in many of his poems, are nearer to the 'school of Donne' than any modern English poet. But poets more classical than they have the same essential quality of transmuting ideas into sensations, of transforming an observation into a state of mind.

> *Pour l'enfant, amoureux de cartes et d'estampes,*
> *L'univers est égal à son vaste appétit.*
> *Ah, que le monde est grand à la clarté des lampes!*
> *Aux yeux du souvenir que le monde est petit!* [26]

In French literature the great master of the seventeenth century—Racine—and the great master of the nineteenth—Baudelaire—are in some ways more like each other than they are like any one else. The greatest two masters of diction are also the greatest two psychologists, the most curious explorers of the soul. It is interesting to speculate whether it is not a misfortune that two of the

22. *The Poetry of Today.*
23. Jules Laforgue (1860–87) at his most chaotic: "O transparent geraniums, warrior spells, / monomaniac sacrileges! / Packing materials, shamelessness, showers! O wine-presses / Of the vintages of evening parties! / Baby-clothes under siege, / Thyrsis in the depths of the woods! / Transfusions, reprisals, / Churchings, compresses and the eternal potion, / Angelus! no more are possible / Nuptial disasters! Nuptial disasters!" From *Derniers Vers* (Last Poems), 1890.
24. "She is far away, she weeps, / The great wind laments also." From "Sur un Défunte" (On a Dead Woman), in *Derniers Vers.*
25. Tristan Corbière (1845–75), French poet and early Symbolist; Eliot wanted to think Corbière and Laforgue into a special affinity with the English Metaphysicals and Jacobean dramatists.
26. From Baudelaire's "Le Voyage": "For the child, in love with maps and prints, / The universe is equal to his vast appetite. / Ah, how big the world is by lamplight! / And how small the world is to the eyes of memory!"

greatest masters of diction in our language, Milton and Dryden, triumph with a dazzling disregard of the soul. If we continued to produce Miltons and Drydens it might not so much matter, but as things are it is a pity that English poetry has remained so incomplete. Those who object to the 'artificiality' of Milton or Dryden sometimes tell us to 'look into our hearts and write.' But that is not looking deep enough; Racine or Donne looked into a good deal more than the heart. One must look into the cerebral cortex, the nervous system, and the digestive tracts.

May we not conclude, then, that Donne, Crashaw, Vaughan, Herbert and Lord Herbert, Marvell, King, Cowley at his best, are in the direct current of English poetry,[27] and that their faults should be reprimanded by this standard rather than coddled by antiquarian affection? They have been enough praised in terms which are implicit limitations because they are 'metaphysical' or 'witty,' 'quaint' or 'obscure,' though at their best they have not these attributes more than other serious poets. On the other hand, we must not reject the criticism of Johnson (a dangerous person to disagree with) without having mastered it, without having assimilated the Johnsonian canons of taste. In reading the celebrated passage in his essay on Cowley we must remember that by wit he clearly means something more serious than we usually mean today; in his criticism of their versification we must remember in what a narrow discipline he was trained, but also how well trained; we must remember that Johnson tortures chiefly the chief offenders, Cowley and Cleveland. It would be a fruitful work, and one requiring a substantial book, to break up the classification of Johnson (for there has been none since) and exhibit these poets in all their difference of kind and of degree, from the massive music of Donne to the faint, pleasing tinkle of Aurelian Townshend—whose *Dialogue Between a Pilgrim and Time* is one of the few regrettable omissions from the excellent anthology of Professor Grierson.

1921

ROBERT BRIDGES
1844–1930

Born in Kent, educated at Eton and Corpus Christi College, Oxford, Robert Bridges went on to study medicine at St. Bartholomew's Hospital, where he took a degree in 1874. Although he continued to practice for seven years thereafter, a poetic career, which he had always planned, claimed the remainder of a very long life. Temporary ill health, combined with the possession of sufficient money to do so, allowed him to give up medical work, move to Berkshire, and devote his life to musical and literary studies and to poetry. Always interested in prosodic theory, he wrote a small but important book, *Milton's Prosody* (1921), championed the poetry of Gerard Manley Hopkins, whom he had known well, and eventually, at the age of eighty-five, published a long philosophical poem in a somewhat cranky, purportedly quantitative meter, *The Testament of Beauty*. His finest poetry remains in his lyrics, however, and in the loose accentual meters with which he tempered impulses toward a late Vic-

27. A theme later developed by F. R. Leavis in his theory of a "Line of Wit."

torian smoothness. The sense of a true classical learning, too, pervades Bridges's best work. He succeeded, in 1913, the unbelievably undistinguished Alfred Austin as Poet Laureate. Bridges published his first volume of poems in 1873; many volumes appeared thereafter, and he lived on, writing, through the dawn of the modern age in literature, not always pleased (if his late "Poor Poll" is indeed the attack on *The Waste Land* it appears to be) with its monuments.

A Passer-by

Whither, O splendid ship, thy white sails crowding,
   Leaning across the bosom of the urgent West,
That fearest nor sea rising, nor sky clouding,
   Whither away, fair rover, and what thy quest?
   Ah! soon, when Winter has all our vales opprest,
When skies are cold and misty, and hail is hurling,
   Wilt thou glide on the blue Pacific, or rest
In a summer haven asleep, thy white sails furling.

I there before thee, in the country that well thou knowest,
10   Already arrived am inhaling the odorous air:
I watch thee enter unerringly where thou goest,
   And anchor queen of the strange shipping there,
   Thy sails for awnings spread, thy masts bare;
Nor is aught from the foaming reef to the snow-capped, grandest
   Peak, that is over the feathery palms more fair
Than thou, so upright, so stately, and still thou standest.

And yet, O splendid ship, unhailed and nameless,
   I know not if, aiming a fancy, I rightly divine
That thou hast a purpose joyful, a courage blameless,
20   Thy port assured in a happier land than mine.
   But for all I have given thee, beauty enough is thine,
As thou, aslant with trim tackle and shrouding,
   From the proud nostril curve of a prow's line
In the offing scatterest foam, thy white sails crowding.
                    1879

London Snow°

When men were all asleep the snow came flying,
In large white flakes falling on the city brown,
Stealthily and perpetually settling and loosely lying,

London Snow Bridges wrote this poem in what he took to be a version of Gerard Manley Hopkins's "sprung rhythm". Hopkins' comments on Bridges' effort can be found on pp. 122–3 of *Letters of Gerard Manley Hopkins to Robert Bridges*, ed. C. C. Abbott (1935).

Hushing the latest traffic of the drowsy town;
Deadening, muffling, stifling its murmurs failing;
Lazily and incessantly floating down and down:
    Silently sifting and veiling road, roof and railing;
Hiding difference, making unevenness even,
Into angles and crevices softly drifting and sailing.
    All night it fell, and when full inches seven
It lay in the depth of its uncompacted lightness,
The clouds blew off from a high and frosty heaven;
    And all woke earlier for the unaccustomed brightness
Of the winter dawning, the strange unheavenly glare:
The eye marvelled—marvelled at the dazzling whiteness;
    The ear hearkened to the stillness of the solemn air;
No sound of wheel rumbling nor of foot falling,
And the busy morning cries came thin and spare.
    Then boys I heard, as they went to school, calling,
They gathered up the crystal manna to freeze
Their tongues with tasting, their hands with snowballing;
    Or rioted in a drift, plunging up to the knees;
Or peering up from under the white-mossed wonder,
'O look at the trees!' they cried, 'O look at the trees!'
    With lessened load a few carts creak and blunder,
Following along the white deserted way,
A country company long dispersed asunder:
    When now already the sun, in pale display
Standing by Paul's° high dome, spread forth below
His sparkling beams, and awoke the stir of the day.
    For now doors open, and war is waged with the snow;
And trains of somber men, past tale of number,
Tread long brown paths, as toward their toil they go:
    But even for them awhile no cares encumber
Their minds diverted; the daily word is unspoken,
The daily thoughts of labour and sorrow slumber
At the sight of the beauty that greets them, for the charm they have broken.

                      1880

Nightingales

Beautiful must be the mountains whence ye come,
    And bright in the fruitful valleys the streams, wherefrom
        Ye learn your song:
Where are those starry woods? O might I wander there,
    Among the flowers, which in that heavenly air
        Bloom the year long!

Paul's St. Paul's Cathedral, until recently one
of the highest points on the London skyline.

Nay, barren are those mountains and spent the streams:°
Our song is the voice of desire, that haunts our dreams,
A throe of the heart,
10   Whose pining visions dim, forbidden hopes profound,
No dying cadence nor long sigh can sound,
For all our art.

Alone, aloud in the raptured ear of men
We pour our dark nocturnal secret; and then,
As night is withdrawn
From these sweet-springing meads° and bursting boughs of May,
Dream, while the innumerable choir of day
Welcome the dawn.

1893

A. E. HOUSMAN
1859–1936

Alfred Edward Housman was born in Fockbury, Worcestershire, on March 26, 1859. He went to Oxford in 1887, and surprisingly failed in his Honors degree examination. In 1892 he took a job in the Patent Office in London, and in his leisure time established a reputation for classical scholarship which served him well, for ten years later he was appointed Professor of Latin at University College, London. His fame as a scholar grew, and by 1911, when he became Professor of Latin at Cambridge, he was recognized as the greatest English classicist since Bentley in the eighteenth century, and among the handful of scholars with unchallenged world reputations. He published his first book of poems, *A Shropshire Lad,* in 1896. Between 1911 and 1936 his work was that of an editor, and his five-volume edition of the difficult Latin astronomical poet Manilius is regarded as his masterpiece. In 1922 he published *Last Poems,* and after his death on April 30, 1936, his writer-brother Laurence brought out another small volume, *More Poems,* and included a few more for the *Additional Poems* in his book, *My Brother, A. E. Housman* (1939).

Housman was a bachelor and something of a recluse, a man of melancholic though excitable temperament. He wanted fame, but had a "horror of being known to like being known"; he sought pleasure in male friendship, but avoided love; he understood food and wine and yet condemned himself for the most part to a life of stoic repression. Among scholars he is famous for the bitter epigrammatic insults he carefully sharpened and used on his enemies and "inferiors." As a poet he sought no fellowship with other poets. Despite many reminiscences of the Greek Anthology and of such Latin poets as Propertius, whom he had edited, the connection in Housman between scholar and poet is not obvious on the surface. He said himself, "The Shropshire Lad is an imaginary figure, with something of my temperament and view of life. . . . I did not begin to write poetry in earnest until the really emotional part of my life was over; and my poetry, as far as I could make out, sprang chiefly from

streams In this and the following stanza, the nightingales answer; their "dark nocturnal secret" may or may not be the Ovidian myth of the transformation of the raped, muted

Philomel into the eloquent, tragic singer of night.
meads fields

physical conditions, such as a relaxed sore throat during my most prolific period, the first five months of 1895." He was then thirty-six; the "emotional part of his life" was his Oxford friendship with Moses Jackson, long since married and emigrated. In this "most prolific period," immediately following the death of his father, he wrote *A Shropshire Lad*.

Some of his feeling about this book can be guessed at from the fact that he refused to accept any royalties from its sale. The book combines a sort of idiosyncratically gloomy urgency about the life of the senses with a dramatically simplified acceptance of fate, the darkness which encloses a life; there is also the notion that to yield to the dark is the right proud thing to do. To make statements of that kind was itself for Housman a sensual experience. In his lecture *The Name and Nature of Poetry* (1933) he speaks of the physical tremor by which he recognizes true poetry, his own or another's. Writing poetry was a quite different experience from writing prose, which he claims to have done with great labor; the poems "came into [his] head" half done, and he had only to finish them (though it often took a long time to do so). Into them went not only the landscapes of Worcestershire and Shropshire but also the poetry in his head—Heine, Arnold, Shakespeare's songs, the "border" ballads, Milton.

There is no marked difference of style between *A Shropshire Lad* and *Last Poems* published twenty-six years later, in the year of *Ulysses* and *The Waste Land*. He prefaced the later volume thus: "I publish these poems, few though they are, because it is not likely that I shall ever be impelled to write any more. I can no longer expect to be revisited by the continuous excitement under which in the early months of 1895 I wrote the greater part of my other book, nor indeed could I well sustain it if it came. . . . About a quarter of this matter belongs to the April of the present year, but most of it dates between 1895 and 1910." The posthumous poetry consists mostly of poems rejected from the two volumes Housman published. Housman produced some good comic verse as well—parodies and nonsense poetry in the tradition of Lewis Carroll and Edward Lear.

From A Shropshire Lad

II

Loveliest of trees, the cherry now
Is hung with bloom along the bough,
And stands about the woodland ride
Wearing white for Eastertide.

Now, of my threescore years and ten,
Twenty will not come again,
And take from seventy springs a score,
It only leaves me fifty more.

And since to look at things in bloom
Fifty springs are little room,
About the woodlands I will go
To see the cherry hung with snow.

XXXV

On the idle hill of summer,
    Sleepy with the flow of streams,
Far I hear the steady drummer
    Drumming like a noise in dreams.

Far and near and low and louder
    On the roads of earth go by,
Dear to friends and food for powder,°
    Soldiers marching, all to die.

East and west on fields forgotten
10   Bleach the bones of comrades slain,
Lovely lads and dead and rotten;
    None that go return again.

Far the calling bugles hollo,
    High the screaming fife replies,
Gay the files of scarlet follow:
    Woman bore me, I will rise.

XL

Into my heart an air that kills
    From yon far country blows:
What are those blue remembered hills,
    What spires, what farms are those?

That is the land of lost content,
    I see it shining plain,
The happy highways where I went
    And cannot come again.

XLVIII

Be still, my soul, be still; the arms you bear are brittle,
    Earth and high heaven are fixt of old and founded strong.
Think rather,—call to thought, if now you grieve a little,
    The days when we had rest, O soul, for they were long.

Men loved unkindness then, but lightless in the quarry
    I slept and saw not; tears fell down, I did not mourn;
Sweat ran and blood sprang out and I was never sorry:
    Then it was very well with me, in days ere I was born.

Now, and I muse for why and never find the reason,
10   I pace the earth, and drink the air, and feel the sun.
Be still, be still, my soul; it is but for a season:
    Let us endure an hour and see injustice done.

food for power Falstaff's description of his
conscripts in 1 *Henry IV* IV.ii.56

Ay, look: high heaven and earth ail from the prime foundation;
  All thoughts to rive the heart are here, and all are vain:
Horror and scorn and hate and fear and indignation—
  Oh why did I awake? when shall I sleep again?

1896

We'll to the Woods No More°

We'll to the woods no more,
The laurels all are cut,
The bowers are bare of bay
That once the Muses wore;
The year draws in the day
And soon will evening shut:
The laurels all are cut,
We'll to the woods no more.
Oh we'll no more, no more
To the leafy woods away,
To the high wild woods of laurel
And the bowers of bay no more.

1922

Her Strong Enchantments Failing

Her strong enchantments failing,
  Her towers of fear in wreck,
Her limbecks° dried of poisons
  And the knife at her neck,

The Queen of air and darkness
  Begins to shrill and cry,
'O young man, O my slayer,
  To-morrow you shall die.'

O Queen of air and darkness,
  I think 'tis truth you say,
And I shall die to-morrow;
  But you will die to-day.

1922

In Valleys Green and Still

In valleys green and still
  Where lovers wander maying

We'll . . . more These prefatory verses to *Last Poems* are translated from a poem by Théodore de Banville (1823–91): *Nous n'irons plus aux bois, / Les lauriers sont coupés.*
limbecks alchemical retorts, for distillation

They hear from over hill
  A music playing.

Behind the drum and fife,
  Past hawthornwood and hollow,
Through earth and out of life
  The soldiers follow.

The soldier's is the trade:
10   In any wind or weather
He steals the heart of maid
  And man together.

The lover and his lass
  Beneath the hawthorn lying
Have heard the soldiers pass,
  And both are sighing.

          1922

When the Eye of Day Is Shut

When the eye of day is shut,
  And the stars deny their beams,
And about the forest hut
  Blows the roaring wood of dreams,

From deep clay, from desert rock,
  From the sunk sands of the main,
Come not at my door to knock,
  Hearts that loved me not again.

Sleep, be still, turn to your rest
10   In the lands where you are laid;
In far lodgings east and west
  Lie down on the beds you made.

In gross marl,° in blowing dust,
  In the drowned ooze of the sea,
Where you would not, lie you must,
  Lie you must, and not with me.

          1922

Tell Me Not Here, It Needs Not Saying

Tell me not here, it needs not saying,
  What tune the enchantress plays
In aftermaths of soft September

marl clayey soil

Or under blanching mays,
For she and I were long acquainted
    And I knew all her ways.

On russet floors, by waters idle,
    The pine lets fall its cone;
The cuckoo shouts all day at nothing
    In leafy dells alone;
And traveller's joy beguiles in autumn
    Hearts that have lost their own.

On acres of the seeded grasses
    The changing burnish heaves;
Or marshalled under moons of harvest
    Stand still all night the sheaves;
Or beeches strip in storms for winter
    And stain the wind with leaves.

Possess, as I possessed a season,
    The countries I resign,
Where over elmy plains the highway
    Would mount the hills and shine,
And full of shade the pillared forest
    Would murmur and be mine.

For nature, heartless, witless nature,
    Will neither care nor know
What stranger's feet may find the meadow
    And trespass there and go,
Nor ask amid the dews of morning
    If they are mine or no.

                1922

Ho, Everyone That Thirsteth°

Ho, everyone that thirsteth
    And hath the price to give,
Come to the stolen waters,
    Drink and your soul shall live.

Come to the stolen waters
    And leap the guarded pale,
And pull the flower in season
    Before desire shall fail.°

It shall not last for ever,
    No more than earth and skies;

Ho, Everyone . . . Thirsteth This poem combines the *carpe diem* theme with biblical texts.

"If any man thirst, let him come unto me,
and drink" (John 7:37).
desire . . . fail Ecclesiastes 12:5

But he that drinks in season
Shall live before he dies.

June suns, you cannot store them
    To warm the winter's cold,
The lad that hopes for heaven
    Shall fill his mouth with mould.

                            1936

To Stand Up Straight

To stand up straight and tread the turning mill,
To lie flat and know nothing and be still,
    Are the two trades of man; and which is worse
I know not, but I know that both are ill.

                            1936

Here Dead Lie We

Here dead lie we because we did not choose
    To live and shame the land from which we sprung.
Life, to be sure, is nothing much to lose;
    But young men think it is, and we were young.

                            1936

WALTER DE LA MARE
1873–1956

A poetry in, but not of, the period of the reign of modernism, de la Mare's work has been admired chiefly by poets themselves. They have always prized his unfailing skill, his pointed ability to intensify a lyrical moment, and his access to the mythologies which the modern movement would either ignore, or enlist in its program of rhetorical debunking of the late nineteenth century. Born in Kent (related to Browning on his mother's side), educated in London, he worked as a clerk for Standard Oil Company there until, in 1908, a pension and government grants enabled him to write all the time. His earliest works were strange evocations of childhood, in poems written for both children and adults. From 1902 until his death he published eighteen volumes of verse—in addition to his fiction (including the remarkable and strangely neglected *Memoirs of a Midget* in 1921) and the anthologies he edited. His mastery of the detail of image forever fixing a moment of transformation—or, more usually, transformation just missed—is as keen as that of the Imagist poets who would have scorned the narratives and dramatic lyrics in which he framed those images, and the lyrical forms in whose chambers they resounded.

Winter

Clouded with snow
The cold winds blow,
And shrill on leafless bough
The robin with its burning breast
Alone sings now.

The rayless sun,
Day's journey done,
Sheds its last ebbing light
On fields in leagues of beauty spread
Unearthly white.

Thick draws the dark,
And spark by spark,
The frost-fires kindle, and soon
Over that sea of frozen foam
Floats the white moon.

1912

All That's Past

Very old are the woods;
And the buds that break
Out of the brier's boughs,
When March winds wake,
So old with their beauty are—
Oh, no man knows
Through what wild centuries
Roves back the rose.°

Very old are the brooks;
And the rills that rise
Where snow sleeps cold beneath
The azure skies
Sing such a history
Of come and gone,
Their every drop is as wise
As Solomon.

Very old are we men;
Our dreams are tales
Told in dim Eden
By Eve's nightingales;
We wake and whisper awhile,
But, the day gone by,

Through . . . rose an observation one might find
n early Yeats, who, in fact, admired these lines

Silence and sleep like fields
Of amaranth° lie.

1912

The Ghost

'Who knocks?' 'I, who was beautiful,
  Beyond all dreams to restore,
I, from the roots of the dark thorn am hither,
  And knock on the door.'

'Who speaks?' 'I—once was my speech
  Sweet as the bird's on the air,
When echo lurks by the waters to heed;
  'Tis I speak thee fair.'

'Dark is the hour!' 'Ay, and cold.'
10   'Lone is my house.' 'Ah, but mine?'
'Sight, touch, lips, eyes yearned in vain.'
  'Long dead these to thine . . .'

Silence. Still faint on the porch
  Brake the flames of the stars.
In gloom groped a hope-wearied hand
  Over keys, bolts, and bars.

A face peered. All the grey night
  In chaos of vacancy shone;
Nought but vast sorrow was there—
  The sweet cheat gone.°

1918

RUDYARD KIPLING
1865–1936

Joseph Rudyard Kipling was born in Bombay, the son of the principal of Lahore Art
School. He was extremely happy during his early childhood, but his life became a
nightmare when he was sent to school in England (at age 6), and the beatings and
humiliations of those six years—though he sometimes spoke of them as a good preparation for life—left a permanent mark on him. Many of his stories are about subtle
and horrible revenges, and the one here included is a masterly example of the kind.
Upon his return to India in 1882 he quickly achieved success as a journalist, and as
a writer of verse and stories (notably *Plain Tales from the Hills*, 1888). During his
second visit to England in 1889 he wrote his first novel, *The Light That Failed* (1890),
not a great success. He married an American and lived for some years in Vermont,

amaranth a mythical undying flower
The sweet cheat gone This phrase may resonate
for the reader because of its use, by C. K.

Scott-Moncrieff, to translate the title (*Albertine
Disparue*) of one of the volumes of Proust's
Remembrance of Things Past.

but the marriage did not work out and he returned once more to England in 1899.

Meanwhile with such verse as *Barrack Room Ballads* (1892), the two *Jungle Books* (1894, 1895), and the stories in *Many Inventions* and *The Day's Work* (1893, 1899) he had become one of the most famous English writers of his time, and one who steadfastly preferred action and machinery to the prevalent Art for Art's Sake. *Stalky & Co.*, a series of school stories often thought brutal, appeared in 1899. His work continued until there was enough of it to fill the thirty-five volumes of the Collected Edition; he was awarded the Nobel Prize in 1907. His (unfinished) auto-biography, *Something of Myself*, was published posthumously in 1937.

Some of the finest and strangest of Kipling's stories are late ones. *Mary Postgate* was published in 1915. England was full of atrocity stories—some true and some not—about the Germans, and Mary Postgate was evidently one who believed them. The power of the tale lies in the way in which she is established as an obedient, patient, passionless woman, already old at forty-four, hardly capable of reacting to a snub, yet concealing, unknown to herself, an appalling ferocity which the destruction of the dead young man's property, the death of the child, and the lie of the doctor some-how bring to the surface. The consequences of this surfacing become a sensual act, leading to the unheard-of break with such routines as that of the hot bath, and the compliments of her employer on her appearance. An act of cruelty and revenge has rejuvenated her, almost as though it were a sexual fulfillment. She even represents it to herself as woman's work. In the later stories it is the richness of ambiguous implications and a kind of masked horror that make them, for some readers, Kipling's best, most disquieting, and most permanent work. Certainly this one appears appro-priately in an anthology that contains so much writing about the great and crucial war of 1914–18.

Mary Postgate

Of Miss Mary Postgate, Lady McCausland wrote that she was 'thoroughly conscientious, tidy, companionable, and ladylike. I am very sorry to part with her, and shall always be interested in her welfare.'

Miss Fowler engaged her on this recommendation, and to her surprise, for she had had experience of companions, found that it was true. Miss Fowler was nearer sixty than fifty at the time, but though she needed care she did not exhaust her attendant's vitality. On the contrary, she gave out, stimulatingly and with reminiscences. Her father had been a minor Court official in the days when the Great Exhibition of 1851 [1] had just set its seal on Civilisation made perfect. Some of Miss Fowler's tales, none the less, were not always for the young. Mary was not young, and though her speech was as colourless as her eyes or her hair, she was never shocked. She listened unflinchingly to every one; said at the end, 'How interesting!' or 'How shocking!' as the case might be, and never again referred to it, for she prided herself on a trained mind, which 'did not dwell on these things.' She was, too, a treasure at domestic accounts,

1. The first international exposition, celebrating British art, industry, and empire. The Crystal Palace was built for it.

for which the village tradesmen, with their weekly books, loved her not. Otherwise she had no enemies; provoked no jealousy even among the plainest; neither gossip nor slander had ever been traced to her; she supplied the odd place at the Rector's or the Doctor's table at half an hour's notice; she was a sort of public aunt to very many small children of the village street, whose parents, while accepting everything, would have been swift to resent what they called 'patronage'; she served on the Village Nursing Committee as Miss Fowler's nominee when Miss Fowler was crippled by rheumatoid arthritis, and came out of six months' fort-nightly meetings equally respected by all the cliques.

And when Fate threw Miss Fowler's nephew, an unlovely orphan of eleven, on Miss Fowler's hands, Mary Postgate stood to her share of the business of education as practised in private and public schools. She checked printed clothes-lists, and unitemised bills of extras; wrote to Head and House masters, matrons, nurses and doctors, and grieved or rejoiced over half-term reports. Young Wyndham Fowler repaid her in his holidays by calling her 'Gatepost,' 'Postey,' or 'Packthread,' by thumping her between her narrow shoulders, or by chasing her bleating, round the garden, her large mouth open, her large nose high in air, at a stiff-necked shamble very like a camel's. Later on he filled the house with clamour, argument, and harangues as to his personal needs, likes and dislikes, and the limitations of 'you women,' reducing Mary to tears of physical fatigue, or, when he chose to be humorous, of helpless laughter. At crises, which multiplied as he grew older, she was his ambassadress and his interpretress to Miss Fowler, who had no large sympathy with the young; a vote in his interest at the councils on his future; his sewing-woman, strictly accountable for mislaid boots and garments; always his butt and his slave.

And when he decided to become a solicitor, and had entered an office in London; when his greeting had changed from 'Hullo, Postey, you old beast,' to 'Mornin' Packthread,' there came a war which, unlike all wars that Mary could remember, did not stay decently outside England and in the newspapers, but intruded on the lives of people whom she knew. As she said to Miss Fowler, it was 'most vexatious.' It took the Rector's son who was going into business with his elder brother; it took the Colonel's nephew on the eve of fruit-farming in Canada; it took Mrs. Grant's son who, his mother said, was devoted to the ministry; and, very early indeed, it took Wynn Fowler, who announced on a postcard that he had joined the Flying Corps [2] and wanted a cardigan waist-coat.

'He must go, and he must have the waistcoat,' said Miss Fowler. So Mary got the proper-sized needles and wool, while Miss Fowler told the men of her establishment—two gardeners and an odd man, aged sixty—that those who could join the Army had better do so. The gardeners left. Cheape, the odd man, stayed on, and was promoted to the gardener's cottage. The cook, scorning to be limited in luxuries, also left, after a spirited scene with Miss Fowler, and took the house-maid with her. Miss Fowler gazetted Nellie, Cheape's seventeen-year-old daughter, to the vacant post; Mrs. Cheape to the rank of cook with occasional cleaning bouts; and the reduced establishment moved forward smoothly.

2. Royal Flying Corps (later, Royal Air Force).

Wynn demanded an increase in his allowance. Miss Fowler, who always looked facts in the face, said, 'He must have it. The chances are he won't live long to draw it, and if three hundred makes him happy——'

Wynn was grateful, and came over, in his tight-buttoned uniform, to say so. His training centre was not thirty miles away, and his talk was so technical that it had to be explained by charts of the various types of machines. He gave Mary such a chart.

'And you'd better study it, Postey,' he said. 'You'll be seeing a lot of 'em soon.' So Mary studied the chart, but when Wynn next arrived to swell and exalt himself before his womenfolk, she failed badly in cross-examination, and he rated her as in the old days.

'You *look* more or less like a human being,' he said in his new Service voice. 'You *must* have had a brain at some time in your past. What have you done with it? Where d'you keep it? A sheep would know more than you do, Postey. You're lamentable. You are less use than an empty tin can, you dowey old cassowary.'

'I suppose that's how your superior officer talks to *you?*' said Miss Fowler from her chair.

'But Postey doesn't mind,' Wynn replied. 'Do you, Packthread?'

'Why? Was Wynn saying anything? I shall get this right next time you come,' she muttered, and knitted her pale brows again over the diagrams of Taubes, Farmans, and Zeppelins.[3]

In a few weeks the mere land and sea battles which she read to Miss Fowler after breakfast passed her like idle breath. Her heart and her interest were high in the air with Wynn, who had finished 'rolling' (whatever that might be) and had gone on from a 'taxi' to a machine more or less his own. One morning it circled over their very chimneys, alighted on Vegg's Heath, almost outside the garden gate, and Wynn came in, blue with cold, shouting for food. He and she drew Miss Fowler's bath-chair,[4] as they had often done, along the Heath foot-path to look at the biplane. Mary observed that 'it smelt very badly.'

'Postey, I believe you think with your nose,' said Wynn. 'I know you don't with your mind. Now, what type's that?'

'I'll go and get the chart,' said Mary.

'You're hopeless! You haven't the mental capacity of a white mouse,' he cried, and explained the dials and the sockets for bomb-dropping till it was time to mount and ride the wet clouds once more.

'Ah!' said Mary, as the stinking thing flared upward. 'Wait till our Flying Corps gets to work! Wynn says it's much safer than in the trenches.'

'I wonder,' said Miss Fowler. 'Tell Cheape to come and tow me home again.'

'It's all downhill. I can do it,' said Mary, 'if you put the brake on.' She laid her lean self against the pushing-bar and home they trundled.

'Now, be careful you aren't heated and catch a chill,' said overdressed Miss Fowler.

'Nothing makes me perspire,' said Mary. As she bumped the chair under the porch she straightened her long back. The exertion had given her a colour, and

---

3. Fighting airplanes and lighter-than-air craft of World War I.
4. Wheelchair.

the wind had loosened a wisp of hair across her forehead. Miss Fowler glanced at her.

'What do you ever think of, Mary?' she demanded suddenly.

'Oh, Wynn says he wants another three pairs of stockings—as thick as we can make them.'

'Yes. But I mean the things that women think about. Here you are, more than forty——'

'Forty-four,' said truthful Mary.

'Well?'

'Well?' Mary offered Miss Fowler her shoulder as usual.

'And you've been with me ten years now.'

'Let's see,' said Mary. 'Wynn was eleven when he came. He's twenty now, and I came two years before that. It must be eleven.'

'Eleven! And you've never told me anything that matters in all that while. Looking back, it seems to me that I've done all the talking.'

'I'm afraid I'm not much of a conversationalist. As Wynn says, I haven't the mind. Let me take your hat.'

Miss Fowler, moving stiffly from the hip, stamped her rubber-tipped stick on the tiled hall floor. 'Mary, aren't you *anything* except a companion? Would you *ever* have been anything except a companion?'

Mary hung up the garden hat on its proper peg. 'No,' she said after consideration. 'I don't imagine I ever should. But I've no imagination, I'm afraid.'

She fetched Miss Fowler her eleven-o'clock glass of Contrexeville.[5]

That was the wet December when it rained six inches to the month, and the women went abroad as little as might be. Wynn's flying chariot visited them several times, and for two mornings (he had warned her by postcard) Mary heard the thresh of his propellers at dawn. The second time she ran to the window, and stared at the whitening sky. A little blur passed overhead. She lifted her lean arms towards it.

That evening at six o'clock there came an announcement in an official envelope that Second Lieutenant W. Fowler had been killed during a trial flight. Death was instantaneous. She read it and carried it to Miss Fowler.

'I never expected anything else,' said Miss Fowler; 'but I'm sorry it happened before he had done anything.'

The room was whirling round Mary Postgate, but she found herself quite steady in the midst of it.

'Yes,' she said. 'It's a great pity he didn't die in action after he had killed somebody.'

'He was killed instantly. That's one comfort,' Miss Fowler went on.

'But Wynn says the shock of a fall kills a man at once—whatever happens to the tanks,' quoted Mary.

The room was coming to rest now. She heard Miss Fowler say impatiently, 'But why can't we cry, Mary?' and herself replying, 'There's nothing to cry for. He has done his duty as much as Mrs. Grant's son did.'

'And when he died, *she* came and cried all the morning,' said Miss Fowler.

5. Mineral water from a French spa.

'This only makes me feel tired—terribly tired. Will you help me to bed, please, Mary?—And I think I'd like the hot-water bottle.'

So Mary helped her and sat beside, talking of Wynn in his riotous youth.

'I believe,' said Miss Fowler suddenly, 'that old people and young people slip from under a stroke like this. The middle-aged feel it most.'

'I expect that's true,' said Mary, rising. 'I'm going to put away the things in his room now. Shall we wear mourning?'

'Certainly not,' said Miss Fowler. 'Except, of course, at the funeral. I can't go. You will. I want you to arrange about his being buried here. What a blessing it didn't happen at Salisbury!'

Every one, from the Authorities of the Flying Corps to the Rector, was most kind and sympathetic. Mary found herself for the moment in a world where bodies were in the habit of being despatched by all sorts of conveyances to all sorts of places. And at the funeral two young men in buttoned-up uniforms stood beside the grave and spoke to her afterwards.

'You're Miss Postgate, aren't you?' said one. 'Fowler told me about you. He was a good chap—a first-class fellow—a great loss.'

'Great loss!' growled his companion. 'We're all awfully sorry.'

'How high did he fall from?' Mary whispered.

'Pretty nearly four thousand feet, I should think, didn't he? You were up that day, Monkey?'

'All of that,' the other child replied. 'My bar [6] made three thousand, and I wasn't as high as him by a lot.'

'Then *that's* all right,' said Mary. 'Thank you very much.'

They moved away as Mrs. Grant flung herself weeping on Mary's flat chest, under the lych-gate, and cried, '*I* know how it feels! *I* know how it feels!'

'But both his parents are dead,' Mary returned, as she fended her off. 'Perhaps they've all met by now,' she added vaguely as she escaped towards the coach.

'I've thought of that too,' wailed Mrs. Grant; 'but then he'll be practically a stranger to them. Quite embarrassing!'

Mary faithfully reported every detail of the ceremony to Miss Fowler, who, when she described Mrs. Grant's outburst, laughed aloud.

'Oh, how Wynn would have enjoyed it! He was always utterly unreliable at funerals. D'you remember——' And they talked of him again, each piecing out the other's gaps. 'And now,' said Miss Fowler, 'we'll pull up the blinds and we'll have a general tidy. That always does us good. Have you seen to Wynn's things?'

'Everything—since he first came,' said Mary, 'He was never destructive —even with his toys.'

They faced that neat room.

'It can't be natural not to cry,' Mary said at last. 'I'm *so* afraid you'll have a reaction.'

'As I told you, we old people slip from under the stroke. It's you I'm afraid for. Have you cried yet?'

'I can't. It only makes me angry with the Germans.'

6. Altimeter (works by barometric pressure).

'That's sheer waste of vitality,' said Miss Fowler. 'We must live till the war's finished.' She opened a full wardrobe. 'Now, I've been thinking things over. This is my plan. All his civilian clothes can be given away—Belgian refugees, and so on.'

Mary nodded. 'Boots, collars, and gloves?'

'Yes. We don't need to keep anything except his cap and belt.'

'They came back yesterday with his Flying Corps clothes'—Mary pointed to a roll on the little iron bed.

'Ah, but keep his Service things. Some one may be glad of them later. Do you remember his sizes?'

'Five feet eight and a half; thirty-six inches round the chest. But he told me he's just put on an inch and a half. I'll mark it on a label and tie it on his sleeping-bag.'

'So that disposes of *that*,' said Miss Fowler, tapping the palm of one hand with the ringed third finger of the other. 'What waste it all is! We'll get his old school trunk to-morrow and pack his civilian clothes.'

'And the rest?' said Mary. 'His books and pictures and the games and the toys—and—and the rest?'

'My plan is to burn every single thing,' said Miss Fowler. 'Then we shall know where they are and no one can handle them afterwards. What do you think?'

'I think that would be much the best,' said Mary. 'But there's such a lot of them.'

'We'll burn them in the destructor,' said Miss Fowler.

This was an open-air furnace for the consumption of refuse; a little circular four-foot tower of pierced brick over an iron grating. Miss Fowler had noticed the design in a gardening journal years ago, and had had it built at the bottom of the garden. It suited her tidy soul, for it saved unsightly rubbish-heaps, and the ashes lightened the stiff clay soil.

Mary considered for a moment, saw her way clear, and nodded again. They spent the evening putting away well-remembered civilian suits, underclothes that Mary had marked, and the regiments of very gaudy socks and ties. A second trunk was needed, and, after that, a little packing-case, and it was late next day when Cheape and the local carrier [7] lifted them to the cart. The Rector luckily knew of a friend's son, about five feet eight and a half inches high, to whom a complete Flying Corps outfit would be most acceptable, and sent his gardener's son down with a barrow to take delivery of it. The cap was hung up in Miss Fowler's bedroom, the belt in Miss Postgate's; for, as Miss Fowler said, they had no desire to make tea-party talk of them.

'That disposes of *that*,' said Miss Fowler. 'I'll leave the rest to you, Mary. I can't run up and down the garden. You'd better take the big clothes-basket and get Nellie to help you.'

'I shall take the wheel-barrow and do it myself,' said Mary, and for once in her life closed her mouth.

Miss Fowler, in moments of irritation, had called Mary deadly methodical. She put on her oldest water-proof and gardening-hat and her ever-slipping

7. Small trucker.

goloshes, for the weather was on the edge of more rain. She gathered fire-lighters from the kitchen, a half-scuttle of coals, and a faggot of brushwood. These she wheeled in the barrow down the mossed paths to the dank little laurel shrubbery where the destructor stood under the drip of three oaks. She climbed the wire fence into the Rector's glebe [8] just behind, and from his tenant's rick pulled two large armfuls of good hay, which she spread neatly on the fire-bars. Next, journey by journey, passing Miss Fowler's white face at the morning-room window each time, she brought down in the towel-covered clothes-basket, on the wheel-barrow, thumbed and used Hentys, Marryats, Levers, Stevensons, Baroness Orczys, Garvices,[9] schoolbooks, and atlases, unrelated piles of the *Motor Cyclist*, the *Light Car*, and catalogues of Olympia Exhibitions; [10] the remnants of a fleet of sailing-ships from nine-penny cutters to a three-guinea yacht; a prep.-school dressing-gown; bats from three-and-sixpence to twenty-four shillings; cricket and tennis balls; disintegrated steam and clockwork locomotives with their twisted rails; a grey and red tin model of a submarine; a dumb gramophone and cracked records; golf-clubs that had to be broken across the knee, like his walking-sticks, and an assegai; [11] photographs of private and public school cricket and football elevens, and his O.T.C.[12] on the line of march; kodaks, and film-rolls; some pewters, and one real silver cup, for boxing competitions and Junior Hurdles; sheaves of school photographs; Miss Fowler's photograph; her own which he had borne off in fun and (good care she took not to ask!) had never returned; a playbox with a secret drawer; a load of flannels, belts, and jerseys, and a pair of spiked shoes unearthed in the attic; a packet of all the letters that Miss Fowler and she had ever written to him, kept for some absurd reason through all these years; a five-day attempt at a diary; framed pictures of racing motors in full Brooklands career, and load upon load of undistinguishable wreckage of tool-boxes, rabbit-hutches, electric batteries, tin soldiers, fret-saw outfits, and jig-saw puzzles.

Miss Fowler at the window watched her come and go, and said to herself, 'Mary's an old woman. I never realised it before.'

After lunch she recommended her to rest.

'I'm not in the least tired,' said Mary. 'I've got it all arranged. I'm going to the village at two o'clock for some paraffin.[13] Nellie hasn't enough, and the walk will do me good.'

She made one last quest round the house before she started, and found that she had overlooked nothing. It began to mist as soon as she had skirted Vegg's Heath, where Wynn used to descend—it seemed to her that she could almost hear the beat of his propellers overhead, but there was nothing to see. She hoisted her umbrella and lunged into the blind wet till she had reached the shelter of the empty village. As she came out of Mr. Kidd's shop with a bottle full of paraffin in her string shopping-bag, she met Nurse Eden, the village nurse, and fell into talk with her, as usual, about the village children. They

8. Cultivable field belonging to a vicarage.
9. Books (chiefly for boys) by adventure novelists.
10. Exhibitions of all kinds held in a large building in West London.
11. Zulu throwing spear (relic of the 19-century Zulu wars).
12. Officers Training Corps.
13. Kerosene.

were just parting opposite the 'Royal Oak' when a gun, they fancied, was fired immediately behind the house. It was followed by a child's shriek dying into a wail.

'Accident!' said Nurse Eden promptly, and dashed through the empty bar, followed by Mary. They found Mrs. Gerritt, the publican's wife, who could only gasp and point to the yard, where a little cart-lodge was sliding sideways amid a clatter of tiles. Nurse Eden snatched up a sheet drying before the fire, ran out, lifted something from the ground, and flung the sheet round it. The sheet turned scarlet and half her uniform too, as she bore the load into the kitchen. It was little Edna Gerritt, aged nine, whom Mary had known since her perambulator days.

'Am I hurted bad?' Edna asked, and died between Nurse Eden's dripping hands. The sheet fell aside and for an instant, before she could shut her eyes, Mary saw the ripped and shredded body.

'It's a wonder she spoke at all,' said Nurse Eden. 'What in God's name was it?'

'A bomb,' said Mary.

'One o' the Zeppelins?'

'No. An aeroplane. I thought I heard it on the Heath but I fancied it was one of ours. It must have shut off its engines as it came down. That's why we didn't notice it.'

'The filthy pigs!' said Nurse Eden, all white and shaken. 'See the pickle I'm in! Go and tell Dr. Hennis, Miss Postgate.' Nurse looked at the mother, who had dropped face down on the floor. 'She's only in a fit. Turn her over.'

Mary heaved Mrs. Gerritt right side up, and hurried off for the doctor. When she told her tale, he asked her to sit down in the surgery till he got her something.

'But I don't need it, I assure you,' said she. 'I don't think it would be wise to tell Miss Fowler about it, do you? Her heart is so irritable in this weather.'

Dr. Hennis looked at her admiringly as he packed up his bag.

'No. Don't tell anybody till we're sure,' he said, and hastened to the 'Royal Oak,' while Mary went on with the paraffin. The village behind her was as quiet as usual, for the news had not yet spread. She frowned a little to herself, her large nostrils expanded uglily and from time to time she muttered a phrase which Wynn who never restrained himself before his women-folk, had applied to the enemy. 'Bloody pagans! They *are* bloody pagans. But,' she continued, falling back on the teaching that had made her what she was, 'one mustn't let one's mind dwell on these things.'

Before she reached the house Dr. Hennis, who was also a special constable, overtook her in his car.

'Oh, Miss Postgate,' he said, 'I wanted to tell you that that accident at the "Royal Oak" was due to Gerritt's stable tumbling down. It's been dangerous for a long time. It ought to have been condemned.'

'I thought I heard an explosion too,' said Mary.

'You might have been misled by the beams snapping. I've been looking at 'em. They were dry-rotted through and through. Of course, as they broke, they would make a noise just like a gun.'

'Yes?' said Mary politely.

'Poor little Edna was playing underneath it,' he went on, still holding her with his eyes, 'and that and the tiles cut her to pieces, you see?'

'I saw it,' said Mary, shaking her head. 'I heard it too.'

'Well, we cannot be sure.' Dr. Hennis changed his tone completely. 'I know both you and Nurse Eden (I've been speaking to her) are perfectly trustworthy, and I can relay on you not to say anything—yet at least. It is no good to stir up people unless——'

'Oh, I never do—anyhow,' said Mary, and Dr. Hennis went on to the country town.

After all, she told herself, it might, just possibly, have been the collapse of the old stable that had done all those things to poor little Edna. She was sorry she had even hinted at other things, but Nurse Eden was discretion itself. By the time she reached home the affair seemed increasingly remote by its very monstrosity. As she came in, Miss Fowler told her that a couple of aeroplanes had passed half an hour ago.

'I thought I heard them,' she replied, 'I'm going down to the garden now. I've got the paraffin.'

'Yes, but—what *have* you got on your boots? They're soaking wet. Change them at once.'

Not only did Mary obey but she wrapped the boots in a newspaper, and put them into the string bag with the bottle. So, armed with the longest kitchen poker, she left.

'It's raining again,' was Miss Fowler's last word, 'but—I know you won't be happy till that's disposed of.'

'It won't take long. I've got everything down there, and I've put the lid on the destructor to keep the wet out.'

The shrubbery was filling with twilight by the time she had completed her arrangements and sprinkled the sacrificial oil. As she lit the match that would burn her heart to ashes, she heard a groan or a grunt behind the dense Portugal laurels.

'Cheape?' she called impatiently, but Cheape, with his ancient lumbago, in his comfortable cottage would be the last man to profane the sanctuary. 'Sheep,' she concluded, and threw in the fusee. The pyre went up in a roar, and the immediate flame hastened night around her.

'How Wynn would have loved this!' she thought, stepping back from the blaze.

By its light she saw, half hidden behind a laurel not five paces away, a bare-headed man sittting very stiffly at the foot of one of the oaks. A broken branch lay across his lap—one booted leg protruding from beneath it. His head moved ceaselessly from side to side, but his body was as still as the tree's trunk. He was dressed—she moved sideways to look more closely—in a uniform something like Wynn's, with a flap buttoned across the chest. For an instant she had some idea that it might be one of the young flying men she had met at the funeral. But their heads were dark and glossy. This man's was as pale as a baby's, and so closely cropped that she could see the disgusting pinky skin beneath. His lips moved.

'What do you say?' Mary moved towards him and stooped.

'Laty! Laty! Laty!' he muttered, while his hands picked at the dead wet leaves. There was no doubt as to his nationality. It made her so angry that she strode back to the destructor, though it was still too hot to use the poker there. Wynn's books seemed to be catching well. She looked up at the oak behind the man; several of the light upper and two or three rotten lower branches had broken and scattered their rubbish on the shrubbery path. On the lowest fork a helmet with dependent strings, showed like a bird's-nest in the light of a long-tongued flame. Evidently this person had fallen through the tree. Wynn had told her that it was quite possible for people to fall out of aeroplanes. Wynn told her too, that trees were useful things to break an aviator's fall, but in this case the aviator must have been broken or he would have moved from his queer position. He seemed helpless except for his horrible rolling head. On the other hand, she could see a pistol case at his belt—and Mary loathed pistols. Months ago, after reading certain Belgian reports together, she and Miss Fowler had had dealings with one—a huge revolver with flat-nosed bullets, which latter, Wynn said, were forbidden by the rules of war to be used against civilised enemies. 'They're good enough for us,' Miss Fowler had replied. 'Show Mary how it works.' And Wynn, laughing at the mere possibility of any such need, had led the craven winking Mary into the Rector's disused quarry, and had shown her how to fire the terrible machine. It lay now in the top-left-hand drawer of her toilet-table—a memento not included in the burning. Wynn would be pleased to see how she was not afraid.

She slipped up to the house to get it. When she came through the rain, the eyes in the head were alive with expectation. The mouth even tried to smile. But at sight of the revolver its corners went down just like Edna Gerritt's. A tear trickled from one eye, and the head rolled from shoulder to shoulder as though trying to point out something.

'Cassée. Tout cassée,[14] it whimpered.

'What do you say?' said Mary disgustedly, keeping well to one side, though only the head moved.

'Cassée,' it repeated. 'Che me rends. [15] Le médicin! Toctor!'

'Nein!' said she, bringing all her small German to bear with the big pistol. 'Ich haben der todt Kinder gesehn.' [16]

The head was still. Mary's hand dropped. She had been careful to keep her finger off the trigger for fear of accidents. After a few moments' waiting, she returned to the destructor, where the flames were falling, and churned up Wynn's charring books with the poker. Again the head groaned for the doctor.

'Stop that!' said Mary, and stamped her foot. 'Stop that, you bloody pagan!'

The words came quite smoothly and naturally. They were Wynn's own words, and Wynn was a gentleman who for no consideration on earth would have torn little Edna into those vividly coloured strips and strings. But this thing hunched under the oak-tree had done that thing. It was no question of reading horrors out of newspapers to Miss Fowler. Mary had seen it with her own eyes on the 'Royal Oak' kitchen table. She must not allow her mind to dwell upon it. Now Wynn was dead, and everything connected with him was lumping and rustling and tinkling under her busy poker into red black dust and grey leaves of ash. The thing beneath the oak would die too. Mary had seen death more than once. She came of a family that had a knack of dying

14. "Broken. All broken."
15. "I giff up. Doctor!"
16. "I've seen the dead child" (quite ungrammatically said).

under, as she told Miss Fowler, 'most distressing circumstances.' She would stay where she was till she was entirely satisfied that It was dead—dead as dear papa in the late 'eighties; aunt Mary in 'eighty-nine; mamma in 'ninety-one; cousin Dick in 'ninety-five; Lady McCausland's housemaid in 'ninety-nine; Lady McCausland's sister in nineteen hundred and one; Wynn burried five days ago; and Edna Gerritt still waiting for decent earth to hide her. As she thought—her underlip caught up by one faded canine, brows knit and nostrils wide—she wielded the poker with lunges that jarred the grating at the bottom, and careful scrapes round the brick-work above. She looked at her wrist-watch. It was getting on to half-past four, and the rain was coming down in earnest. Tea would be at five. If It did not die before that time, she would be soaked and would have to change. Meantime, and this occupied her, Wynn's things were burning well in spite of the hissing wet though now and again a book-back with a quite distinguishable title would be heaved up out of the mass. The exercise of stoking had given her a glow which seemed to reach to the marrow of her bones. She hummed—Mary never had a voice—to herself. She had never believed in all those advanced views—though Miss Fowler herself leaned a little that way—of woman's work in the world; but now she saw there was much to be said for them. This, for instance, was her work—work which no man, least of all Dr. Hennis, would ever have done. A man, at such a crisis, would be what Wynn called a 'sportsman'; would leave everything to fetch help, and would certainly bring It into the house. Now a woman's business was to make a happy home for—for a husband and children. Failing these—it was not a thing one should allow one's mind to dwell upon—but——

'Stop it!' Mary cried once more across the shadows. 'Nein, I tell you! Ich haben der todt Kinder gesehn.'

But it was a fact. A woman who had missed these things could still be useful —more useful than a man in certain respects. She thumped like a paviour [17] through the settling ashes at the secret thrill of it. The rain was damping the fire, but she could feel—it was too dark to see—that her work was done. There was a dull red glow at the bottom of the destructor, not enough to char the wooden lid if she slipped it half over against the driving wet. This arranged, she leaned on the poker and waited, while an increasing rapture laid hold on her. She ceased to think. She gave herself up to feel. Her long pleasure was broken by a sound that she had waited for in agony several times in her life. She leaned forward and listened, smiling. There could be no mistake. She closed her eyes and drank it in. Once it ceased abruptly.

'Go on,' she murmured, half aloud. 'That isn't the end.'

Then the end came very distinctly in a lull between two rain-gusts. Mary Postgate drew her breath short between her teeth and shivered from head to foot. 'That's all right,' said she contentedly, and went up to the house, where she scandalised the whole routine by taking a luxurious hot bath before tea, and came down looking, as Miss Fowler said when she saw her lying all relaxed on the other sofa, 'quite handsome!'

1915   1915

WILFRED OWEN
1893–1918

It is hard for Americans to realize the extent and significance of the toll taken by World War I of the middle classes which had contributed so much to English culture. Such previous wars as those against Napoleon, and those fought all over the globe to maintain "Dominion over palm and pine," as Kipling half-ironically described the Empire, had been paid for with the blood of working-class and rural laboring enlisted men and often aristocratic career officers (the Navy had always drawn its officers from a broader social base). But the publication of the casualty lists of the Battle of the Somme (1916), with their record of decimation of a whole generation of young men of promise, fell across England like the shadow of a scythe. Many talented and brilliant young people who had not yet produced evidence of their gifts enlisted and perished. It is rare to find a young painter or musician who leaves behind, in his twenties, a body of work mature enough to constitute a recognizable though truncated career. It is easier for young mathematicians and poets to bequeath creative work that is more than merely promising.

Wilfred Owen was one such poet. While the popular verses and celebrated physical beauty of Rupert Brooke (1887–1915) were the subject of much patriotic piety, Owen's poems not only provided the prototype for subsequent visions of modern warfare but also came up with some technical developments (such as the off-rhymes of "Strange Meeting") which would influence even the British poetry of the thirties, which was manifestly opposed to Georgian poetry and its stylistic and moral norms. Owen's poetry reveals an ironic distrust of all the traditional ideologies which have kept soldiers fighting, but it informs that distrust with a passion of personal engagement with the direct experience of pain, apocalyptically violent death, and the other sophisticated horrors of a new technology of warfare which the conventional literary language and ethic of battle could not embody. Owen's war poems range from an expression of a private, even an erotic, sense of the being of other men in combat to the most distantly classical of formulations.

Wilfred Owen was born in Shropshire, studied at London University, taught school and tutored privately in France, and enlisted in the army in 1915. He was commissioned in 1916, wounded early the next year, convalesced in Scotland and in England, returned to combat in 1918, and was killed in action exactly one week before the Armistice. His *Collected Poems* was published in 1920; the texts printed below are all from C. Day Lewis's edition of 1963.

Dulce et Decorum Est°

Bent double, like old beggars under sacks,
Knock-kneed, coughing like hags, we cursed through sludge,
Till on the haunting flares we turned our backs
And towards our distant rest began to trudge.

Dulce et Decorum Est a tag from Horace (*Odes* III.2.13), well known to British schoolboys: *Dulce et decorum est pro patria mori*—It is sweet and honorable to die for your country"

Men marched asleep. Many had lost their boots
But limped on, blood-shod. All went lame; all blind;
Drunk with fatigue; deaf even to the hoots
Of tired, outstripped Five-Nines° that dropped behind.

Gas! GAS! Quick, boys!—An ecstasy of fumbling,
Fitting the clumsy helmets just in time;
But someone still was yelling out and stumbling
And flound'ring like a man in fire or lime . . .
Dim, through the misty panes and thick green light,
As under a green sea, I saw him drowning.

In all my dreams, before my helpless sight,
He plunges at me, guttering, choking, drowning.

If in some smothering dreams you too could pace
Behind the wagon that we flung him in,
And watch the white eyes writhing in his face,
His hanging face, like a devil's sick of sin;
If you could hear, at every jolt, the blood
Come gargling from the froth-corrupted lungs,
Obscene as cancer, bitter as the cud
Of vile, incurable sores on innocent tongues,—
My friend, you would not tell with such high zest
To children ardent for some desperate glory,
The old Lie: Dulce et decorum est
Pro patria mori.

1917   1920

Strange Meeting

It seemed that out of battle I escaped
Down some profound dull tunnel, long since scooped
Through granites which titanic wars had groined.°
Yet also there encumbered sleepers groaned,
Too fast in thought or death to be bestirred.
Then, as I probed them, one sprang up, and stared
With piteous recognition in fixed eyes,
Lifting distressful hands as if to bless.
And by his smile, I knew that sullen hall,
By his dead smile I knew we stood in Hell.
With a thousand pains that vision's face was grained;
Yet no blood reached there from the upper ground,
And no guns thumped, or down the flues made moan.
'Strange friend,' I said, 'here is no cause to mourn.'

Five-Nines Shells containing poison gas. This whole poem is about a gas attack, gas being the World War I weapon which raised moral problems (like atomic weapons, or napalm, thereafter).
groined carved out into arches

'None,' said that other, 'save the undone years,
The hopelessness. Whatever hope is yours,
Was my life also; I went hunting wild
After the wildest beauty in the world,
Which lies not calm in eyes, or braided hair,
20   But mocks the steady running of the hour,
And if it grieves, grieves richlier than here.
For of my glee might many men have laughed,
And of my weeping something had been left,
Which must die now. I mean the truth untold,
The pity of war, the pity war distilled.
Now men will go content with what we spoiled,
Or, discontent, boil bloody, and be spilled.
They will be swift with swiftness of the tigress.
None will break ranks, though nations trek from progress.
30   Courage was mine, and I had mystery,
Wisdom was mine, and I had mastery:
To miss the march of this retreating world
Into vain citadels that are not walled.
Then, when much blood had clogged their chariot-wheels,
I would go up and wash them from sweet wells,
Even with truths that lie too deep for taint.
I would have poured my spirit without stint
But not through wounds; not on the cess° of war.
Foreheads of men have bled where no wounds were.
40   I am the enemy you killed, my friend.
I knew you in this dark: for so you frowned
Yesterday through me as you jabbed and killed.
I parried; but my hands were loath and cold.
Let us sleep now. . . .'
1918   1920

Arms and the Boy°

Let the boy try along this bayonet-blade
How cold steel is, and keen with hunger of blood;
Blue with all malice, like a madman's flash;
And thinly drawn with famishing for flesh.

Lend him to stroke these blind, blunt bullet-leads
Which long to nuzzle in the hearts of lads,
Or give him cartridges of fine zinc teeth,
Sharp with the sharpness of grief and death.

For his teeth seem for laughing round an apple.
10   There lurk no claws behind his fingers supple;

cess garbage, refuse
Arms and the Boy a parodic twist on the open-

ing phrase of Virgil's *Aeneid,* "Arms and the
man I sing . . ." (*Arma virumque cano . . .*)

And God will grow no talons at his heels,
Nor antlers through the thickness of his curls.
1918   1920

Fragment: I Saw His Round Mouth's Crimson . . .

I saw his round mouth's crimson deepen as it fell,
  Like a Sun, in his last deep hour;
Watched tho magnificent recession of farewell,
  Clouding, half gleam, half glower,
And a last splendour burn the heavens of his cheek.
  And in his eyes
The cold stars lighting, very old and bleak,
  In different skies.
          1963

Anthem for Doomed Youth

What passing-bells for these who die as cattle?
  Only the monstrous anger of the guns.
  Only the stuttering rifles' rapid rattle
Can patter out their hasty orisons.°
No mockeries now for them; no prayers nor bells,
  Nor any voice of mourning save the choirs,—
The shrill, demented choirs of wailing shells;
  And bugles calling for them from sad shires.

What candles may be held to speed them all?
  Not in the hands of boys, but in their eyes
Shall shine the holy glimmers of good-byes.
  The pallor of girls' brows shall be their pall;
Their flowers the tenderness of patient minds,
And each slow dusk of drawing-down of blinds.
1917   1920

EDWARD THOMAS
1878–1917

Along with Wilfred Owen and Isaac Rosenberg, a third poet of the highest gifts to be killed in World War I was Edward Thomas. Unlike Owen and Rosenberg, however, he had been well known since the early years of the century as an essayist, literary critic, and particularly as a writer about nature and country life. Born in London of Welsh parents, he read History at Oxford, married while still an undergraduate, and took to writing essays and commissioned books, of which he published

orisons prayers

some thirty. It was not until 1914, when he met the American poet Robert Frost, then living in England, that he began writing poems, and these he first submitted to magazines under an assumed name, so hesitant was he about possible presumption in an area for which he had so much respect.

His first published poems appeared, under the pseudonym of "Edward Eastaway", in an anthology he had edited in 1915; volumes appeared in 1917 and (posthumously) 1918, and a *Collected Poems* in 1920. It is possible to detect, here and there, the influence of Frost upon Thomas's verse, particularly in its cadences; but along with Frost, he had read John Clare and other nineteenth-century English poetry which flamed with awareness of nature; and his ability to make the English countryside stand for so much in human life generally parallels, rather than follows, Frost's use of New England. Thomas enlisted in the army in 1915, and was killed fighting at Arras two years later.

The Owl

Downhill I came, hungry, and yet not starved;
Cold, yet had heat within me that was proof
Against the North wind; tired, yet so that rest
Had seemed the sweetest thing under a roof.

Then at the inn I had food, fire, and rest,
Knowing how hungry, cold, and tired was I.
All of the night was quite barred out except
An owl's cry, a most melancholy cry

Shaken out long and clear upon the hill,
10   No merry note,° nor cause of merriment,
But one telling me plain what I escaped
And others could not, that night, as in I went.

And salted was my food, and my repose,
Salted and sobered, too, by the bird's voice
Speaking for all who lay under the stars,
Soldiers and poor, unable to rejoice.

                    1917

Swedes°

They have taken the gable from the roof of clay
On the long swede pile. They have let in the sun
To the white and gold and purple of curled fronds
Unsunned. It is a sight more tender-gorgeous
At the wood-corner where Winter moans and drips

merry note In the great "Winter" song at the end of Shakespeare's *Love's Labour's Lost* the owl's cry is "Tu-whit, Tu-whoo, a merry note." Swedes rutabagas, Swedish turnips

Than when, in the Valley of the Tombs of Kings,
A boy crawls down into a Pharaoh's tomb
And, first of Christian men, beholds the mummy,
God and monkey, chariot and throne and vase,
Blue pottery, alabaster, and gold.

But dreamless long-dead Amen-hotep° lies.
This is a dream of Winter, sweet as Spring.

1917

Liberty

The last light has gone out of the world, except
This moonlight lying on the grass like frost
Beyond the brink of the tall elm's shadow.
It is as if everything else had slept
Many an age, unforgotten and lost—
The men that were, the things done, long ago,
All I have thought; and but the moon and I
Live yet and here stand idle over a grave
Where all is buried. Both have liberty
To dream what we could do if we were free
To do some thing we had desired long,
The moon and I. There's none less free than who
Does nothing and has nothing else to do,
Being free only for what is not to his mind,
And nothing is to his mind. If every hour
Like this one passing that I have spent among
The wiser others when I have forgot
To wonder whether I was free or not,
Were piled before me, and not lost behind,
And I could take and carry them away
I should be rich; or if I had the power
To wipe out every one and not again
Regret, I should be rich to be so poor.
And yet I still am half in love with pain,°
With what is imperfect, with both tears and mirth,
With things that have an end, with life and earth,
And this moon that leaves me dark within the door.

1917

Amen-hotep the Pharaoh Amenhotep IV, called Ikhnaton (reigned 1375?–1357 B.C.), founder of a monotheistic worship that vanished with his death

half . . . pain a deliberate Keatsian echo: "I have been half in love with easeful Death" ("Ode to a Nightingale" l. 52)

The Brook

Seated once by a brook, watching a child
Chiefly that paddled, I was thus beguiled.
Mellow the blackbird sang and sharp the thrush
Not far off in the oak and hazel brush,
Unseen. There was a scent like honeycomb
From mugwort dull. And down upon the dome
Of the stone the cart-horse kicks against so oft
A butterfly alighted. From aloft
He took the heat of the sun, and from below.
10   On the hot stone he perched contented so,
As if never a cart would pass again
That way; as if I were the last of men
And he the first of insects to have earth
And sun together and to know their worth.
I was divided between him and the gleam,
The motion, and the voices, of the stream,
The waters running frizzled over gravel,
That never vanish and for ever travel.
A grey flycatcher° silent on a fence
20   And I sat as if we had been there since
The horseman and the horse lying beneath
The fir-tree-covered barrow on the heath,
The horseman and the horse with silver shoes,
Galloped the downs last. All that I could lose
I lost. And then the child's voice raised the dead.
'No one's been here before' was what she said
And what I felt, yet never should have found
A word for, while I gathered sight and sound.

                                        1918

ISAAC ROSENBERG
1890–1918

Born in Bristol, moved to the East End of London in childhood, educated in local
schools, Rosenberg showed an artistic talent and an interest in poetry while still at
school. Working by day, he took art classes at night at Birkbeck College and finally,
with the help of some patrons, attended the Slade School from 1911 through 1914.
He sold a few pictures and published poems here and there (in 1912 a pamphlet of
early poems; *Youth* in 1915; his verse drama *Moses* the following year). Never in the
best of health, he traveled to South Africa in 1914–15, and upon his return enlisted
in the army. In April of 1918 he was killed in France. A selection of his poems was
published in 1922, and a *Collected Works* appeared in 1937.

    Rosenberg's was an amazingly promising talent, and it is hard to say in what direc-

---

flycatcher a bird that catches insects in mid-air

tion it might have developed had he lived. Certainly he had a remarkable ear, a thoroughly modern economy of setting for his extraordinarily evocative images, and a control of tone of voice which, like Owen's, seemed to be lost to so many of the Georgian poets.

Break of Day in the Trenches

The darkness crumbles away—
It is the same old druid Time as ever.
Only a live thing leaps my hand—
A queer sardonic rat—
As I pull the parapet's poppy
To stick behind my ear.
Droll rat, they would shoot you if they knew
Your cosmopolitan sympathies
(And God knows what antipathies).
Now you have touched this English hand
You will do the same to a German—
Soon, no doubt, if it be your pleasure
To cross the sleeping green between.
It seems you inwardly grin as you pass
Strong eyes, fine limbs, haughty athletes
Less chanced than you for life,
Bonds to the whims of murder,
Sprawled in the bowels of the earth,
The torn fields of France.
What do you see in our eyes
At the shrieking iron and flame
Hurled through still heavens?
What quaver—what heart aghast?
Poppies whose roots are in man's veins
Drop, and are ever dropping;
But mine in my ear is safe,
Just a little white with the dust.

1922

Returning, We Hear the Larks

Sombre the night is:
And, though we have our lives, we know
What sinister threat lurks there.

Dragging these anguished limbs, we only know
This poison-blasted track opens on our camp—
On a little safe sleep.

But hark! Joy—joy—strange joy.
Lo! Heights of night ringing with unseen larks:
Music showering on our upturned listening faces.

10   Death could drop from the dark
As easily as song—
But song only dropped,
Like a blind man's dreams on the sand
By dangerous tides;
Like a girl's dark hair, for she dreams no ruin lies there,
Or her kisses where a serpent hides.

                    1922

A Worm Fed on the Heart of Corinth

A worm° fed on the heart of Corinth,
Babylon and Rome:
Not Paris raped tall Helen,
But this incestuous worm,
Who lured her vivid beauty
To his amorphous sleep.
England! famous as Helen
Is thy betrothal° sung
To him the shadowless,
More amorous than Solomon.

1917   1922

DAVID JONES
1895–

The most remarkable writing about the trench warfare during World War I is *In Parenthesis*. It was done in retrospect, in a strange kind of brief epic that covered not the whole scope of the war, like some later version of Hardy's *The Dynasts*, but one small corner of it. The Richebourg sector of the Western Front is the place, and the time from December of 1915 until July of 1916, when the Battle of the Somme with its astonishing casualty lists brought the whole war, and the twentieth century itself, into new focus.

David Jones, born of Welsh parents in Kent in 1895, was trained as an artist, and served in the trenches until wounded in the Battle of the Somme. He returned to the trenches until demobilization in 1919, and then resumed art studies. After his conversion to Catholicism in 1921, he spent some fruitful years with the community of artists and craftsmen founded at Ditchling (Sussex) by sculptor-essayist Eric Gill and hand-printer-poet Hilary Pepler. In 1929 he began work on *In Parenthesis*, which was published only in 1937, as the clouds of World War II were gathering. Jones

worm Satan, in his attributes of being "shadowless", "amorphous" and, half-echoingly, "amorous"; part-biblical, part-Blakean, this prophecy of the fall of empire ranks perhaps highest among Rosenberg's visionary fragments.

betrothal with the implication that England's marriage to Satan and historically inevitable downfall is not yet consummated, with time yet for moral redemption and escape

created this unique mixture of prose and free verse, held together with collages of quotations, and effecting transitions that would become normal only in film later on, ostensibly to describe the war as he felt it had been. The title referred, he said, to the parenthetical time of life and history in which it was written, and also to the fact that human life on earth is, for an orthodox Christian, parenthetical as well. But other intentions governed the genesis of the work; and although the naturalistic reportage, the fragmentary and intimate glimpses of day-to-day life in the trenches in the months before they had become slaughterhouses, is splendid indeed, the work reaches beyond topical history. A huge body of myth, primarily Welsh but read through subsequent poetic history, is as much a part of the material of the work as its descriptive language.

Arthurian legend, a mainstay of the British imagination, is everywhere. Also, throughout the poem (for such, despite its prose, it is) Jones keeps the reader in mind of Y Gododdin, the sixth-century Welsh epic (attributed to Aneirin) describing the raid of three hundred Welsh from a part of what is now Scotland upon an English kingdom, and the destruction of that raiding force, which left only three survivors, including the poet. Jones invokes the poem in many places and is particularly interested in the relation of Roman Britain to the whole of the European Roman empire, and the implicit contrasts with the split and warring European continent in his own time.

The episode given below is from Part IV, and is entitled "King Pellam's Launde." The name refers to the land laid waste by the dolorous spear-stroke given to King Pellam by Sir Balin in Malory's Morte Darthur. According to the legend, the spear was the one that had pierced the side of Christ, brought to England, with the Holy Grail, by Joseph of Arimathea. Pellam's wound would not heal, and he lay maimed until Galahad, Lancelot's son, eventually cured him as he came by on his quest of the Grail. When Pellam was wounded, "the castle broke roof and walls and fell down to the earth"; later on, Balin "rode forth through the fair countries and cities and found the people dead slain on every side." T. S. Eliot in The Waste Land uses this same story, and Jones follows him in connecting the wounded king with the desolation and dead waste of his kingdom. But this kingdom, the trenches of 1915–16, and the moral life of Europe are connected in a more logical as well as a more mythological way in Jones's work than they are in the more symbolic linking of the Arthurian legend to Eliot's private wasteland of sexual inadequacy.

Jones's own notes to the poem are copious and sometimes digressive; they lead into the mythology (like Eliot, Jones connects his wasteland story with myths of regeneration, such as those of Attis and Adonis). Sometimes they are really part of the work itself, as in this commentary on the phrase "stand to" toward the beginning of the section below:

> Shortly before daybreak all troops in the line stood in their appointed places, their rifles in their hands, or immediately convenient, with bayonets fixed, ready for any dawn action on the part of the enemy. When it was fully day and the dangerous half-light past, the order would come to 'stand-down and clean rifles.' This procedure was strict and binding anywhere in the forward zone, under any circumstances whatever. The same routine was observed at dusk. So that that hour occurring twice in the twenty-four, of 'stand-to,' was one of peculiar significance and there was attaching to it a degree of solemnity, in that one was conscious that from the sea dunes to the mountains, everywhere, on the whole front the two opposing lines stood alertly, waiting any eventuality.

Jones's technique in *In Parenthesis* forms an interesting parallel to the growingly fragmentary assemblages of Ezra Pound's *Cantos*, which Jones had not read. In a later work composed during World War II and titled *The Anathémata* (1952), Jones moved more toward a lyric montage, and toward a total absorption of myth by inner vision. In the earlier war book, the interpenetration of remembered impression and photographic detail with the cadences, however archaic, of old songs of war and peace generate the general truth of its "account" of battle.

From In Parenthesis
King Pellam's Launde

Like an home-reared animal° in a quiet nook, before his day came . . . before entering into the prison of earth . . . around the contest, active and defensive, around the fort, around the steep-piled sods.

So thus he sorrowed till it was day and heard the foules sing, then somewhat he was comforted.°

Stand-to.

Stand-to-arms.

Stealthly, imperceptibly stript back, thinning
night wraps
unshrouding, unsheafing—
and insubstantial barriers dissolve.
This blind night-negative° yields uncertain flux.
At your wrist the phosphorescent dial describes the equal seconds.
    The flux yields up a measurable body; bleached forms emerge and stand.
    Where their faces turned, grey wealed earth bared almost of last clung weeds of night-weft°—
                    behind them the stars still shined.
    Her fractured contours dun where soon his ray would show more clear her dereliction.
    Already before him low atmospheres harbingered° his bright influence.
    The filtering irradiance spread, you could begin to know that thing from this; this nearer from that away over.
    There at ten o'clock from that leaning picket-iron,° where the horizon most invented its character to their eyes straining, a changing dark, variant-textured, shaped to their very watching a wooded gradient.
    Skin off those comforters—to catch with their
cocked ears
the early bird,

Like . . . animal This is quoted from Y *Gododdin* (see Headnote).
So thus . . . comforted quoted from Malory (XIII.19) about Lancelot, lamenting that his adultery with Guinevere prevents him from taking further part in "adventures to seek of holy things," the Grail quest

night-negative The image is of a photographic negative.
night-weft as if the darkness of night were a fabric woven by dark threads (weft) onto the transverse gray warp
harbingered heralded
picket-iron a vertical boundry stake

and meagre chattering of
December's prime
shrill over from
Biez wood.
   Biez wood fog pillowed, by low mist isled, a play of hide and seek arboreal
for the white diaphane.°
   To their eyes seeming a wood moving,
            a moving grove advisioned.
            Stand-to.
            Stand-to,
            Stand-to-arms.
Out there,
get out there
get into that fire trench.
   Pass it along to Stand-to.

   To peel back those eider-ducks me slumberin' lovelies—Prince Charming presents his compliments. Who's this John Moores in his martial cloak—get off it,
wontcher—come away counterfeiting death—cantcher—hear the bird o' dawn-
in'—roll up—it's tomorrow alright.
   Sergeant Charming's through your thorny slumbers, who bends over sweet
Robin's rose cheek.
   Morning sergeant—kiss me sergeant.
   Whose toe porrects° the ritual instrument to
break the spell to
resurrect the traverses.°
   Fog refracted, losing articulation in the cloying damp, the word of command
unmade in its passage, mischiefed of the opaque air, mutated, bereaved of
content, become an incoherent uttering, a curious bent cry out of the smarting
drift, lost altogether—yet making rise again the grey bundles where they lie.
   Sodden night-bones vivify, wet bones live.
   With unfathomed passion—this stark stir and waking—contort the comic
mask of these tragic japers.
   With a great complaining, bay by bay, the furrowed traverses whiten and
agitate.
   In 'P' sap, in 'Q' post,
in the fire-trench,
in Moggs Hole and Cats Post.°
   An eastward alignment of troubled, ashen faces; delicate mechanisms of
nerve and sinew, grapple afresh, deal for another day; ill-matched contesting,
handicapped out of reason, spirits at the ebb bare up; strung taut—by what
volition keyed—as best they may.
   As grievous invalids watch the returning light pale-bright the ruckled counter-

diaphane transparency
porrects tenders, presents (an ecclesiatical
usage)
traverses the embankments projecting above the

trench as a protection against shell bursts or
rifle fire (pronounced "traverses")
Moggs . . . Post parts of the battlefield;
"Mogg," slang for "cat"

pane,° see their uneased bodies only newly clear; fearful to know afresh their ill condition; yet made glad for that rising, yet strain ears to the earliest note— should some prevenient° bird make his kindly cry.

Chance modulations in the fluxing mist, retro-fold° roll, banked up—shield again the waking arborage.°

With the gaining spread grey proto-light,
Morning-star pallid,
with the freshing day,
billowed damp more thickly hung yet whitened marvellously.

Nothing was defined beyond where the ground steepened just in front, where the trip-wire° graced its snare-barbs with tinselled moistnesses.

Cloying drift-damp cupped in every concave place.

It hurts you in the bloody eyes, it grips chill and harmfully and rasps the sensed membrane of the throat; it's raw cold, it makes you sneeze—christ how cold it is.

With each moment passing—the opaque creeping into every crevice creeping, whiter—thick whitened, through-white, argent wall nebulous, took on, gave back, wholly reflected—till transfigured bright in each drenched dew particle— and the last Night-Sentry fidgets expectantly.

Keep on that fire-step.
Keep a sharp look out.
Sights down—watch the wire.
Keep your eyes skinned—it's a likely morning.

Behind them, beyond the brumous° piling the last stars paled and twinkled fitfully, then faded altogether; knowing the mastery and their visitation; this beautiful one, his cloud garments dyed, ruddy-flecked, fleecy stoled; the bright healer, climbing certainly the exact degrees to his meridian. Yet the brume° holds, defiantly, and with winter confident, to shroud the low places.

Even now you couldn't see his line, but it was much lighter. The wire-tangle hanging, the rank grass-tangle drenched, tousled, and the broken-tin glint showed quite clearly. Left and right in the fire-bays you could see: soft service-caps wet-moulded to their heads moving—their drawn upward cloth flaps like home-spun angler-heads—moving in the morning reaches.

Very slowly the dissipating mist reveals saturate green-grey flats, and dark up-jutting things; and pollard boles° by more than timely wood-craftsman's cunning pruning dockt,—these weeping willows shorn.

And the limber-wheel, whose fractured spokes search upward vainly for the rent-off mortised-rim.°

Now his wire thickets were visible as dark surf, before a strand rising to bleached wall of bags in neat layers. The light of day is fully master now, and all along, and from beyond the glistering wall, at irregular intervals, thin blue smoke rises straight, like robber-fire,° to thin-out amber against the eastern bright.

ruckled counterpane rumpled bedspread
prevenient anticipatory
retro-fold folded back on itself
arborage foliage
trip-wire set at shin-height, often in tall grass
brumous misty
brume mist
pollard boles trunks of trees that have been pollarded, or cut back to produce foliage close to the trunk
mortised-rim showing the holes wherein the spokes would be set
robber-fire an allusion to a story in Welsh folklore about a column of smoke unbending in the highest wind in the world, described by one of the protagonists as the fire of a robber

Over Biez Copse, as nainsook,° low vapours yet could draw out tenuous parallels.
Head inclined to head in the bay to the left.
They call from round the traverse wall.
Pass it along to Stand-down.
Stand-down and clean rifles.
Post day-sentries—pass it along.

They stood miserably.
They stretched encumbered limbs to take their rifles, listless, bemused, to slowly scrape away the thicker mire caked, with deadness in their eyes and hands as each to each they spoke—like damned-corpse-gossiping, of hopeless bleedin' dawns—then laught to see themselves so straitened, tricked out in mudded stiffening.
They beat against the padded walls to flow again the ebbing blood. They kicked the oozing sacks above the water surface till their toe-joints ached.

A lean lance-jack,° grey faced with his one night's vicarious office, called over the revetment.°
Get on those rifles at once—get on with it.
Orl right Corp—got any gauze.
Wot we want is gauze.
Wot we want is boiling water,°
            boiling bleedin' water.
Got any boiling water?
Then was great to do and business, then were butt-heel-irons opened, and splintering of thumb nails with the jammed metal, and jack-knife blades shivered.
Got any oil.
Why don't you go to Sergeant and get
for yourselves.
Why didn't you ask the Quarter-bloke
back there.
Only a drop, china, just for the bolt—just a spot—be a kind virgin—he's coming round the bend—he's doing No. 5°—just a spot.
Then was a pulling through of barrels and searching of minute vents and under-facets with pins, and borrowing of small necessaries to do with this care of arms. Then began prudent men to use their stored-up oil freely on bolt and back-sight-flange. And harassed men, and men ill-furnished, complained bitterly. And men improvising and adventurous slipped away along the traverses, to fetch back brimming mess-tin lids, or salvaged jam tins steaming.

How do you get hot water in this place of all water—all cold water up to the knees. These poured quickly lest it should cool off, and eyed their barrels' bright rifling with a great confidence, and boasted to their envious fellows, and offered

nainsook a striped cotton fabric
lance-jack an acting lance corporal (with private's pay)
revetment a retaining wall
boiling water for cleaning fouled rifle barrels,

the fine wire gauze mentioned before being expensive and hard to come by
No. 5 "Field Punishment No. 5," presumably for some minor offense

them the luke-warm left over. So that one way and another they cleaned their rifles—anyway the oil softened the open cracks in your finger-tips.

While these things were being done, while they were at this oiling and tearing off of closely rationed 'four by two,'° conserving carefully each flannel slip, plumbing dexterously with weighted cords, scraping and making their complaint, a message reached them from the right for the Lewis Team with No. 8: to get at once on their day-target, to send a man for S.A.A.° to Pioneer Keep; further, to furnish a report of their night firing. They stood unhappily, and believed themselves to be ill-fortuned above the common lot, for they had barely slept—and a great cold to gnaw them. Their wet-weighted gear pulled irksomely, soaking cloth impeded all their action, adhered in saturate layers when they stood still.

Night-begotten fear yet left them frail, nor was the waking day much cheer for them. They felt with each moment's more ample light, but a measuring, a nearing only, of the noonday hour—when the nescient trouble comes walking.° Their vitality seemed not to extend to the finger-tips nor to enable any precise act; so that to do an exact thing, competently to clean a rifle, to examine and search out intricate parts, seemed to them an enormity and beyond endurance; as one, who, clumsied with fear or unnerved by some grief, seeks to thread needle or turn an exact phrase; for they were unseasoned, nor inured, not knowing this to be much less than the beginning of sorrows. They stood as a lost child stands in his fatigue, and gape-eyed, where tall Guardsmen, their initiators and instructors, moved leisurely about, well pleased with the quiet of the sector.

Presently Mr. Jenkins came with Sergeant Snell and they ported arms for inspection.

He neither blames nor praises,
he whistles low,
he whistles *Dixieland,*
he passes on to Section 4: but
Sergeant Snell checks Jac Jones, checks Jack Float at the ease springs.° Sergeant Snell turns on this going; pokes this right-middle finger at this lance-jack—
instructs him:
Have ready two on 'em—section's rations.
Sergeant Snell gobs in the trench drain; comes to Mr. Jenkins's heel.

It was yet quite early in the morning, at the time of Saturnalia, when men properly are in winter quarters, lighting His birthday candles—
all a green-o.°

'four by two' "Slips of flannelette 4 in. wide cut in lengths of 2 in. from a roll—oiled and drawn through barrel on pull-through to clean bore" (Jones)
S.A.A. "Small Arms Ammunition. Ball cartridge" (Jones)
nescient . . . walking the unknowing (and perhaps, unbelieving) trouble; from Psalm 90 (in the Vulgate), a passage quoted and expounded in Sir Thomas More's *Dialogue of Comfort,* which Jones may have known. The Authorized Version reads: "Thou shalt not be afraid for the terror by night, nor for the arrow that flieth by day, Nor for the pestilence that walketh in darkness, nor for the destruction that wasteth at noonday" (Psalms 91:5–6).

The Vulgate text reads: . . . *A sagitta volante in die, a negotio perambulante in tenebris, ab incursu a demonio meridiano"* ("nor of the arrow flying in the day, nor of the business walking about in the darknesses, nor of the incursion of the devil in the midday," in the Douay-Rheims translation). More is interested in connecting the devil that is called "business" with the devil at noon (the time of the Fall).
ease springs a command at rifle inspection
green-o Jones notes the source as "Two, two, the lily-white boys / Clothèd all in green-o," from "Green Grow the Rushes-o," the well-known counting song, and identifies "boys" as "Our Lord and St. John Baptist."

When children look with serious eyes on brand-new miracles, and red berry sheen makes a Moses-bush,° to mirror in multiplicity the hearth-stones creature of fire.

But John Ball, posted as 1st Day Sentry, sat on the fire-step; and looking upward, sees in a cunning glass the image of: his morning parapets, his breakfast-fire smoke, the twisted wood beyond.

Across the very quiet of no-man's-land came still some twittering. He found the wood, visually so near, yet for the feet forbidden by a great fixed gulf, a sight somehow to powerfully hold his mind. To the woods of all the world is this potency—to move the bowels of us.

To groves always men come both to their joys and their undoing. Come lightfoot in heart's ease and school-free; walk on a leafy holiday with kindred and kind; come perplexedly with first loves—to tread the tangle frustrated, striking—bruising the green.

Come on night's fall for ambuscade.

Find harbour with a remnant.

Share with the prescribed their unleavened cake.

Come for sweet princes by malignant interests deprived.

Wait, wait long for—

with the broken men, nest with badger and the martin-cat till such time as he come again, crying the waste for his chosen.

Or come in gathering nuts and may;°

or run want-wit° in a shirt for the queen's unreason.

Beat boys-bush for Robin and Bobin.°

Come with Merlin in his madness,° for the pity of it; for the young men reaped like green barley,

for the folly of it.

Seek a way separate and more strait.

Keep date with the genius of the place—come with a weapon or effectual branch—and here this winter copse might well be special to Diana's Jack, for none might attempt it, but by perilous bough-plucking.°

Draughtsman at Army° made note on a blue-print of the significance of that grove as one of his strong-points; this wooded rise as the gate of their enemies, a door at whose splintered posts, Janus-wise° emplacements shield an automatic fire.

Moses-bush a burning yet unconsumed bush in which God appeared to Moses (Exodus 3:2)

nuts and may from "Here we go gathering nuts and may / On a cold and frosty morning," children's song; "may," hawthorne

want-wit in madness, like that of Sir Lancelot driven insane by Guinevere's magic (after he had, under another spell and hence unwittingly, slept with Elaine, daughter of the wounded fisher-king Pelles and granddaughter of King Pellam). See Malory XI.3.

Robin and Bobin Welsh version of "The Cutty Wren," a folk song for St. Stephen's Day (December 26), when all over northern Europe a wren was hunted: "We hunted the wren for Robin and Bobin, / We hunted the wren for everyman."

Merlin . . . madness In one story, Merlin, the Arthurian wizard, went mad at a battle and ran wild in the woods.

bough-plucking This refers to the description in Sir James Frazer's *The Golden Bough* of the priest of Diana at Nemi, who became so by killing his predecessor and cutting off the branch of a sacred tree, that branch being identified with the Golden Bough plucked by Aeneas before descending to the Underworld (Virgil, *Aeneid* VI).

Army Army headquarters; the man who drew the maps there, safe and remote from the trenches

Janus-wise looking out backward and forward, like the two heads of Janus, the Roman god of doorways and beginnings

In the mirror: below the wood, his undulating breastworks all along, he sees and loses, thinks he sees again, grey movement for the grey stillness, where the sand-bag wall dipped a little.

He noted that movement as with half a mind—at two o'clock from the petrol-tin.° He is indeterminate of what should be his necessary action. Leave him be on a winter's morning—let him bide. And the long-echoing sniper-shot from down by 'Q' Post alone disturbed his two hours' watching.

His eyes turned again to where the wood thinned to separate broken trees; to where great strippings-off hanged from tenuous fibres swaying, whitened to decay—as swung
immolations
for the northern Cybele.°
The hanged, the offerant:
        himself to himself
        on the tree.
Whose own,
whose grey war-band, beyond the stapled war-net—
(as grey-banded rodents for a shelving warren—cooped in
their complex runnels, where the sea-fret percolates).
Come from outlandish places,
from beyond the world,
from the Hercynian°—
they were at breakfast and were cold as he, they too made
their dole.°
    And one played on an accordion:
        Es ist ein' Ros' entsprungen
        Aus einer Wurzel zart.°
Since Boniface° once walked in Odin's wood.
    Two men in the traverse mouth-organ'd;
four men took up that song.
        Casey Jones mounted on his engine°
        Casey Jones with his orders in his hand.

petrol-tin gasoline can used to take a bearing from
Cybele Originally an Asiatic nature goddess, identified in the west with Rhea, worshiped in wild rites by followers called Corybantes, one of whom would assume the name of her son, Attis (who castrated himself at the foot of a pine when driven mad by a goddess he had spurned); the worshipers would inflict this same, as well as other, wounds on themselves, and Attis was worshiped by an effigy hung on a pine. In Norse mythology human victims were dedicated to Odin, strung up on a tree, and wounded with a spear; and indeed, says Frazer in The Golden Bough, "he is said to have been sacrificed to himself in the ordinary way." Frazer, and Jones in a note, quote an Icelandic poem: "I know that I hung on the windy tree / For nine whole nights, / Wounded myself with the spear, dedicated to Odin, / Myself to myself."

Hercynian forested mountains in south Germany (Caesar's term in his Gallic Wars)
dole See Jones's note on this whole passage: "The German field-grey seemed to us more than a mere colour. It seemed always to call up the grey wolf of Nordic literature. To watch these grey shapes moving elusively among the bleached breast works or emerging from between broken tree-stumps was a sight to powerfully impress us. . . . It would be interesting to know what myth-conception our own ochre coats and saucer hats suggested to our antagonists."
Es ist . . . zart from the German carol usually sung in English as "Lo, how a rose ere blooming" (literally, "It is a rose sprung up from a tender root")
Boniface English missionary (680–754) called the "Apostle to Germany"
Casey . . . engine Jones actually misquotes the line, "Casey Jones mounted to the cabin."

Which nearer,
which so rarely insular,
unmade his harmonies,
honouring
this rare and indivisible
New Light
for us,
over the still morning honouring.
This concertina'd
Good news
of these
barbarians,
them
bastard square-heads.°
    Put the fluence on,°
Rotherhithe°—
drownd the bastards on
Christmass Day in the Morning. Wot's this—
wot type's this of bloody waits°
wot's this he's striking up—
wot type's this of universall Peace
through Sea and Land.°
1929   1937

EDWIN MUIR
1887–1959

A poet of the remote Orkney Islands rather than of the Scottish mainland, Muir
founded his imaginative life more and more on transcendent and on inward realms
—of myth generalized across civilizations, of the repetitions of myth in dream,
and of visions of an integration of life and vision in a lost bucolic world. He moved to
industrial Glasgow at fourteen, educated himself, became a literary journalist, lived
in Europe, and, with his wife Willa, translated Kafka's novels into English. The Muirs
lived in Prague, where he was head of the British Council, from the end of World
War II until the overthrow of the democratic socialist government of Czechoslovakia
(1948). His posthumous Collected Poems, appearing in 1960, took by surprise many
readers who had previously undervalued his accomplishments as a poet. Muir never
became as committed to Scottish literary nationalism as did Hugh MacDiarmid (see
below), and differed with him about the role of dialect in poetry; his sense of place is
located far more in the imagery of his poems, which move from landscape to fable
in a smooth, unmediated way, without the intellectualizations of, for example, W. H.
Auden's equally strong and deeply felt visions of the landscape of the north of England.

square-heads "Term used of the Germans, not
perhaps so commonly as Jerry" (Jones)
Put . . . on cast a spell over
Rotherhithe district of London's dockland
waits carol singers

striking . . . Land (ll. 323–25) quoted from
Milton's "Hymn on the Morning of Christ's
Nativity," l. 52: "She strikes a universal peace
through sea and land."

Muir wrote an *Autobiography* (1954; a revision of the earlier *The Story and the Fable)* and a number of essays on literature and politics. T. S. Eliot in an introduction to a reissue of Muir's *Collected Poems* tried to place Muir's poetic world in a biographical framework. As Eliot wrote, "There is the sensibility of the remote islander, the boy from a primitive offshore community who was then plunged into the sordid horror of industrialism in Glasgow, who struggled to understand the modern world of the metropolis in London and finally the realities of central Europe in Prague. . . ." This is perhaps a bit schematic and a touch condescending, but it will serve to suggest to the reader the kind of imaginative modulations which must have resulted in the difference between the first and last of the poems given below, ostensibly on the same "subject."

Horses

Those lumbering horses in the steady plough,
On the bare field—I wonder why, just now,
They seemed terrible, so wild and strange,
Like magic power on the stony grange.

Perhaps some childish hour has come again,
When I watched fearful, through the blackening rain,
Their hooves like pistons in an ancient mill
Move up and down, yet seem as standing still.

Their conquering hooves which trod the stubble down
10   Were ritual that turned the field to brown,
And their great hulks were seraphim of gold,
Or mute ecstatic monsters on the mould.

And oh the rapture, when, one furrow done,
They marched broad-breasted to the sinking sun!
The light flowed off their bossy sides in flakes;
The furrows rolled behind like struggling snakes.

But when at dusk with steaming nostrils home
They came, they seemed gigantic in the gloam,
And warm and glowing with mysterious fire
20   That lit their smouldering bodies in the mire.

Their eyes as brilliant and as wide as night
Gleamed with a cruel apocalyptic light.
Their manes the leaping ire of the wind
Lifted with rage invisible and blind.

Ah, now it fades! it fades! and I must pine
Again for that dread country crystalline,
Where the blank field and the still-standing tree
Were bright and fearful presences to me.

1925

The Island

Your arms will clasp the gathered grain
For your good time, and wield the flail
In merry fire and summer hail.
There stand the golden hills of corn
Which all the heroic clans have borne,
And bear the herdsmen of the plain,
The horseman in the mountain pass,
The archaic goat with silver horn,
Man, dog and flock and fruitful hearth.
Harvests of men to men give birth.
These the ancestral faces bred
And show as through a golden glass
Dances and temples of the dead.
Here speak through the transmuted tongue
The full grape bursting in the press,
The barley seething in the vat,
Which earth and man as one confess,
Babbling of what both would be at
In garrulous story and drunken song.
Though come a different destiny,
Though fall a universal wrong
More stern than simple savagery,
Men are made of what is made,
The meat, the drink, the life, the corn,
Laid up by them, in them reborn.
And self-begotten cycles close
About our way; indigenous art
And simple spells make unafraid
The haunted labyrinths of the heart,
And with our wild succession braid
The resurrection of the rose.

1956

The Horses

Barely a twelvemonth after
The seven days war that put the world to sleep,
Late in the evening the strange horses came.
By then we had made our covenant with silence,
But in the first few days it was so still
We listened to our breathing and were afraid.
On the second day
The radios failed; we turned the knobs; no answer.
On the third day a warship passed us, heading north,
Dead bodies piled on the deck. On the sixth day

A plane plunged over us into the sea. Thereafter
Nothing. The radios dumb;
And still they stand in corners of our kitchens,
And stand, perhaps, turned on, in a million rooms
All over the world. But now if they should speak,
If on a sudden they should speak again,
If on the stroke of noon a voice should speak,
We would not listen, we would not let it bring
That old bad world that swallowed its children quick
20   At one great gulp. We would not have it again.
Sometimes we think of the nations lying asleep,
Curled blindly in impenetrable sorrow,
And then the thought confounds us with its strangeness.
The tractors lie about our fields; at evening
They look like dank sea-monsters couched and waiting.
We leave them where they are and let them rust:
'They'll moulder away and be like other loam.'
We make our oxen drag our rusty ploughs,
Long laid aside. We have gone back
30   Far past our fathers' land.
                              And then, that evening
Late in the summer the strange horses came.
We heard a distant tapping on the road,
A deepening drumming; it stopped, went on again
And at the corner changed to hollow thunder.
We saw the heads
Like a wild wave charging and were afraid.
We had sold our horses in our fathers' time
To buy new tractors. Now they were strange to us
As fabulous steeds set on an ancient shield
40   Or illustrations in a book of knights.
We did not dare go near them. Yet they waited,
Stubborn and shy, as if they had been sent
By an old command to find our whereabouts
And that long-lost archaic companionship.
In the first moment we had never a thought
That they were creatures to be owned and used.
Among them were some half-a-dozen colts
Dropped in some wilderness of the broken world,
Yet new as if they had come from their own Eden.
50   Since then they have pulled our ploughs and borne our loads,
But that free servitude still can pierce our hearts.
Our life is changed; their coming our beginning.
                    1956

HUGH MACDIARMID
1892–

Hugh MacDiarmid (Christopher Murray Grieve) was born in Dumfries, worked as a journalist, and in the mid-nineteen-twenties began to publish the books of verse with which he attempted to create a Scottish literary Renaissance. Writing both in English and in an artificial literary language of his own which he called "Lallans," he spoke through a complex *persona* derived in some measure from Robert Burns (the language of whose poetry was similarly an artificial one) and from a broader vision of Scottish nationality as representing a version of a "complex fate"—as Henry James described the predicament of being American with respect to British culture.

As with his fifteenth-century forebears, who were closer to France and more in touch with a main line of poetic culture than their English contemporaries, Mac-Diarmid's poetic world and literary program for Scottish poetry were far from provincial or parochial; his work is marked by a cosmopolitanism that rages beneath the relative inaccessibility of some of the language. A very peculiar, personal sort of communism marks his work, as well; it has ranged from a Stalinist orthodoxy on some political matters, to the broad, human revisionism of the end of his *Second Hymn to Lenin,* which is something of a complex self-rebuke for having chosen what Yeats called *rhetoric* (what men make from quarrels with others), as opposed to poetry (which they make from quarrels with themselves). The poet rejects, in effect, the injunctions of "socialist realism" to celebrate the Revolution in verse. The strength of MacDiarmid's language often lies in conflict; he has revived the Scots tradition, as exemplified in poets like Dunbar in the Renaissance, of "flyting" or poetic dispute. And he has contributed to that major movement of the modern in literature, which makes of a regional or private milieu an aspect of a more general condition.

MacDiarmid's early poems hid a lot of Hardy in their heather and thistle garments; his later poems owe something to Lawrence, something to French and German Romantic and modern verse. His "Lallans," made up of Burns's dialect words—both those used in speech and those sleeping in dictionaries—and phonetic spellings, is nevertheless a powerful poetic language, modulating in different poems from the more to the less arcane. Most important, it allows the poet in the closing stanzas of the *Second Hymn to Lenin* to achieve a ruggedness and simplicity, an almost biblical force, which, if attempted in modern, colloquial English, might sound only like propagandistic rant.

Moonlight Among the Pines°

Thraw oot your shaddaws
Owre the heich hillsides,
A' ye lang trees
Quhair the white mune rides.

Moonlight Among the Pines A translation of this early poem in "Lallans" may be helpful: "Threw out your shadows / Over the high hillsides, / All ye tall trees / Where the white moon rides. / My spirit would darken / The sun in the East / For ever, if my love / Laid bare her white breast. / O shadow that hides / In my heart till a sight / Of Love sends it plunging / All else into night!"

My spirit 'ud darken
The sun in the East
For aye, gin my luve
Laid bare her white breist.

O shaddaw that derns
10   In my hert till a sicht
O'Luve sends it plungin'
A' else into nicht! . . .

1925

From Second Hymn to Lenin°

Ah, Lenin, you were richt. But I'm a poet
(And you c'ud mak allowances for that!)
Aimin' at mair than you aimed at
Tho' yours comes first, I know it.

An unexamined life is no' worth ha'in'.°
Yet Burke was richt; owre muckle° concern
Wi' Life's foundations is a sure
Sign o' decay; tho' Joyce in turn

Is richt, and the principal question
10   Aboot a work o' art is frae° hoo deep
A life it springs—and syne° hoo faur
Up frae't it has the poo'er° to leap.

And hoo muckle it lifts up wi' it
Into the sunlicht like a saumon there,
Universal Spring! For Morand's richt°—
It s'ud be like licht in the air—

Are my poems spoken in the factories and fields,
    In the streets o' the toon?°
Gin° they're no', then I'm failin' to dae°
20   *What I ocht to ha' dune.°*

Gin I canna win through to the man in the street,
    The wife by the hearth,
A' the cleverness on earth'll no' mak' up
    For the damnable dearth.

Lenin V. I. Lenin (1870–1924), father of the
Soviet Union, Russian communist in whose
tradition and in whose name a repressive policy
against individual creative imagination in the
arts flourished in opposition to the more humane
one of his exiled follower Leon Trotsky. Mac-
Diarmid, for an orthodox communist, comes
dangerously close to a Trotskyite position in
this poem.
An . . . ha'in' "The unexamined life is not
worth living"—Socrates, in Plato's *Apology*

muckle great
frae from
syne thereafter
poo'er power
Morand's richt "Morand's right:" Paul Morand
(b. 1888), French writer and diplomat
toon town
Gin if
dae do
dune done

'Haud on haud on; what poet's dune that?
    Is Shakespeare read,
Or Dante or Milton or Goethe or Burns?'
    —You heard what I said.

—A means o' world locomotion,
The maist perfected and aerial o' a'.°
Lenin's name's gane owre the haill earth,
But the names o' the ithers?—Ha!

What hidie-hole o' the vineyard d'they scart
Wi' minds like the look on a hen's face,
Morand, Joyce, Burke, and the rest
That e'er wrote; me noo in like case?

Great poets hardly onybody kens o'?
Geniuses like a man talkin' t'm sel'?
Nonsense! They're nocht o' the sort
Their character's easy to tell.

They're nocht but romantic rebels
Strikin' dilettante poses;
Trotsky—Christ, no' wi' a croon o' thorns
But a wreath o' paper roses.

A' that's great is free and expansive.
What ha' they expanded tae?
They've affected nocht but a fringe
O' mankind in ony way.

Barbarian saviour o' civilization
Hoo weel ye kent (we're owre dull witted)
Naething is dune save as we ha'e
Means to en's° transparently fitted.

Poetry like politics maun° cut
The cackle and pursue real ends,
Unerringly as Lenin, and to that
Its nature better tends.

Wi' Lenin's vision equal poet's gift
And what unparalleled force was there!
Nocht in a' literature wi' that
Begins to compare.

Nae simple rhymes for silly folk
But the haill art, as Lenin gied
Nae Marx-without-tears to workin' men
But the fu' course insteed.

o' a'. of all   maun must
ens ends

Organic constructional work,
Practicality, and work by degrees;
First things first; and poetry in turn
'll be built by these.°

.   .   .

Freend, foe; past, present, future;
Success, failure; joy, fear;
Life, Death; and a'thing else,
For us, are equal here.

Male, female; quick or deid,
Let us fike° nae mair;
The deep line o'cleavage
Disna lie there.

Black in the pit the miner is,
150   *The shepherd reid° on the hill,*
And I'm wi' them baith° until
The end of mankind, I wis.

Whatever their jobs a' men are ane
In life, and syne in daith
(Tho' it's sma' patience I can ha'e
Wi' life's ideas o' that by the way)
And he's nae poet but kens it, faith,
And ony job but the hardest's ta'en.

The sailor gangs owre the curve o' the sea,
160   *The hoosewife's thrang° in the wash-tub,*
And whatna rhyme can I find but hub,
And what else can poetry be?

The core o' a' activity,
Changin't in accordance wi'
Its inward necessity
And mede o' integrity.

Unremittin', relentless,
Organized to the last degree,
170   Ah, Lenin, politics is bairns'° play
To what this maun be!

1935

these Eighteen stanzas are omitted here, in
which the poet rejects by degrees the easy
formulation just given.
fike fuss

reid red
baith both
thrang strain of hard work
bairns' children's

Bagpipe Music°

Let me play to you tunes without measure or end,
Tunes that are born to die without a herald,
As a flight of storks rises from a marsh, circles,
And alights on the spot from which it rose.

Flowers. A flower-bed like hearing the bagpipes.
The fine black earth has clotted into sharp masses
As if the frost and not the sun had come.
It holds many lines of flowers.
First faint rose peonies, then peonies blushing,
Then again red peonies, and, behind them,
Massive, apoplectic peonies, some of which are so red
And so violent as to seem almost black; behind these
Stands a low hedge of larkspur, whose tender apologetic blossoms
Appear by contrast pale, though some, vivid as the sky above them,
Stand out from their fellows iridescent and slaty as a pigeon's breast,
The bagpipes—they are screaming and they are sorrowful.
There is a wail in their merriment, and cruelty in their triumph.
They rise and they fall like a weight swung in the air at the end of a string.
They are like the red blood of those peonies.
And like the melancholy of those blue flowers.
They are like a human voice—no! for the human voice lies!
They are like human life that flows under the words.
That flower-bed is like the true life that wants to express itself
And does . . . while we human beings lie cramped and fearful.

1962

ROBERT GRAVES
1895–

Graves's literary career is fascinatingly problematic, although as his earlier works
begin to be reread in the light of his later ones a consistency may emerge which
he himself, up to now, has tended to obscure. He is a poet whose major poetic
work may not be in his poems at all, but rather in a strange, disparate corpus of
mythographic writings in various forms—historical novels, reworkings of classical story,
criticism, and purportedly anthropological studies of mythology and imagination. And
yet he has been insisting for more than forty years that these works of his left hand
were simply day-labor to enable him to support himself for the writing of verse.
Were that verse to exist on its own and without the larger corpus, however, it might
have fewer claims to major importance, representing as it does a continuation of the
tradition of the Georgians. Still, read in context, it is an impressive body of poetry.

Bagpipe Music It is instructive to compare this
beautiful poem, which seems indebted to D.
H. Lawrence, with Louis MacNeice's satirical
piece of the same title; MacDiarmid was the
more committed Communist, and yet there is
not a trace, in this poem touching his deep
Scottish pieties, of the propagandistic writing
known throughout international Communism as
"agitprop."

Born in London, educated at Charterhouse, Robert von Ranke Graves did not go up to Oxford until after World War I. In *Goodbye to All That* (1929) he vividly describes his war service in the Royal Welch Fusiliers; he suffered combat neurosis, and ultimately achieved psychic integration through poetry. Graves taught briefly in Cairo, but in 1929 settled in Majorca where, with the exception of the World War II years, he has lived ever since. His historical novels—*I, Claudius* (1934), *Claudius the God* (1934), *King Jesus* (1946), and many more—are based on vast classical and biblical scholarship; but from the outset (as in his strange, profound, but neglected little biblical fiction, *My Head, My Head,* 1925) he began to weave tendentious interpretations into his treatment of ancient subjects. His two-volume *The Greek Myths* (1955) organizes an encyclopedic body of material around a series of patterns that had only fully emerged in his monumental study, *The White Goddess* (1948).

The thrust of Graves's whole mythographic career has been to build up a great if fragmented vision of The Muse. In an age when such fictions as the Petrarchan Sonnet-Lady were long past possibility, when the romantic feminine demons had been forced to dissolve, as far as their role in a theory of the Imagination was concerned, into systems like Yeats's, Graves began an intense study of what he called the Triple Goddess who had once reigned supreme in a matriarchal culture, until smashed into her components. (These appear in the Greek pantheon, in the phased aspects of, say, Diana the virgin moon goddess, and Hecate, her underground witch-like form.) And yet all mythologies retain the visionary fragments of the original goddess, broken by the encounter with a patriarchy which, in one phase of Graves's hypothesis, invaded the Aegean and brought with it a male sun-god. Throughout his writings, Graves uses historical conjecture, backed up with anthropological data, in the way that other mytho-poetic writers of the past have used a central fiction; he even goes so far, in *The Nazarene Gospel Restored,* as to reconstruct a supposed pre-Pauline Aramaic gospel of a non-divine Jesus, as if to lend truth to his earlier novel, *King Jesus.* His major study of the Feminine as Muse is fascinating; tendentious as historical mythology, it cannot be faulted as a coherent, cyclical vision of the relation between life process and imaginative existence. Along with certain other mythological works of Graves, it will remain (like Yeats's *A Vision* with its attendant doctrinal poems, and Joyce's *Finnegans Wake*) a monument of the imagination.

Graves's poems are many and various; his favorite writers of the past, like Catullus and Skelton (he loathes Milton), were masters of voice and tone, and his whole commitment to lyric poetry would appear to avoid the romantic and the visionary elements so enshrined in his mythical system. His love poems are among the best heterosexual erotic lyrics in modern English, and some of the poems written around the mythology are compellingly direct in a way not chosen by many of his younger contemporaries. As a critic Graves has often been cranky and perverse but never bland, and the primary failure of his essays and lectures, whether in influential early studies or as Professor of Poetry at Oxford, has been a refusal to acknowledge in some of the major traditions of English poetry forces to which his own work has been responsive.

Love Without Hope

Love without hope, as when the young bird-catcher
Swept off his tall hat to the Squire's own daughter,
So let the imprisoned larks escape and fly
Singing about her head, as she rode by.

1920

The Succubus°

Thus will despair
In ecstasy of nightmare
Fetch you a devil-woman through the air,
   To slide below the sweated sheet
And kiss your lips in answer to your prayer
   And lock her hands with yours and your feet with her feet.

Yet why does she
Come never as longed-for beauty
Slender and cool, with limbs lovely to see,
   (The bedside candle guttering high)
And toss her head so the thick curls fall free
   Of halo'd breast, firm belly and long, slender thigh?

Why with hot face,
With paunched and uddered carcase,
Sudden and greedily does she embrace,
   Gulping away your soul, she lies so close,
Fathering you with brats of her own race?
   Yet is the fancy grosser than your lusts were gross?

1930

Sick Love°

O Love, be fed with apples while you may,
And feel the sun and go in royal array,
A smiling innocent on the heavenly causeway,

Though in what listening horror for the cry
That soars in outer blackness dismally,
The dumb blind beast, the paranoiac fury:

Be warm, enjoy the season, lift your head,
Exquisite in the pulse of tainted blood,
That shivering glory not to be despised.

Take your delight in momentariness,

Succubus a demon who assumes a female form
in order to have sexual intercourse with sleeping men
Sick Love The title refers to the Song of Songs

2:5 ("Stay me with flagons, comfort me with
apples: for I am sick of love"), quoted in the
first line. (Originally titled "O Love in Me".)

Walk between dark and dark—a shining space
With the grave's narrowness, though not its peace.

1930

Warning to Children

Children, if you dare to think
Of the greatness, rareness, muchness,
Fewness of this precious only
Endless world in which you say
You live, you think of things like this:
Blocks of slate enclosing dappled
Red and green, enclosing tawny
Yellow nets, enclosing white
And black acres of dominoes,
10 Where a neat brown paper parcel°
Tempts you to untie the string.
In the parcel a small island,
On the island a large tree,
On the tree a husky fruit.
Strip the husk and pare the rind off:
In the kernel you will see
Blocks of slate enclosed by dappled
Red and green, enclosed by tawny
Yellow nets, enclosed by white
20 And black acres of dominoes,
Where the same brown paper parcel—
Children, leave the string untied!
For who dares undo the parcel
Finds himself at once inside it,
On the island, in the fruit,
Blocks of slate about his head,
Finds himself enclosed by dappled
Green and red, enclosed by yellow
Tawny nets, enclosed by black
30 And white acres of dominoes,
With the same brown paper parcel
Still untied upon his knee.
And, if he then should dare to think
Of the fewness, muchness, rareness,
Greatness of this endless only
Precious world in which he says
He lives—he then unties the string.

1930

---

parcel The image of attempting to discover
truth as opening a set of Chinese boxes, one
inside another, or as a Russian doll, is almost
a cliché in modern literature; in André Gide's
The Countefeiters, Aldous Huxley's *Point*
Counter Point, and other novels, the infinite
regression has symbolized the ultimate horror
of the intellect's failure to grasp experience.
Most recently this has been seen in the works
of Jorge Luis Borges.

Down, Wanton, Down!

Down, wanton, down!° Have you no shame
That at the whisper of Love's name,
Or Beauty's, presto! up you raise
Your angry head and stand at gaze?

Poor bombard°-captain, sworn to reach
The ravelin° and effect a breach—
Indifferent what you storm or why,
So be that in the breach you die!

Love may be blind, but Love at least
Knows what is man and what mere beast;
Or Beauty wayward, but requires
More delicacy from her squires.

Tell me, my witless, whose one boast
Could be your staunchness at the post,
When were you made a man of parts°
To think fine and profess the arts?

Will many-gifted Beauty come
Bowing to your bald rule of thumb,
Or Love swear loyalty to your crown?
Be gone, have done! Down, wanton, down!

                                    1933

Recalling War

Entrance and exit wounds are silvered clean,
The track aches only when the rain reminds.
The one-legged man forgets his leg of wood,
The one-armed man his jointed wooden arm.
The blinded man sees with his ears and hands
As much or more than once with both his eyes.
Their war was fought these twenty years ago
And now assumes the nature-look of time,
As when the morning traveller turns and views
His wild night-stumbling carved into a hill.

What, then, was war? No mere discord of flags
But an infection of the common sky
That sagged ominously upon the earth
Even when the season was the airiest May.
Down pressed the sky, and we, oppressed, thrust out

---

down The notion that the male sexual organ has a will or mind of its own is an ancient one, perhaps present even in the etymology of the Latin colloquialism *mentula* (a favorite word of the poet Catullus, in whose mood this poem is written) as derived from *mens:* "mind."
bombard a primitive cannon
ravelin a V-shaped fortification
parts punning on "private parts" and worldliness

Boastful tongue, clenched fist and valiant yard.
Natural infirmities were out of mode,
For Death was young again: patron alone
Of healthy dying, premature fate-spasm.

20   Fear made fine bed-fellows. Sick with delight
At life's discovered transitoriness,
Our youth became all-flesh and waived the mind.
Never was such antiqueness of romance,
Such tasty honey oozing from the heart.
And old importances came swimming back—
Wine, meat, log-fires, a roof over the head,
A weapon at the thigh, surgeons at call.
Even there was a use again for God—
A word of rage in lack of meat, wine, fire,
30   In ache of wounds beyond all surgeoning.

War was return of earth to ugly earth,
War was foundering of sublimities,
Extinction of each happy art and faith
By which the world had still kept head in air.
Protesting logic or protesting love,
Until the unendurable moment struck—
The inward scream, the duty to run mad.

And we recall the merry ways of guns—
Nibbling the walls of factory and church
40   Like a child, piecrust; felling groves of trees
Like a child, dandelions with a switch!
Machine-guns rattle toy-like from a hill,
Down in a row the brave tin-soldiers fall:
A sight to be recalled in elder days
When learnedly the future we devote
To yet more boastful visions of despair.

                              1938

The Thieves

Lovers in the act dispense
With such meum-teum° sense
As might warningly reveal
What they must not pick or steal,°
And their nostrum° is to say:
'I and you are both away.'

meum-teum "mine-yours" (Latin)
pick or steal In the Catechism of the Church
of England there is an injunction to keep one's
hands from "picking and stealing"; Hamlet
alludes to it when he calls his fingers "pickers
and stealers" (III.ii.320).
nostrum "ours" (Latin), with a pun on "nostrum" meaning "remedy"

After, when they disentwine
You from me and yours from mine,
Neither can be certain who
Was that I whose mine was you.
To the act again they go
More completely not to know.

Theft is theft and raid is raid
Though reciprocally made.
Lovers, the conclusion is
Doubled sighs and jealousies
In a single heart that grieves
For lost honour among thieves.

                                    1946

To Juan° at the Winter Solstice

There is one story and one story only
That will prove worth your telling,
Whether as learned bard or gifted child;
To it all lines or lesser gauds belong
That startle with their shining
Such common stories as they stray into.

Is it of trees you tell, their months and virtues,
Or strange beasts that beset you,
Of birds that croak at you the Triple will?°
Or of the Zodiac and how slow it turns
Below the Boreal Crown,
Prison of all true kings that ever reigned?

Water to water, ark again to ark,
From woman back to woman:°
So each new victim treads unfalteringly
The never altered circuit of his fate,
Bringing twelve peers° as witness
Both to his starry rise and starry fall.

Or is it of the Virgin's° silver beauty,
All fish below the thighs?

Juan Graves's young son; the winter solstice was a nodal point in the life and death cycles of many primitive vegetation and sun gods. The sun dies on the shortest day, and is reborn in a new guise or person, as when one of his young priests kills off the older one or one king supplants another. In Graves's mythology, the young poetic acolyte or ephebe must risk this cycle as well, and he chooses the occasion, like an orthodox Jew explaining the story of the Exodus to his sons on Passover, to tell of the Muse who controls these cycles. **Triple will** The White Goddess is the triple queen of female role: mother, bride, and killer-hag. Until Graves revealed her mysteries they were hidden in primitive alphabets made of tree-twigs, in birds' omens, in the constellations.
From . . . woman Born of woman biologically, man returns to woman mythologically (to mother earth, now as the hag of the grave). **twelve peers** an archetypal number of companions (Apostles, etc.)
Virgin's Aphrodite's; some of these attributes are obscure (e.g., the sexual quince held before her, as depicted on Cretan seals).

20   She in her left hand bears a leafy quince;
    When, with her right she crooks a finger smiling,
    How may the King hold back?
    Royally then he barters life for love.

    Or of the undying snake from chaos hatched,°
    Whose coils contain the ocean,
    Into whose chops with naked sword he springs,
    Then in black water, tangled by the reeds,
    Battles three days and nights,
30   To be spewed up beside her scalloped shore?

    Much snow is falling, winds roar hollowly,
    The owl hoots from the elder,
    Fear in your heart cries to the loving-cup:
    Sorrow to sorrow as the sparks fly upward.
    The log groans and confesses
    There is one story and one story only.

    Dwell on her graciousness, dwell on her smiling,
    Do not forget what flowers
    The great boar trampled down in ivy time.
40   Her brow was creamy as the crested wave,
    Her sea-blue eyes were wild
    But nothing promised that is not performed.

                    1946

The White Goddess°

All saints revile her, and all sober men
Ruled by the God Apollo's golden mean—
In scorn of which we sailed to find her°
In distant regions likeliest to hold her
Whom we desired above all things to know,
Sister of the mirage and echo.°

It was a virtue not to stay,
To go our headstrong and heroic way
Seeking her out at the volcano's head,
Among pack ice, or where the track had faded
Beyond the cavern of the seven sleepers:°

snake . . . hatched Ophion, the serpent created out of chaos by Eurynome, dead and reborn like Osiris, Adonis, Blake's Orc (though in simpler form)
The White Goddess See notes on "To Juan at the Winter Solstice"; this poem was originally an epigraph to *The White Goddess*.
sailed to find her primarily the Argonauts, sailing under Jason in the *Argo* for the Golden Fleece, a relic of the earlier, pre-Hellenic, matriarchal cult of the Triple Goddess. Graves began ad-vancing this notion in his prose fiction *Hercules My Shipmate* (1945).
mirage and echo thus the elusiveness of all fictions
cavern . . . sleepers the old myth of the Seven Sleepers of Ephesus, who took to a cave in the year 250 to escape a persecution of Christians, and slept for 230 years. Like most other bits of famous folklore, Graves has an explanation of it in *The White Goddess*, but even the archetypal character of the "seven" of their number will be obvious.

Whose broad high brow was white as any leper's,
Whose eyes were blue, with rowan-berry° lips,
With hair curled honey-coloured to white hips.

The sap of Spring in the young wood a-stir
Will celebrate with green the Mother,
And every song-bird shout awhile for her;
But we are gifted, even in November
Rawest of seasons, with so huge a sense
Of her nakedly worn magnificence
Wo forget cruelty and past betrayal,
Heedless of where the next bright bolt may fall.

1948

ALDOUS HUXLEY
1894–1963

Grandson of Thomas Henry Huxley, the great Victorian scientific theorist, great-nephew of Matthew Arnold, nephew of Mrs. Humphry Ward, the reformer and novelist, brother of the scientist Julian Huxley, and son of the editor of the *Cornhill Magazine*, Aldous Leonard Huxley might have pursued any one of a number of non-literary careers; but since he did not, his entire intellectual inheritance was, it seems, simultaneously available to him.

Born in Surrey in 1894, Huxley went to Eton and to Balliol, the most serious of Oxford colleges, from which he took his degree in 1915. He returned to Eton to teach for a while, flirted with the idea of studying medicine (he read literature rather than biology because of poor vision), wrote a good many poems (his first book of verse was published in Oxford in 1916), and by 1921 had published *Crome Yellow*, the first of a series of clever and brittle novels. Like the much more recherché and weird novels of Ronald Firbank, and like the satirical theatrical pieces and songs of Noel Coward, Huxley's glittering novels later came to represent the historical period they were so committed to denouncing from within. Starting out from a largely aesthetic critique of life style and of ideology in books like *Antic Hay* (1923—perhaps his best novel) and *Those Barren Leaves* (1925), he went on to write the more experimental *Point Counter Point* (1928), which is famous for its fictionalized portraits of the critic John Middleton Murry and D. H. Lawrence, with whom Huxley and his wife maintained a devoted and trusting friendship, particularly toward the end of Lawrence's life. Huxley's equally famous, half-satiric Utopia (or Dystopia), *Brave New World*, appeared in 1932; it is interesting not so much for its anticipation of a drug culture and an erotic life totally divorced from reproduction, as for the remarkable ambivalence felt toward the vision by its author. Huxley, who had struggled since the age of sixteen with near blindness (he was to recover a good portion of his sight in 1939, by a discipline of exercise), was evolving a complex kind of synthetic religion, first to emerge in his *The Perennial Philosophy* (1945) and resulting, after his move to Southern California in 1937, in an attachment to Indian Vedantic thought. At times influenced by Lawrence

---

rowan-berry again, because the rowan or mountain ash is sacred to her mysteries, involving such realms of fable as are dealt with in Sir James Frazer's *The Golden Bough* (1890)

himself, Huxley moved in his later novels and meditative writings beyond skepticism to a kind of humanism open to Eastern influence, but still maintaining a critical relation with Western rationalism.

It may be in his large number of familiar and literary essays that Huxley is at his most profound, elegant, and moving. In such collections as *On the Margin* (1923), *Proper Studies* (1927), *Do What You Will* (1929), from which the essay given below is taken, and *Music at Night and Other Essays* (1931), Huxley demonstrated suppleness and fluency in the handling of a form that we tend to think of as having vanished with the nineteenth century, leaving our day with the philosophical novelist, the post-Symbolist poet, and perhaps, at best, the brilliant aphorist to find forms for wisdom. Without being informed by any particular technical expertise, an essay like "Wordsworth in the Tropics" derives from a widely read, ironically tested humane intelligence.

Wordsworth in the Tropics

In the neighbourhood of latitude fifty north, and for the last hundred years or thereabouts, it has been an axiom that Nature is divine and morally uplifting. For good Wordsworthians—and most serious-minded people are now Wordsworthians, either by direct inspiration or at second hand—a walk in the country is the equivalent of going to church, a tour through Westmorland [1] is as good as a pilgrimage to Jerusalem. To commune with the fields and waters, the woodlands and the hills, is to commune, according to our modern and northern ideas, with the visible manifestations of the 'Wisdom and Spirit of the Universe.'

The Wordsworthian who exports this pantheistic worship of Nature to the tropics is liable to have his religious convictions somewhat rudely disturbed. Nature, under a vertical sun, and nourished by the equatorial rains, is not at all like that chaste, mild deity who presides over the *Gemütlichkeit*,[2] the prettiness, the cozy sublimities of the Lake District. The worst that Wordsworth's goddess ever did to him was to make him hear

> Low breathings coming after me, and sounds
> Of undistinguishable motion, steps
> Almost as silent as the turf they trod; [3]

was to make him realize, in the shape of 'a huge peak, black and huge,' the existence of 'unknown modes of being.' He seems to have imagined that this was the worst Nature *could* do. A few weeks in Malaya or Borneo would have undeceived him. Wandering in the hothouse darkness of the jungle, he would not have felt so serenely certain of those 'Presences of Nature,' those 'Souls of Lonely Places,' which he was in the habit of worshipping on the shores of Windermere and Rydal.[4] The sparse inhabitants of the equatorial forest are all believers in devils. When one has visited, in even the most superficial

1. The northern county which, together with Cumberland, contains the Lake District, Wordsworth's actual and visionary home.
2. German for a kind of spiritual coziness.
3. From Wordsworth's *The Prelude* I.323–25.
4. Two of Wordsworth's lakes.

manner, the places where they live, it is difficult not to share their faith. The jungle is marvelous, fantastic, beautiful; but it is also terrifying, it is also profoundly sinister. There is something in what, for lack of a better word, we must call the character of great forests—even in those of temperate lands—which is foreign, appalling, fundamentally and utterly inimical to intruding man. The life of those vast masses of swarming vegetation is alien to the human spirit and hostile to it. Meredith, in his 'Woods of Westermaine,'[5] has tried reassuringly to persuade us that our terrors are unnecessary, that the hostility of these vegetable forces is more apparent than real, and that if we will but trust Nature we shall find our fears transformed into serenity, joy, and rapture. This may be sound philosophy in the neighbourhood of Dorking,[6] but it begins to be dubious even in the forests of Germany—there is too much of them for a human being to feel himself at ease within their enormous glooms; and when the woods of Borneo are substituted for those of Westermaine, Meredith's comforting doctrine becomes frankly ridiculous.

It is not the sense of solitude that distresses the wanderer in equatorial jungles. Loneliness is bearable enough—for a time, at any rate. There is something actually rather stimulating and exciting about being in an empty place where there is no life but one's own. Taken in reasonably small doses, the Sahara exhilarates, like alcohol. Too much of it, however (I speak, at any rate, for myself), has the depressing effect of the second bottle of Burgundy. But in any case it is not loneliness that oppresses the equatorial traveller: it is too much company; it is the uneasy feeling that he is an alien in the midst of an innumerable throng of hostile beings. To us who live beneath a temperate sky and in the age of Henry Ford,[7] the worship of Nature comes almost naturally. It is easy to love a feeble and already conquered enemy. But an enemy with whom one is still at war, an unconquered, unconquerable, ceaselessly active enemy—no; one does not, one should not, love him. One respects him, perhaps; one has a salutary fear of him; and one goes on fighting. In our latitudes the hosts of Nature have mostly been vanquished and enslaved. Some few detachments, it is true, still hold the field against us. There are wild woods and mountains, marshes and heaths, even in England. But they are there only on sufferance, because we have chosen, out of our good pleasure, to leave them their freedom. It has not been worth our while to reduce them to slavery. We love them because we are the masters, because we know that at any moment we can overcome them as we overcame their fellows. The inhabitants of the tropics have no such comforting reasons for adoring the sinister forces which hem them in on every side. For us, the notion 'river' implies (how obviously!) the notion 'bridge.' When we think of a plain, we think of agriculture, towns, and good roads. The corollary of mountain is tunnel; of swamp, an embankment; of distance, a railway. At latitude zero, however, the obvious is not the same as with us. Rivers imply wading, swimming, alligators. Plains mean swamps, forests, fevers. Mountains are either dangerous or impassable. To travel is to hack one's way laboriously through a tangled, prickly, and venomous

5. A poem by George Meredith (1828–1909) which seeks an almost providential operation in biological phases and cycles.
6. A comfortable town in Surrey, near London.
7. Here taken as the inventor of the assembly line and of mass production.

darkness. 'God made the country,' said Cowper, in his rather too blank verse.[8] In New Guinea he would have had his doubts; he would have longed for the man-made town.

The Wordsworthian adoration of Nature has two principal defects. The first, as we have seen, is that it is only possible in a country where Nature has been nearly or quite enslaved to man. The second is that it is only possible for those who are prepared to falsify their immediate intuitions of Nature. For Nature, even in the temperate zone, is always alien and inhuman, and occasionally diabolic. Meredith explicitly invites us to explain any unpleasant experiences away. We are to interpret them, Pangloss [9] fashion, in terms of a preconceived philosophy; after which, all will surely be for the best in the best of all possible Westermaines. Less openly, Wordsworth asks us to make the same falsification of immediate experience. It is only very occasionally that he admits the existence in the world around him of those 'unknown modes of being' of which our immediate intuitions of things make us so disquietingly aware. Normally what he does is to pump the dangerous Unknown out of Nature and refill the emptied forms of hills and woods, flowers and waters, with something more reassuringly familiar—with humanity, with Anglicanism. He will not admit that a yellow primrose is simply a yellow primrose—beautiful, but essentially strange, having its own alien life apart. He wants it to possess some sort of soul, to exist humanly, not simply flowerily. He wants the earth to be more than earthy, to be a divine person. But the life of vegetation is radically unlike the life of man: the earth has a mode of being that is certainly not the mode of being of a person. 'Let Nature be your teacher,' says Wordsworth. The advice is excellent. But how strangely he himself puts it into practice! Instead of listening humbly to what the teacher says, he shuts his ears and himself dictates the lesson he desires to hear. The pupil knows better than his master; the worshipper substitutes his own oracles for those of the god. Instead of accepting the lesson as it is given to his immediate intuitions, he distorts it rationalistically into the likeness of a parson's sermon or a professorial lecture. Our direct intuitions of Nature tell us that the world is bottomlessly strange: alien, even when it is kind and beautiful; having innumerable modes of being that are not our modes; always mysteriously not personal, not conscious, not moral; often hostile and sinister; sometimes even unimaginably, because inhumanly, evil. In his youth, it would seem, Wordsworth left his direct intuitions of the world unwarped.

> The sounding cataract
> Haunted me like a passion: the tall rock,
> The mountain, and the deep and gloomy wood,
> Their colours and their forms, were then to me
> An appetite; a feeling and a love,
> That had no need of a remoter charm,
> By thought supplied, nor any interest
> Unborrowed from the eye.[10]

8. William Cowper (1731–1800); the quotation is from *The Task* I.749: "God made the country, and man made the town."

9. Dr. Pangloss, Voltaire's optimistic philosopher in *Candide,* who held that this is "the best of all possible worlds," despite much evidence to the contrary.

10. From "Lines Composed a Few Miles Above Tintern Abbey," ll. 76–83.

As the years passed, however, he began to interpret them in terms of a preconceived philosophy. Procrustes-like,[11] he tortured his feelings and perceptions
until they fitted his system. By the time he was thirty,

> The immeasurable height
> Of woods decaying, never to be decayed,
> The stationary blasts of waterfalls—
> The torrents shooting from the clear blue sky,
> The rocks that muttered close upon our ears,
> Black drizzling crags that spake by the wayside
> As if a voice were in them, the sick sight
> And giddy prospect of the raving stream,
> The unfettered clouds and regions of the heavens,
> Tumult and peace, the darkness and the light—
> Were all like workings of one mind, the features
> Of the same face, blossoms upon one tree,
> Characters of the great Apocalypse,
> The types and symbols of eternity,
> Of first, and last, and midst, and without end.[12]

'Something far more deeply interfused' had made its appearance on the
Wordsworthian scene. The god of Anglicanism had crept under the skin of
things, and all the stimulatingly inhuman strangeness of Nature had become as
flatly familiar as a page from a textbook of metaphysics or theology. As familiar
and as safely simple. Pantheistically[13] interpreted, our intuitions of Nature's
endless varieties of impersonal mysteriousness lose all their exciting and disturbing quality. It makes the world seem delightfully cozy, if you can pretend
that all the many alien things about you are really only manifestations of one
person. It is fear of the labyrinthine flux and complexity of phenomena that has
driven men to philosophy, to science, to theology—fear of the complex reality
driving them to invent a simpler, more manageable, and, therefore, consoling
fiction. For simple, in comparison with the external reality of which we have
direct intuitions, childishly simple is even the most elaborate and subtle system
devised by the human mind. Most of the philosophical systems hitherto popular
have not been subtle and elaborate even by human standards. Even by human
standards they have been crude, bald, preposterously straightforward. Hence
their popularity. Their simplicity has rendered them instantly comprehensible.
Weary with much wandering in the maze of phenomena, frightened by the
inhospitable strangeness of the world, men have rushed into the systems prepared for them by philosophers and founders of religions, as they would rush
from a dark jungle into the haven of a well-lit, commodious house. With a sigh
of relief and a thankful feeling that here at last is their true home, they settle
down in their snug metaphysical villa and go to sleep. And how furious they
are when any one comes rudely knocking at the door to tell them that their

11. A giant of Greek myth, who chopped his guests down to, or stretched them out to,
the size of his bed.
12. From *The Prelude* VI.624–40; this is a passage about crossing the Alps. Ll. 627–28:
"And in the narrow rent at every turn / Winds thwarting winds, bewildered and forlorn"
are omitted.
13. Pantheism finds that God is everything everywhere.

villa is jerry-built, dilapidated, unfit for human habitation, even non-existent! Men have been burnt at the stake for even venturing to criticize the colour of the front door or the shape of the third-floor windows.

That man must build himself some sort of metaphysical shelter in the midst of the jungle of immediately apprehended reality is obvious. No practical activity, no scientific research, no speculation is possible without some preliminary hypothesis about the nature and the purpose of things. The human mind cannot deal with the universe directly, nor even with its own immediate intuitions of the universe. Whenever it is a question of thinking about the world or of practically modifying it, men can only work on a symbolic plan of the universe, only a simplified, two-dimensional map of things abstracted by the mind out of the complex and multifarious reality of immediate intuition. History shows that these hypotheses about the nature of things are valuable even when, as later experience reveals, they are false. Man approaches the unattainable truth through a succession of errors. Confronted by the strange complexity of things, he invents, quite arbitrarily, a simple hypothesis to explain and justify the world. Having invented, he proceeds to act and think in terms of this hypothesis, as though it were correct. Experience gradually shows him where his hypothesis is unsatisfactory and how it should be modified. Thus, great scientific discoveries have been made by men seeking to verify quite erroneous theories about the nature of things. The discoveries have necessitated a modification of the original hypotheses, and further discoveries have been made in the effort to verify the modifications—discoveries which, in their turn, have led to yet further modifications. And so on, indefinitely. Philosophical and religious hypotheses, being less susceptible of experimental verification than the hypotheses of science, have undergone far less modification. For example, the pantheistic hypothesis of Wordsworth is an ancient doctrine, which human experience has hardly modified throughout history. And rightly, no doubt. For it is obvious that there must be some sort of unity underlying the diversity of phenomena; for if there were not, the world would be quite unknowable. Indeed, it is precisely in the knowableness of things, in the very fact that they are known, that their fundamental unity consists. The world which we know, and which our minds have fabricated out of goodness knows what mysterious things in themselves, possesses the unity which our minds have imposed upon it. It is part of our thought, hence fundamentally homogeneous. Yes, the world is obviously one. But at the same time it is no less obviously diverse. For if the world were absolutely one, it would no longer be knowable, it would cease to exist. Thought must be divided against itself before it can come to any knowledge of itself. Absolute oneness is absolute nothingness: homogeneous perfection, as the Hindus perceived and courageously recognized, is equivalent to non-existence, is nirvana.[14] The Christian idea of a perfect heaven that is something other than a non-existence is a contradiction in terms. The world in which we live may be fundamentally one, but it is a unity divided up into a great many diverse fragments. A tree, a table, a newspaper, a piece of artificial silk are all made of wood. But

14. In Hindu thought, a total merging of an inner presence with one totally beyond (Atman and Brahman); in Buddhism, a state of total disengagement from the turning wheel of process. Huxley probably means the first of these.

they are, none the less, distinct and separate objects. It is the same with the world at large. Our immediate intuitions are of diversity. We have only to open our eyes to recognize a multitude of different phenomena. These intuitions of diversity are as correct, as well justified, as is our intellectual conviction of the fundamental homogeneity of the various parts of the world with one another and with ourselves. Circumstances have led humanity to set an ever-increasing premium on the conscious and intellectual comprehension of things. Modern man's besetting temptation is to sacrifice his direct perceptions and spontaneous feelings to his reasoned reflections; to prefer in all circumstances the verdict of his intellect to that of his immediate intuitions. 'L'homme est visiblement fait pour penser,' says Pascal; 'c'est toute sa dignité et tout son mérite; et tout son devoir est de penser comme il faut.[15] Noble words; but do they happen to be true? Pascal seems to forget that man has something else to do besides think: he must live. Living may not be so dignified or meritorious as thinking (particularly when you happen to be, like Pascal, a chronic invalid); but it is, perhaps unfortunately, a necessary process. If one would live well, one must live completely, with the whole being—with the body and the instincts, as well as with the conscious mind. A life lived, as far as may be, exclusively from the consciousness and in accordance with the considered judgments of the intellect, is a stunted life, a half-dead life. This is a fact that can be confirmed by daily observation. But consciousness, the intellect, the spirit, have acquired an inordinate prestige; and such is men's snobbish respect for authority, such is their pedantic desire to be consistent, that they go on doing their best to lead the exclusively conscious, spiritual, and intellectual life, in spite of its manifest disadvantages. To know is pleasant; it is exciting to be conscious; the intellect is a valuable instrument, and for certain purposes the hypotheses which it fabricates are of great practical value. Quite true. But, therefore, say the moralists and men of science, drawing conclusions only justified by their desire for consistency, therefore all life should be lived from the head, consciously, all phenomena should at all times be interpreted in terms of the intellect's hypotheses. The religious teachers are of a slightly different opinion. All life, according to them, should be lived spiritually, not intellectually. Why? On the grounds, as we discover when we push our analysis far enough, that certain occasional psychological states, currently called spiritual, are extremely agreeable and have valuable consequences in the realm of social behaviour. The unprejudiced observer finds it hard to understand why these people should set such store by consistency of thought and action. Because oysters are occasionally pleasant, it does not follow that one should make of oysters one's exclusive diet. Nor should one take castor-oil every day because castor-oil is occasionally good for one. Too much consistency is as bad for the mind as it is for the body. Consistency is contrary to nature, contrary to life. The only completely consistent people are the dead. Consistent intellectualism and spirituality may be socially valuable, up to a point; but they make, gradually, for individual death. And individual death, when the slow murder has been consummated, is finally social death. So that the social utility of pure intellectualism and pure spirituality is only apparent

15. "Man is patently made for thinking; it is his entire dignity and his entire virtue, and his only duty is to think correctly." Blaise Pascal (1623–62), Pensées.

and temporary. What is needed is, as ever, a compromise. Life must be lived in different ways at different moments. The only satisfactory way of existing in the modern, highly specialized world is to live with two personalities. A Dr. Jekyll [16] that does the metaphysical and scientific thinking, that transacts business in the city, adds up figures, designs machines, and so forth. And a natural, spontaneous Mr. Hyde to do the physical, instinctive living in the intervals of work. The two personalities should lead their unconnected lives apart, without poaching on one another's preserves or inquiring too closely into one another's activities. Only by living discretely and inconsistently can we preserve both the man and the citizen, both the intellectual and the spontaneous animal being, alive within us. The solution may not be very satisfactory; but it is, I believe now (though once I thought differently), the best that, in the modern circumstances, can be devised.

The poet's place, it seems to me, is with the Mr. Hydes of human nature. He should be, as Blake [17] remarked of Milton, 'of the devil's party without knowing it'—or preferably with the full consciousness of being of the devil's party. There are so many intellectual and moral angels battling for rationalism, good citizenship, and pure spirituality; so many and such eminent ones, so very vocal and authoritative! The poor devil in man needs all the support and advocacy he can get. The artist is his natural champion. When an artist deserts to the side of the angels, it is the most odious of treasons. How unforgivable, for example, is Tolstoy! Tolstoy, the perfect Mr. Hyde, the complete embodiment, if ever there was one, of non-intellectual, non-moral, instinctive life—Tolstoy, who betrayed his own nature, betrayed his art, betrayed life itself, in order to fight against the devil's party of his earlier allegiances, under the standard of Dr. Jesus-Jekyll. Wordsworth's betrayal was not so spectacular: he was never so wholly of the devil's party as Tolstoy. Still, it was bad enough. It is difficult to forgive him for so utterly repenting his youthful passions and enthusiasms, and becoming, personally as well as politically, the anglican tory. One remembers B. R. Haydon's [18] account of the poet's reactions to that charming classical sculpture of Cupid and Psyche. 'The devils!' he said malignantly, after a long-drawn contemplation of their marble embrace. 'The devils!' And he was not using the word in the complimentary sense in which I have employed it here: he was expressing his hatred of passion and life, he was damning the young man he had himself been—the young man who had hailed the French Revolution with delight and begotten an illegitimate child. From being an ardent lover of the nymphs, he had become one of those all too numerous

> woodmen who expel
> Love's gentle dryads from the haunts of life,
> And vex the nightingales in every dell.[19]

Yes, even the nightingales he vexed. Even the nightingales, though the poor birds can never, like those all too human dryads, have led him into sexual

16. "Dr. Jekyll and Mr. Hyde" is Robert Louis Stevenson's story of a benign scientist who, under the influence of a drug, metamorphoses into his bestial *alter ego*.
17. This famous remark is from *The Marriage of Heaven and Hell*.
18. Benjamin Robert Haydon (1786–1846), painter, friend of Wordsworth and other poets.
19. Shelley, "The Woodman and the Nightingale," ll. 68–70.

temptation. Even the innocuous nightingales were moralised, spiritualised, turned into citizens and anglicans—and along with the nightingales, the whole of animate and inanimate Nature.

The change in Wordsworth's attitude toward Nature is symptomatic of his general apostasy. Beginning as what I may call a natural aesthete, he transformed himself, in the course of years, into a moralist, a thinker. He used his intellect to distort his exquisitely acute and subtle intuitions of the world, to explain away their often disquieting strangeness, to simplify them into a comfortable metaphysical unreality. Nature had endowed him with the poet's gift of seeing more than ordinarily far into the brick walls of external reality, of intuitively comprehending the character of the bricks, of feeling the quality of their being, and establishing the appropriate relationship with them. But he preferred to think his gifts away. He preferred, in the interests of a preconceived religious theory, to ignore the disquieting strangeness of things, to interpret the impersonal diversity of Nature in terms of a divine, anglican unity. He chose, in a word, to be a philosopher, comfortably at home with a man-made and, therefore, thoroughly comprehensible system, rather than a poet adventuring for adventure's sake through the mysterious world revealed by his direct and undistorted intuitions.

It is a pity that he never travelled beyond the boundaries of Europe. A voyage through the tropics would have cured him of his too easy and comfortable pantheism. A few months in the jungle would have convinced him that the diversity and utter strangeness of Nature are at least as real and significant as its intellectually discovered unity. Nor would he have felt so certain, in the damp and stifling darkness, among the leeches and the malevolently tangled rattans,[20] of the divinely anglican character of that fundamental unity. He would have learned once more to treat Nature naturally, as he treated it in his youth; to react to it spontaneously, loving where love was the appropriate emotion, fearing, hating, fighting whenever Nature presented itself to his intuition as being, not merely strange, but hostile, inhumanly evil. A voyage would have taught him this. But Wordsworth never left his native continent. Europe is so well gardened that it resembles a work of art, a scientific theory, a neat metaphysical system. Man has re-created Europe in his own image. Its tamed and temperate Nature confirmed Wordsworth in his philosophizings. The poet, the devil's partisan were doomed; the angels triumphed. Alas!

1929

W. H. AUDEN
1907–

The major English poet and man of letters to follow Eliot has been a strange sort of representative of the second generation of modernism. A socialist; a Freudian; a student and transmitter of Germanic rather than Romance Continental literary traditions; a temperament that has always felt a kinship with the scientific imagination, finding itself more at home with Goethe than with Baudelaire; a poetic voice

20. Tropical reed-like palms with pliable stems.

which, no matter how devoted to strategic *personae* and disguises, mastered an expository mode and the art of verse essay at a moment in literary history when these had become most discredited; a devoted composer of occasional poems; a Marxist of sorts who became a Christian; a creator of opera libretti and translator-adapter of opera; a devotee and author of light verse—all of these would seem divergent enough from any career we might have projected for a modern writer of such importance.

Wystan Hugh Auden has been all these and more. He emigrated to the United States in 1934 and became an American citizen, reciprocating in an ironic way the transatlantic displacements of T. S. Eliot and, before him, Henry James. There is a very real sense in which the work of Auden's later years can be called American poetry (language alone, for example: in "The Fall of Rome" he rhymes "clerk" with "work" instead of with "dark"); it is nevertheless part of that same quintessentially English poetic career that started among the members of a particularly self-conscious generation at Oxford in the mid–1920's.

Auden's early work is often spoken of in the context of his literary friendships—with Stephen Spender, Christopher Isherwood, Louis MacNeice, and others; his early poems and, in particular, his remarkable little book called *The Orators* (1930), are full of the almost conspiratorial sense of a strange avant-garde group. Perhaps something should be said of the new spirit that gave this post-World War I generation its sense of itself. Actually, various fashions in generation gaps have succeeded each other ever since the Romantic period invented the condition of adolescence and put a premium on its chronological and moral in-betweenness. Changes of style in the relation of one generation's attitudes toward those of its predecessor have been accompanied by changes of style in the expression of expressing those relations. The French Romantic poet Alfred de Musset had characterized his own generation as played-out and spiritually weakened. The concept of the *poète maudit,* the accursed, alienated artist, had pervaded nineteenth-century French literature before being imported into English tradition first by the writers of the 1890's, then by Eliot. Yet the basic healthiness of society itself, or at least of those principles its institutions were designed, however badly, to embody, had remained an English theme; the Victorian imagination continues to amaze us in the ways it could accompany that theme with both high vision and tough moral perception.

World War I finally ended the possibility of such a view; but even before the war, instances of new versions of a Byronic, ironic youth had begun to appear. The actualities of the life and works of an Aubrey Beardsley were matched by the fictional brilliancies of fierce young gilded youths like Saki's (H. H. Munro's) Clovis or Reginald in his turn-of-the-century sketches. The latter of these young men is reminded by an interlocutor "Some one who Must Not be Contradicted said that a man must be a success by the time he's thirty, or never." "To have reached thirty," said Reginald, "is to have failed in life." Saki built the bridge between the comedy of Oscar Wilde and the post-World War I satiric hilarities of the fiction of Evelyn Waugh, Aldous Huxley, and Ronald Firbank. The role of the pranking doomster, only faintly sinister in the unassailable world of country houses, Continental travel, and aristocratic connections of Saki's stories, took on a new meaning for the intellectual and moral life of young men at Oxford in the 1920's. Many of the cleverest of them became communists, and even those who wished to maintain something of an older, aestheticist tradition, were either revising it along Eliot's lines or adapting it to some fresh social

vision. Unlike Eliot, whose conversion to Anglo-Catholicism was accompanied by professions of commitment to royalism in politics and classicism in literature, Auden's
later reversion to the homely Anglicanism of his boyhood household was influenced
along the way by Søren Kierkegaard's critique of philosophy and by the "crisis theology" of Paul Tillich and Reinhold Niebuhr.

Auden's personal sense of generation was always more of an antithetical cycle,
in some general sense, against an older primary state, than merely a Marxist or an
aestheticist engagement against the bourgeois. Auden was born in York, the son of a
doctor, and showed an early interest in matters mechanical and geological. Prepared
at Gresham's School in Cheshire, he went to Christ Church, Oxford, taught school,
lived in the pre-Hitler Berlin of the Brecht-Weill operas and entertainments, took
literary journeys to Iceland and China, collaborated with Louis MacNeice on a book
about their Iceland trip and with Christopher Isherwood on plays, and then went to
Spain. The Spanish Civil War (1936–38) resulted from the counter-insurgency of the
Spanish Republican government to the military coup of General Francisco Franco, who
was backed in the struggle by weapons and men supplied by Hitler and Mussolini, and
moral support supplied by the Vatican. A whole range of political viewpoints supported the Loyalist or Republican cause: those with a distaste for fascism saw the
Spanish war as a testing ground for a far more general European conflict, while direct
Soviet intervention on the Loyalist side produced some very nasty political results
(such as the murder of anarchists and other factions supposedly allied with them)
which the Stalinist, or official Soviet-communist-sympathizing adherents of the Spanish
cause, refused to admit. It would take the self-searching candor of the socialist George
Orwell to reveal, in Homage to Catalonia (1938), some of the unpleasant realities
which even the committed would have to face. But whether one's will was to "build
the Just City" or to find "the suicide pact, the romantic / Death," as Auden wrote in
a poem in 1937, commitment was obligatory: "I accept, for / I am your choice, your
decision: yes, I am Spain." But the inconclusiveness of such decisions, save in the
death of many young English intellectuals who went to fight there, was typified by
Auden's return to England and then, as the inevitable conflict of World War II drew
nearer, by his emigration to the United States in 1939, a private response to what
seemed increasing social hopelessness.

Auden's earlier poetry was shocking and immediately famous. He drew on many
sources—Anglo-Saxon alliterative verse and its puzzling kennings, balladry, cabaret
and music-hall lyrics, many traditions of complex verse form—and coupled these with
an amazing range of diction—slang, technical, scientific, and philosophical vocabu-
laries of all sorts, and even eighteenth-century personifications. From the beginning he
always used a wide array of metrical forms, rhyme schemes, and structural patterns,
as if to suggest that each kind of form had a different sort of modality, a different
tone. His long poems have included the strange mixed-prose-and-verse of The Orators,
the varied forms of The Sea and the Mirror (a verse commentary on The Tempest of
Shakespeare, published in 1944), The Age of Anxiety (1947)—an eclogue in a Third
Avenue bar, projected in unrhymed alliterative verse—and the tight, highly allusive
name-dropping couplets of his 1941 New Year Letter.

Auden's occasional poetry and his earlier political poems have given way, in later
years, to an almost sermonizing meditative style, but many of the elements that made
him so popular as a young modernist are still present in his imaginative world. He
still admires Byron and dislikes Shelley. His neoclassicism has become more and more

apparent. He has produced an impressive body of prose criticism, *The Enchafèd Flood* of 1950 being perhaps the most remarkable. If his early poems typified the New in England between-the-wars, his reasonable and knowing voice had a strong influence on American poetry of the 1940's and '50's.

Auden has continually revised and rewritten his poems for successive collected editions, and even deleted certain earlier poems (such as his "September 1, 1939," which the editors would like to have reprinted). Auden did this not so much for ideological reasons but because of an awareness that topical or momentarily "relevant" verse always produces what subsequent assessment will see as dated. But what is important throughout his work is the constancy of his major themes: the sanctity of the private heart and the necessity for protecting it even when, to protect the hearts of others, one must act publicly; the natural providence of body and landscape; and the belief in the possibility—especially by a mind technically skilled in the apprehension of the phony—of wisdom.

The Watershed

Who stands, the crux left of the watershed,
On the wet road between the chafing grass
Below him sees dismantled washing-floors,
Snatches of tramline° running to a wood,
An industry already comatose,
Yet sparsely living. A ramshackle engine
At Cashwell raises water; for ten years
It lay in flooded workings° until this,
Its latter office, grudgingly performed.
10 And, further, here and there, though many dead
Lie under the poor soil, some acts are chosen
Taken from recent winters; two there were
Cleaned out a damaged shaft by hand, clutching
The winch a gale would tear them from; one died
During a storm, the fells° impassable,
Not at his village, but in wooden shape
Through long abandoned levels nosed his way
And in his final valley went to ground.
Go home, now, stranger, proud of your young stock,
20 Stranger, turn back again, frustrate and vexed:
This land, cut off, will not communicate,
Be no accessory content to one
Aimless for faces rather there than here.
Beams from your car may cross a bedroom wall,
They wake no sleeper; you may hear the wind
Arriving driven from the ignorant sea

tramline rail lines   fells high hills, and the fields along their sides
workings excavations; here, for a quarry

To hurt itself on pane, on bark of elm
Where sap unbaffled rises, being spring;
But seldom this. Near you, taller than grass,
Ears poise before decision, scenting danger.

1928

Song°

'O where are you going?' said reader to rider,
'That valley is fatal when furnaces burn,
Yonder's the midden° whose odours will madden,
That gap is the grave where the tall return.'

'O do you imagine,' said fearer to farer,
'That dusk will delay on your path to the pass,
Your diligent looking discover the lacking
Your footsteps feel from granite to grass?'

'O what was that bird,' said horror to hearer,
'Did you see that shape in the twisted trees?
Behind you swiftly the figure comes softly,
The spot on your skin is a shocking disease?'

'Out of this house'—said rider to reader,
'Yours never will'—said farer to fearer,
'They're looking for you'—said hearer to horror,
As he° left them there, as he left them there.

1932   1932

Letter to a Wound°

The maid has just cleared away tea and I shall not be disturbed until supper.
I shall be quite alone in this room, free to think of you if I choose, and believe
me, my dear, I do choose. For a long time now I have been aware that you are
taking up more of my life every day, but I am always being surprised to find
how far this has gone. Why, it was only yesterday, I took down all those photographs from my mantelpiece—Gabriel, Olive, Mrs. Marshall, Molim, and the

Song This poem is based on the folk song
called "The Cutty Wren" (see note to "Robin
and Bobin" in David Jones, *In Parenthesis*),
beginning " 'O where are you going?' said
Milder to Malder / 'Where are you going?'
said Festel to Fose.' " It concludes *The Orators*
with rapid instances of escape from one's predicament (social, economic, sexual, imaginative).
midden dungheap
he "Rider," "farer," and "hearer" are all the
same person, the resolved hero. His questioners
are rather like the people called "They" in the
limericks of Edward Lear, the warning father
in Lewis Carroll's "Jabberwocky," and the uncle
in same author's "The Hunting of the Snark."

Wound Manifestly, a cancer; beyond that, the kind of interior "wound," like homosexu-
ality, or even more significantly, an artist's calling, whose discovery demands a reassessment
of priorities; beyond that, the condition of sinfulness that a Christian would equate with
his very humanity. On this prose poem's first publication in *The Orators*, Auden did not
give his own text the last of these readings.

others. How could I have left them there like that so long, memorials to my days of boasting? As it is, I've still far too many letters. (Vow. To have a grand clearance this week—hotel bills—bus tickets from Damascus, presentation pocket-mirrors, foreign envelopes, etc.)

Looking back now to that time before I lost my 'health' (Was that really only last February?) I can't recognize myself. The discontinuity seems absolute. But of course the change was really gradual. Over and over again in the early days when I was in the middle of writing a newsy letter to M., or doing tricks in the garden to startle R. and C., you showed your resentment by a sudden bout of pain. I had outbursts, wept even, at what seemed to me then your insane jealousy, your bad manners, your passion for spoiling things. What a little idiot I was not to trust your more exquisite judgment, which declined absolutely to let me go on behaving like a child. People would have tried to explain it all. You would not insult me with pity. I think I've learned my lesson now. Thank you, my dear. I'll try my hardest not to let you down again.

Do you realize we have been together now for almost a year? Eighteen months ago, if anyone had foretold this to me I should have asked him to leave the house. Haven't I ever told you about my first interview with the surgeon? He kept me waiting three-quarters of an hour. It was raining outside. Cars passed or drew up squeaking by the curb. I sat in my overcoat, restlessly turning over the pages of back numbers of illustrated papers, accounts of the Battle of Jutland,° jokes about special constables and conscientious objectors. A lady came down with a little girl. They put on their hats, speaking in whispers, tight-lipped. Mr. Gangle° would see me. A nurse was just coming out as I entered, carrying a white-enamelled bowl containing a pair of scissors, some instruments, soiled swabs of cotton wool. Mr. Gangle was washing his hands. The examination on the hard leather couch under the brilliant light was soon over. Washing again as I dressed he said nothing. Then reaching for a towel turned, 'I'm afraid,' he said. . . .

Outside I saw nothing, walked, not daring to think. I've lost everything, I've failed. I wish I was dead. And now, here we are, together, intimate, mature.

Later. At dinner Mrs. T. announced that she'd accepted an invitation for me to a whist-drive° at the Stewarts' on Wednesday. 'It's so good for you to get out in the evenings sometimes. You're as bad as Mr. Bedder.' She babbled on, secretly disappointed, I think, that I did not make more protest. Certainly six months ago she couldn't have brought it off, which makes me think what a great change has come over us recently. In what I might call our honeymoon stage, when we had both realized what we meant to each other (how slow I was, wasn't I?) and that this would always be so, I was obsessed (You too a little? No?) by what seemed my extraordinary fortune. I pitied everybody. Little do you know, I said to myself, looking at my neighbour on the bus, what has happened to the little man in the black hat sitting next to you. I was always smiling. I mortally offended Mrs. Hunter, I remember, when she was describing

Battle of Jutland major naval battle of World War I, the question of who actually won it being always and tiresomely in dispute
Mr. Gangle Surgeons in England are called "Mr." (not "Dr.").
whist-drive card party

her son's career at Cambridge. She thought I was laughing at her. In restaurants I found myself drawing pictures of you on the bottom of the table mats.
'Who'll ever guess what that is?' Once, when a whore accosted me, I bowed,
'I deeply regret it, Madam, but I have a friend.' Once I carved on a seat in the
park 'We have sat here. You'd better not.'

Now I see that all that sort of thing is juvenile and silly, merely a reaction
against insecurity and shame. You as usual of course were the first to realize
this, making yourself felt whenever I had been particularly rude or insincere.

Thanks to you, I have come to see a profound significance in relations I never
dreamt of considering before, an old lady's affection for a small boy, the Water-
houses and their retriever, the curious bond between Offal and Snig, the
partners in the hardware shop on the front. Even the close-ups on the films no
longer disgust nor amuse me. On the contrary they sometimes make me cry;
knowing you has made me understand.

It's getting late and I have to be up betimes in the morning. You are so quiet
these days that I get quite nervous, remove the dressing. No I am safe, you are
still there. The wireless says that the frost is coming. When it does, we know
what to expect, don't we? But I am calm. I can wait. The surgeon was dead
right. Nothing will ever part us. Good-night and God bless you, my dear.

Better burn this. °

1932

Paysage Moralisé°

Hearing of harvests rotting in the valleys,
Seeing at end of street the barren mountains,
Round corners coming suddenly on water,
Knowing them shipwrecked who were launched for islands,
We honour founders of these starving cities
Whose honour is the image of our sorrow,

Which cannot see its likeness in their sorrow
That brought them desperate to the brink of valleys;
Dreaming of evening walks through learned cities
They reined their violent horses on the mountains,
Those fields like ships to castaways on islands,
Visions of green to them who craved for water.

They built by rivers and at night the water
Running past windows comforted their sorrow;
Each in his little bed conceived of islands
Where every day was dancing in the valleys
And all the green trees blossomed on the mountains,
Where love was innocent, being far from cities.

Better burn this the usual prudent postscript to a clandestine love-letter

Paysage Moralisé "Moralized landscape"—the
interpretation of pictorial scenes in ethical and
psychological ways, as in 17th- and 18th-century
painting. This sestina (see Glossary) develops
the latent meanings in its terminal words in a
way like that of Sir Philip Sidney's double sestina,
"Ye Goatherd Gods."

But dawn came back and they were still in cities;
20   No marvellous creature rose up from the water;
There was still gold and silver in the mountains
But hunger was a more immediate sorrow,
Although to moping villages in valleys
Some waving pilgrims were describing islands . . .

'The gods,' they promised, 'visit us from islands,
Are stalking, head-up, lovely, through our cities;
Now is the time to leave your wretched valleys
And sail with them across the lime-green water,
Sitting at their white sides, forget your sorrow,
30   The shadow cast across your lives by mountains.'

So many, doubtful, perished in the mountains,
Climbing up crags to get a view of islands,
So many, fearful, took with them their sorrow
Which stayed them when they reached unhappy cities,
So many, careless, dived and drowned in water,
So many, wretched, would not leave their valleys.

It is our sorrow. Shall it melt? Then water
Would gush, flush, green these mountains and these valleys,
And we rebuild our cities, not dream of islands.
1933   1933

Lullaby

Lay your sleeping head, my love,
Human on my faithless arm;
Time and fevers burn away
Individual beauty from
Thoughtful children, and the grave
Proves the child ephemeral:
But in my arms till break of day
Let the living creature lie,
Mortal, guilty, but to me
10   The entirely beautiful.

Soul and body have no bounds:
To lovers as they lie upon
Her tolerant enchanted slope
In their ordinary swoon,
Grave the vision Venus sends
Of supernatural sympathy,
Universal love and hope;
While an abstract insight wakes

Among the glaciers and the rocks
The hermit's carnal° ecstasy.

Certainty, fidelity
On the stroke of midnight pass
Like vibrations of a bell
And fashionable madmen raise
Their pedantic boring cry:
Every farthing° of the cost,
All the dreaded cards foretell,
Shall be paid, but from this night
Not a whisper, not a thought,
Not a kiss nor look be lost.

Beauty, midnight, vision dies:
Let the winds of dawn that blow
Softly round your dreaming head
Such a day of welcome show
Eye and knocking heart may bless,
Find our mortal world enough;
Noons of dryness find you fed
By the involuntary powers,
Nights of insult let you pass
Watched by every human love.
1937   1937

Song

As I walked out one evening,
    Walking down Bristol Street,
The crowds upon the pavement
    Were fields of harvest wheat.

And down by the brimming river
    I heard a lover sing
Under an arch of the railway:
    'Love has no ending.

I'll love you, dear, I'll love you
    Till China and Africa meet
And the river jumps over the mountain
    And the salmon sing in the street.

I'll love you till the ocean
    Is folded and hung up to dry

---

carnal All printed versions of this poem before
1967 had "sensual."

farthing smallest English coin, worth one-quarter
penny (now obsolete)

And the seven stars° go squawking
  Like geese about the sky.

The years shall run like rabbits
  For in my arms I hold
The Flower of the Ages
  And the first love of the world.'

But all the clocks in the city
  Began to whirr and chime:
'O let not Time deceive you,
  You cannot conquer Time.

In the burrows of the Nightmare
  Where Justice naked is,
Time watches from the shadow
  And coughs when you would kiss.

In headaches and in worry
  Vaguely life leaks away,
And Time will have his fancy
  To-morrow or to-day.

Into many a green valley
  Drifts the appalling snow;
Time breaks the threaded dances
  And the diver's brilliant bow.

O plunge your hands in water,
  Plunge them in up to the wrist;
Stare, stare in the basin
  And wonder what you've missed.

The glacier knocks in the cupboard,
  The desert sighs in the bed,
And the crack in the tea-cup opens
  A lane to the land of the dead.

Where the beggars raffle the banknotes
  And the Giant is enchanting to Jack,°
And the Lily-white Boy is a Roarer°
  And Jill goes down on her back.°

O look, look in the mirror,
  O look in your distress;
Life remains a blessing
  Although you cannot bless.

seven stars the Pleiades, referred to through the ancient and mysterious counting song, "Green Grow the Rushes-O": "Seven for the seven stars in the sky and six for the six proud walkers. . . ."
Jack of the folk tale of Jack the Giant-Killer
Roarer "Roaring boy" meant a kind of Eliza-bethan criminal, hell-raising youth; from the same song as above: "Two, two the lily-white boys, clothèd all in green-o" (in Christian reading, they are Christ and John the Baptist).
Jill . . . back for Jack, on the hill, with the pail of water

O stand, stand at the window
    As the tears scald and start;
You shall love your crooked neighbour
    With your crooked heart.'

It was late, late in the evening,
    The lovers they were gone;
The clocks had ceased their chiming
    And the deep river ran on.
    1938   1940

In Memory of Sigmund Freud°
(d. Sept. 1939)

When there are so many we shall have to mourn,
when grief has been made so public, and exposed
    to the critique of a whole epoch
    the frailty of our conscience and anguish,

of whom shall we speak? For every day they die
among us, those who were doing us some good,
    who knew it was never enough but
    hoped to improve a little by living.

Such was this doctor: still at eighty he wished
to think of our life from whose unruliness
    so many plausible young futures
    with threats or flattery ask obedience,

but his wish was denied him: he closed his eyes
upon that last picture, common to us all,
    of problems like relatives gathered
    puzzled and jealous about our dying.

For about him till the very end were still
those he had studied, the fauna of the night,
    and shades that still waited to enter
    the bright circle of his recognition

turned elsewhere with their disappointment as he
was taken away from his life interest
    to go back to the earth in London,
    an important Jew who died in exile.

Freud One of the greatest thinkers of our age (b. 1856), he started his career as a neurologist in Vienna treating girls with hysterical symptoms. From the attempt to understand certain local psychopathologies he moved to a general theory of the human psyche and its development. He died a refugee from Nazism in London, having altered most of the moral and psychological concepts of his time. Auden's ode celebrates Freud as a humane moralist; it deliberately introduces antique personifications ("Hate," "Impulse") and speaks to the general significance of such notions as the relation between instinct and the internalized mechanisms of civilization, and the maintenance of the hidden past in the present inner life. The poem is in syllabic verse, with stanzas of lines of 11–11–9–10 syllables, indented and arranged so as to suggest Horatian odes and German Romantic poets' adaptations of Greek lyric meters.

Only Hate was happy, hoping to augment
his practice now, and his dingy clientele
　　　who think they can be cured by killing
　　　and covering the gardens with ashes.

30 They are still alive, but in a world he changed
simply by looking back with no false regrets;
　　　all he did was to remember
　　　like the old and be honest like children.

He wasn't clever at all: he merely told
the unhappy Present to recite the Past
　　　like a poetry lesson till sooner
　　　or later it faltered at the line where

long ago the accusations had begun,
and suddenly knew by whom it had been judged,
　　　how rich life had been and how silly,
40 　　and was life-forgiven and more humble,

able to approach the Future as a friend
without a wardrobe of excuses, without
　　　a set mask of rectitude or an
　　　embarrassing over-familiar gesture.

No wonder the ancient cultures of conceit°
in his technique of unsettlement foresaw
　　　the fall of princes, the collapse of
　　　their lucrative patterns of frustration:

if he succeeded, why, the Generalised Life
50 would become impossible, the monolith
　　　of State be broken and prevented
　　　the co-operation of avengers.

Of course they called on God, but he went his way
down among the lost people like Dante, down
　　　to the stinking fosse° where the injured
　　　lead the ugly life of the rejected,

and showed us what evil is, not, as we thought,
deeds that must be punished, but our lack of faith,
　　　our dishonest mood of denial,
60 　　the concupiscence of the oppressor.

If some traces of the autocratic pose,
the paternal strictness he distrusted, still
　　　clung to his utterance and features,
　　　it was a protective coloration

cultures of conceit He means not only Western
political and economic structures but also their
bureaucracies and markets internalized in the
psyche of every person living among them.
fosse ditch; the pit of hell, here seen as a
state of crippling neurosis

for one who'd lived among enemies so long:
if often he was wrong and, at times, absurd,
    to us he is no more a person
   now but a whole climate of opinion°

under whom we conduct our different lives:
Like weather he can only hinder or help,
    the proud can still be proud but find it
   a little harder, the tyrant tries to

make do with him but doesn't care for him much:
he quietly surrounds all our habits of growth
    and extends, till the tired in even
   the remotest miserable duchy

have felt the change in their bones and are cheered,
till the child, unlucky in his little State,
    some hearth where freedom is excluded,
   a hive whose honey is fear and worry,

feels calmer now and somehow assured of escape,
while, as they lie in the grass of our neglect,
    so many long-forgotten objects
   revealed by his undiscouraged shining

are returned to us and made precious again;
games we had thought we must drop as we grew up,
    little noises we dared not laugh at,
   faces we made when no one was looking.

But he wishes us more than this. To be free
is often to be lonely. He would unite
    the unequal moieties° fractured
   by our own well-meaning sense of justice,

would restore to the larger the wit and will
the smaller possesses but can only use
    for arid disputes, would give back to
   the son the mother's richness of feeling:

but he would have us remember most of all
to be enthusiastic over the night,
    not only for the sense of wonder
   it alone has to offer, but also

because it needs our love. With large sad eyes
its delectable creatures look up and beg
    us dumbly to ask them to follow:
   they are exiles who long for the future

climate of opinion the phrase of the American   moieties halved parts of the human whole
philosopher Alfred North Whitehead (1861–
1947)

that lies in our power, they too would rejoice
if allowed to serve enlightenment like him,
    even to bear our cry of 'Judas,'
    as he did and all must bear who serve it.

One rational voice is dumb. Over his grave
110 the household of Impulse mourns one dearly loved:
    sad is Eros, builder of cities,
    and weeping anarchic Aphrodite.°
1939   1940

In Memory of W. B. Yeats
(*d. Jan. 1939*)

I

He disappeared in the dead of winter:
The brooks were frozen, the airports almost deserted,
And snow disfigured the public statues;
The mercury sank in the mouth of the dying day.
O all the instruments agree°
The day of his death was a dark cold day.

Far from his illness
The wolves ran on through the evergreen forests,
The peasant river was untempted by the fashionable quays;
10 By mourning tongues
The death of the poet was kept from his poems.

But for him it was his last afternoon as himself,
An afternoon of nurses and rumours;
The provinces of his body revolted,
The squares of his mind were empty,
Silence invaded the suburbs,
The current of his feeling failed: he became his admirers.

Now he is scattered among a hundred cities
And wholly given over to unfamiliar affections;
20 To find his happiness in another kind of wood
And be punished under a foreign code of conscience.
The words of a dead man
Are modified in the guts of the living.

One rational . . . Aphrodite (ll. 109–12) Ultimately, Auden acknowledges that Freud, like Blake and other great Romantic visionaries, were fulfillments of the rationalist tradition of the Enlightenment, rather than destroyers of it. "Eros" here is the Freudian sexual force which in its sublimated form is all creative power (like Venus in Lucretius's *Of the Nature of Things*); "Aphrodite," the destructive but complementary force of Romantic love. Both lament the death of a visionary who knew their relation as no one else in his age did.
O . . . agree In revising this ode for his *Collected Shorter Poems* (1950), Auden qualified the tone of this almost Dryden-like evocation of formal ceremonial diction; the rewritten form, "What instruments we have agree" is used also at l. 30.

But in the importance and noise of tomorrow
When the brokers are roaring like beasts on the floor of the Bourse,°
And the poor have the sufferings to which they are fairly accustomed,
And each in the cell of himself is almost convinced of his freedom;
A few thousand will think of this day
As one thinks of a day when one did something slightly unusual.
O all the instruments agree
The day of his death was a dark cold day.

II

You were silly like us: your gift survived it all;
The parish of rich women, physical decay,
Yourself; mad Ireland hurt you into poetry.
Now Ireland has her madness and her weather still,
For poetry makes nothing happen: it survives
In the valley of its saying where executives
Would never want to tamper; it flows south
From ranches of isolation and the busy griefs,
Raw towns that we believe and die in; it survives,
A way of happening, a mouth.

III

Earth, receive an honoured guest;
William Yeats is laid to rest:
Let the Irish vessel lie
Emptied of its poetry.

Time that is intolerant
Of the brave and innocent,
And indifferent in a week
To a beautiful physique,

Worships language and forgives
Everyone by whom it lives;
Pardons cowardice, conceit,
Lays its honours at their feet.

Time that with this strange excuse
Pardoned Kipling and his views,°
And will pardon Paul Claudel,
Pardons him for writing well.

In the nightmare of the dark
All the dogs of Europe bark,

Bourse the Paris stock exchange, probably used for its alliterative value rather than for any specific quality not shared by, say, Wall Street Pardoned . . . views In 1940, Auden shared the fashionable left-wing view of Kipling as an apologist for imperialism; actually, Kipling's position was far more complex. Paul Claudel (1868–1955), French Catholic poet, was more unambiguously right-wing politically. Both examples are given in acknowledgment that Yeats's flirtations with fascism in the 1930's needed some apology. Auden canceled the three stanzas concluding with this one (ll. 46–57) in the *Collected Shorter Poems.*

60 And the living nations wait,
Each sequestered in its hate;

Intellectual disgrace
Stares from every human face,
And the seas of pity lie
Locked and frozen in each eye.

Follow, poet, follow right
To the bottom of the night,
With your unconstraining voice
Still persuade us to rejoice;

70 With the farming of a verse
Make a vineyard of the curse,
Sing of human unsuccess
In a rapture of distress;

In the deserts of the heart
Let the healing fountain start,
In the prison of his days
Teach the free man how to praise.

                    1940

From For the Time Being°

NARRATOR

Well, so that is that. Now we must dismantle the tree,
Putting the decorations back into their cardboard boxes—
Some have got broken—and carrying them up to the attic.
The holly and the mistletoe must be taken down and burnt,
And the children got ready for school. There are enough
Left-overs to do, warmed-up, for the rest of the week—
Not that we have much appetite, having drunk such a lot,
Stayed up so late, attempted—quite unsuccessfully—
To love all of our relatives, and in general
10 Grossly overestimated our powers. Once again
As in previous years we have seen the actual Vision and failed
To do more than entertain it as an agreeable
Possibility, once again we have sent Him away,
Begging though to remain His disobedient servant,
The promising child who cannot keep His word for long.
The Christmas Feast is already a fading memory,
And already the mind begins to be vaguely aware
Of an unpleasant whiff of apprehension at the thought

For the Time Being This is the closing speech of a Christmas oratorio. In a blend of easy, colloquial language and theological reference, it outlines the concept of the period between Christmas and Easter, two festivals representing events that transcended ordinariness, as a temporary return to that ordinariness again, as though the human significance of religious experience were almost held in abeyance.

Of Lent and Good Friday which cannot, after all, now
Be very far off. But, for the time being, here we all are,
Back in the moderate Aristotelian city°
Of darning and the Eight-Fifteen, where Euclid's geometry
And Newton's mechanics would account for our experience,
And the kitchen table exists because I scrub it.
It seems to have shrunk during the holidays. The streets
Are much narrower than we remembered; we had forgotten
The office was as depressing as this. To those who have seen
The Child, however dimly, however incredulously,
The Time Being is, in a sense, the most trying time of all.
For the innocent children who whispered so excitedly
Outside the locked door where they knew the presents to be
Grew up when it opened. Now, recollecting that moment
We can repress the joy, but the guilt remains conscious;
Remembering the stable where for once in our lives
Everything became a You and nothing was an It.°
And craving the sensation but ignoring the cause,
We look round for something, no matter what, to inhibit
Our self-reflection, and the obvious thing for that purpose
Would be some great suffering. So, once we have met the Son,
We are tempted ever after to pray to the Father;
'Lead us into temptation and evil for our sake.'
They will come, all right, don't worry; probably in a form
That we do not expect, and certainly with a force
More dreadful than we can imagine. In the meantime
There are bills to be paid, machines to keep in repair,
Irregular verbs to learn, the Time Being to redeem
From insignificance. The happy morning is over,
The night of agony still to come; the time is noon:
When the Spirit must practise his scales of rejoicing
Without even a hostile audience, and the Soul endure
A silence that is neither for nor against her faith
That God's Will will be done, that, in spite of her prayers,
God will cheat no one, not even the world of its triumph.

1942   1944

In Praise of Limestone

If it form the one landscape that we the inconstant ones
    Are consistently homesick for, this is chiefly
Because it dissolves in water. Mark these rounded slopes

Aristotelian city the city of Aristotle's golden mean—the world to which reason, reasonableness, and scientific explanation apply, as opposed to the spiritual extremes of "the happy morning" and "the night of agony," to which they do not

You . . . It the difference between the relation of man to God (called "I-Thou") and others (called "I-It"), crucial in the theology of Martin Buber (1878–1965), Jewish existentialist philosopher and scholar

With their surface fragrance of thyme and beneath
A secret system of caves and conduits; hear these springs
That spurt out everywhere with a chuckle
Each filling a private pool for its fish and carving
Its own little ravine whose cliffs entertain
The butterfly and the lizard; examine this region
10   Of short distances and definite places:
What could be more like Mother or a fitter background
For her son, for the nude young male who lounges
Against a rock displaying his dildo,° never doubting
That for all his faults he is loved, whose works are but
Extensions of his power to charm? From weathered outcrop
To hill-top temple, from appearing waters to
Conspicuous fountains, from a wild to a formal vineyard,
Are ingenious but short steps that a child's wish
To receive more attention than his brothers, whether
20   By pleasing or teasing, can easily take.

Watch, then, the band of rivals as they climb up and down
Their steep stone gennels° in twos and threes, sometimes
Arm in arm, but never, thank God, in step; or engaged
On the shady side of a square at midday in
Voluble discourse, knowing each other too well to think
There are any important secrets, unable
To conceive a god whose temper-tantrums are moral
And not to be pacified by a clever line
Or a good lay: for, accustomed to a stone that responds,
30   They have never had to veil their faces in awe
Of a crater whose blazing fury could not be fixed;
Adjusted to the local needs of valleys
Where everything can be touched or reached by walking,
Their eyes have never looked into infinite space
Through the lattice-work of a nomad's comb;° born lucky,
Their legs have never encountered the fungi
And insects of the jungle, the monstrous forms and lives
With which we have nothing, we like to hope, in common.
So, when one of them goes to the bad, the way his mind works
40   Remains comprehensible: to become a pimp
Or deal in fake jewelry or ruin a fine tenor voice
For effects that bring down the house could happen to all
But the best and the worst of us . . .
                                        That is why, I suppose,
The best and worst never stayed here long but sought
Immoderate soils where the beauty was not so external,
The light less public and the meaning of life

dildo literally, an artificial phallus; here, his
own real one
gennels ordinarily, "channels," but in Yorkshire
dialect, "alley-ways"

nomad's comb simply his hair comb, but considered an important possession

Something more than a mad camp.° 'Come!' cried the granite wastes,
  'How evasive is your humour, how accidental
Your kindest kiss, how permanent is death.' (Saints-to-be
  Slipped away sighing.) 'Come!' purred the clays and gravels.
'On our plains there is room for armies to drill; rivers
  Wait to be tamed and slaves to construct you a tomb
In the grand manner: soft as the earth is mankind and both
  Need to be altered.' (Intendant Caesars rose and
Left, slamming the door.) But the really reckless were fetched
  By an older colder voice, the oceanic whisper:
'I am the solitude that asks and promises nothing;
  That is how I shall set you free. There is no love;
There are only the various envies, all of them sad.'

They were right, my dear, all those voices were right
And still are; this land is not the sweet home that it looks,
  Nor its peace the historical calm of a site
Where something was settled once and for all: A backward
  And delapidated province, connected
To the big busy world by a tunnel, with a certain
  Seedy appeal, is that all it is now? Not quite:
It has a worldly duty which in spite of itself
  It does not neglect, but calls into question
All the Great Powers assume; it disturbs our rights. The poet,
  Admired for his earnest habit of calling
The sun the sun, his mind Puzzle, is made uneasy
  By these solid statues which so obviously doubt
His antimythological myth; and these gamins,
  Pursuing the scientist down the tiled colonnade
With such lively offers,° rebuke his concern for Nature's
  Remotest aspects: I, too, am reproached, for what
And how much you know. Not to lose time, not to get caught,
  Not to be left behind, not, please! to resemble
The beasts who repeat themselves, or a thing like water
  Or stone whose conduct can be predicted, these
Are our Common Prayer, whose greatest comfort is music
  Which can be made anywhere, is invisible,
And does not smell. In so far as we have to look forward
  To death as a fact, no doubt we are right: But if
Sins can be forgiven, if bodies rise from the dead,
  These modifications of matter into
Innocent athletes and gesticulating fountains,
  Made solely for pleasure, make a further point:
The blessed will not care what angle they are regarded from,

---

mad camp When this poem was written, "camp" was exclusively a homosexual coterie word to designate overelaborate displays of parodied effeminacy, and, at a higher level, being friv-olous about what meant most to one, being solemn about what mattered least. The term then became general theatrical usage.
lively offers sexual offers of various sorts

90   Having nothing to hide. Dear, I know nothing of
Either, but when I try to imagine a faultless love
     Or the life to come, what I hear is the murmur
Of underground streams, what I see is a limestone landscape.
1948   1951

The Fall of Rome

[*For Cyril Connolly*]
The piers are pummelled by the waves;
In a lonely field the rain
Lashes an abandoned train;
Outlaws fill the mountain caves.

Fantastic grow the evening gowns;
Agents of the Fisc° pursue
Absconding tax-defaulters through
The sewers of provincial towns.

Private rites of magic send
10   The temple prostitutes to sleep;
All the literati keep
An imaginary friend.

Cerebrotonic Cato° may
Extoll the Ancient Disciplines,
But the muscle-bound Marines
Mutiny for food and pay.

Caesar's double-bed is warm
As an unimportant clerk
Writes I DO NOT LIKE MY WORK
20   On a pink official form.

Unendowed with wealth or pity,
Little birds with scarlet legs,
Sitting on their speckled eggs,
Eye each flu-infected city.

Altogether elsewhere, vast
Herds of reindeer move across
Miles and miles of golden moss,
Silently and very fast.
                    1951

Fisc the state treasury
Cerebrotonic Cato "Cato the Censor," Marcus
Porcius Cato (234–139 B.C.), used here as the
type of those who confront social problems
with rigid solutions. The word "cerebrotonic"
comes from Dr. W. H. Sheldon's theory of the
relation between type of physique and personality: according to him, the cerebrotonic type
is "an 'introvert' . . . he is not at home at
social gatherings and he shrinks from crowds."

The Proof°

'When rites and melodies begin
    To alter modes and times,
And timid bar-flies° boast aloud
    Of uncommitted crimes,
And leading families are proud
    To dine with their black sheep,
What promises, what discipline,
    If any, will Love keep?'
      So roared Fire on their right:
      But Tamino and Pamina
      Walked past its rage,
      Sighing O, sighing O,
In timeless fermatas° of awe and delight
    (Innocent? Yes. Ignorant? No.)
      Down the grim passage.

'When stinking Chaos lifts the latch,°
    And Grotte° backward spins,
And Helen's nose° becomes a beak,
    And cats and dogs grow chins,
And daisies claw and pebbles shriek,
    And Form and Colour part,
What swarming hatreds then will hatch
    Out of Love's riven heart.'
      So hissed Water on their left:
      But Pamina and Tamino
      Opposed its spite,
      With his worship, with her sweetness—
O look now! See how they emerge from the cleft
    (Frightened? No. Happy? Yes.)
      Out into sunlight.

      1955

Marginalia

Auden has always been interested in the wisdom of aphorism; his wide reading in German literature had acquainted him early on with the writings of Georg Christoph Lichtenberg (1742–99), that great aphorist of the Enlightenment, and Auden's own

The Proof refers to the testing, in Mozart's *The Magic Flute*, of Prince Tamino and his beloved, Pamina (daughter of an enchantress Queen of the Night named Astrafiammante—"flaming star"), by Priests of Isis, the trials being by the two elements of fire and water.
bar-flies harmless solitary drinkers
fermatas held, extended notes in music
latch that keeps disorder from reclaiming the world again
Grotte or, more properly, Grotti, was a magic

mill belonging to Mägde and turned, at the command of a king, by the two giantesses Fenja and Menja; it ground out Joy, Riches, and Freedom. But to avenge an injury done them they ground it backward to produce bloody warlike weapons, fiery destruction, and a monstrous army that undid the king's realm (from *The Song of the Mill*, in the Old Norse Poetic Edda).
Helen's nose that of Helen of Troy, supposedly perfect

Austrian contemporary Karl Krauss; and the epigraph to *The Orators* was an observation of powerful relevance to more than the private jokes of that volume: *"Private faces in public places / Are wiser and nicer / Than public faces in private places."* In Auden's most recent book he has turned to aphorism himself, combining prose observation with line structures adapted from the Japanese forms called *haiku* and *tanka* (of 17 and 31 syllables, respectively). The first group is a connected sequence; the very last poem refers to the poet himself.

From Marginalia

A dead man
who never caused others to die
seldom rates a statue.

The last king
of a fallen dynasty
is seldom well spoken of.

Few even wish they could read
the lost annals
of a cudgeled people.

The tyrant's device:
*Whatever Is Possible
Is Necessary.*

Small tyrants, threatened by big,
sincerely believe
they love Liberty.

No tyrant ever fears
his geologists or his engineers.

Tyrants may get slain,
but their hangmen usually
die in their beds.

Patriots? Little boys,
obsessed by Bigness,
Big Pricks, Big Money, Big Bangs.

In States unable
to alleviate Distress,
Discontent is hanged.

In semiliterate countries
demagogues pay
court to teen-agers.

When Chiefs of State
prefer to work at night,
let the citizens beware.

The palm extended in welcome:
Look! for you
I have unclenched my fist.

The class whose vices
he pilloried was his own,
now extinct, except
for lone survivors like him
who remember its virtues.

1970

LOUIS MACNEICE
1907–1965

Born in Belfast, educated at boarding school (Marlborough College) and Oxford, Mac-
Neice studied classics and taught them for a while, before becoming a writer for the
British Broadcasting Corporation. In 1936 he went with his friend and fellow poet
W. H. Auden on a journey to Iceland which resulted in their joint volume, *Letters from
Iceland* (1937). MacNeice's poetry and politics were never as doctrinaire in their commitment to the reform of society as those of other poets of the Left, and attempts to
limit his accomplishment by bracketing him with such very different writers as Auden,
Stephen Spender, C. Day Lewis, and that much underrated poet Roy Fuller are useful
only in pointing toward a kind of shared mode of topical poetry—witty, sardonic,
and ironically self-aware of the dangers to poetry, and to the world, of poets' involvement with political causes they may only half-understand. A poem like "Bagpipe
Music" represents that moment in English poetry between the two World Wars when
a parallel emerges with some of the didactic lyric verse of Bertolt Brecht. It is certainly
a moment which political poetry in English has not reached since.

Bagpipe Music°

It's no go the merrygoround, it's no go the rickshaw,°
All we want is a limousine and a ticket for the peepshow.
Their knickers° are made of crêpe-de-chine, their shoes are made of python,
Their halls are lined with tiger rugs and their walls with heads of bison.

John MacDonald found a corpse, put it under the sofa,
Waited till it came to life and hit it with a poker,

Bagpipe Music To a revolutionary socialist the
extremely depressed state of the Scottish economy in the thirties would demand radical solutions, not retreats into a whole range of "opiates"
aside from official religion, including the traditionalism symbolized in the title—which also
characterizes the clever squealing of the poem's
off-rhymes.
rickshaw one in an amusement park
knickers panties (the China silk ones of the
rich)

Sold its eyes for souvenirs, sold its blood for whisky,
Kept its bones for dumb-bells to use when he was fifty.
It's no go the Yogi-Man, it's no go Blavatsky,°
10   All we want is a bank balance and a bit of skirt in a taxi.

Annie MacDougall went to milk, caught her foot in the heather,
Woke to hear a dance record playing of Old Vienna.
It's no go your maidenheads, it's no go your culture,
All we want is a Dunlop tyre° and the devil mend the puncture.

The Laird o' Phelps spent Hogmanay° declaring he was sober,
Counted his feet to prove the fact and found he had one foot over.
Mrs. Carmichael had her fifth, looked at the job with repulsion,
Said to the midwife 'Take it away; I'm through with overproduction.

It's no go the gossip column, it's no go the ceilidh,°
20   All we want is a mother's help and a sugar-stick for the baby.

Willie Murray cut his thumb, couldn't count the damage,
Took the hide of an Ayrshire cow and used it for a bandage.
His brother caught three hundred cran° when the seas were lavish,
Threw the bleeders back in the sea and went upon the parish.°

It's no go the Herring Board,° it's no go the Bible,
All we want is a packet of fags when our hands are idle.

It's no go the picture palace, it's no go the stadium,
It's no go the country cot° with a pot of pink geraniums,
It's no go the Government grants, it's no go the elections,
30   Sit on your arse for fifty years and hang your hat on a pension.

It's no go my honey love, it's no go my poppet;
Work your hands from day to day, the winds will blow the profit.
The glass is falling hour by hour, the glass will fall for ever,
But if you break the bloody glass you won't hold up the weather.

                                                        1937

Whit Monday°

Their feet on London, their heads in the grey clouds,
The Bank (if you call it a holiday) Holiday crowds
Stroll from street to street, cocking an eye

Yogi-Man . . . Blavatsky rejecting the fake solutions of Eastern religions and pseudo-religions: a swami and Madame H. P. Blavatsky, the Russian theosophist (1831–91), stand here for the lot.
Dunlop tyre a bicycle tire
Hogmanay New Year's Eve (Scots)
ceilidh in Scotland, an evening of songs and story telling (pronounced "kay-lee")—a more homely distraction

cran the volume of a herring catch (approximately 750 fish)
upon the parish on welfare
Herring Board national agency set up to aid the failing herring-fishing industry
cot small farm cottage
Whit Monday The Monday after the seventh Sunday following Easter (Whitsuntide) was at the time a bank holiday in England, and a national holiday weekend. But this is London at war.

For where the angel used to be in the sky;
But the Happy Future is a thing of the past and the street
Echoes to nothing but their dawdling feet.
The Lord's my shepherd°—familiar words of myth
Stand up better to bombs than a granite monolith,
Perhaps there is something in them. *I'll not want—*
Not when I'm dead. *He makes me down to lie—*
Death my christening and fire my font—
The quiet (Thames, or Don's or Salween's)° *waters by.*

1941

STEPHEN SPENDER
1909–

Born in London of a literary family, educated at Oxford, Spender was one of the
generation of left-wing writers for whom the Spanish Civil War was an important
confrontation with aspects of the self, as well as what was seen by so many
people as simply a struggle against fascism (see the Headnote to W. H. Auden). More
interested in German poetry than in the French Symbolists that Eliot and his generation
had admired, Spender, like some of his other contemporaries who went to Spain,
published poems in both a public and a spiritually private mode, the latter emerging
as the dominant one. Spender has been active in the literary life of London, co-editing
two important periodicals of the pre- and post-World War II periods, *Horizon* and
Encounter, and is currently Professor of English Literature at University College,
London.

I Think Continually of Those Who Were Truly Great

I think continually of those who were truly great.
Who, from the womb, remembered the soul's history
Through corridors of light where the hours are suns,
Endless and singing. Whose lovely ambition
Was that their lips, still touched with fire,
Should tell of the Spirit, clothed from head to foot in song.
And who hoarded from the Spring branches
The desires falling across their bodies like blossoms.

What is precious, is never to forget
The essential delight of the blood drawn from ageless springs
Breaking through rocks in worlds before our earth.
Never to deny its pleasure in the morning simple light
Nor its grave evening demand for love.

shepherd The italicized words are from a
metrical paraphrase of the 23rd Psalm.
Don's . . . Salween's The Don, in central Russia, and the Salween, flowing through Tibet,
China and Burma. Both, like the Thames, were
the scenes of battles in 1941.

Never to allow gradually the traffic to smother
With noise and fog the flowering of the Spirit.

Near the snow, near the sun, in the highest fields,
See how these names are fêted by the waving grass
And by the streamers of white cloud
And whispers of wind in the listening sky.
20   The names of those who in their lives fought for life,
Who wore at their hearts the fire's centre.
Born of the sun, they travelled a short while toward the sun,
And left the vivid air signed with their honor.

                                        1933

Ultima Ratio Regum°

The guns spell money's ultimate reason
In letters of lead on the Spring hillside.
But the boy lying dead under the olive trees
Was too young and too silly
To have been notable to their important eye.
He was a better target for a kiss.

When he lived, tall factory hooters never summoned him
Nor did restaurant plate-glass doors revolve to wave him in.
His name never appeared in the papers.
10   The world maintained its traditional wall
Round the dead with their gold sunk deep as a well,
Whilst his life, intangible as a Stock Exchange rumour, drifted outside.

O too lightly he threw down his cap
One day when the breeze threw petals from the trees.
The unflowering wall sprouted with guns,
Machine-gun anger quickly scythed the grasses;
Flags and leaves fell from hands and branches;
The tweed cap rotted in the nettles.

Consider his life which was valueless
20   In terms of employment, hotel ledgers, news files.
Consider. One bullet in ten thousand kills a man.
Ask. Was so much expenditure justified
On the death of one so young, and so silly
Lying under the olive trees, O world, O death?

                                        1939

Ultima Ratio Regum "The Ultimate Argument of Kings," a phrase referring to (and engraved on) cannon, by order of Louis XIV; also found on Prussian artillery as late as the early 20th century. This poem refers to the fragile comprehension of the moral and political realities embedded in the violence of the Spanish Civil War that marked the idealistic young Englishmen who enlisted in the Loyalist cause, as well as their Spanish counterparts (the young soldier in the poem might be either). See also the Headnote to W. H. Auden.

EDITH SITWELL
1887–1964

A picturesque and flamboyant literary personage, Edith Sitwell was born at the seaside house of her father, Sir George Sitwell, Baronet, and brought up there and on her family's six-hundred-year-old estate, Renishaw, near Sheffield. Educated privately at home, she and her younger brothers, Osbert and Sacheverell, formed even in their youth a literary community of their own. In 1915 she published her first book of verse, and during the following year began editing, with her brothers, an annual anthology called *Wheels*. With the public performance of *Façade* in London in 1923 her fame was assured; this remarkable suite of poems, spoken rhythmically to amusing musical accompaniments composed by Sir William Walton for chamber orchestra, evidenced all the marks of her subsequent literary and personal style. The influence of French Symbolist poets (Rimbaud, in his *Les Illuminations;* Verlaine's famous dictum about poetry, *De la musique avant toute chose*—"Music before anything else"), the elevation of the brilliant free associations of Victorian nonsense verse (Lewis Carroll's and Edward Lear's) into poetic solemnities, the play with sounds and rhymes and assonances, the vast and curious learning, the fascination with stagey decor, dress, and gesture—all of these mark her poetic and critical works. She was given to eccentric dress, and in many of her portraits, particularly in some of the later photographs by Cecil Beaton, she apparently arranged to look dead. She wrote a novel based on material from the life of Swift (*I Live under a Black Sun*, 1937), a strange biography of Alexander Pope (1930), and a posthumously published autobiography, *Taken Care Of* (1965). She was made Dame Commander of the British Empire in 1953.

The poem from *Façade* given below reflects the satirical turn of many of the nautical poems in the collection; it is as though the archly social world of Victorian seaside resorts fed one half of the poet's childhood imagination, while the richer, dreamier side of her imagination subsisted on the house and books of Renishaw Park, where poetry, to alter Marianne Moore's expression, was a real garden with imaginary toads in it.

Hornpipe°

Sailors come
To the drum
Out of Babylon;
   Hobby-horses
Foam, the dumb
Sky rhinoceros-glum

Watched the courses of the breakers' rocking-horses and with Glaucis°
Lady Venus on the settee of the horsehair sea!°

Hornpipe the traditional sailor's dance. As usual, Walton's score quotes from popular tunes, and the well-known hornpipe theme sounds against the opening sections of the text. This text, incidentally, was written to be recited at breakneck speed, thus ensuring that the internal rhymes all come out clearly.

Glaucis presumably a sea nymph, *glaukos* ("shining," "blue-gray") being used of the sea in Greek literature
horsehair sea Victorian settees were frequently covered and / or stuffed with horsehair.

Where Lord Tennyson in laurels° wrote a gloria free,
10   In a borealic iceberg came Victoria; she
Knew Prince Albert's tall memorial° took the colours of the floreal
And the borealic iceberg; floating on they see
New-arisen Madam Venus for whose sake from far
Came the fat and zebra'd emperor from Zanzibar
Where like golden bouquets lay far Asia, Africa, Cathay,
All laid before that shady lady by the fibroid Shah.
Captain Fracasse° stout as any water-butt came, stood
With Sir Bacchus both a-drinking the black tarr'd grapes' blood
Plucked among the tartan leafage
20   By the furry wind whose grief age
Could not wither°—like a squirrel with a gold star-nut.
Queen Victoria sitting shocked upon the rocking-horse
Of a wave said to the Laureate, 'This minx of course
Is as sharp as any lynx and blacker-deeper than the drinks and quite as
Hot as any hottentot, without remorse!
         For the minx,'
                 Said she,
         'And the drinks,
                 You can see,
30   Are hot as any hottentot and not the goods for me!'
                                                1922

WILLIAM EMPSON
1906–

Although famous when still young for his brilliant and erratic critical work *Seven Types of Ambiguity* (1930), Empson had to await the post-World War II generation of younger poets before his verse achieved wide critical acclaim and influence. It did so not only because of its clean, hard diction, rhetorical directness, and aphoristic knottiness, but also because, apprehended in connection with Empson's own way of reading English literature as expounded in his critical works, it could become a rallying point for the young, clever writers who were to form a new community of university wits. Empson's poetic corpus is quite small (his 1955 *Collected Poems* contained only fifty-six) but it is never diffuse; philosophical and playful by turns and at once, their syntax more elliptically puzzling than their diction, these poems became models of poetic deportment for the fifties generation, which admired D. H. Lawrence's novels and remained unaffected by his poems.

Empson was born in Yorkshire, and educated at Magdalene College, Cambridge, where he was an early student of I. A. Richards, one of the founders of modern

---

Lord Tennyson in laurels that is, as poet laureate. The scene in the poem obliquely invokes Tennyson's reading of *his* 'tall memorial" *(In Memoriam)* to Queen Victoria, also treated comically in Max Beerbohm's drawing from *The Poet's Corner*.
memorial an ornate and rhetorical structure erected by Queen Victoria in Kensington Gardens in 1863.
Fracasse named coined from "fracas" ("uproar")
age . . . wither "Age cannot wither her, nor custom stale / Her infinite variety": proverbially famous description of Cleopatra from Shakespeare, *Antony and Cleopatra*

criticism. Rather more sophisticated in the sciences than most critics of poetry in England, he produced a number of seminal critical works. After the *Seven Types* came *English Pastoral Poetry* (1935), *The Structure of Complex Words* (1951), and *Milton's God* (1961), all of which reflected his pioneering insights into the language of poetry and the interpretive questions raised by the very act of serious reading. He published two collections of verse, *Poems* (1935) and *The Gathering Storm* (1940), many of them written while he was teaching in the Orient—in Japan from 1931 to 1934, and in Peking thereafter. In 1952 he returned to England and held the Chair of English at the University of Sheffield until 1971.

This Last Pain

This last pain for the damned the Fathers° found:
'They knew the bliss with which they were not crowned.'
　　Such, but on earth, let me foretell,
　　Is all, of heaven or of hell.

Man, as the prying housemaid of the soul,
May know her happiness° by eye to hole:
　　He's safe; the key is lost; he knows
　　Door will not open, nor hole close.

'What is conceivable can happen too,'
Said Wittgenstein,° who had not dreamt of you;
　　But wisely; if we worked it long
　　We should forget where it was wrong.

Those thorns are crowns which, woven into knots,
Crackle under and soon boil fool's pots;°
　　And no man's watching, wise and long,
　　Would ever stare them into song.

Thorns burn to a consistent ash, like man;
A splendid cleanser for the frying-pan:
　　And those who leap from pan to fire°
　　Should this brave opposite admire.

Fathers The Church Fathers (early Christian theologians), perfecting the idea of hell for use on earth, framed statements like this one; Satan, in *Paradise Lost*, was keenly aware of their meaning.
her happiness The soul's. The soul is the mistress, and philosophical and scientific man is the housemaid peering at her secrets and joys through holes in bodies (like keyholes), the only access available to him.
Wittgenstein A rewriting of several propositions such as "What is thinkable is also possible" in the *Tractatus Logico-Philosophicus* (1921–22) of Ludwig Wittgenstein (1889–1951), one of the philosophical giants of our age but, when Empson was writing this, still primarily a local

Cambridge presence. In the *Tractatus* Wittgenstein was concerned with, among other things, elementary propositions embodying facts alone; the idea of Empson's poem is, in his own words, "that human nature can conceive of divine states which it cannot attain."
fool's pots Combining (1) Christ's crown of thorns; (2) "As the crackling of thorns under a pot, so is the laughter of a fool" (Ecclesiastes 7:6); (3) "A watched pot never boils" (proverbial). "The folly which has the courage to maintain careless self-deceit is compared to the mock-regal crown of thorns" (Empson).
pan to fire "Out of the frying pan into the fire" is proverbial.

All those large dreams by which men long live well
Are magic-lanterned on the smoke of hell;°
    This then is real, I have implied,
    A painted, small, transparent slide.

These the inventive can hand-paint at leisure,
Or most emporia would stock our measure;
    And feasting in their dappled shade
    We should forget how they were made.

Feign then what's by a decent tact believed
30 And act that state is only so conceived,
    And build an edifice of form
    For house where phantoms may keep warm.

Imagine, then, by miracle, with me,
(Ambiguous gifts, as what gods give must be)
    What could not possibly be there,
    And learn a style from a despair.

1935

Villanelle°

It is the pain, it is the pain, endures.
Your chemic beauty burned my muscles through.
Poise° of my hands reminded me of yours.

What later purge from this deep toxin cures?
What kindness now could the old salve renew?
It is the pain, it is the pain, endures.

The infection slept (custom or change inures)
And when pain's secondary phase was due
Poise of my hands reminded me of yours.

10 How safe I felt, whom memory assures,
Rich that your grace safely by heart I knew.
It is the pain, it is the pain, endures.

My stare drank deep beauty that still allures.
My heart pumps yet the poison draught of you.
Poise of my hands reminded me of yours.

You are still kind whom the same shape immures.
Kind and beyond adieu. We miss our cue.
It is the pain, it is the pain, endures.
Poise of my hands reminded me of yours.

1935

hell "It was done somewhere by missionaries onto a pagan bonfire" (Empson).
Villanelle For a note on this difficult form see the Glossary; notice how subtly the meaning of the refrain is modulated through its repetitions, rather than with bald puns or divided syntax.
Poise weight, balance, posture, and the way in which parts of our bodies feel their own presence

Missing Dates

Slowly the poison the whole blood stream fills.
It is not the effort nor the failure tires.
The waste remains, the waste remains and kills.°

It is not your system or clear sight that mills
Down small to the consequence a life requires;
Slowly the poison the whole blood stream fills.

They bled an old dog dry yet the exchange rills°
Of young dog blood gave but a month's desires;
The waste remains, the waste remains and kills.

It is the Chinese tombs and the slag hills
Usurp the soil, and not the soil retires.
Slowly the poison the whole blood stream fills.

Not to have fire is to be a skin that shrills.
The complete fire is death. From partial fires
The waste remains, the waste remains and kills.

It is the poems you have lost, the ills
From missing dates, at which the heart expires.
Slowly the poison the whole blood stream fills.
The waste remains, the waste remains and kills.

1940

DYLAN THOMAS
1914–1953

Drawing on a Welsh bardic tradition that still manifests itself in poetry competitions in the Welsh language, Dylan Thomas also assimilated in his small but remarkably personal and intense body of work a number of European modernist poetic influences. Always remaining close to an oral poetry (witness his unique attentiveness to sound patterning), he nonetheless manifests in his early poems perhaps more than any other English poet of his stature the effects of Continental surrealism. Gerard Manley Hopkins; the complex cadences and structures of Welsh verse; T. S. Eliot's poems and, in response to the directions of Eliot's criticism, the English devotional poets of the seventeenth century (Donne, Herbert, Vaughan, Crashaw); Joyce's *A Portrait of the Artist as a Young Man* and *Ulysses;* a visionary Welsh religious tradition that informed the Catholicism of his countryman David Jones, and became in Thomas the basis for a kind of pagan use of Christian mythology—elements of all these are present in his poems and in his few moving and intimate prose works.

The . . . kills 1. A. Richards suggested that Empson was echoing, in this refrain, the opening line of another marvelous villanelle, the opening line of Tennyson's "Tithonus": "The woods decay, the woods decay and fall."

rills Brooks, streams; "It is true about the old dog, at least I saw it reported somewhere, but the legend that a fifth or some such part of the soil of China is given up to ancestral tombs is (by the way) not true" (Empson).

Thomas was born in Swansea in Wales and educated at the grammar school there; he then worked as a newspaper reporter, and attracted notice when still quite young for his dense, brilliant, and difficult poetry. Concealed in the meshes of his early verse —the *Eighteen Poems* (1934), *The Map of Love* (1939), and *Deaths and Entrances* (1946; with its title taken from John Donne's last sermon, "Death's Duel")—were an intense sexuality, a linking of sexual themes to religious mythology, and a programmatic modernist obliqueness of reference that use epithet and puzzling kenning (see Glossary) to stand for the object mentioned, and depended upon puns at times almost in the manner of difficult British crossword puzzles. In his poetry published after World War II, and particularly during the last years of his life, when he toured the United States giving flamboyant and resonant readings from his work, a more genial and publicly available mode dominated his work.

Thomas was at home, metrically, both in the iambic rhythms of the seventeenth-century poets he admired, and in a loose accentual "sprung rhythm" (Hopkins's phrase) involving a good deal of internal rhyming and alliterating of phrases. His long *Vision and Prayer* even adopts for its stanzas two graphic patterns in the manner of Herbert. He would let his images evolve through strange and anomalous grammatical constructions—the kind that E. E. Cummings had made familiar in American verse, but which Auden and his followers had never wholeheartedly adopted—ranging from the simple phrase "a grief ago" to all sorts of powerful, but wrenched, verbing of nouns and compoundings. The later pieces in his 1957 *Collected Poems*, his radio play *Under Milk Wood* and some late prose pieces, e.g *A Child's Christmas in Wales* (1955), gained a wide audience for themselves, but not for his earlier and perhaps more interesting work.

When, Like a Running Grave°

When, like a running grave, time tracks you down,
Your calm and cuddled is a scythe of hairs,°
Love in her gear° is slowly through the house,
Up naked stairs, a turtle° in a hearse,
Hauled to the dome,

Comes, like a scissors stalking, tailor age,°
Deliver me who, timid in my tribe,
Of love am barer than Cadaver's° trap
Robbed of the foxy tongue, his footed tape
10   Of the bone inch,

Deliver me, my masters, head and heart,
Heart of Cadaver's candle waxes thin,

When . . . Grave a meditation on love and death, on how each act of love is a death (Thomas is aware of the 17th-century pun on "die," meaning sexual orgasm—as a modern pun would turn on "come")
scythe of hairs both "made of hairs" (pubic)
and "mowing down hairs" (like grass, and the sign of old age)
gear costume
turtle turtledove, emblem of true love
tailor age Age, the shroud tailor
Cadaver's the protagonist of the poem—man, his body, his penis

When blood, spade-handed, and the logic time
Drive children up like bruises to the thumb,
From maid and head,°

For, sunday faced, with dusters° in my glove,
Chaste and the chaser, man with the cockshut° eye,
I, that time's jacket or the coat of ice
May fail to fasten° with a virgin o
In the straight grave,

Stride through Cadaver's country in my force,
My pickbrain masters morsing° on the stone
Despair of blood, faith in the maiden's slime,
Halt among eunuchs, and the nitric stain
On fork° and face.

Time is a foolish fancy, time and fool.
No, no, you lover skull, descending hammer
Descends, my masters, on the entered honour.°
You hero skull, Cadaver in the hangar
Tells the stick,° 'fail.'

Joy is no knocking nation, sir and madam,
The cancer's fusion, or the summer feather
Lit on the cuddled tree, the cross of fever,
Nor city tar and subway bored to foster
Man through macadam.°

I damp the waxlights in your tower dome.
Joy is the knock of dust, Cadaver's shoot°
Of bud of Adam through his boxy shift,
Love's twilit nation and the skull of state,
Sir, is your doom.

Everything ends, the tower ending° and,
(Have with the house of wind), the leaning scene,
Ball of the foot depending from the sun,
(Give, summer, over), the cemented skin,
The actions' end.

All, men my madmen, the unwholesome wind
With whistler's cough contages,° time on track

---

maid and head maidenhead, and thus all young girls

dusters "knuckledusters" (brass knuckles)

cockshut literally, "sunset," the end of day; also with sense of "cocksure" and "cock" in the phallic, slang sense

fasten as with a buttonhole

morsing tapping out Morse code; also "mossing"

fork crotch

honour as Andrew Marvell used "quaint honour" in "To His Coy Mistress" to mean not only chastity but also the sexual organ it protects

stick The aeronautical images in the poem all cluster around the term "joystick," meaning the basic altitude and banking control on older, single-engined planes, and here, of course, the lover's erection.

macadam blacktop paving material named for its inventor; also, literally, "son of Adam"

shoot Words like this and "bud," "boxy," and "country" (in l. 21) are all used with sexual overtones.

tower ending This stanza meditates on detumescence.

contages verb coined from "contagion"

Shapes in a cinder death; love for his trick,
Happy Cadaver's hunger as you take
50   The kissproof° world.

1934

Sonnet°

Let the tale's sailor° from a Christian voyage
Atlaswise° hold half-way off the dummy bay
Time's ship-racked gospel on the globe I balance:
So shall winged harbours through the rockbirds' eyes
Spot the blown word, and on the seas I imagine
December's thorn screwed in a brow of holly.°
Let the first Peter from a rainbow's quayrail°
Ask the tall fish° swept from the bible east,
What rhubarb° man peeled in her foam-blue channel
10   Has sown a flying garden round that sea-ghost?
Green as beginning, let the garden diving
Soar, with its two bark towers,° to that Day°
When the worm° builds with the gold straws of venom
My nest of mercies in the rude, red tree.°

1936

After the Funeral

In memory of Ann Jones°

After the funeral, mule praises, brays,
Windshake of sailshaped ears, muffle-toed tap
Tap happily of one peg in the thick
Grave's foot, blinds down the lids, the teeth in black,
The spittled eyes, the salt ponds in the sleeves,

kissproof probably an ironic adoption of a recently introduced advertising term for a lipstick that would not come off
Sonnet This is one of Thomas's very difficult earlier poems, the last of a sequence of ten loosely connected poems all moving "Altarwise by owl light" (as the first poem begins)— through Christian imagery in a starry night-world—toward a vision of apocalypse implied in this last poem. In the background of this poem are sexual and religious images, frequently superimposed (as in "tall fish"), a vision from an implied shipboard, Crucifixion, St. Peter the fisherman fishing for the fish Christ, and others.
tale's sailor Sinbad, in the *Arabian Nights,* with Christian puns on the two syllables of his name
Atlaswise because the poet-sailor-pilgrim may be holding a celestial globe and turning it (like Atlas bearing the globe of the world), looking at its "seas" of darkness, contemplating the constellations
December's . . . holly a holly wreath for Christ-

mas seen as a Good Friday crown of thorns
quayrail railing on a dock (but "quay," pronounced "key," puns on St. Peter's keys)
fish The Greek acronym for Christ's name and epithet was *ichthus,* "fish," which was an early Christian symbol.
rhubarb perhaps because rhubarb is grown from old roots of its plant, or because its tops are poisonous; also because its stem is red like the flesh of man and his phallus
two bark towers the two trees, in Paradise, of Life and Knowledge
Day Apocalypse
worm the serpent, identified in Revelation with Satan
rude, red tree The pun on "rood" as meaning Christ's cross associates it with the fatal Tree of Knowledge in the manner of old biblical interpretation, picks up the rhubarb phallic image, and closes the poem and the sequence with a vision of first and last things brought together.
Ann Jones Thomas's aunt

Morning smack of the spade that wakes up sleep,
Shakes a desolate boy who slits his throat
In the dark of the coffin and sheds dry leaves,
That breaks one bone to light with a judgment clout,
After the feast of tear-stuffed time and thistles
In a room with a stuffed fox and a stale fern,
I stand, for this memorial's sake, alone
In the snivelling hours with dead, humped Ann
Whose hooded, fountain heart once fell in puddles
Round the parched worlds of Wales and drowned each sun
(Though this for her is a monstrous image blindly
Magnified out of praise; her death was a still drop;
She would not have me sinking in the holy
Flood of her heart's fame; she would lie dumb and deep
And need no druid° of her broken body).
But I, Ann's bard on a raised hearth, call all
The seas to service that her wood-tongued virtue
Babble like a bellbuoy over the hymning heads,
Bow down the walls of the ferned and foxy woods
That her love sing and swing through a brown chapel,
Bless her bent spirit with four, crossing birds.
Her flesh was meek as milk, but this skyward statue
With the wild breast and blessed and giant skull
Is carved from her in a room with a wet window
In a fiercely mourning house in a crooked year.
I know her scrubbed and sour humble hands
Lie with religion in their cramp, her threadbare
Whisper in a damp word, her wits drilled hollow,
Her fist of a face died clenched on a round pain;
And sculptured Ann is seventy years of stone.
These cloud-sopped, marble hands, this monumental
Argument of the hewn voice, gesture and psalm,
Storm me forever over her grave until
The stuffed lung of the fox twitch and cry Love
And the strutting fern lay seeds on the black sill.

1938

A Refusal To Mourn the Death, by Fire, of a Child in London

Never until the mankind making
Bird beast and flower
Fathering and all humbling darkness°
Tells with silence the last light breaking
And the still hour
Is come of the sea tumbling in harness

---

druid priest of an ancient British nature-religion
darkness Read all the foregoing phrases as epithets of darkness: "mankind-making"; "bird-beast-and-flower-fathering"; "all-humbling."

And I must enter again the round
Zion of the water bead
And the synagogue of the ear of corn
Shall I let pray the shadow of a sound
Or sow my salt seed
In the least valley of sackcloth to mourn

The majesty and burning of the child's death.
I shall not murder
The mankind of her going with a grave truth
Nor blaspheme down the stations of the breath°
With any further
Elegy of innocence and youth.

Deep with the first dead lies London's daughter,
Robed in the long friends,
The grains beyond age, the dark veins of her mother,
Secret by the unmourning water
Of the riding Thames.
After the first death, there is no other.

                                    1946

Fern Hill°

Now as I was young and easy under the apple boughs
About the lilting house and happy as the grass was green,
        The night above the dingle° starry,
            Time let me hail and climb
        Golden in the heydays of his eyes,
And honoured among wagons I was prince of the apple towns
And once below a time I lordly had the trees and leaves
            Trail with daisies and barley
        Down the rivers of the windfall light.

10   And as I was green and carefree, famous among the barns
About the happy yard and singing as the farm was home,
        In the sun that is young once only,
            Time let me play and be
        Golden in the mercy of his means,
And green and golden I was huntsman and herdsman, the calves
Sang to my horn, the foxes on the hills barked clear and cold,
            And the sabbath rang slowly
        In the pebbles of the holy streams.

All the sun long it was running, it was lovely, the hay
20   Fields high as the house, the tunes from the chimneys, it was air

stations of the breath echoing the phrase
"stations of the cross," pictured or sculptured
representations of the stages of the Christ's
Passion and Death

Fern Hill the name of Thomas' aunt's farm, remembered from childhood
dingle a wooded valley or dell

And playing, lovely and watery
    And fire green as grass.
And nightly under the simple stars
As I rode to sleep the owls were bearing the farm away,
All the moon long I heard, blessed among stables, the nightjars°
    Flying with the ricks,° and the horses
      Flashing into the dark.

And then to awake, and the farm, like a wanderer white
With the dew, come back, the cock on his shoulder: it was all
    Shining, it was Adam and maiden,
      The sky gathered again
    And the sun grew round that very day.
So it must have been after the birth of the simple light
In the first, spinning place, the spellbound horses walking warm
    Out of the whinnying green stable
      On to the fields of praise.

And honoured among foxes and pheasants by the gay house
Under the new made° clouds and happy as the heart was long,
    In the sun born over and over,
      I ran my heedless ways,
    My wishes raced through the house high hay
And nothing I cared, at my sky blue trades, that time allows
In all his tuneful turning so few and such morning songs
    Before the children green and golden
      Follow him out of grace.

Nothing I cared, in the lamb white days, that time would take me
Up to the swallow thronged loft by the shadow of my hand,
    In the moon that is always rising,
      Nor that riding to sleep
    I should hear him fly with the high fields
And wake to the farm forever fled from the childless land.
Oh as I was young and easy in the mercy of his means,
    Time held me green and dying
    Though I sang in my chains like the sea.

1946

'Do Not Go Gentle into That Good Night'°

Do not go gentle into that good night,
Old age should burn and rave at close of day;
Rage, rage against the dying of the light.

---

nightjars harsh-voiced birds
ricks haystacks
new made as frequently in Thomas, "new-made"
Do Not . . . Night In form this poem is a
villanelle (see the two by William Empson given
above, and the one composed by Stephen Dae-
dulus in Joyce's *A Portrait of the Artist as a
Young Man,* given earlier). This was written for
Thomas' dying father.

Though wise men at their end know dark is right,
Because their words had forked no lightning they
Do not go gentle into that good night.

Good men, the last wave by, crying how bright
Their frail deeds might have danced in a green bay,
Rage, rage against the dying of the light.

10   Wild men who caught and sang the sun in flight,
And learn, too late, they grieved it on its way,
Do not go gentle into that good night.

Grave men, near death, who see with blinding sight
Blind eyes could blaze like meteors and be gay,
Rage, rage against the dying of the light.

And you, my father, there on the sad height,
Curse, bless, me now with your fierce tears, I pray .
Do not go gentle into that good night.
Rage, rage against the dying of the light.
1951   1957

E. M. FORSTER
1879–1970

Edward Morgan Forster was born in London on January 1, 1879. He was the great-grandson of Henry Thornton, the central figure of the Clapham Sect, a Victorian Evangelical group of strong ethical cast and dedicated to reform and philanthropy. Though he was not a Christian, Forster inherited many of their concerns, but he criticized them for their indifference to the evils inherent in the system which produced their wealth, as well as for their lack of "mysticism, a sense of the unseen." He attended Tonbridge, a public school he remembers in his novels—especially in the second, *The Longest Journey* (1907)—as a center of stupidity, false morality, and unspirituality. Cambridge was different; King's College, also celebrated in *The Longest Journey*, was a sort of paradise where friendship and Hellenism ruled.

Forster became a member of the "Apostles," a group founded in 1825 and dedicated to candor, gaiety, and self-effacing honesty. Their sense of the need for these ingredients of true friendship in a very stuffy and hypocritical world was given formal expression by the Cambridge philosopher G. E. Moore (1873–1958) in his *Principia Ethica* (1903). Moore argued, among other things, that the good cannot be identified with anything existent—with evolution, say, or with what benefits the greatest number; rather, it is something in one's head, by which he evaluated the world. He believed also that the "complex wholes" of consciousness in relation to beautiful objects and personal relations are the most valuable things we can know. His followers, translated to London, came to be known as the Bloomsbury group, from the district where most of them lived.

Forster was probably not interested in the technicalities of the *Principia*. He had already acquired, in part from another and very different Cambridge philosopher, J. M. E. McTaggart (1866–1925), a sense of the almost mystical virtues of friendship.

From his friend Goldsworthy Lowes Dickinson he made similar acquisitions, and like Dickinson he especially associated the cult of friendship, candor, and liberty with Greece. On his return after almost two years in Italy and Greece, however, Forster became associated with the so-called Bloomsbury group of Moore's followers, though he was never one of the central figures.

After the death of their father Sir Leslie Stephen (1832–1924), a distinguished man of letters and historian of thought, his children moved to Bloomsbury. It was Sir Leslie's son Thoby who brought the Cambridge ethos to London; but he died young in 1906, and the focus of the group was thenceforth the houses of Thoby's sisters Vanessa (who married the art critic Clive Bell in 1906) and Virginia (later married to Leonard Woolf). The best-known members (Forster apart) are the biographer Lytton Strachey (1880–1932), the economist J. M. Keynes (1883–1946), Leonard Woolf (1880–1969), Roger Fry (1866–1934), and Desmond MacCarthy (1878–1952). The eccentric hostess Lady Ottoline Morrell (1873–1938)—Lawrence's Hermione in *Women in Love*—was also important. Bertrand Russell (1872–1969) was an associate. All these people were extremely talented, and one or two were geniuses. Virginia Woolf (1882–1941) was an important experimental novelist, Keynes transformed twentieth-century economics, and Fry organized the Post-Impressionist exhibition of 1910, one of the most important dates in the history of art in England; Virginia Woolf said that it changed human nature.

Meanwhile the Bloomsbury group, cutting itself off from "good society," made its own rules, talked its own dialect (imitating perhaps the squeaky voice of Lytton Strachey), and attracted dislike and obloquy for many reasons—social, religious, ethical, artistic. Its members believed in freedom: for women, for homosexuals, for the subject races, even for the poor. They saw themselves—much in the manner of that Clapham Sect which lay far behind not only Forster but others of the group—as a sort of elect; and they put personal relations above all else, which is why Forster could make his famous remark (see below) about betraying his country before he would betray his friend, and why Orwell (see below) took great exception to such statements.

Forster has to be understood with reference to this Edwardian development of the old Victorian liberalism; yet he remained very much his own man, with his own voice and his own preoccupations. Between 1905 and 1910 he published four novels, *Where Angels Fear to Tread* (1905), *The Longest Journey* (1907), *A Room with a View* (1908, begun in 1903), and *Howards End* (1910). Though launching himself in a decade of modernism, Forster was not particularly experimental; his modern masters were Wagner, Samuel Butler, Meredith, Hardy, not the late James, Conrad, and Joyce. His novels are, as he said of Meredith's, "contrived": they are very carefully put together, and always mean more than they seem to say, but they are rooted in the contemporary problems of class, and in the difficulties it creates for men and women who are trying to find their true personalities and establish good relations with others and with the world, surrounded as they are by temptations to "sin against passion and truth." Structurally these books have considerable complexity, but nowadays they seem preoccupied with problems one cannot profoundly care about.

In 1912–13 Forster went to India with Lowes Dickinson, and on his return began work on the novel that was to be *A Passage to India*. He broke off, however, to write another novel, *Maurice*, about the happy outcome of a homosexual's search for truth and happiness (which outcome, incidentally, involves the destruction of class barriers). This book he did not publish, though he later revised it; he dedicated it "to a Happier Year," meaning some future, in which he did not really believe, when homosexual relations between men would no longer be forbidden by English law. Although the law was changed during Forster's life, the book did not appear until 1971, after his death. Part of its interest (which is admittedly rather limited) lies in the fact that this was in some ways Forster's true early subject, that in the sinning heroes and heroines of his earlier work he was using substitutes for the homosexual hero, and that now the whole subject of Hellenist freedom and friendship is more clearly defined.

After spending most of World War I as a Red Cross worker in Egypt, Forster returned to journalism. But he returned also to India, and to *A Passage to India,* which was to appear in 1924. *Passage* is an enormous advance on the earlier books—indeed, it is one of the great modern novels. While ostensibly about the relations of the British with the native populations of India, it is fundamentally a highly organized work of art, a limited world commenting on the tragedies and mitigations of the larger one. In 1927 Forster gave the lectures—characteristically whimsical, sly, evasive, unassertive —which were published as *Aspects of the Novel,* one of the most stimulating books ever written on the theory of fiction. In the years between 1927 and his death other books of various kinds appeared: a biography of Lowes Dickinson (1934), and one of Forster's aunt Marianne Thornton (1956), collections of essays—*Abinger Harvest* (1936) and *Two Cheers for Democracy* (1951); but he wrote no more novels.

Forster's reputation has risen and fallen and risen again. But one great book is enough to prove a writer's greatness, and that he wrote in *A Passage to India.* As a more general influence he is harder to assess. His opinions are precisely and characteristically stated in the famous essay given below; and they are not fashionable opinions, though they will always be listened to by intelligent liberals. He spent most of the last years of his life at King's College, Cambridge, and he died there among friends. His private influence on the young has been, within that small circle, considerable, and he has spoken out again and again for the victims of oppression, always in the same mild yet penetrating tones. In a sense he was an Edwardian version of a Victorian sage; but he held a different view of morality, and was also an artist of great strength and delicacy. This last is the attribute that saves him from obsolescence; in him, as in his great book, it is only the surface that looks old-fashioned.

What I Believe, first published in 1939, contains references to the threat of war, which then preoccupied everybody and which was realized in September of the same year. The essay's argument is lucid and unforced, and states Forster's own version of what is recognizably a Bloomsbury position: intelligent skepticism, the supremacy of personal relations over such external loyalties as may be demanded of one. A qualified cheer for democracy as being better than the alternatives is followed by an expression, paralleled elsewhere, of Forster's view that creative work goes on in spite of the "ultimate reality" of force, and that the best we can hope for is that that reality can sometimes, more or less by accident, be overlooked long enough for the work to continue, though hardly at such a moment as the time of writing. Forster's belief in aristocracy—not of birth but of "the sensitive, the considerate and the plucky"—is in the line of the Clapham Sect as well as the secularized Bloomsbury version of vocation and election. These people recognize one another, flash their signal lights through the surrounding dark. The imagery was borrowed soon after by W. H. Auden in his poem "September 1, 1939" (now forbidden the press by its author): "Ironic points of light / Flash out wherever the just / Exchange their messages"; and in 1951 Forster responded, in a review of Auden's *The Enchafèd Flood*, with the words "Because he once wrote 'We must love one another or die' he can command me to follow him."

What I Believe

I do not believe in Belief. But this is an age of faith, and there are so many militant creeds that, in self-defence, one has to formulate a creed of one's own.

Tolerance, good temper and sympathy are no longer enough in a world which is rent by religious and racial persecution, in a world where ignorance rules, and science, who ought to have ruled, plays the subservient pimp. Tolerance, good temper and sympathy—they are what matter really, and if the human race is not to collapse they must come to the front before long. But for the moment they are not enough, their action is no stronger than a flower,[1] battered beneath a military jack-boot. They want stiffening, even if the process coarsens them. Faith, to my mind, is a stiffening process, a sort of mental starch, which ought to be applied as sparingly as possible. I dislike the stuff. I do not believe in it, for its own sake, at all. Herein I probably differ from most people, who believe in Belief, and are only sorry they cannot swallow even more than they do. My law-givers are Erasmus[2] and Montaigne,[3] not Moses and St. Paul. My temple stands not upon Mount Moriah[4] but in that Elysian Field where even the immoral are admitted. My motto is: 'Lord, I disbelieve—help thou my unbelief.'[5]

I have, however, to live in an Age of Faith—the sort of epoch I used to hear praised when I was a boy. It is extremely unpleasant really. It is bloody in every sense of the word. And I have to keep my end up in it. Where do I start?

With personal relationships. Here is something comparatively solid in a world full of violence and cruelty. Not absolutely solid, for Psychology has split and shattered the idea of a 'Person,' and has shown that there is something incalculable in each of us, which may at any moment rise to the surface and destroy our normal balance. We don't know what we are like. We can't know

---

1. "How with this rage shall beauty hold a plea, / Whose action is no stronger than a flower?" Shakespeare, Sonnet LXV.
2. Desiderius Erasmus (c. 1466–1536), humanist famous for his learning, his satire on pedantry, and his defense of the freedom of the will and of the right to doubt and inquire.
3. Michel Eyquem de Montaigne (1533–92), author of *Essays*, written over many years and progressing from a stoical attitude to skepticism (a conviction of the fallibility of the human mind) and thence to the notion of the desirability of free and harmonious use of the human faculties.
4. The hill on which Abraham tried to sacrifice Isaac (Genesis 22) was held to be that on which the Temple later stood.
5. In Mark 9 the father of a sick child asks Jesus to cure him, and when Jesus replies that "all things are possible to him that believeth" the man cries out, "Lord, I believe; help thou mine unbelief" (*help* in the obsolete sense of *cure*). In Forster's parody *help* of course has its modern sense.

what other people are like. How, then, can we put any trust in personal relationships, or cling to them in the gathering political storm? In theory we cannot. But in practice we can and do. Though A is not unchangeably A or B unchangeably B, there can still be love and loyalty between the two. For the purpose of living one has to assume that the personality is solid, and the 'self' is an entity, and to ignore all contrary evidence. And since to ignore evidence is one of the characteristics of faith, I certainly can proclaim that I believe in personal relationships.

Starting from them, I get a little order into the contemporary chaos. One must be fond of people and trust them if one is not to make a mess of life, and it is therefore essential that they should not let one down. They often do. The moral of which is that I must, myself, be as reliable as possible, and this I try to be. But reliability is not a matter of contract—that is the main difference between the world of personal relationships and the world of business relationships. It is a matter for the heart, which signs no documents. In other words, reliability is impossible unless there is a natural warmth. Most men possess this warmth, though they often have bad luck and get chilled. Most of them, even when they are politicians, *want* to keep faith. And one can, at all events, show one's own little light here, one's own poor little trembling flame, with the knowledge that it is not the only light that is shining in the darkness, and not the only one which the darkness does not comprehend. Personal relations are despised today. They are regarded as bourgeois luxuries, as products of a time of fair weather which is now past, and we are urged to get rid of them, and to dedicate ourselves to some movement or cause instead. I hate the idea of causes, and if I had to choose between betraying my country and betraying my friend, I hope I should have the guts to betray my country. Such a choice may scandalise the modern reader, and he may stretch out his patriotic hand to the telephone at once and ring up the police. It would not have shocked Dante, though. Dante places Brutus and Cassius in the lowest circle of Hell because they had chosen to betray their friend Julius Caesar rather than their country Rome. Probably one will not be asked to make such an agonising choice. Still, there lies at the back of every creed something terrible and hard for which the worshipper may one day be required to suffer, and there is even a terror and a hardness in this creed of personal relationships, urbane and mild though it sounds. Love and loyalty to an individual can run counter to the claims of the State. When they do—down with the State, say I, which means that the State would down me.

This brings me along to Democracy, 'even Love, the Beloved Republic, which feeds upon Freedom and lives.'[6] Democracy is not a Beloved Republic really, and never will be. But it is less hateful than other contemporary forms of government, and to that extent it deserves our support. It does start from the assumption that the individual is important, and that all types are needed to make a civilisation. It does not divide its citizens into the bossers and the bossed—as an efficiency-regime tends to do. The people I admire most are those who are sensitive and want to create something or discover something,

6. Fifth line of stanza 38 of *Hertha*, by A. C. Swinburne (1837–1909).

and do not see life in terms of power, and such people get more of a chance under a democracy than elsewhere. They found religions, great or small, or they produce literature and art, or they do disinterested scientific research, or they may be what is called 'ordinary people,' who are creative in their private lives, bring up their children decently, for instance, or help their neighbours. All these people need to express themselves; they cannot do so unless society allows them liberty to do so, and the society which allows them most liberty is a democracy.

Democracy has another merit. It allows criticism, and if there is not public criticism there are bound to be hushed-up scandals. That is why I believe in the Press, despite all its lies and vulgarity, and why I believe in Parliament. Parliament is often sneered at because it is a Talking Shop.[7] I believe in it *because* it is a talking shop. I believe in the Private Member who makes himself a nuisance. He gets snubbed and is told that he is cranky or ill-informed, but he does expose abuses which would otherwise never have been mentioned, and very often an abuse gets put right just by being mentioned. Occasionally, too, a well-meaning public official starts losing his head in the cause of efficiency, and thinks himself God Almighty. Such officials are particularly frequent in the Home Office.[8] Well, there will be questions about them in Parliament sooner or later, and then they will have to mind their steps. Whether Parliament is either a representative body or an efficient one is questionable, but I value it because it criticises and talks, and because its chatter gets widely reported.

So Two Cheers for Democracy: one because it admits variety and two because it permits criticism. Two cheers are quite enough: there is no occasion to give three. Only Love the Beloved Republic deserves that.

What about Force, though? While we are trying to be sensitive and advanced and affectionate and tolerant, an unpleasant question pops up: does not all society rest upon force? If a government cannot count upon the police and the army, how can it hope to rule? And if an individual gets knocked on the head or sent to a labour camp, of what significance are his opinions?

This dilemma does not worry me as much as it does some. I realise that all society rests upon force. But all the great creative actions, all the decent human relations, occur during the intervals when force has not managed to come to the front. These intervals are what matter. I want them to be as frequent and as lengthy as possible, and I call them 'civilisation.' Some people idealise force and pull it into the foreground and worship it, instead of keeping it in the background as long as possible. I think they make a mistake, and I think that their opposites, the mystics, err even more when they declare that force does not exist. I believe that it exists, and that one of our jobs is to prevent it from getting out of its box. It gets out sooner or later, and then it destroys us and all the lovely things which we have made. But it is not out all the time, for the fortunate reason that the strong are so stupid. Consider their conduct

7. The description of Dickens at the time when he was a stenographic reporter in Parliament.
8. See note on Sir William Joynson-Hicks under D. H. Lawrence, *Pornography and Obscenity*.

for a moment in the Niebelung's Ring.[9] The giants there have the guns, or in other words the gold; but they do nothing with it, they do not realise that they are all-powerful, with the result that the catastrophe is delayed and the castle of Walhalla, insecure but glorious, fronts the storms. Fafnir, coiled round his hoard, grumbles and grunts; we can hear him under Europe today; the leaves of the wood already tremble, and the Bird calls its warnings uselessly. Fafnir will destroy us, but by a blessed dispensation he is stupid and slow, and creation goes on just outside the poisonous blast of his breath. The Nietzschean [10] would hurry the monster up, the mystic would say he did not exist, but Wotan, wiser than either, hastens to create warriors before doom declares itself. The Valkyries are symbols not only of courage but of intelligence; they represent the human spirit snatching its opportunity while the going is good, and one of them even finds time to love. Brünnhilde's last song hymns the recurrence of love, and since it is the privilege of art to exaggerate, she goes even further, and proclaims the love which is eternally triumphant and feeds upon freedom, and lives.

So that is what I feel about force and violence. It is, alas! the ultimate reality on this earth, but it does not always get to the front. Some people call its absences 'decadence'; I call them 'civilisation' and find in such interludes the chief justification for the human experiment. I look the other way until fate strikes me. Whether this is due to courage or to cowardice in my own case I cannot be sure. But I know that if men had not looked the other way in the past, nothing of any value would survive. The people I respect most behave as if they were immortal and as if society was eternal. Both assumptions are false: both of them must be accepted as true if we are to go on eating and

9. In the libretto he composed for his four-opera cycle The Ring of the Nibelung (first performances 1869–76), Richard Wagner (1813–83) tells the story of how Alberich steals the gold of the Nibelung and fashions a ring of it. The gods have built a new home named Valhalla, and plan to avoid paying the promised price to the giant builders—Freia, the goddess of youth—by stealing the gold from Alberich and offering that instead. Alberich puts a curse on the stolen ring, but Wotan, king of the gods, gives it to the giants, and Valhalla is occupied. Fafnir, the giant who has the ring, turns himself into a dragon to guard it, but Wotan needs it, lest the race of gods become extinct. The task of recovering the ring falls to Siegfried, son of Siegmund and Sieglinde, the mortal children of Wotan. Siegfried kills the dragon Fafnir, and, because he accidentally tastes his blood, can understand what the birds are saying. He goes to the rescue of the Valkyrie Brunnhilde, who was imprisoned by fire on a rock as a punishment for disobeying Wotan; he passes through the fire, awakes her, and places the ring on her finger. Wotan understands that he cannot save the race of gods, ruined by the immorality brought on by the ring; and Valhalla must be destroyed before the curse of the ring can end. This happens in the last opera, The Twilight of the Gods. Brunnhilde will not give up the ring (now a pledge of Siegfried's love) to the Rhinemaidens who originally owned it. Nor will Siegfried relinquish it. When he is killed by treachery the ring cannot be taken from his finger. But after her last song over Siegfried's corpse Brunnhilde rides her horse into his funeral pyre; and as the Rhine rises to extinguish the flames the Rhinemaidens seize back the ring. Valhalla is seen in the distance in flames.

Forster's private reading involves him in admiring Wotan for carrying on with Valhalla under threat; and in the last sentence of the paragraph he attributes to Brunnhilde the sentiments of his favorite quotation from Swinburne.

10. Friedrich Wilhelm Nietzsche (1844–1900), German philosopher, was at first a fervent Wagnerite but later attacked the composer. Forster is referring to Nietzsche's doctrine of the Superman, beyond good and evil, which came to be identified with the rule of force in Europe.

working and loving, and are to keep open a few breathing holes for the human spirit. No millennium seems likely to descend upon humanity; no better and stronger League of Nations will be instituted; no form of Christianity and no alternative to Christianity will bring peace to the world or integrity to the individual; no 'change of heart' will occur. And yet we need not despair, indeed, we cannot despair; the evidence of history shows us that men have always insisted on behaving creatively under the shadow of the sword; that they have done their artistic and scientific and domestic stuff for the sake of doing it, and that we had better follow their example under the shadow of the aeroplanes. Others, with more vision or courage than myself, see the salvation of humanity ahead, and will dismiss my conception of civilisation as paltry, a sort of tip-and-run game. Certainly it is presumptuous to say that we *cannot* improve, and that Man, who has only been in power for a few thousand years, will never learn to make use of his power. All I mean is that, if people continue to kill one another as they do, the world cannot get better than it is, and that since there are more people than formerly, and their means for destroying one another superior, the world may well get worse. What is good in people— and consequently in the world—is their insistence on creation, their belief in friendship and loyalty for their own sakes; and though Violence remains and is, indeed, the major partner in this muddled establishment, I believe that creativeness remains too, and will always assume direction when violence sleeps. So, though I am not an optimist, I cannot agree with Sophocles that it were better never to have been born.[11] And although, like Horace,[12] I see no evidence that each batch of births is superior to the last, I leave the field open for the more complacent view. This is such a difficult moment to live in, one cannot help getting gloomy and also a bit rattled, and perhaps short-sighted.

In search of a refuge, we may perhaps turn to hero-worship. But here we shall get no help, in my opinion. Hero-worship is a dangerous vice, and one of the minor merits of a democracy is that it does not encourage it, or produce that unmanageable type of citizen known as the Great Man. It produces instead different kinds of small men—a much finer achievement. But people who cannot get interested in the variety of life, and cannot make up their own minds, get discontented over this, and they long for a hero to bow down before and to follow blindly. It is significant that a hero is an integral part of the authoritarian stock-in-trade today. An efficiency-regime cannot be run without a few heroes stuck about it to carry off the dullness—much as plums have be put into a bad pudding to make it palatable. One hero at the top and a smaller one each side of him is a favourite arrangement, and the timid and the bored are comforted by the trinity, and, bowing down, feel exalted and strengthened.

No, I distrust Great Men. They produce a desert of uniformity around them and often a pool of blood too, and I always feel a little man's pleasure when they come a cropper. Every now and then one reads in the newspapers some such statement as: 'The coup d'état appears to have failed, and Admiral Toma's whereabouts is at present unknown.' Admiral Toma had probably every

11. Refers to the closing chorus of *Oedipus the King*.
12. Refers to *Odes* III.vi.46.

qualification for being a Great Man—an iron will, personal magnetism, dash, flair, sexlessness—but fate was against him, so he retires to unknown whereabouts instead of parading history with his peers. He fails with a completeness which no artist and no lover can experience, because with them the process of creation is itself an achievement, whereas with him the only possible achievement is success.

I believe in aristocracy, though [13]—if that is the right word, and if a democrat may use it. Not an aristocracy of power, based upon rank and influence; but an aristocracy of the sensitive, the considerate and the plucky. Its members are to be found in all nations and classes, and all through the ages, and there is a secret understanding between them when they meet. They represent the true human tradition, the one permanent victory of our queer race over cruelty and chaos.[14] Thousands of them perish in obscurity, a few are great names. They are sensitive for others as well as for themselves, they are considerate without being fussy, their pluck is not swankiness but the power to endure, and they can take a joke. I give no examples—it is risky to do that—but the reader may as well consider whether this is the type of person he would like to meet and to be, and whether (going farther with me) he would prefer that this type should *not* be an ascetic one. I am against asceticism myself. I am with the old Scotsman who wanted less chastity and more delicacy. I do not feel that my aristocrats are a real aristocracy if they thwart their bodies, since bodies are the instruments through which we register and enjoy the world. Still, I do not insist. This is not a major point. It is clearly possible to be sensitive, considerate and plucky and yet be an ascetic too; if anyone possesses the first three qualities, I will let him in! On they go—an invincible army, yet not a victorious one. The aristocrats, the elect, the chosen, the Best People—all the words that describe them are false, and all attempts to organise them fail. Again and again Authority, seeing their value, has tried to net them and to utilise them as the Egyptian Priesthood or the Christian Church or the Chinese Civil Service or the Group Movement,[15] or some other worthy stunt. But they slip through the net and are gone; when the door is shut, they are no longer in the room; their temple, as one of them [16] remarked, is the Holiness of the Heart's Affection, and their kingdom, though they never possess it, is the wide-open world.

With this type of person knocking about, and constantly crossing one's path if one has eyes to see or hands to feel, the experiment of earthly life cannot be dismissed as a failure. But it may well be hailed as a tragedy, the tragedy being that no device has been found by which these private decencies can be transmitted to public affairs. As soon as people have power they go crooked and sometimes dotty as well, because the possession of power lifts them into a region

13. This passage is famous as a summary of the Bloomsbury attitude toward personality.
14. In another essay, *Art for Art's Sake* (1949), Forster says of art that it is "the one orderly product that our muddling race has produced". There is no contradiction here, since it was a Bloomsbury doctrine, formulated in the *Principia Ethica* of G. E. Moore (see Headnote) that personal relations were a form of art.
15. The Oxford Group, founded in 1921 by the American Frank Buchman (1878–1961); the purpose was to "change" people's lives by a sort of up-to-date Christian revivalism. Moral Re-Armament is another name for it.
16. Keats.

where normal honesty never pays. For instance, the man who is selling news-papers outside the Houses of Parliament can safely leave his papers to go for a drink and his cap beside them: anyone who takes a paper is sure to drop a copper into the cap. But the men who are inside the Houses of Parliament—they cannot trust one another like that, still less can the Government they compose trust other governments. No caps upon the pavement here, but suspicion, treachery and armaments. The more highly public life is organised the lower does its morality sink; the nations of today behave to each other worse than they ever did in the past, they cheat, rob, bully and bluff, make war without notice, and kill as many women and children as possible; whereas primitive tribes were at all events restrained by taboos. It is a humiliating outlook—though the greater the darkness, the brighter shine the little lights, reassuring one another, signalling: 'Well, at all events, I'm still here. I don't like it very much, but how are you?' Unquenchable lights of my aristocracy! Signals of the invincible army! 'Come along—anyway, let's have a good time while we can.' I think they signal that too.

The Saviour of the future—if ever he comes—will not preach a new Gospel. He will merely utilise my aristocracy, he will make effective the good will and the good temper which are already existing. In other words, he will introduce a new technique. In economics, we are told that if there was a new technique of distribution, there need be no poverty, and people would not starve in one place while crops were being ploughed under in another. A similar change is needed in the sphere of morals and politics. The desire for it is by no means new; it was expressed, for example, in theological terms by Jacopone da Todi [17] over six hundred years ago. 'Ordina questo amore, O tu che m'ami,' he said; 'O thou who lovest me—set this love in order.' His prayer was not granted, and I do not myself believe that it ever will be, but here, and not through a change of heart, is our probable route. Not by becoming better, but by ordering and distributing his native goodness, will Man shut up Force into its box, and so gain time to explore the universe and to set his mark upon it worthily. At present he only explores it at odd moments, when Force is looking the other way, and his divine creativeness appears as a trivial by-product, to be scrapped as soon as the drums beat and the bombers hum.

Such a change, claim the orthodox, can only be made by Christianity, and will be made by it in God's good time: man always has failed and always will fail to organise his own goodness, and it is presumptuous of him to try. This claim—solemn as it is—leaves me cold. I cannot believe that Christianity will ever cope with the present world-wide mess, and I think that such influence as it retains in modern society is due to the money behind it, rather than to its spiritual appeal. It was a spiritual force once, but the indwelling spirit will have to be restated if it is to calm the waters again, and probably restated in a non-Christian form. Naturally a lot of people, and people who are not only good but able and intelligent, will disagree here; they will vehemently deny that Christianity has failed, or they will argue that its failure proceeds from the wickedness of men, and really proves its ultimate success. They have Faith, with a large F. My faith has a very small one, and I only intrude it because

17. Italian Franciscan poet (c.1230–1306); Forster quotes this line several times.

these are strenuous and serious days, and one likes to say what one thinks while speech is comparatively free: it may not be free much longer.

The above are the reflections of an individualist and a liberal who has found liberalism crumbling beneath him and at first felt ashamed. Then, looking around, he decided there was no special reason for shame, since other people, whatever they felt, were equally insecure. And as for individualism—there seems no way of getting off this, even if one wanted to. The dictator-hero can grind down his citizens till they are all alike, but he cannot melt them into a single man. That is beyond his power. He can order them to merge, he can incite them to mass-antics, but they are obliged to be born separately, and to die separately, and, owing to these unavoidable termini, will always be running off the totalitarian rails. The memory of birth and the expectation of death always lurk within the human being, making him separate from his fellows and consequently capable of intercourse with them. Naked I came into the world, naked I shall go out of it! And a very good thing too, for it reminds me that I am naked under my shirt, whatever its colour.

1939

JOHN BETJEMAN
1906–

Modern England's finest exponent of the tradition of "serious" light verse, Betjeman was educated, like Louis MacNeice, at Marlborough and Oxford. He is an authority on Victorian and Edwardian architecture, and has interested himself in the preservation and restoration of ecclesiastical buildings all over England. His verse is frequently satiric, as in the poem given below, which chides the unaltered commitments of a rich London lady at the onset of the Blitz in World War II. He frequently uses that same verse for nostalgic, only vaguely ironic celebrations of the platitudes of upper-middle-class English life. The result is that in certain of his poems, such as the well-known "Subaltern's Love Song" in praise of an athletic "Miss Joan Hunter Dunn," it is difficult to tell whether the transparently cool verse is gently mocking its subject or speaker, or unwittingly, by taking their part, revealing a self-betrayal. In 1972 Betjeman was appointed Poet Laureate, in succession to Cecil Day Lewis.

In Westminster Abbey

Let me take this other glove off
    As the *vox humana*° swells,
And the beauteous fields of Eden
    Bask beneath the Abbey bells.
Here, where England's statesmen lie,°
Listen to a lady's cry.

---

vox humana a particularly throbbing organ stop   statesmen lie in part of the cathedral, under stained-glass windows of biblical scenes

Gracious Lord, oh bomb the Germans.
  Spare their women for Thy Sake,
And if that is not too easy
  We will pardon Thy Mistake.
But, gracious Lord, whate'er shall be,
Don't let anyone bomb me.

Keep our Empire undismembered
  Guide our Forces by Thy Hand,
Gallant blacks from far Jamaica,
  Honduras and Togoland,
Protect them Lord in all their fights,
And, even more, protect the whites.

Think of what our Nation stands for,
  Books from Boots'° and country lanes,
Free speech, free passes, class distinction,
  Democracy and proper drains.°
Lord, put beneath Thy special care
One-eighty-nine Cadogan Square.°

Although dear Lord I am a sinner,
  I have done no major crime;
Now I'll come to Evening Service
  Whensoever I have the time.
So, Lord, reserve for me a crown,
And do not let my shares° go down.

I will labour for Thy Kingdom,
  Help our lads to win the war,
Send white feathers to the cowards
  Join the Women's Army Corps,
Then wash the Steps around Thy Throne
In the Eternal Safety Zone.

Now I feel a little better,
  What a treat to hear Thy Word,
Where the bones of leading statesmen,
  Have so often been interr'd.
And now, dear Lord, I cannot wait
Because I have a luncheon date.

                    1940

Boots' a chain of drugstores with circulating
libraries
proper drains real indoor plumbing (England
has always lagged behind Western Europe in the
technology of comfort)

Cadogan Square an expensive, fashionable address
shares stock

GEORGE ORWELL
1903–1950

Orwell was born Eric Arthur Blair in 1903, in British India. He was brought to England in 1907 and was educated at a private preparatory school and at Eton. On leaving school he joined the Imperial Indian Police and, after serving for five years in Burma, resigned in 1928. He then made his first attempt to explore the life of the English poor, and also worked as a dishwasher in Paris. These experiences formed the subject of his first book, *Down and Out in Paris and London* (1933), for which he chose the pseudonym George Orwell. Three novels followed: *Burmese Days* (1934)—based on his police experience, *A Clergyman's Daughter* (1935), and *Keep the Aspidistra Flying* (1936).

In 1936 he took over a village store, married, and at about the same time was commissioned to write about life among the English unemployed. The result was *The Road to Wigan Pier* (1937), in which he not only produced the kind of reportage he was already well known for, but also developed his own kind of politics: anti-imperialist, anti-capitalist, but not identified with any socialist institution. By January 1937 he was fighting with POUM—an anarchist unit supporting the legal government—in Spain. He was wounded and left Spain that June to write *Homage to Catalonia* (1938), perhaps his best book, certainly one of the best books about the Spanish Civil War, and a clear statement of his independent political position. He developed tuberculosis, and while recovering in Morocco wrote the novel *Coming up for Air* (1939).

Upon returning to England he wrote several now-famous essays on popular culture —on boy's weeklies, seaside postcards, and the like—and critical essays on Dickens, Tolstoy, and Henry Miller. When World War II began he abandoned his view that the Left should not fight, and supported the cause, working for the British Broadcasting Corporation and serving as a Home Guard, but had to relinquish these duties when he became ill again. He became literary editor of the left-wing *Tribune,* and wrote *Animal Farm* (finished by February 1944 but not published till August 1945), an allegory of the failure of Russian socialism under Stalin. In 1945, when his wife died, he settled on the island of Jura off the Scottish coast. His own health grew worse while he was composing *Nineteen-Eighty-Four* (1948). He remarried in October 1949 and died of tuberculosis in January 1950.

Orwell stands in a tradition of English upper-class eccentrics, but also in the more important tradition of plain prose. His behavior and his opinions are individualistic, but they tell because he can always say exactly what he means; a sort of honest completeness of statement characterizes his writing, and that is why, apart from the last two political allegories, his fiction is less effective than his discursive prose. Thus he conveys with rare force the sense of his country as "two nations" (or more than two) but also as one; he sensed this solidarity most strongly at the time of immense national danger, when he wrote "England Your England." This essay has been criticized for mythologizing the English "family" situation—for stressing the tolerance and mildness that coexist with all the social injustice—on the ground that it is not merely superficial class differences that set certain members of the family apart from others, but also the fact that a few of them own almost everything, while most of them own nothing. He makes it easy to laugh at the "ruling class" as comic and inefficient, instead of emphasizing that they are certainly efficient enough to hold on and run the show more or less their way. His images hide the truth. That is the New Left complaint against Orwell; yet he saw the poor, as he saw the population of the colonies, as exploited. On the other hand, he knew the importance of ownership; and when he wrote this essay he saw also that in 1940 the country had been saved by some kind of family solidarity, that the conservatism of rich and poor came together usefully and enabled Britain to hold out. It is by no means clear that the nation would have been better off if this had not happened, and Orwell was too honest and also too patriotic not to realize this and say so.

England Your England

As I write, highly civilised human beings are flying overhead, trying to kill me.[1] They do not feel any enmity against me as an individual, nor I against them. They are 'only doing their duty,' as the saying goes. Most of them, I have no doubt, are kind-hearted law-abiding men who would never dream of committing murder in private life. On the other hand, if one of them succeeds in blowing me to pieces with a well-placed bomb, he will never sleep any the worse for it. He is serving his country, which has the power to absolve him from evil.

One cannot see the modern world as it is unless one recognises the overwhelming strength of patriotism, national loyalty. In certain circumstances it can break down, at certain levels of civilisation it does not exist, but as a *positive* force there is nothing to set beside it. Christianity and international socialism are as weak as straw in comparison with it. Hitler and Mussolini rose to power in their own countries very largely because they could grasp this fact and their opponents could not.

Also, one must admit that the divisions between nation and nation are founded on real differences of outlook. Till recently it was thought proper to pretend that all human beings are very much alike, but in fact anyone able to use his eyes knows that the average of human behaviour differs enormously from country to country. Things that could happen in one country could not happen in another. Hitler's June Purge,[2] for instance, could not have happened in England. And, as Western peoples go, the English are very highly differentiated. There is a sort of backhanded admission of this in the dislike which nearly all foreigners feel for our national way of life. Few Europeans can endure living in England, and even Americans often feel more at home in Europe.

When you come back to England from any foreign country, you have immediately the sensation of breathing a different air. Even in the first few minutes dozens of small things conspire to give you this feeling. The beer is bitterer, the coins are heavier, the grass is greener, the advertisements are more blatant. The crowds in the big towns, with their mild knobby faces, their bad teeth and gentle manners, are different from a European crowd. Then the vast-

1. After the fall of France in mid-June 1940 German aircraft made daylight raids on England: first on ports and airfields, then, in September, on London. Enemy losses were too heavy for daylight bombing to continue, and from mid-September to the spring of 1941 the Germans bombed English cities, especially London, almost nightly. Civilians killed numbered over 30,000, more than half of them in London; and 3,500,000 houses were damaged or destroyed.

2. The murder of Ernst Röhm and his stormtroopers in June 1934.

ness of England swallows you up, and you lose for a while your feeling that the whole nation has a single identifiable character. Are there really such things as nations? Are we not 46 million individuals, all different? And the diversity of it, the chaos! The clatter of clogs in the Lancashire mill towns, the to-and-fro of the lorries on the Great North Road, the queues outside the Labour Exchanges, the rattle of pin-tables in the Soho pubs, the old maids biking to Holy Communion through the mists of the autumn mornings—all these are not only fragments, but *characteristic* fragments, of the English scene. How can one make a pattern out of this muddle?

But talk to foreigners, read foreign books or newspapers, and you are brought back to the same thought. Yes, there *is* something distinctive and recognisable in English civilisation. It is a culture as individual as that of Spain. It is somehow bound up with solid breakfasts and gloomy Sundays, smoky towns and winding roads, green fields and red pillar-boxes.[3] It has a flavour of its own. Moreover it is continuous, it stretches into the future and the past, there is something in it that persists, as in a living creature. What can the England of 1940 have in common with the England of 1840? But then, what have you in common with the child of five whose photograph your mother keeps on the mantelpiece? Nothing, except that you happen to be the same person.

And above all, it is *your* civilisation, it is *you*. However much you hate it or laugh at it, you will never be happy away from it for any length of time. The suet puddings and the red pillar-boxes have entered into your soul. Good or evil, it is yours, you belong to it, and this side the grave you will never get away from the marks that it has given you.

Meanwhile England, together with the rest of the world, is changing. And like everything else it can change only in certain directions, which up to a point can be foreseen. That is not to say that the future is fixed, merely that certain alternatives are possible and others not. A seed may grow or not grow, but at any rate a turnip seed never grows into a parsnip. It is therefore of the deepest importance to try and determine what England *is,* before guessing what part England *can play* in the huge events that are happening.

II

National characteristics are not easy to pin down, and when pinned down they often turn out to be trivialities or seem to have no connection with one another. Spaniards are cruel to animals, Italians can do nothing without making a deafening noise, the Chinese are addicted to gambling. Obviously such things don't matter in themselves. Nevertheless, nothing is causeless, and even the fact that Englishmen have bad teeth can tell one something about the realities of English life.

Here are a couple of generalisations about England that would be accepted by almost all observers. One is that the English are not gifted artistically. They are not as musical as the Germans or Italians, painting and sculpture have never flourished in England as they have in France. Another is that, as Europeans go, the English are not intellectual. They have a horror of abstract thought, they

3. Pillar-shaped red mailboxes in the streets.

feel no need for any philosophy or systematic 'world-view.' Nor is this because they are 'practical,' as they are so fond of claiming for themselves. One has only to look at their methods of town-planning and water-supply, their obstinate clinging to everything that is out of date and a nuisance, a spelling system that defies analysis and a system of weights and measures that is intelligible only to the compilers of arithmetic books, to see how little they care about mere efficiency. But they have a certain power of acting without taking thought. Their world-famed hypocrisy—their double-faced attitude towards the Empire, for instance—is bound up with this. Also, in moments of supreme crisis the whole nation can suddenly draw together and act upon a species of instinct, really a code of conduct which is understood by almost everyone, though never formulated. The phrase that Hitler coined for the Germans, 'a sleepwalking people,' would have been better applied to the English. Not that there is anything to be proud of in being a sleepwalker.

But here it is worth noticing a minor English trait which is extremely well marked though not often commented on, and that is a love of flowers. This is one of the first things that one notices when one reaches England from abroad, especially if one is coming from southern Europe. Does it not contradict the English indifference to the arts? Not really, because it is found in people who have no esthetic feelings whatever. What it does link up with, however, is another English characteristic which is so much a part of us that we barely notice it, and that is the addiction to hobbies and spare-time occupations, the *privateness* of English life. We are a nation of flower-lovers, but also a nation of stamp-collectors, pigeon-fanciers, amateur carpenters, coupon-snippers, darts-players, crossword-puzzle fans. All the culture that is most truly native centres round things which even when they are communal are not official—the pub, the football match, the back garden, the fireside and the 'nice cup of tea.' The liberty of the individual is still believed in, almost as in the nineteenth century. But this has nothing to do with economic liberty, the right to exploit others for profit. It is the liberty to have a home of your own, to do what you like in your spare time, to choose your own amusements instead of having them chosen for you from above. The most hateful of all names in an English ear is Nosey Parker. It is obvious, of course, that even this purely private liberty is a lost cause. Like all other modern peoples, the English are in process of being numbered, labelled, conscripted, 'coordinated.' But the pull of their impulses is in the other direction, and the kind of regimentation that can be imposed on them will be modified in consequence. No party rallies, no Youth Movements, no coloured shirts, no Jew-baiting or 'spontaneous' demonstrations. No Gestapo either, in all probability.

But in all societies the common people must live to some extent *against* the existing order. The genuinely popular culture of England is something that goes on beneath the surface, unofficially and more or less frowned on by the authorities. One thing one notices if one looks directly at the common people, especially in the big towns, is that they are not puritanical. They are inveterate gamblers, drink as much beer as their wages will permit, are devoted to bawdy jokes, and use probably the foulest language in the world. They have to satisfy these tastes in the face of astonishing, hypocritical laws (licensing laws, lottery acts,[4] etc., etc.) which are designed to interfere with everybody but in practice allow everything to happen. Also, the common people are without definite religious belief, and have been so for centuries. The Anglican Church never had a real hold on them, it was simply a preserve of the landed gentry, and the Nonconformist sects only influenced minorities. And yet they have retained a deep tinge of Christian feeling, while almost forgetting the name of Christ. The power-worship which is the new religion of Europe, and which has infected the English intelligentsia, has never touched the common people. They have never caught up with power politics. The 'realism' which is preached in Japanese and Italian newspapers would horrify them. One can learn a good deal about the spirit of England from the comic coloured postcards that you see in the windows of cheap stationers' shops. These things are a sort of diary upon which the English people have unconsciously recorded themselves. Their old-fashioned outlook, their graded snobberies, their mixture of bawdiness and hypocrisy, their extreme gentleness, their deeply moral attitude to life, are all mirrored there.

The gentleness of the English civilisation is perhaps its most marked characteristic. You notice it the instant you set foot on English soil. It is a land where the bus conductors are good-tempered and the policemen carry no revolvers. In no country inhabited by white men is it easier to shove people off the pavement. And with this goes something that is always written off by European observers as 'decadence' or hypocrisy, the English hatred of war and militarism. It is rooted deep in history, and it is strong in the lower-middle class as well as the working class. Successive wars have shaken it but not destroyed it. Well within living memory it was common for 'the redcoats' to be booed at in the street and for the landlords of respectable public-houses to refuse to allow soldiers on the premises. In peace-time, even when there are two million unemployed, it is difficult to fill the ranks of the tiny standing army, which is officered by the county gentry and a specialized stratum of the middle class, and manned by farm labourers and slum proletarians. The mass of the people are without military knowledge or tradition, and their attitude towards war is invariably defensive. No politician could rise to power by promising them conquests or military 'glory,' no Hymn of Hate[5] has ever made any appeal to them. In the 1914–18 war the songs which the soldiers made up and sang of their own accord were not vengeful but humorous and mock-defeatist.[6] The only enemy they ever named was the sergeant-major.

In England all the boasting and flag-wagging, the 'Rule Britannia' stuff, is done by small minorities. The patriotism of the common people is not vocal or even conscious. They do not retain among their historical memories the name of a single military victory. English literature, like other literatures, is full of

4. The English licensing laws prescribe opening and closing hours for public houses (saloons) but not for private clubs. The lottery acts were full of loopholes and did not prevent enormous expenditure on the football pools.

5. The *Hassgesang*, a poem by Ernst Lissauer (1882–1937) which was popular in Germany during World War I; its refrain, *Gott strafe England*, is said to have been used as a greeting, and gave English the verb "to strafe."

6. "For example: 'I don't want to join the bloody Army. / I don't want to go into the war; / I want no more to roam. / I'd rather stay at home / Living on the earnings of a whore.' But it was not in that spirit that they fought." (Orwell)

battle-poems, but it is worth noticing that the ones that have won for themselves a kind of popularity are always a tale of disasters and retreats. There is no popular poem about Trafalgar or Waterloo, for instance. Sir John Moore's army at Corunna, fighting a desperate rear-guard action before escaping overseas (just like Dunkirk! [7]) has more appeal than a brilliant victory. The most stirring battle-poem in English is about a brigade of cavalry which charged in the wrong direction.[8] And of the last war, the four names which have really engraved themselves on the popular memory are Mons, Ypres, Gallipoli, and Passchendaele,[9] every time a disaster. The names of the great battles that finally broke the German armies are simply unknown to the general public.

The reason why the English anti-militarism disgusts foreign observers is that it ignores the existence of the British Empire. It looks like sheer hypocrisy. After all, the English absorbed a quarter of the earth and held on to it by means of a huge navy. How dare they then turn round and say that war is wicked?

It is quite true that the English are hypocritical about their Empire. In the working class this hypocrisy takes the form of not knowing that the Empire exists. But their dislike of standing armies is a perfectly sound instinct. A navy employs comparatively few people, and it is an external weapon which cannot affect home politics directly. Military dictatorships exist everywhere, but there is no such thing as a naval dictatorship. What English people of nearly all classes loathe from the bottom of their hearts is the swaggering officer type, the jingle of spurs and the crash of boots. Decades before Hitler was ever heard of, the word 'Prussian' had much the same significance in England as 'Nazi' has today. So deep does this feeling go that for a hundred years past the officers of the British Army, in peace-time, have always worn civilian clothes when off duty.

One rapid but fairly sure guide to the social atmosphere of a country is the parade-step of its army. A military parade is really a kind of ritual dance, something like a ballet, expressing a certain philosophy of life. The goose-step, for instance, is one of the most horrible sights in the world, far more terrifying than a dive-bomber. It is simply an affirmation of naked power; contained in it,

7. Sir John Moore (1761–1809) led the British retreat to Corunna in the winter of 1808–1809 during the Peninsula War. He began evacuating the troops and repulsed a French attack, but was fatally wounded. The poem on his death is by Charles Wolfe (1791–1823), published 1817. Dunkirk was the scene (from May 26 to June 4, 1940) of the evacuation —in almost a thousand vessels of all kinds—of the main part of the British Expeditionary Force, which had been cut off in northern France by the German advance through the Low Countries.
8. Although they knew they had received wrong orders, the Light Cavalry Brigade charged the Russian guns at Balaclava on September 20, 1854, during the Crimean War. Their heroism was celebrated in the famous poem "The Charge of the Light Brigade," by the Poet Laureate Tennyson, completed during the same year.
9. Mons was the scene of a battle in August 1914. Ypres was a stalemated battle later in the same year and another battle (in which poison gas was used for the first time) in March 1915. Passchendaele was the third and most disastrous Ypres campaign, a stubborn attempt to advance through mud; between June and November 1917 the British suffered, by drowning as well as by enemy action, a quarter-million casualties. Gallipoli was an attempt to open a new front by forcing the Dardanelles and capturing Constantinople. The campaign began well in February 1915 but was a failure by the end of the year.

quite consciously and intentionally, is the vision of a boot crashing down on a face. Its ugliness is part of its essence, for what it is saying is 'Yes, I *am* ugly, and you daren't laugh at me,' like the bully who makes faces at his victim. Why is the goose-step not used in England? There are, heaven knows, plenty of army officers who would be only too glad to introduce some such thing. It is not used because the people in the street would laugh. Beyond a certain point, military display is only possible in countries where the common people dare not laugh at the army. The Italians adopted the goose-step at about the time when Italy passed definitely under German control, and, as one would expect, they do it less well than the Germans. The Vichy government,[10] had it survived, was bound to introduce a stiffer parade-ground discipline into what was left of the French army. In the British army the drill is rigid and complicated, full of memories of the eighteenth century, but without definite swagger; the march is merely a formalised walk. It belongs to a society which is ruled by the sword, no doubt, but a sword which must never be taken out of the scabbard.

And yet the gentleness of English civilisation is mixed up with barbarities and anachronisms. Our criminal law is as out of date as the muskets in the Tower. Over against the Nazi Storm Trooper you have got to set that typically English figure, the hanging judge, some gouty old bully with his mind rooted in the nineteenth century, handing out savage sentences. In England until recently people were still hanged by the neck and flogged with the cat o' nine tails. Both of these punishments are obscene as well as cruel, but there has never been any genuinely popular outcry against them. People accept them (and Dartmoor,[11] and Borstal[12]) almost as they accept the weather. They are part of 'the law,' which is assumed to be unalterable.

Here one comes upon an all-important English trait: the respect for constitutionalism and legality, the belief in 'the law' as something above the State and above the individual, something which is cruel and stupid, of course, but at any rate *incorruptible.*

It is not that anyone imagines the law to be just. Everyone knows that there is one law for the rich and another for the poor. But no one accepts the implications of this, everyone takes it for granted that the law, such as it is, will be respected, and feels a sense of outrage when it is not. Remarks like 'They can't run me in; I haven't done anything wrong,' or 'They can't do that; it's against the law,' are part of the atmosphere of England. The professed enemies of society have this feeling as strongly as anyone else. One sees it in prison-books like Wilfred Macartney's *Walls Have Mouths* [13] or Jim Phelan's *Jail Journey,*[14] in the solemn idiocies that take place at the trials of Conscientious Objectors,[15] in letters to the papers from eminent Marxist professors, pointing out that this

10. After the fall of France the Germans set up a puppet government under Marshal Pétain at Vichy in the unoccupied part of the country.

11. Prison on the Devonshire moors.

12. Generic name for English schools for delinquent boys.

13. Subtitled "A Record of Ten Years Penal Servitude" (1936).

14. Published in 1940.

15. Conscientious objectors to the draft had the right to appear before a tribunal usually consisting of a judge and distinguished local laymen. They pleaded their case of conscience and answered questions such as, "What would you do if you saw a German trying to rape your sister?"

or that is a 'miscarriage of British justice.' Everyone believes in his heart that the law can be, ought to be, and, on the whole, will be impartially administered. The totalitarian idea that there is no such thing as law, there is only power, has never taken root. Even the intelligentsia have only accepted it in theory. An illusion can become a half-truth, a mask can alter the expression of a face. The familiar arguments to the effect that democracy is 'just the same as' or 'just as bad as' totalitarianism never take account of this fact. All such arguments boil down to saying that half a loaf is the same as no bread. In England such concepts as justice, liberty, and objective truth are still believed in. They may be illusions, but they are very powerful illusions. The belief in them influences conduct, national life is different because of them. In proof of which, look about you. Where are the rubber truncheons, where is the castor oil? [16] The sword is still in the scabbard, and while it stays there corruption cannot go beyond a certain point. The English electoral system, for instance, is an all but open fraud. In a dozen obvious ways it is gerrymandered [17] in the interest of the monied class. But until some deep change has occurred in the public mind, it cannot become *completely* corrupt. You do not arrive at the polling booth to find men with revolvers telling you which way to vote, nor are the votes miscounted, nor is there any direct bribery. Even hypocrisy is a powerful safeguard. The hanging judge, that evil old man in scarlet robe and horsehair wig, whom nothing short of dynamite will ever teach what century he is living in, but who will at any rate interpret the law according to the books and will in no circumstances take a money bribe, is one of the symbolic figures of England. He is a symbol of the strange mixture of reality and illusion, democracy and privilege, humbug and decency, the subtle network of compromises, by which the nation keeps itself in its familiar shape.

III

I have spoken all the while of 'the nation,' 'England,' 'Britain,' as though 45 million souls could somehow be treated as a unit. But is not England notoriously two nations, the rich and the poor? Dare one pretend that there is anything in common between people with £100,000 a year and people with £1 a week? And even Welsh and Scottish readers are likely to have been offended because I have used the word 'England' oftener than 'Britain,' as though the whole population dwelt in London and the Home Counties and neither north nor west possessed a culture of its own.

One gets a better view of this question if one considers the minor point first. It is quite true that the so-called races of Britain feel themselves to be very different from one another. A Scotsman, for instance, does not thank you if you call him an Englishman. You can see the hesitation we feel on this point by the fact that we call our islands by no less than six different names, England, Britain, Great Britain, the British Isles, the United Kingdom, and, in very exalted moments, Albion.[18] Even the differences between north and south England loom large in our own eyes. But somehow these differences fade away

16. Huge overdoses of castor oil were used by interrogators.
17. To gerrymander is to rig the constituencies for the benefit of one's own party.
18. Ancient poetic name for Great Britain.

the moment that any two Britons are confronted by a European. It is very rare to meet a foreigner, other than an American, who can distinguish between English and Scots or even English and Irish. To a Frenchman, the Breton and the Auvergnat [19] seem very different beings, and the accent of Marseilles is a stock joke in Paris. Yet we speak of 'France' and 'the French,' recognising France as an entity, a single civilisation, which in fact it is. So also with ourselves. Looked at from the outside, even the cockney and the Yorkshireman have a strong family resemblance.

And even the distinction between rich and poor dwindles somewhat when one regards the nation from the outside. There is no question about the inequality of wealth in England. It is grosser than in any European country, and you have only to look down the nearest street to see it. Economically, England is certainly two nations, if not three or four. But at the same time the vast majority of the people *feel* themselves to be a single nation and are conscious of resembling one another more than they resemble foreigners. Patriotism is usually stronger than class-hatred, and always stronger than any kind of internationalism. Except for a brief moment in 1920 (the 'Hands off Russia' [20] movement) the British working class have never thought or acted internationally. For two and a half years they watched their comrades in Spain slowly strangled, and never aided them by even a single strike.[21] But when their own country (the country of Lord Nuffield [22] and Mr. Montagu Norman [23]) was in danger, their attitude was very different. At the moment when it seemed likely that England might be invaded, Anthony Eden appealed over the radio for Local Defence Volunteers.[24] He got a quarter of a million men in the first twenty-four hours, and another million in the subsequent month. One has only to compare these figures with, for instance, the number of Conscientious Objectors to see how vast is the strength of traditional loyalties compared with new ones.

In England patriotism takes different forms in different classes, but it runs like a connecting thread through nearly all of them. Only the Europeanised intelligentsia are really immune to it. As a positive emotion it is stronger in the middle class than in the upper class—the cheap public schools,[25] for instance, are more given to patriotic demonstrations than the expensive ones—but the

19. Frenchmen from Brittany and from the Auvergne region.
20. In 1920, when there was thought to be some danger of Britain's involving itself with Poland against Soviet Russia, there were demonstrations against intervention. London dockers refused to load a munition ship, and the Trade Unions resolved to take industrial action if necessary.
21. "It is true that they aided them to a certain extent with money. Still, the sums raised for the various aid-Spain funds would not equal 5 per cent of the turnover of the Football Pools during the same period." (Orwell)
22. William Morris, 1st Viscount Nuffield, pioneer British automobile manufacturer—the English Henry Ford.
23. Governor of the Bank of England 1920–44.
24. Eden resigned the office of Foreign Secretary in 1938 as a protest against Chamberlain's appeasement, and became Churchill's War Minister in 1940. In the early summer of 1940, under threat of immediate German invasion, Eden broadcast an appeal for an emergency civilian army, first called the Local Defence Volunteers, later the Home Guard. Eden was prime minister 1955–57.
25. Private, fee-charging schools.

number of definitely treacherous rich men, the Laval-Quisling[26] type, is probably very small. In the working class patriotism is profound, but it is unconscious. The working man's heart does not leap when he sees a Union Jack.[27] But the famous 'insularity' and 'xenophobia'[28] of the English is far stronger in the working class than in the bourgeoisie. In all countries the poor are more national than the rich, but the English working class are outstanding in their abhorrence of foreign habits. Even when they are obliged to live abroad for years they refuse either to accustom themselves to foreign food or to learn foreign languages. Nearly every Englishman of working-class origin considers it effeminate to pronounce a foreign word correctly. During the war of 1914–18 the English working class were in contact with foreigners to an extent that is rarely possible. The sole result was that they brought back a hatred of all Europeans, except the Germans, whose courage they admired. In four years on French soil they did not even acquire a liking for wine. The insularity of the English, their refusal to take foreigners seriously, is a folly that has to be paid for very heavily from time to time. But it plays its part in the English *mystique*, and the intellectuals who have tried to break it down have generally done more harm than good. At bottom it is the same quality in the English character that repels the tourist and keeps out the invader.

Here one comes back to two English characteristics that I pointed out, seemingly rather at random, at the beginning of the last chapter. One is the lack of artistic ability. This is perhaps another way of saying that the English are outside the European culture. For there is one art in which they have shown plenty of talent, namely literature. But this is also the only art that cannot cross frontiers. Literature, especially poetry, and lyric poetry most of all, is a kind of family joke, with little or no value outside its own language-group. Except for Shakespeare, the best English poets are barely known in Europe, even as names. The only poets who are widely read are Byron, who is admired for the wrong reasons, and Oscar Wilde, who is pitied as a victim of English hypocrisy. And linked up with this, though not very obviously, is the lack of philosophical faculty, the absence in nearly all Englishmen of any need for an ordered system of thought or even for the use of logic.

Up to a point, the sense of national unity is a substitute for a 'world-view.' Just because patriotism is all but universal and not even the rich are uninfluenced by it, there can come moments when the whole nation suddenly swings together and does the same thing, like a herd of cattle facing a wolf. There was such a moment, unmistakably, at the time of the disaster in France.[29] After eight months of vaguely wondering what the war was about, the people suddenly knew what they had got to do: first, to get the army away from Dunkirk, and secondly to prevent invasion. It was like the awakening of a giant. Quick!

---

26. Pierre Laval, right-wing French politician, Pétain's prime minister 1942–44, shot as Nazi collaborator in 1945; Vidkin Quisling, Norwegian Nazi collaborator whose name became the generic term for such traitors.
27. British national flag, incorporating the crosses of St. George (England), St. David (Wales), and St. Andrew (Scotland).
28. Hatred of foreigners.
29. During May and June, 1940.

Danger! The Philistines be upon thee, Samson! And then the swift unanimous action—and then, alas, the prompt relapse into sleep. In a divided nation that would have been exactly the moment for a big peace movement to arise. But does this mean that the instinct of the English will always tell them to do the right thing? Not at all, merely that it will tell them to do the same thing. In the 1931 General Election,[30] for instance, we all did the wrong thing in perfect unison. We were as single-minded as the Gadarene swine.[31] But I honestly doubt whether we can say that we were shoved down the slope against our will. It follows that British democracy is less of a fraud than it sometimes appears. A foreign observer sees only the huge inequality of wealth, the unfair electoral system, the governing-class control over the Press, the radio, and education, and concludes that democracy is simply a polite name for dictatorship. But this ignores the considerable agreement that does unfortunately exist between the leaders and the led. However much one may hate to admit it, it is almost certain that between 1931 and 1940 the National Government represented the will of the mass of the people. It tolerated slums, unemployment, and a cowardly foreign policy. Yes, but so did public opinion. It was a stagnant period, and its natural leaders were mediocrities.

In spite of the campaigns of a few thousand left-wingers, it is fairly certain that the bulk of the English people were behind Chamberlain's foreign policy.[32] More, it is fairly certain that the same struggle was going on in Chamberlain's mind as in the minds of ordinary people. His opponents professed to see in him a dark and wily schemer, plotting to sell England to Hitler, but it is far likelier that he was merely a stupid old man doing his best according to his very dim lights. It is difficult otherwise to explain the contradictions of his policy, his failure to grasp any of the courses that were open to him. Like the mass of the people, he did not want to pay the price either of peace or of war. And public opinion was behind him all the while, in policies that were completely incompatible with one another. It was behind him when he went to Munich,[33] when he tried to come to an understanding with Russia, when he gave the guarantee

---

30. The fall of the Labor government as a result of the economic crisis of 1931 was followed by the establishment of a "National" government with representatives of all parties and no effective opposition. This arrangement was overwhelmingly endorsed by a general election. The administration was dominated by the Conservative Party, though Ramsay MacDonald, the Labor leader, was prime minister. He was succeeded by a Tory, Stanley Baldwin, in June 1935, and another general election ensured the continuance of coalition government until the end of the war. Throughout the 'thirties, despite the efforts of Churchill (who held no office) this government delayed rearmament and followed the policy of appeasing the European dictators.

31. When Jesus exorcised the unclean spirits from a madman, he allowed these spirits to pass into the swine of Gadara, which then "ran violently down a steep place into the sea . . . and were choked in the sea" (Mark 5:13).

32. Arthur Neville Chamberlain (1869–1940), who succeeded Baldwin as prime minister in 1937, continued the policy of appeasement culminating in the Munich Agreement of 1938, which sacrificed part of Czechoslovakia to Germany in return for a promise (broken six months later) to make no further demands on that or any other country.

33. Chamberlain's flight to Munich was his third visit to Hitler during September 1938. The agreement was signed on September 29 by Hitler, Mussolini, Chamberlain, and French Premier Daladier.

to Poland,[34] when he honoured it, and when he prosecuted the war half-heartedly. Only when the results of his policy became apparent did it turn against him; which is to say that it turned against its own lethargy of the past seven years. Thereupon the people picked a leader nearer to their mood, Churchill, who was at any rate able to grasp that wars are not won without fighting. Later, perhaps, they will pick another leader who can grasp that only socialist nations can fight effectively.

Do I mean by all this that England is a genuine democracy? No, not even a reader of the *Daily Telegraph* [35] could quite swallow that. England is the most class-ridden country under the sun. It is a land of snobbery and privilege, ruled largely by the old and silly. But in any calculation about it one has got to take into account its emotional unity, the tendency of nearly all its inhabitants to feel alike and act together in moments of supreme crisis. It is the only great country in Europe that is not obliged to drive hundreds of thousands of its nationals into exile or the concentration camp. At this moment, after a year of war, newspapers and pamphlets abusing the Government, praising the enemy and clamouring for surrender are being sold on the streets, almost without interference. And this is less from a respect for freedom of speech than from a simple perception that these things don't matter. It is safe to let a paper like *Peace News* [36] be sold, because it is certain that 95 per cent of the population will never want to read it. The nation is bound together by an invisible chain. At any normal time the ruling class will rob, mismanage, sabotage, lead us into the muck; but let popular opinion really make itself heard, let them get a tug from below that they cannot avoid feeling, and it is difficult for them not to respond. The left-wing writers who denounce the whole of the ruling class as 'pro-fascist' are grossly oversimplifying. Even among the inner clique of politicians who brought us to our present pass, it is doubtful whether there were any *conscious* traitors. The corruption that happens in England is seldom of that kind. Nearly always it is more in the nature of self-deception, of the right hand not knowing what the left hand doeth. And being unconscious, it is limited. One sees this at its most obvious in the English press. Is the English press honest or dishonest? At normal times it is deeply dishonest. All the papers that matter live off their advertisements, and the advertisers exercise an indirect censorship over news. Yet I do not suppose there is one paper in England that can be straightforwardly bribed with hard cash. In the France of the Third Republic [37] all but a very few of the newspapers could notoriously be bought over the counter like so many pounds of cheese. Public life in England has never been *openly* scandalous. It has not reached the pitch of disintegration at which humbug can be dropped.

England is not the jewelled isle of Shakespeare's much-quoted passage, nor

34. In March 1939 German troops marched into Prague and took over the rest of Czechoslovakia. When there were rumors of an imminent attack on Poland in the same month, Chamberlain, stung by Hitler's Munich treachery, offered Poland British support; an Anglo-Polish Agreement was signed on April 6.
35. Conservative newspaper.
36. Newspaper of the Peace Pledge Union, the principal pacifist organization.
37. 1871–1946.

is it the inferno depicted by Dr. Goebbels.[38] More than either it resembles a family, a rather stuffy Victorian family, with not many black sheep in it but with all its cupboards bursting with skeletons. It has rich relations who have to be kow-towed to and poor relations who are horribly sat upon, and there is a deep conspiracy of silence about the source of the family income. It is a family in which the young are generally thwarted and most of the power is in the hands of irresponsible uncles and bedridden aunts. Still, it is a family. It has its private language and its common memories, and at the approach of an enemy it closes its ranks. A family with the wrong members in control—that, perhaps, is as near as one can come to describing England in a phrase.

IV

Probably the battle of Waterloo *was* won on the playing-fields of Eton,[39] but the opening battles of all subsequent wars have been lost there. One of the dominant facts in English life during the past three-quarters of a century has been the decay of ability in the ruling class.

In the years between 1920 and 1940 it was happening with the speed of a chemical reaction. Yet at the moment of writing it is still possible to speak of a ruling class. Like the knife which has had two new blades and three new handles, the upper fringe of English society is still almost what it was in the mid-nineteenth century. After 1832 [40] the old landowning aristocracy steadily lost power, but instead of disappearing or becoming a fossil they simply inter-married with the merchants, manufacturers, and financiers who had replaced them, and soon turned them into accurate copies of themselves. The wealthy ship-owner or cotton-miller set up for himself an alibi as a country gentleman, while his sons learned the right mannerisms at public schools which had been designed for just that purpose. England was ruled by an aristocracy constantly recruited from parvenus.[41] And considering what energy the self-made men possessed, and considering that they were buying their way into a class which at any rate had a tradition of public service, one might have expected that able rulers could be produced in some such way.

And yet somehow the ruling class decayed, lost its ability, its daring, finally even its ruthlessness, until a time came when stuffed shirts like Eden or Halifax [42] could stand out as men of exceptional talent. As for Baldwin,[43] one could not even dignify him with the name of stuffed shirt. He was simply a hole in the air. The mishandling of England's domestic problems during the nineteen-twenties had been bad enough, but British foreign policy between 1931 and 1939 is one of the wonders of the world. Why? What had happened? What was it that at every decisive moment made every British statesman do the wrong thing with so unerring an instinct?

38. Hitler's Minister of Propaganda.
39. Remark attributed to the Duke of Wellington.
40. The First Reform Bill, extending the franchise, was passed that year.
41. Upstarts; newly wealthy or important people.
42. Lord Halifax was Viceroy of India and Foreign Secretary in Chamberlain's adminis-tration.
43. Stanley Baldwin was prime minister 1923–24, 1924–29, 1935–37; responsible for British nonintervention in the Spanish Civil War and held to represent the quietist mood of England between the world wars.

The underlying fact was that the whole position of the monied class had long ceased to be justifiable. There they sat, at the centre of a vast empire and a world-wide financial network, drawing interest and profits and spending them—on what? It was fair to say that life within the British Empire was in many ways better than life outside it. Still, the Empire was undeveloped, India slept in the Middle Ages, the Dominions lay empty, with foreigners jealously barred out, and even England was full of slums and unemployment. Only half a million people, the people in the country houses, definitely benefited from the existing system. Moreover, the tendency of small businesses to merge together into large ones robbed more and more of the monied class of their function and turned them into mere *owners*, their work being done for them by salaried managers and technicians. For long past there had been in England an entirely functionless class, living on money that was invested they hardly knew where, the 'idle rich,' the people whose photographs you can look at in the *Tatler* and the *Bystander*,[44] always supposing that you want to. The existence of these people was by any standard unjustifiable. They were simply parasites, less useful to society than his fleas are to a dog.

By 1920 there were many people who were aware of all this. By 1930 millions were aware of it. But the British ruling class obviously could not admit to themselves that their usefulness was at an end. Had they done that they would have had to abdicate. For it was not possible for them to turn themselves into mere bandits, like the American millionaires, consciously clinging to unjust privileges and beating down opposition by bribery and tear-gas bombs. After all, they belonged to a class with a certain tradition, they had been to public schools where the duty of dying for your country, if necessary, is laid down as the first and greatest of the Commandments. They had to *feel* themselves true patriots, even while they plundered their countrymen. Clearly there was only one escape for them—into stupidity. They could keep society in its existing shape only by being *unable* to grasp that any improvement was possible. Difficult though this was, they achieved it, largely by fixing their eyes on the past and refusing to notice the changes that were going on round them.

There is much in England that this explains. It explains the decay of country life, due to the keeping-up of a sham feudalism which drives the more spirited workers off the land. It explains the immobility of the public schools, which have barely altered since the 'eighties of the last century. It explains the military incompetence which has again and again startled the world. Since the 'fifties every war in which England has engaged has started off with a series of disasters, after which the situation has been saved by people comparatively low in the social scale. The higher commanders, drawn from the aristocracy, could never prepare for modern war, because in order to do so they would have had to admit to themselves that the world was changing. They have always clung to obsolete methods and weapons, because they inevitably saw each war as a repetition of the last. Before the Boer War they prepared for the Zulu War,[45] before 1914 for the Boer War, and before the present war for 1914. Even at this moment hundreds of thousands of men in England are being trained with

44. Papers devoted to "society" gossip.
45. 1879.

the bayonet, a weapon entirely useless except for opening tins. It is worth noticing that the navy and, latterly, the Air Force, have always been more efficient than the regular army. But the navy is only partially, and the Air Force hardly at all, within the ruling-class orbit.

It must be admitted that so long as things were peaceful the methods of the British ruling class served them well enough. Their own people manifestly tolerated them. However unjustly England might be organised, it was at any rate not torn by class warfare or haunted by secret police. The Empire was peaceful as no area of comparable size has ever been. Throughout its vast extent, nearly a quarter of the earth, there were fewer armed men than would be found necessary by a minor Balkan state. As people to live under, and looking at them merely from a liberal, *negative* standpoint, the British ruling class had their points. They were preferable to the truly modern men, the Nazis and Fascists. But it had long been obvious that they would be helpless against any serious attack from the outside.

They could not struggle against Nazism or Fascism, because they could not understand them. Neither could they have struggled against Communism, if Communism had been a serious force in Western Europe. To understand Fascism they would have had to study the theory of socialism, which would have forced them to realise that the economic system by which they lived was unjust, inefficient, and out of date. But it was exactly this fact that they had trained themselves never to face. They dealt with Fascism as the cavalry generals of 1914 dealt with the machine gun—by ignoring it. After years of aggression and massacres, they had grasped only one fact, that Hitler and Mussolini were hostile to Communism. Therefore, it was argued, they *must* be friendly to the British dividend-drawer. Hence the truly frightening spectacle of Conservative M.P.s wildly cheering the news that British ships, bringing food to the Spanish Republican government, had been bombed by Italian aeroplanes.[46] Even when they had begun to grasp that Fascism was dangerous, its essentially revolutionary nature, the huge military effort it was capable of making, the sort of tactics it would use, were quite beyond their comprehension. At the time of the Spanish civil war, anyone with as much political knowledge as can be acquired from a sixpenny pamphlet on socialism knew that if Franco [47] won, the result would be strategically disastrous for England; and yet generals and admirals who had given their lives to the study of war were unable to grasp this fact. This vein of political ignorance runs right through English official life, through Cabinet ministers, ambassadors, consuls, judges, magistrates, policemen. The policeman who arrests the 'Red' does not understand the theories the 'Red' is preaching; if he did, his own position as bodyguard of the monied class might seem less pleasant to him. There is reason to think that even military espionage is hopelessly hampered by ignorance of the new economic doctrines and the ramifications of the underground parties.

The British ruling class were not altogether wrong in thinking that Fascism

---

46. The rejoicing of the Conservative members of Parliament arose from their conviction that a Fascist victory in Spain was preferable to a Republican-Socialist one achieved with Soviet aid.

47. Francisco Franco (b. 1892), leader of the Spanish rebellion.

was on their side. It is a fact that any rich man, unless he is a Jew, has less to fear from Fascism than from either Communism or democratic socialism. One ought never to forget this, for nearly the whole of German and Italian propaganda is designed to cover it up. The natural instinct of men like Simon,[48] Hoare,[49] Chamberlain, etc., was to come to an agreement with Hitler. But— and here the peculiar feature of English life that I have spoken of, the deep sense of national solidarity, comes in—they could only do so by breaking up the Empire and selling their own people into semi-slavery. A truly corrupt class would have done this without hesitation, as in France. But things had not gone that distance in England. Politicians who would make cringing speeches about 'the duty of loyalty to our conquerors' are hardly to be found in English public life. Tossed to and fro between their incomes and their principles, it was impossible that men like Chamberlain should do anything but make the worst of both worlds.

One thing that has always shown that the English ruling class are *morally* fairly sound, is that in time of war they are ready enough to get themselves killed. Several dukes, earls and what-not were killed in the recent campaign in Flanders. That could not happen if these people were the cynical scoundrels that they are sometimes declared to be. It is important not to misunderstand their motives, or one cannot predict their actions. What is to be expected of them is not treachery or physical cowardice, but stupidity, unconscious sabotage, an infallible instinct for doing the wrong thing. They are not wicked, or not altogether wicked; they are merely unteachable. Only when their money and power are gone will the younger among them begin to grasp what century they are living in.

The stagnation of the Empire in the between-war years affected everyone in England, but it had an especially direct effect upon two important sub-sections of the middle class. One was the military and imperialist middle class, generally nicknamed the Blimps,[50] and the other the left-wing intelligentsia. These two seemingly hostile types, symbolic opposites—the half-pay colonel with his bull neck and diminutive brain, like a dinosaur, the highbrow with his domed forehead and stalk-like neck—are mentally linked together and constantly interact upon one another; in any case they are born to a considerable extent into the same families.

Thirty years ago the Blimp class was already losing its vitality. The middle-class families celebrated by Kipling, the prolific lowbrow families whose sons officered the army and navy and swarmed over all the waste places of the earth from the Yukon to the Irrawaddy,[51] were dwindling before 1914. The thing that had killed them was the telegraph. In a narrowing world, more and more

48. John Allsebrook Simon held many high offices and was Lord Chancellor in Churchill's wartime administration.
49. Samuel Hoare, Conservative politician and appeaser, was Foreign Secretary at the time of the Ethiopian crisis of 1935, and British diplomatic representative in Madrid during the Civil War.
50. Colonel Blimp was invented by the cartoonist David Low to ridicule Conservative upper-class "stupidity."
51. Principal river of Burma.

governed from Whitehall, there was every year less room for individual initiative. Men like Clive, Nelson, Nicholson, Gordon [52] would find no place for themselves in the modern British Empire. By 1920 nearly every inch of the colonial empire was in the grip of Whitehall. Well-meaning, overcivilized men, in dark suits and black felt hats, with neatly rolled umbrellas crooked over the left forearm, were imposing their constipated view of life on Malaya and Nigeria, Mombasa and Mandalay. The one-time empire-builders were reduced to the status of clerks, buried deeper and deeper under mounds of paper and red tape. In the early 'twenties one could see, all over the Empire, the older officials, who had known more spacious days, writhing impotently under the changes that were happening. From that time onwards it has been next door to impossible to induce young men of spirit to take any part in imperial administration. And what was true of the official world was true also of the commercial. The great monopoly companies swallowed up hosts of petty traders. Instead of going out to trade adventurously in the Indies one went to an office stool in Bombay or Singapore. And life in Bombay or Singapore was actually duller and safer than life in London. Imperialist sentiment remained strong in the middle class, chiefly owing to family tradition, but the job of administering the Empire had ceased to appeal. Few able men went east of Suez if there was any way of avoiding it.

But the general weakening of imperialism, and to some extent of the whole British morale, that took place during the nineteen-thirties, was partly the work of the left-wing intelligentsia, itself a kind of growth that had sprouted from the stagnation of the Empire.

It should be noted that there is now no intelligentsia that is not in some sense 'Left.' Perhaps the last right-wing intellectual was T. E. Lawrence.[53] Since about 1930 everyone describable as an 'intellectual' has lived in a state of chronic discontent with the existing order. Necessarily so, because society as it was constituted had no room for him. In an Empire that was simply stagnant, neither being developed nor falling to pieces, and in an England ruled by people whose chief asset was their stupidity, to be 'clever' was to be suspect. If you had the kind of brain that could understand the poems of T. S. Eliot or the theories of Karl Marx, the higher-ups would see to it that you were kept out of any important job. The intellectuals could find a function for themselves only in the literary reviews and the left-wing political parties.

The mentality of the English left-wing intelligentsia can be studied in half a dozen weekly and monthly papers. The immediately striking thing about all these papers is their generally negative, querulous attitude, their complete

52. Robert Clive (1725–74) rose in the East India Company to become its leading general; for a time virtual ruler of Bengal. Horatio Viscount Nelson (1758–1805), greatest British admiral, victor and victim of Trafalgar. John Nicholson (1822–57), soldier, administrator in India, killed at siege of Delhi. Charles George Gordon (1833–85) took part in capture of Peking (1860), hence known as "Chinese Gordon." Later, as governor of the Sudan, he was besieged in Khartoum in 1884 and murdered two days before the arrival of Kitchener's relief force.
53. Known as "Lawrence of Arabia" (1888–1935) for his part in stimulating Arab revolt against the Turks during World War I.

lack at all times of any constructive suggestion. There is little in them except the irresponsible carping of people who have never been and never expect to be in a position of power. Another marked characteristic is the emotional shallowness of people who live in a world of ideas and have little contact with physical reality. Many intellectuals of the Left were flabbily pacifist up to 1935, shrieked for war against Germany in the years 1935–39, and then promptly cooled off when the war started. It is broadly though not precisely true that the people who were most 'anti-Fascist' during the Spanish civil war are most defeatist now. And underlying this is the really important fact about so many of the English intelligentsia—their severance from the common culture of the country.

In intention, at any rate, the English intelligentsia are Europeanised. They take their cookery from Paris and their opinions from Moscow. In the general patriotism of the country they form a sort of island of dissident thought. England is perhaps the only great country whose intellectuals are ashamed of their own nationality. In left-wing circles it is always felt that there is something slightly disgraceful in being an Englishman and that it is a duty to snigger at every English institution, from horse-racing to suet puddings. It is a strange fact, but it is unquestionably true, that almost any English intellectual would feel more ashamed of standing to attention during 'God save the King' than of stealing from a poor box. All through the critical years many left-wingers were chipping away at English morale, trying to spread an outlook that was sometimes squashily pacifist, sometimes violently pro-Russian, but always anti-British. It is questionable how much effect this had, but it certainly had some. If the English people suffered for several years a real weakening of morale, so that the Fascist nations judged that they were 'decadent' and that it was safe to plunge into war, the intellectual sabotage from the Left was partly responsible. Both the *New Statesman* and the *News-Chronicle*[54] cried out against the Munich settlement, but even they had done something to make it possible. Ten years of systematic Blimp-baiting affected even the Blimps themselves and made it harder than it had been before to get intelligent young men to enter the armed forces. Given the stagnation of the Empire the military middle class must have decayed in any case, but the spread of a shallow Leftism hastened the process.

It is clear that the special position of the English intellectuals during the past ten years as purely *negative* creatures, mere anti-Blimps, was a by-product of ruling-class stupidity. Society could not use them, and they had not got it in them to see that devotion to one's country implies 'for better, for worse.' Both Blimps and highbrows took for granted, as though it were a law of nature, the divorce between patriotism and intelligence. If you were a patriot you read *Blackwood's Magazine*[55] and publicly thanked God that you were 'not brainy.' If you were an intellectual you sniggered at the Union Jack and regarded physical courage as barbarous. It is obvious that this preposterous convention

54. *The New Statesman* was launched in 1913 as the journal of the Fabian Society (socialism by reform) and still represents the viewpoint of intellectual socialism in England; the *News Chronicle*, a daily of liberal opinions, is now defunct.
55. Edinburgh-based literary journal of conservative cast, founded 1817.

cannot continue. The Bloomsbury highbrow,[56] with his mechanical snigger, is as out of date as the cavalry colonel. A modern nation cannot afford either of them. Patriotism and intelligence will have to come together again. It is the fact that we are fighting a war, and a very peculiar kind of war, that may make this possible.

VI

One of the most important developments in England during the past twenty years has been the upward and downward extension of the middle class. It has happened on such a scale as to make the old classification of society into capitalists, proletarians, and petit-bourgeois (small property-owners) almost obsolete.

England is a country in which property and financial power are concentrated in very few hands. Few people in modern England *own* anything at all, except clothes, furniture, and possibly a house. The peasantry have long since disappeared, the independent shopkeeper is being destroyed, the small businessman is diminishing in numbers. But at the same time modern industry is so complicated that it cannot get along without great numbers of managers, salesmen, engineers, chemists, and technicians of all kinds, drawing fairly large salaries. And these in turn call into being a professional class of doctors, lawyers, teachers, artists, etc., etc. The tendency of advanced capitalism has therefore been to enlarge the middle class and not to wipe it out as it once seemed likely to do.

But much more important than this is the spread of middle-class ideas and habits among the working class. The British working class are now better off in almost all ways than they were thirty years ago. This is partly due to the efforts of the Trade Unions, but partly to the mere advance of physical science. It is not always realised that within rather narrow limits the standard of life of a country can rise without a corresponding rise in real wages. Up to a point, civilisation can lift itself up by its boot-tags. However unjustly society is organised, certain technical advances are bound to benefit the whole community, because certain kinds of goods are necessarily held in common. A millionaire cannot, for example, light the streets for himself while darkening them for other people. Nearly all citizens of civilised countries now enjoy the use of good roads, germ-free water, police protection, free libraries and probably free education of a kind. Public education in England has been meanly starved of money, but it has nevertheless improved, largely owing to the devoted efforts of the teachers, and the habit of reading has become enormously more widespread. To an increasing extent the rich and the poor read the same books, and they also see the same films and listen to the same radio programmes. And the differences in their way of life have been diminished by the mass-production of cheap clothes and improvements in housing. So far as outward

56. A type of intellectual associated with King's College and Trinity College Cambridge, and the Bloomsbury district of London, where Leonard and Virginia Woolf, Lytton Strachey, J. M. Keynes, and others congregated (see E. M. Forster Headnote, above). Their mannerisms and cliquishness, as well as their dissociation from popular thought and practical politics, made them odious to such as Lawrence and Orwell; the designation "highbrow" belonged to them from the start.

appearance goes, the clothes of rich and poor, especially in the case of women, differ far less than they did thirty or even fifteen years ago. As to housing, England still has slums which are a blot on civilisation, but much building has been done during the past ten years, largely by the local authorities. The modern Council house,[57] with its bathroom and electric light, is smaller than the stockbroker's villa, but it is recognisably the same kind of house, which the farm labourer's cottage is not. A person who has grown up in a Council housing estate is likely to be—indeed, visibly *is*—more middle class in outlook than a person who has grown up in a slum.

The effect of all this is a general softening of manners. It is enhanced by the fact that modern industrial methods tend always to demand less muscular effort and therefore to leave people with more energy when their day's work is done. Many workers in the light industries are less truly manual labourers than is a doctor or a grocer. In tastes, habits, manners, and outlook the working class and the middle class are drawing together. The unjust distinctions remain, but the real differences diminish. The old-style 'proletarian'—collarless, unshaven and with muscles warped by heavy labour—still exists, but he is constantly decreasing in numbers; he only predominates in the heavy-industry areas of the north of England.

After 1918 there began to appear something that had never existed in England before: people of indeterminate social class. In 1910 every human being in these islands could be 'placed' in an instant by his clothes, manners and accent. That is no longer the case. Above all, it is not the case in the new townships that have developed as a result of cheap motor cars and the south-ward shift of industry. The place to look for the germs of the future England is in the light-industry areas and along the arterial roads. In Slough, Dagenham, Barnet, Letchworth, Hayes[58]—everywhere, indeed, on the outskirts of great towns—the old pattern is gradually changing into something new. In those vast new wildernesses of glass and brick the sharp distinctions of the older kind of town, with its slums and mansions, or of the country, with its manor-houses and squalid cottages, no longer exist. There are wide gradations of income, but it is the same kind of life that is being lived at different levels, in labour-saving flats or Council houses, along the concrete roads and in the naked democracy of the swimming-pools. It is a rather restless, cultureless life, cen-tering round tinned food, *Picture Post*,[59] the radio and the internal combustion engine. It is a civilisation in which children grow up with an intimate knowl-edge of magnetoes and in complete ignorance of the Bible. To that civilisation belong the people who are most at home in and most definitely *of* the modern world, the technicians and the higher-paid skilled workers, the airmen and their mechanics, the radio experts, film producers, popular journalists, and industrial chemists. They are the indeterminate stratum at which the older class distinc-tions are beginning to break down.

This war, unless we are defeated, will wipe out most of the existing class privileges. There are every day fewer people who wish them to continue. Nor

57. Low-cost housing unit rented from local town council.
58. Towns now virtually absorbed in Greater London.
59. Popular (and intelligent) picture paper, 1938–57.

need we fear that as the pattern changes life in England will lose its peculiar flavour. The new red cities of Greater London are crude enough, but these things are only the rash that accompanies a change. In whatever shape England emerges from the war, it will be deeply tinged with the characteristics that I have spoken of earlier. The intellectuals who hope to see it Russianised or Germanised will be disappointed. The gentleness, the hypocrisy, the thoughtlessness, the reverence for law and the hatred of uniforms will remain, along with the suet puddings and the misty skies. It needs some very great disaster, such as prolonged subjugation by a foreign enemy, to destroy a national culture. The Stock Exchange will be pulled down, the horse plough will give way to the tractor, the country houses will be turned into children's holiday camps, the Eton and Harrow match[60] will be forgotten, but England will still be England, an everlasting animal stretching into the future and the past, and, like all living things, having the power to change out of recognition and yet remain the same.

1940   1941

SAMUEL BECKETT
1906–

Perhaps the greatest living writer in English, and certainly the direct follower of James Joyce in many ways, Beckett was born in Dublin, to a family of middle-class Protestants. He attended the same school as Oscar Wilde, and took a prize degree in Modern Languages at Trinity College, Dublin, in 1927. Thereafter he took a post, in Paris, as a visiting lecturer in English at the *Ecole Normale Supérieure*. In Paris he met Joyce and became part of his circle—indeed, in 1929 he published an essay on Joyce's *Work in Progress* (which was to become part of *Finnegans Wake*). Returning in 1930 to a Lectureship in French at Trinity College, he completed a master's degree in the philosophy of Descartes and his followers; but he abandoned the post in 1931 and wandered about Europe, living in London, France, and Germany. In 1937 he settled in Paris, where he has remained, save for trips abroad, ever since.

Beckett started to publish stories and poems while teaching in Paris; his poem *Whoroscope*, replete with notes that seem to parody those of Eliot's *The Waste Land*, won a prize for a poem on Time in 1930 (it concerned Descartes staring meditatively at his breakfast egg). He brought out a brilliant short book on Marcel Proust in 1931. A collection of short stories, *More Pricks than Kicks,* published in London in 1937, introduced a strange, involuted, meditative protagonist named Belacqua Shuah, whose Christian name comes from that of a slothful figure in Dante's *Purgatorio. Murphy,* a hilarious and profoundly philosophical novel, appeared the next year. Its milieu is London, and its anti-hero, Murphy (the first of several Beckettian protagonists whose names begin with a letter from the middle of the alphabet, the 13th one), starts out by literally and figuratively going off his rocker (a rocking chair, and his mind), ending in an insane asylum (as does the central figure in *Watt*). *Murphy* is concerned in good measure with the philosophical problem of the relation of mind and body, and

60. The annual cricket match between these two aristocratic public schools played in London, and the occasion of much upperclass display.

with Beckett's lifelong humorous fascination with the reductions, diagrams, schematizations, and generalities of human thought. This is evident from its opening sentence, with its almost cosmic shrug about determinism ("The sun rose, having no alternative, on the nothing new"), to its penultimate episode in which the hero's ashes, after his cremation, are mixed with the detritus and dirt on the floor of a pub (a scene Joyce is reputed to have loved). His next novel, *Watt*, is more abstract than *Murphy*, less Joycean in its prose and in the nature of its jokes. It was Beckett's last fictional work written in English, for after World War II he began to compose in French, and during an incredibly creative period between 1945 and 1951 he produced a trilogy of novels, which he himself subsequently translated into English under the titles of *Molloy*, *Malone Dies*, and *The Unnamable* (French, 1951–53; English, 1955–58), and the play for which he is perhaps most famous, *En Attendant Godot* (*Waiting for Godot*, 1954). *Fin de partie* (tr. as *Endgame*, 1958) is easily as great a play: *Krapp's Last Tape* (1959), *Embers* (1959), and *Happy Days* (1961) are all plays originally written in English.

Beckett's later prose comes more and more to seem like parts of an eternal meditative lyrical monologue. In more problematic works like *How it Is* (1961) the writing becomes fragmentary, elusive, and occasionally opaque. *Watt*, despite its strangeness, is a thoroughly comprehensible work, and shows none of the abstruseness of the *récits*, or fictional monologues, which Beckett started writing in French. It was composed during the years 1942–44 when Beckett was in hiding, doing menial work like the hero of *Watt*, in the village of Rousillon in the Vaucluse, in the south of France (he had been a member of a Resistance group in Paris, most of whose members the Gestapo had arrested). *Watt* concerns a meditative hero of that questioning name about whom we know very little (he is first seen getting off a streetcar by a minor character who is not sure whether what he sees is a man or a woman, not sure "that it was not a parcel, a carpet for example, or a roll of tarpaulin, wrapped up in dark paper and tied about the middle with a cord"). But we do know a lot of what Watt thinks. In the almost plotless story, he goes to work for a mysterious householder named Mr. Knott (if Watt is *What?*, then his employer's name suggests *Not* and *Naught* and *Knot* and the German word *Not* meaning "need") who, like the famous Godot, never appears. Watt goes to work on the ground floor of Mr. Knott's house, and the bulk of the middle part of the story concerns his acutely, often hilariously detailed consideration of the not very much that goes on while he works there. Here again is Beckett joking about the schematic, about what the world resembles when stripped to essentials (here, a thinker; something that can be known; and something that can't or, at any rate, isn't). Certainly there is more than a suggestion of the theological parable of Franz Kafka's *The Castle* here, and Mr. Knott is certainly very like the object that results, however unintentionally, from much theological thought. The book employs an array of comic discursive devices; they range from what one critic has called the misplaced literalness which is so basic to the dialogue of the plays ("Poor woman, God forgive her, said Tetty. Faith I wouldn't put it past him, said Mr Hackett") to intense and flamboyant parodies of analysis and philosophical argument. Finally we learn that most of it has been told by Watt to Sam, his fellow inmate in a mental hospital, and at the very end of the book, its by now universalized hero climbs on a tramcar again to go to the end of the line, out of the world of our fiction.

The episode given below, from the beginning of Part II, contains a sort of parody of an event. A piano tuner and his son come to tune Mr. Knott's piano; they have a riotously gloomy conversation and go home, but the event lingers, grows, develops, crystallizes, dissolves, changes, and becomes something else in Watt's mind. In the quasi-theological milieu of Mr. Knott's house (in which Watt is a not-really-suffering servant) we come to feel more and more that the incident of the Galls has many dimensions: event, happening, symbol, myth—indeed, by the end of the section, the blind father and his son seem to have been biblical. The reader should be prepared, throughout Watt, for all manner of unexpected meanings, generated by punning and word-play. And if he has followed the devout attempts in this episode, to wring Truth from what can be known, he will realize that despite all that Watt can try to comprehend of the Galls, father and son, he is brought no closer to final knowledge—that, in fact, what Watt knows is not Knott. Nor ever can be.

From Watt

[The Incident of the Galls, Father and Son]

Mr Knott never left the grounds, as far as Watt could judge. Watt thought it unlikely that Mr Knott could leave the grounds, without it's coming to his notice. But he did not reject the possibility of Mr Knott's leaving the grounds, without his being any the wiser. But the unlikelihood, on the one hand of Mr Knott's leaving the grounds, and on the other of his doing so without exciting the general comment, seemed very great, to Watt.

On only one occasion, during Watt's period of service on the ground floor, was the threshold crossed by a stranger, by other feet that is than Mr Knott's, or Erskine's,[1] or Watt's, for all were strangers to Mr Knott's establishment, as far as Watt could see, with the exception of Mr Knott himself, and his personnel at any given moment.

This fugitive penetration took place shortly after Watt's arrival. On his answering the door, as his habit was, when there was a knock at the door, he found standing before it, or so he realized later, arm in arm, an old man and a middleaged man.[2] The latter said:

We are the Galls, father and son, and we are come, what is more, all the way from town, to choon the piano.

They were two, and they stood, arm in arm, in this way, because the father was blind, like so many members of his profession. For if the father had not been blind, then he would not have needed his son to hold his arm, and guide him on his rounds, no, but he would have set his son free, to go about his own business. So Watt supposed, though there was nothing in the father's face to show that he was blind, nor in his attitude either, except that he leaned on his son in a way expressive of a great need of support. But he might have done this, if he had been halt, or merely tired, on account of his great age. There

1. Erskine is the servant who worked on the ground floor before Watt, and now works on the first one.
2. A master-servant pair, representing a schematic relation between people. Variations of this type are frequent in Beckett's works. Notice how, in this passage, the relation is itself qualified into a step-relation, calling into question even the father-son relation that links the pair.

was no family likeness between the two, as far as Watt could make out, and nevertheless he knew that he was in the presence of a father and son, for had he not just been told so. Or were they not perhaps merely stepfather and stepson. We are the Galls, stepfather and stepson—those were perhaps the words that should have been spoken. But it was natural to prefer the others. Not that they could not very well be a true father and son, without resembling each other in the very least, for they could.

How very fortunate for Mr Gall, said Watt, that he has his son at his command, whose manner is all devotion and whose mere presence, when he might obviously be earning an honest penny elsewhere, attests an affliction characteristic of the best tuners, and justifies emoluments rather higher than the usual.

When he had led them to the music-room, and left them there, Watt wondered if he had done right. He felt he had done right, but he was not sure. Should he not perhaps rather have sent them flying about their business? Watt's feeling was that anyone who demanded, with such tranquil assurance, to be admitted to Mr Knott's house, deserved to be admitted, in the absence of precise instructions to the contrary.

The music-room was a large bare white room. The piano was in the window. The head, and neck, in plaster, very white, of Buxtehude,[3] was on the mantelpiece. A ravanastron[4] hung, on the wall, from a nail, like a plover.

After a short time Watt returned to the music-room, with a tray, of refreshments.

Not Mr Gall Senior, but Mr Gall Junior, was tuning the piano, to Watt's great surprise. Mr Gall Senior was standing in the middle of the room, perhaps listening. Watt did not take this to mean that Mr Gall Junior was the true piano-tuner, and Mr Gall Senior simply a poor blind old man, hired for the occasion, no. But he took it rather to mean that Mr Gall Senior, feeling his end at hand, and anxious that his son should follow in his footsteps, was putting the finishing touches to a hasty instruction, before it was too late.

While Watt looked round, for a place to set down his tray, Mr Gall Junior brought his work to a close. He reassembled the piano case, put back his tools in their bag, and stood up.

The mice have returned, he said.

The elder said nothing. Watt wondered if he had heard.

Nine dampers[5] remain, said the younger, and an equal number of hammers.

Not corresponding, I hope, said the elder.

In one case, said the younger.

The elder had nothing to say to this.

The strings are in flitters, said the younger.

The elder had nothing to say to this either.

The piano is doomed, in my opinion, said the younger.

The piano-tuner also, said the elder.

The pianist also, said the younger.

This was perhaps the principal incident of Watt's early days in Mr Knott's house.

3. Dietrich Buxtehude (1637–1707), Danish baroque composer.
4. A long-necked, single-stringed banjo-like instrument, used in India for thousands of years.
5. Dampers and hammers are part of the internal workings, or "action," of a piano.

In a sense it resembled all the incidents of note proposed to Watt during his stay in Mr Knott's house, and of which a certain number will be recorded in this place, without addition, or subtraction, and in a sense not.

It resembled them in the sense that it was not ended, when it was past, but continued to unfold, in Watt's head, from beginning to end, over and over again, the complex connexions of its lights and shadows, the passing from silence to sound and from sound to silence, the stillness before the movement and the stillness after, the quickenings and retardings, the approaches and the separations, all the shifting detail of its march and ordinance, according to the irrevocable caprice of its taking place. It resembled them in the vigour with which it developed a purely plastic content, and gradually lost, in the nice processes of its light, its sound, its impacts and its rhythm, all meaning, even the most literal.

Thus the scene in the music-room, with the two Galls, ceased very soon to signify for Watt a piano tuned, an obscure family and professional relation, an exchange of judgments more or less intelligible, and so on, if indeed it had ever signified such things, and became a mere example of light commenting bodies, and stillness motion, and silence sound, and comment comment.

This fragility of the outer meaning had a bad effect on Watt, for it caused him to seek for another, for some meaning of what had passed, in the image of how it had passed.

The most meagre, the least plausible, would have satisfied Watt, who had not seen a symbol, nor executed an interpretation, since the age of fourteen, or fifteen, and who had lived, miserably it is true, among face values all his adult life, face values at least for him. Some see the flesh before the bones, and some see the bones before the flesh, and some never see the bones at all, and some never see the flesh at all, never never see the flesh at all. But whatever it was Watt saw, with the first look, that was enough for Watt, that had always been enough for Watt, more than enough for Watt. And he had experienced literally nothing, since the age of fourteen, or fifteen, of which in retrospect he was not content to say, That is what happened then. He could recall, not indeed with any satisfaction, but as ordinary occasions, the time when his dead father appeared to him in a wood, with his trousers rolled up over his knees and his shoes and socks in his hand; or the time when in his surprise at hearing a voice urging him, in terms of unusual coarseness, to do away with himself, he narrowly escaped being knocked down, by a dray [6]; or the time when alone in a rowing-boat, far from land, he suddenly smelt flowering currant; or the time when an old lady of delicate upbringing, and advantageous person, for she was amputated well above the knee, whom he had pursued with his assiduities on no fewer than three distinct occasions, unstrapped her wooden leg, and laid aside her crutch. Here no tendency appeared, on the part of his father's trousers, for example, to break up into an arrangement of appearances, grey, flaccid and probably fistular, or of his father's legs to vanish in the farce of their properties, no, but his father's legs and trousers, as then seen, in the wood, and subsequently brought to mind, remained legs and trousers, and not only legs and trousers, but his father's legs and trousers, that is to say quite different from any of the legs and trousers that Watt had ever seen, and he had

---

6. A horse-drawn cart for carrying heavy loads.

seen a great quantity, both of legs and of trousers, in his time. The incident of the Galls, on the contrary, ceased so rapidly to have even the paltry significance of two men, come to tune a piano, and tuning it, and exchanging a few words, as men will do, and going, that this seemed rather to belong to some story heard long before, an instant in the life of another, ill told, ill heard, and more than half forgotten.

So Watt did not know what had happened. He did not care, to do him justice, what had happened. But he felt the need to think that such and such a thing had happened then, the need to be able to say, when the scene began to unroll its sequences, Yes, I remember, that is what happened then.

This need remained with Watt, this need not always satisfied, during the greater part of his stay in Mr Knott's house. For the incident of the Galls father and son was followed by others of a similar kind, incidents that is to say of great formal brilliance and indeterminable purport.

Watt's stay in Mr Knott's house was less agreeable, on this account, than it would have been, if such incidents had been unknown, or his attitude towards them less anxious, that is to say, if Mr Knott's house had been another house, or Watt another man. For outside Mr Knott's house, and of course grounds, such incidents were unknown, or so Watt supposed. And Watt could not accept them for what they perhaps were, the simple games that time plays with space, now with these toys, and now with those, but was obliged, because of his peculiar character, to enquire into what they meant, oh not into what they really meant, his character was not so peculiar as all that, but into what they might be induced to mean, with the help of a little patience, a little ingenuity.

But what was this pursuit of meaning, in this indifference to meaning? And to what did it tend? These are delicate questions. For when Watt at last spoke of this time, it was a time long past, and of which his recollections were, in a sense, perhaps less clear than he would have wished, though too clear for his liking, in another. Add to this the notorious difficulty of recapturing, at will, modes of feeling peculiar to a certain time, and to a certain place, and perhaps also to a certain state of the health, when the time is past, and the place left, and the body struggling with quite a new situation. Add to this the obscurity of Watt's communications, the rapidity of his utterance and the eccentricities of his syntax, as elsewhere recorded. Add to this the material conditions in which these communications were made. Add to this the scant aptitude to receive of him to whom they were proposed. Add to this the scant aptitude to give of him to whom they were committed. And some idea will perhaps be obtained of the difficulties experienced in formulating, not only such matters as those here in question, but the entire body of Watt's experience, from the moment of his entering Mr Knott's establishment to the moment of his leaving it.

But before passing from the Galls father and son to matters less litigious,[7] or less tediously litigious, it seems advisable that the little that is known, on this subject, should be said. For the incident of the Galls father and son was the first and type [8] of many. And the little that is known about it has not yet all been said. Much has been said, but not all.

7. Here, in the sense of problematic, or argumentative.
8. "Type" is probably being used in both a general sense, and in the technical one of biblical interpretation (see Glossary).

Not that many things remain to be said, on the subject of the Galls father and son, for they do not. For only three or four things remain to be said in this connexion. And three or four things are not really many, in comparison with the number of things that might have been known, and said, on this subject, and now never shall.

What distressed Watt in this incident of the Galls father and son, and in subsequent similar incidents, was not so much that he did not know what had happened, for he did not care what had happened, as that nothing had happened, that a thing that was nothing had happened, with the utmost formal distinctness, and that it continued to happen, in his mind, he supposed, though he did not know exactly what that meant, and though it seemed to be outside him, before him, about him, and so on, inexorably to unroll its phases, beginning with the first (the knock that was not a knock) and ending with the last (the door closing that was not a door closing), and omitting none, uninvoked, at the most unexpected moments, and the most inopportune. Yes, Watt could not accept, as no doubt Erskine could not accept, and as no doubt Arsene and Walter and Vincent [9] and the others had been unable to accept, that nothing had happened, with all the clarity and solidity of something, and that it revisited him in such a way that he was forced to submit to it all over again, to hear the same sounds, see the same lights, touch the same surfaces, and so on, as when they had first involved him in their unintelligible intricacies. If he had been able to accept it, then perhaps it would not have revisited him, and this would have been a great saving of vexation, to put it mildly. But he could not accept it, could not bear it. One wonders sometimes where Watt thought he was. In a culture-park?

But if he could say, when the knock came, the knock become a knock, or the door become a door, in his mind, presumably in his mind, whatever that might mean, Yes, I remember, that is what happened then, if then he could say that, then he thought that then the scene would end, and trouble him no more, as the appearance of his father with his trousers rolled up and his shoes and socks in his hands troubled him no more, because he could say, when it began, Yes, yes, I remember, that was when my father appeared to me, in the wood, dressed for wading. But to elicit something from nothing requires a certain skill and Watt was not always successful, in his efforts to do so. Not that he was always unsuccessful either, for he was not. For if he had been always unsuccessful, how would it have been possible for him to speak of the Galls father and son, and of the piano they had come all the way from town to tune, and of their tuning it, and of their passing the remarks they had passed, the one to the other, in the way he did? No, he could never have spoken at all of these things, if all had continued to mean nothing, as some continued to mean nothing, that is to say, right up to the end. For the only way one can speak of nothing is to speak of it as though it were something, just as the only way one can speak of God is to speak of him as though he were a man, which to be sure he was, in a sense, for a time, and as the only way one can speak of man, even our anthropologists have realised that, is to speak of him as though he were a termite. But if Watt was sometimes unsuccessful, and sometimes successful, as in the affair

9. Watt's predecessors on the ground floor at Mr. Knott's.

of the Galls father and son, in foisting a meaning there where no meaning appeared, he was most often neither the one, nor the other. For Watt considered, with reason, that he was successful, in this enterprise, when he could evolve, from the meticulous phantoms that beset him, a hypothesis proper to disperse them, as often as this might be found necessary. There was nothing, in this operation, at variance with Watt's habits of mind. For to explain had always been to exorcize, for Watt. And he considered that he was unsuccessful, when he failed to do so. And he considered that he was neither wholly successful, nor wholly unsuccessful, when the hypothesis evolved lost its virtue, after one or two applications, and had to be replaced by another, which in its turn had to be replaced by another, which in due course ceased to be of the least assistance, and so on. And that is what happened, in the majority of cases. Now to give examples of Watt's failures, and of Watt's successes, and of Watt's partial successes, in this connexion, is so to speak impossible. For when he speaks, for example, of the incident of the Galls father and son, does he speak of it in terms of the unique hypothesis that was required, to deal with it, and render it innocuous, or in terms of the latest, or in terms of some other of the series? For when Watt spoke of an incident of this kind, he did not necessarily do so in terms of the unique hypothesis, or of the latest, though this at first sight seems the only possible alternative, and the reason why he did not, why it is not, is this, that when one of the series of hypotheses, with which Watt laboured to preserve his peace of mind, lost its virtue, and had to be laid aside, and another set up in its place, then it sometimes happened that the hypothesis in question, after a sufficient period of rest, recovered its virtue and could be made to serve again, in the place of another, whose usefulness had come to an end, for the time being at least. To such an extent is this true, that one is sometimes tempted to wonder, with reference to two or even three incidents related by Watt as separate and distinct, if they are not in reality the same incident, variously interpreted. As to giving an example of the second event, namely the failure, that is clearly quite out of the question. For there we have to do with events that resisted all Watt's efforts to saddle them with meaning, and a formula, so that he could neither think of them, nor speak of them, but only suffer them, when they recurred, though it seems probable that they recurred no more, at the period of Watt's revelation, to me, but were as though they had never been.

Finally, to return to the incident of the Galls father and son, as related by Watt, did it have that meaning for Watt at the time of its taking place, and then lose that meaning, and then recover it? Or did it have some quite different meaning for Watt at the time of its taking place, and then lose that meaning, and then receive that, alone or among others, which it exhibited, in Watt's relation? Or did it have no meaning whatever for Watt at the moment of its taking place, were there neither Galls nor piano then, but only an unintelligible succession of changes, from which Watt finally extracted the Galls and the piano, in self-defence? These are most delicate questions. Watt spoke of it as involving, in the original, the Galls and the piano, but he was obliged to do this, even if the original had nothing to do with the Galls and the piano. For even if the Galls and the piano were long posterior to the phenomena destined to become them, Watt was obliged to think, and speak, of the incident, even at the moment of its taking place, as the incident of the Galls and the piano, if he was to think and speak of it at all, and it may be assumed that Watt would never have thought or spoken of such incidents, if he had not been under the absolute necessity of doing so. But generally speaking it seems probable that the meaning attributed to this particular type of incident, by Watt, in his relations, was now the initial meaning that had been lost and then recovered, and now a meaning quite distinct from the initial meaning, and now a meaning evolved, after a delay of varying length, and with greater or less pains, from the initial absence of meaning.

ENGLISH LITERARY HISTORY IN PROCESS

The history of English poetry since World War II has been marked by the absence of anything like a traceable line of development, however broadly one might draw it. The literature of the past twenty-five years belongs to the realm of the contemporary, rather than specifically to the historical period we can now call Modern; from within the perspective of the contemporary age it is as difficult to agree on the selection of monuments, and to delineate continuities, as it is in any other mode of current experience. Because of the dynamics of literary influence, the ways in which early promise may crystallize, mature, or fizzle out, and the often bewildering spotlight of current fashion, the anthologist of the contemporary cannot attempt to extend the canon of the Modern age down to recent years. He can only remark upon what has seemed prominent, and commend what he thinks excellent.

But a somewhat self-conscious sense of its historical moment by a post-war literary generation in Britain was accompanied by a number of sharply defined intentions on the part of groups of writers who thought of themselves perhaps as analogues rather than descendants of groups like the Auden circle in the nineteen-thirties. Auden himself had gone to the United States at the beginning of World War II and become an American. The new generation of poets was emerging from the universities, where their training had been primarily in literature and literary criticism, and it is not surprising that for several of them the poetry of William Empson should have been as influential as Auden's might otherwise have been. Some of the older of the post-war poets had, indeed, started publishing in the 'thirties, and it is among these that an eclectic range of individual manners and styles can still be observed. Such poets as Vernon Watkins (1906–67), Roy Fuller (b. 1912), Lawrence Durrell (b. 1912), better known for his fiction but author of a group of promising, somewhat surrealist early poems, and others of their generation seem to represent no particular association of interests.

BASIL BUNTING
1900–

The oldest and most anomalous of such poets is Basil Bunting. A professional music critic after World War I, later an associate and follower of Ezra Pound, who published some of his early work in an anthology, he was for a while a diplomat, and after World War II became a journalist, first in Persia, then in his native county of Northumberland. He started publishing obscurely in 1950, but it was not until 1966, when his long autobiographical and mythological poem *Briggflatts* appeared, that he achieved recognition. Championed in a climate which was beginning to encourage the influence of American poetry styles developed by the followers of Pound and William Carlos Williams, *Briggflatts* brought together local Northumbrian allusions and legendary material, astronomical imagery, details of personal narrative, and gnomic aphorism, all informed by an intense, lyrical compression that marks him off strongly from the more expository styles of other post-war poets. The section given below, from the close of Part V, represents the moment of contemplation upon its own completion and upon the life that has both produced and been reflected in it.

Briggflatts

From *Part V*

Light lifts from the water.
Frost has put rowan° down,
a russet blotch of bracken
tousled about the trunk.
Bleached sky. Cirrus
reflects sun that has left
nothing to badger eyes.

Young flutes, harps touched by a breeze,
drums and horns escort
Aldebaran,° low in the clear east,
beckoning boats to the fishing.
Capella° floats from the north
with shields hung on his gunwale.
That is no dinghy's lantern
occulted by the swell—Betelgeuse,°
calling behind him to Rigel.
Starlight is almost flesh.

Great strings next the post of the harp
clang, the horn has majesty,
flutes flicker in the draft and flare.
Orion strides over Farne.°
Seals shuffle and bark,
terns shift on their ledges,

rowan the mountain-ash or service-tree
Aldebaran the first-magnitude orange star in the constellation Taurus, the Bull; followed by Orion, which in turn is followed by the dogs, Canis Minor and Canis Major. Taurus, with the bright Pleiades, leads the magnificent procession of stars across the winter sky.
Capella the fifth or sixth brightest star in the sky, in Auriga, the Chariot

Betelgeuse "Sailors pronounce *Betelgeuse* 'Beetle juice' and so do I. His companion is 'Ridgel,' not 'Rhy-ghel' " (Bunting). This star is the first-magnitude red giant in Orion's shoulder. Rigel is in his left foot.
Farne an island in the North Sea, lying off the English-Scottish border

watching Capella steer for the zenith,
and Procyon° starts his climb.

Furthest, fairest things, stars, free of our humbug,
each his own, the longer known the more alone,
wrapt in emphatic fire roaring out to a black flue.
Each spark trills on a tone beyond chronological compass,
90   yet in a sextant's bubble present and firm
places a surveyor's stone or steadies a tiller.
Then is Now. The star you steer by is gone,
its tremulous thread spun in the hurricane
spider floss on my cheek; light from the zenith
spun when the slowworm° lay in her lap
fifty years ago.

The sheets are gathered and bound,
the volume indexed and shelved,
dust on its marbled leaves.
00   Lofty, an empty combe,°
silent but for bees.
Finger tips touched and were still
fifty years ago.
Sirius° is too young to remember.

Sirius glows in the wind. Sparks on ripples
mark his line, lures for spent fish.

Fifty years a letter unanswered;
a visit postponed for fifty years.

She has been with me fifty years.

10   Starlight quivers. I had day enough.
For love uninterrupted night.

                        1966

Coda

A strong song tows
us, long earsick.
Blind, we follow
rain slant, spray flick
to fields we do not know.

Night, float us.
Offshore wind, shout,

Procyon the first-magnitude star in Canis Minor, rising just before the dog star, Sirius
slowworm the blindworm, a kind of limbless lizard whose stirring in May opens the cyclic vision of Part I of *Briggflatts*
combe a narrow valley

Sirius "Sirius is too young to remember because the light we call by his name left its star only eight years ago; but the light from *Capella*, now in the zenith, set out 45 years ago—as near fifty as makes no difference to a poet" (Bunting). Sirius is the brightest star in the heavens.

ask the sea
what's lost, what's left,
what horn sunk,
what crown adrift.

Where we are who knows
of kings who sup
while day fails? Who,
swinging his axe
to fell kings, guesses
where we go?
1965

STEVIE SMITH
1902–1970

Although the first work of Stevie Smith (Florence Margaret Smith) was published in the late 1930's, she became best known in the post-war period. She was a writer of an almost proverbial eccentricity. Her weighty casualness, apparently haphazard verse forms, and mastery in providing a resonant context for the flat and colloquial, constitute an intense yet improvisatory tone, a blend of the ceremonious and the grotesque.

Not Waving but Drowning

Nobody heard him, the dead man,
But still he lay moaning:
I was much farther out than you thought
And not waving but drowning.

Poor chap, he always loved larking
And now he's dead
It must have been too cold for him his heart gave way,
They said.

Oh, no no no, it was too cold always
(Still the dead one lay moaning)
I was much too far out all my life
And not waving but drowning.
1957

JOHN HEATH-STUBBS
1918–

John Heath-Stubbs was born in London in 1918, studied at Oxford with C. S. Lewis, and took his B.A. in 1942. Despite encroaching blindness he has continued, throughout a career as schoolmaster, free-lance writer, and college teacher, to perfect his intense and elegant poetry, with a voice that has managed to keep faith with an earlier Romantic tradition while speaking in its own accents. With a Byronic urbanity contrasting strongly in tone with that occasionally adopted by W. H. Auden, Heath-Stubbs has avowed a moral commitment to speak out not as a political or theological conscience but as the votary of another muse—sometimes neo-Hellenic, sometimes at her home in the English countryside. "Permit not," he says to her in the epilogue to his *The Triumph of the Muse* (1958), "We should allow the things your wings had taught us, / As in a dream's shame, utterly to vanish, / Through keeping silence."

The Dark Planet

There is a dark planet striking against us. Invisible,
Its venomed arrows whisk through the purple air.
It is the masked dancer, shifting among
The beneficent choir, deflecting
All dulcet influence of Aphrodite the gay,
Ingenious Mercury with his legerdemain,
And Artemis on her silver-sandalled way.

It is because the dark planet decrees,
That the rose discards to the dust her flush-fire mantle.
It is the dark planet's malice that has choked
The song of the bird in its throat, and grinds desire
Down to the bitter ashes, the gritty cinders of time,
Where, with the brazen monument, crumbles the rhyme.

Where the dark planet strikes, nothing is innocent;
My boyhood impulses it caught in a net of fear.
My friends it suborns from me. Now you, my dear,
The dark planet has hit in the thick of the night.
It has turned you away from us all, and away from the light,
And the times we in common possessed, that went by like dreams—
With the unquiet speed of all dreams—must likewise fade,
As memory fades, your image becomes a shade.

In the web of things we perceive, there is nothing the dark planet spares;
For not to our condition is granted ever
Perfection of beauty, intellect, power. They fade like those cold
Prismatic garlands, the abstract blossoms of snow,
In the beams of that black sun, whose visage we may not know.
For it is an envious star. Not one, in their hierarchies,
But must bend to its importunate, to its absolute demands.
Though we turn, in our rage, and upbraid, through our tears, its assaults,
It will yield no retrograde motion, no slackening of its bands.

The dark planet swings through its ebony kingdom above.
Listen, do you not hear the whoosh-whoosh of its wings?
No, it will not cease fire, till every image is emptied

Of all significance, saving only its own.
Ah my dear, has your parting this hypothesis taught me?
Implacable, that sky-wanderer. Its name is Love.

1958

During the early 1950's a number of tendencies began to coalesce among some of the younger poets who had commenced publishing only after the end of the war. A reaction against the complexities engendered in modernist poetry by the influence of French Symbolism combined with a newly rediscovered sense of a native English poetic tradition which had been abandoned since the Georgians. When interwoven with a distrust of gesture and posture, and a revival of concern with the speaking voice, these impulses led to new stylistic directions—certainly not the directions one might expect, say, from poets following Dylan Thomas. A loose affiliation of a number of poets known as "The Movement" was evident in an anthology called *New Lines* edited by Robert Conquest in 1956. Among them were Philip Larkin (b. 1922), Donald Davie (b. 1922), Kingsley Amis (b. 1922), and Thom Gunn (b. 1929).

These poets all spoke in distinctly individual voices, but what they seemed at the beginning to have in common was this new kind of clarity. Metrically iambic and orderly, their poetry generally eschewed experimentation and the cultivation of stylistic idiosyncrasy. Rhetorically smooth even when most intense, the new stylistic trend showed some affinities with eighteenth-century poetic traditions, particularly in that these poets were quite unafraid of writing a poetry of statement, of working in the expository and even essayistic modes which the roots of modernist theory had associated with scientific discourse as the negation of true poetry's irrational music. In the following decade these poets developed in divergent directions, but in many ways Philip Larkin's poetry seems to remain prototypical of its moment, as well as influential.

PHILIP LARKIN
1922–

Philip Larkin, born in Coventry and currently Librarian of the University of Hull, published *The North Ship* in 1945, but it was in *The Less Deceived,* ten years later (and in *The Whitsun Weddings* in 1964), that his exchange (as he later put it) of the influence of Yeats for that of Hardy was confirmed. "Church Going," given below, depicts in an almost completely exemplary way the skeptical and witty terrain, almost bare of metaphor and with low rhetorical contours, that the newer poetry of "The Movement" would inhabit.

Church Going

Once I am sure there's nothing going on
I step inside, letting the door thud shut.
Another church: matting, seats, and stone,
And little books; sprawlings of flowers, cut
For Sunday, brownish now; some brass and stuff
Up at the holy end; the small neat organ;
And a tense, musty, unignorable silence,
Brewed God knows how long. Hatless, I take off
My cycle-clips in awkward reverence,

10   Move forward, run my hand around the font.
From where I stand, the roof looks almost new—
Cleaned, or restored? Someone would know: I don't.
Mounting the lectern, I peruse a few
Hectoring large-scale verses, and pronounce
'Here endeth'° much more loudly than I'd meant.
The echoes snigger briefly. Back at the door
I sign the book, donate an Irish sixpence,
Reflect the place was not worth stopping for.

Yet stop I did: in fact I often do,
20   And always end much at a loss like this,
Wondering what to look for; wondering, too,
When churches fall completely out of use
What we shall turn them into, if we shall keep
A few cathedrals chronically on show,
Their parchment, plate and pyx° in locked cases,
And let the rest rent-free to rain and sheep.
Shall we avoid them as unlucky places?

Or, after dark, will dubious women come
To make their children touch a particular stone;
30   Pick simples° for a cancer; or on some
Advised night see walking a dead one?
Power of some sort or other will go on
In games, in riddles, seemingly at random;
But superstition, like belief, must die
And what remains when disbelief has gone?
Grass, weedy pavement, brambles, buttress, sky,

A shape less recognizable each week,
A purpose more obscure. I wonder who
Will be the last, the very last, to seek
40   This place for what it was; one of the crew
That tap and jot and know what rood-lofts° were?

'Here endeth' The complete phrase is "Here
endeth the Lesson," pronounced after each
reading from Sacred Scripture in the Church
of England services.
pyx case containing Communion wafer

simples herbs; so called because they were used
uncompounded
rood-lofts galleries forming the head of the
screens which separate the nave from the choir
of a church

Some ruin-bibber, randy for antique,
Or Christmas-addict, counting on a whiff
Of gown-and-bands and organ-pipes and myrrh?
Or will he be my representative,

Bored, uninformed, knowing the ghostly silt
Dispersed, yet tending to this cross of ground
Through suburb scrub because it held unspilt
So long and equably what since is found
Only in separation—marriage, and birth,
And death, and thoughts of these—for whom was built
This special shell? For, though I've no idea
What this accoutred frowsty° barn is worth,
It pleases me to stand in silence here;

A serious house on serious earth it is,
In whose blent air all our compulsions meet,
Are recognized, and robed as destinies.
And that much never can be obsolete,
Since someone will forever be surprising
A hunger in himself to be more serious,
And gravitating with it to this ground,
Which, he once heard, was proper to grow wise in,
If only that so many dead lie round.

                    1955

Lines on a Young Lady's Photograph Album

At last you yielded up the album, which,
Once open, sent me distracted. All your ages
Matt and glossy on the thick black pages!
Too much confectionary, too rich:
I choke on such nutritious images.

My swivel eye hungers from pose to pose—
In pigtails, clutching a reluctant cat;
Or furred yourself, a sweet girl-graduate;
Or lifting a heavy-headed rose
Beneath a trellis, or in a trilby hat°

(Faintly disturbing, that, in several ways)—
From every side you strike at my control,
Not least through these disquieting chaps who loll
At ease about your earlier days:
Not quite your class, I'd say, dear, on the whole.

---

frowsty dowdy   **trilby hat** ordinary soft men's felt hat

But o, photography! as no art is,
Faithful and disappointing! that records
Dull days as dull, and hold-it smiles as frauds,
And will not censor blemishes
20   Like washing-lines, and Hall's-Distemper° boards,

But shows the cat as disinclined, and shades
A chin as doubled when it is, what grace
Your candour thus confers upon her face!
How overwhelmingly persuades
That this is a real girl in a real place,

In every sense empirically true!
Or is it just *the past?* Those flowers, that gate,
These misty parks and motors,° lacerate
Simply by being over; you
30   Contract my heart by looking out of date.

Yes, true; but in the end, surely, we cry
Not only at exclusion, but because
It leaves us free to cry. We know *what was*
Won't call on us to justify
Our grief, however hard we yowl across

The gap from eye to page. So I am left
To mourn (without a chance of consequence)
You, balanced on a bike against a fence;
To wonder if you'd spot the theft
40   Of this one of you bathing; to condense,

In short, a past that no one now can share,
No matter whose your future; calm and dry,
It holds you like a heaven, and you lie
Unvariably lovely there,
Smaller and clearer as the years go by.
1955

DONALD DAVIE
1922–

Donald Davie, who comes from Yorkshire and was educated at Cambridge, is a
literary critic of importance as well as a poet, and his sequence of critical writings
reflects in some degree the development of his own poetic concerns. *Purity of Diction in English Verse* (1952) was as influential among his poetic contemporaries as it
was upon his academic colleagues. *Articulate Energy* (1955) gave new impetus to the
study of syntax in English poetry, which a modernist interest in metaphor and image
had largely neglected, and his *Ezra Pound: Poet as Sculptor* (1964), marked his developing involvement in American poetic tradition. After having taught in Dublin, Cam-

Hall's-Distemper an interior wall paint   **motors** cars

bridge, and Essex, Davie moved to the United States, where he now teaches at Stanford University. Most recently, his *Thomas Hardy and British Poetry* (1972) reaffirmed in a more historical way the commitment that Larkin had acknowledged personally two decades earlier. A *Collected Poems* was published in the same year. He is also a student of Slavic languages, and has translated Russian and Polish poetry.

A Winter Talent

Lighting a spill° late in the afternoon,
I am that coal whose heat it should unfix;
Winter is come again, and none too soon
For meditation on its raft of sticks.

Some quick bright talents can dispense with coals
And burn their boats continually, command
An unreflecting brightness that unrolls
Out of whatever firings come to hand.

What though less sunny spirits never turn
The dry detritus° of an August hill
To dangerous glory? Better still to burn
Upon that gloom where all have felt a chill.

1957

Gardens No Emblems

Man with a scythe: the torrent of his swing
Finds its own level; and is not hauled back
But gathers fluently, like water rising
Behind the watergates that close a lock.

The gardener eased his foot into a boot;
Which action like the mower's had its mould,
Being itself a sort of taking root,
Feeling for lodgment in the leather's fold.

But forms of thought move in another plane
Whose matrices no natural forms afford
Unless subjected to prodigious strain:
Say, light proceeding edgewise, like a sword.

1957

spill a twist of paper or splinter of wood   **detritus** debris

KINGSLEY AMIS
1922–

Kingsley Amis, a Londoner, is better known as a comic novelist than as a poet. The influence of American humorists like S. J. Perelman, and of the films of the Marx Brothers, on his fiction was replaced in his poems by a mode of rueful wit more philosophically studious than learned or allusive in its manner. Amis has published many novels and several books of verse, the most recent being *A Case of Samples* (1957) and *A Look Round the Estate* (1967).

A Dream of Fair Women°

The door still swinging to, and girls revive,
Aeronauts in the utmost altitudes
   Of boredom fainting, dive
Into the bright oxygen of my nod;
Angels as well, a squadron of draped nudes,
   They roar towards their god.

Militant all, they fight to take my hat,
No more as yet; the other men retire
   Insulted, gestured at;
10 Each girl presses on me her share of what
Makes up the barn-door target of desire:
   And I am a crack shot.

Speech fails them, amorous, but each one's look,
Endorsed in other ways, begs me to sign
   Her body's autograph-book;
'Me first, Kingsley; I'm cleverest' each declares,
But no gourmet races downstairs to dine,
   Nor will I race upstairs.

Feigning aplomb, perhaps for half an hour,
20 I hover, and am shown by each princess
   The entrance to her tower;
Open, in that its tenant throws the key
At once to anyone, but not unless
   The anyone is me.

Now from the corridor their fathers cheer,
Their brothers, their young men; the cheers increase
   As soon as I appear;
From each I win a handshake and sincere
Congratulations; from the chief of police
30   A nod, a wink, a leer.

A Dream of Fair Women an ironic reference
to Tennyson's vastly chaste poem of the same
title

This over, all delay is over too;
The first eight girls (the roster now agreed)
   Leap on me, and undo . . .
But honesty impels me to confess
That this is 'all a dream,' which was, indeed,
   Not difficult to guess.

But wait; not 'just a dream,' because, though good
And beautiful, it is also true, and hence
   Is rarely understood;
Who would choose any feasible ideal
In here and now's giant circumference,
   If that small room were real?

Only the best; the others find, have found
Love's ordinary distances too great,
   And eager, stand their ground;
Map-drunk explorers, dry-land sailors, they
See no arrival that can compensate
   For boredom on the way;

And, seeming doctrinaire, but really weak,
Limelighted dolls guttering in their brain,
   They come with me, to seek
The halls of theoretical delight,
The women of that ever-fresh terrain,
   The night after to-night.
             1957

THOM GUNN
1929–

The youngest poet of "The Movement" was Thom Gunn. Born in London, educated at Cambridge, he has lived in the United States for the past fifteen years, mostly in California. His *Fighting Terms* (1954) was an early success; *The Sense of Movement* (1957) began to reveal a more idiosyncratic involvement with the American scene. Gunn may have been influenced by some of the ideas of the American critic Yvor Winters (whom he knew at Stanford University), particularly in regard to Winters's notions of clarity and power in the short poem. In his later work Gunn has written in the purely syllabic meters passed on by Auden to many contemporary American poets, but used by hardly anyone in England. The scene of "On the Move," with its colloquial American epigraph and its black-jacketed motorcyclists, contrasts sharply with the almost pious Englishness of Larkin's British bicyclist in "Church Going"; the two poems nevertheless can be heard speaking a common tongue.

On the Move

Man, you gotta Go.

The blue jay scuffling in the bushes follows
Some hidden purpose, and the gust of birds
That spurts across the field, the wheeling swallows,
Have nested in the trees and undergrowth.
Seeking their instinct, or their poise, or both,
One moves with an uncertain violence
Under the dust thrown by a baffled sense
Or the dull thunder of approximate words.

On motorcycles, up the road, they come:
10   Small, black, as flies hanging in heat, the Boys,
Until the distance throws them forth, their hum
Bulges to thunder held by calf and thigh.
In goggles, donned impersonality,
In gleaming jackets trophied with the dust,
They strap in doubt—by hiding it, robust—
And almost hear a meaning in their noise.

Exact conclusion of their hardiness
Has no shape yet, but from known whereabouts
They ride, direction where the tyres press.
20   They scare a flight of birds across the field:
Much that is natural, to the will must yield.
Men manufacture both machine and soul,
And use what they imperfectly control
To dare a future from the taken routes.

It is a part solution, after all.
One is not necessarily discord
On earth; or damned because, half animal,
One lacks direct instinct, because one wakes
Afloat on movement that divides and breaks.
30   One joins the movement in a valueless world,
Choosing it, till, both hurler and the hurled,
One moves as well, always toward, toward.

A minute holds them, who have come to go:
The self-defined, astride the created will
They burst away; the towns they travel through
Are home for neither bird nor holiness,
For birds and saints complete their purposes.
At worst, one is in motion; and at best,
Reaching no absolute, in which to rest,
40   One is always nearer by not keeping still.

1957

"The Movement," tentative as its thematic and stylistic boundaries were, did seem to characterize something of the spirit of the nineteen-fifties in English poetry. But such literary groupings are often misleading and seldom central. Three of the most impressive and interesting of post-war British poets could not be thought of as associated with the tradition of the new, plain style.

CHARLES TOMLINSON
1927–

Charles Tomlinson was born in Staffordshire in 1927, studied at Cambridge and London universities, and teaches at the University of Bristol. He is a poet of considerable stature whose work was marked by a particular openness, at first, to French Symbolist poetry and, later on, to the tradition of American verse stemming from William Carlos Williams. Tomlinson represents more of a continuation of the modernist tradition than do many of his contemporaries, even though the internationalism is in this instance transatlantic in the reverse direction. "Through Binoculars" shows his affinity with Williams (particularly in the earlier Williams), as well as a concern for breaking new formal ground in his use of free verse.

Through Binoculars

In their congealed light
We discover that what we had taken for a face
Has neither eyes nor mouth,
But only the impersonality of anatomy.

Silencing movement,
They withdraw life.

Definition grows clear-cut, but bodiless,
Withering by a dimension.

To see thus
Is to ignore the revenge of light on shadow,
To confound both in a brittle and false union.

This fictive extension into madness
Has a kind of bracing effect:
That normality is, after all, desirable
One can no longer doubt having experienced its opposite.

Binoculars are the last phase in a romanticism:
The starkly mad vision, not mortal,
But dangling one in a vicarious, momentary idiocy.

To dispense with them
20 Is to make audible the steady roar of evening,
Withdrawing in slow ripples of orange,
Like the retreat of water from sea-caves.

1955

TED HUGHES
1930–

Ted Hughes was at Cambridge with Thom Gunn, but his poetry, from the very outset, moved in a rather different direction. Emerging from various kinds of influence—the poems of D. H. Lawrence, Robert Graves, Edward Thomas—Hughes developed in his emblematic nature poems and in his mythological liturgies a powerful sense of communion with his almost totemic subjects. He has lived in the United States and was married to an American poet, the late Sylvia Plath, with whose expressionistic verse his own later poetry shares some characteristics. His recent poems in *Crow* (1971) center on a demonic sort of protagonist, a figure of blackness and negation who cackles and groans throughout the poems' exploration of horror and misery, and through their grotesque reworkings of traditional myth, as in "A Childish Prank."

Pibroch°

The sea cries with its meaningless voice,
Treating alike its dead and its living,
Probably bored with the appearance of heaven
After so many millions of nights without sleep,
Without purpose, without self-deception.

Stone likewise. Stone is imprisoned
Like nothing in the Universe.
Created for black sleep. Or growing
Conscious of the sun's red spot occasionally,
10 Then dreaming it is the foetus of God.

Over the stone rushes the wind,
Able to mingle with nothing,
Like the hearing of the blind stone itself.
Or turns, as if the stone's mind came feeling
A fantasy of directions.

Drinking the sea and eating the rock
A tree struggles to make leaves—
An old woman fallen from space

Pibroch a Scottish bagpipe composition consisting of ornamented variations on a theme

Unprepared for these conditions.
She hangs on, because her mind's gone completely.

Minute after minute, aeon after aeon,
Nothing lets up or develops.
And this is neither a bad variant nor a tryout.
This is where the staring angels go through.
This is where all the stars bow down.

1961

A Childish Prank

Man's and woman's bodies lay without souls,
Dully gaping, foolishly staring, inert
On the flowers of Eden.
God pondered.

The problem was so great, it dragged him asleep.

Crow laughed.
He bit the Worm, God's only son,
Into two writhing halves.

He stuffed into man the tail half
With the wounded end hanging out.

He stuffed the head half headfirst into woman
And it crept in deeper and up
To peer out through her eyes
Calling its tail-half to join up quickly, quickly
Because O it was painful.

Man awoke being dragged across the grass.
Woman awoke to see him coming.
Neither knew what had happened.

God went on sleeping.

Crow went on laughing.

1971

GEOFFREY HILL
1932–

Geoffrey Hill, born in Worcestershire in 1932 and educated at Oxford, may be the most original poet of his generation; certainly his poems are among the most difficult that have appeared in England since the post-war renunciation of the density and obliqueness which modern poetry of previous decades had felt to be almost mandatory for poetic truth. His poems are compressed in their structure and argument, and intense in their visionary, mythological mode. Even a relatively accessible work like "Genesis" is exceedingly problematic in its Blakean sense of the simultaneity of the Fall and Creation, of the impossibility of visualizing an unfallen nature.

Genesis

I

Against the burly air I strode,
Where the tight ocean heaves its load,
Crying the miracles of God.

And first I brought the sea to bear
Upon the dead weight of the land;
And the waves flourished at my prayer,
The rivers spawned their sand.

And where the streams were salt and full
The tough pig-headed salmon strove,
10　Curbing the ebb and the tide's pull,
To reach the steady hills above.

II

The second day I stood and saw
The osprey plunge with triggered claw,
Feathering blood along the shore,
To lay the living sinew bare.

And the third day I cried: 'Beware
The soft-voiced owl, the ferret's smile,
The hawk's deliberate stoop in air,
Cold eyes, and bodies hooped in steel,
20　Forever bent upon the kill.'

III

And I renounced, on the fourth day,
This fierce and unregenerate clay,

Building as a huge myth for man
The watery Leviathan,
And made the glove-winged albatross
Scour the ashes of the sea
Where Capricorn and Zero cross,°
A brooding immortality—
Such as the charmèd phoenix has
30　In the unwithering tree.

Where . . . cross where the tropic of Capricorn
crosses the zero degree of longitude

IV

The phoenix burns as cold as frost;
And, like a legendary ghost,
The phantom-bird goes wild and lost,
Upon a pointless ocean tossed.

So, the fifth day, I turned again
To flesh and blood and the blood's pain.

v

On the sixth day, as I rode
In haste about the works of God,
With spurs I plucked the horse's blood.

By blood we live, the hot, the cold,
To ravage and redeem the world:
There is no bloodless myth will hold.

And by Christ's blood are men made free
Though in close shrouds their bodies lie
Under the rough pelt of the sea;

Though Earth has rolled beneath her weight
The bones that cannot bear the light.

1959

Despite the transitory viability of "The Movement" as a way of classifying writers, it is obvious that modern English literary history, unlike that of France, only rarely lends itself to treatment in terms of schools and movements. The post-war French novel may be studied in terms of successive new waves, but there is nothing closely resembling them in England: novelists are more private and self-cultivated. Lists of the most important will of course vary, but few would omit the names—here set out variously, and covering three generations—of Henry Green, Grahame Greene, Ivy Compton-Burnett, Evelyn Waugh, Kingsley Amis, Anthony Powell, Iris Murdoch, Muriel Spark, William Golding, and Angus Wilson; and some would add C. P. Snow, Anthony Burgess, Richard Hughes, and Sibylle Bedford.

Of these the one who has suffered the most neglect may be the best: Henry Green, author of Living (1929), perhaps the best proletarian novel in English, and Loving (1945), a unique poetic-prosaic masterpiece. Amis's best book is his first, the irreverent Lucky Jim (1954), which, of several rather similar novels published about the same time, best struck the note of change in the attitude of the young toward authority, especially toward the absurdly institutionalized authority in the expanding universities. Iris Murdoch's first novel, Under the Net (1953), is a uniquely gay philosopher's novel; but bringing to her work one of the best minds to engage with English fiction since George Eliot's, she seems not, in the long list of titles that follow the first, ever to have performed the promised wonders. Green is silent, Greene has written no major book for many years, Golding has had a period of seclusion—though The Scorpion God

(1971) reminds us of his extraordinarily original gifts. Powell's long sequence *The Music of Time* has a devoted but restricted following, and for all his elegant humor offers a rather cultish kind of interest. The original blend of the humane and the viciously satirical which made Angus Wilson's early work uniquely valuable in the post-war period survives in the latest novel of this vigorous and inquiring writer, *No Laughing Matter* (1967); but by now he can scarcely do much to surprise us. The virtuosos are Muriel Spark, probably the most gifted English novelist alive, and Anthony Burgess; and of these much more—and that very likely surprising—may be looked for.

It is in the theater that England has a genuine modern movement. One might take 1952, the year of the first London performance of Samuel Beckett's *Waiting for Godot*, as the date when things began to happen; since then a whole new theater has developed. This has its physical center, as such movements tend to, in one theater, the Royal Court, where the English Stage Company still continues its aggressive, experimental way; but it is important to realize that much larger areas of English theater are involved. The first production of *Godot* was by Peter Hall, later director of the Royal Shakespeare Company; and it is in that company that Peter Brook, a director of genius, has shaped his greatest works—the *King Lear* and *A Midsummer Night's Dream*, but also *Marat-Sade*, under the influence of Antonin Artaud. The next historic date, however, had nothing to do with Beckett or Artaud; it was the success of John Osborne's *Look Back in Anger* at the Royal Court in 1956. This play, with its forceful, unconventional, uneuphemistic presentation of modern speech and behavior, created new theatrical standards and exploited new subjects. Osborne has written many more plays, some of them better, but none of such historical importance. The English Stage Company continued its adventures with new playwrights; and important work was going on to the east, where, in a poor district, Joan Littlewood discovered and performed the plays of Shelagh Delaney and Brendan Behan.

The most important of the new writers in this wave is certainly Harold Pinter (b. 1930), whose first major play was *The Birthday Party* (1957) and whose latest and best is *Old Times* (1971). Pinter has studied Brecht and Beckett, but his work is intensely individual, with the appearance of domestic realism, always qualified by imaginative presences, by silence, by the sudden long, broken speech. He is pure playwright; his imagination uses the theater as a painter uses paint, and his work is virtually indescribable. Among his juniors Tom Stoppard, whose *Rosencrantz and Guildenstern Are Dead* was performed by the National Theater Company, comes closest in theatrical genius.

The connections between this theatrical revival and the names of Brecht, Beckett, and Artaud may not be clear. Beckett's work showed how the prose theater could become the medium of a strange new poetry that is much more than merely a doctrinaire Theater of the Absurd; Brecht finally destroyed all obligations to the old illusionist theater; Artaud taught Peter Brook how to realize such a work as Peter Weiss's *Marat-Sade* (1964) in a manner so far transcending any notion of a doctrinaire Theater of Cruelty that the work of the Royal Shakespeare Company, and of serious British writers for the theater, has never been the same since. Experimental theater of all kinds flourishes in England. Some of it may be affected by the American Living Theater; but its health depends on its close association with the major state-subsidized theaters, and the adventurousness of their directors. If the center of the modern literature of contemporary Britain lies so close to the theater, it is perhaps because of English eloquence; manifesting itself in talk, mimetic language, and a national consciousness of the energy and joy of speech, this eloquence continues to provide both a great tradition of stage acting and a love for the theater which affects writers in other genres as well. No matter how experimental Beckett's plays may seem, despite their having been written and produced initially for the French stage, they belong in the line of great English—and Anglo-Irish—prose comedy running from Ben Jonson's *Epicoene* and Congreve's *The Way of the World* through Sheridan, Oscar Wilde, and Shaw. In theater as in poetry, the strands of tradition and innovation are tightly interwoven.

Glossary

A Commentary on Selected Literary and Historical Terms

Allegory   Literally, "other reading"; originally a way of interpreting a narrative or other text in order to extract a more general, or a less literal, meaning from it, e.g. reading Homer's *Odyssey* as the universal voyage of human life—with Odysseus standing for all men—which must be made toward a final goal. In the Middle Ages allegory came to be associated with ways of reading the Bible, particularly the Old Testament in relation to the New. In addition, stories came to be written with the intention of being interpreted symbolically; thus e.g. the *Psychomachia* or "battle for the soul" of Prudentius (b. 348 A.D.) figured the virtues and vices as contending soldiers in a battle (see *Personification*). There is allegorical lyric poetry and allegorical drama well as allegorical narrative. In works such as Spenser's *The Faerie Queene* and Bunyan's *Pilgrim's Progress* allegory becomes a dominant literary form. See also *Dream Vision; Figure; type.*

Alliteration   A repeated initial consonant in successive words. In Old English verse, any vowel alliterates with any other, and alliteration is not an unusual or expressive phenomenon but a regularly recurring structural feature of the verse, occurring on the first and third, and often on the first, second, and third, primary-stressed syllables of the four-stressed line. Thus, from "The Seafarer":

> hréran mid hóndum hrímcælde sǽ
> ("to stir with his hand the rime-cold sea")

In later English verse tradition, alliteration becomes expressive in a variety of ways. Spenser uses it decoratively, or to link adjective and noun, verb and object, as in the line: "Much daunted with that dint, her sense was dazed." In the 18th and 19th centuries it becomes even less systematic and more "musical."

Assonance   A repeated vowel sound, a part-rhyme, which has great expressive effect when used internally (within lines), e.g. "An old, mad, blind, despised and dying king,—" (Shelley, "Sonnet: England in 1819").

Baroque   (1) Originally (and still), an oddly shaped rather than a spherical pearl, and hence something twisted, contorted, involuted. (2) By a complicated analogy, a term designating stylistic periods in art, music, and literature during the 16th and 17th centuries in Europe. The analogies among the arts are frequently strained, and the stylistic periods by no means completely coincide. But the relation between the poetry of Richard Crashaw in English and Latin, and the sculpture and architecture of Gianlorenzo Bernini (1598–1680), is frequently taken to typify the spirit of the baroque. (See Wylie Sypher, *Four Stages of Renaissance Style*, 1955.)

Balade, Ballade   The dominant lyric form in French poetry of the 14th and 15th centuries; a strict form consisting of three stanzas of eight lines each, with an *envoi* (*q.v.*), or four-line conclusion, addressing either a person of importance or a personification. Each stanza, including the *envoi*, ends in a refrain.

Ballad Meter   Or *common meter;* four-lined stanzas, rhyming *abab,* the first and third lines in iambic tetrameter (four beats), and the second and fourth lines in iambic trimeter (three beats). See *Meter.*

Courtly Love   Modern scholarship has coined this name for a set of conventions around which medieval love-poetry was written. It was essentially chivalric and a product of 12th-century France, especially of the troubadours. This poetry involves an idealization of the beloved woman, whose love, like all love, refines and ennobles the lover so that the union of their minds and/or bodies—a union that ought not to be apparent to others—allows them to attain excellence of character.

Dada   A satirical, anti-literary movement in European art and literature, 1916–21, its name having been selected to connote *nothing* (the movement's founders are in dispute over its method of selection). Dadaists engaged in a systematic nullification of reason, religion, and art itself, producing pictures and poems out of the random and the absurd, sculpture out of ordinary objects, and entertainments out of elaborately staged exhibitions that must have been alternately hilarious and tedious. Founded in Zurich by Tristan Tzara, Hans Arp, Hugo Ball, and Richard Huelsenbeck, Dada moved to Paris in 1919, took on a more international character, and was embraced by many young writers who would thereafter become attached to Surrealism (*q.v.*).

Decorum   Propriety of discourse; what is becoming in action, character, and style; the avoidance of impossibilities and incongruities in action, style, and character: "the good grace of everything after his kind" and the "great masterpiece to observe." More formally, a neoclassical doctrine maintaining that literary style—grand, or high, middle, and low—be appropriate to the subject, occasion, and genre. Thus Milton, in *Paradise Lost* (I.13–14), invokes his "adventurous song, / That with no middle flight intends to soar. . . ." See also *Rhetoric.*

Dissenters   In England, members of Protestant churches and sects that do not conform to the doctrines of the established Church of England; from the 16th century on, this would include Baptists, Puritans of various sorts within the Anglican Church, Presbyterians, Congregationalists, and (in the 18th century) Methodists. Another term, more current in the 19th century, is *Nonconformist.*

Elegy   Originally, in Greek and Latin poetry, a poem composed not in the hexameter lines of epic (*q.v.*) and, later, of pastoral, but in the elegiac couplets consisting of one hexameter line followed by a pentameter. Elegiac poetry was amatory, epigrammatic. By the end of the 16th century, English poets were using heroic couplets (*q.v.*), to stand for both hexameters and elegiacs; and an elegiac poem was any serious meditative piece. Perhaps because of the tradition of the pastoral elegy (*q.v.*), the general term "elegy" came to be reserved, in modern terminology, for an elaborate and formal lament, longer than a *dirge* or *threnody*, for a dead person. By extension, "elegiac" has come to mean, in general speech, broodingly sad.

Enjambment   The "straddling" of a clause or sentence across two lines of verse, as opposed to closed, or end-stopped, lines. Thus, in the opening lines of Shakespeare's *Twelfth Night*.

> If music be the food of love, play on!
> Give me excess of it, that, surfeiting
> The appetite may sicken and so die . . .

the first line is stopped, the second enjambed. When enjambment becomes strong or violent, it may have an ironic or comic effect.

The Enlightenment   A term used very generally, to refer to the late 17th and the 18th century in Europe, a period characterized by a programmatic rationalism—i.e. a belief in the ability of human reason to understand the world and thereby to transform whatever in it needed transforming; an age in which ideas of science and progress accompanied the rise of new philosophies of the relation of man to the state, an age which saw many of its hopes for human betterment fulfilled in the French Revolution.

Envoi, Envoy   Short concluding stanza found in certain French poetic forms and their English imitations, e.g. the *ballade* (*q.v.*). It serves as a dedicatory postscript, and a summing up of the poem of which it repeats the refrain.

Epic   Or, *heroic poetry;* originally, oral narrative delivered in a style different from that of normal discourse by reason of verse, music, and heightened diction, and concerning the great deeds of a central heroic figure, or group of figures, usually having to do with a crisis in the history of a race or culture. Its setting lies in this earlier "heroic" period, and it will often have been written down only after a long period of oral transmission. The Greek *Iliad* and *Odyssey* and the Old English *Beowulf* are examples of this, in their narration mixing details from both the heroic period described and the actual time of their own composition and narration. What is called *secondary* or *literary* epic is a long, ambitious poem, composed by a single poet on the model of the older, primary forms, and of necessity being more allusive and figurative than its predecessors. Homer's poems lead to Virgil's *Aeneid,* which leads to Milton's *Paradise Lost,* in a chain of literary dependency. Spenser's *Faerie Queene* might be called *romantic epic* of the secondary sort, and Dante's *Divine Comedy* might also be assimilated to post-Virgilian epic tradition.

Epic Simile   An extended comparison, in Homeric and subsequently in Virgilian and later epic poetry, between an event in the story (the *fable*) and something in the experience of the epic audience, to the effect of making the fabulous comprehensible in terms of the familiar. From the Renaissance on, additional complications have emerged from the fact that what is the familiar for the classical audience becomes, because of historical change, itself fabled (usually, pastoral) for the modern audience. Epic similes compare the fabled with the familiar usually with respect to one property or element; thus, in the *Odyssey,* when the stalwart forward motion of a ship in high winds is described, the simile goes:

> And as amids a fair field four brave horse
> Before a chariot, stung into their course
> With fervent lashes of the smarting scourge
> That all their fire blows high, and makes them rise
> To utmost speed the measure of their ground:
> So bore the ship aloft her fiery bound
> About whom rushed the billows, black and vast
> In which the sea-roars burst . . .
>   (*Chapman translation*)

Notice the formal order of presentation: "even as . . .": *the familiar event, often described in detail;* "just so . . .": *the fabled one.*

Epicureanism   A system of philosophy founded by the Greek Epicurus (342–270 B.C.), who taught that the five senses are the sole source of ideas and sole criterion of truth, and that the goal of human life is pleasure (i.e. hedonism), though this can be achieved only by practicing moderation. Later the term came to connote bestial self-indulgence, which Epicurus had clearly rejected.

Figurative Language   In a general sense, any shift away from a literal meaning of words, brought about by the use of tropes (*q.v.*) or other rhetorical devices. See *Rhetoric.*

Free Verse, Vers Libre   Generally, any English verse form whose lines are measured neither by the number of 1) stressed syllables (see *Meter* §3, accentual verse), 2) alternations of stressed and unstressed syllables (§4, accentual-syllabic verse), or syllables alone (§2, syllabic verse). The earliest English free verse —that of Christopher Smart in *Jubilate Agno* (18th century)—imitates the prosody of Hebrew poetry (reflected also in the translation of the English Bible), in maintaining unmeasured units marked by syntactic parallelism. While many free-verse traditions (e.g. that of Walt Whitman) remain close to the impulses of this biblical poetry, yet others, in the 20th century, have developed new *ad hoc* patternings of their own. *Vers libre* usually refers to the experimental, frequently very short unmeasured lines favored by poets of the World War I period, although the term, rather than the form, was adopted from French poetry of the 19th century.

Gothic   Term (originally pejorative, as alluding to the Teutonic barbarians) designating the architectural style of the Middle Ages. The revival of interest in medieval architecture in the later 18th century produced not only pseudo-Gothic castlese like Horace Walpole's "Strawberry Hill", and more modest artificial ruins on modern estates, but also a vogue for atmospheric prose romances set in medieval surroundings and involving improbable terrors, and known as Gothic novels. The taste for the Gothic, arising during the Age of Sensibility (*q.v.*), is another reflection of a reaction against earlier 18th-century neoclassicism (*q.v*).

Heroic Couplet In English prosody, a pair of rhyming, iambic pentameter lines, used at first for closure—as at the end of the Shakespearean sonnet (*q.v.*)— or to terminate a scene in blank-verse drama; later adapted to correspond in English poetry to the elegiac couplet of classical verse as well as to the heroic, unrhymed, Greek and Latin hexameter. Octosyllabic couplets, with four stresses (eight syllables) to the line, are a minor, shorter, jumpier form, used satirically unless in implicit allusion to the form of Milton's "Il Penseroso," in which they develop great lyrical power. (See *Meter.*)

Irony Generally, a mode of saying one thing to mean another. *Sarcasm*, in which one means exactly the opposite of what one says, is the easiest and cheapest form; thus, e.g. "Yeah, it's a *nice day*–" when one means that it's a miserable one. But serious literature produces ironies of a much more complex and revealing sort. *Dramatic irony* occurs when a character in a play or story asserts something whose meaning the audience or reader knows will change in time. Thus, in Genesis when Abraham assures his son Isaac (whom he is about to sacrifice) that "God will provide his own lamb," the statement is lighted with dramatic irony when a sacrificial ram is actually provided at the last minute to save Isaac. Or, in the case of Sophocles' *Oedipus*, when almost everything the protagonist says about the predicament of his city is hideously ironic in view of the fact (which he does not know) that he is responsible therefor. The ironies generated by the acknowledged use of non-literal language (see *Rhetoric*) and fictions in drama, song, and narrative are at the core of imaginative literature.

Kenning An Old Norse form designating, strictly, a condensed simile or metaphor of the kind frequently used in Old Germanic poetry; a figurative circumlocution for a thing not actually named—e.g. "swan's path" for sea; "world-candle" or "sky-candle" for sun. More loosely, often used to mean also a metaphorical compound word or phrase such as "ring-necked" or "foamy-necked" for a ship, these being descriptive rather than figurative in character.

Macaronic Verse in which two languages are mingled, usually for burlesque purposes.

Meter Verse may be made to differ from prose and from ordinary speech in a number of ways, and in various languages these ways may be very different. Broadly speaking, lines of verse may be marked out by the following regularities of pattern:

    1. *Quantitative Verse*, used in ancient Greek poetry and adopted by the Romans, used a fixed number of what were almost musical measures, called *feet;* they were built up of long and short syllables (like half- and quarter-notes in music), which depended on the vowel and consonants in them. *Stress accent* (the *word* stress which, when accompanied by vowel reduction, distinguishes the English noun "*content*" from the adjective "*content*") did not exist in ancient Greek, and played no part in the rhythm of the poetic line. Thus, the first line of *Odyssey: Andra moi ennepe mousa, polytropon hos mala polla* ("Sing me, O muse, of that man of many resources who, after great hardship . . .") is composed in *dactyls* of one long syllable followed by two shorts (but, as in musical rhythm, replaceable by two longs, a *spondee*).

With six dactyls to a line, the resulting meter is called *dactylic hexameter* (*hexameter*, for short), the standard form for epic poetry. Other kinds of foot or measure were: the *anapest* ($\cup \cup -$); the iamb ($\cup -$); the trochee ($- \cup$); and a host of complex patterns used in lyric poetry. Because of substitutions, however, the number of syllables in a classical line was not fixed, only the number of measures.

2. *Syllabic Verse*, used in French, Japanese, and many other languages, and in English poetry of the mid-20th century, measures only the *number* of syllables per line with no regard to considerations of *quantity* or *stress*. Because of the prominence of stress in the English language, two lines of the same purely syllabic length may not necessarily sound at all as though they were in the same meter, e.g.:

> These two incommensurably sounding
> Lines are both written with ten syllables.

3. *Accentual Verse*, used in early Germanic poetry, and thus in Old English poetry, depended upon the number of strong *stress accents* per line. These accents were four in number, with no fixed number of unstressed. Folk poetry and nursery rhymes often preserve this accentual verse, e.g.

> Sing, sing, what shall I sing?
> The cat's run away with the pudding-bag string

The first line has six syllables, the second, eleven, but they sound more alike (and not merely by reason of their rhyme) than the two syllabic lines quoted above.

4. *Accentual-Syllabic Verse*, the traditional meter of English poetry from Chaucer on, depends upon both numbered *stresses* and numbered *syllables*, a standard form consisting of ten syllables alternately stressed and unstressed, and having five stresses; thus it may be said to consist of five syllable pairs.

For complex historical reasons, accentual syllabic groups of stressed and unstressed syllables came to be known by the names used for Greek and Latin feet—which can be very confusing. The analogy was made between *long* syllables in the classical languages, and *stressed* syllables in English. Thus, the pair of syllables in the adjective "con*tent*" is called an *iamb,* and in the noun "*content*," a *trochee;* the word "classical" is a *dactyll,* and the phrase "of the best," an *anapest.* When English poetry is being discussed, these terms are always used in their adapted, accentual-syllabic meanings, and hence the ten-syllable line mentioned earlier is called "iambic pentameter" in English. The phrase "high-tide" would be a *spondee* (as would, in general, two monosyllables comprising a proper name, e.g. "John Smith"); whereas compound nouns like "highway" would be *trochaic.* In this adaptation of classical nomenclature, the terms *dimeter, trimeter, tetrameter, pentameter, hexameter* refer not to the number of quantitative feet, but to the number of syllable-groups (pairs or triplets, from one to six), composing the line. Iambic pentameter and tetrameter lines are frequently also called *decasyllabic* and *octosyllabic* respectively.

5. *Versification.* In verse, lines may be arranged in patterns called *stichic*

or *strophic,* that is, the same linear form (say, iambic pentameter) repeated without grouping by rhyme or interlarded lines of another form, or varied in just such a way into *stanzas* or *strophes* ("turns"). Unrhymed iambic pentameter, called *blank verse,* is the English stichic form that Milton thought most similar to classic hexameter or *heroic* verse. But in the Augustan period iambic pentameter rhymed pairs, called heroic couplets (*q.v.*), came to stand for this ancient form as well as for the classical elegiac verse (*q.v.*). Taking couplets as the simplest strophic unit, we may proceed to *tercets* (groups of three lines) and to *quatrains* (groups of four), rhymed *abab* or *abcb,* and with equal or unequal li ie lengths. Other stanzaic forms: *ottava rima,* an eight-line, iambic pentameter stanza, rhyming *ababab cc; Spenserian stanza,* rhyming *ababbcbcc,* all pentameter save for the last line, an iambic hexameter, or *Alexandrine.* There have been adaptations in English (by Shelley, notably, and without rhyme by T. S. Eliot) of the Italian *terza rima* used by Dante in *The Divine Comedy,* interlocking tercets rhyming *aba bcb cdc ded,* etc. More elaborate stanza forms developed in the texts of some Elizabethan songs and in connection with the ode (*q.v.*).

Myth   A primitive story explaining the origins of certain phenomena in the world and in human life, and usually embodying gods or other supernatural forces, heroes (men who are either part human and part divine, or are placed between an ordinary mortal and a divine being), men, and animals. Literature continues to incorporate myths long after the mythology (the system of stories containing them) ceases to be a matter of actual belief. Moreover, discarded beliefs of all sorts tend to become myths when they are remembered but no longer literally clung to, and are used in literature in a similar way. The classical mythology of the Greeks and Romans was apprehended in this literary, or interpreted way, even in ancient times. The gods and heroes and their deeds came to be read as allegory (*q.v.*). During the Renaissance, *mythography*—the interpretation of myths in order to make them reveal a moral or historical significance (rather than merely remaining entertaining but insignificant stories)—was extremely important, both for literature and for painting and sculpture. In modern criticism, mythical or *archetypal* situations and personages have been interpreted as being central objects of the work of the imagination.

Neoclassicism   (1) In general the term refers to Renaissance and post-Renaissance attempts to model enterprises in the various arts on Roman and Greek originals—or as much as was known of them. Thus, in the late Renaissance, the architectural innovations of Andrea Palladio may be called "neoclassic," as may Ben Jonson's relation, and Alexander Pope's as well, to the Roman poet Horace. The whole Augustan period in English literary history (1660–1740) was a deliberately neoclassical one.

(2) More specifically, neoclassicism refers to that period in the history of all European art spanning the very late 18th and early 19th century, which period may be seen as accompanying the fulfillment, and the termination, of the Enlightenment (*q.v.*). In England such neoclassic artists as Henry Fuseli, John Flaxman, George Romney, and even, in some measure, William Blake, are close to the origins of pictorial and literary Romanticism itself.

Neoplatonism   See *Platonism.*
Nonconformist   See *Dissenters.*

Octosyllabic Couplet   See *Heroic Couplet; Meter.*
Ode   A basic poetic form, originating in Greek antiquity. The *choral ode* was a public event, sung and danced, at a large ceremony, or as part of the tragic and comic drama. Often called *Pindaric ode,* after a great Greek poet, the form consisted of *triads* (groups of three sections each). These were units of song and dance, and had the form *aab*—that is, a *strophe* (or "turn"), an *antistrophe* (or "counter-turn"), and an *epode* (or "stand"), the first two being identical musically and metrically, the third different. In English poetry, the Pindaric ode form, only in its metrical aspects, became in the 17th century a mode for almost essayistic poetic comment, and was often used also as a kind of cantata libretto, in praise of music and poetry (the so-called *musical ode*). By the 18th century the ode became the form for a certain kind of personal, visionary poem, and it is this form that Wordsworth and Coleridge transmitted to Romantic tradition. A second English form, known as *Horatian ode,* was based on the lyric (not choral) poems of Horace, and is written in *aabb* quatrains, with the last two lines shorter than the first two by a pair of syllables or more.

Paradox   In logic, a self-contradictory statement, hence meaningless (or a situation producing one), with an indication that something is wrong with the language in which such a situation can occur, e.g. the famous paradox of Epimenedes the Cretan, who held that all Cretans are liars (and thus could be lying if— and only if—he wasn't), or that of Zeno, of the arrow in flight: since at any instant of time the point of the arrow can always be said to be at one precise point, therefore it is continually at rest at a continuous sequence of such points, and therefore never moves. In literature, however, particularly in the language of lyric poetry, paradox plays another role. From the beginnings of lyric poetry, paradox has been deemed necessary to express feelings and other aspects of human inner states, e.g. Sappho's invention of the Greek word *glykypikron* ("bittersweet") to describe love, or her assertion that she was freezing and burning at the same time. So too the Latin poet Catullus, in his famous couplet

> I'm in hate and I'm in love; why do I? you may ask.
> Well, I don't know, but I feel it, and I'm in agony.

may be declaring thereby that true love poetry must be illogical.

In Elizabethan poetry, paradoxes were frequently baldly laid out in the rhetorical form called *oxymoron* (see *Rhetoric*), as in "the victor-victim," or across a fairly mechanical sentence structure, as in "My feast of joy is but a dish of pain." In the highest poetic art, however, the seeming self-contradiction is removed when one realizes that either, or both, of the conflicting terms is to be taken figuratively, rather than literally. The apparent absurdity, or strangeness, thus gives rhetorical power to the utterance. Elaborate and sophisticated paradoxes, insisting on their own absurdity, typify the poetic idiom of the tradition of John Donne.

Pastoral   A literary mode in which the lives of simple country people are celebrated, described, and used allegorically by sophisticated urban poets and writers. The *idylls* of Sicilian poet Theocritus (3rd century B.C.) were imitated and made more symbolic in Virgil's *eclogues;* shepherds in an Arcadian landscape stood for literary and political personages, and the Renaissance adapted these narrative and lyric pieces for moral and aesthetic discussion. Spenser's *Shepheardes Calendar* is an experimental collection of eclogues involving an array of forms and subjects. In subsequent literary tradition, the pastoral imagery of both Old and New Testaments (Psalms, Song of Songs, priest as *pastor* or shepherd of his flock, and so on) joins with the classical mode. Modern critics, William Empson in particular, have seen the continuation of pastoral tradition in other versions of the country-city confrontation, such as child-adult and criminal-businessman. See *Pastoral Elegy.*

Pastoral Elegy   A form of lament for the death of a poet, originating in Greek bucolic tradition (Bion's lament for Adonis, a lament for Bion by a fellow poet, Theocritus' first idyll, Virgil's tenth eclogue) and continued in use by Renaissance poets as a public mode for the presentation of private, inner, and even coterie matters affecting poets and their lives, while conventionally treating questions of general human importance. At a death one is moved to ask, "Why this death? Why now?" and funeral elegy must always confront these questions, avoiding easy resignation as an answer. Pastoral elegy handled these questions with formal mythological apparatus, such as the Muses, who should have protected their dead poet, local spirits and other presences appropriate to the circumstances of the life and death, and perhaps figures of more general mythological power. The end of such poems is the eternalization of the dead poet in a monument of myth, stronger than stone or bronze: Spencer's *Astrophel,* a lament for Sir Philip Sidney, concludes with an Ovidian change—the dead poet's harp, like Orpheus' lyre, becomes the constellation Lyra. Milton's *Lycidas* both exemplifies and transforms the convention. Later examples include Shelley's *Adonais* (for Keats), Arnold's *Thyrsis* (for Clough), and Swinburne's *Ave Atque Vale* (for Baudelaire).

Pathetic Fallacy   John Ruskin's term (used in *Modern Painters,* 1856) for the projection of human emotions onto the world in such a way as to personify inanimate things ineptly or falsely.

Personification   Treating a thing or, more properly, an abstract quality, as though it were a person. Thus, "Surely *goodness* and *mercy* shall follow me all the days of my life" tends to personify the italicized terms by reason of the metaphoric use of "follow me." On the other hand, a conventional, complete personification, like *Justice* (whom we recognize by her *attributes*—she is blindfolded, she has scales and a sword) might also be called an *allegorical figure* in her own right, and her attributes *symbols* (blindness = impartiality; scales = justly deciding; sword = power to mete out what is deserved). Often the term "personification" applies to momentary, or *ad hoc,* humanizations.

Platonism   The legacy of Plato (429–347 B.C.) is virtually the history of philosophy. His *Timaeus* was an important source of later cosmology; his doctrine of ideas is central to Platonic tradition. His doctrine of love (especially in the *Symposium*) had enormous influence in the Renaissance, at which time its applicability was shifted to heterosexual love specifically. The *Republic* and the *Laws* underlie a vast amount of political thought, and the *Republic* contains also a philosophical attack on poetry (fiction) which defenders of the arts have always had to answer. Neoplatonism—a synthesis of Platonism, Pythagoreanism, and Aristotelianism—was dominant in the 3rd century A.D.; and the whole tradition was revived in the 15th and 16th centuries. The medieval Plato was Latinized, largely at second-hand; the revival of Greek learning in the 15th century led to another Neoplatonism: a synthesis of Platonism, the medieval Christian Aristotle, and Christian doctrine. Out of this came the doctrines of love we associate with some Renaissance poetry; a sophisticated version of older systems of allegory and symbol; and notions of the relation of spirit and matter reflected in Marvell and many other poets.

Rhetoric   In classical times, rhetoric was the art of persuading through the use of language. The major treatises on style and structure of discourse—Aristotle's *Rhetoric,* Quintilian's *Institutes of Oratory,* the *Rhetorica ad Herrenium* ascribed for centuries to Cicero—were concerned with the "arts" of language in the older sense of "skills." In the Middle Ages the *trivium* (*q.v.*), or program that led to the degree of Bachelor of Arts, consisted of grammar, logic, and rhetoric, but it was an abstract study, based on the Roman tradition. In the Renaissance, classical rhetorical study became a matter of the first importance, and it led to the study of literary stylistics and the application of principles and concepts of the production and structure of eloquence to the higher eloquence of poetry.

Rhetoricians distinguished three stages in the production of discourse: *inventio* (finding or discovery), *dispositio* (arranging), and *elocutio* (style). Since the classical discipline aimed always at practical oratory (e.g. winning a case in court, or making a point effectively in council), *memoria* (memory) and *pronuntiatio* (delivery) were added. For the Renaissance, however, rhetoric became the art of writing. Under the heading of *elocutio,* style became stratified into three levels, *elevated* or high, *elegant* or middle, and *plain* or low. The proper fitting of these styles to the subject of discourse comprised the subject of decorum (*q.v.*).

Another area of rhetorical theory was concerned with classification of devices of language into *schemes, tropes,* and *figures.* A basic but somewhat confused distinction between figures of speech and figures of thought need not concern us here, but we may roughly distinguish between schemes (or patterns) of words, and tropes as manipulations of meanings, and of making words non-literal.

Satire   A literary mode painting a distorted verbal picture of part of the world in order to show its true moral, as opposed merely to its physical, nature. In this sense, Circe, the enchantress in Homer's *Odyssey* who changed Odysseus' men into pigs (because they made pigs of themselves while eating) and would have changed Odysseus into a fox (for he was indeed foxy), was the first satirist. Originally the Latin word *satura* meant a kind of literary grab bag, or medley, and a satire was a fanciful kind of tale in mixed prose and verse; but later a false etymology connected the word with *satyr* and thus with the grotesque. Satire may be in verse or in prose; in the 16th and 17th centuries, the Roman poets Horace and Juvenal were imitated and expanded upon by writers of satiric moral verse, the tone of the verse being wise, smooth, skeptical, and urbane, that of the prose, sharp, harsh, and sometimes nasty. A tradition of English verse satire runs through Donne, Jonson, Dryden, Pope, and Samuel Johnson; of prose satire, Addison, Swift, and Fielding.

Sensibility   (1) In the mid-18th century, the term came to be used in a literary context to refer to a susceptibility to fine or tender feelings, particularly involving the feelings and sorrows of others. This became a quality to be cultivated in despite of stoical rejections of unreasonable emotion which the neoclassicism (q.v.) of the earlier Augustan age had prized. The meaning of the word blended easily into "sentimentality"; but the literary period in England characterized by the work of writers such as Sterne, Goldsmith, Gray, Collins, and Cowper is often called the Age of Sensibility.

(2) A meaning more important for modern literature is that of a special kind of total awareness, an ability to make the finest discriminations in its perception of the world, and yet at the same time not lacking in a kind of force by the very virtue of its own receptive power. The varieties of awareness celebrated in French literature from Baudelaire through Marcel Proust have been adapted by modernist English critics, notably T. S. Eliot, for a fuller extension of the meaning of *sensibility*. By the term "dissociation of sensibility," Eliot implied the split between the sensuous and the intellectual faculties which he thought characterized English poetry after the Restoration (1660).

Sententia   A wise, fruitful saying, functioning as a guide to morally correct thought or action.

Sestina   Originally a Provençal lyric form supposedly invented by Arnaut Daniel in the 12th century, and one of the most complex of those structures. It has six stanzas of six lines each, folllowed by an *envoi* (q.v.) or *tornada* of three lines. Instead of rhyming, the end-words of the lines of the first stanza are all repeated in the following stanzas, but in a constant set of permutations. The *envoi* contains all six words, three in the middle of each line. D. G. Rossetti, Swinburne, Pound, Auden, and other modern poets have used the form, and Sir Philip Sidney composed a magnificent double-sestina, "Ye Goat-herd Gods."

Skepticism   A philosophy that denies the possibility of certain knowledge, and, although opposed to Stoicism and Epicureanism (q.v.), advocated *ataraxy*, imperturbability of mind. Skepticism originated with Pyrrhon (c. 360–270 B.C.), and its chief transmitter was Sextus Empiricus (c. 200 B.C.). In the Renaissance, skepticism had importance as questioning the power of the human mind to know truly (for a classic exposition see Donne's *Second Anniversary*, ll. 254–300), and became a powerful influence in morals and religion through the advocacy of Montaigne.

Sonnet   A basic lyric form, consisting of fourteen lines of iambic pentameter rhymed in various patterns. The *Italian* or *Petrarchan* sonnet is divided clearly into *octave* and *sestet*, the first rhyming *abba abba* and the second in a pattern such as *cdc dcd*. The *Shakespearean* sonnet consists of three quatrains followed by a couplet: *abab cdcd efef gg*. In the late 16th century in England, sonnets were written either independently as short epigrammatic forms, or grouped in sonnet sequences, i.e. collections of upwards of a hundred poems, in imitation of Petrarch, purportedly addressed to one central figure or muse—a lady usually with a symbolic name like "Stella" or "Idea." Milton made a new kind of use of the Petrarchan form, and the Romantic poets continued in the Miltonic tradition. Several variations have been devised, including the additions of "tails" or extra lines, or the recasting into sixteen lines, instead of fourteen.

Stoicism, Stoics Philosophy founded by Zeno (335–263 B.C.), and opposing the hedonistic tendencies of Epicureanism (*q.v.*). The Stoics' world-view was pantheistic: God was the energy that formed and maintained the world, and wisdom lay in obedience to this law of nature as revealed by the conscience. Moreover, every man is free because the life according to nature and conscience is available to all; so too is suicide—a natural right. Certain Stoics saw the end of the world as caused by fire. In the Renaissance, Latin Stoicism, especially that of Seneca (*q.v.*), had a revival of influence and was Christianized in various ways.

Stream of Consciousness A literary technique of modern fiction which attempts to imitate or duplicate, in patterns other than those of discourse, the flow of thoughts, impressions, memories, meditations, musings, and other products of an individual character's consciousness. It can result either in the fragmentation of sentence structure, or the overwhelming of it in long strings of eloquence. In James Joyce's *Ulysses,* where it is called "interior monologue," it operates in different styles to represent the thoughts of different characters, but its most celebrated use is in Molly Bloom's forty-two page soliloquy that concludes the book.

Style See *Decorum.*

Sublime "Lofty"; as a literary idea, originally the basic concept of a Greek treatise (by the so-called "Longinus") on style. In the 18th century, however, the *sublime* -came to mean a loftiness perceivable in nature, and sometimes in art—a loftiness different from the composed vision of landscape known as the *picturesque,* because of the element of wildness, power, and even terror. The *beautiful,* the picturesque, and the sublime became three modes for the perception of nature.

Surrealism (1) A literary and artistic movement, predominantly French but with vast international influence; initiated after World War I by André Breton and others, and enshrining the irrational as the best mode of perceiving and representing reality. Pathological forms of vision, hallucination, psychotic utterance, automatic writing, free association, and other means of nullifying even the structures of Symbolist poetic tradition were celebrated. Poetic form was abandoned as though it were as inauthentic as bookkeeping or scientific language, and the surrealistic "texts" are neither prose nor verse. The unconscious, the impulsive, and particularly the erotic are the domains of the surrealistic imagination, which occupied many European painters including Pablo Picasso at a phase in his career, and particularly and with greatest success, René Magritte. Among French writers associated with the movement were Paul Eluard, Louis Aragon, Philippe Soupault, Antonin Artaud, René Char, and Raymond Queneau.

(2) In a looser sense, "surrealist" has been commonly (and misleadingly) used to describe representations in modern literature of the visionary, the dreamlike, the fantastic in any of its forms.

Symbolism   (1) Broadly, the process by which one phenomenon, in literature, stands for another, or group of others, and usually of a different sort. Clear-cut cases of this in medieval and Renaissance literature are *emblems* or *attributes* (see *Personification; Allegory*). Sometimes conventional symbols may be used in more than one way, e.g. a mirror betokening both truth and vanity. See also *Figure; Emblem*.

(2) In a specific sense (and often given in its French form, *symbolisme*), an important esthetic concept for modern literature, formulated by French poets and critics of the later 19th century following Baudelaire. In this view, the literary symbol becomes something closer to a kind of commanding, central metaphor, taking precedence over any more discursive linguistic mode for poetic communication. The effects of this concept on literature in English have been immense; and some version of the concept survives in modern notions of the poetic *image*, or *fiction*.

Trope   (1) See *Rhetoric*. (2) In the liturgy of the Catholic Church, a phrase, sentence, or verse with its musical setting, introduced to amplify or embellish some part of the text of the mass or the office (i.e. the prayers and Scripture readings recited daily by priests, religious, and even laymen) when chanted in choir. Tropes of this second kind were discontinued in 1570 by the authority of Pope Pius V. Troping new material into older or conventional patterns seems to have been, in a general way, a basic device of medieval literature, and was the genesis of modern drama.

Type, Typology   (1) Strictly, in medieval biblical interpretation, the prefiguration of the persons and events of the New Testament by persons and events of the Old, the Old Testament being fulfilled in, but not entirely superseded by, the New. Thus, the Temptation and Fall of Man were held to prefigure the first Temptation of Christ, pride in each case being the root of the temptation, and a warning against gluttony the moral lesson to be drawn from both. The Brazen Serpent raised up by Moses was held to prefigure the crucifixion of Christ; Isaac, as a sacrificial victim ("God will provide his own Lamb," says Abraham to him) is a *type* of Christ. The forty days and nights of the Deluge, the forty years of Israel's wandering in the desert, Moses' forty days in the desert are all typologically related.

(2) In a looser sense, a person or event seen as a model or paradigm. See also *Figure*.

Villanelle   A lyric form originally used in French Renaissance poetry for pastoral subjects, adopted by 19th-century English writers of light verse, and eventually taken up again by poets such as James Joyce, William Empson, and Dylan Thomas for more than trivial effects. The form consists of five (see *Meter* §5) tercets rhyming *aba*, followed by a quatrain rhyming *abaa*. The first and last line of the first tercet are alternately repeated as refrains at the end of each following tercet. Thus, in Edward Arlington Robinson's famous villanelle beginning

> They are all gone away,
>> The house is shut and still,
> There is nothing more to say.

the first and third line are alternated, finally to follow each other in the last tercet. Modern use of the form depends upon subtle variations of the meaning of the refrain lines at each repetition.

Yorkists   See *Wars of the Roses*.

Zodiac   In astrology, a belt of the celestial sphere, about eight or nine degrees to either side of the ecliptic (the apparent orbit of the sun), within which the apparent motions of the sun, moon, and planets take place. It is divided into twelve equal parts, the signs, through each of which the sun passes in a month. Each division once coincided with one of the constellations after which the signs are named: Aries (Ram)—in Chaucer's time the sun entered this sign on 12 March; Taurus (Bull); Gemini (Twins); Cancer (Crab); Leo (Lion); Virgo (Virgin); Libra (Scales); Scorpio; Sagittarius (Archer); Capricornus (Goat); Aquarius (Water-Carrier); Pisces (Fishes). Each zodiacal sign was believed to govern a part of the human body. See *Astronomy and Astrology*.

Suggestions for Further Reading

The Period in General

Historical Backgrounds The liveliest survey of the period is A. J. P. Taylor's *English History 1914–1945*, 1965 (final volume of the Oxford History of England). See also John A. Lester, Jr., *Journey Through Despair* (1968); Samuel Hynes, *The Edwardian Turn of Mind*, 1969; Julian Symons, *The Thirties*, 1960; Robert Graves and Alan Hodge, *The Long Week-End*, 1940; and the autobiographies of Stephen Spender (*World Within a World*, 1951) and John Lehmann (*In My Own Time*, 1969). Taylor's *Illustrated History of the First World War*, 1964, and Angus Calder's *The People's War*, 1969, give vivid impressions of the two great wars of the period. A. Hamilton, *The Appeal of Fascism*, 1971, studies the record of intellectuals in relation to various forms of Fascism. Useful short histories are L. C. B. Seaman's *Post-Victorian Britain, 1902–51*, 1966, and Arthur Marwick's *Britain in an Age of Total War*, 1968.

Literary Backgrounds Among the many literary surveys of and introductions to modernism are: R. Ellmann and C. Feidelson, Jr., *The Modern Tradition*, 1965, which collects the documents; Stephen Spender, *The Struggle of the Modern*, 1963; Irving Howe, *The Idea of the Modern*, 1968; F. Kermode, *Romantic Image*, 1957, and *Continuities*, 1968; Monroe K. Spears, *Dionysus and the City*, 1971. M. L. Rosenthal's *The New Modern Poetry* (1967), William Y. Tindall's *Forces in Modern British Literature*, 1947, C. K. Stead's *The New Poetic* (1964), A. Alvarez's *Stewards of Excellence*, 1958, Graham Hough's *Image and Experience*, 1960 (seventh and last volume of The Pelican Guide to English Literature), *The Modern Age*, ed. Boris Ford, and J. I. M. Stewart's *Eight Modern Writers*, 1963 (Vol. XII of the Oxford History of English Literature), are introductions and discussions with various perspectives. F. R. Leavis's *New Bearings in English Poetry*, 1932 (repr. 1950), is an important document in itself. See also the essay "On the Modern Element in Modern Literature," in Lionel Trilling's *Beyond Culture*, 1965.

THOMAS HARDY

Editions The collected "Mellstock" (English) edition in 37 volumes includes prose and verse; standard in America is the "Anniversary Edition" of *The Writings of Thomas Hardy*, 1920. The standard edition of the poetry is the *Collected Poems* of 1926 (repr. 1961) exclusive of a posthumous *Winter Words in Various Moods and*

Metres, 1928. There are also *Letters,* ed. C. J. Weber, 1954; *Notebooks,* ed. Evelyn Hardy, 1955; and *A Choice of Thomas Hardy's Poems* by Geoffrey Grigson, 1969.

Critical Studies   The indispensable consideration of the poems, containing a great wealth of biographical and bibliographical information, is by J. O. Bailey, *The Poetry of Thomas Hardy: A Handbook and Commentary,* 1970; *Thomas Hardy and the Cosmic Mind,* 1956, by the same author, offers a reading of *The Dynasts,* as does Walter F. Wright, in *The Shaping of The Dynasts,* 1967. Samuel Hynes's *The Pattern of Hardy's Poetry,* 1961, is a brief general study. Chapters on the poetry in Irving Howe's critical study entitled *Thomas Hardy,* 1967, and in *Thomas Hardy: Distance and Desire* by J. Hillis Miller, 1970, are both good, and the Hardy Centennial Number of *The Southern Review,* VI (1940), contains essays by a number of American critics. Donald Davie's *Thomas Hardy and British Poetry,* 1972, is a fine study of Hardy's influence on poetry down to the present moment. Richard L. Purdy's *Thomas Hardy: A Bibliographical Study,* 1954, is authoritative.

GEORGE BERNARD SHAW

Editions   Publication of the 30-volume Ayot St. Lawrence edition was initiated in 1930; in addition, there are editions of *Nine Plays,* 1931; *Seven Plays,* 1951; a four-volume *Selected Plays,* 1948–57; a *Complete Plays, with Prefaces,* 1962; and a *Selected Prose,* ed. Diarmuid Russell, 1952. Eric Bentley has edited a selection of *Shaw on Music* (1955); and Dan H. Laurence, a *Collected Letters of Bernard Shaw 1874–97,* 1965, and *Collected Letters 1898–1910,* 1972.

Critical Studies   Eric Bentley's *Bernard Shaw, A Reconsideration,* rev. ed., 1955, is very good, as is Richard M. Ohmann, *The Style and the Man,* 1962. Donald P. Costello's *Serpent's Eye* (1965) deals with the filming of Shaw's plays, and Bernard F. Dukore has edited the screenplay of *St. Joan* (1968). Harold Fromm, *Bernard Shaw and the Theatre of the Nineties,* 1967, and Frederick Mayne, *Wit and Satire of George Bernard Shaw,* 1967, represent different critical approaches.

Biography   Hesketh Pearson's *George Bernard Shaw: His Life and Personality,* 1963, may be supplemented by Stanley Weintraub's *Private Shaw and Public Shaw,* 1962, and *Journey to Heartbreak,* 1971.

JOSEPH CONRAD

Editions   The New Collected Edition in 22 volumes, 1946, is standard in England; in America the individual works have been published in careful critical editions. There are also several volumes of correspondence, among them *Letters from Joseph Conrad, 1895–1924,* ed. with introduction and notes by E. Garnett, 1928 (1962). *Last Essays,* 1926, has been reprinted with an introduction by R. Curle, 1970.

Critical Studies   Of many studies the best is Albert J. Guérard's *Conrad the Novelist,* 1958. See also Frederick Karl's *Reader's Guide to Conrad,* 1960, and F. R. Leavis's essays in *The Great Tradition,* 1948. Conrad's voracious use of his own experience in his stories is illuminated by Norman Sherry in *Conrad's Eastern World,* 1966, and *Conrad's Western World,* 1971.

Biography   The standard is Jocelyn Baines's *Joseph Conrad: A Critical Biography,* 1960 (repr. 1967). The autobiographical works of Ford Madox Ford, *Memories and Impressions,* 1911, and Bertrand Russell, *Autobiography,* 1968, 1969, are important sources of information.

WILLIAM BUTLER YEATS

Editions   The unusually complex bibliography is simplified by the posthumous publication of most of Yeats's output in large groupings: for the poetry, *Collected Poems,* 1950; and *Variorum Edition of the Poems of W. B. Yeats,* ed. P. Allt, 1957; for the plays, *Collected Plays,* 1952, and *Variorum Edition of the Plays of W. B. Yeats,* ed. R. K. Alspach, 1966; for the correspondence, *The Letters of W. B. Yeats,* ed. Allan Wade, 1954. For the prose, there are the subject's collections entitled *Autobiographies,* 1938; *Mythologies,* 1959; *Essays and Introductions,* 1961; and *Explorations,* 1962.

Critical Studies   The pioneer analytical introduction is P. Ure's *Towards a Mythology: Studies in the Poetry of W. B. Yeats,* 1946 (repr. 1947). See also his *W. B. Yeats,* 1968, *Yeats the Playwright,* 1963. Of dozens of critical or critico-biographical writings, see L. MacNeice's *Poetry of W. B. Yeats,* 1941; A. N. Jeffare's *W. B. Yeats: Man and Poet,* 1949, and his valuable *Commentary on the Collected Poems,* 1968; T. R. Henn's *The Lonely Tower,* 1950; R. Ellmann's *Yeats: The Man and the Masks,* 1948 (repr. 1962), and *The Identity of Yeats,* 1954; T. R. Parkinson's *W. B. Yeats, Self-Critic,* 1951, and *W. B. Yeats: The Later Poetry,* 1964, both investigating Yeats's revisions, as do Curtis Bradford's *Yeats at Work,* 1965, and Jon Stallworthy's *Between the Lines,* 1963, and *Vision and Revision in Yeats's Poetry,* 1969. Further works are J. Unterecker's *Reader's Guide to William Butler Yeats,* 1959; Virginia Moore's *The Unicorn,* 1954; Giorgio Melchiori's *The Whole Mystery of Art,* 1960; *Images of a Poet,* ed. D. J. Gordon, 1961; T. Whitaker's *Swan and Shadow,* 1964; and Harold Bloom's *William Butler Yeats,* 1970. There is a *Bibliography of the Writings,* by Allan Wade, 1951 (2nd ed. rev., 1958).

Biography   The standard life, *W. B. Yeats,* by J. M. Hone, 1942 (2nd ed., 1962), will be superseded by that of D. Donoghue when it is completed.

JAMES JOYCE

Editions   The early *Stephen Hero* was first published (ed. Theodore Spencer) in 1944, and republished with new material (ed. John J. Slocum and Herbert Cahoon) in 1955. The MS. fragments of *Epiphanies* were edited by O. A. Silverman, 1956. The major works appeared as follows: *Dubliners,* 1914; *A Portrait of the Artist as a Young Man,* 1914; *Ulysses,* 1922; and *Finnegans Wake,* 1939. A *Collected Poems* was published in 1937, and all Joyce's verse is reproduced, together with *Dubliners, A Portrait,* and the play *Exiles,* in Harry Levin's comprehensive *Portable James Joyce* of 1947. *The Critical Writings of James Joyce,* 1959, was edited by Ellsworth Mason and Richard Ellmann; the *Letters,* Vol. I (ed. Stuart Gilbert) appeared in 1957, Vols. II and III (ed. Richard Ellmann), in 1966.

Critical Studies   There are three useful short introductory studies: Harry Levin's *James Joyce: A Critical Introduction* (rev. ed., 1960), still the best, and those of S. L. Goldberg, 1962, and John Gross, 1970, both entitled *James Joyce* and both excellent also. Marvin Magalaner and Richard M. Kain, *Joyce: The Man, the Work, the Reputation*, 1956, is standard, and A. Walton Litz, *James Joyce*, 1966, is very fine. Anthologies of criticism are Seon Givens (Manley), ed., *James Joyce: Two Decades of Criticism*, rev. ed., 1963; and the two volumes of Robert Deming, ed., *James Joyce, the Critical Heritage*, 1970. Clive Hart edited a collections of essays on *Dubliners*, 1969. Particularly good longer studies on *Ulysses* and *Finnegans Wake* are: Stuart Gilbert, *James Joyce's Ulysses*, 1952; S. L. Goldberg, *The Classical Temper*, 1961; Robert Martin Adams, *Surface and Symbol*, 1962; Clive Hart, *Structure and Motif in Finnegans Wake*, 1962; A. Walton Litz, *The Art of James Joyce*, 1961; Bernard Benstock, *Joyce-Again's Wake*, 1965. Weldon Thornton compiled a handbook of *Allusions in Ulysses*, 1968, and William York Tindall, *A Reader's Guide to Finnegans Wake*, 1969. Richard Ellmann, in *Ulysses on the Liffey*, 1972, presents some fascinating and amusing new insights.

Biography   The great biography is the *James Joyce* of Richard Ellmann, 1959; Stanislaus Joyce's *My Brother's Keeper: James Joyce's Early Years*, 1958, and Frank Budgen's *James Joyce and the Making of "Ulysses,"* rev. ed., 1960, are both of great value.

D. H. LAWRENCE

Editions   *Collected Poems*, two vols., ed. V. de S. Pinto and F. W. Roberts, 1964; *Complete Plays*, 1966. The novels are accessible in many formats, as is much of the discursive prose: *Phoenix I*, 1936 (repr. 1961), and *Phoenix II*, 1968, contain generous quantities. Selections are available also in *The Portable D. H. Lawrence*, ed. D. Trilling, 1947; and *Selected Literary Criticism*, ed. A. Beale, 1955. The complete edition of the correspondence is *Collected Letters*, ed. H. T. Moore, two vols., 1961. Lawrence's early versions of *Studies in Classical Literature* (in many ways superior to the later) are included in *The Symbolic Meaning*, ed. A. Arnold, 1962.

Critical Studies   A small selection from a vast output: *Son of Woman*, by Lawrence's onetime friend, J. Middleton Murry, 1931; F. R. Leavis, *D. H. Lawrence*, 1930, and *D. H. Lawrence: Novelist*, 1955; Graham Hough, *The Dark Sun*, 1956; George Ford, *Double Measure*, 1965; H. M. Dalewski, *The Forked Flame*, 1965; Keith Sagar, *The Art of D. H. Lawrence*, 1966; Frank Kermode, *D. H. Lawrence*, 1973: a brief introduction. An important article is M. Kinkhead-Weekes's "The Marble and the Statue," in *Imagined Worlds*, ed. M. Mack and Ian Gregor, 1968. R. Draper's *The Critical Heritage of D. H. Lawrence*, 1970, describes the early reception of his work. A. Alvarez, *Stewards of Excellence*, 1958, deals with the poetry, as does an essay in Harold Bloom's *The Ringers in the Tower*, 1971.

Biography   There are several works of personal reminiscence, the most revelatory being that of "E.T." (Jessie Chambers, the "Miriam" of *Sons and Lovers*), *D. H. Lawrence: A Personal Record*, 1935; and Frieda Lawrence's *Not I but the Wind*, 1934. Biographical material is reproduced or résuméd in *D. H. Lawrence: A Composite Biography*, ed. E. Nehls, three vols., 1957–59. The best life is H. T. Moore's *The Intelligent Heart*, 1955 (repr. 1960).

T. S. ELIOT

Editions   All the canonical verse is collected in *The Complete Poems and Plays*,

1952; the original *Waste Land* text, ed. Valerie Eliot, appeared in 1971. Most but by no means all of the more permanent prose is found in *Selected Essays*, 1932; *The Use of Poetry and the Use of Criticism*, 1934; *Notes Toward the Definition of Culture*, 1949; *On Poetry and Poets*, 1957; and *To Criticize the Critic*, 1965.

Critical Studies   A few of the critical works are F. O. Matthiessen, *The Achievement of T. S. Eliot*, 3rd ed., 1958; *T. S. Eliot*, essays ed. B. Rajan, 1947 (repr. 1966); Helen Gardner, *The Art of T. S. Eliot*, 1950; George Williamson, *A Reader's Guide to T. S. Eliot*, 1953; Grover Smith, *T. S. Eliot's Poetry and Plays*, 1956 (rev. ed., 1962); Hugh Kenner, *The Invisible Poet*, 1959; *The Pound Era*, 1972; and ed. *T. S. Eliot* in (Twentieth Century Views), 1962; Kristian Smidt, *Poetry and Belief in the Work of T. S. Eliot*, 2nd rev. ed., 1961; Northrop Frye, *T. S. Eliot*, 1963; Herbert Howarth, *Notes on Some Figures Behind T. S. Eliot*, 1965; Allen Tate, ed., *T. S. Eliot: The Man and His Work*, 1966; B. C. Southam, *A Student's Guide to the Selected Poems of T. S. Eliot*; Graham Martin, ed., *Eliot in Perspective*, 1970.

ROBERT BRIDGES

Editions   *The Poetical Works of Robert Bridges* in six volumes, 1920, must be supplemented by *New Verse*, 1925, as well as by *The Testament of Beauty*, 1929. There is an enlarged edition of *The Shorter Poems*, 1931, and a selection of poetry and prose edited by John Sparrow, 1955.

Critical Studies   Albert J. Guérard, *Robert Bridges: A Study of Traditionalism in Poetry*, 1942; E. J. Thompson, *Robert Bridges, 1844–1930*, 1945, and G. S. Gordon, *Robert Bridges* (Rede Lecture), 1946. Yvor Winters's essay "Traditional Mastery: The Lyrics of Robert Bridges" was published in *Hound and Horn* in 1932. E. C. Wright's *Metaphor, Sound and Meaning in Bridges' The Testament of Beauty* appeared in 1951.

A. E. HOUSMAN

Editions   There are three volumes of verse: *A Shropshire Lad*, 1896; *Last Poems*, 1922; and the posthumous *More Poems*, 1936; plus a little new material in Laurence Housman's *My Brother, A. E. Housman*, 1938 (repr. 1969). *The Collected Poems*, 1939, was revised in 1953. *Selected Prose*, ed. J. Carter, appeared in 1961; the *Letters*, ed. H. Maas, in 1971.

Critico-biographical Studies   Norman Marlow, *A. E. Housman*, 1958; G. L. Watson, *A. E. Housman: A Divided Life*, 1957; B. J. Leggett, *Housman's Land of Lost Content: A Critical Study of a Shropshire Lad*, 1970; and *A. E. Housman: A Collection of Critical Essays*, ed. C. B. Ricks, 1968, in the series Twentieth Century Views.

WALTER DE LA MARE

There is the massive *Complete Poems*, 1970; an excellent *Selected Poems* chosen by R. N. Green-Armytage, 1954; and *A Choice of De la Mare's Verse*, ed. with introduction by W. H. Auden, 1963. Prose works include *Pleasures and Speculations*, 1940; *Private View*, 1953; and the novel *Memoirs of a Midget*, 1921. There are critical studies—all entitled *Walter de la Mare* with appropriate subtitles—by Forrest Reid, 1929; H. C. Duffin, 1949; and Kenneth Hopkins, 1953.

RUDYARD KIPLING

Editions   The definitive collection in England is the Sussex Edition, in 35 vols., 1937–39. For the poetry see T. S. Eliot, ed., *A Choice of Kipling's Verse*, 1941. Randall Jarrell's *Best Short Stories of Rudyard Kipling*, 1961, contains the important briefer fiction.

Critical Studies   There are good essays by Edmund Wilson in *The Wound and the Bow*, 1941; George Orwell in *Critical Essays*, 1946; and Lionel Trilling in *The Liberal Imagination*, 1950. J. M. S. Tompkins, *The Art of Rudyard Kipling*, 1959; C. A. Bodelsen, *Aspects of Kipling's Art*, 1964; and Bonamy Dobrée, *Rudyard Kipling, Realist and Fabulist*, 1967, are the leading books; a collection of essays entitled *Kipling's Mind and Art* is edited by Andrew Rutherford, 1964.

Biography   Charles Carrington, *Life of Rudyard Kipling*, 1955. Richard Faber's *The Vision and the Need* (1966) is useful on Kipling's imperialism, as are, in their way, studies by J. I. M. Stewart, *Rudyard Kipling*, 1966, and T. R. Henn, *Kipling*, 1968. R. L. Green compiled *The Reader's Guide to Kipling's Works*, 1961.

WILFRED OWEN

Poems, with an Introduction by Siegfried Sassoon, appeared in 1920; a later edition carried commentary by Edmund Blunden, 1931. The best edition is the scholarly text entitled *The Collected Poems of Wilfred Owen*, 1964, with introductory notes by C. Day Lewis and a memoir by Edmund Blunden. Owen's *Letters,* ed. Harold Owen and John Bell, 1967, complements the three-volume biography by Harold Owen, *Journey into Obscurity: Wilfred Owen 1893–1918*, 1963–65. D. S. R. Welland's *Wilfred Owen: A Critical Study,* was published in 1960.

EDWARD THOMAS

The *Collected Poems* was published in 1936, with a foreword by Walter de la Mare; from 1949 on, reprintings have contained one additional poem. John Moore's *The Life and Letters of Edward Thomas,* 1939, is a biographical study; it may be supplemented with memoirs by the poet's widow, Helen Thomas, *As It Was,* 1926, and *World Without End,* 1931. There are critical studies by H. Coombes, 1956, and Vernon Scannell, 1963, both entitled *Edward Thomas.*

ISAAC ROSENBERG

Collected Works, ed. Gordon Bottomley and Denys Harding, 1937, is abridged in a *Collected Poems* of 1949. The *Poems* of 1922 has a prefatory memoir by Laurence Binyon, and the *Collected Works,* an essay on Rosenberg by Siegfried Sassoon. John H. Johnston, *English Poetry of the First World War,* 1964, includes valuable background material for the study of Rosenberg, Wilfred Owen, and Edward Thomas.

DAVID JONES

In Parenthesis, published in 1937, was reprinted, with an introductory note by T. S. Eliot, in 1961; *The Anathémata*, his remarkable long poem, was first published in 1952. A collection of his prose writing, entitled *Epoch and Artist*, was edited by Harman Grisewood in 1959. Subsequent poetry includes *The Fatigue*, 1965, and *The Tribune's Visitation*, 1969. There is a good chapter on *In Parenthesis* in John H. Johnston, *English Poetry of the First World War*, 1964. Robin Ironside edited and introduced the Jones volume of the Penguin Modern Painters, 1949. David Balmires's *David Jones: Artist and Writer*, 1972, is a full-view study.

EDWIN MUIR

Editions available are *Collected Poems*, 2nd ed., 1965, with a preface by T. S. Eliot; *Essays on Literature and Society*, 2nd ed., 1965; *The Estate of Poetry*, 1962. *An Autobiography*, 1964, continues and expands *The Story and the Fable*, 1940. P. H. Butter's *Edwin Muir, Man and Poet*, 1966, is biographical; the same author's critical study appeared in 1962 (repr. 1967). Other recent works include D. G. Hoffman, *Barbarous Knowledge*, 1967; and E. Huberman, *The Poetry of Edwin Muir*, 1971.

HUGH MACDIARMID
(*Christopher Murray Grieve*)

Collected Poems was published in 1962, and a second edition, with an expanded glossary, appeared in 1967. An autobiography, *The Company I've Kept*, 1966, and *Selected Essays*, ed. Duncan Glen, 1970, comprise his published prose. A volume of essays in his honor, *Hugh MacDiarmid: A Festschrift*, ed. K. Duval and S. G. Smith, appeared in 1962, and, in 1964, studies by Kenneth Buthlay (*Hugh MacDiarmid*), and by Duncan Glen, entitled *Hugh MacDiarmid and the Scottish Renaissance*.

ROBERT GRAVES

Editions   Since Graves has published more than 120 books, and has been regathering his verse into *Collected Poems* volumes since 1926, the bibliographical problems are immense. The 1959 *Collected Poems* was followed by another in 1965; then a *Poems, 1965–1968*, appeared in 1969. *The White Goddess* originally appeared in 1948, but was expanded in 1952. The memoir of World War I, *Goodbye to All That*, 1929, was revised and extended in 1957. Of the novels the most remarkable are *I, Claudius*, 1934, *Claudius The God*, 1934, *Antigua, Penny, Puce*, 1936, and *Hercules My Shipmate*, 1944. His (frequently annoying) essays on poetry are included in *The Common Asphodel*, 1948, *The Crowning Privilege*, 1955, and a *Collected Talks and Essays*, 1969.

Critical Studies   There are critical studies—all entitled *Robert Graves*—by Martin Seymour-Smith, 1956 (rev. ed., 1965); J. M. Cohen, 1960; George Stade, 1967; and Michael Kirkham, *The Poetry of Robert Graves*, 1969; Lionel Trilling has an excellent essay on Graves in *A Gathering of Fugitives*, 1956. Douglas Day's *Swifter Than*

Reason, 1963, deals with the critical writings as well. F. H. Higginson brought out his *Bibliography of the Works of Robert Graves* in 1966.

ALDOUS HUXLEY

The most important novels are *Crome Yellow,* 1921; *Antic Hay,* 1923; *Brave New World,* 1932; *Eyeless in Gaza,* 1936; *After Many a Summer,* 1939; *Time Must Have a Stop,* 1944; *Ape and Essence,* 1948 (a horrific antithetical alternative to *Brave New World*); *Collected Essays,* 1959, a selection; *Collected Letters,* ed. Grover Smith, 1969; *Collected Poetry,* 1971. Useful studies, all entitled *Aldous Huxley,* are by Jocelyn Brooke, 1954; J. A. Atkins, 1956; and Peter Bowering, 1969. See also George Woodcock, *Dawn and the Darkest Hour,* 1971.

W. H. AUDEN

Editions From the *Collected Poems* of 1945 onward, the poet has revised and re-written his selections from past books. Subsequent volumes were *The Age of Anxiety,* 1947; *Nones,* 1951; *The Shield of Achilles,* 1955; *Homage to Clio,* 1960; *About the House,* 1965; and *City Without Walls,* 1969. A new *Collected Shorter Poems* in 1966 was followed by a *Collected Longer Poems,* 1969; a shorter *Selected Poetry* was published in 1959. *The Enchafèd Flood,* 1951, is a long essay on "the romantic iconography of the sea"; and *The Dyer's Hand,* 1962, a generous selection of critical essays. Auden's commonplace book, entitled *A Certain World,* appeared in 1970. Of his many collaborations, two plays written with Christopher Isherwood are available, *The Ascent of F6* and *On the Frontier,* new ed. 1958; with Chester Kallmann, a translation of *The Magic Flute,* 1957; and narration for *The Play of Daniel,* ed. Noah Greenberg, 1959. The opera libretti with Kallmann, for *The Rake's Progress* (Stravinsky), *Elegy for Young Lovers* and *The Bassarids* (Hans Werner Henze) are not published as books. A co-translation with Paul B. Taylor of a selection from *The Elder Edda,* 1970, is to be followed by further versions of Icelandic poetry.

Critical Studies The best comprehensive critique is by Monroe K. Spears, *The Poetry of W. H. Auden,* 1963. Appearing earlier were Richard Hoggart's *Auden: An Introductory Essay,* 1951; and a somewhat tendentious bibliographical study by Joseph Warren Beach, *The Making of the Auden Canon,* 1957. Current studies include J. G. Blair, *The Poetic Art of W. H. Auden,* 1965; George W. Bahlke, *The Later Auden,* 1970; John Fuller, *A Reader's Guide to W. H. Auden,* 1970; and a (forthcoming) study of the early poetry, by Frederick Buell.

LOUIS MACNIECE

The complete poetry canon is contained in *Collected Poems,* ed. E. R. Dodds, 1967. Prose works include *Modern Poetry: A Personal Essay,* 1938; *The Poetry of William Butler Yeats,* 1941; *Varieties of Parable,* 1965; and the unfinished, posthumously published autobiographical *The Strings Are False,* 1966. There are critical studies (both under the subject as title) by John Press, 1965 (2nd ed. 1967); and Elton E. Smith, 1970. An essay on MacNeice appears in F. O. Matthiessen's *The Responsibilities of the Critic,* 1952.

STEPHEN SPENDER

Collected Poems, 1928–1953, 1955, actually a carefully pruned selection; there are also *Selected Poems,* 1964, and *The Generous Days,* 1971. Prose works include *The Destructive Element,* 1934; the autobiographical *World Within World,* 1953; *The Creative Element,* 1954; *The Making of a Poem,* 1955; *The Struggle of the Modern,* 1963; and *Year of the Young Rebels,* 1969. There is material on Spender in Derek Stanford's monograph, *Pylon Poets,* 1969.

EDITH SITWELL

The basic work is contained in *Collected Poems,* 1930; an enlarged *Collected Poems,* 1954, contains explanatory and introductory notes by the poet herself. *The Outcasts,* 1962, and its slightly expanded U.S. version, *Music and Ceremonies,* 1963, prints poems not in the collected edition. Of the prose works, her *Alexander Pope* appeared in 1930, *The English Eccentrics* in 1933, and an autobiography, *Taken Care of,* after her death in 1965. There is a brief study by John Lehmann, 1952, and a longer one by Ralph J. Mills, Jr., 1966, both entitled *Edith Sitwell.* John Lehmann's *A Nest of Tigers,* 1968, concerns the Sitwell family.

WILLIAM EMPSON

The *Collected Poems,* 1955, contains slightly more material than the previous collection of 1949. Of his critical works, *Seven Types of Ambiguity* appeared in 1930 (rev. ed., 1947); *Some Versions of Pastoral* (also known as *English Pastoral Poetry*) in 1935; and *The Structure of Complex Words* in 1951. Essays on Empson's poetry are included in John Wain's *Preliminary Essays,* 1957, and A. Alvarez, *Stewards of Excellence,* 1958. In June 1963 *The Review* devoted a double number (Nos. 6–7) to Empson.

DYLAN THOMAS

Editions The expanded edition of the 1952 *Collected Poems,* published in 1957, is the standard. Prose works include *Portrait of the Artist as a Young Dog,* 1940; *Adventures in the Skin Trade,* 1955; and *Quite Early One Morning,* 1954. Thomas's popular radio play, *Under Milk Wood,* was published also in 1954; and his *Notebooks* were edited by Ralph N. Maud in 1967.

Critical Studies Interpretive works range from the early one by Henry Treece, *Dylan Thomas: Dog Among the Fairies,* 1949 (revised 1956), to those by Elder Olson, *The Poetry of Dylan Thomas,* and Derek Stanford, *Dylan Thomas: A Literary Study,* both in 1954; and G. S. Fraser, *Dylan Thomas,* 3rd ed., 1965; and William T. Moynihan, *The Craft and Art of Dylan Thomas,* 1966. Ralph N. Maud's *Entrances to Dylan Thomas's Poetry* (1963) is probably the best of these.

Biography The standard is Constantine FitzGibbon's *The Life of Dylan Thomas,* 1965, which was preceded by John Malcolm Brinnin's *Dylan Thomas in America,* 1955. Bill Read's *The Days of Dylan Thomas,* 1964, contains valuable photographs.

E. M. FORSTER

Editions   Apart from the novels the most important books are *Aspects of the Novel*, 1927, and the two collections of essays *Abinger Harvest*, 1936, and *Two Cheers for Democracy*, 1951. There is also the book on his second Indian visit, *The Hill of Devi*, 1953.

Critical Studies   Of several full-length essays the best are by Lionel Trilling, 1943; (2nd ed. rev., 1965); F. C. Crews, *E. M. Forster: The Perils of Humanism*, 1962; and Wilfred Stone, *The Cave and the Mountain*, 1966. There is an extensive survey (under his subject's name) by Laurence Brander, 1968; and *Forster: A Collection of Critical Essays*, ed. Malcolm Bradbury, in the series Twentieth Century Views. See also J. K. Johnstone's *The Bloomsbury Group*, 1954; and Quentin Bell's *Bloomsbury*, 1968. At this writing, P. N. Furbank is at work on an authorized biography.

JOHN BETJEMAN

A *Collected Poems* (rev. ed., 1970) preserve all that the poet wishes to keep from earlier volumes; its first publication was followed by *High and Low* in 1966. A previous *Selected Poems*, 1948, and *A Few Late Chysanthemums*, 1953, are still in print. *Slick But Not Streamlined*, 1947, an earlier selection, had an introduction by W. H. Auden. *Summoned by Bells*, 1960, is a verse autobiography. Among his architectural prose works are *The American's Guide to English Parish Churches*, 1959, and *Ghastly Good Taste*, 1933. There are analyses by Derek Stanford, *John Betjeman: A Study*, 1961, and Jocelyn Brooke, *Ronald Firbank and John Betjeman*, 1962.

GEORGE ORWELL

The novels are published in various editions; the nonfiction titles, *The Road to Wigan Pier, Homage to Catalonia*, and *Down and Out in London and Paris*, are supplemented by the standard collection of his shorter pieces, *Collected Essays, Journalism and Letters*, ed. S. Orwell and I. Angus, four vols., 1968. There is a useful *Orwell Reader*, ed. R. Rovere, 1956. Studies include George Woodcock, *The Crystal Spirit*, 1966; and Raymond Williams's briefer *George Orwell*, 1971.

SAMUEL BECKETT

There is a *Collected Works* published in 16 vols., 1970, and available in America. The past fifteen years have seen the accumulation of a vast amount of criticism of Beckett; among the best of the critiques are Hugh Kenner, *Samuel Beckett, A Critical Study*, 1961; Ruby Cohn, *Samuel Beckett*, 1962; John Fletcher, *The Novels of Samuel Beckett*, 1964; Raymond Federman, *Journey into Chaos*, 1965, on Beckett's earlier fiction. Stanley Cavell's "Ending the Waiting Game," in *Must We Mean What We Say?*, 1969, is a brilliant study of *Endgame* by a philosopher whose techniques are analytic rather than existential. Lawrence E. Harvey's *Samuel Beckett: Poet and Critic* (1970) is thoroughly detailed in documenting the background to the poems. Martin Esslin edited *Samuel Beckett: A Collection of Critical Essays* in 1965.

THE CONTEMPORARY PERIOD

Critical Essays and Anthologies   For the study of post-war poetry: G. S. Fraser, *Vision and Rhetoric*, 1959; John Press, *Rule and Energy*, 1963; Robert Conquest, ed., *New Lines*, 1956, and *New Lines* II, 1963; and A. Alvarez, *The New Poetry*, 1966. Perhaps the most useful volumes are John Press, *A Map of Modern English Verse*, 1969, with extensive quotation of entire poems, and the tasteful and broadly inclusive anthology of Edward Lucie-Smith, *British Poetry Since 1945*, 1970. A good general treatment of developments in the theatre is John Russell Taylor, *The Angry Theatre: New British Drama*, 1969.

Basil Bunting   *Poems*, 1950, *Briggflatts*, 1966, *Collected Poems*, 1968.

Stevie Smith   *Selected Poems*, 1962; *The Frog Prince*, 1966; *The Best Beast*, 1969; among her novels are *Novel on Yellow Paper*, 1937, and *Harold's Leap*, 1950.

John Heath-Stubbs   *The Charity of the Stars*, 1944; *The Triumph of the Muse*, 1958; *Selected Poems*, 1966; *Satires and Epigrams*, 1968.

Donald Davie   *New and Selected Poems*, 1961; *Essex Poems*, 1969; *Collected Poems*, 1972. Criticism: *Purity of Diction in English Verse*, 1952; *Articulate Energy*, 1955 (repr. 1971).

Philip Larkin   *The North Ship*, 1945 (rev. ed., 1966); *The Less Deceived*, 1955; *The Whitsun Weddings*, 1964.

Kingsley Amis   *A Case of Samples*, 1957; *A Look Round the Estate*, 1967. Novels: *Lucky Jim* (1954); *The Anti-Death League*, 1967; *The Green Man*, 1970 (among several fictional titles); the critical piece *What Became of Jane Austen?* 1971.

Charles Tomlinson   *The Necklace*, 1955; *Seeing is Believing*, 1960; *A Peopled Landscape*, 1963; *American Scenes*, 1966; *The Way of a World*, 1969.

Thom Gunn   *Fighting Terms*, 1954 (rev. ed., 1962); *The Sense of Movement*, 1957; *My Sad Captains*, 1961; *Positives*, 1966; *Touch*, 1967. Gunn also edited and introduced a selection of Fulke Greville poetry in 1969.

Ted Hughes   *The Hawk in the Rain*, 1957; *Lupercal*, 1960; *Wodwo*, 1967; *Crow*, 1970.

Geoffrey Hill   *For the Unfallen*, 1959; *King Log*, 1968; *Mercian Hymns*, 1971.

Other poets working during the post-World War II period are **Roy Fuller**, with a *Collected Poems*, 1962, and a subsequent *New Poems*, 1968; **George Barker**, *Collected Poems*, 1957, and *The True Confessions of George Barker*, 1965. **Keith Douglas** (killed in the war) had a posthumous *Collected Poems*, 1966, ed. J. Waller, G. S. Fraser and J. C. Hall.

Author and Title Index

First-Line Index